THE CATECHISM

OF

THOMAS BECON,

WITH OTHER PIECES.

THE

Catechism

OF

THOMAS BECON, S. T. P.

CHAPLAIN TO ARCHBISHOP CRANMER, PREBENDARY
OF CANTERBURY, &c.

WITH OTHER PIECES WRITTEN BY HIM IN THE
REIGN OF KING EDWARD THE SIXTH.

WIPF & STOCK · Eugene, Oregon

Wipf and Stock Publishers
199 W 8th Ave, Suite 3
Eugene, OR 97401

The Catechism of Thomas Becon, S.T.P. Chaplain to Archbishop Cranmer, Presbendary of Canterbury, &c.
With Other Pieces Written by Him in the Reign of King Edward the Sixth.
By Becon, Thomas
ISBN 13: 978-1-60608-437-3
Publication date 7/9/2009
Previously published by Cambridge University Press, 1844

CONTENTS.

PAGE

The Catechism 1

The Jewel of Joy 411

The Principles of Christian Religion 477

A Fruitful Treatise of Fasting 523

The Castle of Comfort 552

The Solace of the Soul 569

The Fortress of the Faithful 581

The Christian Knight 620

An Homily against Whoredom 641

ERRATA AND ADDENDA.

PAGE

116 margin, *for* A go, *read* A good.
253 note 9 line 3 from end, *for* Tit. lxi. *read* Tit. xli.
256 All the references in note 2 may be found Cassandr. Op. Par. 1616. Liturg. cap. xxvi. pp. 55, 6.
273 note 2 line 7, *insert* Alex. The passage referred to was more probably the following: Sed diligenter hic animadvertendum, quod etsi corporis sui præsentiam hinc subduxerit, majestate tamen divinitatis semper adest: sicut ipse a discipulis abiturus pollicetur: Ecce ego vobiscum sum omnibus diebus usque ad consummationem seculi.—Cyril. Alex. Op. Lat. Par. 1604-5. In Joan. Evang. Lib. VI. cap. xiv. Tom. I. p. 562.
284 note 4 lines 3, 8—10, *transpose* Ibid. and Decret. &c.
288 note 8 line 4, *insert* Tom. IV.
289 note 9 line 9, *for* Theophyl. *read* Theophil.
535 note 3 line 3 from end, *read* putatur.
578 last line but 1, *omit* [which].

A NEW CATECHISM,

SET FORTH

DIALOGUE-WISE IN FAMILIAR TALK BETWEEN THE FATHER AND THE SON,

MADE BY

THOMAS BECON.

DIEU ET MON DROIT

¶ A new Catechisme sette forth Dialoge wise in familiare talke betwene the father and the son, lately made and now fyrst of all published by Thomas Becon.

Psal. xxxiiii.

O come hither ye children, and heare me: for I wil teache you the feare of the Lorde.

Deute. xxxii.

Set your hartes vpon all the wordes, which I testify vnto you this day, and ye shall commaunde them vnto your children, that they may obserue, and do al the woordes of this lawe.

Ephe. vi.

Ye Fathers prouoke not your children to wrath: but bryng them vp in the doctrine and informacion of the Lord.

ARISE FOR IT IS DAY.

TO THE READER THE BOOK SPEAKETH.

Though I be small in quantity,
Yet despise me not, good reader;
For perchance thou shalt find in me
That wanteth in many greater.

Though I be without eloquence,
Rude and barbarous to behold,
Yet much true divine sapience
Have I forth brought, and here enroll'd.

No subtile logic, nor sophistry,
Shalt thou in me find and perceive;
But Christ and his doctrine plainly,
Which can no man living deceive.

To teach thee Christ is mine intent,
And all that to him do belong,
That thou mayest keep his commandment,
And in the christian faith be strong.

Approach, therefore, O gentle reader,
Pray to God for understanding;
So shalt thou in all things prosper,
And enjoy life everlasting.

Mark x.

¶ Suffer the children to come unto me: forbid them not. For unto such doth the kingdom of God appertain.

THE

PREFACE OF THE AUTHOR

UNTO HIS CHILDREN,

THEODORE AND BASIL HIS TWO SONS, AND RACHEL HIS ONLY DAUGHTER[1]:

GRACE, MERCY, AND PEACE, FROM GOD THE FATHER, AND FROM THE LORD JESUS CHRIST OUR LORD AND ALONE SAVIOUR, THROUGH THE MIGHTY OPERATION OF THE HOLY GHOST, BE WITH YOU, MY DEAR CHILDREN, BOTH NOW AND EVER. AMEN.

AFTER that it pleased the Lord my God to call me unto the holy state of honourable matrimony, and to bless me with the increase of you, not of you only, but also of two more your brethren, named Theodore and Christophile, which now rest in glory with our head Christ; I thought no charge more straitly to be laid upon me of the Lord our God, than with all diligence to provide and aforesee, that you, my most dear and sweet children, may be brought up, even from your very cradles (as they use to say), in the knowledge and doctrine of the one alone true and everlasting God, and of his Son Christ Jesus, our most mighty Lord and alone sufficient Saviour: which knowledge, learned out of the holy scriptures, bringeth to the faithful believers everlasting life.

John xvii. Wisd. xv.

And as I judged this to be my duty and office committed unto me of God, if I would in any point answer his good will and pleasure, and satisfy my vocation or calling; so likewise to the uttermost of my power I have ever travailed godly and virtuously to bring you up in the knowledge of God and of his holy word, even from your tender years, that at the last you, being now young children, may wax ancient in Christ, and through him obtain everlasting life.

Rom. vi.

Wicked parents.

For in mine opinion, howsoever the wicked world judgeth in this behalf, those fathers, which only study to enrich their children with worldly possessions, and neglect their duty in the virtuous education and godly bringing up of their youth, are rather to be counted fathers of the body than of the mind, of the flesh than of the soul, and may right well be resembled, likened, and compared to unreasonable and brute beasts, which are also led with this care, and so affected toward their younglings, that with all diligence they travail and labour for the fostering and feeding of them, by this means providing that they lack nothing concerning the safe state and harmless conservation of the body. These parents are beastly parents: these fathers and mothers are ungodly fathers and mothers, and altogether unworthy of this great blessing of God, I mean the gift of children, whom God hath given unto them for this purpose and end, that they in this world should be godly and virtuously brought up in the doctrine and knowledge of his holy word, lead a good life, call on his holy name, be thankful for his benefits, study to profit the commonweal, and to do good to all men; that, when they shall be called out from this vale of misery, they may be made citizens of the heavenly kingdom, and there for ever reign and remain with their head Christ, in the glory of his Father. And would God we had not too too many of these ungodly parents in this our age! Verily unto such corruption of manners and lewd disposition of life are we come now-a-days, that all parents almost seek rather how to avance their children in worldly than in godly things; how to beautify them rather with the vain and flitting goods of the corruptible body, than with the true, constant, and immortal goods of the uncorruptible mind; how to get them rather the favour of men, than the good will of God; how they may increase rather in worldly studies, than in the knowledge of God; and in fine, how they may rather become in this world men of great renown and of innumerable possessions, than after this life glorious and well-accepted citizens of that most glorious

To what end God giveth children.

[[1] The principal part of the information we have of Becon's family is obtained from this preface. The biographical memoir of him prefixed to the former volume of his works may be consulted, p. xiv.]

and heavenly kingdom. Certes the greatest multitude of our parents at this day, although they profess Christ, and glory to be called Christians, are much inferior to the heathen, which knew not God nor any point of godliness rightly, if we should respect the good and virtuous bringing up of youth.

To whom is this unknown, that the very gentiles spared neither cost nor labour that their children might be brought up learnedly and virtuously, and at the last become worthy citizens of the commonweal? Read we not, that when it was objected unto Lycurgus, that noble prince of the Lacedemonians, that he gave too much a liberal stipend to the teacher and bringer up of his children, he answered on this manner: "If any man will take upon him to bring up my children, and to render them unto me better than he received them, I will not only give him large sums of money, but also the half of all my goods"? Read we not, that Philip, king of the Macedonians, when his son Alexander was born, wrote letters unto Aristotle, the philosopher, in the which he gave thanks unto God, not only because he had given him a son, which should succeed him in his kingdom, but also that it chanced him to be born in the time of so noble a philosopher, which should bring him up in virtue, learning, and knowledge, and make him a prince worthy of such a father and of so flourishing a kingdom[2]? Read we not, that a certain noble woman of Rome, called Cornelia, when a strange lady, which lodged in her house, shewed unto her her ornaments and jewels, yea, and those so precious and goodly as none could be found more precious nor more goodly, prolonged the talk with her until her children came home from school, and then brast out into these words, *Et hæc ornamenta mea sunt*[3]? That is in English: "And these," saith she, "are my ornaments and jewels;" signifying by this her answer, that nothing is so precious and goodly a jewel to a discreet, wise, and sober matron, as children virtuously and learnedly brought up. Read we not, that when Alphonsus, king of the Aragones, was demanded how it came to pass that he had so flourishing a realm, whether it was that he was so excellently learned, or of so good success in martial affairs, whereof he also had singular knowledge, he answered on this manner: "Of books I learned both armours and the law of armours[4]"?—hereby confessing, that learning was the alone occasion of all his good success and of so flourishing a commonweal: so truly is it said of Plato, that blessed, fortunate, and happy is that commonweal, wherein either philosophers do bear rule, or else kings that be studious of philosophy and of good letters do reign.

[Margin: The earnest study of the gentiles for the virtuous bringing up of their youth. Lycurgus. — Philip, king of the Macedonians. — Cornelia. — Alphonsus, king of the Aragones. — Plato.]

But wherefore do I tarry so long in rehearsing these profane and heathenish histories concerning the good and virtuous bringing up of youth, seeing that in the holy bible, which containeth the words of everlasting life, examples do abound?

As I may pass over with silence those holy, grave, and ancient patriarchs, Adam, Seth, Enos, Henoch, Noha, Thare, Abraham, Isaac, Jacob, Joseph, &c., which lived before Moses, of whose industry and diligence in the godly and virtuous bringing up of their younglings to doubt, I think it more than double wickedness; who is able to express what study and care that most excellent and prince-like prophet David, the most worthy and most noble grandfather of our Lord and alone Saviour Jesu Christ, took for the godly and honest education of his children, specially of Salomon, that for his godliness, learning, and wisdom he might be counted of all men worthy to enjoy the imperial crown after him? He was so diligent in exhorting his son Salomon unto virtue and true religion, that, lying upon his death-bed, he ceased not continually to put him in remembrance of his duty toward the Lord his God. Among other were not these his words: "I go the way of all the world: be strong therefore, and shew thyself a man. Keep thou the watch of the Lord thy God, and see that thou walk in his ways, and keep his statutes and his precepts, his judgments and his testimonies, even as it is written in the law of Moses, that thou mayest prosper in all that thou doest, and in every thing that thou meddlest withal; that the Lord also may make good his word, which he spake unto me, saying, If thy children take

[Margin: The earnest study of God's people in times past for the godly bringing up of their children. David, king of Israel. — 1 Kings ii.]

[[2] A. Gell. Noctes Attic. Lib. IX. cap. iii.]

[[3] Valer. Max. Lib. IV. cap. iv. 1.]

[[4] Alphonso V.—Anton. Panorm. De Dict. et Fact. Alphons. Reg. Arag. et Neap. Witeb. 1585. Lib. IV. 19. p. 87. It is to this monarch that a saying, erroneously attributed in the former volume, p. 398, to the king of Castile, really belongs.]

heed to their way, that they walk before me in truth with all their hearts, and with all their souls, then shalt thou not be without a man on the seat of Israel, &c."

Tobias. Tob. i. [Vulgate] Tob. iv.

Tobias also, that ancient father and faithful servant of God, taught his young son Tobias, even from his tender age, to fear God, and to refrain from all sin. His admonitions which he gave to his son are so godly and profitable, so avancing virtue and repressing vice, that they may justly seem worthy to be written in letters of gold; and would God they were so surely graven in the hearts of all men that they might never fall out of remembrance!

Hist. Sus. The parents of Susanna.

The noble parents likewise of that most noble lady Susanna, beautiful in body, but more beautiful in mind, goodly in the lineaments of the body, but more goodly in the virtues of the soul, brought up their aforesaid daughter Susanna, from her very young age, in all godliness and honesty according to the law of God given by Moses: which godly, virtuous, and honest bringing up so greatly prevailed in her, that she rather choosed to suffer any kind of cruel torments, yea, most cruel death, than she would once turn aside from those godly lessons and virtuous instructions which she had learned of her godly and virtuous parents in her young and tender years; so profitable a thing is it even from the very cradles, as they use to say, to drink in godliness and honesty.

Acts xxi. Philip the evangelist.

But what shall I speak of Philip the evangelist, which, having four daughters, brought them up so godly and learnedly that they were able to prophesy, that is to say, to understand the holy scriptures according to the meaning of the Holy Ghost, and to render a perfect accompt of their faith in Christ Jesu our Lord? I pass over

Timothy. 2 Tim. iii.

the godly bringing up of bishop Timothy, which from his very infancy and childhood learned and understood, as St Paul writeth, the holy scriptures, which alone are "able sufficiently and even to the uttermost to instruct the man of God unto salvation through faith in Christ Jesu."

Many and divers other histories are contained in the holy scriptures, which abundantly remember what studious diligence and diligent study, what painful labour and laborous pain, the holy fathers in times past did take to bring up their children

Deut. iv. xi. Ecclus. vii. x. xxx. xlii. Eph. vi. Col. iii. Tit. ii.

godly and honestly according to the doctrine and commandment of the Lord our God, that they might truly be counted fathers not only of the body, but also of the mind, and by this means satisfy the good pleasure of God, which requireth nothing more earnestly of fathers and mothers, than that they should godly and holily bring up their children which he hath given them, that not only in this world, but in the world to come, they may celebrate, praise, and magnify his holy and glorious name.

Provoked with these and such like examples, my most dear and sweet children, I have done mine endeavour to the uttermost of my power, from time to time, as your age requireth, to sow in your tender breasts the wholesome seed of God's most holy word, that from your very cradles ye may learn to know your Lord God, which made you and gave you unto me, which also conserveth and nourisheth you by me; and to believe in him the alone true God; to call on his holy name, from whom

James i.

alone cometh all goodness; to fear and reverence him as your most beneficial Lord; to love him as your most gentle and kind Father; to be thankful unto him for his benefits as your most bounteous and merciful Saviour; and to reverence and honour the magistrates and all that be in authority; again, to shew yourselves humble, lowly, and obedient to the faithful ministers of God's holy word: Item, to be gentle, loving, and helping to all men; and in fine, so to train your lives according to the rule of God's holy commandment, that, in this world being good and profitable members of the christian commonweal, in the world to come ye may be made citizens of that glorious and heavenly kingdom. And according to this my doctrine, yea, rather God's doctrine, ye for your little strengths daily do your endeavour to bring forth the fruits of this good seed, which, by the help of God's Spirit, I have sown in your young and tender breasts: which thing delighteth me so greatly, that I can none otherwise than daily offer unto God the sacrifice of praise and thanksgiving, which by his Holy Spirit hath wrought so good things in you, yea, and that in so young and tender age; most humbly beseeching him to continue his fatherly favour toward you, that he may bring unto a fortunate and blessed end that which he most mercifully hath begun in you, unto the glory and praise of his holy name.

And forasmuch as I your father, from my youth up even unto this day, have ever been attempted with the cruel assaults of envious fortune, which for the most part is always an unmerciful stepdame to all such as are truly studious of virtue and learning, and contrariwise a bounteous mistress to such as are dissolute and careless livers, without all fear of God, without all care of godliness, without all honest and godly disposition, &c.; and by this means have no worldly possessions to leave unto you, whereby ye may be the more able to resist the fierce and cruel darts of froward, frowning fortune; I, in this behalf leaving you to the merciful and bounteous providence of God, which never leaveth them succourless that cleave unto him with strong faith, and labour to "serve him in holiness and righteousness all the days of their life," have thought it good to study how I may enrich you, not with the flitting goods of fliring[1] fortune, or with the trifling treasures of the wicked world, (after the which all degrees of people in this our age, without exception, run headlong, and so inordinately hunt after them, as though they should continue in this vale of misery for ever, utterly forgetting that they are "strangers and pilgrims," and can "have no long abode here," but must give over to nature and depart hence, as their ancestors and elders have done before them, and leave their pelf, for the which they have so swinked[2] and sweat, they cannot tell to whom, as we read in the gospel of a certain ungodly rich man; and as the psalmograph saith, the covetous, rich worldling "heapeth treasure upon treasure, and knoweth not for whom he gathereth his treasure";) but with such riches, goods, treasures, and possessions, as neither fire can bren, nor water overwhelm, nor wind blow away, nor tempest disquiet, nor old age consume, nor froward fortune remove, neither any adversity put to flight; I mean the goods and riches of the mind; as doctrine, learning, knowledge, the right understanding of the holy scriptures, sincerity of judgment, wisdom, discretion, and such other godly and virtuous qualities, wherewith whosoever is endued, he may worthily be counted rich, although he were utterly destitute and void of all those things which the madness of men hath in these our days in so great admiration and price; yea, where these honourable treasures of the mind are, there the frail goods of most frail fortune offer themselves, and willingly give their service, not suffering the possessor of them extremely to lack, as divers histories do evidently declare.

B. and Dr. Luke i.

The insatiable covetousness of this our age.

1 Pet. ii. Heb. xiii.

Luke xii. Psal. xxxix.

Therefore to the end that you may the more plentifully abound with these immortal, constant, and unmoveable riches, and by this means become richer than king Crœsus, even in the midst of your poverty; I thought it not unseemly, nor unworthy either of my vocation or of your young years, to give unto you this little book, which of late I made; wherein is contained whatsoever is necessarily required unto the perfect instruction of a christian man; that you, exercising yourselves diligently in the reading of it, may become learned in the rules of your profession, and attain unto such knowledge of God's doctrine in this your tender age, that at the last ye may become ancient and perfect in Christ, and so in fine obtain that which is the end of our hope, I mean everlasting felicity.

This book I commend unto you, my most sweet and dear children, as a noble and singular treasure, profitable both for the body and for the soul, and necessary for the right institution of your life: according to the doctrine whereof if you frame your life, ye shall not only wax and become learned in your profession (whereof to be ignorant is too much ungodliness), but also not attempt any thing at any time that shall either be displeasant to God, or to godly men, or to yourselves.

Take it, therefore, with joyful hearts as a testimony of your father's good will toward you; yea, receive it as your patrimony, left of your father unto you, which otherwise is not able to enrich you; and glory no less in this my gift, than other children do in the riches of this world. And I shall most humbly beseech God to be your father and defender, and to give you his Holy Spirit, which may govern you in all your doings, that ye may walk blameless in his sight, and be found in the number of God's elect.

The Lord Jesus Christ be with your spirit! Amen.

[[1] Fliring: fleering.] [[2] Swinked: laboured, toiled.]

THE CATECHISM,

SET FORTH

DIALOGUE-WISE IN FAMILIAR TALK BETWEEN THE FATHER AND THE SON.

Deut. iv. xi. *Father*. FORASMUCH, my dear child, as all parents are commanded of God diligently
Ecclus. vii. x. xxx. xlii. to bring up their children in the knowledge of his most holy and blessed will, that
Eph. vi. Col. iii. they, even from their very cradles, may learn to fear God and to walk in his ways,
Tit. ii. neither declining on the right hand nor on the left; I have, to the uttermost of my power, not only by myself, but also by other godly and virtuous learned men, (as I may speak nothing of my diligence in bringing thee unto the temple to hear the preachings of God's law, and the godly prayers which are there used unto the glory of God and the edifying of such as be present, whereby thy knowledge in the Lord's ordinances may not only be confirmed, but also increased,) travailed to bring thee up even from thy very infancy and tender age in the doctrine of holy letters; following in this behalf not only the commandment of God, but also the examples both of the ancient patriarchs and of many other godly men, whose names as they be registered in the book of life, so likewise are they honourably remembered in the holy bible. Wherefore my desire is at this present to have some taste, by familiar talk between thee and me, of thy knowledge in the Lord Jesu, and how thou hast profited in matters of everlasting life; that by this means I may know whether thou hast satisfied my expectation, and no less prospered in the study of godliness, than my opinion is that thou hast done.

Son. I can none otherwise, most loving father, than acknowledge and confess your fatherly good will toward me, which have neither spared labour nor cost to bring me unto the knowledge of God, and of my salvation in the Lord Jesu.

Father. Son, that hath been ever my desire. For he is not worthy the name
Psal. xxxii. of a christian man, but rather may justly be resembled to "an horse or mule," that have not this knowledge.

John xvii. "This is everlasting life," saith our Saviour Christ, "that they know thee (that thou only art the true God), and whom thou hast sent, Jesus Christ." Hereto pertaineth
Wisd. xv. the saying of the wise man: "To know thee, O God, is perfect righteousness; yea,
Wisd. xiii. to know thy righteousness and power is the root of immortality." "Vain are all men,
Matt. xxii. which have not the knowledge of God." "Ye err," said Christ to the Sadducees,
John v. "because ye know not the scriptures." Again: "Search the scriptures, for ye think ye have everlasting life in them, and the same are they which testify of me; and ye will not come unto me, that ye might have life."

But come off, let me now have some experience of thy good success in matters of christian religion.

Son. I am ready, most gentle father, at your commandment. Only I shall most humbly desire you to consider my young age, and the small continuance which, by the reason of my few and tender years, I have had in the studies both of godliness and letters.

Father. This thing is not unknown unto me. Thy age is young, thy years are few, thy continuance in study is small, for as yet art thou not six years old. Therefore my mind is only at this present to talk with thee, not of things which far exceed both thy age and capacity, but of such matters as be meet for children to know, wherein also thou hast heretofore (as thy age hath suffered) been exercised, both by me thy father, and also by the preacher, and by thy schoolmaster.

Son. Do you mean such matters, as be contained in my catechism? *Father*. The very same. *Son*. If it shall be your good pleasure to examine me in them, I trust, by the help of God and by the assistance of his Holy Spirit, to make such answers as shall not only not displease you, but also most highly please you, content your mind, and satisfy your expectation; so that you shall think both your labour and cost to have been not unfruitfully employed and bestowed upon me.

Father. If thou performest no less in deed than thou promisest in word, thou shalt not only content me, but also deserve at my hand both praise and a continuance of my fatherly favour and liberality toward thee. And forasmuch as our whole communication at this time shall be altogether of the doctrine contained in the catechism, I first of all demand of thee, what thou meanest by this word *Catechism.* For many have this word *Catechism* in their mouth, but few understand what it meaneth.

Son. As I remember, I heard our schoolmaster say, that it is a Greek word, and signifieth a doctrine taught of the wise and learned to the younglings of Christ's religion, in the which, after a brief and goodly order, is comprehended whatsoever is necessarily required unto the right institution of a christian man; so that whosoever hath and understandeth this doctrine, hath and understandeth the whole sum of all things necessary unto salvation contained in the old or new testament. What this word *catechism* signifieth.

Father. Is not this kind of teaching younglings new, and lately invented? *Son.* No, verily. It is rather old, and of long time used in the church of Christ, as the monuments of the ancient writers testify. For in the primitive church there were not only bishops and pastors that preached the gospel of Christ to the people, which were already graffed by baptism and the Holy Ghost in Christ Jesu, but also certain teachers, called *catechistæ*[1], which taught not only the young children that were already baptized, but also such as being in age came and were contented to forsake gentility and to take upon them christianity, and to turn from idolatry unto the worshipping of that one and alone true, living, immortal, and everlasting God, the principles of christian religion, before they received baptism, and were openly admitted into the congregation of the faithful. And as these teachers were called *catechistæ*, that is to say, instructors, or teachers; so likewise were the younglings called *catechumeni*, that is to say, persons instructed or taught. And the office of the catechist was not only to instruct and teach, but also to examine such as they taught how they profited and increased in the knowledge of God's mysteries; and if they failed in any point, diligently to instruct and teach them, till they were well exercised in the doctrine of Christ. The custom of teaching the catechism is old and ancient.

Father. They then do evil which report, that the teaching of the catechism, that is to say, the elements or principles of Christ's doctrine, to the young lambs of Christ's flock, I mean the children, is a late invention, and newly crept into the church of Christ, through the device of certain backsliders and runaways from the catholic church. *Son.* The true catholic and apostolic church hath had the catechism taught in it from the beginning. It is no late invention, but before many hundred years used of Christ and of his apostles, and also of the ancient fathers, both in the Greek and Latin church. Of this kind of teaching speaketh St Paul in his epistle unto the Galatians on this manner: "Let him that is taught with the word minister in all good things unto him that teacheth him." Gal. vi

Father. Let this suffice concerning this word catechism. Declare now unto me of how many parts the doctrine of the catechism consisteth. *Son.* Of six parts. The parts of the catechism.

Father. Which are they? *Son.* Repentance, faith, law, prayer, sacraments, and the offices of all degrees.

Father. Is the whole sum of Christ's doctrine contained in these six parts? *Son.* Yea, verily.

[1 The office or duty of the catechists, in the primitive church, was precise and well-defined; but it does not appear that they were a distinct *order*. See Bingham, Orig. Eccles. Book III. chap. x.]

THE FIRST PART OF THE CATECHISM.

OF REPENTANCE.

Repentance. *Father*. AND is repentance the first part of that doctrine which is taught in the catechism? *Son*. So have I learned. For our catechist declared unto us, that, when John Baptist, Christ, and his apostles began to teach, they preached first of all repentance.

Father. Where readest thou that John Baptist began his doctrine of repentance? *Son*. In the third chapter of St Matthew's gospel, where we read on this manner:
Matt. iii. "In those days came John Baptist preaching in the wilderness of Jewry, and saying, Repent, for the kingdom of heaven is at hand." Again, in the first chapter of blessed
Mark i. Mark: "John baptized in the wilderness, preaching the baptism," that is to say, the doctrine, "of repentance unto the remission of sins." The very same thing read we in
Luke iii. the gospel of Luke.

Father. Began Christ also his preaching of repentance? *Son*. So write the
Matt. iv. evangelists. Matthew hath in his gospel thus: "Jesus began to preach and to say,
Mark i. Repent, for the kingdom of heaven is at hand." Mark hath these words: "Jesus came into Galilee, preaching the gospel of the kingdom of God, and saying, The time is fulfilled, and the kingdom of God is at hand: repent, and believe the gospel." Hereof learn we, that both John Baptist and Christ began their preaching of repent-
Luke xxiv. ance. And in the gospel of Luke we read, that Christ gave in commandment to his disciples, that they should preach repentance and forgiveness of sins unto all nations. And according to the commandment of Christ the apostles taught. For in the Acts of the Apostles we read that, when Peter laid their sins before the Jews, they were greatly dismayed and stricken with an inward sorrow, so that they brast out into
Acts ii. these words: "Ye men and brethren, what shall we do? Peter said unto them, Repent ye of your sins, and be baptized every one of you in the name of Jesus Christ for the remission of sins, and ye shall receive the gift of the Holy Ghost." Again:
Acts iii. "Repent, and turn, that your sins may be put away." In another place of the same
Acts xxvi. book we read, that St Paul maketh mention of his doctrine which he taught "to the Jews and to the gentiles, which is, that they should repent, turn unto God, and do works worthy such as do repent." All these testimonies of the holy scripture do abundantly declare, that the doctrine of repentance ought to have the first place in the institution of a christian man, if we will observe that order which John Baptist, Christ with his apostles, and St Paul used.

What repentance is. *Father*. What is repentance? *Son*. Repentance is an inward and true sorrow of the heart, unfeignedly conceived in the mind by earnest consideration of our sins and wickednesses, which heretofore most unkindly we have committed against the Lord our God, of whom we have freely received so many, so great, and so noble benefits, with a perfect detestation and utter abhorring of our former wicked life; whereunto is also added a fervent and inward desire from henceforth to live godly and virtuously, and to frame our life in all points according to the holy will of God expressed in the divine scriptures. Of this repentance speaketh St Paul in his second epistle to the
2 Cor. vii. Corinthians on this manner: "A godly sorrow causeth repentance unto salvation, not to be repented of; when the worldly sorrow causeth death. For behold this thing, what diligence this godly sorrow that ye took hath wrought in you; yea, it causeth you to clear yourselves: it caused indignation, it caused fear, it caused desire, it caused a fervent mind, it caused punishment."

Father. Thou confessest then the doctrine of repentance to be necessary for the right institution of a christian man? *Son*. Yea, so necessary, that without it the other parts of christian doctrine do not much profit.

For the doctrine of repentance bringeth a man unto the knowledge of himself, without the which no man shall ever know God aright, nor his salvation, which he re-
Matt. ix. ceiveth of God through Jesus Christ. "I came not," saith Christ, "to call the right-

eous, but sinners unto repentance." "For such as are whole need no physician, but they that are sick." What brought the people of Israel, David, Manasses, Mary Magdalene, &c. unto the knowledge of themselves and of their sins, and enforced them to run unto God for mercy, but the doctrine of repentance? The doctrine of repentance setteth before the sinner the greatness and weight of his sins, the heavy anger of God against the sinner for his sin, everlasting damnation for committing the sin, and so combereth the conscience of the sinner with the terrors of God's judgment, that in himself he can find no rest, no ease, no consolation, no remedy; but is compelled with all humility and submission of mind to confess his sin, to grant himself a most damnable sinner, and to seek comfort not of himself, nor of his own good works, but of God and of his great mercies. The fruit of the doctrine of repentance.

Moreover, the doctrine of repentance enarmeth a man against the assaults of Satan, against the enticements of the flesh, against the pleasures of the world, against the sting of sin, against the dart of desperation, and admonisheth him afterward so warily and circumspectly to live, that he fall no more into the same sins, nor be snarled again with the like snares; but rather from henceforth so frame his life, that he shall not need to be combered with the like shame and sorrow for committing the like wickedness, while he endeavoureth himself to the uttermost of his power to garnish his conversation with all kind of spiritual virtues and godly works, as St John Baptist saith: "Bring forth fruits worthy of repentance." "For even now is the axe laid at the Matt. iii.
root of the tree: every tree that bringeth not forth good fruit is hewn up and cast into the fire.'

Father. They then that truly and with a faithful heart receive this doctrine of repentance, whereof thou hast hitherto spoken, are not excluded from the grace, favour, and mercy of God, but may well persuade themselves to receive remission of sins, and to be made inheritors of everlasting glory. *Son.* Yea, verily. For thus saith God himself by the prophet: "As surely as I live, I desire not the death of a sinner, Ezek. xxxiii.
but rather that he should turn and live." And the prophet Esay saith: "Let the Isai. lv.
ungodly man forsake his own ways, and the unrighteous his own imaginations, and turn again unto the Lord; so shall he be merciful unto him. For he is such a God as is ready to forgive." "If the ungodly," saith God by the prophet Ezechiel, "will turn away Ezek. xviii.
from all his sins that he hath done, and keep all my commandments, and do the thing that is equal and right, doubtless he shall live and not die. As for all his sins that he did before, they shall not be thought upon, but in his righteousness that he hath done he shall live. For have I any pleasure in the death of a sinner, saith the Lord God, and not rather that he should convert and live?" "Be converted, and turn you from all your wickedness; so shall there no sin do you harm. Cast away from you all your ungodliness that ye have done. Make you new hearts and a new spirit. Wherefore will ye die, O ye house of Israel, seeing I have no pleasure in the death of him that dieth, saith the Lord God? Turn ye then, and ye shall live." Doth not Christ in the gospel call lovingly unto him all such as be diseased and Matt. xi.
laden with the burden of sin, and promise that he will ease and comfort them? Saith he not that he came "to save such as were lost"? What other thing do we learn Luke xix.
of the parables of the lost sheep and of the prodigal son, than that sinners repenting be received unto mercy and favour? And are not these Christ's words? "I say Luke xv.
unto you, that there shall be joy in heaven before the angels of God over one sinner, more than over ninety and nine righteous that need no repentance." There is no sin that giveth not place to repentance.

Such as sin and afterward repent are not excluded from grace and remission of their sins.

Father. And is this repentance the gift of nature or of grace? *Son.* It is the gift of God, and cometh not of ourselves. For what good thing either have we, or can we do, except we first receive it of God? This testifieth St Paul, saying: "What 1 Cor. iv.
hast thou that thou hast not received? If thou hast received it, why dost thou glory as though thou hadst not received it?" Hereto pertaineth the saying of St James: "Every good gift and every perfect gift is from above, and cometh down James i.
from the Father of lights." Forasmuch therefore as repentance is a good gift, therefore cometh it from God. Repentance is the gift of God.

Father. Came the repentance of Caim, Esau, Saul, Judas, and such like, from

The repentance of the reprobate is no true repentance. 2 Cor. vii.

God also? *Son.* It came from themselves, and from the devil, author of all sin and wickedness. For this repentance leadeth unto desperation and finally unto damnation, and is that "worldly sorrow," which, as St Paul writeth, "causeth death." But that repentance, which is wrought by the Spirit of God in the hearts of men, doth not only contain in it an hearty sorrow for the sin committed, with an earnest intent and full purpose to live from henceforth according to the will of God, but also an assured faith and undoubted persuasion that God for our mediator Jesu Christ's sake will be merciful unto us, forgive us our sins, and make us inheritors of everlasting glory. And this repentance, I say, cometh not of ourselves, but it is the gift of God.

True repentance hath faith to her companion. True repentance is the gift of God.

Father. Prove that by the word of God. *Son.* By the prophet Ezechiel God speaketh on this manner: "I will pour clean water upon you, and ye shall be clean; yea, from all your uncleannesses and from all your idols shall I cleanse you. A new heart also will I give you, and a new spirit will I put into you. As for that stony heart, I will take it out of your body, and give you a fleshly heart. I will give you my Spirit among you, and cause you to walk in my commandments, to keep my laws, and to fulfil them. And ye shall be my people; and I will be your God." The prophet Jeremy prayeth on this manner: "Convert thou me, O Lord, and I shall be converted; for thou art my Lord God. As soon as thou turnedst me I repented, and as soon as thou shewedst me my sins, I smote my thigh: yea, I was confounded and right greatly ashamed." Again: "O Lord, turn thou us unto thee, and so shall we be turned." St Paul, in his epistle unto Timothy, by most manifest and expressed words sheweth repentance to be the gift of God. "The servant of God," saith he, "must inform them that resist, if that God at any time will give them repentance, for to know the truth, and that they may come to themselves again out of the snare of the devil, which are holden captive of him at his will."

Ezek. xxxvi. Jer. xxxi. Lam. v. 2 Tim. ii.

Father. That therefore is the alone true repentance, which, being the gift of God, and wrought in the hearts of men by the Holy Ghost, doth not only contain in it an inward sorrow of the mind for the sins tofore committed against God, with a full determined purpose from henceforth to amend and to lead a new life, but also a perfect faith to be forgiven for Christ's sake. *Son.* Repentance not accompanied with faith driveth rather unto desperation than unto salvation; as we may see in Caim, Esau, Saul, Judas, and in such like. But repentance combined with faith lifteth up the wearied and cast down soul, comforteth the troubled heart, rejoiceth the sorrowful mind, and quieteth the restless conscience; as we have for examples in the holy scripture David, Manasses, Mary Magdalene, Peter, &c. And therefore in a most goodly and seemly order followeth the second part of the doctrine of the Catechism, which entreateth of faith. For after the doctrine of repentance, the doctrine of faith necessarily is to be set forth unto such as will be rightly and truly instructed in the rules of christianity.

THE SECOND PART OF THE CATECHISM.

OF FAITH.

Father. Observed Christ and his apostles that order of teaching also? *Son.* So teach the evangelical history. For Christ began his preaching on this manner: "Repent, and believe the gospel." Mark i.

First he taught repentance, and afterward faith. And after his resurrection, when he sent forth his apostles to preach, he commanded them to "preach in his name repentance and remission of sins to all nations." Luke xxiv. What other thing is it to preach remission of sins, than to publish and set forth the doctrine of faith, which faith alone obtaineth the favour of God and forgiveness of sin? What it is to preach remission of sins. Where faith in the Son of God is, there is everlasting life; but where this faith is not, there is eternal death and damnation, as the scripture saith: "He that believeth on the Son (of God) hath everlasting life; but he that believeth not on the Son (of God) shall not see life, but the wrath of God abideth upon him." John iii.

And according to this commandment of their Master Christ, the apostles observed and kept this order of teaching in their sermons. The order of the apostles' doctrine. First they taught repentance, and afterward faith, as we may see in the chronicle of the apostles' acts, where we read that St Peter answered to this demand of the Jews, "What shall we do, ye men and brethren?" Acts ii. on this manner: "Repent ye of your sins, and let every one of you be baptized in the name of Jesu Christ," &c. What is it to be baptized in the name of Jesus Christ, What it is to be baptized in the name of Christ. but first stedfastly to believe, and undoubtedly to be persuaded that through the might and power of Christ our sins be forgiven, and we received and taken into the number of God's sons; and afterward in token of this grace and favour, which we through faith have obtained of God, to receive the sacrament of baptism, whereby we do profess that we pertain no more unto the kingdom of Satan, but unto the kingdom of Christ, and will from henceforth serve him, and seek his glory all the days of our life? Again, in the same book: "Repent and turn, that your sins may be put away." Acts iii. Is it any other thing to turn, than to forsake incredulity and to believe, than to cast away the service of idols and to serve the living God in such "holiness and righteousness," Luke i. as are accepted before him? In another place of the same book we read, that St Paul taught "repentance toward God and faith toward our Lord Jesus Christ." Acts xx. And in his epistle to the Hebrews, where he maketh mention of the principles of christian religion, he first of all nameth repentance, and afterward faith. His words are these: "Let us leave the doctrine pertaining to the beginning of a christian man, Heb. vi. and let us go unto perfection, and now no more lay the foundation of repentance from dead works, and of faith toward God, of baptism, of doctrine, and of laying on of hands, and of resurrection from death, and of eternal judgment."

Thus see we, that the order which Christ and his apostles observed in their sermons was first to teach the doctrine of repentance, and then of faith.

Father. Let this suffice for the order of the doctrine contained in the catechism. Tell me now what faith is. *Son.* "Faith," as the apostle defineth it, "is a sure confidence of things which are hoped for, and a certainty of things which are not seen." Heb. xi.

Father. This definition seemeth to be somewhat hard. What teacheth the apostle here? *Son.* Verily, that faith is a certain, assured, and an undoubted persuasion of the mind, What faith is. conceived of the word of God through the operation of the Holy Ghost, concerning the performance and enjoying of such heavenly things as God hath promised in his holy scriptures to the faithful. Which things although reason cannot comprehend them, yet faith embraceth them, and believeth them to be most true and most certain; nothing doubting but that God in his time will most assuredly accomplish, perform, and bring to pass whatsoever he hath promised.

Father. But what are those things which, being not seen, are hoped for? *Son.* The things which are not seen, and yet be hoped and looked for of the faithful

at God's hand, are deliverance from the tyranny of Satan, from the curse of the law, and from everlasting damnation, remission of sins, the gift of the Holy Ghost, hearing and granting of our prayers, regeneration unto a new birth, justification, resurrection of the dead, everlasting life, and whatsoever good, godly, precious, heavenly, comfortable, and glorious things are promised us of God in the holy scriptures. These
1 Cor. ii. things "the natural and unregenerate man understandeth not, neither can he comprehend them;" but faith, wrought in our hearts by the Holy Ghost, without any doubting believeth, hopeth, and looketh for the very same things, nothing despairing but that God, which in his holy word hath mercifully promised these things, as he is able, so will most liberally perform the same things in his time, although reason, which is altogether blind in matters of God, seeth not how it may be brought to pass.

Faith is the gift of God. 2 Cor. iii. *Father.* Cometh not faith then of ourselves, but it is rather the gift of God? *Son.* Of ourself? What cometh of ourselves that good is, which are not able of ourselves
Hos. xiii. once to think a good thought? Our destruction cometh of ourselves, but our salvation
John vi. cometh only of God. "No man can come unto me," saith Christ, "except my Father
Isai. liv. Jer. xxxi. draweth him." "For it is written in the prophets, All shall be taught of God. Every one therefore, that hath heard of the Father and learned, cometh unto me."

Father. Prove by the word of God, that faith is the gift of God, and cometh not of ourselves. *Son.* When Christ demanded of his disciples who he was, Peter, in the name
Matt. xvi. of himself and of his fellows, answered: "Thou art Christ, the Son of the living God. Christ answered and said, Blessed art thou, Simon the son of Jonas; for flesh and blood hath not shewed this thing unto thee, but my Father which is in heaven." In the gospel of St John we read, that when the Jews asked of Christ what they should
John vi. do, that they might work the works of God, he answered: "This is the work of God, that ye believe in him whom he hath sent." And in the Acts of the Apostles we read,
Acts xiii. that when Paul and Barnabas preached, "so many as were tofore ordained unto everlasting life, believed." Again, of a certain woman called Lydia, blessed Luke writeth,
Acts xvi. "that the Lord opened her heart to give attendance to these things that Paul spake."
Phil. i. And blessed St Paul, writing to the Philippians, saith: "It is given to you, not only to believe in Christ, but also to suffer for him." And in another place he confesseth
1 Cor. xii. Rom. xii. Eph. ii. faith to be given unto men of God through the Holy Ghost. These testimonies of the holy scripture declare sufficiently that faith cometh "not of ourselves, but is the gift of God;" only given to them which are the vessels of mercy, and tofore ordained unto
2 Thess. iii. everlasting life. For, as the apostle saith, "All have not faith." To obtain therefore this most precious and noble gift of faith, we have need to pray with the father of the
Mark ix. Luke xvii. diseased child: "Lord, help mine unbelief." And with the apostles: "Lord, increase our faith."

Heb. xi. *Father.* Is faith so necessary a thing unto salvation? *Son.* "Without faith it is not possible to please God. For he that cometh to God must believe that God is,
John iii. and that he is a rewarder to them that seek him." "He that believeth not on the Son (of God) shall not see life, but the wrath of God abideth on him." The godless and heathenish people wrought in times past many notable and worthy acts, and outwardly glistered with goodly virtues; so that in outward appearance they might seem not
All virtues without faith are very sins before God. Rom. xiv. unjustly to compare with the Christians: notwithstanding, forasmuch as they wanted this faith, whereof we now speak, all that ever they did was nothing but hypocrisy and abomination before God. "For whatsoever is not grounded on faith, the same is sin."
Luke xvi. And, "That which is worthy greater commendation before men is abominable before God."

The fruits of faith. *Father.* Why, what commodities bringeth faith to man? *Son.* By faith we be made the sons of God.

John i. *Father.* How provest thou that? *Son.* In the gospel of St John it is written: "As many as received him, to them he gave power to be the sons of God, even to them that believe on his name; which were born not of blood, nor of the will of the flesh, nor of
Gal. iii. the will of man, but of God." And St Paul also writeth: "All ye are the sons of God, because ye have believed in Christ Jesu."

Father. What more? *Son.* By faith we, which afore were sinners and unrighteous, are justified and counted righteous before God for Christ's sake.

Father. Where is that proved? *Son.* St Paul saith: "We plainly affirm, that a man is justified by faith, without the works of the law." (Rom. iii.) Again: "We, being justified by faith, have peace toward God through our Lord Jesus Christ." (Rom. v.) Also in another place he saith: "We know that a man is not justified by the deeds of the law, but by the faith of Jesu Christ. And we have believed on Jesu Christ, that we might be justified by the faith of Christ, and not by the deeds of the law; forasmuch as by the deeds of the law no flesh shall be justified." (Gal. ii.)

Father. Have we any other profit by faith? *Son.* Yea, many and divers.

Father. What are they? *Son.* By faith are we espoused and married unto Christ, as Christ himself testifieth by the prophet Ose: "I will marry thee unto myself in faith," saith he, "and thou shalt know the Lord." (Hos. ii.) Faith is that wedding-garment also, wherewith we be married unto Christ, according to the parable which we read in the gospel. (Matt. xxii.)

Furthermore, by faith Christ's fulfilling of the law is counted our fulfilling, as St Paul witnesseth, saying: "Christ is the fulfilling of the law, to justify all that believe." (Rom. x.) Again: "Christ hath delivered us (he speaketh of the faithful) from the curse of the law, inasmuch as he was made accursed for our sake." (Gal. iii.) And in the Acts of the Apostles we read thus: "Be it known unto you, ye men and brethren, that through this man (Christ) is preached unto you the forgiveness of sins, and that by him all that believe are justified from all things, from the which ye could not be justified by the law of Moses." (Acts xiii.) The wise man also saith: "In all thy works believe faithfully with all thy soul; for that is the keeping of the commandments. He that believeth on God giveth attendance to the commandments, and he that trusteth in him shall not be confounded." (Ecclus. xxxii.)

Moreover, by faith our prayers are accepted and heard of God, as Christ himself saith: "All things whatsoever ye ask in prayer, if ye believe, ye shall receive them." (Matt. xxi.) Hereunto pertaineth the saying of St James: "Let him that pray ask in faith, and doubt not. For he that doubteth is like a wave of the sea, which is tossed of the winds, and carried with violence. Neither let that man think that he shall receive any thing of the Lord." (James i.) Item, by faith our works are allowed before God as righteous for Christ's sake: as we read of Abel, whose sacrifice was approved of God, because it was done in faith. (Gen. iv.) And so likewise were all the sacrifices which the holy patriarchs and other godly men offered in the old law. "Thine eyes, O Lord, look upon faith," saith the preacher Hieremy. (Jer. v.)

Finally, by faith we obtain everlasting life, as Christ witnesseth, saying, "As Moses lifted up the serpent in the wilderness, so must the Son of man be lifted up, that every one that believeth on him may not perish, but have everlasting life." (John iii.) Again: "This is the will of him that sent me, that every one which seeth the Son, and believeth on him, have everlasting life." (John vi.) Also in another place: "I am the resurrection and life. He that believeth in me, although he be dead, yet shall he live: and every one that liveth and believeth in me, he shall never die." (John xi.)

Father. I commend thee, my dear child, that thou rememberest these things so well. But where are those things contained which we must believe, if we will receive the foresaid commodities and profits which thou hast rehearsed? *Son.* In the holy scriptures; but briefly and in a short sum, they are contained in the Apostles' creed, as they call it. For in that is comprehended in few words whatsoever is taught throughout the whole bible in many, necessarily to be believed unto everlasting salvation.

(In the holy scriptures only are all those things contained which of necessity are to be believed.)

Father. Why is it called the Apostles' creed? *Son.* Either because the apostles, as some say, did make it together with one consent, and delivered it to the congregation of the faithful both to teach and to believe: or else, because it is agreeable in all points to the doctrine which the apostles taught by mouth, and left in writing unto their posterity; so that whosoever believeth and confesseth this doctrine, which is contained in this creed, may right well be counted in the number of the faithful Christians, and taken for a member of Christ's church.

(Of the Apostles' creed. Why it is called the Apostles' creed.)

Father. How many articles of the christian faith are there? *Son.* Twelve.

Father. Which are they?

Son. 1. I believe in God, the Father Almighty, maker of heaven and of earth.
2. And in Jesus Christ, his only Son, our Lord.
3. Which was conceived by the Holy Ghost, born of the virgin Mary.
4. Suffered under Ponce Pilate, was crucified, dead, and buried: he descended unto hell.
5. The third day he rose again from death.
6. He ascended into heaven, and sitteth on the right hand of God the Father Almighty.
7. From thence he shall come to judge the quick and the dead.
8. I believe in the Holy Ghost.
9. The holy universal church, which is the fellowship or company of saints.
10. The forgiveness of sins.
11. The rising again of the body.
12. And everlasting life. Amen.

Father. Into how many parts is this symbol or creed of the apostles divided? *Son.* Into four.

The creed divided into four parts.

Father. Which are they? *Son.* The first part is of God and of the creation; and comprehendeth only one article. The second part is of Christ the Son of God, and of our redemption; and consisteth of six articles. The third part is of the Holy Ghost; and containeth one article. The fourth part is of our sanctification, and of the fruits and effects of faith; and comprehendeth four articles. And thus is this creed finished.

Father. Recite the first article.

The first part of the christian faith.

Son. "I believe in God, the Father Almighty, maker of heaven and of earth."

Heb. xi.

Father. Why beginnest thou on this manner, "I believe in God"? *Son.* For "he that cometh to God must believe that God is, and that he is a rewarder to them that seek him." And "without faith it is not possible to please God." Yea, "whatsoever is not grounded on faith, the same is sin."

Rom. xiv.

Father. What meanest thou when thou sayest, "I believe in God"? *Son.* I assuredly, undoubtedly, and most certainly am persuaded in my heart, that there is but one only true, living, immortal, and everlasting God, in whom alone I repose and set all mine affiance, trust, and confidence, and of whom only and of none other I hope and look for all good things, pertaining unto the soul or unto the body.

Father. What is God? *Son.* To define God, which is infinite, and whose majesty is unsearchable, it lieth not in my power. But I will make a certain description of God, as I have learned.

What God is. John iv.

Father. Let me hear. *Son.* "God is a spirit," everlasting, infinite, almighty, true, most wise, righteous, gentle, merciful, kind, liberal, the fountain of all goodness, an essence of himself, without beginning or ending, unchangeable, abiding alway in one state, favouring the good, punishing the evil, "in whom we live, move, and have our being:" the Father, which from everlasting begat his Son, like unto himself: the Son, which is the true and lively "image" of the Father, being of the same eternity, might, power, and majesty: the Holy Ghost, which proceedeth from the Father and the Son: three Persons, and one alone true God.

Acts xvii. Heb. i. Psal. cx. John xv. xvi. 1 John v.

Of three Persons in the Godhead.

Father. Why, are there three Persons in the Godhead, and yet but one God? *Son.* Yea, most certainly.

Father. Prove that by the scriptures. *Son.* When man should be made, God the Father said to the Son and to the Holy Ghost, "Let us make man like unto our own similitude and image." In these two words, *us* and *our*, is declared the plurality of Persons; and in these two words, *similitude* and *image*, is expressed the unity or singularity of the Godhead in the Trinity of Persons. The holy scripture testifieth, that Abraham saw three, and worshipped one: that is to say, three in the propriety of persons, and one in the unity of the divine substance. The prophet Esay heard seraphin crying: "Holy, holy, holy, the Lord God of hosts." By the thrice repetition of this word "holy," the three Persons in the Trinity are expressed unto us; but by the one denomination of God, one Deity, or one only divine substance of

Gen. i. Gen. xviii. Isai. vi.

those three Persons is declared unto us: likewise as by the one naming of the Lord of hosts, the lordship, kingdom, majesty, power, and authority of this one God is understanded to be all one and the same. The psalmograph also writeth on this manner: "By the Word of the Lord were the heavens made sure, and with the Spirit of his mouth all the power of them." Here likewise is set forth unto us, that there be three Persons in the Godhead. The Father is called the Lord, the Son the Word, and the Holy Ghost the Spirit. In the evangelical history we read that, when Christ was baptized, the Father from heaven was heard saying, "This is my well-beloved Son, in whom I have a great delight." We read also, that the Holy Ghost came down from heaven in the likeness of a dove, and rested upon Christ. Here is it most evident, that in that most blessed, glorious, and everlasting Godhead there are three Persons, the Father, the Son, and the Holy Ghost. And when our Saviour Christ sent forth his apostles to preach, he commanded them also to "baptize all nations in the name of the Father, and of the Son, and of the Holy Ghost." The unity of the divine essence is set forth in this, that Christ saith, "in the name," and not in the names; as likewise by these three names, the Father, the Son, and the Holy Ghost, is declared, that there are three Persons in the divine substance. To be short, St John in his epistle doth in few words comprehend all this matter, saying: "They are they[1], which give witness in heaven, the Father, the Word, and the Holy Ghost; and these three are one."

Psal. xxxiii. Matt. iii. Mark i. Luke iii John i. Matt. xxviii. 1 John v.

Father. Thou affirmest then, that in the divine essence, although there be three distinct Persons, yet is there but one God. *Son.* I do not only affirm and confess it with my mouth, but I also most certainly do believe it with my heart. "It is the Lord that made the heavens," which is the true and alone God; "as for the gods of the heathen, they are devils," as the psalmograph saith. And therefore in the confession of my faith I say, "I believe in God," and not in gods. For there is but one God, even the Father of our Lord Jesus Christ, as God himself testifieth, saying: "Behold, I am alone, and there is none other God besides me."

1 Cor. viii. Eph. iv. Deut. xxxii.

Father. Wherefore dost thou call God Father in the confession of thy faith, saying, "I believe in God the Father?" *Son.* For two causes. First, to declare that in the Godhead there are three distinct Persons, as we heard before, of the which God the Father is the first, which is the true and natural Father of his Son Jesus Christ our Lord, begotten from everlasting, very God of very God, and of the same substance with the Father. Secondly, to express, that as Jesus Christ is the Son of this first Person in the Deity by natural substance, so likewise through this Christ am I his son also, not by nature, but by adoption; so that God the Father is now also become my father, and hath made me by grace his son, and inheritor of his heavenly kingdom. And while I am in this world, he conserveth and keepeth me: he nourisheth and comforteth me: yea, and as a most loving and gentle father he blesseth me with all good things necessary both for soul and body.

Why we call God Father. Psal. cx.

Father. Prove me out of the holy scriptures, that God is the father of the faithful. *Son.* Moses saith: "Give praise unto our God. Is not he thy father, that hath made and created thee?" The prophet Esay saith: "Thou, O Lord, art our Father and Redeemer. Thy name is from everlasting." God himself saith by the prophet Jeremy: "Thou shalt call me, dear Father, and thou shalt turn no more away from me." Our Saviour Christ saith: "Call no man your father upon the earth; for one is your Father, which is in heaven." St Paul saith: "As many as are led by the Spirit of God, they are the sons of God. For ye have not received the spirit of bondage to fear any more, but ye have received the Spirit of adoption, whereby we cry, Abba, dear Father. The same Spirit certifieth our spirit, that we are the sons of God. If we be sons, we are also heirs, the heirs, I mean, of God, and fellow-heirs with Christ." St John crieth out on this manner: "O behold, what a wonderful love God hath given to us, that we should be called the sons of God!" In fine, God saith: "I will be a father unto you; and ye shall be my sons and daughters."

Deut. xxxii. Isai. lxiii. Jer. iii. Matt. xxiii. Rom. viii. 1 John iii. 2 Cor. vi.

Father. But wherefore dost thou call God not only a Father, but also Almighty?

Why God is called almighty.

[[1] A misprint probably for *three*.]

Psal. cxv. Luke i. *Son.* He is called Almighty, because he is able to do whatsoever his good pleasure is; and no man is of power to resist his godly will and determination. And this word, Almighty, is a great comfort unto me. For hereof I learn, that as God being my loving father hath a good mind and will graciously to help and succour me, so likewise hath he power and ability to aid and comfort me in all my troubles and necessities; so that in him there is both will and power.

Father. Declare unto me by the holy scriptures, that God is almighty. *Son.* God Gen. xvii. said unto Abraham: "I am the Almighty God: walk before me, and be thou Jer. xxxii. perfect." By the prophet Jeremy he saith also: "Behold, I am the Lord God of all flesh. Is there any thing too hard for me? Shall any thing be unpossible in my Matt. xix. sight, saith the Lord of hosts?" Our Saviour Christ saith also: "With God all Luke i. things are possible." And the angel Gabriel said to Mary the virgin: "With God shall nothing be unpossible."

Father. Thou believest with thy heart, and confessest with thy mouth, not only that God is a Father and Almighty, but also the creator and maker both of heaven and of earth. *Son.* I both believe and confess.

Why God the Father is called maker of heaven and earth.

Father. Why callest thou God the Father maker of heaven and of earth? *Son.* I call God not only a Father, but also almighty. And in that he is almighty, he made both heaven and earth, and all things contained in them, both visible and invisible, yea, and that of nothing. And as he at the beginning made them of nothing, so likewise doth he now still defend, govern, and keep them, even with the same might and power, wherewith he made them at the beginning.

Father. Shew unto me by the word of God, that God created all things. *Son.* Gen. i. Jer. xxxii. Moses saith: "In the beginning God made heaven and earth." Jeremy saith: "It is thou, O Lord God, that hast made heaven and earth with thy great power and outstretched arm. For there is nothing too hard for thee." The psalmograph saith: Psal. cii. "Thou, O Lord, at the beginning madest the earth; and the heavens are the works of Acts xvii. thy hands." St Paul saith: "God made the world, and all things that are in it." Eph. iii. Again: "God made all things."

Father. What comfort or doctrine dost thou gather of this, that God is the maker of heaven and earth? *Son.* Great comfort, and much doctrine.

For in believing on this God, which made both heaven and earth, I am right well assured, that I am free from the number of them which do believe, honour, and serve strange and false gods, yea, rather idols and devils; and that I am the servant, yea, the son by adoption, through Christ Jesu our Lord, of that one and alone true and everlasting God.

Again, by the consideration of God's creatures I am taught to know God, his omnipotency, goodness, and providence, whose majesty otherwise I could never comprehend, nor attain unto any part of the knowledge of the same. But in them, as in a certain clear mirror or pleasant glass, I see and behold him, and learn partly to Rom. i. know him, as the apostle saith: "That which may be known of God is manifest among them: for God did shew it unto them: so that his invisible things, that is to say, his eternal power and Godhead, are understand and seen by the works from the creation of the world. So that they are without excuse; inasmuch as, when they knew God, they glorified him not as God, neither were thankful, but waxed full of vanities in their imaginations, and their foolish hearts were blinded." Hereto ap-Psal. xix. pertaineth the saying of the psalmograph: "The heavens declare the glory of God; and the very firmament sheweth his handy-work."

Moreover, hereof I learn that God created me and all his other creatures, both spiritual and corporal, both heavenly and earthly, of nothing, by his mighty power; and that I have my being, body, soul, wit, reason, discretion, wisdom, knowledge, health, wealth, riches, wife, children, and all that ever I have, of the bounteous liberality of this creator and maker of heaven and earth; which, as he by his power hath made me, so likewise by his wisdom and providence doth preserve, keep, govern, and defend me and all that I have.

1 Cor. iv. James i. And here am I taught that whatsoever good thing I have, it is the gift of God, the author of all goodness; and that therefore I ought not to be proud, nor to stand in mine

own conceit, which have nothing of myself that good is, no, not so much as once to think a good thought, much less to do any good work, but rather to humble myself before the presence of God's majesty, and to magnify and exalt his glorious name, for the benefits which he most graciously hath bestowed upon me without my deserts, and to labour unto the uttermost of my power to use his gifts unto the glory of his holy name, the profit of my neighbour, and the salvation of my soul. 2 Cor. iii. John xv.

Finally, this comfort have I also, that, forasmuch as I believe in that God the Father, which through his omnipotency and almighty power hath made all things contained in heaven and in earth, I shall lack no good thing necessary either for my body or for my soul; but, while I live in this world, my body shall have sufficient food and raiment for the conservation and maintenance of the same, and after this life my soul, being delivered from the prison of the body, shall enjoy the blessed inheritance of God's glorious and heavenly kingdom. For my wealth and comfort, for my joy and solace, hath God my Father created heaven and earth, and whatsoever is contained in them.

Father. Thou sayest well. But come off, tell me, why dost thou rather say, "I believe in God," than I believe that God is? *Son.* To believe that God is is common not only to the faithful but also to the unfaithful, yea, to the very devils, as St James saith: "Thou dost believe that there is but one God. Thou doest well. But the devils believe that also, and tremble." But to "believe in God" is to put our whole trust and confidence, not in any creature in heaven or in earth, not in any work or ceremony, but only and alone in this one true and everlasting God, which is the Father of our Lord Jesus Christ by nature, and the Father of the faithful by grace, of such omnipotency and almighty power, that at the beginning he made of nothing both heaven and earth, and whatsoever is contained in them; to look for assuredly all good things at his hands, meat, drink, clothe, wife, children, house, health, &c., remission of sins, quietness of conscience, the gift of the Holy Ghost, everlasting life, &c.; to depend only on him; in all necessities and troubles to flee unto him, as unto the only and alone haven of health; to yield ourselves to him both body and soul; to cleave to him and to his promises both in prosperity and adversity; and in fine, so wholly to repose, settle, and quiet our minds in him, that we honour him as our alone God, love him as our most gentle Father, and obey him as our most gracious Lord, which both can and also will help, aid, succour, preserve, and defend us, suffering us to want no good thing either for the body or for the soul, but giving us largely all good things, himself being the highest good, and the fountain or well-spring of all goodness. This faith, this persuasion, this trust, this confidence of God's goodness and mercy, have neither the unfaithful nor the devils; and therefore they "believe and tremble." The faithful have only this faith and confidence; and therefore they do believe and rejoice, as St Paul saith: "We, being justified by faith, are at peace with God through our Lord Jesus Christ: by whom we have a way in through faith unto this grace wherein we stand, and rejoice in the hope of the glory of God," &c. James ii. What it is to believe in God. James ii. Rom. v

Father. Let this suffice at this present for the first part of the christian faith, concerning God the Father. Let us now go in hand with the second part. What followeth?

Son. "And in Jesus Christ, his only Son, our Lord."

Father. What meanest thou by that? *Son.* I said unto you before, that there are three distinct and several Persons in the Godhead, the Father, the Son, and the Holy Ghost, and yet one only God. Of the first Person in the Deity, which is God the Father, you have heard the confession of my faith. Now in most goodly order followeth the second part of the christian faith, concerning the second Person in the Godhead, which is here called Jesus Christ, the only Son of God, and our Lord. The second part of the christian faith.

Father. What believest thou of this second Person in the Deity, Jesus Christ? *Son.* As with my heart I do believe, and with my mouth confess the first Person in the Godhead, that is to say, the Father Almighty, which made heaven and earth, to be very God; so likewise with my heart do I believe, and with my mouth confess, that the second Person in the Deity, that is to say, Christ Jesus, is very God, begotten after an unoutspeakable manner of God the Father from everlasting, without any diminution of his divine substance, being of the same perfection, omnipotency, majesty, wisdom, eternity, glory, &c. And therefore, as I believe and put my whole trust and confidence in God the Father, and most certainly look for all good things at his hand, so in like manner do I believe and set all mine affiance and trust in God the Son, hoping to receive all prosperous things also of him, being the Son of God, and of the same might and power with God his Father.

That Christ is God. *Father*. Prove by the holy scriptures that Jesus Christ is God. *Son*. Nothing is more easy. And although there be many, and almost innumerable, both sentences and histories in the holy scriptures, which do most evidently prove and declare that Christ Jesus is very God, yet may it seem for this present sufficient, out of so great a multitude, to select and choose out these few that follow.

Father. Agreed.

Isai. ix. *Son*. The prophet Esay saith: "Unto us a child is born, and unto us a son is given: upon his shoulder doth the kingdom lie, and he is called with his own name Wonderful, the Giver of Counsel, the Mighty God, the Everlasting Father, the Prince of Peace," &c. Isai. xxv. Again he saith: "In that day it shall be said, Lo, this is our God; we have waited for him, and he shall save us. This is the Lord, in whom we have hoped. We shall be merry and rejoice in the salvation that cometh of him." Also in another Isai. xxxv. place he saith: "They shall see the glory of the Lord, and the majesty of our God, &c. Behold that God cometh to take vengeance; and you shall see the reward that God giveth. God cometh his own self, and will deliver you. Then shall the eyes of the blind be lightened, and the ears of the deaf opened. Then shall the lame man leap as an hart, and the dumb man's tongue shall be loosened." Baruch also saith: Bar. iii. "This is our God, and there shall none other be compared unto him. It is he that hath found out all wisdom, and hath given her unto Jacob his servant, and to Israel his beloved. Afterward did he shew himself upon earth, and dwelt among men." Psal. xlv. The psalmograph also saith: "Thy seat, O God, endureth for ever: the sceptre of thy kingdom is a right sceptre."

Father. Let these testimonies of Christ's divinity suffice concerning the old testament. Recite me some out of the new testament. *Son*. All the books of the new testament do largely bear witness of the Deity of Christ. St Matthew, speaking of Christ, hath these words: "His name shall be called Emanuel, that is to say, God with us," or God and man. St John writeth that, when Thomas the apostle saw John xx. Christ risen from death, he cried out and said, "My Lord, and my God." And in John i. the beginning of his gospel he setteth forth the divinity of Christ plenteously. "In the beginning," saith he, "was the Word, and the Word was with God, and God was the Word. He was at the beginning with God: all things were made by him; and without him nothing was made that is made," &c. Christ, speaking of himself, John viii. John vi. saith: "Verily, I say unto you, before Abraham was, I am." Again: "I am that living bread which came down from heaven. If any man eat of this bread, he shall live John viii. for ever." Item: "Except ye believe that I am (God), ye shall die in your sins." John xvii. "I and my Father are one." Also in another place: "This is everlasting life, even to know thee the alone true God, and whom thou hast sent, Jesus Christ." St Paul Rom. ix. saith, that "Christ came of the fathers as concerning the flesh; which (Christ) is God, Col. ii. in all things worthy to be praised for ever. Amen." Again: "In Christ dwelleth all the fulness of the Godhead corporally," that is to say, naturally, truly, and effectually. Tit. ii. Item: "We look for that blessed hope, and glorious appearing of the great God and Col. i. our Saviour Jesu Christ." In other places St Paul calleth Christ the "image of the Heb. i. invisible God, first-begotten before all creatures," the "brightness of his glory, and 1 John v. the very image of his substance." And St John, speaking of Christ, saith: "The same is very God and everlasting life." Furthermore, the restoring of the blind to their sight, the raising up of the dead unto life, the cleansing of the lepers, the healing of them that were diseased with the palsy, the restoring of men possessed with devils and unclean spirits to their whole mind, the making of the deaf to hear and the dumb to speak, with the other miracles that Christ wrought, do evidently prove that Christ is very God.

Father. These things are more open than they may be denied. Now then, seeing it is manifestly declared and proved by the holy scriptures, that Christ Jesus, the second Person in the Godhead, is equal God with God the Father, dost thou also believe in him, repose thine affiance, put all thy trust and confidence in him, and look for all good things at his hand? *Son.* Yea, verily; and therefore, as I said before, "I believe in God the Father," so likewise say I now: "And I believe in Jesus Christ, his only Son, our Lord:" declaring my faith to be all one, both in God the Father, and in God the Son, which although they be two distinct and several Persons in the Deity, yet are they not two Gods, but one God. Our Lord and Saviour Christ saith: "Ye believe in God (the Father): believe ye also in me." For "I and my Father are one." "He that seeth me seeth the Father also." "I am in my Father, and he is in me." And St John saith: "This is the commandment of God, that we believe in the name of his Son Jesus Christ." For "he that believeth on the Son hath everlasting life: but he that believeth not on the Son shall not see life; but the wrath of God abideth on him." John xiv. John x. John xiv. 1 John iii. John iii.

Father. And out of this faith mayest thou boldly cry unto this second Person in the Deity, and crave all good things at his hand? *Son.* No less than unto the Father. For it is written: "All that believe on him (Christ) shall not be ashamed;" "for there is one Lord of all, rich enough for all that call on him; so that every one that calleth on the name of the Lord shall be saved." And that we may be certain and not doubt, but that salvation cometh also unto us from this second Person in the Godhead, he is called Jesus. For so soundeth the article: "And in Jesus Christ, his only Son, our Lord." Isai. xxviii. Rom. x. Joel ii. Acts ii.

Father. What signifieth this name *Jesus?* *Son.* Jesus is an Hebrew word, and signifieth a Saviour. What Jesus signifieth.

Father. Who gave the Son of God this name? *Son.* God the Father himself, as we read in the gospel. For Matthew writeth thus: "Behold, the angel of the Lord appeared unto Joseph in a dream, saying, Joseph, the son of David, fear not to take unto thee Mary thy wife. For that which is conceived in her is of the Holy Ghost. She shall bring forth a son; and thou shalt call his name Jesus: for he shall save his people from their sins." "And the angel said unto Mary, Lo, thou shalt conceive in thy womb, and shalt bear a son, and shalt call his name Jesus." Matt. i. Luke i.

Father. Why was this name *Jesus* appropriated and given to Christ of God the Father? *Son.* To declare unto us that he alone is our Saviour, and that we ought to seek salvation only at his hand, as St Peter saith: "There is salvation in none other but in the Lord Jesus. Neither is there any other name under heaven given unto men, wherein we must be saved," but only the name of Jesu. And here is another noble and notable testimony of Christ's divinity. For in this that he is a Saviour, and saveth his people from their sins, it is evident that he is true and natural God. For none saveth, delivereth from sin, and giveth everlasting life, but God alone. But all these things doeth Christ. Therefore is Christ very God. Why this name *Jesus* was given to Christ. Acts iv.

Father. Is Christ Jesus alone a Saviour? *Son.* Yea, verily. So teach the holy scriptures. And Christ himself saith by the prophet: "I, I am the Lord, and besides me there is no Saviour." Again: "Thy destruction, O Israel, cometh of thyself; but thy salvation cometh only of me." Neither angel in heaven, nor man in earth, nor any work that we do, seemeth it never so holy, perfect, and righteous, can save us, but this Lord Christ alone, which is called Jesus. Whosoever therefore seeketh salvation at the hand of any other, deceiveth himself, and, as much as in him is, robbeth Christ both of his name and glory. And whosoever presumeth to save other by his own holiness, virtue, or righteousness, he denieth Christ to be Jesus, and is led with the spirit of antichrist. Christ calleth all them that are grieved and heavy loaden with the burden of sin unto him, and promiseth to ease them. He sendeth them not to other for to be eased. He "came to seek that was lost," and to give his life a ransom for many. "This is a true saying," saith St Paul, "and by all means worthy to be received, that Christ Jesus came into the world to save sinners." And St John saith: "To this end hath the Son of God appeared, that he should destroy the works of the devil." Again: "In this appeared the love of God toward us, that he sent his Isai. xliii. Hos. xiii. Matt. xi. Matt. xviii. Luke ix. 1 Tim. i. 1 John iii. 1 John iv.

only-begotten Son into the world, that we might live through him. In this is love; not that we loved God, but that he first loved us, and sent his Son to make agreement for our sins." Christ is so alone Jesus, that he only saveth, delivereth from sin, and giveth everlasting life. Whosoever falleth away from this Saviour, and hunteth after other, he doeth nothing else than throw himself headlong into everlasting damnation. Against such backsliders this Son of God, this Jesus, this alone Saviour of the world, crieth out by the prophet on this manner: "Be astonied, O ye heavens, be afraid, and be abashed at such a thing, saith the Lord. For my people hath done two evils; they have forsaken me, the well of the water of life, and digged them pits, yea, vile and broken pits, that hold no water." "Cursed is he," saith Jeremy, "that putteth his trust in man, and taketh flesh for his arm; and he whose heart departeth from the Lord. He shall be like the heath that groweth in the wilderness. As for the good thing that is to come, he shall not see it, but dwell in a dry place of the wilderness, in a salt and an unoccupied land. But O! blessed is the man that putteth his trust in the Lord, and whose hope the Lord himself is. For he shall be as a tree that is planted by the water side, which spreadeth out the root unto moistness, whom the heat cannot harm, when it cometh; but his leaves are green," &c.

Jer. ii. Jer. xvii. Psal. i.

Father. But this second Person in the Godhead is not only called Jesus, but also Christ. *Son*. So is it.

What Christ is.

Father. What is Christ to say? *Son*. Christ, in the Greek tongue, soundeth in our English speech, Anointed.

Why Jesus is called Christ.

Father. Why is he called Christ, or Anointed? *Son*. As God the Father would declare unto us by this name Jesus, that his Son is our alone Saviour, and therefore true and natural God, so that we should seek our salvation of none, but of him alone; so likewise by this name *Christ* he teacheth us, that his Son is our alone king, priest, and prophet.

Father. Why was Jesus anointed also with oil, after the manner of kings, priests, and prophets in the old law? *Son*. The oil wherewith they were anointed was corruptible, as they themselves were corruptible and mortal; but the oil wherewith Christ was anointed was uncorruptible, immortal, heavenly, and spiritual.

Father. Of what oil speakest thou? *Son*. Of that oil which the psalmograph calleth the oil of gladness, saying: "Thou hast loved righteousness and hated wickedness; therefore hath God, even thy God, anointed thee with the oil of gladness more than all thy fellows."

Psal. xlv.

Father. What is this oil of gladness? *Son*. The Holy Ghost. With this oil, I mean the Holy Ghost, Christ is most abundantly anointed of God the Father, whereas the other faithful are anointed with this oil according to the measure which God hath given them; as St John Baptist saith: "God giveth not the Spirit by measure unto him," that is to say, Christ. But "of his fulness," and of the overflowing abundance of his Spirit, "have we all received."

John iii. John i.

Christ's kingdom is spiritual.

Father. Hath God anointed Christ to be our king? *Son*. Yea, verily. But as his anointing is spiritual, so likewise is he a spiritual king; and his kingdom also is spiritual, as he said to Pilate: "My kingdom is not of this world." He ruleth not with the sword of the flesh, but with "the sword of the Spirit, which is the word of God." Therefore saith the prophet: "Behold, thy king cometh unto thee, meek, poor, humble, or lowly, sitting upon an ass," &c. He ruleth in the hearts of the faithful with his Spirit and word, defending them from the tyranny of the devil, from the captivity of sin, from the curse of the law, from the sting of death, from the torments of hell, and from everlasting damnation. For this cause he is called "the Prince of peace." Neither is his kingdom temporal, but perpetual, as the angel saith: "He shall be great, and shall be called the Son of the Highest. And the Lord God shall give unto him the seat of his father David; and he shall reign over the house of Jacob for ever, and of his kingdom shall be none end." For he is "the King of kings, and Lord of lords."

John xviii. Eph. vi. Zech. ix. Luke i. Mic. iv. Dan. vii. Rev. xix.

The profit of Christ's kingdom.

Father. What profit have we by this kingdom of Christ? *Son*. Great and much. You heard before that Christ, being anointed of God his Father to be our king, preserveth and governeth us by his word and Spirit, and leadeth us in the way of holiness and righteousness. Again, he defendeth us from the cruelty of Satan, from the raging lusts of the flesh, from the vain pleasures of the world, from the thraldom of sin, from the curse of the law, from the sting of death, from the pains of hell, and from eternal damnation, and hath gotten for us an heavenly and everlasting kingdom. And through this his kingdom he hath also made us kings and conquerors of all our enemies; so that we may triumphantly and with rejoicing hearts say: "Death, where is thy sting? Hell, where is thy victory? The sting of death is sin; and the strength of sin is the law: but thanks be unto God, which hath given us the victory, through our Lord Jesus Christ." Hereto pertaineth the saying of St Paul: "Christ through death did put him down, that had lordship over death, that is to say, the devil, that he might deliver them which through fear of death were all their lifetime in danger of bondage." 1 Cor. xv. Hos. xiii. Heb. ii.

Father. Is Christ also our priest? *Son*. Yea, the one and alone priest of the new testament, whose priesthood as it is most high and most excellent, so is it everlasting and perpetual, as the psalmograph saith: "Thou art a priest for ever after the order of Melchisedech." Christ alone is our priest. Psal. cx. Heb. vii.

Father. Why is Christ called a priest? *Son*. First, because he, being the true paschal lamb without spot, offered himself on the altar of the cross, a sweet-smelling sacrifice unto God the Father, for the sins of the whole world, and, by the virtue of that one and alone sacrifice once offered for all, he "hath made perfect for ever them that are sanctified;" so that now we have no need of any other oblations or sacrifices to be offered unto God for our sins. For this our Bishop, with the one and alone sacrifice of his blessed body, hath fully and unto the uttermost finished and brought to pass whatsoever is necessary for our salvation, as the apostle saith: "We are sanctified and made holy by the offering up of the body of Jesu Christ done once for all." Secondly, because he being our alone mediator, advocate, and intercessor, and sitting on the right hand of God the Father, doth continually pray for us, and appeaseth the wrath of God daily kindled against us through sin, as St John testifieth: "If any man," saith he, "sin, we have an advocate with the Father, Jesus Christ the righteous. And he it is that obtaineth mercy for our sins; not for our sins only, but for the whole world's." Exod. xii. John i. Eph. v. Heb. ix. x. Heb. x. 1 Tim. ii. Rom. viii. Heb. x. 1 John ii.

Father. What doth this priesthood of Christ profit us? *Son*. Very much. For in this that he is our alone high and everlasting priest, he hath offered sacrifice, as ye have heard, to God his Father, which sacrifice is he himself; and by this means hath he pacified the Father's wrath, satisfied for our sins, reconciled us unto God, made us his sons, and fellow-heirs with him of everlasting glory. Again, through this his priesthood, he is made unto God the Father our mediator, advocate, and intercessor, prayeth for us, pleadeth our cause, appeaseth God's wrath, and obtaineth for us all good things necessary either for body or for soul. Moreover, by this his priesthood he hath made us priests to offer spiritual sacrifices acceptable to God through him, that is to say, ourselves, our souls and bodies, to be a lively, holy, and well-pleasing sacrifice unto God; again, our prayers, praises, thanksgivings, and such other good works, even the fruits of our faith, as St Paul saith: "By Christ offer we the sacrifice of praise alway to God, that is to say, the fruit of those lips which confess his name. To do good and to distribute forget not; for with such sacrifices God is well pleased." "Ye are an holy priesthood," saith St Peter, "for to offer up spiritual sacrifices acceptable to God by Jesus Christ." Again: "Ye are a chosen generation, a royal priesthood, an holy nation, and a peculiar people, that ye should shew the virtues of him that called you out of darkness into his marvellous light." The profit of Christ's priesthood. 1 Pet. ii. Rom. xii. Heb. xiii. 1 Pet. ii.

Father. Is Christ also a prophet? *Son*. Yea, verily, even the very same prophet, of whom it is thus written: "I will raise them up a prophet from among their brethren like unto thee, and will put my words in his mouth; and he shall speak unto them all that I shall command him. And whosoever will not hearken unto my words which he shall speak in my name, I will be avenged of him." That Christ is this very prophet, the people also at his coming confessed, saying: "Of a truth this is that prophet that should come into the world." Christ is our prophet. Deut. xviii. Acts vii. John vi.

Father. What profit have we by this, that Christ is a prophet? *Son*. In that he is that prophet, which God so many years before his coming promised to send, we are well assured that he is a schoolmaster sent from God unto us, and hath the words of God in his mouth, and teacheth us the truth, which we ought both diligently to hear, and stedfastly to believe, according to this saying: "This is my well-beloved Son, for whose sake I am well pleased with man; hear him." Of his prophecy, doctrine, or preaching, Christ himself speaketh on this manner by the prophet: "The Spirit of the Lord is upon me, because he hath anointed me, and sent me to preach good tidings unto the poor, that I might bind up the wounded hearts, that I might preach deliverance to the prisoners, and open the prison to them that are bond, that I might declare the acceptable year of the Lord, and the day of the avengeance of our God, that I might comfort all them that are in heaviness, that I might give unto them that mourn in Sion beauty in the stead of ashes, joyful ointment for sighing, pleasant raiment for an heavy mind; that they might be called excellent in righteousness, a planting of the Lord for him to rejoice in." Hereunto belongeth the saying of the woman of Samaria: "I know that Messias shall come, which is called Christ; and that, when he cometh, he will shew and declare unto us all things." Furthermore, in that Christ is a prophet, he doth also anoint us with the oil of gladness, which is the Holy Ghost, and giveth us also the gift of prophecy, that we both can understand the holy scriptures, and also teach them to other unto the edifying of his church, as he himself saith by the prophet: "I will pour out of my Spirit upon all flesh; and your sons and your daughters shall prophesy." Again: "I will put my laws in their minds, and in their hearts I will write them; and I will be their God, and they shall be my people. And they shall not teach every man his neighbour, and every man his brother, saying, Know the Lord: for they shall know me from the least to the most of them."

Matt. xvii. Isai. lxi. Luke iv. John iv. Joel ii. Acts ii. Jer. xxxi. Heb. viii.

Why Christ is called the only Son of God.

Father. Let these things suffice concerning the names of Christ and his office. Why dost thou call him the only Son of God? *Son.* I am taught by the word of God, which is an infallible verity, so to do.

Father. Prove by the word of God, that Christ is the Son of God. *Son.* God himself saith: "Out of Egypt have I called my Son." Again: "I will be his Father, and he shall be my Son." Item: "Thou art my Son; this day have I begotten thee." Peter, with his fellow apostles, John Baptist, Nathaniel, Martha, with all the faithful of the new testament (as I may speak nothing of the wicked and damnable spirits), confessed Christ to be the Son of God. Christ said to the blind man, whom he had restored unto his sight: "Dost thou believe in the Son of God? He answered and said, Who is he, Lord, that I may believe in him? Jesus said unto him, Thou hast seen him, and he it is that talketh with thee. And he said, I believe, O Lord; and worshipped him." And the eunuch said unto Philip: "I believe that Jesus Christ is the Son of God." God the Father himself with an open voice from heaven twice pronounced Christ to be his Son, saying: "This is my well-beloved Son, in whom I have a singular delight; hear him." St Paul also saith: "Christ was begotten of the seed of David as pertaining to the flesh, and declared to be the Son of God with power," &c. Again: "God in times past diversly and many ways spake unto the fathers by the prophets; but in these last days he hath spoken unto us by his Son, whom he hath made heir of all things, by whom also he made the world: which Son also is the brightness of his glory, and the very image of his substance," &c. Moreover St John saith: "These things are written, that ye may believe that Jesus is Christ, the Son of God, and that ye thus believing might have life through his name."

Hos. xi. Matt. ii. 2 Sam. vii. Heb. i. Psal. ii. Matt. xvi. John vi. John i. John xi. Mark i. Matt. viii. Mark v. Luke viii. John ix. Acts viii. Matt. iii. Matt. xvii. 2 Pet. i. Rom. i. Heb. i. John xx.

Father. Thou hast proved sufficiently, that Christ Jesus is the Son of God; but thy creed teacheth that he is the only Son of God. Declare that also by the word of God. *Son.* Christ himself saith: "God hath so dearly loved the world, that he gave his only-begotten Son, that every one that believeth on him may not perish, but have everlasting life. For God sent not his Son into the world to condemn the world, but that the world should be saved by him. He that believeth on him is not condemned: but he that believeth not is already condemned, because he hath not believed on the name of the only-begotten Son of God." St John Baptist also saith: "No man hath seen God at any time. The only-begotten Son, which is in the bosom of the Father, he hath declared him." St John the evangelist also writeth

John iii. John i.

1 John iv.

in his epistle: "In this appeareth the love of God toward us; because that God sent his only-begotten Son into the world, that we might live through him."

Christ is the Son of God by nature; but the faithful are the sons of God by adoption.

Father. If Christ be the only Son of God, how cometh it then to pass, that the faithful are also called the sons of God in so many places of the holy scripture? *Son.* Christ Jesus is the true and natural Son of God, begotten of his Father from everlasting, before all worlds, of the same substance, majesty, might, and power, with his Father. The elect and faithful people are also the sons of God, not by nature, but by adoption.

What adoption signifieth.

Father. What meanest thou by this word adoption? *Son.* I call adoption when one doth take a child, which is not his own proper child, begotten of his own body, for his own proper and legitimate child, giving unto him all rights and titles, as though he were truly and naturally his child, not as though he were bound unto it, but doeth it of his own free goodness, and of the very love that he beareth toward him. Even so be we the sons of God by Jesus Christ, in whom and for whose sake God doth love us, adopt, choose, and receive us for his children, and maketh us inheritors of his everlasting and glorious kingdom, as St Paul saith: "Blessed be God the Father of our Lord Jesus Christ, which hath blessed us with all manner of spiritual blessings in heavenly things by Christ, according as he had chosen us in him before the foundation of the world was laid, that we should be holy and without blame before him through love, and ordained us before through Jesus Christ to be sons and heirs unto himself, according to the good pleasure of his will, to the praise of the glory of his grace, wherewith he hath made us accepted in his well-beloved Son, by whom we have redemption through his blood, even the forgiveness of sins, according to the riches of his grace," &c. Again: "Not of the deeds of righteousness which we wrought, but of his mercy hath God saved us, by the fountain of the new birth and the renewing of the Holy Ghost, which he shed on us abundantly through Jesus Christ our Saviour, that we, being justified by his grace, should be heirs of everlasting life through hope."

Eph. i. Tit. iii.

Therefore, when the scripture calleth Christ the Son of God, it is to be understand that he is the Son of God by nature and by the divine substance. But when it nameth the faithful to be the sons or children of God, it is meant by grace and adoption. And so are these sentences to be understand: "So many as received him (Christ), to them he gave power to be the sons of God," &c. "As many as are led by the Spirit of God, they are the sons of God. For ye have not received the spirit of bondage to fear any more, but ye have received the Spirit of adoption, whereby we cry, Abba, dear Father. The same Spirit certifieth our spirit that we are the sons of God. If we be sons, we are also heirs, the heirs, I mean, of God, and fellow-heirs with Christ." "Ye are all the sons of God, because ye have believed in Christ Jesu." "Behold, what love the Father hath shewed on us, that we should be called the sons of God."

John i. Rom. viii. Gal. iii. 1 John iii

Father. What learnest thou of this, that Christ is the only-begotten Son of God? *Son.* By this I am fully and most certainly persuaded, that Jesus Christ, the second Person in the Deity (in whom I do believe as in the Father), is true, perfect, immortal, and everlasting God, begotten of God the Father before all worlds, of the same majesty, nature, substance, might, and power with the Father. For even as of the substance of a true man there is none born but a true man, so likewise of the substance of the true God there is none born but true God. Every thing begetteth the thing that is like unto itself in nature and substance.

What the Godhead of Christ profiteth.

Father. What doth it profit thee, that Christ is the Son of God, yea, God himself? *Son.* Very much. For in that he is God, or the Son of God, he is able to forgive me my sins, to beget me of new by his Holy Spirit, to defend me from mine enemies, to save me, to give me all good things necessary both for body and soul, to make me the son of God and heir of everlasting glory.

1 Tim. vi. Rev. xvii xix.

Father. But wherefore callest thou Christ our Lord? *Son.* For he is the "Lord of lords, and King of kings." I with my heart therefore believe, and with my mouth confess Christ also to be our Lord.

Isai. xlii.

Father. Prove by the word of God, that Christ is our Lord. *Son.* Christ himself saith by the prophet: "I am the Lord; this is my name: my glory will I give to

John xiii. none other, neither mine honour to graven images." Again: "Ye call me master
1 Cor. i. and Lord, and ye say well; for so am I in deed." St Paul also saith: "God is faithful, by whom ye are called unto the fellowship of his Son Jesus Christ, our
Rom. i. Lord." Again: "Grace be unto you, and peace from God the Father, and our Lord
1 Cor. viii. Jesus Christ." Item: "There is but one Lord, even Jesus Christ; by whom are all things, and we by him."

What profit we have in this, that Christ is our Lord.

Father. What profit have we by this, that Christ is our Lord? *Son*. In that he is our Lord, we are taught, first of all, that we ought to serve, honour, magnify, and praise him above all things, and to seek his glory in all our life and conversation, and by no means to commit any thing, whereby the majesty of his name should be
Deut. vi. Matt. iv. obscured or hindered, according to this commandment: "Thou shalt honour the Lord thy God, and him alone shalt thou serve." Secondly, he is called our Lord, that is to say, the Lord of the faithful, because that he through his almighty power doth mightily defend us, and deliver us from the tyranny of all our enemies, sin, death, devil, and hell, and careth and provideth for us, as a bounteous lord and master doth for his true and faithful servants; so that no good thing shall want unto us, profitable either for body or for soul.

Father. Hitherto have we heard of the divinity of Christ, that is to say, that Christ is the only-begotten Son of God, and therefore true God: again, that he is our Lord, our buckler, our shield, our strong and mighty tower, yea, our horn of plenty and fountain of all goodness. But come off: is this second Person in the Godhead, whom thou in thy creed callest Jesus Christ, only God, and not also man? *Son*. My Lord and Saviour Christ Jesus is not only God, but also man, as the next article of the christian faith doth right well declare.

Father. What is that? Rehearse it. *Son*. This is it:

"Which was conceived by the Holy Ghost, born of the virgin Mary."

Of the humanity of Christ.

Father. What dost thou believe and confess in this article? *Son*. That Christ Jesus, the natural Son of God, at the time appointed of his heavenly Father from everlasting, became man, not after the common order of men, but after a supernatural manner, even by the marvellous working of the Holy Ghost, taking his perfect humanity of the substance of the most pure and undefiled virgin Mary; and when the time of her deliverance came, he was truly and naturally born of her, and brought forth into this world; so that, as he is true God of the nature and substance of his Father before all worlds, even from everlasting, so likewise is he true man of the nature and substance of his mother Mary.

Father. Are there then two natures in the Lord Christ? *Son*. Yea, verily, the nature of God, and the nature of man.

Father. And are both these natures in one person? *Son*. Yea, and that without any confusion or separation, so that whole Christ is very God and very man in one and unseparable person.

Father. How dost thou prove by the word of God, that Christ was conceived in the virgin Mary's womb without the seed of man, only by the supernatural and wonderful operation of the Holy Ghost? *Son*. The holy scriptures are evident. For
Luke i. thus writeth blessed Luke: "The angel Gabriel was sent from God unto a city of Galilee, named Nazareth, to a virgin spoused to a man, whose name was Joseph, of the house of David; and the virgin's name was Mary. And the angel went in unto her, and said, Hail, full of grace, the Lord is with thee: blessed art thou among women. And when she saw him, she was abashed at his saying, and cast in her mind what manner of salutation that should be. And the angel said unto her, Fear not, Mary; for thou hast found grace with God. Lo, thou shalt conceive in thy womb, and shalt bear a son, and shalt call his name Jesus. He shall be great, and shall be called the Son of the Highest. And the Lord God shall give unto him the seat of his father David; and he shall reign over the house of Jacob for ever; and of his kingdom shall be none end. Then said Mary unto the angel, How shall this be, seeing I know not a man? And the angel answered and said, The Holy Ghost shall come upon thee, and the power of the Highest shall overshadow thee. Therefore also that holy thing, which shall be

born, shall be called the Son of God." St Matthew also hath these words: "When Mary, Christ's mother, was betrothed to Joseph, before they came together, she was found with child of the Holy Ghost. Then Joseph, her husband, being a just man, and loth to defame her, was minded to put her away secretly. While he thus thought, behold, the angel of the Lord appeared unto him in a dream, saying, Joseph, the son of David, fear not to take unto thee Mary thy wife: for that which is conceived in her is of the Holy Ghost. She shall bring forth a son; and thou shalt call his name Jesus; for he shall save his people from their sins. All this was done to fulfil that which was spoken of the Lord by the prophet, saying, Behold, a maid shall be with child, and shall bring forth a son; and they call his name Emmanuel, which is by interpretation, God with us," or God and man. Matt. i. Isai. vii.

Father. What doth it profit us, that Christ received his perfect humanity and manhead of the virgin Mary without the company of man, only by the marvellous and above-natural working of the Holy Ghost? *Son*. The commodity and profit hereof is greater than it can be expressed. It is not unknown unto you, that all we sinned, and justly for our sin were condemned unto everlasting damnation in Adam; so that both we and all our acts are altogether filthy, unpure, and unclean. Our generation, our conception, our birth, our life, our working, our thinking, our breathing, and whatsoever besides we are, have, or do, it is altogether unpure and unclean. For "that is born of flesh is flesh." "A corrupt tree cannot bring forth good fruits." "By nature we all are the children of wrath." And therefore David shamed not thus to write of himself and of his being: "Behold, my father begat me in wickedness, and my mother conceived me in sin." Rom. v. John iii. Matt. vii. Eph. ii. Psal. li.

Now to be delivered from this filthy uncleanness and unclean filthiness, it was requisite that one should be born free and utterly estranged from this filthy generation and conception, wherein all we the children of Adam are wrapped, which, by his pure, clean, and holy conception, and blessed nativity and birth, should put away and cleanse the filthiness of our most filthy generation, conception, and birth, which we received of old sinful Adam. And because none among all creatures was found, either in heaven or in earth, of such purity and cleanness, that might work and bring this most noble and excellent benefit of everlasting salvation unto mankind, therefore the heavenly Father of his unoutspeakable clemency, goodness, mercy, charity, and love, sent his only-begotten Son into this world, to take upon him the nature of man, but yet not after the common order of nature, but far otherwise, without the help of man, even by the wonderful virtue and power of the Holy Ghost, by this means becoming man, and yet not of the seed of man, (for so should his conception and nativity have profited us nothing at all; for of the unclean what can be cleansed?) and "like unto us in all things, sin alone except." Heb. iv.

Father. It was necessary then, that the Son of God should be incarnate by the Holy Ghost, and not by any workman? *Son*. Yea, verily, for this incarnation of the Son of God wrought by the Holy Ghost is after a certain manner our regeneration; so that through it we, which before were the cursed children of Adam, begotten and conceived of unclean seed, are purified, and made in Christ of carnal spiritual, of filthy clean, of unrighteous righteous, of the fire-brands of hell the sons of God, and heirs of his everlasting glory.

Father. As Christ was conceived by the Holy Ghost, so was he born of the maid Mary. *Son*. So saith the article of our faith.

Father. But how is that proved by the scriptures? *Son*. That the Lord Christ should be born of a maid, it was prophesied many years before Christ was born. For thus saith the prophet Esay: "Behold, a maid shall conceive or be with child, and shall bring forth a son; and they shall call his name Emmanuel." St Matthew saith: "Jacob begat Joseph the husband of Mary, of whom Jesus was born, which is called Christ." The angel Gabriel said unto Mary: "Behold, thou shalt conceive in thy womb and bear a son, and shalt call his name Jesus." St Paul saith: "When the time was full come, God sent his Son, made of a woman, and made bond unto the law." Isai. vii. Matt. i. Luke ii. Gal. iv.

Father. What is meant when we say, Christ was born of the virgin Mary? *Son*.

Nothing else, than that Christ is true, perfect, and natural man, taking this his humanity or manhood of the pure and undefiled virgin Mary; so that, as he is true, perfect, and natural God of the substance of God the Father, so likewise is he true, perfect, and natural man of the substance of Mary his mother. And as Christ from everlasting was begotten very God of God his Father, without any mother; so likewise was he born at the time appointed very man of the virgin Mary his mother, without any father, only by the virtue and power of the Holy Ghost.

Father. This is then a certain and undoubted verity, that Christ brought not his body with him from heaven, and so passed through the virgin Mary, as the water goeth through the conduit, but received his perfect humanity of the substance of Mary his mother; so that as of God his Father he is true and natural God, so likewise of Mary his mother he is true and natural man. *Son*. This is so certain, as nothing is more Heb. ii. certain. For St Paul saith, speaking of Christ: "He in no condition taketh on him the angels, but the seed of Abraham taketh he on him." Again: "Forasmuch as the children Rom. i. were partakers of flesh and blood, he also himself took part with them." Item: "Jesus Christ the Son of God was begotten of the seed of David, as pertaining to the flesh." Rom. ix. Also in another place: "Christ, as concerning the flesh, came of the Israelites." For Gen. iii. Matt. xv. Luke i. Matt. xvi. this cause in the holy scriptures is Christ called "the seed of the woman," "the Son of David," "the fruit of Mary's womb," "the Son of man," &c.

Heb. iv. What profit we have by the humanity of Christ. *Father*. What profit have we by this, that Christ is true and perfect man, and "like unto us in all things, sin alone except"? *Son*. Very much. For in that he is not only God, but also man, yea, and that pure and undefiled man, conceived, born, and living without all sin, he is of sufficient dignity, worthiness, and perfection before God the Father, to be our Mediator and peace-maker, to be our high priest and everlasting bishop, to be a sweet-smelling sacrifice for our sins, to be head of the congregation, to be the Lord of the faithful, to subdue Satan, to destroy hell, to deliver us from the bond of sin and from the curse of the law, and to enrich us with all heavenly and spiritual blessings; for whatsoever we have offended in our wicked and sinful flesh, that same hath Christ the Lord recompensed and satisfied in his most blessed, pure, and holy flesh. And his recompence and satisfaction is accepted of God the Father for Isai. ix. our own recompence and satisfaction, as the prophet saith: "A child is born to us, and a son is given to us;" that is to say, to our singular commodity and great profit.

Father. How cometh this to pass? *Son*. By his passion and death, as the article following declareth.

Father. Rehearse it.

Son. "Suffered under Ponce Pilate, was crucified, dead, and buried: He descended unto hell."

Father. What doth this article teach thee? *Son*. I learn of this article two things. First, my too much misery and wretchedness, into the which I was cast both by mine own sin and Adam's; which misery and wretchedness was so great and unrecompensable, that from it neither I myself, nor no creature for me, either in heaven or in earth, could deliver me; so that remediless I must perish and everlastingly be damned. Secondly, the exceeding great and unmeasurable mercy and love of my heavenly Father toward me, which without all my deserts, even of his own mere goodness, so greatly tendered my salvation, that he, having but one only-begotten Son, was content to give him unto the death for my sake; so that I, believing on him, and looking for health and everlasting life at my heavenly Father's hand through the passion and death of this his dearly-beloved Son, might be delivered from this my wretchedness, be made free from the tyranny of Satan, and become partaker of everlasting glory, as the Lord Christ John iii. himself witnesseth, saying: "As Moses lifted up the serpent in the wilderness, even so must the Son of man be lift up, that none that believeth on him perish, but have everlasting life. For God loved the world so dearly, that he gave his only-begotten Son, that none that believe in him should perish, but have everlasting life." Hereto Rom. v. belongeth the saying of St Paul: "God doth wonderfully set forth his love that he hath to us, seeing that, while we were yet sinners, Christ died for us. Much more then now, seeing we are justified in his blood, shall we be saved from wrath through him. For if, when we were yet enemies, we were reconciled to God by the death of his Son; much more, seeing we are reconciled, we shall be preserved by his life. Not only so, but we also joy in God by the means of our Lord Jesus Christ, by whom we have now received the atonement."

Father. Whatsoever therefore Christ suffered in his body, did he suffer it for thee and for thy salvation? *Son*. That is my belief. All that ever Christ did or suffered in his humanity, was altogether done and suffered for my sake. He came down from heaven for my sake. He was incarnate by the Holy Ghost and born of the virgin Mary for my sake. He was circumcised and baptized for my sake. He fasted, prayed, preached, wrought miracles for my sake. He suffered his passion and death for my sake. He rose again for my sake. He is ascended into the kingdom of his Father for my sake. He at the last day shall come again unto the judgment for my sake, and place me with him in the glory of his Father, where I shall most blessedly remain worlds without end. For Christ is mine: how then can it be, but that, whatsoever Christ hath, the same is mine also?—as St Paul saith: "God spared not his own Son, but gave him for us all: how shall he not with him give us all things also?" Rom. viii.

Father. Declare unto me by the word of God that Christ suffered under Ponce Pilate. *Son*. In the prayer, which the apostles after Christ's ascension made unto God the Father, these words are contained: "Of a truth, O Lord, against thy holy child Jesus, whom thou hast anointed, both Herod and also Ponce Pilate, with the gentiles, and the people of Israel, gathered themselves together in this city, for to do whatsoever thy hand and thy counsel determined before to be done." St Paul unto bishop Timothy writeth on this manner: "I give thee charge in the sight of God, which quickeneth all things, and before Jesu Christ, which under Ponce Pilate witnessed a good witnessing, that thou keep the commandment, and be without spot." David also saith: "The kings of the earth stood up, and the rulers took counsel together against the Lord, and against his Anointed." The evangelical history sheweth most evidently, that Christ suffered under Ponce Pilate. And the Lord Jesus himself divers times before his passion said unto his disciples, that he should "be betrayed to the heathen, and mocked, and scourged, and spitted on, and slain," &c. Acts iv. 1 Tim. vi. Psal. ii. Matt. xxvii. Mark xv. Luke xxiii. John xix. Matt. xx. Mark x. Luke xviii.

Father. What profit hast thou by this, that Christ suffered such and so great torments and pains? *Son*. I am not able to express it. The pains, plagues, and punishments, which I both in body and soul ought most worthily to have suffered even in hell-fire, for my great and innumerable sins committed against the majesty of God, those did my Lord and Saviour Christ Jesus most willingly suffer in his most blessed, innocent, guiltless, and pure body, at the will of his Father, to deliver me from everlasting pains and torments, which most justly were due unto me; so that it is truly said of the Lord Christ by the psalmograph: "The rebukes of them which rebuked thee fell on me." Again: "I am fain to pay the things which I never took." What profit we have by the passion of Christ.

Father. Prove by the scriptures that the pains which Christ suffered, he suffered them for thy sake, for thy profit and salvation. *Son*. Christ Jesus is that immaculate and unspotted "Lamb of God," "which never committed any sin, neither was there any guile found in his mouth." For himself there was no need to suffer. For us therefore and for our sins he suffered whatsoever he suffered. And that this is true, the holy scriptures declare manifestly. Esay the prophet speaketh on this manner: "We reckoned him so simple and so vile, that we hid our face from him. Howbeit, of a truth, he took away our infirmities, and bare our sorrows and pains. And yet we judged him as though he had been plagued and cast down of God (for his sins): whereas he notwithstanding was wounded for our offences, and smitten for our wickedness. For the pain of our punishment was laid upon him; and with his stripes are we made whole. As for us, we all have gone astray like sheep, every one hath turned his own way. But through him the Lord hath pardoned all our sins." And a little after the prophet, speaking in the person of God, saith: "The punishment came upon him for the sins of my people." St Peter also saith: "Christ hath once suffered for sins, the just for the unjust, for to bring us to God." Again: "Christ hath suffered for us in the flesh." These scriptures with many more do most plainly Exod. xii. John i. 1 Pet. ii. Isai. liii. 1 Pet. iii. 1 Pet. iv.

declare, that those pains which the Lord Christ suffered, he suffered them not for his own (which were utterly none), but for our sins, that we, through the temporal pains of his most innocent and pure body, might be delivered from the eternal and everlasting pains of hell-fire.

Father. Was Christ compelled to suffer these pains, either suffered he them gladly and willingly? *Son.* It pleased the heavenly Father of his mere mercy toward mankind, that his only-begotten Son should become man, and suffer those pains which were due unto man for his sin, that by this means the justice of God might be both pacified and satisfied, and man delivered from his most miserable captivity, and made free from the bitter torments of hell. The Son of God, taking upon him the nature of man, and like to man in all things, sin alone except, shewed himself in all things conformable to
Phil. ii. the will of his heavenly Father, and most willingly "obeyed him unto the death, even the death of the cross," that by this means he, suffering temporal pains in his innocent body, might deliver mankind from the everlasting pains both of body and soul.

Isai. liii. For thus writeth the prophet of Christ: "He was offered, because it was his good
Isai. l. pleasure." And by the same prophet he himself saith: "I offered my back unto the smiters, and my cheeks to the nippers: I turned not my face from shame and spitting."
Psal. liv. And by the psalmograph he saith: "I will offer sacrifice unto thee willingly." He
Psal. xl. speaketh of the sacrifice of his body. Again: "Sacrifice and offering thou wouldst not have, but a body hast thou ordained me. Burnt offerings and sin-offerings hast thou not allowed. Then said I, Lo, I come: in the beginning of the book it is written
Isai. liii. of me, that I should do thy will, O God." The prophet also saith of him: "When he was pained and troubled, he did not once open his mouth. He was led as a sheep to be slain, yet was he as still as a lamb before the shearer, and did not once open his
Matt. xx. Mark x. Luke xviii. mouth." His voluntary going up unto Jerusalem, when the time of his passion began to draw nigh, declareth evidently that the passion of Christ was willing and not constrained. When he was apprehended in the garden, and Peter fought for his
Matt. xxvi. defence, were not these his words unto thee, Peter? "Put up thy sword into his place: for all that take the sword shall perish with the sword. Or thinkest thou, that I cannot pray my Father now to send me more than twelve legions of angels? But how then should the scriptures be fulfilled? For thus must it be." Doth not the evangelical
John xviii. history plainly declare, that those which were sent to take Christ could not abide the speech of him, but fell down as dead before him, and could lay no hand on him till he
John x. suffered them? Are not these the words of Christ? "Therefore doth my Father love me, because I give over my life, that I may take it again. No man taketh it from me; but I give it over of myself. I have power to give it over, and I have power to take it again."

Father. Where suffered Christ these pains? *Son.* Upon the cross. For so hath our article: "He suffered under Ponce Pilate, was crucified," that is to say, fastened to the cross. As through the fruit of a tree mankind perished, so through pains suffered on a tree mankind is restored to his former blessed state. The one tree brought death and damnation; the other, life and salvation.

Father. Declare unto me by the word of God, that Christ was crucified and fastened
Num. xxi. to the cross. *Son.* It was figured by the brasen serpent, which Moses set up in the wilderness at the commandment of God, that Christ should also be lifted up and nailed
John iii. on the cross. For so doth Christ himself apply this figure, saying: "Like as Moses lifted up the serpent in the wilderness, even so must the Son of man be lifted up, that whosoever believeth in him should not perish, but have everlasting life." The evangelists
Luke xxiii. write on this manner: "After they came into that place, which is called Calvary, there they crucified Jesus and the two thieves; one on his right hand, the other on his left
John xix. hand." When "Pilate said unto the Jews, Behold your king! they cried, Away with him, away with him, crucify him, crucify him! Pilate said unto them, Shall I crucify your king? The bishops answered, We have no king, but an emperor. Then he delivered
John xx. [Matt. xxviii.] 1 Cor. i. Phil. ii. Jesus unto them to be crucified." The angel said to the women: "Ye seek Jesus crucified." St Paul saith: "We preach Christ crucified." Again: "Christ Jesus became obedient to his Father unto the death, even the death of the cross."

What profit we have in this, that *Father.* What profit have we by this, that Christ was crucified or fastened to the cross? *Son.* The profit is great and incomparable.

First, in that Christ was crucified and nailed on the cross, and there suffered most intolerable pains, he by his bitter torments and punishments took away that damnation which we most righteously in Adam had deserved by eating of the forbidden fruit, and whatsoever besides we of ourselves have committed worthy the pains of hell-fire. "For as by the sin of one (Adam) condemnation came on all men, even so by the justifying of one cometh the righteousness that bringeth life upon all men. For as by one man's disobedience many became sinners, so by the obedience of one (Christ) shall many be made righteous." Christ was fastened to the cross. Rom. v.

Secondly, Christ, being crucified and fastened to the tree, became accursed for our sake, and by this means delivered us from the curse of the law, as St Paul testifieth, saying: "Christ hath delivered us from the curse of the law, and was made accursed for us. For it is written, Cursed is every one that hangeth on tree." Gal. iii. Deut. xxi.

Thirdly, the crucifying or fastening of Christ unto the cross preacheth to us, that as he was lifted up on the cross, so likewise, by the virtue of his passion, shall he lift us up unto the kingdom of his Father, as he himself saith: "Now is the judgment of this world: now shall the prince of this world be cast out. And I, if I were lift up from the earth, will draw all men unto me. This said Jesus (writeth the evangelist), signifying what death he should die." John xii.

Fourthly, in that Christ was fastened to the cross, we are taught, that as Adam through a tree did sin, and by that means cast both himself and all his posterity under the power of the devil; so likewise Christ Jesus through a tree delivered us from the tyranny and power of the devil, and set us again at liberty to serve the living God "in holiness and righteousness all the days of our life." Luke i.

Fifthly and finally, Christ crucified hath not only "put out the hand-writing that was against us contained in the law written, and fastened it to his cross, and hath spoiled rule and power, and hath made a shew of them openly, and hath triumphed over them in his own person," but he hath also "reconciled all things unto God, and through the blood of his cross he hath set at peace both things in heaven, and things in earth;" so that we, which afore were reputed "aliens from the commonweal of Israel, and utterly without Christ," are now "no more strangers and foreigners, but citizens with the saints, and of the household of God, and are built upon the foundation of the apostles and prophets, Jesus Christ being the head corner-stone, in whom every building coupled together groweth unto an holy temple in the Lord." Col. ii. Eph. ii.

Father. Christ was not only crucified for us, but he also died for us and for our sins. *Son*. That is most certain. For this is the article of our faith:

"He suffered under Ponce Pilate, was crucified, dead, and buried."

Father. Prove by the word of God, that Christ died. *Son*. Daniel prophesied of Christ's death on this manner: "After those sixty-two weeks shall Christ be slain; and they shall have no pleasure in him." Christ himself, long before he died, many and divers times told his disciples that he should be slain and suffer death at Jerusalem. Bishop Caiphas also prophesied of Christ's death, when he said: "It is more expedient for us, that one die for the people, than that all the people should perish." "This spake he," saith the evangelist, "not of himself, but, forsomuch as he was high priest of the same year, he prophesied. For Jesus must die for the people, and not for the people only, but that he should gather together the children of God, which were scattered abroad." "Jesus," saith St Matthew, "cried with a loud voice, and gave up the ghost." Blessed Luke writeth thus: "Jesus, crying with a loud voice, said, O Father, I commend my spirit into thy hands. And immediately he gave up the ghost." St John writeth thus: "When Jesus knew that all was performed, that the scripture might be fulfilled, he said, I am athirst. There stood a vessel full of vinegar. They filled a sponge with vinegar, and wound it about with hyssop, and held it to his mouth. Now when Jesus had received the vinegar, he said, It is finished; and bowed his head, and gave up the ghost." Dan. ix. Matt. xvi. xvii. xx. Mark x. Luke ix. xviii. John xi. Matt. xxvii. Luke xxiii. John xix.

The apostles of Christ, in their sermon, spake on this manner to the Jews: "Ye men of Israel, hear these words: Jesus of Nazareth, the man approved of God among you with miracles, wonders, and tokens, which God did by him in the midst of Acts ii.

you, as ye yourselves know also, him (after that he was delivered by the determinate counsel and foreknowledge of God), have ye taken by the hands of unrighteous persons, and crucified him, and slain him," &c.

Of Christ's death St Paul maketh mention almost in all his epistles. I will re-
Rom. v. hearse certain sentences out of his writings. "God," saith he, "doth wonderfully set forth his love toward us, in that Christ died for us when we were yet sinners." Again:
1 Cor. xv. "I delivered unto you that which I also received, which is, that Christ died for
Phil. ii. our sins." Also in another place: "Let the same mind be in you that was in Christ Jesu, which, being in the shape of God, thought it no robbery to be equal with God, but made himself of no reputation, and took upon him the shape of a servant, became like another man, and was found in his apparel as a man: he humbled himself, and became obedient unto the death, even the death of the cross." Hereto appertaineth the saying
1 Pet. iii. of St Peter: "Christ died once for our sins, the righteous for the unrighteous," &c.

What profit we have by the death of Christ. *Father.* What profit have we by the death of Christ? *Son.* Christ by his temporal death hath for our sake overcome everlasting death, whereunto through sin we were
Hos. xiii. subject and thrall, as Christ himself saith by the prophet: "O death, I will be thy
1 Cor. xv. death." Like unto this is that which St Paul writeth: "Death is swallowed up into victory. Death, where is thy sting? Hell, where is thy victory? The sting of death is sin: the strength of sin is the law: but thanks be unto God, which hath given us the victory through our Lord Jesus Christ." Again, Christ by his death hath overcome
Heb. ii. him which had the rule of death, as St Paul testifieth, saying: "Christ through death destroyed him that had the rule of death, that is to say, the devil; and hath set them at liberty, which through the fear of death all their life-time were subject unto bondage." Furthermore, Christ by his death hath made a full and perfect satisfaction to God the Father for all our sins, and hath offered unto him such a sacrifice for all our wickednesses and trespasses, that it sufficeth without either any repetition of the same, or without any other sacrifice to be added thereunto, for all the offences that have been
Heb. x. or shall be committed unto the world's end, as St Paul saith: "With one only oblation hath he (Christ) made perfect for ever them that are sanctified." Again: "We are made holy by the offering of the body of Jesus Christ done once for all." Moreover, by the death of Christ we are not only delivered from all our sins, but also reconciled unto God, received into his favour, and made his sons and inheritors of
Rom. v. everlasting glory, as St Paul saith: "If we were reconciled unto God by the death of his Son, when we were yet enemies, much more shall we be saved by him now
2 Tim. i. that we are reconciled." Again: "Our Saviour Jesus Christ (by his death) hath taken away the power of death, and hath brought life and immortality."

Father. Great are the benefits, I confess, which we have obtained by the death of
Gal. vi. Christ; so that it is not without a cause said of the holy apostle St Paul: "God forbid that I should rejoice in any thing, but in the cross," that is to say, the passion and death, "of our Lord Jesu Christ." But what was done with the body of Christ, after that it was crucified and dead? *Son.* It was buried. For so is the article of our faith:

"He suffered under Ponce Pilate, was crucified, dead, and buried."

Father. Declare unto me by the word of God, that Christ was buried. *Son.* The
Isai. liii. prophet Esay speaketh of Christ's burial on this manner: "His grave shall be given him with the condemned, and his crucifying with the thieves." The four evangelists
Matt. xxvii. Mark xv. Luke xxiii. John xix. write that, when Christ was once dead, "Joseph of Aramathia, a good, just man, which was a disciple of Jesus, and one that consented not unto the wicked counsel and deed of the Jews, but waited for the kingdom of God, went unto Pilate, and besought him that he might take down the body of Jesus. And Pilate gave him licence. Then took he down the body of Jesus." "There came also Nicodemus, (which afore came unto Jesus by night,) and brought of myrrh and aloes mingled together about an hundred pound weight. They took the body of Christ, and wound it in fine linen clothes, and laid it in a new sepulchre, wherein was never man laid afore, hewn out of a rock; and they rolled a great stone to the door of the sepulchre, and
1 Cor. xv. went their way." St Paul also saith: "Christ died for our sins according to the scriptures, and was buried."

Father. What doth it profit us that Christ was buried? *Son.* First, in that Christ was buried, it doth evidently declare unto us, that his passion and death were not fantastical, but true, certain, and unfeigned. Again, that as his body was covered in the grave, so likewise should the sins of the faithful be covered for his sake, and never be imputed unto them nor laid unto their charge. Thirdly, the burying of Christ hath brought this to pass, that our grave, which before was the dungeon of hell, should be translated and turned into a sweet, quiet, and holy dormitory, or resting-place, in the which the godly rest, abiding the joyful day of their resurrection. Finally, Christ was buried, that we also, being dead through repentance, and buried with him by baptism, should through grace from henceforth rise out of sin and walk in a new life. What profit we have by Christ's burial. Rom. vi.

Father. What followeth in the creed?

Son. "He went down unto hell."

Father. How provest thou that Christ went down unto hell? *Son.* Christ himself by the prophet David saith: "Thou shalt not leave my soul in hell, neither shalt thou suffer thy Holy One to see corruption." St Peter also saith: "Christ hath once suffered for our sins, the just for the unjust, for to bring us unto God, and was slain after the flesh, but quickened after the Spirit; in the which Spirit he also went and preached unto the spirits that were in prison," &c. Psal. xvi. Acts ii. 1 Pet. iii.

Father. What profit have we by Christ's descension and going down unto hell? *Son.* By this means are we well assured, that Christ hath overcome the devil, broken the serpent's head, destroyed the gates of hell, vanquished the infernal army, and utterly delivered us from everlasting damnation, as Christ himself saith by the prophet: "O death, I will be thy death. O hell, I will be thy destruction." So that now with joyful hearts and triumphant voices we may well say with the apostle: "Death is swallowed up into victory. Death, where is thy sting? Hell, where is thy victory? The sting of death is sin: the strength of sin is the law: but thanks be unto God, which hath given us the victory through our Lord Jesus Christ." What profit we have by Christ's descension unto hell. Hos. xiii. 1 Cor. xv.

Father. Suffered Christ pains also in hell? *Son.* Nothing less. For whatsoever pains were to be suffered for our sins and wickednesses, he suffered them all in his blessed body on the altar of the cross. He went not down unto hell as a guilty person to suffer, but as a valiant prince to conquer, and as a most puissant and glorious king to triumph over his enemies, and to make us also lords and conquerors of Satan and of all his infernal army.

Father. When Christ by his passion and death had wrought this most noble work of our redemption, paid our ransom, satisfied for our sins, appeased God's wrath, and reconciled us unto his favour, what did he then?

Son. "The third day he rose again from death."

Father. How provest thou that by the word of God? *Son.* Long before the coming of Christ into the flesh it was prophesied not only that Christ should suffer and die (as we afore have heard), but also that he should rise again unto life, yea, and that on the third day. By the prophet speaketh Christ himself on this manner: "He shall make us alive after two days, and on the third day he shall raise us up again, and we shall live before him." Was not the swallowing up of Jonas into the whale's belly, and the deliverance of him again unto the land the third day, a very figure of Christ's death and of his resurrection? "Jonas," saith the scripture, "was in the belly of the fish three days and three nights." "And the Lord spake unto the fish; and it cast out Jonas again upon the dry land." Certes Christ applieth it unto himself, saying: "As Jonas was in the whale's belly three days and three nights, so shall the Son of man be in the heart of the earth three days and three nights." The prophet David, speaking in the person of Christ, saith: "I laid me down and slept, but I rose up again; for the Lord sustained me." Again: "My flesh shall rest in hope. For thou shalt not leave my soul in hell, neither shalt thou suffer thy Holy One to see corruption. But thou shalt shew unto me the way of life, and make me full of joy with thy countenance." Of the resurrection of Christ. Hos. vi. Jonah ii. Matt. xii. Luke xi. Psal. iii. Psal. xvi. Acts ii. xiii.

Christ divers times before his passion declared unto his disciples, that he should rise again on the third day from death unto life. Christ himself, many times before his passion and death, declared unto his disciples that, after he was slain, he should rise again unto life the third day following. The evangelists rehearse his words on this manner: [Matt. xvi.] "From that time," saith blessed Matthew, "began Jesus to declare unto his disciples, that he must go unto Jerusalem, and suffer many things of the elders, and of the scribes, and of the head priests, and be slain, and rise again on the third day." [Matt. xx.] Again: "Jesus, going up unto Jerusalem, took his twelve disciples with him secretly, and said unto them, Behold, we go up unto Jerusalem; and the Son of man shall be betrayed to the chief priests and scribes; and they shall condemn him unto the death, and they shall deliver him to the heathen to mock, scourge, and crucify him; and on the third day he shall rise again." [Mark x. Luke xviii.] The like words read we in Mark and Luke.

Moreover (as I may let pass the history of Christ's resurrection, lively and largely described of the four evangelists), the angel of God beareth witness of Christ's resurrection on this manner, speaking to the women which came to Christ's sepulchre for to anoint his body: [Matt. xxviii. Mark xvi. Luke xxiv.] "I know that ye seek Jesus, which was crucified. He is not here, but is risen again, as he told you afore." Again: "Why seek ye the living with the dead? He is not here, but is risen. Remember how he said unto you, when he was yet in Galilee, that the Son of man must be betrayed into the hands of sinful men, and be crucified, and on the third day rise again." [Matt. xvii. Mark ix. Luke ix.]

[Acts ii.] Furthermore, the apostles testify of Christ's resurrection on this wise: "God hath raised up again Jesus, whereof all we are witnesses." St Paul also maketh many times mention of Christ's resurrection. In a certain sermon, as blessed Luke writeth, he spake these words: [Acts xiii.] "God raised up Jesus from the dead on the third day, which was seen many days of them which went up with him from Galilee unto Jerusalem," &c. In his epistles he hath these sentences, and many such like: [Rom. iv.] "Jesus Christ died for our sins, and rose again for our justification." [Rom. viii.] "It is Christ which died, yea rather, which is risen again." [1 Cor. xv.] "I delivered that unto you which I received, that Christ died for our sins according to the scriptures, and that he was buried, and rose again on the third day according to the scriptures." [2 Tim. ii.] "Remember that Jesus Christ, which came of the seed of David, rose again from the dead."

Father. These testimonies of the holy scripture concerning Christ's resurrection may seem abundantly for this present to suffice. But come off, tell me, what profit have we by Christ's resurrection? *Son*. Such and so great, that without it all is in vain whatsoever Christ hath done for us. [1 Cor. xv.]

[What profit we have by Christ's resurrection.]

For, first of all, by his glorious resurrection he hath shewed himself a most noble and valiant conqueror of death, devil, and hell, and by this his most victorious conquest hath he delivered us from the cruelty and tyranny of our enemies; I mean, death, devil, and hell; so that now we be no more captives and bond-slaves unto them, but sons and heirs of God, yea, and fellow-heirs with the Lord Jesu of his Father's kingdom; [Rom. viii.] so that we may triumphantly say with St Paul: [1 Cor. xv.] "Death, where is thy victory? Death, where is thy sting? The sting of death is sin; and the power of sin is the law: but thanks be unto God, which hath given us the victory through our Lord Jesus Christ."

Secondly, by Christ's resurrection we be justified and made righteous before God, as St Paul saith: [Rom. iv.] "Christ Jesus died for our sins, and rose again for our justification," or righteous-making.

Thirdly, Christ by his resurrection hath made us certain and sure of the resurrection of our bodies and of everlasting life, as Christ himself saith: [John xi.] "I am the resurrection and life. He that believeth in me, although he be dead, yet shall he live; and every one that liveth and believeth in me, he shall not die everlastingly." St Paul also saith: [1 Cor. xv.] "As by Adam all die, so likewise by Christ all shall be made alive." Again: [1 Thess. iv.] "If we believe that Jesus Christ died and rose again, even so shall God also bring with him again those which are fallen asleep by Jesus." Item: [Phil. iii.] "Our conversation is in heaven, from whence we look for a Saviour, even the Lord Jesus Christ, which shall transfigure and change this our vile body, that he may make it like to his own glorious body, according to the power wherewith he is able to make all things subject unto himself."

Fourthly and finally, Christ by his glorious resurrection hath given us power, through the Holy Ghost, to shake off the miserable yoke of dead works, and the bondage of wicked and ungodly conversation, and to garnish ourselves with all kind of godly virtues; so that from henceforth we should walk in a new life, and pass over the time of this our pilgrimage in holiness, righteousness, and truth, doing alway that which is acceptable before the majesty of the Lord our God, as St Paul saith: "We are buried together with Christ through baptism into death, that as Christ was raised up from the dead through the glory of his Father, so likewise we should walk in a new life." Again: "If ye be risen again together with Christ, seek for those things which are above, where Christ is sitting on the right hand of God. Be careful about heavenly, and not earthly things. For ye are dead; and your life is hid in Christ with God. Whensoever Christ your life shall appear, then shall ye also appear with him in glory. Mortify therefore your earthly members," &c. Once again he saith: "If one died for all, then were all dead; and he died for all, that they which live should no more from henceforth live to themselves, but to him which died for them and rose again." Rom. vi. Col. iii. 2 Cor. v.

Father. What did Christ after his resurrection? *Son*. After that the Lord Christ had shewed himself alive certain days to his disciples, declaring by divers most certain arguments that he was unfeignedly and truly risen again from death, by this means shewing himself to be an Almighty God, and Lord over sin, devil, death, and hell, he by the power of his Godhead, leaving this world, ascended into heaven visibly and corporally, yea, and that in the presence of his disciples, where he now remaineth, and shall remain unto the day of judgment, sitting on the right hand of God his Father. For so is the article of our faith, as it followeth in order: Of Christ's ascension. Mark xvi. Luke xxiv. Acts i.

"He ascended into heaven, and sitteth on the right hand of God the Father Almighty."

Father. Prove me by the word of God, that Christ after his resurrection ascended and went up into heaven. *Son*. We have many and divers testimonies in the holy scriptures of Christ's ascension unto the kingdom of his Father.

Father. Let me hear.

Son. That prince-like prophet David writeth of Christ's ascension, yea, rather prophesieth on this manner: "Thou art gone up on high, and hast led captivity captive, and hast received gifts for men." Again: "God is gone up with great rejoicing, yea, the Lord is ascended with the sound of a trumpet." Blessed St Mark writeth of Christ's ascension on this manner: "After the Lord had spoken these things, he was taken up into heaven, and sat down on the right hand of God." St Luke hath these words: "Jesus led out his disciples unto Bethania, and, lifting up his hands, he blessed them. And it came to pass that when he had blessed them, he departed from them, and was carried up into heaven." In the chronicle of the apostles' acts we read thus: "And when Jesus had spoken these things, while they beheld, he was taken up; and a cloud received him up out of their sight. And while they looked stedfastly up to heaven, as he went, behold, two men stood by them in white apparel, which also said, Ye men of Galilee, why stand ye gazing up into heaven? This same Jesus, which is taken up from you into heaven, shall so come, even as ye have seen him go into heaven." Psal. lxviii. Psal. xlvii. Mark xvi. Luke xxiv. Acts i.

Christ in his last sermon maketh mention divers times of his ascension. "I go my way," saith he, "unto him that sent me; and none of you asketh me, Whither goest thou? But because I have said such things to you, your hearts are full of sorrow. Nevertheless I tell you the truth, it is expedient for you that I go my way: for if I go not away, that Comforter will not come unto you," &c. Again: "I went out from the Father, and came into the world; and I leave the world again, and go to the Father." John xvi.

The blessed apostle St Paul writeth on this manner: "God hath raised up Christ from death, and set him on his right hand in heavenly things, above all rule, power, might, and dominion, and above all names that are named, not in this world only, but also in the world to come; and hath put all things under his feet, and hath made him above all things the head of the congregation, which is his body and fulness of Eph. i.

Psal. lxviii. him that filleth all in all." Again: "He is gone up on high, and hath led captivity
Eph. iv. captive, and hath given gifts unto men. That he ascended, what meaneth it, but that he also descended first of all into the lowest parts of the earth? He that descended is even the same also that ascended up above all heavens to fulfil all things." Item:
Heb. ix. "Christ is not entered into the holy places that are made with hands, which are but figures of true things; but he is entered into the very heaven, for to appear now in the sight of God for us."

Father. In the article which thou recitedst, there is not only contained, that Christ "ascended into heaven," but also that he "sitteth on the right hand of God" his Father. This latter part of the article would I have proved by the holy scriptures, I mean, that Christ sitteth on the right hand of God.

Son. Like as the psalmograph prophesied of the ascension of Christ, so likewise
Psal. cx. speaketh he of Christ's sitting on the right hand of God on this manner: "The Lord said unto my Lord, Sit on my right hand, till I make thine enemies thy footstool."
Matt. xxvi. Mark xiv. Christ himself saith: "Ye shall see the Son of man sitting on the right hand of power."
Rom. viii. St Paul hath these testimonies concerning this matter: "It is Christ that died, yea, rather that rose again, which also is on the right hand of God, and maketh intercession
Col. iii. for us." "If ye be risen with Christ, seek after those things that are above, where
Heb. i. Christ is sitting on the right hand of God." Christ "in his own person hath cleansed
Heb. x. our sins, and is set on the right hand of the Majesty on high." "This man (Christ), after he had offered one sacrifice for sins, sat him down for ever on the right hand of God, and from henceforth tarrieth till his foes be made his footstool." St Peter
1 Pet. iii. also saith: "Jesus Christ is on the right hand of God, and is gone into heaven, angels, power, and might subdued unto him."

Father. What profit have we by the ascension of Christ? *Son*. Great and large.

Father. What is it?

What profit we have by the ascension of Christ.

Son. First of all, in that Christ ascended into heaven, he hath not only subdued our enemies, the devil, the world, the flesh, sin, death, hell, damnation, &c., gloriously triumphing over them for our sake; but he hath also given us many noble and precious gifts, as the Holy Ghost, faith, love, hope, joy, quietness of conscience, patience, long-suffering, temperance, goodness, meekness, continence, &c., which thing David
Psal. lxviii. expresseth very aptly in this verse: "Thou art gone up on high, and hast led captivity captive, and given gifts unto men."

Secondly, in that Christ is gone up into heaven, we are well assured that he is gone, being our head, to prepare a place for us, being his members, as he himself saith:
John xiv. "Ye believe in God; believe also in me. In my Father's house there are many mansions. If it were otherwise, I would have told you. I go to prepare you a place. And if I go away to prepare you a place, I will come again, and take you unto myself, that where I am you also may be with me."

Thirdly, in that Christ is ascended into heaven, he is become our Mediator, Advocate, and Intercessor, pleadeth our cause before God his Father, and obtaineth all good
Rom. viii. things of him abundantly for us. "Christ," saith St Paul, "is on the right hand of
1 John ii. God, and maketh intercession for us." "If any man sinneth," saith St John, "we have an Advocate with the Father, Jesus Christ that righteous one. And he it is that obtaineth mercy for our sins; not for our sins only, but also for all the world's."

Fourthly, by the ascension of Christ we have a most certain and sure testimony of our ascension into the kingdom of heaven, and that we shall there remain for ever
Isai. lxiv. 1 Cor. ii. both body and soul with our head Christ, having such joys as "eye never saw the like, ear never heard the like, no tongue is able to express the like, nor heart able to conceive and think the like." And this is it, that Christ hath in his prayer unto
John xvii. his heavenly Father: "O Father, whom thou hast given me, I will that, where I am, they also be with me, that they may see my glory which thou gavest me."

Father. But what meaneth the scripture to remember and affirm, that Christ sitteth on the right hand of God the Father, when God the Father hath neither right nor left hand? *Son*. Truth it is, that God the Father, the first Person in the Godhead, ☞ hath neither hand nor foot, neither any other corporal member, as we have, (for, as

Christ saith, "God is a spirit," and "a spirit hath neither flesh nor bones;)" therefore the scriptures in this behalf are to be understand, not as the bare letter sound, but as it may agree with the other scriptures. John iv. Luke xxiv.

Father. What is it then to sit on the right hand of God? *Son*. To sit on the right hand of God is nothing else, than Christ, God and man, to be of the same might and power, of the same glory and majesty with God the Father, to be king, Lord, ruler, and governor over all things both in heaven and in earth, as he himself saith: "All power is given unto me in heaven and in earth;" so that the same honour and praise is due to Christ, God and man, which is due to God his Father. What it is to sit on the right hand of God. Matt. xxviii.

Father. What doth it profit us, that Christ sitteth on the right hand of God the Father? *Son*. Very much. It certifieth us, that we have a king and a Lord in heaven, which hath a care for us, loveth and tendereth us, and defendeth us from our enemies, and giveth us all good things; so that we need not fear devil, world, flesh, sin, death, hell, curse, law, damnation, and whatsoever is contrary or enemy to our health, commodity, and salvation: moreover it assureth us, that we, after this our exile and banishment from our native country, which is heaven, shall also be citizens of that blessed kingdom, enjoy the glory of heaven, and behold the majesty of God face to face, sitting with our head Christ in the glorious palace of his Father, worlds without end, noble, triumphant, and victorious conquerors over all our enemies, as St Paul saith: "God, which is rich in mercy, through his great love wherewith he hath loved us, even when we were dead by sin, hath quickened us together in Christ (for by grace are ye saved), and hath raised us up together, and made us sit together with him in heavenly things through Christ Jesus," &c. What profit we have by Christ's sitting on the right hand of God. Eph. ii.

Father. Remaineth there any other thing concerning our Lord and Saviour Christ Jesus in the articles of the christian faith? *Son*. Christ Jesus, as we have heard, for our salvation took flesh, and was born of the undefiled and pure maid Mary through the wonderful operation of the Holy Ghost, suffered death, rose again from death unto life, ascended by the power of his Godhead into heaven, where he sitteth now at the right hand of God his Father. As he hath done all these things aforesaid for us and for our salvation, so likewise at the end of this wretched and transitory world shall he come again to give judgment over all flesh, and to render unto every one according to his deeds, rewarding the righteous with everlasting glory, and the unrighteous with everlasting punishment. For thus soundeth the article which followeth:

"From thence shall he come to judge both the quick and the dead."

Father. Let me hear it proved by the holy scriptures, that Christ shall come from heaven to judge the quick and the dead. *Son*. As I may let pass the testimonies of the old testament concerning Christ's coming unto the judgment, which indeed are very many, Christ himself describeth his manner of coming unto the judgment on this wise: "As the lightning cometh out of the east, and shineth unto the west, so shall the coming of the Son of man be." "Then shall all the kindreds of the earth mourn, and they shall see the Son of man come in the clouds of heaven with power and great glory. And he shall send his angels with the great voice of a trumpet; and they shall gather together his chosen from the four winds, and from the one end of the whole world to the other." Again: "When the Son of man cometh in his glory, and all the holy angels with him, then shall he sit on the seat of his glory; and before him shall be gathered all nations. And he shall separate them one from another, as a shepherd divideth the sheep from the goats. And he shall set the sheep on the right hand, and the goats on the left," &c. Hereto appertaineth the saying of St Paul: "The Lord himself shall come down from heaven with a shout, and the voice of the archangel, and trumpet of God; and the dead in Christ shall arise," &c. Again: "The day of the Lord shall come, even as a thief in the night. When they shall say, Peace and no danger, then cometh on them sudden destruction, as the travailing of a woman with child; and they shall not escape." Of Christ's coming unto the judgment. Matt. xxiv. Matt. xxv. 1 Thess. iv. 1 Thess. v.

Now have we heard the manner of Christ's coming unto the judgment lively described and set forth. I will also rehearse a few sentences out of the new testament concerning Christ's judgment. Christ himself saith: "The Son of man shall come in the glory of Matt. xvi.

his Father with his angels, and then shall he reward every man according to their
John v. deeds." Again he saith: "The Father judgeth no man, but hath given all the judgment
Acts x. to the Son; that all should honour the Son, as they honour the Father." "Christ," saith St Peter in a certain sermon, as blessed Luke writeth, "commandeth us, that we should preach to the people, and testify that it is he which was appointed of God to be the judge of the quick and the dead." And in his epistle he writeth on this manner:
1 Pet. iv. "All men shall render an accompts unto him", that is to say, Christ, "which shall judge
Rom. xiv. both the quick and the dead." St Paul also saith: "We shall all appear before the
2 Cor. v. judging-place of Christ." Again: "We must all appear before the judging-seat of Christ, that every man may receive his reward according unto that which he hath done in his body, whether it be good or evil." Hitherto appertaineth the saying of the holy apostle Judas in his epistle: "Behold, the Lord shall come with thousands of saints to give judgment over all men."

What is meant by the quick and the dead.

Father. What meanest thou by "the quick and the dead"? *Son.* By "the quick" I understand them which shall be alive in this world, when Christ shall come unto the judgment; and by "the dead", such as have slept in the heart of the earth from the beginning of the world unto the last day.

Father. Why, shall any live in this world when Christ shall come to the judgment?
1 Cor. xv. *Son.* Yea, verily. For thus writeth St Paul: "Behold I shew you a mystery. We shall not all sleep, but we shall all be changed, and that in a moment, in the twinkling of an eye, at the sound of the last trump. For the trump shall blow, and the dead shall rise again incorruptible, and we all shall be changed. For this corruptible must
1 Thess. iv. put on incorruption, and this mortal must put on immortality." Again, he saith: "This say we unto you in the word of the Lord, that we, which live and are remaining in the coming of the Lord, shall not come yer[1] they which sleep. For the Lord himself shall descend from heaven with a shout, and the voice of the archangel, and trump of God. And the dead in Christ shall arise first: then shall we which live and remain be caught up with them also in the clouds to meet the Lord in the air. And so shall we ever be with the Lord."

What profit we have by Christ's coming unto the judgment.

Father. What profit shall the coming of Christ unto the judgment bring unto us? *Son.* This world, which is altogether set on wickedness, shall then have an end. The wicked and bloody tyrants of this world, with all the ungodly of the same, shall come
1 John v. unto confusion, their tyranny and wickedness being made open to the whole world.
Wisd. v. Yea, these wicked themselves shall confess: "O, these be they whom we sometime had in derision, and thought their ways to be very foolishness." The faithful and godly
Luke xxii. shall then be wholly delivered and made free from the tyranny of the devil, the world, and the flesh, and receive that which long tofore they hoped and looked for, I mean,
1 Cor. xiii. 1 John iii. Rev. vi. everlasting salvation. They shall see God "face to face," "even as he is." They shall be clad with the white vesture of immortality. They shall receive the crown of glory.
Isai. lxiv. 1 Cor. ii. Finally, they shall have such joys as "eye[2] never saw the like, ear never heard the like, no tongue is able to express the like, nor any heart is able to conceive or think the like."

The third part of the christian faith.

Father. Hitherto thou hast not altogether unaptly declared the two first parts of the christian faith, concerning God the Father and God the Son. It remaineth that we approach unto the third part of the christian belief, which concerneth the third Person in the Godhead, I mean, the Holy Ghost. What saith the article of our faith in this behalf?

Son. "I believe in the Holy Ghost."

Of the Holy Ghost.

Father. Why sayest thou, "I believe in the Holy Ghost"? *Son.* When I say, "I believe in the Holy Ghost", it is thus much in effect: I believe with my heart, and confess with my mouth, that the Holy Ghost, the third Person in the Deity, is equal God with God the Father and God the Son, in essence, power, and majesty, of whom also, as of the Father and of the Son, one true, living, immortal, and everlasting God, I look for all good things appertaining unto the body or unto the soul.

[1 Come yer, or come er: come ere, or before, anticipate.] [2 Folio, *ye*.]

Father. How provest thou that the Holy Ghost is God? *Son*. Because I say no less, "I believe in the Holy Ghost," than, "I believe in God the Father, and in Jesus Christ his only Son." For we may believe in none but in God alone. But I believe in the Holy Ghost; therefore the Holy Ghost is God. That the Holy Ghost is God.

Father. I would hear gladly this thing proved by the word of God. *Son*. Nothing is more easy. In the first book of Moses we read on this manner: "In the beginning God made heaven and earth. And the earth was void and empty; and darkness was upon the deep. And the Spirit of God moved upon the water." Here see we, that the Spirit of God, which otherwise we call the Holy Ghost, was in the beginning at the creation of things, not a spirit then made with other creatures, but a Spirit from everlasting, proceeding from the Father and the Son, maker of all things with the Father and the Son, being also of like majesty and power, as David witnesseth, saying: "The heavens were made through the word of the Lord, and all the host thereof through the Spirit of his mouth." Here are the three Persons in the Godhead lively set forth in the work of the creation, the Lord, the Word, and the Spirit. Hereof doth it follow that as the Lord, whereby is signified the Father, is God, and as the Word, whereby is understand the Son, is God, so likewise is the Spirit, which is the Holy Ghost, God. Therefore in the creation of man it is not in vain said thus: "God spake, Let us make man." He saith not, I will make man, or let me make man, but he saith, "Let *us*, *us*, *us*," namely, the Father, the Son, and the Holy Ghost, true God, one in divine essence, and three in Persons. Gen. i. Gen. i.

So likewise read we of Abraham, which saw three persons, but worshipped one. Gen. xviii.

Again, in a certain psalm we read on this manner: "Whither shall I go from thy Spirit? or whither shall I fly from thy presence? If I climb up into heaven, thou art there: if I go down to hell, thou art there also," &c. This sentence of the psalmograph proveth manifestly and truly the Holy Ghost to be God. For none can be in all places at one time, but God alone. The Holy Ghost is in all places at one time; therefore is the Holy Ghost God. Psal. cxxxix.

The prophet Esay also saith: "Who hath reformed[3] the Spirit of the Lord? or who is of his counsel to teach him? At whom hath he asked counsel to make him understand, and to learn him the way of judgment; to teach him science, and to instruct him in the way of understanding? Behold all people are in comparison of him as a drop to a bucket-full, and are counted as the least thing that the balance weigheth," &c. These words of the prophet testify also abundantly that the Holy Ghost is very God; forasmuch as he is reformed of no man, asketh counsel of no man, craveth understanding, doctrine, knowledge, &c., of no man, but hath all these things in himself and of himself: yea, all these things flow out of him unto other, as out of a most rich and plenteous fountain or head-spring; so that, whatsoever goodness we have, it cometh from this Spirit and Holy Ghost, the author, giver, and worker of all good things. Isai. xl.

Father. Are there any testimonies of the divinity of the Holy Ghost contained in the new testament? *Son*. Very many; yea, and those both noble and notable.

Father. Rehearse one or two. *Son*. In the baptism of Christ, when the Father made himself open by a voice from heaven, and the Son by taking man's nature upon him, the Holy Ghost shewed himself in the likeness of a dove, to declare that the Holy Ghost is of all one majesty with the Father and the Son, and yet a distinct Person from them both. Our Saviour Christ commanded his disciples to "teach all nations, and to baptize them in the name of the Father, and of the Son, and of the Holy Ghost." Except the Holy Ghost were true God, truly giving everlasting salvation, he should not be joined in the works of our salvation with the Father and the Son. But forasmuch as we be baptized in the name of the Holy Ghost, so must it needs follow, that he is undoubtedly very true God. Moreover, in the chronicle of the apostles' acts we read that the Holy Ghost filled the whole house, and sat upon each one of the apostles severally; so that they were all filled with the Holy Ghost. But this thing can no creature do, I mean, be in divers places at once, as we read here of the Holy Ghost: Matt. iii. Mark i. Luke iii. Matt. xxviii. Acts ii.

[[3] Reformed: informed.]

therefore followeth it necessarily that he is true God, of like might, power, and majesty,
1 John v. with the Father and the Son. St John also saith: "There are three which bear witness in heaven, the Father, the Word, and the Holy Ghost; and these three are one." Who seeth not also by this testimony of St John, that the Holy Ghost is very God, and of the same power, might, and majesty with the Father and the Son?

What profit the Deity of the Holy Ghost bringeth.

Father. These testimonies may suffice for this present concerning the divinity of the Holy Ghost. But come off, tell me, what doth it profit thee that the Holy Ghost is God, and that thou dost believe in him? *Son.* So greatly, that otherwise I cannot be saved.

First, in that the Holy Ghost is God, he maketh me which believe in him, of a wretched unclean creature, an holy creature. For he is called the Holy Ghost, not only because he is holy for himself and in himself, or that there may be a difference between him and the wicked and unholy spirits; but also because he sanctifieth and maketh the elect people of God holy, pure, and clean. For as the Father hath created me, and the Son hath redeemed me, so likewise hath the Holy Ghost sanctified me; without whom I am nothing else but a lump of unholiness, and a very monster of
Rom. viii. wickedness, as St Paul saith: "If any man hath not the Spirit of Christ, he is not
John iii. of God." And Christ himself saith: "That which is born of flesh is flesh, and that which is born of the Spirit is spirit." Therefore prayeth the prophet David on this
Psal. li. manner: "Make me a clean heart, O God, and renew a right spirit within me. Cast me not away from thy presence, and take not thy Holy Spirit from me. O give me the comfort of thy help again, and stablish me with thy free Spirit."

John xiv. Secondly, this Holy Spirit is a comforter unto us, whensoever either Satan, or the law, or the wrath of God, or sin, or the fear of everlasting damnation, troubleth and disquieteth us and our weak conscience. He also encourageth us valiantly to resist the assaults of Satan, studiously to mortify the lusts of the flesh, stoutly to contemn and despise both the tyranny and flattery of the world, and with a good courage through the strength of faith and innocency of life to walk before the Lord our God.

1 Cor. ii. Thirdly, forasmuch as we of ourself are nothing but beast-like, rude, gross, ignorant, and utterly without knowledge of God and of his holy mysteries, this Holy Ghost is a teacher and schoolmaster unto us, informing us of all things appertaining unto our salvation, and leading us into all truth necessary for our profession, as Christ said
John xiv. to his disciples: "The Comforter, that Holy Spirit, whom the Father shall send in my name, he shall teach you all things, and bring to your remembrance all that ever I
John xvi. have said unto you." Again: "When he, which is the Spirit of truth, shall come, he shall lead you into all truth."

Fourthly, this Holy Ghost altereth the whole man, making him of the bond-slave of Satan the free servant of God; of the child of wrath the dearly-beloved son of God; of the firebrand of hell the inheritor of everlasting glory; as St Paul saith:
Rom. viii. "They that are led with the Spirit of God, they are the sons of God." Again: "Where the Spirit of the Lord is, there is liberty."

Fifthly, he garnishes us with many glorious and heavenly gifts, which we cannot
Gal. v. have of ourselves, as faith, hope, love, patience, long-suffering, peace, joy, meekness, temperance, pureness, innocency, gentleness, goodness, mercy, liberality, &c.

Sixthly, if at any time through the contemplation of our own frailness, or the consideration of God's high justice, we should fear to have access to the merciful throne of God's grace, this Holy Spirit helpeth, comforteth, assisteth us, yea, and prayeth for us; not only that, but he also through his most sweet and comfortable motions encourageth our minds, that we ourselves also have a certain reverent boldness with our prayers to approach unto the glorious throne of his divine majesty, even as
Rom. viii. loving children unto their most loving and dear father, as the apostle saith: "Whosoever are led by the Spirit of God are the sons of God. For ye have not received the spirit of bondage to fear any more, but ye have received the Spirit of adoption, whereby we cry, Abba, dear Father. The same Spirit certifieth our spirit that we are the children of God. If we be children, then are we heirs also, I mean, the heirs of God and fellow-heirs with Christ." Again: "The Spirit helpeth our weakness. For we know not what we should desire as we ought: nevertheless the Spirit

itself maketh intercession mightily for us with unoutspeakable groanings. Howbeit he that searcheth the heart knoweth what the mind of the Spirit is; for he maketh intercession for the saints according to the pleasure of God."

To end, if any end may be found in so overflowing, unsearchable, and bottomless sea of all good and heavenly things, this Holy Ghost is "the earnest of our inheritance," whereby we are assured in our heart of God's good will toward us, that he loveth us, keepeth and defendeth us, blesseth us with all both ghostly and bodily benefits, and hath made us his sons and heirs of his most glorious kingdom. Eph. i.

Father. Hitherto hast thou declared unto me thy faith concerning that true, living, immortal, and everlasting God, one in divine substance, and yet in that divine substance three several Persons, God the Father, which made thee; God the Son, which redeemed thee; and God the Holy Ghost, which sanctifieth thee. What now remaineth? *Son.* The fourth part of the christian faith, which comprehendeth four articles. Rom. viii. The fourth part of the christian faith.

Father. Rehearse the first.

Son. "I believe that there is an holy universal church, which is the fellowship or company of saints." Of the church.

Father. But wherefore sayest thou rather, "I believe that there is one holy universal church," than on this manner, I believe in the holy universal church? *Son.* My faith and my belief must be set and reposed in God alone, forasmuch as salvation cometh from him alone, and not in creatures, be they never so holy and perfect. For vain is the salvation that cometh from man, yea, "cursed be he that putteth his trust and confidence in man, and maketh flesh his arm." If I should say, I believe in the holy universal church, then must I also grant that the church is God, and by this means make four persons in the Godhead, which God forbid. My belief is not in the body, but in the head, which is Christ Jesus our Lord and alone Saviour. Psal. iii. Jer. xvii.

Father. What meanest thou by this word "church"? *Son.* Nothing else than a company of people gathered together, or a congregation. And this word "church" in the holy scriptures is taken not only for the fellowship or company of the good and faithful, but also of the wicked and unfaithful. St Paul, beside many other places, speaking of that church, which is the company of saints, hath these words: "Christ loved the church, and gave himself for it to sanctify it, and cleansed it in the fountain of water by the word, to make it unto himself a glorious church, having no spot, nor wrinkle, nor any such thing, but that it should be holy and without blame." Of that church, which is the company of the wicked, ungodly, and unfaithful, speaketh that prince-like prophet David on this manner: "I hate and utterly abhor the church of the malignant and wicked: as for the ungodly, I will by no means keep company with them." What this word *church* signifieth. Eph. v. Psal. xxvi.

Father. Why dost thou call the church of Christ "holy"? *Son.* To discern it from other churches, which are unholy. The ethnicks, the Jews, the Mahometans, the anabaptists, the Arians, with all the rabble of heretics and sectaries, have their churches also; but all those churches are the synagogues of Satan, unpure, filthy, stinking, vile, abominable, full of all sin and wickedness. The church of Christ alone, alone is holy, pure, "without spot or wrinkle," as it is written: "Thou art all fair, O my love; and no spot is there in thee." In this church all goodness is to be found: without this church is nothing but sin, wrath, and damnation. Again, the church of Christ is called holy, not for the holiness of itself, (for what member of that church hath not also his infirmity in this life? as it is written, "If we say we have no sin, we deceive ourselves, and the truth is not in us." Item: "All we offend in many things,") but for the holiness of Christ, the Son of God, which is the head of the church, which also hath given to his church his holiness, innocency, righteousness, and whatsoever good thing he hath more, himself being the fountain of all goodness, and hath with all these things clothed, decked, adorned, garnished, and trimmed the church, as his most dear spouse; so that now, being clothed with Christ's holiness, she may right well be called holy, and without spot or wrinkle. The church of Christ is also called holy, because it is sanctified and made holy of the Holy Ghost, which governeth, ruleth, defendeth, and saveth her, and moveth her continually with his Why the christian church is called holy. Eph. v. Cant. iv. 1 John i. James iii. Eph. i. Col. i.

heavenly inspiration unto the fervent study, exercise, and increase of all virtue and godliness.

Why the christian church is called catholic or universal. John iv. Mark xvi. Luke xxiv. Matt. xxiv.

Father. Why is this church called "catholic" or universal? *Son.* Because it is not bound to one certain place, kingdom, or empire, but is dispersed throughout the whole world; so that in all places God hath his elect and chosen people, which believe in him, call on his holy name, and worship him according to his word, even "in spirit and truth", according to this commandment of Christ: "Go throughout the whole world, and preach the gospel to every creature." Again: "Ye shall be witnesses of me, even unto the furthermost part of the world." Item: "The gospel of the kingdom shall be preached throughout the whole world for a witness unto all nations."

Christ's church is but one only church. Cant. vi. 1 Tim. iii. Matt. xvi. Eph. ii. Matt. vii. Luke xxii. Matt. xxiv. John x.

Father. Why dost thou rather say and confess, that there is one holy catholic or universal church, than many churches; seeing there are in the world so many companies, fellowships, or congregations of the faithful, that call on the name of the Lord? *Son.* As there is but one head of this holy catholic or universal church, which is the Lord Christ Jesus alone, so likewise is there but one holy church, as it is written: "One is my dove and my darling. She is the only beloved of her mother, and dear unto her that bare her. When the daughters saw her, they said she was blessed." And, although this holy church in her members be dispersed and scattered abroad throughout the world, so that there be in divers countries divers companies, that profess and confess Christ and his holy gospel; yet, forasmuch as they are gathered and linked together in one faith and one doctrine, under one head Christ, into whose name alone they are consecrate and sworn, all those so great and so many multitudes are counted and called but one church, which church "is the house of the living God, the pillar and ground of truth," so stedfastly founded on the rock Christ, that "the very gates of hell shall never be able to prevail against her;" so surely "built upon the foundation of the apostles and prophets," that though abundance of rain descend, and the winds blow, yet can they not move her; yea, though Satan goeth never so much about to sift her, yet shall her faith never fail, but remain perfect, whole, and sound. For this church is that holy congregation or fellowship of God's elect, which cannot err, nor be brought into error, much less perish and be damned.

Certain signs whereby the church of Christ may be known from the synagogue of antichrist.

Father. There is at this present day great contention concerning the church, every sect sweating to prove that they are the church of God, and that all other, which dissent from them, are synagogues of Satan: come off, tell me therefore, how the true church of Christ may be known from the malignant and wicked churches, which are led with the spirit, not of God, but of the devil. *Son.* Albeit many signs, tokens, and marks might here be rehearsed, whereby we may easily discern the church of Christ from the synagogue of antichrist, the people of God from the bond-slaves of Satan, the vessels of mercy from the vessels of wrath; yet will I recite at this present only four tokens, or marks, whereby we may truly and undeceivably know the true catholic and apostolic church.

John viii. John x.

Father. Which are those four? *Son.* The first is, the sincere, true, and uncorrupt preaching of God's word, without the intermixtion or mingling of man's doctrine, in the which God, that mighty Lord, hath opened himself, his will, his mercy, and favour to his faithful congregation, as it is written: "He that is of God heareth the words of God." Again: "My sheep hear my voice;" "as for a stranger, they follow him not, but fly from him; for they know not the voice of strangers."

1 Cor. xi.

The second is, the true administration of the sacraments according to the institution and ordinance of Christ, as we read of St Paul entreating of the supper of the Lord: "That which I delivered unto you received I of the Lord. For the Lord Jesus, the same night in the which he was betrayed, took the bread," &c.

The third is, fervent prayer and the diligent invocation of God in the name of our alone Mediator Jesus Christ, with continual thanksgiving for his benefits.

The fourth is, ecclesiastical discipline according to the prescript and appointment of God's word.

Although many other signs, notes, tokens, and marks, might here be rehearsed, whereby also the church of Christ may easily be discerned from the synagogue of antichrist, yet these be the principal and chief; so that, in whatsoever congregation these aforesaid signs be found, there may we well affirm and say the true church of Christ to be, and the faithful people of God.

Father. But what dost thou mean by calling the holy universal church "the company or fellowship of saints"? *Son*. These words, "The company or fellowship of saints" or holy men, do nothing else in a manner than declare what the holy universal church is; verily, a company of saints or of holy and godly-disposed persons knit together by one Spirit, in one faith, in one hope, in one love, in one baptism, in one doctrine, having one head, which is Christ Jesus, and serving one God, which is the Father of our Lord Jesus Christ, "in holiness and righteousness all the days of their life." For this fellowship of saints, although they be dispersed never so far abroad, yea, in all quarters under the sun, not only in Europa, but also in India, Persia, &c., be they Jews or gentiles, barbarous or Scythians, have, hold, and maintain one baptism, one faith, one God and Lord, one doctrine, and are led with one Spirit, and make one flock, whereof Christ Jesus is the pastor and shepherd. And in this company or fellowship of saints all things appertaining unto everlasting salvation are common, as the favour of God, remission of sins, quietness of conscience, the gift of the Holy Ghost, and everlasting life; yea, in this holy fellowship there is such a love and hearty good will one toward another (for they are members all of one body, and therefore like affected and minded), that there is also, as I may so speak, a certain community of temporal things among them, as we read in the Apostles' Acts of Christ's church at the beginning; so that the rich have not too much, nor the poor too little, but a certain equality is among them, no man wanting, that is of that holy fellowship, but having sufficient to satisfy his necessity; such and so great care one for another reigneth in them, provoked thereunto by the Holy Ghost, which ruleth and governeth that holy congregation and fellowship of saints.

Why the church is called the company or fellowship of saints.

Luke i.

Acts iv.

2 Cor. viii.

Father. I cannot disallow that thou speakest. But as concerning this word "saint," methink it ought rather to be appropriated unto the saints departed and reigning in glory with Christ, than unto us, which live in this world and are subject to many infirmities. *Son*. The holy scriptures, both of the old and new testaments, do rather ascribe this word "saint" unto us in this world, which believe in Christ, than unto the godly, which are now in glory with their head Christ. And we are termed saints by the Holy Ghost in the divine scriptures, first, to put us in remembrance that we are made saints, that is to say, holy, pure, and blameless, by the free grace of God through faith for Christ's sake, and so recounted just and righteous before God for the righteousness not of ourselves, but of our Mediator Christ Jesus: secondly, that we should endeavour ourselves unto the uttermost of our power in all our manners, life, and conversation, to answer to our name, that is to say, to be saints, I mean holy, pure, blameless, good, righteous, merciful, gentle, liberal, and altogether virtuous, "putting on that new man which is shapen after the image of God in true righteousness and holiness," as it is written: "Even as he which hath called you is holy, even so be ye holy also in your conversation; for it is written, Be ye holy, for I am holy."

Saint.

Why the faithful in this world are called saints.

Eph. iv. Col. iii. 1 Pet. i. Lev. xix.

Father. What doth it profit thee to believe that there is an holy universal church, which is the company or fellowship of saints, that is to say, of godly and virtuous persons? *Son*. Very much. For in believing that there is such an holy church, I am well ascertained and fully persuaded, that I also am a member of the same church, and partaker of all the goods of the church, having Christ my head, my bridegroom, and most loving friend, and with him all that ever he hath.

What it profiteth to believe that there is an holy universal church.

Father. What good things are these, which thou hast or hereafter shalt have, because thou art a member of this holy church? *Son*. Even those that are contained in the three last articles of the christian faith now next ensuing.

Rom. viii.

Father. Rehearse them.

Son. "The forgiveness of sins."

I believe that I, being a member of this holy church, shall have through the blood of Christ remission and forgiveness of all my sins, be they never so many, great, and grievous; yea, and that not only before or at the time of baptism, but also after

Of the forgiveness of sins.

baptism, even all my life-time and unto the very death, sin I never so oft through the frailness of nature or of ignorancy, or otherwise, if I repent, bewail my sins, crave remission and forgiveness of them through the blood of Christ, with strong faith in the merciful promises of God, that Father of mercies and God of all consolation, yea, and that "not only seven times, but seventy times seven times." For as there is no time wherein we do not sin, even so is there no time wherein the grace and benefit of forgiving our sins is barred and shut up from us of God, if we crave it in the name of Christ, as St John testifieth: "If we say we have no sin, we deceive ourselves, and the truth is not in us. But if we confess our sins, God is faithful and righteous to forgive us our sins and to cleanse us from all wickedness."

Matt. xviii. ☞ 1 John i.

There is no forgiveness of sins, but only in the church of Christ.

Father. Is there remission of sins in none other congregation, but in the congregation or church of Christ only? *Son*. No, verily. For to him that is no member of this holy church sin is not remitted but retained.

Father. Prove by the holy scriptures, that there is remission of sins laid up in God's treasure-house for all sinners that repent in faith. *Son*. Are not these the words of God by the prophet? "If the ungodly will turn away from all his sins that he hath done, and keep all my commandments, and do the thing that is equal and right, doubtless he shall live and not die. As for all his sins that he did before, they shall not be thought upon, but in his righteousness that he hath done he shall live. For I have no pleasure in the death of a sinner, saith the Lord God, but rather that he convert and live." Again: "As truly as I live, saith the Lord God, I have no pleasure in the death of the wicked, but much rather that the wicked turn from his way and live. Turn you, turn you from your ungodly ways, O ye of the house of Israel. O, wherefore will ye die?" Also in another place: "It is commonly said, if a man putteth away his wife, and she goeth from him and marrieth with another, should he resort any more unto her after that? Is not this field then defiled and unclean? But as for thee, thou hast played the harlot with many lovers; yet turn again unto me, saith the Lord." Item: "Thou shrinking Israel, turn again, saith the Lord, and I will not turn my face from you; for I am merciful, saith the Lord, and I will not alway bear displeasure against you," &c. "O ye shrinking children, turn again, saith the Lord; and I will be married with you."

Ezek. xviii. Ezek. xxxiii.

As I may pass over almost innumerable testimonies of the old testament, which do most manifestly declare, that there is plenty of mercy and abundance of remission of sins laid up in store with God for all sinners that repent and unfeignedly turn unto their Lord God; to whom is it unknown, how lovingly and mercifully Christ Jesus the Lord calleth unto him all such as are grieved and heavy loaden with the burden of sin, and promiseth that he will ease them and give them rest? How oft doth he call them that thirst, and promiseth to give them of the water of life freely! How oft doth he confess that he came "to call sinners unto repentance," and "to seek up that which was lost"! What other thing do the parables of the stray sheep, of the lost groat, and of the riotous son preach unto us, than that there is mercy in store for all penitent sinners? Are not these the words of Christ? "Verily I say unto you, there shall be joy in heaven before the angels of God over one sinner that repenteth, more than over ninety and nine which need no repentance." What other thing also do the histories of Matthew the publican, of Mary Magdalene, of Simon Peter, of Zache the publican, of the thief, of the incestuous Corinthian, of Paul, of Onesimus, and of such like, than preach unto us, that there is grace, favour, mercy, and remission of sins laid up in store in God's treasure-house for all sinners that repent in faith, being members of this holy universal church? Therefore I may right well say: "I believe the forgiveness of sins."

Matt. xi. Isai. lv. John vii. Rev. xxii. Matt. ix. Luke xix. Luke xv. Matt. ix. Luke vii. Matt. xxvi. Luke xix. xxiii. 2 Cor. ii. Philem.

All men are sinners. James iii. Luke xvii. Rom. iii. Psal. xiv. Prov. xx. Isai. lxiv. Psal. cxliii.

Father. We then are all sinners? *Son*. Yea, verily. For "in many things we all offend." "We are all unprofitable servants." "There is no difference. All have sinned, and want the glory of God." "There is no man so righteous on the earth which sinneth not." "Who is able to say, My heart is clean, and I am free from sin?" "All our righteousnesses are as a defiled cloth." If God should enter into judgment with us, and deal with us according to our deserts, no man that liveth should be found righteous in his sight.

Father. We may then, although never so sinful, believe, hope, and look for remission of our sins boldly at the hand of God, if we unfeignedly repent and turn unto the Lord our God. *Son.* Nothing is more true. And therefore our Saviour Christ taught us daily to pray on this wise: "And forgive us our trespasses, as we forgive them that trespass against us." Matt. vi.

Father. Who forgiveth sins? *Son.* God alone, as it is written: "No man can forgive sins, but God alone." And God himself saith: "I am he, yea, I am he indeed, which putteth away thy sins, yea, and that for my own sake, and I will remember them no more." "The Lord," saith the psalmograph, "is full of compassion and mercy, long-suffering, and of great goodness. He will not alway be chiding, neither will he keep his anger for ever. He dealeth not with us after our sins, neither rewardeth he us according to our wickedness. For look how high the heaven is in comparison of the earth, so great is his mercy also toward them that fear him. Look how wide the east is from the west, so far doth he set our sins from us. Yea, like as a father pitieth his own children, even so is the Lord merciful unto them that fear him. For he knoweth whereof we be made, he remembereth that we are but dust." "Who is like unto thee, O God," saith the prophet Miche, "which pardonest wickedness, and forgivest the offences of the remnant of thine heritage? Thou keepest not thine anger for ever. And why? thy delight is to have compassion. Thou shalt turn again, and be merciful unto us; yea, thou shalt put down our wickednesses, and cast all our sins into the bottom of the sea." God alone forgiveth sins. Matt. ix. Mark ii. Psal. ciii. Mic. vii.

Father. What moveth God to be so gentle and merciful unto us, that he will so bounteously forgive us all our sins, when we repent and turn unto him? *Son.* His own nature, which is altogether good and gracious, and "hateth nothing of all those things that he hath made." "He hath saved me," saith David, "because it was his pleasure." Again: "Freely, and for none of their deserts, shalt thou save them, O Lord." "It lighteth not," saith St Paul, "in any man's will or running, but in the mercy of God." And God himself saith: "I shew mercy to whom it pleaseth me to shew mercy, and have compassion on whom it is my pleasure to have compassion." Again: "I am he, yea, I am he indeed, which putteth away thy sins, yea, and that for mine own sake." Item: "Thy destruction cometh of thyself, O Israel; but thy salvation cometh only of me." What moveth God to forgive us our sins. Wisd. xi. Psal. xviii. Rom. ix. Exod. xxxiii. Isai. xliii. Hos. xiii.

Father. But seeing that God is not only gracious but also righteous, not only a rewarder but also a revenger, not only a Saviour but also a condemner, how cometh it to pass, that his mercy excelleth his justice, and his judgment giveth place to grace and favour, so that we be not punished according unto justice, but forgiven according unto mercy? *Son.* Christ Jesus is that dearly-beloved Son of God, for whose sake God the Father is well pleased with man. He is our peace-maker. "He by his blood hath pacified all things both in heaven and earth." He hath reconciled us unto God his Father, and set us at one. He is "the perfect fulfilling of the law to justify every one that believeth." He is that "Lamb of God, which taketh away the sin of the world." He is that "Mediator between God and man, which gave himself a ransom for all men." He is that Advocate, which pleadeth our cause before God the Father, and easily obtaineth pardon and forgiveness of our sins. He is that high and everlasting Bishop, "which sitteth on the right hand of God, and maketh intercession for us." He is that Saviour, which "came into the world to save sinners." He is that mighty and valiant conqueror, which hath delivered us from the tyranny of Satan, from the captivity of sin, from the curse of the law, from the danger of desperation, from the dart of death, and finally from the torments of everlasting damnation. To be short, he is our "wisdom, righteousness, sanctification, and redemption, that, as it is written, He that rejoiceth should rejoice in the Lord." God the Father giveth us all good things for Christ's sake. Matt. iii. Eph. ii. Col. ii. Eph. ii. Rom. x. John i. 1 Tim. ii. 1 John ii. 1 Cor. i. Jer. ix.

Father. How or by what means do we obtain and come ye[1] this exceeding great grace, favour, and mercy, concerning the remission of our sins at the hand of God for Christ's sake? *Son.* By faith, as St Paul saith: "Of grace are ye saved through faith, and that not of yourselves; for it is the gift of God, and cometh not of works, lest any By faith we obtain all good things of God. Eph. ii.

[[1] Perhaps a mere error for *come by*.]

Acts x. man should boast himself." St Peter also saith: "Of Christ all the prophets bear witness, that through his name all they that believe in him shall receive forgiveness Acts xiii. of sins." St Paul agreeth with this, as blessed Luke testifieth, saying: "Be it known, ye men and brethren, that through this man (Christ) is preached unto you the forgiveness of sins; and from all the things whereby ye might not be justified by the law of Rom. iii. Moses, by this man (Christ) every one that believeth is justified." Item: "There is no difference: all have sinned, and want the glory of God; but freely are they made righteous even by his grace through the redemption that is done by Christ Jesu, whom God hath set for a mercy-seat through faith in his blood, to shew the righteousness which availeth before him, in that he forgiveth the sins which were done before under the sufferance of God, which he suffered, that at his time he might shew the righteousness which availeth before him, that he only might be righteous, and the righteous-maker of him which is of the faith of Jesu."

What profit we have by believing remission of sins. 1 Cor. ii. *Father*. What doth it profit thee that thou believest the forgiveness of sins? *Son*. By this I am certified and well assured in my conscience, that I am a member of Christ's church. For none doth rightly believe but such as appertain unto the holy congregation of the Christians. Again, that I am partaker of all the merits of Christ's passion and death. Thirdly, that by the blood of Christ all my sins are washed away and utterly forgiven, so that they shall never more be imputed unto me, nor laid unto my charge: not only that, but also that, as all evils be taken away from me by the death and blood of Christ, so likewise by the same are all good things given unto me, 1 Cor. vi. as it is written: "Ye are washed, ye are sanctified, ye are made righteous, by the name of the Lord Jesu, and by the Spirit of our God."

Father. Let this suffice for this present concerning the article of the forgiveness of sins. What followeth?

Son. "I believe the resurrection of the body."

Of the resurrection. *Father*. What meanest thou by this? *Son*. I believe with my heart, and confess with my mouth, that God by his almighty power at the last day shall raise up from death unto life the bodies of all men, women, and children, that have lived and died from the time of Adam's creation unto the day of judgment, be they good or bad, faithful or unfaithful, and by whatsoever death they perished, whether they were consumed unto ashes by fire, or devoured of wild beasts, or eaten of the fowls of the air, or swallowed up of the fishes in the waters. Those very same bodies, wherein they lived sometime here upon earth, shall be restored unto them; so that, body and soul linked Rom. xiv. together, they shall "all stand before the judging-place of Christ," and there receive their reward according to the works which they have done, be they good or bad.

Father. Let me hear it proved by the word of God, that the bodies of the dead shall rise again, and be restored to life at the last day. *Son*. The scriptures are plentiful in this behalf.

Job xix. The holy man Job speaketh on this manner: "I know, and am fully persuaded, that my Redeemer doth live, and that at the last day I shall rise out of the earth, and be clothed again with my skin, and shall see God in my flesh, whom I myself shall see, and mine eyes shall behold, and none other. This hope lieth buried up in my breast." Isai. xxvi. The prophet Esay saith: "Thy dead shall live again, our bodies shall rise again. Awake and rejoice, ye that dwell in the dust: for thy dew is the dew of life and light." The Ezek. xxxvii. prophet Ezechiel saith: "The hand of the Lord came upon me, and carried me out in the Spirit of the Lord, and let me down in a plain field that lay full of bones; and he led me round about by them; and behold, the bones that lay upon the field were very many, and marvellous dry also: then said he unto me, Thou son of man, thinkest thou these bones may live again? I answered, O Lord God, thou knowest. And he said unto me, Prophesy thou upon these bones, and speak unto them, Ye dry bones, hear the word of the Lord. Thus saith the Lord God unto these bones: Behold, I will put breath into you that ye may live. I will give you sinews, and make flesh grow upon you, and cover you with skin, and so give you both that ye may live, and know that I am the Lord. So I prophesied, as he had commanded me. And as I was prophesying, there came a noise and a great motion; so that the bones ran every one to another.

Now, when I had looked, behold, they had sinews, and flesh grew upon them, and above they were covered with skin; but there was no breath in them. Then said he unto me, Thou son of man, prophesy thou toward the wind: prophesy and speak to the wind, Thus saith the Lord God, Come, O thou air, from the four winds, and blow upon these slain, that they may be restored to life. So I prophesied, as he had commanded me. Then came the breath unto them; and they received life, and stood up upon their feet, a marvellous great sort." And a little after: "Thus saith the Lord God: Behold, I will open your gates, O my people, and take you out of your sepulchres, and bring you into the land of Israel again. So shall ye know that I am the Lord, when I open your graves and bring you out of them. My Spirit also will I put in you; and ye shall live." The prophet Daniel saith also: "Many of them that sleep in the Dan. xii. dust of the earth shall awake; some to everlasting life, some to perpetual shame and reproof."

As I may at the last come to the testimonies of the new testament, are not these the words of our Saviour Christ unto the Sadducees, which denied the resurrection of the dead and the immortality of the soul? "As concerning the resurrection of the dead, have ye Matt. xxii Exod. iii. not read what is spoken unto you of God, which saith, I am the God [of] Abraham, and Matt. xxii the God of Isaac, and the God [of] Jacob? Now is not God the God of the dead, but of the living." Christ said unto Martha of her brother Lazarus that was dead: "Thy brother shall rise again. Martha answered, I know that he shall rise again in John xi. the resurrection at the last day." In another place the Lord Christ, appointing whom Luke xiv. we should call unto our table, namely, the poor, the halt, the lame, the blind, &c. saith, that although they be not able to make us amends, yet shall we be recompensed in the resurrection of the righteous. And that we should not be doubtful of the resurrection of the dead, we read that our Saviour Christ, that most mighty conqueror of sin, devil, death, and hell, raised up certain that were dead unto life, as the widow's son of Naim, Luke vii. the daughter of Jairus, and Lazarus, with divers other. We read also that, after Christ's Luke viii John xi. resurrection, "the graves did open, and the bodies of many saints which slept arose, Matt. xxvii. and came out of the graves, and came into the holy city, and appeared to many." Blessed Luke in the chronicle of the apostles' acts writeth, that St Peter raised up Acts ix. from death unto life a certain woman named Tabitha, otherwise called Dorcas; again, that St Paul likewise wrought the like miracle upon a certain young man that was Acts xx. dead, named Eutychus.

Father. Are there no testimonies of the resurrection of the dead in the epistles of St Paul? *Son*. St Paul in all his epistles writeth of nothing so oft and so largely as of the resurrection of the dead. In his epistle unto the Romans he writeth on this manner: "If we be dead with Christ, we believe also that we shall live with him." Rom. vi. Again: "If we be engraft in death like unto him, then shall we also undoubtedly be partakers with him of the resurrection." In his first epistle to the Corinthians he writeth this: "God hath raised up the Lord (Jesus), and he shall raise up us also 1 Cor. vi. by his power. Know ye not, that your bodies are the members of Christ?" If our bodies be the members of Christ, then must they also be glorified with their head, Christ. In the fifteenth chapter of the foresaid epistle, the blessed apostle doth prove the resur- 1 Cor. xv. rection of the dead with so manifest reasons and invincible arguments, that it is wonder that the very godless epicures should doubt of it; which chapter I would wish that all true Christians should diligently commend to memory. I will only give you a taste of it, and of that judge you the residue.

Father. It is well said, my son. Let me hear.

Son. "If there be no resurrection of the dead, then is Christ not risen. If Christ 1 Cor. xv. be not risen, then is our preaching in vain, and your faith also is in vain; yea, and we are found false witnesses of God, because we have testified against God, that he hath raised up Christ, whom he hath not raised up, if the dead rise not again. For if the dead rise not again, then is Christ also not risen again. But if Christ be not risen again, then is your faith in vain, and ye are yet in your sins: they also that are fallen asleep in Christ are perished. If in this life only we have hope in Christ, then are we of all men most miserable. But now is Christ risen from the dead, and is become the first-fruits of them that sleep. For by one man cometh death, and by one man the resurrection of the dead. For as they all die in Adam, so shall they all be made alive in Christ," &c.

2 Cor. iv. In his second epistle to the Corinthians he writeth thus: "We know that he which raised up the Lord Jesus, shall raise us up also by the means of Jesus." Also to the Phil. iii. Philippians: "Our conversation is in heaven, from whence we look for a Saviour, even the Lord Jesus Christ, which shall change this our vile body, that he may make it like unto his own glorious body, according to the working whereby he is able also to subdue 1 Thess. iv. all things unto himself." Item to the Thessalonians: "We would not, brethren, that ye should be ignorant concerning them which are fallen asleep, that ye sorrow not as other do, which have no hope. For if we believe that Jesus died and rose again, even so them also which sleep by Jesus shall God bring with him. For this we say unto you in the word of the Lord, that we which live and are remaining in the coming of the Lord, shall not come ere they which sleep. For the Lord himself shall come down from heaven with a shout, and voice of the archangel, and with the trump of God; and the dead in Christ shall arise first: then shall we, which live and remain, be caught up with them also in the clouds to meet the Lord in the air, and so shall we ever be with the Lord. Wherefore comfort yourselves one another with these words."

Father. We have heard testimonies concerning the resurrection of the dead out of the holy scriptures abundantly. But shall the wicked and ungodly rise again also at the day of judgment, no less than the faithful and godly? *Son.* Yea, verily.

Father. Where doth that appear in the holy scripture? *Son.* In divers and sundry places.

Father. Let me hear.

Dan. xii. *Son.* The prophet Daniel saith: "Many of them that sleep in the dust of the earth shall awake; some to everlasting life, some to perpetual shame and reproof." Our John v. Saviour Christ saith also: "The hour cometh, in the which all that are in the graves shall hear the voice of the Son of God, and shall come forth; they that have done good, unto the resurrection of life; but they that have done evil, unto the resurrection of Matt. xxv damnation." And in the gospel of St Matthew, where Christ describeth and setteth forth the form and manner of his judgment, we read that at the last day, "when he shall come in his glory, and all the holy angels with him, he shall sit upon the seat of his glory; and all people shall be gathered before him. And he shall separate them one from another, as a shepherd divideth the sheep from the goats. And he shall set the sheep on his right hand, and the goats on his left. Then shall he say unto them that shall be on his right hand, Come hither, ye blessed of my Father, inherit ye the kingdom which was prepared for you from the beginning of the world, &c. Then shall he say unto them also that shall be on the left hand, Depart from me, ye cursed, into the everlasting fire, which is prepared for the devil and his angels, &c. And these shall go into everlasting pain, but the righteous into everlasting life."

Here is it evident, that all men, both good and bad, faithful and unfaithful, righteous and unrighteous, shall rise again at the day of judgment, and come before the high judge Christ, there to receive a reward according unto their deeds, as Christ himself Rev. xxii. saith: "Behold, I come out of hand, and my reward with me, that I may give to 2 Cor. v. every one according unto his works." Hereto agreeth the saying of St Paul: "We must all appear before the judgment-seat of Christ, that every one may receive in his body, according to that he hath done, whether it be good or bad."

Father. With what bodies shall the dead rise again? *Son.* Even with the very same bodies wherein sometime they lived in this world.

Father. What, mortal, corruptible, heavy, weak, sick, diseased, &c.? *Son.* Nothing less; but immortal, uncorruptible, light, or quick, strong, heathful, perfect, &c.

Father. How can it be the same body, when it is so altered? *Son.* The very same body, wherein we have lived here, shall be restored unto us through the mighty power of God, with all the parts and members of the same. The alteration of the body shall be not in substance, but in quality. Our bodies are now mortal and corruptible; but at the resurrection they shall be immortal and uncorruptible.

Father. Declare by the word of God, that the very same bodies, which we have now, shall be restored unto us at the day of judgment. *Son.* The holy man Job saith: "I know, and am fully persuaded, that my Redeemer doth live, and that at the last day I shall rise out of the earth, and be clothed with my skin, and shall see God in my flesh; whom I myself shall see, and mine eyes shall behold, and none other. This hope lieth buried up in my breast." These words are so plain, that nothing can be spoken more plainly. St Paul also saith: "This corruptible must put on uncorruption, and this mortal must put on immortality. But when this corruptible shall put on uncorruption, and this mortal shall put on immortality, then shall the word be fulfilled that is written: Death is swallowed up into victory. Death, where is thy sting? Hell, where is thy victory? The sting of death is sin: the strength of sin is the law: but thanks be unto God, which hath given us the victory through our Lord Jesus Christ."

Job xix. 1 Cor. xv. Isai. xxv. Hos. xiii. Heb. ii.

Moreover, we read, that in times past, in the Aquilian and Carthagian church, men did use to pronounce this article on this manner: "I believe the resurrection even of this body[1]." They added to the article these words, "Even of this," to the intent that it might be plainly and evidently expressed, that none other body like unto this shall be raised up or made, but even this very self-same body, wherein we now live, stand, sit, hear, see, walk, sleep, wake, &c.; yea, and which useth itself here with the soul in all manner of good works.

Father. What doth it profit thee, that thou dost believe the resurrection of this body? *Son.* First, it putteth me in remembrance, that in this world I am nothing else but a stranger and a pilgrim, and must away from hence, and that therefore I ought not to set my mind upon the things of this world, but rather "seek after those things which are above, where Christ sitteth on the right hand of God."

What profit we have by believing the resurrection of the body. Col. iii.

Secondly, so often as I say or remember this article of the christian faith, it beateth into my heart a certain reverent fear toward the Lord my God, wherewith I am provoked to be ware and circumspect, that I commit none unclean thing with this my body, which, being dead, shall once rise again and stand before the judgment-seat of Christ, there to render an accompts, even before the whole world, of all things that it hath done, be it good or bad; but rather so order it in all my doings, that in this world it may be the temple of the Holy Ghost, and after this life reign with our head Christ in the glory of his Father worlds without end.

Thirdly, it encourageth me greatly to suffer in this my body, both patiently and thankfully, whatsoever cross is laid upon me for the glory of my Lord God, and for the testimony of his truth, yea, although it were very death; being perfectly persuaded that this my body, thus afflicted for the Lord's sake, shall once again be restored unto me after a more perfect and blessed state, than I ever had it in this world, even in all points "like to the glorious body of our Lord and Saviour Jesus Christ."

Phil. iii.

Fourthly, it occasioneth me patiently to bear the departing of my friends, and of such as I most tenderly love, seeing that I am well assured in my heart by the word of God, that they shall live again, not only in soul, which is immortal and never dieth, but in body, although taken away by death, and resolved into earth, dust, and ashes.

Fifthly and finally, it provoketh me to be studious of good works, always attempting some good and godly deed in this my body, seeing my labour shall not be vain, but at the resurrection of the righteous, whatsoever good deed I have wrought, it shall abundantly be recompensed me both in body and in soul.

Father. What remaineth of the articles of the christian faith? *Son.* One only article, which is this:

Of everlasting life.

"And I believe everlasting life. Amen."

Father. What meanest thou by that? *Son.* I believe with my heart, and con-

[1 Et ideo satis caute ecclesia nostra fidem symboli docet, quæ in eo quod a ceteris traditur 'carnis resurrectionem,' uno addito pronomine tradidit 'hujus carnis resurrectionem.'—Symbolum Ruffini in Hieron. Op. Par. 1693—1706. Tom. V. col. 144. Ruffinus was a presbyter of the church of Aquileia; but his exposition of the creed was formerly attributed to Cyprian, and is generally now appended to that father's works. Hence, perhaps, the Carthaginian church was understood to have adopted the same addition to the article. See for further authorities as to the church of Aquileia, Pearson's Exposition of the Creed, Art. xi.]

fess with my mouth, that after this transitory and miserable life, which is rather a shadow of a life, if not a death, both my body and soul being linked again together, through the mighty power of God, shall live for ever in the kingdom of God, without all trouble, pain, sickness, or taste of death any more, in such perfect joy and
Isai. lxiv. 1 Cor. ii. Wisd. iii. true felicity, as "eye never saw the like, ear never heard the like, no tongue is able to express the like, nor any heart is able to conceive or think the like." The righte-
Matt. xxii. ous shall glister as the shining of heaven, yea, "they shall be as the angels of
1 John iii. God." They shall see God "face to face," even "as he is," with all the holy angels and blessed saints of God, which have been from the beginning of the world unto the end of the same; and with them shall they rejoice, glory, and triumph with an unoutspeakable gladness, praising the most high majesty of God, worlds without end.

Father. Declare unto me by the word of God, that there is an everlasting life after this transitory, frail, and short life, which we lead in this world. *Son.* The prophet
Dan. xii. Daniel saith: "Many of them that sleep in the dust of the earth shall awake; some to everlasting life, some to perpetual shame and reproof. The wise, such as have taught other, shall glister as the shining of heaven; and those that have instructed the multitude unto godliness shall be as the stars world without end." Esdras also
2 Esdr. ii. hath these words: "I say unto you, O ye heathen, that hear and understand: Look for your shepherd, he shall give you everlasting rest. For he is nigh at hand, that shall come in the end of the world. Be ready to the reward of the kingdom. For the everlasting light shall shine upon you for evermore. Flee the shadow of this world: receive the joyfulness of your glory: I testify my Saviour openly. O receive the gift that is given you, and be glad, giving thanks unto him that hath called you to the
Matt. xxv. heavenly kingdom." The Lord Christ saith also: "The righteous shall go into ever-
John iii. lasting life." Again: "God hath so dearly loved the world, that he gave his only-begotten Son, to the end that all that believe in him should not perish, but have everlasting life." Again, in the same chapter: "He that believeth on the Son hath
John x. everlasting life." Also in another place: "My sheep hear my voice, and I know them, and they follow me, and I give them everlasting life, and they shall never perish, neither shall any man pluck them out of my hand. My Father, which gave me them, is greater than all; and no man is able to pluck them out of my Father's hand. I
John xvii. and the Father am one." Item: "O Father, my hearty desire is, that they, whom thou hast given me, may be with me where I am, that they may see my glory,
2 Cor. v. which thou hast given me." The blessed apostle St Paul saith: "We know surely that, if our earthy house of this dwelling were destroyed, we have a building ordained of God, an house not made with hands, but everlasting in heaven."

Father. Is this everlasting life the free gift of God, or is it deserved by our own good deeds? *Son.* Deserved? What deserve we of ourselves, or by our own works, but the wrath of God and everlasting damnation, if God should deal with us accord-
Rom. vi. ing to our deserts? "Everlasting life," as Paul saith, "is the gift of God through
Luke xii. Jesus Christ our Lord." And Christ himself saith: "Fear not, ye little flock; for it
John x. is your Father's good pleasure to give you a kingdom." Again: "My sheep hear my voice, and I know them, and they follow me, and I give them everlasting life."
Rev. ii. Item: "Be thou faithful unto the death; and I will give thee the crown of life."
1 John v. Hereto appertaineth the saying of St John: "This is the witness, that God hath given us everlasting life, which life is in his Son." "He that hath not the Son hath not life." Again: "We know that the Son of God is come, and hath given us a mind to know the true God; and we are in him which is true, even in his Son Jesus Christ. This is the true God, and everlasting life."

Father. Is this everlasting life given of God to all men indifferently? I mean, so well to the bad as to the good, and to the unfaithful as to the faithful? *Son.* Ever-
Rev. xxi. lasting life is only given to the faithful: as for the unfaithful, they "have their portion
Matt. xxii. in that lake which brenneth with fire and brimstone," "where is weeping and gnashing
Isai. lxvi. of teeth," and "where the worm" that gnaweth the conciences of the damned, "shall
John iii. never die." Our Saviour Christ saith: "As Moses lifted up the serpent in the wilderness, so must the Son of man be lifted up, that every one that believeth in him

may not perish, but have everlasting life." Again: "Verily, verily, I say unto you, John v.
Whosoever heareth my word, and believeth on him that sent me, he hath everlasting
life, and cometh not into judgment, and is removed from death unto life." Also in
another place: "Verily, verily, I say unto you, He that believeth on me hath ever- John vi.
lasting life." Item: "He that believeth on the Son hath everlasting life: he that John iii.
believeth not on the Son shall not see life, but the wrath of God abideth upon him."
These aforesaid scriptures, with many other, do manifestly declare, that everlasting life
is only laid up in God's treasure-house for the faithful, and not for the unfaithful;
so that as the one sort, that is to say, the faithful, shall enjoy everlasting life, so
likewise the other part, I mean, the unfaithful, shall be cast headlong into "that
lake that brenneth with fire and brimstone."

Father. And shall the bodies of the faithful enjoy this everlasting life, no less than the souls? *Son.* Both joined together by the mighty power of God shall be partakers alike of this everlasting life.

Father. How can that be, when the holy apostle saith, "Flesh and blood cannot 1 Cor. xv.
inherit the kingdom of God"? And the Lord Christ saith: "No man goeth up into John iii.
heaven, but he that came down from heaven, even the Son of man, which is in heaven."
Son. Truth it is, that our bodies, as we received them of Adam, (for "that is born John iii.
of flesh is flesh," and "by nature we are all the children of wrath,") cannot inherit Eph. ii.
the kingdom of God: for so are they sinful, mortal, and corruptible. But being
regenerate, and born anew by the Spirit of God and holy baptism, and the qualities
being changed at the resurrection of the righteous, I mean, corruption into uncorrup- 1 Cor. xv.
tion, and mortality into immortality, the very same bodies, wherein we have lived,
without any alteration of the substance, shall enjoy the kingdom of God, as St Paul 2 Cor. v.
declareth in divers places of his epistles, and as we have abundantly heard heretofore. 1 Thess. iv.

Father. What is this everlasting life? *Son.* The perfect fruition, sight, and know-
ledge of God's majesty in his glorious kingdom. "We now see God through a glass 1 Cor. xiii.
in a dark speaking, but then shall we see him face to face. We now know God
unperfectly, but then shall we know him, even as he now knoweth us." We now
behold the majesty of God only with the eyes of our faith, and "it hath not yet 1 John iii.
appeared what we shall be; but we know that, when Christ the Lord shall appear,
we shall be like him, and shall see him even as he is." We now, being clad with
this mortal and corruptible body, are not at home with the Lord; but "when this
mortality shall be swallowed up of immortality, and this corruption of uncorruption,"
then shall we be at home with the Lord, and dwell in "an house not made with 2 Cor. v.
hands, but everlasting in heaven."

Father. What doth it profit thee to believe everlasting life? *Son.* So greatly, that without this faith the belief of all the other articles profit me nothing at all. So oft as I consider this blessed, glorious, immortal, and everlasting life, it maketh me to fight valiantly against the devil, the world, and the flesh, to seek the glory of the Lord my God unfeignedly, to obey his holy word, will, and commandment, to frame my life according to his pleasure, to do good to all men, yea, even to my very enemies, to bear all kind of adversity, not only patiently but also thankfully; in fine, to wish for to be loosened out of this miserable and wretched body, and to be with my Lord and Saviour Christ in the kingdom of his Father, where I shall see face to face the glorious majesty of the Lord my God, the Father, the Son, and the Holy Ghost, and understand those heavenly mysteries and secrets, which I, being clad with this gross, mortal, corruptible, and sinful body, can by no means attain unto; where also I shall have the company of the blessed angels, and of all the elect and chosen people of God, which have lived from the beginning unto the end of the world, and with them rejoice in the Lord our God worlds without end.

Father. Wherefore dost thou at the end of the articles of the christian faith say, "Amen"? *Son.* To declare that even from the very heart I do believe all those articles of the christian faith to be true, which I have now rehearsed, and that whatsoever is contained in them is a most undoubted verity, and hath or shall come to pass unfeignedly, as is in them contained. And thereunto I say once again, Amen.

Father. We have now handled the two first parts of the Catechism, wherein thou hast not only satisfied, but also overcome my expectation. And I thank my Lord God for thee, my dear child, that he hath through his holy Spirit, in this thy tender age, so graciously endued thee with the knowledge of his holy word. And I beseech him for his mercies' sake to continue his fatherly favour toward thee, and daily more and more to increase the knowledge of his blessed will in thee, that thou mayest at the last become a perfect man in Christ, and serve the Lord thy God in holiness and righteousness all the days of thy life. *Son.* God give me grace so to do!

THE THIRD PART OF THE CATECHISM.

OF THE LAW.

Father. Now followeth the third part of the Catechism, which thou saidst, as I remember, is the law. *Son.* Truth it is.

Father. Of what law speakest thou? *Son.* Not of man's, but of God's law.

Father. What is this law of God? *Son.* It is a doctrine containing the certain and unchangeable will of God, teaching what things are holy and pleasant to God, and contrariwise what things are ungodly and displeasant unto him; again, commanding what we ought to do, and forbidding what we ought to leave undone. What the law is.

Father. Give me examples of this thing. *Son.* Among the precepts which God will have to be done of us, these are comprehended: "Thou shalt love the Lord thy God with all thy heart, with all thy mind, and with all thy strengths." Again: "Remember that thou keep holy the sabbath-day." The contrary commandments, I speak of such as forbid us those things which we ought not to do, are these and such like: "Thou shalt have no strange gods in my sight." "Thou shalt not take the name of the Lord thy God in vain." "Thou shalt not steal," &c. Deut. vi. Exod. xx.

Father. To whom did God give his law? *Son.* He first of all gave it generally to all men, writing it in their hearts, whereby every man did know when he did well or otherwise, his conscience either commending or condemning him for his act: afterward the Lord our God gave it to the people of Israel, when he was determined to erect and stablish a new commonweal among the Israelites; that by this means they might know the certain and express will of God, and frame their lives according to the same.

Father. By whom did God deliver his law to the people of Israel? *Son.* By his servant Moses.

Father. Where? *Son.* In the mount Sinai. Exod. xix.

Father. At what time? *Son.* The third month after that the people of Israel were delivered out of Egypt; in the year 430 after the promise made to Abraham concerning that blessed seed; and after the flood in the year 797; and from the beginning of the world, in the year 2454. At what time the law was given.

Father. After what manner was this law of God given? *Son.* With great glory, written with the finger of God in two tables of stone. For when this law of God should be given and published to the people of Israel, God himself, that mighty Lord, came down into the mount Sinai with fire; and there was heard great thundering and much lightning seen in the air. And there was a thick cloud upon the mount, and a noise of a trumpet exceeding mighty, insomuch that the people which were in the tents were wonderful afraid; for the smoke of the mount went up as the smoke of a furnace; so that the whole mount was exceeding terrible, and the noise of the trumpet was wonderful mighty.

Father. To what end did God give his law to the people of Israel? *Son.* Not only to the Israelites in times past gave God his law, (I speak not of the ceremonial or judicial, but of the moral law;) but to us also, and to so many as profess godliness, is that law given, and we owe now no less obedience to it, than heretofore the Jews did; so that we also, which are called Christians, ought diligently to do whatsoever is there commanded, and leave undone whatsoever is there forbidden.

Father. I grant. But my question is, to what end, or for what purpose God gave this law?

Son. First, that it should be unto us a certain, sure, and undoubted doctrine, opening and declaring the everlasting and unchangeable will of God, whereof we may learn both how to frame our life according to the good pleasure of God, and also what works we ought to do, wherewith we may please God, and serve him according to his holy will; lest we, following our own foolish fancies, corrupt judgments, blind zeals, and fleshly good intents, should attempt and do those things which are dis- Why God gave his law.

Deut. xii. pleasant and unacceptable to the Lord our God; seeing it is written: "Ye shall not do every man what seemeth him good in his own eyes." Again: "That I command thee, do thou only to the Lord: neither put thou any thing thereto, nor take ought Deut. iv. therefrom." Item: "Ye shall put nothing to the word which I command you, neither do ought therefrom, that ye may keep the commandments of the Lord thy God, Eph. ii. which I command you." The holy apostle also saith: "We are the workmanship of God, created in Christ Jesu unto good works, which God hath prepared that we should walk in them."

The names of the law of God in the holy scripture. And for this cause hath the law of God divers names in the holy scriptures, which tend unto this end. The prophet Esay and the psalmograph also call the law of God "a witness", because it testifieth, sheweth, and declareth unto us the good will and Isai. viii. pleasure of God. Esay writeth thus: "If any man want light, let him look upon Psal. xix. the law and witness," &c. David saith: "The witness of the Lord is true, and giveth wisdom even unto babes."

Moreover, David, Salomon, and our Saviour Christ calleth the law of God "a light." For as the light doth shew to him that walketh in darkness the way perfectly, and how he may safely walk, and without jeopardy; so likewise the law of God sheweth a christian man how he ought to direct his ways, and to walk according to the will of God, neither declining on the right hand nor on the left. And as "he that walketh in darkness knoweth not whither he goeth," yea, for want of light he goeth out of his way, stumbleth, falleth, hurteth himself, and many times casteth himself into great danger; so, in like manner, he that walketh in the blind darkness and dark blindness of carnal reason, not having the light of God's law, whereunto he may direct his footsteps, falleth into most filthy errors and heresies, embraceth idolatry and superstition in the stead of the true worshipping of God, and, forsaking the alone true God, honoureth idols and false gods: as we may see in the kingdom of the pope, where, for lack of the light of God's word, who is able to express, what false religion, what superstition, what idolatry, what hypocrisy, what heresy, what monstrous sects, what errors, what wicked opinions, what kinds of all abominations do reign? Contrariwise, where the light of God's word reigneth, there is an whole sea of good and godly things; but where the darkness of men's traditions bear rule, there is a world of all evils. Without this light of God's law we utterly know not how we ought to Exod. xiii. direct our pathways according to the will of God. Look what the "pillar of fire" was to the children of Israel, when they passed through the Red sea, in the night time; the very same unto us, which are tossed with the troublous waves of this Psal. cxix. world, is the law and word of God. The psalmograph saith: "Thy word, O Lord, Prov. vi. is a lantern to my feet, and a light to my pathways." Salomon also saith: "The Psal. xix. commandment is a lantern, and the law a light." David once again saith: "The commandment of the Lord is bright, and giveth light to the eyes." Hither pertaineth John iii. the saying of our Saviour Christ: "This is condemnation, that light is come into the 2 Pet. i. world, and men have loved darkness more than light." St Peter also saith: "We have a sure word of prophecy; and ye do well that ye take heed thereunto, as unto a light that shineth in a dark place, until the day dawneth, and the day-star arise in your hearts."

James i. Furthermore, St James compareth the law of God to a glass. For as in a glass we see what is fair or foul in our face, so likewise when we look in the law of God, we easily see and perceive what is well or evil in our doings; so that through the benefit of this glass, I mean the law of God, we are provoked to amend those things that are amiss, which otherwise should remain and continue in us unto our damnation.

Secondly, forasmuch as man of himself is nothing else than a very lump of pride, and soon forgetteth his vileness, nakedness, corrupt and sinful nature, boasting himself even before God to be somewhat, when he is nothing else than mere vanity, and worthy of praise, when he is most worthy of everlasting damnation; as we may see Luke xviii. in the parable or history of the proud Pharisee and sinful publican, and in divers other of the holy scripture; God, willing to paint, shew, and set forth man to himself, as it were in his native colours, gave unto him his law, that by the consideration thereof he might learn to know himself, his misery, weakness, impiety, sin, and his unableness to fulfil the law of God, seeing the law is spiritual, and we are carnal; as St Paul testifieth: "By the law," saith he, "cometh the knowledge of sin." Again: "I know not sin, but by the law. For I had not known concupiscence or lust (to be sin), except the law had said, Thou shalt not covet, or lust. But sin took an occasion by the means of the commandment, and wrought in me all manner of concupiscence. For verily without the law sin was dead. I once lived without law: but when the commandment came, sin revived; and I was dead. And the very same commandment, which was ordained unto life, was found to be unto me an occasion of death. For sin took occasion by the means of the commandment, and so deceived me, and by the self commandment slew me. Wherefore the law is holy, and the commandment holy, just, and good. Was that then which is good made death unto me? God forbid! Nay, it was sin, that it might appear, how that sin, by the means of that which is good, had wrought death in me; that sin, by the means of the commandment, might be out of measure sinful. For we know that the law is spiritual; but I am carnal, sold under sin, because I allow not that which I do. For what I would, that do I not; but what I hate, that do I. If I do now that which I would not, I grant to the law that it is good. So then now it is not I that do it, but sin that dwelleth in me. For I know that in me (that is to say, in my flesh) dwelleth no good thing," &c. Rom. vii. Rom. iii. Rom. vii. Exod. xx. Deut. v.

This end of the law is necessary to be known. For without this knowledge, we esteem of ourselves, of our strengths, of our free will, might, and power, more than becometh us: yea, we think ourselves through our own good works and merits worthy of the favour of God, remission of sins, the gift of the Holy Ghost, and everlasting life, when we be least of all worthy of those things. But the law uttereth and sheweth us unto ourselves, and maketh evident, plain, and open before our eyes, our own wickedness, misery, and wretchedness; as we may see in Adam, Heva, Cain, David, Saul, Mary Magdalene, Peter, &c. Yea, the law accuseth, condemneth, killeth, and casteth us down headlong into hell-fire, with all our works and merits, because we do not fulfil the law with such purity of heart, as the law doth require, according to this saying of our Saviour Christ: "Did not Moses give you a law, and yet none of you keepeth the law?" Hereto belongeth the saying of St Peter: "Why tempt ye God, that ye would put a yoke on the disciples' necks, which neither our fathers nor we were able to bear?" Neither differeth the saying of Moses from this purpose: "Cursed be every one that abideth not in all things which are written in the book of the law, and fulfilleth them." In consideration whereof the law is called "the killing letter," "the ministry of death and damnation," "the power of sin," &c. John vii. Acts xv. Deut. xxvii. Gal. iii. Rom. iv. 2 Cor. iii. 1 Cor. xv.

Thirdly, God hath given us his law unto this end, that, after we have perfectly learned of the law our corruption, our wicked nature, our impiety, our pronity unto sin, our slackness unto all goodness, and finally, our feebleness, yea, our nothing in fulfilling the holy, good, and righteous law of God, (lest we, beholding our damnation for not satisfying the will of God, should despair, and be made by this means inheritors of hell-fire,) it should be unto us a schoolmaster to point and lead us unto Christ, which is "the end and perfect fulfilling of the law, to make righteous so many as believe on him;" that we, apprehending and laying hand through strong faith on his perfection and fulfilling of the law, might be counted righteous before God, and so become heirs of everlasting glory. For by this means, namely, through faith in Christ, we obtain that of God, which cannot be obtained of the law through works, that is to say, the favour of God, remission of sins, quietness of conscience, the gift of the Holy Ghost, and in fine, everlasting life, as these scriptures following do abundantly testify. Rom. x.

Our Saviour Christ saith: "Think not that I am come to break the law or the prophets. No, I am not come to break, but to fulfil." All things written in the law or in the prophets Christ hath unto the uttermost fulfilled, not for himself, but for us, that his fulfilling should be recounted our fulfilling, if we believe on him. This witnesseth St Paul, saying: "Christ is the perfect fulfilling of the law, to justify every one that believeth on him." Again: "Christ hath delivered us from the curse of the law, while he was made accursed for our sake: for it is written, Cursed is every Matt. v. Rom. x. Gal. iii. Deut. xxi.

Gal. iii. one that hangeth on the tree." Item: "The law was our schoolmaster to drive us unto Christ, that we might be made righteous by faith. But after that faith is come, now are we no longer under a schoolmaster. For ye are all the sons of God by the Heb. vii. faith which is in Christ Jesus." Also in another place: "The law made nothing perfect, but was an introduction of a better hope; by which hope we draw nigh unto Gal. iv. God." Once again he saith: "When the time was full come, God sent his Son, born of a woman, and made bond unto the law, to redeem them which were under the law; that we through election might receive the inheritance that belongeth unto the natural sons." Hereto appertaineth part of St Paul's sermon, which blessed Luke re- Acts xiii. citeth in his chronicle of the apostles' acts: "Be it known unto you, ye men and brethren, that through this man (Christ) is preached unto you the forgiveness of sins, and that by him all that believe are justified from all things, from which ye could not be justified by the law of Moses."

Fourthly, God ordained his law, that it should be a bit or a bridle to restrain the evil and disobedient persons from their evil and disobedience, and by this means at the least compel them to walk in an order, and do that which is good and righteous, if not for the love of God, yet for the fear of punishment, as the poet saith:

"Oderunt peccare boni virtutis amore;
Oderunt peccare mali formidine pœnæ.[1]"

1 Tim. i. Of this use or end of the law speaketh St Paul, saying: "We know that the law is good, if a man use it lawfully; understanding this, how that the law is not given unto a righteous man, but unto the unrighteous and disobedient, to the ungodly Rom. xiii. and to sinners," &c. Again: "Rulers are not to be feared for good works, but for evil. Wilt thou be without fear of the power? Do well then; and so shalt thou be praised of the same: for he is the minister of God for thy wealth. But if thou do evil, then fear; for he beareth not the sword for nought, but is the minister of God to take vengeance on them that do evil."

These are the principal and chief causes, which I have now rehearsed, wherefore God hath given us his law, as I have learned of the holy scriptures.

Father. How many commandments doth this law of God contain? *Son*. Ten: whereof four appertain unto God, teaching what our duty is toward the Lord our God, how we ought to serve, honour, and worship him; again, how we ought to call upon, praise, and glorify his holy name, and behave ourself in all things that concern the glorious majesty of God. The other six teach us what our duty is toward our neighbour, and how we ought to behave ourselves toward him, both in thought, word, and deed. Exod. xx. And for this cause God gave this his law written in two tables of stone: the one containing, as ye have heard, our duty toward God; the other, toward our neighbour.

Father. Rehearse the first commandment.

The first commandment. *Son*. "I am the Lord thy God, which have brought thee out of the land of Egypt, even out of the house of bondage. Thou shalt have no strange gods in my sight."

Why God is called the Lord. *Father*. Wherefore doth God use so solemn and noble preface in the beginning of his commandments? Why calleth he himself "the Lord"? *Son*. The Lord is a name of great majesty and wonderful high excellency, which name is properly due unto our God alone, as he saith by the prophet: "I am the Lord: this is my name. I will give my glory to none other, nor my honour to graven images." And he calleth himself by this name, "the Lord," to declare and set forth unto us his might, power, and authority, which he of right hath to command all creatures, of whom he alone is the creator, that by this means we may diligently address ourselves unto the perfect accomplishment of his holy and blessed will.

Why God calleth himself our God. *Father*. Why doth he call himself "our God"? *Son*. In calling himself "our God," he giveth us to understand, that he alone is and will be our high goodness, comfort, help, defence, health, treasure, abundance of all good things, horn of plenty, and bottomless fountain, out of the which we may abundantly draw whatsoever is necessary either

[[1] Hor. Epist. I. xvi. 52, 53.]

for the soul or for the body, both in this world and in the world to come; as he said to Abraham: "I am the Almighty God (or as some read, *El Shadai*, that is, a God mighty in power, abundant in riches, sufficient to reward plentifully, and lacking of nothing): walk before me, and be without spot. I will make my covenant between me and thee, and thy seed after thee, throughout their posterities, that it may be an everlasting covenant; so that I will be the God of thee, and of thy seed after thee." Again: "Fear not: I am thy shield, and thy exceeding great reward." Gen. xvii. xv.

Father. For what cause is mention made here of the deliverance out of Egypt, seeing not we, which are called Christians, but the Jews, were delivered out of Egypt, that house of bondage, even from the tyranny of that most wicked king, Pharao? *Son.* Their corporal deliverance was a figure of our spiritual deliverance, manumission, and freedom. For as the Israelites were delivered from the captivity of the cruel Egyptians by the out-stretched arm and mighty hand of that most mighty God; even so likewise are we, which are of the household of faith, delivered and made free from the power of the devil, and from the bondage of the world, and from the yoke of sin, death, and damnation, by the passion and death of our Lord and Saviour Jesus Christ; yea, and that of God's mere mercy and undeserved liberality, which hath chosen us a peculiar and several people unto himself, and given us the liberty of his most dear sons and the fellowship of everlasting life. In the preface therefore of his law, God maketh mention of the Israelites' deliverance out of Egypt to this end, that we thereby should be put in remembrance of our deliverance out of the spiritual Egypt, that is to say, the tyranny of Satan and hell-fire, and by this means be provoked the more earnestly to embrace the law of God, and to frame our lives according to the same. Of the deliverance out of Egypt. Exod. xiv.

Father. What doth God require of us in this first commandment, "Thou shalt have no strange gods in my sight"? *Son.* First, in that we are forbidden to have any strange gods in his sight, he signifieth plainly unto us, that he is the one and alone true God, and that there is none other God but he alone, neither in heaven, nor in earth, nor under the earth. What God requireth of us in the first commandment.

Father. How provest thou that by the holy scripture? *Son.* Moses saith: "Take heed, and imprint it well in your heart, that the Lord is God, both above in heaven, and beneath upon the earth, and that there is none other God." Again: "The Lord is God, and there is none other God but he only." Item: "Hear, O Israel, the Lord our God is one Lord only." God himself saith: "See now that I, I am, and there is none other God but I." Again: "Hear, O my people, for I assure thee, O Israel, if thou wilt hearken unto me, there shall be no strange god in thee, neither shall thou worship any other God. I am the Lord thy God, which brought thee out of the land of Egypt." By the prophet Esay he saith also: "I am, I am the Lord, and there is none other Saviour. I am the Lord, and besides me there is none other God. Consider, that I am he, before whom there was never any God, neither shall there be any after me. I am only the Lord." Again: "I am the Lord, and besides me there is no God." Hereto agreeth the saying of St Paul: "We know that there is none other God but one. For although there be that are called gods (as there be gods many, and lords many), yet have we but one God, even that Father, of whom are all things, and we in him, and one Lord Jesus Christ, by whom are all things, and we by him." Deut. iv. Deut. vi. Psal. lxxxi. Isai. xliii. Isai. xlv. 1 Cor. viii.

Father. Of this matter we heard abundantly afore in the declaration of the articles of the christian faith. Go forth to express the will of God concerning the first commandment, as thou begannest. *Son.* Secondly, as I am commanded here to believe, confess, and grant, that there is but one only true and everlasting God, so likewise is it required of me that I put my faith, hope, trust, and confidence in no creature either in heaven or in earth, but in this one God alone; looking for all good things at his hand, be they worldly or heavenly; and thanking him for all the benefits that I receive, whether they appertain unto the body or unto the soul, with this confession, that whatsoever I have, being good and godly, I have it altogether of his mere mercy and undeserved liberality. For, as St Paul saith: "What hast thou, that thou hast not received? If thou hast received it, why dost thou glory as though thou hadst not received it?" St James also saith: "Every good gift and every perfect gift is from above, and cometh down from the Father of lights." 1 Cor. iv. James i.

Father. How provest thou that thy whole faith, trust, and confidence ought to depend on this God alone? *Son*. Salomon saith: "Have thy faith, or put thy trust and confidence, in the Lord with all thy heart, and lean not to thine own wisdom." The prophet Jeremy pronounceth that man "accursed, which trusteth in man, maketh flesh his strength, and suffereth his heart to depart from the Lord." But he calleth that man "blessed, which setteth his faith and putteth his confidence in the Lord," depending wholly on him, and looking for all good things at his hand. St Paul also saith: "Without faith it is not possible to please God. For he that cometh unto God must believe that God is, and that he is a rewarder of them that seek him." To be short, our Saviour Christ saith: "Have your faith and confidence in God."

Prov. iii. Jer. xvii. Heb. xi. Mark xi.

Father. Requireth God in this commandment nothing else but faith in him? *Son*. Not only faith, but also love, which issueth and proceedeth out of faith, as fruit out of the tree, yea, and that "from a pure heart, and a good conscience, and a faith unfeigned," as St Paul saith, doth God require in this commandment.

Gal. v. Psal. i. 1 Tim. i.

Father. Declare that by the scriptures. *Son*. Moses saith: "Hear, O Israel, the Lord our God is one Lord only. And thou shalt love the Lord thy God with all thy heart, with all thy soul, and with all thy might." In the gospel we read that a certain scribe demanded of Christ: "Which is the chiefest commandment of all?" To whom he answered on this manner: "Hear, O Israel, the Lord our God is one God; and thou shalt love the Lord thy God with all thy heart, with all thy soul, with all thy mind, and with all thy strength." "And the scribe said unto him, Master, verily thou hast said right. For there is but one God, and there is none other besides him. And to love him with all thy heart, with all thy mind, with all thy soul, and with all thy strength, is more than brent-offerings and sacrifices."

Deut. vi. Mark xii. Deut. vi. xxx.

Father. What requireth God in this commandment besides faith and love? *Son*. Fear: yea, and that not servile or thrall, but childish and reverent. For God is to be believed as God, loved as a father, feared as a Lord.

Father. Let me hear that proved by the scriptures. *Son*. Moses saith: "Now, Israel, what requireth the Lord thy God of thee, but that thou fear the Lord thy God; and that thou walk in all his ways, and love him, and serve the Lord thy God with all thy heart, and with all thy soul; and that thou keep the commandments of the Lord and his ordinances, which I command thee this day, that thou mayest prosper?" Salomon also saith: "Fear the Lord, and depart from evil: so shall thy navel be whole, and thy bones strong." God himself saith by the prophet: "A son honoureth his father, and a servant his master. If I now be a father, where is my honour? if I be the Lord, where is my fear?"

Deut. x. Prov. iii. Mal. i.

Father. Requireth God in this precept any other thing, besides faith, love, and fear? *Son*. Yea.

Father. What is that? *Son*. Honour and service.

Father. Where is that proved? *Son*. Moses saith: "Thou shalt honour the Lord thy God, and serve him alone."

Deut. vi.

Father. What is the true honour and service of God? *Son*. To honour and serve him according to his word, and to do those works, not which carnal reason and blind zeal fancieth, but which God himself commandeth. Of this honour and service speaketh the Lord Christ in the gospel on this manner: "The true worshippers shall worship the Father in spirit and truth; for the Father will have such to worship him. God is a spirit, and they that worship him must worship him in spirit and truth." Zachary the priest also saith: "God hath delivered us from the power of our enemies, that we should serve him in holiness and righteousness before him all the days of our life."

John iv. Luke i.

Father. May we not also honour and serve other, as angels, saints, or images, as we do God? *Son*. God forbid! God himself saith by the prophet: "I am the Lord: this is my name. I will give my glory to none other, nor mine honour to graven images." We read in the holy scriptures, that when Cornelius the centurion, esteeming more of Peter than he ought to judge of a man, "fell down before Peter, and worshipped him, Peter took him up again, and said, Arise; for I am a man also." The people of Lystra, for a miracle which was wrought among them, called Paul and Barnabas gods, and

Isai. xlii. Acts x. Acts xiv.

would have worshipped them as gods. "But Paul rent his clothes, and cried out, saying, Ye men, why do ye these things? We are mortal men also like unto you, and preach unto you the gospel, that ye should turn from these vain things unto the living God, which made heaven and earth," &c. St John also fell down before the angel to worship him; but the angel forbad him, saying: "Look, that thou do it not. I am the fellow-servant of thee and of thy brethren, which have the testimony of Jesu. Worship God." All the angels, saints, and blessed spirits cry with one voice: "Not to us, O Lord, not to us, but to thy name give the glory, for thy mercy and truth's sake." They all with one accord cast their crowns before the throne of God's majesty, praising and honouring him both day and night, worlds without end, and saying: "Thou art worthy, O Lord our God, to take the glory, honour, and power; for thou hast made all things, and by thy will they are and were created." How grievously did the prophet Helias rebuke the Israelites, which worshipped both God and Baal! Were not these his words, "How long will ye halt on both sides? If the Lord be God, follow him: if Baal be he, follow him"?

Rev. xix. xxii.

Psal. cxv.

Rev. iv.

1 Kings xviii.

Father. God then in this his first commandment requireth of us faith, love, fear, and honour. *Son.* Yea, verily, and that from the very bottom of the heart only and alone, as he saith by Salomon: "O son, give me thy heart." For as "God is a spirit," so will he be worshipped in spirit and truth. And the law of God requireth not only of us outward honest and godly works, but also the pure affects and uncorrupt motions of the mind, with a perfect consent to the law of God concerning the full and due accomplishment of the same. Such as honour and worship God otherwise, God rejecteth and casteth them away by his prophet, saying: "This people draweth nigh unto me, and honoureth me with their lips; but their heart is far from me. Verily, they worship me in vain."

Prov. xxiii. John iv.

Isai. xxix. Matt. xv.

Father. Hitherto have we heard, what we ought to do concerning the accomplishment of this first commandment. Declare now also what we are forbidden here to do, that we fall not into the transgression and breaking of this commandment, and so displease the Lord our God. *Son.* We are forbidden to believe, love, fear, and honour those whom the gentiles and heathen have heretofore through ignorance reputed and taken for gods, when indeed they are nothing but idols, yea devils, as the psalmograph saith: "The gods of the heathen are devils: it is the Lord that made the heavens." We are forbidden also to use the art of magic, witchcraft, sorcery, charms, incantations, conjurations, &c.; to set our affiance and trust in any creature; to glory in ourselves, blood, kindred, wisdom, strength, riches, beauty, cunning, learning, eloquence, &c.; to seek health either of body or soul, as the giver thereof, at any creature in heaven or in earth, but only at the mighty hand of God, from whom alone "cometh every good and perfect gift;" again, to receive or set forth any doctrine that fighteth with the word of God; in fine, to do any thing whereby the glory of God may be obscured, or his holy religion evil reported.

Psal. xcvi.

James i.

Father. In forbidding us to have strange gods, why doth God use these words, "in my sight"? *Son.* There is nothing hidden from the face of God, which "searcheth the hearts and reins;" to whose eyes also "all things are open and naked:" therefore doth God require of us in this precept not only an outward reverence of the body, but also the inward honour of the mind, yea, and that a pure and faithful mind, utterly estranged from all idolatry, superstition, hypocrisy, &c.

Psal. vii. Jer. xi. xvii. Rev. ii. Heb. iv.

Father. Rehearse the second commandment.

Son. "Thou shalt make thee no graven or carved image, nor likeness at all of any thing that is in heaven above, or in earth beneath, or in the waters under the earth. Thou shalt not bow before them, nor worship them. For I the Lord thy God am a strong and jealous God, punishing the wickedness of the parents in the children until the third and fourth generation of them that hate me; and shew mercy until thousands unto those that love me, and keep my commandments."

The second commandment.

Father. There are some writers, yea, and those of no obscure fame, (as I may speak nothing of the long custom used in the church, which hath utterly left out this commandment, and to supply the number hath divided the tenth commandment into two, that is, into the ninth and tenth, contrary to the mind of the lawgiver, whose words, and the order also of the same, ought by no means either to be corrupted, altered, or changed,) which thrust out of the decalogue or ten commandments this second commandment, as a ceremonial law, serving for the time, but now of none effect concerning us Christians, to whom it is, say they, lawful to have the images of Christ and of saints in churches, private houses, or elsewhere, without any offence or breach of God's commandment; and therefore, to supply the number of the ten commandments, they also divide, as I said before, the tenth commandment into the ninth and tenth, making of one two, according to the custom used in the pope's church. *Son.* As touching the custom of reciting the ten commandments according to the appointment of the bishop of Rome, in the which is utterly omitted this second commandment concerning the forbidding either of making or worshipping of images, it cannot be denied but it is wicked and ungodly, and left out of the pope and of his adherents of a set purpose for the maintenance of images in churches, brought in by the devil and antichrist contrary to the word of God; and therefore ought this custom utterly to be broken, and every commandment to be restored to his proper place, and so to be recited of the Christians, as it is now used in the best reformed churches.

And as for the judgments, or rather opinions and fancies, of certain learned men in this our age, which in this behalf remain still infected with the dirty dregs of that whore of Babylon, I can by no means approve and allow them. For whereas they say, that the second commandment concerning images is ceremonial, and only served for the people of Israel, and not for us, so that it is lawful for us to have images in our temples, chapels, houses, &c. notwithstanding this commandment; I utterly deny this their doctrine, and affirm it to be most wicked and utterly estranged from the truth of God's word. For if this law be ceremonial, and we set without the limits thereof, then followeth it, that as it is lawful for us to have images in our churches, so is it lawful also to reverence, worship, or honour them: which is so great an absurdity, that I think they themselves will not allow it, except they be sworn chaplains to pope Gregory III., which made a law, that images should not only be had in churches, as laymen's books, according to the doctrine of pope Gregory I., but that they also should be worshipped and had in greater reverence than ever they were before, and that whosoever were of a contrary opinion, he should be excommunicate and condemned for an heretic[1]. For throughout the whole course of God's law there is not one commandment so fortressed and confirmed with the testimonies of the holy scripture, and so urged to be observed and kept of God's people, as this is, concerning the not having or worshipping of images. Therefore as the first, so likewise the second commandment abideth moral, and requireth like obedience. And whereas they exclude it from the number of the ten commandments, and rack that one tenth commandment into two for to supply the number, they do most unjustly, and contrary to the doctrine of the ancient fathers and old catholic doctors of Christ's church.

Images not lawful in the temples of the Christians.

For as our catechist declared unto us, Athanasius, Origenes, Chrysostomus, Gregorius Nazianzenus, Hieronymus, Ambrosius, with divers other, both of the ancient and late writers, number this precept among the ten commandments; and hold that it is a moral law, no less appertaining unto us Christians now, than it did in times past unto the Jews. He said, moreover, unto us, that in the church of God among the Jews, in the old law, there was no image suffered neither of God nor of any saint; although who knoweth not, what a great number of godly persons there lived before the coming of Christ, both patriarchs, judges, kings, priests, Levites, prophets, matrons, virgins, &c.? He added furthermore, that, almost five hundred years after Christ's ascension, images could not be suffered to have any place in the temples of the Christians. He told us also an history of a certain holy bishop named Epiphanius, which, coming into a church to pray, saw a veil there hanging, wherein was painted the image of Christ, or of some saint. So soon as he saw it, being greatly offended thereat, he cut the image away, and said, that "it is contrary to the authority of the holy scrip-

Images in temples destroyed. Epiphanius.

[[1] In a council held at Rome, A.D. 732. See Concil. Stud. Labbei. Lut. Par. 1671—2. Tom. VI. cols. 1463, 4, 85.]

tures to have the image of any man in the church of Christ[2]." He told us moreover of one Serenus, bishop of Massilia[3], which did not only take away images out of the churches throughout all his diocese, but he also brake them on pieces, and brent them.

Serenus.

He brought forth also unto us certain laws and decrees of most noble and virtuous emperors[4]; again, certain councils[5], in the which it was decreed and enacted, that all images should be taken out of the churches and burnt openly; and that from henceforth no man should presume to make an image either of Christ or of any saint, nor cause it to be painted on the walls of the church where christian men come together for to pray.

Laws and decrees of princes and bishops against the having of images in churches.

He alleged unto us the sentence of the great and ancient clerk Lactantius, which saith, that "God cannot be truly worshipped in that place where an image is[6]." Again: "If your saints (saith he), if the holy mother of Christ be in heaven, why do ye not lift up your eyes unto heaven? Why do ye rather look unto walls and unto stocks, than unto that place where ye believe that they are? What mean the temples, the tabernacles, yea, and (to be short) what mean those images[7]?" In fine, he said, that the use of images came from the heathen unto us, and alleged Eusebius[8] with certain other for his authors; and that therefore they ought by no means to be placed in the temples, chapels, oratories, or houses of the Christians.

Lactantius.

Placing of images in churches came from the old idolaters.

Eusebius.

Father. I can none otherwise but praise thee for thy good remembrance concerning the doctrine of your catechist, a man both godly and learned. But the image-mongers object and say, that they are laymen's calendars, and are the very same to the lewd, simple, and ignorant people, that books are to the wise, discreet, and learned men. *Son.* What wisdom, knowledge, or learning can a man get of that thing which is a very block or stone, and utterly without sense? Can the dumb teach to speak? the blind to see? the deaf to hear? the lame to go? the dead to live? Can that which hath no understanding, no wisdom, no learning, teach us to understand, to be wise and learned? O unprofitable schoolmasters! O rude teachers! O too much beast-like instructors! "They have mouths," as the psalmograph saith, "and speak not: eyes have they, but they see not. They have ears, and hear not: noses have they, but they smell not. They have hands, and handle not: feet have they, but they cannot go; neither can they speak through their throat." They are not able to wipe away the dust from their faces. They have sceptres and swords in their hands,

The objections of the image-mongers answered.

Images are not profitable books for the lay.

Psal. cxv.

Bar. vi.

[[2] Præterea quod audivi quosdam murmurare contra me, quia quando simul pergebamus ad sanctum locum, qui vocatur Bethel, ut ibi collectam tecum ex more ecclesiastico facerem, et venissem ad villam, quæ dicitur Anablatha, vidissemque ibi præteriens lucernam ardentem, et interrogassem, quis locus esset, didicissemque esse ecclesiam, et intrassem ut orarem: inveni ibi velum pendens in foribus ejusdem ecclesiæ tinctum atque depictum, et habens imaginem, quasi Christi, vel sancti cujusdam: non enim satis memini, cujus imago fuerit. Cum ergo hoc vidissem, in ecclesia Christi contra auctoritatem scripturarum hominis pendere imaginem, scidi illud, et magis dedi consilium custodibus ejusdem loci, ut pauperem mortuum eo obvolverent et efferrent. Illique contra murmurantes dixerunt: Si scindere voluerat, justum erat, ut aliud daret velum, atque mutaret. Quod cum audissem, me daturum esse pollicitus sum......Nunc autem misi quod potui reperire, et precor ut jubeas presbyteros ejusdem loci suscipere velum a latore, quod a nobis missum est; et deinceps præcipere, in ecclesia Christi ejusmodi vela, quæ contra religionem nostram veniunt, non appendi.—Epiphan. Op. Par. 1622. Epist. ad Joan. Episc. Hieros. Hieron. Interp. Tom. II. p. 317.]

[[3] Præterea indico dudum ad nos pervenisse, quod fraternitas vestra, quosdam imaginum adoratores aspiciens, easdem in ecclesiis imagines confregit atque projecit. Et quidem zelum vos, ne quid manu factum adorari posset, habuisse laudavimus; sed frangere easdem imagines non debuisse indicamus. Idcirco enim pictura in ecclesiis adhibetur, ut hi qui literas nesciunt, saltem in parietibus videndo legant quæ legere in codicibus non valent.—Gregor. Magni Papæ I. Op. Par. 1705. Lib. IX. Indict. ii. Epist. cv. Ad Serenum Massiliens. Episc. Tom. II. col. 1006.]

[[4] See below, page 71, note 2.]

[[5] See below, page 71, note 5.]

[[6] Quare non est dubium, quin religio nulla sit, ubicumque simulacrum est.—Lactant. Op. Lut. Par. 1748. Divin. Instit. Lib. II. De Orig. Error. cap. xix. Tom. I. p. 185.]

[[7] Nempe ideo timetis, quod eos esse in cœlo arbitramini: neque enim, si dii sunt, aliter fieri potest. Cur igitur oculos in cœlum non tollitis? et advocatis eorum nominibus, in aperto sacrificia celebratis? Cur ad parietes, et ligna, et lapides potissimum, quam illo spectatis, ubi eos esse creditis? Quid sibi templa, quid aræ volunt? quid denique ipsa simulacra?—Id. ibid. cap. ii. p. 116.]

[[8] Καὶ θαυμαστὸν οὐδὲν τοὺς πάλαι ἐξ ἐθνῶν εὐεργετηθέντας πρὸς τοῦ Σωτῆρος ἡμῶν ταῦτα πεποιηκέναι· ὅτε καὶ τῶν ἀποστόλων αὐτοῦ τὰς εἰκόνας Παύλου καὶ Πέτρου, καὶ αὐτοῦ δὴ τοῦ Χριστοῦ, διὰ χρωμάτων ἐν γραφαῖς σωζομένας ἱστορήσαμεν· ὡς εἰκὸς τῶν παλαιῶν ἀπαραφυλάκτως, οἷα σωτῆρας, ἐθνικῇ συνηθείᾳ παρ' ἑαυτοῖς τοῦτον τιμᾷν εἰωθότων τὸν τρόπον.—Hist. Eccles. Script. Amst. 1695—1700. Euseb. Pamph. Lib. VII. cap. xviii. p. 216.]

but they are not able to defend themselves. They have candles brenning before them, but they see none of them, neither take they any pleasure of the light. If the house bren over their heads, they are not able to flee that they may escape the danger of brenning. If they fall down to the ground, they cannot rise up again. If any man striketh them, they cannot revenge their quarrel. If the worms eat them, they feel it not. If the owls, sparrows, doves, or any other fowls or beasts file[1] upon their heads, they perceive it not, neither are they angry at the matter. In fine, they be utterly unprofitable both to themself and to all other; so far is it off, that such idle idols and mumming mawmets can teach us any good thing. By the lessest creature that ever God made may we learn better to know God than by these dumb images, seem they never so glorious in the eyes of the foolish.

Psal. xix. Rom. i. "The heavens," saith David, "shew forth the glory of God; and the very firmament declareth his handy-works." Hereto appertaineth the saying of St Paul: "That which may be known of God is made open to men. For God hath shewed it unto them, that the invisible things of God (that is, his everlasting power and Godhead) might be seen, while they are considered by the works from the creation of the world; so that they are without excuse, inasmuch as they knew that there is a God, and have not praised him as God, nor thanked him, but became vain in their imaginations, and their foolish heart was blinded. When they counted themselves wise, they became fools, and turned the glory of the incorruptible God into the similitude of the image of a corruptible man," &c.

How unmeet a schoolmaster a blind idol, a dumb mawmet, a popish puppet, a dead image is to teach us any good thing, these words of the prophet declare manifestly: Hab. ii. "What profiteth a graven image which the workman hath fashioned? a vain cast idol, and false lying image? Because the workman hath put his trust in it, therefore maketh he dumb images. But wo be unto him which saith to a block, Awake; and to a dumb stone, Arise! Can such one teach, or give any good instructions? Behold, it is laid over with gold and silver, and there is no breath in it. But the Lord in his holy temple is he whom all the world should fear." The prophet Esay Isai. xliv. also saith, that "images are profitable for nothing;" and addeth moreover, that the labour in making them is utterly lost. How then can they be profitable to teach? Wisd. xiv. How can they then be the books of the lewd people? "The seeking out of images," saith the wise man, "is the beginning of whoredom; and the bringing up of them is the destruction of life. But they were not from the beginning, neither shall they continue for ever. The wealthy idleness of men hath found them out upon earth: therefore shall they come shortly to an end." If the seeking out of images be the beginning of whoredom, that is to say, idolatry, which in the scripture is called whoredom, how can we be taught and brought unto God by them? If the bringing up of them be the destruction of life, how can they then bring us unto everlasting salvation? and how can they edify us and teach us the way of truth? Vain and unprofitable schoolmasters are these blind and dumb images.

When God determined to erect and set up the commonweal of the Israelites, he gave them not his image to look upon, that by the sight thereof they might learn to know him and to do his will (no, he only spake to them, any similitude of him they saw not, lest by this means they should have gone about to make his image, and have committed idolatry or spiritual whoredom with the same); but he gave them Deut. vi. his holy word, charging and commanding them to hear and read that diligently, and to write it upon the gates and posts of their houses, that it might be always before their eyes, that they might the better frame their lives according to the same, and do that which is pleasant in the sight of God.

The prophet Esay sendeth not them that want the knowledge of God and of his holy word unto idols, images, and mawmets; but he commandeth them to make Isai. viii. haste unto the holy scriptures, saying: "To the law and witness; if they speak not according unto this, they shall not have the morning light." The psalmograph calleth not them blessed, which stand all the whole day gazing and looking on images, to see

[[1] File: defile.]

what they can pick out and learn of them; but he calleth them blessed and happy, which "delight in the law of the Lord, and exercise themselves in the studying, reading, and hearing of that day and night." Again, he calleth not them blessed, which hunt and seek after images, but them which "search the testimonies of the Lord, and seek him with their whole heart."

Psal. i.

Psal. cxix.

Furthermore, Christ, our Lord and Saviour, commandeth all those that will come unto the true knowledge of him, not to behold images, but to search the scriptures, saying: "Search the scriptures; for they are those that testify of me." He saith also: "My sheep hear my voice." He saith not, My sheep look upon my image. Again: "He that is of God heareth the word of God." He saith not, He that is of God beholdeth the image of the Trinity, or of the crucifix.

John v.

John x.

John viii.

Moreover, when the wisdom of God was determined to call all nations of the earth unto the knowledge of the way of salvation, Christ commanded not painters and carvers to be set a work in making images throughout the world, that the people by beholding them may turn from their idolatry unto the worshipping of the true God; but he sent forth his apostles to preach the gospel to every creature, that they believing might be baptized in the name of the Father, and of the Son, and of the Holy Ghost, and so obtain everlasting salvation. For, as St Paul saith: "Faith cometh by hearing; but hearing cometh by the word of God." We are made faithful by hearing and believing the word of God, and not by looking and tooting[2] upon images; which rather draw men from the true faith of God than allure them unto it; so far is it off, that they be meet schoolmasters to lead us unto God.

Matt. xxviii. Mark xvi.

Rom. x

If the blessed apostle St John had thought images to be profitable books to bring men unto the knowledge either of God or of themselves, he would never have commanded us to "beware and to keep ourselves from images." But he knew right well, that nothing doth so much pluck away the minds of men from the honour of the true and living God (as daily experience teacheth, and as we have manifestly seen under the kingdom of the pope in the time of darkness, when the people went on pilgrimage unto images, sought their salvation of them, gilded them, costly arrayed them, gave gifts unto them, set up brenning candles before them, kneeled before them, made vows unto them, prayed unto them, asked all good things of them necessary either for the body or for the soul, gave thanks unto them, censed them, imputed working of miracles unto them, yea, and honoured them as gods, rather going for help unto them with the feet of the body, than repairing unto the alone true helping God with the feet of the mind), as these dumb and deaf idols; and therefore he chargeth us above all things to avoid images, and by no means to have any thing to do with them, but to flee from them as from the plague and pestilence, yea, as from the devil and from everlasting damnation.

1 John v.

"Let them all therefore," as the psalmograph saith, "be confounded, and be brought unto utter confusion and shame, that worship carved idols, and glory in their images." And let us that fear God cast away all such fond fancies and doting dreams, and give diligent attendance to the hearing, reading, and preaching of God's word, and of that learn to know the way of salvation: so shall we be blessed, and come to the true knowledge of that alone true God and of his Son Jesus Christ; which thing bringeth unto us everlasting life, as the Lord himself saith: "This is everlasting life, even to know thee the alone true God, and whom thou hast sent, Jesus Christ."

Psal. xcvii.

John xvii.

Father. Thou hast right well answered to the first and principal objection which the image-mongers make for the defence of their vain images, which doctrine they learned of pope Gregory I. as we have tofore heard[3]. But they say moreover, that images are not only profitable books for the lewd people, but that they also move the beholders of them marvellously unto devotion and true godliness. *Son*. This is so vain, as nothing is more vain; so false, as that which is most false; so foolish, as it may worthily be counted the self foolishness. Can that move unto devotion, which itself is without all motion and devotion? Can the dead corpse of a captain encourage the soldiers unto battle? Can a featherless eagle teach other birds to fly? Can a water-

Images move not unto devotion.

[2 Tooting: prying, peeping.]

[3 See before, pp. 60, 1; notes 1, 3.]

less whale teach other fishes to swim upon the dry land? No more can these blockish idols, which are utterly without all senses, affects, and motions, move us unto devotion and unto the true worshipping of God, they themselves also being utterly godless,
1 Cor. iii. and most estranged from all that is godly. The holy apostle saith: "Neither he that planteth, nor yet he that watereth, is any thing worth; but the Lord God is altogether, which giveth the increase." If neither the planter nor the waterer (whereby are understand the preachers of God's word) profit nothing, except God giveth the increase, that is to say, worketh with their preaching through the influence of his holy Spirit (which thing to be true, divers places of the holy scripture declare manifestly); what are images then able to do, which have mouths, and speak not; eyes, and see not; noses, and smell not; hands, and feel not; feet, and go not?

Father. But God is able, say they, to work no less with the beholding of images in the hearts of men, than with the preaching of his word. *Son.* What God is able to do, we will not dispute now; although I know this to be an old refuge of the papists, and a sanctuary unto the which they flee in all their straits.

But let them shew by the word of God, that the beholding of images is no less an ordinary way appointed of God to bring men unto the knowledge of God and unto everlasting salvation, than the preaching of the word is, whereof St Paul speaketh
Rom. x. on this manner: "Faith cometh by hearing; but hearing cometh by the word of God."
Psal. li. The prophet David saith also: "I will teach the wicked thy ways; and the ungodly
Psal. xviii. shall turn unto thee." Again: "The people, whom I knew not, have served me: through the hearing of the ear they were obedient unto me." And God himself saith
Isai. lv. by the prophet: "Like as the rain and snow cometh down from heaven, and returneth not thither again, but watereth the earth, maketh it fruitful and green, that it may give corn and bread unto the sower; so the word also, that cometh out of my mouth, shall not turn again void unto me, but shall accomplish my will, and prosper in the
Jer. i. thing whereto I send it." Again: "I will watch diligently upon my word, to perform
Rom. i. it." Moreover, St Paul calleth "the gospel of Christ the power of God unto salvation for all that believe it." And St James saith, that the word of God is of such efficacy,
James i. strength, virtue, might, and power, that "it is able to save the souls" of so many as
John xv. receive it with meekness. Saith not also the Lord Jesus on this manner, "Now are ye clean, because of the word which I have spoken unto you"? Let the image-mongers prove by the holy scriptures, that the beholding of images worketh this conversion, this repentance, this faith, this newness of life, this salvation, &c., in the gazers of them, that the word of God doth in the faithful believers; and we will admit them, their doctrine, and images, and suffer them to have place in our churches. But this can they not do: therefore vain are they, vain is their doctrine, and vain are their images, yea, stumbling-blocks are they, thorns and pricks in the eyes of the simple, provoking rather unto abomination than unto devotion, unto wickedness than unto godliness, unto superstition than unto true religion, unto hypocrisy and idolatry than unto pure worshipping and serving of God, as experience hath heretofore taught us.

John xiv. Again, our Saviour Christ saith: "I am the way, the truth, and the life. No man cometh unto the Father but by me." If no man cometh unto the Father but by Christ, what help then images in this behalf? What make they unto the furtherance of true godliness and true religion? How move they unto devotion? Again, he saith:
John vi. "No man can come unto me, except my Father draw him." If no man can come unto Christ, except the heavenly Father draweth him by his holy Spirit, what profiteth then in this behalf the beholding of images? Are they of such inward working in the hearts of men, that they are able to convert them unto God, and to bring them unto Christ? Yea, they lead away men from Christ unto vain spectacles, from the living God unto dumb idols, from true religion unto wicked superstition; so far is it off, that they move any man unto godly devotion or devout godliness. It is the office of the Holy Ghost to bring us unto Christ, and not the part of dumb idols. The Holy Ghost is appointed of God to be our schoolmaster for to lead us into all truth, and not idle images and monstrous mawmets. To place images therefore in the temples of the Christians to this end, that they should be the books of the lewd people, or that they should move us unto devotion, is nothing else than to make the Holy Ghost, as

they use to say, Jack out of office, and to place a rabblement of vile and abominable idols in the stead of God's Spirit to be the teachers and schoolmasters of the faithful. Perish mought all those vain mawmets from the face of the earth, with all such as glory and rejoice in them, that all the honour may be given to our Lord, that living God alone, whose name be praised for ever!

Father. Amen. But these image-mongers have yet another defence for their idols, and say, that images are to be placed in churches, if for nothing else, yet for the adorning, decking, trimming, beautifying, and garnishing of the temples: which temples otherwise, say they, are more like barns than churches. *Son.* I answer with St Paul: "How agreeth the temple of God with images?" What concord is there between God's service and idol-service? Can God be worthily called upon in that place where so many mawmets stand, contrary to the commandment of God? Can God be worshipped there in spirit and truth, where so many idols are seen, which have neither spirit nor truth? What garnishing of the church is this, to see a sort of puppets standing in every corner of the church, some holding in their hands a sword, some a sceptre, some a spit, some a butcher's knife, some a gridiron, some a pair of pinsons[1], some a spear, some an anchor of a ship, some a shoemaker's cutting-knife, some a shepherd's hook, some a cross, some a cup, some a boot, some a book, some a key, some a lamb, some an ox, some a pig, some a dog, some a basket of flowers, some a crosier-staff, some a triple cross, some an arrow, some an horn, some an hawk, &c.; some bearded, some unbearded, some capped, some uncapped, some weeping, some laughing, some gilded, some painted, some housed, some unhoused[2], some rotten, some worm-eaten, some coated, some cloked, some gowned, some naked, some censed, some perfumed, some with holy water sprinkled, some with flowers and garlands garnished, &c.?

Images garnish not the churches of the Christians.

2 Cor. vi.

But why do I tarry in reciting these vain trifles and trifling vanities, wherewith the churches of the papists are stuffed? I think verily, that in the temples of the old pagans there was never found so much vanity and so many childish sights, as there be at this present day in those churches which are under the yoke and tyranny of that bloody bishop of Rome. These vain idols therefore do not adorn, but deform; not polite, but pollute; not deck, but infect, the temples of the Christians, and make them of the churches of God the synagogues of Satan; of houses of prayer, the vile cages of all filthy and unclean birds. For, as we heard before, Lactantius, that ancient and noble clerk, affirmeth plainly, that "God cannot be truly worshipped in that place where an image is[3]."

The primitive church knew no such kind of beautifying and garnishing their temples: all things were then simple, plain, and homely, and altogether without such vain sights, which rather pluck away men's minds from God, than allure them unto the true worshipping of him. For as "God is a spirit, so will he be worshipped in spirit and truth." The more simply all things are done in the church of Christ, the better is God served: "for that which before men seemeth to be of great estimation is before God great abomination." The temples of the Christians are then best garnished, when the people that are in them be gathered together in the unity of the Holy Ghost, with strong faith toward God, and with fervent love one toward another, to hear the word of God, to call on the name of the Lord, to thank him for his benefits, to eat the supper of the Lord, to make collections for the poor, and to exercise themselves in such works as are pleasant to God and profitable to the brethren. All other superfluous deckings and trimmings, as they be the daughters of foolish fancy, so likewise serve they rather the fond desires of carnal and superstitious people, than make any thing at all unto the true honour of the Lord our God, to whom alone be all glory for ever.

John iv.

Luke xvi.

Father. Amen. Let these things suffice for this present concerning the objections of the image-mongers for the maintenance of their idols in churches, and to declare that this precept of not making nor worshipping images appertaineth no less now unto us Christians than it did in times past unto the Jews. But come off, tell me, what

[1 Pinsons: pincers.]

[2 With, or without, *housings*, a kind of stocking or boot.]

[3 See before, page 61, note 6.]

What God requireth of us in this second commandment. Gen. vi. viii.

is the good pleasure of God in the second commandment? *Son.* God, which is the searcher of the heart, and knoweth the corrupt, froward, and wicked nature of man, and how even from his cradle he is prone, bent, and wholly given unto all that is ungodly, and specially unto new, strange, and counterfeit worshipping of God, invented of his own idle brain, blind zeal, good intent, corrupt judgment, contrary to God's holy ordinance and appointment, which willeth none otherwise to be served, honoured, and worshipped, than he himself hath prescribed in his blessed law; to bridle this evil and corrupt affection of man, and to keep him within the limits of his godly commandments, that he run not a whore-hunting after strange idols, but worship him according to his own appointment, and none otherwise, first of all in this his second commandment—forasmuch as nothing doth so alienate, estrange, and pluck away the heart of man from God and from all godliness, as idols, mawmets, images, and puppets, which be made and set forth before the eyes of the simple and unlearned people, to preach and represent unto them the majesty of God, which by no means can be counterfeit, seeing itself is both infinite and incomprehensible, and cannot be feigned nor set forth, no, not so much as shadowed by the art of man, although never so cunning either of graving or painting, in any corporal substance—chargeth and straitly commandeth his people, even so many as take him for their Lord and God, that they make no graven or carved image, nor the likeness of any thing that is in heaven above, as the sun, moon, stars, &c.; or in earth beneath, as men, beasts, birds, worms, &c.; or in the waters under the earth, as fishes, and whatsoever liveth in the waters; lest by the making of such things they should go about after the manner of the heathen to counterfeit the majesty of God, and so, by beholding the same, at the last conceive an opinion on godhead and divine power to be in those images, and so fall to the worshipping of them, (as we read of divers nations both in God's and man's histories,) and by this means provoke God unto anger, which is both "a jealous God, and a consuming fire." (Deut. xii. — Deut. iv.)

It is not lawful to make the image of God.

Father. Is it not then lawful to make an image of God? *Son.* By no means: for it is plainly forbidden of God in this second commandment.

Father. Are there no more scriptures in the holy bible, which bear witness of this thing? *Son.* Yes, forsooth, very many.

Father. Recite part of them. *Son.* Moses, that most excellent prophet of God, saith: "The Lord spake unto you out of the midst of the fire. The voice of his words ye heard; nevertheless ye saw no image, but heard the voice only. And he declared unto you his covenant, which he commanded you to do, namely, the ten verses, and wrote them upon two tables of stone. And the Lord commanded me at the same time to teach you his ordinances and laws, that ye might do thereafter in the land into the which ye go to possess it. Keep well your souls therefore, (for ye saw no manner of image in the day when the Lord spake unto you out of the fire upon mount Horeb,) that ye destroy not yourselves, and make you any image that is like a man, or woman, or beast upon earth, or feathered fowl under the heaven, or worm upon the ground, or fish in the water under the earth; that thou lift not up thine eyes toward heaven, and see the sun, and the moon, and the stars, and the whole host of heaven, and be deceived, and worship and serve them, which the Lord thy God hath created to serve all nations under the whole heaven." (Deut. iv.)

Again: "Take heed unto yourselves, that ye forget not the covenant of the Lord your God, and that ye make no images of any manner of fashion, as the Lord thy God hath commanded. For the Lord thy God is a consuming fire and a jealous God. If when ye have begotten children, and childer's children, and have dwelt in the land, ye mar yourselves, and make you images of any manner of fashion, and do evil in the sight of the Lord your God to provoke him, I call heaven and earth to record over you this day, that ye shall shortly perish from the land into the which ye go over Jordan to possess it. Ye shall not dwell long therein, but shall utterly be destroyed."

Lev. xix. Deut. vii.

Also in another place: "Ye shall not turn yourselves unto images, and ye shall make you no gods of metal; for I am the Lord your God." Item: "Thus shall ye do with those nations unto whom the Lord your God shall send you: ye shall overthrow their altars, break down their pillars, cut down their groves, and burn their images with fire. For thou art an holy people unto the Lord thy God. Thee hath the Lord thy God chosen, that thou shouldest be his own peculiar people from among all nations that are upon earth." Again: "These are the ordinances and laws which ye shall keep, that ye do thereafter in the land which the Lord God of thy fathers hath given thee to possess, as long as ye live upon earth. Destroy all the places wherein the heathen, whom ye shall conquer, have served their gods, whether it be upon high mountains, upon hills, or among green trees. And overthrow their altars, and break down their pillars, and burn their groves with fire, and hew down the images of their gods, and bring the names of them to nought out of the same place." Once again he saith: "Cursed be he that maketh any carved image, or molten idol (an abomination unto the Lord, a work of the hands of the craftsman), and putteth it in a secret place. And all the people shall answer and say, Amen." Deut. xii. Deut. xxvii.

The prophet Esay also saith: "To whom will ye liken God? or what similitude will ye set up unto him? Shall the carver make him a carved image? and shall the goldsmith cover him with gold, or cast him into a form of silver plates? &c. Know ye not this? heard ye never of it? hath it not been preached unto you since the beginning? have ye not been informed of this since the foundation of the earth was laid, that he (God) sitteth upon the circle of the world, and all the inhabiters of the world are, in comparison of him, but as grasshoppers," &c.? Isai. xl.

God himself saith by the aforesaid prophet: "To whom now will ye liken me? and whom shall I be like, saith the Holy One?" Again: "Whom will ye make me like in fashion or image, that I may be like him? which take out silver and gold out of your purses and weigh it, and hire a goldsmith to make a god of it, that men may kneel down and worship it. Yet must he be taken on men's shoulders, and borne, and set in his place, that he may stand and not move. Alas, that men should cry unto him which giveth no answer, and delivereth not the man that calleth upon him from his trouble! Consider this well, and be ashamed. Go into your own selves, O ye runagates; remember the things which are past since the beginning of the world, that I am God, and that there is else no God, yea, and that there is nothing like unto me." Isai. xlvi.

The prophet Esay saith once again: "All carvers of images are but vain, and their labour lost. They must bear record themselves that, seeing they can neither see nor understand, they shall be confounded. Who should now make a god, or fashion an idol that is profitable for nothing? Behold, all the fellowship of them must be brought to confusion. Let all the work-masters come and stand together from among men: they must be abashed and confounded one with another. The smith taketh iron, and tempereth it with hot coals, and fashioneth it with hammers, and maketh it with all the strength of his arms: yea, sometime he is faint for very hunger, and so thirsty that he hath no more power. The carpenter (or image-carver) taketh the timber and spreadeth forth his line: he maketh it with some colour: he planeth it: he ruleth it, and squareth it, and maketh it after the image of a man, and according to the beauty of a man, that it may stand in a temple. Moreover, he goeth out to hew down cedar-trees: he bringeth home elms and oaks and other timber of the wood, or else the fir-trees which he planted himself, and such as the rain hath swelled, which wood serveth for men to burn. Of this he taketh and warmeth himself withal: he maketh a fire of it to bake bread, and afterward maketh a god thereof to honour it, and an idol to kneel before it. One piece he burneth in the fire: with another he roasteth flesh, that he may eat roast his bellyful: with the third he warmeth himself, and saith, Aha! I am well warmed, I have been at the fire. And of the residue he maketh him a god, and an idol for himself. He kneeleth before it, he worshippeth it, he prayeth unto it, and saith, Deliver me, for thou art my God. Yet men neither consider nor understand, because their eyes are stopped that they cannot see, and their hearts that they cannot perceive. They ponder not in their minds (for they have neither knowledge nor understanding) to think thus: I have brent one piece in the fire; I have baked bread with the coals thereof; I have roasted flesh withal, and eaten it: shall I now of the residue make an abominable idol, and fall down before a rotten piece of wood? Thus he doth but lose his labour, and his heart, which Isai. xliv.

is deceived, doth turn him aside, so that none of them can have a free conscience to think: May not I err? Consider this, O Jacob and Israel; for thou art my servant: I have made thee, that thou mightest serve me. O Israel, forget me not. As for thine offences, I drive them away like the clouds, and thy sins as the mist. Turn thee again unto me; and I will deliver thee."

Jer. x. The prophet Jeremy saith also: "They hew down a tree in the wood with the hands of the workman, and fashion it with the axe: they cover it over with gold or silver: they fasten it with nails and hammers, that it move not. It standeth as stiff as the palm-tree: it can neither speak nor go, but must be borne. Be not ye afraid of such; for they can do neither good nor evil. But there is none like unto thee, O Lord: thou art great; and great is the name of thy power."

Hos. xiii. God him[self] saith by the prophet Osee: "Of their silver they make them molten images, like the idols of the heathen; and yet all is nothing but the work of the craftsman, &c. Therefore they shall be as the morning cloud, and as the dew that early passeth away, and like as dust that the wind taketh away from the floor, and as smoke that goeth out of the chimney. I am the Lord thy God, which brought thee out of the land of Egypt, that thou shouldest know no God but me only, and that thou shouldest have no Saviour but only me."

As I may at the last cease to gather the testimonies of the old testament, which both forbid and condemn the making of such images, as pluck the minds of men from the living God unto dumb mawmets, I would wish all men diligently to read and remember the thirteenth, fourteenth, fifteenth, and sixteenth chapters of the book of Wisdom, and the sixth chapter of the prophet Baruch; which lively paint and set forth in their true colours these images, idols, and mawmets, which many have in so great admiration, with all the vanities and abominations of them.

Father. Doth not also the new testament judge of images even as the old? *Son*. Yes, verily. The Holy Ghost varieth not in his doctrine. Paul and Barnabas said

Acts xiv. unto the people: "We preach unto you, that ye should turn from these vanities (they speak of images and of image-service) unto the living God, which made heaven and earth, and the sea, and all things that are therein." St Peter[1] likewise said to the con-

Acts xv. gregation of God: "My judgment is, that we trouble not them which from among the gentiles are turned to God, but that we write unto them, that they abstain themselves

1 John v. from the filthiness of images." St John saith: "Babes, keep yourselves from images."

Father. But come off, my dear child, tell me, Is it not lawful for the Christians in no condition to have images? *Son*. There be some that so think, of whose judg-

Of images lawful to be had. ment I am not. All such may worthily be resembled to the Turks, which, as they say, take this commandment of God so straitly, that they can by no means suffer any image to be made, no, not in profane and civil things.

Father. Is it then lawful in politic, civil, and worldly matters to have images? *Son*.

Matt. xxii. It is not forbidden, which thing we may right well be learned in that gospel, where we read, that certain men came unto Christ, demanding of him, whether it were lawful to pay tribute unto Cæsar, or not. Christ, willing them to shew him a piece of the money, asked, whose image and superscription that was which was graven on the coin? And when they said, "The emperor's," he answered, "Give unto the emperor that which is the emperor's, and give unto God that which is God's." We read not here that Christ did condemn the image that was graven in the coin, neither that he said, Cast away this money for the image sake; for it is unlawful even in civil and profane things to have images: but, to declare that the use of images in profane and worldly matters is not unlawful, he approved the money, notwithstanding the image. And it is not to be doubted, but that money also, which he commanded Peter to take out of the fish's mouth, and to give it for tribute unto the emperor's officers, was also such money as was then customably paid to the emperor for tribute, having the emperor's image upon it. Again, the money, which the disciples of Christ carried about with them for their relief and for the comfort of the poor which followed Christ, was also without all doubt of that money which was coined with the image

[[1] An oversight, it would appear, for St James.]

and superscription of the emperor. All these things declare manifestly that in politic, civil, profane, and worldly things the use of images is not unlawful.

Father. If in politic and worldly matters, why not also in divine and holy things? *Son.* In the one is no peril; in the other, great danger, as we have learned too much by experience.

Father. Did not God command Moses, after that he had given this law concerning images, to make the brasen serpent, and to set it up in the wilderness for the people of Israel to behold? *Son.* I grant. Notwithstanding, that was but a figurative image, serving for the time, prefiguring Christ, as we may see in the gospel, and therefore is now utterly abolished: as all figures, clouds, and shadows of the old testament vanished, when Christ, which is the very truth and light, came. Yea, long before the coming of Christ, that noble and godly king Ezechias, when he saw the people abuse this image, kneel unto it, honour it, and burn incense unto it, he threw it down and utterly destroyed it, although set up at the commandment of God: which thing he would never have done, if he had known that commandment of setting up the brasen serpent to be moral (for every moral law is the certain, undoubted, unchangeable, and everlasting will of God); but being well assured that it was but a ceremonial law, serving for the time, and a figure or shadow of a better thing to come, when he saw it abused, so that by that means the glory of God was obscured, yea, and that honour given to an image which alone is due to the living God, he plucked it down, burnt it, and utterly destroyed it. For this is diligently to be noted, that no particular commandment taketh away the virtue of a general or universal law, as this law of images is in the book of God.

Num. xxi. John iii. 2 Kings xviii.

Father. Thou holdest then, that although it be tolerable, yea, and lawful in politic and worldly things, to have images, yet in matters appertaining unto godliness and religion it is neither tolerable nor lawful. *Son.* Not only I, but the holy fathers also of the primitive church were of that opinion, as we have tofore heard: "God is a spirit; and they that worship him must worship him in spirit and truth." Now, saith Lactantius, "God is never truly worshipped in that place where an image is"[2]: which thing made that holy bishop St Epiphanius, when he saw an image in the church, to take it away, and to cut it in pieces, affirming, that it is contrary to the authority of God's word to have images in the church of Christ[3]: which thing also made many noble princes and holy bishops to give commandment, that all images of God, of Christ, of angels, and of saints, should be taken out of churches, and burnt openly, and from henceforth that no images should be made and brought into such places as christian men use to resort unto for to pray unto their Lord God: if any did presume to do the contrary, he should suffer such punishments as was appointed by the law for such and so grievous offenders[4].

John iv.

Father. If it be not lawful to make images for religion sake, then is it not lawful for us to honour and worship them, as the custom was, and yet is, in the pope's church. *Son.* No, verily. For as God in this commandment saith, "Thou shalt make thee no graven image," &c.; so likewise saith he, "Neither shalt thou bow down before them, nor worship them."

It is neither lawful to make images for religion sake, nor to worship them.

Father. Here then are we forbidden in the way of religion not only to make images, but also to worship them. *Son.* Truth it is.

Against the worshipping of images.

Father. Declare unto me by other scriptures also, that it is not lawful to worship images. *Son.* God saith by his servant Moses: "I am the Lord your God: ye shall make you no idols, nor image in your land, to bow yourselves thereto. For I am the Lord your God." Moses also saith: "Beware, that thou make no covenant with the indwellers of the land, that thou comest into, lest they be the cause of thy ruin in the midst of it; but their altars shalt thou overthrow, and break down their gods, and root out their groves. For thou shalt have none other God, (for the Lord is called Jealous, because he is a jealous God;) lest, if thou make any agreement with the indwellers of the land, when they go a whoring after their gods, and do sacrifice unto their gods, they call thee, and thou eat of their sacrifice, and lest thou take their daughters unto thy sons to wives, and the

Lev. xxvi. Exod. xxxiv.

[[2] See before, page 61, note 6.] [[3] See before, page 61, note 2.] [[4] See below, page 71, notes 2 and 5.]

same go a whoring after their gods, and make thy sons to go a whoring after their gods Deut. xi. also." Again: "Beware, that your heart be not deceived, that ye go aside and serve other gods, and worship them; and then the wrath of the Lord wax hot upon you, and he shut up the heaven that there come no rain, and the earth give not her increase, and Deut. xiii. ye perish shortly from the good land which the Lord hath given you." Item: "If there rise up a prophet or dreamer among you, and give thee a token or wonder, and that token or wonder, which he spake of, come to pass, and then say, Let us go after other gods (whom thou knowest not), and let us serve them; thou shalt not hearken unto the words of such a prophet or dreamer. For the Lord your God proveth you, to wete, whether ye love him with all your heart and with all your soul. For ye shall walk after the Lord your God, and fear him, and keep his commandments, and hearken unto his voice, and serve him, and cleave unto him. As for that prophet or dreamer, he shall die; because he hath spoken to turn you away from the Lord your God."

Psal. xcvii. The psalmograph also saith: "Confounded be all they that worship carved images, Wisd. xiv. and they that delight in vain gods." The wise man saith: "The honouring of abominable images is the cause, the beginning, and the end of all evil." God himself saith by Isai. xlii. the prophet Esay: "I am the Lord, this is my name. I will give my glory to none 1 Cor. x. other, nor my honour to graven images." Hereto pertaineth the saying of St Paul: "Be 1 Cor. vi. not worshippers of images." "For no worshippers of images shall inherit the kingdom Rev. xxi. of God:" yea, as St John saith: "They shall have their part in that lake that burneth with fire and brimstone, which is the second death."

Besides these sentences of the holy scripture, which utterly condemn the honouring and worshipping of images, we have manifest examples in the word of God of certain holy men, which did rather choose to suffer death, than they would serve, honour, or worship images. What a number of prophets and godly men did that most wicked woman, queen Jesebel, kill and murder, because they would not bow their knee to that Dan. iii. foul idol, Baal! Read we not also in the book of Daniel the prophet, that three young men did rather choose to be put into a fiery furnace, and there to be burnt unto ashes, than they would once fall down before the golden image at the commandment of king Nabuchodonosor? Was not this their answer to the king, "O Nabuchodonosor, we ought not to consent unto thee in this matter. For why? our God whom we serve is able to keep us from the hot burning oven, O king, and can right well deliver us out of thy hands. And though he will not, yet shalt thou know, O king, that we will not serve thy gods, nor do reverence to the image which thou hast set up." Read we not again that B. & Dr. Daniel was commanded of the king to worship a certain image at Babylon called Bel? But Daniel answered and said, "I may not worship things that are made with hands, but the living God, which made heaven and earth, and hath power upon all flesh."

What shall I speak of all the holy martyrs which were in the primitive church, and many years after, that suffered most bitter torments, yea, and very death, because they would not bow down before images, and honour them?

Image service is such and so great abomination not only before God, but also in the sight of all good men, that we read of certain noble princes, which could by no means abide such wickedness to be used in their kingdoms, and therefore utterly destroyed all those idols, images, puppets, and mawmets, that plucked away the people's hearts 2 Kings xviii. from the honour of the living God unto image-service. Read we not, that king Ezechias put away the high places, and brake down the pillars, and rooted out the groves, and brake the brasen serpent, which Moses had made? "For unto that time had the children 2 Kings xxiii. of Israel burnt incense unto it." Read we not also, that king Josias destroyed and utterly took away the images and idols, and all the abominations which were seen in the land of Juda and at Jerusalem; and that he commanded all the vessels to be taken out of the temple, which were made for Baal, and for the grove, and for all the host of heaven, and that he burnt them without Jerusalem in the valley of Cedron, and caused the dust of them to be carried unto Bethel? Again, that he did break down the altars which Manasses had made in the two courts of the house of the Lord, and caused the dust of them to be cast into the brook of Cedron; and the altar at Bethel, and the high place that Jeroboam made, which both he destroyed and made them unto dust, and burnt up the grove, &c.?

2 Chron. xxxiii. Read we not, moreover, that the wicked king Manasses, because that he walked after

the abominations of the heathen, builded the high places, which his father Ezechias had broken down, set up altars, made grevous[1], worshipped all the host of heaven, caused carved images and idols to be made and set up in the house of the Lord, shed much innocent blood, and did that which was evil in the sight of the Lord, was taken of the host of the king of the Assirians, bound with chains, and so led away prisoner unto Babylon? Which Manasses being in trouble, after that he had humbled himself and prayed unto the Lord his God, his prayer was heard, and the Lord "brought him again to Jerusalem, even to his kingdom; so that Manasses knew that the Lord is God. Afterward put he away the strange gods and idols out of the house of the Lord, and all the altars which he had builded upon the mount of the house of the Lord, and in Jerusalem, and cast them out of the city, &c."

What shall I speak of Constantine the Great, of Leo III., of Valens and Theodosius, of Philip, of Constantine, &c., most noble and worthy emperors, and of Sabanus, king of the Bulgarians[2], with divers other godly princes, which all banished idols, images, or mawmets out of their dominions, and would by no means suffer them to be remaining in those places, where christian men resort and come together to pray; lest the people should fall from the honour of the one and alone true living God, and be allured unto the vain worshipping of most vain images, and so heap the wrath and vengeance of God upon them, which as all sins, so likewise the sin and abomination of image-service, most highly doth detest and abhor?

What shall I here rehearse the most godly and virtuous acts of the reverend and holy bishops, Epiphanius, bishop of Cyprus[3], and Sirenus, bishop of Massilia[4], and such like, which by no means could abide either images or image-service in their diocese?

I pass over the most holy and christian councils, Agathense, Tolitane, Elibertine[5], &c., which decreed that all pictures or images should be had out of the churches, and that nothing that is honoured or worshipped should be painted on the church-walls.

[1 The true reading is no doubt *groves*.]

[2 The following authorities may be adduced in regard to the princes above named:

Ἐπιτείνας δ' ἔτι μᾶλλον ὁ βασιλεὺς τὴν πρὸς τὸν Θεὸν ὁσίαν, διδασκαλίαν κατὰ τῆς εἰδωλολατρίας πλάνης τῶν πρὸ αὐτοῦ κεκρατηκότων τοῖς κατὰ πᾶν ἔθνος ἐπαρχεώταις κατέπεμπε.—Hist. Eccles. Script. Græc. Amst. 1695—1700. Euseb. Pamph. de Vit. Constant. Lib. II. cap. xlvii. p. 383.

Relatum est in veterum annalibus de Leonis Augusti imperio, et ejus moribus; quodque is Theodosio Imper. defuncto in Byzantio urbe, quæ Constantinopolis dicitur, factus imperator, edicto cavit, ut omnes quidem sanctorum imagines, quæ in Christianorum fanis ac templis forent, abolerentur..... Sed libitum est verba ex libris Augustalibus referre, quo id totum melius innotescat; quoniam et Valens et Theodosius Augusti Imp. præfecto prætorio ad hunc modum scripserunt: Cum sit nobis cura diligens in rebus omnibus superni numinis religionem tueri, signum salvatoris Christi nemini quidem concedimus, coloribus, lapide, aliave materia fingere, insculpere, aut pingere. Sed quodcunque reperitur tolli jubemus, gravissima pœna eos mulctando, qui contrarium decretis nostris et imperio quicquam tentaverint.—Petr. Crinit. De Honest. Discip. Lugd. 1585. Lib. IX. cap. ix. pp. 278, 9.

At Constantinus [Papa] habita synodo, non modo Philippici et Joannis monachi opiniones improbat, verum etiam decernit, ut sanctorum patrum imagines, qui sex conciliis ab omnibus probatis interfuerant, in porticu beati Petri depingerentur, cum intellexisset eas a Philippico e parietibus sanctæ Sophiæ ignominiæ causa abrasas fuisse.—Plat. De Vit. Pont. Rom. Col. 1568. Constantinus I. p. 107. See also Cent. Eccles. Hist. Magd. Basil. 1560—74. Cent. VIII. cap. iii. col. 31.

Nam Leo anno imperii sui nono, consilio cujusdam nomine Beser, et episcopi Nacoliæ, decretum promulgavit, ne in ulla ecclesia cujuslibet sancti, aut martyris, aut angeli imago habeatur.—Cent. Magd. ibid. col. 33.

Imperator [Constantinus Copronymus] ergo edicta proponit quibus imagines adorari vetat: et synodi decreta suscipi jubet, et reliquias sanctorum igni tradit.—Id. ibid. col. 37.

Bulgares contra Sabinum regem suum arma capiunt, propter imaginum adorationem defendendam; quam ille, a Constantino imperatore et a recte sentientibus doctoribus persuasus, damnabat, et abolere nitebatur.—Id. ibid. col. 39. See also Paul. Diac. Hist. Miscell. Lib. XXI. capp. xvii. xviii. Lib. XXII. capp. xxiv. xxxix. Lib. XXIII. cap. vii.]

[3 See before, page 61, note 1.]

[4 See before, page 61, note 2.]

[5 Placuit, picturas in ecclesia esse non debere; ne quod colitur, et adoratur, in parietibus depingatur.—Concil. Eliberit. in Concil. Stud. Labbei. Lut. Par. 1671-2. can. xxxvi. Tom. I. col. 974.

The 11th canon of the 12th council of Toledo is probably that intended by the author, in which we find: Cultores idolorum, veneratores lapidum, accensores facularum, et excolentes sacra fontium vel arborum admonemus.—Id. Tom. VI. col. 1234. See also the 2nd canon of the 16th council of Toledo.—Id. ibid. col. 1337.

As respects the council of Agde, the canons, as printed by Labbè, do not seem to contain any thing to the point. Durandus, however, says: Concilium Agathen. de consec. distin. 3. cap. *placuit*, inhibet picturas in ecclesiis fieri, et quod colitur et adoratur in parietibus depingi.—Gul. Durand. Rat. Div. Offic. Venet. 1609. Lib. I. cap. iii. 4. fol. 9. 2. But as these words are almost identical with the canon of Elvira, quoted above, Durandus was perhaps in error.]

All these things heretofore rehearsed do evidently declare, what is to be thought both of images made for religion sake, and also of the worshipping and honouring of the same.

What it is to bow down before an image.

Father. Now, my good child, forasmuch as in this second commandment of God we are not only forbidden to make images, but also to bow down to them, and to worship them; tell me what is meant or understand by the bowing down unto an image. *Son*. To bow down to, or before an image, which in Greek is *προσκυνεῖν*, and in the Latin *adorare*, is reverently with the body to fall down before it, to kneel unto it, to set it in a place where we use to worship God, to garnish it with costly array and precious jewels, to kiss it, to put off our cap unto it, and to shew any gesture of reverence outwardly unto it. All these things doth God forbid to be given to images in this his second commandment.

Father. Yet all these things are done to images in the pope's churches. *Son*. Truth it is. For in divers popish books we read on this manner: "To all them that say this prayer following before the image of the crucifix, pitifully beholding the same, and devoutly kneeling upon their knees, are granted as many days of pardon, by divers popes of Rome, as be gravel stones in the sea, or grasses on the earth[1]." Moreover, who knoweth not this to be a custom in the synagogues of the pope both on Good Friday, as they call it, and on Easter-day in the morning, to creep unto the cross, to kneel unto it, to kiss it, to offer gifts unto it, &c., while the priests and the clerks sing on this manner, *Crucem tuam adoramus, Domine, &c.*[2] "We worship thy cross, O Lord;" which is plain and manifest idolatry, and a work directly against the commandment of God?

O abomination!

St Ambrose writeth on this manner: "Helene found a title or superscription, but she worshipped the king, and not the tree; for this is an heathenish error, and the vanity of the ungodly; but she worshipped him that did hang on the tree, written in the title, &c."[3] With what conscience then can the papists compel, as they do, the simple Christians to worship the cross, contrary to the doctrine both of the holy scriptures and of the ancient godly writers? This kind of worshipping required the devil at Christ's hand; but he answered: "Avoid, Satan. For it is written, Thou shalt worship the Lord thy God, and him alone shalt thou serve." This worship refused Simon Peter to be given unto him of Cornelius the centurion. "Stand up," saith he, "I am a man also." This worship also refused the angel, when John fell down at his feet, and said unto John: "See that thou do it not. For I am thy fellow-servant, and one of thy brethren, and of them that have the testimony of Jesus. Worship thou God." If the apostle of Christ and the angel of God refused to be worshipped with falling down before them, and with kneeling unto them, is it reason that this worship, I mean, kneeling and bowing of the body, should be given to dumb idols and vain images? "Confounded and put to utter confusion and shame mought all they be," saith the psalmograph, "which worship," that is to say, kneel down before, "graven images," or do any outward reverence unto them.

Matt. iv. Deut. vi.

Acts x.

Rev. xix. xxi.

Psal. xcvii.

What it is to honour or worship images.

Father. We are not only commanded of God in this his second commandment, that we should not bow down before any image, but also that we should not worship nor honour them. What is meant by worshipping or honouring of images? *Son*. As by bowing down before an image is understand all outward reverence, which with our body we give unto it, whether it be by setting it in that place where we come together to honour God, as in churches, chapels, oratories, &c., or by kneeling unto it, or putting off our cap unto it, or garnishing it, or kissing it, &c.; so likewise by worshipping an image is meant to pray unto it, to offer gifts and sacrifices unto it, to go on pilgrimage

[1 Bishop Burnet, in the Collection of Records appended to his History of the Reformation, has printed, Vol. II. Book I. No. 26, several extracts exhibiting the chief indulgences in the English offices. Among them are some which resemble that in the text, though not couched in precisely the same words.]

[2 The hymn thus commencing may be found repeatedly used in the Romish services. See Missale ad Us. et Consuetud. Sarum. Par. 1527. In die Parasc. fol. 89. 2. Also, In Invent. Sanct. Cruc. iii. Maii.; and In Exalt. Sanct. Cruc. xiv. Sept. See also Portifor. seu Breviar. ad Us. Eccles. Sarisbur. Par. 1510. In Exalt. Sanct. Cruc. &c. It is common in modern books of Romish worship.]

[3 Invenit ergo titulum, regem adoravit, non lignum utique; quia hic gentilis est error, et vanitas impiorum: sed adoravit illum, qui pependit in ligno, scriptus in titulo.—Ambros. Op. Par. 1686—90. De Obit. Theodos. Orat. 46. Tom. II. col. 1211.]

unto it, to seek health, help, and salvation at it, to flee unto it in our necessities, to put our faith, hope, and confidence in it, and to make it, as I may so speak, a very God; which is plain idolatry and image-service.

Father. These things also are done at this present day in the kingdom of the pope. *Son*. It is the more to be lamented. All good and godly men ought to study, unto the uttermost of their power, to banish these so great and grievous pestilences from the bounds of Christendom, that all the worship, honour, glory, and praise may be given to God alone, as he himself saith by the prophet: "I am the Lord: this is my name. I will give my glory to none other, nor my honour to graven images." In the Acts of the Apostles we read, that when the men of Lystra, with Jupiter's priest, brought oxen and garlands, and would have done sacrifice to Paul and Barnabas, because of the miracle that Paul wrought among them, in healing a man which was impotent of his feet, and a cripple even from his mother's womb, and cried out with a loud voice, saying, "The gods are become like unto men, and are come down unto us; calling Barnabas Jupiter, and Paul Mercurius, because he was the preacher;" the apostles rent their clothes, and ran in among the people, crying and saying: "Ye men, why do ye this? We are mortal men also like unto you, and preach unto you the gospel, that ye should turn from these vain things unto the living God, which made heaven, and earth, and the sea, and all that therein is." If the apostles of Christ refused to be honoured, to have gifts and sacrifices offered unto them, &c., is it then seemly that such honour should be given to dumb images, idols, and mawmets? Neither outward worship nor inward honour ought to be given unto such vanities. "Blessed is that man," saith the psalmograph, "whose hope, affiance, and trust is in the name of the Lord, and that hath not regarded these vanities and foolish fond fantasies." These image-mongers may justly be resembled to the priests of Baal, which called on the name of Baal from the morning unto the noon-day, and yet were not heard. So likewise these new Baalites and idolaters, though they cry never so much upon these idols and images, yet shall they never be heard. "For they have ears and hear not, &c. They that make them are like unto them, and so are all such as put their trust in them. But let Israel trust in the Lord; for he is their succour and defence."

Isai. xlii.
Acts xiv.
Psal. xl.
1 Kings xviii.
An apt comparison.
Psal. cxv.

Father. Hitherto have we heard what the good will and pleasure of God is in this his second commandment, concerning images. Go forth now, and declare unto me that which followeth in this precept. *Son*. The words that follow are these:

"For I the Lord thy God am a strong and a jealous God, punishing the wickedness of the parents in the children, until the third and fourth generation of them that hate me, and shew mercy until thousands, unto those that love me and keep my commandments."

Father. Why doth the Lord our God call himself "a strong God"? *Son*. To declare that his divine majesty is so great, infinite, unmeasurable, and incomprehensible, so excellent and far passing the reach and compass of man's wit or reason, that it can by no means be expressed or set forth by any similitude, likeness, or image, that man can devise. For seeing that heaven and earth, and all that ever is contained in them, cannot represent God, much less are vile and vain images able to do this, which are made with man's hand, and have neither life nor moving, nor any thing at all that is like our most strong and mighty God, as both Esay and Baruch do right well testify. He is also called a strong God, to declare that he is of sufficient might and power to help and to defend all those that put their trust in him, with whatsoever kind of adversity they be assailed; and that, as he is able, so likewise he will alway be present with his saving health unto all such as unfeignedly cleave unto him, refusing utterly all false gods, idols, images, mawmets, puppets, &c., and seeking their health and salvation both of body and of soul at his merciful hand only and alone.

Why the Lord is called a strong God.
Isai. xliv.
Bar. vi.

Father. But why doth he call himself "a jealous God"? *Son*. To declare that he by no means can abide that that glory which is due from us to him alone should be given to any creature, although never so excellent, either in heaven or in earth, much less to vain images, dumb idols, monstrous mawmets, and popish puppets; no, nor any part of that glory; as he saith by the prophet: "I am the Lord: this is my name:

Why the Lord is called a jealous God.
Isai. xlii.

I will give my glory to none other, nor my honour to graven images." As of God we receive all good things appertaining either unto the body or unto the soul, so likewise owe we unto God alone all our faith, love, fear, service, honour, glory, praise, &c., as Moses saith: "Thou shalt honour the Lord thy God, and serve him alone." And as a true wedded husband, that loveth his wife dearly, tendereth her above all creatures, resteth in her love only, rejoiceth and delighteth in her alone, cherisheth her, and maketh sufficient provision for her in all things, so that at his hand she hath abundantly all good things, yea, and that without any lack, cannot abide that his wife should give her love, or any part of her love to any other man, but to him alone; so in like manner cannot God suffer, which hath taken us to his spouse, and married us unto him in faith, that we should set our love upon any other but upon him alone, of whom we receive all good things necessary both for body and soul, or that we should give the glory and praise of our salvation to any but to him alone. Therefore to declare how impatient he is of any rival or paramour, and how vehement his love is toward us, and how fervently again he requireth of us to be loved, he compareth himself to a jealous lover or husband, and us to a wife; signifying by this comparison how pure, chaste, and unspotted, yea, and utterly estranged from all other creatures, our love toward God ought to be. This perceived the psalmograph right well, when he said: "Thou destroyest all them that run a whore-hunting from thee. But it is good for me to cleave hard to God, and to put my trust in the Lord God."

Deut. vi. Matt. iv. Eph. v. Hos. ii. 1 Cor. iv. James i. Psal. lxxiii.

What is it to run a whore-hunting from God.

Father. What is it to run a whore-hunting from God? *Son*. To forsake the Lord our God, and to follow creatures; to pluck our faith and love from God, and to give it unto strange gods; to seek health and salvation, remission of sins and everlasting life, at the hand of any, either in heaven or in earth, saving only at the hand of the Lord our God, which alone is the author, beginner, and finisher of our salvation. And to pluck us away from this whore-hunting and spiritual whoredom, which is nothing else than idolatry or image-service, he doth not only call himself a jealous God, but he also addeth, that he will punish the wickedness of the parents "in the children, until the third and fourth generation of them that hate him."

Father. What wickedness is that which God will so extremely punish? *Son*. Every sin is wickedness. God will by no means suffer the transgression and breaking of his holy commandments unpunished: as it is written: "Wo be unto them that sin, and keep not my commandments, saith the Lord; for I will not spare them." Again: "Cursed is every one which abideth not in all things that are written in the book of the law, that he may do them." And albeit all kind of sins do greatly offend the majesty of God, so that he will leave none of them unpunished; yet this sin of idolatry or image-service do most highly displease him: neither will he by any means suffer the transgression and breaking of this second commandment, which forbiddeth idolatry and image-service, to escape without punishment, as divers histories of the holy scripture do manifestly declare. And therefore it is here to be noted by the way, that God calleth the idolaters, image-servants, or worshippers of strange gods, his enemies and such as hate him. Is it to be thought that such can escape unpunished? It is not therefore without a cause, that God, tendering our health and salvation, in this his second commandment forbiddeth both the making and worshipping of images. If we will avoid the worshipping of images, let us cease to make them, and place them in our temples, chapels, oratories, &c.; and so shall we easily escape from the danger of idolatry or image-service, which is so grievous an offence, and so wicked and abominable sin before the Lord our God, that he threateneth to punish it in the children of the idolatrous fathers, until the third and fourth generation.

Isai. v. Deut. xxvii. Gal. iii.

Father. This seemeth to me very lamentable, that God should punish the wickedness of the parents in their children's children. *Son*. This on this wise is to be understand. If the children of the parents, which were wicked idolaters, commit that same idolatry which their fathers have committed, and continue in the same wickedness wherein their forefathers have lived, then will God not only punish the parents which have so offended, but also their children, yea, and their children's children, which commit the like offence, yea, and that so much the more grievously, because they be the idolatrous children of idolatrous fathers, and have more pleasure to walk in the wicked steps of their most wicked fathers, than to give ear to the righteous laws of the most righteous God.

Father. But what if the parents be wicked and the children godly, as it sometime chanceth, and as we also find in the holy scriptures, shall the children notwithstanding be plagued and punished for their fathers' offences? *Son*. God forbid. For it is written: "The soul that sinneth shall die. If a man be godly, and do the thing **Ezek. xviii.** that is equal and right (he eateth not upon the hills: he lifteth not his eyes up to the idols of Israel: he defileth not his neighbour's wife: he meddleth with no menstruous woman: he grieveth nobody: he giveth his debtor his pledge again: he taketh none other man's good by violence: he parteth his meat with the hungry: he clotheth the naked: he lendeth nothing upon usury: he taketh nothing over: he writhed[1] with his hand from doing wrong: he handleth faithfully betwixt man and man: he walketh in my commandments, and keepeth my laws, and performeth them faithfully); this is a righteous man: he shall surely live, saith the Lord God. If he now beget a son that is a murderer and a shedder of blood; if he do one of these things (though he do not all); he eateth upon the hills; he defileth his neighbour's wife; he grieveth the poor and needy; he robbeth and spoileth; he giveth not the debtor his pledge again; he lifteth up his eyes unto idols, and meddleth with abominable things; he lendeth upon usury, and taketh moreover; shall this man live? he shall not live. Seeing he hath done all these abominations, he shall die: his blood shall be upon him. Now if this man beget a son also, that seeth all his father's sins which he hath done, and feareth, neither doth such like; namely, he eateth not upon the mountains; he lifteth not his eyes up to the idols of Israel; he defileth not his neighbour's wife; he vexeth no man; he keepeth no man's pledge; he neither spoileth nor robbeth any man; he dealeth his meat with the hungry; he clotheth the naked; he oppresseth not the poor; he receiveth no usury, nor any thing over; he keepeth my laws, and walketh in my commandments; this man shall not die in his father's sin, but shall live without fail. As for his father, because he oppressed and spoiled his brother, and did wickedly among his people, he is dead in his own sin. And yet say ye: Wherefore then should not this son bear his father's sin? Therefore, because the son hath done equity and right, hath kept all my commandments and done them; therefore shall he live in deed. The soul that sinneth shall die. The son shall not bear the father's offences, neither shall the father bear the son's offence. The righteousness of the righteous shall be upon himself; and the wickedness of the wicked shall be upon himself also."

Of these words, which I have borrowed out of the prophet Ezechiel, is it plain and evident, that, although the parents be wicked and idolatrous, yet if their children be not polluted and defiled with the same wickedness and idolatry, but lovers of God, studious of his holy word, and diligent walkers in his laws and commandments; they shall be free from those plagues and punishments which their wicked and ungodly fathers have most justly deserved, and be no partakers of God's displeasure, indignation, and vengeance in this behalf. Therefore, where it is said that God will punish the wickedness of parents "in the children, until the third and fourth generation," it is to be understand of those children which, having wicked fathers, follow the steps of their fathers, committing the same wickedness which they tofore have committed, without repentance or amendment of life. The other, which are free from the wickedness of their parents, are also free from the curses and plagues of God, and be in the number of those which are mentioned in the end of this second commandment.

Father. What is that? *Son*. "And shew mercy until thousands, unto those that love me and keep my commandments."

Father. What learnest thou of these words? *Son*. Verily, that as God is righteous and severe in punishing the wicked doers, which transgress his commandments, so likewise is he merciful, gentle, and liberal to all such as love him, and study to frame their lives according to his holy word; as the apostle saith: "Unto them that are **Rom. ii.** contentious, and not obedient to the truth, but obey unrighteousness, shall come indig-

[[1] Writhed with: turned away.]

nation and wrath, trouble and anguish, upon all the souls of men that do evil, of the Jew first, and also of the Greek. But unto all them that do good (shall come) praise and honour and peace, unto the Jew first, and also the Greek. For there is no respect of persons before God."

Father. What is meant by this, that God, in plaguing the wickedness of the parents in the children, will only extend his punishment until the third and fourth generation, yea, and that none otherwise, except they follow the wickedness of their fathers, as we heard tofore; but in shewing mercy unto those that love him and keep his commandments, he saith, that he will extend and stretch forth his merciful kindness and kind mercy until thousands, that is to say, infinite generations? *Son.* This declareth unto us, that the mercy of God is greater than his anger, and that he is more bent to loving-kindness than to severe justice. And with this agreeth the saying of that blessed virgin Mary: "His mercy," saith she, "endureth throughout all generations upon them that fear him." The psalmograph also saith: "The Lord is full of compassion and mercy, long-suffering, and of great goodness. He will not alway be chiding, neither will he keep his anger for ever. He will not deal with us after our sins, nor reward us according to our wickedness. For look how high the heaven is in comparison of the earth; so great is his mercy also toward them that fear him. Look how wide the east is from the west; so far will he set our sins from us. Yea, like as a father pitieth his own children, even so is the Lord merciful unto them that fear him, &c. The merciful goodness of the Lord endureth for ever and ever upon them that fear him, and his righteousness upon their childer's children; even such as keep his covenant, and think upon his commandments to do them."

The mercy of God is greater than the anger of God.

Luke i.

Psal. ciii.

Father. We have largely talked of all things concerning this second commandment of God; whereof we have learned, that we ought to make no image of God, nor of any other thing for religion sake, nor yet give any adoration or worship to them, but serve the Lord our God "in spirit and truth;" forasmuch as he is a spirit, and is chiefly delighted with spiritual things. Go forth now, and recite unto me the third commandment.

John iv.

The third commandment. Exod. xx. Deut. v.

Son. "Thou shalt not take the name of the Lord thy God in vain. For the Lord will not hold him guiltless that taketh his name in vain."

What God requireth of us in the third commandment.

Father. What is the will of God in this law? What requireth he of us? *Son.* First, he forbiddeth us to abuse his holy name through false, light, or vain swearing, or to call his name unto witness in any matter, except it be godly, charitable, true, grave, weighty, and necessary. Again, he chargeth us straitly, that we do not usurp his glorious name in any kind of superstition, sorcery, enchantment, witchcraft, conjuration, invocation of devils and wicked spirits: Item, that we do not dishonour the name of the Lord our God through our evil behaviour. Secondly, he requireth of us that in matters of faith, or in grave and weighty causes of controversies, where an oath is necessarily required, and ministered unto us by them which are in authority, we swear not by the name of any creature that is in heaven or in earth, but only by his blessed and glorious name: again, that in all our necessity, sickness, sorrow, and care, we flee unto the name of no creature neither in heaven nor in earth, but only unto his holy name for aid, help, and succour, which is "a strong tower" for all them that resort unto it; seeing that "there is no name given unto men under the cope of heaven wherein they may receive salvation" either of body or of soul, but this one only name of that most mighty Lord our God. Also, that in our prosperity, when all things go well with us, we shew ourselves thankful unto him, laud, praise, magnify, and extol his holy, blessed, and glorious name: Item, that we set forth, preach, and declare his holy word, and avaunce his pure and true religion, without the intermixtion or mingling of any man's doctrine. Finally, that we to the uttermost of all our power, even with our whole strength both of body and soul, seek continually the avancement, glory, and honour of God's most glorious and honourable name, never attempting, either in word, deed, or thought, that may in any point before men obscure or deface the majesty of the Lord our God.

Prov. xviii.

Acts iv.

Pray in adversity: praise in prosperity.

Father. How provest thou by the word of God, that we are forbidden in this third commandment falsely, lightly, or vainly to swear by the name of God? *Son.* God saith by his servant Moses: "Ye shall not swear falsely by my name, neither shalt thou unhallow the name of thy God; for I am the Lord." By the prophet Zachary he also saith: "The things that ye shall do are these: speak every man the truth unto his neighbour: execute judgment truly and peaceably within your gates: let none of you imagine evil in his heart against his neighbour; and love no false oaths; for all these are the things that I hate, saith the Lord." Jesus the son of Syrach writeth on this manner: "Hear me, O ye children: I will give you a doctrine, how ye shall order your mouth: whoso keepeth it shall not perish through his lips, nor be hurt through wicked works. As for the sinner, he shall be taken in his own vanity: he that is proud and cursed shall fall therein. Let not thy mouth be accustomed with swearing; for in it there are many falls. Let not the naming of God be continually in thy mouth; for like as a servant which is oft punished cannot be without some sore, even so whatsoever he be that sweareth and nameth God shall not be clean purged from sin. A man that useth much swearing shall be filled with wickedness; and the plague shall never go from his house. If he beguile his brother, his fault shall be upon him: if he knowledgeth not his sin, he maketh a double offence; and if he swear in vain, he shall not be found righteous, for his house shall be full of plagues. The words of the swearer bringeth death, (God grant that it be not found in the house of Jacob!) but they that fear God eschew all such things, and lie not weltering in sin."

Lev. xix. Zech. viii. Ecclus. xxiii.

Our Saviour Christ also forbiddeth all manner of vain and light swearing in these words: "Ye have heard how it was said to them of old time, Thou shalt not forswear thyself, but shalt perform thy oath to God. But I say unto you, Swear not at all; neither by heaven, for [it] is God's seat; nor yet by the earth, for it is his footstool; neither by Jerusalem, for it is the city of the great King: neither shall thou swear by thy head, because thou canst not make one hair white or black. But your communication shall be yea, yea, nay, nay; for whatsoever is more than that cometh of evil." St James also saith: "Above all things, my brethren, swear not; neither by heaven, neither by earth, neither by other oath. Let your yea be yea, and your nay, nay; lest ye fall into dissimulation."

Matt. v. Lev. xix. Exod. xx. Deut. x. James v.

Father. Where are we forbidden in the holy scripture to usurp the name of the Lord, of God, in any kind of superstition, sorcery, enchantment, &c.? *Son.* God saith: "Ye shall not turn yourselves to the soothsayers, neither shall ye ask any thing at the expounders of tokens, that ye be not defiled by them; for I am the Lord your God." Again: "If any soul turn him to the soothsayers and expounders of tokens, so that he goeth a whoring after them, I will set my face against that soul, and will root him out from among his people. Sanctify yourselves therefore, and be holy; for I am holy, even your God. And keep ye my statutes, and do them; for I am the Lord that sanctified you." Moses also saith: "When thou comest into the land which the Lord thy God shall give thee, thou shalt not learn to do the abominations of these nations, that there be not found among you that maketh his son or daughter go through the fire, or a prophesier, or a chooser out of days, or that regardeth the birds' crying, or a witch, or a conjurer, or soothsayer, or an expounder of tokens, or that asketh any thing of the dead. For whosoever doth such is abomination unto the Lord." The prophet Esay also saith: "If they say unto you, Ask counsel at the soothsayers, witches, charmers, and conjurers, then make them this answer: Is there a people anywhere that asketh not counsel at his god, whether it be concerning the dead or the living? If any man want light, let him look upon the law and testimony," &c.

Lev. xix. Lev. xx. Deut. xviii. Isai. viii.

Father. Are we also forbidden here to dishonour the name of the Lord our God through our wicked and evil behaviour? *Son.* Yea, verily. For God himself complaineth in the holy scripture, that his name is greatly dishonoured and evil spoken of among the heathen, because of the corrupt manners and ungodly conversation of such as profess his name. Therefore the holy apostle St Peter exhorteth us, that we "lead an honest conversation among the heathen; that whereas they backbite us as evil-doers, they, judging us of our good works, may glorify God in the day of

Isai. lii. Ezek. xxxvi. Rom. ii. 1 Pet. ii.

Matt. v. visitation." And our Saviour Christ commandeth us, that our "light should so shine before men, that they may see our good works, and glorify our Father which is in heaven." For as nothing in this world doth more dishonour the name of God Tit. i. than the wicked life of such as with their mouth "profess God, and with their deeds deny him;" so likewise nothing in this life doth more avance and set up the glorious majesty of the name of the Lord our God, than when such as profess his holy name live godly, virtuously, and honestly.

Father. Is it lawful for a christian man in any case to swear? *Son*. Yea, in all such cases as I tofore rehearsed.

Heb. vi. *Father*. How is that proved? *Son*. St Paul saith: "An oath is the end of all Jer. iv. controversy, or strife." And God himself saith: "O Israel, if thou wilt turn thee, then turn unto me, saith the Lord. And if thou wilt put away thine abominations out of my sight, thou shalt not be moved; and shalt swear, The Lord liveth, in truth, Jer. xii. in equity, and in righteousness." Again: "If they (that trouble my people) will learn the ways of them to swear by my name, The Lord liveth, like as they have learned my people to swear by Baal, then shall they be reckoned among my people. But if they will not obey, then will I root out the same folk, and destroy Deut. vi. x. them, saith the Lord." Moses also saith: "Thou shalt fear the Lord thy God, and him only shalt thou serve, and swear by his name." The psalmograph also saith: Psal. lxiii. "All they that swear by him (that is to say, God) shall be commended." Again: Psal. xv. "He shall dwell in the tabernacle of God, and rest upon his holy hill, that sweareth unto his neighbour, and disappointeth him not." It is so far off from sin to swear in a true and necessary cause, that we read, that God himself did swear. The psal- Psal. cx. mograph hath these words: "The Lord sware, and will not repent, Thou art a priest for ever after the order of Melchisedech." In the books of the prophets we Ezek. xxxiii. read that the manner of swearing which God used was this: "As truly as I live." John iii. iv. vi. viii. The evangelical history declareth, that Christ's oath was this: "Verily, verily, I say Rom. i. ix. unto you." St Paul also did swear, as we may see in his epistles. What shall I Gen. xxi. xlii. & xlvii. speak of Abraham and Abimelech, of Joseph, of the princes of Israel, of Josue, of Josh. ix. David, and such like? All these histories do evidently declare, that it is not for- 1 Sam. xx. xxiv. bidden by God's law for a christian man to swear by the name of the Lord his God, 1 Kings i. ii. and to call God for a witness in a true and just cause, and specially when it is required of the magistrates and head rulers for the avoiding of controversies, that peace and quietness may be had among their subjects.

Father. May magistrates then lawfully require an oath of their subjects? *Son*. Yea, most lawfully.

Gen. xxiv. *Father*. Where is that declared in the word of God? *Son*. We read, that Abraham required an oath of his servant; and the servant sware at his master's commandment. Gen. xxi. King Abimelech required an oath of Abraham, which was a stranger in his land; Gen. xxvi. and Abraham did swear. Abimelech also, king of the Philistines, required an oath of Isaac, that he should do him and his people no harm; and Isaac agreed to his request, Gen. xxxi. Gen. xlvii. and sware. Jacob sware unto Laban, when he was required. Jacob, otherwise called Israel, required of his son Joseph an oath, that he should not bury him in Egypt, but among his fathers; and Joseph sware. Divers such like examples are to be found in the holy scriptures, which do plainly declare, that christian men may lawfully take an oath, when it is required of them by such as are in authority. Are not Exod. xxii. these the words of the law of God? "If a man deliver his neighbour money or vessels to keep, and it be stolen from him out of his house; if the thief be found, he shall restore double. But if the thief be not found, then shall the good man of Psal. lxxxii. John x. the house be brought before the gods" (that is to say, before the magistrates, or head rulers), and "shall swear that he hath not put his hand unto his neighbour's good."

Father. Doth this third commandment of God require of us also, that in all our adversity and trouble we flee unto the name of God, as unto a strong tower, for help and succour, and diligently with strong faith call upon it? *Son*. Yea, verily. For Psal. l. this is the commandment of God: "Call on me in the day of thy trouble, and I will deliver thee, and thou shalt honour me." And as we are commanded to call on the name of God in our trouble, so likewise are we most graciously promised to be heard, as it is written: "Every one that calleth on the name of the Lord shall be saved." Joel ii. Acts ii. Rom. x. And God himself saith by the psalmograph: "Because he hath put his trust in me, I will deliver him: I will defend him, because he hath known my name. When he calleth upon me, I will hear him: yea, I am with him in his trouble, and I will deliver him, and bring him to honour. With long life will I satisfy him, and shew him my salvation." Psal. xci.

Father. Is it also required of us in this commandment that we be thankful to the name of the Lord our God for his benefits? *Son.* Is it not reason that we be thankful to him and praise his name, of whom we receive all that we have, appertaining either unto the body or unto the soul, that good is or godly? 1 Cor. iv. James i.

Father. It is indeed reason and right. *Son.* This is the commandment of God by the psalmograph: "Offer unto God the sacrifice of praise or thanksgiving." And Psal. l. God himself saith: "Whoso offereth unto me thanks and praise, he honoureth me; and this is the way whereby I shall shew him the salvation of God." The psalmograph himself also saith: "I will praise the name of God with a song, and magnify it with Psal. lxix. thanksgiving; and it shall please God better than a bullock that hath horns and hoofs."

Father. Are we commanded also in this law to confess and set forth the true religion and doctrine of God to other, whensoever the glory of God doth require, and the salvation of the brethren, although the cross, yea, death itself should follow? *Son.* Yea, that is our duty; and whosoever doth it not, he transgresseth this commandment of God, and hath no portion in the inheritance of God's kingdom, as our Saviour Christ testifieth, saying: "Whosoever confesseth me before men, him will I confess Matt. x. Luke xii. also before my Father which is in heaven. But whosoever denieth me before men, him will I also deny before my Father which is in heaven." Again: "Whosoever Mark viii. Luke ix. is ashamed of me and of my sayings before this whorish and sinful generation, of him shall the Son of man also be ashamed, when he cometh in the glory of his Father with the holy angels." Not to confess the truth of God, when the glory of God and the salvation of our neighbour require, is none other thing than to deny the truth and to blaspheme the name of God, and to envy God his glory and praise. And "what Matt. xvi. doth it profit a man to win the whole world, and at the last to lose his own soul? Or what can a man give to redeem his soul withal?" In God's cause, and in the matter of truth, they are not to be feared that slay the body, and that done, they can Matt. x. do no more; but that Lord is to be feared which is able to destroy both body and soul in hell-fire. "For the truth strive thou unto the death," saith the wise man, Ecclus. iv. "and God shall fight for thee against thine enemies."

Father. Besides these things heretofore rehearsed, are we bound by this commandment to seek the glory of God's most holy name above all things, and not to attempt any thing either in thought, word, or deed, that may in any point obscure the honour of it? *Son.* Who doubteth of that? For this thing only ought to be the alone study of a true Christian, even to the uttermost of his power to avance the glory of God's most glorious name. Therefore thus stirreth up the psalmograph himself, and saith: "Magnify the Lord, O my soul, and all that is within me praise his holy name. Psal. ciii. Praise the Lord, O my soul, and forget not all his benefits; which forgiveth all thy sins, and healeth all thine infirmities; which saveth thy life from destruction, and crowneth thee with mercy and loving-kindness," &c.

Father. But what mean these words that follow in the commandment? "For the Lord will not hold him guiltless that taketh his name in vain." *Son.* In these words the Lord our God, which is a mighty and jealous God, yea, and a consuming Deut. iv. Exod. xx. fire, declareth how greatly he is angry with them that do abuse his holy name, and honour it not on such sort as is above specified. And although God gave ten commandments, which he will diligently to be observed of all men, yet to none of them all specially doth he add any threatenings but only to the second and third commandments: by this signifying unto us, that although his godly majesty detesteth, abhorreth, and hateth all sins, yet the sin of idolatry and the abusing of his holy name most chiefly; and that whosoever transgresseth these two commandments, he will most extremely plague and punish them; in this world temporally, and in the world to come eternally, except they repent and amend.

Father. Are there any sentences in the holy scripture which also declare the anger, wrath, and vengeance of God against all such as transgress this commandment, and abuse his holy name? *Son.* Many and divers.

Father. Rehearse some of them. *Son.* God himself saith by the prophet Moses: "Whosoever blasphemeth his God shall bear his sin; and he that blasphemeth the name of the Lord shall die the death. The whole congregation shall stone him. As the stranger, so shall he of the household be also. If he blaspheme the name (of God), he shall die." And in the prophet Zachary we read on this manner: "I turned me, lifting up mine eyes, looked, and behold, a flying book. And he said unto me, What seest thou? I answered, I see a flying book, of twenty cubits long, and ten cubits broad. Then said he unto me, This is the curse that goeth forth over the whole earth. For all thieves shall be judged after this book, and all swearers shall be judged according to the same. I will bring it forth, saith the Lord of hosts, so that it shall come to the house of the thief, and to the house of him that falsely sweareth by my name, and shall remain in his house, and consume it with the timber and stones thereof." The wise man also saith: "Let not thy mouth be accustomed with swearing; for in it there are many falls. Let not the naming of God be continually in thy mouth; for like as a servant which is oft punished cannot be without some sore, even so whatsoever he be that sweareth and nameth God shall not be clean purged from sin. A man that useth much swearing shall be filled with wickedness; and the plague shall never go from his house, &c. The words of the swearer bring death."

Lev. xxiv. Zech. v. Ecclus. xxiii.

Father. These authorities of the holy scripture declare evidently, how greatly God abhorreth the abuse of his holy name, either through false, vain, or light swearing, or otherwise; so that it is not without a cause said in this precept, that "the Lord will not hold him guiltless that taketh his name in vain." But let us go forth and hear the fourth commandment. *Son.* The fourth commandment of God is this:

The fourth commandment. Exod. xx. Deut. v.

"Remember that thou keep holy the sabbath-day. Six days shalt thou labour, and do all thy work. But the seventh day is the sabbath of the Lord thy God. In it shalt thou do no manner of work, neither thou, nor thy son, nor thy servant, nor thy maid, nor thy cattle, nor thy stranger that is within thy gates. For in six days the Lord made heaven, and earth, and the sea, and all that in them is, and rested on the seventh day. Therefore the Lord blessed the seventh day, and hallowed it."

What God requireth of us in the fourth commandment.

Father. What is the will of God in this commandment? *Son.* God in this his law requesteth of us two things: First, that we keep holy the sabbath-day: Secondly, that on the seventh day we rest from all worldly and bodily business, labours, and works, that we may the more freely serve the Lord our God, and consider the things which appertain unto the salvation of our souls.

Father. What signifieth this word *sabbath?* *Son.* Rest, and ceasing from servile labour and outward works.

What it is to sanctify the sabbath-day.

Father. What is it to sanctify the sabbath-day? *Son.* Not to pass over that day idly in lewd pastimes, in banqueting, in dicing and carding, in dancing and bear-baiting, in bowling and shooting, in laughing and whoring, and in such like beastly and filthy pleasures of the flesh; nor yet in bargaining, buying and selling, as they do which run to fairs and markets on the sabbath-day and on other holy and feastful days (for this is not to sanctify, but to profanate, not to hallow, but to defile the sabbath-day); but, all such madnesses and wickednesses laid aside, and the mind utterly sequestered from all worldly things, and the body free from all servile works, to address ourselves, and to apply our whole mind and body unto godly and spiritual exercises; as unto the consideration of the mighty power of God in creating all things both in heaven and in earth, yea, and that of nothing, through his word, for the wealth and commodity of man: again, unto the consideration of God's unoutspeakable goodness in preserving and maintaining those his creatures for the use and profit of man: Item, unto the humble and reverent hearing or reading of God's holy word; unto the faithful and diligent calling on the name of God by fervent prayer; unto the unfeigned and hearty thanksgiving to God for his benefits no less diversly than plenteously declared unto us; unto the worthy receiving of the holy mysteries of the body and blood of our Lord and Saviour Christ Jesu; unto the visiting, counselling, comforting, and helping of the poor and miserably afflicted persons; unto the utter giving over of all the studies, devices, and works of the old man; unto the earnest embracing of the fruits of the Spirit; and in fine, unto the whole giving over of ourselves unto the good will of God, to work in us by his holy Spirit whatsoever his blessed pleasure shall be, that he alone may live, rule, reign, and triumph in us.

Father. Are there any sentences in the holy scripture, which confirm this law of the sabbath-day? *Son.* Yea, many and divers. *Father.* Rehearse part of them.

Son. God said to Moses: "Speak unto the children of Israel, and say: Keep my sabbath; for it is a token between me and you and your posterities, that ye may know how that I am the Lord which halloweth you: therefore keep my sabbath; for it shall be holy unto you. Whoso unhalloweth it shall die the death. For whoso doeth any work therein shall be rooted out from among his people. Six days shall men work; but upon the seventh day is the sabbath, that is to say, the holy rest of the Lord. Whoso doeth any work upon the sabbath-day shall die the death. Therefore shall the children of Israel keep the sabbath, that they may keep it also among their posterities for an everlasting covenant. An everlasting token is it between me and the children of Israel. For in six days made the Lord heaven and earth, but upon the seventh day he rested, and was refreshed." Again he saith unto Moses: "Speak unto the children of Israel, and say unto them: These are the feasts of the Lord, which ye shall call holy days. Six days shalt thou work; but the seventh day is the rest of the sabbath, and shall be called holy. Ye shall do no work therein; for it is the sabbath of the Lord, wheresoever ye dwell."

Exod. xxxi. Num. xv. Lev. xxiii.

By the prophet Esay God also saith: "Keep equity, and do right, &c. Blessed is the man that doth this, and the man's child, which keepeth the same; even he that taketh heed that he unhalloweth not the sabbath, that is, he that keepeth himself that he do no evil, &c. Unto them that keep my sabbath, and hold greatly of the thing that pleaseth me, and keep my covenant, will I give in my household and within my walls a better heritage and name, than if they had been called sons and daughters. I will give them an everlasting name that shall not perish, &c. All they which keep themselves, that they unhallow not the sabbath, namely, that they fulfil my covenant; them will I bring unto my holy mountain, and make them joyful in my house of prayer." Again, God by the same prophet saith: "If thou on the sabbath-day turnest thy foot away from doing thine own will and pleasure in my holy day, then shalt thou be called unto the pleasant, holy, and glorious sabbath of the Lord, where thou shalt be in honour; so that thou do not after thine own imagination, neither seek thine own will, nor speak thine own words. Then shalt thou have thy pleasure in the Lord, which shall carry thee high above the earth, and feed thee with the heritage of Jacob thy father; for the Lord's own mouth hath so promised."

Isai. lvi. Isai. lviii.

By the prophet Jeremy God speaketh also on this manner: "Take heed for your lives, that ye carry no burden upon you in the sabbath-day, to bring it through the gates of Jerusalem: ye shall bear no burden also out of your houses in the sabbath. Ye shall do no labour therein, but hallow the sabbath, as I commanded your fathers. Howbeit, they obeyed me not, neither hearkened they unto me, but were obstinate and stubborn, and neither obeyed me, nor received my correction. Nevertheless if ye will hear me, saith the Lord, and bear no burden into the city through this gate upon the sabbath; if ye will hallow the sabbath, so that ye do no work therein; then shall there go through the gates of this city kings and princes, that shall sit upon the seat of David, &c. But if ye will not be obedient unto me, to hallow the sabbath, so that ye will bear your burdens through the gates of Jerusalem upon the sabbath; then shall I set fire upon the gates of Jerusalem, and it shall burn up the houses of Jerusalem, and no man shall be able to quench it."

Jer. xvii.

Again, by the prophet Ezechiel he saith: "Walk not in the statutes of your fore-fathers: keep not their ordinances, and defile not yourselves with their idols; for I am the Lord your God. But walk in my statutes: keep my laws and do them:

Ezek. xx.

hallow my sabbaths; for they are a token betwixt me and you, that ye may know how that I am the Lord."

Whether the Christians be bound unto the observation of the sabbath-day as the Jews were.

Father. Are the Christians also no less bound unto the observation and keeping of the sabbath-day than the Jews were in times past? *Son*. As concerning the seventh day, which was the Jews' sabbath, wherein they were commanded to rest and cease from all outward labour, we be free from that law, and are no more bound to the restful keeping thereof than of any other day. In consideration whereof, the godly fathers of Christ's church turned the Jews' sabbath-day into the Sunday, which is now called the sabbath of the Christians, to declare, that we Christians are free from the ☞ keeping of the aforesaid Jewish sabbath, and that it is in the liberty of the christian magistrates to appoint what day they will to be the sabbath of the Christians; and therefore we shall note, that the law concerning the sabbath-day is partly ceremonial, and partly moral. It is ceremonial, as touching the external rest, and the self seventh day, which now is abrogated with all the other Mosaical ceremonies through the coming of Christ; so that in this behalf we be free from that law. Notwithstanding, as touching the keeping of the public ministry, I mean, the Christians to repair together unto their temples on some certain day in the week at the appointment of the godly christian rulers, to pray unto God, to give thanks to God for his benefits, to hear God's word, to receive the holy mysteries of the body and blood of our Saviour Christ, &c., and, that they may do these things the more conveniently, to sequester both their bodies and minds from all worldly things and servile works, &c.; in this behalf this law concerning the sabbath abideth moral, and is to be observed also of the Christians, not only spiritually, but also corporally, except some grave, weighty, urgent, and necessary cause persuadeth to the contrary, that by this means they may learn the better to exercise themselves in matters of God and godliness, and seek by that temporal rest, how they may attain unto the perpetual rest of the world to come.

The law of the sabbath is partly ceremonial, and partly moral.

Note well.

Father. Declare to me by the word of God, that the Christians are free from the sabbath of the Jews. *Son*. Our Saviour Christ said unto the Pharisees (when they found fault with his disciples, because that "they being hungry plucked of the ears of the corn, and did eat on the sabbath-day, saying unto him, Behold, thy disciples do that which is not lawful to do upon the sabbath), Have ye not read, what David did, when he was hungry, and they also that were with him? How he entered into the house of God, and did eat the shew-breads, which were not lawful for him to eat, neither for them that were with him, but only for the priests? Or have ye not read in the law, how that the priests in the temple break the sabbath, and yet are blameless? But I say unto you, that there is one here greater than the temple. But if ye knew what this were, I have pleasure in mercy and not in sacrifice, ye would not have condemned innocents. For the Son of man is Lord even over the sabbath." In another place he also saith: "The sabbath was made for man, and not man for the sabbath. Therefore is the Son of man Lord even over the sabbath." St Paul also saith: "Seeing ye now know God (yea, rather are known of God), how is it that ye turn you back again unto the weak and beggarly traditions, whereunto ye desire again afresh to be in bondage? Ye observe days, and months, and times, and years. I am in fear of you, lest I have bestowed labour on you in vain." Again: "Let no man trouble your consciences about meat, or drink, or for a piece of an holy day, as the holy day of the new moon, or of the sabbath-days, which are the shadow of the things that were to come." Item: "Bodily exercise profiteth little; but godliness is profitable unto all things, as a thing which hath promises of the life that now is, and of the life to come."

Matt. xii. 1 Sam. xxi. Hos. vi. Mark ii. Gal. iv. Col. ii. 1 Tim. iv.

Father. It appeareth by the words of the apostle in his epistle to the Hebrews, that we Christians have also a sabbath. *Son*. What are those words?

Heb. iv.

Father. Thus saith he: "There remaineth yet a sabbath or rest unto the people of God. For he that is entered into the rest of God ceaseth from his works, as God doth from his. Let us make haste, therefore, to enter into that rest, lest that any man fall after the same example of unbelief."

The sabbath of the Christians.

Son. This sabbath or rest, whereof the apostle here speaketh, is not corporal, but spiritual; not worldly, but ghostly; not outward, but inward; consisting rather in the quietness or rest of the mind than of the body, being a very figure of that godly and everlasting quietness and rest, which through Christ we shall have after this life in the kingdom of God the Father. For a christian man being at quiet with God in his conscience, by ceasing from doing evil works, and by conforming of himself unto the will of God, even in this world hath heaven in his breast, as I may so speak: even as the faithful man, which believeth in Christ, hath everlasting life even in this world, as it is written: "He that believeth on the Son hath everlasting life." John iii. The sabbath therefore of the Christians is spiritual and everlasting, not to be observed one day in the week only, after the manner of the Jews, but every day so long as we live, by ceasing to do evil, and by studying to do good, as it is written: "There Isai. lxvi. shall be a new moon for the other, and a new sabbath for the other; and all flesh shall come to worship before me, saith the Lord."

Father. Notwithstanding these things, which thou hast spoken of the spiritual, Feastful days appointed by the magistrates are to be observed. inward, and everlasting sabbath of the Christians, thou dost not take away the sabbaths and feastful days, which are appointed of the rulers of Christ's church to be observed of their subjects, that they may the more quietly give themselves to spiritual and godly exercises. *Son.* God forbid. For so should I sin both against faith and charity. Against faith: because I should directly strive against God's word, Rom. xiii. 1 Pet. ii. Heb. xiii. which commandeth not to resist but humbly to obey the godly and righteous ordinances of the high powers, forasmuch as "there is no power but of God;" and "he that resisteth the power resisteth the ordinance of God, and purchaseth to himself everlasting damnation." Against charity: because I should transgress and break that good and godly order, which is both confirmed by public authority, and also received with the common consent of all faithful congregations, avancing greatly both the glory of God, and making not a little to the increase of our knowledge in the mysteries of our salvation through the blood of Christ.

Father. And is it lawful for us upon our sabbaths and feastful days in any case Of labour on the feastful days. Luke vi. to labour? *Son.* "It is lawful," as our Saviour Christ saith, "to do good even on the sabbath-day." We read, that on the sabbath-day Christ healed divers persons that were diseased, and restored them to their health, to give us an example to do the like, when either faith, charity, or necessity requireth. For to the true godly, every day is the sabbath-day; forasmuch as they spend every day in holy works, and have nothing to do with such deeds, as be uncomely to be done of true Christians; forasmuch also as every day they lift up their minds unto God, call on his holy name by fervent prayer, praise his glorious majesty, and have their meditation in the law of the Lord, yea, and that in the midst of their godly travails and labours. Notwithstanding, except great necessity or urgent causes do require that we should work on the sabbath-day, or on other feastful days appointed by public authority unto holy exercises, we ought not to break that godly quietness on such holy days, but diligently apply our minds (all worldly business set apart) unto such heavenly and godly studies and actions, as the solemnity of those feasts requireth. If any man without necessary cause attempteth the contrary, he greatly offendeth, as I have heretofore said.

Father. But wherefore doth God in this law make mention of labour, commanding Of labour. us to work six days in the week, and to rest on the seventh? *Son.* God at the beginning, so soon as man had transgressed and broken his holy commandment in paradise, and had eaten of the forbidden fruit, enjoined Adam, and in him all his posterity, this penance, that in the sweat of his brows and in the labour of his hands Gen. iii. he should eat his bread, and get his living, until he returned into the earth: for earth he was, and unto earth he should return. Therefore, whereas the Lord our God had from the beginning laid this yoke of labour upon all men's neck, commanding them to work and to travail for their living so long as they remained in this vale of misery, no day excepted, and is now determined to erect and set up a comely order in the public weal of the Israelites, wherein he will have his wonderful works considered, his word preached, his glorious name called upon and praised, his people brought unto the knowledge of his holy will, matters of their soul-health regarded, spiritual exercises practised, &c.; he reneweth here his former penance of labour laid

upon man for his disobedience, commanding him not to live idly, dissolutely, and slothfully, but diligently to travail by all lawful means to get his living with the labour of his hands and the sweat of his brows, yea, and that six days in the week: notwithstanding, that such godly exercises, whereof I have tofore spoken, may the more conveniently be brought to pass, he exempteth man from labour and servile occupations on the sabbath-day, commanding him on that day to rest, and to give himself to corporal quietness, that he may the more freely give his mind to spiritual and godly things, and on that day no less to seek after things pertaining unto the salvation of his soul, than he the six days past laboured for the things which concern the health and preservation of his body. And to provoke man the more earnestly both unto labour and also unto the hallowing of the sabbath-day, God setteth forth himself an example unto us of them both, that is to say, of labour on the six days, and of rest on the sabbath, which is the seventh day; affirming that "in six days he made heaven, and earth, and the sea, and all that in them is, and rested on the seventh
Gen. ii day," so that "he blessed the seventh day, and hallowed it."

Father. We are then commanded of God in this precept two things: first, six days to labour; secondly, to rest from labour on the seventh day, yea, and that unto this end, that we may pass over that day in godly and spiritual exercises. *Son*. So is it.

Father. Are there any other places of the holy scripture, which command us to labour with our hands, and to get our living with the sweat of our brows? *Son*. We have plenty, both of sentences and of examples. God said unto Adam immedi-
Gen. iii. ately after his fall: "In the sweat of thy face shalt thou eat thy bread, until thou dost return unto the earth, out of the which thou art taken. For earth thou art, and
Psal. cxxviii. to earth shalt thou return." The psalmograph saith: "Thou shalt eat the labours of thy hands: so shalt thou be blessed, and it shall go well with thee." That mirror
Job v. of patience saith: "A man is born to labour, and a bird to fly." The wise man
Prov. vi. saith: "Go to the emmet, thou sluggard, consider her ways, and learn to be wise. She hath no guide, nor overseer, nor ruler; yet in the summer she provideth her meat, and gathereth her food together in the harvest. How long wilt thou sleep, thou sluggish man? When wilt thou arise out of thy sleep? Yea, sleep on still a little; slumber a little; fold thine hands together yet a little, that thou mayest sleep: so shall poverty come unto thee, as one that travelleth by the way, and necessity like a weaponed man." But if thou be not slothful, thy harvest shall come as a springing
Prov. x. well, and poverty shall flee far from thee. Again: "Whoso gathereth in summer is wise; but he that is sluggish in harvest bringeth himself to confusion." "An idle hand maketh poor; but a quick labouring hand maketh rich." Also in another place: "Whoso is slothful and slack in his labour is the brother of him that is a
Prov. xx. waster." Item: "Delight not thou in sleep, lest thou come unto poverty; but open thine eyes, that thou mayest have bread enough." "A slothful body will not go to plough for cold of the winter: therefore shall he go a begging in summer, and have nothing."

Eph. iv. St Paul also saith: "Let him that stole steal no more, but let him rather labour with his hands the thing which is good, that he may give unto him that needeth."
1 Thess. iv. Again: "We beseech you, brethren, that ye increase more and more, and that ye study to be quiet, and to meddle with your own business, and to work with your own hands, as we commanded you; that ye may behave yourselves honestly toward
2 Thess. iii. them that are without, and that nothing be lacking unto you." Item: "When we were with you, this we warned you of, that if any would not work, the same should not eat. For we have heard say, that there are some which walk among you inordinately, working not at all, but being busy-bodies. Them that are such we command and exhort by our Lord Jesus Christ, that they work with quietness, and eat their own bread."

Examples of labour. Gen. ii. *Father*. Rehearse some examples of labour out of the holy scripture. *Son*. Adam, even in paradise, was commanded of God to keep and to till the garden. Cain was
Gen. iv. a plowman. Abel was a shepherd. Thubal exercised music. Thubal-cain was a
Gen. ix. worker in brass and iron. Noe was an husbandman, and planted a vineyard.
Gen. xiii. xxvi. xxix. xxxvii. Abraham, Isaac, Jacob, and many of the ancient patriarchs were keepers of sheep.

Joseph was a magistrate and ruler in the commonweal. Moses was a shepherd, and Gen. xli.
afterward a governor in the public weal of Israel. The children of Israel laboured Exod. iii. Exod. i.
painful in the land of Egypt. David kept sheep, and afterward was king over 1 Sam. xvi.
Israel. The prophet Elizeus was a plowman and tilled the earth. The prophet Amos 1 Kings xix. Amos i.
was a shepherd and kept sheep.

Joseph, the husband of Mary the virgin was a carpenter. Christ likewise was a Matt. xiii. Mark vi.
carpenter, and laboured for his living, till he came to the office of preaching. Many Matt. iv. John xxi.
of Christ's disciples were fishermen. Matthew the evangelist was a custom-gatherer. Matt. ix.
Luke the evangelist was a physician. Tabitha, otherwise called Dorcas, made coats Col. iv. Acts ix.
and garments with her own hands for the poor people. A certain godly and religious Acts xvi.
woman, called Lydia, was a seller of purple. Aquila and Priscilla his wife were makers Acts xviii.
of tents: of the which occupation St Paul also was, which lived not idly, nor yet of the sweat of other men's brows, but got his living with the labours of his own hands, because he would be chargeable to no man, as these his words do manifestly declare: "We labour and work with our own hands." Again: "Ye yourselves know, 1 Cor. iv. 2 Thess. iii.
how ye ought to follow us. For we behaved not ourselves inordinately among you: neither took we bread of any man for nought; but wrought with labour and sweat night and day, because we would not be chargeable to any of you: not but that we had authority, but to make ourselves an ensample unto you, to follow us. For when we were with you, this we warned you of, that if any would not work, the same should not eat." Also in another place he saith: "I have desired no man's silver, Acts xx.
gold, or vesture: yea, ye yourselves know, that these hands have ministered unto my necessities, and to them that were with me."

Father. Is it not lawful then for christian men to cease from work on those six days, seeing that God saith, "Six days shalt thou labour, and do all thy work"? *Son.* Even as on the sabbath-day, wherein we are commanded to cease from bodily labour, it is lawful, when charity or necessity requireth, to work, as we have tofore heard; so likewise is it lawful on the other six days to abstain also from labour, when the glory of God, or any other necessary cause, doth require.

Father. As God setteth forth himself unto us an example of labour for six days; so doth he of rest for the seventh day. "For in six days the Lord made heaven, and earth, and the sea, and all that in them is, and rested on the seventh day." *Son.* Truth it is.

Father. Of the sabbath-day and of the sanctifying thereof, we have tofore sufficiently heard. Rehearse therefore the next commandment.

Son. "Honour thy father and thy mother, that thy days may be long in the land, The fifth commandment.
which the Lord thy God giveth thee."

Father. This commandment pertaineth not unto the person of God, as the other four, which we have tofore heard. *Son.* No, verily. For the law of God was written Exod. xxxi.
with the finger of God in two tables of stone. The first table containeth four commandments, and those pertain unto the worshipping and honouring of God. The other table comprehendeth six, and those concern our duty toward our neighbour. Of the which six this is the first, which I have now rehearsed.

Father. Why is the commandment concerning our duty toward our parents set next in order to the precepts, which concern our office and duty toward God? *Son.* To declare that, next unto God, we owe the chief honour, worship, and reverence to our father and mother.

Father. What is it to "honour thy father and thy mother"? *Son.* Not only to give What it is to honour our father and mother.
them outward reverence, to rise up unto them, to give them place, to put off our caps, to kneel unto them, to ask them blessing, &c., but also honourably to esteem them, godly to think of them, heartily to love them, humbly to obey them, diligently to pray for them, charitably to conceal and hide their faults, in all honest things to gratify them, in their need to help and succour them, and in fine, at all times to do all good things for them, whatsoever lieth in our power.

Father. Are there other testimonies contained in the holy scripture, which also require this duty of us toward our parents? *Son.* Yea, very many.

Lev. xix. *Father*. Rehearse some of them. *Son*. Moses saith: "Let every one reverence his father and mother." Ecclus. iii. Jesus, the son of Syrach, writeth on this manner: "Hear me, your father, O my dear children, and do thereafter, that ye may be safe. For the Lord will have the father honoured of the children; and look, what a mother commandeth her children to do, he will have it kept. Whoso honoureth his father, his sins shall be forgiven him; and he that honoureth his mother is like one that gathereth treasure together. Whoso honoureth his father shall have joy of his own children; and when he maketh his prayer, he shall be heard. He that honoureth his father shall have long life; and he that is obedient for the Lord's sake, his mother shall have joy of him. He that feareth the Lord honoureth his father and mother, and doeth them service, as it were to the Lord himself Honour thy father in deed, in word, and in all patience, that thou mayest have God's blessing; and his blessing shall abide with thee for ever. The blessing of the father buildeth up the houses of the children; but the mother's curse rooteth out the foundations. Rejoice not when thy father is reproved; for it is not honour unto thee, but a shame. For the worship of a man's father is his own worship; and where the father is without honour, it is the dishonesty of the son. My son, make much of thy father in his age, and grieve him not as long as he liveth. And if his understanding fail, have patience with him, and despise him not in thy strength. For the good deed that thou shewest to thy father shall not be forgotten; and when thou thyself wantest, it shall be rewarded thee (and for thy mother's offences thou shalt be recompensed with good, yea, it shall be found for thee in righteousness), and in the day of trouble thou shalt be remembered. Thy sins also shall melt away, like as the ice in the fair warm weather. But he that forsaketh his father shall come to shame, and he that despiseth his mother is cursed Ecclus. vii. of God." Again he saith: "Honour thy father from thy whole heart; and forget not the sorrowful travail that thy mother had with thee. Remember that thou was born through them; and how canst thou recompense them the things that they have Tob. iv. done for thee?" Old Toby said to his son: "Hold thy mother in honour all the days of thy life. For thou oughtest to remember what and how great perils she suffered for thee in her womb." Our Saviour Christ also hath these words in the Matt. xv. gospel: "God commandeth, saying, Honour father and mother; and he that curs-Eph. vi. eth father and mother, let him die the death." St Paul likewise saith: "Ye children, obey your fathers and mothers in the Lord; for that is right. Honour thy father and mother (the same is the first commandment in the promise); that thou mayest prosper, Col. iii. and live long on earth." Again: "Ye children, obey your fathers and mothers in all things; for that is well-pleasing unto the Lord."

Father. Are there any ensamples contained in the holy scriptures of such as practised this obedience toward their parents? *Son*. Yea, verily.

Examples of obedience unto the parents. *Father*. Recite part of them. *Son*. Isaac shewed such obedience to his father Abraham, that when he at the commandment of God should have been offered for a Gen. xxii. sacrifice unto the Lord, he did not once resist his father, but willingly suffered himself to be bound, and to be laid on the altar above upon the wood, being ready also to be slain of his father, if God had not otherwise provided. Likewise read we of young Tobias, which, when his father sent him unto a far country about certain businesses of his, refused not to take so great a journey upon him, but meekly answered his father, Tob. v. and said: "Father, all that thou hast commanded me will I do, and that diligently." As I may let pass the other examples; have we not Christ Jesus our Lord and Saviour a perfect example in this behalf? First, in as much as he is the only-begotten Son Phil. ii. of God, he so obeyed the good will and pleasure of his heavenly Father, that "when he was God and equal with God, he made himself of no reputation, taking on him the shape of a servant, and became like unto men, and was found in his apparel as a man. He humbled himself and became obedient unto the death, even the death of the cross." Again, in that he is man, and the son of Mary the virgin, read we not, that he, being a child, was obedient to Mary his mother, and to Joseph her husband? Are Luke ii. not these the words of blessed Luke? "Jesus went down with them, and came to Nazareth, and was obedient unto them."

Father. Owe we such honour and obedience to our fathers and mothers, that we are bound by the commandment of God to obey them in all things, and to do whatsoever they command us? *Son.* The honour and obedience is great, I confess, which the children owe to their parents: notwithstanding, if they command any thing contrary to the word of God, in this behalf they are not to be obeyed. The honour due unto parents is so far to be executed, as it may stand with the honour of God. If it doth in any point obscure that, then is it utterly to be rejected and cast away. And we may right well and with a good conscience say: "We must obey God more than men." Therefore the apostle saith very aptly: "Ye children, obey your fathers and mothers in the Lord; for that is right." Fathers and mothers are none otherwise to be obeyed, than in the Lord, that is to say, than their obedience may stand with the Lord's pleasure and with his holy word. If they command contrary to this, they are by no means to be obeyed. The Father of the spirit and of the new man is more to be honoured and obeyed, than the father of the flesh and of the old man. The honour and obedience toward God, which the law of the first table requireth of us, is more to be regarded, than the honour and obedience toward man, which the law of the second table requireth of us.

How far parents are to be obeyed

Acts v.

Eph. vi.

Father. Give me an ensample of such things, as wherein we may not obey our parents. *Son.* Let it so be, that our parents were so wicked and ungodly, that they would command us to forsake the true living God and his pure religion, and to follow strange gods, and the trifling traditions of men: in this behalf they are not to be obeyed, but we must rather obey God, which saith by Moses his servant, "Thou shalt honour the Lord thy God, and him alone shalt thou serve." Again: "That I command thee, do that only to the Lord: look thou neither put ought thereunto, nor pluck any thing from it." Moreover, let this be the case, that some evil-disposed father and mother would entice their daughter for lucre's sake to play the whore, and to make her body common to other: in this behalf she may by no means obey the commandment of her parents, but she must rather obey God, which saith, "Thou shalt not play the whore: there shall be no whoremonger among the sons of Israel, nor no whore among the daughters of Israel."

Deut. vi.

Deut. xii.

Deut. xxiii.

Father. Prove by the word of God, that the wicked commandments of ungodly parents are not to be obeyed. *Son.* God saith by the prophet: "Walk not in the commandments of your fathers: keep not their ordinances, and defile not yourselves with their idols; for I am the Lord your God. But walk in my statutes: keep my laws, and do them." Again he saith by another prophet: "Be ye not like your fathers, unto whom the prophets cried aforetime, saying, Thus saith the Lord God of hosts: Turn you from your evil ways and from your wicked imaginations. But they would not hear, nor regard me, saith the Lord." Hereto pertaineth the saying of that most noble and virtuous king Ezechias: "Be not ye like your fathers and your brethren, which trespassed against the Lord God of their fathers, which gave them up to be destroyed, as ye see. And now be not ye stiff-necked, like as were your fathers, but yield yourselves unto the Lord, and enter into his holy place, which he hath sanctified for ever, and serve the Lord your God; and the fierceness of his wrath shall turn away from you." Our Saviour Christ saith also: "Think not that I am come to send peace into the earth. I came not to send peace, but a sword. For I am come to set a man at variance against his father, and the daughter against her mother, and the daughter-in-law against her mother-in-law. And a man's foes shall be they that are of his own household. He that loveth father or mother more than me is not worthy of me."

Ezek. xx.

Zech. i.

2 Chron. xxx.

Matt. x.

Father. Hitherto hast thou right well declared, what it is to honour father and mother, and how far honour and obedience is to be shewed unto them. Now declare unto me what is meant by the words that follow: "That thy days may be long in the land, which the Lord thy God giveth thee." *Son.* That we, which of ourselves and of our own nature are too much ingrate, unthankful, ungentle, unkind, yea, churlish, and very unmindful of benefits, those specially, which come from our parents, whom we think to do too little for us, when they be most beneficial toward us, may be provoked, moved, and stirred the more diligently to satisfy this commandment, I mean, to honour our father and mother, God addeth to this his precept a pleasant, bounteous, and liberal promise; which is this, that such as honour their parents from the bottom of their heart, and seek to pleasure them to the uttermost of their power, shall have in this world many good and cheerful days, long, yea, and that quiet and joyful life, good success in all their affairs, abundance of worldly substance, health, peace, rest, comfort, joy, glory, honour, &c. and see their children's children unto the third and fourth generation, as it is written: "Behold, thus shall the man be blessed that feareth the Lord. The Lord from out of Sion shall so bless thee, that thou shalt see Jerusalem in prosperity all thy life long; yea, that thou shalt see thy childer's children, and peace upon Israel."

Psal. cxxviii.

Children disobedient to their parents ought to be punished.

Father. And shall all these good things chance to those children also, that unreverently behave themselves toward their parents? *Son.* Nothing less. For of such children speaketh the holy scripture on this manner. First, God the Father saith: "If any man hath a son, that is stubborn and disobedient, that he will not hearken unto the voice of his father and the voice of his mother, and they have chastened him, and he would not hearken unto them; then shall his father and his mother take him, and bring him out to the elders of that city, and unto the gate of the same place, and say unto the elders of the city, This our son is stubborn and disobedient, and will not hearken unto our voice; he is a rioter, and a drunkard. And all the men of that city shall stone him with stones unto death. And thou shalt put evil away from thee; and all Israel shall hear and fear." Again: "Whosoever he be, that curseth his father or his mother, let him die; for he that curseth his father and mother, his blood be upon him." And again: "He that smiteth his father or mother, let him be slain for it." Also in another place: "Cursed be he that curseth his father and his mother; and all the people shall say, Amen."

Deut. xxi. Lev. xx. Exod. xxi. Deut. xxvii.

The wise man also saith: "He that hurteth his father, and shutteth out his mother, is a shameful and an unworthy son." "Whoso curseth his father and mother, his light shall be put out in the midst of darkness." "Whoso laugheth his father to scorn, and setteth his mother's commandment at nought; the ravens pick out his eyes in the valley, and devoured be he of the young eagles." What miserable end abideth those children which dishonour and disobey their parents, the histories of Heli the priest's children, and of Absolom David's son, do sufficiently declare.

Prov. xix. Prov. xx. Prov. xxx. 1 Sam. iv. 2 Sam. xviii.

Father. It is good therefore, my dear child, that all children give ear to this admonition of the wise man: "Be obedient to thy father that begot thee, and despise not thy mother when she is old." "Do so that thy father and mother may be glad of thee; and that she that bare thee may rejoice."

Prov. xxiii.

But come off, tell me, doth this fifth commandment of God bind us only unto the honour, reverence, service, and obedience of our parents? *Son.* Our schoolmaster, and also our catechist, taught us that this commandment of God doth not only require of us honour and obedience toward our fathers and mothers, but also toward the temporal magistrates, and the ministers of God's word, and toward our elders and all such as be our superiors and governors. For if it be meet and convenient, that we should honour and obey them which are the parents of this our body; is it not also seemly, that we do honour and obey the temporal magistrates, through whose benefit this our body is well governed and enjoy peace and quietness? again, that we reverence the spiritual magistrates, I mean the preachers of God's word, which beget us anew, not with mortal and corruptible seed, but with immortal and uncorruptible seed, I mean, the precious word of God, that word of life and everlasting salvation? Is it not also comely, that we honour and reverence such as excel us, not only in age, but also in learning, wisdom, knowledge, counsel, experience, &c.? All these aforesaid to honour, reverence, and obey, this commandment of God bindeth us: which thing to neglect is great wickedness.

Of honour and obedience toward our superiors.

Of honouring the magistrates. Prov. xxiv.

Father. Prove by the word of God, that we ought to honour and obey the temporal magistrates, no less than our carnal parents. *Son.* Salomon saith: "My son, fear thou the Lord and the king, and keep no company with them that slide back from his fear." Moses saith: "Thou shalt not rail upon the gods (he meaneth the magistrates, which exercise the office of God in the commonweal, and represent the majesty of God), neither blaspheme the ruler of the people." Our Saviour Christ saith: "Give

Exod. xxii. Matt. xxii.

the temporal ruler the things that appertain unto the temporal ruler." St Paul saith: "Let every soul submit himself unto the authority of the higher powers. For there is no power but of God: the powers that be are ordained of God. Whosoever therefore resisteth power resisteth the ordinance of God. But they that resist shall receive to themselves damnation, &c. Wherefore ye must needs obey, not only for fear of vengeance, but also because of conscience. And even for this cause pay ye tribute. For they are God's ministers, serving for the same purpose. Give to every man therefore his duty; tribute, to whom tribute belongeth; custom, to whom custom is due; fear, to whom fear belongeth; honour, to whom honour pertaineth." Again he saith: "Warn them that they submit themselves to rule and power, that they obey the officers," &c. St Peter also saith: "Submit yourselves unto all manner ordinance of man, for the Lord's sake; whether it be unto the king, as unto the chief head; either unto rulers, as unto them that are sent of him for the punishment of evil-doers, but for the praise of them that do well." Again: "Fear God: honour the king." Rom. xiii. Tit. iii. 1 Pet. ii.

Father. Have we any examples in the holy scripture of this honour and obedience toward the higher powers? *Son.* Very many, both in the old and new testament. The Israelites, specially such as were the faithful people of God, were obedient always to Moses their magistrate, and to the other rulers appointed by him, not only men of the temporalty, but also of the spiritualty, as they say; I mean, the priests and the Levites. When Josua in Moses' stead was appointed ruler by God over the Israelites, and commanded them to do certain things at the appointment of God; they answered all with one voice, and said: "All that thou hast commanded us, we will do; and whithersoever thou sendest us, we will go. Even as we obeyed Moses in all things, so will we obey thee: only the Lord thy God be with thee, as he was with Moses. And whosoever he be, that doth disobey thy mouth, and will not hearken unto thy words in all that thou commandest him, let him die. Only be strong and of a good courage." And as the Israelites obeyed Moses and Josua, so likewise did they obey the judges and kings that succeeded them according to the law of God. Examples of obedience to the magistrates. Exod. xxxii. Josh. i.

And this obedience toward the higher powers, as I said before, was not only practised of the temporalty, but also of the spiritualty, to declare that all degrees of estates owe obedience to the temporal power; for Aaron the high priest was obedient to Moses, whom God appointed ruler over his people, and did whatsoever he commanded him. Achimelech the high priest and all the other priests of the Lord were obedient to king Saul, and called themselves his servants, and him their lord, not once resisting the fury of the most furious king, but rather choosing to suffer death patiently under so great a tyrant, than once to resist him disobediently. What shall I speak of David, Salomon, Ezechias, Josaphat, Josias, &c., which had the bishops, priests, and Levites and other spiritual ministers always humble subjects, and obedient unto them without any resistance? The spiritualty is not exempted from obedience to the magistrates. Exod. xxxii. 1 Sam. xxii.

As I may at the last come to the new testament; did not Mary the mother of Christ, and Joseph her husband, obey the commandment of Augustus the emperor, when the whole world should be taxed, and went into their city Bethlehem? Did not Christ teach obedience toward the high powers? Did he not pay tribute? Was not he content to die under the temporal rulers, and confess that their power was given them from above? Did not the apostles of Christ so in like manner both teach and do? Did not Paul willingly ever obey the public magistrates, Festus and Felix, with such like? These histories do sufficiently declare, what honour, reverence, and obedience we owe to the temporal rulers. Luke ii. Matt. xvii. Matt. xxii. Mark xiv. Luke xxii. John xix. Acts xxv.

Neither lack we in the holy scriptures histories also, which do manifestly declare, what a great sin disobedience is, and how grievously God hath punished it. To whom are the histories of Dathan and Abiron, of Zamri and Baasa unknown? of the which the two first, for their sedition, conspiracy, and disobedience against the higher powers were swallowed up alive of the earth, with all that ever they had, so that they went down quick unto hell; the other two most miserably perished. I pass over the histories of Miriam, Aaron's sister, of Theudas, and of Judas Galileus and such like, whom God, for their disobedience toward the higher powers, suffered not to escape unpunished. It is good to follow the example of David, which shewed such honour and reverence Disobedience punished. Num. xvi. 1 Kings xvi. Num. xii. Acts v.

1 Sam. xxvi. to king Saul, being both a wicked ruler, and also his mortal enemy, that he would not once hurt him, nor yet suffer any other to do it, although he had sufficient opportunity and occasion at divers times to have slain him, if he had been minded. "The Lord forbid," saith he, "that I should lay my hand on him." Again: "Kill him
2 Sam. i. not. For who," saith he, "shall lay hands on the Lord's anointed, and be not guilty? The Lord liveth, he dieth not, except the Lord smite him, or that his day be come to die, or else go to battle, and there perish."

How far princes are to be obeyed.

Father. What if the princes be wicked, and command us to do wicked things? Shall we then also obey them? *Son.* In this behalf we owe them no honour, no reverence, no obedience. So long as they are the ministers of God, that is to say, seek the glory of God, the avancement of his holy religion, the increase of virtue, and the
Rom. xiii. suppression of vice, we are bound by the commandment of God to obey them, not only for fear of punishment, but also for conscience sake: but if they cease to be the ministers of God, the promoters of his true religion, the avancers of virtue, and the suppressers of vice, we owe them no honour, no reverence, no obedience in this behalf; but with a
Acts v. good conscience we may say unto them with the apostles: "We must obey God more than men."

Father. How provest thou by the word of God, that magistrates commanding wicked things are not to be obeyed? *Son.* God is the highest magistrate, and his will is to be tendered before the fancy of any inferior magistrate. Therefore if the ☞ inferior magistrate commandeth any thing that is contrary to the commandment of the highest magistrate, I mean God, it is not to be obeyed, but utterly to be rejected and cast away, as these examples of the holy scripture do manifestly prove.

Exod. i. That wicked king Pharao gave out this most wicked commandment to midwives of Egypt, that they should kill all the men-children of the Israelites, and by no means suffer them to live. But the midwives fearing God would not in any condition obey
1 Sam. xxii. this commandment of the king, but suffered the men-children to live. When king Saul commanded his footmen that stood about him to kill the priests of the Lord, the king's servants would not once move their hands to fall upon the priests of the Lord,
Dan. iii. neither would they once touch them. King Nabuchodonozor caused a golden image to be made, and commanded that all his subjects should fall down before it and worship it. Notwithstanding, the servants of God, Sidrach, Misach, and Abednago would by no means worship that idol, but rather choosed to be cast into an hot brenning oven, and so to be consumed unto ashes, than they would once obey the most wicked com-
Dan. vi. mandment of so wicked a king. King Darius made a law, that whosoever did ask any petition either of any god or man within thirty days, except it were only of him, the same person should be cast into the lions' den. But Daniel the servant of God would by no means obey this commandment of the king, but choosed rather to be cast into the lions' den, and so be devoured, than he would cease so long time to
1 Macc. ii. pray unto the Lord his God. Mathathias, when he was commanded of king Antiochus' commissioners to do sacrifice, and to burn incense unto idols, and to forsake the law of God, as many of Juda and Jerusalem had done according to the king's commandment, utterly refused it, and stoutly brast out into the words, saying: "Though all nations obey the king Antiochus, and fall away every man from keeping of the law of their fathers, though they consent to his commandments, yet will I and my sons and my brethren not fall from the law of our fathers. God forbid we should: that were not good for us, that we should forsake the law and ordinances of God, and to agree unto the commandments of king Antiochus. Therefore we will do no such sacrifice, neither break the statutes of our law, to go another way." And when he had spoken these words, there came one of the Jews, which openly in the sight of all did sacrifice unto the idols upon the altar, in the city of Modin, according to the king's commandment. When Mathathias saw this, it grieved him at the heart, so ☞ that his reins shook withal, and his wrath kindled for very zeal of the law. With that he start up, and killed the Jew beside the altar, and slew the king's commissioner, that compelled him to do sacrifice, and destroyed the altar at the same time:
Num. xxv. such a zeal had he unto the law of God, like as Phinehes did unto Zamri, the son of Salom.

What shall I speak of that most noble woman and of her seven sons, which all did rather choose not only to suffer most grievous torments, but also most cruel and bitter death, than they would once obey the king's commandment in eating swine's flesh against the law of God? I pass over the most notable history of that most worthy and ancient father Eleazarus, which, refusing also to obey the king's commandment in eating swine's flesh, desired rather to die gloriously than to live with shame, and so offered himself willingly to the martyrdom, yea, to the very death.

2 Macc. vii.

2 Macc. vi.

The noble enterprise of the apostles is more known, than it needeth here to be recited; which, when they were commanded that they should no more preach in the name of Christ, would not obey the head rulers in this behalf, but continued still in preaching the gospel of Christ diligently. And when they were convented before the magistrates, and demanded why they shewed themselves so disobedient to their commandment, they stoutly and boldly answered: "Whether it be right in the sight of God to hear you rather than God, judge ye. We can none otherwise than speak those things which we have seen and heard." Again: "We must obey God more than men." O courageous hearts!

Acts iv.

Acts v.

And as I may interlace one history, although not mentioned in the sacred bible, yet worthy to be remembered, our catechist, entreating on a certain time of obedience due unto princes, told us this history. "The Roman emperor Diocletian," said he, "commanded one of his captains called Maurice, being a christian man, to prepare an army against the Christians, and utterly to destroy them, except they would give over the faith of Christ, and worship the gods of the Romans, and do sacrifice unto them. But Maurice, valiant not only in body but also in mind, strong in arms, but stronger in faith, courageous in martial affairs, but more courageous in matters of God, stoutly and boldly answered on this manner: 'O emperor, I am ready to serve thee in all thy righteous and honest affairs, neither have I at any time refused to do thee service. Notwithstanding in this behalf, know thou, O emperor, I neither may nor will obey thy commandment, being both wicked and ungodly. For I myself also am a christian man, and must obey God on whom I believe, and of whom I look for the crown of everlasting glory, more than thee, O emperor, of whom I have only mortal and transitory rewards. Therefore be it known unto thee, O emperor, that I will rather suffer my blood to be shed, than once according to thy commandment attempt to hurt any that profess Christ, being linked and joined with me in one faith, baptism, and doctrine[1].'"

The history of St Maurice.

Father. Of the temporal magistrates and of the honour and obedience due to them, we have sufficiently heard. But come off, tell me, doth this fifth commandment of God require of us also, that we honour, reverence, and obey the ministers of God's word? *Son*. Yea, no less than the temporal ministers. For as the one conserveth the body, so doth the other the soul: yea, both of them watch for the safeguard of the body and of the soul.

Of honour and obedience to the minister of God's word.

Father. Declare by the word of God, that we owe no less honour, reverence, and obedience to the ministers of God's word, than we do to the temporal rulers or to our corporal parents. *Son*. The names which be appropriated to the ministers of God's word, do abundantly declare in what great honour and reverence we ought to have them.

The names of the spiritual ministers.

Father. Which are they? *Son*. They be called in the holy scriptures "shepherds," "watchmen," "overseers," "feeders of the Lord's flock," "angels of the Lord," "embassadors of God," "salt of the earth," "light of the world," "fishers of men," "servants of God," "apostles of Christ," "God's labourers," "Christ's ministers," "stewards of the secrets of God," "elders," "prophets," "teachers," "ensamples to the flock," &c. Who, hearing the ministers of God's word to be called with such honourable names, is

Ezek. xxxiv. Ezek. xxxiii. Mal. ii. Matt. v. Matt. iv. Rom. i. 1 Cor. iii. 1 Cor. iv. 1 Pet. v. 1 Cor. xii. 1 Tim. iv. 1 Pet. v.

[[1] The story referred to is that noted one of Mauritius, or Maurice, and the Theban legion. These are said to have perished, to the number of 6660, rather than take any part in the persecution of their brother Christians. There is an account at length extant under the name of Eucherius, bishop of Lyons, though it probably was not from his pen. The speech (of which that in the text seems to be an abstract) is there fully given, as made by the soldiers to Maximian, the colleague of Diocletian. See Acta Sanct. Martyr. Agaunens. Auct. Sanct. Eucherio Lugd. Episc. in Max. Biblioth. Vet. Patr. Lugd. 1677. Tom. VI. p. 867.]

not straightways moved to give honour and reverence unto them, and to esteem them as precious jewels and noble treasures?

Father. But let me hear what the holy scripture speaketh in this behalf. *Son*. The
Ecclus. vii.
wise man saith: "Fear the Lord with all thy soul, and honour his ministers. Love thy Maker with all thy strength, and forsake not his servants. Fear the Lord with all
Deut. xii.
thy soul, and honour his priests." God the Father saith: "Beware that thou forsake not the Levite (he meaneth the minister of his word), as long as thou livest upon the
Matt. x. Luke x.
earth." Our Saviour Christ saith: "He that receiveth you receiveth me; and he that receiveth me receiveth him that sent me. He that heareth you heareth me; and he that despiseth you despiseth me; but he that despiseth me despiseth him that sent me."
1 Thess. iv.
St Paul saith: "He that despiseth despiseth not man (he meaneth the preacher of God's
1 Thess. v.
word) but God, which hath given his holy Spirit into you." "We beseech you, brethren, that ye know them which labour among you, and have the oversight of you in the Lord, and give you exhortation; that ye have them in high reputation, through
1 Tim. v.
love for their work's sake, and be at peace with them." Again: "The elders that rule well are worthy of double honour; but most specially they which labour in the word
Deut. xxv. 1 Cor. ix. Matt. x.
and teaching. For the scripture saith: Thou shalt not muzzle the mouth of the ox, that treadeth out the corn. And, The labourer is worthy of his reward. Against an elder receive none accusation, but under two or three witnesses." Also in another place
Heb. xii.
he saith: "Obey them that have the oversight of you, and submit yourselves unto them; for they watch for your souls, even as they that must give accompts, that they may do it with joy, and not with grief. For that is a profitable thing for you."

Father. If any man sheweth disobedience to the ministers of God's word, and will not honour nor reverence them according to the commandment of God, shall they
Luke x.
escape unpunished? *Son*. Heard ye not before what Christ saith? "He that despiseth you despiseth me; and he that despiseth me despiseth him that sent me." Can there be any greater dishonour be done to a prince, than when his embassador is evil entreated? Can that king take in good part the disobedience of those subjects which disobey and resist his commission, published for their wealth by his officers? No more can God abide that his embassadors and commissioners, I mean the preachers of his holy word, should be contemned, despised, and not regarded, or their sermons, which are the
Disobedience punished.
infallible oracles of God, neglected and nothing set by. Yea, such despisers of God's preachers, and of their doctrine, did never, nor never shall, escape unpunished.

Gen. iii.
What drove Adam and Heva out of paradise into this vale of misery, making them of immortal mortal, of uncorruptible corruptible, of God's friends God's enemies, of the inheritors of everlasting glory firebrands of hell, &c., but disobedience to God and
Gen. vii.
to his holy word? What caused the whole world once to be drowned, eight persons only excepted, but disobedience to the preachers and to their doctrine? Again, what
Gen. xix.
provoked God to consume Sodom and Gomorre, and certain other cities, with fire and brimstone from heaven, but that they contemned the preacher of God's word, and his heavenly doctrine? What was the occasion that God did so oftentimes plague with hunger, sword, fire, and pestilence, the Israelites, but that they despised the prophets of God and their preachings? How came it to pass that whole Jewry came to havoc, and finally both destruction and desolation, certain years after Christ's ascension, but that they did nothing regard the doctrine of Christ and of his apostles, but utterly sought the decay and utter confusion of them both? How doth our Saviour Christ cry out against certain cities, which despised the preachers and the doctrine that they taught!
Matt. xi. Luke x.
Are not these his words? "Wo unto thee, Chorasin! wo unto thee, Bethsaida! for if the miracles which were shewed in you had been done in the city of Tyre or Sidon, they had repented of their sins long agone in sackcloth and ashes. Nevertheless, I say unto you, it shall be easier for Tyre and Sidon at the day of judgment, than for you. And thou, Caparnaum, which art lift up unto heaven, shall be brought down to hell. For if the miracles which have been done in thee had been shewed in Sodom, they had remained until this day. Nevertheless, I say unto you, it shall be easier for the land of Sodom at the day of judgment, than for thee."

How far the spiritual ministers are to be obeyed.
Father. What if they which take upon them to be the ministers of Christ and the preachers of his word, teach false doctrine, and the traditions of men, corrupting rather

than correcting our minds with their wicked doctrine, and labouring to bring us rather unto the perdition than salvation of our souls? Shall we also in this behalf honour, reverence, and obey them? *Son.* Nothing less. For they are now no more the ministers of Christ, but the servants of antichrist; no more the angels of light, but the messengers of darkness; no more the sons of God, but the bond-slaves of the devil. Therefore have we nothing to do with them. For they sit not in the chair of Moses, but in the chair of pestilence; so that, if they require any obedience of us because they occupy the place, and yet not the office, of Christ's ministers, we may with a good conscience refuse so to do, and say with the apostles, "We must obey God more than men." Christ sent forth his disciples to preach, not their own fancies, nor the traditions of their forefathers, but the gospel. "Go and preach the gospel," saith he, "to every creature." "Wo be unto me," saith St Paul, "if I preach not the gospel!" The aforesaid apostle in a certain epistle writeth on this manner: "Though we ourselves or an angel from heaven preach any other gospel unto you, than that which we have preached unto you, hold it accursed. As we said before, so say I now again: If any man preach unto you any other gospel than that ye have received, hold it accursed." St John also saith: "If there come any unto you, and bring not this learning, him receive not to house, neither bid him God speed. For he that biddeth him God speed is partaker of his evil deeds." Such therefore as will be counted true ministers of Christ, and zealous preachers of his holy word, must observe this rule of St Peter: "If any man speak, let him so speak, that it be agreeable to God's word;" and so are they worthy to be honoured, reverenced, and obeyed, as spiritual fathers, according to the commandment of God: otherwise there is neither honour, reverence, nor obedience due unto them, as our Saviour Christ saith: "Ye are the salt of the earth. But if the salt have lost his saltness, what shall be seasoned therewith? It is thenceforth good for nothing, but to cast out, and to be trodden down of men."

Matt. xxiii. Psal. i. Acts v. Matt. xxviii. Mark xvi. Luke xxiv. John xx. 1 Cor. ix. Gal. i. 2 John. 1 Pet. iv. Matt. v.

Father. As I remember, thou saidst that your schoolmaster and also your catechist taught you, that not only corporal fathers and mothers, magistrates, and preachers are commanded to be honoured, reverenced, and obeyed, but also our elders, and all such as be our superiors and governors. *Son.* Truth it is.

Of honour and obedience to our elders, governors, and superiors.

Father. What meanest thou by elders? *Son.* Such as do excel us in age, wisdom, discretion, knowledge, learning, experience, &c.

Father. How provest thou by the holy scripture, that we ought to reverence our elders? *Son.* God saith by his servant Moses: "Thou shalt rise up before the hoar-headed, and reverence the face of the old man, and dread thy God; for I am the Lord." The wise man also saith: "Keep company with the multitude of such elders as have understanding, and consent unto their wisdom with thine heart, that thou mayest hear all godly sermons, and that the worthy sentences escape thee not. And if thou seest a man of discreet understanding, get thee soon unto him, and let thy foot tread upon the steps of his doors." Again: "Think scorn of no man in his old age; for we wax old also, &c. Despise not the sermons of such elders as have understanding, but acquaint thyself with the wise sentences of them; for of them thou shalt learn wisdom, and the doctrine of understanding, and how to serve great men without complaint. Go not from the doctrine of the elders; for they have learned it of their fathers. For of them shalt thou learn understanding, so that thou mayest make answer in the time of need." Also in another place he saith: "If thou be among men of higher authority, desire not to compare thyself unto them; and when an elder speaketh, make not thou many words." Hereto agreeth the saying of St Paul: "Rebuke not an elder rigorously, but exhort him as a father; the younger men as brethren; the elder women as mothers; the younger as sisters with all pureness."

Lev. xix. Ecclus. vi. Ecclus. viii. Ecclus. xxxii. 1 Tim. v.

Father. But what if our elders require those things to be done of us, which manifestly fight with the word of the Lord, and be contrary to the glory and honour of God? Shall we then hearken unto them, and obey them? *Son.* Yea, we shall rather say with the apostles, as we heard afore: "We must obey God more than men."

How far our superiors are to be obeyed. Acts v.

Father. What meanest thou by superiors and governors, whom this commandment also, as thou sayest, bindeth us to honour, reverence, and obey? *Son.* Schoolmasters, teachers, tutors, patrons, masters of occupations, &c. For St Paul saith: "Obey them

Heb. xiii.

that have the oversight of you, and submit yourselves unto them." And that servants ought to honour and obey their bodily masters, appear plainly by these exhortations of St Paul: "Ye servants," saith he, "obey them that are your bodily masters, with fear and trembling, even with the singleness of your heart, as unto Christ; not doing service unto the eye, as they that go about to please men; but as the servants of Christ, doing the will of God from the heart, with a good will, serving the Lord and not men; knowing this, that whatsoever good thing any man doeth, the same shall he receive again of God, whether he be bond or free." Again: "Let as many servants as be under the yoke count their masters worthy of all honour, that the name of God, and his doctrine, be not evil spoken of. See that they which have believing masters despise them not because they are brethren, but rather do service; forasmuch as they are believing and beloved, and partakers of the benefit." Also in another place: "Exhort servants to be obedient unto their own masters, and to please them in all things, not answering again, neither to be pickers, but that they shew all good faithfulness, that they may do worship to the doctrine of God our Saviour in all things." St Peter also saith: "Ye servants, obey your masters with fear, not only if they be good and courteous, but also though they be froward. For it is thankworthy, if a man for conscience toward God endure grief, and suffer wrong undeserved."

Eph. vi. Col. iii. — 1 Tim. vi. — Tit. ii.

Father. If the schoolmasters, teachers, tutors, patrons, masters of occupations, or any other of our superiors and governors should command us that which striveth with the glory, honour, and word of God, is it to be obeyed? *Son.* You heard before what I said concerning honour, reverence, service, and obedience due unto men, of whatsoever degree or estate they be. If it may not stand with the honour, reverence, service, and obedience, which we owe unto God, it is utterly to be rejected and cast away. For the honour of God is to be considered before the honour of man. Therefore in this behalf, if they require of us any honour, reverence, service, and obedience, that cannot stand with our duty toward God, we may with a good conscience answer with the apostles, and say: "Whether it be right in the sight of God to hear you rather than God, judge ye." "We must obey God more than men."

Acts iv. v.

Father. Thou hast satisfied me right well in this fifth commandment. Come off, rehearse unto me the next precept, as it followeth in order.

The sixth commandment.

Son. "Thou shalt not kill."

What God requireth in the sixth commandment.

Father. What doth God require of us in this his commandment? *Son.* First of all, that no private person shall kill another, although injuried and wronged.

Lev. xix. — Prov. xx. — Rom. xii. — Deut. xxxii. — Prov. xxv.

Father. Prove that by the word of God. *Son.* God saith: "Thou shalt not avenge thyself, nor be mindful of wrong against the children of my people, but shalt love thy neighbour even as thyself." The wise man also saith: "Say not thou, I will recompense evil; but put thy trust in the Lord; and he shall defend thee." Hereto agreeth the saying of the apostle: "Recompense to no man evil for evil. Provide aforehand things honest, nor only before God, but also in the sight of all men. If it be possible (so much as is in you), live peaceably with all men. Dearly beloved, avenge not yourselves, but rather give place unto wrath. For it is written, Vengeance is mine, I will reward, saith the Lord. Therefore if thine enemy hunger, feed him: if he thirst, give him drink: for in so doing thou shalt heap coals of fire on his head. Be not overcome of evil, but overcome evil with goodness."

Wilful and pretensed murder unpardonable.

Father. What if any man, overcome with ire and madness for the avengement of his own private cause, killeth his neighbour? Shall he be pardoned, and not rather suffer death? *Son.* Whosoever committeth wilful and pretensed murder ought not to be pardoned, but rather to be killed, as he hath killed.

Gen. ix. — Lev. xxiv.

Father. How provest thou that by the word of God? *Son.* God saith: "Whoso sheddeth man's blood, his blood shall be shed again. For in the image of God did God make man." Again: "He that killeth any man, let him die the death." "And if a man maim his neighbour, as he hath done, so shall it be done to him again; broke[1] for broke, eye for eye, and tooth for tooth: even as he hath maimed a man,

[[1] Broke: breach.]

so shall he be maimed again." Also in another place: "He that smiteth a man, that he die, shall be slain for it." Our Saviour Christ said unto Peter: "Put up thy sword into his sheath; for all they that take the sword shall perish with the sword." Exod. xxi. Matt. xxvi.

Father. Is it not lawful by any means to kill? *Son*. For a private man it is not lawful: for a temporal magistrate it is lawful. The magistrates may lawfully kill offenders.

Father. Where findest thou that in the word of God? *Son*. God speaking to the temporal ruler saith: "Thou shalt have no pity on him (the murderer), but thou shalt require soul for soul, eye for eye, tooth for tooth, foot for foot, hand for hand." David, that most noble king, saith in a certain psalm: "I shall soon destroy all the ungodly that are in the land, that I may root out all wicked doers from the city of the Lord." The apostle also saith: "Rulers are not to be feared of them that do well, but of them that do evil. Wilt thou be without fear of the power? Do well then, and so shalt thou be praised of the same: for he is the minister of God for thy wealth. But if thou do that which is evil, then fear; for he beareth not the sword for nought. For he is the minister of God to take vengeance on him that doeth evil." St Peter also saith, that the "rulers are ordained of God for the punishment of the evil-doers, but for the praise of them that do well." Psal. ci. Rom. xiii. 1 Pet. ii.

Father. What doth God require more of us in this his precept? *Son*. Secondly, he requireth of us not only that we should not kill, but also that we should bear no hatred, anger, nor malice in our hearts against our neighbour.

Father. For this cause then is the law called of St Paul "spiritual," because it requireth not of us only outward and civil righteousness, but also inward and spiritual justice, even pure and uncorrupt motions of the mind; so that the law must be fulfilled both with the inward and outward man, both with body and soul. *Son*. Yea, verily; and so doth our Saviour Christ interpret and expound the whole law of God contrary to the doctrine of the scribes and Pharisees. Rom. vii. Why the law of God is called spiritual. Matt. v.

Father. Let me hear it proved by the word of God, that we are forbidden to bear any hatred, anger, malice, envy, displeasure, &c. in our hearts against our neighbour. *Son*. God saith: "Thou shalt not stand against the blood of thy neighbour: I am the Lord. Thou shalt not hate thy brother in thy heart, but shalt in anywise rebuke thy neighbour, that thou bear not sin for his sake." The wise man saith: "There are six things which the Lord doth hate, and the seventh he utterly abhorreth: a proud look; a lying tongue; hands that shed innocent blood; an heart that goeth about with wicked imaginations; feet that be swift in running to do mischief; a false witness that bringeth up lies; and such one as soweth discord among brethren." Our Saviour Christ saith: "Ye have heard that it was said to them of the old time, Thou shalt not kill; for whosoever killeth shall be in danger of judgment. But I say unto you, that whosoever is angry with his brother shall be in danger of judgment; and whosoever saith unto his brother, Racha, shall be in danger of a council; but whosoever saith, Thou fool, shall be in danger of hell-fire. Therefore if thou offerest thy gift at the altar, and there rememberest, that thy brother hath ought against thee; leave there thine offering before the altar, and go thy way first, and be reconciled to thy brother, and then come and offer thy gift. Agree with thine adversary quickly, whiles thou art in the way with him; lest at any time thy adversary deliver thee to the judge, and the judge deliver thee to the minister, and then thou be cast into prison. Verily, I say unto thee, Thou shalt not come out thence, till thou hast paid the uttermost farthing." St Paul saith: "Let all bitterness, and fierceness, and wrath, and roaring, and cursed speaking be put away from you, with all maliciousness. Be ye courteous one to another, merciful, forgiving one another, even as God for Christ's sake hath forgiven you." Hereto appertaineth the saying of St John: "He that loveth not his brother abideth in death. Whosoever hateth his brother is a manslayer; and ye know that no manslayer hath eternal life abiding in him." Lev. xix. Prov. vi. Matt. v. Eph. iv. 1 John iii.

Father. I perceive now right well, that we may not only not kill, hurt, or noy our neighbour in any condition, either with hand, weapon, tongue, &c., but also that we may not so much as once hate him, or bear malice or anger in our hearts toward him, although it should never brast out either into word or deed: if we do, we are transgressors of the law of God, and before the majesty of God plain murderers and manslayers. *Son.* So is it.

Father. Who can so warely and circumspectly walk in the pathways of christian charity, or so continue in brotherly love, but that sometime he falleth into anger and displeasure with his neighbour? *Son.* We are all frail indeed, and ready at every hour to fall. Therefore if at any time we pass the bounds of charity, and slip into the rage
Psal. iv. Eph. iv. of anger, it is good to follow this most wholesome counsel of the apostle: "Be angry and sin not. Let not the sun go down upon your wrath, neither give place unto the backbiter."

Father. We may not then continue in anger, nor seek to be revenged? *Son.* No,
Matt. v. verily, but seek rather to be reconciled, as our Saviour commandeth us in the gospel.
Ecclus. xxviii. For the wise man saith: "He that seeketh vengeance shall find vengeance at the Lord's hand, which shall surely keep him his sins. Forgive thy neighbour the hurt that he hath done thee; and so shall thy sins be forgiven thee also when thou prayest. A man that beareth hatred against another, how dare he desire forgiveness of God? He that sheweth no mercy to a man, which is like himself, how dare he ask forgiveness of his sins? If he that is but flesh beareth hatred and keepeth it, who will entreat for his sins? Remember the end, and let enmity pass, which seeketh death and destruction; and abide thou in the commandments. Remember the commandments; so shalt thou not be rigorous over thy neighbour. Think upon the covenant of the Highest, and forgive thy neighbour's ignorance. Beware of strife, and thou shalt make thy sins fewer. For an angry man kindleth variance, and the ungodly disquieteth friends, and putteth discord among them that be at peace."

Father. What is required of us more in this precept? *Son.* Thirdly, God requireth of us not only that we should not kill, hurt, noy, or bear secretly in our hearts any anger or displeasure against our neighbour, but also that we should patiently suffer whatsoever is unjustly done against us, and for evil recompense goodness; when we are evil spoken of, speak well; when we are cursed, bless; when we are railed upon, give good words; when we are injuried, forgive; when we have displeasure done unto us, do good, &c.

Father. Where are these things taught in the holy scripture? *Son.* That we ought patiently to suffer, whatsoever is unjustly done against us, we have our master Christ, whose disciples we profess ourselves to be, for a most manifest example, of whom
1 Pet. ii. St Peter writeth on this manner: "Christ suffered for us, leaving us an ensample that ye should follow his steps; which did no sin, neither was there guile found in his mouth; which, when he was reviled, reviled not again; when he suffered, he threatened not, but commit the vengeance to him that judgeth righteously." St Paul also exhorteth
Eph. iv. us, that "with all lowliness and meekness, and with all humbleness of mind, we should forbear one another through love, and be diligent to keep the unity of the Spirit through
Col. iii. the bond of peace:" again, that we should "forgive one another, if any man have a quarrel against another, even as Christ hath forgiven us."

Father. Where are we taught to recompense evil with good? *Son.* St Paul saith:
1 Thess. v. "See that none recompense evil for evil unto any man; but ever follow that which is
Rom. xii. good, both among yourselves and to all men." Again: "Recompense to no man evil for evil, &c. Avenge not yourselves, but rather give place unto wrath. For it is
Deut. xxxii. Prov. xxv. written, Vengeance is mine, I will reward, saith the Lord. Therefore if thine enemy hunger, feed him; if he thirst, give him drink: for in so doing, thou shalt heap coals of fire on his head. Be not overcome of evil, but overcome evil with goodness."

Father. Where readest thou, that when we are evil spoken of, we should speak well, &c.? *Son.* Our Saviour Christ, that most perfect schoolmaster of all perfect righte-
Matt. v. Exod. xxi. Deut. xix. ousness, saith: "Ye have heard that is said, An eye for an eye, and a tooth for a tooth. But I say unto you, that ye resist not evil. But whosoever giveth thee a blow on the right cheek, turn to him the other also. And if any man will sue thee at the law, and take away thy coat, let him have thy cloke also. And whosoever will compel thee to go a mile, go with him twain. Give to him that asketh thee, and from him that would borrow, turn not thou away. Ye have heard that is said, Thou shalt love thy neighbour, and hate thine enemy. But I say unto you, Love your

enemies: bless them that curse you: do good to them that hate you: pray for them which hurt you and persecute you; that ye may be children of your Father which is in heaven. For he maketh his sun to arise on the evil and on the good, and sendeth rain on the righteous and on the unrighteous. For if ye love them which love you, what reward have ye? do not the publicans also even the same? And if ye make much of your brethren only, what singular thing do ye? do not also the publicans likewise? Ye shall therefore be perfect, even as your Father which is in heaven is perfect." St Paul also saith: "Bless them which persecute you: bless, I say, and curse not." Rom. xii. Hereto agreeth the saying of St Peter: "Be ye all of one mind, of one heart, love 1 Pet. iii. as brethren, be pitiful, be courteous, meek, not rendering evil for evil, or rebuke for rebuke; but contrariwise, bless, knowing that ye are thereunto called, even that ye should be heirs of the blessing. For he that doth long after life, and loveth to see Psal. xxxiv. good days, let him refrain his tongue from evil, and his lips that they speak not guile: let him eschew evil, and do good: let him seek peace, and ensue it."

Father. Declare now in few words what God forbiddeth, and what he requireth, in this his sixth commandment, that we may proceed with the residue. *Son*. God forbiddeth us that outwardly we should kill, hurt, noy, hinder, strike, or smite our neighbour, or yet speak and report evil of him, or hinder his good name, or ungently entreat either him or any that do belong unto him. That same God forbiddeth us that inwardly we should malign, envy, or hate our neighbour. And the same Lord our God requireth of us, that [we] patiently suffer whatsoever is unjustly done against us; that we speak well of our neighbour; that we maintain his good name; that we further his commodity and profit; and seek all means possible, as to love him with our heart unfeignedly, so most readily to do for him and his to the uttermost of his power, that we may satisfy the will of God, which saith: "Thou shalt love thy Lev. xix. neighbour as thyself." Again: "What ye would other men would do to you, do you Matt. xxii. Rom. xiii. the same to them." Matt. vii. Luke vi.

Father. Let us hear the next commandment. *Son*. The next is the seventh in order, and soundeth thus:

"Thou shalt not commit adultery." The seventh commandment.

Father. What doth God forbid, or what requireth he, in this commandment? *Son*. First, forasmuch as God is the institutor and ordainer of the holy state of Gen. ii. Matt. xix. honourable wedlock, he utterly forbiddeth that such as profess that godly order, and What God forbiddeth in the seventh commandment. have chosen that kind of life, should in any point defile themselves with whoredom, adultery, or with any kind of filthy uncleanness or unclean filthiness; but that they 1 Cor. vii. should live together in all godliness, purity, cleanness, and honesty all the days of Heb. xiii. their life, according to their promise made of one to the other, without the knowledge Of married persons. of any strange flesh, that God may bless them and their marriage, and make them joyful parents of many children, which in this world may be good members of the christian commonweal, and in the world to come blessed citizens of that glorious and heavenly Jerusalem.

Father. Declare unto me by the word of God, that such as be married ought not to break their marriage vow, nor defile themselves with adultery or any other uncleanness.

Son. God saith: "The man that breaketh wedlock with another man's wife, even Lev. xx. he that breaketh wedlock with his neighbour's wife, let him be slain, both the advouterer and the advouteress." Again: "Cursed be he that lieth with his neighbour's Deut. xxvii. wife; and all the people shall say, Amen." The wise man saith: "Keep thee from Prov. vi. the evil woman, and from the flattering tongue of the harlot, that thou lust not after her beauty in thy heart, and lest thou be taken with her fair looks. An harlot will make a man to beg his bread; but an honest married wife will hunt for the precious life. May a man carry fire in his bosom, and his clothes not be brent? Or can one go upon hot coals, and his feet not be hurt? Even so whosoever goeth in to his neighbour's wife, and toucheth her, cannot be unguilty. Men do not utterly despise a thief that stealeth to satisfy his soul, when he is hungry; but if he may be gotten, he restoreth again seven times as much, or else he maketh recompence with all the

The fruits of whoredom. goods of his house: but whoso committeth adultery with a woman, he is a fool, and bringeth his life to destruction. He getteth himself also shame and dishonour, such as shall never be put out. For the jealousy and wrath of the man will not be entreated: no, though thou wouldest offer him great gifts to make amends, he will not receive Tob. iv. them." The ancient father Tobie said to his son: "My son, keep thee well from whoredom; and beside thy wife see that no fault be known of thee." Job also saith: Job xxxi. "I made a covenant with mine eyes, that I would not look upon a damsel. For how great a portion shall I have of God, and what inheritance from the Almighty on high? As for the ungodly, and he that joineth himself to the company of wicked doers, shall not destruction and misery come upon him? &c. If my heart hath lusted after my neighbour's wife, or if I have laid wait at his door; O then let my wife grind unto another man, and let other men lie with her. For this is a wickedness and sin, that is worthy to be punished; yea, a fire that should utterly consume and root out all my Ecclus. xli. substance." Jesus, the son of Sirach, saith: "Be ashamed of whoredom before father and mother. Be ashamed of lying before the prince and men of authority; of sin before the judge and ruler; of offence before the congregation and people; of unrighteousness before a companion and friend; of theft before thy neighbours. As for the truth of God and his covenant, be not ashamed thereof. Be ashamed to lie with thine elbows upon the bread: be ashamed to look upon harlots: be ashamed to turn away thy face from thy friend. Be ashamed to take and not to give: be ashamed also to look upon another man's wife, and to make many trifling words with her maiden, or to stand by her bedside. Be ashamed to upbraid thy friend: when thou givest any thing, cast him not in the teeth withal."

Of unmarried persons. *Father*. Are such only as are married forbidden to lead an incontinent life? *Son*. Both the married and unmarried are forbidden in this precept to exercise any corporal uncleanness in their life and conversation: whether they be linked with the chain of matrimony, or free from it, this commandment forbiddeth them to practise any kind of incontinency in their manners. Not only adultery, which (as they say) is committed between two married persons unlawful, or between a married and a single person, is here Deut. xxiii. forbidden; but also fornication, which is the sin of uncleanness committed between two single or unmarried persons, as some writeth. To be short, God, speaking on this manner, "Thou shalt not commit adultery," forbiddeth all unlawful knowledge of man and woman, be they married or unmarried.

Father. Prove by the word of God, that not only adultery, but fornication also and Deut. xxiii. all other uncleanness, is forbidden. *Son*. God saith: "There shall be no whore of the Lev. xix. daughters of Israel, nor whore-keeper of the sons of Israel." Again: "Thou shalt not make thy daughter common, that thou wouldest cause her to be an whore, lest the land Prov. ii. also fall to whoredom, and be full of wickedness." The wise man saith: "When wisdom entereth into thine heart, and thy soul delighteth in knowledge, then shall counsel preserve thee, and understanding shall keep thee;" "that thou mayest be delivered from the strange woman, and from her that is not thine own; which giveth sweet words, forsaketh the husband of her youth, and forgetteth the covenant of her God. For her house is inclined unto death, and her paths unto hell. All they that go in unto her come not again, neither take they hold of the word of life. Therefore walk thou in the way of such as be virtuous, and keep the paths of the righteous. For the just shall dwell in the land, and they that be perfect shall remain in it; but the ungodly shall be rooted out Prov. v. of the land, and the wicked doers shall be rooted out of it." Again: "Apply not thyself to the deceitfulness of a woman. For the lips of an harlot are a dropping honeycomb, and her throat is more glistering than oil: but at the last she is as bitter as wormwood, and her tongue as sharp as a two-edged sword. Her feet go down unto ☞ death, and her steps pierce through unto hell, &c. Keep thy way far from her, and come not nigh the doors of her house; that thou give not thy strength unto other, and thy years to the cruel; that other men be not filled with thy goods, and that thy labours come not in a strange house; yea, that thou mourn not at the last, when thou hast spent thy body and lusty green youth, and then say, Alas! why hated I nurture? why did my heart despise correction? wherefore was I not obedient unto the voice of my teachers, and hearkened not unto them that informed me? I am come almost into all misfortune, in the midst of the multitude and congregation, &c. Be glad with the wife of thy youth. Loving is the hind, and friendly is the roe. Let her breasts always satisfy thee, and hold thee ever content with her love. My son, why wilt thou have pleasure in an harlot, and embrace the bosom of another woman? For every man's ways are open in the sight of the Lord; and he pondereth all their goings. The wickedness of the ungodly shall catch himself, and with the snares of his own sins shall he be trapped," &c. "Hear me now, therefore, O my children, and mark the words of my mouth. Let not thine heart wander in the ways of an whore, and be not thou deceived in her paths. For many one hath she wounded and cast down: yea, many a strong man hath been slain by the means of her. Her houses are the way unto hell, and bring men down into the chambers of death." Prov. vii.

The holy apostle St Paul saith: "If any that is called a brother (that is to say, a Christian) be an whoremonger, or a covetous person, or a worshipper of images, either a railer, either a drunkard, or an extortioner; with him that is such see that ye eat not." Again: "Know ye not, that your bodies are the members of Christ? Shall I now take the members of Christ, and make them the members of an harlot? God forbid. Do ye not know, that he which coupleth himself with an harlot is become one body? For two, saith he, shall be one flesh. But he that is joined to the Lord is one spirit. Flee fornication. Every sin that a man doeth is without the body: but he that is a fornicator sinneth against his own body. Either know ye not, how that your bodies are the temple of the Holy Ghost, which dwelleth in you, whom ye have of God, and how that ye are not your own? For ye are dearly bought. Therefore glorify God in your bodies, and in your spirits, which are God's." "Be not deceived. For neither fornicators, neither worshippers of images, neither advouterers, neither weaklings, neither abusers of themselves with mankind, neither thieves, neither covetous persons, neither drunkards, neither cursed speakers, neither pillers shall inherit the kingdom of God." Again: "Let us not be defiled with fornication, as some of them (the Israelites) were defiled with fornication, and fell in one day twenty-three thousand." "For this is the will of God, even your holiness, that ye should abstain from fornication, and that every one of you should know how to keep his vessel in holiness and honour, and not in the lust of concupiscence, as do the heathen, which know not God, &c. For God hath not called us unto uncleanness, but unto holiness." Also in another place: "Mortify your earthy members, fornication, uncleanness, unnatural lust, evil concupiscence," &c. Item: "Wedlock is honourable among all persons, and the bed undefiled. But whoremongers and adulterers God shall judge." 1 Cor. v. 1 Cor. vi. Gen. ii. Matt. xix. Mark x. 1 Cor. x. Num. xxv. 1 Thess. iv. Col. iii. Heb. xiii.

Father. Doth God forbid us none other thing in this commandment, but only to abstain from the gross sin of adultery, fornication, incest, and such other corporal uncleanness? *Son*. All filthy talk, wanton countenances, singing of bawdy ballads, reading of amorous books, idle jesting, vain pastimes, and whatsoever maketh unto the provocation of fleshly appetite, as idleness, banqueting, wanton company-keeping, &c. is here also forbidden. All enticements to uncleanness are forbidden.

Father. Is it not then lawful to use merry talk, singing of pleasant ballads, reading of amorous books, &c.? *Son*. By no means. For St Paul saith: "Let no filthy communication proceed out of your mouth, but that which is good to edify withal, as oft as need is, that it may minister grace unto the hearers. And grieve not ye the Holy Spirit of God, by whom ye are sealed unto the day of redemption." Again: "Let your speech be always well-savoured, and powdered with salt, that ye may know how ye ought to answer every man." Also in another place: "As for fornication, and all uncleanness, or covetousness, let it not be once named among you, as it becometh saints; or filthiness, or foolish talking, or jesting, which are not comely, but rather giving of thanks. For this ye know, that no whoremonger, either unclean person, or covetous person (which is a worshipper of images) hath any inheritance in the kingdom of Christ and of God. Let no man deceive you with vain words: for because of such things cometh the wrath of God upon the children of [un]belief. Be not ye therefore companions of them." Eph. iv. Col. iv. Eph. v.

Father. Are we only forbidden in this precept the uncleanness of the body? *Son*. Not only. For God forbiddeth us here also the impurity and uncleanness of the mind.

7—2

The law of God, as you know, is spiritual, and must be fulfilled not only outwardly
but also inwardly, even with pure affects and clean motions of the heart. For even
as he is very murderer and manslayer before God, which beareth hatred and malice in
his heart against his neighbour, although he never lay hand on him, nor hurt him
outwardly; so likewise is he a very adulterer and whoremonger before God, which
nourisheth fleshly lusts in his heart, although he never commit the outward uncleanness.
John iv. For as "God is a Spirit," so judgeth he all things of the spirit. If our hearts be once
polluted and defiled with the evil lust and filthy concupiscence of any woman, we are
straightways no less adulterers and fornicators before God, than we are before men,
when we have outwardly committed the very act. And as I am guilty and worthy
☞ before men, when I have so wickedly behaved myself, of punishment, yea, of very death;
so likewise am I before God guilty and worthy of everlasting damnation, so soon as the
evil concupiscence entereth into my heart, and I with delight consent to the same.

Matt. v. *Father.* How provest thou this? *Son.* By the words of Christ, which saith: "Ye
have heard, that it was said to them of old time, Thou shalt not commit adultery: but
I say unto you, that whosoever looketh on another man's wife to lust after her, hath
committed adultery with her already in his heart. Therefore if thy right eye hinder
thee, pluck him out, and cast him from thee. For better is it unto thee, that one member
perish, than that thy whole body should be cast into hell." "And if thy right hand
hinder thee, cut him off, and cast him from thee. For better it is unto thee, that one
Matt. xv. of thy members perish, than that all thy body should be cast into hell." Again: "Those
things which proceed out of the mouth come from the heart, and they defile the man.
For out of the heart proceed evil thoughts, murders, breaking of wedlock, whoredoms,
thefts, false witness, blasphemies. These are the things which defile a man." St Paul
Col. iii. also saith: "Mortify your earthy members, fornications, uncleanness, unnatural lust,
1 Pet. ii. evil concupiscence," &c. Hereto agreeth the saying of St Peter: "Dearly beloved, I
beseech you as strangers and pilgrims, abstain from fleshly lusts, which fight against
the soul; and see that ye have honest conversation among the gentiles, that, whereas
they backbite you as ill-doers, they may see your good works, and praise God in the
day of visitation."

Father. Hath God at any time plagued this sin of adultery, whoredom, &c.? *Son.*
Whoredom plagued. Yea, very oft, and that most grievously.

Father. Shew me that out of the holy scripture. *Son.* To whom is this unknown,
Gen. vi. that the whole world was once drowned, eight persons only except? Was not whoredom
Gen. xix. one of the chief causes why the world was thus plagued with waters? Sodom with
certain other cities were consumed with fire and brimstone from heaven: was not un-
cleanness of life a great occasion hereof? Were not the citizens of Sichem slain, because
Gen. xxxiv. their prince deflowered Dina, Jacob's daughter? Were there not slain in the wilderness
Num. xxv. 1 Cor. x. twenty-three thousand men for whoredom? Was not the whole tribe of Benjamin after-
Judg. xx. ward almost utterly destroyed for abusing a Levite's wife? Perished not the sons of Heli
1 Sam. ii. the priest in battle, because of their too much unshamefaced wickedness committed with
2 Sam. xi. women? Who knoweth not, into what great miseries David fell, and his kingdom also,
for the adultery which he committed with Urias' wife? How was Salomon plagued
1 Kings xi. for his too much licentious living with women? Was not his most excellent wisdom
turned into most extreme foolishness, when at the enticement of women he fell from
honouring the true God unto the worshipping of idols? So true is it, which the prophet
Hos. iv. hath: "Whoredom, wine, and drunkenness take away the heart." Many other and
1 Cor. vi. Eph. v. divers histories are found in the holy bible, which do sufficiently declare, how grievously
1 Thess. iv. Heb. xiii. God hath plagued adultery, whoredom, and all uncleanness, in every age; as I may speak
nothing of the most grievous plague, which is everlasting damnation.

Father. Seeing that God doth so greatly detest and abhor this abominable vice of
uncleanness; come off, tell me how it may be eschewed, that we provoke not God
unto anger, and procure unto us his heavy displeasure, seeing, as the apostle saith,
Heb. x. "it is a dreadful thing to fall into the hands of the living God." *Son.* To lead an
honest, pure, and continent life, is the gift of God, and cannot be obtained by our own
Wisd. viii. strengths, as the wise man saith: "I know that I cannot be chaste, except God giveth
Matt. xix. the gift:" and as our Saviour Christ saith: "All men cannot away with this saying

(he meaneth, to lead a single life and unmarried) but they to whom it is given." Notwithstanding, certain remedies may be devised against these most abominable sins of adultery and whoredom, which to practise it shall neither be ungodly nor unprofitable.

Father. Which are they? Let me hear them. *Son*. First, when Satan, that old adversary of mankind, which, as St Peter saith, "goeth about like a roaring lion, seeking whom he may devour," goeth about to attempt us unto incontinency, adultery, whoredom, incest, or unto any other uncleanness, which fighteth with the word of God; it shall be necessary to set before our eyes, not the desire of the flesh, not the filthy and short pleasure of the body, whereof followeth everlasting damnation, but the commandment of God, which saith, "Thou shalt not commit adultery:" and again, "Flee whoredom:" once again, "There shall be no whore among the daughters of Israel, nor no whore-keeper among the sons of Israel;" and cleave with tooth and nail, as they use to say, to these commandments of God, which he hath most straitly commanded to be observed and kept. For there is no weapon more apt to resist "the fiery darts" of Satan, than the word of God, as St Paul teacheth, and as we have our Saviour Christ for an ensample. "Thy words have I hidden within my heart," saith the psalmograph, "that I should not sin against thee." Again: "Wherewithal shall a young man cleanse his way? even by ruling himself after thy word." It shall not be unprofitable also to set before our eyes the grievous plagues, which God in every age poureth out upon the adulterers, fornicators, and all unclean persons; again, everlasting damnation both of body and soul after this life, if repentance, joined with faith, cometh not.

Remedies against whoredom. 1 Pet. v. Psal. cxix. Eph. vi. Matt. iv. Psal. cxix.

Secondly, forasmuch as we of ourselves are able to do no good thing, no, not so much as once to think a good thought ("it is God that worketh in us both the will and the deed"), it shall be necessary that, so soon as we begin to feel that the devil and the flesh begin to assail and to provoke us unto the breach of God's commandment, and by this means to fall into whoredom, adultery, incest, &c., we straightways give ourselves unto prayer, according to this commandment of Christ: "Watch and pray, that ye fall not into temptation. The spirit is ready, but the flesh is weak." For there is not a better armour against Satan and his subtile suggestions, than faithful and continual prayer. "The fervent prayer of a righteous man," saith St James, "availeth much." "Call on me," saith God, "in the time of thy trouble, and I will deliver thee, and thou shalt honour me." It shall be good to pray with the wise man and to say: "O Lord, thou Father and God of my life, let me not have a proud look, but turn away all voluptuousness fro me. Take fro me the lusts of the body: let not the desires of uncleanness take hold upon me," and "give me not over into an unshamefaced and obstinate mind." Pray also with the psalmograph on this manner: "O turn away mine eyes, lest they behold vanity; and quicken thou me in thy way. O stablish thy word in thy servant, that I may fear thee." Again: "Make me a clean heart, O God, and renew a right spirit within me. Cast me not away from thy presence, and take not thy holy Spirit from me. O give me the comfort of thy help again; and stablish me with thy free Spirit."

2 Cor. iii. Phil. ii. Matt. xxvi. James v. Psal. l. Ecclus. xxiii. Psal. cxix. Psal. li.

Thirdly, idleness above all things is to be eschewed, and some virtuous and honest labour is continually to be practised, that our enemy find us not idle. For idleness is the chief "mistress of vices all," as a certain ballad hath. Nothing doth so open both windows and doors to the tempter, as sluggish idleness. It is truly said of the poet:

Idleness is to be eschewed.

"Otia si tollas, periere Cupidinis arcus."

"If thou takest away idleness," saith he, "Cupid the god of love shooteth his arrows in vain." Again that same poet saith:

"Quæritur, Ægistus quare sit factus adulter:
In promptu causa est, desidiosus erat[1]."

"If any man will know," saith he, "how it came to pass that Ægistus fell into adultery; it may soon be known, he was idle." Read we not that Dina, Jacob's Gen. xxxiv.

[[1] Ovid. Remed. Amor. 139, 161, 2.]

daughter, through idleness, when she went out to see the daughters of the land, was ravished and deflowered of Sichem, the son of Hemar, the Hevite, lord of that country? 2 Sam. xi. Read we not that David, when he was once free from the persecution of Saul, and possessed his kingdom quietly, and by this means fell into idleness, committed adultery? 1 Kings xi. What did so greatly cause Salomon to dote in the love of so many women, as wealth Ecclus. xxxiii. and idleness? It is truly said of the wise man: "Idleness bringeth much evil." Who knoweth not, what too much abominable uncleanness was practised of the most filthy Sodomites? And was not idleness one of the principal causes thereof? These are the Ezek. xvi. words of the prophet: "Behold, the sins of thy sister Sodoma were these, pride, fulness of meat, abundance, and idleness: these things did she and her daughters. Besides that, they reached not their hand to the poor and needy, but were proud, and did abominable things before me. Therefore I took them away, as pleased me."

The company of the wicked is to be eschewed. Fourthly, as idleness above all things is to be eschewed, so likewise the company and communication of wanton and unhonest persons is utterly to be abhorred, if we 1 Cor. xv. purpose to lead a godly, pure, and honest life. For "evil words corrupt good man- Psal. xviii. ners." "With the holy thou shalt be holy, and with a perfect man thou shalt be perfect. With the clean thou shalt be clean, and with the froward thou shalt learn frowardness," Ecclus. xiii. saith the psalmograph. "Whoso toucheth pitch," saith Jesus the son of Sirach, "shall be filled withal; and he that is familiar with the proud shall clothe himself with pride." Ecclus. ix. Again: "Look not upon a woman, that is desirous of many men, lest thou fall into her snares. Use not the company of a woman that is a player and a dancer, and hear her not, lest thou perish through her enticing. Behold not a maiden, that thou be not hurt in her beauty. Cast not thy mind upon any harlots in any manner of thing, lest thou destroy both thyself and thine heritage. Go not about gazing in every lane of the city; neither wander thou abroad in the streets thereof. Turn away thy face from a beautiful woman, and look not upon the fairness of other. Many a man hath perished through the beauty of women; for through it the desire is kindled as it were fire. An advouterous woman shall be trodden under foot, as mire, of every one that goeth by the way. Many a man wondering at the beauty of a strange woman hath ☞ been cast out; for her words kindled as fire. Sit not with another man's wife by any means: lie not with her upon the bed: make no words with her at the wine, lest thy heart consent unto her, and so thou with thy blood fall into destruction."

1 Kings xi. Became not Salomon an idolater by keeping company with idolatrous women? Num. xxv. Became not the children of Israel wicked and ungodly by companying with wicked Matt. xxvi. and ungodly people? Became not Peter, which, so long as he continued with Christ and his disciples, was faithful, constant, and stedfast in the love and service of Christ, a very denier and forswearer of his master, when he once accompanied himself with Gen. xxi. the servants of the high priest? Sara, Abraham's wife, could by no means abide that her son Isaac should play and keep company with Ismael her handmaid's son, but Gen. xxviii. drove both him and his mother out of the doors. Jacob would by no means keep company with his ungodly brother Esau. Notable is this saying of Sara, young Tobias' Tob. iii. wife: "Thou knowest, O Lord, that I never had desire unto man, and that I have kept my soul clean from all uncleanly lust. I have not kept company with those that pass their time in sport; neither have I made myself partaker with them that Tob. ii. walk in light behaviour." Old Tobias would keep company with none, but with such Tob. iv. as feared God; and he commanded his son, young Tobias, that he should keep no 1 Cor. v. company, neither eat nor drink, with the sinners. St Paul also chargeth us, that we should not eat nor keep company with such as are whoremongers and of a lewd disposition. If therefore we intend to have pure minds and chaste bodies, wherein as in 1 Cor. iii. vi. 2 Cor. vi. a most sacred temple the Holy Ghost doth delight to dwell, let us diligently avoid the wicked company of wicked doers.

Fifthly, to avoid uncleanness both of body and mind, it shall not a little help, if we be temperate and sober in our diet, considering with ourselves, that we live not to eat, but we eat to live; and nature is content with a little. It was wittily said of the poet: *Sine Cerere et Baccho friget Venus;*[1] that is to say: "Temperance in

[[1] Ter. Eun. iv. v. 6.]

eating and drinking cooleth and abateth the courageous lust of the flesh." The wise man saith: "Look not thou upon the wine, how red it is, and what a colour it giveth in the glass. It goeth down softly; but at the last it biteth like a serpent, and stingeth as an adder. So shall thine eyes look unto strange women; and thine heart shall muse upon froward things." What a great provocation unto uncleanness intemperancy of diet is, the history of Loth the patriarch doth plainly declare, which, not once giving place to the filthy Sodomites in any point of their abominations all the time of his being among them, at the last through drunkenness fell into such horrible wickedness, that he deflowered and defiled his own daughters. Was not the excess of eating and drinking one of the causes that the world was once drowned, and that Sodom and Gomorre with certain other cities were consumed with fire and brimstone from heaven? Prov. xxiii Gen. xix. Gen. vii. Luke xvii. Ezek. xvi. Gen. xix.

It shall be good, therefore, if we intend to lead an honest and godly life, utterly estranged from the filthy sin of most filthy whoredom and adultery, to follow the most godly counsel of our Saviour Christ and of his apostles. Christ saith: "Take heed to yourselves, lest at any time your hearts be overcome with surfeiting and drunkenness." St Paul saith: "Let us walk honestly, as it were in the daylight, not in eating and drinking, neither in chambering and wantonness; but put ye on the Lord Jesus Christ; and make not provision for the flesh to fulfil the lusts of it." Again: "Be not drunk with wine, wherein is excess, but be ye filled with the Spirit." St Peter also saith: "Forasmuch as Christ hath suffered for us in the flesh, arm ye yourselves likewise with the same mind. For he which suffereth in the flesh, ceaseth from sin; that he henceforward should live (as much time as remaineth in the flesh) not after the lusts of men, but after the will of God. For it is sufficient for us, that we have spent the time that is past of the life after the will of the gentiles, walking in wantonness, lusts, in excess of drinking, in drunkenness, and in abominable idolatry." Luke xxi. Rom. xiii. Eph. v. 1 Pet. iv.

Sixthly, forasmuch as matrimony is an honourable state of living, ordained of God, sanctified by the Holy Ghost, and beautified with the first-fruits of Christ's miracles; to the end that we may avoid all uncleanness in our life and conversation, and lead an honest and virtuous life before God and man, it shall be very meet and convenient for all such as have not received of God the gift of continency to take upon them the holy state of honourable wedlock, and to join unto them a wife in the fear of God, and so to live christianly and quietly together, as St Paul saith: "To avoid whoredom, let every man have his own wife, and every woman her own husband. Let the husband give unto the wife due benevolence: likewise also the wife unto the husband. The wife hath not power of her own body, but the husband. And likewise the husband hath no power of his own body, but the wife. Withdraw not yourselves one from another, except it be with consent for a time, for to give yourselves to fasting and prayer. And afterward come together again, lest Satan tempt you for your incontinency." Again: "If any cannot abstain, let them marry. For it is better to marry than to burn." Also in another place: "This is the will of God, even your holiness, that ye should abstain from fornication, and that every one of you should know how to keep his vessel in holiness and honour, and not in the lust of concupiscence, as do the heathen, which know not God." Item: "Wedlock is honourable among all men, and the bed undefiled. But adulterers and whoremongers God shall judge," that is to say, punish, plague, and condemn. To embrace therefore holy matrimony in the fear of God, if the gift of continency be not given, is the most sure way to avoid all uncleanness, both of the mind and body. And hereunto ought all kind of persons the more diligently to apply themselves, because it is the holy ordinance of God appointed unto that end. Of matrimony. Gen. ii. ix. Matt. xix. Heb. xiii. John ii. 1 Cor. vii. 1 Cor. vii. 1 Thess. iv. Heb. xiii.

Father. Hitherto have we heard, what God forbiddeth in this his seventh commandment: declare unto me now, what he also requireth in the same. *Son*. That will I do, yea, and that in few words.

First, whereas God saith, "Thou shalt not commit adultery," he declareth evidently, that he approveth and alloweth the holy state of honourable wedlock, and the godly life of the same; so that the very act of matrimony between the man and the wife, done in the fear of God, and unto that end for the which God did What God requireth of us in this precept.

Heb. xiii. ordain it, is also pure and clean in the sight of God, as St Paul witnesseth: "Wedlock is honourable among all persons, and the bed undefiled."

The duty of married persons. And forasmuch as matrimony is an holy state of life, God in the aforesaid precept requireth of all married persons, that they lead a pure, clean, and blameless life, that they be faithful and loving one to the other, that they break not the marriage vow, that they know not the company of any strange flesh, that they defile not themselves in mind with evil lusts and in the body with uncleanness; but that they be pure both in body and spirit, utterly estranged from all adultery, incest, whoredom, and whatsoever is unclean in the sight of God, living together in all godliness and honesty. And that the married folk may the better this do, God requireth also of them in this precept, that they suffer no fleshly thoughts to rise and rule in their hearts, but that they suppress them straightways through earnest and hearty prayer, and through the diligent consideration of God's holy will, and through the fervent meditation of the sacred scripture: again, that they frequent the company of no lewd and evil-disposed persons, whereby they may be the rather provoked unto the breach of this commandment and unto dissolution of life: Item, that they avoid all wanton pastimes, all filthy communication, all uncomely gestures, all nice and lascivious apparel, all reading of wanton books, all beholding of unpure images or pictures, all banqueting and excess of eating and drinking, and besides, whatsoever may entice or move unto the filthy pleasure of the flesh; and finally, that in all their words and deeds there appear nothing in them but gravity, modesty, and honest behaviour, unto the good ensample of such as be their youngers and inferiors.

The duty of unmarried persons. Moreover, God also requireth, in this his precept, of all single and unmarried persons, that they fly the lascivious lusts of frail youth, eschew all vain and foolish pastimes, abhor all wanton talk, despise all wicked counsels, refrain all ungodly company, contemn the reading or singing of bawdy ballads, refuse riot and all excess both in diet and apparel, and in fine, so utterly reject and cast away whatsoever is contrary to the purity of the mind or to cleanness of the body, that they, in their single life being free from all corruption of manners, may bring with them unto the holy state of honourable matrimony (if God afterward call them unto it) both pure minds and chaste bodies, and so continually be made the temples of the Holy Ghost, which delighteth to dwell in such bodies and hearts, as be pure, holy, virtuous, and given to the study of godliness and honesty.

Father. God make us such! *Son.* Amen.

Father. Let me now hear the eighth commandment. *Son.* It is this:

The eighth commandment. "Thou shalt not steal."

What God forbiddeth in the eighth commandment. *Father.* Tell me now, my dear child, what God forbiddeth, and what he requireth, in this his precept. *Son.* First, God forbiddeth here, that we by no means take away unjustly our neighbour's goods, whether it be openly by force and violence, or secretly by craft or subtilty. For all this is termed theft in this commandment of God.

Father. Let me hear some authorities of the holy scripture, which forbid theft
Lev. xix. and the unjust taking away of our neighbour's goods. *Son.* God saith: "Ye shall not steal, neither lie, neither deal falsely one with another." The wise man
Prov. xxix. saith: "Whoso keepeth company with a thief hateth his own soul: he heareth
Eph. iv. blasphemies, and telleth it not forth." The holy apostle saith also: "Let him that stole steal no more, but let him rather labour with his hands the thing which is
Divers thieves and divers kinds of theft. good, that he may give unto him that needeth." But we shall note that there be divers kinds of thieves, and therefore divers kinds also of theft.

Father. Why, are not they thieves only, which either violently take or craftily steal away other men's goods? *Son.* No, verily. There be many thieves besides these, which steal, rob, poll, pill, and spoil, no less than the other, although before the world they be more glorious thieves, and not of so great infamy.

Father. Which are they? *Son.* Such as in buying and selling beguile and circumvent their neighbour with craft and subtilty, and use false weights and false measures: these also are thieves, and transgress this commandment of God, "Thou shalt not steal."

Father. Where is that forbidden? *Son.* God saith: "Thou shalt not do thy neighbour wrong, neither rob him violently." "If thou sellest ought to thy neighbour, or buyest of thy neighbour's hand, ye shall not deceive one another." The apostle saith: "This is the will of God, even your holiness, that no man oppress and defraud his brother in bargaining; because that the Lord is the avenger of all such things." And as concerning false weights and false measures, God saith: "Ye shall do no unrighteousness in judgment, in meteyard, in weight, or in measure. True balances, true weights, a true epha, and a true hin shall ye have: I am the Lord your God." Again: "Thou shalt not have in thy bag two manner of weights, a great and a small: neither shalt thou have in thy house divers measures, a great and a small. But thou shalt have a right and just weight, and a perfect and a just measure shalt thou have, that thy days may be lengthened in the land which the Lord thy God giveth thee. For all that do such things, and all that do unright, are abomination unto the Lord thy God." God saith also by the prophet: "Should I not be displeased for the unrighteous good that is in the houses of the wicked, and because the measure is minished? Or should I justify the false balances, and the bag of deceitful weights, among those that be full of riches unrighteously gotten; where the citizens deal with falsehood, speak lies, and have deceitful tongues in their mouths? Therefore I will take in hand to punish thee, and to make thee desolate because of thy sins." The wise man also saith: "A false balance is an abomination unto the Lord; but a true weight pleaseth him:" Again: "A true measure and a true balance are the Lord's judgment: he maketh all weights." Item: "To use two manner of weights, or two manner of measures, both these are abominable unto the Lord." Again: "The Lord abhorreth two manner of weights; and a false balance is an evil thing."

Lev. xix. Lev. xxv. 1 Thess. iv. Lev. xix. Deut. xxv. Mic. vi. Prov. xi. Prov. xv Prov. xx.

Father. Ought satisfaction to be made unto all such as are thus deceived and wronged? *Son.* Yea, verily. For whatsoever is gotten with craft and subtilty, with unrighteous bargaining, with false weights and unjust measures, is before God plain theft; and therefore it ought to be restored.

Satisfaction.

Father. How provest thou that by the word of God? *Son.* Is not this the commandment of God, that if any man steal an ox or a sheep, and kill it, or sell it, he shall restore for one ox five oxen, and for one sheep four sheep? Are not these also the words of God? "A thief shall make restitution: if he have not wherewith, he shall be sold for his theft." So likewise saith Salomon: "A thief, if he may be gotten, restoreth again seven times as much; or else he maketh recompence with all the good of his house." Were not these the words of Zacheus unto Christ? "Behold, Lord, the half of my goods I give to the poor; and if I have done any man wrong, I restore him fourfold."

Exod. xxii. Prov. vi. Luke xix.

Father. What other are there, which, transgressing this commandment, are also thieves before God? *Son.* Such as unjustly retain in their hands the reward or wages that is due to workmen or servants for their labour, pain, and travail.

Retaining of men's wages unjustly is theft.

Father. Are these thieves also? *Son.* Yea, verily: for they break the commandment of God.

Father. Why, what saith God in this behalf? *Son.* Thus saith he: "Thou shalt not do thy neighbour wrong, neither rob him violently: neither shall the workman's labour abide with thee until the morning." Again: "Thou shalt not defraud an hired servant that is needy and poor, whether he be of thy brethren or of the stranger that are in the land within thy gates; but thou shalt give him his hire the same day, and let not the sun go down thereon; (for he is needy and therewith sustaineth his life;) lest he cry against thee unto the Lord, and it be sin unto thee." Saint James also saith: "Go to now, ye rich men, weep and howl on your wretchedness that shall come upon you. Your riches is corrupt: your garments are moth-eaten: your gold and silver is cankered; and the rust of them shall be a witness unto you, and shall eat your flesh as it were fire. Ye have heaped treasure together, even wrath to yourselves in your last days. Behold, the hire of the labourers, which

Lev. xix. Deut. xxiv. James v.

have reaped down your fields, (which hire is of you kept back by fraud,) crieth; and the cries of them which have reaped are entered into the ears of the Lord of hosts. Ye have lived in pleasure on the earth, and been wanton: ye have nourished your hearts as in a day of slaughter: yea, ye have condemned and killed the righteous, and he hath not resisted you."

Unmerciful rich men are thieves before God.

Father. Remain there any other, that be guilty of theft through the transgression of this commandment? *Son*. Yea, very many. The rich men also, to whom God hath committed the goods of this world, not only of them to live themselves, but also to distribute some reasonable portion of the same to the poor and needy, and yet are so unfaithful to God and unmerciful to their poor neighbours, that they will consider nothing at all the miserable state of other, when necessity requireth, are very thieves and robbers; yea, and very murderers, as the wise man saith: "The bread of the needy is the life of the poor; but he that defraudeth him of it is a manslayer." And these covetous and unmerciful rich men may be sure to obtain no mercy at the hand of God, but with that unpitiful rich glutton to be cast into hell-fire, even into that "lake that burneth with fire and brimstone." For as they are "blessed which are merciful, and shall obtain mercy" at the hand of God at that great day of judgment; so likewise "shall the judgment be without mercy to him that hath shewed no mercy." It is a point of wisdom therefore for all rich men to follow this counsel of our Saviour Christ: "Make you friends of wicked mammon, that, when you fail, they may receive you into everlasting tabernacles." Again: such as they commonly call usurers, which are they that oppress their debtors with receiving too much gain for the loan of their money, corn, cattle, &c., are also thieves, and transgress this commandment.

Ecclus. xxxiv. Luke xvi. Rev. xxi. Matt. v. James ii. Matt. xxv. Luke xvi. Usurers.

Father. Where is it forbidden in the word of God, that we may not commit usury, that is to say, receive such unreasonable gain for the loan of our money, corn, cattle, &c., as we can get, although it be to the great damage, loss, yea, and almost utter undoing, of our debtors? *Son*. God saith by his servant Moses: "If thy brother be waxen poor, and fallen in decay with thee, thou shalt relieve him, both the stranger and sojourner, that he may live with thee. And thou shalt take none usury of him, or vantage. But thou shalt fear thy God, that thy brother may live with thee. Thou shalt not give him thy money upon usury, nor lend him thy corn for increase. I am the Lord your God," &c. Again he saith: "If thou lend money to any of my people that is poor by thee, thou shalt not be as tyrant unto him; neither shalt thou oppress him with usury." Also in another place: "Thou shalt not hurt thy neighbour by usury of money, or by usury of corn, nor by usury of any thing that he may be hurt withal."

Lev. xxv. Exod. xxii. Deut. xxiii.

Father. Of these authorities aforesaid, which thou hast alleged, methink I may right well gather two things: one is, that if I lend unto my neighbour such things as God hath blessed me with, to do him pleasure and profit thereby, for any gain or avantage, as it shall be covenanted and agreed upon between him and me, I may not so let him out my things, that I shall grieve or oppress him by taking any commodity for the loan thereof, but suffer him so to have the use thereof for a reasonable gain, that I may not disprofit but profit him, not hinder but promote him, not drive him unto poverty but rather help that he may be able to live. *Son*. You say truth.

Father. The other is, that if my neighbour be fallen into poverty, I ought to lend him part of such goods, as God hath lent unto me, freely and without any avantage, looking for no gain at his hand, that by this means he may be delivered from the heavy yoke of poverty, and be able to live. *Son*. To such as be poor we are not only bound by the commandment of God freely and without any avantage to lend, but also to give. For thus are we taught of our Saviour Christ in the gospel: "Give to every man that asketh of thee." (He speaketh of the poor and needy, which have not of their own, whereof to live.) "And as ye would that men should do to you, do ye also to them likewise. Lend, looking for nothing again; and your reward shall be great, and ye shall be the children of the Highest: for he is kind to the unkind and to the evil."

Luke vi.

Labourers. Artificers. Servants.

What shall I speak of the labourers, of artificers, and men of occupation, of servants, and such other like, which, being hired diligently to do their work, negligently behave themselves in their business, idly and unfruitfully spending their time, which they ought faithfully and truly, yea, painfully and earnestly to bestow upon such works as are appointed unto them by such as have hired them? These also are thieves, and transgress the commandment of God.

Moreover, what shall I speak of those magistrates, princes, rulers, common officers, and governors of the public weal, which without just cause do overcharge their subjects with rents, services, tributes, customs, toll, subsidies, pensions, &c. and exact of them more than is needful to the maintenance of the common charges, and so impoverish and oppress them, whom they ought from all injury and wrong to save and defend? Again, which do not bestow the goods, which they receive for the maintenance of the commonweal, as they ought to do, but spend them away in riot and unlawful pleasures, or in things of vanity? These also are thieves before God, and shall grievously be punished of God for their misbehaviour; and they be of that company, of the which the prophet speaketh on this manner: "Thy princes are wicked, and companions of thieves. They love gifts altogether, and gape for rewards. As for the fatherless, they help him not to his right: neither will they let the widow's causes come before them. Therefore saith the Lord God of hosts, the mighty governor of Israel, Out upon ye: I will ease me of mine enemies, and I will avenge me of mine adversaries." The prophet Ezechiel saith also: "Thy rulers in thee are like ravening wolves to shed blood, and to destroy souls for their own covetous lucre." Hereto belongeth the saying of the prophet Micheas: "Hear, O ye princes," saith he; "should not ye know what were lawful and right? But ye hate the good, and love the evil. Ye pluck off men's skins, and the flesh from their bones. Ye eat the flesh of my people, and flay off their skin. Ye break their bones; ye chop them in pieces as it were into a caldron, and as flesh into a pot." The prophet Sophonie saith also: "Wo to that abominable, filthy, and cruel city, which will not hear, nor be reformed! Her trust is not in the Lord, neither will she hold her to her God. Her rulers within her are as roaring lions: her judges are as wolves in the evening, which leave nothing behind them till the morrow."

Magistrates. Isai. i. Ezek. xxii. Zeph. iii.

Again, what shall I speak of those subjects, which, contrary to the law of God and good conscience, either grudge to pay, or else unjustly withhold, such taxes, tributes, customs, subsidies, tenths, pensions, &c. as are due to the magistrates or common officers for the conservation of the public weal, that they may be the more able to sustain and bear the charges of the common administration? These also are thieves, and grievously offend God, which by his apostle giveth this commandment: "Give to every man his duty, tribute to whom tribute belongeth, custom to whom custom is due, fear to whom fear belongeth, honour to whom honour pertaineth."

Subjects. Rom. xiii.

Furthermore, what shall I speak of bishops, pastors, curates, preachers, and such other spiritual ministers, which, contrary to their profession and calling, steal away from the people of God the nourishment both of their souls and bodies, while they neither feed them with the true and sincere word of God, which is the food of the soul, nor yet with corporal sustenance for the comfort of their bodies; but like bellied hypocrites and voluptuous epicures give themselves to the pleasures of the flesh, to eating and drinking, to dicing and carding, to hunting and hawking, &c. being led with no care toward the flock of Christ, whom he hath so dearly purchased, even with his own dear and precious blood; but so framing their life, as though there were no life after this, or as though they should never render accompts of their pastoral office to the high pastor and shepherd Christ? These are also thieves, and deserve at the hand of God most grievous punishment. Against these sluggish, unmerciful, and thievish pastors God crieth out by his prophet, saying: "Wo be unto the shepherds of Israel that feed themselves! Should not the shepherds feed the flock? Ye have eaten up the fat: ye have clothed you with the wool: the best fed have ye slain; but the flock have ye not nourished. The weak have ye not holden up: the sick have ye not healed: the broken have ye not bound together: the outcasts have ye not brought again: the lost have ye not sought; but churlishly and cruelly have ye ruled them," &c. Yea, these are those hirelings, thieves, robbers, and murderers, which enter not into the sheepfold by the door, but climb up some other way; which, when they see the wolf coming, leave the sheep and fly away. For they came only into the sheepfold to steal,

Bishops. Pastors. Curates. Acts xx. 1 Pet. i. John x. Ezek. xxxiv. John x.

to kill, and to destroy, and not to teach, to comfort and to edify, which is the very proper and true office of a faithful and godly pastor. "Wo be unto me," saith St Paul, "if I preach not the gospel."

1 Cor. ix.

Parishioners.

Those parishioners also, which do detain and withhold such duties and payments, as by order of law are due to the ministers of God's word for their labour, travail, and pain in the ministry, are thieves before God, and transgressors of his holy law. For "the Lord hath ordained, that they which preach the gospel should live of the gospel." "The workman is worthy his reward." The priests "that rule well are worthy of double honour, but most specially they which labour in the word and doctrine. For the scripture saith: Thou shalt not muzzle the mouth of the ox, that treadeth out the corn." And St Paul saith: "Let him that is taught in the word of God minister unto him that teacheth him all good things. Be not deceived: God is not mocked."

1 Cor. ix. Matt. x. 1 Tim. v. Deut. xxv. Gal. vi.

Lawyers. Advocates. Attorneys. Proctors.

Again, what shall I speak of those lawyers, advocates, attorneys, proctors, &c., which for their own gains do counsel a man to wage the law, making him to believe, that his matter is good, when in deed they think it naught; which also for money do so craftily handle or plead a matter, that they with their shifts and colours will purposely hide the truth, and make a good cause to seem bad, and a bad cause to appear good? Of those judges, which for bribes or any corruption do wittingly and willingly give wrong judgment? Of those merchantmen, brokers, chapmen, merchants' factors, which require unreasonable gains in selling of their merchandise; utter corrupt and naughty wares for good; deceive their neighbour with false weight and measure, &c.? Of husbandmen in the country, which for worldly lucre sell their corn, cattle, or any other victual, at unreasonable prices, and seek to make a dearth of things, where no need is? Of those gentlemen, which either take of their tenants such fines and incomes, or else so stretch out the prices and annual rents of their farms, that their farmers must either go on begging, or else sell their corn, hay, cattle, butter, cheese, &c. at such unreasonable prices, as shall turn unto the utter impoverishment of the buyers? Of those debtors, which, although they be able, yet for their own lucre will not pay their debts, nor at the day appointed restore that money which they have borrowed? Of such, as do not render the things which they have found, so far as they can come to knowledge of the true owners? Of them that do not give again such things as be committed to their custody for a time? Of gamesters, as dicers, and carders, &c., which direct their play only to this end, by unlawful pastimes, yea, by craft and subtilty, to deceive their neighbour, and to win away their substance? Of prodigal persons, which, lashing[1] out their goods without discretion or measure, afterward fall into beggary, and from beggary many times unto thievery, and from thievery come to the pillory, yea, to the halter? Of valiant and sturdy beggars, which, being able to labour and to get their living with the sweat of their brows and with the labour of their hands, walk up and down idly from door to door, and without all shame, through their importune begging, get that unto them, which is due to such as be in deed poor, and are not able to work for the infirmity and weakness of their body?

Judges. Merchants. Chapmen. Husbandmen. Gentlemen. Debtors. Finders of things. Gamesters. Dicers. Carders. Prodigal parents. Beggars.

To conclude, what shall I speak of all them that do hawk and hunt for other men's goods against the will of the owners, or do hurt them in any part of the same, &c.? All these aforesaid are thieves before God, although the world doth not so judge them, nor punish them for the same.

Father. There is a great number of thieves by thy reckoning. *Son*. The world is full of privy thieves. For there is almost no state or kind of life, from the highest to the lowest, of the which there be not many that have broken this commandment. Whosoever dealeth with his neighbour unjustly or untruly, and otherwise than he would that his neighbour should deal with him, he is before God a very thief and a robber. For this is the commandment of Christ: "Whatsoever ye would that men should do unto you, do ye the very same unto them." "For look with what measure ye mete unto other, with the same shall it be mete again to you."

Matt. vii. Luke vi.

[1 Lashing: lavishing.]

Father. Why, will God punish them also that transgress this commandment? *Son*. Why should they escape unpunished?

Father. Let me hear it proved by the word of God, that the transgressors of this commandment shall not escape free from punishment. *Son*. God commanded in the law of Moses, that if any person among the Israelites did steal a man, and sell him, the same should suffer death. Again, if any did steal an ox or a sheep, that he should restore five oxen for an ox, and four sheep for a sheep. Item, that it should be lawful for a man taking a thief in his house before daylight to kill him. The wise man saith: "He that is partaker with a thief hateth his own soul." St Paul writeth, that "thieves, extortioners, robbers, pollers, &c., shall not inherit the kingdom of God." He addeth, moreover, that "if any man oppress or defraud his brother in bargaining, the Lord will be avenged of him." Jesus the son of Sirach saith: "Shame and sorrow goeth over the thief." Theft punished. Exod. xxi. Deut. xxiv. Exod. xxii. Prov. xxix. 1 Cor. vi. 1 Thess. iv. Ecclus. v.

The prophet Esay crieth out against the thief on this manner: "Wo be to thee that spoilest! for thou shalt be spoiled again." So likewise doth the prophet Micheas, saying: "O wo be unto them that imagine to do harm, and devise ungraciousness upon their beds to perform it in the clear day! for their power is against God. When they come to have land, they take it by violence: they rob men of their houses. Thus they oppress a man for his house, and every man for his heritage. Therefore thus saith the Lord: Behold, against this household I have devised a plague, whereout ye shall not pluck your necks. Ye shall no more go so proudly; for it will be a perilous time." Again: "Should I not be displeased for the unrighteous good in the houses of the wicked, and because the measure is minished? Or should I justify the false balances, and the bag of the deceitful weights, among those that be full of riches unrighteously gotten; where the citizens deal with falsehood, speak lies, and have deceitful tongues in their mouths? Therefore I will take in hand to punish thee, and to make thee desolate, because of thy sins." Isai. xxxiii. Mic. ii. Mic. vi.

The prophet Habacuc crieth out in like manner, saying: "Wo be unto him that heapeth up other men's goods! How long will he load himself with thick clay? O how suddenly shall they stand up that shall bite, and awake that shall tear thee in pieces! yea, thou shalt be their prey. Seeing that thou hast spoiled many nations, therefore shall the remnant of the people spoil thee; because of men's blood, and for the wrong done in the land, in the city, and unto all them that dwell therein. Wo be unto him that covetously gathereth together evil-gotten goods into his house, that he may set his nest on high, to escape from the power of misfortune! Thou hast devised the shame of thine own house; for thou hast slain too much people, and hast wilfully offended, so that the very stones of thy wall shall cry out of it, and the timber that lieth betwixt the joints of the building shall answer. Wo be unto him that buildeth the town with blood, and maintaineth the city with unrighteousness!" Read we not, that the prophet Zachary saw a flying book of twenty cubits long and ten cubits broad, in the which was written the curse that shall fall upon all thieves? "I will bring it forth, saith the Lord of hosts, so that it shall come to the house of the thief, and shall remain in his house, and consume it with the timber and stones thereof." The wise man also saith: "Whoso hoardeth up riches with the deceitfulness of his tongue, he is vain and a fool, and like unto them that seek their own death. The robberies of the ungodly shall be their own destruction; for they will not do the thing that is right." Hab. ii. Zech. v. Prov. xxi.

Moreover, in the book of Josua we read, that Achan the son of Zereth stole and conveyed away a goodly Babylonish garment, and two hundred sicles[2] of silver, and a tongue of gold of fifty sicles[2] weight, and that therefore at the commandment of God he was stoned unto death; and his stolen good with all that ever he had besides, his sons and his daughters, his oxen and his asses, his sheep and his tent, &c. were brent with fire. Was not Gehezi, the servant of Elisa the prophet, stricken with leprosy even unto his dying day, both he and his seed for ever, because with craft and subtilty in his master's name he took of Naaman the Syrian two talents of silver, and two change of garments? Josh. vii. 2 Kings v.

[[2] Sicles: shekels.]

2 Macc. i. I pass over with silence king Antiochus, which, when he with his army entered into the temple, purposing to have spoiled it, and to take out of it great sums of money, was slain both he and his company, and hewn in pieces. What shall I here rehearse, 2 Macc. iii. how that king Saleucus, understanding that there were great sums of gold and silver in the temple of Jerusalem, sent Heliodorus his steward thither to take away the money, and to bring it unto him? But when the aforesaid Heliodorus with his men of war brast into the temple, and were about the treasure, the Spirit of God shewed himself openly, so that all they which presumed to obey Heliodorus fell through the power of God into great fearfulness and dread. "For there appeared unto them an horse with a terrible man sitting upon him decked in goodly array, and the horse smote at Heliodorus with his fore feet. Now he that sat upon the horse had harness of gold upon him. Moreover there appeared two fair and beautiful young men in goodly array, which stood by him, scourged him of both the sides, and gave him many stripes without ceasing. With that fell Heliodorus suddenly unto the ground. So they took him up (being compassed about with great darkness), and bare him out upon a bier. Thus he, that came with so many runners and men of war into the said treasure, was borne out, where as no man might help him; and so the power of God was manifest and known. He lay still dumb also by the power of God, destitute of all hope and life."

These and such like ensamples contained in the holy scripture declare evidently, how greatly God detesteth and abhorreth robbing, stealing, spoiling, polling, picking, and all unrighteous dealing, aud that he will by no means suffer it to escape unpunished.

Of propriety of goods. *Father*. Thou sayest truth, my child. Here learn we also moreover, that all things that we do possess are not common, and at liberty to take them for all other also, and to do with them what they lust without check; but that there is a propriety and ownership of things among the people of God. *Son*. If it were otherwise, this commandment of God, "Thou shalt not steal," were given in vain, and it were no theft nor robbery to take from my neighbour what I lusted, and to do withal what I would, seeing all things be common among the Christians, and nothing proper.

But the word of God teacheth us, that a christian man may with a good conscience have riches, enjoy, and possess them, and use them as his own. For riches is the good Prov. x. gift of God, as Salomon saith: "The blessing of the Lord maketh men rich." And Ecclus. xi. Sirach saith, that "both riches and poverty cometh from God." St Paul wrote not unto bishop Timothy, that he should command the rich men of this world, that they should not be rich, nor have any riches and possessions, but rather cast away their goods from 1 Tim. vi. them as things unlawful to be possessed; but he chargeth him to "command the rich men, that they be not high-minded, nor trust in uncertain riches, but in the living God, which giveth us abundantly all things to enjoy them; that they do good, that they be rich in good works, that they be ready to give, and gladly to distribute, laying up in store for themselves a good foundation against the time to come, that they may obtain everlasting life." It is not forbidden the Christians to have riches, but to set their whole heart Psal. lxii. upon the riches, as the psalmograph saith: "If ye have abundance of riches, set not Ecclus. xxxi. your heart upon them." "Blessed is the rich," saith Sirach, "which is found without blemish, and hath not gone after gold, nor put his trust in money and treasures. Where is there a such one? and we shall commend him, and call him blessed; for great things doeth he among his people."

Matt. xix. *Father*. Doth not our Saviour Christ say, that "it is more easy for a cable-rope to go through the eye of a needle, than for a rich man to enter into the kingdom of heaven"? *Son*. I grant. But Christ speaketh there of such rich men as are mammonists and the slaves of mammon, as put not their trust in the living God, but in uncertain riches, as glory not in God, but have all their rejoicing in the goods of this world, as St Mark doth right well declare, which reporteth the Mark x. words of Christ on this manner: "Little children, it is a very hard thing for them that put their confidence in money to enter into the kingdom of God."

Gen. xx. Gen. xxiv. Gen. xxvi. Gen. xxxi. Abraham was rich, and brought great possessions with him out of Egypt. Isaac, his son, was wonderful rich, and had great abundance of cattle. Jacob brought with him from Laban great multitudes of sheep and very much substance; for the Lord Gen. xli. had blessed him. Joseph was a noble magistrate and a mighty ruler in Egypt, and was endued with great possessions. Job was exceedingly rich; for "he had of his own fourteen thousand sheep, six thousand camels, and a thousand yoke of oxen, and a thousand she asses," and a very great family. Tobias also was so rich, that he was able daily to give and distribute almose to the poor. What shall I speak of the noble kings, David, Salomon, Ezechias, Josias, &c., and of the virtuous women Judith, Hester, &c., and such like; which all had great possessions and very many goods and riches; and yet were they the dearly beloved servants of God, and are now inheritors of everlasting glory?

Job xlii.
Tob. i. ii.

Christ saith not simply, that the poor are blessed, and that unto them belongeth the kingdom of heaven, but the poor in spirit. "Blessed are the poor in spirit," saith he, "for unto them doth the kingdom of heaven belong." Christ crieth not wo upon all rich men without exception, but upon such only as repose all their consolation and comfort, all their joy and hope, in their riches. Riches, therefore, forasmuch as they are the gift and blessing of God, may right well be possessed of the true Christians: neither do the possessions of this world hinder or let any thing unto the obtaining of everlasting life, if we set not our heart upon them, if like good stewards we give and distribute them gladly, when necessity requireth, to the poor and needy members of Christ, and follow this counsel of the apostle: "The time is short," saith he: "it remaineth that they which have wives be as though they had none; and they that weep be as though they wept not; and they that rejoice be as though they rejoiced not; and they that buy be as though they possessed not; and they that use this world be as though they used it not. For the fashion of this world passeth away."

Matt. v.
Luke vi.
Prov. x.
Ecclus. xi.
1 Cor. vii.

Father. Hitherto have we heard, my dear son, what God forbiddeth in this his law, "Thou shalt not steal," and how grievously he will punish all such as transgress this commandment. Now it remaineth, that thou declarest unto me, what God requireth of us to be done in this law. *Son*. In this law God requireth of us, that we should not only not steal or unjustly convey away our neighbour's goods by any means from him, and turn them unto our own use and commodity; but also that we should seek all means possible to save, keep, and defend his goods, to help him, to study how we may, either in word or in deed, pleasure him, that his goods through us may not be diminished, but increased. Verily, so great care ought we to have for our neighbour, and for all things that appertain unto him, as we have for ourselves and for ours.

What God requireth in the eighth commandment.

Father. How provest thou this? *Son*. It is soon proved. God saith: "Thou shalt love thy neighbour even as thyself." Again he saith: "Whatsoever ye would that men should do to you, do ye so even to them also. For this is the law and the prophets." And in the law of Moses God gave this commandment, saying: "Thou shalt not see thy brother's ox or sheep go astray, and withdraw thyself from them; but shalt bring them again unto thy brother. And if thy brother be not nigh unto thee, or if thou know him not, then bring it to thine own house; and it shall remain with thee, until thy brother ask for them; and then deliver him them again. In like manner shalt thou do with his ass, and so shalt thou do with his raiment; and with all the lost things of thy brother, which he had lost and thou hast found, shalt thou do likewise; for thou mayest not hide it. Thou shalt not see thy brother's ass or ox fall down by the way, and withdraw thyself from them, but shalt help him to heave them up again." Again he saith: "If thou meet thine enemy's ox or ass going astray, thou shalt bring them to him again. If thou see thine enemy's ass sink under his burden, thou shalt not pass by and let him alone, but shalt help him to lift him up again."

Lev. xix.
Matt. xxii.
Rom. xiii.
Gal. v.
James ii.
Matt. vii.
Luke vi.
Deut. xxii.

Here are we commanded of God to do good to our neighbour, to help, save, and defend our neighbour's goods, that nothing of them perish; yea, and that not only if he be our friend, but also if he be our enemy, that we may be the children of our Father, which is in heaven; "for he maketh his sun to arise on the evil and on the good, and sendeth rain on the righteous and on the unrighteous": so far is it off, that we ought unjustly to take away his goods, or in any point to hinder him. What we ought to be to our neighbour, the parable of the wounded man and of the Samaritan

Matt. v.

do manifestly set forth unto us in the gospel of St Luke; which I would wish all men at all times to have before their eyes.

Father. What is that parable? Rehearse it unto me. *Son*. St Luke describeth it on this manner: "A certain man (saith he) descended from Jerusalem to Jericho, and fell among thieves, which robbed him of his raiment, and wounded him, and departed, leaving him half dead. And it chanced that there came down a certain priest that same way, and when he saw him he passed by. And likewise a Levite, when he went nigh to the place, came and looked on him, and passed by. But a certain Samaritan, as he journeyed, came unto him; and when he saw him, he had compassion on him, and went to him, and bound up his wounds, and poured in oil and wine, and set him on his own beast, and brought him to a common inn, and made provision for him. And on the morrow when he departed, he took out two pence, and gave them to the host, and said unto him: Take cure[1] of him, and whatsoever thou spendest more, when I come again, I will recompense thee."

Luke x.

Father. This parable setteth forth our duty right well to our neighbour. *Son*. It teacheth us, that we should be ready at all times both with our heart, body, and goods to help and succour our neighbour: so far is it off, that we ought to envy him the good success of things, or the felicity of worldly goods, or unjustly by any manner of means to convey his goods unto us and unto our use; but rather rejoice, when all things go prosperously with our neighbour, and to the uttermost of our power labour that he and whatsoever pertaineth unto him may be safely preserved without all peril and danger. For charity and true neighbourly love seeketh not her own, but the commodity and profit of other.

The duty of the rich.

Father. What requireth God of us more in this law? *Son*. That such as be rich should deal mercifully and liberally with the poor, helping their necessity and relieving their poverty. For unto this end hath God blessed them with worldly substance, that they should be merciful and bounteous to the poor, and gladly and willingly minister unto them all good things, as faithful and trusty stewards of the Lord's treasures.

Father. Let me hear it proved by the word of God, that the Lord our God requireth of the rich men this mercy and liberality to the poor. *Son*. The holy scripture is large in this behalf. God saith: "There shall be no needy person nor beggar among you, that the Lord thy God may bless thee." Again: "If any of the brethren among you be poor within any of thy gates, in the land which the Lord God giveth thee, thou shalt not harden thine heart, nor shut thine hand from thy poor brother; but open thine hand unto him, and lend him sufficient for his need which he hath. Beware, that there be not a wicked point in thine heart, that thou wouldest say, The seventh year, the year of freedom, is at hand; and therefore it grieveth thee to look on thy poor brother, and givest him nought, and he then cry unto the Lord against thee, and it be sin unto thee; but give him, and let it not grieve thine heart to give unto him; because that for this thing the Lord thy God shall bless thee in all thy works, and in all that thou puttest thine hand to. The land shall never be without poor. And therefore I command thee, saying: Thou shalt open thine hand unto thy brother that is needy and poor in the land." The wise man saith: "Withdraw no good thing from them that have need, so long as thine hand is able to do it. Say not unto thy neighbour, Go thy way and come again: to-morrow will I give thee; whereas thou hast now to give him."

Deut. xv.

Prov. iii

Ecclus. iv.

Jesus the son of Sirach saith: "My son, defraud not the poor of his alms, and turn not away thine eyes from him that hath need. Despise not an hungry soul, and defy not the poor in his necessity. Grieve not the heart of him that is helpless, and withdraw not thy gift from the needful. Refuse not the prayer of one that is in trouble: turn not away thy face from the needy: cast not thine eyes aside from the poor for any evil will, that thou give him none occasion to speak evil of thee. For if he complain of thee in the bitterness of his soul, his prayer shall be heard; even he that made him shall hear him. Be courteous unto the company of the poor. Let it not grieve thee to bow down thine ear unto the poor; but pay the debt, and give

[[1] Cure: care. It is still used, as in *cure* of souls.]

him a friendly answer, and that with meekness. Let not thine hand be stretched out to receive, and shut when thou shouldest give." Again he saith: "The bread of the needy is the life of the poor: he that defraudeth him thereof is a man-slayer. Whoso robbeth his neighbour of his living doth as great a sin, as though he slew him to death." Ecclus. xxxiv.

The prophet Esay saith: "Loose him out of bondage, that is in thy danger. Break the oath of wicked bargains. Let the oppressed go free, and take from him all manner of burdens. Deal thy bread to the hungry, and bring the poor wayfaring man home into thine house: when thou seest the naked, cover him, and hide not thy face from thy neighbour, and despise not thine own flesh. Then shall thy light break forth as the morning, and thy health flourish right shortly: thy righteousness shall go before thee, and the glory of the Lord shall embrace thee." And the prophet Zachary saith: "Execute true judgment: shew mercy and loving-kindness every man to his brother. Do the widow, the fatherless, the stranger, and poor no wrong; and let no man imagine evil against his brother in his heart." Isai. lviii. Zech. vii.

Tobias saith: "Give alms of thy goods, and turn never thy face from the poor; and so shall it come to pass, that the face of the Lord shall not be turned away from thee. Be merciful after thy power. If thou hast much, give plenteously: if thou hast little, do thy diligence gladly to give of that little. For so gatherest thou thyself a good reward in the day of necessity. For mercy delivereth from all sin and from death, and suffereth not the soul to come in darkness. A great comfort is mercy before the high God unto all them that shew it." "Look that thou never do unto another man the thing that thou wouldest not another man should do unto thee." "Eat thy bread with the hungry and poor, and cover the naked with thy clothes." Tob. iv.

Moreover Christ our Saviour saith: "Give to him that asketh thee, and from him that would borrow turn not thou away." "Lay not up for yourselves treasure upon earth, where the rust and the moth do corrupt, and where thieves break through and steal. But lay up for you treasures in heaven, where neither rust nor moth doth corrupt, and where thieves do not break through nor steal. For where your treasure is, there will your heart be also." "Be ye merciful, even as your heavenly Father is merciful. Give, and it shall be given unto you: good measure, and pressed down, and shaken together, and running over shall men give into your bosoms. For with the same measure that ye mete withal, shall other men mete to you [a]gain." "Sell that ye have, and give alms: and prepare you bags that wax not old, even a treasure that faileth not in heaven, where no thief cometh, neither moth corrupteth." "When thou makest a feast, call the poor, the feeble, the lame, and the blind, and thou shalt be happy: for they cannot recompense thee; but thou shalt be recompensed at the resurrection of the righteous." "Make you friends of unrighteous mammon, that, when ye shall have need, they may receive you into everlasting habitations." Matt. v. Matt. vi. Luke vi. Luke xii. Luke xiv. Luke xvi.

The blessed apostle St Paul saith: "Distribute unto the necessity of the saints. Be ready to harbour." "If thine enemy hunger, feed him: if he thirst, give him drink. For in so doing thou shalt heap coals of fire on his head. Be not overcome of evil; but overcome evil with goodness." "Let us not be weary of well doing: for when the time is come, we shall reap without weariness. While we have therefore time, let us do good unto all men, but specially unto them which are of the household of faith." And to bishop Timothy he writeth thus: "Charge them which are rich in this world, that they be not high-minded, nor trust in uncertain riches, but in the living God, which giveth us abundantly all things to enjoy them; that they do good; that they be rich in good works; that they be ready to give, and gladly to distribute, laying up in store for themselves a good foundation against the time to come, that they may obtain everlasting life." Rom. xii. Gal. vi. 1 Tim. vi.

St James also saith: "The judgment shall be without mercy unto him that sheweth no mercy; and mercy rejoiceth against judgment. What availeth it, my brethren, though a man saith he hath faith, if he have no deeds? Can faith save him? If a brother or a sister be naked and destitute of daily food, and one of you say unto them, Depart in peace; God send you warmness and food; notwithstanding ye give them not those things which are needful to the body, what shall it help? &c." James ii.

1 John iii. St John saith likewise: "Whoso hath the goods of this world, and seeth his brother have need, and shutteth up his compassion from him, how dwelleth the love of God 1 John iv. in him?" "And this commandment have we of him, that he which loveth God should love his brother also."

Matt. xxv. In the gospel we read, that the merciful at the day of judgment shall receive this mercy at the hand of God, that they shall be made inheritors of the heavenly kingdom. Contrariwise, the unmerciful shall for their portion have everlasting damna- Rev. xxi. Luke xvi. tion in that lake that burneth with fire and brimstone; as we have the unmerciful rich glutton for an example.

Father. What is more required of us in this commandment of God? *Son*. God requireth also of us in this his law, that we should be content with that we have, and not falsely and unjustly go about to be rich with the incommodity and hindrance of our neighbour, but be well pleased with our own, whether it be much or little, avoiding covetousness, which is the root of all evils, in all our life and conversation.

Father. Where are we taught to be content with our own? *Son*. The blessed 1 Tim. vi. apostle saith: "Godliness is great riches, if a man be content with that he hath. For we brought nothing into the world, neither may we carry any thing out. But when we have food and raiment, we must therewith be content. They that will be rich fall into temptation and snares of the devil, and into many foolish and noisome lusts, which drown men into perdition and destruction. For covetousness of money is the root of all evil: which while some lusted after, they erred from the faith, and tangled themselves with many sorrows. But thou, man of God, fly such things. Follow righteousness, godliness, faith, love, patience, meekness," &c. Also in another Heb. xiii. place he saith: "Let your conversation be without covetousness, and be content with Josh. i. such things as ye have already. For he hath said, I will not fail thee, neither Psal. cxviii. forsake thee: so that we may boldly say, The Lord is my helper; and I will not Ecclus. xxix. fear what man may do unto me." Hereto agreeth the saying of Sirach: "Be it little or much that thou hast, hold thee content withal; and thou shalt not be blamed as a vagabond; for a miserable life is it to go from house to house."

Father. What requireth God more of us in this precept? *Son*. He requireth that every man in his vocation and calling shall so live, that he shall not only not hurt his neighbour either in thought, word, or deed, but also do good to all men, so much as lieth in him.

Magistrates. The magistrate ought not to take too much of his subjects, nor to overcharge them with intolerable payments, but only to lay such burdens upon them, as they may well and conveniently bear, yea, and that for the maintenance of the commonweal; ever setting before their eyes, that they are the ministers of God, appointed to bear rule not for their own profit and commodity, but for the wealth and profit of Rom. xiii. God's people; as St Paul saith: "The magistrate is the minister of God for thy Ecclus. xxxii. wealth." Hereto agreeth the saying of Jesus, the son of Sirach: "If thou be made a ruler, pride not thyself therein, but be thou as one of the people. Take diligent care for them, and look well thereto; and when thou hast done all thy duty, sit thee down, that thou mayest be merry with them, and receive the crown of honour."

Subjects. The subjects ought not to withhold any thing unjustly that is due to the temporal rulers, but gladly and willingly to give, whatsoever is required of them for the maintenance of the commonweal.

Bishops. Pastors. John xxi. 1 Pet. v. 1 Tim. iii. 1 Tim. iv. The bishops, pastors, and curates ought diligently to feed the flock of Christ with the true and pure word of God, to maintain hospitality for the relief of the poor and miserably afflicted Christians, and to be an example to the flock in all godliness and honesty.

Parishioners. 1 Cor. iv. Gal. iv. 1 Cor. iv. 1 Tim. v. Gal. vi. 1 Thess. v. The parishioners ought to reverence the spiritual ministers, as fathers that begat them in Christ through the gospel, as the angels of God, as the stewards of the mysteries of God, and to give them double honour, and to provide and aforesee, that they lack no good thing necessary for their estate, that their ministry be not hindered.

Men of law. Such as be officers in the law ought above all things to seek equity and justice, to give counsel according to right, to boult out the truth, to judge indifferently without respect of persons, not to prolong for filthy lucre's sake the causes of their clients; but with all expedition and convenient haste to dispatch them, yea, and that according to right and conscience, ever setting before their eyes this notable admonition, which the most noble king Jehosaphat gave to the judges: "Take heed," saith he, "what ye do; for ye execute not the judgment of man, but of God, which is with you in judgment. Let the fear of the Lord be therefore upon you; and take heed, and see that ye do the thing that pleaseth him. For there is no unrighteousness with the Lord your God, that he should have respect of persons or take rewards." Isai. i. Jer. vii. xxii. Zech. vii. viii. 2 Chron. xix.

They that exercise themselves in merchandise, in buying and selling, in husbandry, in manual arts and handy occupations, &c., ought so to travail in their mysteries, that, all craft and subtilty, all falsehood and dissimulation set apart, they may deal truly and faithfully with all men, having ever an eye not so much unto their own private profit, as to the commodity of the country wherein they dwell; remembering also, that we be not born for ourselves, but to do good to other and to serve other. Merchants. Husbandmen. Artificers.

The gentlemen and landlords ought so to let out their farms, lands, tenements, lordships, &c., for a reasonable price, that their tenants may be able to live under them, to nourish their family, to bring up their children in good arts, to maintain hospitality, to help to bear the charges of the commonweal, to sell their corn, cattle, and all other victuals, for a mean and indifferent price, and to do good unto such as have need of their help. Gentlemen. Landlords.

Such as are indebted ought truly and faithfully at the day appointed to pay their debts, and to live of their own. Debtors.

Such as live after an unlawful and wicked means, as dicers, carders, jesters, counterfeit fools, &c., ought to cast away this licentious kind of living, and to practise some honest and seemly art, wherewith they may be able not only to eat their own bread with a good conscience, but also to profit other, as the apostle saith: "Let him that stole steal no more, but let him rather labour with his hands the thing which is good, that he may give unto him that needeth." Again: "We require you, brethren, by the name of our Lord Jesu Christ, that ye withdraw yourselves from every brother that behaveth himself inordinately, and not after the institution which he received of us. For ye yourselves know how ye ought to follow us. For we behaved not ourselves inordinately among you: neither took we bread of any man for nought; but wrought with labour and sweat night and day, because we would not be chargeable to any of you: not but that we had authority; but to make ourselves an ensample unto you to follow us. For when we were with you, this we warned you of, that, if any would not work, the same should not eat. For we have heard say that there are some which walk among you inordinately, working nothing at all, but being busybodies. Them that are such we command and exhort by our Lord Jesus Christ, that they work with quietness, and eat their own bread." Dicers. Carders. Jesters, &c. Eph. iv. 2 Thess. iii.

They also that are called beggars, and get their living by asking alms from door to door, if they have their limbs, and be able to work, ought not to run up and down idly, but to labour with their hands for their living, and with the sweat of their faces to eat their own bread, and to be able also to give somewhat unto the needy. For let them know this to be a most certain truth, that, if they be able to labour and will not, they are thieves before God; and every morsel of bread or meat, that they eat by this their begging, turneth to their own damnation; forasmuch as they eat away the living of the poor needy man, which is feeble, sick, lame, &c. Beggars. Psal. cxxviii. Gen. iii. Eph. iv. 2 Thess. iii.

Servants, workmen, day-labourers, and such other like, ought diligently to labour and to serve their bodily masters, which have hired them, and of whom they take wages, "not with eye-service only as men-pleasers, but as the servants of Christ, doing the will of God from the heart with a good will, serving the Lord and not men, knowing this, that whatsoever good thing a man doeth, the same shall he receive again of God, whether he be bond or free." Servants. Workmen. Day-labourers, &c. Eph. vi. Col. iii. Tit. ii. 1 Pet. ii.

In fine, all persons of every degree ought so to frame their lives according to the will of God, that they should not at any time attempt any thing toward their neighbour, that they would gladly refuse to be done to themselves; but live with such an upright mind toward all men, that they should be no less careful for their neighbour's commodity, than they are for their own; so far is it off that any enterprise to the contrary ought to be attempted of them that profess godliness.

If all men on this manner would endeavour themselves to frame their lives according to the rule of God's word, sin should soon decrease, and virtue increase; self-love should shortly be banished, and neighbourly love take place; private profit should quickly cease, and common commodity rise, grow, prosper, flourish, reign, triumph.

Father. God make us true professors and faithful practisers of his holy will! *Son*. Amen, good Lord.

Father. Now have we passed over eight of God's commandments. Let me now hear the ninth. *Son*. This is it:

The ninth commandment.

"Thou shalt not bear false witness against thy neighbour."

Father. What is the will of God in this law? *Son*. In the four last commandments, which concern our duty toward our neighbour, first, we have learned how we ought to behave ourselves toward our parents, superiors, and elders; secondly, what our duty is toward our neighbour concerning his body; thirdly, how we ought to behave ourselves toward our neighbour concerning his wife; fourthly, what our duty is toward our neighbour concerning his goods. Now followeth the fifth commandment of the second table, which is the ninth precept in order, wherein we are taught, how we should behave ourselves toward our neighbour concerning his good name and fame. For he doth no less offend, which oppresseth his innocent neighbour with false witness, than he which killeth him with weapon. Neither is that thief more worthy of punishment, which with open violence or with subtile and crafty means spoileth a man of his goods, than that person, which with lying and false witness-bearing robbeth a man of his good name and fame: which good name doth so far excel all the riches of this world, as the sun in quantity and brightness surmounteth and passeth the least star in the firmament. The wise man saith: "Like as the clearness of the eyes rejoiceth the heart, so doth a good name feed the bones." Again he saith: "A good name is more worth than great riches; and loving favour is better than silver and gold." Item: "A good name is more worth than precious ointment." Jesus the son of Sirach saith: "Labour to get thee a good name; for that shall continue surer by thee than a thousand great treasures of gold. A good life hath a number of days; but a good name endureth ever." Therefore, forasmuch as "the tongue," as St James saith, "although a little member, boasteth great things, is a fire and a world of wickedness, defileth the whole body, and setteth a-fire all that we have of nature, and is itself set a-fire even of hell," being "an unruly evil, and full of deadly poison;" God in this his law declareth unto us, how we should behave ourselves toward our neighbour in tongue and speech, as he hath taught us in his laws aforesaid, how we should behave ourselves toward him in body and in bodily acts. And as we are forbidden, in the four commandments above rehearsed, to hurt our neighbour with our body or with the deeds thereof; so likewise in this precept are we forbidden to hurt our neighbour with our tongue, or with any word that proceedeth from the same. And in this behalf God commandeth us here expressly, that we bear not false witness against our neighbour.

A good name passeth all worldly riches. Prov. xv. Prov. xxii. Eccles. vii. Ecclus. xli. James iii.

What God forbiddeth in this commandment.

Father. What doth God forbid, or what requireth he, in this commandment? *Son*. First, he forbiddeth, that, when any matter being in controversy is brought before the judge, and we be called of him to be witnesses in this behalf, we, contrary to our conscience and knowledge, either for favour toward the one part, or for displeasure toward the other part, should bear false witness or give wrong evidence against our neighbour, to the impoverishment and loss of his goods, or to the appairing[1] of his good name, estimation, and fame.

Father. Is this bearing of false witness forbidden in other places also of the holy scripture? *Son*. Yea, verily. God saith by his servant Moses: "Thou shalt not accept a vain tale, neither shalt thou put thy hand with the wicked, to be an unrighte-

Exod. xxiii.

[[1] Appairing: impairing.]

ous witness (against thy neighbour). Thou shalt not follow a multitude to do evil, neither answer in a matter of plea, that thou wouldest (to follow many) turn away from the truth," &c. Again: "Thou shalt not go up and down as a privy accuser among Lev. xix. thy people, neither shalt thou stand against the blood of thy neighbour: I am the Lord." Also in another place: "Cursed be he that hindereth the right of the stranger, Deut. xxvii. fatherless, and widow; and all the people shall say, Amen." "Cursed be he that taketh a reward to slay the soul of innocent blood; and the people shall say, Amen." The wise man saith: "Be not a false witness against thy neighbour, and speak no false- Prov. xxiv. hood with thy lips." Again: "Whoso beareth false witness against his neighbour, he Prov. xxv. is a very club, a sword, and a sharp arrow." Our Saviour Christ saith: "Thou shalt Matt. xix. not speak false witness." Again: "Out of the heart come false witnesses and evil speak- Matt. xv. ings: these defile a man."

Father. Is God angry with such as bear false witness against their neighbour? *Son.* Who doubteth of that? Gave he not this commandment by his servant Moses to the people of Israel? "If any unrighteous witness rise up against a man to accuse Deut. xix. him of trespass, then both the men which strive together shall stand before the Lord, before the priests and the judges which shall be in those days; and the judges shall make diligent inquisition. And if the witness be found false, and that he hath given false witness against his brother, then shall ye do unto him as he had thought to do unto his brother; and thou shalt put evil away from thee. And other shall hear and fear, and shall henceforth commit no more any such wickedness among you. And thine eye shall have no compassion, but soul for soul, eye for eye, tooth for tooth, hand for hand, foot for foot." This thing read we practised in the two elders, which gave false witness against the virtuous and chaste lady Susanna; also in those princes Hist. Sus. and lords, which sought the destruction of Daniel the prophet. Furthermore, the wise Dan. vi. man saith: "The Lord hateth a false witness that bringeth up lies." Again: "A Prov. vi. false witness shall not remain unpunished; and he that speaketh lies shall not escape." Prov. xix. Also in another place he saith: "A false witness shall perish; but he that is a true Prov. xxi. man boldly speaketh that he hath heard."

Father. Is false witness-bearing only forbidden in this precept? *Son.* Not only that, but also all other vices and abuses of the tongue.

Father. Where is lying forbidden in the word of God? *Son.* God saith by his Of lying. servant Moses: "Ye shall not lie." The wise man saith: "God hateth a lying tongue." Lev. xix. Prov. vi. Jesus the son of Sirach hath these words: "In no wise speak against the word of Ecclus. iv. truth; but be ashamed of the lies of thine own ignorance. Shame not to confess thine error, and submit not thyself unto every man because of sin." Again: "Make no lies Ecclus. vii. against thy brother, neither do the same against thy friend. Use not to make any manner of lie; for the custom thereof is not good." Once again he saith: "A lie is Ecclus. xx. a wicked shame in a man, yet shall it be ever in the mouth of the unwise. A thief is better than a man that is accustomed to lie; but they both shall have destruction to heritage." The psalmograph saith: "Thou, O Lord, shalt destroy all them that Psal. v. speak leasing: the Lord will abhor both the blood-thirsty and deceitful man." The holy apostle saith: "Put away lying, and speak every man truth unto his neighbour; Eph. iv. forasmuch as we are members one of another." Again: "Put away wrath, fierceness, Col. iii. maliciousness, cursed speaking, filthy communication out of your mouth. Lie not one to another; seeing that ye have put off the old man with his works, and have put on the new man, which is renewed into the knowledge and image of him that made him."

Father. Will God punish them also that are liars? *Son.* Heard you not even now out of the words of Salomon, that "God hateth a lying tongue"? Again, of Prov. vi. Jesus the son of Sirach, that "the liar shall have destruction for his heritage"? Item Ecclus. xx. of the psalmograph, that "God will destroy them that speak lies"? Moreover Salo- Psal. v. mon saith: "Lying lips are abomination unto the Lord; but they that labour for Prov. xii. truth please him." Again he saith: "The mouth that lieth slayeth the soul." Read Wisd. i. we not also in the last chapter of St John's Revelations, that "such as make leas- Rev. xxi. ings shall have their portion with enchanters, and whoremongers, and murderers, and idolaters, in that lake that brenneth with fire and brimstone"? The devil is a liar Gen. iii.

John viii. and the father of all lying. Therefore whosoever followeth him in this behalf shall
Matt. xxv. with him feel the like and very same torments in hell-fire.

Father. A reward worthy such an act. But come off, tell me, is false witness-
Of slandering. bearing and lying only forbidden in this precept? *Son.* Not only: for slandering, evil reporting, backbiting, defaming of our neighbour, with all other vices of the tongue, are here also forbidden.

Father. What saith the holy scripture of these things?

Lev. xix. *Son.* God saith: "Thou shalt not go up and down as a privy accuser among thy people: neither shalt thou stand against the blood of thy neighbour: I am the Lord. Thou shalt not hate thy brother in thine heart," &c. Jesus the son of Sirach saith:
Ecclus. v. "Be not a privy accuser as long as thou livest, and use no slander with thy tongue. For shame and sorrow goeth over the thief, and an evil name over him that is double-tongued; but he that is a privy accuser of other men shall be hated, envied, and con-
Ecclus. xxi. founded." Again: "A privy accuser of other men shall defile his own soul, and be hated of every man; but he that keepeth his tongue and is discreet shall come to
Ecclus. xxviii. honour." Also in another place: "Beware of strife, and thou shalt make thy sins fewer. For an angry man kindleth variance, and the ungodly disquieteth friends, and putteth discord among them that be at peace." "A tongue that beareth false witness bringeth death. The slanderer and double-tongued is cursed; for many one that be
Rom. xii. friends setteth he at variance." St Paul saith: "Bless them which persecute you:
Eph. iv. bless (I say) and curse not." Again: "Let all bitterness, and fierceness, and wrath, and roaring, and cursed speaking be put away from you with all maliciousness. Be ye courteous one to another, merciful, forgiving one another, even as God for Christ's sake hath forgiven you."

Father. Fall these also into the displeasure of God? *Son.* Yea, verily. Heard
Ecclus. xxi. ye not afore, that "he which is a privy accuser of other men defileth his own soul"?
Matt. xv. "Out of the heart," saith our Saviour Christ, "proceed evil thoughts, murders, breaking of wedlock, whoredoms, thefts, false witness, blasphemies, or evil speakings. These
Matt. xii. are the things which defile a man." Again he saith: "Of every idle word that men shall speak, they shall give accompts in the day of judgment. For out of thy words shalt thou be justified, and out of thy words thou shalt be condemned." St Paul saith,
1 Cor. vi. that "cursed speakers shall not inherit the kingdom of God."

Father. Now that we have heard what God forbiddeth in this his law, declare also unto me what he requireth of us, that we may learn to know and to do his blessed will and pleasure.

What God requireth in this commandment. *Son.* First, he requireth of us, that we boldly and without fear (whensoever we be called of any temporal ruler to bear witness in any matter) testify the truth, and by no means, neither for love nor for hatred, dissemble and cloke that which we know to be true, but freely utter it, although displeasure at the hands of the ungodly should
Ecclus. iv. follow; as the wise man saith: "For righteousness take pains with all thy soul, and for the truth strive thou unto the death; and God shall fight for thee against thine
Exod. xxiii. enemies." This is God's commandment. "Thou shalt not hinder (saith he) the right of the poor in their suit. Keep thee far from a false matter; and the innocent and righteous see thou slay not; for I will not justify the wicked. Thou shalt take no
Lev. xix. gifts; for gifts blind the sight, and pervert the words of the righteous." Again: "Ye shall not do unrighteousness in judgment. Thou shalt not favour the poor, nor honour the mighty; but in righteousness shalt thou judge thy neighbour." The wise man also
Prov. xii. saith: "A just man will tell the truth, and shew the thing that is right; but a false witness deceiveth. A slanderous person pricketh like a sword; but a wise man's tongue is wholesome. A true mouth is ever constant; but a dissembling tongue is soon changed."

Secondly, God requireth of us, that we should not only not backbite, slander, and defame our neighbour, but also that we speak well of him, defend his good name, set forth his good report, maintain his honest estimation, and rather cover, cloke, and dissemble our neighbour's faults, than accuse and publish them unto his hindrance and
Prov. x. destruction, as Salomon saith: "Evil will stirreth up strife; but love covereth the mul-
1 Pet. iv. titude of sins." Hereto pertaineth the saying of St Peter: "Above all things have fervent love among yourselves; for love shall cover the multitude of sins."

Thirdly, it is required of us, not only that we shall not through our misreports and slanderous words set neighbours together at variance, but also, if any be at dissension among themselves, to help to reconcile them, to make them friends, to set them at one, and to link them together again in true amity and unfeigned love, that we may be of that number of whom our Saviour Christ speaketh on this manner: "Blessed are they which make peace; for they shall be called the sons of God." Matt. v.

Fourthly, God requireth of us, that we should at all times so use our tongue, that it may profit, not disprofit our neighbour, quiet, not disquiet him, further, not hinder, his good name and estimation; and in fine, so to use our tongue, that it may be the organ of the Holy Ghost, ready at all times to set forth the glory of God and the commodity of our neighbour.

And that we may the more conveniently this do, it shall not be unprofitable at all times to set before our eyes these sayings of the holy scripture. David saith: "What man is he that lusteth to live, and would fain see good days? Keep thy tongue from evil, and thy lips that they speak no guile. Eschew evil and do good, seek peace and ensue it." "For a man full of words shall not prosper upon the earth: evil shall hunt the wicked person to overthrow him." Therefore prayeth that prince-like prophet on this manner: "Set a watch, O Lord, before my mouth, and keep the door of my lips." Salomon hath these golden sentences: "Where much babbling is, there must needs be offence; but he that refraineth his lips is wise." "A wise man useth but few words; and he is a man of understanding, that maketh much of his spirit. Yea, a very fool, when he holdeth his tongue, is counted wise, and to have understanding, when he shutteth his lips." "A word spoken in due season is like apples of gold in a graven work of silver." Jesus the son of Sirach saith: "Learn before thou speak." "Who shall set a watch before my mouth, and a sure seal upon my lips, that I fall not with them, and that my tongue destroy me not?" The holy apostle saith: "Let no filthy communication proceed out of your mouth, but that which is good to edify withal, as oft as need is; that it may minister grace to the hearers." Again: "Let your speech be always well savoured and powdered with salt, that ye may know how ye ought to answer every man." St James saith: "Let every man be swift to hear, but slow to speak, and slow to wrath." "If any man among you seemeth to be devout, and refraineth not his tongue, but deceiveth his own heart, this man's devotion is in vain." "The tongue is a little member, and boasteth great things: it is a fire and a world of wickedness: it defileth the whole body, and setteth a-fire all that we have of nature, and is itself set a-fire even of hell:" it is "an unruly evil, full of deadly poison," &c. St Peter also saith: "Render not evil for evil, or rebuke for rebuke; but contrariwise, bless, knowing that ye are thereunto called, even that ye should be heirs of the blessing. For he that doth long after life, and loveth to see good days, let him refrain his tongue from evil, and his lips that they speak no guile. Let him eschew evil and do good: let him seek peace and ensue it. For the eyes of the Lord are over the righteous; and his ears are open unto their prayers." Again: "The face of the Lord is over them that do evil." And to be short, it shall not a little profit, but help greatly, to remember this saying of our Saviour Christ: "Of every idle word that men shall speak they shall render accompts at the day of judgment."

[Margin: Psal. xxxiv. Psal. cxl. Psal. cxli. Prov. x. Prov. xvii. Prov. xxv. Ecclus. xviii. Ecclus. xxii. Eph. vi. Col. iv. James i. James iii. 1 Pet. iii. Psal. xxxiv. Matt. xii.]

Father. Thou hast satisfied mine expectation concerning the ninth commandment. Rehearse me now the tenth commandment, as it followeth in order. *Son.* It is this:

"Thou shalt not covet thy neighbour's house. Thou shalt not covet thy neighbour's wife, his servant, his maid, his ox, his ass, nor any thing that is thy neighbour's." The tenth commandment.

Father. What is the good pleasure of God in this commandment? *Son.* Forasmuch as the words of the aforesaid commandments seem by outward appearance to require nothing of us, but politic, civil, and external justice or righteousness; lest that any man should think to have fulfilled the law by bringing forth, after a certain manner, the outward works of the law, and so think himself to be somewhat, when indeed he is nothing, and by this means glory of his own perfection and righteousness, whereas all his glory ought to be only in the Lord our God, as it is written, 2 Cor. x. Jer. ix. 1 Cor. i. "He that glorieth, let him glory in the Lord;" God, willing to shew man unto himself, what he is, with all the strengths of his free will, with all his perfection and righteousness, with all his good works and merits, in this his law requireth of us not only politic, civil, and outward justice, but also spiritual and inward justice, with the full and perfect consent of the mind, with the unspotted cleanness of the heart, with the pure thoughts, godly desires, and holy affects of the spirit; yea, and that without any grudging or concupiscence to the contrary: which thing is impossible 1 Cor. ii. for any natural man to do, which "understandeth not the things that belong unto 2 Cor. iii. God:" which of himself is not able so much as to think a good thought: whose Eph. ii. Psal. li. heart (as of him which by nature is the child of wrath, begotten, conceived, and Jer. xvii. Gen. vi. viii. born in sin) is lewd and unsearchable: whose "imaginations of the thoughts of his heart Isai. lxiv. are evil continually even from his youth:" whose "righteousness and best works are as Rom. vii. a cloth defiled[1];" forasmuch as "the law is spiritual," and he "carnal, sold under sin," 2 Cor. iii. yea, and the very bond-slave of Satan, not able of himself either to think, breathe, speak, or do, that is praiseworthy before God.

And here must all flesh with all humility and reverence fall down before the Rom. iii. majesty of God, and confess themselves most grievous sinners, and worthy of everlasting damnation, forasmuch as they are justly proved transgressors of the law of Deut. xxvii. Gal. iii. God; seeing it is written: "Cursed be every one that continueth not in all things which are written in the book of the law to fulfil them." For no man liveth which ☞ fulfilleth the law of God with such purity of mind, with such obedience of heart, with such free will of the spirit, and with such pure and uncorrupt motions of the inward man, as the law requireth, according to this saying of our Saviour Christ: John vii. Rom. vii. "Moses gave you a law; and yet none of you keepeth the law." "We know," saith St Paul, "that the law is spiritual; but I am carnal, sold under sin."

Father. God, therefore, in this his tenth and last commandment requireth of us not only outward justice, but also inward righteousness, so that we may not once What God requireth of us in his law. lust or covet against the law of God. *Son*. Not only in this last commandment, but in all the other also God requireth that we shall not only, after a certain manner, fulfil them outwardly, but also inwardly, with a full and perfect consent of a pure and uncorrupt heart, without any grudging or concupiscence to the contrary.

Father. Prove by the word of God, that we may not so much as once lust or covet against the will of God, and that concupiscence is sin before God. *Son*. That Rom. vii. concupiscence is sin, it is manifest by these words of the apostle: "I had not known," saith he, "what lust had meant, except the law had said, Thou shalt not lust. But sin took an occasion by the means of the commandment, and wrought in me all manner of concupiscence."

Now, that we are forbidden to lust or covet contrary to the commandment of God, and that, if we do otherwise, I mean, nourish any evil concupiscence or lust in our heart, although it never brast out into outward work, we are transgressors of the law of God, and worthy of everlasting damnation, it appeareth manifestly by Matt. v. these words of Christ: "Whosoever looketh on another man's wife to lust after her hath committed adultery with her already in his heart." Here is it evident, that God requireth not only an outward cleanness of the body, but also an inward purity of the mind; so that we must be unspotted both in body and in mind. For as he is an adulterer before man, which is apprehended in the very act of gross adultery; so likewise is he an adulterer before God, which only in his heart lusteth after another man's wife, although he never commit the act, no, nor once make mention John iv. of it so much as by word. "God is a Spirit," and he judgeth all things of the ☞ spirit. If the spirit and inward man be once polluted with filthy lusts and fleshly concupiscences, we are straightways before God transgressors and breakers of his law, and worthy to be condemned unto everlasting fire, although we appear never so holy, pure, and honest before the blind world, which only seeth and considereth the outward deeds, and cannot behold the secrets of our heart, which only are known

[[1] Two words are omitted.]

unto God. Therefore Christ, the Wisdom of the Father, and the true interpreter of the law, in the aforesaid sentence pronounceth him not only an adulterer, which committeth the gross act of adultery, but also which only in his heart nourisheth fleshly and unclean lusts; to declare unto us, that the law of God, as St Paul saith, "is spiritual," Rom. vii.
and requireth not only an outward cleanness of the body, but also a perfect purity of the mind, utterly estranged from all evil, wicked, and ungodly concupiscences and lusts. Hereto pertaineth the saying of Jesus, the son of Sirach: "Thou shalt not lust after Ecclus. xxv.
the beauty of a woman, lest thou be provoked in desire toward her."

And as our Saviour Christ expoundeth this commandment spiritually, "Thou Matt. v.
shalt not commit adultery," declaring that not only pure bodies but also clean minds, uncorrupt affects, godly motions, &c., are required unto the perfect fulfilling thereof; so likewise doeth he in the other. This kind of doctrine used also both the apostles and prophets; as for an ensample, let us take this commandment: "Thou shalt not kill." Exod. xx. Deut. v.
Whereas the words seemeth only to forbid gross manslaughter, the mind of the lawgiver, which is the Lord our God, is that we shall not only not kill our neighbour, but also bear no malice nor envy against him in our heart, but rather love him, and seek to preserve him to the uttermost of our power. For Moses writeth on this manner: "Thou shalt not hate thy brother in thine heart." "Thou shalt not Lev. xix.
avenge thyself, nor be mindful of wrong against the children of my people; but thou shalt love thy neighbour even as thyself." St John also saith: "He that loveth 1 John iii.
not his brother abideth in death. Whosoever hateth his brother is a manslayer: and ye know that no manslayer hath everlasting life abiding in him."

Of these authorities of the holy scripture do we learn, that this commandment of God, "Thou shalt not kill," forbiddeth us not only to abstain from gross manslaughter, but also from all malice, envy, hatred, and all manner of displeasure-bearing against our neighbour; so that before God he is not only a manslayer, which with weapon killeth his brother, but he also which in his heart hath conceived malice, hatred, and displeasure against his neighbour, although it never brasteth into outward and gross manslaughter, as the history of Caim doth evidently declare: in the which we read that, before he murdered his brother Abel, God would not once vouchsafe to Gen. iv.
look neither unto Caim nor unto his gifts. Why so? Because of the malice and hatred 1 John iii.
which he had already conceived in his heart against his brother Abel. He was now before God a bloody murderer, and had transgressed this commandment of God, "Thou shalt not kill," and therefore worthy of everlasting damnation. The wise man also saith: "The bread of the needy is the life of the poor: he that defraudeth Ecclus.
him of it is a plain murderer." Here the unmerciful man is called a murderer, not xxxiv.
that he hath with any weapon slain the poor man, but because he hath withdrawn that from the poor and needy, through the covetous affection which is in his heart, that should sustain the miserable life of the poor. The blind world recounteth the unmerciful man no murderer; but before God such one is both a murderer and the heir of everlasting damnation, as St James saith: "The judgment shall be James ii.
without mercy to him that hath shewed no mercy." Thus may we see, that all Matt. xxv. Luke xvi.
the commandments of God require of us not only an outward and civil righteousness, but also an inward and spiritual justice, with pure affects and clean motions of the mind, utterly sequestered from all carnality and imperfection.

Father. Let me hear more sentences of the holy scripture, wherein we are forbidden to nourish evil concupiscences and wicked lusts in our hearts: for many be of this mind, that evil lusts and ungodly thoughts defile not man. *Son.* That which in the holy scriptures is forbidden is plain sin. Evil concupiscence in the word of God is forbidden; therefore is evil concupiscence sin. And as touching wicked and unclean thoughts, thus saith the holy scripture: "God hateth and utterly ab- Prov. vi.
horreth an heart that goeth about with wicked imaginations." Again: "Froward Wisd. i.
thoughts separate from God." Item: "Inquisition shall be made for the thoughts of the ungodly; and the report of his words shall come unto God, so that his wickedness shall be punished." Our Saviour Christ saith also: "Out of the heart Matt. xv.
proceed evil thoughts: these are the things which defile man." Now as concerning

the sentences, which forbid the filthy raging lusts of the heart, the scripture is full
Prov. iv. of them in every place. Salomon saith: "Keep thine heart with all diligence; for
Ecclus. v. thereupon hangeth life." Jesus the son of Sirach saith: "Follow not the lusts of
Ecclus. xviii. thine own heart." Again: "Follow not thy lusts, but turn thee from thine own
will: for if thou givest thy soul her desires, it shall make thine enemies to laugh
Ecclus. xli. thee to scorn." Also in another place: "Be ashamed to desire another man's wife,
and to make many trifling words with her maiden, or to stand by her bedside."
Ecclus. xxv. Item: "Look not too narrowly upon the beauty of a woman, lest thou be pro-
Prov. vi. voked in desire toward her." Salomon saith again: "Lust not after the beauty
of a strange woman in thine heart, lest thou be taken with her fair looks." The
Zech. vii. prophet Zachary saith: "Let no man imagine evil against his brother in his heart."
Zech. viii. Again: "Speak every man the truth unto his neighbour: execute judgment truly
and peaceably within your ports. None of you imagine evil in his heart against
his neighbour, and love no false oaths; for all these are the things that I hate,
saith the Lord."

Mark iv. Our Saviour Christ saith: "The cares of this world, and the deceitfulness of riches,
and the lusts of other things, do so choke the word of God, that it is made unfruit-
Luke xxi. ful." Again: "Take heed that your hearts be not overwhelmed with the cares of
Rom. xiii. this life." St Paul saith: "Make not provision for the flesh to fulfil the lusts of
Col. iii. it." Again: "Mortify your earthy members; fornication, uncleanness, unnatural lust,
1 Tim. vi. evil concupiscence," &c. Also in another place: "Godliness is great riches, if a man
be content with that he hath. For we brought nothing into the world, neither may
we carry any thing out. But when we have food and raiment, we must therewith
be content. They that will be rich fall into temptation and snares of the devil,
and into many foolish and noisome lusts, which drown men into perdition and de-
struction. For the covetousness of money is the root of all evil, which while some
lusted after, they erred from the faith, and tangled themselves with many sorrows.
But thou, man of God, flee such things. Follow righteousness, godliness, faith, love,
Heb. xiii. patience, meekness." Item: "Let your conversation be without covetousness, and be
Josh. i. content with such things as ye have already. For he hath said, I will not fail thee,
Psal. xxvii. neither forsake thee: so that we may boldly say, The Lord is my helper, and I will
James i. not fear what man may do unto me." St James saith: "Let no man say, when he
is tempted, that he is tempted of God. For as God cannot be tempted with evil,
so neither he himself tempteth any man unto evil. But every man is tempted, when
he is drawn away and enticed of his own concupiscence. Then when lust is conceived,
she bringeth forth sin; and sin, when it is finished, bringeth forth death." St John
1 John ii. also saith: "See that ye love not the world, neither the things that are in the
world. If any man love the world, the love of the Father is not in him. For all
that is in the world, as the lust of the flesh, and the lust of the eyes, and the pride
of life, is not of the Father, but of the world. And the world passeth away and
the lust thereof; but he that doeth the will of God abideth for ever."

Evil lusts punished. *Father*. Doth evil concupiscence or lust also so displease God, that he will punish
Prov. vi. it? *Son*. We heard afore out of the mouth of Salomon, that God hateth and utterly
abhorreth that heart, which goeth about with wicked imaginations; and that God
Wisd. i. will punish the wickedness of an ungodly mind. The like thing heard we of the
Zech. vii. viii. prophet Zachary. St Paul also saith, that "if we live after the flesh, we shall
Rom. viii. die," that is to say, be damned for ever. And in the first book of Moses we read,
Gen. iv. that Caim was found a murderer before God, before he slew his brother, because
1 John iii. Jude. of the malice and hatred that he had conceived in his heart against his brother;
so that God would neither look upon him nor upon his offerings. Therefore was
he cursed, and all his life-time was he a fugitive and a vagabond, and is now a
Gen. xii. damned soul in hell-fire. In the aforesaid book also read we, that God smote Pharao
and his house with great plagues, because in his heart he brenned with evil concu-
piscence and fleshly lust toward Sara, Abraham's wife; whom notwithstanding he had
not touched, neither knew he that she was Abraham's wife. The like thing read we
Gen. xx. of king Abimelech.

Father. What requireth God then of us in this his last commandment? *Son.* That we, having contented minds with such things as wherewith God hath blessed us, should not desire unlawfully any thing that appertaineth unto our neighbour, but rather do our diligence, that whatsoever is his may remain his, unto his own commodity and profit; yea, and if we be able further to pleasure him or his, to do it unto the uttermost of our power, being no less godly and profitably affected toward him, than we are toward ourselves, yea, and that from the very heart. In fine, God requireth of us both in this last precept and in all other, that we bring unto the fulfilling of his law, not only outward, but also inward righteousness, not only the innocency of the body, but also the purity of the mind; so that both our bodies, and souls, hearts, minds, desires, and thoughts be pure, clean, and without spot, according to this saying of St Paul: "Ye are dearly bought; therefore glorify God in your bodies and in your spirits, which belong unto God."

What God requireth of us in the tenth commandment.

1 Cor. vi.

Father. Rehearse me the sum briefly of all the commandments of God, that we may know, in few words, what is our duty to do both toward God and our neighbour. *Son.* Christ saith: "Hear, O Israel: The Lord our God is Lord only. And thou shalt love the Lord thy God with all thy heart, and with all thy soul, and with all thy mind, and with all thy strength. This is the first commandment. And the second is like unto this: Thou shalt love thy neighbour as thyself. In these two commandments hang all the law and the prophets." "Whatsoever ye would that men should do to you, do ye even so to them also: for this is the law and the prophets." St Paul saith: "Owe nothing to any man, but this, that ye love one another. For he that loveth another hath fulfilled the law. For these commandments, Thou shalt not commit adultery, Thou shalt not kill, Thou shalt not steal, Thou shalt not bear false witness, Thou shalt not lust, and so forth, if there be any other commandment, it is all comprehended in this saying, namely, Love thy neighbour as thyself. Love hurteth not his neighbour: therefore is love the fulfilling of the law." Again he saith: "All the law is fulfilled in one word, which is this: Thou shalt love thy neighbour as thyself." Also in another place: "The end of the commandment is love, out of a pure heart, and of a good conscience, and of faith unfeigned." St John saith: "This is God's commandment, that we believe on the name of his Son Jesus Christ, and that we love one another." "For this commandment have we of him, that he which loveth God should love his brother also."

The sum of the law.

Mark xii. Matt. xxii.

Matt. vii. Luke vi.

Rom. xiii.

Gal. v.

1 Tim. i.

1 John iii.

1 John iv.

Father. Well, now have we heard, my dear son, what the law is; to what end the law was given; and how many commandments of the law there are; and what is required of us that we should do concerning the fulfilling of them. This law of God seemeth unto me a very heavy yoke and a burden almost intolerable, if the righteousness of Christ in this behalf did not help us, which (as St Paul saith) is "the perfect fulfilling of the law to justify all that believe." Now, forasmuch as a new life requireth new manners, and our faith and love toward God is to be declared in the obedience of his law, and in the framing of our life according to his holy commandment; which thing of ourselves and of our own strengths we by no means are able to perform, seeing we be not able so much as to think a good thought, much less to accomplish the will of God with such purity and innocency of heart, as is required of us; come off, tell me, what is now to be done, that we may obtain some both will and strength, whereby we may be able to shew ourselves not altogether negligent in conforming ourselves to the blessed will of God, but that our "light may so shine before men, that they may see our good works and glorify our Father which is in heaven." *Son.* This question, O my dear father, is asked in due time. To obtain will and strength to walk in the law of God, there is none other way but only to fly unto faithful and hearty prayer, and to crave of the Lord our God by humble supplication the help of his holy Spirit, which may renew our hearts, and engraff in us new affects and new motions, that by this means we may become new creatures, unto the glory, praise, and honour of his holy name. And the order of the doctrine of the catechism requireth now, that we speak of prayer, which is the fourth part of the catechism, as you heard.

Rom. x.

2 Cor. iii.

Matt. v.

Of prayer.

Father. Well said, my son. For we have passed over the first three parts; that is to say, repentance, faith, and law. Now remaineth the fourth part to be entreated of, which thou sayest is prayer. *Son*. Yea, verily.

Father. What order wilt thou take in this treatise of prayer? *Son*. I will, first, by the grace of God and through the help of his holy Spirit, declare what prayer is. Secondly, how we ought to address ourselves unto prayer. Thirdly, I will declare and expound the Lord's prayer; forasmuch as that of all prayers is the best and most excellent, both because of the maker of it, which is the Lord Jesus, and also because in few words it containeth abundantly whatsoever is necessary to be desired either for the body or for the soul.

Father. I allow thy order well. Tell me therefore, my son, what prayer is.

THE FOURTH PART OF THE CATECHISM.

OF PRAYER.

Son. Our preacher and also our catechist hath declared unto us divers definitions of prayer.

Father. Let me hear one or two of them. *Son.* Prayer is a lifting up of a pure mind unto God, in the which we ask somewhat of him according to his will. (What prayer is.) Or thus: Prayer is an earnest talk with God, proceeding from a very inward, deep, and brenning or fervent affection of the heart, craving somewhat at the hand of God. Or else thus: Prayer is a mourning, or a longing and a desire, of the spirit to God-ward, for that which she lacketh; as the sick mourneth and sorroweth in his heart, longing for health.

Father. Of these definitions of prayer I learn three things. First, that prayer is the work and exercise of the mind, heart, or spirit, I mean, the inward man. Secondly, that in our prayer we must ask and crave somewhat. Thirdly, that that thing which we desire to have, we must require it at the hand of God. *Son.* Truth.

Father. How provest thou, that prayer is the work of the spirit? *Son.* I am so taught by the word of God. (Prayer is the work of the spirit. John iv.) Our Saviour Christ saith: "The hour cometh, and now it is, when the true worshippers shall worship the Father in spirit and truth: for the Father seeketh such that should worship him. God is a Spirit; and they that worship him must worship him in spirit and truth." St Paul also saith: "God is my witness, whom I worship in my spirit." (Rom. i.) Likewise saith the psalmograph: "O my soul, praise thou the Lord, and all that is within me, praise his holy name. (Psal. ciii.) O my soul, praise thou the Lord, and forget not all his benefits." Again: "My heart is fixed, O God, my heart is fixed: I will sing and give praise." (Psal. lvii.) The history of Moses, when he led the people of Israel out of Egypt, declareth manifestly, that prayer is the work and exercise of the spirit. (Exod. xiv.) For when he by reason saw no way how to escape either from the bloody hands of that most bloody tyrant Pharao, or else from drowning, he only groaned and lamented in his heart unto God, desiring his help for their safe deliverance; and God said unto him, "What criest thou unto me?" His crying was not the voice of the mouth, but the affection of the heart. He cried with a sorrowful mind unto God, and he was heard, although the mouth kept silence, and obtained that he desired. Likewise Anna the wife of Helcana, when she had been long barren, prayed unto God for to give her children. (1 Sam. i.) But what saith the scripture of her prayer? "She spake in her heart: her lips only moved, but her voice was heard nothing at all." Who seeth not now, that prayer is the work of the mind, heart, spirit, and inward man? Not without a cause, therefore, saith the blessed apostle St Paul: "Speak among yourselves in psalms, hymns, and spiritual songs, singing and making melody in your hearts to the Lord." (Eph. v.)

Father. What sayest thou then of those prayers, which are only uttered with the lips and tongue, yea, and that without the affection of the spirit? *Son.* Even that, which Christ speaketh in the gospel, alleging it out of the prophet Esay: "This people," saith he, "draweth nigh unto me, and honoureth me with their lips, howbeit their heart is far from me; but in vain do they honour me." (Isai. xxix. Matt. xv.)

Father. Dost thou then utterly contemn and condemn prayers that come from the mouth, tongue, and lips? *Son.* If they proceed from the heart, and rise of the affection of the mind, they are not to be discommended, but rather commended, inasmuch as the tongue doth nothing but utter the fervent desire of the mind, the prayer still remaining the work of the inward man. (Mouth prayer proceeding from the heart is also commendable.) The outward speaking or singing of prayers, the kneeling or prostrating of ourselves, the lifting up of hands and eyes, the knocking of the breast, and such other like gestures in praying, are not discommendable, so long as they spring of the fervent affection of the mind. For all these things have many godly men used in their prayers heretofore, and yet do. "Let us," saith the prophet Jeremy, "lift up our hearts with our hands to the Lord even unto the heavens." (Lam. iii.) St Paul also saith: "I will that men pray in every place, lifting up pure hands without (1 Tim. ii.)

wrath and contention." The psalmograph saith: "I will magnify the Lord at all times: his praise shall be always in my mouth." Moses and the prophets, Christ and his apostles, prayed with expressed words, as the scripture doth declare. Moreover, we [Matt. xxvi. Acts xx. Luke xviii.] read that Christ fell flat upon the ground, when he prayed. Paul and so many as were with him kneeled at a certain time, when they prayed. The publican knocked his breast, when he prayed.

Father. The second thing, which I noted in the definitions of prayer, is that whosoever intendeth to pray with fruit, he must in his prayer ask somewhat. *Son.* It is truth. For unto what end should we pray, if in our prayer we ask nothing? Is not the office of prayer to ask that which we lack? Which of the godly ever prayed, not setting before the eyes of their mind the cause of their prayer? Otherwise to pray is nothing else than to mock and scorn God.

Father. Yet many there are, which persuade themselves to pray, yea, and to merit greatly for their praying, when they, notwithstanding, neither know what nor wherefore they pray. *Son.* The ignorancy and blindness of such is greatly to be lamented. [Matt. xii.] And if at the day of judgment, as Christ affirmeth, we shall render an accompts of every idle word that we have spoken, what is then to be thought of those words, which be not only vainly and idly, but also superstitiously and dissemblingly, uttered [Matt. xxiii.] in prayer? To pretend to pray, and not to pray, is double wickedness, and deserveth the greater damnation.

Father. I gather also of the definitions of prayer, that whensoever we ask any thing, [Of God only all good things are to be asked.] we must ask it of God only. *Son.* Is it not meet and right so to do? Whither should the sick man go for counsel, but unto the physician? Whither shall the thirsty hart repair to slake her thirst, but unto the water-brooks? So likewise, whither shall we go to obtain any good thing by prayer, but unto God, which is the fountain and well- [James i.] spring of all goodness? "Every good gift and every perfect gift," saith St James, "is from above, and cometh down from the Father of lights." Unto whom prayed all the holy patriarchs and the godly men, which lived under the old testament, but unto [Psal. xxii.] God? as David saith: "Our fathers trusted in thee; they trusted in thee, and thou deliveredst them. They cried unto thee, and they were saved: they trusted in thee, and they were not confounded." And as all the godly of the old testament directed their prayers only unto God, so likewise did all the holy men of the new testament. We also in every age ought to make our prayers unto God alone, according to their [Psal. l.] example; yea, according to the doctrine of the holy scripture. "Call upon me," saith God, "in the day of thy trouble, and I will deliver thee, and thou shalt honour me." [Psal. cxx.] "When I was in trouble," saith David, "I cried unto the Lord; and he graciously [Psal. xxv.] heard me." Again: "Mine eyes are continually unto the Lord; for he shall pluck my feet out of the snare." Item: "The eyes of the Lord are upon the righteous, and his ears are bent unto their prayers."

Father. Notwithstanding, some there are, which offer their prayers unto creatures, and crave of them all good things necessary both for the body and for the soul.

Son. These walk a wrong way, and may right well be resembled, likened, and com- [1 Kings xviii.] pared to the priests of Baal, which cried continually unto their idol, "O Baal, hear [Psal. xciv.] us, O Baal, hear us;" and yet notwithstanding they were not heard. "Take heed," saith the psalmograph, "ye unwise among the people: O ye fools, when will ye understand? He that planted the ear, shall he not hear? Or he that made the eye, shall he not see? The Lord knoweth the thoughts of man." He that flieth unto any creature, either in heaven or in earth, for succour, or asketh remission of his sins and everlasting life, or whatsoever good thing it be besides, except of God alone, he is a thief, and robbeth God of his honour, and grievously offendeth against the first commandment of God, and is of the number of those, against whom God complaineth [Jer. ii.] by the prophet on this manner: "Be astonied, O ye heavens, be afraid and abashed at such a thing, saith the Lord. For my people have done two evils: they have forsaken me, the fountain of the water of life, and digged them pits, yea, vile and [Deut. vi. Matt. iv. Mark i. Luke iv.] broken pits, that can hold no water." "Thou shalt worship the Lord thy God (saith Moses), and him alone shalt thou serve." Can there be any greater service done, or more honour shewed unto God, than in the time of adversity to fly unto his holy name for succour, by faithful and earnest prayer, as unto a strong tower? Again, in the time of prosperity, to praise and to magnify his glorious name for the benefits received? as the psalmograph saith: "What reward shall I give unto the Lord for Psal. cxvi. all the benefits that he hath done unto me? I will receive the cup of salvation, and call upon the name of the Lord. I will pay my vows in the presence of all his people."

Father. Thou holdest then, that whatsoever good thing we have need of, appertaining unto the body or unto the soul, we ought to ask it only of God, the alone fountain of all goodness. *Son*. Yea, verily, and that in the name only of his most dear Son Jesus Christ, our alone Mediator, Advocate, and Intercessor. "For there is one Lord 1 Tim. ii. of all, which is plentifully rich unto all that call upon him. For whosoever doth call 1 John ii. Rom. viii. on the name of the Lord, he shall be safe." "God is able," saith St Paul, "to do Joel ii. Rom. x. exceeding abundantly above all that we ask or think, according to the power that Acts ii. xxii. Eph. iii. worketh in us." "The hand of the Lord is not so shortened, that it cannot help: neither Isai. lix. is his ear so stopped, that it cannot hear:" nor yet are his eyes so dim, that they Psal. xciv. can no more see. "Blessed is the man, that putteth his trust in the name of the Psal. xl. Lord, and regardeth not vanities and false imaginations." "Thou, O God, art our Father," saith the prophet Esay: "Abraham knoweth us not; neither is Israel ac- Isai. lxiii. quainted with us. But thou, Lord, art our Father and Redeemer, and thy name is everlasting."

Father. We have talked sufficiently for this present concerning the definition of prayer. Let me hear now, how we ought to address and prepare ourselves unto the exercise of prayer, that we may pray with fruit; seeing it is written, "Before thou Ecclus. xviii. prayest, prepare thy soul, and be not as one that tempteth God:" lest, if we pray unworthily, we be found in the number of those, to whom God speaketh on this manner by the prophet: "When ye hold out your hands, I will turn mine eyes from Isai. i. you; and when ye make many prayers, I will not hear you; for your hands are full of blood." *Son*. Prayer is a precious treasure in the sight of God, and easily obtaineth The virtue of prayer. whatsoever it asketh, so that it be made according to the will of God. But if it be framed contrary to the good pleasure of God, it bringeth not salvation but destruction, not pleasure but displeasure, not commodity but incommodity, not favour but wrath, not life but death, yea, and finally everlasting damnation. If God could not abide that the Jews should presume to receive the law, which notwithstanding is "the 2 Cor. iii. ministration of death," which also accuseth, judgeth, condemneth, woundeth, killeth, Rom. vii. yea, and casteth down headlong into the dungeon of hell-fire all men without exception for their imperfection and wickedness, if they were not delivered from that damnation by faith in the blood of Christ, before they were sanctified and cleansed; is it to be thought, that God will hear our prayer, although proceeding from a corrupt, filthy, and unpure heart? Can that prayer be accepted of God, and obtain good things at the hand of God, which cometh from an heart void of faith, charity, mercy, &c. and overwhelmed with all beastly and carnal affects? The psalmograph saith: "If I in- Psal. lxvi. cline unto wickedness with my heart, the Lord will not hear me." "We be sure," John ix. saith the blind man, "that God heareth not sinners: (he speaketh of the unpenitent Prov. i. sinners, and of such as glory in their sin, and delight when they have done evil.) But if any man be a worshipper of God, and obedient to his will, him heareth he." St Paul also straitly chargeth us, that we "lift up pure hands" unto God. And our 1 Tim. ii. Saviour Christ saith, that "they which will worship God the Father must worship John iv. him in spirit and truth." Hereunto appertaineth the saying of the psalmograph: "The Lord is nigh unto all that call on him, yea, unto all that call on him in Psal. cxlv. truth."

Father. Seeing then that wickedness must be cast out of our heart, seeing pure Psal. lxvi. hands must be lifted up unto God, seeing God heareth not sinners, but such as 1 Tim. ii. John ix. labour to be obedient unto his holy will, seeing God must be worshipped in spirit John iv. Psal. cxlvi. and truth, in fine, seeing that God is not otherwise to be called upon, but as he hath prescribed in his holy word; come off, tell me, what is to be done, that we may not come altogether unworthily unto the throne of God's majesty, but rather offer up such prayers unto his glorious name, as he shall be well content to accept them for his

How we shall prepare ourselves to pray. mercy's sake in the blood of Christ. *Son.* That we may not altogether unworthily come with our prayers unto the gracious and merciful throne of God's majesty, it shall not be unprofitable to mark these few things, which I shall now rehearse.

The cause which moveth us to pray is diligently to be considered. First of all, if we will pray with fruit, we must diligently and earnestly consider, weigh, and ponder the cause, which moveth us to pray. For whosoever addresseth himself unto prayer, not having an urgent, grave, weighty, and necessary cause to pray, doth none other thing, than after the manner of the popinjay recite a multitude of words without the affection of the mind and the desire of the heart; and so is his prayer a very derision and mocking of God: yea, it is nothing else than hypocrisy and feigned holiness, and therefore also double wickedness.

Father. Few observe this order. *Son.* Few therefore pray before God.

Father. Many think that they do God good service when they pray after this manner, although they know not what nor wherefore they pray. *Son.* Such do nothing less than pray. The godly both of the old and new testament never addressed themselves unto prayer, before some grave and weighty matter provoked them to pray, as divers examples in the holy scripture evidently declare.

Father. Rehearse me some of them. *Son.* Abraham, the father of the faithful,
Gen. xx. prayed for Abimelech and for his household, that God would turn away his wrath
Gen. xxiv. from them. He prayed also for the life of his son Ismael. Abraham's servant prayed
Gen. xxv. for a good and prosperous journey. Isaac prayed that his wife Rebecca might be
Gen. xxx. fruitful and bring forth children. Lia and Rachel, the wives of Jacob, prayed that their barrenness might be taken from them, and that they might become fruitful.
Gen. xxxii. Jacob prayed that he might be delivered from the tyranny of his brother Esau.
Exod. viii. xvii. xxxii. &c. Moses prayed divers times for divers sundry causes. Josua prayed that the sun and
Josh. x. the moon might stand still by the space of an whole day, until he was revenged of
1 Sam. i. his enemies. Anna, the wife of Helcana, prayed that she might conceive and bring
2 Sam. vii. Psal. li. forth children. The Israelites prayed for victory against their enemies. David oftentimes prayed, yea, and that for sundry purposes. I pass over the residue of the godly, both men and women of the old testament, (lest I should seem to be too long,) which always prayed unto God, when they had an urgent and necessary cause.

What shall I speak of them which are remembered in the new testament? The
Matt. viii. lepers prayed that they might be cleansed from their leprosy: the blind that they
Matt. ix. Matt. xv. might be restored to their sight: the woman of Canaan for her daughter: the
Matt. viii. Luke xviii. centurion for his servant: the publican for remission of his sins: Christ himself
John xvii. Acts iv. for his disciples, and for the whole congregation: the apostles for the good success of
Acts vii. the gospel: St Stephen for his enemies. The congregation of Christ prayed for the
Rom. i. deliverance of Peter out of prison. St Paul prayed for the churches of Christ, that
Col. i. 1 Thess. i. they might abide constant and stedfast in the faith of Christ unto the coming of Christ. To be short, none of all the godly at any time attempted to pray unto God, but provoked with some urgent, grave, weighty, and necessary cause, which compelled them to fly unto God for aid, help, and succour. After their examples ought we to behave ourselves.

☞ Therefore, before we pray, let us consider wherefore we will pray, and what moveth us to offer up our prayers unto God, lest that we become like unto those hypocrites,
Matt. vi. which think that they shall be heard for their much babbling sake, howsoever they pray, although they neither know what or wherefore they pray. Let us diligently ponder our necessity, and weigh our cause, and warely aforesee, that our cause, which moveth us to pray, be godly, righteous, and honest, yea, and in all points such as shall not be thought unworthy the ears of God's majesty; I mean, made unto this end, that God thereby may be glorified, we ourselves comforted, and our neighbour not endamaged.

Now, as concerning the causes which ought to move us for to pray, they be infinite and innumerable, whether we respect the body or the mind. If we consider also our state, vocation, or calling, causes many shall abundantly offer themselves unto us, which justly and necessarily ought to provoke us unto prayer. If we weigh the great company of our adversaries, which daily and hourly go about like ravening wolves to devour us; if we ponder our infirmity and weakness, and how unable we be to stand against their power, &c. we shall find abundance of causes wherefore we ought to pray; so that we need not to come slackly and dissolutely, but rather diligently and earnestly, unto prayer.

Father. This then is thy counsel, that, before we attempt to pray, we first of all diligently consider with ourselves, wherefore we will pray, and unto what end we will direct our prayer, that we seem not rather to mock God than to pray God: again, that the cause, which moveth us to pray, be godly, just, honest, and not unworthy the ears of God. *Son.* So is it.

Father. What is requisite more unto the worthy preparation unto prayer? *Son.* Secondly, after that we have diligently considered our necessity, and pondered the cause that moveth us to pray, and have found it good, godly, just, honest, necessary, and not unworthy the hearing of God, so that we find in ourselves, whether we respect the body or the mind, plenty of causes, which justly ought to provoke us to fly unto God, and by faithful and earnest prayer to crave help and succour at his hand, that we may either be delivered from so great evils, or else endued with such benefits from God, as we greatly desire, hunger, and thirst after; it shall be expedient, that we straightways set before the eyes of our mind the commandment of God, which willeth and commandeth us to pray, to call upon his glorious majesty, and to fly unto his holy name, as unto a strong tower and mighty fortress in all our necessities, troubles, adversities, and miseries. The commandment of God to pray.

This commandment of God to pray is earnestly to be weighed, pondered, and considered. For although we have never so many and necessary causes, yea, and those godly, good, righteous, honest, &c., yet, if we had not a commandment from God to pray, who durst so much as once be bold to open his lips for to pray unto God, which is "a consuming fire," which hateth both the wicked and his wickedness, which hath prepared hell-fire to be a reward unto such as transgress his holy law; of the which number we all are without exception, being worthy for our disobedience not only not to be heard, but also to have our miseries increased, and finally to be rewarded with the torments of that "lake which brenneth with fire and brimstone?" Deut. iv. Heb. xii. Rev. xxi.

Come off, tell me, what traitor is so without all shame, that he dare appear in the presence of that prince, and to crave pardon of him, whom he hath most traitorously offended, and whose honour he hath sought utterly to deface and obscure? Yea, rather fleeth not that traitor from the face of that prince so far as his legs are able to bear him, and wisheth that that prince were dead, that by this means he might be free from that punishment which he most righteously hath deserved for his wicked and abominable treason? Now was there never traitor that hath at any time so grievously offended his prince, as we (ah, wretches that we are!) through our infidelity and wicked conversation have offended the Lord our God, that Prince of Glory, yea, that "King of kings, and Lord of lords." How then dare we be bold to shew ourselves before that God, which is "a consuming fire," whom we have so often most grievously offended, and to offer and to present unto his most excellent majesty our prayers for pardon and remission of our sins, or to ask any thing at all of him? Verily, if God had not given us a commandment to pray unto him, we would sooner have put our heads in a bush with Adam, or taken us unto our legs with Caim, or have hanged up ourselves with that traitor Judas, than we would once have opened our lips to pray unto him. And who therefore seeth not here the exceeding great, marvellous, and unspeakable kindness of the Lord our God toward us vile and wretched sinners, which, being hedged round about with the thorns both of so many miseries and wickednesses, and not knowing how to be delivered from them, are notwithstanding commanded of this our most gentle God boldly to come unto him, frankly to lament our miseries unto him, largely to pour out the sighings and groanings of our heavy hearts before him, and frankly and with a good courage to ask all good things of him? O the deep and bottomless seas of God's wonderful mercies toward mankind! An example. 1 Tim. vi. Rev. xvii. xix. Deut. iv. Heb. xii. Gen. iii. Gen. iv. Acts i. Matt. xxvii.

All the commandments therefore of God, wherewith we are provoked unto prayer, are to be embraced as most precious jewels, and to be reposed in the lowest part of our memory as incomparable treasures, that we never forget them; of the which

Psal. l. sort these are that follow. "Call upon me," saith God, "in the time of thy trouble." Here have we a commandment of God to fly unto him with our prayers Matt. vii. in all our troubles, necessities, and miseries. Christ our Saviour saith also: "Ask:" Matt. xxvi. "Seek:" "Knock." Again: "Watch and pray, that ye fall not into temptation." Col. iv. St Paul also saith: "Continue in prayer, and watch in the same with thanksgiving." 1 Thess. v. Again: "Pray continually: in all things give thanks; for this is the will of God."

For no man is able to express what great consolation and comfort, what joy and gladness these commandments to pray bring to troubled and weak consciences. For who now will be afraid even with a good courage to go unto the throne of God's majesty with his prayers, seeing he hath so many commandments to stir him up and to prick him forward to pray; yea, and that out of the mouth of God, which Psal. cxlv. is "faithful in all his words and holy in all his works;" which is not only true, but John xiv. also the self truth?

Let no man object his indignity or unworthiness to pray. Our unworthiness ought to be no let unto us, that we should not be bold to call upon God, so that we repent and turn unto God with full purpose from henceforth to train our life according to the rule of God's word. For God neither for our worthiness nor for our unworthiness heareth us; but for his commandment and promise sake. He hath commanded us to ☞ pray; therefore ought we to pray. For if we should never pray till we were worthy of ourselves before God to pray, so should we never pray: but we therefore pray, because God hath commanded us so to do. Our worthiness is the humble confession of our unworthiness; and our obedience unto the commandment of God to pray maketh us most worthy.

He that will not pray, because he thinketh himself unworthy to pray, might with the same reason be a thief or an adulterer all his life-time, and excuse himself by saying on this manner: I am not worthy to keep these commandments of God, Exod. xx. Deut. v. "Thou shalt not steal," "Thou shalt not commit adultery." But all men are bound to keep all the ten commandments of God: so likewise are they bound to observe Matt. vii. and keep this commandment of praying: "Ask:" "Seek:" "Knock:" &c. For as he falleth into the danger of everlasting damnation, which violateth and breaketh this commandment, "Thou shalt have no strange gods in my sight;" so likewise doth he make himself the son of Satan and the inheritor of hell-fire, which neglecteth and transgresseth this commandment of God, "Watch and pray." For he that said, "Thou shalt not steal;" the same saith also, "Thou shalt pray:" and we owe like obedience to both commandments; and the transgression or breaking of any of these commandments deserveth like pain. He that killeth a man, or he that defileth his neighbour's wife, sinneth not more before God, than he which prayeth not. For as this commandment, "Thou shalt not kill," is a precept negative; so likewise is this commandment, "Thou shalt pray," a precept affirmative; and God requireth the same and like obedience to all his commandments. Let us therefore, when we intend to pray, not be discouraged from prayer, although we feel in ourselves an unworthiness to pray; but rather consider the commandment of God, which willeth us to pray, and according to his will fall to prayer, and ask all good things of him, which is both the only fountain of all goodness, and also the alone horn of plenty.

The promise to hear. *Father*. What is more to be done? *Son*. Thirdly, we must consider the loving gentleness of the Lord our God toward us, which hath not only commanded us to pray, but hath also promised most graciously to hear us. And this maketh unto our great consolation and comfort, that we are not only commanded to pray, but also promised to be heard. Therefore, when we intend to pray, as we set before our eyes the commandment of God, wherein we are willed to pray, that by this means we may with the better courage come unto the throne of God's majesty with our prayers; so likewise must we call to remembrance the most loving, sweet, and comfortable promises of God, which he hath annexed and joined to his commandment, having ever this consideration in ourselves, that we are both commanded to pray, and also promised to be heard.

And here again appeareth the singular and exceeding great goodness of God toward us. For what should it have profited us to pray, if we had not been heard? The pro-

mises therefore, which God hath made unto us, that he will hear us, are most earnestly to be considered; of the which sort these are: "Call on me," saith God, "in the time of trouble, and I will deliver thee, and thou shalt glorify me." Here have we a commandment of God both to call on him, and also a promise that he will hear us. Again, by the prophet Hieremy he saith: "Call on me, and ye shall live: Jer. xxix.
pray unto me, and I will graciously hear you: seek me, and ye shall find. When ye shall seek me with all your heart, I will be found of you, saith the Lord." And our Saviour Christ saith: "Ask, and it shall be given unto you. Seek, and ye shall Matt. vii.
find. Knock, and it shall be opened unto you. For whosoever asketh receiveth; and whosoever seeketh findeth; and to him that knocketh it shall be opened." Here have we to every commandment a promise annexed. We are commanded to ask; and we are promised to have. We are commanded to seek; and we are promised to find. We are commanded to knock; and we are promised to be let in. It followeth: "Is there any man among you (saith Christ) which, if his son ask bread, will offer Matt. vii.
him a stone? or he if he ask fish, will he proffer him a serpent? If ye then, Luke xi.
when ye are evil, can give your children good gifts; how much more shall your Father which is in heaven give good things, if ye ask of him!" In another place Christ also saith: "Ask, and ye shall receive, that your joy may be perfect." John xvi.

These and such other comfortable promises are diligently to be retained in memory, both against the assaults of Satan, and against the infirmities of our flesh. For whensoever we intend earnestly to pray (I speak of experience, God comfort me!) Satan on the one side, and the flesh on the other side, saith unto us: Tush, man, what wilt thou do? Wilt thou pray unto God? Thou labourest in vain. Thou comest, or thou be welcome. Knowest thou not these words of the scripture? "God John ix.
heareth not sinners." Again: "Salvation is far from sinners." Hast thou not sinned? Psal. cxix.
If thou deniest it, thy conscience shall bear witness against thee. Thy conscience shall accuse thee, prove thee guilty, and condemn thee. If thou confessest that thou art a sinner, then mayest thou be well assured that God will not hear thee; for the scripture saith: "God heareth not sinners." If thou then, seeing thou art a sinner, lookest for help at the hand of God, thou art utterly deceived. For the scripture, which is the word of truth, and cannot lie, saith: "Salvation is far from sinners." O subtile Satan! O frail flesh!

Indeed it is most true, that God heareth not sinners; but those sinners are unpenitent, unfaithful, and obstinate or stubborn sinners. Salvation also without doubt is far from sinners; but yet from such sinners as have cast away both God and the study of all godliness. If sinners repent, believe, and amend, although they be never so notable and grievous sinners, yet God receiveth them into favour for Christ's sake. If they pray, God heareth them. If they seek salvation at the hand of God, they shall surely find it. For to such sinners are all the comfortable promises of God made, which are found in the holy scripture. Are not these the words of Christ our Saviour? "I came not to call the righteous, but sinners unto repentance." Again: Matt. ix.
"The Son of man is come to seek and to save that was lost." Whom calleth Christ Luke xix.
unto him in these words, but sinners? "Come unto me all ye that labour and Matt. xi.
are heavy loaden, and I shall refresh you." St Paul also saith: "This is a true 1 Tim. i.
saying, and worthy of all men to be received, that Jesus Christ came into the world to save sinners."

Against these assaults therefore of Satan, and against the weakness of the flesh, it shall not a little profit always to set before the eyes of our mind the most sweet and comfortable promises of God in hearing us, although never so great sinners, when in faith we repent and pray unto him; and to consider that God heareth not us for our dignity and innocency, but for his promise sake, for his faith and truth's sake, that he may be found faithful in all his words, and such a God as neither will nor can lie. No: "let God be true, and all men liars." Rom. iii. Psal. cxvi.

Why God heareth our prayers.

All the saints in time past, both of the old and new testament, whensoever they did pray, did not set before their eyes and consider their own dignity and worthiness, their own works and merits, but the commandment and promise of God, which both commanded them to pray, and also promised to hear them, and to grant them their

petitions. They depended wholly on the most loving and merciful promises of God; and being comforted and encouraged with them, they feared not to have access with their prayers unto the glorious throne of God's most glorious majesty. Hear what
Dan. ix. Daniel saith, both in his own name, and in the name of all the godly: "Not in our own righteousnesses," saith he, "lay we forth our prayers before thy face, but in
Psal. lxxix. thy great and manifold mercies." David also prayeth on this manner: "Help us, O God our Saviour, and for the glory of thy name, O Lord, deliver us, and forgive our
Psal. xxv. sins for thy holy name's sake." Again: "For thy name's sake, O Lord, be merciful unto my sin; for it is great." Jacob, in his prayer unto God for his deliverance from
Gen. xxxii. the hand of his brother Esau, confesseth that he is "unworthy of all the mercies which God had shewed unto him:" notwithstanding, setting before his eyes the promises which God had made him, he feareth nothing even to ask greater things of him, which he also obtained.

A Christian, although never so unworthy in his own sight, may be bold to ask whatsoever God hath commanded and promised. For God giveth not us any thing for our worthiness, but for his promise, name, mercy, and truth's sake, that this sen-
Psal. xxv. tence of David may for ever and ever abide true and constant: "All the ways of the Lord are mercy and truth." It is the great and infinite mercy of the Lord, that he freely and without our merits and deserts promiseth unto us so many and so great good things. It is the truth of the Lord, in that he performeth truly and faithfully those things which he mercifully hath promised.

Let us therefore, whensoever we intend to pray, diligently consider the promises of God, and embrace them as most precious treasures and heavenly jewels, and depend wholly upon them, and not upon our worthiness and innocency, not upon our merits and good works, not upon our satisfactions and works of supererogation, nor upon the mediations and intercessions of saints in heaven. For whosoever, in asking any thing of God, dependeth upon any creature, either in heaven or in earth, but upon the merciful promise of God alone, he shall obtain nothing of God, although he prayeth so earnestly that he sweateth drops of blood.

Father. Blessed be God for his sweet and comfortable promises that he hath made us; and God give us grace to enjoy them! *Son.* Amen.

Father. Is there none other thing to be considered, when we intend to pray, but only the commandment and promise of God? *Son.* Fourthly, it is required of us,
Faith in prayer. if we will pray with fruit, that we give an earnest and undoubted faith to the promise of God, believing stedfastly, that we shall abundantly receive of God what-
Heb. xi. soever he hath mercifully promised. For without this faith nothing is obtained of God. The commandment of the Lord to pray, and the promise of God to hear and to grant those things for the which we pray, profit nothing at all, if faith be absent: yea, whatsoever good thing God promiseth, he promiseth it only to the faithful; so that whosoever presumeth to pray without faith, that is to say, without a full and certain persuasion of the mind to obtain the thing which he asketh, he doth none other thing than deride and mock God, yea, and recounteth God a liar, forasmuch as he doubteth of the truth, faith, constancy, and power of God; and by this means
Psal. cix. Prov. xxviii. Rom. xiv. Heb. xi. is his prayer become sin and abomination to the Lord, and to himself sin and damnation. "For whatsoever is not of faith is sin," saith St Paul. Again: "Without faith it is unpossible to please God: for he that cometh unto God must believe that God is, and that he is a rewarder of such as seek him." Now he that doubteth whether God be a rewarder to them that seek him, cometh not to God aright; but this do they, which do not believe that they shall obtain the thing which they ask of God: therefore come they not rightly unto God, and so consequently they obtain ☞ nothing of God. No, verily; for where faith wanteth in prayer, no good thing is obtained, although they pray so fervently, that they sweat both water and blood.

That faith is necessarily required in prayer, very many both sentences and his-
James i. tories of the holy scripture do most manifestly declare. St James saith: "If any of you lack wisdom, let him ask of him that giveth it, even God, which giveth to all men indifferently, and casteth no man in the teeth; and it shall be given him. But let him ask in faith, and waver not: for he that doubteth is like a wave

of the sea, which is tossed of the winds, and carried with violence. Neither let that man think that he shall receive any thing of the Lord. A wavering-minded man is unstable in all his ways." Our Saviour Christ saith also: "Whatsoever ye desire when ye pray, believe that ye shall have it; and it shall be done to you." Mark xi.

Faith obtaineth easily all things of God. For "all things are possible to him that believeth." And without faith nothing is obtained of God, but wrath, vengeance, the curse of God, and everlasting damnation. Therefore in the histories of the gospel we read, that when any benefit was asked of Christ, Christ made inquisition of their faith, demanding of the askers, whether they did believe that he was able to grant them their requests, and to satisfy their desires. In the gospel of Matthew we read, that when two blind men desired Christ, that he would restore unto them their sight, "Christ said unto them, Do ye believe that I am able to do this thing?" They answered: "We believe, Lord." Then said Christ: "According to your faith be it unto you." Likewise read we, that when the father of that child, which was possessed of a dumb spirit, desired Christ to have pity on his son and to heal him, "Jesus said unto him: If thou canst believe, all things are possible to him that believeth. The father of the child even with tears cried out and said: I believe; O Lord, help my incredulity." And straightways his son was made whole. Again, to whom is this unknown, that the woman of Canaan making intercession for her daughter, which was possessed of a devil, received of Christ many hard, and (as I may so speak) unfriendly answers: notwithstanding she with a strong and unshaken faith continued still praying, never ceasing from prayer, till at the last Christ, being overcome with the faithful prayer of her, said: "O woman, great is thy faith: be it unto thee even as thou desirest." How often read we in the scripture, "Thy faith hath saved thee!" [Mark ix.] [Matt. ix.] [Mark ix.] [Matt. xv.]

Faith is so mighty a thing before God, that it many times obtaineth a benefit of God before it be asked. Read we not, that certain men brought a man diseased of the palsy unto Christ? We read not, that they made any petition unto Christ for his health: notwithstanding Christ healed him, and said unto him, "Son, be on a good comfort: thy sins are forgiven thee. Rise, take up thy bed, and go thy way into thy house." How came this to pass? Verily, through the faith both of the man diseased of the palsy, and of them also which brought the man. For thus writeth St Matthew: "When Jesus saw their faith, he said to the man diseased of the palsy, Be on a good comfort, son: thy sins are forgiven thee." They believed in their hearts, that Christ both was able and also would heal the sick man, of the which thing the sick man himself was also fully persuaded; and this their faith was so acceptable unto Christ, that without any asking, yea, before they opened their mouth to speak, he granted them their desire. And here see we that true, which God speaketh by the prophet: "It shall be that, or ever they call, I shall answer them: while they are yet but thinking how to speak, I shall hear them." This we see also proved true in David, which writeth on this manner: "I said, I will confess my sins unto the Lord; and so thou forgavest the wickedness of my sin. For this shall every one that is godly make his prayer unto thee, in a time when thou mayest be found." It is truly also said of Moses: "What other nation is so great, that gods come so nigh unto, as the Lord our God is nigh unto us in all things, as oft as we call unto him?" [Matt. ix.] [Isai. lxv.] [Psal. xxxii.] [Deut. iv.]

Forasmuch therefore as we have so gentle, so loving, and so liberal a Father, which hath not only commanded us, that we should pray unto him, but also hath promised that he will hear us, and grant us our petitions; let us bring with us, whensoever we intend to pray, a sure, constant, and unshaken faith, nothing doubting of the promises of God; but being surely persuaded that, whatsoever he most graciously hath promised us, the same will he also most bounteously perform and give unto us.

Father. God give us this faith! *Son.* Let us crave it of God, and pray with the apostles, saying: "O Lord, increase our faith." Luke xvii.

Father. Is there any other thing behind, concerning the due preparation unto prayer? *Son.* Yea, verily. Fifthly, after we have diligently considered the cause wherefore we will pray, and have earnestly pondered the commandment of God, which willeth us to pray, and have also most deeply weighed the promise of God, that he will both hear us and grant us our petitions, again, that to the promise of God, we must annex and adjoin a sure and stedfast faith, being thoroughly persuaded, that whatsoever God hath promised, he will abundantly perform; this followeth next in order to be considered, that whatsoever we ask of God, it must be asked of him in the name of his most dear and only-begotten Son, Christ Jesus. For albeit our cause be never so good and godly, and although our consideration about both the commandment and promise of God be never so earnest, and albeit we bring never so great faith by believing the promises of God; yet, if the prayers, which we do make, if the petitions which we do ask, be not made and asked in the name of Christ, all the aforesaid things profit nothing at all.

Prayer must be made in the name of Christ.

Whosoever therefore intendeth to pray aright, let him fully determine with himself, before he pray, to ask nothing of God, but only in the name of Christ: otherwise he shall not only pray in vain, but also with his prayers provoke and kindle the wrath and vengeance of God against himself. For whatsoever we obtain of God, we obtain it not for our worthiness, nor for the holiness of any creature either in heaven or in earth, but only for Christ's sake, for Christ's innocency, dignity, and holiness; in whom, and for whose sake, God the Father is well pleased with us. For, as St Paul saith, "All the promises of God by Christ are yea, and by him Amen;" that is to say, in Christ and for Christ's sake God most certainly fulfilleth whatsoever he hath most graciously promised. For Christ is that dearly-beloved Son, for whose sake God the Father is well pleased with man. Christ is that door, by the which we have free access unto God the Father. Christ is that way, by the which whosoever doth not walk, he cannot come unto the Father, as he himself testifieth: "I am the way, the truth, and the life. No man cometh unto the Father, but by me." Christ is that high and everlasting bishop, by whom we must offer our prayers, praises, and thanksgivings unto God the Father, as the apostle saith: "By him (Christ) do we offer sacrifice of praise alway to God, that is to say, the fruit of those lips which confess his name." Whosoever striveth to approach unto God with his prayers by any other mean than by Christ alone, he is a thief, a robber, and a spoiler of the glory of Christ. And against such Christ-robbers this saying of Christ shall stand for ever, as an invincible bulwark and mighty fortress: "I am the way, the truth, and life. No man cometh unto the Father, but by me." Whosoever therefore will address himself unto prayer aright, he must direct his prayers unto God the Father, not in his own name, nor in the name of any other creature either in heaven or in earth, but only in the name of Jesus Christ, our alone Mediator, Advocate, and Intercessor.

Matt. iii. xvii. 2 Pet. i. 2 Cor. i. Mark i. ix. Luke iii. ix. John x. Rom. v. John xiv. Heb. xiii. John xiv.

What it is to pray in the name of Christ.

Father. What is it to pray in the name of Christ? *Son*. To pray in the name of Christ is to believe and to acknowledge Christ alone to be our Mediator, Advocate, and Intercessor unto God the Father; and in the dignity, virtue, and power of his mediation and intercession to offer up our prayers and praises unto God, and to ask of him all good things necessary for the body or for the soul, only for the excellency, majesty, and honour of this our alone Mediator, Christ Jesu. Whosoever prayeth on this manner, I mean, in the name of Christ, he may be well assured, that he shall suffer no repulse at the hand of God, but shall abundantly obtain whatsoever he asketh, as our Saviour Christ saith: "Whatsoever ye shall ask in my name, that will I do, that the Father may be glorified by the Son. If ye shall ask any thing in my name, that will I do." To make us certain and sure that, whatsoever we ask of God in the name of Christ, we shall easily obtain it, Christ in the aforesaid words promiseth twice, that he will bring to pass, that we shall enjoy the things which we have asked in his name. Again he saith: "Verily, verily, I say unto you, whatsoever things ye shall ask the Father in my name, he shall give you." As Christ afore promised twice that he will bring to pass, that we shall obtain of God the Father whatsoever we ask in his name; so likewise now, because we should not doubt of his truth, he addeth unto his promise an oath, and sweareth, that whatsoever we ask of the Father in his name he shall give us: "Verily, verily, I say unto you, whatsoever ye shall ask the Father in my name, he shall give you." O unoutspeakable comfort!

John xiv. John xvi.

Col. iii.

St Paul also commandeth us, that "whatsoever we do in word or in deed, we should do all things in the name of the Lord Jesu." For nothing is acceptable unto God, that is not done in the name of Christ. Our prayings, our preachings, our watchings, our fastings, our almose-deeds, with all our other good works, are vile and filthy, yea, they stink before the face of God, if they be not done in the name of Christ, be they otherwise never so much seasoned and powdered either with the merits and intercessions of saints, or with our own righteousness and good works. For what other thing are "all our righteousnesses," yea, even of the most perfectest, but "as a polluted and defiled cloth," if Christ's righteousness be laid aside? All our righteousnesses, prayings, fastings, watchings, almose-deeds, good works, satisfactions, merits, and whatsoever besides even the most holy among us have, are none other thing before God, without Christ, than dunghills of abominations. It is not therefore without a cause required of him, which intendeth to pray aright, that he offer his prayers unto God in the name of Christ Jesus our Lord. Isai. lxiv.

It is truly said of St Austin: "The prayer which is not made through Christ (that is to say, in the name of Christ) doth not only not put away sin, but the very prayer itself is made sin[1]." Notable, golden, and precious is this sentence of St Ambrose, and worthy to be reposed in the lowest part of our memory: "Christ alone is our mouth, whereby we speak to the Father; our eye, whereby we see the Father; our right hand, whereby we offer unto the Father; which Christ except he maketh intercession for us, neither we, nor all the saints, have any thing to do with God[2]." In Psal. cviii. Libr. de Isaac et anima.

And here fall down flat to the ground, yea, to the very hell, all the prayers of the Jews, of the Mahometists, and of all other sectaries. For albeit that all these after a certain manner call upon God, and offer prayers and praises unto him; yet, forasmuch as they pray not in the name of Christ, they rather with their prayers provoke God unto anger, than make him their good and gracious Lord.

For as concerning the Jews, although at this present day they boast themselves alone to be the peculiar people of God, they pray, they fast, &c., yet, because they do not believe in Christ, neither acknowledge Christ to be God and man, to be their Saviour, Mediator, Reconciliator, and Atonement-maker, &c., nor offer their prayers unto God in his name, God doth utterly detest and abhor both them and their prayers, as it is written: "He that believeth on the Son hath everlasting life. But he that believeth not on the Son shall not see life, but the wrath of God abideth on him." Neither is it sufficient that the Jews do acknowledge God the Father, pretend a certain faith toward him, pray unto him, and call upon his holy name, except they also believe and confess that Christ is the Son of God, yea, God himself, equal with the Father, of the same majesty, might, virtue, and power, to the uttermost; for whose sake alone God is at one with them, forgiveth them their sins, and accepteth their prayers; which thing because they do not, whatsoever they boast of the favour and good will of God toward them, it is but a vain ostentation and brag, seeing they cast away Christ, and the saving health, which is laid up in him for all the faithful. For, as St John saith: "Whosoever denieth the Son, he hath not the Father." Again: "He that hath the Son hath life: he that hath not the Son of God hath not life." The Jews. John iii. 1 John ii. 1 John v.

The same is to be said of the Mahometists, that we have spoken of the Jews. For neither they call on God in the name of Christ: therefore are their prayers also sin, wickedness, and plain abomination before God. Mahometists.

But what shall we speak of the papists? Do they call upon God in the name of Christ? yea, rather in the merits, mediations, intercessions, dignities, wounds, blood, passion, and death of saints. Let the popish portasses[3] and mass-books be searched, and it shall soon be perceived how idolatrous the prayers of the papists are, formed and made in the names, merits, and intercessions of saints, as though there were so great dignity in the merits and intercessions of saints, that God for their sake were bound both to hear their prayers and to grant their requests. I could bring forth ensamples too many of this matter, if time did serve. But to whom are they un- Papists.

[[1] August. Op. Par. 1679–1700. Enarrat. in Psalm. cviii. v. 7. Tom. IV. col. 1219.—See Vol. I. page 149, note 3.]

[[2] Ambros. Op. Par. 1686–90. De Isaac et Anim. Lib. cap. viii. 75. Tom. I. col. 380.—See Vol. I. page 150, note 2.]

[[3] Portasses: breviaries.]

known? Whosoever therefore will prepare himself to pray aright, let him fully determine with himself to offer and present his prayers to God only, only in the name of Christ, in the virtue and power of Christ, in the dignity and excellency of Christ; and desire to be heard, and his prayers to be accepted of God, for Christ's sake our only Medi-
Heb. xiii. ator, as St Paul saith: "By him (Christ) we offer sacrifice of praise alway to God, that is to say, the fruit of those lips which confess his name." If any man presume to pray otherwise, he shall find at God's hand all one reward with the Jews, Mahometists, papists, and such other sectaries.

Father. God give us all grace in the unity of his holy Spirit truly to call upon the Lord our God, in the name of his most dear Son Jesus Christ, our alone Mediator. But if there be yet remaining any thing that is necessarily required unto the worthy

All things are to be asked according to the will of God.

preparation unto prayer, I would gladly hear it. *Son*. Sixthly, it is required of us, if we will pray aright, that we have also this consideration in us, I mean, that in our prayer we ask nothing of God but that which is agreeable to his holy will. For our will is wicked and naught, desirous rather of ungodly than godly things, and for the most part wishing that which should rather hurt us than profit us.

And here may we see the corruption of our nature, which we have sucked out of the breast of our old mother Heve; which hath so infected and poisoned us, yea, and every part of us, that, whether we respect the body or the soul, nothing can be found whole, nothing sound, nothing perfect in us; so truly is it said of the prophet:
Isai. i. "The whole head is sick, and the heart is heavy. From the sole of the foot unto the head there is no whole part in all your body; but all are wounds, botches, sores, and stripes," &c. The heart of man is unpure, filthy, lewd, and so stuffed full of all
Jer. xvii. Prov. xx. kind of wickedness, that it is utterly unsearchable, except of him alone which searcheth the hearts and the reins. All the senses and thoughts of man are not only prone unto
Gen. vi. viii. evil, but also evil in deed even from the very cradles. The free will of man is so wounded and made weak, that in things appertaining unto the Spirit of God and
John xv. unto our salvation it can of itself do nothing at all, as Christ saith: "Without me
Phil. ii. ye can do nothing." Also St Paul: "It is God that worketh in us both the will and
2 Cor. iii. the deed." Again: "We are not able of ourselves so much as to think a good thought." Moreover, the strengths of man are so weak, yea, so none, that, being once thrown down, we are not able to rise up again.

Luke x. Luke xv. Such misers and wretches are we, that we suffer ourselves as miserable bond-slaves to be led captive of the devil, the world, and the flesh, and to be handled as it
Luke x. pleaseth them. We are so spoiled of our garments, that our miserable nakedness is
Gen. iii. easy to be perceived; neither can we of ourselves cover that evil-favoured nakedness
1 Cor. ii. of ours. Beastly are we, not understanding the things which belong unto the Spirit of God. Hypocrites are we, and a very lump of wickedness, yea, the wickedness
2 Cor. iii. itself. We cannot so much as once think well; so unable are we either to ask or to do any good thing. What would such a monster of wickedness do in prayer, if it were suffered to ask according to his own will, and to enjoy the requests which it would ask? What would that monster (I mean man) desire? what would he ask? what would he wish? Being a covetous man, he would wish with king Midas, that whatsoever he touched might straightways be made gold. Being a carnal and voluptuous man, he would wish with Jupiter, that Phœbus would prolong the time of going forth with his fiery cart many hours, that he, being in darkness, might without all shame use his venerous pastime at his pleasure. Being an ambitious man, he would
Dan. iii. wish with king Nabuchodonosor to have all nations under the heavens subject unto him, and himself to be taken for a god upon the earth. Being an idolater, he would
1 Kings xviii. wish with Jesabel, that no god might be worshipped but Baal, and that no ministers should be had in honour but only the priests of Baal. Being an hog of Epicure's flock, he would wish with Epicurus none other thing but worldly and fleshly pleasures, eating and drinking, quietness, rest, dicing, carding, &c. Are not these meet and worthy things to be asked of God? O miserable blindness of most miserable man!

Rom. viii. It is truly said of St Paul: "We know not what to desire as we ought." It is not therefore without a cause required, that whosoever intendeth to pray aright should determine with himself only to ask that in his prayer which is agreeable to the will

of God. For it is not lawful for us to ask what we think good in our carnal judgments, but that only which we know to be acceptable in the sight of God; or else we pray in vain, and without fruit: or if we do obtain at any time that which we ungodly require, we obtain it unto our destruction and damnation; and better were it for us never to have obtained it. The will of God above all things is to be considered in our prayers, and according unto that ought we to pray; which thing if we do, we may be sure to pray profitably, and to obtain that we ask, as St John testifieth, saying: "This is the trust that we have in God, that if we ask any thing 1 John v.
according to his will, he heareth us. And if we know that he heareth us, whatsoever we ask, we know that we have the petitions that we desire of him."

That things asked contrary to the will of God are vainly asked and without fruit, it appeareth by divers histories of the holy scripture. In the gospel of St Mark we Mark x.
read, that James and John, the sons of Zebedeus, came unto Christ, and said: "Master, we will that, whatsoever we shall ask, thou grant us. Christ said unto them, What will ye have me to do for you? They said, Grant us, that one may sit on thy right hand, the other on the left hand, in thy glory. But Jesus answered: Ye know not what ye ask." James and John, the dearly beloved disciples of Christ, persuaded themselves, that they should easily obtain whatsoever they asked of so loving and gentle master, without any respect or exception. They dreamed that Christ (as the blind Jews do at this present day) should have an earthly kingdom in this world, and reign like a most triumphant and glorious prince over all nations: therefore desired they of Christ, that one of them might sit on his right hand in his kingdom, the other on his left hand, that is to say, bear the chief rule about him; and, as I may so speak, one to be lord chancellor, and the other to be lord treasurer. These two disciples prayed, but not according to the will of God. Therefore said Christ unto them: "Ye know not what ye ask." The will of God was, not that they should reign in this world as earthly princes, which thing they greatly desired; but that they should prepare themselves to the cross, and be content to suffer for the gospel of his Son, and so to enter into glory, not of the world, but of heaven.

St Paul also prayed that the unquietness through the flesh, even the messenger 2 Cor. xii.
of Satan, wherewith he was continually buffeted, might depart from him; but he obtained not his desire, although he desired it of the Lord thrice, that is to say, oftentimes. Why so? Because he prayed not according to the will of God. Therefore was it answered him on this manner: "My grace is sufficient for thee."

Many in times past have prayed, and were not heard. Many also pray at this day, and are not heard. How cometh it to pass? Because they pray not according to the will of God.

Plato in his prayer unto Jupiter hath a notable sentence, which is this: "O king Jupiter, give us good things both when we pray, and when we do not pray. As concerning things which are evil, give them by no means unto us, although we ask them[1]." The noble philosopher Socrates affirmed that we should ask nothing of the immortal gods, but only that they should give us good things, forasmuch as they do best know what is most profitable for every man: as for us, we many times in our prayers ask that which were better for us not to have it granted[2]. Here even of the very ethnicks may we learn, that nothing ought to be asked of God, but that only which is good: again, that in all our prayers we submit our will to the good will and pleasure of God, according to this our common prayer: "Thy will be Matth. vi.
done in earth, as it is in heaven." Luke xi.

Father. What is to be done that we may pray according to the will of God? *Son*. God hath opened unto us his blessed will in the holy scripture, wherein he hath

---

[1 *Ζεῦ βασιλεῦ, τὰ μὲν ἐσθλὰ καὶ εὐχομένοις καὶ ἀνεύκτοις*
ἄμμι δίδου, τὰ δὲ δεινὰ καὶ εὐχομένοις ἀπαλέξειν.
These lines are quoted in Plat. Alcibiad. Secund.]

[2 Socrates humanæ sapientiæ quasi quoddam terrestre oraculum, nihil ultra petendum a Diis immortalibus arbitrabatur, quam ut bona tribuerent; quia ii demum scirent quid unicuique esset utile: nos autem plerumque id votis expetere, quod non impetrasse melius foret.—Valer. Max. Lib. VII. cap. ii.]

declared what we ought to ask. Whatsoever we find in them to be the will of God, that may we be bold to ask and to crave. And whatsoever we ask, so praying, we may be sure to obtain it, forasmuch as we pray according to the will of God. As for an example: St Paul writeth this to be the will of God, that "all men should be saved, and come to the knowledge of the truth." Whosoever therefore prayeth that he may be saved, and come to the knowledge of the truth, he prayeth according to the will of God. Jeremy the prophet prayed unto God that he might obtain everlasting salvation, saying: "Heal thou me, O Lord, and I shall be healed: save thou me, and I shall be saved." The thief also prayed for the same on this manner: "O Lord, remember me when thou comest into thy kingdom." Also St Paul: "I wish to be loosened, and to be with Christ." For the knowledge of God's truth David prayed thus: "Shew me thy ways, O Lord, and teach me thy paths. Direct me in thy truth, and teach me; for thou art God my Saviour." Again, he saith: "Give me understanding, O Lord, that I may know thy testimonies." All these prayed according to the will of God, and were heard.

(1 Tim. ii.; Jer. xvii.; Luke xxiii.; Phil. i.; Psal. xxv.; Psal. cxix.)

Moreover, the holy scripture declareth this to be the will of God, that no man should perish, but that all should repent and live. For so writeth St Peter: "The Lord is patient toward us, while he will none to perish, but to receive all unto repentance." God himself saith by the prophet: "As surely as I live, saith the Lord, I will not the death of a sinner, but rather that he turn and live." Christ also saith: "I say unto you, that there shall be joy in heaven over one sinner that repenteth, more than over ninety and nine righteous, that need no repentance." Whosoever therefore prayeth unto God for repentance, he prayeth according to the will of God, and may be sure to be heard.

(2 Pet. iii.; Ezek. xviii. xxxiii.; Luke xv.)

Likewise as for repentance, so for faith also, the good will of God is, that we should pray; forasmuch as without faith repentance before God is of no valor: yea, repentance without faith driveth unto desperation, and desperation unto damnation, as we may see in Caim, Judas, and such like. And forasmuch as both repentance and faith is the gift of God, therefore must they both be asked of him. For Christ said not only, "repent," but he added, "and believe the gospel." Repentance and faith must go together as companions inseparable, even as the sun and light, fire and heat. For the will of God is, not only that we should repent, but also that we should believe, as our Saviour Christ saith: "This is the will of him that sent me, that all that see the Son and believe on him should have everlasting life." Whosoever therefore prayeth for faith, that he may have everlasting life through Christ, he prayeth according to the will of God. So read we of the apostles, which prayed unto God for faith on this manner: "O Lord, increase our faith."

(Gen. iv.; Matt. ii.; Matt. xxvii.; Acts i.; Mark i.; John vi.; Luke xvii.)

Furthermore, "this is the will of God (saith St Paul), even your sanctification, that ye abstain from whoredom, and that every one of you know how to possess his own vessel with holiness and honour, and not in the lust of concupiscence, as do the heathen, which know not God." Again, this is the will of God, saith he, "that no man oppress and defraud his brother in bargaining, because that the Lord is the avenger of all such things." Whosoever therefore prayeth that he may be holy in all his conversation, that he may not pollute his vessel, that is to say, his body, with fornication, adultery, or with any other kind of uncleanness, but keep it in holiness and honour; again, whosoever prayeth that he may deal justly and truly with all men, with whom he hath to do, either in bargaining, buying, or selling, he prayeth according to the will of God, and may be sure to be heard. To be short, look whatsoever we find in the holy scripture to be the will of God, that may we freely and with a good conscience ask; and so asking we pray according to the will of God, and we may be sure both to be heard and also to enjoy our requests.

(1 Thess. iv.)

Father. We may then lawfully pray for the enlarging of Christ's kingdom, for the avancement of his holy word, for the true understanding of the sacred scripture, for constancy and stedfastness in the religion of Christ, for remission of our sins, for the gift of the Holy Ghost, for the increase of faith, for fervent love toward our neighbour, yea, even toward our enemy, for peace and quietness of conscience, for long-suffering, for modesty, for patience in adversity, for humility in prosperity, and for such other like spiritual gifts and fruits of the Holy Ghost: and as we pray for them, so shall we enjoy them. *Son.* Yea, verily.

Father. But what concerning bodily and worldly things? must we ask them also of God? Do we pray according to the will of God, when we crave at his hand all things necessary for the sustentation of this our poor and needy life? *Son.* I am not altogether ignorant what some writers judge in this behalf. Notwithstanding, this have I learned, that we may with a good conscience ask of God all things necessary as well for the body as for the soul; as meat, drink, clothe, health of body, long life, defence from miseries, deliverance from tribulations, prosperous success in all our labours and travails, a quiet commonweal, public peace, a good wife, obedient children, quiet subjects, good magistrates, and such like, as we have divers examples in the holy scripture. And our Saviour Christ taught us to ask of God the Father "our daily bread," that we may know that all good things, Matt. vi.
both for the body and for the soul, come from God, and by this means learn to be thankful unto God for all his benefits.

But this is to be noted, that as all spiritual things appertaining either unto the glory of God or unto the salvation of our souls are to be asked of God without any condition, so likewise are all corporal things to be desired of God with a condition, which knoweth better what is expedient for us, than we ourselves do. As Note well.
for an example: When we pray for the forgiveness of sins, we shall not pray on this manner: 'O heavenly Father, forgive us our sins, if it be thy will.' No, but without any condition we shall say: 'O heavenly Father, forgive us our sins for Christ's sake.' For God hath declared unto us in his holy word, that it is his good will and pleasure that we should so pray. "As surely as I live (saith he) I will Ezek. xxxiii. Jer
not the death of a sinner, but rather that he turn and live." But if we pray to be delivered from any corporal incommodity or disease, as from an ague, from the plague, from banishment, from imprisonment, from poverty, from sickness, from death, &c., then ought we to submit our will to God's will, which best knoweth what is most profitable for us; as a certain man saith: "What is most profitable for the sick man, the physician knoweth better than he that is diseased." As for an example, if we should pray to be delivered from sickness, we must pray after this manner: 'O God and heavenly Father, which for our sins and wickedness hast worthily cast upon us this grievous cross of sickness, wherewith we be greatly enfeebled, made weak and brought low; we most humbly beseech thee, that thou wilt now at the last, after so many and so great troubles, pains, and adversities, take away mercifully from us this our sickness, and liberally restore unto us the benefit of health, that we, as in mind, so likewise in body, being made sound and strong, may live and glorify thy holy name. Notwithstanding, O heavenly Father, thy will, and not ours, be done in this thing.'

For concerning temporal and corporal matters we must so pray, that all things be left unto the counsel, determination, and will of God, to give unto us what he will, when he will, and how much he will. So teacheth us Christ in our common prayer: "Thy will be done in earth as it is in heaven." And as he taught us thus Matt. vi.
to pray, so likewise did he himself practise this manner of praying. For when the time of his passion began to draw nigh, he prayed unto his Father on this manner: "O my Father, if it be possible, let this cup depart from me. Notwithstanding, not Matt. xxvi.
as I will, but as thou wilt." Here Christ prayed his Father, that he might not Mark xiv. Luke xxii.
drink of the cup of his passion: notwithstanding he submitted his will to the will of his Father. Likewise prayed the leper: "Lord," saith he, "if thou wilt, thou art Matt. viii.
able to make me clean." The leper wished to be cleansed from his leprosy: notwithstanding he referred the matter to Christ, and to his holy will, to do with him as he thought best. Again, those three young men, which at Nabuchodonosor's commandment were cast into the hot brenning furnace, because they would not worship the golden image, said to the king: "We may not consent unto thee in this Dan. iii.
matter. For behold, our God, whom we serve, is able to keep us from the hot burning oven, O king, and can right well deliver us out of thy hands. And though he will not, yet shalt thou know, O king, that we will not serve thy gods, nor do reverence unto that image which thou hast set up." Furthermore David desired to 2 Sam. xv.

be restored to his kingdom, when he was put out of it by Absolon his son; yet he wished it none otherwise then it should seem good in the sight of God. His words are these: "If I shall find favour in the eyes of the Lord, he will bring me again. But if the Lord thus say, I have no lust unto thee; behold, here am I, let him do with me what seemeth good in his eyes." Note here, how obedient David shewed himself to the will of God. He wisheth to be restored to his kingdom: notwithstanding, if it shall otherwise seem good unto God, he is content also to obey his holy will.

All these examples teach us, that in all corporal and temporal things we ought to submit our will to the good will and pleasure of God, and to be content to receive of him whatsoever his good will shall be, whether it be riches or poverty, health or sickness, life or death, &c. He is our Father, and we are his sons. Let us not doubt therefore, but that he will give us that which he knoweth to be best and most profitable for us. Only let us do our endeavour to pray according to his will, and ask those things which we are taught in the holy scripture to ask, that is to say, those things which belong unto the glory of God, the salvation of our souls, and the commodity of our neighbour; and let us not doubt, but that we shall be heard, and obtain our desires, whether they pertain unto the soul or unto the body. God without doubt will accomplish our desire, if we go about to satisfy his godly pleasure, and frame our prayers according to his blessed will; as the psalmograph witnesseth, saying: "He will accomplish the desire of them that fear him, and hear their prayer, and save them." Hereto belongeth the saying of St John: "Dearly beloved, if our heart do not condemn us, we have trust to God-ward; and whatsoever we ask, we receive of him, because we keep his commandments, and do those things which are pleasing in his sight."

Psal. cxlv.
1 John iii.

Father. God give us all grace, both in our prayers and in all other exercises either of the body or of the soul, only to do those things which are acceptable in his sight! *Son*. Amen.

Father. What remaineth there yet behind concerning the worthy preparation unto prayer? *Son*. Seventhly, although the aforesaid things, whereof we have hitherto spoken, are so necessary to the worthy preparation unto prayer, that whosoever cometh not so instructed unto prayer, he prayeth unprofitably and in vain; yet this matter also, whereof we shall now entreat, is so necessary unto him that intendeth to pray with fruit, that without it all the other profit nothing at all.

Father. What is that, my son? *Son*. It is the frank and free forgiving of them, which have offended us either in word or in deed.

Father. Is this thing so necessary? *Son*. Yea, verily, as you shall hear hereafter. Therefore whosoever intendeth to pray, if he will pray aright, let him consider with himself, how he is affected toward his neighbour, although his enemy. Let him search his conscience, and look in the book of his heart, whether all things in him be friendly, loving, and charitable toward not only his friends, but also his enemies. For, as our Saviour Christ saith: "If ye love them which love you, what thanks have ye? For sinners also love their lovers. And if ye do good for them which do good for you, what thank have ye? For sinners also do even the same." Whosoever therefore intendeth to pray with fruit, let him see in himself whether he hath a cankered, malicious, hateful, despiteful, and envious heart against any man, or not. If he have, let him know that he is a right bird of Caim's nest, and a very image of Satan, although he speak with the tongues of angels, and understood all the mysteries both of God and God's word; yea, although he were so fervent in prayer, that his knees were made like to the knees of camels through kneeling, as we read of St James, the bishop of Jerusalem[1].

Forgiving our offenders.
Matt. v.
Luke vi.
Gen. iv.
1 John iii.
1 Cor. xiii.

If any man therefore findeth in himself an hateful heart toward any man, let him not presume once to open his mouth for to pray. If he do, the first word of his prayer turneth unto his own damnation. And the more he prayeth, being so affected, the more doth he heap the hot wrath and fierce vengeance of God against himself. Neither shall such a monster of wickedness obtain any grace or favour at the hand

[[1] Euseb. Hist. Eccles. Lib. II. cap. xxiii. p. 50. Amst. 1695. See Vol. I. p. 143.]

of God, as the wise man testifieth, saying: "He that seeketh vengeance shall find vengeance at the Lord's hand, which shall sure keep him his sins. Forgive thy neighbour thy hurt that he hath done thee; and so shall thy sins be forgiven thee also, when thou prayest. A man that beareth hatred against another, how dare he desire forgiveness of God? He that sheweth no mercy to a man, which is like himself, how dare he ask forgiveness of his sins? If he that is but flesh beareth hatred and keepeth it, who will entreat for his sins? Remember the end, and let enmity pass, which seeketh death and destruction, and abide thou in the commandments (of God). Remember the commandments (of God): so shalt thou not be rigorous over thy neighbour, &c." Ecclus. xxviii.

Here hear we, that except we forgive them that have offended us, although we pray never so much, yet shall not our prayers be heard of God, I mean unto our salvation: our sins shall never be forgiven us, but God shall reserve and keep them unto our damnation; and albeit heaven and earth, and all that ever are in them, with one voice should pray for us, yet should not their prayers for us be heard, so vile misers and damnable wretches are we in the sight of God, so long as we continue in this malicious mind and despiteful hatred. For God loveth, alloweth, and regardeth nothing that proceedeth from an envious, hateful, and malicious heart. Let us remember Caim. He offered sacrifices unto God, praying and praising God outwardly with no less holiness and devotion, than his brother Abel did. But what saith the scripture? "God looked unto Abel, and unto his gifts; but unto Caim and unto his gifts he looked not." Gen. iv. Why so? Because his heart was void both of faith toward God, and of love toward his brother. His heart burned with envy and hatred against his brother Abel. Therefore his prayers, praises, and sacrifices were abomination unto God.

O, with what face dare we be bold once to open our mouth, and to say the Lord's prayer, calling the heavenly Father our Father, when we hate one another, and speak evil one of another? Is God the Father the father of the malicious, of the envious, of the hateful, and of the uncharitable? Or is he rather the father of the friendly, of the loving, of the charitable, and of the well-willing? "God is charity," saith St John, "and he that dwelleth in charity dwelleth in God, and God in him." 1 John iv. Now he that dwelleth in hatred, in whom dwelleth he? verily, in the devil, and the devil in him. Is such a monster of malice a meet person to call upon God the Father? A malicious and envious person to call God father, is none other thing than to call God envious, malicious, hateful, despiteful, and the father of all tyrants and bloodthirsty people. And how great an impiety that is, who knoweth not?

Again, with what forehead (except we have too much rubbed our forehead, I mean, except we be past all shame) dare we say in the Lord's prayer, "Forgive us our trespasses, as we forgive them that trespass against us," Matt. vi. Luke xi. if we do not forgive them which have offended us? So to pray, is it any other thing than to ask vengeance upon ourselves? If we retain hatred in our minds; if we seek to be revenged; if we devise how we may hurt them that have hurted us; yea, if we labour not to be reconciled even to our very enemies; and if we cannot be content to forgive them, to love and favour them, to speak well of them, to pray for them, and to do for them whatsoever lieth in our power, and no less to seek their commodity and profit, than we do our own; when we pray this prayer, we do none other thing than beseech God that he will not forgive us our sins, but rather deal with us according to our deservings, with all kind of rigour and severity. For except we forgive other, it is vain to look for remission and forgiveness of our sins at the hand of God, as our Saviour Christ witnesseth, saying: "Forgive, and it shall be forgiven you." Luke vi. Again: "If ye forgive men their faults, your heavenly Father will also forgive you. But if ye will not forgive men their faults, neither will your Father forgive you your sins." Matt. vi. The demand which Peter asked of Christ, how often he should forgive his brother, is not unknown. St Matthew writeth, that "Peter said unto Christ on this manner: Matt. xviii. Lord, how often shall my brother sin against me, and I shall forgive him? Seven times? Christ answered: I say not unto thee seven times, but seventy times seven times:" that is to say, so often as he sinneth, forgive him. The parable, which Christ immediately after put forth, declareth evidently, that except we forgive them that have offended us, yea, and that from the very heart, we shall never obtain remission of our sins at the hand of God.

Col. iii. Are not these the words of blessed St Paul, "Forgive ye one another: if any man have a quarrel against another, even as Christ forgave you, even so do ye?" Can any better or more apt example be brought forth, whereby we may be provoked one to forgive another, than the example of Christ? To whom is his free forgiving

Rom. v. of our sins unknown? When we were yet his enemies, he did not only forgive us our sins, but he also gave himself even unto the death to be a ransom for our sins, and to reconcile us unto God his Father, that through his pains we might be deli-

1 Cor. xv. Heb. ii. vered from the pains of hell, and by his death be made free from everlasting death, and be made inheritors of everlasting life.

Father. It is meet and convenient, that if we will find favour at the hand of God, we shew also favour to our neighbour, and be the very same unto him that we would wish God should be unto us. And forasmuch as we are but frail vessels, and cannot so live in this world, but sometime displeasure shall chance among us, it is our duty one of us to forgive another, to bear one with another, to take all things into the best part, not soon to be provoked unto anger, not straightways to bear any displeasure against any man, not to shew ourselves hard to be entreated, but easy to

Rom. xii. be reconciled, and to seek all men. *Son.* This is the office and duty of a christian man. For if any do behave himself otherwise, he is no meet man to pray unto God.

Father. Remaineth there any more to be spoken of, concerning the worthy prepa-

In prayer no time of granting is to be appointed unto God. ration unto prayer? *Son.* Finally, it is requisite, that whensoever we intend to pray, we appoint not God the time when he shall help us, and perform our desires; but commit this thing unto his godly wisdom, as unto him which best knoweth when our petitions ought to take place, and to be brought unto effect. For as the way and the place to help us are not to be assigned unto God, no more is the time to be appointed unto him when he shall help us, and bring our requests unto a fortunate end; but in this behalf we must be content to receive the benefits of our desires at the hand of God, not when we will, but at what time it shall be his good pleasure to give them unto us; which thing without all doubt shall then come to pass, when it shall be most unto our great joy and singular comfort.

And although we do not perceive that God doth straightways grant us our petitions, yet let us not faint in our faith, nor despair of our hope, nor yet conceive an evil opinion of God, as though he were angry with us, or unfaithful in his words, and not true in his promises; but rather cleave unto him with a strong faith, and wholly depend upon his promises, nothing doubting, but that in his time he will liberally perform and abundantly give whatsoever we have asked, yea, more than we can or

Hab. ii. dare be bold to ask, as the prophet Habacuc saith: "If the Lord maketh tarriance, abide thou his leisure; for he will undoubtedly come, and will not tarry." The pro-

Isai. xxx. phet Esay saith: "In silence and hope shall your strength be." Jeremy also saith:

Lam. iii. "It is good with silence to tarry for the saving health of God."

For God many times deferreth to give us our requests, not because he is angry or hateth us, or because he is unfaithful in his words and not constant in his promises; but unto this end, that he may prove our faith, and try whether we be faithful and constant in giving credit to his promises, or not: again, that we, after long desire enjoying his benefits, should the more fervently be kindled to embrace them, and to make much of them: again, that we should the more earnestly be provoked heartily to praise and magnify the name of God for his fatherly benefits, so liberally and lovingly bestowed upon us. For things soon given soon wax vile; but things long desired, and at the last obtained, are highly esteemed and had in great price. All the godly therefore in times past, although they did not straightways enjoy their desires, ceased not still to pray unto God: neither were they any thing at all dismayed, but patiently abode the Lord's leisure, being content to receive when it should be his good pleasure

Psal. cxxiii. to give, as David saith: "Behold, even as the eyes of servants look unto the hand of their masters; and as the eyes of a maiden unto the hand of her mistress; even so our eyes wait upon the Lord our God, until he have mercy upon us." Here David appointed God no certain time, when he shall shew his mercy on him and grant him his requests, neither ceaseth he from lifting up his eyes unto the Lord his God, because he doth not straightways obtain his desires; but he goeth forth in his prayers, and continueth calling on the name of God, even so long until the Lord hath pity on him, and grant him his desire. O blessed David! O worthy ensample to be followed of all them which are led with the earnest love of prayer, and heartily wish to have their petitions accepted of God!

And this is it that our Saviour Christ saith in the gospel: "Men ought alway to pray, and not to be weary." "For God will tender the supplications of them which night and day cry unto him, although for a time he defer them." Such patient abider of the Lord's leisure was Job also, which saith: "Although he killeth me, yet will I put my trust in him." Likewise said Moses unto the children of Israel, when Pharao pursued them, and they saw no way to escape, but either to perish with waters, or else to fall into the hands of the enemy. "Fear not," saith he, "stand still, and behold the wonderful works of God, which he will do this day." Moses commandeth the people of Israel not to fear, but to stand still, that is to say, not to prescribe unto God either the way, or the place, or the time of their deliverance, but with strong faith to cleave to the promises of God, and patiently to abide their deliverance, when his good pleasure shall be.

Luke xviii. Job xiii. Exod. xiv.

The patient abiding of the Lord's leisure doth so greatly please God, that nothing can more haste or provoke his benefits; as, on the contrary part, nothing doth more displease and offend God, than through impatiency to prescribe unto him the time when he shall help us; as we may perceive by the words which the godly matron Judith spake unto the citizens of Bethulia, which, when Holofernes besieged their city, prescribed unto God five days' respite to help them. If no help came from God by that time, they were full determined to yield and give over the city to the enemy. But how earnestly that stout-stomached and courageous matron Judith rebuked them for this their impatiency, incredulity, and tempting of God, these her words do evidently declare: "What thing is this (saith she) wherein Osias hath consented, that, if God help not within five days, he will give over the city to the Assyrians? What are ye, that ye tempt the Lord? This device obtaineth no mercy of God, but provoketh him to wrath and displeasure. Will ye set the mercy of the Lord a time, and appoint him a day after your will? Nevertheless, forasmuch as the Lord is patient, let us rather repent, pouring out tears and beseeching him of grace. For God threateneth not as a man, neither will he be provoked unto wrath as the children of men. And therefore let us heartily fall down before him, and serve him with a meek spirit, and with weeping eyes say unto the Lord, that he deal with us according to his own will and mercy."

Judith viii. [Vulgate.]

Therefore, whensoever we intend to pray, let us determine with ourselves patiently to abide the Lord's leisure, and by no means to prescribe unto him either the time, or the place, or the way, or any other circumstance, concerning our requests, but to submit all our desires to his fatherly providence; being content to receive of him what, when, and how, it shall be his good pleasure to give us; and yet notwithstanding, still continuing to cry unto the Lord with our prayers both day and night, after the example of the widow of whom we read in the gospel of Luke, with this sure persuasion, that God in his time will either give unto us those things which we presently ask, or else better things. Whosoever on this manner offereth his prayers unto God, he may be sure to be welcome unto the majesty of God, and to obtain his requests, unto the salvation both of his body and soul. And thus much have I spoken concerning the due and worthy preparation unto prayer, as I have heretofore learned of our preacher and catechist.

Luke xviii.

Father. I greatly commend thee, my sweet and dear son, that thou dost so well remember the good and godly doctrine which heretofore thou hast learned of thy teachers. Let me hear now, according to thy promise, the declaration of the Lord's prayer, that in this behalf also I may have a taste of thy diligence. *Son*. The Lord's prayer beginneth on this manner:

The preface of the Lord's prayer with the first petition.

"Our Father, which art in heaven, hallowed be thy name."

Father. This is the first petition contained in the Lord's prayer? *Son*. Yea, verily.

Father. How many petitions are there in the Lord's prayer? *Son*. They commonly number seven.

Why it is called the Lord's prayer.

Father. Why is it called the Lord's prayer? *Son*. Because the Lord Christ himself made it, and taught it his disciples, and willed them so to pray.

Father. Where teacheth the holy scripture that? *Son*. In the gospel of Luke we read, that one of the disciples came unto Christ, and said unto him: "Lord, teach us to pray, even as John taught his disciples. And Christ said unto them, When ye pray, say: Our Father, which art in heaven, hallowed be thy name," &c. (Luke xi.)

The excellency of the Lord's prayer.

Father. Is this prayer of all other most excellent? *Son*. Yea, forsooth; both because of the maker of it, as I said before, which is the Lord Jesus; and also because in few words it containeth abundantly whatsoever is necessary to be desired, either for the glory of God or for the safeguard of the body and soul of man. For the three first petitions concern the glory of God and the avancement of his kingdom: the other four petitions, which follow in order, entreat of our necessities, and pertain unto our commodity and profit, whether we respect the body or the soul, or both.

Father. Why dost thou direct thy prayer unto God, and not rather unto men, ☞ or unto the blessed spirits in heaven? *Son*. Vain is the salvation that is looked for from man. To save is the office of God alone, from whom "cometh down every good and perfect gift;" (James i.) therefore unto God alone are our prayers to be directed, according to this commandment: "Call on me," saith God, "in the day of trouble, and I will deliver thee." (Psal. l.) To invocate and call upon the saints in heaven, as it is not commanded in the word of God, so likewise is it injurious to the majesty of God, seeing we give that honour to creatures, which is due to God alone; neither have we any promise in the holy scripture, that we shall be heard and enjoy our petitions, if we pray unto saints departed. To pray unto God, and to ask all good things of him in the name of our alone Mediator Christ Jesu, we are not only commanded, but also promised that we shall be heard. Therefore to leave that which is certain, and to embrace that which is uncertain, is mere folly, as I may speak nothing more sharply.

Father. But what if we do both? *Son*. What mean you?

Father. Pray both unto God and unto the saints in heaven? *Son*. Then is your faith divided; and therefore no true and perfect faith. Then also do you steal away that honour and glory from God and give it unto creatures, which alone is due unto ☞ God. For there can be no greater glory and honour given to God, than in our adversity and trouble to flee unto his holy name as unto a strong bulwark, (Prov. xviii.) to call upon it, and to ask all good things of the Lord our God, which is "a jealous God," (Exod. xx. Deut. v.) and speaketh by the prophet on this manner: "I am the Lord, this is my name: my glory will I give to none other." (Isai xlii.) And his servant Moses saith: "Thou shalt honour the Lord thy God, and him alone shalt thou serve." (Deut. vi. Matt. iv. Luke iv.) The saints themselves also cry and say: "Not to us, O Lord, not to us, but to thy name give the glory, for thy mercy and truth's sake." (Psal. cxv.) Against all such half worshippers of God, the prophet Elias thundereth on this manner: "How long will ye halt on both knees? If the Lord be God, follow him: if Baal be he, follow him." (1 Kings xviii.) And God himself saith to such halting hypocrites and double dissemblers: "I know thy works, that thou art neither cold nor hot: I would thou were cold or hot. But because thou art between both, and neither cold nor hot, I will spue thee out of my mouth." (Rev. iii.) As God alone giveth all good things, so is he alone to be called upon in all our adversities and troubles.

Superstitious worshippers of saints.

Father. What is to be thought of them which, when they pray unto the saints in heaven, use to say this prayer of the Lord, "Our Father which art in heaven," &c. and use to say it oftentimes in the honour of such saints as they most fancy? *Son*. Their blindness is much to be lamented; and it is to be wished that such people were better taught. Is it a meet thing to call any saint in heaven, Father? to desire that his name may be sanctified? and that he will forgive us our sins, &c.? They which thus pray do rather dishonour than honour the heavenly spirits; and indeed, so praying, they do nothing else than blaspheme God, and provoke God unto anger; so that by this means, where they seem to seek salvation, they fall into the danger of everlasting damnation.

Father. Thou holdest then, that this prayer ought to be said unto God alone. *Son.* Yea, verily, if we intend to pray it with fruit.

Father. Let us then fall in hand with this prayer of the Lord, and boult out every parcel thereof. *Son.* Content.

Father. In the beginning of this prayer thou callest God "Father". *Son.* So is it. Why we call God Father.

Father. Why callest thou God thy Father? *Son.* I have learned so to do out of the word of God.

Father. Let me hear some testimonies of the holy scripture concerning this matter. *Son.* Moses saith to every faithful man: "Is not the Lord thy Father, and thine Deut. xxxii. owner? Hath he not made thee and ordained thee?"

Father. But why dost thou rather say "our Father," than "my Father"? *Son.* To declare that God is the common Father of all the faithful, and not of one only.

Father. How provest that by the word of God? *Son.* The prophet Esay saith: "Thou, O God, art our Father. For Abraham knoweth us not, neither is Israel Isai. lxiii. acquainted with us. But thou, Lord, art our Father and Redeemer; and thy name is everlasting." Again: "Thou, O Lord, art our Father: we are thy clay, and thou art our potter, and we all are the work of thy hands." The prophet Malache saith: "Have we not all one Father? Hath not God made us? Why doth every one of Mal. ii. us then despise his own brother?" God himself saith by the same prophet: "Should Mal. i. not the son honour his father, and a servant fear his master? If I be now a Father, where is my honour? If I be a Lord, where is my fear?" In another place he also saith: "I will be a Father unto you; and ye shall be my sons and daughters." Our 2 Cor. vi. Saviour Christ saith: "Call no man your father on the earth; for one is your Father, Matt. xxiii. which is in heaven." St Paul also saith: "As many as are led by the Spirit of God, Rom. viii. they are the sons of God. For ye have not received the spirit of bondage to fear any more, but ye have received the Spirit of adoption, whereby we cry, Abba, dear Father. The same Spirit certifieth our spirit, that we are the sons of God. If we be sons, then are we also heirs; the heirs (I mean) of God, and fellow-heirs with Christ." Again: "Because ye are sons, God hath sent the Spirit of his Son into our hearts, Gal. iv. crying, Abba, dear Father. Wherefore now thou art not a servant, but a son. If thou be a son, thou art also an heir of God through Christ." St John also saith: "Behold, 1 John iii. what exceeding great love the Father hath shewed unto us, that we should be called (and be in deed) the sons of God."

Father. How cometh it to pass, that God is our Father, seeing that we are flesh How God is our Father. and blood, corruption and dust? *Son.* God is our Father two manner of ways: first, in that he hath created and made us, as we tofore heard; secondly, in that he hath begotten us anew, "not of mortal, but of immortal seed," in that he hath given us 1 Pet. i. his Spirit, and we believe in his Son Christ Jesu, as St John saith: "As many as John i. received him (Christ), to them gave he power to be the sons of God, even them that believed in his name; which were born not of the blood, nor of the will of the flesh, nor yet of the will of man, but of God." St Paul also saith: "Ye are all the children Gal. iii. of God, because ye believe in Christ Jesu." Again: "As many as are led by the Rom. viii. Spirit of God, they are the sons of God."

Father. Then are not we the sons of God by nature? *Son.* No, verily, but by Christ alone is the Son of God by nature, we by adoption. adoption. One only is the natural Son of God, even Christ Jesus the Lord: the faithful are the sons of God only by adoption and grace, as we tofore abundantly heard in the declaration of the second article of the christian belief.

Father. Thou sayest truth, my child. But what profit hast thou in this, that God What it profiteth us that God is our Father. is thy Father? *Son.* What profit have I not, whether I respect the body or the soul? In that God is my Father, I am well assured, that I shall want no good thing necessary both for the body and for the soul. For as a good father hath a special care to provide and aforesee, that his son lack no good thing that is necessary for him; so likewise my heavenly Father, which by adoption and grace hath chosen me to be his son, will suffer me to lack no good thing, but abundantly minister and give unto me whatsoever is needful either for the body or for the soul, as God said unto Abraham: "Fear not: I am thy defence and mighty shield; and thy reward shall be exceeding Gen. xv. great." By the psalmograph he also saith: "I am the Lord thy God, &c.: open thy Psal. lxxxi.

mouth wide, and I shall fill it." And if at any time I seem to lack, in that God is my Father, I may be bold to come unto him, and to crave of him whatsoever thing I have need of, with this perfect persuasion and assured hope, that he will grant me my petitions no less, yea, much more (for he is almighty, and an horn of plenty) than any natural father will labour to satisfy the desires of his son; as our Saviour Christ saith: "Is there any man among you, which, if his son ask bread, will offer him a stone? or if he ask fish, will he proffer him a serpent? If ye then (when ye are evil) can give your children good gifts, how much more shall your Father which is in heaven give you good things, if ye ask of him?" Therefore in that I am taught by him, which is the self truth, to call God Father, I may be bold to come unto him, to lament my miseries unto him, to crave at his hand help, succour, defence, and whatsoever besides I have need of, with this faith, that I shall not be denied of my requests; forasmuch as he tendereth me no less, yea, much more, than a most loving father pitieth his most dear child.

Matt. vii. Luke xi. John xiv.

What we learn by calling God our Father.

Father. What learnest thou of this, that thou sayest not "my Father," but "our Father"? *Son.* In that I call God "our Father," I am put in remembrance, that God is the Father of us all, (I mean the faithful,) and that we be his sons, and therefore brethren ☞ also. Now, forasmuch as we all have one Father, and be all brethren and fellow-heirs of one and the same kingdom, I am here taught to love my brethren, and to do them good unto the uttermost of my power, to seek no less their commodity and profit than mine own, as St Paul saith: "Let no man seek his own commodity, but the profit of other." Again: "Charity or love seeketh not her own." He that hath not this love toward his christian brethren, he is not the son of God, neither is God his Father. "In this thing," saith Christ, "shall all men know that ye are my disciples, if ye love one another."

Phil. ii. 1 Cor. xiii. John xiii.

Father. Thou dost not only call God "our Father", but thou sayest moreover that he "is in heaven". *Son.* Yea, verily.

God is in heaven. Isai. lxvi. Psal. ciii. Psal. cxv. Psal. cxxiii. Matt. xxiii.

Father. How provest thou that God is in heaven? *Son.* God himself saith by the prophet: "Heaven is my seat." The psalmograph also saith: "The Lord hath prepared his seat in heaven." Again: "Our God is in heaven." Item: "Unto thee lift I up mine eyes, which dwellest in the heavens." Likewise saith our Saviour Christ: "Call no man father on the earth; for one is your Father, which is in heaven."

Psal. cxxxix. 1 Kings viii. Jer. xxiii.

Father. How canst thou truly and properly say that God is in heaven, when he is in all places at once, and filleth heaven and earth with his presence; forasmuch as he is infinite and incomprehensible? as the psalmograph saith: "Whither shall I go from thy Spirit? or whither shall I go from thy presence? If I climb up into heaven, thou art there: if I go down to hell, thou art there also. If I take the wings of the morning, and remain in the uttermost parts of the sea, even there also shall thy hand lead me, and thy right hand shall hold me. If I say, Peradventure the darkness shall cover me; then shall my night be turned to day. Yea, the darkness is no darkness with thee; but the night is as clear as the day: the darkness and the light to thee are both alike." Salomon also in his prayer said unto God: "Behold, the heavens and heavens of all heavens are not able to contain thee." And God himself saith by the prophet: "I fill both heaven and earth." *Son.* I know and confess that the majesty of God is infinite, unmeasurable, incomprehensible, filleth heaven and earth, occupieth all places at once, and cannot be compassed within certain limits (as all creatures are); forasmuch as he is the Maker of all things, and not a thing made: notwithstanding, the holy scripture most commonly termeth him to be and to dwell in heaven, yea, and that for divers causes.

God is infinity, and cannot be comprehended within certain limits.

Why it is said that God is in heaven. 1 John v.

First, to set forth unto us his majesty, highness, might, and power; while we consider that his dwelling is not in this world, which is a vale of miseries and a sink of all evils, but in the most high and glorious palace of heaven, where all joy and everlasting felicity is, where all goodness and virtue do abound, where nothing is that is not most delectable, most sweet, most pleasant; and that he hath there placed himself, not only that it should be his mansion, but ours also, forasmuch as he is our Father, and we are his children; so that whatsoever glory, joy, and felicity our Father hath and enjoyeth, the very same shall we his children, after this our banishment, likewise have and enjoy, as our inheritance freely given us of our most loving, gentle, and bounteous Father.

Secondly, to declare that our heavenly Father, being in so high a place, doth lovingly behold us and all ours, consider our necessities, hear our prayers, grant our requests, defend us, save us from our enemies, and give us all good things; as the psalmograph saith: "The Lord is high above all heathen, and his glory above the heavens. Who is like unto the Lord our God, that hath his dwelling so high, and yet humbleth himself to behold the things that are in heaven and earth? He taketh up the simple out of the dust, and lifteth the poor out of the mire; that he may set him with the princes, even with the princes of his people. He maketh the barren woman to keep house, and to be a joyful mother of children." Psal. cxiii.

Thirdly, to teach us, that as the heaven by unmeasurable wideness of compass containeth all places, the earth and the sea; and no place is there, that may be hid from the large reach of heaven, sith it is at every instant of time to every thing present; so likewise God is present to each thing in each place. He seeth, heareth, understandeth, and perceiveth all things, he being himself a spirit, and most far from all earthy and mortal state. This witnesseth God himself by the prophet, saying: "Am not I a God near unto you? and am not I a God far off? Shall any man be able to shroud himself in such a corner that I cannot espy him?" John iv. Jer. xxiii.

Fourthly, to signify unto us, that if we will have any thing to do with this our heavenly Father, we must have our minds free and utterly estranged from vicious affects, sinful lusts, and worldly desires, and fixed only upon God, and upon heavenly and everlasting things, as the apostle saith: "If ye be risen again with Christ, seek those things which are above, where Christ sitteth on the right hand of God. Set your affection on heavenly things, and not on earthy things." Col. iii.

Fifthly and finally, we call God our heavenly Father, to discern him from our fathers which be upon earth. For our fathers which we have in earth are but miserable, poor, needy, and mortal men, and of themselves neither able to save themselves nor us. But our Father which we have in heaven is omnipotent, almighty, rich, sufficiently able of himself to help us in all our necessities, immortal and ever living, at all times ready in this world to give us what is needful for body and soul, and after our departure from this world to place us in his heavenly kingdom, there to remain with him for ever in eternal felicity and joy.

Father. God make us all partakers of that heavenly glory! Now that thou hast declared why we call God our Father, and what is meant when the scripture saith he is in heaven; come off, rehearse unto me the first petition of the Lord's prayer. *Son.* The first petition is this:

"Hallowed be thy name." The first petition.

Father. What desire we of God in this petition? *Son.* Forasmuch as the name, that is to say, the majesty, glory, honour, fame, wisdom, power, goodness, mercy, justice, truth, knowledge, &c., of God, is divers ways profanated, polluted, and defiled in this world by many and sundry sects, by divers heresies and wicked opinions, by manifold superstition and idolatry, by the drowsy dreams and trifling traditions of men; we most humbly beseech our heavenly Father, that he will take away out of the earth all these abominations and filthy uncleannesses, wherewith not only the glory of his most glorious name among men is greatly obscured and defaced, but the souls of many are brought also into great errors, and in fine unto everlasting damnation. And as we desire of our heavenly Father in this first petition, that all things may be taken away wherewith either the glory of his holy name is diminished, or the salvation of men's souls is hindered; so likewise we pray, that he alone may be known, not only among the Christians, but also among all the nations of the earth, to be the only true God, the alone Saviour of the world, the mighty defender of his people, the plentiful rewarder of all them that trust in him, the merciful comforter of the faithful penitent sinners, the joyful receiver of such as turn unto him, and the strong avenger and punisher of all those that run from him a whore-hunting after strange What we desire in the first petition.

gods, and the wicked imaginations and inventions of their own hearts: again, that all nations of the world without exception may fear, reverence, honour, worship, glorify, call upon, and praise the glorious name of our heavenly Father, and in all things seek the avancement and honour thereof, preferring the glory of it before all creatures either in heaven or in earth, yea, more than our own goods and life, as it is written:
Psal. xliv. Rom. viii. "For thy sake," that is to say, for the glory and hallowing of thy name, "we are killed all day long, and are counted as sheep appointed to be slain." Daniel crieth
Dan. ix. out on this manner, and saith: "O Lord, to us, to our kings and princes, to our forefathers, yea, even to us all that have offended thee, belongeth nothing but open shame. But unto thee, O Lord our God, pertaineth righteousness, mercy, and forgive-
Psal. cxv. ness." All the saints of God cry out on this wise: "Not to us, O Lord, not to us, but to thy name give the glory, for thy mercy and truth's sake."

Father. Methink the words of this first petition do so sound, as though the name of God might yet be made more holy and more glorious than it is now,
Rev. xxii. as it is written: "He that is righteous, let him be more righteous; and he that is holy, let him be more holy." *Son.* God forbid, that any man should so think, that the name of God may be made more holy, glorious, and honourable than it is already, which is in all points in itself and of itself so holy, that no holiness can be put unto it; so glorious, that no glory can be added; so honourable, that more honourable it cannot be made; being of itself full of all holiness, glory, and honour: neither do we pray, that the name of our heavenly Father may be sanctified and hallowed unto this end, that in itself it may be made more holy, which is already most holy, but that it may be hallowed of all men in this world, and that the holiness of his name may be known among all nations, that they with one consent may believe and repose their whole affiance, trust, and confidence in it, call upon it
Prov. xviii. and fly unto it as unto a strong and mighty bulwark in their adversity, praise and magnify it in their prosperity, and at all times have it in great honour and reverence; so that in all their thoughts, words, and deeds, the glory of God's most glorious name
1 Cor. x. may be set forth by them, as the apostle saith: "Whatsoever ye do, do all to the
Col. iii. glory and praise of God." Again: "Whatsoever ye do in word or deed, do all in the name of the Lord Jesu, giving thanks to God the Father by him."

Of this hallowing of his name among all nations, God speaketh by the prophet on
Ezek. xxxix. this manner: "I will make the name of my holiness to be known among my people of Israel; and I will not let my holy name be evil spoken of any more; but the very heathen also shall know that I am the Lord, the Holy One of Israel. Behold, it cometh, and shall be fulfilled indeed, saith the Lord God." Hereto belongeth the saying of the
Psal. lxxxvi. psalmograph: "Among the gods there is none like unto thee, O Lord: there is not one that can do as thou doest. All nations, whom thou hast made, shall come and worship thee, O Lord, and shall glorify thy name."

Moreover, we do not only pray that the name of God may be sanctified, hallowed, called upon, praised, magnified, and perfectly known among all nations, yea, among the very heathen, which as yet have no perfect and true knowledge of God and of his holy name; but also that his name may be hallowed and magnified of us, which are his people, which have dedicated ourselves to his holy religion, which are baptized in the name of his Son Christ, and of him are called Christians, which profess godliness, and which are dead unto the world, and live unto Christ, lest, through our corrupt manners, wicked life, and ungodly conversation, the name of the Lord God be evil spoken of, slandered, railed upon, and blasphemed among the enemies of the truth,
Isai. lii. and his holy law condemned for heresy, as God himself complaineth by the prophet.
Rom. ii. And St Paul saith: "The name of God is evil spoken of among the gentiles through ☞ you." For as there can be no greater dishonour done unto God in this world, nor no greater ignominy unto his holy name, than when such as profess godliness practise ungodliness, unto the great slander of our profession, and unto the utter condemnation of ourselves; so likewise can there be no greater honour and glory shewed unto the Lord our God, and unto his blessed name, than when we, which profess godliness in
Tit. i. word, practise the same in deed, that we be not of the number of them which "profess that they know God, but with their deeds deny him, seeing they are abominable and

disobedient, and unapt unto every good work;" nor like unto the five foolish virgins, Matt. xxv. which had lamps and no oil, and therefore were shut out of the bridegroom's chamber, and when they knocked, and would have been let in, answer was made, "I know you not; depart from me, ye workers of iniquity;" nor like to that son, which promised his Psal. vi. father that he would work in his vineyard, and yet did not; nor yet like unto that Matt. xxi. fig-tree, which had leaves, but no fruit, and therefore was accursed of Christ, so that Mark xi. it withered away, and never brought forth fruit after.

In consideration whereof our Saviour Christ exhorteth us unto good works, saying: "Let your light so shine before men, that they may see your good works, and glorify Matt. v. your Father, which is in heaven." St Peter also saith: "Dearly beloved, I beseech you 1 Pet. ii. as strangers and pilgrims, abstain from fleshly lusts, which fight against the soul; and have your conversation honest, that whereas they backbite you as evil doers, they, judging you of your good works, may glorify God in the day of visitation." Again: "This is the will of God, that with well doing ye may stop the mouths of foolish and ignorant men; as free, and not as having the liberty for a cloke of maliciousness, but even as the servants of God." Likewise St Paul in divers places of his epistles exhorteth us, that by well doing we should "garnish the doctrine of God our Saviour," Tit. ii. walk worthy of the gospel of Christ, and so live, that we may be "such as no man Phil. i. Phil. ii. can complain on, and unfeigned sons of God, without rebuke in the midst of a crooked and perverse nation, among whom we ought so to shine as the lights of the world, holding fast the word of life."

Father. In this first petition, therefore, we ask of our heavenly Father, that his name, that is to say, his majesty, glory, honour, fame, wisdom, power, goodness, mercy, justice, truth, knowledge, &c., might be known, reverenced, honoured, and magnified throughout the world; and that all things, which in any part may seem to hinder the glory of God's most glorious name, or let the salvation of men's souls, although there be never so great shine and outward appearance of holiness, may utterly be extirped and rooted out of the earth, that the Lord our God may be known among all the nations of the world, to be the alone true and everlasting God, the alone Saviour of them that trust in him, and the plentiful fountain of all goodness, in adversity to be called on, in prosperity to be thanked and praised, and at all times to be most humbly reverenced, worshipped, and honoured: again, that such as profess his holy name may so frame their lives according to his blessed word, that God may be glorified, even among the very heathen, through their godly conversation and honest life, and his most glorious name praised among all the nations of the world. *Son.* So is it.

Father. Let me now hear the second petition. *Son.* This is it:

"Thy kingdom come." The second petition.

Father. What do we require of God in this second petition? *Son.* It is not Of Satan. What we desire in the second petition. unknown how great, how mighty, and of what puissance the kingdom of Satan is, which, as St Peter saith, "goeth about like a roaring lion, seeking whom he may 1 Pet. v. devour;" which Satan, in the holy scriptures, is termed the "prince and god of this John xiv. 2 Cor. iv. world," "the ruler of darkness," "the strong armed man," and "the accuser of the Eph. vi. Luke xi. brethren," and such one indeed as feared not, even in the state of their innocency and Rev. xii. Gen. iii. sinless life, to assault our grand parents, Adam and Heva, and with his sugared eloquence to allure them from the obedience of God's most blessed word unto the wicked transgression of his holy commandmant and perfect will; not only that, but he also feared not (such is his impudency and unshamefacedness) to attempt the Lord Jesus, Matt. iv. Mark i. that innocent Lamb of God, "in whom was never sin, and in whose mouth no guile Luke iv. 1 Pet. i. at any time was found," that he should despair of his heavenly Father's good will 1 Pet. ii. Isai. liii. toward him, and obey to his subtile persuasions and wicked temptations. There is no 1 John iii. ravening wolf that so earnestly seeketh greedily to devour his prey, as this enemy of 2 Cor. v. Rev. xii. mankind: that old serpent hunteth and studieth every moment of an hour, how he 1 Pet. v. Eph. vi. may destroy and bring to everlasting damnation mortal men, that they may fall from the favour of God, and "have their portion with him in that lake that burneth Isai. lxvi. with fire and brimstone." As this god of the world, I mean Satan, is a great king Rev. xxi.

Eph. ii. and mighty prince, and strongly ruleth in the children of unbelief and in the vessels of wrath, so is his kingdom ample and large; which kingdom this prince of darkness ceaseth not daily more and more to amplify, to enlarge, and to make very populous, that he might be the chief ruler of this world, and his kingdom the alone monarchy on the earth.

Of the world. And as Satan and his kingdom is mighty, large, and great, so likewise is the world a mighty prince, and ruleth strongly and stoutly in very many; whose kingdom also is most ample and populous, stuffed in every part with infinite numbers of people, compassed about with all wickedness. The guard of this prince is so great, that in this earth no potentate, no ruler, no governor is able to compare with it. For from the highest to the lowest, from the magistrate to the subject, from the priest to prophet, from the bishop to the deacon, all in a manner are worldlings, and under the kingdom of this mighty prince, the world. The world at this present hath so blinded the eyes of all men, that without any consideration they follow the world and the vanities thereof, being snarled with them, even as the fish is with the line and hook. They
Jer. iv. Phil. ii. from the least to the greatest are miserable mammonists and wretched money-slaves, serving their goods, and not their goods them, which is the greatest slavery and the most detestable bondage that can be found on the earth. And in serving such a vile ☞ idol, they are utterly fallen away from the faithful service which they owe unto the one and alone true God, whom above all things they ought to fear, reverence, serve, honour, worship, praise, magnify, and obey, yea, and that with all their heart, with all their soul, with all their mind, and with all the powers both of their soul and body, that the Lord our God may reign king, ruler, and governor alone, and that his kingdom
Psal. cxiii. may be enlarged "from the rising of the sun unto the going down of the same;" again, that his holy name may be known and praised among all the nations of the world.

The world so ruleth in the hearts almost of all men, that they utterly forget
Gen. xlvii. Psal. xxxix. 1 Pet. ii. 1 Tim. vi. themselves to be "strangers and pilgrims" in this life; neither do they consider, that they "brought nothing into this world, neither shall they carry any thing out of it;" so far is it off, that at any time they call to remembrance these sayings of the holy
James iv. scripture: "Ye adulterers and adulteresses, know ye not that the friendship of the world is enmity with God? Whosoever therefore will be a friend of the world is made the
1 John ii. enemy of God." Again: "See that ye love not the world, neither the things that are in the world. If any man love the world, the love of the Father is not in him. For all that is in the world (as the lust of the flesh, and the lust of the eyes, and the pride of life) is not of the Father, but of the world. And the world passeth away, and the lust thereof; but he that fulfilleth the will of God abideth for ever." Also
1 John v. in another place: "We know that we are of God, and the world is altogether set on wickedness." Item: "The time is short: it remaineth that they which buy be as though they possessed not, and they that use this world be as though they used
Heb. xiii. it not." Once again: "Let your conversation be without covetousness, and be con-
Josh. i. tent with such things as ye have already: for he hath said, I will not fail thee,
Psal. cxviii. neither forsake thee; so that we may boldly say, The Lord is my helper, and I will
Heb. xiii. not fear what man may do unto me." "Here have we no continuing city, but we seek one to come."

Of the flesh. Again, what shall I speak of the flesh? Is her kingdom small and little? Ruleth she in few, or rather in many? This flesh also seeketh and deviseth all means possible to enlarge her kingdom and empire, and studieth with all her wits how she may allure and entice the people of this world from the works of God's Spirit unto her
Gal. v. filthy lusts and fleshly pleasures, as the apostle saith: "Walk in the Spirit, and fulfil not the lusts of the flesh. For the flesh lusteth contrary to the Spirit, and the Spirit
Rom. viii. contrary to the flesh. These are contrary one to the other." "They that are carnal are carnally minded: but they that are spiritual are ghostly minded. To be carnally minded is death; but to be spiritually minded is life and peace: because the fleshly mind is enemy against God; for it is not obedient to the law of God, neither can be; so that they which are in the flesh cannot please God." The kingdom of this flesh, as it hath been in all ages, so likewise now in these our days, wherein

men are rather "lovers of pleasure than of God," is very large and ample, and comprehendeth infinite numbers of people, which willingly offer themselves subjects, servants, and slaves to this vile strumpet, the flesh; and the flesh again as a most mighty empress ruleth in them, and carrieth them as bond-slaves whither she willeth, and enforceth them as miserable captives to follow her lust and pleasure in all points; so that the flesh also is a mighty ruler and governor of the people of this world, and her kingdom is wide, large, and populous. 2 Tim. iii.

Now at the last cometh also antichrist and his kingdom; which antichrist with his false belief, superstition, hypocrisy, false worshipping of God, men's traditions, wicked counsels, devilish constitutions, ungodly doctrines, &c., stoutly and strongly ruleth in the hearts of the children of unbelief, deceiving them through the superstitious visor of feigned holiness, and throwing them into everlasting damnation; forasmuch as they reject and cast away, despise and condemn the true faith, religion, and doctrine of our Saviour Christ, and embrace, maintain, and defend the trifling traditions of this most abominable antichrist, that adversary of God and of all godliness. The kingdom also of this antichrist is very ample, large, mighty, and strong, and containeth in it infinite multitudes of people, even so many as are fallen away from the faith and doctrine of Christ, and are not led with the Spirit of God. "For they only are the sons and children of God, which are led with the Spirit of God." Of antichrist. 2 Thess. ii. Rom. viii.

All these princes and rulers, I mean the devil, the world, the flesh, and antichrist, labour with all main daily and continually to plant their kingdoms and to rule in the hearts of men, that, God and his holy Spirit through unbelief and wickedness of life chased out of their minds, they only may reign and possess them as their slaves, impelling and moving them unto what lewdness they lust. And this their labour they do not only employ about the wicked (whom they have already in their nets), but also, yea, much more, about us, which are the children of light, which profess godliness, and in our baptism have utterly forsaken and given over the devil, the world, and the flesh, with all their vain pomps, beastly pleasures, and wicked works, and have wholly renounced and cast away antichrist with all his antichristian traditions, and dedicated ourselves to God, to God's doctrine, and to his holy religion. Who seeth not now then, how necessary this second petition is, wherein we pray that the kingdom of our heavenly Father may come and rule in us?

Father. What meanest thou? For I do not perfectly understand thee. *Son.* Forasmuch as we are environed, besieged, compassed, and set round about with so many adversaries, as we have tofore heard, which studiously and diligently labour to possess our hearts, to rule in us, and to make us their subjects, servants, bondmen, captives, and slaves in this present world, and after this life to make us firebrands of hell and inheritors of everlasting damnation; our Lord and Master Christ Jesus—the alone teacher of truth, and the alone wisdom also of the Father, tendering our health and salvation of body and soul both in this world and in the world to come, knowing also how unable we be of ourselves to resist and withstand so great multitudes of adversaries, which, being strong and valiant, strongly and valiantly seek our destruction—commandeth us to flee unto our heavenly Father with faithful and earnest prayer, and to crave of him succour and aid against so fierce and cruel enemies, lest we fall into their hands, and so become their preys, and at the last be swallowed up of hell-mouth, and made heirs of everlasting damnation.

And in this behalf we first of all desire of our heavenly Father, that the kingdom of the devil, that sworn enemy of mankind, "that old serpent," that wily fox, that ravening wolf, which at all hours seeketh our destruction, may utterly be subdued, destroyed, and brought to nought, with all his wicked temptations and poisonful persuasions, that we never give place unto them, nor yet be overcome of them, but with strong faith manfully resist them, that Satan may not rule in us, nor we become his kingdom. We also desire of our heavenly Father, that the kingdom of the wicked world with all his vain pleasures, lusts, pomps, and vanities, may be dispersed and brought unto confusion, that we, which profess godliness, be by no means snarled or seduced by them; but that we, considering how vain, transitory, flitting, and soon passing away they be, may embrace those pleasures which Gen. iii. Rev. xii. 1 Pet. v.

are immortal, those goods which are constant, those riches which never fail, and by this means bid adieu both to the world and to his kingdom, setting always before our remembrance, that we are selected and "chosen aside from the world;" yea, that by our profession we are dead to the world, and our "life is hid with Christ in God."

John xv. Col. iii.

Again, we desire of our heavenly Father, that the kingdom of the wicked flesh, with all her carnal concupiscences and filthy lusts, which fight against the soul, may be so extirped and plucked up by the roots, that we, being made free from all the uncleannesses thereof, may no more be seduced with the venomous and poisonful enticements of this most venomous and poisonful mermaid, the flesh, nor by any means hereafter consent to her beast-like desires and filthy lusts; but so live, being clad with this weak and mortal flesh, that the lusts thereof may not rule in us, but that we rather may subdue them, and "put on the new man, which is shapen and made in righteousness, holiness, and truth."

Eph. iv. Col. iii.

Item, we desire of our heavenly Father, that antichrist with his kingdom, which hath seduced, and daily doth seduce, an infinite number of miserable and poor wretched souls through his glistering and painted visor of counterfeit, false, and feigned holiness, may shortly be slain and brought unto confusion "with the breath of the Lord's mouth, and utterly be abolished with the brightness of his coming;" that "that sinful man, the son of perdition, which is an adversary, and is exalted above all that is called God, or that is worshipped," may no longer "sit in the temple of God, boasting himself to be God," nor be "drunken" any more "with the blood of the saints and with the blood of the martyrs of Jesu," nor yet sell the souls of men, nor utter any more of his false and counterfeit merchandise to the simple ones; that the kingdom may be his alone, which is "King of kings and Lord of lords."

Isai. xi. Dan. viii. 2 Thess. ii. Rev. xvii. Rev. xviii. Rev. xix.

And as we pray unto our heavenly Father, that we, through his mighty power, may be delivered from these our aforesaid enemies and from their tyranny (so that they rule not us, but we rather rule and subdue them); even so in like manner do we desire of him, that he will vouchsafe to make us his kingdom, and to rule in us by his mighty power, that we may be his inheritance, and he our owner; he our Lord, and we his people; he our Father, and we his children.

And forasmuch as we of ourselves are feeble and weak, of no force and strength, ready at all times to be cast down even of the least of our enemies, if we were not underpropped and stayed up by the strong hand of God; we in this petition crave of our heavenly Father, that he will pour out his holy Spirit into our hearts, which may rule and govern us, and direct us in all our ways, and so at all times work and shew his mighty power in us, that we may be and continue the obedient people of God, "serving him in holiness and righteousness all the days of our life." For "the kingdom of God," as St Paul saith, "is righteousness, peace, and joy in the Holy Ghost;" and God hath delivered us "from the power of our enemies, that we should serve him in holiness and righteousness all the days of our life." Christ, that most high and everlasting bishop, "through the everlasting Spirit, offered himself without spot to God, that he might purge our conscience from dead works for to serve the living God." For "God hath not called us unto uncleanness, but unto holiness."

Luke i. Rom. xiv. Heb. ix. 1 Thess. iv.

Again, forasmuch as we of ourselves, of our own nature and natural strengths, although otherwise never so prudent and worldly-wise, are not able to perceive and understand those things which belong unto the Spirit of God and unto our salvation, but are miserable, poor, and blind, and without any true knowledge of God; we desire our heavenly Father, that, all our ignorance and blindness wiped away, and all the dark dreams and dreaming darkness of antichrist utterly dispelled, removed, and put aside, the glorious light of Christ's gospel, which is "the mighty power of God to save so many as believe," which is the food of the soul, which is the undefiled word of the Lord, which "turneth souls," which "is pure and giveth wisdom unto the simple," which "rejoiceth the hearts," which "giveth light unto the eyes," which is an "armour," or weapon, "not carnal, but mighty in God to cast down strongholds, and to overthrow counsels, and every high thing that exalteth itself against the knowledge of God, and bringeth into captivity all imagination to the obedience of Christ," which is "the sword of the Spirit," &c., may shine among us, lighten our

Matt. xi. 1 Cor. ii. Rom. i. Matt. iv. Psal. xix. 2 Cor. vi. Eph. vi.

dark hearts, illumine our senses, polish our wits, fine our understanding, and bring us unto the true knowledge, faith, and doctrine of him (I mean God the Father) which "hath delivered us from the power of darkness, and hath translated us into the king- Col. i.
dom of his dear Son, by whom we have redemption through his blood, even the forgiveness of sins." For where this gospel of Christ is truly preached, and through the working of the Holy Ghost received into the hearts of the hearers, there is faith, joy, peace, quietness of conscience, new godly affects, spiritual motions, heavenly desires, correction of manners, newness of life, continual study of innocency, with all the fruits of the Holy Ghost, as St Paul saith: "If any man be in Christ, he is a new 2 Cor. v.
creature." Again: "They that appertain unto Christ have crucified the flesh with Gal. v.
the affects and lusts thereof."

Contrariwise, where the gospel of Christ is not preached nor received, there remaineth unbelief, grief of mind, trouble of heart, disquietness of conscience, old corrupt affects, carnal motions, worldly desires, continuance in sin, wickedness of life, disposition unto all evil, with all the works of the flesh, as Salomon saith: "When the preaching of Prov. xxix.
God's word faileth, the people perish." Again: "Where the knowledge of God's word Prov. xix.
is not, there is no goodness for the soul." Item: "Vain are all they which have no Wisd. xiii.
knowledge of God."

Therefore in this petition also we ask of our heavenly Father, that his holy gospel may reign among us, all man's doctrines utterly set apart, and that it may bring forth such fruits in us, that we may be the kingdom of God, his holy Spirit continually ruling and governing us, and "leading us into all truth." John xvi.

Moreover, forasmuch as there be yet divers nations and kingdoms which know not the true, and him the one and alone God, but walk after the vanities of their own mind, or else after the trifling traditions of men; we beseech our heavenly Father, that he will have mercy on all people, and "shew unto them also the light of his Psal. lxvii.
countenance, that all nations on the earth may know his ways, and his saving health Isai. lxi.
throughout the world;" that, as we altogether have one Creator and Maker, so likewise Mal. i.
we may have "one faith, one hope, one baptism," one doctrine, and one life everlast- Eph. iv.
ing, there worlds without end to magnify and praise our heavenly Father. For by this means shall it come to pass, that the kingdom of Satan, of the world, of the flesh, of sin, and of antichrist, shall greatly be diminished and soon brought to nought, and the glorious kingdom of God shall most triumphantly prosper, grow, increase, wax strong, and flourish; so that with one voice all nations of the earth shall praise the blessed name of the Lord our God, and be made his kingdom and possession, knowing him and his saving health even "from the least to the greatest, insomuch that it Jer. xxxi.
shall not be needful one to say unto another, Know the Lord; for," when the Heb. viii.
kingdom of God shall so be enlarged, "all shall know God, even from the highest to the lowest."

Finally, in this our petition we do not only ask and desire of our heavenly Father, that the kingdom of Satan, of the world, of the flesh, and of antichrist, may be destroyed and brought to nought, so that from henceforth we neither serve them, neither they rule in us: again, that God through his Holy Ghost and blessed word should only have dominion and power over us, yea, and rule in our hearts, so that, all sin and wickedness set apart, we shall be plentiful of all good works, and abound in all godliness and honesty: Item, that the kingdom of our heavenly Father may be so enlarged, that all nations of the world may know him to be the alone true God, and embrace his blessed gospel, and, so believing, become with us the people and servants of God; but also, that after this life we may come to that kingdom, where all true joy and immortal felicity is, which is the end of our faith, and the consummation and perfect fulfilling of our hope, I mean the glorious palace of that most high God, where we shall see the blessed Trinity, not "in a dark speech or in a glass," or with 1 Cor. xiii.
the eyes of our faith, as we do now, but we shall see him "face to face, and know him, as we are known," according to this saying of St John: "Dearly beloved, now 1 John iii.
are we the sons of God, and yet it doth not appear what we shall be: but we know that, when it shall appear, we shall be like him; for we shall see him as he is. And every one that hath this hope in him purifieth himself even as he is also pure."

1 Cor. xiii. Hereto belongeth the saying of St Paul: "Now we see in a glass, even in a dark speaking; but then shall we see face to face. Now I know unperfectly, but then shall I know even as I am known."

Father. God give us grace so to behave ourselves in this world, that after this mortal and transitory life we may come unto his heavenly kingdom, and enjoy the immortal and everlasting life! *Son*. Amen.

Father. Rehearse the third petition contained in the Lord's prayer.

The third petition. *Son*. "Thy will be done in earth, even as it is in heaven."

What we desire in the third petition. Gen. vi. viii. Phil. ii. *Father*. What is that? *Son*. Forasmuch as our will is alway evil, or at the least prone unto evil, even from our cradles upward, fleshly, and disobedient to the most holy and perfect will of God, seeking her own, and not that which is Christ's, coveting evermore worldly and not godly things, wholly bent unto things which lead not unto salvation but unto damnation; in this third petition we desire our heavenly Father, that he will mortify this our carnal, worldly, and devilish will, and make it obedient and conformable to his most godly and blessed will, that we in nothing resist his holy pleasure, but shew ourselves ready to follow and to accomplish unto the uttermost of our power, without any resistance, that which in the holy scripture we have learned unfeignedly to be his good and fatherly will.

Father. Are not we able of ourselves, without craving this at the hand of God, to frame our will to the will of God, and to perform whatsoever the good pleasure
The will of man is naturally bent unto evil. of God is? *Son*. Our will of itself is a captive, bond, and thrall will, subject unto sin, estranged from all goodness, and altogether unapt either to consent unto the will of God or to perform the same; so little, or rather none, are the strengths of our will, whose liberty or freedom was not only grievously wounded, but in a manner wholly lost and perished in the fall of Adam, insomuch that the best and most perfectest
Rom. vii. among the children of men may right well say with St Paul: "The law," that is to
Rom. viii. say, the will of God, "is spiritual, but I am carnal, sold under sin." Again: "The fleshly mind is enemy against God; for it is not obedient to the law of God, neither
John iii. can it be; so that they which are in the flesh cannot please God." For "that which
1 Cor. ii. is born of flesh is flesh;" and "a natural man perceiveth not the things that belong to the Spirit of God: for they are but foolishness unto him; neither can he perceive
2 Cor. iii. them, because they are spiritually examined." "We be not able of ourselves to think any (good) thing, as of ourselves; but if we be able unto any (good) thing, the same
James i. cometh of God." For "every good gift and every perfect gift is from above, and cometh
John xv. down from the Father of lights." "Without me," saith Christ, "ye can do nothing."
Phil. ii. "It is God that worketh in us both the will and the deed, even of good will." Who seeth not now therefore, what great need we have to cry unto God, that it may please him to reform our will, which is altogether naught and given to wickedness, and to make it obedient and conformable to his will, which is most holy, just, and perfect? This considered the Lord Jesu, which is the wisdom of his Father, when he taught
Matt. vi. us in this most perfect prayer to say: "Thy will be done in earth, even as it is in
Psal. cxliii. heaven." This thing also was not unknown to the psalmograph, when he prayed on this manner: "Teach me, O Lord, to do thy will; for thou art my God."

Father. But what meaneth this that we are taught to pray, that God's will may be fulfilled here "in earth, as it is in heaven"? Is not God able to bring to pass whatsoever his good pleasure is here in earth among the children of men, as well as he is able to do it in heaven among the holy angels and blessed saints? *Son*. God is almighty, and able to perform abundantly whatsoever he determineth; neither is any thing impossible unto him; so that without our help or without our prayer he can right well bring to pass whatsoever his good will and pleasure shall be, as he himself
Isai. xlvi. saith by the prophet: "My device standeth stedfastly stablished, and I fulfil all my
Jer. xxxii. pleasure." Again: "Behold, I am the Lord God of all flesh: is there any thing
Isai. xiv. then too hard for me?" The prophet Esay also saith: "If the Lord of hosts determine a thing, who is able to disannul it? And if he stretch forth his hand, who may hold
Psal. xxxiii. it in again?" Likewise saith the psalmograph: "He spake, and it was done: he commanded, and it stood fast. The Lord bringeth the counsel of the heathen to nought,

and maketh the devices of the people to be of none effect: but the counsel of the Lord shall endure for ever, and the thoughts of his heart from generation to generation." Again he saith: "Our God is in heaven: he hath done whatsoever pleased him." Psal. cxv.

We pray not, therefore, that God's will may be done here in earth "as it is in heaven," unto this end, as though it had need of our prayer, that it may have good success, which in and of itself is almighty; but we pray, that God's good will, which he hath revealed and shewed unto us in his holy word, may effectually be done in us through the working of the Holy Ghost, and obediently fulfilled by us, both privately and openly, both in word and in deed, unto the glory of his holy name; which otherwise can never be brought to pass of us nor in us, so great is our infirmity, so corrupt is our nature, so malicious and disposed to all evil is our heart, so carnal, wicked, and ungodly is our own will, and so slender, yea, rather so none, are all the strengths of our free will, which, as the apostle saith, "of ourselves are not able to think a good thought." 2 Cor. iii.

Father. But what meaneth this, when we pray that the will of God may "be done in earth, as it is in heaven"? Why is mention made here of the fulfilling of God's will in heaven? *Son.* Our Saviour Christ, in teaching us so to pray, setteth before our eyes a goodly exemplar or pattern to follow. Who knoweth not that the glorious angels and blessed spirits in heaven do most obediently and readily accomplish and fulfil the holy will of God, and by no means resist his godly pleasure? as it is written: "O praise the Lord, ye angels of his, ye that excel in strength, ye that fulfil his commandment, and hearken unto the voice of his words." The Lord commanded his angel to plague the Israelites with pestilence; and he plagued them straightways, so that there died in three days seventy thousand men. And when the Lord bade him hold his hand, the angel striked no more, so that the plague ceased. The Lord's angel also at his commandment slew in one night an hundred fourscore and five thousand of the Assyrians. Raphael the angel, at the Lord's commandment, accompanied young Tobias in all his journey. Again, Gabriel the angel, at the commandment of God, came from heaven unto the virgin Mary, to declare unto her the good pleasure of God concerning his Son's incarnation, which through the power of the Holy Ghost should be brought to pass in her. Many other histories have we in the holy scripture, which do evidently declare how obediently and diligently the angels accomplish the will of God; so that not without a cause they are called of St Paul "ministering spirits, that are sent to minister for their sakes which shall be heirs of salvation." After the example of these holy angels and blessed spirits ought we here in earth with all diligence to endeavour ourselves to accomplish the good pleasure of God. Psal. ciii. 2 Sam. xxiv. 2 Kings xix. Tob. v. xii. Luke i. Heb. i.

Father. Have we any examples in the holy scriptures, that men, living here in this world, have in this behalf followed the angels by practising and executing the will of God? *Son.* Many are found in the word of God; but let this one example of our Lord and Saviour Christ suffice for this present, of whom we read, that it was his meat and greatest desire to fulfil the will of his heavenly Father, insomuch that, to obey his blessed pleasure and determinate counsel, he was content to suffer "death, yea, even the death of the cross." He prayed unto his heavenly Father, that if it were possible, the cup of his passion and death might pass away from him; yet he added: "Not as I will, but as thou wilt, O Father." In all things he gladly obeyed the will of his Father, and performed the same, to give us an example, which of Christ are called Christians, that we also should labour to practise the like obedience to the will of God in our life and conversation, as St John saith: "He which saith that he dwelleth in Christ ought to walk even as he hath walked." And the Lord Jesus himself saith: "I have given you an example, that even as I have done, so ye likewise should do." John iv. Phil. ii. Matt. xxvi. Mark xiv. Luke xxii. 1 John ii. John xiii.

Father. Seeing we pray in this third petition, that we may have so fervent a desire to accomplish the will of God in all things here on earth, as the holy angels and blessed saints have in heaven; come off, tell me what the will of God is. *Son.* Although we have partly touched this matter before, when we entreated of the worthy What the will of God is.

preparation unto prayer; yet, forasmuch as your pleasure is to ask me this question, I answer that the will of God is whatsoever in his holy word he commandeth us to do.

Father. What willeth he us to do? What commandeth he? *Son.* Forasmuch
Eph. ii. Psal. li. as by nature we are the "children of wrath," and bond unto everlasting damnation,
Repentance. God, tendering our health and salvation, hath commanded us to repent and to better our life, that by this means we might be received into favour.

Father. Where hath he expressed this his will? *Son.* In divers places of the
Jer. [Ezek. xxxiii.] holy scripture. By the prophet he saith: "I have no pleasure in the death of a sinner;
1 Tim. ii. but rather that he should turn and live." St Paul also saith: "God will all men to
Matt. iii. iv. Mark i. be saved, and to come unto the knowledge of the truth." St John the Baptist, Christ,
Luke iii. Acts ii. and his apostles, call us all unto repentance and unto the amendment of our life;
Rev. ii. whereof also we may learn, that the good will of God is, that although heretofore we have been never so great and grievous sinners, yet we should now repent, correct our manners, and amend our life.

Secondly, forasmuch as repentance and amendment of life are things unperfect con-
Faith. cerning everlasting life, except faith be annexed, therefore the good will of God is not only that we should repent, but also believe, I mean, in our hearts to be perfectly
1 Tim. ii. persuaded that for Christ's sake, our alone Mediator, all our sins be forgiven us. Therefore Christ and his apostles taught not only repentance and amendment of life, but
Mark i. also faith. "Repent and believe the gospel," saith our Saviour Christ. God's good pleasure therefore is, not only that we should repent, but also believe, and so be saved,
John vi. as Christ saith: "This is the will of him that sent me, that every one which seeth the Son, and believeth on him, should have everlasting life." Again: "This is the work of God (which he requireth of you), that ye should believe on him whom he hath sent."

Thirdly, after we be engraffed in Christ through faith, God, willing us to shew ourselves no more to be the sons of Satan, or of the world, but the sons of God,
A new life. and new-born children of the Holy Ghost, commandeth us from henceforth not to obey the lust of the flesh, but the desire of the Spirit; not to walk any more in our old sinful life, but to lead a new conversation, and to practise new manners, yea, and
2 Cor. v. those godly, pure, and christian, as St Paul saith: "If any man be in Christ, he is
Gal. v. a new creature." "They that pertain unto Christ have crucified the flesh with the
Rom. vi. affects and lusts thereof." Again: "Let not sin reign in your mortal body, that ye should thereunto obey by the lusts of it: neither give ye your members as instruments of unrighteousness unto sin; but give over yourselves unto God, as they that of dead
1 Thess. iv. are alive." Also in another place: "This is the will of God, even your sanctification, that ye abstain from whoredom, and that every one know to possess his vessel with holiness and honour, &c. For God hath not called us unto uncleanness, but unto
1 Pet. ii. holiness." Likewise saith St Peter: "This is the will of God, that by well doing ye should stop the mouth of foolish and ignorant men; as free, and yet not having the freedom as a cloke of maliciousness, but as the servants of God."

Fourthly and finally, this also is the good will and pleasure of God, that we shall not only repent, believe, and lead a new life, garnished with all good works; but also that we both obediently, patiently, and thankfully bear and suffer whatso-
Cross. ever cross, trouble, sickness, persecution, or any other kind of adversity God layeth upon us, being thoroughly persuaded, that this visitation of God cometh not from an angry and displeasant heart, but rather from a fatherly affection and singular good will toward us, yea, and that not for our destruction and damnation, but rather for our
Prov. iii. edification and salvation, as it is written: "My son, despise not the chastening of the Lord, neither faint when thou art rebuked of him. For whom the Lord loveth, him he chasteneth, and yet delighteth in him, even as the father in his own son." God
Rev. iii. himself saith: "As many as I love I rebuke and chasten." "If ye endure chasten-
Heb. xii. ing," saith St Paul, "God offereth himself unto you as unto sons. What son is he, whom the father chasteneth not? If ye be not under correction, whereof all are partakers, then ye are bastards, and not sons," &c. "No manner chastising for the present time seemeth to be joyous, but grievous; nevertheless, afterward it bringeth

the quiet fruit of righteousness unto them which are exercised thereby." "Blessed is the man," saith St James, "that endureth temptation; for when he is tried, he shall receive the crown of life, which the Lord hath promised to them that love him." Hereto belongeth the saying of the psalmograph: "It is highly for my profit that thou hast chastened me, that I may learn thine ordinances." For "those which God knew afore, he also ordained afore, that they should be like fashioned unto the shape of his Son." "The disciple is not above his master, nor the servant above his lord." Our elder brother Christ first suffered, and afterward entered into glory. "By many tribulations must we enter into the kingdom of God." "All that will live godly in Christ Jesu shall suffer persecution." "If we be dead with Christ, we shall also live with Christ: if we suffer with Christ, we shall also reign with Christ." And our Saviour Christ himself saith: "Whosoever will follow me, let him forsake himself, and take up his cross, and follow me. For whosoever will save his life shall lose it; but whosoever shall lose his life for my sake and the gospel's, the same shall save it." Forasmuch therefore as it is God's good pleasure to keep his children under the cross, whom he hath appointed to be inheritors of his everlasting glory, it shall become as many as wish to be glorified with Christ, to bear also the cross with Christ, and to shew themselves in all kind of adversity and trouble conformable to the will of God, and both obediently, patiently, gladly, and thankfully to bear whatsoever God layeth upon their shoulders, even unto the very death.

James i. Psal. cxix. Rom. viii. Matt. x. Luke xxiv. Acts xiv. 2 Tim. iii. 2 Tim. ii. Matt. xvi. Mark viii. Luke ix.

Father. Have we any examples in the holy scripture, which declare that certain in times past have been so obedient to the will of God in this behalf, that they have patiently, and without any murmuring or grudging (against God), borne and suffered whatsoever kind of adversity hath been cast upon them? *Son.* You heard before the example of the Lord Jesu. But besides this we have divers other. To whom is it unknown, with how many great and grievous kinds of adversity that mirror of perfect patience, I mean Job, was afflicted? Notwithstanding, how conformable he shewed himself to the will of God, how patiently he suffered that heavy cross, these his words do most manifestly declare: "Naked came I out of my mother's womb, and naked shall I turn thither again. The Lord gave, and the Lord hath taken away. Even as it hath pleased the Lord, so is it come to pass. Blessed be the name of the Lord." Again: "Shall we receive prosperity at the hand of God, and not receive adversity?" "In all these things," saith the historiograph, "Job did not offend, nor murmured foolishly against God." To whom also is the history of old Tobias unknown? whom God deprived of his sight, that he might try his patience and conformity to his godly will. "He grudged not," saith the scripture, "against God, because the plague of blindness had chanced unto him, but remaineth still stedfast in the fear of God, and praising God all the days of his life." What shall I speak of king David, which, being grievously and mortally pursued of his ungodly and disobedient son Absolon, committed himself wholly unto the hands of God, ready to receive whatsoever the good pleasure of God should be, whether it were restitution unto his kingdom, or an utter loss of the same?

Examples of patience. Job i. Job ii. Job i. Tob. ii. [Vulgate.] 2 Sam. xv.

I pass over Moses and the prophets, Paul and the apostles, which patiently, joyfully, and thankfully bare whatsoever cross God laid upon their back, never grudging against the will of God. The history of Lazarus is more known than it needeth here to be recited, which, suffering quietly the great pains of many mortal diseases, besides the extreme famine, with whose dart he was most miserably pierced, and never grudging against the good will of God, was at the last of the glorious angels carried up into the bosom of Abraham. I pass over the history of the leper, which although he desired to be cleansed from his leprosy, yet he referred the matter to Christ, to do with him whatsoever his good pleasure should be, either to be made clean, or to remain still in his leprosy. Thus all good men from time to time in every age have patiently and thankfully borne the cross that God hath laid upon them, and submitted their will to the good will of God, being fully persuaded that "all things work for the best unto them that love God," seeing that nothing chanceth to the godly without the good will and the determinate counsel and singular providence of God.

Luke xvi. Matt. viii. Rom. viii.

Father. Doth God send such afflictions and troubles as chance unto men in this

☞ world? *Son.* To the godly, and to such as fear God, nothing cometh by fortune or by chance, but by the determination and will of God, be it never so grievous and troublous cross.

Isai. xlv. God saith by the prophet: "I am the Lord, and there is else none. It is I that created light and darkness. I make peace and trouble: yea, even I the Lord do all these things." (Lam. iii.) Jeremy also saith: "What is he that saith, there should something be done without the Lord's commandment? Out of the mouth of the Most Highest goeth not evil and good?" By evil he meaneth adversity; by good he understandeth prosperity. (Matt. x.) Likewise saith our Saviour Christ: "Are not two little sparrows sold for a farthing? and one of them shall not light on the ground without your Father;" that is to say, without the consent and good will, without the counsel and determination of your Father. (Psal. xxxiv. Psal. civ. Psal. xxxiv. Wisd. xiv.) "The Lord keepeth all the bones of the righteous, so that not one of them shall be broken." For he giveth his angels charge of them to keep them in all their ways, which shall pitch their tents round about the godly, and shall deliver them. By the providence of God all things are governed, and at his appointment all things chance to the godly; neither can any thing happen to such as fear God without both the determination and permission of God. (Gen. xxvii. xxxii. xxxiii.) Esau burneth with an immortal hatred against his brother Jacob, purposing in his heart to kill him: but God so mollified his heart, that when he met with his brother Jacob, he lovingly embraced him, friendly kissed him, and for very joy wept upon him. Saul persecuted David cruelly, purposing to kill him; but his labour was in vain. (1 Kings xix.) Jesabel threatened and sware, that she would slay the prophet Helias; but the Lord preserved him. (Job ii.) Satan could do nothing to Job, till God licensed him; neither exercised he his cruelness any further against Job than he was appointed of God. (John xix.) Christ said unto Pilate: "Thou couldest have no power at all against me, except it were given thee from above." The devils had no power to enter into the swine, till Christ gave them leave. (Matt. viii.) "If thou cast us out of this man," said they, "suffer us to enter into the herd of swine." Christ answered, "Go ye;" and they went.

Seeing then that nothing chanceth to the godly without the singular providence and determinate counsel of the Lord our God; again, whatsoever chanceth unto them is for the best, and for their great commodity and profit; it is our duty in prosperity not to wax proud against God, nor in adversity to murmur or grudge against him; but like obedient children to surrender and give up unto him ourselves, our wills, our affections, our lusts, and whatsoever we have besides, humbly desiring him, that not our own will, nor the will of Satan, or of the world, but his most godly and blessed will may be done in us; yea, and that with no less fervent desire and greedy affection than it is accomplished and fulfilled of the glorious angels and blessed spirits in the kingdom of heaven; so that from henceforth even unto our life's end there may no motion of lust be felt in us, but such only as shall wholly consent with his will; nor that we will any thing of ourself, but as the Holy Ghost will in us, by whose secret instruction we may learn to love and to do those things that be pleasant to him, and to hate and abhor whatsoever displeaseth him.

Father. God for his mercy's sake mought vouchsafe to bring to pass this thing in us, unto the glory of his holy name! *Son.* Amen.

Father. Let me now, my son, hear the fourth petition.

The fourth petition.

Son. "Give us this day our daily bread."

Father. To what end do we direct this prayer unto God? *Son.* You heard afore, that the Lord's prayer containeth in it seven several petitions, whereof the three first petitions concern the glory of God and the avancement of his kingdom; the other four, which follow in order, entreat of our necessities, and appertain unto our commodity and profit; of the which this is the first: "Give us this day our daily bread." After that we have most humbly desired of our heavenly Father, that his holy name may be sanctified in us; that the glorious kingdom of his holy Spirit and gospel may come unto us; and that his most blessed will may be done and fulfilled of us here in earth, with no less desire than it is done and accomplished of the holy angels in heaven; forasmuch as we cannot live in this world to enjoy these most precious and

inestimable benefits, for the which we have tofore prayed, without bodily food (for man being made of two parts must have a double nourishment; he is made of soul, whose food is the word of God; he is also made of body, which must needs Deut. viii. Matt. iv.
be fed with corporal sustenance); therefore, as "in him we live, move, and have our Luke iv. Acts xvii.
being," so likewise in this petition do we crave of him all things necessary for the maintenance of this our poor and needy life, as that alone fountain of all goodness, "from whom descendeth every good and perfect gift;" and as that alone most bounteous James i.
Lord, which "giveth food to all flesh, and filleth every living creature with his blessing." Psal. cxlv.
And of this order of praying we learn a good and profitable lesson, even this, A good lesson.
that we should first of all pray unto our heavenly Father for spiritual and heavenly things, and afterward for such things as are necessary for the preservation of the body, as our Saviour Christ saith: "Seek first the kingdom of God and the righteousness Matt. vi.
thereof; and all these things shall be cast unto you." "For man shall not live with Matt. iv. Deut. viii.
bread alone, but with every word that cometh out of the mouth of God."

Father. But come off, let us examine every word of this petition in order. *Son*. Agreed.

Father. Wherefore sayest thou unto God, "give"? Can we not have whereof Give.
to live by our own policy, wit, industry, and labour, except we ask it of God? *Son*. No, verily. Except the Lord blessed our labours, pains, and travails, all that ever we do is in vain, as the psalmograph saith: "Except the Lord build the house, Psal. cxxvii.
their labour is but lost that build it. Except the Lord keep the city, the watchman waketh but in vain." "The blessing of the Lord maketh men rich: as for careful Prov. x.
travail, it doth nothing thereto." And therefore are we taught of our Saviour Christ Matt. vi.
to crave daily food of our heavenly Father. For except he give it us, our travail is vain and but lost, as the psalmograph saith: "All creatures wait upon thee, O Lord, Psal. civ. Psal. cxlv.
that thou mayest give them meat in due season. When thou givest it them, they gather it; and when thou openest thy hand, they are filled with plenteousness. But when thou hidest thy face, they are troubled; and when thou takest away their breath, they die, and are turned again to their dust." "It is the Lord that giveth meat to Psal. cxlvi.
the hungry." "They that fear the Lord shall have no scarceness: they which seek Psal. xxxiv.
the Lord shall want no good thing." "The eyes of the Lord are upon them that fear Psal. xxxiii.
him, and upon them that trust in his mercy; that he may deliver their lives from death, and nourish them in the time of hunger." "In this world we lead a poor life; Tob. iv.
notwithstanding we shall have plenty of all good things, if we fear the Lord, depart from all sin, and do good." For good and evil, life and death, poverty and riches are of God, "in whose sight it is an easy thing quickly to enrich a poor Ecclus. xi.
man."

Whosoever trusteth in God and laboureth according to his vocation or calling, ever crying unto God for good success in his labours, he may be well assured never to want, as David saith: "The lions do lack and suffer hunger; but they which seek Psal. xxxiv.
the Lord shall want no manner of thing that is good." Again: "I have been young, Psal. xxxvii.
and now am old; and yet saw I never the righteous forsaken, nor his seed begging their bread on the earth. He is merciful all his life-time, and lendeth, and yet hath his children after him God's plenty and enough." Let us therefore "cast all our care 1 Pet. v.
upon the Lord; for he careth for us." "Lay thy care upon the Lord," saith David, Psal. lv.
"and he shall nourish thee."

Father. It is then God alone which giveth us all good things, when we call upon him. *Son*. Yea, verily. This considered Jacob right well, when he said on this manner: "If God will be with me, and will keep me in this journey which I go, and will give Gen. xxviii.
me bread to eat, and clothes to put on, so that I come again unto my father's house in safety, then shall the Lord be my God." Neither was this thing unknown to Salomon, when he thus prayed: "Two things have I required of thee, O Lord, that Prov. xxx.
thou wilt not deny me before I die. Remove from me vanity and lies: give me neither poverty nor riches: only grant me a necessary living; lest if I be too full, I deny thee, and say, Who is the Lord? and lest I, being constrained through poverty, fall unto stealing, and take the name of my God in vain."

Father. But wherefore in this petition do I rather say, praying by myself alone, Us.

Matt. vi. Luke xi.

"give us," than "give me"? *Son.* This prayer, which the Lord Christ both taught and commanded us to say, is a common and general prayer, serving for the use of the whole church or congregation of God, in the which we pray one for another, the prince for the subject, and the subject for the prince; the lord for the servant, the servant for the lord; the rich for the poor, and the poor for the rich, &c. and not every man for himself only; yea, and that both in spiritual and corporal things. Therefore in the beginning of this prayer, we say not, "My Father which art in heaven," but "Our Father which art in heaven." So likewise in this petition we say not, "give me this day my daily bread," but "give us this day our daily bread;" wishing not only from our heavenly Father good things every man to himself privately and only, but generally and universally to all men indifferently; declaring hereby, that as we be members all of one body, and children of one heavenly Father, so are we careful one for another, gentle and loving one to another, and pray generally one for another, wishing indifferently all good things to all men without exception, and without any respect had to private profit and singular commodity.

Rom. xii. Phil. ii. 1 Cor. xii. 2 Cor. xi.

And this is it that St Paul saith: "Be of like affection one toward another." Again: "If there be any consolation in Christ, if there be any comfort of love, if there be any fellowship of the Spirit, if there be any compassion and mercy, fulfil ye my joy, that ye be like-minded, having one love, being of one accord, and of one mind; that nothing be done through strife, or of vain glory; but in meekness of mind let every man esteem another better than himself. Look not ye every man on his own things, but every man on the things that are other men's. Let the same mind be in you that was also in Christ Jesu," &c. Also in another place: "Members (all Christians are members one of another's body) should indifferently care one for another. And if one member suffer, all suffer with him: if one member be had in honour, all members be glad also. Ye are the body of Christ, and members one of another." Of this christian and brotherly affection toward the congregation of Christ was blessed St Paul, as these his words plainly declare: "I am cumbered daily, and do care for all the congregations. Who is weak, and I am not weak? Who is offended, and I burn not?"

Lev. xix. 1 Cor. xiii.

☞ *Father.* It is then the duty of so many as profess Christ, one to be careful for another; one to pray and provide for another, according to this commandment of God: "Thou shalt love thy neighbour as thyself." *Son.* Yea, verily. For "love is gentle and courteous," and "seeketh not her own."

Father. They then which are led with no careful and friendly affection toward other, neither have any regard whether their neighbour sink or swim, but only are studious of themselves and of their own gain, say not this prayer aright. *Son.* They do nothing else than mock God, and their prayer is to themselves sin and damnation; so far is it off, that it please God, or obtain any thing at the hand of God, which requireth a loving and charitable heart in all them that pray.

Every man may lawfully pray to God for his own necessities.

Father. But tell me, my son, is it not lawful for a christian man to pray for himself only, and for his own necessities unto God? *Son.* Yes, verily, so that the affection of neighbourly love be not quenched in us. For whether we respect ghostly or bodily things, we find sufficient examples in the holy scripture, which plainly shew that divers men have lamented their private and singular state unto God, craving at his hand aid and succour against their own miseries, and have obtained their requests. Jacob and Salomon, as we heard, desired of God corporal sustenance. David, Manasses, Mary Magdalene, Peter, the thief, the publican, &c., craved of God remission of their sins; and every one of these severally obtained their requests at the hand of God. It is therefore lawful for every man to lament his private cause unto God, as his necessity shall require.

Gen. xxviii. Prov. xxx. Psal. li. 2 Chron. xxxiii. Luke vii. Matt. xxvi. Luke xxiii. Luke xviii.

This day.

Psal. xxxix. 2 Esdr. xvi. 1 Pet. ii. Heb. xiii. James iv. Job vii.

Father. Why do we use this word in our petition, "this day"? "Give us this day our daily bread." *Son.* Forasmuch as in this world we are "strangers and pilgrims," as our forefathers were before us, and "have here none abiding city, but seek one to come;" forasmuch also as nothing is more certain than death, and nothing more uncertain than the hour of death, to the which death our life at all hours, yea, at every moment of an hour is subject and ready to give place; our Saviour Christ,

willing to give us an occasion not to forget, but to have those things continually in our remembrance, teacheth us to ask of our heavenly Father food and sustenance of the body, not for many days, months, or years to come, being uncertain whether we shall live so long or not, but for that one present day wherein we live; that we may learn not to be careful after the manner of the worldlings, in making provision aforehand for this uncertain life, but to be content with the meat of the present time, so that, leaving to the providence of God, we care not for the morrow, seeing that "the morrow-day shall care for itself;" and again, "sufficient unto the day is the Matt. vi.
travail thereof." For what is our life, that we should make provision for it so many days, months, or years aforehand? Verily, this "our life," as St James saith, "is even James iv.
a vapour, that appeareth for a little time and then vanisheth away." "A man that Job xiv.
is born of a woman hath but a short time to live, and is full of misery. He cometh up and is cut down like a flower. He flieth as it were a shadow, and never continueth in one state." His "days are more swift than a runner: they pass away as Job ix.
the ships that be good under sail, and as the eagle that flieth to the prey."

Father. Few consider this thing; but many, flattering themselves with hope of long life, make provision aforehand for a great number of years to come. *Son.* These may justly be resembled to that rich man of whom we read in the gospel of Luke, which, having great abundance of goods, and not knowing where to bestow them, said, "This will I do: I will destroy my barns and build greater, and therein will Luke xii.
I gather all my goods that are grown unto me; and I will say unto my soul, Soul, thou hast much goods laid up in store for many years: take thine ease, eat, drink, and be merry. But God said unto him, Thou fool, this night will they fetch away thy soul again from thee. Then whose shall those things be which thou hast provided?"

Father. The like thing chanceth to many in these our days; but few regard it. *Son.* No marvel; for the world and the love of worldly things hath so blinded their eyes, that they cannot consider the things that belong unto their salvation. They forget themselves to be strangers and pilgrims on earth. They consider not how in Psal. xxxix. 2 Esdr. xvi.
this world they have none abiding city, and that therefore they ought to seek one to 1 Pet. ii. Heb. xiii.
come. They call not unto remembrance that they brought nothing into this world, 1 Tim. vi.
neither shall they carry any thing out of it; and that therefore having meat, drink, and clothe, they ought to be content; forasmuch as naked they came out of their Job i.
mother's womb, and naked they shall depart again.

That we ought not to be so careful in making provision aforehand for long time to come, not only the shortness and uncertainty of our life teacheth us, but also the manner of feeding the Israelites which God used in the wilderness. For when God sent the people of Israel meat from heaven, which in the book of Moses is called "manna," or heavenly bread, and in the book of Psalms the "bread of angels," and Exod. xvi. Psal. lxxviii.
in the book of Wisdom "angels' food and bread from heaven, very pleasant and of Wisd. xvi
good taste"; he commanded them that they should gather no more of it every day than should serve and suffice them for that one present day, and so every day gather new, except on the sixth day; then was it lawful to gather by the commandment of God so much as should serve them that day and the day following, which was the sabbath of the Lord and a day of rest. If any presumed, of a greedy, careful, Exod. xvi.
and covetous mind, to gather more than should suffice for that present day, it waxed full of worms and stank: whereby we may evidently learn, that as God will not forsake them that depend on his fatherly providence and put their trust in him, but daily give them all things necessary for their use, yea, and that abundantly; so likewise he utterly abhorreth, condemneth, and cursed the sorrowful carefulness of the flesh, which, mistrusting the providence and help of God, leaneth only unto her own wisdom, forecast, and provision. "Covetousness is the root of all evils, and it causeth 1 Tim. vi.
many to wander from the faith, and to snarl themselves with many sorrows"; and yet the covetous man, "heaping treasure upon treasure, cannot tell for whom he Psal. xxxix.
gathereth his treasure."

Father. Truth it is; but let us go forward. Wherefore do we use this word "our," saying, "Give us this day our daily bread", and not rather "my" daily bread? Our.

Son. For two causes. First, to declare our good will toward our neighbours, while we wish no less abundance of good things to them than to ourselves, and be led with no less careful affection toward them and their profit, than we are toward ourselves and our own commodity. For this mind ought to rule in all that profess God, have one heavenly Father, and be called by one name, I mean Christians, that they should be careful one for another, provide one for another, one seek another's commodity and profit, and in all points be the same to other that they are to themselves, according to this commandment of God: "Thou shalt love thy neighbour even as thyself." Again: "Whatsoever ye would that other men should do to you, do ye the same unto them." But of this thing we spake afore, when we entreated of this word "us."

Lev. xix.
Matt. vii.

No man ought to live idly.

Father. Thou sayest truth. Let me now hear the second cause. *Son.* The second cause why we say "our bread" is to put us in remembrance that we live not idly, nor of the labour of other men's hands, nor of the sweat of other men's brows, nor yet that we eat our bread and get our living unjustly, or by any unlawful means; but that we eat our own bread justly and truly, labouring every man some good thing according to his vocation and calling, avoiding idleness as an extreme pestilence, both of ourselves and of the commonweal wherein we dwell.

For God, shortly after the transgression of his holy commandment in paradise, gave this charge not only to Adam, but to all his posterity, that they by no means should live idly as unprofitable burdens of the earth, or as monsters only "born to consume the good fruits of the earth"[1]; but that they should exercise some good art, some profitable occupation, whereby they may be able to eat their own bread, and not to be any burden without cause to other. "In the sweat of thy face (saith God) shalt thou eat thy bread, till thou be turned again into the ground; for out of it wast thou taken, inasmuch as thou art dust, and into dust shalt thou be turned again." "As the bird is born to fly, so is man to labour," saith Job. The psalmograph also saith: "Thou shalt eat the labours of thine own hands, and so shall it go well with thee." Likewise saith the blessed apostle St Paul: "We beseech you, brethren, that ye increase more and more, and that ye study to be quiet, and to meddle with your own business, and to work with your own hands, as we commanded you; that ye may behave yourselves honestly toward them that be without, and that nothing be lacking unto you." Again: "We require you, brethren, by the name of our Lord Jesu Christ, that ye withdraw yourselves from every brother that behaveth himself inordinately, and not after the institution which he received of us. For ye yourselves know how ye ought to follow us: for we behaved not ourselves inordinately among you; neither took we bread of any man for nought; but wrought with labour and sweat night and day, because we would not be chargeable to any of you: not but that we had authority; but to make us an ensample unto you to follow us. For when we were with you, this we warned you of, that if any would not work, the same should not eat. For we have heard say that there are some which walk among you inordinately, working not at all, but being busy-bodies. Them that are such we command and exhort by our Lord Jesus Christ, that they work with quietness, and eat their own bread." And according to this commandment of God all the holy men both of the old and new testament behaved themselves, practising always some honest and godly exercise, that by this means they might both avoid idleness, and also eat their own bread, as we tofore heard in the declaration of the fourth commandment.

Gen. iii.
Job v.
Psal. cxxviii.
1 Thess. iv.
2 Thess. iii.

Dicers. Carders. Usurers.

Father. What thinkest thou then of such as live by unlawful gaming, as dicing, carding, &c., or by usury? *Son.* I count them nothing else than thieves, robbers, and spoilers of the commonweal; forasmuch as they eat not their own bread, but by fraud and subtilty, by craft and oppression, they unlawfully get from other wherewith they maintain themselves. And of such speaketh St Paul on this manner: "Let him that stole steal no more; but let him rather labour with his hands the thing which is good, that he may give unto him that needeth."

Eph. iv.

[[1] Fruges consumere nati, Hor. Epist. I. ii. 27.]

Father. What is thy judgment of those rich men, which either defraud the poor men of their almose, or keep back the wages from the labourers? *Son*. These also are thieves and murderers. Against the one sort of these ungodly rich men speaketh the wise man on this manner: "The bread of the needy is the life of the poor: he that defraudeth him of it is a manslayer." Against the other speaketh St James thus: "Go to now, ye rich men, weep and howl on your wretchedness that shall come upon you. Your riches is corrupt: your garments are moth-eaten: your gold and silver is cankered; and the rust of them shall be a witness unto you, and shall eat your flesh as it were fire. Ye have heaped treasure together, even wrath to yourselves in your last days. Behold, the hire of the labourers which have reaped down your fields (which hire is of you kept back by fraud) crieth; and the cries of them which have reaped are entered into the ears of the Lord of hosts." Against them both crieth out the word of God on this manner: "Wo to thee that spoilest or robbest; for thou also shalt be spoiled and robbed!" "Wo unto him that heapeth up other men's goods! How long will he load himself with thick clay? O how suddenly will they stand up that shall bite, and awake that shall tear thee in pieces! yea, thou shalt be their prey. Seeing thou hast spoiled many people, therefore shall the remnant of the people spoil thee, because of men's blood, and for the wrong done in the land, in the city, and to all them that dwell therein. Wo unto him that covetously gathereth evil-gotten goods into his house, that he may set his nest on high, to escape from the power of misfortune! Thou hast devised the shame of thine own house; for thou hast slain too much people, and hast wilfully offended; so that the very stones of the wall shall cry out of it, and the timber that lieth betwixt the joints of the building shall answer. Wo unto him that buildeth the town with blood, and maintaineth the city with unrighteousness!"

Ungodly rich men. Ecclus. xxxiv. James v. Isai. xxxiii. Hab. ii.

These ungodly and unmerciful rich men in praying this prayer do none other thing than mock God and abuse his holy name, seeing both their affects and deeds are contrary to their words. Of such it may right well be verified, that our Saviour Christ hath in the gospel, borrowing it out of the prophet: "This people draweth nigh unto me with their mouth, and honoureth me with their lips; howbeit their heart is far from me. In vain verily do they serve me." For they desire of God "our bread," that is to say, things necessary not only for themselves, but also for other; and they themselves, contrary to their prayer, go about with all diligence to deprive the poor of that which is their living, being indeed before God thieves, robbers, murderers, manslayers, and blood-soupers. Therefore whatsoever they pray in this behalf, it is nothing else than a mocking of God, and to themselves sin and everlasting damnation.

Isai. xxix. Matt. xv.

Father. Many, I grant, are so worldly-minded, that, seeking their own commodity, they little esteem the profit of other. God amend that is amiss! But, my dear son, tell me what is meant by this word "daily," which followeth in order. For thus pray we: "Give us this day our daily bread." *Son*. This word "daily" putteth us in remembrance of two things. The first is, which I partly touched afore in speaking of this word "this day," that we should not be led with too much carefulness for living in time to come, but be content with the present blessing of God, nothing doubting but that that liberal God, our heavenly Father, which feedeth us this day, is both able and also will feed us to-morrow and the next day and so forth so long as we live, as Christ himself witnesseth, saying: "Be not careful for your life, what ye shall eat or drink, nor yet for your body, what raiment ye shall put on. Is not the life more worth than meat, and the body more of value than raiment? Behold the fowls of the air; for they sow not, neither do they reap, nor carry into the barns; and yet your heavenly Father feedeth them. Are ye not much better than they? Which of you by taking careful thought can add one cubit unto his stature? And why care ye for raiment? Consider the lilies of the field, how they grow. They labour not, neither do they spin; and yet I say unto you, that even Salomon in all his royalty was not arrayed like unto one of these. Wherefore if God so clothe the grass of the field, which, though it stand to-day, is to-morrow cast into the furnace, shall he not much more do the same for you, O

Daily. Matt. vi.

ye of little faith? Therefore take no thought, saying, What shall we eat, or what shall we drink, or wherewith shall we be clothed? After all these things do the heathen seek. For your heavenly Father knoweth that ye have need of all these things. But rather seek ye first the kingdom of God and the righteousness thereof; and all these things shall be ministered unto you. Care not then for the morrow; for the morrow-day shall care for itself. Sufficient unto the day is the travail thereof."

1 Tim. vi. "Godliness," saith St Paul, "is great riches, if a man be content with that he hath. For we brought nothing into the world, neither may we carry any thing out. But when we have food and raiment, we must therewith be content. They that will be rich fall into temptation and snares of the devil, and into many foolish and noisome lusts, which drown men into perdition and destruction. For covetousness of money is the root of all evil; which while some lusted after, they erred from the faith, and tangled themselves with many sorrows. But thou, man of God, fly such things."

Gen. xxviii. Prov. xxx. 1 Kings xix. Jacob desired of God only food and raiment. Salomon prayed unto God for no more, but for things necessary for his living. When the prophet Elias fled from the face of wicked Jesabel which sought his life, and was hungry in the wilderness, God by his angel sent him not great plenty of dainty dishes or costly wines, but only bread and a cup of water; to declare that we should not hunt after superfluous things, but be content with things present; and if we have necessaries, and so much as will suffice nature, which is content with little, we should desire no more; as St Paul saith (Heb. xiii.): "Let your conversation be without covetousness; and be content with such things as ye have already. For he hath said (Josh. i.), I will not fail thee, neither forsake thee."

Father. But come off, tell me, my son, is it not lawful for a christian man in any condition (Note well.) to provide aforehand, and to lay up in store necessaries for themselves, and for such as belong unto them, seeing it is written (1 Tim. v.), "If any make not provision for his, he hath denied the faith, and is worse than an infidel"? *Son.* God forbid else! Godly, righteous, and necessary provision is not forbidden; but greedy carefulness and insatiable covetousness of worldly things, which riseth of mistrust toward the providence of God, and of unfaithfulness toward his promise, as though God would not satisfy his promise, but suffer us to perish for hunger if we did not provide for ourselves, is here reproved and condemned as a thing unworthy the children of God, which ought to look for all good things with a strong faith at the hands of their heavenly Father, nothing doubting but that he will abundantly perform whatsoever he hath mercifully promised.

2 Cor. xii. St Paul saith: "The children ought not to lay up for the fathers and mothers, but the fathers and mothers for the children." Here the holy apostle evidently declareth that it is the office and duty of parents (The duty of parents.) to provide in the fear of God, and to lay up in store all things necessary for their children, and to aforesee that they want nothing. Joseph (Gen. xli.) is greatly commended in the word of God, because in the time of plenty he provided and laid up in store abundance of corn against the time of dearth, which after certain years followed, by this means preserving the commonweal from famine. In the history of the gospel we read that, when Christ had fed certain thousands, and there remained part of the meat uneaten (Matt. xiv. Mark vi. Luke ix. John vi.), he said unto his disciples: "Gather up the broken meat which remaineth, that nothing be lost. And they gathered it together," &c. Moreover, upon the sixth day God commanded the Israelites that they should gather and lay up in store so much of manna as should suffice them to eat on the sabbath day. And it is not to be doubted (Acts vi.) but that the seven deacons, whom the apostles and the congregation appointed to minister unto the poor, and to foresee that they lack nothing, had in store both money and victuals, and made provision aforehand for such things as the necessity of the poor required.

After this manner may every householder, or whosoever hath care over other, make provision aforehand, and lay up in store things necessary for them and theirs. And this carefulness is not wicked nor unrighteous, but godly and righteous; forasmuch as it riseth not of false faith or mistrust toward God, but of an honest care toward those over whom God hath appointed him ruler and overseer. The wise man saith:

"Go to the emmet, thou sluggard, consider her ways, and learn to be wise. She [Prov. vi.] hath no guide, nor overseer, nor ruler; yet in the summer she provideth her meat, and gathereth her food together in the harvest." Again: "Whoso gathereth in summer [Prov. x.] is wise; but he that is sluggish in harvest bringeth himself to confusion."

Father. Thou hast both godly and learnedly answered to my question. Let me now hear the second cause why we use this word "daily" in our prayer: "Give us this day our daily bread." *Son.* In so praying we are admonished that our life is not maintained and preserved by our own wisdom, forecast, counsel, labour, travail, &c. Neither that the things which be needful for the feeding and conservation of this our mortal body are gotten only by our own provision; but that all these things come unto us by the appointment, counsel, and determination of God, through whose blessing all good things chance unto us, as the wise man saith: "The blessing of [Prov. x.] the Lord maketh men rich: as for careful travail, it doth nothing thereto:" and that therefore, as we have need of our daily food, so ought we daily to crave and ask it at the hand of our heavenly Father, "from whom cometh every good and perfect gift;" [James i.] which heavenly Father, when he openeth his hand, filleth all living creatures with [Psal. civ. Psal. cxlv.] plenteousness; but when he hideth his face, then are they troubled, and nothing availeth their labour; so truly is it said of our Saviour Christ: "No man's life [Luke xii.] standeth in the abundance of the things which he possesseth." For "except the Lord [Psal. cxxvii.] build the house, their labour is but lost that build it: except the Lord keep the city, the watchman waketh but in vain."

Father. Daily therefore must we ask of our heavenly Father our daily bread. *Son.* Yea, verily.

Father. And he will give it us. *Son.* Nothing is more certain than that, if we pray in faith and according to his will. "The Lord will not let the soul of the [Prov. x.] righteous suffer hunger." For the Son of God would never have taught us to call on God his Father for all good things, if he would not have granted us our requests. "If ye," saith he, "when ye are evil, can give your children good gifts, how much [Matt. vii.] more shall your Father which is in heaven give good things, if ye ask of him?" Likewise saith St Paul: "The Lord is at hand. Be careful for nothing; but in all [Phil. iv.] prayer and supplication let your petitions be manifest unto God with giving of thanks." And our heavenly Father himself saith: "I am the Lord thy God: open thy mouth [Psal. lxxxi.] wide, and I shall fill it."

Father. Are there any examples in the holy scripture which may ascertain us of this liberality and lent[1] good will of God toward us, when we call upon him? *Son.* Very many; which all at this present to recite, were almost an infinite labour. But I will rehearse certain, and omit the residue.

God at the beginning, willing to shew his fatherly care in making provision for [Gen. i.] man, before he created and made man, prepared all things necessary for man, and then making man, he brought man into paradise, a place already garnished with all most pleasant fruits, and stuffed full of all things necessary for the conservation of man, and there placed him, so to have continued, if he had not been disobedient to the voice of God. But after that God for his disobedience had cast him out of [Gen. iii.] paradise into this world, what lacked man here, that might in any point serve his necessary use? Of an earth flowing with the abundance of all good things made God man ruler and possessor, that we may learn God to be a careful God for man his creature, and that he will not suffer him to want any good thing.

What shall I speak of Adam's posterity, specially of the ancient patriarchs Abraham, [Gen. xii. xiv. xx. xxiv. xxxi. xxxix. xli.] Isaac, Jacob, &c.? How did God provide for them, yea, and that in strange countries! How richly did he bless them, and give them favour in the eyes of unknown men! How liberally dealt he with the Israelites, after that he had brought them out of [Exod. xvi. xvii. Num. xi. Psal. lxxviii. Wisd. xvi.] Egypt into the wilderness, where he fed them by the space of forty years with meat from heaven, and gave them most sweet and pleasant waters even out of the hard rock! How lovingly handled he their children, bringing them into a land that flowed with [Josh. xiii.] milk and honey! How miraculously did he increase the oil and meal of Helias' [1 Kings xvii.]

[[1] Lent: if correct, perhaps it is used in the sense of *offered*.]

B. & Dr. Matt. xv. Mark viii. John vi. John ii. hostess, the widow of Sarepta! How mercifully provided he for Daniel, being in the den of lions! How bounteously fed he certain thousands with few loaves and fishes! How friendly did he turn water into wine at a certain marriage, when wine wanted!

These and divers histories do abundantly declare, that the Lord our God is plentifully "rich to so many as call on him in truth;" so that, if we daily ask of him our daily bread, we may be sure daily to be heard and daily to be fed, so that we shall lack no good thing, as David saith: "Fear the Lord, all ye his saints; for they that fear him shall have no scarceness." Again: "The rich have wanted and suffered hunger; but they that seek after the Lord shall want no good thing."

Rom. x. Psal. xxxiv.

Father. God give us all grace to seek the Lord unfeignedly, that, our minds sequestered from the unrighteous and unnecessary cares of this world, we may wholly depend on the merciful providence of God, live according to our vocation, and do that which is righteous in the sight of God! *Son.* Amen.

Bread. What bread signifieth in the holy scripture.

Father. This petition beginneth to haste unto an end. Tell me therefore what thou understandest by this word "bread"? For thus pray we: "Give us this day our daily bread." *Son.* By "bread" I understand not only that which we commonly call bread, but also all other things necessary for the body and for this present life; as meat, drink, apparel, health, peace, tranquillity, strength to labour, wisdom to govern our things, a quiet household, a loving wife, obedient children, faithful servants, a flourishing commonweal, wholesomeness of air, seasonable weather, rain in due time, a fruitful year, abundance of all things, safeguard from enemies, long life, joyful days, house, land, cattle, good magistrates, righteous officers, painful teachers, diligent tutors, and whatsoever is necessary to the maintenance and conservation of our life. As bread, after the Hebrew phrase and manner of speaking, signifieth all these things aforesaid, so are we taught of our Saviour Christ in this petition to ask all these things of God alone, "from whom cometh every good and perfect gift;" which also is rich enough even unto the full to help so many as "in spirit and truth" call upon him; again, whose "eye is upon them that fear him, and upon them that put their trust in his mercy, to deliver their lives from death, and to feed them in the time of dearth."

James i. Rom. x. John iv. Psal. xxxiii.

Father. I have heard that this word "bread", in this petition, signifieth not only the nourishment of the body, but also the food of the soul; so that as man is made of two parts, that is to say, of body and soul, so likewise we ask here of God daily sustenance for them both. *Son.* By an allegory it may be used unto this end; but after the doctrine of our catechist the more simple, sincere, and right sense is, that "bread" in this place should only signify the food of the body, for the which we also here pray. Notwithstanding both our preacher and catechist have not so concealed this exposition also from us, but that they also have declared unto us the minds of certain writers in this behalf.

Christ the food of the soul. John vi.

Father. What have they said? *Son.* This have they said, that some expositors understand by this word "bread" in this place Christ Jesus, our Lord and alone Saviour, which undoubtedly is the food of our soul and the bread of everlasting life, as he testifieth of himself, saying: "I am the bread of life. He that cometh to me shall not hunger; and he that believeth on me shall never thirst." Again: "I am that living bread which came down from heaven. If any man eat of this bread, he shall live for ever." St Paul also calleth the Lord Christ a "spiritual meat", which the fathers of the old testament through faith did eat, while they, through the word of God's promise, and through the outward figures and ceremonies which painted forth Christ, believed, saw, and laid hand on Christ, believing him to be their alone Saviour, and therefore the alone food and meat also of their souls. "Our fathers," saith he, "were all under the cloud, and all passed through the sea, and were all baptized under Moses in the cloud and in the sea, and did all eat of one spiritual meat, and drink all one manner of spiritual drink," &c. For look, what corporal sustenance is to the hungry body, the same is Christ Jesus the Lord to the hungry soul. And as the eating of material bread comforteth and maketh both strong and merry the body that was hungry; so likewise doth the Lord Christ through his holy Spirit, and through true faith in him, in his passion and death, in his merits and deserts,

1 Cor. x. 1 Cor. x.

comfort and make joyful that soul which cometh unto him hungering and thirsting after righteousness, as it is written: "He hath filled the hungry with good things; but the rich he hath sent empty away." Again: "Blessed are they which hunger and thirst after righteousness; for they shall be filled." Luke i. Matt. v.

The word of God. Some understand by "bread" in this petition the word of God, that is to say, the law and the gospel; affirming that this word of God is as necessary for the consolation and conservation of the soul, as the material bread is for the comfort and preservation of the body, alleging this text of the holy scripture: "Man shall not live by bread alone, but by every word that cometh out of the mouth of God." Deut. viii. Matt. iv.

The supper of the Lord. Some say that "bread" in this place signifieth the mystical bread and cup of Christ's body and blood, which St Paul calleth "the Lord's supper." Thus this word "bread" is of divers diversely expounded. 1 Cor. xi.

I will strive with no man, so that his exposition dissent not from the analogy and true proportion of the christian faith and doctrine, that this rule of St Peter may be observed: "If any man speak, let him so speak that it be agreeable to the words of God": again, that this commandment of the heavenly Father may be obeyed, *ipsum audite:* "hear him," that is to say, my Son Christ and his doctrine, in whose mouth I have put my words, that ye may hear and hearken unto them, lest, if any presume to do the contrary, I take vengeance on him, plague, punish, and condemn him. For as it is godly and our bounden duty to desire of God meat, drink, and all other necessaries for the conservation and maintenance of this our frail and needy life; so likewise is it most godly and our most bounden duty to crave at the hand of our Lord God that he will give us his Son Christ, which is the true food of the soul, to feed upon by strong faith, being perfectly persuaded that he alone is our Redeemer, Mediator, Advocate, Intercessor, Peace-maker, Law-fulfiller, Saviour, Wisdom, Righteousness, Sanctification, &c. For except the heavenly Father give us this faith and knowledge, whereby we may spiritually feed upon his Son Christ, we shall still in spirit and mind remain and continue miserably famished, and never be fed with that heavenly meat, and so at the last die the death everlasting, as Christ himself testifieth, saying: "No man can come to me, except the Father which sent me draw him; and I will raise him up at the last day. It is written in the prophets, They shall all be taught of God. Every one therefore that hath heard, and hath learned of the Father, cometh unto me: not that any man hath seen the Father, save he which is of God, the same hath seen the Father. Verily, verily, I say unto you, He that putteth his trust in me hath everlasting life. I am that bread of life." "Verily, verily, I say unto you, Except ye eat the flesh of the Son of man, and drink his blood, ye have no life in you. Whoso eateth my flesh and drinketh my blood hath everlasting life; and I will raise him up at the last day, &c. But I say unto you, That no man can come unto me, except it be given unto him of my Father." 1 Pet. iv. Matt. xvii. Deut. xviii. John vi. Hos. xiii. 1 Tim. ii. 1 John ii. Eph. ii. Rom. x. Gal. iii. Matt. i. Acts iv. 1 Cor. i. John vi. Psal. xliv. Jer. xxxi. Psal. liv. [Isai. liv?]

Again, forasmuch as man doth not consist of body only, but also of soul, and God hath appointed his holy word to be the nourishment and food of the soul, and this food of his blessed word can we not come by, but only through the benefit of our heavenly Father; therefore is it meet and convenient that we crave at his hand this spiritual and heavenly nourishment of the soul, which is the word of God, that it may be truly preached unto us, and that we again may earnestly hear it and faithfully believe it, yea, and plentifully bring forth the fruits of the same in patience, unto the glory of his holy name. For little doth the sound of the outward letter profit, whether it be by reading or hearing, as we may see in Jews and Turks, except God inwardly teach us by his holy Spirit, as the apostle saith: "Neither he that planteth nor he that watereth is any thing, but God which giveth the increase;" otherwise our heart shall still continue hardened, stony, and uncircumcised, and we hearing shall not hear, neither understand. When Lydia, a seller of purple, heard Paul preach, the scripture saith that "the Lord opened her heart, that she attended unto the things which Paul spake." And God himself saith: "I will put my laws in their minds, and in their hearts I will write them; and I will be their God, and they shall be my people." Deut. viii. Matt. iv. Luke iv. Luke viii. 1 Cor. iii. Acts xvi. Heb. viii.

The supper of the Lord is a Now as touching the supper of the Lord, which is also a certain kind of spiritual

spiritual nourishment. 2 Cor. iii. Phil. ii. nourishment for the soul, if it be received in faith and with a good conscience toward God; and this of ourselves we cannot do, except God give us the gift (for "of ourselves we are not able to think a good thought"; "it is God that worketh in us both the will and the deed"); and, otherwise receiving it, we do none other thing than eat and drink our own damnation: it is not unfitting, but convenient and necessary, that we desire of God his Spirit and grace, that whensoever we come unto that heavenly banquet, we may worthily eat that mystical bread and drink of that mystical cup, and so be made worthy partakers of Christ's blessed body and precious blood, and of all the merits of his death and passion, whereby he hath purchased to all sinners that repent in faith remission of sins, the favour of God, quietness of conscience, the gift of the Holy Ghost, and finally everlasting life. They therefore, which teach that in this petition we, asking of our heavenly Father bread, desire of him the food of his Son Christ, the nourishment of his holy word, and the worthy participation of the holy mysteries of Christ's body and blood, which all three are the meat of the soul, teach nothing contrary to the word of God; so that this their exposition may well be received of the faithful, although it seem to some enforced, and not agreeable to the mind of Christ in that place.

1 Cor. xi. Eph. i. Col. i. ii.

Father. I cannot disallow any thing that thou hast spoken, but commend it as godly and good. And forasmuch as we may seem abundantly to have spoken of this petition, let me hear what followeth. *Son.* The next that followeth in order is the fifth petition, and soundeth on this manner:

The fifth petition.

"And forgive us our trespasses, as we forgive them that trespass against us."

Father. What crave we of our heavenly Father in this petition? *Son.* In the former petition we desired of our heavenly Father meat, drink, clothe, and whatsoever besides is necessary unto the conservation and maintenance of this our present life, without the which we cannot live, neither be able to do those things either unto God or unto our neighbour, which the law of God requireth of us. In this present petition we pray our heavenly Father to give us that which is the consolation and conservation of our souls, yea, of both our bodies and souls unto everlasting life.

What we ask of God in the fifth petition.

Father. What is that? *Son.* Forgiveness of our sins.

Father. Is that so great a comfort to the soul? *Son.* Yea, verily. For where remission and forgiveness of sins is, there is the favour of God, the gift of the Holy Ghost, quietness of conscience, rest of spirit, joy of heart, and assurance of everlasting life. They that obtain this great and singular benefit at the hand of God are called in the holy scripture blessed and happy. For so is it written by that prince-like prophet: "Blessed are they whose unrighteousnesses are forgiven, and whose sins are covered. Blessed is that man to whom the Lord will not impute sin."

Of the forgiveness of sin. Psal. xxxii. Rom. iv.

Father. May we be so bold to ask of our heavenly Father forgiveness of our sins? *Son.* David saith: "I will knowledge my sin unto thee, and mine unrighteousness have I not hid. I said, I will confess my sins unto the Lord; and so thou forgavest the wickedness of my sin. For this (that is to say, for the forgiveness of sins) shall every one that is godly make his prayer unto thee in a time when thou mayest be found." Likewise saith St John: "If we confess our sins, God is faithful and just to forgive us our sins, and to cleanse us from all unrighteousness." And in this petition are we taught of our Saviour Christ to ask of our heavenly Father forgiveness of our sins.

Psal. xxxii. 1 John i.

Father. This is great comfort to a penitent sinner. *Son.* Nothing can be greater. ☞ For if we have our sins forgiven, we have also an assurance both of God's favour and also of everlasting life. But many things offer themselves to be spoken of in this petition.

Father. What are they? *Son.* First of all, that so many of us as are clad with this mortal flesh, and breathe upon the earth, are without exception sinners and offenders.

Father. How provest thou that? *Son.* It is soon proved. For who knoweth not that we all are begotten, conceived, born, nourished, and live in sin? We are "all the children of wrath by nature," saith St Paul, Christ Jesus only excepted, that

All are sinners without exception. Psal. li. Eph. ii.

blessed Seed of the woman, which was "the Lamb of God," "innocent, faultless, and without spot"; which "never committed sin, and in whose mouth no guile or deceit was found": all other that have lived, do live, or shall live unto the end of the world, may justly be counted in the number of sinners. Gen. iii. Gal. iii. John i. Exod. [xii.]

Father. Let me hear some testimonies of the holy scripture concerning this matter.

Son. The psalmograph saith: "They are corrupt and become abominable in their doings: there is not one that doth good, no, not one. The Lord looked down from heaven upon the children of men, to see if there were any that would understand and seek after God. But they are all gone out of the way: they are all together become abominable: there is none that doth good, no, not one." The wise man saith: "There is not one just upon the earth, that doeth good and sinneth not." The prophet saith: "We have gone all astray, like sheep: every one hath turned his own way." Salomon saith: "Who is able to say, My heart is clean, and I am free from sin?" St Paul saith: "There is no difference: all have sinned, and want the glory of God." St James saith: "In many things we offend all." St John saith: "If we say we have no sin, we deceive ourselves, and the truth is not in us. But if we confess our sins, God is faithful and just to forgive us our sins, and to cleanse us from all unrighteousness. If we say we have no sin, there is no truth in us." Psal. xiv. Rom. iii. Eccles. vii. Isai. liii. Prov. xx. Rom. iii. James iii. 1 John i.

Father. These sentences of the holy scripture do manifestly declare that all men are sinners. Are there also any histories contained in the holy bible, which make this thing evident? *Son.* Very many, both in the old and new testament.

Father. Rehearse me part of them. *Son.* Adam and Eve, of whom we had our beginning, sinned against God in paradise, by eating the forbidden fruit; and in them have all we sinned, and worthily deserved everlasting damnation. Noah, that noble and ancient patriarch, was drunken, so that he lay sleeping, his privities uncovered. Lot was not only drunken, but he also lay with his own daughters, and committed the vile sin of incest. Abraham, which in the scripture is called the father of the faithful, denied his wife twice, and put her in danger of defiling. Divers of the patriarchs, besides other sins, conspired to put Joseph their brother unto death. Moses committed manslaughter. David was both an adulterer and a murderer. Salomon his son was an idolater. Matthew the evangelist was a toll-gatherer. Peter both denied and forsware Christ. The apostles of Christ were ambitious, and contended which among them should be greatest. They were "foolish in heart, and slow to believe." They forsook their Master Christ in his chief trouble. Mary Magdalene was a famous sinner. The thief that was saved, hanging on the cross with Christ, was a seditious person and a murderer. Paul persecuted the congregation of God, consented to the death of the blessed martyr St Stephen, blasphemed Christ and his glorious gospel, &c. Gen. iii. Rom. v. Gen. ix. Gen. xix. Rom. iv. Gen. xii. xx. Gen. xxxvii. Exod. ii. 2 Sam. xi. 1 Kings xi. Matt. ix. Matt. xxvi. Luke xxii. Luke xxiv. Matt. xxvi. Luke vii. Luke xxiii. Acts viii. ix. xxii. 1 Tim. i.

These histories, with divers other contained in the holy bible, declare manifestly that all the children of men are sinners without exception; so truly is it said of our Saviour Christ, "There is none good but God alone." Again: "When ye have done all the things that are commanded you, say, We are unprofitable servants." It is not without a cause said of Job: "Behold, God found no truth in his servants, and in his angels there was folly: how much more in them that dwell in houses of clay, and whose foundation is but dust!" &c. Again: "If I will justify myself, mine own mouth shall condemn me. If I will put forth myself for a perfect man, God shall prove me a wicked doer." "If I wash myself with snow-water, and make my hands never so clean at the well, yet shalt thou, O God, dip me in the mire, and mine own clothes shall defile me." Also in another place: "What is man, that he should be clean? What hath he that is born of a woman, whereby he might be righteous? Behold, he doth not trust his saints; yea, the very heavens are not clean in his sight. How much more then an abominable and vile man, which drinketh wickedness like water!" Item: "How can he be clean that is born of a woman? Behold, the moon shineth nothing in comparison to him, and the stars are unclean in his sight. How much more then man, that is but corruption; and the son of man, which is but a worm!" "All our righteousnesses," saith the prophet, "are as a cloth defiled[1]." Matt. xix. Luke xvii. Job iv. Job ix. Job xv. Job xxv. Isai. lxiv.

[[1] Two words are omitted.]

Rom. vii. St Paul likewise saith: "I know that in me, that is to say, in my flesh, there Rom. xi. dwelleth no good thing." Again: "God hath comprehended all under sin, that he might have mercy of all." The perfectest amongst the children of men may pray on Psal. cxliii. this manner: "Enter not into judgment with thy servant, O Lord; for none that Psal. cxxx. liveth shall be righteous in thy sight." Again: "If thou, O Lord, shouldest narrowly look upon our iniquities, O Lord, who were able to abide it? But there is mercy with thee in store; yea, with the Lord there is mercy, and plenteous redemption Mary the mother of Christ. with him." The glorious virgin Mary, although of all creatures most holy, most pure, most innocent (Christ Jesus her Son only excepted), in her song, considering certain imperfections to remain and abide in her, which she received of old Adam from her father and mother, confesseth and granteth God, and not herself, to be her Saviour. Luke i. "My soul," saith she, "magnifieth the Lord; and my spirit hath rejoiced in God my Saviour." She calleth God her Saviour, to declare that there was somewhat in her, from the which she must be saved by the mercy and goodness of God. Now if so pure, godly, and virtuous a virgin would not justify herself before God, but humbly confessed God to be her Saviour, and magnified him; who is so far estranged from the knowledge both of God and of himself, that he will not humble himself before the majesty of God, and grant himself to be (as he is indeed) a sinner, but rather Job xv. justify himself before God, in whose sight the very angels in heaven are not pure and clean?

The wicked opinion of the anabaptists. *Father.* Seeing we be all sinners, and grievously offend the Lord our God, insomuch that through our dissolution of life we deserve the loss of everlasting life, tell me if there be any hope of the remission of our sins at the hand of God. For there lack not at this present day, which affirm that a man sinning after baptism shall never be forgiven. *Son.* This is an old heresy lately renewed by the wicked anabaptists. If those sins were unpardonable which be commit after baptism, then had Christ taught us in vain daily to pray for the daily remission of our daily sins. But Christ teacheth nothing in vain; therefore are sins also committed after baptism forgiven. If God could not as well forgive sins after baptism as afore, so were he not almighty: then is this article of our faith false, "I believe in God the Father Almighty." But God is almighty; therefore is he able at all times to forgive and to remit sin. And that he doth at all times forgive sin to such as repent in faith and call unto him for mercy, innumerable places of the holy scripture, both in the old and new testament, do evidently shew and declare.

Jer. iii. iv. xviii. xxiii. xxv. Ezek. xviii. xxxiii. Hos. ii. Joel ii. Jonah iii. iv. Zech. i. How oftentimes doth God call sinners unto him, and will them to convert and turn unto him, and promise that he will receive them, take them again into his favour, and forgive them their sins! How oftentimes doth he protest by the prophets, that at whatsoever hour a sinner turneth unto him, repenteth him of his former life, and intendeth to become a new man, he shall be safe, his sins shall be forgiven and forgotten, yea, so forgiven and forgotten that they shall never more be remembered Psal. lxviii. Isai. lix. nor laid to his charge! God is called "the God of saving health;" and is his hand so shortened, and his power so abated, that he can only save and forgive sins before baptism, and not after baptism also? Is he not a "God of saving health" at all times and at all hours? The mercies of God are like and one at all seasons without exception. So often as a sinner with all his heart repenteth and turneth unto God, so often is he forgiven and pardoned of all his offences.

Joel ii. "Turn you unto the Lord your God," saith the prophet; "for he is gracious and merciful, long-suffering, and of great compassion, and ready to pardon wickedness." Matt. xviii. Luke xvii. Our Saviour Christ commanded us in the gospel to forgive our neighbours that have offended us so often as they come unto us and grant their offence, offend they never Matt. vi. Luke vi. so often; and promised again, that we shall find the like kindness at our heavenly Father's hand. How dare then the wicked anabaptists teach, that the sins committed after baptism are not pardonable? Who doubteth but that the apostles of Christ were baptized? And yet who knoweth not that after baptism they both offended Matt. xvi. and were forgiven? Did not Peter so offend his Master Christ, that he called him Matt. xxvi. Satan? Did not Peter afterward forsake his Master and run away from him, yea, Gal. ii. utterly deny and forswear him? Did not Peter after that also so halt in matters of the gospel, that Paul openly reproved him? Were not all those sins forgiven Peter? James and John, the sons of Zebedeus, were so ambitious that they would have been Matt. xx. in authority above all their fellow-apostles, insomuch that Christ reproved them sharply Mark x. for this their ambition. The very same apostles also were so replenished with anger against the Samaritans, because they would not receive their Master Christ, that they Luke ix. wished fire to come down from heaven upon them and utterly to consume them. The other apostles of Christ had also their infirmities and imperfections; and yet were they all forgiven, and are now most glorious saints in the kingdom of God. Sins therefore are forgiven after baptism.

The incestuous Corinthian was baptized, and in profession a Christian, yet fell he 1 Cor. v. afterward so grievously from the rule of christian doctrine, that by the apostle's commandment he was excommunicate; and yet notwithstanding afterward he was forgiven, 2 Cor. ii. when he repented, and was received into the fellowship of God's saints. Sinners then after baptism are forgiven.

To whom wrote St John those words? "If we say we have no sin, we deceive 1 John i. ourselves, and the truth is not in us. But if we confess our sins, he is faithful and just to forgive us our sins, and to cleanse us from all unrighteousness. If we say we have not sinned, we make him a liar, and his word is not in us. My little babes, 1 John ii. these things write I unto you, that ye sin not. But if any man sin, we have an advocate with the Father, Jesus Christ, that righteous one. He it is that obtaineth mercy for our sins, not for our sins only, but also for the sins of all the world." Wrote not St John these words to the Christians that were baptized? See we not then here, that though the Christians do sin after baptism, if they confess their sins, God for his faithfulness and righteousness' sake will forgive them; yea, and that so much the more, because Jesus Christ is our advocate, which for his dignity and worthiness, for his perfection and righteousness, easily obtaineth of God the Father for us not only remission and forgiveness of our sins, but also all other good things, both bodily and ghostly?

Our Saviour Christ calleth unto him all that are grieved and laden with the Matt. xi. burden of sin, and promiseth that he will refresh and ease them. He appointed no time, no age, before baptism, or after baptism. Only he biddeth them come, and whensoever they come, he promiseth to ease them of their burdens, be they never so grievous and many. Christ is that "Lamb of God which taketh away the sin of John i. the world." Note that he saith, "taketh away," and not have taken away, to declare, that the virtue of Christ's passion and death abideth still before God of such dignity and price, that it continually sufficeth at all times, and in all ages, to put away the sins of the world, whether they be committed before or after baptism. For as the apostle saith, "The blood of Christ speaketh better than the blood of Abel." Heb. xii.

Christ in the holy scripture is called our Mediator and Advocate, and is reported 1 Tim. ii. to live with God to this end, that he may at all times make intercession for us unto 1 John ii. Heb. vii. the Father. And is it to be thought that this his intercession serveth only for the sins committed before baptism, and not rather generally for all sins, whensoever they be done? The apostle writeth that Christ Jesus, that most high and everlasting Bishop, is "able at the full and even unto the uttermost to save them that come unto Heb. vii. God through him." But this could he not do, if he saved us only from the sins committed before baptism. Who seeth not now the fond and foolish, the vain and wicked doctrine of the anabaptists to be directly contrary to God's most holy and blessed word, while they teach that sins committed after baptism are unpardonable, when the truth of the holy scriptures plainly teacheth that, through faith in Christ, sins not only before, but also after baptism committed, are forgiven to the penitent sinner at all times?

Father. As the doctrine of the anabaptists is utterly uncomfortable, and leadeth unto desperation; so likewise is the doctrine of the holy scripture most comfortable to a penitent sinner, and openeth the way unto everlasting salvation. But tell me, my son, seeing we be all sinners, and notwithstanding there is hope of the forgiveness of our sins, who forgiveth these sins? *Son*. God our heavenly Father. For thus pray we: "And forgive us our trespasses."

God alone forgiveth sin. *Father*. But doth God alone, and none but God only, forgive sin? *Son*. Only God, and God alone, forgiveth sin.

Father. Let me hear it proved by the word of God. *Son*. God himself by the prophet Esay speaketh on this manner: "I am, I am he which putteth away thy sins, yea, and that for mine own sake, and I will remember them no more." God in this aforesaid sentence, because he would not have us to doubt, but to be most certainly persuaded that he alone forgiveth sin, doubleth, and saith twice: "I am, I am he which putteth away thy sins." By the same prophet he saith also: "O Israel, forget me not. As for thine offences, I have driven them away like the clouds, and thy sins as the mist: turn thee again unto me." By the prophet Jeremy God also saith: "From all misdeeds wherein they have offended against me I will cleanse them, and all their blasphemies which they have done against me, when they regarded me not, I will forgive them." By the prophet Osee God also saith: "Thy destruction, O Israel, cometh of thyself: only of me cometh thy salvation." The prophet Micheas speaketh unto God on this manner: "Where is there such a God as thou, that pardonest wickedness, and forgivest the offences of the remnant of thine heritage? He keepeth not his wrath for ever; and why? His delight is to have compassion: he shall turn again, and be merciful to us: he shall put down our wickednesses, and cast all our sins into the bottom of the sea."

Isai. xliii. Isai. xliv. Jer. xxxiii. Hos. xiii. Mic. vii.

Psal. ciii. The psalmograph also saith: "Praise the Lord, O my soul, and all that is within me, praise his holy name. Praise the Lord, O my soul, and forget not all his benefits; which forgiveth all thy sins, and healeth all thine infirmities; which saveth thy life from destruction, and crowneth thee with mercy and loving-kindness," &c. "The Lord is full of compassion and mercy, long-suffering and of great goodness. He will not alway be chiding, neither keepeth he his anger for ever. He hath not dealt with us after our sins, nor rewarded us according to our wickedness. For look how high the heaven is in comparison of the earth; so great is his mercy also toward them that fear him. Look how wide also the east is from the west; so far hath he set our sins from us. Yea, like as a father pitieth his own children, even so is the Lord merciful unto them that fear him. For he knoweth whereof we be made: he remembereth that we are but dust."

As I may at the last come unto the new testament, we read in the gospel that our Saviour Christ said to a certain man sick of the palsy: "Son, be of good cheer; thy sins are forgiven thee. And behold, certain of the scribes said within themselves, This man blasphemeth: who can forgive sins, but God alone?" The scribes judged Christ to be only man, and not God. Now, if he had been man only, and not God also, so had he spoken blasphemies; forasmuch as he challenged that to him which is alone due to God, that is to say, forgiveness of sins. But forasmuch as Christ is not only man, but also very God, therefore not Christ but the Jews blasphemed. Here is it evident, even by the testimony of Christ's enemies, that God alone forgiveth sin.

Matt. ix. Mark ii. Luke v. To forgive sin is proper to God alone.

Neither read we, in any part either of the old or new testament, that any other forgiveth sin but God alone. For "who can be made clean of him that is unclean?" who can make him clean which is conceived of unclean seed, but God alone? All the saints of the old and new law did always fly unto God for the remission of sins, as it is written: "For this," that is to say, for the remission of sins, "shall every saint pray unto thee in time convenient." He therefore doth nothing else, whatsoever he be, than blaspheme God, which taketh upon him to forgive sin; seeing that he only must forgive the sin against whom the sin is committed. Now is the sin committed against God, whose commandment is transgressed and broken: God therefore must forgive the sin, and none other.

Job xiv. Psal. xxxii.

The bishop of Rome. *Father*. The bishop of Rome hath taken upon him by his bulls and pardons to forgive sin. *Son*. Unjustly hath he this done. For not only the holy scriptures, but also the ancient fathers of Christ's church, affirm plainly that God alone forgiveth sin.

In serm. de Lapsis. "The Lord alone," saith St Cyprian, "may shew mercy, and forgive the sins which are committed against him: he alone can grant pardon, which bare our sins, which sorrowed for us, whom God delivered unto the death for us. Man cannot be greater than God, neither can he forgive and pardon the servants of that which through grievous sin is committed against the Lord[1]."

St Ambrose saith: "To forgive sin, and to give the Holy Ghost, is only in the power of God[2]." Again: "He alone forgiveth the sins, which alone died for our sins[3]." In 2 Cor. cap. xii.

St Austin saith: "No man taketh away the sins of the world, but Christ alone, which is the Lamb that taketh the sins of the world. He taketh away, both in forgiving those sins that are done, and in helping that they may be no more done, and in bringing unto life, when they can by no means be any more done[4]." Contra Julianum, lib. ii.

Cyril, the Greek doctor, saith: "Inwardly to quicken a sinner, it is the gift of him alone which saith by the prophet, 'I am he which putteth away thine iniquities'[5]." In Joan. cap. xi.

Chrysostom saith: "To deliver from the filthiness of sin, it is without doubt the mighty power of Christ." Again: "The bondage of sin is most grievous, from the which God alone is able to deliver. No man hath power to forgive sin but God[6]." In Matt. cap. viii. Hom. 53.

Theophylact saith: "It belongeth to God alone to forgive sin. Therefore he saith, 'Every one that doth sin is the servant of sin'; and ye therefore are servants, because ye are sinners. Moreover, forasmuch as it was like that they would say, Although we be bound to such thraldom, yet have we sacrifices, we have also priests, which shall purge and make us clean from sin; he saith, that they also are sinners. 'For all have sinned and want the glory of God.' And your priests, forasmuch as they are also servants, have no power to forgive other men their sins; which thing St Paul declareth manifestly, saying, 'The priest hath as much need to offer for himself as for the people, seeing that he also is compassed about with infirmities and diseases'[7]." Again he saith: "Christ could not otherwise have been known to be God, except he had forgiven the people their sins. For it belongeth to God to forgive sins[8]." In Joan. cap. viii. Rom. iii. Heb. v. In Lucam, cap i.

The bishop of Rome in taking upon him to forgive sin sheweth himself to be "that sinful man, that son of perdition, that adversary, which exalteth himself above all that is called God, or that is worshipped; so that he doth sit in the temple of God, boasting himself to be God." 2 Thess. ii.

[1 Solus Dominus misereri potest. Veniam peccatis, quæ in ipsum commissa sunt, solus potest ille largiri, qui peccata nostra portavit, qui pro nobis doluit, quem Deus tradidit pro peccatis nostris. Homo Deo esse non potest major: nec remittere aut donare indulgentia sua servus potest, quod in Dominum delicto graviore commissum est.—Cypr. Op. Oxon. 1682. De Lapsis. p. 129.]

[2 This passage will be given more fully afterwards. See the Index.]

[3 See below, page 174, note 1.]

[4 Ac per hoc, nemo tollit peccatum, quod nec lex, quamvis sancta et justa et bona, potuit auferre, nisi ille de quo dictum est, Ecce Agnus Dei, ecce qui tollit peccata mundi. Tollit autem et dimittendo quæ facta sunt, ubi et originale comprehenditur, et adjuvando ne fiant, et perducendo ad vitam ubi fieri omnino non possint.—August. Op. Par. 1679—1700. Op. Imperf. cont. Julian. Lib. II. lxxxiv. Tom. X. col. 986.]

[5 Vivificare autem interius peccatorem solius Dei munus est, qui per prophetam dicit: Ego sum qui deleo iniquitates vestras.—Cyril. Alex. Op. Lat. Par. 1604—5. In Joan. Evang. Lib. VII. cap. xxiii. Tom. I. p. 591. These are not the genuine words of Cyril. Only fragments of the 7th and 8th books of that father's commentary on St John have been discovered; and these, with the 5th and 6th books, were first printed after Becon's time. In their place four books had been previously inserted by Judocus Clichtoveus. See Cave's Script. Eccles. Hist. Lit. Oxon. 1740—3. Vol. I. pp. 391, 2.]

[6 There appears to be an error in the reference, as above given. The latter passage is found elsewhere: 'Αλλ' οὐ τοῦτο ἐσπούδαζε δεῖξαι, δούλους ἀνθρώπων γενομένους· ἀλλὰ τῆς ἁμαρτίας, ἥπέρ ἐστι καὶ χαλεπωτάτη δουλεία, ἧς Θεὸς μόνος ἀπαλλάξαι δύναται. τὸ γὰρ ἀφεῖναι ἁμαρτίας οὐδενὸς ἑτέρου ἐστί.—Chrysost. Op. Par. 1718—38. In Joan. Hom. liv. Tom. VIII. p. 316.]

[7 Τὸ γὰρ ἀφεῖναι ἁμαρτίας, Θεοῦ μόνου. διό φησι, πᾶς ὁ ποιῶν τὴν ἁμαρτίαν, δοῦλός ἐστι τῆς ἁμαρτίας, καὶ ὑμεῖς οὖν δοῦλοί ἐστε, καθὸ ἁμαρτωλοί. εἶτα ἐπεὶ εἰκὸς ἦν ἐκείνους εἰπεῖν, ὅτι εἰ καὶ τοιαύτῃ δουλείᾳ ὑποκείμεθα, ἀλλὰ θυσίας ἔχομεν, ἀλλ' ἱερεῖς, οἳ καθαρίσουσιν ἡμᾶς ἐκ τῶν ἁμαρτιῶν, φησὶν, ὅτι καὶ ἐκεῖνοι δοῦλοί εἰσι. πάντες γὰρ ἥμαρτον, καὶ ὑστεροῦνται τῆς δόξης τοῦ Θεοῦ. καὶ λοιπὸν δοῦλοι κἀκεῖνοι ὄντες οἱ ἱερεῖς ὑμῶν, οὐκ ἔχουσιν ἐξουσίαν ἀφιέναι ἄλλοις ἁμαρτίας. ὃ καὶ αὐτὸς ὁ Παῦλος σαφέστερόν φησιν, ὅτι ὀφείλει ὁ ἱερεὺς ὑπὲρ ἑαυτοῦ προσφέρειν, καθὰ καὶ ὑπὲρ τοῦ λαοῦ, ἐπεὶ καὶ αὐτὸς περίκειται ἀσθενείαις.—Theophyl. Op. Venet. 1754—63. In Joan. Comm. cap. viii. Tom. I. p. 623.]

[8 Οὐκ ἂν γὰρ ἄλλως ἐπεγνώσθη Θεὸς εἶναι ὁ Κύριος, εἰ μὴ ἀφῆκε τὰς ἁμαρτίας τῷ λαῷ· Θεοῦ γὰρ τὸ ἀφιέναι ἁμαρτίας.—Id. In Luc. Comm. cap. i. Tom. I. p. 284.]

Priests. *Father.* Priests also in their private absolutions challenged to themselves authority and power to forgive sin. *Son.* St Ambrose saith: "The word of God forgiveth the sins: the priest is the judge[1]", that is to say, declareth and sheweth that sins are forgiven to such as repent by the mighty power of God; and contrariwise, that their sins are retained and not forgiven, which do not repent. St Augustine also saith, that "the priests do not forgive sin, but the Holy Ghost through them, as it is said,
Matt. x. 'Ye are not they that speak, but the Holy Ghost which is in you'.[2]" Theophylact
In Joan. cap. viii. likewise said: "Your priests, forasmuch as they are servants, have no power to forgive sins." The priest executeth his commission, that is to say, he preacheth the word
☞ of God, and declareth that whatsoever sinner repenteth him of his sin, and believeth the promise of God made to all penitent sinners in Christ's blood, the same hath all his sins forgiven him: but whosoever will not receive the word, nor believe it, neither repent him of his former life: as the priest declareth to the other that is penitent and faithful remission of his sins, so likewise doth he pronounce to him that is impenitent and unfaithful, that his sins are not forgiven him, but that the
John iii. wrath and vengeance of God abideth upon him. God alone forgiveth the sin.

Father. Doth God forgive all the sins together, or but part of them, and reserve the residue still unforgiven? *Son.* God is no botcher. He either forgiveth all or none, according to this old saying:

☞

> Summa Dei pietas veniam non dimidiabit:
> Aut nihil, aut totum, te pœnitente dabit.

That is,

> God unto goodness so greatly is bent,
> That he forgiveth not unperfectly:
> For rather all or none, when thou repent,
> Shall thy sins be forgiven through God's mercy.

Father. Doth God also forgive the pain with the fault? *Son.* Why ask you that question?

God forgiveth both the fault and the pain together. *Father.* I have heard some say that God, forgiving the fault, reserveth the pain, and punisheth it afterward, sometime in this world, and sometime in the world to come. *Son.* That is a wicked doctrine and unworthy the majesty of God. To remit the sin and to retain the pain or punishment due for the sin is nothing else than to make God of a most merciful Father a merciless tyrant. The teachers of this doctrine
Proud antichrist. make God inferior to the pope in goodness and mercy. For the pope in his pardons maketh men clean, and granteth them remission of all their sins, *a pœna et culpa, toties quoties.* The pope for a little money delivereth men from all their sins, both from the fault, and from the pain due for the fault, yea, and that so often as they buy his pardons; and shall not God, that Father of mercy, and God of all consolation and comfort, for the most dear and precious blood of his Son Christ, shew the like favour to his creatures when they repent, believe, and amend?

Isai. xliii. God saith by the prophet that he will so forgive us our sins that he will "never remember them more": when then will he punish them? He saith also that he will
Mic. vii. "cast all our sins into the bottom of the sea": how shall then the remembrance of them so come before the presence of God's majesty, that he will punish them? The
Luke xxiii. thief that did hang on Christ's right hand was forgiven both the fault and the pain;

[1 It is probable that the author cited this passage and the one referred to before (see above, page 173, note 3.) from the Liber Sententiarum, where we read: Item Ambrosius: Verbum Dei dimittit peccata, sacerdos est judex. Sacerdos quidem officium suum exhibet, nullius potestatis jura exercet. Idem, Ille solus peccata dimittit, qui solus pro peccatis nostris mortuus est.—Pet. Lomb. Lib. Sentent. Lib. IV. Dist. xviii. The first passage here quoted appears to be the following: Remittuntur peccata per Dei verbum, cujus Levites interpres et quidem executor est.—Ambros. Op. Par. 1686—90. De Cain et Abel. Lib. II. cap. iv. 15. Tom. I. col. 212. The Benedictine editors remark on it in a note: Gratianus, De Pœn. Dist. i. c. Verbum Dei, et Magister Sent. in 4. Dist. 18. in hoc loco citando nec verba nec sensum Ambrosii exhibent. The second passage does not occur in the place indicated.]

[2 Cum vero interpositum est, Hoc cum dixisset, insufflavit, et ait illis, Accipite Spiritum sanctum, et deinde illatum, per eos vel remissionem vel retentionem fieri peccatorum; satis ostenditur, non ipsos id agere, sed per eos utique Spiritum sanctum, sicut alio loco dicit, Non enim vos estis qui loquimini, sed Spiritus sanctus qui in vobis est.—August. Op. Par. 1679—1700. Cont. Epist. Parmen. Lib. II. 24. Tom. IX. col. 41.]

and shall God deal less mercifully with us? The sheep that went astray, and the wasteful child, being forgiven and received into favour, were not afterward punished, as we read; except this be to punish, namely, to bring the wandering sheep home upon shoulders most tenderly, and to have compassion of the lost child, to kiss him, to clothe him with the best garment, to put a ring on his hand and shoes on his feet, to make a banquet for the joy of his return, to call the neighbours together, to be merry, to have minstrelsy and dancing, &c. Luke xv.

The psalmograph saith: "With the Lord there is mercy in store, yea, with him there is plenteous redemption." But what singular mercy is this, or what plenteous redemption and deliverance is this, to have the sin forgiven, and the pain reserved? Far be this from God! God, I grant, in this world many times sendeth to the godly and faithful people afflictions; but these are none other thing than exercises and trials of their faith and patience, that through them they may be the more provoked to call upon God, to mortify the old man, and to be renewed in the spirit of their mind. But as for the life to come, the faithful shall there taste no more sorrow, labour, pain, trouble, torment, weeping, mourning, lamenting, &c. but rather all joy, all comfort, all glory, all pleasure, all felicity, &c. as it is written: "They shall hunger no more, neither thirst, neither shall the sun light on them, neither any heat. For the Lamb which is in the midst of the seat shall feed them, and lead them unto fountains of living waters; and God shall wipe away all tears from their eyes." Again: "I heard a voice from heaven," saith St John, "saying unto me, Blessed are the dead that die in the Lord. For even out of hand, saith the Spirit, they rest from their labours, pains, or travails." The wise man saith, that "the souls of the righteous are in the hand of God, and the pain of death shall not touch them. In the sight of the unwise," saith he, "they appear to die, and their end is taken for very destruction; but they are in peace." Psal. cxxx. Afflictions. Rev. vii. Rev. xiv. Wisd. iii.

Father. It is to be thought that the inventors of this doctrine had no true judgment of God's mercy, and that they never thoroughly tasted of the sweetness of God's tender goodness. *Son*. It is to be thought that the authors of this doctrine were of the number of them "whose god their belly is." Phil. iii.

Father. Whom meanest thou? *Son*. Purgatory-rakers and soul-carriers, which for the maintenance of their idle bellies devised first of all this wicked doctrine, contrary to the word of God, unto the great discomfort, yea, almost desperation of the simple Christians, by this means procuring to themselves one kingdom more than God himself hath. Purgatory-rakers.

Father. What is that? *Son*. Purgatory. Purgatory.

Father. Away with purgatory and with all the purgatory-rakers, and tell thou me what moved God to be so beneficial and merciful to mankind that he is ready at all times to forgive us our sins, whensoever we turn unto him. *Son*. His alone free goodness and mere mercy is the only and alone cause of this his benefit, and of all other toward mankind, for his Son Christ Jesus' sake, and not our works, merits, and deserts, as the apostle saith: "Not by the works of righteousness which we wrought, but according to his mercy hath he saved us, by the fountain of the new birth and renewing of the Holy Ghost, which he shed on us abundantly through Jesus Christ our Saviour; that we justified by his grace should be made heirs according to hope of everlasting life." God himself saith by the prophet: "I am, I am he only which put away thy wickednesses, yea, and that for mine own sake, and will remember them no more. Put me now in remembrance (for we will reason together), and tell me if thou hast any thing wherewith thou mayest be justified." Again: "For my name's sake I will withdraw my wrath, and it shall be for mine honour's sake if I patiently bear thee, and root thee not out," &c. "Even for mine own sake I will do this." The psalmograph saith: "He saved me because he would have me." Again: "For nothing, O Lord, shalt thou save them." Why God is so merciful to us. Tit. iii. Isai. xliii. Isai. xlviii. Psal. xviii. Psal. lxvi.

Now that God saveth us only of his mere mercy for his Son Christ's sake, the scriptures shew plentifully in every place. God from the high heavens testified with an open voice that his Son Christ is the alone cause that he is so merciful and bounteous unto us. "This is my well-beloved Son," saith he, "for whose sake I am well pleased" with man. St Paul saith that Christ is "our peace," because he hath made an atone- Christ. Matt. iii. xvii. 2 Pet. i. Eph. ii.

ment between God and us; forasmuch as "it pleased the Father that in him should all fulness dwell, and by him to reconcile all thing to himself, and to set at peace by him through the blood of his cross both things in heaven and things in earth." Again:
Eph. i. "By Christ we have redemption through his blood, even the forgiveness of sins, according to the riches of grace. For by Christ hath he set up all things perfectly, both the things which are in heaven, and the things which are in earth: yea, by Christ are we made heirs of everlasting life according to the purpose of his own will."
Rom. v. Once again: "God setteth out his love toward us, seeing that, while we were yet sinners, Christ died for us. Much more then now, we that are justified by his blood shall be saved from wrath through him. For if when we were enemies we were reconciled to God by the death of his Son, much more, seeing we are reconciled, we shall be preserved by his life."

Father. What is the mean whereby we obtain of God, for Christ's sake, this
Faith. benefit of the remission and forgiveness of sins? *Son.* Faith only, whereby alone we
John iii. be justified and saved. For so saith our Saviour Christ: "God so loved the world that he gave his only-begotten Son, that whosoever believeth in him should not perish, but have everlasting life. For God sent not his Son into the world to condemn the world, but that the world through him might be saved." Again: "He that believeth on the Son hath everlasting life; but he that believeth not on the Son shall not see life, but the wrath of God abideth on him."

Rom. v. St Paul saith: "We being justified by faith are at peace with God, through our Lord Jesus Christ; by whom also it chanced unto us to be brought in through faith unto this grace, wherein we stand, and rejoice in the hope of the glory of God."
Eph. ii. Also in another place he saith: "By grace are ye made safe through faith, and that not of yourselves. It is the gift of God, and cometh not of works, lest any man
Acts x. should boast himself." And in the Acts of the Apostles we read these words: "To Christ give all the prophets witness, that through his name whosoever believeth in
Acts xiii. him shall receive remission of sins." Again: "Be it known unto you, that through this man (Christ) is preached unto you the forgiveness of sins, and that by him all that believe are justified from all things, from the which ye could not be justified by the law of Moses."

Thus see you, that God of his own mere mercy and free goodness, for Christ's sake, through faith, forgiveth us our sins without all our good works, merits, and deserts; again, that no one neither in heaven nor in earth forgiveth sin, but God alone.

Father. Thou hast fortressed and confirmed all these things so strongly with the authorities of the holy scriptures, my most dear son, that he can none otherwise be
Question. than a plain antichrist that shall deny this doctrine. But as we may proceed with this our petition, why do we rather say, "Forgive us," than forgive me, seeing one
Answer. alone many times saith this prayer privately by himself? *Son.* As in the former petition we desired of God all things necessary for this our present life, not only for ourselves, but also for other (christian charity binding us so to do); even in like manner in this present prayer we crave of God our heavenly Father not only for ourselves, but also for the whole company of the Christians, remission of sins, the favour of God, the gift of the Holy Ghost, quietness of conscience, and everlasting
Lev. xix. life, according to this commandment of God: "Thou shalt love thy neighbour as thyself."

Father. Are we then bound to seek the salvation of our christian brethren?
☞ *Son.* If we be bound to care for the health and prosperity of our neighbour's body, much more are we bound to be careful for the salvation of his soul; seeing the one is but earth, dust, and ashes, the other is made like unto the image of God. And
Ecclus. xvii. the wise man saith that "God hath given every man charge of his neighbour." And
Ezek. iii. is not this the saying of God by the prophet? "If I say unto thee concerning the ungodly man, that without doubt he must die, and thou givest him not warning, nor speakest unto him, that he may turn from his evil way, and so to live; then shall the same ungodly man die in his own unrighteousness, but his blood will I require at thy hand."

Every godly and charitable person ought to be no less careful for the health and

salvation of other than for his own, seeing we are "members one of another's body," Rom. xii.
and have one heavenly Father, one Saviour, one Redeemer, one Mediator, one Lord; Matt. xxiii. 1 Tim. ii.
and be baptized with one baptism, profess one gospel, eat and drink of one mystical Eph. iv. 1 Cor. x.
food, have one faith, one hope, and look for one inheritance of God's most glorious Rom. viii.
kingdom.

The holy scripture setteth forth unto us divers godly persons which were thus Examples of
affected toward other. To whom is it unknown that, when God was determined love toward other.
utterly to consume and to destroy the people of Israel for making and worshipping Exod. xxxii.
the golden calf, Moses sought all means possible to appease the wrath of God, and wished himself not to live, yea, to be wiped out of the book of life, except those people which had so greatly offended might also live and be saved with him? Are not
these his words? "O, this people have sinned a great sin, and have made them Moses.
gods of gold. And now, I pray thee, either forgive them their sin, or if thou wilt not, wipe me out of thy book which thou hast written." Here was fervent love even toward the enemies both of God and of himself. Here is a spectacle, wherein we may see that a Christian hath no less care for other, yea, though they be his enemies, than he hath for himself, and prayeth no less unto God for the remission of
their sins than for his own. In like manner, when the Lord God sent a great plague 2 Sam. xxiv. 1 Chron. xxi.
throughout all the coasts of Israel, insomuch that there died of it seventy thousand David.
men, David, being sore troubled in his heart for the death of such a multitude, and greatly wishing that the wrath of God might be appeased and the plague cease, fell straightways unto prayer, and said: "It is I that have sinned and done evil indeed; and what have these sheep done? Let thine hand, O Lord my God, be on me and on my father's house; but not on thy people, that they should be punished." David brenned with so fervent love toward his people, that he had rather die himself and all that were his kinsfolk, than his subjects should so miserably be slain with plague.

What shall I speak of the holy apostle St Paul, which did not only continually Paul.
pray unto God for the forgiveness of the sins of the Israelites, but he also even from Rom. ix.
the very heart wished to be accursed and utterly banished from Christ, so that they might be saved?

Of these histories and such like we may easily learn, how one of us ought to be affected toward another both in bodily and ghostly things; and that we ought to pray one for another, that not only abundance of all worldly things may be given us, but also that we may have remission of sins, the favour of God, quietness of con-
science, and in fine, everlasting life, as St James saith: "Pray one for another, that James v.
ye may be saved." In consideration whereof our Saviour Christ taught us to say, "Forgive us our trespasses," and not, Forgive me my trespasses.

Father. Is it not therefore lawful for a man privately to lament his miserable Question.
state unto God, and to desire a redress of the same? *Son.* It is most lawful, as we Answer.
have divers examples in the holy scripture. David prayed for the remission of his
own sins only, when he said: "Have mercy on me, O Lord, according to thy great Psal. li.
mercy; and according to the multitude of thy tender compassions, put away my wickedness. O, wash me yet more, O Lord, from mine iniquity, and cleanse me
from my sin." So likewise read we of king Manasses and of divers other. 2 Chron. xxxiii.

In the new testament we have manifest examples likewise. Mary Magdalene secretly in her heart lamented her most miserable state, her most wicked and sinful life, yea, and that not without tears brasting out from the sorrow of the heart; and
she heard at the mouth of Christ these most comfortable words: "Thy sins are for- Luke vii.
given thee. Thy faith hath saved thee. Go in peace." The lost son, coming home again to his father, prayed on this manner for a redress of his most miserable state:
"Father, I have sinned against heaven and before thee, and am no more worthy to Luke xv.
be called thy son: make me as one of thy hired servants." What shall I here recite the thief, which did hang on the cross with Christ? Prayed not he for himself on
this wise, speaking to the Lord Christ? "O Lord, remember me when thou comest Luke xxiii.
into thy kingdom." Christ answered him: "This day shalt thou be with me in paradise." I pass over the apostles of our Saviour and many other godly persons, which prayed unto God for their own private causes, and were most graciously heard.

Psal. l. "Call on me," saith God, "in the time of thy trouble, and I will deliver thee, and thou shalt honour me."

Debts. *Father.* What be these trespasses, or rather debts, which we desire to be forgiven of our heavenly Father in this petition? *Son.* God in his holy law hath given us ten commandments, which we are bound to observe and keep. Now, forasmuch as none of us all fulfilleth them all, no, not one of them all with such perfection as the law
Rom. vii. requireth, being indeed spiritual, and we carnal, as our Saviour Christ said unto the
John vii. Jews, "Did not Moses give you a law, and yet none of you keepeth the law?" therefore are we all debtors unto God; so that in this petition we desire him to forgive us these debts, yea, the pain and punishment also, which is due to us for not paying our debts, and not to lay unto our charge those our sins which we daily commit in thought, word, and deed; but rather most graciously both to forgive and to forget them.

We all are debtors to God. *Father.* We therefore are all debtors unto God? *Son.* Every one of us is that indebted servant, of whom we read in the gospel, which, when his master called him
Matt. xviii. unto accompts, was found to owe him ten thousand talents: neither was he able to pay so great a debt, though both wife, children, household, and all that ever he had should be sold. After this sort are we all. We owe unto God a most certain and sure debt, even the fulfilling of his ten commandments. But this debt are we not able to pay; therefore owe we also unto our Lord and Master ten thousand talents, neither are we able to pay them; no, not the most richest, the most holiest, the most per-
Justiciaries. fectest of us all: albeit there want not, which so pride themselves by the reason of their good works and merits, that they shame not to boast that they have good works enough, not only to save themselves, but other also. And these works they call
O proud Lucifers! *Opera supererogationis:* they might more justly call them *Opera superarrogantiæ.* For too much and too great pride is this, vile, corruptible, and stinking flesh so to lift up his horns in the presence of God's majesty, that by his own righteousnesses and good
Isai. lxiv. works, which before God are more unpure, unclean, and filthy, than a cloth polluted[1],
2 Thess. ii. he will take upon him both to justify himself and other also. Is not this to "sit in the temple of God, and to boast himself as God"? Is not this to say with that
Isai. xiv. most arrogant and proud king of Babylon, "I will climb up into heaven, and exalt my throne above besides the stars of God; I will climb up above the clouds, and will be like the Highest of all"? But, O thou vile, stinking, and unrighteous flesh, thou shalt be brought down to the deep of hell.

1 Pet. v. God is an enemy to the proud; but to the humble and lowly-spirited he is a
Luke i. most dear and loving friend. "He putteth down the mighty from their seat; but he exalteth the humble and meek." The holiest and perfectest company of God's saints
Psal. cvi. that ever lived in this world may justly say, as it is written: "We have sinned
Bar. i. with our forefathers, we have dealt unrighteously, and committed wickedness." "There-
Psal. cxxx. fore to the Lord our God be righteousness; but to us confusion and shame." "If thou, O Lord, shouldest narrowly look upon our wickednesses, O Lord, who were able to abide it?" saith the psalmograph. Every one of us, when we be most holy and per-
Psal. cxliii. fect, may right well pray on this manner: "Enter not into judgment with thy servant,
1 John i. O Lord; for no man that liveth is righteous in thy sight." "If we say we have no sin," saith St John, "we deceive ourselves, and the truth is not in us." For, as St
James iii. James saith: "All sort of us offend in many things." Who seeth not now, that we all be debtors unto God, and have grievously offended him?

Father. What is then to be done, that we may be delivered from this debt? *Son.* As our Saviour Christ, which is the wisdom of the Father, teacheth us here.

How we may obtain forgiveness of our sins. *Father.* What is that? *Son.* Humbly to knowledge ourselves God's debtors, transgressors and breakers of God's most holy law, and therefore worthy, if we should be handled according to our merits and deserts, not only of temporal punishment, but also of everlasting damnation. Again, forasmuch as we of ourselves, with all our good works, merits, and righteousnesses, are not able to pay so great a debt, to desire
Matt. iii. xvii. our heavenly Father, for his Son Christ Jesus' sake, (in whom he is well pleased

[[1] Two words are omitted.]

with man, and for whose sake he gladly giveth and granteth whatsoever is asked in his name, as it is written, "Whatsoever ye shall ask the Father in my name, he shall give it you; ask, and ye shall have,") to remit and forgive us whatsoever we owe him, and to deliver us out of that servitude and bondage whereunto we are most miserably cast through sin; that we, being set at liberty from that debt, may frankly and freely and with a good courage "serve him in holiness and righteousness all the days of our life." John xvi. Luke i.

Father. If we thus humble ourselves before God, and with all submission of heart crave the forgiveness of our debts, will God be merciful unto us, and forgive us our debts, and set us free from all our sins, and from all the pains due unto us for those sins? *Son.* Yea, most certainly. For he delighteth not in the death of a sinner, but is at all times most ready to pardon and forgive whatsoever is done against him, if with humble hearts we fly unto the throne of his majesty, and desire mercy and favour; as we have an example in that servant which ought his lord and master ten thousand talents. So soon as that servant humbled himself before his master, and desired favour at his hand, his master forgave him all the debt so clearly as though he had never ought him one farthing, as it appeareth by the words of the master: "I forgave thee all that debt, when thou desiredst me." So likewise will our heavenly Father do with us, if we confess the debt, and desire forgiveness of the same. Ezek. xviii. Matt. xviii.

Father. Well said, my son. God grant us of his grace! And blessed be the Lord our God for his clemency and goodness toward us his miserable and sinful creatures. But what is meant by this that followeth in our petition? "As we forgive them that trespass against us," or, "as we forgive our debtors." *Son.* Whosoever will obtain at the hand of God grace, favour, and remission of his sins, he must also forgive them that have offended him. And verily of this nature are the sons of God, which are regenerate and born anew by the Holy Ghost, "not of mortal seed, but of immortal, by the word of God, which liveth and lasteth for ever," that they wish in all things to resemble the manners of their heavenly Father, and to be the same unto other that God is unto them, according to this commandment of our Saviour Christ: "Be ye merciful, as your heavenly Father is merciful." St Paul also saith: "Be ye the followers of God, and walk in love, as Christ hath loved us." Of forgiving our debtors. 1 Pet. i. Eph. v.

Of this affection and mind were divers godly persons which are mentioned in the holy scripture. King David unjustly was persecuted of Saul, and his life very narrowly sought; yet the Spirit of God was so strong in David that he did not only not seek to be revenged, but he also forgave his enemy Saul, and never either did or procured any evil against him; insomuch that when he might have slain him, he would not once touch him; yea, when Abisai said to David, "God hath delivered thine enemy into thine hand this day; now therefore let me smite him once with my spear to the earth, and I will not smite him the second time," David answered, "Destroy him not. For who can lay his hand on the Lord's anointed, and be guiltless?" Examples of forgiving other. David. 1 Sam. xxiv. 1 Sam. xxvi.

St Stephen in like manner did so little malign his enemies, that he did not only freely forgive them, but he also prayed unto God for them, saying: "Lord, lay not this sin unto their charge." Stephen. Acts vii.

But wherefore do I cease to rehearse him, and his unoutspeakable love, which is the mirror of all goodness, and of whom we are named, I mean Christ? This precious pearl of perfect patience shewed so great charity even unto his most cruel and bloody enemies, that he himself did not only most frankly and freely forgive them, but he also, hanging on the cross, and even in the midst of his torments, prayed unto his heavenly Father, that he would forgive them. Christ. Luke xxiii.

After this manner ought all Christians to be affected, not to revenge, but ready to forgive; not to curse, but to bless; not to render evil for evil, but to overcome evil with goodness, leaving all vengeance to God, which saith: "Vengeance is mine: I will reward." Whosoever is otherwise minded, let him look for no favour at the hand of God. Rom. xii. Deut. xxxii.

Father. Let me hear it proved by the word of God, that I ought to forgive them that have offended me, and that doing otherwise I shall find no favour at the hand of

God, but rather displeasure, wrath, vengeance, plagues, and everlasting damnation. *Son.* Jesus the son of Sirach writeth on this manner: "He that seeketh vengeance shall find vengeance at the Lord's hand, which shall surely keep him his sins. Forgive thy neighbour the hurt that he hath done to thee; and so shall thy sins be forgiven thee also, when thou prayest. A man that beareth hatred against another, how dare he desire forgiveness of God? He that sheweth no mercy to a man which is like himself, how dare he[1] ask forgiveness of his sins? If he that is but flesh beareth hatred, and keep it, who will entreat for his sins? Remember the end, and let enmity pass, which seeketh death and destruction; and abide thou in the commandments. Remember the commandments; so shalt thou not be rigorous over thy neighbour. Think upon the covenant of the Highest, and forgive thy neighbour's ignorance."

Ecclus. xxviii.

Our Saviour Christ saith also: "Forgive, and it shall be forgiven to you. If ye forgive other men their trespasses, the heavenly Father shall forgive you. But if ye will not forgive men their trespasses, no more shall your Father forgive you your trespasses." Again: "When ye stand and pray, forgive, if ye have ought against any man, that your Father also which is in heaven may forgive you your trespasses."

Luke vi. Matt. vi.

And unto what other end did Christ put forth the similitude and parable of the servant that ought his lord ten thousand talents, which were all forgiven him, and notwithstanding afterward the whole debt required of him again, because he so cruelly handled his fellow-servant, so that he was cast into prison till he should pay all that was due unto his lord; but only to shew, that as we handle our neighbours and such as are debtors unto us, even so will God handle us again? This evidently appeareth by the conclusion of the parable, where Christ speaketh on this wise: "So likewise shall my heavenly Father do also unto you, if ye from your hearts forgive not every one his brother their trespasses." Hereto belongeth the saying of St Paul: "As the chosen of God, holy and beloved, put on tender mercy, kindness, humbleness of mind, meekness, long-suffering, forbearing one another, and forgiving one another, if any man have a quarrel against another; as Christ forgave you, even so do ye."

Matt. xviii. Col. iii.

How we ought to behave ourselves toward them that have offended us, the examples of our Saviour Christ, and of the most blessed martyr St Stephen, do plainly declare.

Luke xxiii. Acts vii.

Father. What if any man presume to pray unto God, or to do any other good work, not being in love and charity, but bearing malice against his christian brother, so that he by no means will forgive him, but seek all means possible to be revenged; is that his prayer, or any other good work that he doth, acceptable to God? *Son.* So acceptable as though he offered swine's blood unto him, or committed manslaughter. What pleasure God hath in the prayers, gifts, and sacrifices of the wicked, the history of Cain sheweth openly. Therefore our Saviour Christ giveth this commandment to all his people, saying: "If thou offerest thy gift at the altar, and there rememberest that thy brother hath ought against thee; leave there thine offering before the altar, and go thy way first, and be reconciled to thy brother, and then come, and offer thy gift." Whosoever saith either ☞ the Lord's prayer or any other for the remission of his sins, not being in love and charity, doth nothing else than ask vengeance of himself, and hasteth the wrath of God to fall upon him. For such as we are to them that have offended us, even such shall we find God to us again. If the merciful shall receive mercy, then shall the unmerciful receive no mercy, as St James saith: "The judgment shall be without mercy to him that hath shewed no mercy."

Isai. lxvi. Gen. iv. Matt. v. Matt. v. James ii.

The parable of the indebted servant, whereof we spake before, declareth openly what they may look for at the hand of God, which are unmerciful to their neighbours. His lord and master had forgiven that servant all the debt. "And he, straightways going out, found one of his fellows, which ought him an hundred pence, and laid hands on him, and took him by the throat, saying, Pay that thou owest. And his fellow fell down, and besought him, saying, Have patience with me, and I will pay thee all. And he would not, but went and cast him into prison, till he should pay the debt."

Matt. xviii.

[1 The folio reads *ye*.]

"His lord, understanding this, called that malicious and cruel servant unto him, and said, O thou ungracious servant, I forgave thee all that debt, when thou desiredst me. Shouldest not thou also have had compassion on thy fellow, even as I had pity on thee? And his lord was wroth, and delivered him to the jailors, till he should pay all that was due unto him."

St John saith: "Whosoever hateth his brother is a manslayer. And ye know that no manslayer hath everlasting life abiding in him." Here may we see that, if we desire to have forgiveness at the hand of God, it is necessarily required of us, that we also forgive them that have offended us: otherwise our desire is in vain, yea, so much in vain, that we shall not only not obtain remission of our sins, but we shall also after this life have our "portion in that lake that burneth with fire and brimstone." Our Saviour Christ saith of that evil servant which ungently and churlishly entreateth his fellow servants: "The same servant's lord shall come in a day when he looketh not for him, and in an hour that he is not ware of, and shall hew him in pieces, and give him his portion with the hypocrites: there shall be weeping and gnashing of teeth."

1 John iii.

Rev. xxi.

Matt. xxiv.

Father. Seeing it is so necessarily required unto the forgiveness of our sins at the hand of God, that we also must forgive them that offend us, or else we shall never be forgiven; it followeth, as methinketh, that the cause why God forgiveth us our sins is because we have first forgiven them that have sinned against us. *Son*. Nothing less, my dear father. For so should it follow, that the remission of our sins should not come of the free favour and mere mercy of God, but rather of our deserts. But that were contrary to the wholesome doctrine of the holy scripture, which teacheth that we are "saved by grace through faith, and that it is the gift of God, and cometh not of works, lest any man should boast himself." "Not by the deeds of righteousness, which we wrought," saith St Paul, "but according to his mercy hath he saved us, by the fountain of the new birth, and renewing of the Holy Ghost which he shed on us abundantly through Jesus Christ our Saviour, that we, being justified by his grace, should be made heirs, according to the hope of everlasting life." God himself saith by the prophet: "Thy destruction, O Israel, cometh of thyself; but thy salvation cometh of me only." Our Saviour Christ saith: "Ye have not chosen me, but I have chosen you." And St John saith: "Herein is love, not that we loved God, but that he loved us, and sent his Son to be the satisfaction for our sins."

The forgiving of our neighbour is not the cause why God forgiveth us.

Eph. ii.

Tit. iii.

Hos. xiii.

1 John iv.

Likewise saith St Paul: "God setteth out his hand toward us, seeing that while we were yet sinners, Christ died for us: much more then now, we that are justified by his blood shall be saved from wrath through him. For if, when we were enemies, we were reconciled to God by the death of his Son, much more, seeing we are reconciled, we shall be preserved by his life."

Rom. v.

All these and many such like sentences of the holy scripture should be found false and untrue, yea, the order of God's doctrine should not only be perverted, but also subverted, if that your supposition might be found true. For God forgiveth not us our sins because we forgive them that have offended us, so that, through our benefit first shewed unto our neighbour, we should provoke him to be beneficial again to us, and forgive us our debts and trespasses; but he forgiveth us frankly and freely, without respect either of our former or latter good works, of his own free favour, gracious goodness, and mere mercy, for his Son Christ Jesus' sake, in whom, or for whose sake, he is well pleased with man; as he saith by the prophet: "I am, yea I am he which putteth away thy sins, yea, and that for mine own sake, and I will remember thy faults no more. Tell me, if thou have any thing, wherewith thou mayest be made righteous, &c."

Note.

James i.

Isai. xliii.

In consideration whereof David prayeth for the forgiveness of his sins on this manner: "For thy name's sake, O Lord, forgive me my sin, for it is much." Again: "Have mercy on me, O God, according to thy great mercy; and according to the multitude of thy tender compassions do away my wickedness." David desireth not forgiveness of his sins at the hand of God, because he had first of all forgiven such as had offended him; but for God's own name's sake, and for his great mercy and tender compassions' sake, he craveth to be forgiven. For what thing can we work, although

Psal. xxv.

Psal. li.

never so good and godly, that may worthily deserve the least of all God's benefits, when "all our righteousnesses are like to a polluted and defiled cloth"? As Jacob said to God in his prayer: "O Lord, I am not worthy of the least of all the mercies and truth, which thou hast shewed unto thy servant." The prophet Daniel prayeth also on this manner: "O my God, incline thine ear, and hearken: at the least for thine own sake open thine eyes. Behold, how we be desolate; yea, and the city also, which is called after thy name; for we do not cast our prayers before thee in our own righteousness, but only in thy great mercies. O Lord, hear. O Lord, forgive. O Lord, consider: tarry not overlong, but for thine own sake do it."

Isai. lxiv. Gen. xxxii. Dan. ix.

That God doth not forgive us our sins, because we have first forgiven our offenders, but rather that we ought to forgive such as have offended us, because God hath first of all forgiven us our offences, the order of the parable of the indebted servant shew most evidently. For in that we read, that when the servant was not able with all that he had to discharge the debt, and his lord and master, moved with mercy, pity, and compassion toward him, frankly and freely forgave it him, is plainly declared, that God first of all forgiveth our sins, debts, and trespasses. Again, whereas we read that the lord was angry with his servant, whom he had forgiven so great a debt, because he so cruelly handled his fellow-servant for so little and slender a debt, and shewed him no favour at all, and therefore most worthily for his unmercifulness he was cast into the prison at his lord's commandment; it is plainly set forth unto us, that it is our duty, which have received so great a benefit of God, even remission of all our sins, to be beneficial again to our fellow-servants, and according to our Lord's commandment to forgive them, as he hath already forgiven us; yea, and that so much the more, because the debt which we forgive our debtors is but little and almost of no valor, whereas the debt which we owe unto our Lord and Master is great and infinite. "O thou ungracious servant," said the lord, "I forgave thee all that debt, when thou desiredst me; shouldest not thou also have had compassion on thy fellow, even as I had pity on thee?"

Matt. xviii.

Every man ought to be that to his neighbour that God is to him.

The obedience and love, which we owe unto God and unto his holy law, ought to move us to be the same to our neighbour that God is to us. Hath God dealt mercifully with us, and forgiven us our debts? Even so ought we lovingly to deal with our debtors, and not to be cruel against them; yea, and that so much the more, because God, our most merciful, gentle, loving, bounteous, and liberal Father, hath in his holy word commanded us so to do. When "Simon Peter came unto Christ, and said unto him, Lord, how oft shall I forgive my brother, if he sin against me? till seven times? Jesus said unto him, I say not unto thee, until seven times, but seventy times seven times." Again he saith: "If thy brother trespass against thee, rebuke him; and if he repent, forgive him. And though he sin against thee seven times in a day, and seven times in a day turn again to thee, saying, It repenteth me; thou shalt forgive him."

Matt. xviii. Luke xvii.

Why we ought to forgive our neighbour.

Thus see we, that we are bound by the commandment of God to forgive them that sin against us, not to this end, that through our forgiving we should deserve at the hand of God to be forgiven, (for that were nothing else than to disannul the free grace of God, and to make the merits of Christ vain and of none effect;) but to declare our obedient love and loving obedience toward the blessed will and holy commandment of our most merciful Father, which hath commanded us to forgive such as trespass against us, even as he of his great goodness hath already pardoned and forgiven us all our sins: again, that it should be a sure certificate and an undoubted testimony unto our consciences, that our sins are forgiven us of our heavenly Father, that we are at peace with him, that he loveth us, and in fine, that he hath chosen us to be his sons and heirs, yea, and fellow-heirs of his glorious kingdom with his Son Christ Jesus.

Rom. viii.

A short rehearsal of the things entreated of in this petition.

Father. I perceive now by thy words, that remission of our sins cometh unto us from God freely, and without all merits and works on our behalf, for Christ Jesus' sake through faith; and that our forgiving of such as offend us is not the cause why God forgiveth us our sins, but his own mere mercy, gracious goodness, and free favour: again, that we, which have already received forgiveness of all our debts at the hand of our heavenly Father, should forgive likewise our offenders their debts and trespasses for two causes: the first is, because God hath commanded us so to do, whose commandment to disobey is more than double wickedness: the second is, that we in forgiving our neighbour should be perfectly assured and certified in our conscience, without all doubting, that our heavenly Father hath also forgiven us all our debts, sins, and wickednesses; which will always be the same to us that we are to our neighbour; so that, if we gladly and freely forgive them that trespass against us, it is a most manifest argument and undoubted assurance, that we are forgiven of God; but contrariwise, if we be unmerciful, cruel, and vengeance-thirsty against our neighbour, so that we will not forgive him, but seek to be revenged, and to reward evil for evil, by this means neglecting and nothing regarding the blessed will of God, which hath commanded us to forgive our offenders; then it is a most sure sign, that our sins are not forgiven, but that the hot wrath and fierce vengeance of God abideth still upon us, and that we remain in a most damnable state; seeing that the property of such as be in the favour of God, and have obtained remission of their sins, is to be the very same to their neighbour that they feel in their conscience God is unto them. *Son.* You say truth. For, as St John saith: "Every one that loveth is born of God, and knoweth God[1]. But he that loveth not knoweth not God; for God is love. If any man say, I love God, and hate his brother, he is a liar. For he that loveth not his brother, whom he hath seen, how can he love God, whom he hath not seen? And this commandment have we of him, that he which loveth God should also love his brother." 1 John iv.

And verily, if we did consider the great goodness of God in forgiving us our debts, being indeed great, many, yea, and innumerable, we should easily be moved to forgive those small and slender debts which other owe unto us. For look how much ten thousand talents are in number and weight being compared with an hundred pence; even so far do our debts, which we owe unto God, surmount and pass the debts which our neighbour owe unto us. And who will not gladly forgive an hundred pence, to be discharged of the debt of ten thousand talents? Note.

Father. Well said, my son. We have sufficiently conferred of this petition. Let me now hear what followeth. *Son.* The next petition is the sixth in number, and this is it:

"And lead us not into temptation." The sixth petition.

Father. Wherefore hath our Saviour Christ taught us thus to pray? *Son.* You remember that in the last petition we heard that we are all sinners and debtors unto the Lord our God, and owe his divine majesty so much, that we neither are, nor never shall be, with all our good deeds and merits, able to satisfy him; insomuch that of necessity we are enforced to fly unto God's mercy for the release of this our so great debt, which he freely forgiveth us for his dear Son Christ Jesus' sake through faith.

Now, lest we should lose so great a benefit, I mean remission of our sins, and fall again into the old captivity and misery, wherein we were most miserably detained of Satan before we received and tasted so great kindness at the hand of God, and so become worse than we were afore; (for "of whom a man is overcome," saith St Peter, "unto the same he is brought in bondage: For if they, after they have escaped from the filthiness of the world through the knowledge of the Lord and Saviour Jesu Christ, are yet tangled again therein, and yet overcome, then is the latter end worse with them than the beginning: For it had been better for them not to have known the way of righteousness, than, after they have known it, to turn from the holy commandment that was given unto them: But the same is happened to them that is used to be spoken by the true proverb: The dog is turned to his own vomit again; and the sow that was washed is turned again to her wallowing in the mire;") we are taught in this petition to pray unto our heavenly Father, that he will most graciously assist and aid us with the power of his holy Spirit against all our enemies, and preserve us in that most blessed state, wherein he hath set us by forgiving us our debts, that from henceforth we 2 Pet. ii. Prov. xxvi.

[[1] The folio reads *not*.]

may live with free consciences, glad minds, and cheerful hearts, and serve the Lord our God "in holiness and righteousness all the days of our life." Luke i.

Father. What enemies are these, of whom thou speakest? *Son*. Do you ask what enemies? As though a christian man in this world wanted enemies, which continually assault him, and seek his destruction. The life of a Christian in this world is called of holy Job a "knighthood" or "warfare." (Job vii. [marg.]) And not without a cause. For as they that are worldly warriors have enemies, that come against them, fight with them, and seek all means possible to vanquish them, and to make them their captives and slaves, or else to make havoc of them, and utterly to destroy them; so likewise is it with the true Christians in this world.

Satan. Think you that Satan, whom the holy scripture termeth the "prince" and "god of this world," (John xiv. 2 Cor. iv.) is a slender enemy, and of small force? Never was there wolf that so greedily sought the destruction of any beast, as Satan seeketh our damnation. Are not these the words of St Peter? (1 Pet. v.) "Be ye sober, and watch. For your adversary the devil goeth about like a roaring lion, seeking whom he may devour." Did not Satan assault our first parents Adam and Heva in paradise, (Gen. iii. Rom. v.) yea, and also overcome them, unto the great dismaying not only of themselves, but also of all their posterity? Provoked not he David (1 Chron. xxi.) to number the people of Israel, whereby he displeased God? What mischief hath there been done since the beginning of the world, whereof he hath not been the author? How many hath he moved unto idolatry, unto perjury, unto disobedience, unto murder, unto whoredom, unto theft, unto false witness-bearing, unto the transgression and breaking of all the commandments of God, unto desperation, and by this means have brought them also unto everlasting damnation? And what marvel, seeing he feared nothing at all to enter battle with our most puissant and mighty Captain, the Lord Christ? (Matt. iv. Luke iv.) If he made this enterprise against our most valiant, victorious, and triumphant Emperor, which is the Lord of glory, and "mighty in battle;" (Psal. xxiv.) shall we think that he will be afraid of us, and leave us unassaulted? So little, yea, rather so none are our strengths, if we be left unto ourselves, that in comparison of him, I mean Satan, we are most weak, most feeble, most miserable, most easy to be overcome.

Of the flesh. Another of our enemies is the flesh, which is an adversary so much the more to be feared, because she is domestical and one of household, yea, nourished and brought up even in our own breast. This enemy ceaseth neither night nor day to allure us into her nets, yea, and that not tyrant-like, but friend-like, while she with her honey-like, yet hell-like and poisonful pleasures go about to infect us, and to allure us from godliness to beastliness, from virtue to sin, as St Paul saith: (Gal. v.) "The flesh lusteth against the Spirit, and the Spirit against the flesh: these are always contrary one to the other. But they that belong unto Christ have crucified the flesh with the affects and lusts thereof." This grievous enemy, the flesh, hath deceived many good and godly men in times past, as Sampson, David, Salomon, &c., and still doth at this present; so that she reigneth now not as a vice, but as a lady, queen, and empress.

Of the world. The third enemy is the world, which both with his pleasures and riches doth so entangle men in this our age, that he seemeth to reign alone like a god. All follow the world, even from the highest to the lowest, from the king to the subject, and from the bishop to the deacon. They are all mammonists and worldlings. They all embrace the frail and transitory things of this world, and utterly neglect the constant and immortal treasures of the world to come. They "all seek those things that appertain unto themselves, but not that belong unto Jesus Christ." (Phil. ii.) They are "lovers rather of pleasure than of God." (2 Tim. iii.) They follow covetousness, and by this means they have "made shipwreck of all godliness," whom notwithstanding the Holy Ghost calleth us away from the love of the world and worldly things. St John saith: (1 John ii.) "Love not the world, nor those things that are in the world. If any man love the world, the love of the Father is not in him. For all that is in the world, as the concupiscence of the flesh, the lusts of the eyes, and the pride of the life, is not of the Father, but of the world. And the world passeth away, and the lust thereof. But he that doth the will of God abideth for ever." Likewise saith St Paul: (1 Cor. vii.) "The time is short: it remaineth that they which have wives be as though they had none; and that they which weep be as though they wept not; and that they also which rejoice be as though they rejoiced not; and that they which buy be as though they possess not; and that they which use this world be as though they used it not. For the fashion of this world passeth away."

I pass over all the other infernal army, malicious devils, wicked spirits, damned souls, cruel tyrants, bloody antichrists, &c., which daily do nothing else than seek our destruction. These, these go about to bring us unto villany[1]. These with their wicked and deceitful temptations labour unto the uttermost of all their powers to bring us again into the pestiferous puddle of sin, and to defile ourselves with those most ungodly abominations, from the which God of his great mercy hath purged and cleansed us by the blood of his Son through faith.

Now, forasmuch as we have so many and so grievous enemies, which, seeking our destruction, daily tempt and move us unto wickedness, that by this means we may fall from the favour of God into the dreadful pit of everlasting damnation, and lose that most gracious benefit which was for Christ's sake given us of our heavenly Father, I mean remission of sins; our Saviour Christ teacheth us in this petition to flee unto our heavenly Father with fervent and faithful prayer, and humbly to crave of him aid and help against these our most grievous enemies, that we be not overcome with their temptations, and so become their miserable captives and slaves; but rather that we, overcoming them through strong faith in the power of our Captain Christ, may become valiant, victorious, and triumphant conquerors, unto the glory and praise of God's most blessed name.

Father. Doth not God also tempt us? *Son*. I grant; but yet far otherwise than Satan tempteth us.

Father. What difference is there? *Son*. Very much and great. Satan tempteth unto this end, that he may accuse, condemn, and destroy; and therefore he is called "the tempter," "the calumniator or quarrel-picker," and "the accuser of the brethren." He tempted Adam and Heva unto disobedience, Cain unto manslaughter, the people of the old world unto oppression and lewd living, the Sodomites unto unnatural lusts, the Israelites unto idolatry, David unto whoredom and murder, Salomon unto the worshipping of false gods, Manasses unto the shedding of innocent blood, Judas to the betraying of his Master Christ, Simon Magus unto counterfeit religion, Ananias and Saphira unto dissimulation, with innumerable thousands more; so that the temptation of Satan tendeth only unto evil, and the end thereof, if it be obeyed and followed, is everlasting damnation. But it is far otherwise with that temptation wherewith God assaileth us. For it tendeth not unto evil, but unto good; not unto desperation, but unto consolation; not unto damnation, but unto salvation; as St James saith: "Let no man say when he is tempted (unto evil), that he is tempted of God. For as God cannot be tempted with evil, so neither he himself tempteth any man (unto evil). But every man is tempted, when he is drawn away and enticed of his own concupiscence. Then when lust hath conceived, she bringeth forth sin; and sin, when it is finished, bringeth forth death."

The temptations of God and Satan, how they differ. Rev. xii. Gen. iii. Gen. iv. Gen. vi. Gen. xix. Exod. xxxii. 2 Sam. xi. 1 Kings xi. 2 Kings xxi. Matt. xxvi. Acts viii. Acts v. James i.

And forasmuch as this temptation of God bringeth rather good than evil, light than darkness, life than death, it may not unjustly be called a probation or trial of the faithful, seeing that by it the wheat is known from the tares, the sons of the kingdom from the children of that evil, the true Christians from the dissembling hypocrites, the vessels of mercy from the vessels of wrath. This temptation bringeth to the faithful rather gladness than sadness. Therefore saith St James: "Brethren, count it for an exceeding joy when ye fall into divers temptations, knowing this, that the trial of your faith bringeth forth patience; but let patience have her perfect work, that ye may be perfect and sound, lacking nothing." Again: "Blessed is he that endureth temptation; for when he is tried he shall receive the crown of life, which the Lord hath promised to them that love him."

Matt. xiii. James i.

Of this temptation speaketh David also on this manner: "Examine me, O Lord, and prove me: try out my reins and my heart. For thy loving-kindness is before mine eyes; and I will walk in thy truth." Again: "Try me, O God, and seek the ground of mine heart: prove me, and examine my thoughts." Once again: "With fire hast thou tried me; and yet was there none unrighteousness found in me." St Peter also saith: "Dearly beloved, marvel not that ye are proved by fire, which thing is to try you, as though some

Psal. xxvi. Psal. cxxxix. 1 Pet. iv.

[[1] Villany: servitude.]

strange thing happened unto you; but rejoice, inasmuch as ye be partakers of Christ's passions; that when his glory appeareth, ye may be merry and glad."

☞ Whosoever determineth to profess Christ aright, and to be a true Christian, he must determine with himself to suffer temptation, and not to look to live in wealth, joy, and pleasure, as the wise man saith: "My son, if thou wilt come into the service of God, stand fast in righteousness, and fear, and prepare thy soul unto temptation." For in this exercise hath God from the beginning trained up his people, whom he hath loved, that he might prove and try their faith, love, hope, constancy, obedience, &c., as the virtuous matron Judith saith: "Call to remembrance how our fathers in times past were tempted, that they might be proved, if they worshipped their God aright. They ought to remember how our father Abraham, being tempted and tried through many tribulations, was found a lover and friend of God. So was Isaac, so was Jacob, so was Moses; and all they that pleased God, being tried through many troubles, were found stedfast in faith. Again, they that received not their temptations with the fear of God, but put themselves forth with unpatience and murmuring against God, perished of the destroyer, and were slain of serpents." The author of the book of Wisdom saith: "God proveth them, and findeth them meet for himself; yea, as the gold in the furnace doth he try them, and receiveth them as a burnt-offering, and when the time cometh they shall be looked upon."

Ecclus. ii. Judith viii. [Vulgate.] Wisd. iii.

Job saith of himself thus: "He tried me as the gold in the furnace." The psalmograph likewise, speaking of himself and of all the other faithful, saith: "Thou, O God, hast proved us: thou also hast tried us, like as silver is tried. Thou broughtest us into the snare, and laid trouble upon our loins. Thou sufferedst men to ride over our heads: we went through fire and water, and thou broughtest us out into a wealthy place." In the history of Toby we read that God suffered the temptation of blindness to fall upon him, that he should be an example of patience to his posterity. Again, in that same book it is written: "Remember how our fathers were tempted, that they might be proved." For, as the wise man saith: "What knoweth he that is not tempted?" "Vexation giveth understanding," saith the prophet.

Job xxiii. Psal. lxvi. Tob. ii. [Vulgate.] Ecclus. xxxiv. Isai. xxviii.

Thus see we how God in all ages, even from the beginning, hath sent temptations to all good and godly men, not to destroy them, as Satan goeth about with his temptations, but to prove, try, and examine them, whether they be constant in faith, love, hope, patience, obedience, &c., that by this means they might be found the more perfect and glorious, as St Peter saith: "Ye are kept by the power of God through faith unto salvation, which is prepared all ready to be shewed in the last time; in the which ye rejoice, though now for a season, if need require, ye are in heaviness through manifold temptations, that the trial of the faith, being much more precious than gold that perisheth, though it be tried with fire, might be found unto praise, glory, and honour at the appearing of Jesus Christ."

1 Pet. i.

God tempteth us two manner of ways.

Father. How doth God tempt us? *Son*. Sometime by prosperity, and sometime by adversity.

The temptation of prosperity.

Father. How by prosperity? *Son*. God many times blessed his people with the abundance both of corporal and worldly things, to tempt, prove, and try them, whether they will continue still in that humbleness of mind that becometh true Christians, knowledge the liberality of God, live worthy his kindness, use these gifts unto the glory of his name, and at all times be thankful for his benefits.

Father. Should we not thus do? *Son*. We should do it indeed; but who doth it? So corrupt is our nature, so wicked is our disposition, so bent unto evil are all our senses even from our very cradles, that, as experience teacheth, the most part of the world greatly abuseth the benefit of God, insomuch that they forget God, so far is it off that they walk worthy of his great kindness and liberality; yea, to say the truth, the ☞ temptation of prosperity hath plucked more from God, and allured them unto wickedness, than the temptation of adversity; as both the writings of God and men, besides daily experience, abundantly declare.

Gen. viii.

Are not these the words of Moses concerning the people of Israel? "He that should have been upright, when he waxed fat, spurned with his heel. Thou art well fed: thou art grown thick: thou art even laden with fatness. And he forsook God his Maker, and regarded not the God of his salvation. They provoked him to anger with

Deut. xxxii.

strange gods; even with abominations provoked they him. They offered unto devils, and not to God; even to gods whom they knew not; to new gods, that came newly up, whom their fathers feared not." The prophet Jeremy also saith, in the person of God: "I have fed them to the full; and they have fallen to whoring, and played the ruffians in harlots' houses. In the desire of uncleanly lust, they are become like the stoned horse: every man neigheth at his neighbour's wife. Should I not correct this, saith the Lord? Should I not be avenged of every people that is like unto this?" Again: "They are waxen fat and wealthy, and they have utterly set at nought my words." Jer. v.

The histories of the holy bible shew plainly, that, so long as the people of Israel were assaulted with the temptation of adversity, and were kept low, and nurtured under the cross, they called upon God, and walked in the obedience of his holy word; but when they had peace and quietness, health and wealth, riches and abundance of all things, then ran they on whoring after strange gods, fell to banqueting, to dancing, to adultery, to idleness, to oppression of the poor, and most wickedly lived without the fear of God, in all carnal security and fleshly quietness; so great an adversary unto true godliness is the too much abundanee of worldly things, except it be thoroughly tempered with the love and fear of God: which thing we read also of other. What was the destruction of the Sodomites, of the Gomorrians, and of other that dwelt about them, but wealth and plenty of all things, as the prophet saith? Saul at the beginning, when he was made king, was good, and pleased God; but after that he grew to wealth, he waxed proud, and lost the Spirit of God. David, so long as he was under the cross, walked in the ways of the Lord; but when he came once unto prosperity, and to live wealthily and idly and without care, he straightways forgat God, and became both an adulterer and a manslayer. What brought Salomon unto such dissolution of life, that he had seven hundred queens and three hundred concubines, as I may speak nothing of his idolatry and worshipping of false gods? Was it not too much prosperity and abundance of all things? Hieroboam, before he was exalted to be a king, was well commended and favoured; but, coming once unto the crown of Israel, he straightways wrought abomination in the sight of the Lord. Prosperity more dangerous than adversity. Ezek. xvi. 1 Sam. xiii. 2 Sam. xi. 1 Kings xi. 1 Kings xii.

I let pass Roboam, Amasias, Ozias, Manasses, Nabuchodonozor, Aman, Ptolomeus, Antiochus, Herod, the rich glutton, with divers other mentioned in the holy scripture, which through the too much wealth and abundance of things fell into intolerable pride, and afterward into many great absurdities and inconveniences.

It is truly said of St Paul: "They that have a desire to be rich fall into temptation and snares (of the devil), and into many foolish and noisome lusts, which drown men into perdition and destruction. For the desire of money is the root of all evil; which while some lusted after, they erred from the faith, and tangled themselves with many sorrows. But thou, man of God, fly such things. Follow righteousness, godliness, faith, love, patience, meekness." "Godliness is great riches, if a man be content with that he hath. For we brought nothing into the world, neither may we carry any thing out. But when we have food and raiment, we must therewith be content." King Salomon therefore, wishing to be overcome neither with the temptation of prosperity or adversity, prayed to God on this manner: "Two things have I required of thee, O Lord, that thou wilt not deny me before I die. Remove from me vanity and lies: give me neither poverty nor riches: only grant me a necessary living: lest if I be too full, I deny thee, and say, Who is the Lord? and lest I, being constrained through poverty, fall unto stealing, and take the name of my God in vain." 1 Tim. vi. Prov. xxx.

Father. What and how great a let wealth is unto true godliness, the history of the young man of whom we read in the gospel, maketh plain and evident. For when Christ said unto him, "Go thy way, sell all that thou hast, and give to the poor, and thou shalt have treasure in heaven, and come, follow me, and take up my cross upon thy shoulders; he was discomforted," saith the evangelist, "because of that saying, and went away mourning; for he had great possessions." *Son.* It is not, therefore, without cause that Christ compared riches to thorns, and saith that they smother up the word of God; and that "no man can serve both God and Matt. xix. Mark x. Luke xviii. Matt. xiii. Matt. vi.

mammon; but either he shall hate the one, and love the other; or else lean to the one, and despise the other."

How worldly things are to be used. *Father*. But forasmuch as health of body, riches, public peace, tranquillity, victory over the enemies, wealth, abundance of all things, and such like gifts appertaining unto this mortal life, are the benefits of God, and his good blessings; tell me how we ought to use them, that we do not abuse them, nor be overcome of them. *Son*. Among all the bodily and worldly gifts wherewith God blesseth many, I will take

Of riches. riches for an example. Is any man endued with riches? Let him consider, that God hath not only enriched him with the goods of this world, that he should be the lord and owner of them, but also to tempt, try, and prove him, whether he will use them rightly and truly, according to his holy will, or rather suffer himself to be overcome with the inordinate and unlawful desire and detaining of them. Now if this man do so use, yea, rather abuse, his goods, that he either spend them away wastefully, prodigally, and riotously, in banqueting, in superfluous building, in costly clothing, in

Luke xv. vain playing, in wicked company-keeping, (as we read in the gospel of the wasteful son,) or else in oppressing his poor and needy neighbour; then is he overcome of his riches, and become a miserable money-slave, and shall be damned. But contrariwise, if he use his substance and riches aright, and unto that end for the which God gave them unto him, that is to say, unto the nourishing of God's ministers, which preach and set forth his holy word, and unto the relief and succour of the poor and needy Christians, which are of the household of faith, and unto the doing of such good, godly, and charitable acts, and in fine, knowledgeth God to be the giver of them, and therefore is thankful to him for them, and in all points study to dispose them according to his blessed pleasure and holy commandment; then is he not overcome of his riches, neither are they to him any temptation unto evil, but rather an allurement unto all goodness and godliness. And so likewise of all the other gifts and benefits wherewith God blesseth men in this world.

Experience in our time. But forasmuch as many are not only tempted, but also overcome with the temptation of prosperity, as we have also at this present day (alas, for pity!) too many for an example, yea, and that among them which in the time of the cross were so zealous for the Lord's cause, that their very life was not dear unto them, much less the pelf of this world, and now contrariwise are so drowned with the pleasures and riches of this world, that they may justly seem to be very worldlings and epicures; therefore, lest they should so go forth and perish, God assayeth them another way, and assaileth them with another kind of temptation.

The temptation of adversity. *Father*. What is that? *Son*. The temptation of adversity, as sickness of body, poverty, infamy, war, pestilence, famine, persecution, imprisonment, torments, &c.

Father. Why doth God send these evils unto us? *Son*. Not [to] destroy us, but either to admonish us of our sin, or to try our faith, love, obedience, patience, &c., or for certain other causes, whereof we will speak hereafter. And with this kind of temptation God doth ofter try and prove his people than with the temptation of prosperity. For as our grand Captain Christ in this world was tempted with many and divers kinds of temptation, and yet not with the temptation of prosperity, but

Luke xxiv. of adversity, according as it is written, "The Son of man must first suffer, and afterward enter into glory"; so likewise is it convenient, that his soldiers follow their Master Christ, take the cross upon them, and so strive to enter into the glory of

Acts xiv. their Lord and Master. For, as St Paul saith: "By many tribulations must we enter into the kingdom of God."

And verily this kind of temptation is more profitable to them that be of the household of faith than the temptation of prosperity. For prosperity maketh not ☞ only the reprobate, but also the very elect and chosen people of God many times, to forget God and to commit these things which be most unworthy their profession, as we tofore heard of David and Salomon, and of such like. But adversity keepeth the godly in order, and suffereth them not to run astray; and as for such as wander

Luke xv. 2 Chron. xxxiii. Dan. iv. abroad, and keep no rule, it bringeth them home again, as we read in the gospel of the lost son, and in the histories of Manasses, of Nabuchodonozor, and of such like.

God, by the prophet Osee, saith: "In their adversity they shall early seek me, Hos. vi. and say, Come, let us turn again to the Lord; for he hath smitten us, and he shall heal us: he hath wounded us, and he shall bind us up again, &c., so that we shall live in his sight. Then shall we have understanding, and endeavour ourselves to know the Lord." The psalmograph saith: "When he slew them, they sought him, and Psal. lxxviii. turned them early, and sought after God. And they remembered that God was their strength, and that the high God was their redeemer." The prophet Esay, in his prayer unto God, saith on this manner: "Lord, in trouble have they visited thee: Isai. xxvi. they poured out their prayer when thy chastening was upon them." Likewise saith the prophet Jeremy: "Thou hast chastened me, O Lord, and I was nurtured as an Jer. xxxi. untamed calf. Convert thou me, and I shall be converted; for thou art my Lord God. Yea, as soon as thou turnest me, I shall reform myself; and when I understand, I shall smite upon my thigh. For verily I have committed shameful things." And St Paul saith, that "when we are judged of the Lord, we are chastened, 1 Cor. xi. that we should not be damned with the world."

Father. When God thus trieth sinners with the temptation of adversity, and they turn unto him, will he receive them, and accept their conversion and amendment? *Son.* Unto this end doth God lay his cross upon sinners, not to destroy Why God layeth his cross upon us. them, and to make havoc of them, but to call them home again, which have run astray like wandering and lost sheep; and in that he layeth upon them his cross, adversity, trouble, &c., it declareth evidently that God loveth them, wisheth their salvation, and willeth by no means that they should perish, as he himself saith: "As many as I love, I rebuke and chasten." God delighteth not in the death Rev. iii. and destruction of sinners: his desire is, that "all men should be saved, and Ezek. xviii. 1 Tim. ii. come unto knowledge of the truth." At whatsoever hour a sinner repenteth Ezek. xviii. him of his wickedness, God putteth all his sins out of his remembrance, as he saith by the prophet: "Turn ye unto me, and I will turn me unto you." How Zech. i. greatly had Manasses, of whom we spake afore, sinned against the Lord his God! 2 Kings xxi. Did he not evil in the sight of the Lord, even after the abominations of the heathen, whom the Lord cast out before the children of Israel? Built not he up the hill-altars, which Hezechiah his father had destroyed? Reared he not up altars for Baal, and made idol-groves, and worshipped all the host of heaven, and served them? Offered he not his sons in fire unto idols, and gave heed unto witchcraft and sorcery, and maintained workers with spirits, and tellers of fortunes? Shed he not innocent blood exceeding much, till he replenished Hierusalem from corner to corner? He wrought exceeding much wickedness in the sight of the Lord; not only he himself, but he led the people also out of the way, to do more wickedly than did the heathen people, whom the Lord destroyed before the children of Israel. The Lord therefore brought him to great misery, so that he was taken prisoner, 2 Chron. xxxiii. bound with chains, and carried away to Babylon. Now doth God prove and try this king Manasses with the temptation of adversity, which worketh so fruitfully in him, that he falleth unto repentance, humbleth himself exceedingly before the God of his fathers, beseecheth the Lord his God, and maketh intercession unto him; insomuch that "the Lord was entreated of him, and heard his prayer, and brought him again to Hierusalem, into his kingdom."

Father. This is a comfortable history, and a good hearing. *Son.* Yea, of this history may we learn not only the great goodness and unoutspeakable mercies of the Lord our God toward sinners, but also what our duty is again toward God, when he most justly What we ought to do in adversity. assaileth us for our sins with the temptation of adversity.

Father. What is that? *Son.* Not to murmur or grudge against God, not to think God unrighteous, not impatiently to bear the visitation of God, not to go forth to sin of malice and obstinacy, not to defy God; but humbly and even from the very heart to submit ourselves to the blessed will of God, to grant our sins, to confess that we have not only deserved those afflictions and troubles which God hath laid upon us, but also innumerable more, yea, the very pains of hell, and to desire God, for his mercies' sake, to give us grace patiently, quietly, and thankfully to bear that his cross, and when his good pleasure is, either to take it away, or else so to mitigate and ease it, that we may with patient and thankful hearts suffer it, and alway do that thing that may be pleasant and acceptable in his godly sight.

Father. God give us all grace so to do! For such as murmur and grudge against ☞ God shall not escape unpunished. The patient and thankful sufferer shall obtain all good Isai. xxx. things at the hand of God, as God saith by the prophet: "If ye will return and be quiet, ye shall be safe: for in silence and hope shall that strength be;" or as the common English translation hath: "In repentance and in rest shall ye be safe: in quiet- Lam. iii. ness and sure confidence shall be your strength." The prophet Jeremy also saith: "The Lord is good to them that trust in him, and to the soul that seeketh after him. It is good with silence and patience to tarry for the saving health of the Lord." Hereto agreeth Job xiii. the saying of Job: "Behold, though God slay me, yet will I put my trust in him." *Son.* This can we not do of ourselves, except it be given us from above. For of ourselves in all our afflictions we can none otherwise do, than with impatiency murmur and grudge against the Lord God, yea, and blaspheme his holy name. And this is nothing else than to be overcome with the temptation of adversity, from the which we desire God in this 1 Cor. x. our petition to be delivered. But "God is faithful, which will not suffer us to be tempted above our strength; but will in the midst of the temptation make a way that he may be able to keep it."

Father. Well said, my son. But doth God assail sinners only with this temptation of adversity? *Son.* Before God the holiest and most perfect of all men are sinners; Prov. xx. neither can any man say, "My heart is clean, and I am pure from sin;" and, to say Note. the truth, sin is the principal and chief cause of all the plagues and punishments that God layeth upon us, as the holy scriptures testify in many places: notwithstanding, God many times assaileth his dear people and well-beloved servants, (without any respect had to sin,) with this kind of temptation unto this end, that he may prove and try their faith, love, and obedience toward him, and that they may be an example of patience and of long-suffering to other.

Father. Whom did God so handle? *Son.* The word of God remembering[1] divers. But as I may let pass Abraham, Isaac, Jacob, Joseph, with many other, which were all the true and faithful servants of God, let us consider Job, that most precious pearl of perfect Job i. patience. The holy scripture describeth him to be "a perfect and just man, such one as feared God, and eschewed evil." Now mark how God dealt with him, that he might prove his faith and patience. All that ever Job had, both in goods and cattle, was destroyed with fire from heaven, or carried away by enemies. His children also, as they were making merry together, were slain, the house through a mighty great wind Job ii. falling down upon them. Moreover, Job was smitten with marvellous sore boils, from the sole of his foot unto his crown, so that he sat upon the ground in the ashes, and scraped off the filth of his sores with a potsherd. Who, beholding this most miserable state of Job, will not think him to be thus stricken of God for his sins? Notwithstanding, even by the report of God's own mouth, there was none like Job in the land. For he was "a perfect and a just man, such a one as feared God, eschewed evil, and continued still in his godliness;" yea, and that not only in prosperity, but also in adversity. Wherefore then did God thus plague him?

Why God layeth his cross upon the faithful. Verily, first of all, to prove and try his faith and love to God-ward, which remaineth perfect and constant, even in the midst of his plagues.

Secondly, to make him an example of patience to his posterity. For Job in all his troubles offended not God, neither in word nor in deed; no, he did not once murmur against God, but quietly and patiently brasted out into these and such like words: Job i. "Naked came I out of my mother's womb, and naked shall I turn thither again. The Lord gave, and the Lord hath taken away: even as it hath pleased the Lord, so is it Job ii. come to pass: blessed be the name of the Lord." Again: "If we have received prosperity at the hand of God, ought we not also to receive adversity?"

Thirdly, to declare how merciful, gentle, loving, kind, bounteous, and liberal God is to them that patiently abide his good pleasure in temptations and troubles. For the Job xlii. scripture declareth, that when God had tried the faith and patience of Job, he afterward

[1 Perhaps a misprint for *remembereth,* meaning makes mention of.]

made him richer than ever he was before, both in goods, cattle, and children, and he lived after his trouble an hundred and forty years, so that he saw his children, and his children's children into the fourth generation. Of this Job St James speaketh thus: "Ye have heard of the patience of Job, and have known what end the Lord made. For the Lord is very pitiful and merciful." And of the holy prophets he speaketh on this manner likewise: "Take the prophets for an ensample of suffering adversity, and of patience, which spake in the name of the Lord. Behold, we count them happy which endure." James v.

Thus see we, that God doth not only tempt the sinners with adversity, to call them unto repentance and amendment of life; but he also with the same temptation proveth the godly and righteous, that by this means they, being tried as gold in the furnace with many and divers temptations and troubles, may the more gloriously set forth their faith and love, which they have to God; submit their will to God's good will and pleasure; bear patiently, thankfully, and obediently, whatsoever cross God layeth upon them; confess the name and truth of God boldly and stoutly, come life, come death; not murmur or grudge against God; not think that that temptation, trouble, or adversity chanceth to them any otherwise than by the determinate counsel and singular providence of God; not suffer their hearts to depart from God and from his holy word for the loss of any worldly thing, although never so precious and dear; but both in prosperity and adversity at all times unto the uttermost of their power avance and set forth the glory of God and of his true religion. How we ought to behave ourselves in adversity.

Father. Come these things to the faithful to their profit, or rather for their disprofit? *Son.* For their most high profit and singular avantage, as the psalmograph saith: "It is for my great commodity, that thou hast brought me low, that by this means I may learn thine ordinances." For hereof cometh it to pass, as we have heard, that the faith, love, constancy, obedience, &c. of the godly is tried, even as gold is in the furnace, and made much more glorious, not only in the sight of God, but also before men, unto the glory and praise of our heavenly Father. Psal. cxix.

Father. This trial then of the faithful which is here called "temptation," although it be never so grievous to the old man, and contrary to his fleshly lusts and filthy desires, is no token of God's anger toward such as be thus tempted. *Son.* It is rather a most certain argument and sure token of God's dear favour and singular good will toward them. "For whom the Lord loveth, him he chasteneth; yea, he scourgeth every son that he receiveth," as God himself saith: "As many as I love, I rebuke and chasten." "By many tribulations must we enter into the kingdom of God." "All that will live godly in Christ Jesu shall suffer persecution." "Many are the troubles of the righteous; but the Lord shall deliver them from them all. For the Lord keepeth all their bones, so that not one of them shall be bruised." "If ye endure chastening," saith St Paul, "God offereth himself unto you as unto sons. What son is he, whom the father chasteneth not? If ye be not under correction, whereof all are partakers, then ye are bastards, and not sons, &c. God nurtureth us for our profit, to the intent that he may minister of his holiness unto us. No manner chastising for the present time seemeth to be joyous, but grievous: nevertheless, afterward it bringeth the quiet fruit of righteousness unto them which are exercised thereby." Therefore saith the wise man: "My son, despise not the chastening of the Lord, neither faint thou when thou art rebuked of him." Jesus, the son of Sirach, also saith: "My son, if thou wilt come into the service of God, stand fast in righteousness, and fear, and arm thy soul to temptation." Prov. iii. Heb. xii. Rev. iii. Acts xiv. 2 Tim. iii. Psal. xxxiv. Heb. xii. Prov. iii. Ecclus. ii.

Father. How may I persuade myself that this temptation from God cometh of a love and good will toward me? *Son.* If you do consider the end thereof, you shall easily persuade yourself that the temptation wherewith God proveth you proceedeth from God's hearty good will toward you.

Father. Declare unto me how. *Son.* First, forasmuch as the remnants of sin do yet abide in us, and still rage in our flesh, continually labouring to reign and rule in us as lords and emperors, and to subdue the Spirit, with all the godly motions thereof, and so at the last utterly to pluck us from the favour of God, and to throw us headlong into the whorle-pit of everlasting damnation; God, tendering our salvation, Why God tempted us.

tempteth us with some adversity, and layeth his cross upon us, that by this means the old man, with all his affects and lusts, may be mortified and slain in us; and contrariwise, the new man with his motions increase, grow, prosper, flourish, reign, and triumph, as the apostle saith: "Though our outward man perish, yet the inward man is renewed day by day. For our tribulation, which is short and light, prepareth an exceeding and everlasting weight of glory unto us, while we look not on things which are seen, but on the things which are not seen. For the things which are seen are temporal; but things which are not seen are eternal." (2 Cor. iv.)

Now he that is thus tempted of God, and beareth this temptation obediently, quietly, patiently, and thankfully, without any murmuring or grudging against God, ever submitting his will to the good pleasure of God, and hereof take an occasion to amend his manners and to better his life, can none otherwise do than confess, that this temptation came unto him from the singular good will of God, yea, and that unto his great commodity and unoutspeakable profit, as the psalmograph saith: "It is for my great commodity that thou hast brought me low, that by this means I may learn thine ordinances." "Vexation giveth understanding," saith the prophet. And the wise man saith: "What knowledge hath he that is not tempted?" (Psal. cxix. Isai. xxviii. Ecclus. xxxiv.)

Secondly, God tempteth us, that he may prove and try by some outward adversity, whether we be truly his or not; whether our faith, love, fear, obedience, &c. toward him be constant and stedfast, or otherwise. And with this temptation he hath proved all good men from the beginning, as that noble matron Judith said in her oration unto the citizens of Bethulia: "Call to your remembrance how our fathers in times past were tempted, that they might be proved, if they worshipped their God aright. Call to remembrance how our father Abraham, being tempted and tried through many tribulations, was found a lover and friend of God. So was Isaac, so was Jacob, so was Moses; and all they that pleased God, being tried through many troubles, were found stedfast in faith. Again, they that received not their temptations with the fear of God, but put themselves forth with unpatience and murmuring against God, perished of the destroyer, and were slain with serpents." (Judith viii. Num. xi. xxi. 1 Cor. x.)

He, which in this temptation is not driven back from God and from his holy word, but abideth constant and stedfast in his profession, is greatly blessed; and this temptation hath chanced to him for his great commodity and profit. For by it he is now found the faithful servant of God, and well assured in his conscience that he is inheritor of everlasting glory, as St James saith: "Blessed is the man that endureth temptation; for when he is tried, he shall receive the crown of life, which the Lord hath promised to them that love him." (James i.)

Thirdly, God tempteth us, that we, patiently and thankfully abiding his loving visitation, should be an example to other, how they ought to behave themselves toward God, when the like thing chance to them, as it is written of Tobias: "This temptation did God suffer to chance unto him, that they which came after might have an example of his patience, like as of holy Job. For insomuch as he ever feared God from his youth up, and kept his commandments, he grudged not against God that the plague of blindness chanced unto him, but remained stedfast in the fear of God, praising God all the days of his life." So likewise read we of the Thessalonians, which, although tempted and proved with many and divers afflictions for the word's sake, yet remained "constant and stedfast in the faith of the Lord, with joy of the Holy Ghost; so that they became an ensample to all that believed in Macedonia and Achaia." Hereto belongeth the saying of St James: "Take, my brethren, the prophets for an ensample of suffering adversity and of patience, which spake in the name of the Lord. Behold, we count them blessed that endure. Ye have heard of the patience of Job, and have known what end the Lord made. For the Lord is very pitiful and merciful." (Tob. ii. [Vulgate.] 1 Thess. i. James v.)

Fourthly, God tempteth us, that we, feeling the merciful hand of God and his present help in our temptation, may be made the more able through the help of the Holy Ghost to succour, help, and comfort such as fall into temptation, as St Paul writeth of our Saviour Christ: "In that," saith he, "that it fortuned Christ himself to be tempted, he is able to succour them also that are tempted." Likewise saith St Paul (Heb. ii.)

himself: "Blessed be God the Father of our Lord Jesus Christ, which is the Father 2 Cor. i.
of mercy, and the God of all comfort, which comforteth us in all our tribulation, insomuch that we are able to comfort them which are in any manner of trouble, with the same comfort wherewith we ourselves are comforted of God. For as the afflictions of Christ are plenteous in us, even so is our consolation plenteous by Christ."

Fifthly and finally, God tempteth us, that we may be made like unto his own Son, which first suffered before he entered into glory, with this perfect persuasion and Luke xxiv.
assured hope, that "if we suffer with Christ, we shall reign with Christ; if we die 2 Tim. ii.
with Christ, we shall live with Christ;" although "the afflictions of this life are not Rom. viii.
worthy of the glory which shall be shewed upon us."

Whosoever diligently considereth these things, he shall easily perceive that the temptations wherewith God proveth and trieth us are most certain arguments and sure tokens of God's good will toward us; so that we may well and justly persuade ourselves, that we are in the favour of God when we are thus tempted, and not in the hatred and displeasure of God, as the wicked world most wickedly judgeth.

Father. It pleaseth me right well, whatsoever thou hast said in this behalf. But it is too heavy a burden for us to bear such temptations, except God aid us with his holy Spirit, and strengthen us with power from above. *Son*. It is truth. But "God is faithful," saith St Paul, "which will not suffer you to be tempted above 1 Cor. x.
your strength, but shall in the midst of the temptation make a way that ye may be able to bear it." God "knoweth whereof we are made: he remembereth that we Psal. ciii.
are but dust." And therefore mercifully will he deal with us.

Father. But the temptations of the devil, the world, and the flesh are grievous and intolerable. *Son*. Although they be never so grievous and intolerable, yet God is both able, and also will make them easy and light, if we earnestly call upon him for help and succour, according to this his promise: "Call on me in the time of thy Psal. l.
trouble, and I will deliver thee." Again: "Forasmuch as he hath put his trust in Psal. xci.
me, I will deliver him: I will defend him, because he hath known my name. He hath cried unto me, and I will graciously hear him: I am with him in his trouble: I will deliver him, and glorify him." For unto this end hath God commanded us to pray in this petition for aid and succour unto him against our adversaries, that in our conflict with the devil, or with the world, or with the flesh, we should not doubt of the victory, nor despair of the triumph over our enemies; but with strong faith in Christ, and with fervent prayer unto our heavenly Father, buckle and strive with them manfully and stoutly, ever setting before the eyes of our mind, that our grand captain Christ hath subdued all our enemies, the devil, the world, the flesh, &c. and hath most victoriously and gloriously triumphed over them; and his victory, glory, and triumph is our victory, our glory, and our triumph.

Furthermore, this thing ought also greatly to comfort us, yea, and to encourage us to encounter with our enemies; I mean, to consider that these enemies, which are left only to try our faith, are of no puissance or strength, but miserable captives and bond- Note well.
slaves, and can do no more unto us, that be God's elect and chosen people, than God doth both suffer and appoint: but as a hunter hath his greyhounds in a leash, so that they cannot run when they will, but when the hunter lusteth; so likewise the devil, the world, the flesh, &c. cannot rage so fiercely against us, nor take their scope so far abroad as they would, but so much shall they do, and so far shall they rage, as God's good will and pleasure shall be, and no further. For God hath them in leash. Yea, God is their Lord, and they are his slaves. The devil could do no more to Job Job i. ii.
than God both suffered and appointed. The legion of devils, which Christ cast out Matt. viii.
of a certain man, had no power to enter into the herd of swine, till Christ gave them licence. If so great company of devils could do nothing to a sort of filthy swine, till they had obtained licence of Christ; what shall they be able to do unto us, which Note.
are the elect and chosen people of God, enarmed with the Spirit of God, with faith, and with prayer? Only let us "be sober, and watch": only let us not give place, 1 Pet. v.
but manfully fight with faith, with prayer, and with "the sword of the Spirit, which Eph. vi.
is the word of God"; and we shall surely obtain a glorious victory, and put them to flight like miserable cowards, as St James saith: "Resist the devil, and he will James iv.

flee from you." Therefore, whensoever the enemy assail us, let us not fear, but boldly in the name of our alone Mediator Jesus Christ cry unto our heavenly Father, and say: "O thou Father, which art in heaven, lead us not into temptation."

Mark well. *Father.* Well said, my son. But methink the words of this petition so sound as though God led us into temptation, and that he is the cause that our enemies, the devil, the world, and the flesh tempt us; so that, if God were not, we should be free from temptation, and so in fine from damnation. And hereof then should it follow, that God is the author both of our temptation and also of our damnation. *Son.* God forbid! God forbid that we should so unreverently think of the majesty of God, which "will the death of no sinner; but rather that he should turn and live": which "will have all men to be saved, and to come to the knowledge of the truth." The Lord our God can abide no wickedness: he hateth all them that work ungodliness; neither shall such abide in his sight.

Ezek. xviii. 1 Tim. ii. Psal. v.

Now, that God tempteth no man unto evil, neither is the occasion thereof, ye heard before out of the testimony of St James. That we are tempted unto evil, we ourselves, whose nature is always prone unto evil, and the devil, which naturally is bent to seek our destruction, is the cause thereof, and not God; as St James saith: "Let no man say when he is tempted, that he is tempted of God. For as God cannot be tempted with evil, so neither he himself tempteth any man (unto evil). But every man is tempted, when he is drawn away and enticed of his own concupiscence: then when lust is conceived, she bringeth forth sin; and sin, when it is finished, bringeth forth death."

James i. James i.

☞ Now, that God should be the author of our damnation, that is so far from the truth that nothing can be more false, as these his words by the prophet do most manifestly declare: "Thy destruction, O Israel, cometh of thyself: only of me cometh thy health and salvation." And St Peter saith: "Be ye sober, and watch; for your adversary the devil like a roaring lion goeth about, seeking whom he may devour." Of these testimonies of the holy scripture it plainly appeareth, that not God, but we ourselves and the devil are the occasion of our damnation; so that, if we perish and be damned, we ourselves and the devil are the alone authors of our destruction.

Hos. xiii. 1 Pet. v.

Father. How then are the words of this petition to be understand? *Son.* Forasmuch as the devil, the world, and the flesh, are the sworn and immortal enemies of mankind, daily sweating and swinking to destroy us and to make us fellow-inheritors with him of everlasting damnation in "that lake that burneth with fire and brimstone," in "that darkness, where weeping and gnashing of teeth shall be," in those torments, "where the worm" that shall gnaw their conscience "shall never die, and the fire shall never be quenched"; and we of ourselves are so feeble, weak, lame, impotent, and without all strength, that we are able to do nothing against so puissant, strong, mighty, prudent, active, expert, exercised, and practised adversaries in all kind of mischief; we, knowledging our imbecility and weakness, our little, yea, our no strengths, most humbly and from the very heart pray and beseech our most dear and loving heavenly Father, that he of his great mercy and tender goodness will vouchsafe to aid and preserve us against such and so great enemies, to send us strength from his high tower, to endue us with virtue and power from above, to enrich us with the graces and gifts of his holy Spirit, that we never give place neither to the flattering enticements nor to the menacing terrors of our enemies; but being clad with the armour of God, manfully resist them, stoutly defend our quarrel, courageously maintain our title and right, that by this means we being made noble and triumphant conquerors through the puissance of our most noble and triumphant captain, Christ Jesus the Lord, may at the last receive the uncorruptible crown and the immortal laurel of eternal glory.

Note. Rev. xxi. Matt. xxii. Isai. lxvi.

Father. But tell me, my sweet son, what if in this temptation we, being negligent and uncircumspect in our affairs, and making very slender provision against our enemies, their crafts and policies, should chance to be circumvented and overcome? what is then to be done? *Son.* In this petition we do not only desire of our heavenly Father that he will so aid us with his holy Spirit against the assaults of our enemies, that we be not overcome of them; but also our prayer is, that if we at any time chance to give place to our adversaries, and to lose the victory, it may please his majesty through his mighty and strong power to deliver and set us at liberty again from the bondage of our enemies, and to strengthen us with power from above, that we, once again being lifted up and delivered from their hands, may from henceforth become the more circumspect in our affairs, and so for ever after courageously fight with our adversaries, that at the last we may obtain the glorious crown of immortality in heaven.

Father. There is then hope of recovering God's favour, though sometime we be overcome with the grievous temptations of our enemies. *Son.* Yea, verily, so we return, ask mercy for our fault, crave help from above, and continually afterward labour not only valiantly to fight with our enemies, but also through the mighty power of God gloriously to triumph over them.

Father. Blessed be God for his inestimable goodness toward man! And God give us grace to walk worthy of this his kindness! But let me now hear the seventh petition.

Son. This is it:

"But deliver us from the evil." The seventh petition.

Father. What desire we of our heavenly Father in this petition? *Son.* As in the last petition we sued unto God, that he will rule, govern, and strengthen us by his holy Spirit, that we may be able to fight against sin, and to withstand all the perilous temptations of the devil, the world, and the flesh, and to overcome them, that we may be found valiant soldiers in the camp of Christ; so likewise in this seventh and last petition we desire of our heavenly Father that he will deliver us from that wicked evil, which is the original and only cause of all evils that chance unto us, whether we respect the body or the soul.

Father. What is this evil? *Son.* Our arch-enemy the devil, author of all evil, which, as St Peter saith, "walketh about like a roaring lion, seeking whom he may devour." 1 Pet. v.

Father. Where is he termed "the evil," in any other place of the holy scripture? *Son.* St Paul so calleth him in his epistle to the Ephesians, where he hath these words: "Above all things take to you the shield of faith, wherewith ye may be able to quench the fiery darts of the evil," or wicked. And this Satan may justly be termed "the evil;" for as there is nothing in him but evil, so likewise is he the only occasion of all evil, that from the fall of Adam (whereof he also was the author) unto this day have reigned in this wicked world, or shall reign unto the end of the same. For "through the envy of the devil death, and with it all kind of evils, entered into the world." And as he first of all sought the destruction of man, which through his subtile persuasions he craftily brought to pass; so likewise goeth he forth continually to bring us out of God's favour, that we may lose the benefit of our redemption, which we obtained by Christ: therefore we desire our heavenly Father in this petition, that he will deliver us from this evil, that is to say, the devil. Eph. vi. Gen. iii. Wisd. ii.

Father. Why do we rather desire to be delivered from the devil than from the world or from the flesh? Are not they also grievous enemies of mankind? Have not we also need to crave God's help against them? *Son.* I grant. Notwithstanding, forasmuch as the devil is our arch-enemy, and above all other seeketh our destruction, and without him all our other enemies are able to do nothing, as receiving all their power of him (for he is "the god" and "prince of this world," "the power of darkness," "the ruler of the flesh," &c.); therefore in this petition we principally direct our prayers unto God against him, as against the chief captain of all evil, and the most extreme foe of our health and salvation, whom once vanquished, all the other our enemies straightways fly away like cowards and heartless monsters. John xii. Eph. vi.

Father. Do we not also in this petition desire to be delivered from the world and the flesh? *Son.* Not only from the world and the flesh, but also from all other evils both of body and soul, wherewith Satan goeth about daily to molest, trouble, disquiet, hurt, grieve, punish, plague, and destroy us.

Father. Give me examples of these evils. Name some of them unto me. *Son.* The evils of the soul, wherewith Satan laboureth continually to plague us, that by this means he may wrest us out of the favour of God, and make us fellow-inheritors with him of everlasting damnation, are incredulity, misbelief, doubting, desperation, The evils of the soul.

idolatry, superstition, false worshipping of God, invocation of creatures, confidence in good works, trust in other men's merits, hypocrisy, strange religion, counterfeit holiness, blind zeals, good intents, ignorance, contempt of God, hate of Christ's gospel, blindness of heart, unrepentance, rejoicing in sin, glorying in wickedness, presumption, impatiency, grudging against the will of God, uncircumcision of heart, corruption of judgment, error, heresy, schisms, controversies in religion, sects, pride of the mind, obstinacy in wickedness, fleshly lusts, and whatsoever besides can be reckoned that defileth the soul of man. Now, that we may be delivered from these such and so great evils, plagues, and pestilences, whereby the salvation of our soul is greatly endangered, yea, and also perisheth, if we persevere in them without repentance and faith unto the last end, we most humbly pray unto our heavenly Father in this petition, which alone is able to deliver us from these evils; and as he is able, so likewise will he do it for his mercies' sake.

Father. Which are the evils of the body, wherewith Satan laboureth to plague us, and from the which we desire of our heavenly Father to be delivered? *Son*. Sudden death, plague, pestilence, unwholesome weather, too much abundance of waters, famine, hunger, battle, dearth, beggary, loss of goods, infamy, shame, confusion, madness, insurrections, tumults, commotions, tyranny of princes, disobedience of subjects, dissolution of commonwealths, discord between realms, private lucre, singular commodities, raising of rents, enhancement of farms, joining of houses together, havoc-making of villages, towns, cities, &c., destruction of hospitality, desolation of countries, and whatsoever can be rehearsed besides that is hurtful to the body, or to the things that appertain unto the body. From these evils also we desire our heavenly Father that he will deliver us, that we, through his mighty defence, being safe and sound both in body and in soul, may live in his fear, and glorify his holy name.

The evils of the body.

Father. As we desire in this petition of our heavenly Father, that he will deliver us from the aforesaid evils both of the body and of the soul, are not we here also humble suitors unto him for the good treasures, gifts, and benefits both of the soul and of the body? *Son*. Yes, verily. For in that we pray our heavenly Father to take from us all evils, we crave at his hand all good things, and that it will please him to enrich us with the treasures both of the soul and the body; that we, being free from all evil, and furnished with all good, may be the more able to resist our enemies, and to "serve the Lord our God in holiness and righteousness all the days of our life."

Luke i.

Father. Which are the treasures of the mind, that we desire of our heavenly Father? *Son*. The fruits of the Holy Ghost, as faith, hope, charity, repentance, joy, peace, long-suffering, gentleness, goodness, faithfulness, meekness, temperancy, righteousness, holiness, truth, mercy, humility, kindness, patience in adversity, thankfulness in prosperity, knowledge of God, pureness of life, liberality to the poor, mortification of the old man, vivification of the new man, &c.

Gal. v.

Father. Which are the gifts or benefits of the body, that we require here of our heavenly Father? *Son*. Health, long life, prosperity, joy, quietness, seasonable weather, abundance of all necessary things, a quiet and prosperous commonwealth, righteous magistrates, good officers, learned schoolmasters, studious scholars, loving parents, obedient children, faithful servants, &c. And, finally, we pray here our heavenly Father that he will give us a joyful and prosperous departure out of this miserable world at the hour of death; that we may with strong faith commend our souls into his merciful hands, and so, through his grace, come unto that heavenly kingdom, where we shall not only be delivered from all evil, but also enjoy for ever all good things, yea, the glorious sight of the most glorious majesty of God, and there remain with him in joy and glory, worlds with[out] end.

Father. God grant it us! *Son*. Amen.

Father. But what are those words which follow the end of these seven petitions, and are the conclusion of the Lord's prayer? *Son*. The words are these:

"For thine is the kingdom, the power, and the glory, for ever and ever. Amen."

Father. Why are these words added to the petitions that go before? *Son*. To our great comfort, and to the confirmation of our faith. For in that we ascribe unto our heavenly Father the kingdom and the power, we are well ascertained that, as he is a most mighty and most glorious king, so is he sufficiently able even to the uttermost both to vanquish our enemies, the devil, the world, and the flesh, &c., and also to grant us all that we ask, yea, and more than we dare be bold to ask, as St Paul saith: "God is able to do exceeding abundantly above all that we ask or think." Eph. iii.

Father. How provest thou that the kingdom and the power is God's? *Son*. Thus is it written in the holy scripture: "Blessed be thou, Lord God of Israel, our Father, 1 Chron. xxix. for ever and ever. Thine, O Lord, is greatness and power, glory, victory, and praise; for all that is in heaven and in earth is thine, and thine is the kingdom, O Lord, and thou excellest above all, even as the head of all. And riches and honour come of thee, and thou reignest over all, and in thine hand is power and strength, and in thy hand it is to make great and to give strength unto all. And now, our God, we thank thee, and praise thy glorious name." The psalmograph also saith: "Thy king- Psal. cxlv. dom is an everlasting kingdom, and thy dominion endureth throughout all ages." Again: "The kingdom is the Lord's, and he is the governor among the people." Also in Psal. xxii. another place: "The Lord hath prepared his seat in heaven, and his kingdom ruleth Psal. ciii. over all."

Father. Why do we not only ascribe unto God the kingdom and the power, but also the glory? *Son*. As of our heavenly Father we receive all good things both for the body and for the soul, so likewise is the glory, praise, and honour for those benefits due to him alone. Therefore, as we grant that whatsoever good thing we 1 Cor. iv. have, we receive it at the most excellent, mighty, and powerful hand of God, from whom "cometh every good and perfect gift," which also "giveth abundantly to them James i. that ask of him in faith, and casteth no man in the teeth;" so, in like manner, we freely confess that all the glory, all the praise, all the honour is due to none, neither in heaven, nor in earth, but to this our heavenly Father alone; which as he is able, so likewise he will, and as he will, so likewise he doth both mercifully and plentifully enrich us daily with his both spiritual and corporal gifts.

Father. How provest thou that all glory, praise, and honour is due to God alone? *Son*. The apostle saith: "To the alone wise God be honour and praise, through Jesus Rom. xvi. Christ, for ever and ever." Again: "Unto God, King everlasting, immortal, invisible, 1 Tim. i. wise only, be honour and praise for ever and ever." In the Revelation of St John we read that "the twenty-four elders fell down before him that sat on the throne, Rev. iv. and worshipped him that liveth for ever, and cast their crowns before the throne, saying, Thou art worthy, O Lord, to receive glory, and honour, and power; for thou hast created all things, and for thy will's sake they are, and were created." Again: "Blessing, honour, glory, and power be unto him that sitteth upon the seat, and Rev. v. unto the Lamb for evermore." Item: "Blessing, and glory, and wisdom, and thanks, Rev. vii. and honour, and power, and might be unto our God for evermore."

Father. Wherefore dost thou say, "for ever and ever"? *Son*. By these words I plainly declare and signify that the kingdom and power of our heavenly Father is not like the kingdom and power of earthly princes, which endureth a short time; but his kingdom and his power, his dominion and his might, abideth for ever and ever; that is to say, everlastingly, and worlds without end, as the psalmograph saith: "Thy kingdom is an everlasting kingdom, and thy dominion endureth throughout Psal. cxlv. all ages." Again, that the glory, praise, honour, and worship of our heavenly Father is not like the glory, praise, honour, and worship of worldly kings and rulers, which soon vanish away, with all their glory and renown; but it is everlasting, and never shall have end, as David witnesseth: "Blessed," saith he, "are they which dwell Psal. lxxxiv. in thy house; for they shall praise thee worlds without end."

Father. Wherefore dost thou close up the Lord's prayer with this word, "Amen"? Amen. *Son*. By saying "Amen", I plainly and manifestly declare that I most certainly do believe, and am most assuredly persuaded, that my heavenly Father, for Christ's sake, in whose name I have offered these my humble supplications unto him, hath both graciously heard me, accepted my prayers, and also as he is able, so likewise he will grant me these my petitions and requests; yea, that he hath already given and granted me my desires, and at all times will do, whensoever I call upon him in the name of his dearly-beloved Son Christ Jesu our Lord and alone Saviour, according to this his Son's promise: "Whatsoever ye ask in my name, that will I do, that the Father may be glorified by the Son. If ye shall ask any thing in my name, I will do it." (John xiv.) Again: "Verily, verily I say unto you, Whatsoever ye shall ask the Father in my name, he will give it you." "Ask, and ye shall receive, that your joy may be full." (John xvi.)

Father. God give us his holy Spirit, that he may lighten our dark senses, and teach us so to pray, that we may at all times pray with fruit, even unto the glory of his holy name, and unto the salvation of our souls! *Son.* Lord, let it so come so to pass!

Father. Now have we examined, my dear son, the four first parts of the Catechism. It remaineth that we go in hand with the fifth part of the same. Whereof doth that entreat? *Son.* Of the sacraments: for so were we taught of our catechist.

Father. Let us then now begin with that, in the name of God. *Son.* Let it so be, my most loving father.

THE FIFTH PART OF THE CATECHISM.

OF THE SACRAMENTS.

Father. How many sacraments are there? *Son.* I know that in the church of the pope there are numbered seven.

Father. Which are they? *Son.* Baptism, confirmation, order, penance, eucharist, matrimony, and extreme unction.

Father. Confessest thou all these to be sacraments? *Son.* Our preacher and our catechist taught us, that there are but two only which may properly and truly be called sacraments. Sacraments two only in number.

Father. Which are they? *Son.* Baptism, and the Lord's supper, otherwise called the eucharist, or the sacrament of the body and blood of Christ.

Father. What thinkest thou of the other five? *Son.* They said that matrimony, and the ministry concerning the preaching of God's word and the administration of the sacraments, are holy orders of life, instituted and ordained of God to be used in his church. As touching confirmation, and extreme unction, they are ceremonies, said they, brought into the church by man, and not worthy to be numbered among sacraments. And as concerning penance, which ought more justly to be termed repentance, [it] is a continual exercise of a true Christian, said they, so long as he liveth, and may more justly be reckoned among the fruits of the Holy Ghost than among sacraments.

Father. Why are baptism and the Lord's supper properly called sacraments? *Son.* Because they only have those things which are necessarily required in a sacrament, yea, and that of the institution of Christ.

Father. Which are they? *Son.* The outward sign, and the promise of grace added to the sign. What is necessarily required in a sacrament.

Father. Give me an example hereof. *Son.* Baptism hath his outward sign, which is water. It hath also his promise annexed to his outward sign, which is this: "Whosoever shall believe and be baptized, he shall be saved." Likewise the supper of the Lord hath his signs, that is to say, bread and wine. It hath also promises annexed to these signs, which are these: "which shall be betrayed for you," "which shall be shed for you." Mark xvi. Matt. xxvi.

Father. Tell me now, my child, what a sacrament is. *Son.* A sacrament is an holy action and exercise of Christ's church, in the which the redemption and partaking of our Lord Jesus Christ is given to us through the word and the signs instituted for this purpose of God. Or thus: A sacrament is an outward sign or visible token, comprehending in it a gracious, comfortable, and healthful promise of God. Or on this wise: A sacrament is properly an outward sign, wherein God representeth and witnesseth his good will toward us, to sustain the weakness of our faith. Or another way, more short and also more plain: A sacrament is a witness of God's favour, declared by an outward sign. What a sacrament is.

Father. Wherefore are the sacraments instituted and ordained? *Son.* First, that they should be unto us testimonies, pledges, signs, or seals of God's grace, favour, and mercy, to teach us that God is merciful unto us, and will forgive us our sins, justify and save us for Christ's sake, and that all the benefits of Christ doth both belong and are freely given unto us of God the Father, if with faith we come and receive those holy mysteries. As for an ensample, baptism beareth witness unto us, that we are washed in the blood of Christ; that all our sins be put away and cleansed by the death and passion of Christ; and that Christ by his blood hath so purified us, that he hath "made us unto himself a glorious congregation, without spot or wrinkle, or any such thing, that we should be holy and without blame." Likewise, the supper of the Lord doth put us in remembrance of the grace, mercy, and favour of God, and of the free remission of all our sins, and testify unto us that all the benefits of the passion and death of Christ appertain unto us, and that we, in the Why sacraments are ordained. Eph. v.

worthy receiving of the Lord's supper, are made partakers of them all, if we believe that Christ's body was broken and his blood shed for our sins.

Secondly, that they should be certain tokens and marks, whereby the church of Christ may be discerned from the synagogue of antichrist, and from all other sects. For God will have his church to be known, seen, and heard throughout all mankind,
Psal. xix. as it is written: "The sound of them went out through all the world." And therefore hath he ordained certain noble ceremonies, which should be evident signs of his church, and discern that from other congregations. For where baptism and the Lord's supper is, there is the church of Christ; forasmuch as they are sacraments and tokens of Christ's church only, and belong not unto the congregations of the ethnicks and infidels.

Thirdly, that they should be signs, tokens, and marks of our confession, in the which we outwardly profess what we inwardly think and believe. As for an ensample, when we come unto baptism or unto the Lord's supper, we openly confess and profess that we utterly reject and cast away all strange doctrine and all false religion, and that we only cleave to the true religion of the alone true and everlasting God, and that we embrace even from the very heart the doctrine of the gospel of Christ, of the which doctrine baptism and the Lord's supper are most certain signs and seals: as they which in the old law were circumcised, and did eat of the paschal lamb, did openly declare by those outward sacraments, that they utterly refused all the wicked doctrines of the heathen, and only embraced the law and ordinances of the God of Israel.

Fourthly, that they should be as sinews and bonds to link and knit together the congregations of God publicly and openly, whereby they may be known to be of one company, and of one spirit, of one faith, and of one doctrine and profession. For God will that his people should oftentimes resort and come together, yea, and that not only privately, but also publicly, to pray unto him, to give thanks unto him, to hear his holy word, to confer of matters concerning religion, to edify and comfort one another, and to occupy themselves in such godly and spiritual exercises. Therefore, as the Lord appointed that his sacraments should be sinews and bonds openly to knit together in holy actions his people, even so many as profess his holy name; even so ought those sacraments publicly and openly to be administered; as we see in the administration of baptism there is a common resort. First, there is the minister; secondly, the person that shall be baptized; thirdly, the witnesses; fourthly, divers other of Christ's congregation. For baptism ought then to be administered, when the faithful do most assemble and meet together. Likewise the Lord's supper ought to be administered in a multitude and company of God's people, and not privately, or where one alone is present to receive it, as it is used in the pope's church. Thus St
1 Cor. x. Paul saith: "The cup of thanksgiving for the which we give thanks, is it not the partaking of the blood of Christ? The bread which we break, is it not the partaking of the body of Christ? Because that we, although we be many, are yet one bread and one body, inasmuch as we all are partakers of one bread and of one cup." Again:
1 Cor. xi. "When ye come together to eat (the Lord's supper), tarry one for another."

Fifthly, that they should be unto us memorials, to put us in remembrance what mutual benevolence, what love, and hearty friendship one to another ought to reign among us. For seeing we all are partakers of the same mysteries, baptized with one baptism, and eat together of one bread, and drink together of one cup, by this means protesting openly that we are members one of another's body, whereof Christ Jesus is the head; who seeth not how far all enmity, debate, strife, malice, envy, and all displeasure ought to be from us? Again, what fervent charity, love, concord, amity, good will, friendship, peace, quietness, gentleness, &c. ought to rule in our hearts one
Eph. iv. to another? as Saint Paul saith: "I exhort you that ye walk worthy of the vocation wherewith ye are called, with all lowliness and meekness, with humbleness of mind, forbearing one another through love; and be diligent to keep the unity of the Spirit through the bond of peace, being one body and Spirit, even as ye are called in one hope of your calling; one Lord, one faith, one baptism, one God and Father of all, which is above all, and through all, and in you all."

Sixthly, that they should be testimonials unto us, to testify and witness how nigh Christ join himself unto us, that he giveth himself whole unto us, and that he will dwell in us, and endow us with all his benefits and riches, so that whatsoever is Christ's, the same is ours. For in taking upon us baptism, we take Christ upon us, with all his holiness and righteousness, as St Paul saith: "All ye that are baptized have put on Christ." Likewise, in receiving the sacrament of the body and blood of Christ we receive not only the sacrament, but also Christ himself, with all the fruits, benefits, and merits of his glorious passion and healthful death, as Christ himself saith: "This is my body, which is betrayed or broken for you." "This is my blood, which is shed for you unto the remission of your sins."

Gal. iii.

Matt. xvi. Mark xiv. Luke xxii. 1 Cor. xi.

Seventhly, that they should be unto us a singular consolation and an exceeding great comfort in all our troubles, perils, dangers, and adversities, while in receiving them we do behold and consider the merciful good will of God toward us, with this persuasion, that that God, which hath instituted these sacraments, delivered them unto us as pledges of his most hearty good will toward us, and hath also commanded us to use them for our comfort, will not leave us succourless, but in his time deliver us from all those miseries, and bring us into the haven of quietness, according to this his promise: "Call on me in the day of trouble, and I will deliver thee, and thou shalt honour me." Again: "Forasmuch as he put his trust in me, I will deliver him: I will defend him, because he hath known my name. He cried unto me, and I will hear him: I am with him in trouble: I will deliver him, and glorify him. Yea, with long life will I satisfy him, and shew him my saving health."

Psal. l.

Psal. xci.

Many other causes might here be alleged, why did God institute and ordain his sacraments; but these are the chief and principal, and for this present they may seem abundantly to suffice.

Father. What need have we of sacraments, seeing we have the Holy Ghost and the sacred scriptures of God to lead us into all necessary truth, which can abundantly inform us of the grace, favour, mercy, and good will of God toward us? *Son.* Christ, the Wisdom of the Father, knowing our grossness and dulness in understanding matters that belong unto our salvation, wishing our health and commodity, and minding to remedy and help this our great infirmity, and to bring us into some knowledge of God's mysteries, that we may be saved, hath not only given us his holy Spirit to inform, instruct, and teach our inward man; but, to make us perfect both in body and soul, he hath also given us his word to serve our ears, and his sacraments to serve our eyes. For whatsoever the Holy Ghost saith inwardly unto us, the very same doth the word of God to our ears, and the sacraments to serve our eyes, preach, declare, and set forth outwardly, that we may be taught both corporally and spiritually. Again, who knoweth not that things seen with eyes are more surely fixed in the minds of men than those things which are only heard? And therefore a sacrament may right well be called a visible word. For whatsoever the word is to the ear, the very same thing is the sacrament to the eye. The word of God saith to mine ear, The body of Christ was broken for thee: the blood of Christ was shed for thee. The very same thing doth the sacrament preach unto mine eye, while in the holy action of the Lord's supper I see the bread broken and the wine shed. Therefore Christ the Lord, to inform and instruct our outward senses, ordained these outward signs and sacraments, that by the consideration and beholding of them that thing might the more easily slide into our minds, which hath been inculked and beaten into our ears through the voice of the preacher. If we had been without bodies, Christ would have given unto us those spiritual gifts nakedly and simply, which are given to the faithful in the deliverance of the sacraments; but forasmuch as we have bodies joined to our souls, therefore in sensible things he doth communicate unto us the gifts of grace. And this hath been the property of God not only in the new, but also in the old testament. For as in the old law he gave to the Jews circumcision and the passover, so likewise in the new law hath he given to us Christians baptism and the Lord's supper.

John xvi.

1 Cor. ii.

Father. What difference is there between the sacraments of the old and of the new testament? *Son.* The sacraments of the old testament were figures and shadows

The difference between the sacraments of the old and new testament. of Christ to come: but the sacraments of the new testament do signify, declare, and set forth unto us that Christ is come, and have perfectly fulfilled in his flesh whatsoever was prefigured and afore shadowed of him in the old sacraments and ceremonies.

Father. Let us then fall in hand with the sacraments of the new testament; and first of all, with the sacrament of baptism: for of that we have our beginning, when we come unto the profession of Christ. Tell me therefore, my dear child, what baptism is.

OF BAPTISM.

What baptism is. Tit. iii. *Son.* Baptism, after the definition of St Paul, is "the fountain of the new birth, and renewing of the Holy Ghost." Or thus: Baptism, as St Peter doth define it, is
1 Pet. iii. "not the putting away of the filthiness of the flesh, but a good conscience consenting to God by the resurrection of Jesus Christ." Or on this manner: Baptism is an holy sacrament instituted of the Lord Jesu to this end, that so many as will shake off the cruel yoke of Satan, the world, and the flesh, and become his faithful soldiers and trusty servants, should be washed with water in the name of the Father, and of the Son, and of the Holy Ghost.

Of how many parts baptism consisteth. *Father.* Of how many parts doth the sacrament of baptism consist? *Son.* Of two.

Father. Of which two? *Son.* Of the word, and of the water.

Father. Is not the water sufficient to make the sacrament of baptism perfect without the word? *Son.* Neither the water without the word, nor the word without the water, can make a perfect sacrament. The word and the element must concur and go together, and so is it a sacrament. In baptism the word and the water must be joined and linked together. So likewise in the Lord's supper bread and wine, which are the elements, and the words of institution must also go together; otherwise there is no perfect sacrament. Take away the word; and water remaineth water, and no sacrament. Take away the word; and bread abideth bread, and wine continueth wine, and no sacrament. But if the word be joined to the element, so is it made a sacrament.

Father. How provest thou, that water alone without the word maketh not perfect baptism? *Son.* St Paul, speaking of baptism, joineth the word and the water
Eph. v. together. His words are these: "Christ loved the congregation, and gave himself for it, to sanctify it, and cleansed it in the fountain of water through the word, to make it unto himself a glorious congregation, without spot or wrinkle or any such thing; but that it should be holy and without blame."

Father. Which callest thou the word? *Son.* The institution and commandment
Matt. xxviii. of Christ, which are comprehended in these words: "Go ye and teach all nations, baptizing them in the name of the Father, and of the Son, and of the Holy Ghost."
Mark xvi. "He that believeth and is baptized, he shall be saved."

Father. Of how many baptisms doth the holy scripture make mention? *Son.* Of two.

Father. Which are they? *Son.* The baptism of water, and the baptism of the Spirit, that is to say, of the Holy Ghost.

Father. Where is that found in the word of God? *Son.* John Baptist, son of
Matt. iii. Mark i. Luke iii. Zachary the priest, said to them which came unto his baptism: "I have baptized you with water, but he (Christ) shall baptize you with the Holy Ghost." And Christ
Acts i. said unto his apostles after his resurrection: "John baptized with water, but ye shall be baptized with the Holy Ghost after these few days." Of both these two baptisms
Tit. iii. speaketh St Paul on this manner: "Not by the deeds of righteousness which we wrought, but according to his mercy hath God saved us, by the fountain of the new birth, and renewing of the Holy Ghost, which he shed on us abundantly through Jesus Christ our Saviour; that we, justified by his grace, should be made heirs according to the hope of everlasting life."

What it is to be baptized with the Holy Ghost. *Father.* What is it[1] to be baptized with the Holy Ghost? *Son.* To be regenerate, to be born anew, to be made of earthly heavenly, of carnal spiritual, of the bond-slaves of the devil the sons of God, of the inhabitants of this wretched world the citizens of that glorious and heavenly kingdom.

[[1] Folio, *it is.*]

Father. Is this baptism of the Spirit necessary unto everlasting salvation? *Son.* So necessary, that without it the baptism of water profiteth nothing. As in the old testament the circumcision of the flesh profited the Jews nothing at all without the circumcision of the Spirit; so likewise in the new testament the baptism of the water availeth nothing without the baptism of the Spirit. "He is not a Jew," saith St Paul, "which is a Jew outward; neither is it circumcision, which is outward in the flesh. But he is a Jew, which is hid within, and the circumcision of the heart is the true circumcision, which consisteth in the spirit, and not in the letter, whose praise is not of men, but of God." And St Peter saith: "Baptism now saveth us; not the putting away of the filthiness of the flesh, but a good conscience consenting unto God by the resurrection of Jesus Christ." What did it profit Simon Magus that he was baptized with water, not being also through his hypocrisy baptized with the Holy Ghost? Verily, nothing at all. "They that are led with the Spirit of God, they are the sons of God." "If any man have not the Spirit of Christ, he belongeth not unto God." The wicked and the unfaithful have the element of the sacrament, which is water; but the godly and the faithful have both the sacrament, and also the virtue and strength of the sacrament, which is the Holy Ghost; as Christ saith: "Except a man be born of water and of the Spirit, he cannot enter into the kingdom of God. For that which is born of the flesh is flesh; and that which is born of the Spirit is spirit."

Rom. ii. 1 Pet. iii. Acts viii. Rom. viii. John iii.

Father. But, my son, let us now return unto the outward baptism, and tell me who did institute it. *Son.* God the Father did first of all institute it, and commanded John, Zachary the priest's son, to practise it among his people the Jews, even among so many as repented them of their sinful life, and purposed henceforth to live in the fear of God.

Who first instituted baptism.

Father. Where readest thou that? *Son.* In the gospel of St John, where we read on this manner: "John bare record of Christ, saying, I saw the Spirit descend from heaven like unto a dove, and abode upon him; and I knew him not. But he that sent me to baptize in water, the same said unto me, Upon whom ye shall see the Spirit descend, and tarry still upon him, the same is he which baptizeth with the Holy Ghost." Moreover God the Son, Christ Jesus our Lord, a little before his ascension into the kingdom of his Father, ordained this holy sacrament of baptism, when he said on this manner to his apostles[2]: "Go ye and teach all nations, baptizing them in the name of the Father, and of the Son, and of the Holy Ghost." "He that believeth and is baptized, he shall be saved: but he that believeth not shall be condemned." And as the Lord Christ commanded that all such should be baptized with water, that believe in him and appertain unto his holy congregation; so likewise was he himself baptized, as the evangelical history plainly declareth: whereof we may learn what an holy and precious mystery baptism is, and that it ought not to be neglected nor despised, but rather, as they say, to be embraced with meeting arms, and to be had in great reverence. "I have given you an ensample," saith Christ, "that as I have done, so likewise ye should do."

John i. Matt. xxviii. Mark xvi. Matt. iii. Mark i. Luke iii. John xiii.

Father. What is it to be baptized in the name of the Father, and of the Son, and of the Holy Ghost? *Son.* To be admitted and received into the family and household of God, the Father, the Son, and the Holy Ghost, and from henceforth to be reckoned, yea, and also to be, the son and heir of God, serving him in "holiness and righteousness all the days of our life."

What is to be baptized in the name of the Father, and of the Son, and of the Holy Ghost.

Father. To what end art thou baptized? *Son.* First, that baptism (which thing I have partly touched before) should be unto my conscience a sure testimony and witness of God's favour toward me through his Son Christ, against the subtile assaults of Satan, the world, and the flesh, and against the curse of the law, the sting of death, and the dreadful dart of damnable desperation; wherewith I may be bold at all times to comfort myself against mine enemies even in the midst of all my troubles and temptations.

Why we are baptized.

Father. Of what favour from God is baptism a sign and testimony unto thee? *Son.* Baptism declareth evidently unto me, that God doth so dearly love and favour

The fruit of baptism.

[[2] Folio, *apostle.*]

me, that whereas before I was an heathen, I am now become a Christian; whereas before I was by nature the child of wrath and a very firebrand of hell, I am now the son of God and heir of everlasting glory; where before I was a member of Satan, I am now a member of that holy congregation and body whereof Christ is the head; whereas before I was stuffed full of all sin, yea, I was nothing else but a very lump of sin, both body and soul, I am now cleansed from all sin, delivered from all wickedness, purged from all uncleanness, and adorned with most beautiful amd goodly virtues; Eph. v. as St Paul saith: "Christ loved the congregation, and gave himself for it, to sanctify it, and cleansed it in the fountain of water through the word, to make it unto himself a glorious congregation, without spot or wrinkle or any such thing; but that it Tit. iii. should be holy and without blame." Again: "After that the kindness and love of our Saviour God toward man appeared, not by the deeds of righteousness which we wrought, but according to his mercy he saved us, by the fountain of the new birth, and renewing of the Holy Ghost, which he shed on us abundantly through Jesus Christ our Saviour; that we, justified by his grace, should be made heirs according to the hope of everlasting life."

Father. Camest thou then a sinner unto baptism? *Son*. Yea, and stuffed full Psal. li. of sin, begotten, conceived, brought forth, nourished, and living in sin, and the very Eph. ii. child of wrath by nature.

Father. And art thou delivered from the whole lump of ungodliness at thy baptism? *Son*. Yea, verily.

Mark xvi. *Father*. How provest thou that? *Son*. Christ our Saviour saith: "He that believeth and is baptized, he shall be saved." The citizens of Hierusalem said unto Peter, when he reproved them in his sermon for their wickedness against the Lord Christ, Acts ii. the alone author of our salvation: "What shall we do? Peter said unto them, Repent of your sins, and be baptized every one of you in the name of Jesus Christ for the remission of sins, and ye shall receive the gift of the Holy Ghost." And Ananias Acts xxii. said to Paul: "Why tarriest thou? Arise, and be baptized, and wash away thy sins in calling on the name of the Lord." And we heard before out of the mouth of St Eph. v. Paul, that "Christ hath sanctified and cleansed his congregation in the fountain of water through the word, to make it unto himself a glorious congregation, without spot or wrinkle or any such thing; that it should be holy and without blame." And again 1 Cor. vi. he saith: "Such were you sometime (he meaneth, fornicators, worshippers of images, advouterers, weaklings, thieves, covetous persons, drunkards, cursed speakers, pillers, extortioners, and polluted with all kind of sin); but ye are washed (from these your sins by baptism), but ye are sanctified, but ye are justified, by the name of the Lord Jesus, and by the Spirit of our God."

Father. In baptism then we receive both remission of our sins, and the Holy Ghost. *Son*. Yea, and with the Holy Ghost the fruits also of God's Spirit, which St Paul Gal. v. remembereth in his epistle to the Galatians. And this is it which Christ said to his Acts i. disciples: "John baptized with water, but you shall be baptized with the Holy Ghost." Matt. iii. Mark i. Luke iii. So likewise said John the Baptist: "I baptize you with water unto repentance; but he that shall come after me is mightier than I: he shall baptize you with the Holy Ghost and with fire."

Father. If sin be remitted and forgiven us, yea, and put away in baptism, how cometh it then to pass, that we feel in ourselves such cruel and raging lusts, which without ceasing move and provoke us unto the transgression of God's most holy will? *Son*. That concupiscence is left unto us to be an exercise of our faith, that we should daily labour through [the] Spirit of God to repress it, and by little to quench it, that at the last we may wax perfect in Christ.

James i. *Father*. Doth not that concupiscence condemn us? *Son*. No, verily, except we willingly give over the Spirit of God, and give place to those fleshly lusts, and so fall away from the grace that was given us in our baptism. For not only the gross sins, but also the concupiscence of the flesh is forgiven in baptism; not that it should not be, but that it should not be reckoned to us for sin. For, as St Paul saith: Rom. viii. "There is no damnation to them which are in Christ Jesu, which walk not after the flesh, but after the Spirit. For the law of the Spirit of life through Jesus Christ

hath made me free from the law of sin and death. For what the law could not do, inasmuch as it was weak because of the flesh, that performed God, and sent his Son in the similitude of sinful flesh, and by sin damned sin in the flesh, that the righteousness of the law might be fulfilled in us, which walk not after the flesh, but after the Spirit." So long as we live in this mortal body, we shall find in ourselves a continual strife, yea, a mortal war between the flesh and the Spirit, as St Paul saith:
"The flesh lusteth contrary to the Spirit, and the Spirit contrary to the flesh. These Gal. v.
are contrary one to the other, so that ye cannot do whatsoever ye would." Likewise
saith St Peter: "Dearly beloved, I beseech you as strangers and pilgrims, abstain 1 Pet. ii.
from fleshly lusts, which fight against the soul, and see that ye have honest conversation among the gentiles; that, whereas they backbite you as evil-doers, they may see your good works, and praise God in the day of visitation." And St Paul com-
mandeth us so to frame our lives, that "sin reign not in our mortal bodies, that we Rom. vi.
should thereunto obey by the lusts of it:" again, that we should "not make pro- Rom. xiii.
vision for the flesh, to fulfil the lusts of it."

Father. What other thing doth baptism preach unto thee? *Son*. Baptism doth not only declare unto me, that I am in the favour of God, have obtained remission of all my sins, and that I am the son and heir of God; but also that I am dead unto sin, that I have crucified the old man with his concupiscences and lusts, that I have given over the devil, the world, and the flesh, with all their works, pomps,
vanities, pleasures &c., that I have put off old Adam with all his deeds, and that I Col. iii.
am buried with Christ, so that from henceforth "the world should be crucified unto Rom. vi. Gal. vi.
me, and I unto the world."

Father. How provest thou this? *Son*. St Paul saith: "Know ye not, that all Rom. vi.
we which are baptized into Jesus Christ are baptized to die with him? We are buried then with him by baptism for to die, that likewise as Christ was raised up from death by the glory of the Father, even so we also should walk in a new life. For if we be graft in death like unto him, even so shall we be partakers of the resurrection; knowing this, that our old man is crucified with him also, that the body of sin might utterly be destroyed, that henceforth we should not be servants unto sin. For he that is dead is justified from sin. Wherefore if we be dead with Christ, we believe that we shall also live with him; knowing that Christ being raised from death dieth no more: death hath no more power over him. For as touching that he died, he died concerning sin once; and as touching that he liveth, he liveth unto God. Likewise consider ye also that ye are dead as touching sin, but are alive unto God
through Jesus Christ our Lord." Likewise saith St Peter: "Baptism now saveth us, 1 Pet. iii.
not the putting away of the filthiness of the flesh, but in that a good conscience consenteth to God by the resurrection of Jesus Christ, which is on the right hand of God, and is gone into heaven, angels, powers, and might subdued unto him."

Father. What learnest thou more of thy baptism? *Son*. Baptism preacheth unto me not only the mortification of the flesh, but also the vivification of the Spirit.

Father. What meanest thou? Speak more plainly. *Son*. Baptism teacheth me, that I should not only put off the old man with all his lusts and works, mortify the flesh with all her affects and concupiscences, and utterly die and be buried unto sin;
but also that I should "put on the new man, which is renewed into the knowledge Col. iii.
and image of him that made him, in righteousness and true holiness;" that I should Eph. iv.
"walk in a new life;" that I now, "being delivered from the power of mine enemies, Rom. vi.
should serve the Lord my God in such holiness and righteousness" as are accepted Luke i.
before him, "all the days of my life;" and in fine, so form[1] my life and compose my manners in all points, that it may be garnished with good works and with the fruits
of the Holy Ghost, unto the glory and praise of God. For "how shall we, that are Rom. vi.
dead as touching sin, live any longer therein? We are buried with Christ by baptism for to die (unto sin), that likewise as Christ was raised up from death by the glory
of the Father, even so we also should walk in a new life." "If any man be in Christ, 2 Cor. v.
he is a new creature." "So many as are baptized have put on Christ." Yea, "they Gal. iii. Gal. v.

[[1] The folio reads *in synne, so from.*]

that belong unto Christ have crucified the flesh with the affects and lusts thereof."
Col. iii. "If ye be risen again with Christ," saith St Paul, "seek those things which are above, where Christ sitteth on the right hand of God. Set your affection on heavenly things, and not on earthy things. For you are dead, and your life is hid with Christ in God."

Father. So many therefore as are baptized ought to address themselves unto a new life, and to walk worthy this kindness of God, which they have received in their baptism. *Son.* Yea, verily. For they that are baptized in Christ Jesu have not only remission of all their sins, but they receive also of God the gift of the Holy Ghost, which worketh in them new affects and new motions, yea, and those godly and spiritual, out of the which issueth, through the power of God's Spirit, a virtuous life
Gal. iii. and a christian conversation; so that it is truly said of St Paul: "All ye that are baptized have put on Christ."

What is to put on Christ. *Father.* What is it to put on Christ? *Son.* Not only to clothe ourselves with his saving health, but also to garnish our lives with his godly virtues, which he used
1 Pet. ii. in all his life, when he was in this wretched world, to give us "an ensample that
John xiii. we should follow his steps," as he saith: "I have given you an ensample, that as I
1 John ii. have done, so likewise ye should do." "He that saith that he dwelleth in Christ,"
1 John i. saith St John, "ought to walk as Christ hath walked." Again: "If we say that we have fellowship with God, and walk in darkness, we lie, and do not the truth. But if we walk in light, even as he is in light, then have we fellowship with him,
2 Cor. v. and the blood of Jesus Christ his Son cleanseth us from all sin." "If any man be in Christ," saith St Paul, "he is a new creature." They therefore which have taken on them holy baptism, ought to answer and to live agreeable to their baptism, I mean, to die unto sin, and to live unto righteousness; and not only to clothe themselves with the merits of Christ, embracing him with strong faith as their true and alone Saviour, but also to garnish their life and conversation with the virtues of Christ, that they may be Christ's both in heart, word, and deed.

Gross gospellers. *Father.* What sayest thou then to those Christians, which brag much of Christ and of Christ's gospel, and yet lead a life spotted and defiled with all kind of sin and wickedness? *Son.* These are fallen from the grace which they received in their baptism, and have lost the Holy Ghost, wherewith they were renewed in the fountain of re-
Tit. i. generation; and although "with their mouth they profess God, yet with their deeds they deny him, seeing they are abominable and disobedient, and unapt unto every good work:" neither are such the servants of Christ, though they brag never so much of Christ and of Christ's gospel, but rather bond-slaves of Satan, and miserable captives
Rom. vi. of the world and of the flesh. "Know ye not," saith St Paul, "that to whomsoever ye commit yourselves as servants to obey, his servants ye are to whom ye obey; whether it be of sin unto death, or of obedience unto righteousness?" Likewise saith
2 Pet. ii. St Peter: "Of whom a man is overcome, unto the same is he brought in bondage. For if they (after they have escaped from the filthiness of the world through the knowledge of the Lord and the Saviour Jesu Christ) are yet tangled again therein, and overcome, then is the latter end worse with them than the beginning. For it had been better for them not to have known the way of righteousness, than, after they have known it, to turn from the holy commandment that was given unto them. But the same is happened unto them that is used to be spoken by the true proverb,
Prov. xxvi. The dog is turned to his own vomit again, and the sow that was washed is turned again to her wallowing in the mire."

Gen. xix. These backsliding Christians may justly be compared to Lot's wife, which, after she was delivered out of stinking Sodom, and commanded no more to look back unto it, but with all expedition to fly far from it, looked back again unto Sodom, contrary to the commandment of God, and for her disobedience she was turned into a
Matt. xxi. pillar of salt. They may also be truly resembled unto that son which promised his father to work in his vineyard, and yet wrought nothing at all. They are those
Matt. xxv. foolish virgins which had lamps and no oil; and therefore were they shut out of the
Matt. xxvi. bridegroom's chamber. Yea, they may not without a cause be likened to Judas Iscarioth
Acts viii. the traitor, and to Simon Magus, which both fell away from their profession which
Luke ix. they made at baptism. "No man that putteth his hand to the plough, and

looketh back, is meet for the kingdom of God." "He that continueth unto the end, he shall be saved." "God hath delivered us from the power of our enemies, that we should serve him in holiness and righteousness all the days of our life." "The blood of Christ hath purged our conscience from dead works to serve the living God." "God hath not called us unto uncleanness, but unto holiness." "Be faithful unto the death," saith Christ, "and I will give thee the crown of life." Matt. x. Luke i. Heb. ix. 1 Thess. iv. Rev. ii.

Father. God make us all true Christians both in word and in work! But come off, my child, what thinkest thou of those ceremonies which are used in the pope's church at the ministration of baptism, as salt, oil, cream, spittle, candle, hallowed font, holy water, crossing of the child, chrism, conjuring the devil out of the child, laying the child down upon the ground before the high altar, while the priest read the gospel against the falling sickness, and such like? Dost thou think that these things are necessary unto the administration of baptism? *Son*. I think them neither necessary nor commendable. For they are but the idle inventions of the most idle papists, thrust into the church without the authority of God's word, not garnishing but rather obscuring the dignity of holy baptism. St John the Baptist, Christ and his apostles, and the ancient primitive church knew no such beggarly ceremonies; neither doth the word of God make any mention of them. The more simply and the more agreeably to the institution of Christ the sacraments are ministered, the more doth it please God. In the Acts of the Apostles we read that Philip baptized the eunuch, chamberlain to the queen of Candace. This eunuch did confess Jesus Christ to be the Son of God, which is the sign of our faith, and desired baptism; and Philip, at the next water they came unto, washed him "in the name of the Father, and of the Son, and of the Holy Ghost." Here was neither hallowed font, nor holy water, salt, oil, cream, spittle, candle, or any other point of papistry; and yet I am sure, that no man will deny, but that the manner of baptizing which Philip used here was both good and perfect. And to say truth, it were better that these popish ceremonies were rooted out of the church, than that they should be suffered to continue: for they have been and yet are the occasion of much superstition and false belief. Of ceremonies used at baptism in the pope's church. Acts viii.

Father. It is truly said. For many people at this present day die so superstitious and so far from true belief, that they are fully persuaded, that if any of those ceremonies, whereof we spake tofore, do lack in the ministration of baptism, that the baptism is not perfect, nor the child fully and sufficiently christened. *Son*. Truth it is. And verily it is greatly to be lamented, that such blind popish errors have crept into the church of Christ. These are those tares, which the enemy hath sown in the Lord's field, while the men slept. But "every plant that the heavenly Father hath not planted shall be plucked up by the roots." Matt. xiii. Matt. xv.

Father. Forasmuch as now we entreat of baptism, I would gladly hear thine opinion and learning concerning the baptism of infants. For there wanteth not a swarm of heretics in this our age, which both deny and condemn the baptism of infants, and teach that such as were baptized in their infancy received no profit by their baptism; and that therefore they must be baptized again, when they come to age, and be able to confess their faith. *Son*. These are the anabaptists, whom the devil, that old enemy of mankind, hath raised up now of late to trouble and to disquiet the church of Christ with their most pestilent and schismatical errors and heresies. Of the baptism of infants. Anabaptists.

Father. Is it then lawful to baptize young children in their infancy, and before they be able openly to confess their faith? *Son*. Yea, verily.

Father. How provest thou that? *Son*. When our Saviour Christ sent forth his disciples to convert the world from vain superstition unto true religion, from false gods unto the one and alone living God, he commanded them to baptize all nations generally, excepting no state nor age. Under this general commandment are the infants contained; therefore ought the children also to be baptized. Matt. xxviii.

Father. But the children cannot profess their faith; therefore, say the adversaries, they ought not to be baptized. *Son*. As concerning the profession of faith, that doth God require only of such as are grown up in age, and are already instructed in the mysteries of Christ's religion; of the which sort there were many about the beginning of Christ's church after Christ's ascension, which, after they were taught the gospel, confessed their faith, and so were baptized, as we read in divers places of the holy scripture. But this toucheth not the infants, which as they lack speech, so want they the use of reason, whereby (God assisting them with his grace) they should attain unto the knowledge of God's doctrine and of christian faith; and yet notwithstanding they are not excluded from baptism, but are comprehended under the general commandment of baptizing all nations. For as the infants of the Hebrews were not secluded and put away from circumcision, which was also a sacrament or sign of God's grace, mercy, and favour to the Jews, even as baptism is now to the Christians, although they could not profess their faith, but were commanded of God notwithstanding to be circumcised, and by this outward sign to be received into the congregation of God's people, and so to be counted for the promise sake the sons and heirs of God; even so in like manner ought the infants of the Christians to be admitted unto the sacrament and sign of grace, (I mean baptism,) although they cannot by the reason of their tender age profess their faith; forasmuch as God is now no less the God of the Christians and of their children, than he was in times past the God of the Jews and of their children.

Gen. xvii. For this gracious promise of God, "I will be thy God, and the God of thy seed," appertaineth no less unto us Christians and unto our children, than it belonged heretofore unto the Jews and unto their children. For there is one God both of the believing Jew and of the faithful gentile; neither is there any respect of persons before him. And is it to be thought, that the grace of God is now diminished toward the children of the Christians, and not so plenteous in this time of the new testament, after that the Lord Christ hath taken upon him our nature and clothed himself with our flesh, and all figures and clouds be utterly dispelled and put away, so that now the true light of God's most glorious truth shineth, as it was in the law of Moses? God blessed the children of the Jews even in their mothers' womb, and gave them his holy Spirit, yea, and that before they were born; and is it to be thought, that his hand is now so shortened, that he neither can nor will shew the like merciful kindness to the children of the Christians, whom he hath taken unto him to be his people, yea, to be his sons and heirs of everlasting glory? God envied not the children of the Jews his sacrament and sign of grace, (I mean circumcision,) although they could neither speak nor had the use of reason; and shall we think that he disdaineth that our children should be enabled with his sacrament and sign of grace, (I mean baptism,) now in the new testament?

The children of the old testament were endued with the Holy Ghost even from
Jer. i. their cradles, yea, before they were born, as we read of Jeremy the prophet, and of
Luke i. St John Baptist; and shall we be persuaded that the like mercy is not shewed to our children in the new testament, a time of all grace, favour, mercy, and loving kindness? The children of the old testament, after they had received the Holy Ghost even in their mother's womb, were admitted unto circumcision, yea, and that by the commandment of God; and shall the children of the new testament be barred and shut out from baptism, which have now received the Holy Ghost no less than they did in the old law? The best and the chiefest baptism is given to the infants; and shall we deny them[1] the inferior and baser baptism? God hath baptized them with the Holy Ghost; and shall we disdain to baptize them with water? St Peter saith:
Acts x. "Can any man forbid water, that these should not be baptized, which have received
Rom. viii. the Holy Ghost as well as we?" "They that are led with the Spirit of God," saith St Paul, "are the sons of God." The infants of the Christians are led with the Spirit
Jer. i. of God, as we heard before of the prophet Jeremy and of St John Baptist; and St
Luke i. 1 Cor. vii. Paul likewise calleth the children of the Christians holy and pure: therefore are they the sons of God. Now, if the infants of the Christians be pure and holy and the sons of God, shall any man be so rigorous to take that from them which God hath appointed and ordained for his sons?

God hath instituted baptism as a most certain pledge of his love, mercy, and favour toward his people, and hath commanded it to be received of all that appertain unto him; and shall we, contrary to the commandment and will of God, deny it to the
Matt. xix. Mark x. infants whom Christ commanded to be brought unto him; whom Christ most lov-

[[1] Folio, *then.*]

ingly embraced in his arms; whom Christ most graciously blessed; whom Christ pronounced to belong unto the kingdom of God; whose angels Christ affirmeth to see the face of our heavenly Father? Who seeth not here therefore the madness of those apish anabaptists, which, contrary to the commandment and expressed will of God, forbid baptism to be given unto the infants? Our Saviour Christ saith: "Except a man be born of water and of the Spirit, he cannot enter into the kingdom of God." What other thing then do the anabaptists, by forbidding the water of baptism to be given unto infants, than utterly seclude and put away the young children, so much as in them is, from the inheritance of God's kingdom, and so to become for ever heirs of everlasting damnation? O most damnable sect! O bloody murderers, both of souls and bodies! As they are of the devil their father, so do these wicked anabaptists satisfy the desires of the devil their father, "which was a murderer from the beginning, and abode not in the truth, because there is no truth in him."

Luke xviii. Matt. xviii. John iii. John viii.

Moreover, do we not read that the apostles baptized whole households? and is it to be thought that there were no children among them? If it were lawful at that time to baptize children, is it unlawful now in these our days? If it were then lawful to dedicate young children to God, and to receive them into the church of Christ by baptism, that they might be one body with the elders, and partakers of the same glory, shall it be counted now unlawful? If the apostles of Christ and the primitive church thought it an holy deed and acceptable before the presence of God's majesty to offer their infants by humble prayers and by the administration of holy baptism unto God, obeying the general commandment of Christ to baptize all nations without exception, and trusting on this merciful promise of God, "I will be thy God, and the God of thy seed;" shall we be so far estranged from all sense and feeling of godliness, that through the fleshly, wicked, ungodly, and devilish persuasions of these most fleshly, most wicked, most ungodly, and most devilish anabaptists, we shall cease to do that for the salvation of our infants, which both the apostles of Christ and the primitive church most gladly and most willingly practised?

Acts xvi. 1 Cor. i. Matt. xxviii.

Father. But the anabaptists utterly deny that the apostles of Christ and the primitive church baptized any infants. *Son*. It is an easy thing to deny. But let them prove their denial with the manifest words of the holy scripture, as we have proved our purpose by the authority of the same; and we will gladly give place straightways unto them. If they cannot so do (as I am right well assured they cannot), let them give over their damnable errors, lean to the truth, and come again unto the church of Christ, out of the which there is no salvation. But that children were baptized in the time of the apostles and of the primitive church, not only the holy scriptures, but also the most ancient fathers do testify.

Origen, that ancient father and doctor of Christ's church, which lived in the year of our Lord two hundred and thirty, affirmeth plainly, that the baptism of infants was the doctrine of the apostles, and that to baptize young children was no new invention, but an observation used of the apostles, and by them commended to the church of Christ[2].

Origen. In sext. cap. ad Rom. Lib. v.

St Cyprian, that ancient father and most constant martyr of Christ, which lived about the year of our Lord two hundred and five and fifty, affirmeth plainly the baptism of infants, and saith that the young speechless children ought not to be kept from baptism and grace. Again, whereas a certain priest called Fidus held this opinion, that the infants of the Christians ought not to be baptized before the eighth day, as the children of the Hebrews were not circumcised before the eighth day; St Cyprian, with sixty-six bishops gathered together in a council, consented and agreed that the infants might be baptized at all times, yea, even so soon as they are born, and not of necessity to defer their baptism until the eighth day. For "spiritual circumcision," said he, "ought not to be hindered by carnal circumcision[3]."

Cyprian. Lib. iii. cap. 8. ad Fidum.

[[2] Pro hoc et ecclesia ab apostolis traditionem suscepit, etiam parvulis baptismum dare. Sciebant enim illi quibus mysteriorum secreta commissa sunt divinorum, quod essent in omnibus genuinæ sordes peccati, quæ per aquam et Spiritum ablui deberent.—Orig. Op. Par. 1733-59. In Epist. ad Rom. Lib. v. Tom. IV. p. 565.]

[[3] Quantum vero ad causam infantium pertinet, quos dixisti intra secundum vel tertium diem, quo nati sint, constitutos, baptizari non oportere, et con-

Hierome. Ad Lætam et adversus Pelagian.

St Hierome, that old and learned doctor of Christ's church, which lived about the year of our Lord three hundred and seventy, in divers of his books, both approveth, and proveth with manifest scriptures and grounded reasons, the baptism of infants[1].

Ambrose. De Voc. Gent. Lib. ii. cap. 8.

St Ambrose, that both ancient, learned, and courageous doctor of Christ's church, which lived about the year of our Lord three hundred and threescore, maketh mention also of the baptism of infants, affirming that it ought necessarily to be given also unto young children[2].

Austin. Adversus Donatist. Lib. iv. cap 4.

What shall I speak of St Augustine, which lived also in the time of St Ambrose and of St Hierome? Verily, he is so stout in the defence of the baptism of infants, that he doth not only affirm the baptism of young children to come from the apostles unto us, and not to be enacted and stablished by any council of men, but also, that all infants ought of necessity to be baptized, and that otherwise they are in great danger of their salvation[3].

I pass over the other ancient fathers and doctors both of the Greek and Latin churches, which in all their writings allow the baptism of infants, as a doctrine coming from Christ and his apostles unto us.

Hyginus.

But one thing I may not pass over, how a certain bishop of Rome called Higinus, which lived in the year of our Lord a hundred and eleven, as some write, commanded that infants, when they were brought to be baptized, should have at the least one godfather and godmother[4]: whereby we may also learn, that the baptism of children is no new invention, but an ancient godly custom coming unto us from the apostles, and so from their days unto this time continued in the church of Christ.

Mark xvi.

Father. But the adversaries object and say, that children ought not to be baptized, because they have no faith. For these are the words of Christ: "He that believeth and is baptized shall be saved." Faith, say they, goeth before baptism: if any man therefore putteth baptism before faith, he perverteth the order of Christ's words. Forasmuch therefore as infants and speechless children have not faith, say they, therefore ought they not to be baptized. *Son*. If the adversaries do so greatly rejoice in this one sentence, which you have alleged out of St Mark, what will they say to this sentence written in the gospel of St John, which also are the words of our Saviour Christ?

---

siderandam esse legem circumcisionis antiquæ, ut intra octavum diem eum qui natus est baptizandum et sanctificandum non putares; longe aliud in concilio nostro omnibus visum est...neminem putamus a gratia consequenda impediendum esse...nec spiritalem circumcisionem impediri carnali circumcisione debere...Porro autem, si etiam gravissimis delictoribus et in Deum multum ante peccantibus, cum postea crediderint, remissa peccatorum datur, et baptismo atque a gratia nemo prohibetur; quanto magis prohiberi non debet infans, qui recens natus nihil peccavit, nisi quod secundum Adam carnaliter natus contagium mortis antiquæ prima nativitate contraxit?—Cypr. Op. Oxon. 1682. Epist. lxiv. Ad Fidum. pp. 158-161.]

[1 Hoc unum dicam, ut tandem finiatur oratio: aut novum vos debere symbolum tradere, ut post Patrem et Filium et Spiritum Sanctum baptizetis infantes in regnum cœlorum; aut unum et in parvulis et in magnis habetis baptisma, etiam infantes in remissionem peccatorum baptizandos in similitudinem prævaricationis Adam.—Hieron. Op. 1693–1706. Lib. III. Dial. adv. Pelag. Tom. IV. Pars II. col. 546. Jerome is here summing up his argument against the Pelagians, who, though they allowed infant baptism, yet denied that it was for the remission of sins.]

[2 Ambros. Op. Par. 1614. Tom. IV. cols. 545-7. The chapter referred to is headed: Quare tanta multitudo non regeneratorum infantium a perpetua alienetur salute. The necessity of infant baptism is of course implied.]

[3 Nullus Christianorum dixerit eos [parvulos] inaniter baptizari. Et si quisquam in hac re auctoritatem divinam quærat, quamquam quod universa tenet ecclesia, nec conciliis institutum, sed semper retentum est, non nisi auctoritate apostolica traditum rectissime creditur; tamen veraciter conjicere possumus, quid valeat in parvulis baptismi sacramentum, ex circumcisione carnis.—August. Op. Par. 1679—1700. De Bapt. cont. Donatist. Lib. IV. 30, 1. Tom. IX. col. 140.]

[4 It is possible that the following ascribed to Hyginus may be the decree intended: In catechismo et in baptismo et in confirmatione unus patrinus fieri potest, si necessitas cogat.—Hygin. Papæ Decr. in Concil. Collect. Par. 1644. Tom. I. p. 220. Or perhaps the following, which stands next below it in Gratian, may have been confounded with it: Non plures ad suscipiendum de baptismo infantem accedant, quam unus sive vir, sive mulier.—Ex Decr. Leon. Papæ in Decret. Gratiani, Par. 1583. Decr. Tert. Pars, De Consecr. Dist. IV. can. 101. cols. 2481, 2. See however Polyd. Verg. de Rer. Invent. Lib. IV. c. iv. p. 306, Basil. 1570. Iginius Romanus pontifex statuit, ut unus, quem compatrem vocant, uti testis interesset.—The date of Hyginus is generally placed later than that assigned in the text.]

Father. What words are those? *Son.* "Verily, verily I say unto thee, Except John iii. a man be born of water and of the Spirit, he cannot enter into the kingdom of God." Here is mention made, first of water, and afterward of the Spirit. Hereof then may we gather, that children may be baptized before they have faith. For water is put here before the Spirit, which Spirit, (I mean the Holy Ghost,) is the author and giver of faith. If baptism may be ministered to the speechless children before they believe, then do the anabaptists plain wrong to the infants, when they deny them baptism. And look what authority the wicked anabaptists may deny baptism to the infants by the virtue of this text, "He that believeth and is baptized shall be saved;" even with Mark xvi. the same authority will we grant baptism to the infants by the virtue of this text, "Verily, verily I say unto thee, Except a man be born of water and of the Spirit, John iii. he cannot enter into the kingdom of God."

Father. How then is that text, which the adversaries allege out of St Mark, Mark xvi. to be understand, which mentioneth faith before baptism, as though no man ought to be baptized before he believeth? *Son.* It may be answered two manner of ways.

First, we shall consider what goeth before. Thus writeth the evangelist: "Go ye into all the world, and preach the gospel to every creature. He that believeth and is baptized shall be saved: but he that believeth not shall be damned." Here our Saviour Christ gave commandment to his apostles to preach the gospel to all reasonable creatures. Now if any that heard the preaching of the gospel (I speak of them which through their age had the use of reason) believed the doctrine of the gospel preached unto them, he commanded that they should be baptized, in token that they were of the household of God, and inheritors of everlasting glory. For when the apostles began first to preach the gospel, their hearers were for the most part heathen, and ignorant both of God and of his godly mysteries; and therefore so many as believed the doctrine of the apostles, and desired to be recounted among the Christians, first confessed their sins, afterward protested their faith, and so consequently they were admitted unto holy baptism. Thus see we, that faith went before baptism, according to the saying of Christ,—I mean in them that had the use of reason, and were able to confess their faith.

Another way it may be answered thus: Infants and speechless children have faith; therefore they also ought to be baptized, that they may be saved, according unto Christ's saying: "He that believeth and is baptized shall be saved." So that this Mark xvi. sentence of our Saviour Christ, which the ungodly anabaptists wrest and wring for the condemnation of the baptism of infants, make nothing for them, but rather stablisheth the baptism of young children against them and against their most devilish doctrine.

Father. What, hath infants faith? St Paul saith: "Faith cometh by hearing, Of the faith of infants. and hearing cometh by the word of God." How can infants have faith, when they Rom. x. understand not the preaching of God's word? *Son.* Whether infants have faith or no (I speak of the infants which are the children of the Christians), we shall afterward consider. But I will first answer to the words of St Paul. It is truth that "faith cometh by hearing." But this is to be understand of such as have age, and are endued with reason, and can discern good from evil. The ordinary way, which God useth to call such unto faith, is the preaching of his holy word, as we may see throughout the holy scripture. God saith by the psalmograph: "A people whom I Psal. xviii. knew not have served me: through the hearing of the ear they obeyed me." And the psalmograph himself saith: "I will teach the wicked thy ways, and the ungodly Psal. li. shall turn unto thee." So likewise read we that, when the apostles preached the gospel of Christ among the heathen, "so many as were tofore appointed unto ever- Acts xiii. lasting life believed," and with great joy received the doctrine of the gospel; so that "faith cometh by hearing, and hearing cometh by the word of God," as God saith by the prophet: "Like as the rain and snow cometh down from heaven, and returneth Isai. lv. not thither again, but watereth the earth, maketh it fruitful and green, that it may give corn to the sower and bread to him that eateth; so the word also that cometh out of my mouth shall not turn void again unto me, but shall accomplish my will, and prosper in the thing whereto I send it." For, although God is able by his holy

Spirit to turn the hearts of all men, to plant faith in the minds of all men, and to
John xvii. bring all men unto the knowledge of him and of his Son Christ Jesu, which knowledge bringeth everlasting life; as he is able to feed the whole world without meat,
Matt. iv. Luke iv. drink, or bread, as our Saviour Christ saith, "Man shall not live with bread alone, but with every word that cometh out of the mouth of God:" yet, as his ordinary way to feed his creatures is to give them corporal sustenance, so likewise to plant faith and true religion in the hearts of men his ordinary way is the preaching of his
Rom. i. holy word; so that it is not without a cause said of St Paul: "I am not ashamed of the gospel of Christ; for it is the power of God unto salvation to every one that believeth."

God was able to have converted all, both Jews and gentiles, without the preaching of any man, unto the faith: notwithstanding in the old law to turn the Jews he sent his prophets, priests, and Levites to preach unto them; and in the new law to turn both the Jews and gentiles he sent his apostles, that by this means they might believe and be saved. God was able to have converted the city of Corinth without Paul's preaching: notwithstanding he used his ordinary mean to call them unto the faith, and
Acts xviii. therefore said unto Paul: "Fear not, but speak, and hold not thy peace; for I have much people in this city." The like examples find we in other places of the holy
Acts viii. Acts ix. Acts x. scripture, as of Philip and the chamberlain, of Saul and Ananias, of Peter and Cornelius, &c.

The ordinary way to call such as are grown up in age, and have the use of reason, unto faith and unto the true knowledge of God, is the preaching of God's word, as
Rom. x. St Paul saith: "Faith cometh by hearing, and hearing cometh by the word of God."
Psal. cxix. And as the psalmograph saith: "The declaration of thy word, O Lord, giveth light,
Psal. xix. and openeth understanding to the little ones." Again: "The law of the Lord turneth souls, giveth wisdom to the humble, maketh merry the hearts, lighteneth the eyes,.... and is worthy more to be desired than gold and precious stone; yea, it is sweeter than the honey and the honey-comb."

Father. But this ordinary way useth not God toward the infants, which have neither speech nor use of reason, to bring them unto the faith. *Son*. No, verily.

Faith is the work of God. *Father*. How then do they obtain faith? *Son*. By the Holy Ghost. For true and christian faith is the work and fruit of the Holy Ghost; without whose divine inspiration all the preaching in the world cannot bring faith to a man, as St Paul
1 Cor. iii. saith: "Neither he that planteth, nor he that watereth is any thing; but God which
John vi. giveth the increase." And our Saviour Christ saith: "This is the work of God, that ye believe in him whom he hath sent." Again: "No man can come unto me, except
Isai. liv. Jer. xxxi. Phil. i. my Father draweth him." "It is written in the prophets, All shall be taught of God." And St Paul, writing to the Philippians, saith: "It is given to you, not only that ye should believe in him, but also that ye should suffer for him." Likewise writeth
Acts xvi. St Luke of a certain woman called Lydia, "whose heart," saith he, "the Lord opened, that she attended to the things which Paul spake."

Father. I grant that faith is the great and singular gift of God. But how canst thou prove, that the infants and speechless children have this gift of faith in them?
Heb. xi. *Son*. St Paul saith: "Without faith it is impossible to please God." But children do please God. Therefore children have faith.

Father. The first part of thine argument I cannot deny. But how provest thou the second part, I mean, that children please God? *Son*. By the histories of the sacred bible, in the which we read that Jacob, Jeremy the prophet, John Baptist, and such like, pleased God.

Mal. i. *Father*. What saith the scripture of Jacob? *Son*. God himself saith thus: "I have loved Jacob, and hated Esau." Of Jeremy the prophet God speaketh thus:
Jer. i. "Before I fashioned thee in thy mother's womb, I did know thee. (That is to say, I favoured and loved thee.) And or ever thou wast born, I sanctified thee." Of John Baptist the angel of the Lord spake unto Zacharias the priest his father on this manner:
Luke i. "He shall be filled with the Holy Ghost, even from his mother's womb." Blessed Luke also writeth that, when Elizabeth, John's mother, the priest's wife, heard the salutation of Mary, "the babe sprung in her womb." And Elizabeth herself said unto

Mary her cousin, Christ's mother: "Behold, as soon as the voice of thy salutation sounded in my ears, the babe sprung in my womb for joy." St Mark also telleth in his evangelical history, how Christ "rebuked them that forbade the children to come unto him," and commanded that they should come unto him; again, how "he took the children in his arms, laid his hands upon them, and blessed them." Are not all these things manifest signs and evident tokens of Christ's dear love toward children? If he commanded the children to come unto him, if he embraced them in his arms, if he blessed them, is it not a good argument that they pleased him? If they pleased him, then doth it consequently follow, that they were not without faith: for "without faith it is impossible to please God," saith St Paul; and "whatsoever is not of faith is sin." Who doubteth now of the faith of infants? If they have faith, with what forehead dare the impudent anabaptists deny infants their baptism, and recount them in the number of the unfaithful? Moreover, how can the infants be without faith, when they have the Holy Ghost? Dwelleth the Holy Ghost in the hearts of the unfaithful? "What fellowship hath righteousness with unrighteousness? Or what company hath light with darkness? Or what concord hath Christ with Belial?"

Mark x. Heb. xi. Rom. xiv. 2 Cor. vi.

Father. How provest thou that children have the Holy Ghost? *Son.* St Paul saith: "If any man have not the Spirit of Christ, he is none of God's." But children are God's, and dearly beloved of God, as we have tofore heard. Therefore children have the Spirit of Christ.

Rom. viii.

The histories also of Jacob, of Jeremy the prophet, of John Baptist, &c., whereof we spake before, declare evidently that children have the Holy Ghost. We read that God loved Jacob, yea, and that before he was born. But God loveth none that hath not his Spirit, as we heard before out of St Paul. It therefore followeth, that Jacob had the Spirit of God, yea, and that before he was born. Of Jeremy the prophet the scripture saith, that before he was fashioned in his mother's womb, God knew him, that is to say, favoured and loved him; again, or that ever he was born, God sanctified him. Wherewith was Jeremy sanctified, but by the Holy Ghost and faith? So doth it then follow, that Jeremy had both the Holy Ghost and faith. Of John Baptist we read, that he was filled with the Holy Ghost even from his mother's womb; again, that, being in his mother's womb, he sprung for joy so soon as Mary the mother of Christ saluted his mother Elizabeth, rejoicing without all doubt that the time of grace was come, wherein Christ the Saviour of the world, so oft promised and so long looked for, should be born, unto the great comfort of all people. Thus see we that infants also have the Holy Ghost, as these aforesaid ensamples of Jacob, of Jeremy, of John Baptist, &c., do manifestly declare.

Gen. xxv. Rom. ix. Mal. i. Rom. viii. Jer. i. Luke i.

Furthermore, God himself saith by the prophet Joel: "I will pour out of my Spirit upon all flesh; and your sons and your daughters shall prophesy, and your young men shall see visions," &c. Now if the infants have the Spirit of God, as it is already proved by the holy scripture, then are they also the sons of God, as St Paul saith: "They that are led with the Spirit of God are the sons of God. If they be sons, then are they also heirs; the heirs, I mean, of God, and heirs annexed with Christ." Again, St Paul calleth them holy, and our Saviour Christ pronounceth them to pertain unto the kingdom of heaven; and God himself saith, that he will be their God, that is to say, their Saviour and mighty defender. If young children then be favoured of God, sanctified in their mother's womb, have the Holy Ghost, be endued with faith, are the sons and heirs of God, are holy, belong unto the kingdom of heaven, have God their Saviour and mighty defender, &c.; how can baptism be justly denied them, seeing that baptism appertaineth unto the people of God, whereof the children are not the lessest part? For God himself numbereth the young infants among his people. "I will be their God," saith he, "and the God of thy seed." And the prophet Joel saith: "Call the congregation, and gather the people together, warn the congregation, gather the elders, bring the children and sucklings together," &c.

Joel ii. Acts ii. Rom. viii. 1 Cor. vii. Matt. xix. Mark x. Gen. xvii. Gen. xvii. Joel ii.

Father. But the adversaries object and say, We see no fruits of faith in the infants, neither in word or in work; therefore we may right well doubt of their faith, yea, we may conclude that they have no faith. *Son.* That the infants have faith, we have tofore heard. Now, whereas the adversaries say, that the infants shew no fruits of faith, and therefore they have no faith; this is no good argument. St Paul (who knoweth not?) was a diligent preacher of the Lord's word, and had a strong faith in Christ. Shall we notwithstanding say, that when St Paul after his great and unrestful labours gave himself to rest, and to the quietness of sweet sleep for the comfort of his wearied body, and for the recovery of his wasted strengths, and ceased to preach, to pray, to make provision for the poor, &c., he had no faith? Faith without all doubt remained in St Paul being asleep, although he brought not forth the works and fruits of faith. Even so likewise dwelleth faith in children through the secret ministry of the Holy Ghost, although they be not yet come unto the time of declaring of faith by their works. And God, which kept the faith of St Paul, when he was at rest, doth also keep and nourish the treasure of faith in the young ones by his holy Spirit, until the time come of bringing forth the fruits of faith; and in the mean time they are counted faithful before God. Is there any man so fond or so foolish, that will call a young gryft[1] of the first year's gryfting fruitless and barren, when as it cannot for lack of time and age bring forth as yet any fruit? If we cannot call a tree unfruitful, until the time come of bringing forth of fruit; so ought we not to call a child unbelieving and faithless, until he come unto the time of declaring his faith. As a child both is and also may be called a reasonable creature, although for lack of time and age he cannot use reason; so likewise may a child have faith and be called faithful, although for lack of time and age it can shew as yet no good works, which are the tokens and fruits of faith. A Christian in the holy scripture is resembled, compared, and likened to "a tree planted by the rivers' side, that will bring forth his fruit in due season," or as some read, "in his time." "The kingdom of God," saith our Saviour Christ, "is even as if a man should sow seed in the ground, and should sleep; and notwithstanding it riseth up night and day, and the seed springeth and groweth up while he is not aware." What can be more plainly spoken against the wisdom of man's reason, than that Christ saith here? Reason cannot see how infants can have faith and believe. But of these words of Christ we learn, that faith, even when we know not, yea, when we are asleep, groweth and increaseth in us; so that every faithful Christian may say, "I sleep, and yet my heart watcheth."

Psal. i. Mark iv. Cant. v.

Father. Thou holdest then, that the infants of the Christians have both the Holy Ghost and faith; and that therefore they ought of right to be baptized according to the commandment of Christ, and the practice of the primitive church. *Son*. Yea, verily.

Father. What sayest thou of the infants of the heathen and unbelieving? *Son*. Forasmuch as they belong not unto the household of faith, neither are contained in this covenant, "I will be thy God, and the God of thy seed;" again, "I will pour out my Spirit upon thy seed, and my blessing upon thy buds;" therefore I leave them to the judgment of God, to whom they either stand or fall. With the children of the faithful God hath made a sure and an everlasting covenant, that he will be their God and Saviour, yea, their most loving Father, and take them for his sons and heirs, as St Peter saith: "The promise was made to you and to your children."

Gen. xvii. Isai. xliv. Rom. xiv. Acts ii.

Of children dying without baptism.

Father. Hitherto thou hast right well set forth the baptism of infants, confirming the same both by the holy scriptures, and by the testimonies of the ancient fathers of Christ's church; as I may speak nothing of thy answers to the objections of the anabaptists, wherewith they go about to impugn the baptism of infants. But now, come off, and tell me what thou thinkest of those children of the Christians, which, prevented with death, come not unto baptism, but depart unbaptized. Judgest thou them damned or saved? Let me hear thine opinion in this behalf. *Son*. I know how hard and rigorous divers fathers of Christ's church are to such infants as die without baptism, whose names I pass over with silence. And although I reverence both them and their writings, yet their judgment in this behalf I can by no means allow; forasmuch (so far as I have learned) it is not only injurious to the grace of God, but also it utterly dissenteth from the verity of God's word, which we all are bound to defend

[[1] Gryft: graft.]

against all men, and all men's inventions, that the victory may be God's and his Son Christ's; yea, that "God may be true, and all men liars." John iii. viii. Psal. cxvi. Rom. iii.

Father. How provest thou that the doctrine which generally condemneth all that die without baptism is injurious to the grace of God? *Son.* First, I here protest that, as you have already heard, I utterly abhor and detest, I wholly contemn and condemn the wicked doctrine of the anabaptists, which deny the baptism of infants, as a thing unprofitably used in the church of Christ; and I believe with my heart, and confess with my mouth, that baptism is an holy sacrament, and a most certain sign of God's grace, favour, and mercy toward the faithful, instituted of the Lord Jesu to be frequented and used in his church, and reverently to be received of all degrees and estates, of whatsoever age they are; so that whosoever may have convenient time to be baptized, and yet refuse to take that holy sacrament, and willingly reject and cast away baptism, as I believe them not to be led with the Spirit of God, but with the spirit of error, not with the Spirit of Christ, but with the spirit of antichrist; so likewise I am fully persuaded that they have no portion in the inheritance of God's kingdom. And this also do I speak of all such parents as will not suffer their children to be baptized, being infected with the pestiferous plague of anabaptism. Notwithstanding this protestation, I plainly confess, that I neither do nor can allow the doctrine of them which generally condemn all such, and seclude them from the kingdom of God, that die without the baptism of water, whether they be infants or of a more ripe age. For, as I said before, this doctrine is not only injurious to the grace of God, but also it utterly dissenteth from the verity of God's word.

The protestation of the author concerning the baptism of infants.

Father. Let me hear it proved that this doctrine is injurious to the grace of God. *Son.* The holy scripture in every place attributeth our salvation to the free grace of God, and not either to our own works, or to any outward sign or sacrament. St Paul saith: "There is [no] difference; for all have sinned, and have need of the glory of God; but are justified freely by his grace through the redemption that is in Christ Jesu, whom God hath set forth to be the obtainer of mercy through faith by the means of his blood, to declare his righteousness in that he forgiveth the sins that are passed, which God did suffer, to shew at his time his righteousness; that he might be counted righteous, and the righteous-maker of him which believeth on Jesus." Again: "If (our salvation) be of grace, then is it not now of works; for then grace is no more grace. But if it be of works, then is it now no grace." Also in another place: "By grace are ye saved through faith, and that not of yourselves. It is the gift of God, and cometh not of works, lest any man should boast himself." Item: "Not by the deeds of righteousness which we wrought, but according to his mercy he saved us." St Peter also saith: "We believe that we shall be saved by the grace of our Lord Jesus Christ." Once again, St Paul saith: "God hath saved us, and called us with an holy calling, not according to our deeds, but according to his own purpose and grace, which was given us through Christ Jesu before the world began." And in another place he saith: "By the grace of God I am that I am." Here the blessed apostle granteth that whatsoever he is, or whatsoever he hath that is good, appertaining unto body or soul, whether it be his election, vocation, creation, reparation, justification, glorification, &c., it cometh altogether of the free grace of God.

Rom. iii. Rom. xi. Eph. ii. Tit. iii. Acts xv. 2 Tim. i. 1 Cor. xv.

If our election, vocation, creation, reparation, justification, glorification, and whatsoever maketh unto the salvation either of body or soul, come of the free grace and mere mercy of God, is it not injurious to the grace and kindness of the Lord our God, so to embrace it, that without the help of an external sign and outward ceremony it cannot save us? Hath God so bound and made himself thrall to a sacrament, that without it his power of saving is lame, and of no force to defend from damnation? Rom. viii.

In the old testament it was not lawful to circumcise the male children of the Hebrews before the eighth day: who doubteth but that many of their infants died before that time, and so departed without circumcision? Shall we now say that all those children perished and were damned? Where is then this promise of God become? "I will be thy God, and the God of thy seed." God saved not the Jews and their children for the circumcision sake, but for his gracious and merciful promise sake. "For he is not a Jew," as St Paul saith, "which is a Jew outward; neither is it

Gen. xvii Rom. ii.

circumcision, which is outward in the flesh. But he is a Jew, which is hid within; and the circumcision of the heart is the true circumcision, which consisteth in the Gal. v. spirit, and not in the letter; whose praise is not of men, but of God." Again: "In Christ Jesu neither is circumcision any thing worth, neither yet uncircumcision; but 1 Cor. vii. faith, which worketh by love." Once again: "Circumcision is nothing, and uncircumcision is nothing, but the keeping of God's commandments."

Deut. x. Jer. iv. Acts vii. For this cause the holy scripture calleth the disobedient and ungodly Jews "uncircumcised," and exhorteth them to circumcise the heart, and to mortify their carnal affects, which fight against the soul, and to become new men in their life and con- Phil. iii. versation, which is the true circumcision, and not the cutting away of the foreskin. "We Col. ii. are the circumcision," saith St Paul, "which serve God in the spirit." Again: "By Christ are ye circumcised with circumcision which is done without hands; forasmuch as ye have put off the sinful body of the flesh through the circumcision that is in Christ, in that ye are buried with him through baptism, in whom ye are also risen again through faith, that is wrought by the operation of God, which raised him from death."

Hereof then doth it follow, that if God saved not the fathers of the old testament ☞ for circumcision, but for his gracious and merciful promise; again, if God received unto his glory the children of the Hebrews, before they were comprehended in the covenant which God made with their fathers, although they died uncircumcised; neither doth he save us for the outward baptism, which is the washing of the body by water, but for his gracious promise: again, that he will receive the children of the Chistians, because they be members of his church, unto everlasting life, though it so chance that they die without baptism. For it is not to be thought that God will deal less mercifully with the Christians, and with their children, than he did with the Isai. l. fathers, and with their infants, in the time of the old testament. The hand and mighty power of God is not so shortened, that it cannot now also help: neither is his ear so stopped, that it cannot now hear. He is a saving God at all times alike.

And, moreover, look of what price and dignity baptism is now with us Christians; even of the same price and dignity was circumcision with the Jews, into whose place baptism hath succeeded. And look of what necessity baptism is required now of us Christians; even of the very same necessity was circumcision required of the fathers in Note. the old testament. But God by his grace, for his merciful promise sake, saved the infants of the Hebrews, although they departed before the eighth day, and so were uncircumcised: in like manner God by his grace, for his merciful promise sake, saveth the young children of the Christians, although by the providence of God they are taken away from this life before they be baptized.

St Paul calleth circumcision not the self righteousness, or the righteous-making, but Rom. iv. "a seal of righteousness." And to declare that righteousness, that is to say, forgiveness of sins, salvation, and everlasting life cometh not of any outward sign, sacrament, ceremony, or work, but of the free grace of God through faith, the blessed apostle St Paul expresseth with manifest words that Abraham was justified and accepted for righteous before God through faith, before he was circumcised. His words are these: Rom. iv. Gen. xv. "We say that faith was reckoned to Abraham for righteousness. How was it then reckoned? when he was in the circumcision, or when he was in the uncircumcision? Not in the time of circumcision, but when he was yet uncircumcised. And he received the sign of circumcision, as a seal of the righteousness of faith, which he had yet being uncircumcised, that he should be the father of all them that believe, though they be not circumcised, that righteousness might be imputed to them also; and that he might be the father of circumcision, not unto them only which came of the circumcised, but unto them also that walk in the steps of the faith that was in our father Abraham before the time of circumcision. For the promise, that he should be the heir of the world, happened not to Abraham or to his seed through the law, but through the righteousness of faith. For if they which are of the law be heirs, then is faith but vain, and the promise of none effect."

Forasmuch therefore as baptism is unto the Christians even the very same in effect that circumcision was to the Jews, I mean, not the self righteousness, or righteous-making, but only "a seal of righteousness," and a sign or token of God's favour toward us, (for the outward baptism doth neither give us the Spirit of God, neither yet grace, that is to say, the favour of God, by any power or influence that it hath; otherwise should it come to pass, that whosoever were baptized, although he were an infidel and utterly without faith, should receive this precious gift, that is, the Spirit and grace of God, which is not so;) it followeth, that not the outward washing in water saveth us, but the free grace and mere mercy of God. And as the enjoining[1] of this outward baptism doth not save, so likewise the wanting of it (if it be not contemned of any man that is grown up in age, but he would gladly have it, if he might obtain it; as many holy martyrs in times past, prevented by death through the cruelty of tyrants, died without baptism of water, being indeed baptized inwardly with the Holy Ghost, and outwardly with their own blood; or if an infant of the Christian taken away by death, either before the birth, or in the birth, or immediately after the birth, should depart before the baptism of water can be ministered unto the child) doth not condemn.

This considered St Peter right well, when he wrote on this manner: "Baptism now saveth us, not the putting away of the filthiness of the flesh, but in that a good conscience consenteth to God, by the resurrection of Jesus Christ, which is on the right hand of God, and is gone into heaven, angels, power, and might subdued unto him." 1 Pet. iii.

Hereof then may we truly conclude, that, forasmuch as the outward baptism, which is done by water, neither giveth the Holy Ghost, nor the grace of God, but only is a sign and token thereof; if any of the christian infants, prevented by death, depart without baptism (necessity so compelling), they are not damned, but be saved by the free grace of God; forasmuch as we tofore heard, they be contained in the covenant of grace, they be members of God's church, God promiseth to be their God, they have faith, and be endued with the Spirit of God, and so finally "sons and heirs of God, and heirs annexed with Christ Jesu." Rom. viii.

Who seeth not now, that the doctrine which generally condemneth all such, be they young or old, that die without the baptism of water, is injurious to the grace of God, whereby alone we be saved? For if the baptism of water saveth either in part or in whole, so resteth not all our salvation only and alone in the free grace of God, neither is God a perfect and sufficient Saviour. But as God in the old law saved many both young and old, which were never circumcised; so likewise it is not to be doubted, but many also in this time of grace, both young and old, God saveth, although, prevented by death, and not of any contempt, they die unbaptized, seeing God is as merciful unto us, which are of the spiritual Israel, as he was unto carnal Israel. For as St Paul saith: "They are not all Israelites, which are of Israel; neither are they all children straightways, that are the seed of Abraham. They which are the children of the flesh are not the children of God; but they which be the children of promise are counted the seed," &c. Rom. ix.

The difference between the sacraments of the old and new law.

Father. I have heard some say, that there is great difference between the sacraments of the old law, and the sacraments of the new law. *Son.* It is truth. For the Jews had circumcision, in whose place the Christians have baptism. The Jews had the paschal lamb, in whose stead the Christians have the Lord's supper. The Jews' sacraments prefigured and tofore taught Christ to come. The sacraments of the Christians do plainly declare and shew unto us that Christ is come, and hath perfectly fulfilled whatsoever was written of him in the law, in the psalms, and in the prophets. The Jews' sacraments had specially in outward appearance promises of corporal benefits annexed unto them: the sacraments of the Christians have adjoined unto them promises of spiritual and heavenly benefits, as the grace, favour, and mercy of God, remission of sins, the gift of the Holy Ghost, quietness of conscience, and the assurance of everlasting life. The sacraments of the old testament only appertained unto the nation of the Jews; but the sacraments of the new testament belong both unto the Jew and unto the gentile, yea, unto the whole world, even unto so many as turn from idolatry unto the true worshipping of that one and alone living God, and with sure faith embrace the gospel of our Saviour Jesus Christ.

[[1] Perhaps *enjoying*.]

Father. My meaning is this. The sacraments of the old law were only signs and tokens of God's grace and favour to the Jews; but the sacraments of the new testament, as I have heard say, are not only signs and tokens, notes and marks, testimonies and seals of God's grace, but they also give grace to such as receive them. *Son.* This your hearsay hath sounded no truth in your ears. For this doctrine is contrary to the word of God, brought lately into the church by the papists, and is greatly injurious both to the grace of God, and to the blood of Christ, and also to the dignity of faith. If our sacraments, which of themselves are nothing else than (as St Paul termeth them) the "seals of righteousness," or of our righteous-making by faith, and witnesses of God's favour toward us, were of such virtue, that they could give grace, that is, the favour of God, remission of sins, justification, the Holy Ghost, everlasting life, &c. by the work wrought, as they say, or by any power that remaineth in the outward signs; so should it follow, that our justification depend not only of the free grace of God, but of works; which is most false: "If it be of grace," as St Paul witnesseth, "then is it not now of works: for then grace is no more grace." Again: "By grace are ye saved through faith, and that not of yourselves; it is the gift of God, and cometh not of works, lest any man should boast himself." Also in another place: "Not by the works of righteousness which we wrought, but according to his mercy he saved us, &c., that we, justified by his grace, should be made heirs according to hope of everlasting life."

Sacraments of themselves give not grace.

Rom. iv.

Rom. xi.

Eph. ii.

Tit. iii.

If sacraments of themselves, by any power or influence that is in them, could give grace and the Spirit of God, then should Simon Magus and Judas the traitor have been endued with the grace and Spirit of God; which is most false. For although Simon Magus, the filthy sorcerer and dissembling hypocrite, received the outward sign of baptism, (I mean water,) as a great number of false Christians likewise have done; yet received he neither the grace nor the Spirit of God, as both divine and human histories declare. Likewise Judas the traitor received the sacrament of Christ's body and blood with the other disciples, (I mean the bread and the wine,) yet received he neither the Spirit nor the grace of God, but the devil and damnation, as the holy scriptures bear witness. Are not these also the words of the apostle, concerning all such as unworthily come unto the holy communion of the body and blood of the Lord? "Let a man examine himself, and so let him eat of the bread and drink of the cup. For he that eateth and drinketh unworthily eateth and drinketh his own damnation." And as concerning the outward baptism of water, saith not St Peter on this manner? "Baptism saveth us now, not the putting away of the filthiness of the flesh, but in that a good conscience consenteth to God, by the resurrection of Jesus Christ."

Acts viii.

John vi. John xiii.

John xvii.

1 Cor. xi.

1 Pet. iii.

Who seeth not now evidently by the testimonies of these two apostles, that the outward sacraments of themselves give not grace, justify not, neither bring the Holy Ghost, which only are the works of the Almighty God? "I baptize you with water unto repentance," saith St John; "but he that shall come after me (he speaketh of Christ) shall baptize you with the Holy Ghost and with fire." Of these words of the holy Baptist, it is manifest that washing with water bringeth not the Holy Ghost, but it is the gift of God.

Matt. iii. Mark i. Luke iii.

Man baptizeth with water; but God baptizeth with his Spirit and grace. Without the inward baptism of the Holy Ghost, the outward baptism of the water profiteth nothing, as St Austin saith: "Moses sanctifieth not for the Lord, but Moses with invisible sacraments through his ministry, and the Lord with invisible grace through the Holy Ghost sanctifieth; where is the whole fruit also of the visible sacraments. ☞ For without this sanctifying of the invisible grace what do the visible sacraments profit?" And afterward in the same place he sheweth, that the invisible sanctifying may both be present and also profit without the visible sign, as in the thief; and again, that the visible sign without the invisible sanctifying may be present and profit nothing, as in Simon Magus[1]. Again he saith: "The Lord hath granted to many

Lib. Quæst. 3. quæst. 83.

Luke xxiii.

Acts viii. In Scal. Parad. cap. 3.

[[1] Quomodo ergo et Moyses sanctificat et Dominus? Non enim Moyses pro Domino; sed Moyses visibilibus sacramentis per ministerium suum, Dominus autem invisibili gratia per Spiritum sanctum, ubi est totus fructus etiam visibilium sacramentorum. Nam sine ista sanctificatione invisibilis gratiæ visibilia

the office of baptizing; but the power and authority in baptism to forgive sins hath he retained to himself alone[2]."

St Ambrose also saith: "To forgive sins (in baptism), and to give the Holy Ghost, is the office of God alone. If God therefore give the effect of health, there is no glory of man in this behalf. For we know that the Holy Ghost was given of God without laying on of hands, and that he, which was not baptized, obtained remission of sins[3]." In 1 Cor. cap. 3. Acts x.

Friar Bonaventure, a writer numbered among the school doctors, and canonized of the pope for a saint, writeth on this manner: "It is by no means to be said, that grace is contained in the sacraments essentially, as water in a vessel, or medicine in a box; yea, thus to think is erroneous. But the sacraments are said to contain grace, because they signify it, and because, except there be a default of the receiver's part, in them grace is always given; yet so understanding the matter, that grace is in the soul, and not in the visible signs: in consideration whereof they are called the vessels of grace. They may also be called vessels in another respect. For as that which is in the vessel is not of it, nor of the substance thereof, but yet is drawn from it; so likewise grace is not of the sacraments, nor out of the sacraments, but it springeth from the everlasting fountain, and is drawn from that of the very soul in the sacraments[4]". In iv. Lib. Sentent. dist. 1. quæst. 3.

Another friar, called Franciscus Maronis, hath these words also: "If the very sacraments by their own virtue should cause grace, then such ministers as minister the sacraments should give the Holy Ghost"[5]. In iv. Lib. Sentent.

Who seeth not, that the sacraments by themselves and by their own power do not give grace, nor the Spirit of God, neither justify they the receiver? "If righteousness come by works, then died Christ in vain." "By faith doth God purify our hearts," and by the grace of the Lord Jesu are we saved. "Neither he that planteth, nor yet he that watereth, is any thing worth, but God which giveth the increase." "In Christ Jesu neither circumcision nor uncircumcision is any thing worth; but faith which worketh by love." In consideration whereof our Saviour Christ, when he speaketh of baptism, joineth the water and the Spirit together, or baptism and faith, which is the fruit of the Spirit, to declare that outward baptism without the Spirit and faith availeth nothing. These are his words: "Except a man be born of the water and of the Spirit, he cannot enter into the kingdom of God." Again: "He that believeth and is baptized shall be saved." So likewise do the apostles of Christ, as the holy scriptures do evidently declare. For when the Jews, hearing Peter's sermon, wherein he rebuked them for their cruel murdering of Christ, were pricked in their hearts, and said Gal. ii. Acts xv. 1 Cor. iii. Gal. v. John iii. Mark xvi.

---

sacramenta quid prosunt?.....Nihil quippe profuit Simoni Mago visibilis baptismus, cui sanctificatio invisibilis defuit.....Hoc et de latrone illo, cui secum crucifixo Dominus ait, Hodie mecum eris in paradiso. Neque enim sine sanctificatione invisibili tanta felicitate donatus est. Proinde colligitur invisibilem sanctificationem quibusdam affuisse atque profuisse sine visibilibus sacramentis, quæ pro temporum diversitate mutata sunt, ut alia tunc fuerint, et alia modo sint: visibilem vero sanctificationem, quæ fieret per visibilia sacramenta, sine ista invisibili posse adesse, non posse prodesse.—August. Op. Par. 1679—1700. Quæst. in Heptateuch. Lib. III. Quæst. lxxxiv. Tom. III. Pars I. col 524.]

[[2] Officium baptizandi Dominus concessit multis, potestatem vero et auctoritatem in baptismo remittendi peccata sibi soli retinuit.—Id. Scal. Parad. Tom. VI. Appendix, col. 164. This is not a genuine work of Augustine.]

[[3] Plantare est evangelizare, et ad fidem adtrahere: rigare vero baptizare solemnibus verbis: peccata autem dimittere, et Spiritum dare, Dei solius. Si ergo effectum salutis Deus dat, nulla gloria in hac re hominis est. Scimus enim et Spiritum sanctum sine manus impositione datum a Deo, et non baptizatum consequutum remissionem peccatorum. Numquid non hic invisibiliter baptizatus est; quando donum baptismatis consequutus est?—Ambros. Op. Par. 1686-90. Comm. in Epist. ad Cor. prim. cap. iii. v. 6. Tom. II. Appendix, col. 121.]

[[4] Sed tamen, sicut ostensum est per plures rationes, non est aliquo modo dicendum quod gratia contineatur in ipsis sacramentis essentialiter tamquam aqua in vase, vel medicina in pyxide: immo hoc intelligere est erroneum. Sed dicuntur continere gratiam, quia ipsam significant; et quia nisi ibi sit defectus ex parte suscipientis, in ipsis gratia semper confertur, ita intelligendo quod gratia sit in anima, non in signis visibilibus: pro tanto etiam dicuntur vasa gratiæ. Possunt etiam dici vasa alia ratione, quia sicut quod est in vase non est de ipso, nec ex ipso, sed tamen ab ipso hauritur; sic gratia non est a sacramentis, nec de sacramentis, sed oritur a fonte æterno, et ab illo hauritur ab ipsa anima in ipsis sacramentis.—Bonavent. Op. Mogunt. 1609. In Lib. IV. Sentent. Dist. i. Quæst. 3. Tom. V. pp. 7, 8.]

[[5] The precise words of the text have not been discovered in the work of Francisc. de Mayronis upon the Lib. Sentent.]

Acts ii. unto him and unto the other apostles, "Ye men and brethren, what shall we do? Peter said unto them, Repent ye of your sins, and let every one of you be baptized in the name of Jesu Christ unto the remission of sins; and ye shall receive the gift of the Holy Ghost." When "the eunuch said unto Philip, Behold water; what letteth that I may not be baptized? Philip answered, If thou believest from thy whole heart, it is lawful. And the eunuch said, I believe that Jesus Christ is the Son of God." Likewise St Paul, when he should baptize the keeper of the prison, said unto him: "Believe thou in the Lord Jesus, and thou shalt be saved." And in his epistle unto bishop Titus he writeth thus: "God according to his mercy hath saved us by the fountain of the new birth and renewing of the Holy Ghost, which he shed on us abundantly through Jesus Christ our Saviour, that we, justified by his grace, should be made heirs according to hope of everlasting life."

Acts viii. Acts xvi. Tit. iii.

Father. Thou hast abundantly satisfied me in this point. Let me hear it now proved by the holy scripture, that that doctrine, which teacheth that christian infants dying without the outward baptism of water perish and are damned, utterly dissenteth from the verity of God's word, as thou hast already proved that it is injurious to the grace of God. *Son.* First, as we have tofore heard, God hath promised not only to be God of the ancient believers, but also of their children. Now what other thing is it to be the God of the faithful people's children, than to be their Saviour and blessed-maker? If God, which is faithful in all his words, which also is not only true, but also the self truth, saveth the children for his promise sake; is it to be thought, that the want of a little water (when necessity compelleth) can make God to fall from his truth, and his promise to be both vain and void, so that without the water he cannot save the christian infants, whom notwithstanding he hath promised to save? What other thing is this, than to make God servant to his sacraments, and to bind his grace and Spirit to an outward ceremony or sign? Which thing, what is it but to deny God to be omnipotent? But that God both is able, and also will, yea, and doth save without the help of any outward sacrament or sign, we have tofore sufficiently heard.

Gen. xvii. Psal. cxlv. John xiv.

John iii. Again, that the grace and Spirit of God cometh where and when it pleaseth God, yea, and that they be not bound to any external ceremony, as to be present and to be given when the sacraments are ministered, and otherwise not, so that the Spirit and grace of God must wait and attend upon those outward signs, as servants do attend and wait upon their lords and masters, (which is nothing else than to bring God into bondage of his creatures, and to make him not master of his own,) the history of Cornelius the centurion doth evidently declare. For Cornelius and all his household (as blessed Luke testifieth) received the Holy Ghost before they were baptized; insomuch that Peter said: "May any man forbid that these should be baptized with water, which have received the Holy Ghost as well as we? And so he commanded them to be baptized in the name of the Lord." Here may we see, that the Spirit of God lighteth where he will, neither is he bound to any thing. Hereof also may we learn, that the sacraments are given to be an outward witness unto all the congregation of the grace, which is given before privately unto every man; so that through baptism the congregation of God receiveth the infant into the church of Christ, which was received before of God through the grace of his promise.

Acts x.

Who seeth not now that baptism itself bringeth not grace, but doth testify unto the congregation, that he which is baptized hath already received grace and the Spirit of God, and is accepted of God for his merciful promise sake a dear child and heir of everlasting glory? Again, who knoweth not that many even among the gentiles, as Job and such like, under the old law, were the elect and chosen people of God, yea, and had the Spirit and grace of God, and were saved, although outwardly they were not circumcised, being notwithstanding inwardly circumcised through the Spirit of God, which indeed is the true circumcision, and most regarded of God, as St Paul testifieth, saying: "He is not a Jew, which is a Jew outward; neither is that circumcision, which is outward in the flesh; but he is a Jew which is hid within; and the circumcision of the heart is the true circumcision, which consisteth in the spirit, and not in the letter; whose praise is not of men, but of God."

Rom. ii.

And it is not to be doubted but that, even among the Turks and the other heathen, there are many spiritually baptized, and so are saved, although their bodies want the water of baptism. For he is not a Christian only, which is washed with water; neither is that baptism only, which is outward in the flesh; but that is the very baptism, which God alloweth, even to be baptized in heart through the Spirit of God, as St Peter saith: "Baptism now saveth us, not the putting away of the filthiness of the flesh, but in that a good conscience consenteth to God, by the resurrection of Jesus Christ." St Paul also saith: "We are the circumcision, which serve God in the spirit." Again: "By Christ are ye circumcised with circumcision which is done without hands; forasmuch as ye have put off the sinful body of the flesh through the circumcision that is in Christ, in that ye are also buried with him through baptism, in whom ye are also risen again through faith that is wrought by the operation of God, which raised him from death."

1 Pet. iii. Phil. iii. Col. ii.

Item, who doubted that many and divers infants of the Israelites died without circumcision? Shall we say that all these perished and were damned for lack of circumcision? God forbid! God saved not these infants for the circumcision sake, but for his merciful promise sake, and because they were comprehended in the covenant of grace, which he had made with Abraham and his posterity.

And is it to be thought that this Lord our God, that Father of mercies and God of all consolation and comfort, will be less merciful to the infants of the Christians than he was to the young children of the Hebrews, seeing that the very same promise of grace, mercy, and favour is made to us that was made to them? The infants of the Hebrews dying without circumcision were saved because of the promise; and shall our children (whom in our hearts we have consecrated and commended to God, whom also we have greatly wished to have been baptized, if they had not been taken away by sudden death), dying without baptism, be damned, seeing that the same gracious promise doth no less appertain unto them, than it doth to the other? Who seeth not now, how greatly their doctrine dissenteth from the truth of God's word, which teach that the infants of the Christians dying without baptism perish and are damned?

Moreover, doth not St Paul call the children of the Christians pure and clean? If they be pure and clean, can the lack of a little water make them so unpure and so unclean, that they shall be cast out of the favour of God, and have their portion with the damned spirits in that "lake that burneth with fire and brimstone?" "They that be pure shall see God." "The children are pure." The children therefore shall see God. The angels, which as ministers attend upon the children for their health and safeguard, see the face of our heavenly Father; and shall the infants, upon whom they wait at the appointment of God, be cast from the sight of that heavenly Father, because they depart unbaptized? The infants of the Christians are so dearly beloved of God, that he sendeth his angels to attend upon them; and shall the lack of an outward sign be of such force, that it shall quench this love of God toward the infants, seeing whom God once loveth, he loveth unto the end? seeing also that "the gifts and calling of God are such, that it cannot repent him of them."

1 Cor. vii. Rev. xxi. Matt. v. 1 Cor. vii. Matt. xviii. John xiii. Rom. xi.

Furthermore St Paul saith: "They that are led with the Spirit of God are the sons of God." The infants of the Christians are led with the Spirit of God, as we tofore heard of Jacob, Jeremy, and John Baptist. Therefore are the infants of the Christians the sons of God. "If they be sons, then are they also heirs; the heirs, I mean, of God, and heirs annexed with Christ." How can these sons and heirs of God then be damned, if through the providence of God they be suddenly called away from this life before they can attain unto baptism, seeing "there is no damnation to them which are in Christ Jesu?"

Rom. viii. Rom. viii. Rom. viii.

Besides all these things, what shall we say of God's election? Can the lack of outward baptism destroy and make of none effect the election of God; so that whom God hath chosen unto everlasting salvation, the want of an external sign shall cast down unto everlasting damnation? St Paul saith: "Whom God appointed before, them also he called: and whom he hath called, them also he justified; and whom he justified, them also he glorified. What shall we then say to these things? If God be on our side, who can be against us? Which spared

Of God's election. Rom. viii.

not his own Son, but gave him for us all; how can it be, that with him he should not give us all things also? Who shall lay any thing to the charge of God's elect and chosen? It is God that justifieth: who is he that can condemn? It is Christ which died, yea, rather which is risen again, which is also on the right hand of God, and maketh intercession for us. Who shall separate us from the love of God? &c. I am sure that no creature shall be able to pluck us from the love of God, which is in Christ Jesu our Lord." Our Saviour Christ saith also: "All that the Father giveth me shall come to me; and him that cometh to me I cast not away. For I came down from heaven, not to do that I will, but that he will which hath sent me. And this is the Father's will which sent me, that of all which he hath given me I shall lose nothing, but raise them up again at the last day." Again he saith: "My sheep hear my voice, and I know them, and they follow me, and I give unto them everlasting life, and they shall never perish, neither shall any man pluck them out of my hand. My Father which gave them me is greater than all; and no man is able to take them out of my Father's hand."

John vi.

John x.

If the election of God be certain, as it is most certain, who learneth not then of these aforesaid sentences, that God's elect can by no means perish? To be elected is to be saved. The infants are elected: the infants therefore are saved. "God," saith St Paul, "did choose us in Christ, before the foundations of the world were laid, that we should be holy and without blame before him through love; which ordained us before through Jesus Christ to be heirs unto himself, according to the good pleasure of his will, to the praise of the glory of his grace, wherewith he hath made us accepted through the Beloved; by whom we have redemption through his blood, even the forgiveness of sins, according to the riches of his grace." Of this sentence also of St Paul who learneth not, that our salvation dependeth only of the election of God, and not of any outward sacrament? Neither are we then first elected, when we be washed with the water of baptism; but we were "elected in Christ Jesu," saith St Paul, "before the foundations of the world were laid;" that we may certainly know that our whole salvation dependeth not of any external work, but of the free election and undoubted grace of God.

Eph. i.

Who seeth not now, that the doctrine of them which teach that christian infants, dying without the outward baptism of water, perish and are damned, utterly dissenteth from the verity of God's word? They, therefore, that teach and hold this doctrine, are not only enemies to the salvation of the infants, but they also utterly obscure, yea, and quench the grace and election of God, and the secret operation of the Holy Ghost in the tender breasts of the most tender infants, and attribute to an external sign more than right is.

John iii. *Father*. What sayest thou then to these words of Christ? "Verily, verily I say unto thee, Except a man be born of water and of the Spirit, he cannot enter into the kingdom of God." Are not these words plain enough? Doth it not evidently appear here that, except a man be born not only of the Spirit, but also of water, he cannot be saved? How can infants then be saved, if they be not born of water? *Son*. The like manner of speaking almost read we in the holy scripture concerning circumcision, when God said unto Abraham: "See thou keep my testament, both thou and thy seed after thee, in their generations. This is my testament, which ye shall keep, between me and you, and thy seed after thee: Every man-child among you shall be circumcised. Ye shall circumcise the flesh of your foreskin; and it shall be a token of the bond between me and you; and every man-child of eight days old shall be circumcised among you, and such as be in your generations, and born at home, and he that is bought with money of any stranger, which is not of thy seed. He that is born in thine house, and he also that is bought with money, must needs be circumcised; and my testament shall be in your flesh for an everlasting bond. And the uncircumcised man-child, in whose flesh the foreskin is not circumcised, that soul shall perish from his people, because he hath broken my testament."

Gen. xvii.

Who seeth not here what strait charge God giveth concerning circumcision? "He must needs," saith he, "be circumcised." Again: "The uncircumcised man-child's soul shall perish." Who perceiveth not now by these words, how strait God here requireth circumcision; so that, as the words do import outwardly, the man-child of necessity must be circumcised, otherwise his soul perisheth? &c.

What shall we then say to those infants which died before the eighth day? are they damned? Where then is this promise of God become? "I will be thy God, and the God of thy seed." (Gen. ii.) What shall we say of God's election and predestination? Are they made frustrate and void, because the flesh of the foreskin is not circumcised? What shall we then say to these words of the apostle? "Whom God appointed before, them also he called: and whom he hath called, them also he justified; and whom he justified, them also he glorified. What shall we then say to these things? If God be on our side, who can be against us?" (Rom. viii.) Again: "God did elect and choose us in Christ Jesu, before the foundations of the world were laid." (Eph. i.) And a little after he saith: "God hath predestinate and tofore ordained us through Jesus Christ to be heirs unto himself, according to the good pleasure of his will." What shall we also say to the operation of the Holy Ghost in the tender breast of the infant? Is that also vain, if circumcision be absent, specially when necessity compelleth? But how standeth that with this saying of St Paul? "They that are led with the Spirit of God are the sons of God." (Rom. viii.) If the infants be led with the Spirit of God, as we have tofore heard, so followeth it that they are the sons of God. If they be the sons of God, then are they also the heirs of God. If they be the heirs of God, then are they also heirs annexed with Christ. If they be fellow-heirs with Christ, how can the lack of an outward ceremony condemn them, seeing it is written, "There is no condemnation to them which are in Christ Jesu?" (Rom. viii.)

Who doubteth but that there were many infants whom that most bloody tyrant Herod slew, when he pursued the Lord Jesus, that new-born King of the Jews, which in that persecution died without circumcision? (Matt. ii.) Shall we say that these all perished, and are damned? and not rather (as the church of Christ believeth and confesseth) that they are blessed saints and glorious martyrs in the kingdom of God?

King Pharao gave commandment to the midwives of the Hebrews' women, that in the birth-time they should kill all the male children of the Hebrews, and by no means to suffer them to live. (Exod. i.) What if this bloody commandment of this most bloody king had been obeyed of the midwives, so that they had slain the infants before they had been circumcised; is it to be thought that they had so fallen away from the favour of God, that, notwithstanding his merciful promise and covenant made with them and with their fathers, they had perished and be damned?

The holy scripture declareth that all the time that the people of Israel were in the wilderness, which was the space of forty years, there was no circumcision used among them. (Josh. v.) Is it not to be supposed that many in the meantime both of the younger and of the elder sort died? Shall we now say that all such were damned, because they died uncircumcised? God forbid!

Therefore, as the young children of the Hebrews many times died before they were circumcised, and yet notwithstanding for God's election and promise sake they were saved; so likewise the infants of the Christians, prevented by death, remain still in the favour of God and state of salvation, although (necessity so compelling) they die without baptism; forasmuch as the gracious and merciful promise of God pertaineth now no less to the infants of the Christians, than it did in times past to young children of the Hebrews. (Gen. xvii.)

Father. But what is to be said to this sentence of Christ? "Except a man be born of water and of the Spirit, he cannot enter into the kingdom of God." (John iii.) *Son*. The like manner of speaking read we in the gospel of St John; and they also are the words of Christ: "Verily, verily I say unto you, Except ye eat the flesh of the Son of man, and drink his blood, ye have no life in you." (John vi.) Some of the ancient fathers, understanding these words literally, thought that whosoever died without the receiving of the sacrament of the body and blood of Christ, was in great danger of damnation; and therefore they ordained, that the young infants also, so soon as they were baptized, should receive the sacrament of the body and blood of Christ, lest that they, departing without it, should fall from the favour of God, and so perish; when, to say the truth, these words of Christ are not to be understand literally, but spiritually, not of the sacramental, but of the spiritual eating and drinking of Christ's body and blood, which is done by faith.

John vi. And as these fathers grated too hard upon this sentence of Christ, "Except ye eat the flesh of the Son of man, and drink his blood, ye have no life in you;" so likewise did those fathers cleave too much to these words of Christ, "Except a man be born of water and of the Spirit, he cannot enter into the kingdom of God," when they taught that the children, dying without the baptism of water, perish and are not saved. For as many of the people of God are saved, which never received the sacrament of the body and blood of Christ, so likewise are many saved, though they were never outwardly baptized with water; forasmuch as the regeneration of a Christian consisteth rather in the spirit than in the flesh; even as the circumcision also of the Jews consisted not in the letter, but in the spirit, not in the circumcision of the flesh, but in the circumcision of the heart.

John iii.

John iii This text therefore of Christ, "Except a man be born of the water and of the Spirit," &c. is to be understand of such as may conveniently be baptized, and yet notwithstanding contemptuously refuse baptism, and in this behalf despise the ordinance of Christ, and by this means seclude themselves from the company of God's people. These shall not enter into the kingdom of God. For this contempt of the outward sacrament is an evident argument and a sure sign, that such despisers of God's ordinance have not the Spirit of God, without the which no man can be saved, as St Paul saith: "If any man have not the Spirit of Christ, he is none of God's;" and so doth it consequently follow, that they have no portion in the inheritance of Christ and of God. But as touching the young infants, whom their parents would gladly offer unto God by baptism, (and in their hearts they have already dedicated them to God by prayer and a free willing spirit,) if they had not been prevented by death, they are free from this sentence of damnation; not only they, but also all other persons, of whatsoever age they are, if they do not contemn the ordinance of God, but rather in the hearts most desirously wish to receive that outward baptism of water according to the institution of Christ, if they might come by it.

Read the seventy-seventh epistle of St Bernard[1]. Rom. viii.

Such as are thus affected toward holy baptism are without doubt led with the Spirit of God; and though baptism of water be denied, yet, inwardly being baptized with the Holy Ghost, they cannot perish, but have everlasting life; as we read of a certain emperor called Valentinianus, which, being desirous to be baptized, and notwithstanding prevented by death, came not unto baptism, and yet died in the Lord, and is saved, as St Ambrose abundantly proveth[2]. And who knoweth not, that in the primitive church many were suddenly taken away through the tyranny of wicked rulers from this life, before that they could attain unto the sacrament of baptism, and suffered martyrdom for the testimony of the Lord Jesus? Shall we say that all these perished, because they lacked the water of baptism? God forbid!

Read St Ambrose de Morte Valentiniani.

John iii. Who seeth not now then that this sentence of Christ, "Except a man be born of the water and of the Spirit, he cannot enter into the kingdom of God," is not so straitly to be taken, that we should judge all those damned which die without the baptism of water? The thief died without baptism; yet the thief was saved, as these words of Christ spoken unto him declare manifestly: "This day shalt thou be with me in paradise."

Luke xxiii.

Contra Donatist. Lib. iv. It is notably said of St Augustine: "Then is it fulfilled invisibly, when not the contempt of religion, but the article of necessity, excludeth the mystery of baptism[3]."

Epist. 77. And St Bernard likewise saith: "The will is taken for the deed, when necessity excludeth the deed[4]."

[[1] Bernard. Op. Par. 1690. Vol. I. Tom. II. cols. 625-36.]

[[2] Sed audio vos dolere, quod non acceperit sacramenta baptismatis. Dicite mihi, quid aliud in nobis est, nisi voluntas, nisi petitio? Atqui etiam dudum hoc voti habuit, ut et antequam in Italiam venisset, initiaretur, et proxime baptizari se a me velle significavit; et ideo præ ceteris causis me accersendum putavit. Non habet ergo gratiam, quam desideravit: non habet quam poposcit? Certe quia poposcit, accepit.—Ambros. Op. 1686-90. De Ob. Valentin. Consol. 51. Tom. II. col. 1188.]

[[3] Sed tunc impletur invisibiliter, cum ministerium baptismi non contemptus religionis, sed articulus necessitatis excludit.—August. Op. Par. 1679—1700. De Bapt. cont. Donatist. Lib. IV. 29. Tom. IX. col. 139.]

[[4] Quid planius, quod voluntas pro facto repute-

This thing considered right well certain fathers of Christ's church, which affirm the baptism is divided into three kinds, that is to say, the baptism of the Holy Ghost, the baptism of blood, and the baptism of water[5]; and of all these three the baptism of water is the most inferior, forasmuch as we read that divers so baptized have notwithstanding perished. But whosoever is baptized with the Holy Ghost, and so dieth, he cannot perish. For without this baptism the baptism of the water profiteth nothing. Again, such as confess Christ boldly, and seal the confession with their blood, and, through the cruelty of the most cruel persecutors prevented by death, cannot come unto baptism, are no less dear and acceptable to God than [if] they were baptized with water. For they are baptized with the Holy Ghost and with their own blood; so that in them is fulfilled this saying of the apostle: "With the heart it is believed unto righteousness, but with the mouth confession is made unto salvation. For the scripture saith, Whosoever believeth on him shall not be confounded." Three kinds of baptism. Rom. x. Isai. xxviii.

Moreover, the words of Christ, which he spake after his resurrection to his disciples concerning baptism, are diligently to be noted. The words are these: "He that believeth and is baptized shall be saved; but he that believeth not shall be damned." He saith not, He that is not baptized (with water) shall be damned; but only, "He that believeth not shall be damned;" hereby declaring that our salvation hangeth not of the water, but of the faith; as it is written: "He that believeth on the Son hath everlasting life: but he that believeth not on the Son shall not see life; but the wrath of God abideth on him." Mark xvi. John iii.

Of these aforesaid authorities, both of the holy scripture and also of the ancient fathers, I gather and conclude, that both the infants of the Christians, and also other of more ripe age, being of the number of the faithful, if they be prevented by death, are saved, and inheritors of everlasting life, although they depart without baptism: the infants, both because they are contained in the number of God's people, and are concluded within this most gracious promise, "I will be thy God, and the God of thy seed," and also because they are prevented by death, and by this means of necessity excluded from the sacrament of baptism; the elder, because they believe in God, confess their faith, and most desirously wish to be baptized, if they might attain thereunto. Gen. xvii.

Father. I cannot disallow thy doctrine in this behalf. But methink thou makest three baptisms, which is contrary to this saying of the apostle: "One Lord, one faith, one baptism, one God," &c. *Son*. There is but one baptism. Notwithstanding, because this one baptism is of divers diversely taken, as we have tofore heard, therefore the ancient fathers of Christ's church have thus made a partition of baptism, sometime calling it the baptism of water, sometime the baptism of the Holy Ghost, and sometime the baptism of blood; forasmuch as all that are contained in the visible church are not baptized alike. With water alone are the ungodly and wicked hypocrites baptized, which outwardly feign repentance and faith, when inwardly they have nothing less; and therefore the baptism profiteth them nothing at all, but rather turneth unto their damnation. With the Spirit or Holy Ghost they are baptized, which do truly repent and believe, and fix the eyes of their mind on the commandment of God, and the promise annexed to baptism. To them is the baptism of water wholesome and profitable. With blood are they baptized, which, prevented of death through the cruelty of the persecutors, cannot come unto the baptism of water, although greatly wished; and yet notwithstanding boldly and stoutly confess Christ and his holy gospel before the tyrants of this world, yea, and confirm with their death and seal with their blood this their confession. These are holy martyrs and blessed witnesses of Christ; and therefore they are as acceptable and dear unto God, as though they were baptized with water. Eph. iv.

tur, ubi factum excludit necessitas?—Bernard. Op. Par. 1690. Epist. lxxvii. seu Tract. de Bapt. ad Hug. de S. Vict. cap. ii. 8. Vol. I. Tom. II. col. 629.]

[5 This distinction may be frequently found made or implied by ancient writers. See Cypr. Op. Oxon, 1682. Præfat. ad Fortunat. De Exhort. Martyr. pp. 168, 9; Epist. lxxiii. ad Jubaian. pp. 198, &c.: also Cyril. Hieros. Op. Par. 1720. Cateches. III. 9, 10. p. 44. See also Polyd. Verg. De Rer. Inventor. Basil. 1570. Lib. IV. cap. IV. p. 308.]

Father. And are these three kinds of baptism approved of God's word? *Son.* Yea, verily.

Father. Where? Let me hear. *Son.* Of the baptism of water Christ our Saviour speaketh on this manner: "Baptize all nations in the name of the Father, and of the Son, and of the Holy Ghost." "He that believeth and is baptized shall be saved." Of the baptism of the Holy Ghost, or of the Spirit, Christ also said thus to his apostles: "John baptized with water; but ye shall be baptized with the Holy Ghost." And of the baptism of blood the Lord Christ hath these words spoken unto James and John, which desired to be highest in authority with Christ: "Can ye drink of the cup which I shall drink, and be baptized with the baptism wherewith I shall be baptized?" Again he saith: "I must be baptized with a baptism; and how am I pained till it be ended!"

Matt. xxviii. Mark xvi. Acts i. Matt. xx. Mark x. Luke xii.

Father. I perceive now right well, that baptism is an holy mystery and blessed sacrament. *Son.* Nothing is more true. For it is an holy ordinance instituted of God, and no practice of man's imagination, put in use in Christ's time, and after his resurrection commanded to be ministered unto all that believe, whether they were Jews or gentiles. For although it appeareth outwardly never so base a thing to be washed with water, yet it is an honourable mystery, and ought to be had in great reverence and price, because it was commanded of God to be done; insomuch that whosoever contemneth this holy sacrament, and refuse to be baptized, when opportunity serveth, is not of God, neither appertaineth he unto the kingdom of God. For he that despiseth the ordinance of God, despiseth God himself.

Whether baptism may be twice ministered to one person.

Father. What judgest thou of them that minister baptism twice to one person? *Son.* You speak of the anabaptists, which, condemning the baptism of infants as a thing both vain and unprofitable (such is their madness), because they cannot openly protest their faith before the world, teach that they ought to be baptized again, when they come to age and have the use of reason, being able to confess their own faith. This doctrine of the wicked anabaptists I utterly both contemn and condemn as a doctrine pestiferous and poisonful, which plainly dissenteth from the word of God and from the practice of the primitive church; forasmuch as we have tofore heard, the baptism of infants is grounded on the word of God, pleaseth him, and is acceptable unto him, even no less than is the baptism of the elder sort. Whosoever therefore is once baptized, of whatsoever age he be, according to the institution and word of God, which abideth for ever, he ought not to be baptized again. For to be baptized again is none other thing than to mock and blaspheme God, to recount God a liar, as one which either will not, or else is not able to keep his word uttered in baptism, to doubt of his ordinance, to call our salvation into question, &c.

Isai. xl. Matt. v.

Whether the unworthiness of the minister hindereth the worthiness of baptism.

Father. What thinkest thou of baptism, if it be ministered of a wicked and ungodly minister? *Son.* It is to be wished, that such as are appointed to be spiritual ministers in the church of Christ should be men both in doctrine and life godly and virtuous, that they might be no stumbling-blocks to the congregation of God, but edify God's people both with sound learning and christian conversation. But if it so chanceth, that the life of him which, being admitted unto the public ministry, baptizeth, be evil, wicked, and ungodly; yet notwithstanding, the aforesaid minister ministering baptism truly, and according to the institution of Christ, his wicked life and ungodly conversation hindereth baptism nothing at all.

For the sacraments, when they be lawfully and duly ministered, are not of force and strength for the worthiness of the minister, but for the institution and ordinance of God, that the promise may be certain. For it is Christ himself which truly and properly baptizeth, and not man, whose ministry, as an hand, Christ useth in baptizing. Man baptizeth outwardly; but Christ baptizeth inwardly. Man washeth the body with water; but Christ cleanseth the soul with his holy Spirit.

In serm. de Baptismo.

For, as St Cyprian saith: "Whether Judas or Paul baptizeth, Christ washeth, absolveth, and putteth away the sin[1]."

[[1] ....quoniam sive Judas sive Paulus baptizet; Christus peccatum lavat, absolvit, et delet.—Cypr. Op. Oxon. 1682. De Baptism. Christ. This is one of the treatises of Arnold, abbot of Bonavalla, p. 31.]

"To forgive sins in baptism, and to give the Holy Ghost," saith St Ambrose, "is the office of God alone. If God therefore give the effect of health, then is there no glory of man in this behalf. For we know that the Holy Ghost was given of God without laying on of hands, and that he which was not yet baptized obtained remission of sins[2]." In 1 Cor. iii. Acts x.

"As concerning the visible ministry, both good and bad baptize; but invisibly he by them baptizeth, whose both the visible baptism and the invisible grace is. Both good and bad may baptize; but to wash the conscience, that can none do, but he which is alway good," saith St Austin[3]." Again he saith: "To minister and to distribute the word and sacrament the minister is somewhat; but to make clean and to justify he is nothing. For this thing worketh he only in the inward man, by whom the whole man is made[4]." Contra Crescon. Lib. ii. cap. 21. Contra Petil. Lib. ix. cap. 54.

Father. Whether is it requisite and necessary that the infant which should be baptized be plunged down into the water; or is it sufficient that a little water be poured upon his head or upon his face? *Son.* It appeareth by the writings of the ancient fathers, Tertullian, Damasus, Cyril, Austin, Ambrose, Basil, Theophylact[5], and divers other, that in times past, both in the Greek and Latin church, the custom was to dip such as should be be baptized thrice into the water, in token that they are baptized in the name of the glorious Trinity, the Father, the Son, and the Holy Ghost, one alone true and everlasting God. And the plunging into the water signified that we are buried with Christ, as the plucking of us out of the water preacheth unto us that we be risen again with Christ; which thing St Paul also teacheth in these words: "Know ye not that all we which are baptized into Jesus Christ are baptized to die with him? We are buried then with him by baptism for to die; that likewise as Christ was raised up from death by the glory of the Father, even so we also should walk in a new life. For if we be graft in death like unto him, even so shall we be partakers of the resurrection; knowing this, that our old man is crucified with him also, that the body of sin might utterly be destroyed, that henceforth we should not be servants unto sin." But to dip them thrice into the fount, as the manner was then, I think it not to be of necessity; but it may seem to suffice, if water be poured upon their head or upon their face. Whether infants in their baptism ought to be plunged down into the water. Rom. vi. Note.

Christ commanded to baptize all men; but he left the manner of baptizing free to his church, whether they would wash the whole body, or some part thereof. Moreover, as all the people of the Jews was counted to be sprinkled with the blood of the covenant, because it was accustomed to be sprinkled upon all, when notwithstanding not their whole bodies, but some part of them was imbrued with the blood; so likewise a man or an infant is taken to be wholly baptized, dipped, and cleansed, when some one member only is overflowed with water, dipped, or cleansed. For this lawish sprinkling[6] was a figure of the blood of Christ, wherewith the consciences are sprinkled, and of our baptism. Furthermore, seeing that the virtue and power of

[2 See before, page 219, note 3.]

[3 Baptizant ergo, quantum adtinet ad visibile ministerium, et boni et mali: invisibiliter autem per eos ille baptizat, cujus est et visibile baptisma et invisibilis gratia. Tinguere ergo possunt et boni et mali; abluere autem conscientiam non nisi ille qui semper est bonus.—August. Op. Par. 1679—1700. Cont. Crescon. Donatist. Lib. II. 26. Tom. IX. col. 423.]

[4 Ad ministrandum et dispensandum verbum ac sacramentum aliquid est [minister Christi]: ad mundandum autem et justificandum non est aliquid; quia hoc non operatur in interiore homine, nisi per quem creatus est totus homo.—Id. Cont. Litt. Petil. Lib. III. 66. cols. 331, 2.]

[5 See Tertull. Op. Lut. Par. 1641. Advers. Prax. cap. xxvi. p. 659; Joan. Damasc. Op. (perhaps Damasus in the text is an error) Basil. 1575. Orthodox. Fid. Lib. IV. cap. x. p. 296; Cyril. Hieros. Op. Par. 1720. Catecheş. Myst. II. 4. p. 312; August. in Decret. Gratiani, Par. 1583. Decr. Tert. Pars, De Consecr. Dist. iv. can. 78. cols. 2473, 4; Ambros. Op. Par. 1686-90. De Sacram. Lib. II. cap. vii. 20. Tom. II. col. 359; Basil. Op. Par. 1721-30. De Spir. Sanct. cap. xxvii. Tom. III. p. 55; Theophyl. Op. Venet. 1754-63. Comm. in Naum, cap. i. Tom. IV. p. 221. The practice was at length relinquished, because certain Arians chose to interpret the three immersions as denoting a difference or division in the three divine Persons. Gregory the Great, being consulted thereupon, pronounced against it; and some time after the fourth council of Toledo decreed that only one immersion should be used.—See Greg. Leandr. Episc. Hisp. Lib. I. Epist. xli. in Decret. Gratiani, Decr. Tert. Pars, De Consecr. Dist. iv. can. 80. cols. 2475, 6; and Concil. Tolet. 4. c. 5, in eod. can. 85. cols. 2477, 8.]

[6 Lawish sprinkling: that sprinkling which was prescribed and practised under the law.]

cleansing the minds cometh not from the water, it is all one matter, whether the whole body, or some part thereof, as the head, be washed. It is therefore sufficient, if the signification of spiritual baptism be observed.

That to "baptize" signifieth not to plunge the whole man into the water, it may easily be gathered both of St Mark's and St Luke's gospel, where we read thus: Mark vii. *Reversi a foro non comedunt nisi prius baptizati;* that is: "The Pharisees, when they come home from the market, eat not, except they first be baptized," that is to say, wash Luke xi. their hands. Again: *Mirabatur Pharisæus, quod Christus non baptizatus accumbat mensæ;* that is: "The Pharisee marvelled that Christ was not baptized," that is to say, washed not his hands, "before he sat down at the table."

Of god-fathers and god-mothers. *Father.* What thinkest thou of those which promise for the infant in his baptism, whom they call god-fathers and god-mothers? *Son.* The custom is old and ancient in the church of Christ, and hath from time to time been used among the Christians above fourteen hundred years; and it is no less commendable than ancient, if the god-fathers and god-mothers satisfy their promise, and do according as they have said, in bringing up the young infant in the nurture and doctrine of the Lord, in the faith, Fathers ought to be present at the baptism of their children. fear, and love of God, in the obedience of God's holy law, &c. But this I greatly discommend in the church of the papists, that they will by no means suffer the fathers of the infants to be present at the baptism of their children, whom God above Eph. vi. all other hath commanded to instruct and to bring up their children in the knowledge of his holy law, and of them will require a strait accompts concerning the education and bringing up of their young ones. Therefore, as I do not discommend the custom of having god-fathers and god-mothers, which should openly promise for their god-children that they shall mortify the root of sin, which springeth in the bodies, and subdue their lusts under the law of God; again, that they will instruct and bring up their god-children in the faith of Christ; so likewise do I utterly discommend this use, that fathers cannot be suffered to be present at the baptism of their own children, and there also promise, before God and his holy congregation, that they will, unto the uttermost of their power, provide and see that their children shall so be brought up, that even from their cradles they shall drink in the principles of christian religion, and learn to know and serve God, that their whole life may be agreeable to their profession.

Father. It were good, in my opinion, that the parents should be present at the baptism of their children, and so there promise, and afterward do, as thou hast said. For it should put them well in remembrance of the duty which they owe by the word of God unto their children.

Well, my son, we have now sufficiently conferred of the holy sacrament of baptism, and of the principal things pertaining unto the same. Let us now somewhat talk of the other sacrament, I mean the holy supper of the Lord, otherwise called the sacrament of the body and blood of Christ. *Son.* Let it so be, my most loving and dear father.

OF THE LORD'S SUPPER.

What the Lord's supper is. *Father.* Tell me, first of all, what the Lord's supper is. *Son.* After the definition of St Paul, it is the partaking of the body and blood of Christ.

1 Cor. x. *Father.* Why, what saith St Paul in this behalf? *Son.* Thus saith he: "Is not the bread which we break the partaking of the body of Christ? And is not the cup of thanksgiving, for the which we give thanks, the partaking of the blood of Christ?"

Father. Let me hear other definitions of the Lord's supper, if thou hast any in store. *Son.* The Lord's supper is an holy and heavenly banquet, in the which the faithful Christians, besides the corporal eating of the bread, and the outward drinking of the wine, do spiritually through faith both eat the body of Christ and drink his blood, unto the confirmation of their faith, the comfort of their conscience, and the salvation of their souls.

Or thus: The supper of the Lord is a spiritual food, in the which Christ Jesus the Son of God witnesseth that he is the living bread, wherewith our souls are fed unto everlasting life. John vi.

Or on this manner: The supper of the Lord is an holy sacrament instituted of the Lord Jesu, to be a commemoration and a perpetual remembrance of his body-breaking and blood-shedding, yea, of his passion and death on the altar of the cross, that the faithful communicants, eating and receiving those holy mysteries, (I mean the bread and wine sanctified in the body and blood of Christ,) should earnestly set before their eyes the death of Christ and all the benefits which they have received through the same; that is to say, the grace, favour, and mercy of God, remission of sins, quietness of conscience, freedom from the captivity of Satan, from the curse of the law, from the sting of death, and from everlasting damnation, the gift of the Holy Ghost, and assurance of eternal life; and that by this means they should be provoked and stirred up to magnify and praise our heavenly Father, for this his unoutspeakable kindness and exceeding great love.

Or on this wise briefly: The supper of the Lord is a memorial of Christ's death.

Father. Who instituted and ordained this holy and heavenly banquet, which is called the supper of the Lord? *Son.* Not angel nor archangel; not king nor patriarch, nor yet mere man; but Christ Jesus the Lord, both God and man, King of kings, and Lord of lords. Who did institute the Lord's supper.

Father. Where readest thou that? *Son.* In the evangelist and in St Paul. Matt. xxvi. Mark xiv. Luke xxii.

Father. Let me hear the words of the institution of the Lord's supper. *Son.* St Paul reciteth them on this manner:

"The Lord Jesus the same night in which he was betrayed took bread; and when he had given thanks, he brake it, and said, Take ye, and eat: this is my body, which is broken for you: this do ye in the remembrance of me. After the same manner also he took the cup, when supper was done, saying, This cup is the new testament in my blood: this do, so oft as ye drink it, in remembrance of me." 1 Cor. xi.

Father. To what use, or for what purpose did the Lord Christ institute this his holy supper? *Son.* First, that it should be an holy memorial and worthy remembrance of his passion and death, of his body-breaking and blood-shedding, which he suffered on the altar of the cross; where "he offered himself an acceptable oblation and a sweet-smelling sacrifice unto God" the Father, for us and for our sins, that by his temporal death we might be delivered from everlasting death. Why Christ instituted his supper. Eph. v. Rom. iv. 1 Cor. xv. Heb. ii. Hos. xiii.

Father. How provest thou, that Christ ordained this his supper to be a memorial of his death and passion? *Son.* It is evident both by the word of Christ and also of St Paul. For thus saith the Lord Jesu: "This do in the remembrance of me." And St Paul saith: "So oft as ye shall eat this bread, and drink of this cup, ye shall shew the Lord's death till he come." Again, in that the Lord's supper is a sacrament, that is to say, a sign of an holy thing (bread is the sign of Christ's body, and the wine is the sign of his blood), it doth sufficiently instruct and teach us, that it was ordained of Christ to be a memorial of his death and passion. For sacraments are instituted unto this end, to put us in remembrance of other things, which are signified by them; as the water of baptism, wherewith the body is outwardly washed, preacheth unto us that our souls are inwardly washed by the blood of Christ, and cleansed and sanctified by the Holy Ghost. Luke xxii. 1 Cor. xi.

Father. Was it of necessity that Christ should die for us? *Son.* Otherwise could we never have been saved. For there was nothing found, neither in heaven nor in earth, of such and so great price, dignity, and worthiness in the sight of God, that could pacify the wrath of God, and satisfy his justice, and pay our ransom for our sins, and so reconcile us to God, and make an everlasting agreement between him and us, but Christ alone, that "Lamb of God," without spot, "which taketh away the sin of the world." For all creatures were found spotted in the sight of God, and unapt to accomplish the work of our salvation; so that of necessity the Son of God must by himself alone fulfil this work of our redemption, as it is written: "The blood of The necessity of the death of Christ. Exod. xii. John i. Heb. x.

oxen and of goats cannot take away sins. Wherefore when he (Christ) cometh into
Psal. xl. the world, he saith, Sacrifice and offering thou wouldest not have; but a body hast thou ordained me. Burnt offerings also for sin hast thou not allowed. Then said I, Lo, I am here. In the beginning of the book it is written of me, that I should do thy will, O God. Above," saith St Paul, "when he saith, Sacrifice and offering and burnt sacrifices and sin offerings thou wouldest not have, neither hast thou allowed them, (which yet are offered by the law); then said he, Lo, I am here to do thy will, O God. He taketh away the first to stablish the latter; by which will we are made holy, even by the offering of the body of Jesu Christ once for all."

Father. Though sufficient dignity, worthiness, and perfection could not be found in the sacrifices of beasts and fowls to pacify the wrath of God kindled against man for sin; was there neither angel nor man in heaven or in earth of such worthiness and integrity, that might perfectly have finished this work of our salvation? *Son.*
Rom. iii. Psal. xiv. As concerning men, it is thus written: "There is no difference: all have sinned. There is none righteous, no, not one. All are gone out of the way: they are all unprofit-
Rom. xi. able: there is none that doth good, no, not one." "God hath wrapped all nation
Gal. iii. in unbelief, that he might have mercy on all." "The scripture hath concluded all things under sin, that the promise by the faith of Jesus Christ should be given unto them
Eph. ii. Rom. v. that believe." "We are all by nature the children of wrath." "Through the sin of one
Isai. ix. lxiv. (Adam) death went over all men; forasmuch as all have sinned." We are all hypocrites, unclean, sheep that run astray, and "all our righteousnesses are as a cloth
Prov. xx. defiled[1]." The perfectest of us all is not able to say, "My heart is clean, and I am
Eccles. vii. Psal. cxliii. free from sin." "There liveth none, even the most righteous, that sinneth not." "No living creature is righteous before the eyes of God." Seeing then that the whole kind of man is unpure, wicked, unrighteous, defiled with sin, estranged from all goodness, and a very lump of lewdness, what can such a monster of wickedness do unto the reconciliation
Ecclus. xxxiv. either of himself or of other unto God? "Of the unclean, what can be cleansed?" Who
Job xiv. can make him clean that is conceived of unclean seed, but God alone?

And as touching the angels, neither are they so pure in the sight of God, that they were of sufficient worthiness and worthy sufficiency to make an agreement between
Job iv. God and man. For even in them also was there found folly, as Job saith: insomuch
2 Pet. ii. that "God spared not the angels that sinned," as St Peter writeth, "but cast them down into hell, and delivered them into chains of darkness (to be punished) to be kept unto judgment." In angels then also was there found imperfection; so that they were no meet mediators between God and man, to set a love-day between them, and to bring them unto an unity.

Who seeth not now then, how necessary the death of Christ was? without the which no reconciliation could have been made between God and man. Yea, not only things in earth, but also things in heaven are made at one with God through the passion and
Eph. i. death of Christ, as St Paul testifieth, saying: "God hath restored and made all things perfect by Christ, both the things which are in heaven, and the things which are in
Col. i. earth." Again: "It pleased the Father, that in Christ should all fulness dwell, and by him to reconcile all thing unto himself, and to set at peace by him, through the blood of his cross, both things in heaven and things in earth."

Father. By the death of Christ then are we delivered from our sins, and from
Rom. iv. the captivity of Satan. *Son.* Yea, verily, Christ was delivered unto the death for
1 Cor. vi. our sins. "We are washed, we are made holy, we are justified and made righteous by the name of the Lord Jesu, and through the Spirit of our God." In Christ God made agreement between the world and himself, and imputed not their sins unto them. Yea,
2 Cor. v. "God made Christ, which knew no sin, to be sin for us (that is to say, a sacrifice for sin), that we by his means should be made that righteousness," which before God is allowed.
Eph. i. "By Christ we have redemption through his blood, even the forgiveness of sins." By the
Eph. ii. means of Christ Jesus "we, which were sometime far off, are made nigh by the blood of Christ; for he is our peace; so that now we are not strangers and foreigners, but
Eph. v. citizens with the saints, and of the household of God." "Christ loved us, and gave

[[1] Two words are omitted.]

himself for us, an offering and a sweet-smelling sacrifice to God." "We are made holy by the offering of the body of Jesus Christ done once for all;" so that "Christ is able even unto the full to save them which come unto God by him." Heb. x. Heb. vii.

Father. And to remember this his passion and death, by the which we have received so many noble and precious benefits, the Lord Christ instituted this holy sacrament, which the apostle calleth "The Lord's Supper." *Son.* Yea, verily. And therefore they, that will worthily and with fruit come unto this holy and heavenly banquet, must diligently consider, remember, and set before the eyes of their mind the passion and death of our Lord and Saviour Christ Jesu, and the merits and benefits thereof; that by this means they may the more earnestly be stirred up both unto thanksgiving, and also unto a continual meditation of a better life.

Father. Is there any other cause, why the Lord Jesu did ordain this his holy supper? *Son.* You have heard the chief and principal cause, which is the remembrance of Christ's death. Another end why this holy banquet was instituted is, that it should be a sign and a token of the unity and concord, of the hearty good will and singular friendship, and of the perfect agreement in doctrine and religion that ought to be among them that profess Christ. And this is that which St Paul writeth: "We, though we be many, yet are one bread and one body; inasmuch as we all are partakers of one bread." 1 Cor. x.

Father. They then, which will approach unto the table of the Lord, ought not only to shew themselves mindful of the Lord's passion and death, but also provide that they bring with them charitable, friendly, and loving hearts toward all men, and minds settled in the truth of God's word, and in the unity of his true religion. *Son.* So is it. For whosoever presume to come unto the table of the Lord with uncharitable hearts, and with minds dissenting from the truth of God's word, and estranged from the unity of God's holy congregation, they shall find nothing there but the wrath and anger of God, the displeasure and vengeance of God, and finally (except repentance conjoined with true faith come) everlasting death and damnation. For this holy table of the Lord abhorreth no sin so greatly as envy, hatred, malice, anger, displeasure, distraction of minds, dissension in religion, &c.

In consideration whereof the ancient fathers of Christ's church in times past were wont to call this holy banquet or supper of the Lord *Agape*[2], that is to say "love," to put men in remembrance, that none should come unto that heavenly table, where the blessed sacrament of love is ministered and set forth, but such as came with hearts inflamed with true love and unfeigned charity toward all men. They, therefore, which presume otherwise to come, are companions with Judas, into whom Satan entered so soon as he had unreverently and unworthily tasted of these holy mysteries, never forsaking him till he had brought him unto desperation, destruction, and damnation. John xiii. Matt. xxvi.

Seeing we be members all of one body, and have one head, even the Lord Christ Jesus; seeing also we have all one heavenly Father, one elder brother, one inheritance in the kingdom of heaven; again, seeing we all be baptized with one baptism, and eat of one bread, and drink of one cup; what thing should be of so great force to dissolve this unity, and to break that concord and amity, which we ought continually to have among us, both in doctrine and manners? "In this thing shall all men know," saith Christ, "that ye are my disciples, if one of you love another." And the blessed apostle St Paul exhorteth us, by the name of our Lord Jesus Christ, that we "all speak one thing, and that there be no dissension among us, but that we may be an whole body, of one mind, and of one meaning;" yea, and that the same affection may reign in us one toward another, that was in Christ Jesu, so that, "if one member suffer, all should suffer with him; and if one member be had in honour, all members should be glad also," "forasmuch as we be members one of another," and have one head, even the Lord Jesu. John xiii. 1 Cor. i. Phil. ii. 1 Cor. xii.

[2 Οὐκ ἐξόν ἐστιν χωρὶς τοῦ ἐπισκόπου οὔτε βαπτίζειν οὔτε ἀγάπην ποιεῖν.—Ignat. ad Smyrn. 8. in Patr. Apostol. Oxon. 1838. Tom. II. p. 414. It ought to be observed, that Ignatius is by some supposed to mean here not the Lord's supper itself, but the *Agape*, or feast of charity which accompanied it; of which our author afterwards makes mention. See below, page 251.]

Father. What other causes are there of the institution of the Lord's supper? *Son.* The Lord Christ ordained this holy supper also, that we, worthily enjoying the same, should the better be confirmed in our faith, and nothing doubt of the promise and good will of God toward us; but faithfully and constantly be persuaded, that whatsoever our heavenly Father hath promised us in Christ, and for Christ's sake,
Hos. xiii. 1 Cor. xv. that will he abundantly perform; so that we need not fear the tyranny of Satan, the
Eph. ii. Col. ii. curse of the law, the horror of death, the dart of desperation, the pains of hell, nor
Heb. ii. any other thing, whatsoever is most contrary to our health and salvation, which all
Rom. viii. be taken away by the death of Christ. "If God be on our side," saith St Paul, "who can be against us? which spared not his own Son, but gave him for us all: how can it be, that with him he should not give us all things also?" For who
Rom. iv. knoweth not, that sacraments are the seals of God, annexed to his most comfortable promises, which he hath most graciously made to all sinners that repent and believe, that through the contemplation and beholding of them, yea, through the enjoying and using of them, their faith may be stirred up, increased, and confirmed?

Again, this holy sacrament was instituted of the Lord Jesu, to preach unto us that his blessed body and his precious blood is the true nourishment of the faithful soul; and that through this meat, which is received by faith, our souls be relieved, comforted, sustained, made strong, joyful, and merry, and preserved unto everlast-
John vi. ing life, as Christ himself testifieth, saying: "I am the bread of life: he that cometh to me shall not hunger; and he that believeth on me shall never thirst." "And this is the will of him that sent me, that every one which seeth the Son, and believeth on him, have everlasting life; and I will raise him up at the last day." "Verily, verily, I say unto you, He that putteth his trust in me hath everlasting life." "I am that living bread, which came down from heaven. If any man eat of this bread, he shall live for ever. And the bread that I will give is my flesh, which I will give for the life of the world." "Whoso eateth my flesh, and drinketh my blood, hath everlasting life; and I will raise him up at the last day. For my flesh is meat indeed, and my blood is drink indeed. He that eateth my flesh, and drinketh my blood, dwelleth in me, and I in him. As the living Father hath sent me, and I live for the Father; even so he that eateth me shall live by the means of me."

Furthermore, another cause of the institution of this heavenly banquet is to move us to be thankful unto our heavenly Father for the death and passion of his Son, and for the inestimable benefits, fruits, and commodities, which we have plentifully obtained by the same, as deliverance from Satan, freedom from the curse of the law, forgiveness of sins, quietness of conscience, the gift of the Holy Ghost, victory against sin, death, and hell, righteousness before God, salvation, and everlasting life. And to this end the ancient fathers of Christ's church called the supper of the Lord *Sacramentum Eucharistiæ*[1], that is to say, the "sacrament of thanksgiving." So likewise read we
Acts ii. of the primitive and apostolic church: "All that believed," saith blessed Luke, "continued daily with one accord in the temple, and brake bread from house to house, and did eat their meat together with gladness and singleness of heart, praising God."
1 Cor. x. And St Paul saith: "Is not the cup of thanksgiving, for the which we give thanks, partaking of the blood of Christ?" &c.

Father. Now that thou hast declared unto me, what the Lord's supper is, who did institute it, and for what purpose and end it was ordained and commanded to be frequented and used in the church of Christ, come off, tell me how we ought to prepare ourselves unto the worthy receiving of so worthy and holy mysteries, that we, coming worthily and reverently unto them, may be made partakers of all those heavenly benefits, which Christ hath purchased of God the Father for us by his glorious passion and blessed death. *Son.* This thing is also necessary to be known.
1 Cor. xi. And unto this doth the apostle exhort us, saying: "Whosoever shall eat of this bread, or drink of the cup of the Lord unworthily, shall be guilty of the body and blood of the Lord. But let a man examine himself, and so let him eat of the bread, and

[[1] This name is found given to the Lord's supper in Justin. See below, page 239, note 2. Other authorities might easily be added.]

drink of the cup. For he that eateth or drinketh unworthily, eateth and drinketh his own damnation; because he maketh no difference of the Lord's body."

The Lord our God can by no means abide that any man should come unto his holy sacraments with unwashed feet, as they use to say; that is, unreverently and unworthily, as we may see also in the old law. Was not this the commandment of God, that when the people of Israel did eat the Lord's passover, otherwise called the paschal lamb (which was the sacrament and figure of the true paschal Lamb, even Christ Jesus, "which taketh away the sin of the world"), they should eat sweet and unleavened bread, and suffer no leaven to be in their houses, nor yet taste of any leavened bread by the space of seven days; and if any did the contrary, that that soul should be plucked out from Israel? Was not Uzza stricken of God even unto the death, because he unworthily touched the ark of the Lord? Was not a certain man taken from the table, bound hand and foot, and cast into utter darkness, where weeping and gnashing of teeth shall be, because he presumed to come unto the marriage of a certain noble king's son without the wedding garment? Did not the devil enter into Judas immediately after he had unworthily received the holy mysteries of the body and blood of Christ? Writeth not St Paul, that the Corinthians were both grievously and diversly plagued of God, because they came unreverently unto the Lord's table? And who doubteth but that even at this present time many plagues are cast upon us for abusing this holy sacrament? It is therefore convenient, that we learn how we may come unto so holy mysteries not unworthily, but worthily, not unto our damnation, but unto our salvation; lest, where we seem to seek remedy and comfort, we find destruction and displeasure.

Exod. xii. John i. 2 Sam. vi. Matt. xxii. John xiii. 1 Cor. xi.

Father. Well said, my son. Let me therefore now hear, how we ought to prepare ourselves worthily to come unto the table of the Lord, lest, where we seek consolation, we find desolation. *Son*. Whosoever intendeth with fruit to come unto the table of the Lord, and worthily to receive the holy mysteries of the body and blood of our Saviour Christ, he must first of all even from the very heart repent him of his former wicked life, lament earnestly his corrupt manners, abhor his old ungodly conversation, and be heartily sorry that ever he hath committed such wickedness against the Lord his God, and so disobediently transgressed and broken his holy and blessed commandments.

How we shall prepare ourselves unto the Lord's table.

Repentance.

Father. Is this repentance so necessary for the worthy preparation unto the coming to the Lord's table? *Son*. It is so necessary, that whosoever presumeth to come unto the supper of the Lord without this repentance, he shall not only not receive any benefit at the Lord's table, but he also shall be guilty of the body and blood of Christ, and get unto himself everlasting damnation. The unpenitent sinners are meet guests for the table of the devil; but such doth not the Lord admit unto his table, as St Paul saith: "I would not that ye should have fellowship with the devils. Ye cannot drink of the cup of the Lord, and of the cup of the devils. Ye cannot be the partakers of the Lord's table, and of the table of the devils." If any man therefore intendeth to come unto the Lord's table worthily, let him bring repentance with him, yea, and that not feigned, but hearty repentance; as we read of David, Peter, Mary Magdalen, the thief, and such like. For true repentance is an acceptable sacrifice unto God, as David witnesseth: "A sacrifice to God is a troubled spirit; a broken and a contrite heart, O God, shalt thou not despise." And the Lord himself saith by the prophet: "Which of them shall I regard? Even him that is poor, and of a lowly troubled spirit, and standeth in awe of my words." To the penitent and sorrowful-hearted is Christ a Saviour, and not to such as glory and delight in their sin. "Repent," saith the scripture, "for the kingdom of God," that is to say, remission of sins, "is at hand." "Repentance" goeth before, and "remission of sins" followeth; so that without repentance remission of sins is looked for in vain; as Christ saith: "Except ye repent, ye shall all perish." And the apostle saith: "Godly sorrow causeth repentance unto salvation not to be repented of." St Peter also saith: "God resisteth the proud, but he favoureth the humble and lowly."

1 Cor. x. 2 Sam. xxiv. 1 Chron. xxi. Matt. xxvi. Luke vii. Luke xxii. Psal. li. Isai. lxvi. Matt. iv. Mark i. Luke xxiv. Luke xiii. 2 Cor. vii. 1 Pet. v.

Father. What followeth? *Son*. Out of this hearty and earnest repentance must also an humble confession of the repented sins unto God issue; so that we do not dissemble nor cloke our sins, but with all humility and lowliness of heart confess them, and frankly and freely grant that we have most wickedly disobeyed the Lord our God, and transgressed his holy and blessed will.

Confession unto God.

Father. Is the confession of sins also necessary for them that will worthily come unto the Lord's table? *Son*. Yea, verily.

Father. And doth it profit also unto everlasting life? *Son*. Who doubteth of that? Hear what the psalmograph saith: "I will knowledge my sin, O Lord, unto thee, and mine unrighteousness will I not hide. I said, I will confess my sins unto the Lord; and thou forgavest the wickedness of my sin." Hear also what St John saith: "If we say that we have no sin, we deceive ourselves, and the truth is not in us. But if we confess our sins, God is faithful and righteous to forgive us our sins, and to cleanse us from all unrighteousness. If we say we have not sinned, we make him a liar, and his word is not in us." David, guilty both of whoredom and manslaughter, after he had repented him and confessed that he had sinned against the Lord, heard these sweet and comfortable words at the mouth of the prophet Nathan: "The Lord hath put away thy sin: thou shalt not die." The prodigal son, which had riotously and wickedly spent his father's goods, after that he fell to repentance, humbled himself before his father, and confessed his sins, saying, "O father, I have sinned against heaven and in thy sight, and am no more worthy to be called thy son," was clearly forgiven; so that his father had compassion on him, ran unto him, fell on his neck, and kissed him, and caused the best garment to be brought forth and to be put on him, and a ring to be put on his hand, and shoes on his feet, and a fat calf to be killed, that they might eat and make merry, because his son which was dead was alive again, and he that was lost was found again. The poor publican, which was so ashamed of his sins, that he durst not look up unto heaven, but stood afar off, and smote upon his breast, saying, "O God, be merciful to me a sinner," went home to his house more justified than the proud Pharisee for all his glistering works. For Christ "came not to call the righteous," that is to say, such as justify themselves, "but sinners unto repentance." "There is more joy in heaven over one sinner that repenteth, than over ninety and nine just persons that need no repentance."

Psal. xxxii. 1 John i. 2 Sam. xii. Luke xv. Luke xviii. Matt. ix. Luke xv.

Father. Is repentance and confession of sins unto God sufficient for the worthy preparation unto the Lord's table? *Son*. That which followeth is so necessary, that without it both repentance and confession profit nothing at all.

Faith.

Father. What is that? *Son*. Faith.

Father. What is that to say? *Son*. A sure and an undoubted persuasion or belief of heart, that though the sins of them that intend to come unto the Lord's table be never so great and many, yet notwithstanding that they shall be freely and fully forgiven of God the Father for his Son Christ Jesus' sake, for his passion and death, for his blessed body-breaking and precious blood-shedding, for the dignity and worthiness of that one and alone sweet-smelling sacrifice, which he offered once for all, sufficient to the uttermost for the salvation of the whole world, unto God his Father on the cross.

Eph. v. Heb. vii. ix. x.

Father. Is this faith necessary to the faithful communicant? *Son*. So necessary, that without it all other preparations are frustrate and vain. For "he that believeth on the Son of God," saith the scripture, "hath everlasting life: but he that believeth not on the Son of God shall not see life, but the wrath of God abideth upon him." Faith is the wedding-garment, wherewith whosoever is not clad, and yet presumeth to come unto the marriage of the Son of God, he shall be bound hand and foot, and cast into utter darkness, where weeping and gnashing of teeth shall be. And these are they (I speak of the unfaithful), which most unworthily come unto the Lord's table, and are guilty of the body and blood of the Lord; yea, and whatsoever they receive there, they receive it unto the damnation both of their body and soul. Therefore such as intend with fruit to come unto the Lord's table, they may not only bring with them repentance and confession of their sins, but also this faith, wherewith they are most assuredly persuaded that they have obtained full and perfect remission of all their sins through the blood and death of Christ, and that whatsoever Christ

John iii. Matt. xxii.

suffered on the altar of the cross, he suffered it altogether for them and for their sins: again, whatsoever he won, got, and purchased by his passion and death, he got it altogether for them and for their salvation; so that whole Christ, with all the benefits, merits, profits, fruits, and commodities, which he obtained of God his Father in his humanity, is altogether theirs, their own, and their right; forasmuch as they believe in Christ, and with strong faith embrace him as their alone perfect and omnisufficient Saviour, as St Paul saith: "Christ is the perfect fulfilling of the law to justify every one that believeth." Again: "Christ is our wisdom, and righteousness, and sanctification, and redemption, that, according as it is written, He that rejoiceth should rejoice in the Lord." And the prophet saith: "Whosoever believeth on him shall not be confounded." Rom. x. 1 Cor. i. Jer. ix. Isai. xxviii.

To stir up and to confirm the faith of the faithful communicants in that behalf, it shall be necessary diligently to weigh, ponder, and consider these sweet and comfortable promises, which are annexed to the holy mysteries of the body and blood of our Saviour Christ; even these: "Which shall be betrayed for you," "which shall be shed for you and for many, unto the remission of sins." For in them doth our greatest consolation and comfort consist, if we believe them. Little doth it profit us to believe that Christ's body was broken, and his blood shed, except we believe that his body was broken and his blood shed for our sins, for our wealth and commodity, for our profit and singular benefit; even as it pleasureth us nothing to believe that Christ was born, except we also believe that he was born for us and for our salvation, as the prophet saith: "A child is born TO US, and a son is given TO US." For this must be our faith, belief, and undoubted persuasion, that Christ gave up his body to be crucified, and his blood to be shed, that he might purchase unto us remission and forgiveness of all our sins, the grace, favour, and mercy of God, quietness of conscience, the gift of the Holy Ghost, and in fine, everlasting salvation, as St Paul saith: "God made him to be sin (that is to say, a sacrifice for sin) FOR US, which knew no sin, that we by his means should be made that righteousness," which before him is allowed. Again: "Christ loved us, and gave himself FOR US, an offering and a sweet-smelling sacrifice to God." Matt. xxvi. Isai. ix. 2 Cor. v. Eph. v.

Father. If the communicants bring with them unto the Lord's table repentance, confession, and faith, is it then sufficient? *Son.* Out of this repentance and faith, whereof I have hitherto spoken, must true, fervent, christian, vehement, and brenning charity or love toward our neighbour spring; so that we must also diligently consider how the matter standeth between us and our neighbour. For this supper of the Lord, as it abhorreth all sin, so likewise doth it most chiefly detest hatred, malice, envy, rancour, displeasure, and whatsoever is contrary to christian charity and brotherly love; being itself, as we tofore heard, a sacrament of love, unity, and concord. Charity.

Father. Is charity and love so necessary also to them that intend worthily to come unto the table of the Lord? *Son.* So necessary, that without it, whatsoever we do at the Lord's table, it turneth unto damnation. To speak with the tongues of men and of angels; to prophesy and to understand all secrets and all knowledge; to have all faith, so that we could move mountains out of their places; to bestow all our goods to feed the poor; yea, to give our bodies to be burned; profiteth nothing, without charity and love. 1 Cor. xiii.

"Every one that loveth," saith St John, "is born of God, and knoweth God. But he that loveth not knoweth not God; for God is love." "If any man say, I love God, and yet hate his brother, he is a liar. For how can he, that loveth not his brother whom he hath seen, love God whom he hath not seen?" "Every one that hateth his brother is a manslayer." "In this," saith the Lord Jesu, "shall all men know that ye are my disciples, if one of you love another." 1 John iv. 1 John iii. John xiii.

Such therefore as intend worthily to approach unto the Lord's table, let them not only consider how the matter standeth between them and God, but also between them and their neighbours. And if they shall find any displeasure among themselves one toward another, let them, before they come unto the Lord's table, seek to be reconciled one to another, according to this commandment of our Lord and Saviour Christ: "If thou offerest thy gift at the altar, and there rememberest that thy brother hath ought Matt. v.

against thee, leave there thine offering before the altar, and go thy way first, and be reconciled to thy brother, and then come and offer thy gift." How greatly those things displease God, although in outward appearance they glister and shine never so holy
Gen. iv. and virtuous, which come from an hateful and malicious heart, the history of Cain
1 Pet. iv. declareth abundantly. "Above all things," saith St Peter, "have fervent charity among you. For charity covereth the multitude of sins." And let this their love be no fleshly
1 Tim. i. nor worldly love, but such love as cometh "out of a pure heart, and of a good conscience, and of faith unfeigned." Such love is the end, that is to say, the fulfilling of the law;
Rom. xiii. Exod. xx. Deut. v. as St Paul saith: "He that loveth his neighbour hath fulfilled the law. For these commandments, Thou shalt not commit adultery, Thou shalt not kill, Thou shalt not steal, Thou shalt not bear false witness, Thou shalt not lust, and so forth; if there
Lev. xix. Matt. xxii. be any other commandment, it is all comprehended in this saying, namely, Love thy neighbour as thyself. Love hurteth not his neighbour: therefore is love the fulfilling of the law."

Father. If this repentance, confession, faith, and love, whereof thou hast hitherto spoken, be found in the communicants, may they then with a free conscience come unto the Lord's table, as persons not altogether unworthy to be partakers of so holy mysteries?

Disposition unto amendment of life. *Son.* Besides these things whereof we have hitherto spoken, it is required of the Lord's guests, that they have within themselves an hearty and unfeigned disposition to lead a better life for ever after, and earnestly to provide, that they fall no more into those sins, wherewith heretofore they have most grievously offended the majesty of God; whereof also they are now greatly ashamed and sore repent them. For without this meditation and earnest study of a new life, I see not what all the aforesaid things profit.

2 Cor. v. Gal. v. Matt. iii. "If any man," saith St Paul, "be in Christ, he is a new creature." Again: "They that are Christ's have crucified the flesh with the affections and lusts." "Bring forth the fruits that belong to repentance," saith St John the Baptist. "For even now is the axe also put unto the root of the trees; so that every tree which bringeth not forth good fruit is hewn down and cast into the fire." And Christ said unto the Jews:
John viii. "If ye were Abraham's children, ye would do the works of Abraham." Even so, if we be God's children, as we profess by our outward coming unto the Lord's supper,
John vi. we must do the works of God. The works which God requireth of us, are to believe in the name of his only-begotten Son, to love one another, and to walk in a new life.
Luke i. For unto this end hath God the Father by the death of his Son "delivered us from the power of our enemies, that we should serve him in holiness and righteousness all
1 Thess. iv. the days of our life." "God hath not called us unto uncleanness, but unto holiness."
Eph. ii. "We are God's workmanship, created in Christ Jesu unto good works, which God
Tit. ii. ordained, that we should walk in them." "The grace of God, which bringeth salvation unto all men, hath appeared, teaching us that we should deny ungodliness and worldly lusts, and that we should live soberly and righteously and godly in this present world, looking for that blessed hope and glorious appearing of the great God and of our Saviour Jesu Christ, which gave himself for us, to redeem us from all unrighteousness, and
Heb. ix. to purge us a peculiar people unto himself, fervently given unto good works." "Christ, which through the eternal Spirit offered himself without spot to God, hath purged our conscience from dead works, for to serve the living God."

Father. The faithful communicants then ought to bring with them unto the Lord's ☞ table unfeigned repentance, humble confession of their sins unto God, constant faith in the merciful promises of God, fervent charity toward their neighbour, and an hearty disposition unto amendment of life. *Son.* Yea, verily. And all these things ought to brast out into good works, into godliness of life, into a new conversation, into uncorrupt manners; so that from henceforth our life be altered, our conversation be changed, and our manners be framed according to the rule of God's holy word, that ever
Phil. ii. after we may be "such as no man can complain on, and unfeigned sons of God, without rebuke in the midst of a crooked and perverse nation, shining as lights in the world,
Matt. v. and holding fast the word of life." "Let your light so shine before men," saith our Saviour Christ, "that they may see your good works, and glorify your Father which
Tit. iii. is in heaven." And St Paul saith: "Let ours (that is to say, Christians) learn to excel in good works, as far forth as need requireth, that they be not unfruitful."

Father. And must this disposition unto innocency of life continue in them so long as they live? *Son*. They may not only dispose themselves unto good works, but also practise good works diligently all the days of their life, that they be not wording gospellers, but working gospellers; not favourers only, but also followers of God's word. For it is not sufficient to begin well, except we continue well; neither it is sufficient for a while to continue well, except we end well. "He that continueth unto the end shall be saved." "No man that putteth his hand to the plough, and looketh back, is meet for the kingdom of God." "No man is crowned, except he strive lawfully." "Be faithful unto the death," saith Christ, "and I will give thee the crown of life." Our Saviour Christ in the gospel commandeth us to "remember Lot's wife;" by the which he goeth about to put us in remembrance, that it is not sufficient to begin well, except we continue well, and also end well. Lot's wife began well, when she came out of Sodom; but because she continued not well, but, contrary to the commandment of God's angel, looked back again to Sodom, she was punished and turned into a salt pillar.

Matt. x. Luke ix. 2 Tim. ii. Rev. ii. Luke xvii. Gen. xix.

The wise men, which came from the east parts to seek Christ, that new-born King of the Jews, after they had departed from that bloody tyrant king Herod, and had worshipped Christ, were commanded by the angel of God that they should no more return unto king Herod, but go home into your country another way. For all such as have dedicated themselves to God by taking on them the holy sacrament of baptism, and by receiving the holy and blessed mysteries of the body and blood of our Saviour Christ, have openly professed, that from henceforth they will never have to do with the devil, the world, and the flesh, but utterly renounce and forsake them, with all their works, pomps, and vanities, serving their Lord God "in holiness and righteousness all the days of their life."

Matt. ii. Luke i.

Now, if any fall from this their profession, and join familiarity again with the devil, the world, and the flesh, obeying their lusts, and satisfying their desires, then have they utterly given over God and all godliness; yea, then are they become mockers of God and of his holy mysteries, and get to themselves everlasting damnation. "For of whom a man is overcome," saith St Peter, "unto the same is he brought in bondage. For if they (after they have escaped from the filthiness of the world, through the knowledge of the Lord and Saviour Jesu Christ) are yet tangled again therein, and overcome, then is the latter end worse with them than the beginning. For it had been better for them not to have known the way of righteousness, than after they have known it to turn from the holy commandment that was given unto them. But the same is happened to them that is used to be spoken by the true proverb, The dog is turned to his vomit again; and the sow that was washed is turned again to her wallowing in the mire." To whom is this saying of the Lord Jesu unknown? "When the unclean spirit is gone out of a man, he walketh through dry places, seeking rest. And when he findeth none, he saith, I will return again unto my house, whence I came out. And when he cometh, he findeth it swept and garnished. Then goeth he and taketh to him seven other spirits worse than himself; and they enter in and dwell there: and the end of that man is worse than the beginning."

2 Pet. ii. Prov. xxvi. Luke xi.

Therefore whosoever intendeth to prepare himself worthily unto the Lord's table, let him first of all fall unto hearty repentance; secondly, let him humble himself before the majesty of God by confessing his sins; thirdly, let him stedfastly believe, and be perfectly persuaded, that all his sins are forgiven him of God the Father for Christ's sake; fourthly, let him nourish fervent love in his heart toward his neighbour; fifthly and finally, let him for ever after so dispose himself to walk in a new life, that from henceforth he "have no more to do with the unfruitful works of darkness," but in all points so behave himself as it becometh the professor of godliness.

Eph. v.

Father. Hitherto thou hast declared what the Lord's supper is, who did institute it, unto what end it was ordained, and how we ought to prepare ourselves worthily to come unto the Lord's table: I would now gladly hear, if any abuses have crept into the church of Christ concerning the Lord's supper. Have your preacher or catechist opened nothing unto you in this behalf? *Son*. Yes, verily. They have declared certain notable abuses brought into the church of Christ in times past by antichrist and his adherents.

Certain abuses of the Lord's supper.

Father. Which are they? Let me hear part of them. *Son*. First, whereas the Lord Christ ordained this his holy supper to be received of many, antichrist and his complices, contrary to the institution and commandment of Christ, have made a private ☞ breakfast of it; as we may see in the popish mass, where the mumbling massmonger eateth and drinketh all alone, and giveth no man part with him, except this be any part, to bless the people with an empty cup, when he hath drunk up altogether, as the manner is in all the pope's churches at principal and high feasts, as they term them.

The Lord's supper ought [not] to be private repast, but an holy banquet for many.

Father. Let me hear it proved by the word of God, that the Lord's supper ought not to be a private repast (as the papists abuse it in their masses), but rather a common banquet for many to receive it together. *Son*. The institution itself declareth evidently that it ought to be the food of many together, and not of one alone. For thus read we: "When they were eating, Jesus took bread, and when he had given thanks, he brake it, and gave it to the disciples, and said, Take ye, eat ye: this is my body, which is betrayed for you. And he took the cup, and thanked, and gave it them, saying, Drink ye all of this. For this is my blood (which is of the new testament), that is shed for many for the remission of sins. This do in the remembrance of me."

Matt. xxvi. Mark xiv. Luke xxii. 1 Cor. xi.

Here is it evident that Christ did not eat and drink the sacrament of his body and blood alone, nor yet gave it to one of his disciples only; but he distributed it to all his disciples, that they should eat and drink of it together, and not one alone. "Take ye: eat ye." He saith not, Take thou, eat thou alone by thyself. Again: "Drink ye all of this." He saith not, Drink thou alone of this. And the blessed apostle St Paul saith: "Is not the bread which we break (he saith not, which I break) partaking of the body of Christ? Is not the cup of thanksgiving, for the which we gave thanks, (he saith not, I give thanks) partaking of the blood of Christ?" And a little after he saith: "We all are partakers of one bread, and of one cup." Again he saith: "When ye come together into one place, the Lord's supper cannot be eaten. For every one beginneth afore to eat his own supper." Also in the same place he saith: "My brethren, when ye come together to eat (the Lord's supper), tarry one for another. If any man hunger, let him eat at home, that ye come not together unto condemnation." And blessed St Luke, describing the manner and custom of the primitive church, saith: "All that believed kept themselves together, and had all things common, and sold their possessions and goods, and parted them to all men, as every man had need. And they continued daily with one accord in the temple, and brake bread from house to house, and did eat their meat together with gladness and singleness of heart, praising God." Again: "Upon one of the sabbath days, when the disciples came together for to break bread," &c.

1 Cor. x.

1 Cor. xi.

Acts ii.

Of these authorities of the holy scripture is it evident, that the Lord's supper ought to be the banquet of many together, and not of one alone, as the papists abuse it.

The doctrine of the old fathers concerning the Lord's supper.

In Epist. i.

Father. But what is the doctrine of the ancient fathers in this behalf? *Son*. In all points like to the doctrine of the holy scripture. Of the order used in the old Latin church concerning the receiving of the holy communion of the body and blood of the Lord Jesu, Anacletus, bishop of Rome, writeth on this manner: "When the consecration is once done, let all communicate that will not be excommunicate. For so did the apostles ordain, and the holy church of Rome doth still observe and maintain the same[1]." Here it is plain, that the manner of the Latin church, otherwise called the west church, was that many, yea "all," saith Anacletus, should eat the Lord's supper together. Again, that all which would not be partakers of the Lord's supper should be excommunicate. He addeth moreover, that it was the ordinance of the apostles, and that the church of Rome did observe, keep, and maintain that ordinance

---

[[1] Peracta consecratione omnes communicent, qui noluerint ecclesiasticis carere liminibus. Sic enim et apostoli statuerunt, et sancta Romana tenet ecclesia.—Anaclet. Papa, Epist. i. in Decret. Gratiani, Par. 1583. Decr. Tert. Pars, De Consecr. Dist. ii. can. 10. cols. 2363, 4. The decretal epistles ascribed to the early bishops of Rome are not genuine.]

of the apostles; that is to say, that, when the Lord's supper was ministered, not one alone, as the manner is now, but many together were partakers of the same.

Father. The private masses were not then in use, as it seemeth. *Son.* Antichrist and the devil brought in those private, that is to say, thievish masses, many hundred years after, for lucre's sake, as the ancient histories do evidently prove. The old catholic church of Rome knew no private masses.

Father. But what sayest thou of the Greek church, otherwise called the east church? What order observed they? *Son.* Even the very same that the old Latin or west church observed. For the Greeks even from the apostles' time until these our days have ever observed and kept the order that was used in the primitive church, neither would they at any time receive these private masses into their churches; but whensoever they celebrate the Lord's supper, not one alone (as the use is in the pope's church), but many together are partakers of the same, according to this saying of St Paul: "We all are partakers of one bread, and of one cup." The Greeks have no private masses. 1 Cor. x.

Father. Canst thou prove this by ancient writers of the Greek church? *Son.* Yea, forsooth, very easily.

Father. Let me hear. *Son.* The ancient Greek writer, Justinus Martyr, hath these words: "After that he which is the ruler (in the ministry) hath given thanks, and all the people hath blessed, they which are called with us deacons, do give to every one of them that are present bread, wine, and water to receive; which with thanksgiving are consecrate; and they also carry it unto them that are absent. And this meat is called with us *Eucharistia*[2]," that is to say, thanksgiving. In secund. Apologia.

And Dionysius Areopagita, in his book *De Ecclesiastica Hierarchia*, sheweth evidently that in his time also the bread and the cup was not received of the minister alone, but that they were distributed to all men; so that many were partakers of those holy mysteries, and not one alone, as it is used in the popish masses[3]. Cap. 3. part 2.

St John Chrysostom in a certain homily hath these words: "Forasmuch as it is the dominical supper, that is to say, the Lord's, it ought to be common. For those things that are the Lord's, belong not to this or that servant (only), but they are common to all. That therefore which is the Lord's, even the very same is also common. For if it be thy Lord's, as it is indeed, thou oughtest not to take those things as proper to thee, but to set them forth as the Lord's things commonly to all; for this is the Lord's. But now thou dost not suffer it to be the Lord's, when thou dost not suffer it to be common, but eatest to thyself[4]." In 1 Cor. cap. xi. Hom. 27.

Clement, bishop of Rome, commandeth that there should so many hosts be offered on the altar, as should suffice the people. He saith not, as should serve the priest alone[5]. Epist. 2.

Bishop Durande writeth on this manner: "In the primitive church all that were present at the celebration of the masses (he meaneth, the Lord's supper) were wont every day to communicate, because all the apostles did drink of the cup, according to this saying of the Lord, 'Drink ye all of this.' For they offered a great loaf of bread, and sufficient for all; which thing the Grecians are reported to keep at this day[6]." In Rat. Div. Off. Lib. 4. Matt. xxvi.

Albertus, in his book *De Missæ Mysteriis*, declareth, that the use in times past

---

[[2] *Εὐχαριστήσαντος δὲ τοῦ προεστῶτος, καὶ ἐπευφημήσαντος παντὸς τοῦ λαοῦ, οἱ καλούμενοι παρ' ἡμῖν διάκονοι διδόασιν ἑκάστῳ τῶν παρόντων μεταλαβεῖν ἀπὸ τοῦ εὐχαριστηθέντος ἄρτου καὶ οἴνου καὶ ὕδατος, καὶ τοῖς οὐ παροῦσιν ἀποφέρουσι. καὶ ἡ τροφὴ αὕτη καλεῖται παρ' ἡμῖν εὐχαριστία.*—Just. Mart. Op. Par. 1742. Apol. i. p. 83.]

[[3] *Καὶ τὰς ἱερὰς θεουργίας ὁ Ἱεράρχης ὑμνήσας ἱερουργεῖ τὰ θειότατα, καὶ ὑπ' ὄψιν ἄγει τὰ ὑμνημένα διὰ τῶν ἱερῶς προκειμένων συμβόλων· καὶ τὰς δωρεὰς τῶν θεουργιῶν ὑποδείξας, εἰς κοινωνίαν αὐτῶν ἱερὰν αὐτός τε ἔρχεται, καὶ τοὺς ἄλλους προτρέπεται. μετασχὼν δὲ καὶ μεταδοὺς τῆς θεαρχικῆς κοινωνίας, εἰς εὐχαριστίαν ἱερὰν καταλήγει.*—Dionys. Areop. Op. Antv. 1634. De Eccles. Hierarch. cap. iii. 2. Tom. I. p. 284. See also 3. pp. 298, 9. It is hardly necessary to say that the works which go under the name of the Areopagite are not really his.]

[[4] *Ὅτι τὸ κυριακὸν δεῖπνον, τουτέστι, τὸ δεσποτικὸν, ὀφείλει κοινὸν εἶναι. τὰ γὰρ τοῦ δεσπότου οὐχὶ τοῦδε μέν ἐστι τοῦ οἰκέτου, τοῦδε δὲ οὐκ ἔστιν, ἀλλὰ κοινῇ πάντων. τὸ οὖν κυριακὸν τοῦτό φησι τὸ κοινόν. εἰ γὰρ τοῦ δεσπότου σου ἐστὶν, ὥσπερ οὖν καὶ ἔστιν, οὐκ ὀφείλεις ὡς ἴδια ἀποσπᾷν, ἀλλ' ὡς τοῦ Κυρίου καὶ τοῦ δεσπότου ὄντα, κοινῇ πᾶσι προτιθέναι. τοῦτο γάρ ἐστι κυριακόν. νῦν δὲ οὐκ ἀφίῃς αὐτὸ εἶναι κυριακὸν, μὴ ἀφεὶς εἶναι κοινὸν, ἀλλὰ καθ' ἑαυτὸν ἑστιώμενος.*—Chrysost. Op. Par. 1718-38. In Epist. I. ad Cor. Hom. xxvii. Tom. X. p. 244.]

[[5] See below, page 251, note 10.]

[[6] Ceterum in primitiva ecclesia omnes, qui celebrationi missarum intererant singulis diebus com-

was, that so many as came together in the church should communicate together[1]. The ancient Grecians call the Lord's supper *Synaxin*[2], that is to say, the communion or fellowship of many, or a partaking together of many.

But wherefore do I gather together so many authorities out of the ancient writers, to declare that the massing papists do utterly abuse the Lord's supper, while they make it a private breakfast, admitting no man unto the partaking of those holy mysteries but themselves alone; seeing that even of the very words, which they yet use in their mass, it may easily be gathered, that in times past, before antichrist sat as god in the consciences of men, and with his devilish decrees had driven away God's holy ordinances out of the church, the use and manner was, that many should communicate together with the priest, and not the priest alone? I will rehearse some of the words, as they be mentioned in their mass-book, and as the massmongers in the kingdom of antichrist say them at this present day in their masses. At their post-communion they say thus: *Quod ore sumpsimus, Domine, pura mente capiamus, &c*[3]. That is to say: "That which we have taken with the mouth, O Lord, grant that we may receive it with a pure mind, and that it may be made unto us of a temporal gift an everlasting remedy." Again: *Hæc nos communio purget a crimine, et cœlestis remedii faciat esse consortes*[4]. Which is thus Englished: "This communion mought purge us from sin, and make us partakers of the heavenly remedy." And in another place of their mass the massmongers desire God that so many as shall receive the holy body and blood of Christ may be filled with all heavenly blessing and grace[5].

All these words tofore rehearsed declare evidently, that in times past, before this devilish private mass brast in, the minister and the people together did receive the holy mysteries of the body and blood of Christ, and not the priest alone, as the manner is now in antichrist's kingdom. Neither do we find any mention made of the private mass in the writings of the ancient doctors, before the time of pope Gregory the First. As for the Grecians, the Armenians, the Indians, &c., they know not these private masses, but they use the Lord's supper in their churches, according to the institution of the Lord Jesu; not one alone, but many communicating together, as St Jerome saith: "The Lord's supper ought to be common to all; for he delivered the sacraments to all his disciples that were present equally[6]." (In 1 Cor. cap. xi.)

Father. I see now, that the Lord's supper is greatly abused of the papists in their private masses, while, contrary to the institution of Christ, they make that singular and private, which ought to be universal and common. But go forth to rehearse the abuses of the Lord's supper brought in by the papists.

(The second abuse.) *Son*. Secondly, the papists greatly abuse, yea, they alter, mangle, and deform the holy institution of the Lord's supper, while they, contrary to the commandment of Christ, take away half the sacrament of the body and blood of our Saviour Christ from the communion of the lay people, ministering the sacrament unto them, not under both kinds, according to the institution of Christ, but under one kind only, contrary to the commandment of Christ.

Father. What meanest thou by that? *Son*. Christ, giving for us and for our salvation not only his blessed body to be crucified, but also his most precious blood to be shed on the altar of the cross, that by this means we might be perfectly made

municare solebant, eo quod apostoli omnes de calice biberunt, Domino dicente, Bibite ex hoc omnes. De consecr. dist. 2. Non iste. Offerebant enim magnum panem, et omnibus sufficientem, quod adhuc Græci servare dicuntur.—Durand. Rat. Div. Offic. Venet. 1609. Lib. IV. cap. liii. 3. fol. 132.]

[1 Primum enim institutum fuit quod omnes in ecclesia convenientes omni die communicarent.—Albert. Mag. Opus Tripartit. Col. 1503. Summ. de Offic. Missæ, cap. xxi. fol. 39.]

[2 ..... ἐνιαίως ἀνηγόρευται Κοινωνία τε καὶ Σύναξις.—Dionys. Areop. Op. Antv. 1634. De Eccles. Hierarch. cap. iii. 1. Tom. I. p. 282.]

[3 Quod ore sumpsimus, Domine, pura mente capiamus: et de munere temporali fiat nobis remedium sempiternum.—Missal. ad Us. ac Consuet. Sarum. Par. 1527. Canon Missæ, fol. 164. 1.]

[4 Id. ibid.]

[5 Supplices te rogamus, omnipotens Deus: jube hæc perferri per manus sancti angeli tui in sublime altare tuum, in conspectu divinæ majestatis tuæ: ut quotquot ex hac altaris participatione sacrosanctum Filii tui corpus et sanguinem sumpserimus, omni benedictione cœlesti et gratia repleamur.—Id. ibid.]

[6 Cæterum dominica cœna omnibus debet esse communis: quia ille omnibus discipulis suis qui aderant, æqualiter tradidit sacramenta.—Hieron. Op. Par. 1693—1706. Comm. in Epist. I. ad Cor. cap. xi. Tom. V. col. 997.]

whole both in body and soul, willing that a remembrance of this his healthful benefit should for ever after be continued in his church until he return unto the judgment, that the most noble work of our redemption might perpetually remain in our memories, and never be forgotten, and we thereby provoked unto humble and hearty thanksgiving to God the Father for the live-making death of his most dearly-beloved Son, instituted an holy sacrament, which St Paul calleth "the Lord's supper," even the sacrament of his body and blood, consisting of bread and wine—not of bread only, nor of wine only, but of bread and wine together—and commanded them to be received together of the faithful in the holy action of his supper, the bread to be a memorial of his body-breaking, and the wine a remembrance of his blood-shedding; that we, according to his holy institution eating the bread and drinking the wine, should be admonished and put in remembrance of our perfect salvation concerning both body and soul, gotten by the passion and death, by the body-breaking and blood-shedding of Christ, the Son of God, and the son of Mary the virgin. Now therefore, whereas the papists, contrary both to the institution and commandment of Christ, administer this holy sacrament to their communicants only under one kind, that is to say, the kind of bread, and steal from them the cup of the mystery of Christ's blood, they greatly abuse the Lord's supper; yea, as I said afore, they alter, change, mangle, corrupt, and utterly deform the holy institution of these blessed mysteries; as I may speak nothing of the extreme injury and wrong, of the theft and bribery, yea, of the sacrilege and health-robbing, which these antichrists do and commit against the people of God, contrary to all truth, contrary to all right.

1 Cor. xi.

Father. Ought the lay people also to receive the mysteries of the body and blood of Christ under both kinds, no less than the ministers of the church? *Son.* Did not Christ give his body to be crucified and his blood to be shed for the salvation of the layman so well as he did for the minister?

Of receiving the sacrament under both kinds.

Father. Who doubteth of that? *Son.* Are not the lay people also members of Christ's church?

Father. I grant. *Son.* And the Lord Jesus instituted his holy supper to be received of his whole church, I mean so many as are able to discern this mystical meat from the common food, and to prepare themselves worthily to come unto it.

Father. I confess. *Son.* With what forehead then, except they have too much rubbed their forehead, and be past all shame, dare they infringe and break both the institution and commandment of Christ, taking most unjustly that from the laity which the Lord Jesus hath most freely given unto them, yea, and hath commanded them so to receive and take it; I mean, not only the bread, but also the cup?

Father. Let me hear where Christ commanded that not only the bread, but also the cup, should be ministered. *Son.* Concerning the bread, which is the mystery of his body, Christ saith: "Take ye, eat ye." And as touching the mystery of his blood he saith: "Drink ye all of this." And in the words of the cup it is to be noted, that Christ hath this word, "all," which he hath not in the words belonging to the mystery of his body: "Drink ye all of this," saith he, aforeseeing, without doubt, in the Spirit, that there should arise false prophets and false anointed, which presumptuously would deny the mystery of his blood to some certain men, as the papists do to the laity, yea, and to their own priests also, except they sacrifice and be clothed with their missal and mystical, with their histrionical and scenical robes; by this means transgressing the commandment of God for the maintenance of their wicked trifling tradition. Therefore with express, evident, and plain words Christ saith: "Drink ye all of this." "All," saith he, excepting none. With what therefore imprudenty, shall I say, or rather impudency, dare the adversaries of God's truth, against so evident words and express commandment of Christ, take away the holy mystery of the blood of Christ from the lay people? "Drink ye all of this," saith he.

Matt. xxvi.

Matt. xv.
Mark vii.

Father. And did the disciples drink of this cup according to the commandment of Christ? *Son.* So testifieth blessed Mark, saying: "They all drank of it."

Mark xiv.

Father. But here it is objected, Christ spake these words to his disciples, which were consecrate priests, and not to laymen; and therefore the priests alone ought to receive the cup of the mystery of Christ's blood. *Son.* So likewise spake Christ

Objection.

Answer. of the mystery of his body these words only to his disciples: "Take ye, eat ye." Therefore look, with what authority the papists may take away the mystery of the blood of Christ from the laity, with the very same authority may they also take from them the mystery of Christ's body. For he that said, "Take and eat;" the very same said:
Luke xxii. "Take and drink," "Divide this cup among you."

If "take and eat" belong unto the common people, so likewise doth "take and drink" appertain unto the common people. If "take and drink" belong not unto them, neither do "take and eat" appertain unto them. But "take and eat" appertain unto the laity; therefore "take and drink" belong unto them also. For who knoweth not that the apostles of Christ in that holy supper represented the whole church of Christ?
☞ and Christ, in delivering unto them the holy mysteries of his body and blood, and commanding them to receive those from time to time, even unto the world's end, in the remembrance of him, of his passion and death, of his body-breaking and blood-shedding, delivered them to his whole church, and gave commandment that his people should from age to age, yea, in every age, use those holy mysteries unto his glorious return unto the
1 Cor. xi. judgment, as St Paul saith: "So often as ye shall eat this bread, and drink of this cup, ye shall shew the Lord's death till he come." And thus did both the apostles of Christ, and Christ's primitive church, and all the ancient fathers many hundred years after, understand, take, and use the Lord's supper, as both divine and human letters manifestly declare.

1 Cor. x. Are not these the words of blessed St Paul? "Is not the cup of thanksgiving, for the which we give thanks, partaking of the blood of Christ? Is not the bread, which we break, partaking of the body of Christ? Because that we (though we be many) yet are one bread, and one body; inasmuch as we all are partakers of one bread and of one cup." Of whom speaketh the holy apostle here? of consecrate priests, as they term them, or rather of the whole congregation of God? Verily, of the whole congregation of God. And forasmuch as he maketh mention here, not only of the bread, but also of the cup; who seeth not evidently, that in the time of the blessed apostle St Paul all the Christians, so well the temporalty as the spiritualty, as I may speak after the common manner, received the holy communion of the body and blood of Christ under both kinds, according to the institution and commandment of the Lord Jesu? which thing he declareth afterward manifestly, when he entreateth at large of the Lord's supper, joining ever together the bread and the cup. Are not these his words? "As often as ye shall eat this bread, and drink of this cup." Again: "Whosoever shall eat of this bread, or drink of the cup of the Lord." Item: "Let him eat of the bread, and drink of the cup." And a little after: "He that eateth or drinketh unworthily eateth and drinketh his own damnation."

Here see we that the apostle, entreating of the Lord's supper, joineth always the bread and the cup together, to declare that it cannot be the Lord's supper, except there be distribution both of the bread and of the wine. And hereof may we learn that the Corinthians, which I am sure were not all consecrate priests, but the greatest part of them were lay people, received in the days of St Paul the holy sacrament of the body and blood of Christ under both kinds, and not under the kind of bread alone, as the manner is in the kingdom of the pope. And verily, it is unto me great wonder that ever the pope durst so presumptuously (but what dare not antichrist, having a
Rev. xiii. 2 Thess. ii. mouth full of blasphemies even against the Most Highest, and "exalting himself above all that is called God, or that is worshipped, so that he doth sit in the temple of God, boasting himself to be God?") alter and change, yea, corrupt and mangle the holy testament of our Lord and Saviour Jesus Christ, that King of kings and Lord of lords,
Gal. iii. which he sealed with his most precious blood. "Though it be but a man's testament," saith St Paul, "yet, if it be allowed, no man despiseth it, or addeth any thing thereto." How intolerable then is it for a sinful man to alter and change, to corrupt and mangle the blessed testament of God's only-begotten Son, which he confirmed with his death, and left it unto his church to be kept inviolably or unchangeably, as I may so speak!

Father. And was the receiving of the sacrament of Christ's body and blood under both kinds used in the church of Christ after the apostles' time? *Son*. Yea, many hundred years after the time of the apostles, as we may see in the books of the ancient writers, wherein we read that both the bread and cup was given not only to the strong in age, but also to the young infants, yea, and that of necessity, as some thought, being moved with this sentence of our Saviour Christ, as it may seem: "Verily, verily, I say unto you, Except ye eat the flesh of the Son of man, and drink his blood, ye have no life in you." Notwithstanding, as we may easily gather of the ancient writings, the devil in all ages, from time to time, went about in his members to corrupt and to alter this godly institution of the Lord Jesus, and to take away the mystery of the Lord's blood from the communion of the laity, contrary to the institution of Christ; so greatly in no age ceaseth Satan to obscure the glory of Christ, and to pervert his holy ordinances. John vi.

In the time of St Cyprian, that blessed martyr, the like thing was attempted, as it may easily be gathered of these his words: "How do we teach or provoke them to shed their blood in the confession of the name (of Christ), if we do deny them, when they go unto the battle, the blood of Christ? Or how do we make them meet and apt unto the victory of martyrdom, if we do not first admit them that would rightly communicate in the church to drink of the Lord's cup[1]?" Ad Cornel. Epist. 2.

The like enterprise was attempted also in the days of these two bishops of Rome, Gelasius the first and Julius the first: but they both manfully resisted this wicked enterprise; so that pope Gelasius commanded that the whole sacrament should be received in both kinds severally, according to the institution of Christ, or else that whosoever would attempt the contrary, taking only the mystery of Christ's body, and abstain from the cup, should be restrained from the whole sacrament. He addeth moreover, that the "division of one and the same mystery cannot be done without great sacrilege[2]." And the gloss of the aforesaid decree of Gelasius hath these words: "The sacrament is not superfluously received under both kinds. For the kind of bread is referred unto the flesh, and the kind of wine unto the soul; when one[3] is the sacrament of the blood, in the which is the seat of the soul. And therefore is the sacrament received under both kinds, that it may be signified that Christ took both, the flesh and the soul, and that the participation of the sacrament is profitable as well for the soul as for the body; so that, if it should be taken only under one kind, it should be signified that it profiteth unto the tuition and preservation of the one only." De Consec. Dist. 2. Can. Comperimus. Ibidem.

And pope Julius commanded that the people should receive the holy communion according to Christ's institution, both the bread and cup, one several from the other[4], as the apostle saith: "Let a man examine himself, and so eat of that bread and drink of that cup." De Consec. Dist. 2. Can. Cum omne. 1 Cor. xi.

Moreover Gelasius, of whom we afore spake, wrote to certain bishops[5], and commanded all such to be excommunicate and accursed, which receiving the body of Christ abstained from the communion of the cup. Gelasius lived about the year of our Lord four hundred and ninety-two. And Julius lived about the year of our Lord three hundred and thirty-six.

Furthermore, this use of ministering the Lord's supper to the lay people under both kinds, according to the institution of Christ, endured in the church of Christ unto the time of pope Urban the fourth, and long after; which pope Urban lived about the year

---

[1 Nam quo modo docemus aut provocamus eos in confessione nominis sanguinem suum fundere, si eis militaturis Christi sanguinem denegamus? aut quo modo ad martyrii poculum idoneos facimus, si non eos prius ad bibendum in ecclesia poculum Domini jure communicationis admittimus?—Cypr. Op. Oxon. 1682. Epist. lvii. ad Cornel. p. 117.]

[2 Comperimus autem, quod quidam sumpta tantummodo corporis sacri portione a calice sacri cruoris abstineant. Qui proculdubio (quoniam nescio qua superstitione docentur obstringi) aut integra sacramenta percipiant, aut ab integris arceantur: quia divisio unius ejusdemque mysterii sine grandi sacrilegio non potest provenire.—Gelas. Papa in Decret. Gratiani, Par. 1583. Decr. Tert. Pars. De Consecr. Dist. ii. can. 12. cols. 2363-6.]

[3 Qu. *wine*?—Nec superflue sumitur sub utraque specie. Nam species panis ad carnem, et species vini ad animam refertur, cum vinum sit sacramentum sanguinis, in quo est sedes animæ. ideoque sumitur sub utraque specie, ut significetur quod utrumque Christus assumpsit, et carnem et animam; et quod tam animæ quam corporis participatio valeat. unde si sub una tantum specie sumeretur, ad tuitionem alterius tantum valere significaretur.—Ibid.]

[4 Illud vero, quod pro complemento communionis intinctam tradunt eucharistiam populis, nec hoc prolatum ex evangelio testimonium recipit, ubi apostolis corpus suum et sanguinem commendavit. Seorsum enim panis, et seorsum calicis, commendatio memoratur.—Jul. Papa in eod. can. 7. cols. 2361, 2.]

[5 The canon quoted above was addressed by Gelasius: Majorico et Joanni episcopis.]

of our Lord one thousand two hundred and sixty-three. In his days lived Thomas de Aquino, the black friar, which died about the year of our Lord one thousand two hundred and seventy-four. In his writings it evidently appeareth, that in his time both kinds of the sacrament were delivered to the lay people at the ministration of the Lord's supper, according to the institution of Christ; and he rendereth a reason and sheweth a cause, why the sacrament ought to be received under both kinds. These are his words: "Though whole Christ be under both kinds, yet is he not given in vain under both kinds: for this is the true use of the sacrament, that the body of Christ be exhibited and given apart to the faithful for meat, and the blood for drink. For the body (of Christ) is given for the salvation of the body, and the blood (of Christ) for the salvation of the soul[1]."

3 Par. q. 80. Art. 12.

☞

In 1 Cor. cap. xi.

The like words hath St Ambrose: "That we receive," saith he, "availeth unto the tuition of body and soul; for the flesh of Christ is offered for the salvation of the body, and the blood (of Christ) for our soul, as Moses prefigured: The flesh, saith he, is offered for your body, the blood for the soul[2]."

The council of Constance.

And this use of receiving the holy sacrament under both kinds continued in the church unto the council of Constance, which was holden and kept in the year of our Lord one thousand four hundred and fifteen; in the which council and thirteenth session it was decreed, that from that time forward the cup of the mystery of Christ's blood should no more be given to the laity, but that the lewd people should hold themselves content with one kind, and half of the sacrament, and think that they, so communicating after the determination of our mother holy church like obedient children, did receive enough for their salvation; forasmuch as under the kind of bread both the body and blood of Christ is contained[3].

Here drove antichrist, with his wicked tradition, Christ and his holy ordinance out of place; so that now whosoever shall presume to teach that the faithful ought to communicate under both kinds, according to Christ's institution, he himself is an heretic, and his doctrine plain heresy. And thus from that wicked council hitherto (in the which council most unjustly that most famous clerk John Wickliffe, our countryman, was condemned for an heretic, and the two godly learned men, Johannes Husse and Hieronymus de Praga, were most cruelly murdered and brent of the bloody papists, notwithstanding the emperor's safe conduct, for denying the popish article of transubstantiation, and for maintaining the receiving of the sacrament under both kinds, according to the doctrine of Christ), contrary to the practice of the primitive church, and contrary to the teaching of the ancient doctors, the cup of the mystery of Christ's blood hath been taken away in the kingdom of the pope from the communion of the laity. Notwithstanding this may we evidently see, that for the space of fourteen hundred years and fifteen after Christ the use was from time to time, that the lay people received the sacrament under both kinds, according to Christ's ordinance; so that this order of communicating the laity under one kind, as the custom is now under the pope's kingdom, hath only endured in the church an hundred years and forty-five in this year of our Lord one thousand five hundred and sixty. Who seeth not now, how this tradition is no less new than wicked? new, because it is lately invented and brought

[1 Ad primum ergo dicendum, quod quamvis totus Christus sit sub utraque specie, non tamen frustra. Nam primo, &c.......Secundo, hoc est conveniens usui hujus sacramenti, ut seorsum exhibeatur fidelibus corpus Christi in cibum et sanguis in potum. Tertio, quantum ad effectum, secundum quod supra dictum est, quod corpus exhibetur pro salute corporis, et sanguis pro salute animæ.—Thom. Aquinat. Op. Venet. 1506. Summ. Theol. Tert. Pars. Quæst. lxxvi. Art. 2. Tom. XII. fol. 245, 6. See also Quæst. lxxx. Art. 12. fol. 267.]

[2 In cujus typum nos calicem mysticum sanguinis ad tuitionem corporis et animæ nostræ percipimus......Caro enim Salvatoris pro salute corporis, sanguis vero pro anima nostra effusus est, sicut prius præfiguratum fuerat a Moyse; sic enim ait: Caro pro corpore vestro offertur, sanguis vero pro anima.—Ambros. Op. Par. 1686–90. Comm. in Epist. ad Cor. prim. cap. xi. 26. Tom. II. Appendix, col. 149.]

[3 Et sicut hæc consuetudo ad evitandum aliqua pericula et scandala est rationabiliter introducta, quod licet in primitiva ecclesia hujusmodi sacramentum reciperetur a fidelibus sub utraque specie, postea a conficientibus sub utraque, et a laicis tantummodo sub specie panis suscipiatur; cum firmissime credendum sit, et nullatenus dubitandum, integrum Christi corpus et sanguinem tam sub specie panis, quam sub specie vini veraciter contineri. Unde cum hujusmodi consuetudo ab ecclesia et sanctis patribus rationabiliter introducta et diutissime observata sit, habenda est pro lege, quam non licet reprobare, aut sine ecclesiæ auctoritate pro libito mutare.—Concil. Constant. in Concil. Stud. Labbei. Lut. Par. 1671–2. Sess. xiii. Tom. XII. col. 100.]

into the church; wicked, forasmuch as it fighteth with the ordinance of God, which to violate and to break is more than double wickedness.

Moreover, who knoweth [not] that the churches of the Greeks, of the Ethiopes, of the Rutenes[4], of the Bohems, &c. (as histories make mention) have unto this day always observed and kept the ancient and apostolic manner of receiving the sacrament under both kinds, according to the institution and ordinance of the Lord Christ, and by no means would obey the new and wicked decree of the bishop of Rome in this behalf? All the reformed churches throughout Europe also, even so many as have shaken off the cruel and heavy yoke of antichrist in this our age, have utterly rejected and cast away this wicked decree of the pope, and receive now generally the Lord's supper, according to the appointment of Christ, under both kinds. This thing also is not to be passed over with silence, that in a certain general council holden at Basil, after that wicked council tofore gathered at Constance, it was concluded, that according to Christ's institution the lay people also should receive the sacrament of the body and blood of Christ under both kinds[5]. And this decree was not only established by the authority of the emperor Sigismund, with the consent of the other nobles and learned men; but also confirmed, approved, and allowed by pope Eugenius the fourth, about the year of our Lord one thousand four hundred and thirty-six. I speak nothing of the council Toletane, in the which we may easily see, that at that time also the lay people used the sacrament under both kinds[6].

But wherefore do I tarry so long in setting forth so clear a matter, seeing this one sentence of Chrysostom, which I shall now recite, may seem abundantly to declare what is to be thought in this behalf? "Not as in the old law," saith he, "the priest did eat part and the people part; but one body and one cup is set forth to all. Those things which belong unto the eucharist (that is to say, the Lord's supper) are common all between the priest and the people[7]." In 2 Cor. cap. xviii. Hom. 18.

In the canon of the popish mass also we may plainly perceive, that before the private mass took place, the people did receive the sacrament with the minister, yea, and that under both kinds[8].

Father. Great abuses, I see right well, have of late years brast into the church of Christ, and specially about the Lord's supper. But, my dear son, if there be any other notable abuses behind concerning the sacrament of the body and blood of Christ, let me hear them also.

Son. Thirdly, the papists greatly abuse the supper of the Lord, while they make it of a commemorative sacrifice, or a sacrifice of thanksgiving, a sacrifice propitiatory, expiatory, satisfactory, &c. The third abuse.

[4 Probably the Russians. Illyricus Flac. con. Prim. Petr. et Paul. cap. vi. p. 48. 1667. Quin ne Græcæ quidem ecclesiæ, Asiaticæ, Rudenicæ, Moscoviticæ, Valachicæ, et aliæ, quæ vicinæ sunt, etiam hodierna die, Papam audiunt.]

[5 It appears to have been a modified consent that the council of Basil gave to the Bohemian petition on communion under both kinds. The following are the words of the decree: Decernit et declarat eadem sancta synodus, quod fideles laici sive clerici communicantes, et non conficientes, non adstringuntur ex præcepto Domini ad suscipiendum sub utraque specie, panis scilicet et vini, sacrum eucharistiæ sacramentum. Sed ecclesia quæ regitur Spiritu veritatis secum manente in æternum, et cum qua Christus manet usque ad consummationem sæculi, (sicut ait divina scriptura,) ordinare habet, quomodo ipsis non conficientibus ministretur, prout pro reverentia ipsius sacramenti et salute fidelium viderit expedire. Sive autem sub una specie, sive sub duplici quis communicet, secundum ordinationem seu observantiam ecclesiæ, proficit digne communicantibus ad salutem.—Concil. Basil. Sess. xxx. in Concil. Stud. Labbei. Tom. XII. cols. 600, 1. But Bellarmine is obliged to admit that a consent *was* given: Concessit eam facultatem (teste Æneа Sylvio in historia Bohemica, cap. 52.) cum ea conditione, ut crederent communionem sub una esse licitam, et proinde non esse contra jus divinum.—Bellarm. Op. Col. Agrip. 1617—20. De Sacr. Euchar. Lib. iv. cap. xxvi. Tom. III. col. 768.]

[6 The eleventh council of Toledo, held A.D. 675, is in all probability meant. Solet enim humanæ naturæ infirmitas, in ipso mortis exitu prægravata, tanto siccitatis pondere deprimi, ut nullis ciborum illationibus refici, sed vix tantumdem illati delectetur poculi gratia sustentari. Quod etiam in multorum exitu vidimus, qui optatum suis votis sacræ communionis expetentes viaticum, collatam sibi a sacerdote eucharistiam rejecerunt; non quod infidelitate hoc agerent, sed quod præter dominici calicis haustum, traditam sibi non possent eucharistiam deglutire.—Concil. Tolet. xi. in Concil. Stud. Labbei. cap. xi. Tom. VI. col. 552.]

[7 Ἔστι δὲ ὅπου οὐδὲ διέστηκεν ὁ ἱερεὺς τοῦ ἀρχομένου· οἷον, ὅταν ἀπολαύειν δέῃ τῶν φρικτῶν μυστηρίων. ὁμοίως γὰρ πάντες ἀξιούμεθα τῶν αὐτῶν. οὐ καθάπερ ἐπὶ τῆς παλαιᾶς, τὰ μὲν ὁ ἱερεὺς ἤσθιε, τὰ δὲ ὁ ἀρχόμενος. καὶ θέμις οὐκ ἦν τῷ λαῷ μετέχειν ὧν μετεῖχεν ὁ ἱερεύς. ἀλλ' οὐ νῦν· ἀλλὰ πᾶσιν ἓν σῶμα πρόκειται, καὶ ποτήριον ἕν.—Chrysost. Op. Par. 1718–38. In Epist. II. ad Cor. Hom. xviii. Tom. X. p. 568.]

[8 See before, p. 240, notes 3, 5.]

Against the sacrifice of the mass. *Father*. What meanest thou by that? *Son*. It is not unknown to the godly learned, that the Lord Jesus instituted the holy mysteries of his body and blood to this end, that they should be a memorial of his body-breaking and blood-shedding, of his passion and death, which he suffered on the altar of the cross for our redemption, as these his words evidently prove: "Take ye, eat ye: this is my body which is broken for you: do this in the remembrance of me." Again: "Drink ye all of this: this cup is a new testament in my blood. Do this, so oft as ye shall drink it, in the remembrance of me." So likewise saith the holy apostle: "So oft as ye shall eat this bread, and drink of the cup, ye shall shew the Lord's death till he come." But the papists cannot be content with this doctrine, that the supper of the Lord (which they more gladly term "the mass"), should be a memorial or remembrance of that sacrifice which Christ himself offered on the cross; but they will have it the self-same sacrifice, of the same virtue, strength, efficacy, might, and power, to save the souls both of the quick and dead.

Luke xxii.

O blasphemous doctrine! *Father*. How can that be? *Son*. They say that they offer up Christ the Son of God unto his heavenly Father, for a sacrifice both for the sins of the quick and of the dead.

Father. Is it so? *Son*. Nothing less. For the holy scripture declareth plainly in many places, that not another, but Christ himself offered himself a sacrifice unto God his Father to appease his wrath kindled against mankind through sin; and that, by the virtue of that his one and alone sacrifice God is at peace with man, favoureth, and loveth man, and accepteth man for righteous in his sight. St Paul hath these words: "Christ loved us, and gave up himself for us an oblation and sweet-smelling sacrifice to God." Again: "Christ through the everlasting Spirit offered himself undefiled unto God." Also in another place: "Christ did that, when he offered himself." And the prophet saith: "He offered up himself, because it was his pleasure." And although the papists have shewed themselves very arrogant and proud in matters of salvation; yet in this one point, that they will take upon them to offer Christ in their masses to be a propitiatory sacrifice unto God the Father for the sins of the quick and of the dead, they shew themselves to be more proud than Lucifer, as they say, or than that most proud king, which said in his heart: "I will climb up into heaven, and exalt my throne above, beside the stars of God. I will sit also upon the holy mount toward the north. I will climb up above the clouds, and will be like the Highest of all." And verily this is "that man of sin, the son of perdition, which is an adversary, and is exalted above all that is called God, or that is worshipped; so that he doth sit in the temple of God, boasting himself to be God: whom the Lord shall consume with the spirit of his mouth, and shall destroy with the appearance of his coming."

Eph. v. Heb. ix. Isai. liii. Isai. xiv. 2 Thess. ii. Isai. xi.

For what other thing is it, to presume for to offer Christ, than the massing papists to make themselves equal in dignity with Christ; yea, than to excel Christ in dignity? For he that offereth sacrifice unto God is greater and of more dignity before God than the sacrifice that is offered (for for the offerer's sake is the offering accepted of God, and not contrariwise): it therefore followeth that the massing papists, presuming to offer Christ for a sacrifice, are greater and of more dignity before God than Christ the Son of God. O intolerable pride!

Gen. iv. Who knoweth not that Habel was greater and of more dignity before God than the firstlings of his sheep, which he offered for a sacrifice? To whom also is it unknown, that Noah was more acceptable unto God, and of greater dignity before him, than all the clean beasts and clean fowls that he offered for a sacrifice? Was not Abraham of more excellency before God than the ram which he offered up for a sacrifice? The sacrificer is greater than the sacrifice. Who seeth not then, that the mass-mongers sacrificing Christ are greater and of more worthiness before God than Christ, whom they offer? Is not this to be like the Highest of all?

Gen. viii. Gen. xxii. Isai. xiv.

But if there be none other remedy, but that the massing priests will sacrifice Christ in their masses, and so obtain remission of sins unto them for whom they offer; then doth it also follow that they must needs murder, kill, and slay Christ, and shed Christ's blood. For "without shedding of blood," saith the apostle, "there is no remission of sins." But what read we in St Paul? "Christ," saith he, "being raised from death, dieth no more. Death hath no more power over him. For as

Heb. ix. Rom. vi.

touching that he died, he died as concerning sin once; and as touching that he liveth, he liveth unto God." If Christ dieth no more, then is he sacrificed no more. If he be sacrificed no more, then obtain the papists no remission of sins, either for the quick or for the dead, by the virtue of their popish mass, though they make it a sacrifice never so much propitiatory, expiatory, satisfactory, &c. But these massing papists are those "false prophets and false teachers," "which deny the Lord that bought them, 2 Pet. ii.
and bring upon themselves swift damnation; and many follow their damnable ways, by whom the way of truth is evil spoken of, and through covetousness with feigned words they make merchandise of their captives; whose judgment is not far off, and their damnation sleepeth not."

The missal sacrifice is injurious to the blood of Christ.

Moreover, this doctrine of the sacrifice of the mass is plainly injurious to the blood of Christ, obscureth the price of Christ's death, and disannulleth the virtue of Christ's sacrifice, which he offered on the altar of the cross for our sins, and maketh Christ no perfect Saviour and Redeemer. For if any of our sins be put away through the sacrifice of the popish mass, then was not our redemption perfect in the death of Christ, neither were all our sins washed away by the blood of Christ. But if all our sins be put away by the death of Christ, according to the doctrine of Christ and of his apostles, then is their doctrine of the missal sacrifice vain, false, wicked, and worthy to be hissed out of the church of Christ; seeing it so greatly embaseth the dignity of the sacrifice of Christ's death, and plucked away our trust and confidence from the merits of Christ's passion and death unto the trifling traditions and devilish doctrines of men. For to stablish a new sacrifice to take away sin is nothing else than to affirm and grant that the old sacrifice (I mean the death of Christ) is either of no force, or else it is imperfect. For if the death of Christ be of full force, and sufficiently perfect, yea, and to the uttermost able to take away the sins of the whole world (as it is indeed,) what need we the missal sacrifice, lately brought in by the devil and antichrist?

Father. Christ then offered himself a sacrifice to God the Father for our sins. *Son.* Yea, verily. He was both the offerer and the offering, the sacrificer and the sacrifice. For there was found neither patriarch nor prophet, neither priest nor Levite, neither angel nor archangel, neither any other creature in heaven or earth, that was of sufficient dignity to offer this our sacrifice, I mean the Lord Jesus. Much less are the filthy and ungodly papists, whose life is full of all uncleanness, and whose doctrine swimmeth with divers errors and heresies, meet men to offer up the Son of God a sacrifice for sin to the heavenly Father. And therefore "Christ offered him- Eph. v.
self a sweet-smelling sacrifice to God the Father."

The omnisufficiency of Christ's sacrifice.

Father. And was this his one sacrifice, which he offered on the altar of the cross, sufficient for the sins of the whole world, once offered, so that it needeth no more to be reiterated or offered again, being and remaining of sufficient force for ever and ever to purge the wickednesses of the people? *Son.* Christ is an everlasting priest; and as his priesthood is everlasting, so likewise is his sacrifice everlasting, I mean it endureth for ever in full virtue and perfect strength to put away at all times all the sins of all people that do unfeignedly repent and believe: so that it needeth not for any imbecillity, weakness, or imperfection to be repeated or offered again, as the papists presume, being of itself most perfect and most full for the abolishing of sin even unto the uttermost; yea, and that even to the world's end, when sin shall altogether cease, as the apostle saith: "Jesus Christ yesterday and to-day, and the same continueth Heb. xiii.
for ever. Be not carried about with divers and strange learning."

Father. Let me hear it proved by the word of God, that that one and alone sacrifice, which Christ himself offered once for all on the altar of the cross, is sufficient without any repetition or offering again to put away the sins of the world; so that we may be thoroughly persuaded that the sacrifice of the popish mass, whereof the papists do so greatly brag, and wherewith they have almost seduced the whole world, and too much bleared the eyes of the simple and ignorant, is vain and wicked. *Son.* St Paul saith: "Jesus was a stablisher of a better testament. For among them many Heb. vii.
were made priests, because they were not suffered to endure by the reason of death. But this man (Christ), because he endureth for ever, hath an everlasting priesthood. Wherefore he is able also ever to save them to the uttermost that come unto God by

him, seeing he ever liveth to make intercession for us. For such an high priest became us to have, which is holy, harmless, undefiled, separate from sinners, made higher than heaven; which needeth not daily, as yonder high priests, to offer up sacrifice, first for his own sins, and then for the people's sins: for that he did once, when he offered up himself."

Heb. ix. Again: "Christ, being an high priest of good things to come, came by a greater and more perfect tabernacle, not made with hands, that is to say, not of this building; neither by the blood of goats and calves, but by his own blood, he entered in once into the holy place, and found everlasting redemption." And a little after: "Christ is not entered into the holy places that are made with hands, (which are similitudes of true things;) but he is entered into the very heaven, for to appear now in the sight of God for us: not to offer himself often, as the high priest entereth into the holy place every year with strange blood; for then must he have often suffered since the world began. But now, in the end of the world, hath he appeared once to put sin to flight by the offering up of himself. And as it was appointed unto all men that they shall once die, and then cometh the judgment; even so Christ was once offered to take away the sins of many; and unto them that look for him shall he appear again without sin unto salvation."

Heb. x. Once again he saith: "By the will of (Christ) we are made holy, even by the offering of the body of Jesu Christ once for all. And every priest (he speaketh of the priests of the old law) is ready daily ministering, and offering oftentimes one manner of oblation, which can never take away sins. But this man (Christ), after he hath offered one sacrifice for sins, is set down for ever on the right hand of God, and from henceforth tarrieth till his foes be made his footstool. For with one offering hath he made perfect for ever them that are sanctified."

1 Pet. ii. Hereto belongeth the saying of St Peter: "Christ his own self bare our sins in his body on the tree, that we, being delivered from sin, should live unto righteousness."
Rev. i. St John also saith: "Christ loved us, and washed us from our sins in his own blood, and made us kings and priests unto God his Father." And God the Father himself
Isai. liii. saith by the prophet: "For the wickedness of my people have I stricken him," which
Rom. viii. indeed had deserved the punishment, as St Paul saith: "God spared not his own Son,
Rom. iv. but gave him (unto the death) for us all." Again: "Christ died for our sins." Item:
Eph. i. "By Christ we have redemption through his blood, even remission of sins." And
Isai. liii. the prophet saith: "He only (Christ) hath taken on him our infirmities, and borne our pains. He was wounded for our offences, and smitten for our wickedness. For the chastisement of our peace was laid upon him; and with his stripes are we healed. As for us, we have gone all astray (like sheep); every one hath turned his own way: but the Lord hath heaped together upon him the iniquity of us all." "Yet hath it pleased the Lord thus to burst him with plagues, and to smite him with infirmities, that, when he had made his soul an offering for sin, he might see long-lasting seed." Again: "He shall justify the multitude, for he shall bear away their sins." Item: "He hath taken away the sins of the multitude, and made intercession for the mis-
Isai. lxiii. doers." And Christ himself saith by the prophet: "I have trodden down the winepress myself alone, and of all people there is not one with me."

All these sentences aforesaid do evidently declare, that by that one and alone sacrifice, which Christ, that high and everlasting Bishop, offered once for all upon the altar of the cross, we are made righteous, holy, pure, and perfect; so that, after that one and alone sacrifice done by Christ on the tree, no sacrifice, no offering for sin remain to be offered for the sins of the people, of any person either in heaven or in earth, all sins being already taken away by that one sacrifice of Christ: so far is it
Phil. iii. off that we have need of that missal sacrifice whereof the massing papists, "whose God the belly is," do so greatly brag; wherein also they stoutly affirm that they offer for a propitiatory sacrifice unto God the Father, for the sins of the quick and of the dead, the Son of God, Christ Jesus the Lord; when as tofore we have abundantly heard that Christ (and not any other) offered himself on the altar of the cross, "a sweet-smelling sacrifice unto God his Father" for the sins of the whole world, yea, and that once for all; so that with that one and alone oblation, without any repetition or renewing of the same, all that are sanctified are made perfect for ever and ever.

And this is that which the Lord Jesus, hanging on the cross, said a little before his death: "It is finished:" as though he should say, "Whatsoever is necessary for the salvation of man is perfectly, and even unto the uttermost, and at the full, accomplished and fulfilled in this one and alone sacrifice of my body, which I now offer unto my heavenly Father here hanging upon the cross." John xix.

For upon the cross, and not upon the popish altar, was Christ Jesus offered, and there abundantly he finished the work of our redemption, as the apostle saith: "Now by the means of Christ Jesu ye which sometime were far off were made nigh by the blood of Christ; for he is our peace, which hath made of both one, and hath broken down the wall that was a stop between us, and hath also put away through his flesh the cause of hatred, even the law of commandments contained in the law written, for to make of twain one new man in himself, so making peace, and to reconcile both unto God in one body through the cross, and slew hatred thereby, and came and preached peace to you that were afar off, and to them that were nigh. For through him we both (Jew and gentile) have an entrance in one Spirit unto the Father." Eph. ii. Again: "It pleased the Father that in him (Christ) should all fulness dwell, and by him to reconcile all thing unto himself, and to set at peace by him through the blood of his cross both things in heaven and things in earth." Col. i. St Peter also saith: "Christ his own self bare our sins in his body on the tree, that we being delivered from sin should live unto righteousness: by whose stripes ye were healed." 1 Pet. ii.

Father. What shall we then say to the ancient fathers of Christ's church, which in many places call the supper of the Lord a sacrifice? *Son.* "Even as images are wont to be called (as St Austin saith) by the names of those things whereof they are images, as when we behold a table or wall painted we say, That is Cicero, that is Sallustius[1];" so likewise, forasmuch as the celebration of the Lord's supper is a certain representative image of the passion of Christ, which is the alone true sacrifice, therefore the holy fathers many times call the Lord's supper a sacrifice. Now, if the Lord's supper be not properly a sacrifice, but only a memorial of the true sacrifice, which is the passion and death of Christ; how can the massing papists brag that their mass (in the which many things are done contrary to the institution of Christ) is a propitiatory, satisfactory, and expiatory sacrifice for the sins of the quick and of the dead?

Father. How provest thou that this was the meaning of the fathers? *Son.* St John Chrysostom saith: "Do we not offer every day? We offer indeed, but yet that we do is unto the remembrance of his death, &c. This that we do is done in the remembrance of that which was done. 'This do ye,' saith he, 'in the remembrance of me.' Not another sacrifice, as the bishop did, but the self-same do we alway; yea, rather we work a remembrance of the sacrifice[2]." In Heb. Hom. 17. Luke xxii.

The very same words in effect hath St Ambrose. "In Christ," saith he, "a sacrifice was once offered, mighty enough unto everlasting salvation. What do we then? Do not we also offer every day? Yea, but unto the remembrance of his death[3]." In Heb.

St Austin also saith: "The flesh and blood of this sacrifice before the coming of Christ was promised by the sacrifices of similitudes: in the passion of Christ it was performed by the self truth: after the ascension of Christ it is celebrated by the sacrament of remembrance[4]." Contra Faustum, Lib. xx. cap. 21.

[1 ...omnes fere imagines earum rerum quarum imagines sunt, appellari nominibus solent.....velut cum intuentes tabulam aut parietem, dicimus, Ille Cicero est, ille Sallustius.—August. Op. Par. 1679-1700. De Div. Quæst. ad Simplic. Lib. II. Quæst. iv. 2. Tom. VI. col. 116.]

[2 Τί οὖν; ἡμεῖς καθ' ἑκάστην ἡμέραν οὐ προσφέρομεν; προσφέρομεν μὲν, ἀλλ' ἀνάμνησιν ποιούμενοι τοῦ θανάτου αὐτοῦ ...... τοῦτο εἰς ἀνάμνησιν γίνεται τοῦ τότε γενομένου. τοῦτο γὰρ ποιεῖτέ, φησιν, εἰς τὴν ἐμὴν ἀνάμνησιν. οὐκ ἄλλην θυσίαν, καθάπερ ὁ ἀρχιερεὺς τότε, ἀλλὰ τὴν αὐτὴν ἀεὶ ποιοῦμεν· μᾶλλον δὲ ἀνάμνησιν ἐργαζόμεθα θυσίας.—Chrysost. Op. Par. 1718-38. In Epist. ad Hebr. cap. x. Hom. xvii. Tom. XII. pp. 168, 9.]

[3 In Christo autem e contrario semel oblata est hostia potens ad salutem sempiternam. Quid ergo nos? nonne per singulos dies offerimus? Offerimus quidem, sed recordationem facientes mortis ejus.—Ambros. Op. Par. 1614. Comm. in Epist. ad Heb. cap. x. Tom. III. col. 651.]

[4 Hujus sacrificii caro et sanguis ante adventum Christi per victimas similitudinum promittebatur: in passione Christi per ipsam veritatem reddebatur: post adscensum Christi per sacramentum memoriæ celebratur.—August. Op. Cont. Faust. Lib. xx. cap. xxi. Tom. VIII. col. 348.]

In Senten. Prosper hath these words: "The heavenly bread, which is the flesh of Christ, after his manner is called the body of Christ, when it is in very deed the sacrament or holy sign of the body of Christ; and that immolation or offering of the flesh, which is done with the hands of the priest, is the passion, death, and crucifying of Christ, not in the truth of the thing, but in a signifying mystery[1]."

Lib. Sent. iv. Dist. 13. Petrus Lombardus, the master of the sentences, writeth on this manner: "That which is offered and consecrated of the priest is called a sacrifice and an offering, because it is a remembrance and representation of the true sacrifice and of the holy offering done on the altar of the cross. And Christ was once offered on the cross, and there he was offered in himself; but he is daily offered in the sacrament, because in the sacrament a remembrance is made of that which was once done[2]."

In Heb. And the ordinary gloss hath these words: "In the altar there is no reiteration or doing again of (Christ's) sacrifice; but there is made a daily remembrance of

Luke xxii. one sacrifice once done on the cross, according to the saying of Christ, 'Do this in the remembrance of me'[3]."

De Consec. Dist. 2. But wherefore do I tarry so long in gathering together the testimonies of the old fathers, seeing we find these words written in the pope's old law, "Christ was once offered in himself; and yet is he daily offered in the sacrament?" Upon these words thus saith the gloss: "He is offered, that is to say, the offering of him is represented, and there is made a memory of the passion of Christ[4]."

Again: "Because we fall daily, Christ mystically is offered up for us daily; and the passion of Christ is set forth in a mystery." Now saith the gloss: "The offering up of Christ done for us is represented in the sacrament of his body and blood[5]."

And Thomas Aquinas himself calleth the sacrifice of the mass a memorial of the Lord's passion[6].

The death of Christ is the alone sacrifice for sin. *Father.* Thou hast sufficiently proved both by the scriptures and by the ancient fathers, that there is but one sacrifice which purchaseth remission of sins for all faithful penitent sinners, which is the death of Christ, once for all offered of Christ himself on the altar of the cross; whose virtue, power, and strength is so great and in all points perfect, that it needeth no more to be offered, being of itself for ever sufficient to put away the sins of the whole world: again, that the Lord's supper, although an holy institution or ordinance of Christ, is not a sacrifice to put away sin, but a memorial of that one and alone true sacrifice, which Christ himself offered on the cross for the abolishing of the world's sin: and hereof thou hast also sufficiently proved

[1 Sicut ergo cœlestis panis, qui vere Christi caro est, suo modo vocatur corpus Christi, cum revera sit sacramentum corporis Christi, illius videlicet, quod visibile, palpabile, mortale, in cruce est suspensum, vocaturque ipsa immolatio carnis, quæ sacerdotis manibus fit, Christi passio, mors, crucifixio, non rei veritate, sed significante mysterio; sic sacramentum fidei, quod baptismus intelligitur, fides est.—Id. in Lib. Sent. Prosp. in Decret. Gratiani. Par. 1583. Decr. Tert. Pars. De Consecr. Dist. ii. can. 48. cols. 2387, 8.]

[2 Ad hoc breviter dici potest, illud quod offertur et consecratur a sacerdote vocari sacrificium et oblationem: quia memoria est et repræsentatio veri sacrificii, et sanctæ immolationis factæ in ara crucis. Et semel Christus mortuus in cruce est, ibique immolatus est in semetipso: quotidie autem immolatur in sacramento, quia in sacramento recordatio fit illius, quod factum est semel.—Pet. Lomb. Lib. Sentent. Col. Agrip. 1576. Lib. IV. Dist. xii. fol. 357.]

[3 This is the comment of Nic. de Lyra: Sed adhuc diceres: sacramentum altaris quotidie offertur in ecclesia. ergo, &c. Dicendum quod non est ibi sacrificii reiteratio: sed unius sacrificii in cruce oblati quotidiana commemoratio. propter hoc dicitur Lucæ xxii. b. Hoc facite in meam commemorationem.—Bibl. cum Gloss. Ord. et Expos. Nic. de Lyra. Basil. 1502. Ad Heb. cap. x. Sext. Pars. fol. 152. The ordinary gloss conveys the same sense; but the expressions are somewhat different: Et si nos quotidie offerimus, recordatio mortis ejus est; et hæc hostia una est. non multæ: quia semel tantum oblata est.... Quod nos agimus recordatio sacrificii est. Id. ibid.]

[4 Semel immolatus est Christus in semetipso, et tamen quotidie immolatur in sacramento.—Lib. Sent. Prosp. in Decret. Gratiani, Decr. Tert. Pars. De Consecr. Dist. ii. can. 52. cols. 2389, 90. On this the gloss is: *Immolatur:* id est, ejus immolatio repræsentatur, et fit memoria passionis.—Ibid. col. 2390.]

[5 Et ideo, quia quotidie labimur, quotidie Christus pro nobis mystice immolatur: et passio Christi in mysterio traditur.—Paschas. in Lib. de Corp. et Sang. Christ. in eod. can. 71. cols. 2403, 4. The gloss is: *Immolatur:* Christi immolatio facta pro nobis in sacramento corporis et sanguinis ejus repræsentatur.—Ibid. col. 2404.]

[6 ..... in sacramento eucharistiæ commemoratur mors Christi, in quantum ipse Christus passus exhibetur nobis.—Thom. Aquinat. Op. Venet. 1595. Summ. Theol. Tert. Pars. Quæst. lxvi. Art. 9. Tom. XII. fol. 210. 2.]

that the mass, which is but the invention of man, and containeth in it many absurdities, abuses, and errors, is no propitiatory, expiatory, or satisfactory sacrifice, as the adversaries brag, to put away the sins of the quick and of the dead, or, as some write, necessary *ad salutem*. *Son.* It is truth.

Father. Remain there yet any other abuses of the Lord's supper undeclared?

Son. Fourthly, the papists have greatly abused the Lord's supper, while they, contrary to the institution of Christ and the practice of the primitive church, reserve the sacramental bread, and keep it in boxes and pixes, and hang it up, yea, and so long reserve it, that it corrupt, putrify, waxeth mould, stinketh, is eaten of worms, so that they are compelled to burn it according to their decree.

The fourth abuse.

Against the popish reservation of the sacramental bread.

Father. Is it not lawful by the word of God to reserve the sacramental bread? *Son.* Christ, in delivering the bread to his disciples, said: "Take ye, eat ye." He said not, Take ye, reserve ye. The sacrament was instituted of Christ to be received, and not to be reserved; to be eaten, and not to be hanged up with a rope; to be meat of the faithful, and not to be devoured of worms. They therefore, that reserve the sacramental bread after the Lord's supper be done, enterprise that which is not found in the word of God.

Father. Was it not used in the primitive church to reserve the sacramental bread? *Son.* No. The primitive, which is the apostolic church, walked in the steps of Christ, and observed that which their Lord and Master commanded. And what if some, (I know not with what spirit provoked,) kept of that mystical bread, certain years after the apostles' time, and reserved it in their chests or coffers at home, (I cannot tell for what purpose,) as the nature of man is always more bent unto superstition and counterfeit worshipping of God than unto the simplicity of God's holy ordinance? Their error ought to be no precedent to the true Christians, whose delight is to hear the voice of their Shepherd, and whose only study is to walk in the holy ways of their Lord God.

Father. What was the use among the old churches? *Son.* In the primitive church, if any of the bread or of the wine remained after the Lord's supper was ended, the communicants making a common feast together did either eat and drink it up themselves, or else they gave it to the poor; as it may be truly gathered of these authorities of the ancient fathers.

St Jerome saith: "After the communion, whatsoever things were remaining unto them of the sacrifices, even there in the church they, eating the common supper together, consumed and spent them[7]." **1 Cor. xi.**

Of this common supper or banquet writeth both Chrysostom[8] and Tertullian[9].

The old bishop Clement saith also: "Verily, so many sacrifices shall be offered on the altar as ought to suffice the people. If there remain any, let them not be reserved till to-morrow, but with the fear and trembling of the clerks let them be spent[10]." **Epist. 2.**

Origen also saith: "The bread which the Lord gave to his disciples and said, 'Take and eat,' he deferred not, neither commanded he that it should be kept till to-morrow[11]." **In Levit. Hom. 5. c. 7.**

[7 ...et post communionem quæcumque eis de sacrificiis superfuissent, illic in ecclesia communem cœnam comedentes, pariter consumebant.—Hieron. Op. Par. 1693-1706. Comm. in Epist. I. ad Cor. cap. xi. Tom. V. col. 998.]

[8 *Καὶ ἐπειδὰν συνέβαινε τοὺς μὲν πένητας εἶναι, τοὺς δὲ πλουσίους, τὰ μὲν ἑαυτῶν οὐ κατετίθεντο πάντα εἰς μέσον, κοινὰς δὲ ἐποιοῦντο τὰς τραπέζας ἐν ἡμέραις νενομισμέναις, ὡς εἰκὸς, καὶ τῆς συνάξεως ἀπαρτισθείσης μετὰ τὴν τῶν μυστηρίων κοινωνίαν, ἐπὶ κοινὴν πάντες ᾔεσαν εὐωχίαν, τῶν μὲν πλουτούντων φερόντων τὰ ἐδέσματα, τῶν δὲ πενομένων καὶ οὐδὲν ἐχόντων ὑπ' αὐτῶν καλουμένων, καὶ κοινῇ πάντων ἑστιωμένων. ἀλλ' ὕστερον καὶ τοῦτο διεφθάρη τὸ ἔθος.*—Chrysost. Op. Par. 1718-38. In Epist. I. ad Cor. Hom. xxvii. Tom. X. p. 240.]

[9 Cœna nostra de nomine rationem sui ostendit. Id vocatur quod dilectio penes Græcos. Quantiscunque sumptibus constet, lucrum est pietatis nomine facere sumptum. siquidem inopes quosque refrigerio isto juvamus, non qua penes vos parasiti affectant ad gloriam famulandæ libertatis sub auctoramento ventris inter contumelias saginandi; sed qua penes Deum major est contemplatio mediocrium.—Tertull. Op. Lut. 1641. Apologet. 39. pp. 35, 6.]

[10 Certe tanta in altario holocausta offerantur, quanta populo sufficere debeant. Quod si remanserint, in crastinum non reserventur, sed cum timore et tremore, clericorum diligentia consumantur.—Clement. Papæ I. Epist. ii. ad Jacob. in Epist. Decret. Sum. Pont. Rom. 1591. Tom. I. p. 16.]

[11 Nam et Dominus panem, quem discipulis dabat, et dicebat eis, Accipite et manducate, non distulit, nec servari jussit in crastinum.—Orig. Op. Par. 1733-59. In Levit. Hom. v. 8. Tom. II. p. 211.]

De Trinit. Lib. iii. c. 10. And St Austin saith: "The bread appointed for this purpose is consumed and spent in receiving the sacrament[1]."

Lib. iv. c. 36. Evagrius, in his Ecclesiastical History, declareth that "the old custom was, when much of the holy parcels of the undefiled body of Christ our God remained, the young children, which were wont to go to school, were called for to eat them[2]".

In Levit. In the time of Origen and Hesychius (as their commentaries testify) the bread that remained after the communion was wont to be brent[3].

Contra Nicetam. And a certain man called Humbertus writeth on this manner: "We read not that the Lord himself did deliver to his disciples an unperfect, but a perfect commemoration, the bread being blessed, and straightways broken and distributed. For he did not only bless it, and so reserved it to be broken till to-morrow; neither did he break it only, and keep it in store; but he distributed it straightways so soon as it was broken. In consideration whereof blessed Alexander, the martyr and fifth[4] pope from the apostle Peter, putting the passion of the Lord in the canon of the mass, saith: 'So oft as ye shall do this,' that is to say, bless, break, and distribute, 'ye shall do it in the remembrance of me.' For every one of these three done without the residue, that is to say, either the blessing without the breaking and distribution, or the breaking without the blessing and distribution, representeth not a perfect remembrance of Christ, as neither do the distribution without blessing and breaking[5]."

Dist. 2. de Consec. John vi. Paschasius also hath these words: "Christ, willing to set forth the fruit of this sacrament, said: 'He that eateth my flesh, and drinketh my blood, he shall live for ever.'" And afterward: "Christ willing that his disciples should be made partakers of the fruit of this sacrament, after he had consecrated his body, he stood not still in the consecration, neither gave it he to his disciples, that they should reserve and keep it honourably; but he gave it them for that purpose for the which he did institute it, saying, 'Take ye, and eat[6].'"

Of these authorities, gathered out of the writings of the ancient fathers, it is evident that the church of Christ, when it was most pure, and most diligently walked in the steps of the doctrine of Christ and of his apostles, knew no reservation of the Lord's bread, as it is now used in the church of the pope. Neither is this use of reserving and keeping, of boxing and pixing, of hiding and closing the sacramental

---

[1 ...panis ad hoc factus in accipiendo sacramento consumitur.—August. Op. Par. 1679-1700. De Trin. Lib. III. 19. Tom. VIII. col. 803.]

[2 Ἔθος παλαιὸν βούλεται ἀνὰ τὴν βασιλεύουσαν, ὅτ' ἂν πολύ τι χρῆμα τῶν ἁγίων μερίδων τοῦ ἀχράντου σώματος Χριστοῦ τοῦ Θεοῦ ἡμῶν ἐναπομείνοι, παῖδας ἀφθόρους μεταπέμπτους γίγνεσθαι παρὰ τῶν ἐς χαμαιδιδασκάλου φοιτώντων, καὶ ταῦτα κατεσθίειν.—Evagr. Schol. in Hist. Eccles. Script. Amst. 1695-1700. Lib. IV. cap. XXXVI. pp. 410, 11.]

[3 Sed hoc quod reliquum est de carnibus et panibus, in igne incendi præcepit. Quod nunc videmus etiam sensibiliter in ecclesia fieri, ignique tradi quæcunque remanere contigerit inconsumpta, non omnino ea quæ una die, vel duabus, aut multis servata sunt: sicut enim apparet, non hoc legislator præcepit: sed quod reliquum est, incendi jubet.—Isych. Presb. Hieros. in Levit. Basil. 1527. Lib. II. in cap. viii. fol. 49, 2......quod idem habes in Origene super Leviticum, licet idem sit liber qui duobus ascribitur.—Loc. Com. Pet. Mart. Heid. 1613. Class. IV. cap. x. 51. p. 862.]

[4 A correction is here made from the passage as given below of Humbert. The folio reads *master and first.*]

[5 Nempe hic, in panis fractione et communicatione, non nisi perfectam actionem missæ debemus accipere; quemadmodum et ipsum Dominum legimus non imperfectam, sed perfectam commemorationem suis discipulis tradidisse, in pane a se benedicto et mox fracto atque distributo. Non enim benedixit tantum et servavit frangendum in crastinum, nec fregit tantum et reposuit, sed fractum statim distribuit. Unde B. Alexander martyr et papa V. ab apostolo Petro, passionem Domini inserens Canoni Missæ, non ait, Hoc quotiescunque feceritis; sed, 'Hæc quotiescunque feceritis,' id est, benedixeritis, fregeritis et distribueritis, 'in mei memoriam facietis:' quia quodlibet horum trium, si sine reliquis fiat, scilicet, benedictio sine distributione, aut fractio sine benedictione et distributione, perfectam Christi memoriam non repræsentant, sicut distributio nulla sine benedictione et fractione.--Humbert. cont. Nicet. in Mag. Biblioth. Vet. Patr. Col. Agrip. 1618-22. Tom. XI. p. 333.]

[6 Ad idem Pascasius canone immediate præcedente: Hinc frequenter Christus volens exprimere fructum hujus sacramenti dixit: Qui manducat carnem meam et bibit sanguinem meum habet vitam eternam. Manducatio et potio hujus sacramenti est usus. Hinc et volens discipulos suos Christus fructus hujus sacramenti participes fieri, postquam corpus suum consecravit, non sistebat in consecratione. Neque dedit discipulis ut ipsum honorifice conservarent: sed dedit in sui usum dicens, Accipite et manducate.—Gab. Biel. Canon. Missæ Expos. Basil. 1515. Lect. XXXVI. fol. 83. 2. This passage does not appear in Gratian in the canon named.]

bread, so greatly old. Verily it was the invention of pope Innocent the third, about the year of our Lord one thousand two hundred and fifteen[7].

Father. God give us all grace to use Christ's holy sacraments aright, and according to his institution! *Son*. Amen.

Father. Is there any other abuse that hath crept into the church concerning the Lord's supper?

Son. Fifthly, the papists greatly abused the Lord's supper, while they made of it a gazing-stock, by carrying it about in public processions, or by heaving and lifting it up above their heads to make it a spectacle to the people; by this means provoking them unto the worshipping of it, and so to fall unto idolatry, unto the great danger of their soul health. For this sacrament was not ordained of the Lord Jesu to be carried about like a puppet, as the manner is in the pope's wicked kingdom, nor to be made an heave-offering, as the papists use in their masses; but to be meat unto the faithful, to be broken and eaten in the remembrance of Christ's passion and death, as Erasmus Roterodamus very godly writeth: "Christ," saith he, "is in that sacrament, under this manner of meat and drink, that he should be received with high purity of mind; not that he should be shewed abroad, or carried about in plays and common pageants, or that he should be carried about the fields on horseback. This was not the manner of the primitive church, but in this thing the foolish affections of the multitude hath been too much served and obeyed[8]". Neither is this custom so greatly old, but brought in, as it may appear, of pope Honorius the third, about the year of our Lord one thousand two hundred and twenty-two[9].

The fifth abuse.

In Lib. de Amab. Conc.

Sixthly, this was also a great abuse among the papists, that the sacrament of the body and blood of Christ was always ministered to the common people in a strange and unknown tongue, which the simple and rude common people understood not, and so were not edified, neither received they any profit by the words that were spoken, although never so good and godly.

The sixth abuse.

All things ought in churches to be spoken in that tongue which the common people understand.

Father. Was this also an abuse? *Son*. Yea, verily, and a great abuse, and directly contrary both to the doctrine of Christ, and the ancient practice of Christ's church.

Father. How provest thou that? *Son*. St Paul saith: "Brethren, if I come unto you speaking with tongues, what shall I profit you, except I speak to you either by revelation, or by knowledge, or by prophesying, or by doctrine? Moreover, when things without life give sound (whether it be a pipe or an harp) except they make a distinction in the sounds, how shall it be known what is piped or harped? For if the trump give an uncertain voice, who shall prepare himself to the war? Even so likewise when ye speak with tongues, except ye speak words that have signification, how shall it be understand what is spoken? For ye shall but speak in the air." And a little after he saith: "When thou blessest with the spirit (that is to say, givest thanks in a strange tongue), how shall he that occupieth the room of the unlearned say Amen at thy giving of thanks, seeing he understandeth not what thou sayest? Thou verily givest thanks well; but the other is not edified, &c. I had rather in the congregation to speak five words with my understanding to the

1 Cor. xiv.

[7 Statuimus, ut in cunctis ecclesiis chrisma et eucharistia sub fideli custodia clavibus adhibitis conserventur; ne possit ad illa temeraria manus extendi, ad aliqua horribilia vel nefaria exercenda.—Concil. Lat. iv. cap. xx. in Concil. Stud. Labbei. Lut. Par. 1671-2. Tom. XI. Pars i. col. 172.]

[8 Quamquam Christus in eo sacramento est sub ratione cibi ac potus, ut summa cum animi puritate sumatur, non ut ostentetur, aut in ludis publicisque pompis circumferatur, aut in equo circum arva vehatur. Id nequaquam est veteris exempli, sed in hoc multitudinis affectui plus satis indultum est.—Des. Erasm. Op. Lugd. Bat. 1703—6. De Amab. Eccles. Concord. Enarr. Psalm. lxxxiii. Tom. V. cols. 503, 4.]

[9 Ne propter incuriam sacerdotum divina indignatio gravius exardescat, districte percipiendo mandamus, quatenus a sacerdotibus eucharistia, in loco singulari, mundo, et signato semper honorifice collocata, devote, ac fideliter conservetur. Sacerdos vero quilibet frequenter doceat plebem suam, ut cum in celebratione missarum elevatur hostia salutaris, se reverenter inclinet, idem faciens, cum eam defert presbyter ad infirmum. Quam in decenti habitu, superposito mundo velamine, ferat, et referat manifeste ac honorifice ante pectus, cum omni reverentia et timore, semper lumine præcedente, cum sit candor lucis æternæ: ut ex hoc apud omnes fides et devotio augeatur. Prælati autem hujusmodi mandati graviter punire non differant transgressores, si et ipsi divinam et nostram volunt effugere ultionem.—Hon. III. in Decretal. Greg. IX. Taurin. 1621. Lib. iii. De Celebr. Missar. Tit. lxi. col. 1378. See also Const. Ric. Episc. Sar. (temp. Hon. III.) in Concil. Stud. Labbei. cap. xxxix. Tom. XI. col. 259.]

information of other, than ten thousand words with the tongue." Again he saith: "If when all the congregation is come together, and all speak with tongues, there come in they that are unlearned, or they which believe not, will they not say that ye are out of your wits? But and if all prophesy, and there come in one that believeth not, or one unlearned, he is rebuked of all men, and is judged of every man; and so are the secrets of his heart opened, and so falleth he down on his face and worshippeth God, and saith that God is in you of a truth, &c. Let all things be done unto edifying. If any man speak with tongue, let it be by two, or at the most by three, and that by course, and let another interpret it. But if there be no interpreter, let him keep silence in the congregation, and let him speak to himself and to God."

Who seeth not evidently by these words of the holy apostle, that whatsoever things be spoken in the congregation, whether it be in praying or in preaching, all things ought to be uttered in that language which the people understand, and that all things ought to be done unto edifying? which thing cannot be brought to pass if the administration of God's mysteries be done in a foreign and strange tongue, as the papists do in all their churches. The papists therefore have greatly abused themselves in the administration of God's holy mysteries, while they have uttered all things to the people in such a tongue as they understand not.

Father. Was the use in the church of Christ also after the apostles' time, that all things both in preaching and praying should be done in that speech which the common people understood? *Son.* Yea, forsooth, many hundred years after, till that antichrist, the bishop of Rome, sitting now in the consciences of men, and calling himself "Christ's vicar," "Peter's successor," and "supreme head of the universal church of Christ," devised and commanded the contrary; so that so many as submitted their necks to the tyranny of that Romish bishop from that time forward were compelled to use the Roman, that is to say, the Latin tongue in all their divine service, as they use to call it, contrary to the doctrine of God, and contrary to the practice of Christ's ancient church, yea, and that without all edifying or profit.

Father. And was this Romish order universally received of all Christians throughout all Christendom? *Son.* Nothing less. For many christian nations even unto this day would never obey the tyranny of that Romish bishop, nor knowledge him to be "Christ's vicar," "Peter's successor," "supreme head of the universal church of Christ," &c., nor yet to have any more power than any other ordinary bishop hath; but whatsoever authority or jurisdiction he challengeth more and obtaineth, they[1] affirm it to be false and usurped, yea, and contrary to the word of God and the doctrine of the ancient fathers of Christ's church.

Therefore, as the Jews from the beginning used no strange tongue in their temples, neither yet do at this present, but their own language, that is to say, the Hebrew tongue; so likewise, even from the beginning of Christ's profession, the Greeks, the Indians, the Armenians, the Illyricks, the Slavones, the Moscovites, the Liburnians, with divers other, have ever used their own country speech in the celebration of God's mysteries, and not a strange tongue (as the manner is in the pope's church), which they understand not. Whosoever hath travailed either in the reading of histories or of ancient writers, he right well knoweth these things to be true which I now speak.

Father. I grant, my son. But let me hear an authority or two out of the old writers, which testify this thing to be true. *Son.* St Ambrose saith: "If ye come together to edify the congregation, those things ought to be spoken which the hearers may understand. For what doth it profit that any man speak with a tongue which he alone knoweth, that he which heareth may have no profit? Therefore he ought to hold his peace in the congregation, that they may speak which may profit the hearers[2]."

In 1 Cor. cap. xiv.

St John Chrysostom saith: "If I shall not speak that which may plainly and easily be understand of you, but only shew myself to be endued with the gift

In 1 Cor. cap. xiv. Hom. 53.

[[1] Folio, *there.*]

[[2] Si utique ad ædificandam ecclesiam convenitis, ea debent dici, quæ intelligant audientes. Nam quid prodest ut quis lingua loquatur, quam solus scit; ut qui audit, nihil proficiat? Ideo tacere debet in ecclesia, ut ii loquantur, qui prosint audientibus.—Ambros. Op. Par. 1686—90. Comm. in Epist. ad Cor. prim. cap. xiv. 17. Tom. II. Appendix, col. 157.]

of tongues, I believe ye shall go away receiving no fruit of those things which ye understand not. For what profit can there be of a voice not understand[3]?"

Cassiodorus saith: "The speech is unprofitably uttered that is not understand. Not only singing, but also understanding, we ought to give thanks. For no man doth any thing wisely that he understandeth not[4]."

Haymo also saith: "Your speech ought to be understand, that the soldier may prepare himself unto the spiritual battle of Christ[5]." In 1 Cor. cap. xiv.

To whom is the godly law of the emperor Justinian unknown, in the which he commandeth that all bishops and priests, both in the time of divine service, and also in the ministration of the holy sacraments, should with so open and clear voice utter all things in the tongue which the people understand, that the hearers may thereby be the better edified, and also be the more fervently stirred up unto devotion and praying unto God[6]?

Many authorities out of the old writers might here be alleged to declare, that all things spoken in the church, both in preaching and praying, ought to be uttered in that tongue which the people understand; but let these for this present suffice.

Father. Contented, my child. But remaineth there yet any other abuse in the administration of the Lord's supper brought in by that bishop of Rome?

Son. Seventhly, this also is a great abuse in the pope's church, that the papists at the celebration of the Lord's supper do not only suffer the communicants to be present at the participation of those holy mysteries of the body and blood of Christ, (which ought of right so to be,) but also they admit other not communicating to be present, only idle gazers and vain beholders of those things, whereof they will not be partakers; whereas of right they ought to be excluded, put out, and utterly banished from that company in the time of that holy action. The seventh abuse. None ought to be present at the ministration of the Lord's supper, but the communicants only.

Father. Why, is it lawful for other to be present at the ministration of the Lord's supper which are not communicants? *Son*. No, verily.

Father. Why so?

Son. First, we read not that any were present at the table, when the Lord Jesus instituted and delivered the blessed sacraments of his body and blood, but only his disciples, which all were communicants; to declare unto us, that none should be present at that holy action, but such only as be partakers of those holy mysteries.

Secondly, we read that the ancient fathers of Christ's church would by no means suffer that any should be present at the ministration of the Lord's supper, but such only as would communicate. The other were commanded to depart, and by no means to remain among those that came unto that holy and heavenly banquet.

Father. How provest thou that? *Son*. Micrologus, in the book *de Ecclesiasticis observationibus*, hath these words: "It is to be known according to the use of the ancient fathers, that the communicants alone were wont to be present at the divine mysteries. In consideration whereof before the oblation (he meaneth the receiving of Cap. xxvi.

[3 Ὁ δὲ λέγει τοῦτό ἐστιν, ἐὰν μή τι εἴπω δυνάμενον ὑμῖν εὔληπτον γενέσθαι, καὶ δυνάμενον εἶναι σαφὲς, ἀλλ' ἐπιδείξομαι μόνον, ὅτι γλωττῶν ἔχω χάρισμα, γλωττῶν ὧν ἀκούσαντες, οὐδὲν κερδάναντες ἀπελεύσεσθε. πῶς γὰρ ἀπὸ φωνῆς, ἧς οὐ συνίετε;—Chrysost. Op. Par. 1718—38. In Epist. i. ad Cor. Hom. xxxv. Tom. X. p. 323.]

[4 Adjecit, Psallite sapienter; ut non solum cantantes, sed intelligentes psallere debeamus. Nemo enim sapienter quicquam facit quod non intelligit.—Cassiodor. Op. Rotom. 1679. Expos. in Psal. xlvi. v. 7. Tom. II. p. 157.]

[5 Vester autem sermo intelligi debet, ut possit ad spiritale bellum Christi se miles præparare.—Haymo in Div. Paul. Epist. Interp. 1528. Ad Cor. I. cap. xiv. fol. A. v.]

[6 Ad hæc jubemus, ut omnes episcopi pariter et presbyteri non tacito modo, sed clara voce, quæ a fideli populo exaudiatur, sacram oblationem et preces in sancto baptismate adhibitas celebrent, quo majore exinde compunctione in depromendis Domini Dei laudibus audientium animi efferantur. Ita enim et divus apostolus docet, dicens in prima ad Corinthios epistola: Enimvero si solummodo benedicas spiritu, quomodo is qui privati locum implet, dicet ad gratiarum actionem tuam Deo ipsum Amen; quandoquidem quid dicas, non videt? Tu quidem pulchre gratias agis, alter autem non ædificatur. Et rursus in epistola ad Romanos sic inquit: Corde quidem creditur ad justitiam, ore autem fit confessio ad salutem. His igitur de causis convenit, ut inter ceteras preces et ea quæ in sancta oblatione dicuntur, clara voce a religiosissimis episcopis et presbyteris Domino nostro Jesu Christo Deo nostro cum Patre et sancto Spiritu proferantur: scituris religiosissimis sacerdotibus, quod si quid horum neglexerint, et in horrendo judicio magni Dei et Servatoris nostri Jesu Christi de his rationem reddent, neque nos hæc cognoscentes conquiescemus, relinquemusque inulta.—Justin. Princ. Novell. Constit. Basil. 1561. Const. cxxxvii. (al. cxxiii.) pp. 409, 10.]

the sacrament), according to the canons, both they which were called *Cathecumeni*, that is to say, persons newly instructed or trained up in the principles of christian religion, and also *Pœnitentes*, that is, such as for their looseness of life were not yet meet to be admitted unto the participation of those holy mysteries, were commanded to go out, so that it was not lawful for them there to remain[1]."

In Expos. Ord. Rom.

St Gregory also bishop of Rome testifieth, that "this was the manner in times past, that whensoever the holy communion of the body and blood of Christ should be ministered, the deacon turned him to the people, and cried out on this sort: *Si quis non communicat, exeat.* That is to say: 'If any do not communicate, let him go out.' For in this respect is the communion called *Missa*, because all such are to be sent out by the deacon, which are not partakers of the sacrifice or of the holy communion," &c. And in another place he declareth, that when the gospel was once read, the deacon came and openly commanded all such to depart as had not prepared themselves to be partakers of the holy communion. For it was not lawful for such to be present at the celebration of those holy mysteries. Again he saith: "Except such as do not communicate be commanded to go out at the voice of the deacon, according to the custom and manner of our ancestors, the service or office, which commonly is called *Missa*, cannot truly and perfectly be done." Once again he saith: "The exorcist must cast out devils, and say unto the people, that all such as will not communicate must depart and go away[2]."

Lib. i. de Ord. Rom.

Lib. de Divin. Off. sec. Ord. Rom. de Off. Exorcistæ.

And Dionysius Areopagita writeth, that after the gospel was once read, all that did not communicate were put out of the church, and by no means suffered to see those holy mysteries, nor to be present at the ministration of the same[3].

Moreover, in the liturgy of the Ethiopes, we read thus: "So soon as the gospel is ended, the deacon saith: 'All ye that will not receive the sacrament or eucharist, get ye out.' And again after the creed is sung, the deacon saith: 'Ye that will not communicate, depart and go your way; but ye that will communicate, embrace and kiss one another[4].'"

In the liturgy of the Armenians we find these words: "The deacon a little before the preface saith: 'They that are not worthy to communicate and to be partakers of this holy oblation of God, let them go out and stand before the church door, and there pray[5].'"

In Liturg. Chrysost.

And in the liturgy of St John Chrysostom we read that, when the communicants prepared themselves unto the Lord's table, the archdeacon commanded the deacon that stood without, to shut the chancel doors, that none might there remain but the communicants only[6].

[1 Sciendum est autem, juxta antiquos patres, quod soli communicantes divinis mysteriis interesse consueverunt, unde et ante oblationem juxta canones jubebantur exire catechumeni, et pœnitentes, videlicet qui nondum se paraverunt ad communicandum.—Microlog. de Eccles. Observat. in Mag. Biblioth. Vet. Patr. Col. Agrip. 1618—22. cap. li. Tom. XI. p. 392.]

[2 The substance of these references may be found as follows. Expositor Ord. Rom. B. Gregorius papa testatur, moris fuisse diacono proclamare: Si quis non communicat, exeat; et propter hoc certe dicitur Missa, quando mittendi sunt foras per diaconum, qui non participant sacrificio vel communione sancta.—Cassandr. Op. Par. 1616. Liturg. cap. xvii. pp. 35, 6.—Iterum admonentur ab archidiacono his verbis Catechumeni recedant: Si quis catechumenus est, recedat. Omnes catechumeni exeant foras.—Ord. Rom. I. in Mus. Ital. a Mabill. Lut. Par. 1687-9. Tom. II. p. 24. See also vii. p. 81.—Exorcistam oportet ejicere dæmones, et dicere populo qui non communicat, ut det locum.—Ord. Rom. De Offic. Div. De Exorcist. in Max. Biblioth. Vet. Patr. Lugd. 1677. Tom. XIII. col. 703.]

[3 Ἑξῆς δὲ, διὰ τῶν λειτουργῶν ἢ τῶν ἁγιογράφων δέλτων ἀνάγνωσις ἀκολούθως γίνεται· καὶ μετὰ ταύτας, ἔξω γίγνονται τῆς ἱερᾶς περιοχῆς οἱ κατηχούμενοι, καὶ πρὸς αὐτοῖς οἱ ἐνεργούμενοι, καὶ οἱ ἐν μετανοίᾳ ὄντες, μένουσι δὲ οἱ τῆς τῶν θείων ἐποψίας καὶ κοινωνίας ἄξιοι.—Dionys. Areop. Op. Antv. 1634. De Eccles. Hierarch. cap. iii. 2. Tom. I. p. 284.]

[4 *Diaconus.* Orate pro pace perfecta, et amica salutatione apostolica. Amplectimini invicem: Qui non communicatis, exite: qui communicatis, amplectimini invicem in plenitudine cordis vestri: qui communicaturus est custodiat se a malo.—Lit. Com. Æthiop. in Liturg. Orient. Coll. Stud. Eus. Renaudot. Par. 1716. Tom. I. p. 513. This is what was uttered after the creed. Of the warning after the gospel, Renaudot says in his note: Quod in versione Latina statim post recitationem evangelii legitur. Exite fores qui non vultis accipere sacramentum, sive eucharistiam: ite catechumeni, non legitur in editione Æthiopica.—p. 531.]

[5 Diaconus monet, Salutate invicem in osculo sancto. Qui non sunt digni communicare hanc oblationem Dei, exeant foras ante fores ecclesiæ, et ibi orent.—Ord. Cel. Myst. ex Lit. Armen. in Cassandr. Op. Liturg. cap. xii. p. 30.]

[6 Καὶ ὁ διάκονος περιπτύσσεται τὸ ὠράριον αὐτοῦ, καὶ προσκυνεῖ τρὶς, καὶ ἐπισυνάπτει ἐκφώνως. Τὰς θύρας, τὰς θύρας, ἐν σοφίᾳ πρόσχωμεν.

And in a certain homily he hath these words: "Whosoever is not partaker of the mysteries, he standeth by impudent and lewd. Therefore they that are in sin are first cast out. For even as it is not lawful for them to approach and to draw nigh unto the table, where their master sit, which have offended him, and to be present among the servitors, but is driven out from among them; so likewise is it in this place, while the oblation is offered, while Christ that Lamb of the Lord is offered up for a sacrifice[7]." Again he saith: "When the mysteries be once done, thou mayest come and see; but, so long as the mysteries be in hand, get thee hence: for thou hast nothing here to do[8]." Hom. 3. ad Ephes. Ad Pop. Antioch. Hom. 61.

Father. I perceive now right well that the papists, suffering other to be present at the ministration of the holy communion of the body and blood of our Lord and Saviour Christ Jesu, which do not communicate, nor be partakers of those blessed mysteries, err greatly from the ways and usages of the ancient christian churches. *Son.* You say truth.

Father. Is there any other abuse behind, crept into the church of Christ, concerning the holy supper of the Lord?

Son. This is another great abuse, that, whereas the Lord Christ Jesus would have the holy communion of his blessed body and precious blood to be oftentimes received of the faithful for a remembrance of his death and passion, and for the worthy, diligent, and earnest consideration of his inestimable benefits, which we have obtained of God the Father through the same his passion and death; the custom in the pope's church is, that the people receive that sacrament usually but once in the year, that is to say, at Easter, and that but under one kind and manner, contrary to the institution of Christ; so that by this means the commandment of Christ is broken, the sacrament is neglected, the death of Christ is not earnestly remembered, the people become unthankful, dissolution of life brasteth in, vice increaseth, virtue decreaseth. The eighth abuse.

Father. Is it the will of Christ that the faithful should oftentimes come unto those holy mysteries? *Son.* Who doubteth of that? To what end was the Lord's supper instituted, but that it should be frequented and used? To what end doth God give his commandment, but that it should be put in execution and practice? Is not this the commandment of Christ concerning his holy supper in the use of the same? "This do ye in the remembrance of me." Are not these the words of blessed St Paul? "The Lord Jesus the same night in which he was betrayed took bread; and when he had given thanks, he brake it, and said, Take ye, and eat: this is my body, which is broken for you: this do ye in the remembrance of me. After the same manner also he took the cup, when supper was done, saying, This cup is the new testament in my blood. This do, as oft as ye drink it, in remembrance of me. For as often as ye shall eat this bread, and drink of this cup, ye shall shew the Lord's death till he come." Luke xxii. 1 Cor. xi.

Here hear we both the commandment to receive, and also mention made of the often receiving. How is this put in practice in the pope's church, where the people receive the Lord's supper but once in a year? "As often," saith Christ. "As often," saith St Paul. But "as seldom," saith antichrist. They take away from the people the mysteries of Christ's body and blood, and feed them with holy bread and holy water, beggarly ceremonies of their own invention.

Father. Was the use in the time of the apostles to come often unto the Lord's tables? *Son.* Yea, verily. For thus read we in the Acts of the Apostles: "They that gladly received his (Peter's) preaching, were baptized; and the same day there were added unto them about three thousand souls. And they continued in the apostles' Acts ii.

—Div. Miss. S. Joan. Chrysost. in Rit. Græc. Op. Jac. Goar. Lut. Par. 1647. p. 75. See Goar's note, p. 134. Further remarks on the custom may be found in Renaudot, Tom. II. pp. 71, 601.]

[7 Πᾶς γὰρ ὁ μὴ μετέχων τῶν μυστηρίων, ἀναίσχυντος καὶ ἰταμῶς ἑστηκώς. διὰ τοῦτο πρότεροι ἐκβάλλονται οἱ ἐν ἁμαρτήμασι. καθάπερ γὰρ ἐπὶ τραπέζης παραγενομένου τοῦ δεσπότου οὐ δεῖ τοὺς προσκεκρουκότας τῶν οἰκετῶν παρεῖναι, ἀλλ' ἐκποδὼν γίνονται· οὕτω δὴ καὶ ἐνταῦθα, ἐκφερομένης τῆς θυσίας, καὶ τοῦ Χριστοῦ τεθυμένου, καὶ τοῦ προβάτου τοῦ δεσποτικοῦ.—Chrysost. Op. Par. 1718—38. In Epist. ad Ephes. cap. i. Hom. iii. Tom. XI. p. 23. A part of the homily numbered in the Latin editions Ad Pop. Ant. lxi. is found as just quoted among those on Ephesians. See Catalogus prefixed by Fronto Ducæus to his edition of Chrysostom. Par. 1621—24.]

[8 Ἔξεστι μετὰ ταῦτα προσελθεῖν, καὶ ἰδεῖν· ὅταν μέντοι παρῇ, ἄπιθι. οὐκ ἔξεστί σοι μᾶλλον, ἢ τῷ κατηχουμένῳ.—Id. ibid. p. 24.]

doctrine and fellowship, and in breaking of bread, and in prayers." Again: "All that believed kept themselves together, and had all things common, and sold their possessions and goods, and parted them to all men, as every man had need. And they continued daily with one accord in the temple, and brake bread from house to house, and did eat their meat together with gladness and singleness of heart, praising God," &c. Here hear we of daily continuance of breaking bread, whereby is understand the Lord's supper; and not of coming unto the Lord's tables once in the year, as the manner is in the pope's kingdom.

Father. And what was the use in the primitive church after the apostles' time? Came the Christians then also often unto the Lord's table? *Son.* That is not to be (In Rat. Div. Off. lib. iv.) doubted. For Guilhelmus Durandus saith, that in the primitive church all that were present at the celebration of the Lord's supper were wont every day to communicate[1].

And Platina, in his book of the lives of the Romish bishop[s], writeth that Anacletus bishop of Rome made a decree, that the Christians should receive the eucharist, that is to say, the sacrament of the body and blood of Christ, every day, and that those which would not communicate should be excommunicate[2].

And many years after, as we may perceive by reading the ancient writers, this often receiving of the sacrament continued in the church of Christ. For in the time (Ad Janua. epist. 2. In Joan. cap. vi. Trac.) of St Augustine, as he himself writeth, some did communicate every day; some but certain days in the week; some only upon the Saturday and Sunday; some not at all but only upon the Sunday[3].

(In epist. ad Lucian.) So likewise was the custom in the days of St Hierome[4].

(De Eccle. Dog. cap. 53.) And St Augustine hath a notable sentence in this behalf, which is this: "Daily to receive the communion of the eucharist I neither commend nor discommend; notwithstanding I would wish and exhort men to communicate every Sunday[5]."

In the time of St John Chrysostom also the Lord's supper was greatly frequented.

Among the Grecians, even at this present day, if any man absent himself from the Lord's table by the space of fourteen days (except he can render a reasonable cause of his absence), he is excommunicate, and put from the company of the faithful[6].

In all those mighty, large, and populous kingdoms which are under that most puissant king, Precious John[7], the holy communion of the body and blood of the Lord hath been from the beginning daily ministered to the people, and yet is at this present day, as histories make mention.

Moreover, unto the often receiving of the holy mysteries of Christ's body and blood all the ancient writers do diligently exhort. But blessed Ignatius hath these words: (In Epist. ad Ephes.) "Make haste oftentimes to come unto the eucharist and glory of God. For when this thing is busily done, the powers of Satan are expelled[8]."

(In Orat. de B. Philogonio.) St John Chrysostom saith: "He that hath a pure conscience ought every day to come unto the communion[9]." This aforesaid doctor in divers places of his writings

[1 See before, page 239, note 6.]

[2 Omnibus quoque fidelibus præcepit, ut peracta consecratione communicarent; qui vero nollent, e sacris ædibus eliminarentur.—Plat. De Vit. Pont. Rom. Col. 1568. Anacletus I. p. 15. See also before, page 238, note 1.]

[3 Alii quotidie communicant corpori et sanguini Domini, alii certis diebus accipiunt: alibi nullus dies prætermittitur, quo non offeratur, alibi sabbato tantum et dominico, alibi tantum dominico.—August. Op. Par. 1679—1700. Ad Inquis. Januar. Lib. I. Epist. liv. 2. Tom. II. col. 124. Hujus rei sacramentum, id est, unitatis corporis et sanguinis Christi, alicubi quotidie, alicubi certis intervallis dierum in dominica mensa præparatur, et de mensa dominica sumitur.—Id. In Johan. Evang. cap. vi. Tractat. XXVI. 15. Tom. III. Pars II. col. 500.]

[4 De sabbatho quod quæris, utrum jejunandum sit; et de eucharistia, an accipienda quotidie, quod Romana ecclesia et Hispaniæ observare perhibentur, scripsit quidem et Hippolytus vir disertissimus.—Hieron. Op. Par. 1693—1706, Epist. lii. ad Lucin. Tom. IV. Pars II. col. 579.]

[5 Quotidie eucharistiæ communionem percipere nec laudo nec vitupero. Omnibus tamen dominicis diebus communicandum suadeo et hortor, si tamen mens in affectu peccandi non sit.—August. Op. De Eccles. Dogm. cap. xxiii. Tom. VIII. Appendix, col. 78. This treatise is certainly not Augustine's: it is usually attributed to Gennadius.]

[6 Apud Græcos quoque, illi qui duas dominicas vel tres sine communione transierint, excommunicari dicuntur.—Wal. Strab. in Mag. Biblioth. Vet. Patr. Col. Agrip. 1618—22. De Reb. Eccles. cap. xx. Tom. IX. Pars I. p. 956.]

[7 Prester John, as he was usually called; the sovereign of Abyssinia.]

[8 Σπουδάζετε οὖν πυκνότερον συνέρχεσθαι εἰς εὐχαριστίαν Θεοῦ καὶ εἰς δόξαν· ὅτ' ἂν γὰρ πυκνῶς ἐπὶ τὸ αὐτὸ γίνεσθε, καθαιροῦνται αἱ δυνάμεις τοῦ Σατανᾶ.—Ignat. Epist. ad Ephes. cap. xiii. in Patr. Apost. Oxon. 1838. Tom. II. p. 284.]

[9 Καὶ καθάπερ τὸν οὐδὲν ἑαυτῷ συνειδότα φαῦλον καθ' ἑκάστην δεῖ προσιέναι τὴν ἡμέραν· οὕτω

both sharply and grievously reproveth his audients for their slack coming unto the Lord's table, and exhorteth them many times in the year, yea, daily (if they have Hom. 61. ad Pop. Antioch. pure minds) to come unto the holy communion[10].

Theophylact also admonisheth us that we should not come this or that day unto In 1 Cor. cap. xi. the holy mysteries of the body and blood of Christ, but at all times, whensoever we find ourselves pure and worthy[11].

St Ambrose, speaking of the Lord's supper, saith: "Receive (the Lord's bread) Lib. v. de Sacra. cap. 4. daily, which may profit thee daily. So live that thou mayest deserve to receive it daily[12]," &c. Again: "If so oftentimes as the blood of Christ is shed it is shed Lib. iv. de Sacra. cap. 6. unto the remission of sins, I ought to receive it alway, that my sins may alway be forgiven me. I that alway sin ought alway to have the medicine[13]." The medicine, saith he, is the heavenly and worshipful sacrament.

Hereto appertaineth the saying of St Bernard: "He that hath a wound seeketh a medicine: we have a wound while we are under sin; the medicine is the sacrament: daily receive, daily thou shalt be healed[14]."

St Hierome also saith: "Would God we were able at all times to receive the Ad Lucin. eucharist without the condemnation of ourselves and without a pricking conscience, and to hear the psalmist saying, 'Taste and see how sweet the Lord is[15].'" Psal. xxxiv.

Many other histories and authorities might here be alleged to declare, that when the church of Christ was most pure, the sacrament of the body and blood of Christ was most often received of the Christians; again, that we, which at this time live and profess Christ, ought to frequent the holy sacrament, and oftentimes to be partakers of those holy mysteries, lest that we, abstaining from so wholesome medicine, acquire and get to ourselves wounds incurable. Who seeth not then, what and how great an abuse this is in the pope's church, the lay people commonly to receive the Lord's supper but once in the year, yea, and that under one kind, contrary to the institution of Christ? I greatly marvel that the papists observe not so much as the decree of their father the pope! For pope Fabian made a decree, and gave out a commandment, De Consec. dist. 2. that all men should at the least thrice in the year receive the holy communion; that is to say, at Easter, and at Whitsuntide, and at Christmas[16]. The very same thing was enacted in the council Agathense, of the which we read on this manner: "The secular Lib. Concil. people which do not communicate at Christmas, Easter, and Whitsuntide, let them not be counted catholics, nor taken among the catholics[17]."

Thus see we, that the papists in abusing the supper of the Lord are utterly fallen

---

τὸν ἐν ἁμαρτήμασι προκατειλημμένον, καὶ μὴ μετανοοῦντα, οὐδὲ ἐν ἑορτῇ προσιέναι ἀσφαλές.—Chrysost. Op. Par. 1718—38. De B. Philogon. cont. Anom. Hom. vi. Tom. I. p. 499.]

[10 Μετὰ ταύτης [καθαρότητος] ἀεὶ πρόσιθι, χωρὶς ταύτης μηδέποτε...ὢ τῆς συνηθείας, ὢ τῆς προλήψεως, εἰκῇ θυσία καθημερινὴ, εἰκῇ παρεστήκαμεν τῷ θυσιαστηρίῳ, οὐδεὶς ὁ μετέχων...σκόπει, παρακαλῶ· τράπεζα πάρεστι βασιλικὴ, ἄγγελοι διακονούμενοι τῇ τραπέζῃ, αὐτὸς πάρεστιν ὁ βασιλεὺς, καὶ σὺ ἕστηκας χασμώμενος; ῥυπαρά σοι τὰ ἱμάτια, καὶ οὐδείς σοι λόγος; ἀλλὰ καθαρά ἐστιν; οὐκοῦν ἀνάπεσον, καὶ μέτεχε.—Id. In Epist. ad Ephes. cap. i. Hom. iii. Tom. XI. pp. 22, 3.]

[11 Δίκασον οὖν τῷ συνειδότι σου, καὶ οὕτω πρόσιθι, μὴ ὅταν ἑορτὴ ᾖ, ἀλλ' ὅταν καθαρὸν σεαυτὸν καὶ ἄξιον εὕρῃς.—Theophyl. Op. Venet. 1754—63. Comm. in I. Epist. ad Cor. cap. xi. 28. Tom. II. p. 192.]

[12 Accipe quotidie, quod quotidie tibi prosit. Sic vive, ut quotidie merearis accipere.—Ambros. Op. 1686—90. De Sacram. Lib. v. cap. iv. 25. Tom. II. col. 378. It is very doubtful whether this be a genuine work of Ambrose. See Cave's Script. Eccles. Hist. Lit. Oxon. 1740—3. Tom. I. p. 263.]

[13 Si quotiescumque effunditur sanguis, in remissionem peccatorum funditur, debeo illum semper accipere, ut semper mihi peccata dimittantur. Qui semper pecco, semper debeo habere medicinam.—Id. Ibid. Lib. IV. cap. vi. 28. col. 372.]

[14 The precise words have not been discovered; but the idea is not unfrequent in the works ascribed to this father. See especially Bernard. Op. Par. 1690. De Excell. Sanctiss. Sacram. Serm. (it is uncertain who the author of the treatise is) 10. Vol. II. Tom. v. col. 672; and Guerr. Abbat. De Res. Dom. Serm. ii. 4. Tom. VI. col. 1001.]

[15 Atque utinam omni tempore jejunare possimus......eucharistiam quoque absque condemnatione nostri, et pungente conscientia, semper accipere, et psalmistam audire, dicentem: Gustate et videte, quoniam suavis est Dominus.—Hieron. Op. Epist. lii. ad Lucin. Tom. IV. Pars II. col. 579.]

[16 Etsi non frequentius, saltem in anno ter laici homines communicent (nisi forte quis majoribus quibuslibet criminibus impediatur) in pascha videlicet, et pentecoste, et natali Domini.—Fabian. in Decret. Gratiani, Par. 1583. Decr. Tert. Pars, De Consecr. Dist. ii. can. 16. cols. 2367, 8.]

[17 Sæculares, qui in natali Domini, pascha, et pentecoste non communicaverint, catholici non credantur, nec inter catholicos habeantur.—Ex Concil. Agathens. can. 18, in eod. can. 19. ibid. See also Conc. Stud. Labbei. Par. 1671—2. Tom. IV. col. 1386.]

from their own law and decrees, while they commonly minister the sacrament of the body and blood of Christ to the laity but once in the year; whereas the commandment of Christ, the practice of the apostolic and primitive church, the use of those churches which until this day have continued in the doctrine of the apostles, the doctrine of the ancient fathers, and the best reformed churches in these our days, teach the contrary.

Father. There have been (it cannot be denied) great abuses, and yet are in the pope's church, concerning the supper of the Lord; and this rare and seldom coming of the common people unto the receiving of the sacrament of the body and blood of Christ is not one of the lessest. But notwithstanding, because the people should not be altogether without some outward thing to put them in remembrance of the body-breaking and blood-shedding of Christ, the papists have brought into the church two ceremonies, that is to say, holy bread and holy water; and they every Sunday minister them to the common people, instead of the honourable sacrament of the body and blood of Christ, by giving them the bread to eat, and by casting the water on their faces. *Son.* It may justly be said unto them as Christ answered the Pharisees and scribes: "Well prophesied Esaias of you, O ye hypocrites, as it is written, This people honoureth me with their lips, but their heart is far from me; howbeit in vain do they serve me, teaching the doctrines and commandments of men. For ye lay the commandment of God apart, and observe the constitutions of men, &c. Ye cast away the commandment of God to maintain your own traditions."

Matt. xv. Mark vii. Isai. xxix.

Errors crept into the church about the Lord's supper.

Father. Besides these abuses, have there not also crept in certain errors into the church of Christ about the matter of the Lord's supper, through the ungodly doctrine of the papists? *Son.* Yes, verily, divers, but three principally.

Father. Which are they? *Son.* The first is the doctrine of transubstantiation. The second is the doctrine of the corporal presence of Christ in the sacrament, as he hanged on the cross. The third is, that the godless and wicked people, receiving the sacrament, eat and drink the body and blood of Christ no less than the godly and the faithful people.

Of transubstantiation.

Father. Why, what thinkest thou of transubstantiation? *Son.* I think it to be a papistical, wicked, and devilish error.

Father. Why dost thou call it a papistical error? *Son.* Because it was thrust into the church of Christ through the violent tyranny and tyrannical violence of the pope, and made of full force with the articles of the christian belief.

Father. What pope brought it in? *Son.* Pope Innocent the third.

Father. Where? *Son.* At Rome, in a certain council called Concilium Latronense, in the which were gathered together wonderful swarms of smeared, spiritual, shorling[1] sorcerers, to the number of twelve hundred and odd; whereof the greatest part were monks, friars, canons, and such other idle monsters, which "devour widows' houses, under the pretence of long prayer," which "have an outward appearance of godly living, but have denied the power thereof," which "think lucre godliness," which also, being damnable sects, "deny the Lord that bought them;" forasmuch as they are the "enemies of the cross of Christ, and have the belly for their god."

Matt. xxiii. 2 Tim. iii. 1 Tim. vi. 2 Pet. ii. Phil. iii.

Father. At what time came transubstantiation into the church? *Son.* Pope Innocent the third, with his adherents, hatched this cockatrice's egg, (I mean the horrible monster of transubstantiation,) in the year of our Lord one thousand two hundred and fifteen, while he sat in the chair not of Moses, but of pestilence.

Father. This doctrine then of transubstantiation is but new. *Son.* New indeed, and as I may so speak, yesterday's doctrine.

Father. And doth pope Innocent make this his new doctrine of equal authority with the articles of the christian faith? *Son.* Yea, as we may see in his devilish decree[2].

De summa Trinitate, cap. Firmiter.

[[1] Shorling: a sheep that has been shorn; here, shaveling.]

[[2] Una vero est fidelium universalis ecclesia, extra quam nullus omnino salvatur. In qua idem ipse sacerdos et sacrificium Jesus Christus, cujus corpus et sanguis in sacramento altaris sub speciebus panis et vini veraciter continentur, transsubstantiatis pane in corpus, et vino in sanguinem potestate divina, ut ad perficiendum mysterium unitatis accipiamus ipsi de suo, quod accepit ipse de nostro.—Innocent. III. Op. Col. 1575. Concil. Lat. Decr. De Trin. cap. i. Tom. I. p. 461. See also Concil. Stud. Labbei. Lut. Par. 1671—2. Tom. XI. Pars I. col. 143.]

Father. Why callest thou this doctrine of transubstantiation a wicked error? *Son*. Because it is not grounded upon the word of God, but rather it is contrary to the word of God. For whereas the holy scripture calleth the sacrament of the body and blood of Christ, bread and wine, this doctrine of transubstantiation teacheth plainly that there is neither bread nor wine; which are two such repugnancies and contraries, as darkness is not more contrary to light, nor death to life. And as the holy scripture affirmeth bread and wine to remain in the sacrament, so likewise do all the ancient writers and old doctors of Christ's church; so that this doctrine of transubstantiation is no less contrary to the teaching of the holy scripture and of the godly fathers, than it is new.

And St Ambrose saith: "We lawfully condemn all new things which Christ hath not taught; for to the faithful Christ is the way. If Christ therefore have not taught that thing which we teach, even we ourselves also judge and recount it detestable." Again he saith: "Whatsoever is not of the apostles, it is full of wickedness[3]." Tract. 4. de Virg.

St Hierome saith: "That is the doctrine of the Holy Ghost, which is set forth in the canonical letters; against the which doctrine if councils establish any thing, I judge it unlawful and wicked[4]." In Epist. ad Galat.

Panormitanus also saith: "We ought more to believe a simple layman alleging the holy scripture than an whole council" (without the scripture). Once again he saith: "More credit is to be given to such one as is perfectly learned in holy letters, and bringeth for him universal authority, than to a general council." Item: "In matters concerning faith, the word even of one private man is more to be regarded than the saying of the pope, if he be moved with better authorities of the new and old testament than the pope[5]." De Elect. cap. Significasti.

"It is needful," saith Origen, "that we call the holy scriptures in to witness. For our devices and expositions without these witnesses are not to be believed[6]." In Hiere.

St Cyprian saith: "Adulterous and whorish is it, ungodly is it, yea, plain sacrilege and God-robbing is it, whatsoever is appointed through the madness of man, that God's ordinance should be violated and broken[7]." Ad Felicem. Epist. 8.

For the authority of the holy scripture is greater than all the perspicacity or quick sight of man's wit[8], as St Augustine saith.

Father. But wherefore dost thou call the doctrine of transubstantiation a devilish error? *Son*. Because the devil, "which is a liar and the father of all lies," first of all invented this prodigious monster of transubstantiation, to corrupt the true doctrine of the Lord's supper left unto us in the holy scriptures and in the godly monuments of the ancient fathers, and breathed it into the breast of his chaplain, pope Innocent John viii.

[[3] Nos enim nova omnia, quæ Christus non docuit, jure damnamus; quia fidelibus via Christus est. Si igitur Christus non docuit quod docemus, etiam nos id detestabile judicamus.—Ambros. Op. Par. 1686—90. De Virgin. Lib. cap. vi. 28. Tom. II. col. 220.]

[[4] Spiritus sancti doctrina est, quæ libris canonicis est prodita: contra quam, si quid statuant concilia, nefas duco.—Hieron. in Epist. ad Gal. in Catal. Test. Verit. Genev. 1608. col. 201. In Jerome's works the editor has not succeeded in discovering the passage.]

[[5] Uni fideli privato, si meliorem scripturæ auctoritatem aut rationem habeat, plus credendum est, quam toti concilio vel papæ.—Panorm. in Catal. Test. col. 1889. This sentence does not seem to be in Panormitan's work in the chapter mentioned.

Perhaps the following is the second passage intended:...Puto tamen quod si papa moveretur melioribus rationibus et auctoritatibus quam concilium, quod standum esset sententiæ suæ; nam et concilium potest errare.—Panorm. (N. de Tudesch.) sup. Decretal. Lib. Venet. Nur. et Basil. 1476-8. Lib. I. Tit. vi. Tom. I. fol. k. 2.

Nam in concernentibus fidem etiam dictum unius privati esset præferendum dicto papæ, si ille moveretur melioribus auctoritatibus novi et veteris testamenti quam papa.—Id. ibid.]

[[6] Μάρτυρας δεῖ λαβεῖν τὰς γραφάς. ἀμάρτυροι γὰρ αἱ ἐπιβολαὶ ἡμῶν καὶ αἱ ἐξηγήσεις ἄπιστοί εἰσιν.—Orig. Op. Par. 1733—59. In Jer. Hom. i. Tom. III. p. 129.]

[[7] Adulterum est, impium est, sacrilegum est, quodcunque humano furore instituitur, ut dispositio divina violetur.—Cypr. Op. Oxon. 1682. Epist. xliii. p. 83.]

[[8] Passages to the effect of that cited in the text are very frequent in the voluminous works of Augustine; so that it is difficult to decide, when no reference is given, which precisely the author had in his mind. The following contains the substance of his quotation: Sed si divinarum scripturarum, earum scilicet quæ canonicæ in ecclesia nominantur, perspicua firmatur auctoritate, sine ulla dubitatione credendum est. Aliis vero testibus vel testimoniis, quibus aliquid credendum esse suadetur, tibi credere vel non credere liceat, quantum ea momenti ad faciendum fidem vel habere vel non habere perpenderis.—August. Op. Par. 1679—1700. Lib. ad Paulin. seu Epist. clxvii. 4. Tom. II. col. 475.]

the third, which, being conceived with this most ungracious monster, was delivered thereof at the council Latronense; at the birth whereof were present more than a thousand papists, which gave this monster this monstrous name, "transubstantiation."

What this word "transubstantiation" meaneth. *Father*. What meanest thou by this word "transubstantiation?" *Son*. A conversion or changing of a thing from his own natural substance unto the substance of another creature, as if chalk should be changed into cheese, or a fox into a friar.

Father. Is the like thing found in the sacrament of Christ's body and blood? *Son*. So say the papists.

Father. What say they? *Son*. Thus say they, that by the virtue of these five words, *Hoc est enim corpus meum*, "this is my body," they at their masses convert and turn the substance of bread into the substance of the natural body of Christ: again, that by the virtue of those words, *Hic est enim calix sanguinis mei*, &c. "this is the cup or chalice of my blood," &c., the substance of wine is turned into the substance of that very blood of Christ which he shed for our sake on the altar of the cross; so that now there remaineth no more bread or wine, but the very natural, real, and substantial body and blood of Christ, which he received of the holy virgin Mary.

Reason denieth the doctrine of transubstantiation. *Father*. Whatsoever the papists for their belly's sake prattle in this behalf, I am sure reason saith that there remaineth both bread and wine. For after the words of consecration, as they term them, we see, feel, taste, smell, savour, and receive ☞ both bread and wine. Yea, the bread after the consecration, if it be long kept, will mould, and stink, and breed full of worms: the wine also will lose her taste and colour, and wax sour and pale, as experience hath sufficiently taught. In consideration whereof, as I have heard, it is agreed among the papists, and set forth in their doctrine, that if the body of Christ (so term they the sacramental bread) should chance through the negligence of the priest to corrupt and putrify, a fire should be made, in the which that corrupt and rotten stuff should be consumed unto ashes, and the ashes to be reposed in the sacrary among the other reliques: again, that if the blood of Christ should fall upon the ground, the priest should lick it up with his tongue, and scrape the place where the blood fell, and, the scrapings gathered together, burn them in the fire, and the ashes thereof also laid up among the reliques; and that the priest for this his negligence should do penance by the space of forty days: when who knoweth not that the true body of Christ is immortal, uncorruptible, and can by no means be any more subject to mortality or corruption? so far is it off that it can be consumed with fire and brent unto ashes, Rom. vi. as St Paul saith: "Christ being raised from death dieth no more: death hath no more power over him. For as touching that he died, he died concerning sin once: and as touching that he liveth, he liveth unto God."

The old fathers never knew the popish doctrine of transubstantiation. *Son*. Not only reason, but also the word of God and the ancient fathers of Christ's church, affirm both bread and wine to remain in the sacrament, and by no means know or grant any such monstrous transubstantiation as the papists feign.

Father. First tell me what the holy scripture saith in this behalf. *Son*. Christ, in the institution of the holy sacrament of his blessed body and precious blood, as both Matt. xxvi. Mark xiv. Luke xxii. 1 Cor. xi. the evangelists and also St Paul testify, "took bread and gave thanks, brake it, and gave it to the disciples, and said, Take, eat: this is my body which is betrayed for you. Do this in the remembrance of me." Now, who seeth not evidently that that which Christ took was very bread? That which he took he also brake. And that which he took and brake, he gave to his disciples. And of that which he took, brake, and gave to his disciples, he said, "Take, eat: this is my body which is betrayed for you." Here is it manifest and plain, that Christ both took, brake, and gave bread to his disciples, and they did eat of it, remaining still bread in substance, without any alteration or changing; and called the bread his body, as the manner of the scripture Note well. is to call the signs by the names of the things signified, that the things which the signs represent may the more stedfast remain and abide in the minds of the faithful receivers. If the substance of bread remain, where is then their transubstantiation?

Father. The papists grant that that was bread which Christ took into his hands; but they utterly deny that that was bread which he brake and delivered to his disciples.

Son. What was it then? *Father.* Christ's very natural body, say they, as it was born of Mary the virgin, and hanged on the cross.

Son. How became it the natural body of Christ? *Father.* Through the virtue and power of certain words which Christ spake.

Son. Which are they? *Father.* The papists are not yet fully agreed among themselves in this matter.

Son. It is a common thing for liars to vary in their tales, and one to tell one thing, and another another thing[1]. But what say they? *Father.* Some affirm that Christ had consecrate the bread, and made it his body, with certain words which are not mentioned in the scripture, before he delivered the sacrament to his disciples, and said, "Take, eat; this is my body." For how could he have delivered his body to be eaten, if it had not been his body afore? Or how could he have said, "Take, eat; this is my body," if it had not been his body before he spake? Innocentius. Comestor. Thomas.

Son. At what time should Christ have spoken these words, wherewith he made the bread his body? *Father.* When he blessed or gave thanks, as they say. *Son.* But the words of Christ's blessing or thanksgiving are not contained in the word of God: it therefore followeth, that we have not the words of consecration which Christ used: it followeth also that these words, whereunto the papists stick with tooth and nail, *Hoc est enim corpus meum*, are not the very right words of the consecration; and therefore brag they of their transubstantiation in vain.

Father. Some say that Christ in his blessing or thanksgiving rehearsed these words, *Hoc est enim corpus meum*, first secretly and privately to himself, and so consecrated the bread and made it his body; and afterward, when he brake it and delivered it to his disciples, commanding them to take and eat, he openly pronounced those words again to his disciples, (I mean, *Hoc est enim corpus meum*,) both to certify them of the presence of his body, and also to declare unto them what words they also should afterward use in the consecration of the bread. *Son.* This thing is sooner said than proved. For whatsoever they speak in this behalf, it cometh out of their own idle brain, and not out of the word of God: and St Hierome saith, "That which hath not authority of the scriptures is despised with the same facility or easiness wherewith it is proved[2]." In Matt. xxiii.

[[1] *Benedixit.* Cum ad prolationem verborum istorum, Hoc est corpus meum, Hic est sanguis meus, sacerdos conficiat, credibile judicatur, quod et Christus eadem verba dicendo confecit. Porro quidam dixerunt, quod Christus confecit, cum benedixit, literam construentes hoc ordine: Accepit panem, benedixit, subaudiendum est, 'dicens, Hoc est corpus meum,' et tunc fregit, et dedit, et ait: Accipite et comedite, et iteravit: Hoc est corpus meum. Prius ergo protulit illa verba, ut eis vim conficiendi tribueret: deinde protulit eadem, ut apostolos formam conficiendi doceret. Alii vero dixerunt, quod et sacramentum confecit, et formam instituit post benedictionem, cum dixit, Hoc est corpus meum; intelligentes illam benedictionem fuisse vel aliquod signum quod super panem impressit, vel aliquod verbum, quod super panem expressit. Quibus illud videtur obsistere, quod prius fregerit, quam dixerit, Hoc est corpus meum. Nec etiam est credibile, quod prius dederit quam confecerit. Sane dici potest, quod Christus virtute divina confecit; et postea formam expressit, sub qua posteri benedicerent. Ipse namque per se virtute propria benedixit: nos autem ex illa virtute, quam indidit verbis.—Innocent. III. Op. Col. 1575. Myst. Miss. Lib. IV. cap. vi. Tom. I. p. 377.

Et nota quod in canone cum proferuntur hæc verba, Hoc est corpus meum, Hic est sanguis meus, ex virtute horum verborum fit transubstantiatio. Unde credibile est, cum Dominus eadem verba dixit, mutasse panem et vinum in carnem et sanguinem. et tunc eandem vim contulit Dominus verbis illis in posterum. Et propterea sic construenda est litera. Benedixit: subaudi: dicens, Hoc est corpus meum. Et tunc fregit et dedit discipulis suis: et ait, Comedite. Et iteravit: Hoc est corpus meum. Vel forte tunc benedixit benedictione nobis non tradita: sed post ad institutionem apostolorum vis benedicendi tradita est a Domino verbis istis, Hoc est corpus meum.—Hist. Scolast. Pet. Comest. Par. 1513. Hist. Evang. cap. clii. fol. 237.

Quidam enim dixerunt, quod Christus, qui habebat potestatem excellentiæ in sacramentis, absque omni forma virtute divina confecit, et postea verba protulit, sub quibus alii deinceps consecrabant......alii dicunt, quod confecit quidem sub aliqua forma verborum, non autem sub his, sed sub aliis verbis ignotis...... alii dicunt, quod confecit sub eisdem verbis, sed ea bis protulit, primo tacite, cum benedixit; secundo aperte, cum distribuit, ut formam consecrandi aliis traderet......alii dicunt, et melius, quod Christus ea semel tantum protulit, et eis semel prolatis consecravit, et formam consecrandi dedit. hoc enim participium, *dicens*, non importat concomitantiam solum ad hoc verbum, *dedit*; sed ad hoc cum aliis prædictis, ut sit sensus, Dum benedixit, et fregit, et dedit discipulis, hæc verba protulit, Accipite, &c. Vel secundum quosdam, evangelista non observat ordinem verborum quo a Domino fuerunt prolata. ordo enim fuit talis: Accepit panem, et benedixit, dicens, Accipite, &c.—Thom. Aquin. Op. Venet. 1595. In Lib. Sentent. IV. Dist. viii. Quæst. ii. Art. 1. Tom. VII. fol. 42. See also Tert. Pars Summ. Theol. Quæst. lxxv. Art. 7. Tom. XII. fols. 243, 4.]

[[2] Hoc quia de scripturis non habet auctoritatem, eadem facilitate contemnitur, qua probatur.—Hieron. Op. 1693—1706. Comm. Lib. IV. in Matt. cap. xxiv. Tom. IV. Pars I. col. 112.]

In Titum. Again: "Without authority of the scriptures, garrulity or prattling and vain jangling hath no faith, or is not to be credited[1]." This dream, therefore, of the papists is of no force to prove their prodigious transubstantiation.

Father. Some say that Christ made the bread his body by rehearsing these words, *Hoc est enim corpus meum*, once for all; yea, and that with a clear, evident, and open voice; and yet so that neither this word *hoc*, nor this word *est*, nor this word *enim*, nor this word *corpus*, nor yet this syllable *me*, doth much in the matter; but this last syllable *um* maketh up all the market, in the which, say they, all the virtue of the consecration dependeth and resteth; so that, *um* being once pronounced, the matter is full finished, the bread is dispatched, a transubstantiation is made, the substance of bread is turned into the substance of Christ's corporal, real, substantial, and natural body[2]; so that, although that was bread which Christ took in his hands, yet that which he brake and delivered to his disciples was not bread, say they, but the very natural body of Christ, and is now handled of the priest's hands, broken, and torn on pieces with the teeth of the faithful, according to the doctrine of pope Nicolas the second[3].

Son. That it was very bread which Christ brake, the order of the text doth most evidently declare. But that bread remaineth in the action of the Lord's supper not only before, but also after the consecration, as they term it, St Paul proveth manifestly by these his words: "The bread which we break," saith he, "is it not the communion," that is to say, the partaking, "of the body of Christ?" Here the holy apostle calleth the mystery of Christ's body "bread," and saith, "that we break bread;" meaning that in the Lord's supper we both break and eat bread. The blessed apostle knew nothing of this prodigious monster, "transubstantiation," which the papists, more than a thousand years after, brought forth, and delivered it to the church of Christ; and therefore he termeth bread, bread; yea, and that after it is made the mystery of Christ's body. Likewise in another place, where he entreateth largely of the sacrament of the body and blood of Christ, he calleth after the words of consecration the mystery of Christ's body "bread," three times; which thing he would never have done, if he had known that there had been any transubstantiation after the words of consecration, I mean, changing of the substance of bread into the substance of the natural body of Christ. But not only St Paul, but blessed Luke also termeth the mystery of the Lord's body "bread," whensoever he maketh mention of the supper of the Lord in his chronicle of the apostles' acts.

1 Cor. x.

St Paul knew not the popish doctrine of transubstantiation.

1 Cor. xi.

Acts ii. xx.

Now, as touching the wine, it is most manifest also that there is no transubstantiation, (I mean, changing of the substance of wine into the substance of the natural blood of Christ,) by the virtue of these words, *Hic est enim calix sanguinis mei*, &c. For Christ himself, after the words of consecration, as I may speak after the accustomed manner, called the mystery of his blood "the fruit of the vine-tree." Now, who knoweth not, that not the blood of Christ, but wine, is the fruit of the vine? If the ☞ mystery, therefore, of Christ's blood be the fruit of the vine-tree, then is it not the natural blood of Christ, as the papists teach, but natural wine. And here falleth down to the ground, yea, even unto hell, from whence it first of all came, the wicked doctrine of transubstantiation. For we have learned of the very words of Christ and of St Paul, and likewise of blessed Luke, that there is transubstantiation neither in the bread nor yet in the wine.

Matt. xxvi.

[1 Et quidem sine scripturarum auctoritate garrulitas non haberet fidem, nisi viderentur perversam doctrinam etiam divinis testimoniis roborare.—Id. Comm. in Epist. ad Tit. cap. i. col. 420.]

[2 See Decret. Gratiani, Par. 1583. Decr. Tert. Pars, De Consecr. Gloss. in Dist. ii. can. 40. col. 2381. *Significatur*, et licet verba successive proferantur; non tamen successive consecratio fit: sed in uno instanti corrumpitur panis, scilicet in ultimo instanti prolationis verborum: et licet panis sit corpus compositum, momentanea est tamen ejus corruptio.]

[3 Berengarius was compelled to recant before a council held at Rome (A. D. 1059) under Nicolas II. In his abjuration we find: Ego Berengarius...... profiteor de sacramento dominicæ mensæ eam fidem me tenere, quam dominus et venerabilis papa Nicolaus, et hæc sancta synodus auctoritate evangelica et apostolica tenendam tradidit, mihique firmavit: scilicet panem et vinum, quæ in altari ponuntur, post consecrationem non solum sacramentum, sed etiam verum corpus et sanguinem Domini nostri Jesu Christi esse: et sensualiter, non solum sacramento, sed in veritate, manibus sacerdotum tractari, et frangi, et fidelium dentibus atteri.—Concil. Rom. in Concil. Stud. Labbei. Lut. Par. 1671—2. Tom. IX. col. 1101. See also Pet. Lombard. Lib. Sentent. Col. Agrip. 1576. Lib. IV. Dist. xii. fol. 356.]

Father. Some affirm that the disciples had received both bread and wine, before Christ had recited the words of consecration, as they call them: and then must it needs follow, that those elements of bread and wine, which the disciples had already received, were not transubstantiated, nor turned into the natural body and blood of Christ; except the adversaries will say that Christ did consecrate and transubstantiate them after they were received of the disciples.

Son. Of the mystery of Christ's blood it is plain and evident, by the words of blessed St Mark, that the disciples received it before the words of consecration were pronounced. For thus writeth he: "He took the cup, and when he had given thanks, he took it to them; and they all drank of it. And he said unto them, This is my blood of the new testament, which is shed for many. Verily I say unto you, I will drink no more of the fruit of the vine, until that day that I drink it new in the kingdom of God." And the same may also be thought of the mystery of Christ's body, I mean, that they did eat the mystery of Christ's body before the words of consecration, as they call them, were pronounced. But howsoever it was, they cannot stablish nor ground their doctrine of transubstantiation by the word of God, as we have sufficiently tofore heard. Mark xiv.

Father. Do not the ancient writers and doctors of Christ's church teach and allow this doctrine of transubstantiation? *Son.* Nothing less. For they did never so much as once dream of it, but always taught the contrary, as we may see in their books which yet remain.

Father. Let me hear some authorities alleged out of the ancient writers concerning this matter. *Son.* First of all Origen, that ancient writer in the Greek church, cometh and offereth himself unto us as an enemy of this wicked doctrine of transubstantiation, whose words these are: "If any thing enter into the mouth, it goeth away into the belly, and is avoided into the draught; yea, and that meat which is sanctified by the word of God and prayer, concerning the matter thereof, it goeth away into the belly, and is avoided into the draught. But for the prayer which is added unto it, for the proportion of the faith, it is made profitable, making the mind able to perceive and see that which is profitable. For it is not the material substance of bread, but the word which is spoken upon it, that is profitable to the man that eateth it not unworthily. And this I mean of the typical and symbolical body[4]." Whether the old doctors taught transubstantiation. In Matt. cap. xv.

Here Origen affirmeth plainly, that in the Lord's supper the bread, which he calleth the typical and symbolical, that is to say, the figurative and the sacramental body of Christ, remaineth, yea, and that after it is sanctified by the word of God and prayer; and that the material substance thereof is received, digested, and avoided, as the material substance of other bread and meat is; which could not be, if there were no material substance of bread at all remaining. Who seeth not now, how directly Origen confoundeth, yea, condemneth the fantastical doctrine of the papists, concerning that monster of transubstantiation, which deny any substance of bread to remain in the sacrament?

That golden-mouthed doctor, St John Chrysostom, cometh next in order, and saith: "Before the bread be hallowed, we call it bread; but, the grace of God sanctifying it by the means of the priest, it is delivered now from the name of bread, and esteemed worthy to be called Christ's body, although the nature of the bread tarry in it still[5]." Ad Cæsar. Monach.

Here the holy doctor saith plainly, that the nature of bread remain still in the

[4 Εἰ δὲ πᾶν τὸ εἰσπορευόμενον εἰς τὸ στόμα, εἰς κοιλίαν χωρεῖ, καὶ εἰς ἀφεδρῶνα ἐκβάλλεται, καὶ τὸ ἁγιαζόμενον βρῶμα διὰ λόγου Θεοῦ καὶ ἐντεύξεως κατ' αὐτὸ μὲν τὸ ὑλικὸν εἰς τὴν κοιλίαν χωρεῖ, καὶ εἰς ἀφεδρῶνα ἐκβάλλεται· κατὰ δὲ τὴν ἐπιγενομένην αὐτῷ εὐχὴν, κατὰ τὴν ἀναλογίαν τῆς πίστεως, ὠφέλιμον γίνεται, καὶ τῆς τοῦ νοῦ αἴτιον διαβλέψεως, ὁρῶντος ἐπὶ τὸ ὠφελοῦν· καὶ οὐχ ἡ ὕλη τοῦ ἄρτου, ἀλλ' ὁ ἐπ' αὐτῷ εἰρημένος λόγος ἐστὶν ὁ ὠφελῶν τὸν μὴ ἀναξίως τοῦ Κυρίου ἐσθίοντα αὐτόν. καὶ ταῦτα μὲν περὶ τοῦ τυπικοῦ καὶ συμβολικοῦ σώματος.—Orig. Op. Par. 1733—59. Comm. in Matt. Tom. XI. cap. xv. Tom. III. pp. 499, 500.]

[5 Sicut enim antequam sanctificetur panis, panem nominamus; divina autem illum sanctificante gratia, mediante sacerdote, liberatus est quidem ab appellatione panis, dignus autem habitus Dominici corporis appellatione, etiamsi natura panis in ipso permansit, et non duo corpora, sed unum corpus Filii prædicamus.—Chrysost. Op. Par. 1718—38. Epist. ad Cæsar. Monach. Tom. III. p. 744. The genuineness of this epistle has been, but without sufficient ground, impugned.]

Lord's supper, although it be called Christ's body. If the nature of bread remain still, where is then the popish transubstantiation become? O too much vain and false doctrine!

Contra Eutychen. Dialog. 1.

Theodoretus, an eloquent and great learned man, writeth on this manner: "He that called his natural body corn and bread, and also named himself a vine-tree, even the same hath honoured the symbols (that is, the sacramental signs) which are seen, with the names of his body and blood; not changing indeed the nature itself, but adding grace to the nature[1]." Again he saith: "Neither do the mystical signs after the consecration depart from their nature. For they abide still in their former substance, both in figure and form, and may be both seen and touched even as before[2]." What can be spoken more plainly against the doctrine of the popish transubstantiation? If the nature and substance of bread remain still after the consecration, who seeth not how falsely the papists lie, which affirm that the substance of bread in the sacrament abide not, but is altered and changed into the substance of the natural body of Christ?

Dialog. 2.

Divers other Greek writers might here be alleged for the confirmation of our doctrine against the papists' monstrous and misshapen child transubstantiation, begotten and born at Rome; but let these suffice for this present. Only this one thing I will add, that the Greeks with all the east church could never be allured, moved, enticed, and brought to receive this doctrine of transubstantiation, being so lewd, unsavoury, unreasonable, monstrous, wicked, worthy to be laughed at, and so utterly estranged from the writings both of the apostles and of the ancient fathers, although divers ways and at divers times attempted of the subtile and wily papists. For at a certain council holden at Florence under Eugenius the fourth, bishop of Rome, about the year of our Lord a thousand four hundred thirty and one, the pope with his adherents sought all means possible to bring the Greeks and all the east church to confess with the church of Rome the doctrine of transubstantiation, and that after the words of consecration the substance of bread and wine is turned into the substance of the natural body and blood of Christ, no bread nor wine remaining, but only the accidents of bread and wine: notwithstanding, the Greeks utterly refused it, and would by no means receive, admit, approve, and allow such and so new and strange doctrine, brought in of late without the authority of the holy scriptures, and hitherto unknown in those churches which were founded and edified by the apostles and by the fathers of the primitive church; insomuch that, in the letters of mutual consent concerning the proceeding of the Holy Ghost, made between the Greek and Latin churches, the Greeks above all things did most earnestly take heed, and gave diligent warning, that there should be no mention made in those letters of any agreement or consent between them and the Romanists in the late-invented doctrine of transubstantiation[3].

Father. This declareth evidently that transubstantiation is but a new invention, and unknown of the best and purest churches; and therefore right well worthy to be banished out of all churches. *Son*. It is truth.

Father. But what say the ancient fathers of the Latin church? Do they allow this doctrine of transubstantiation? *Son*. Nothing less. For this matter was also

---

[1 See below, page 288, note 6, where this passage is more fully given.]

[2 *Οὐδὲ γὰρ μετὰ τὸν ἁγιασμὸν τὰ μυστικὰ σύμβολα τῆς οἰκείας ἐξίσταται φύσεως. μένει γὰρ ἐπὶ τῆς προτέρας οὐσίας, καὶ τοῦ σχήματος, καὶ τοῦ εἴδους, καὶ ὁρατά ἐστι, καὶ ἁπτὰ, οἷα καὶ πρότερον ἦν.*—Theodoret. Op. Lut. Par. 1642-84. Inconfus. Dial. II. Tom. IV. p. 85.]

[3 Ceterum concilio huic objicimus generale et œcumenicum concilium Florentiæ habitum sub Eugenio quarto Pontifice Romano, qui ibi interfuit: et aderat una imperator Græcorum, cum Patriarcha Constantinopolitano et multis episcopis orientalibus. In quo concilio Græca Latinæ est conjuncta, et consenserunt in dissidio de Spiritu Sancto. Atque in gestis illius concilii videre licet, posteaquam inter orientales et Latinos convenisset de quibusdam articulis, voluisse papam ulterius progredi, et illos adigere ad transubstantiationem tractandam, et recipiendam ut Latini sentiebant. Ibi Græci reluctati sunt, et de ea re agere noluerunt, neque perpelli ullis argumentis potuerunt, ut de ea consensus iniretur. Cumque unionis literæ essent formandæ et publicandæ, prorsus caverunt, ut hujus rei nulla mentio fieret; quod et observatum est, ut patet in bulla Eugenii, quæ incipit, Exultent cœli, et lætetur terra.—Loc. Com. Pet. Mart. Heid. 1613. Class. IV. cap. x. 59. pp. 867, 8. See also Concil. Flor. in Concil. Stud. Labbei. Lut. Par. 1671—2. Tom. XIII. cols. 491, &c.; and Covel, Account of the Greek Church, Camb. 1722. chap. v. pp. 138-9. The full history of this council may be seen in Vera Hist. Union. non Veræ, sive Conc. Flor. Narr. per Sylv. Sguropulum, a Creyghton. Hagæ-Com. 1660.]

unknown to them, as we may see in their writings. Ireneus, that learned and ancient father, saith thus: "The bread wherein we give thanks, which is of the earth, receiving the calling of God, is now no common bread, but the eucharist," that is to say, the bread of thanksgiving, "consisting of two things, earthly and heavenly[4]." Again he saith: "When the cup mingled and the bread broken receive the word of God, it is made the eucharist (or sacrament) of the body and blood of Christ, of which the substance of our flesh is stayed and increased[5]." Here saith Ireneus plainly, that the sacrament of the body and blood of Christ consisteth of two things, one heavenly and the other earthly. What is this earthly thing, but very bread? Which thing he declareth manifestly, in that he saith, it is of the earth, and nourisheth our bodies, as other bread doth. If the bread of thanksgiving be an earthly thing, and feedeth our bodies no less than all other bread doth which we use, who seeth not then that the substance of bread remaineth? except peradventure the papists will say, that we be fed with the accidents of bread, which is a thing impossible and against both nature and reason. If bread remain, where is then their transubstantiation?

Adversus Hæreses, Lib. iv. cap. 34.

Lib. v. cap. 57.

St Cyprian, that old doctor and blessed martyr, saith: "The Lord calleth the bread, being compact together of many corns, his body; and he nameth the wine, being pressed out of many grapes, and made into wine, his blood[6]." Again he saith: "The hallowed bread entered into the wicked mouth[7]." Item: "Drink sanctified into the blood of Christ brast out of the defiled bowels[8]." Here St Cyprian openly affirmeth that that which Christ called his body was very bread, even such bread as is made of corn: again, that that which he named his blood was very wine, even such wine as is pressed out of many grapes. What can be spoken more plainly against the wicked doctrine of transubstantiation?

Ad Magnum, Lib. i. epist. 6.

In serm. de Cœna Dom.

Moreover Gelasius, a bishop of Rome—of Rome, I say, but yet before Rome was infected with the pestiferous breath of that most poisonful old serpent, the father of all errors and lies—writeth of the sacrament of the body and blood of Christ against the heretic Eutyches on this wise: "The sacrament of the body and blood of Christ which we receive is a godly thing, for the which also through the same we are made partakers of the divine nature; and yet nevertheless the substance or nature of bread and wine do not cease or depart and go away[9]." Can any thing be spoken more plainly against the error of the popish transubstantiation, than this which a bishop of Rome writeth? Would God all his successors had walked in the same simplicity of God's Spirit, and had with no less dexterity and uprightness[10] handled the holy scriptures! Then should never so many pestilent errors and heresies have crept into the church. For what can any man say more to overthrow the doctrine of the papistical transubstantiation, than this bishop of Rome uttereth? which with most manifest words affirmeth, that in the sacrament of the body and blood of Christ the substance of bread and wine remaineth, and goeth not away. If the substance of bread and wine remain, and do not depart, where is then transubstantiation become?

Contra Eutych.

Again, St Austin, one of the best writers among the doctors of Christ's church, saith thus: "That which ye have seen is the bread and the cup, which also your

In serm. ad Infantes.

[4 Ὡς γὰρ ἀπὸ γῆς ἄρτος προσλαμβανόμενος τὴν ἔκκλησιν τοῦ Θεοῦ, οὐκέτι κοινὸς ἄρτος ἐστὶν, ἀλλ' εὐχαριστία, ἐκ δύο πραγμάτων συνεστηκυῖα, ἐπιγείου τε καὶ οὐρανίου.—Iren. Cont. Hær. Lib. Quinque. Par. 1710. Lib. iv. cap. xviii. 5. p. 251.]

[5 Ὁπότε οὖν καὶ τὸ κεκραμένον ποτήριον, καὶ ὁ γεγονὼς ἄρτος ἐπιδέχεται τὸν λόγον τοῦ Θεοῦ, καὶ γίνεται ἡ εὐχαριστία σῶμα Χριστοῦ, ἐκ τούτων δὲ αὔξει καὶ συνίσταται ἡ τῆς σαρκὸς ἡμῶν ὑπόστασις.—Id. Lib. v. cap. ii. 3. p. 294.]

[6 Nam quando Dominus corpus suum panem vocat de multorum granorum adunatione congestum; populum nostrum, quem portabat, indicat adunatum: et quando sanguinem suum vinum appellat, de botris atque acinis plurimis expressum atque in unum coactum; gregem item nostrum significat, commixtione adunatæ multitudinis copulatum.—Cypr. Op. Oxon. 682. Epist. lxix. ad Magn. p.182.]

[7 Necdum Judas ad veterem vitam pertinens, diabolo invadente et occupante animum ejus egredi cogebatur, sed ubi sacrum cibum mens perfida tetigit, et sceleratum os panis sanctificatus intravit, parricidialis animus vim tanti sacramenti non sustinens, quasi palea de area exsufflatus, et præceps cucurrit ad proditionem et pretium, ad desperationem et laqueum.—Id. De Cœn. Dom. (Arnold. Abbat. Bonavall.) Appendix, p. 39.]

[8 Sanctificatus in Domini sanguine potus, de pollutis visceribus erupit.—Id. de Laps. p. 132.]

[9 Certe sacramenta quæ sumimus corporis et sanguinis Christi, divina res est, propter quod et per eadem divinæ efficimur consortes naturæ, et tamen esse non desinit substantia vel natura panis et vini.—Gelas. Episc. Rom. adv. Eutych. et Nestor. in Mag. Biblioth. Vet. Patr. Col. Agrip. 1618—22. Tom. V. Pars III. p. 671.]

[10 The folio reads *unrightness*.]

eyes do shew you. But that faith requireth to be instructed, the bread is the body of Christ, and the cup his blood[1]." Again he saith: "The sacrifice of the church consisteth of two things, of the visible kind of the element, and of the invisible flesh and blood of our Lord Jesu Christ, both of the sacrament, and of the thing signified by the sacrament; even as the person of Christ consisteth of God and man, forasmuch as he is very God and very man. For every thing containeth in it the very nature of those things whereof it consisteth. Now the sacrifice of the church consisteth of two things, of the sacrament, and of the thing thereby signified, that is to say, the body of Christ. Therefore there is both the sacrament, and the thing of the sacrament, which is Christ's body[2]." St Austin saith here plainly, that that which we see at the Lord's table with our corporal eyes is bread; and that, as the person of Christ consisteth of two natures, that is to say, of his manhood and of his Godhead; even so the sacrament consisteth of two natures, of the elements of bread and wine, and of the body and blood of Christ. If the elements of bread and wine remain, if that which we see with our eyes be bread, who then perceiveth not evidently the manifest error of the popish transubstantiation, and that whatsoever the papists teach in this behalf is plain falsehood and lies?

In Sentent. Prosperi.

Bertramme, a great learned man, among many other, hath these words, writing of the Lord's supper: "As touching the substance of the creatures" (he speaketh of the mysteries of Christ's body and blood), "look what they were before the consecration, even the very same do they remain still afterward. Bread and wine were they before; in the which kind also, being now consecrate, they are seen to continue and remain[3]." What can be spoken more plainly against the popish transubstantiation, than to affirm that bread and wine do remain and continue in the sacrament, not only before the consecration, but also after the consecration?

Many more, yea, almost infinite authorities might be gathered out of the books of the godly ancient learned writers, which do manifestly impugn and condemn this wicked error of the papistical transubstantiation; but these tofore alleged may seem to any indifferent person abundantly to suffice. And wherefore should I labour so greatly with the testimonies of the best and most ancient writers to subvert and overthrow this monstrous transubstantiation, seeing that the papists themselves in their popish mass call the sacrament "bread," yea, and that after the consecration[4]? Neither is this to be passed over with silence, that certain among the papists themselves could very hardly brook and digest this strange doctrine of so monstrous transubstantiation.

For that subtile doctor, Joannes Scotus, otherwise called Duns, one of the subtilest disputers and chief champions among the papists, freely confesseth that the article of transubstantiation is neither expressed in the creed of the apostles, nor yet in the other ancient and old creeds; but now in these latter times declared, set forth, defined, and determined of the church (he speaketh of the Romish synagogue) under pope Innocentius the third, in the council Latronense, in the year of our Lord one thousand two hundred and fifteen. And he saith moreover, that "the words of the scripture might be expounded more easily and more plainly without transubstantiation; but the church did choose this sense (which is more hard), being moved thereto (as it seemeth) chiefly because that of the sacraments men ought to hold as the holy church of Rome holdeth;

In Sentent. dist. xi. lib. iv. quæst. 3.

[1 Quod ergo videtis, panis est et calix; quod vobis etiam oculi vestri renuntiant: quod autem fides vestra postulat instruenda, panis est corpus Christi, calix sanguis Christi.—August. Op. Par. 1679—1700. Serm. cclxxii. ad Infant. Tom. V. cols. 1103, 4.]

[2 Hoc est quod dicimus: hoc modis omnibus approbare contendimus, sacrificium scilicet ecclesiæ duobus confici, duobus constare, visibili elementorum specie, et invisibili Domini nostri Jesu Christi carne et sanguine, sacramento, et re sacramenti, id est corpore Christi, sicut Christi persona constat et conficitur Deo et homine; cum ipse Christus verus sit Deus, et verus homo: quia omnis res illarum rerum naturam et veritatem in se continet, ex quibus conficitur. Conficitur autem sacrificium ecclesiæ sacramento et re sacramenti, id est corpore Christi. Est igitur sacramentum et res sacramenti, id est corpus Christi.—Id. in Lib. Sent. Prosp. in Decret. Gratiani. Par. 1583. Decr. Tert. Pars. De Consecr. Dist. ii. can. 48. cols. 2387, 8.]

[3 Nam secundum creaturarum substantiam, quod fuerunt ante consecrationem, hoc et postea consistunt. Panis et vinum prius extitere, in qua etiam specie jam consecrata permanere videntur.—Ratramn. Lib. De Corp. et Sang. Dom. Oxon. 1838. cap. liv. p. 27.]

[4 Hic quinque cruces fiant...Quarta super panem tantum. (This is after the consecration.) Missal. ad Us. et Consuet. Sarum. Par. 1527. Canon Miss. fols. 158, 9.]

but it holdeth that bread is transubstantiated or turned into the body, and wine into the blood of Christ, as it is shewed[5]."

Furthermore, Gabriel Biel, one of the chief captains among the school writers, agreeth with Duns, speaking on this manner: "It is to be noted that, although it be plainly taught in the scripture that the body of Christ is truly contained and received of the faithful under the kinds of bread and wine, yet, how the body of Christ is there, whether by conversion of any thing into it, or without conversion the body is there with the bread, both the substance and accidents of bread remaining there still, it is not found expressed in the canon of the bible. Notwithstanding, forasmuch as of the sacraments men must hold as the holy church of Rome holdeth, as it is written, *De hæreticis, Ad abolendam;* and that church holdeth and hath determined that the bread is transubstantiated into the body of Christ, and the wine into his blood; therefore is this opinion received of all catholics, that the substance of bread remaineth not, but really and truly is turned, transubstantiated, and changed into the substance of the body of Christ[6]."

In Decre. de summa Trinitate, et Fide Cath. cap. Firmiter.
In Can. Missæ. Lect. 40.

Again, Comeracensis, a school writer, affirmeth plainly, that it is more probable and more to be allowed, yea, and more agreeable to the truth of God's word, to grant that in the eucharist, that is to say, in the sacrament of the body and blood of Christ, there remain very bread and very wine, and not the accidents alone, than otherwise, if the church (he meaneth the Romish church) had not determined the contrary[7]. Note.

Who seeth not now evidently, that the doctrine of transubstantiation is new and lately sprung up, not taught in the holy scriptures, unknown to the ancient fathers, not heard of in the godly old councils, lately thrust into the church of Christ of the Romish bishop and of his adherents by violence and tyranny, and now defended and maintained still of the papists, not with the holy scriptures and ancient authorities, but with fire and fagot, sword and halter?

Notwithstanding the papists themselves, namely, such as had any judgment at all, grant and confess, that it is more easy, more plain, more probable, more to be allowed, yea, and more agreeable to the truth of God's word, to affirm and believe that the substance of bread and wine remaineth in the sacrament, than otherwise, if the church of Rome had not determined the contrary; from whose trifling traditions to dissent they thought it more than double wickedness.

[[5] Respondeo, quod communiter tenetur, quod nec panis manet......nec annihilatur, vel resolvitur in materiam primam......sed convertitur in corpus Christi......Principaliter autem videtur movere, quod de sacramentis tenendum est, sicut tenet sancta Romana ecclesia, sicut habetur Extrà de hæreticis, *Ad abolendum.* Nunc autem ipsa tenet panem transubstantiari in corpus, et vinum in sanguinem, sicut manifeste habetur Extrà de Sum. Trinit. et fide, cap. Firmiter credimus, §. Una vero......dicendum quod ecclesia declaravit istum intellectum esse de veritate fidei in illo symbolo edito sub Innocent. III. in Concilio Lateranensi. Firmiter credimus, &c. sicut allegatum est superius; ubi explicite ponitur veritas aliquorum credendorum, magis explicite quam habebatur in symbolo apostolorum, vel Athanasii, vel Niceni. Et breviter, quidquid ibi dicitur esse credendum, tenendum est esse de substantia fidei: et hoc post istam declarationem solemnem factam ab ecclesia. Et si quæras quare voluit ecclesia eligere istum intellectum ita difficilem hujus articuli, cum verba scripturæ possent salvari secundum intellectum facilem, et veriorem secundum apparentiam de hoc articulo: dico, &c.—Joan. Duns Scot. Op. Lugd. 1639. In Lib. IV. Sentent. Dist. xi. Quæst. 3. Tom. VIII. pp. 616, 18, 19. See also Tom. XI. Pars II. p. 670.]

[[6] Circa quod notandum quod quamvis expresse tradatur in scriptura, quod corpus Christi veraciter sub speciebus panis continetur et a fidelibus sumitur: ut patuit lectione præcedente: tamen quomodo ibi sit Christi corpus, an per conversionem alicujus in ipsum, an sine conversione incipiat esse corpus Christi cum pane, manentibus substantia et accidentibus panis: non invenitur expressum in canone bibliæ. Unde de hoc antiquitus fuerunt diversæ opiniones......Sed nunc opinio tertia ab omnibus doctoribus catholicis acceptatur: scilicet quod substantia panis non manet: sed realiter veraciter in substantiam corporis Christi convertitur, transsubstantiatur seu commutatur. Tum quia de sacramentis tenendum est sicut tenet sancta Romana ecclesia: ut habetur de hæreticis *Ad abolendam.* Nunc autem ipsa tenet et determinavit panem transsubstantiari in corpus Christi et vinum in sanguinem.—Gab. Biel. Canon. Missæ Expos. Basil. 1515. Lect. xl. fol. 94. 2.]

[[7] Tertia opinio fuit quod substantia panis remanet: et hoc potest dupliciter imaginari......quicquid tamen sit de hoc, patet quod ille modus est possibilis, nec repugnat rationi nec auctoritati bibliæ. imo est facilior ad intelligendum, &c. ...... Quarta opinio communior est, quod substantia panis non remanet sed simpliciter desinit esse. Cujus possibilitas patet, quia non est Deo impossibile quod illa substantia subito desinat esse: quamvis non esset possibile creata virtute. Et licet ita esse non sequatur evidenter ex scriptura, nec etiam videre meo ex determinatione ecclesiæ; quia tamen magis favet ei, et communi opinioni sanctorum et doctorum; ideo teneo eam.—Quæst. Pet. de Alliaco Card. Camerac. sup. Lib. Sentent. Par. Lib. IV. Quest. vi. Art. 2. fol. 265.]

But how can this their doctrine of transubstantiation stand with this saying of ☞ St Austin? "The word cometh unto the element, and thereof is made a sacrament[1]." Here learn we of St Austin, that every sacrament doth consist of two things, that is to say, of the word and of the element. Now is the Lord's supper a sacrament: it followeth therefore that it consisteth of the word and of the element. The word of this sacrament is this: "Take, eat: this is my body, which is betrayed for you. Do this in the remembrance of me." Now must this word have his element, which indeed is bread, and not the accidents of bread, as the papists teach. Again, the word of the other part of the sacrament is this: "Take, drink of this, all ye. This cup is a new testament in my blood," &c. Now must this word also have his element, which indeed is wine, and not the accidents of wine, as the papists hold. And who knoweth not that an element is a thing, that is to say, a substance, and not the accident of a thing? Who perceiveth not now that the papists, teaching this doctrine of transubstantiation, do utterly corrupt and destroy the sacrament, and make it no sacrament in deed; forasmuch as they take away the element, which is bread and wine, from the word? He that would take away water from the sacrament of baptism, which is the element of that sacrament, should he leave baptism a perfect sacrament? Even so in like manner he, that goeth about to pluck from the sacrament of the body and blood of Christ the substance of bread and wine, destroyeth utterly the aforesaid sacrament, and, to say the truth, maketh it no sacrament. We may therefore conclude truly and justly, that the doctrine of transubstantiation, as I said before, is a papistical, wicked, and devilish error.

Every sacrament consisteth of the word and of the element.

The doctrine of transubstantiation destroyeth the sacrament of Christ's body and blood.

Father. God root out all errors once out of his church, that we may walk only in the truth of his holy word! *Son*. Amen. I nothing doubt of this matter. For this prophecy of the Lord Jesu shall unfeignedly be fulfilled, yea, and that shortly: "Every plant that my heavenly Father hath not planted shall be plucked up by the roots."

Matt. xv.

Father. What is the second error? *Son*. The second error is the doctrine of the papists concerning the corporal presence of Christ in the sacrament, as he was born of Mary the virgin, and hanged on the cross.

Of the corporal presence of Christ in the sacrament.

Father. This must needs follow of the doctrine of transubstantiation. For if the substance of bread and wine be turned into the substance of the natural body and blood of Christ, then must this doctrine also be true, that Christ is in the sacrament really, naturally, substantially, corporally, &c.; yea, that the sacrament is the true, real, natural, corporal, and substantial body of Christ. *Son*. You say truth. But as the doctrine of transubstantiation is vain and false, as we have even now heard both by the holy scriptures, and also by the authorities of the ancient fathers; so likewise the doctrine of Christ's corporal presence in the sacrament [is] most vain, false, and erroneous.

Father. In that the papists say it is the very same body, that was born of Mary the virgin and hanged on the cross, methink they greatly overshoot themselves. For who knoweth not that the body of Christ, which he received of Mary the virgin, and died for us on the altar of the cross, was a mortal body? But that body is now become immortal, uncorruptible, glorious, &c. If they then deliver that self-same body, as it was born of Mary the virgin and hanged on the cross, to the communicants, so followeth it that they deliver a mortal body; and by this means should it come to pass that Christ hath two bodies, one mortal here in earth at the distribution of the sacrament, and another immortal in heaven, sitting on the right hand of God the Father. *Son*. The papists mean, that in the sacrament is contained the very self-same body, that was born of Mary the virgin and died for us on the altar of the cross, the qualities only changed, as mortality into immortality, corruption into uncorruption, &c.

Father. And is Christ in the sacrament with his glorified and immortal body, as he is in heaven? *Son*. Nothing less. For that manifestly fighteth with the truth of Christ's body, and plainly stablisheth the heresy of the Marcionites. It is proper to

[1 August. Op. Par. 1679—1700. In Johan. Evang. cap. xv. Tractat. lxxx. 3. Tom. III. Pars II. col. 703. See Vol. I. page 12, note 1.]

God alone to be in all or in divers places at once; which property no creature hath, no, not angel. Therefore, forasmuch as the body of Christ, although immortal and glorified, is, remaineth, and abideth still a creature, and is not swallowed up, as I may so speak, of the divine nature, but, being joined to the divine nature, abideth still a creature, and very man; it therefore followeth most certainly that Christ's body, taken up into heaven, neither is, neither can be, both in heaven and in earth at once.

And we are taught in the articles of the Christian faith, and throughout the whole bible, that as Christ is ascended into heaven, so likewise shall he there remain, as concerning his corporal presence, unto the day of judgment, as St Peter saith: "Jesus Christ must receive heaven, until the time that all things, which God hath spoken by the mouth of all his holy prophets since the world began, be restored again." And the angels said to the apostles at Christ's ascension: "Ye men of Galilee, why stand ye gazing up into heaven? This Jesus, which is taken up from you into heaven, shall so come even as ye have seen him go into heaven." And St Paul, entreating of the sacrament, saith: "As often as ye shall eat this bread, and drink of this cup, ye shall shew the Lord's death till he come." In this one sentence of the holy apostle it manifestly appeareth, that Christ is not corporally in the sacrament, as the papists teach. For he commandeth us to eat and drink those holy mysteries in remembrance of the Lord's death till he come, meaning, unto the judgment: whereby we may plainly learn that Christ is not there corporally, really, substantially, naturally, &c., as the adversaries teach, but in heaven only, and there shall remain in the glory of his Father, until that great and fearful day of judgment come. And in the mean season, as often as we shall be partakers of that holy bread and cup, we shall call to remembrance the death of the Lord Christ, and all the benefits that we have received thereby, and give most humble thanks for the same to God the Father.

Acts iii. Acts i. 1 Cor. xi.

Father. Is this then a true doctrine, that Christ is corporally in heaven only, and in none other place? *Son.* Yea, verily.

Christ's natural body is only in heaven.

Father. Let me hear it proved by the word of God. *Son.* Our Saviour Christ himself saith: "Ye have the poor always with you; but me shall ye not have always." "I go to prepare a place for you. And if I go to prepare a place for you, I will come again and receive you even unto myself, that where I am, there ye may be also." "If ye loved me, ye would rejoice, because I said, I go unto the Father." "Now I go my way to him that sent me, and none of you asketh me whither I go. But because I have said such things unto you, your hearts are full of sorrow. Nevertheless I tell you the truth: it is expedient for you that I go away. For if I go not away, the Comforter will not come unto you. But if I depart, I will send him unto you." "I went out from the Father, and came into the world: again, I leave the world, and go to the Father." St Mark saith: "When the Lord had spoken unto them, he was received into heaven, and is set down on the right hand of God." Blessed Luke saith: "It came to pass, as Christ blessed them, he departed from them, and was carried up into heaven." St Paul saith: "It is Christ which died, yea, rather which is risen again, which is also on the right hand of God." "God the Father raised Christ from the dead, and set him on his right hand in heavenly things, above all rule, power, and might, and dominion, and above all names that are named, not in this world only, but also in the world to come." "Christ is gone up on high, and hath led captivity captive, and hath given gifts unto men." If ye be risen again with Christ, seek those things which are above, where Christ sitteth on the right hand of God." "Whensoever Christ, which is our life, shall appear, then shall you also appear with him in glory." "This man Christ, after he hath offered one sacrifice for sins, is set down for ever on the right hand of God, and from henceforth tarrieth till his foes be made his foot-stool." St Peter saith: "Jesus Christ is on the right hand of God, and is gone into heaven, angels, power, and might subdued unto him."

Matt. xxvi. John xiv. John xvi. Mark xvi. Luke xxiv. Rom. viii. Eph. i. Eph. iv. Col. iii. Heb. x. 1 Pet. iii.

All these scriptures, with divers other, evidently declare that Christ corporally dwelled only in heaven. Heaven is his resting-place concerning his body, and shall be until he come unto the judgment.

Father. Christ's body then is not in every pix, and in every altar, and in every massmonger's hands, as the papists hold? *Son.* No, verily. As touching his bodily presence, Christ is in heaven, yea, in heaven only. Of them which teach us the contrary Christ biddeth us take heed, saying: "If any man say unto you, Lo, here is Christ, or there is Christ; believe it not. For there shall arise false anointed, and false teachers, and shall shew great miracles and wonders; insomuch that, if it were possible, the very elect should be deceived. Behold, I have told you afore. Wherefore if they say unto you, Behold, he is in the desert; go not ye forth: behold, he is in the secret places; believe it not. For as the lightning cometh out of the east, and appeareth unto the west; so shall the coming of the Son of man be."

Matt. xxiv.

Father. How then are these sentences to be understanded? "Where two or three are gathered together in my name, there am I in the midst of them." Again: "Behold, I am with you continually, until the end of the world." *Son*. These sentences and such like are to be understanded not of Christ's corporal, but of his spiritual presence. For Christ, in that he is man, abideth only in heaven; but in that he is God, he is everywhere, at all times present with his church by his almighty power and heavenly Spirit; as Christ, when he should with his body ascend into the kingdom of his Father, promised that he would "not leave his disciples succourless," but that he would "send unto them another Comforter, which should abide with them for ever, even the Spirit of truth," &c.

Matt. xviii. Matt. xxviii. Christ in his manhood is in one place only at one time; but in his Godhead he is in all places at one time. John xiv.

Father. Thou holdest then that Christ, as concerning his bodily presence, is only in heaven; but, as touching his godly presence, he is everywhere. *Son*. So am I taught by the word of God, as you have heard.

Father. Yea, but what say the ancient fathers of Christ's church? Do they also affirm this thing? *Son*. Most constantly, yea, and that with one voice.

Father. Let me hear some of their sayings. For it delighteth me greatly to hear ☞ the doctrine and consent of the ancient fathers, that we boldly say: Our doctrine is both grounded of the word of God, and also confirmed of the old writers. *Son*. To recite all the authorities of all the ancient fathers that make for our purpose, I mean, that evidently declare that Christ in his corporal substance is only in heaven, and not in the sacrament, as the papists teach, were an infinite labour. But I will rehearse so many as may seem for this present to suffice.

Father. Agreed.

Son. First of all I will allege the mind of the ancient writer Origen. Upon Matthew he hath these words: "Let us first of all inquire of his journey to a strange country, namely because it seemeth to be contrary to that which he promiseth of himself to his disciples, saying: 'Where two or three be gathered together in my name, there am I in the midst of them.' Again: 'Behold, I am with you continually, even unto the end of the world.' And also contrary to that which John Baptist speaketh of him, shewing that he is in every place, on this manner: 'In the midst of you standeth he whom ye know not. He it is that cometh after me.' Therefore will some man say, If he stand even in the midst of them that know him not; if, wheresoever two or three be gathered together in his name, he be among them; if, so long as the disciples live, he be with them even unto the world's end; how then is he set forth in this parable to take his journey into a far country? Entreating of this matter, we ought to consider that which Paul speaketh of himself: 'I verily, absent in body, but present in spirit, have determined already (as though I were present), concerning him that hath done this deed, in the name of our Lord Jesus Christ, when ye are gathered together, and my spirit with you, with the power of the Lord Jesus Christ, to deliver him unto Satan for the destruction of the flesh, that the spirit may be saved in the day of the Lord Jesus.' If that he be ever present with all his, how do his parables bring him in to be gone into a far country? Thus may this question be answered. He that saith unto his disciples, 'Behold, I am with you unto the end of the world;' and again, 'Where two or three be gathered together in my name, there am I in the midst of them;' and he also, that standeth in the midst of them that know him not, is the only-begotten Son of God, God the Word, and Wisdom, and Righteousness, and Truth, which is not inclosed about with any bodily compass. ☞ After this nature of his divinity he is not departed into another country; but he is gone away after the dispensation of the body which he took, after the which also he

In Matt. cap. xxiii. Hom. 33. Matt. xviii. Matt. xxviii. John i. Matt. xviii. Matt. xxviii. 1 Cor. v. Matt. xviii. Matt. xxviii. John i.

was troubled, and became heavy, saying, 'Now is my soul troubled;' and again: John xii.
'My soul is heavy unto the death.' And speaking these things, we divide not his Matt. xxvi.
humanity (for St John writeth, 'Every spirit that divideth Jesus is not of God'), 1 John iv.
but we reserve to both his natures their own properties[1]."

Of these words of the ancient writer Origen we plainly are taught, that the Lord Christ, as touching his divinity, is present at all times and in every place, neither can he be comprehended in any one several place only; but as concerning his humanity, or bodily presence, he is not in all places, neither is he here with us on the earth, but he is gone hence into a far country, that is to say, into heaven. If Christ's body be not here on earth, but is gone hence and estranged from us, with what forehead dare the papists affirm that they have him inclosed in a wafer cake, break him with their fingers, and tear him with their teeth? Can one and the same thing be both absent and present at one time and in one place? A monstrous doctrine!

Father. Do any other of the ancient fathers agree with Origen in this behalf? *Son.* All, without exception. For Cyrillus, a Greek writer, also agreeth with Origen in all points, saying: "Although Christ took away from hence the presence of his body, yet In Joan. Lib. vi. cap. 4.
in the majesty of his godhead he is ever here, as he promised to his disciples at his departure, saying: 'Behold, I am with you continually, even unto the world's end[2].'" Matt. xxviii.
Here have we plainly also of Cyrillus, that Christ, as concerning his bodily presence, is not here among us; but, as touching his godhead, he is never away from us, but remaineth with us continually.

I will now recite unto you some of the ancient Latin writers, that by this means you may hear and understand, what time[3] concord and perfect amity hath from the beginning continued in the church of Christ in all ages and in all places concerning the truth of God's religion, till this monstrous beast of many heads, (I mean papism,) in the which be more than an hundred sects, brast in and overflowed the world. And forasmuch as by the judgment of all godly learned men St Austin is the best and most sincere expositor of the holy scripture among the ancient writers, I will first of all declare his mind in this behalf.

"As concerning his divine majesty, as concerning his providence, as concerning his In Joan. Tract. l.
infallible and invisible grace," saith St Augustine, "these words be fulfilled which he spake: 'Behold, I am with you unto the world's end.' But as concerning the flesh Matt. xxviii.
which he took in his incarnation, as concerning that which was born of the virgin, as concerning that which was apprehended by the Jews and crucified upon a tree, and

[1 Ergo primum quæramus de peregrinatione ipsius, maxime quia peregrinationi ejus videtur esse contrarium quod ipse de se discipulis suis promittit, dicens: Ubi fuerint duo vel tres congregati in nomine meo, ibi sum in medio eorum. Item illud: Ecce ego vobiscum sum omnibus diebus, usque ad consummationem sæculi. Et quod Baptista dicit de eo, ubique eum esse demonstrans, ita: In medio autem vestrum stat quem vos nescitis; ipse est qui post me venit. Propterea dicet aliquis: Si in medio etiam nescientium se stat; si ubicumque duo vel tres congregati fuerint in nomine ejus, inter eos habetur; si per omnes dies vitæ discipulorum cum eis est usque ad consummationem sæculi; quomodo in ista parabola proponitur peregrinans? Tractantes autem assumere debemus et illud quod Paulus ait de se: Ego autem absens corpore, præsens autem spiritu, jam judicavi ut præsens, congregatis vobis et meo spiritu cum virtute Domini Jesu, eum qui talis est tradere Satanæ in interitum carnis, ut spiritus ejus salvus sit in die Domini nostri Jesu Christi. Si enim virtus Jesu congregatur cum his qui congregantur in nomine ejus, non peregrinatur a suis, sed semper præsto est eis. Quod si semper omnibus suis est præsens, quomodo introducunt eum parabolæ ejus peregrinantem? Vide si possumus solvere hoc modo quod quæritur. Qui enim dicit discipulis suis, Ecce ego vobiscum sum usque ad consummationem sæculi; et item, Ubi fuerint duo vel tres congregati in nomine meo, et ego sum in medio eorum, et cætera; et qui in medio etiam nescientium se consistit, Unigenitus Dei est, Deus Verbum, et sapientia, et justitia, et veritas, qui non est corporeo ambitu circumclusus. Secundum hanc divinitatis suæ naturam non peregrinatur, sed peregrinatur secundum dispensationem corporis quod suscepit; secundum quod et turbatus est, et tristis factus est, dicens, Nunc anima mea turbatur; et iterum: Tristis est anima mea usque ad mortem. Hæc autem dicentes non solvimus suscepti corporis hominem, cum sit scriptum apud Joannem: Omnis spiritus qui solvit Jesum, non est ex Deo; sed unicuique substantiæ proprietatem servamus.—Orig. Op. Par. 1733—59. In Matt. Comm. Ser. 65. Tom. III. pp. 882, 3.]

[2 Denique quum de se dixit, Me autem non semper habebitis, loquebatur Dominus de præsentia corporis sui. Nam secundum majestatem suam, secundum providentiam, secundum ineffabilem et invisibilem divinitatis gratiam, impletur quod ab eo dictum est: Ecce ego vobiscum sum omnibus diebus usque ad consummationem seculi.—Cyril. Alex. Op. Lat. Par. 1604—5. In. Joan. Evang. Lib. VIII. cap. vii. Tom. I. p. 597.]

[3 Folio, *tyme*. Probably, *true*.]

taken down from the cross, lapped in linen clothes, and buried, and rose again, and appeared after his resurrection; as concerning the flesh, he said: 'You shall not ever have me with you.' Wherefore seeing that, as concerning his flesh, he was conversant with his disciples forty days, and they accompanying, seeing, and following him, he went up into heaven, both he is not here (for he sitteth on the right hand of his Father); and yet he is here, for he departed not hence as concerning the presence of his divine majesty. As touching the presence of his majesty, we have Christ ever with us; but as concerning the presence of his flesh, he said truly to his disciples: 'Ye shall not ever have me with you.' For as concerning the presence of his flesh, the church had Christ but a few days; but now it holdeth him fast by faith, it seeth not him with eyes[1]." Again he saith: "How shall I lay hand on him being absent, or seeing he is gone? How shall ☞ I put my hand into heaven, that I may lay hand on him sitting there? Send thy faith, and thou hast laid hand on him. Thy fathers have laid hand on him in the flesh; but lay thou hand on him with thy heart. For Christ, although he be absent, yet is he present: except he were present, we could not lay hand on him. But because that is true which he saith, 'Behold, I am with you continually unto the world's end'; he is both gone away, and he is also here: he is both gone again, and yet hath he not forsaken us. He hath carried away his body into heaven, yet notwithstanding he hath not taken away his majesty from the world[2]."

Matt. xxvi. Note. Matt. xxviii.

Hereto agreeth the saying of St Hierome: "Wherefore said the Lord after his resurrection unto his disciples, 'Behold, I am with you unto the end of the world;' and now he saith, 'You shall not have me always'? Methink that in this place he speaketh of his corporal presence, that he shall not be with them after his resurrection, as he is now, living with them familiarly; which thing the apostle considering saith: 'Although we have known Christ after the flesh, now yet henceforth know we him so no more[3].'"

In Matt. cap. xxvi. 2 Cor. v.

Likewise saith St Ambrose: "O Lord Jesu, we ought not to seek thee upon the earth, nor in the earth, nor after the flesh, if we will find thee. For 'we know now Christ no more after the flesh.' Stephen sought thee not upon the earth, which saw thee standing on the right hand of God: but Mary, which sought thee on the earth, could not touch thee. Stephen touched thee, because he sought thee in heaven[4].'"

In Luc. Lib. x. cap. 24. 2 Cor. v. Acts vii.

And St Gregory writeth thus: "Christ is not here by the presence of his flesh, and yet is he absent nowhere by the presence of his majesty[5]." Again he saith: "The Word

In Hom. Pasch. In Hom. Pentecost.

[1 Nam secundum majestatem suam, secundum providentiam, secundum ineffabilem et invisibilem gratiam, impletur quod ab eo dictum est, Ecce ego vobiscum sum usque in consummationem sæculi. Secundum carnem vero quam Verbum assumsit, secundum id quod de virgine natus est, secundum id quod a Judæis prehensus est, quod ligno confixus, quod de cruce depositus, quod linteis involutus, quod in sepulcro conditus, quod in resurrectione manifestatus, non semper habebitis vobiscum. Quare? Quoniam conversatus est secundum corporis præsentiam quadraginta diebus cum discipulis suis, et eis deducentibus videndo, non sequendo, adscendit in cœlum, et non est hic. Ibi est enim, sedet ad dexteram Patris: et hic est, non enim recessit præsentia majestatis. Aliter: Secundum præsentiam majestatis semper habemus Christum: secundum præsentiam carnis, recte dictum est discipulis, Me autem non semper habebitis. Habuit enim illum ecclesia secundum præsentiam carnis paucis diebus: modo fide tenet, oculis non videt.—August. Op. Par. 1679—1700. In Johan. Evang. cap. xii. Tractat. l. 13. Tom. III. Pars II. col. 634.]

[2 Quomodo tenebo absentem? Quomodo in cœlum manum mittam, ut ibi sedentem teneam? Fidem mitte, et tenuisti. Parentes tui tenuerunt carne, tu tene corde: quoniam Christus absens etiam præsens est. Nisi præsens esset, a nobis ipsis teneri non posset. Sed quoniam verum est quod ait, Ecce ego vobiscum sum usque ad consummationem sæculi: et abiit, et hic est; et rediit, et nos non deserit: corpus enim suum intulit cœlo, majestatem non abstulit mundo.—Id. ibid. 4. cols. 630, 1.]

[3 Alia oboritur quæstio, quare Dominus post resurrectionem dixerit ad discipulos, Ecce ego vobiscum sum usque ad consummationem mundi, et nunc loquatur, Me autem non semper habebitis. Sed mihi videtur in hoc loco de præsentia dicere corporali: quod nequaquam cum eis ita futurus sit post resurrectionem, quomodo nunc in omni convictu et familiaritate. Cujus rei memor apostolus ait: Et si noveramus Jesum Christum secundum carnem, sed nunc jam non novimus eum.—Hieron. Op. Par. 1693—1706. Comm. Lib. IV. in Matt. cap. XXVI. Tom. IV. Pars I. col. 126.]

[4 Ergo non supra terram, nec in terra, nec secundum carnem te quærere debemus, si volumus invenire; nunc enim secundum carnem jam non novimus Christum. Denique Stephanus non supra terram quæsivit, qui stantem te ad dexteram Dei vidit: Maria autem quia quærebat in terra, tangere non potuit. Stephanus tetigit, quia quæsivit in cœlo.—Ambros. Op. Par. 1686—90. Expos. Evang. sec. Luc. Lib. x. 160. Tom. I. col. 1538.]

[5 Surrexit, non est hic. Non est hic, dicitur, per præsentiam carnis, qui tamen nusquam deerit per

incarnate both tarrieth and goeth away: he goeth away in his body, but he tarrieth in his godhead[6]."

Likewise saith Beda: "He (Christ), being God and man, was taken up in his humanity, which he took of the earth; but, as concerning his divinity, he abideth still with his saints on the earth, wherewith he filleth earth and heaven[7]." Also in another place he saith: "He, after his resurrection going up into heaven, forsook them corporally, which notwithstanding never failed them concerning the presence of his divine majesty[8]." In Hom. Pasch. Hom. in Vigil. Pent.

Moreover Vigilius, that blessed bishop and holy martyr, writing against Eutyches, that heretic, which denied the humanity of Christ, hath these words: "Christ said to his disciples: 'If ye loved me, ye would rejoice; for I go unto my Father.' And again he said: 'It is expedient for you that I go; for if I go not, the Comforter shall not come to you.' And yet surely the eternal Word of God, the Virtue of God, the Wisdom of God, was ever with his Father and in his Father, yea, even at the same time when he was with us and in us. For when he did mercifully dwell in this world, he left not his habitation or dwelling in heaven; for he is every where whole with his Father, equal in divinity, whom no place can contain. For the Son filleth all things, and there is no place that lacketh the presence of his divinity. From whence then and whither did he say that he would go? Or how did he say that he went to his Father, from whom doubtless he never departed? But that was to go to the Father and to depart from us, even to take from this world that nature which he received of us. Thou seest therefore, that it was the property of that nature to be taken away and to go from us, which in the end of the world shall be rendered again to us, as the angels witnessed, saying: 'This Jesus, which is taken from you, shall come again, like as you saw him going up into heaven.' For look upon the miracle, look upon the mystery of both the natures. The Son of God, as concerning his humanity, went from us: as concerning his divinity, he said unto us, 'Behold, I am with you all the days unto the world's end.'" And a little after he saith: "He is both with us, and he is not with us. For those whom he left, and went from them, as concerning his humanity, those he left not, nor forsook them not, as touching his divinity. For as touching the form of a servant (which he took away from us into heaven), he is absent from us; but by the form of God (which goeth not from us), he is present with us in earth; and nevertheless, both present and absent, he is all one Christ[9].'" Lib. i. John xiv. John xvi. Acts i. Matt. xxviii.

And a certain bishop called Justus Orgelitanus, writing upon Salomon's ballads, bringeth in Christ speaking to the faithful soul on this manner: "Desire thou not to In Cantica Canticorum.

---

præsentiam majestatis.—Gregor. Magni Papæ I. Op. Par. 1705. In Evang. Lib. II. Hom. xxi. Die Sanct. Pasch. Tom. I. col. 1527.]

[6 Sed Verbum incarnatum et manet et recedit: recedit corpore, manet divinitate.—Id. Lib. II. Hom. xxx. Die Sanct. Pentecost. col. 1576.]

[7 Quia enim ipse Deus et homo est, assumptus est in cœlum humanitate, quam de terra susceperat: manet cum sanctis in terra divinitate, qua terram pariter implet et cœlum.—Ven. Bed. Op. Col. Agrip. 1612. Hom. Fer. Sext. Pasch. Tom. VII. col. 14.]

[8 Verum quia ille post resurrectionem ascendens in cœlum eos corporaliter deseruit, quibus tamen divinæ præsentia majestatis nunquam abfuit, recte de hoc paracleto, id est, Spiritu sancto subjunxit: Ut maneat vobiscum in æternum.—Id. Hom. in Fest. Sanct. Pentecost. col. 38.]

[9 Ait namque discipulis suis, Si diligeretis me, gauderetis, quia vado ad Patrem, quia Pater major me est. Et iterum: Expedit vobis ut ego eam. Si enim ego non abiero, Paracletus ad vos non veniet. Et certe Verbum Dei, Virtus Dei, Sapientia Dei, semper apud Patrem et in Patre fuit, etiam quando in nobis nobiscum fuit. Neque enim cum terrena misericorditer incoluit, de cœlesti habitatione recessit. Cum Patre enim ubique est totus pari divinitate, quem nullus continet locus. Plena sunt quippe omnia Filio, nec est aliquis locus divinitatis ejus præsentia vacuus. Unde ergo et quo se iturum dicit, aut quomodo se ad Patrem perrecturum adserat, a quo sine dubio nunquam recessit? Sed hoc erat ire ad Patrem et recedere a nobis, auferre de hoc mundo naturam, quam susceperat ex nobis. Vides ergo eidem naturæ proprium fuisse ut auferretur et abiret a nobis, quæ in fine temporum reddenda est nobis, secundum attestantium vocem angelorum, Hic Jesus qui receptus est a vobis, sic veniet, quemadmodum vidistis eum euntem in cœlum. Nam vide miraculum, vide utriusque proprietatis mysterium: Dei Filius secundum humanitatem suam recessit a nobis, secundum divinitatem suam ait nobis, Ecce ego vobiscum sum omnibus diebus usque ad consummationem sæculi. Si nobiscum est, quomodo ait, Venient dies quando desideretis diem unum Filii hominis, et non videbitis? Sed et nobiscum est, et non est nobiscum; quia quos reliquit et a quibus discessit humanitate sua, non reliquit nec deseruit divinitate sua. Per formam enim servi, quam abstulit a nobis in cœlum, absens est nobis: per formam Dei, quæ non recedit a nobis, in terris præsens est nobis; tamen et præsens et absens ipse unus idemque est nobis.—Vigil. adv. Eutych. in Cassandr. Op. Par. 1616. Lib. I. p. 518.]

see me always in the body, whom thou seest better in the spirit through faith. For to this end went I up into heaven, that thou shouldest see me no more compassed in a place; which notwithstanding do so replenish and fill all things with the presence of my divinity, that I am in every place, and contain all things, and am contained of no place[1]."

Breath should fail me, if I should go forth to recite the sayings of all the ancient Greek and Latin writers, which most constantly affirm, that as the Lord Christ, in that he is God, is every where and filleth all places at all times; so likewise, in that he is man, he is only in heaven, and in no place else, where he shall remain until the day of judgment, according to the scriptures. Now if this doctrine be true and certain, as it is most true and most certain, then is the doctrine of the papists most false and most vain, which teach the contrary, being through the spirit of error deceived themselves, and also deceiving other.

Father. The papists deny not, that the natural body of Christ is in heaven; but they say moreover, that as he is in heaven, so likewise is he on earth in the sacrament, although invisibly; insomuch that, whensoever the bread and wine be once consecrate, there straightways, under the accidents of bread and wine, the real, corporal, natural, and substantial body of Christ is contained, even the very self-same body that was born of Mary the virgin, and died on the cross. They add moreover, that, look in how many thousand thousand places the sacrament is, in so many thousand thousand places is the natural body of Christ. *Son.* O monstrous doctrine! What any other thing is it thus to teach, than to affirm, with the old heretics, that Christ had no true, but a fantastical body; no natural, but a celestial body; or, as some later heretics have taught, that the body of Christ is now not only glorified, but also deified, and swallowed up of the divine nature, insomuch that, wheresoever the deity of Christ is, there is also his humanity? O wicked and most detestable doctrine! Is this any other thing than to destroy and utterly to make nothing the humanity of Christ?

Father. There is, they say, great difference between the mortal and immortal, the passible and unpassible, the humbled and glorified body of Christ. *Son.* I grant. For the glorified body of Christ, which is now in heaven, and sitteth on the right hand of God, is immortal, and delivered from all mortal qualities, as St Paul saith:
Rom. vi. "Christ, being raised from death, dieth no more. Death hath no more power over him. For as touching that he died, he died concerning sin once; and as touching that he liveth, he liveth unto God." Notwithstanding, though the qualities of mortality be changed, yet the very same substance and nature of Christ's body remaineth still, and is not altered nor changed; so that, as in his mortality his body was local, and occupied a place, and was not in all places at once, but at one time in one only place; so likewise now, in his immortality, his body is local, and occupieth a place, even heaven, and is not in all places at once, as some hold.

Father. Prove me by the word of God, that the body of Christ, although glorified and immortal, is not in divers places at once. *Son.* The angel of God said to certain
Matt. xxviii. women which came to anoint the body of Jesus: "I know that ye seek Jesus, which was crucified. He is risen. He is not here. Behold the place where they laid him." "He goeth before you into Galilee: there shall ye see him, as he told you."

Of these words of the angel it is plain and evident, that as tofore the mortal and humbled, so likewise now the immortal and glorified body of Christ can be but in one place at once. For if the body of Christ, now clad with immortality and uncorruption, might have been in all places at one time, then had not the angel spoken
Acts iii. truly when he said: "He is not here," &c. St Peter saith plainly, that "Christ must receive heaven, until the time that all things which God hath spoken by the mouth of all his holy prophets, since the world began, be restored again." And all the holy scriptures openly testify that Christ, as concerning his corporal presence, is

[1 Non me semper in corpore conspiciendum requiras, quem Spiritu per fidem melius cernis. Idcirco etenim in cœlos ascendi, ut non semper localis tibi appaream qui sic omnia (divinitatis meæ præsentia) repleo, ut ubique adsim, cunctaque contineam et a nullo loco continear.—Just. Orgel. in Cant. Explic. 137. in Mag. Biblioth. Vet. Patr. Col. Agrip. 1618—22. Tom. VI. Pars I. p. 515.]

in heaven only, and that there he shall remain in the glory of his Father, till he come again to judge the quick and the dead; neither read we in all the bible, that Christ since the time of his ascension hath occupied with his body any other place than heaven. Moreover, doth not Christ plainly forbid us to believe such, which Matt. xxiv. teach us that Christ is in this place, and that place; in the wilderness, and in secret places, &c.? as some say that his body is in all places, wheresoever his godhead is; some again affirm that Christ's natural body is in the pix, is between the priest's hands at mass, is eaten of the mouse, rat, cat, dog, &c. This monstrous kind of doctrine the holy scripture knoweth not, neither was it ever taught of the ancient fathers of Christ's church; but it is a new doctrine, crept into the church of Christ through the subtilty of Satan, and maintained by the cruel tyranny of antichrist and his adherents.

Father. Let me then hear also, what the doctrine of the old doctors and holy fathers is in this behalf. Teach they also, that the natural body of Christ, although immortal and glorified, is only in heaven, and occupieth one place only at one time? *Son.* Yea, verily. For the holy fathers of Christ's church, led with the Spirit of Christ, could teach nothing, but that which is agreeable to the doctrine of Christ; namely, if we respect the principal points of christian religion. Therefore in this behalf they also agree with the doctrine of the holy scripture, and with one accord affirm that Christ, as concerning his corporal presence, is in heaven only, and occupieth but one place at one time; so that he is not in many and divers places at once, as the adversaries teach. And that you may be well assured that this is their doctrine, I will here allege certain testimonies out of their own writings.

That ancient doctor and courageous bishop of Christ's church hath these words, I mean St Ambrose: "Christ is to be sought neither upon earth, nor in earth, but In Lucam, Lib. x. cap. 24. in heaven, where he sitteth at the right hand of his Father[2]." Again he saith: "Here De Off. Lib. iv. cap. 48. the shadow, here the image; there the truth. Shadow in the law, image in the gospel; truth in heaven. Before the lamb was offered, the calf was offered: now is Christ offered; but he is offered as man, as receiving passion; but he offereth himself as a priest, that he may forgive our sins: here in image, there in truth, where as an advocate he maketh intercession for us unto the Father[3]."

Next in order followeth St Austin, that most worthy and faithful doctor, whose words are these: "Doubt not but that Jesus Christ, as concerning the nature of his Ad Dard. Epist. lvii. manhood, is now there, from whence he shall come. And remember well, and believe the profession of a christian man, that he rose from death, ascended into heaven, sitteth at the right hand of his Father, and from that place, and from none other, shall he come to judge the quick and the dead. And he shall come (as the angels said), Acts i. as he was seen go into heaven; that is to say, in the same form and substance, unto the which he gave immortality, but changed not nature. After this form (he speaketh of Christ's human nature) we may not think that he is every where. For we must beware that we do not so stablish his divinity, that we take away the verity of his body. For it followeth not that the thing, which is in God, should be in every place, as God is. For the scripture doth truly testify unto us, 'that we live, move, and be Acts xvii. in him;' and yet are we not in every place, as he is. But man is otherwise in God, and God otherwise in man, by a certain proper and singular way. For God and man is one person, and both of them one Christ Jesus, which is in every place in that he is God, and in heaven in that he is man[4]." Again in the same place he saith:

[2 See before, page 274, note 4.]

[3 Hic umbra, hic imago, illic veritas. Umbra in lege, imago in evangelio, veritas in cœlestibus. Ante agnus offerebatur, offerebatur et vitulus, nunc Christus offertur: sed offertur quasi homo, quasi recipiens passionem; et offert se ipse quasi sacerdos, ut peccata nostra dimittat: hic in imagine, ibi in veritate, ubi apud Patrem pro nobis quasi advocatus intervenit. —Ambros. Op. Par. 1686—90. De Offic. Minist. Lib. I. cap. xlviii. 248. Tom. II. col. 63.]

[4 Noli itaque dubitare ibi nunc esse hominem Christum Jesum, unde venturus est, memoriterque recole, et fideliter tene Christianam confessionem, quoniam resurrexit a mortuis, adscendit in cœlum, sedet ad dexteram Patris, nec aliunde quam inde venturus est ad vivos mortuosque judicandos. Et sic venturus est illa angelica voce testante, quemadmodum ire visus est in cœlum, id est in eadem carnis forma atque substantia; cui profecto immortalitatem dedit, naturam non abstulit. Secundum hanc formam non est putandus ubique diffusus. Cavendum est enim, ne ita divinitatem adstruamus hominis, ut

"Doubt not but that our Lord Jesus Christ is every where as God, and that he is in a certain place of heaven, because of the measure of a true body[1]." Once again in the same place he saith: "Take away the spaces of places from the bodies, and so shall they nowhere be; and forasmuch as they shall be nowhere, neither shall they be. Take away the self bodies from the qualities of the bodies, and there shall be no place where they may be; and so it followeth of necessity that they are not[2]." And writing upon the gospel of St John, he saith thus: "The Lord is alone[3], but yet his truth is here. For his body, wherein he rose, must be in one place; but his truth is dispersed in all places[4]." Again: "As concerning the presence of his majesty, we have Christ ever with us; but as concerning the presence of his flesh, he said truly to his disciples: 'Ye shall not ever have me with you.' For as concerning the presence of his flesh, the church had Christ but a few days; yet now it holdeth him fast by faith, though it see him not with eyes[5]." Also in another place he saith: "Where and how the body of the Lord is in heaven, it is a thing both curious and vain to demand. Notwithstanding, this must we believe, that the body of Christ is only in heaven[6]."

Tract. xxx. Tract. l. De Fide et Symb. c. vi. ☞

Saint Gregory also saith: "Christ is not here by the presence of his flesh; and yet is he absent nowhere by the presence of his majesty[7]."

In Hom. Pasch.

The very same in effect writeth Beda on this manner: "Christ, after his resurrection ascending into heaven, left his disciples corporally; whom notwithstanding he never forsook concerning the presence of his divine majesty[8]."

In Hom. in Vigil. Pent.

With these aforesaid ancient writers agreeth the noble clerk Fulgentius, whose words are these: "One and the self-same Christ of mankind was made a man, compassed in a place, who of his Father is God, without measure or place. One and the self-same person, as concerning his man's substance, was not in heaven when he was in earth, and forsook the earth when he ascended into heaven; but, as concerning his godly substance (which is above all measure), he neither left heaven when he came from heaven, nor he left not the earth, when he ascended into heaven; which may be known by the most certain word of Christ himself, who, to shew the placing of his humanity, said to his disciples: 'I ascend up to my Father and your Father, to my God and your God.' Also, when he had said of Lazarus that he was dead, he added, saying: 'I am glad for your sakes, that you may believe. For I was not there.' But to shew the unmeasurable compass of his divinity, he said to his disciples: 'Behold, I am with you always unto the world's end.' Now, how did he go up into heaven, but because he is a very man, contained within a place? Or how is he present with faithful people, but because he is very God, being without measure[9]?"

Ad Trasi. Lib. ii. John xx. John xi. Matt. xxviii.

---

veritatem corporis auferamus. Non est autem consequens, ut quod in Deo est, ita sit ubique ut Deus. Nam et de nobis veracissima scriptura dicit, quod in illo vivimus, movemur et sumus, nec tamen sicut ille ubique sumus: sed aliter homo ille in Deo, quoniam aliter et Deus ille in homine, proprio quodam et singulari modo. Una enim persona Deus et homo est, et utrumque est unus Christus Jesus; ubique per id quod Deus est, in cœlo autem per id quod homo.—August. Op. Par. 1679—1700. Lib. ad Dard. seu Epist. clxxxvii. 10. Tom. II. col. 681.]

[1 Christum autem Dominum nostrum unigenitum Dei filium æqualem Patri, eumdemque hominis filium, quo major est Pater, et ubique totum præsentem esse non dubites tamquam Deum, et in eodem templo Dei esse tamquam inhabitantem Deum, et in loco aliquo cœli propter veri corporis modum.—Id. ibid. 41. col. 692.]

[2 Nam spatia locorum tolle corporibus, nusquam erunt; et quia nusquam erunt, nec erunt. Tolle ipsa corpora qualitatibus corporum, non erit ubi sint, et ideo necesse est ut non sint.—Id. ibid. 18. col. 683.]

[3 Perhaps the true reading here is *above*.]

[4 Sursum est Dominus: sed etiam hic est veritas Dominus. Corpus enim Domini, in quo resurrexit, uno loco esse potest: veritas ejus ubique diffusa est.—Id. In Johan. Evang. cap. vii. Tractat. xxx. 1. Tom. III. Pars II. col. 617. This passage is cited by Lombard in somewhat different words: in uno loco esse oportet.—Lib. Sentent. Col. Agrip. 1576. Lib. IV. Dist. x. fol. 351.]

[5 See before, page 274, note 1.]

[6 Sed ubi et quomodo sit in cœlo corpus dominicum, curiosissimum et supervacaneum est quærere; tantummodo in cœlo esse credendum est.—Id. Lib. de Fid. et Symb. 13. Tom. VI. col. 157.]

[7 See before, page 274, note 5.]

[8 See before, page 275, note 8.]

[9 Unus idemque homo localis ex homine, qui est Deus immensus ex Patre: unus idemque, secundum humanam substantiam, absens cœlo, cum esset in terra, et derelinquens terram, cum ascendisset in cœlum: secundum divinam vero immensamque substantiam, nec cœlum dimittens, cum de cœlo descendit, nec terram deserens, cum ad cœlum ascendit. Quod ipsius Domini certissimo potest cognosci sermone; qui ut localem ostenderet humanitatem suam, dicit discipulis suis: Ascendo ad Patrem meum et ad

Vigilius also, a valiant defender of the christian verity, hath these words: "If the Word and the flesh were both of one nature, seeing the Word is every where, why is not then the flesh every where? For when it was in earth, then verily it was not in heaven; and now, when it is in heaven, it is not surely in earth. And it is so sure that it is not in earth, that as concerning it we look for him to come from heaven, whom as concerning his eternal Word we believe to be with us in earth. Therefore by your doctrine (the author speaketh unto the heretic Eutyches, who taught that the divinity and humanity in Christ was but one nature), either the Word is contained in a place with his flesh, or else the flesh is every where with the Word. For one nature cannot receive in itself two diverse and contrary things. But these two things be diverse and far unlike, that is to say, to be contained in a place and to be every where. Therefore, inasmuch as the Word is every where, and the flesh is not every where, it appeareth plainly that one Christ himself hath in him two natures; and that by his divine nature he is every where, and by his human nature he is contained in a place; that he is created, and hath no beginning; that he is subject to death, and cannot die. Whereof one he hath by the nature of his Word, whereby he is God; and the other he hath by the nature of his flesh, whereby the same God is man also. Therefore one Son of God, the self-same was made the Son of man, and he hath a beginning of the nature of his flesh, and no beginning by the nature of his godhead. He is comprehended in a place by the nature of his flesh, and not comprehended in a place by the nature of his godhead. He is inferior to angels in the nature of his flesh, and is equal to his Father in the nature of his godhead. He died by the nature of his flesh, and died not by the nature of his godhead. This is the faith and catholic confession, which the apostles taught, the martyrs did corroborate, and faithful people keep unto this day[10]."

Contra Eutychen, Lib. iv.

I could rehearse divers other, both old and new writers, which with one consent teach, that as the godhead of Christ is every where, and cannot be shut up in one certain place, so likewise the manhood of Christ is only in heaven, and occupieth one certain place, and cannot be in more places than in one at once: but let these suffice for this present. For even of them learn we sufficiently, that the body of Christ is now only in heaven, and so in heaven that it is in none other place, neither shall be until the day of judgment; so far is it off from the truth that the papists teach, affirming that the natural body of Christ lurketh under the kinds of bread and wine, is upon every altar at every mass, is handled, touched, and broken with the priest's hands, is received with the bodily mouth of the priest and of the people, is crushed on pieces with the teeth of the communicants, is devoured of mice, rats, dogs, owls, flittermouses, &c.

Patrem vestrum, Deum meum et Deum vestrum: De Lazaro quoque cum dixisset, Lazarus mortuus est, adjunxit dicens: Et gaudeo propter vos, ut credatis, quoniam non eram ibi. Immensitatem vero suæ divinitatis ostendens discipulis dicit: Ecce ego vobiscum sum omnibus diebus, usque ad consummationem sæculi. Quomodo autem ascendit in cœlum, nisi quia localis et verus est homo? Aut quomodo adest fidelibus suis, nisi quia idem immensus et verus est Deus?—Fulgent. Op. Venet. 1742. Ad Trasimund. Lib. II. cap. xvii. p. 50.]

[10 Deinde si verbi et carnis una natura est, quomodo, cum verbum ubique sit, non ubique inveniatur et caro? Namque quando in terra fuit, non erat utique in cœlo: et nunc quia in cœlo est, non est utique in terra; et in tantum non est, ut secundum ipsam Christum spectemus venturum de cœlo, quem secundum verbum nobiscum esse credimus in terra. Igitur secundum vos, aut verbum cum carne sua loco continetur, aut caro cum verbo ubique est, quando una natura contrarium quid et diversum non recipit in seipsa. Diversum est autem et longe dissimile circumscribi loco, et ubique esse; et quia verbum ubique est, caro autem ejus ubique non est, apparet unum eundemque Christum utriusque esse naturæ, et esse quidem ubique secundum naturam divinitatis suæ, et loco contineri secundum naturam humanitatis suæ: creatum esse, et initium non habere: morti subjacere, et mori non posse: quod unum illi est ex natura verbi, qua Deus est, aliud ex natura carnis, qua idem Deus homo est. Igitur unus Dei Filius, idemque hominis factus Filius, habet initium ex natura carnis suæ, et non habet initium ex natura divinitatis suæ: creatus est per naturam carnis suæ, et non est creatus per naturam divinitatis suæ: circumscribitur loco per naturam carnis suæ, et loco non capitur per naturam divinitatis suæ: minor est etiam angelis per naturam carnis suæ, et æqualis est Patri secundum naturam divinitatis suæ: mortuus est natura carnis suæ, et non est mortuus natura divinitatis suæ. Hæc est fides et confessio catholica, quam apostoli tradiderunt, martyres roboraverunt, et fideles nunc usque custodiunt.—Vigil. adv. Eutych. in Cassandr. Op. Par. 1616. Lib. IV. pp. 546, 7.]

Father. The opinion of the papists, I confess, is gross and too much unsavoury: notwithstanding, in my judgment, it greatly derogateth the omnipotency and almighty power of Christ, (which being God is able to do all things,) to affirm that Christ's body is so inclosed in heaven, that it can be in none other place, or to say, that the body of Christ can be but in one place at once. *Son.* First, as touching the omnipotency and almighty power of Christ, in that he is God, this thing derogateth nothing the glory, majesty, and virtue of the Lord Jesus, to teach, as we are taught of the holy scriptures, and have received from the most ancient fathers of Christ's church; namely, that Christ in his humanity hath forsaken the earth, and is gone up into the glorious kingdom of his Father, where he shall remain until he return unto the judgment. For Christ, being God, is not therefore called almighty because he is able to do all things without exception, but because he is of sufficient power to do whatsoever his good pleasure is to do; as the psalmograph saith: *Omnia quæcunque voluit fecit;* "He hath done whatsoever his good pleasure was to do." For there are many things which God cannot do. He cannot lie. He cannot deny himself. He cannot save the unfaithful. He cannot condemn the faithful. He cannot deny mercy to them that be merciful. He cannot make the damned inheritors of everlasting salvation. He cannot make one of like dignity with himself. He cannot love wickedness, nor abhor righteousness. He cannot delight in the death of sinners; and, as some write, he cannot restore virginity once violated; neither can he sin, nor do any thing against his word or determinate purpose, &c.

Of the omnipotency and almighty power of God.

Neither doth this thing any whit at all hinder the omnipotency of God, or prove God to be the less omnipotent or almighty. For, as I said before, God is called almighty, because he is able to do whatsoever his godly pleasure is, and because there is no superior power above him, but that he may do all that he will; and all that his pleasure is to do, that may he bring to pass, and no power is able to resist him, as he saith by the prophet: "I will work, and who shall be able to turn it away?" Likewise saith the psalmograph: "The Lord breaketh the counsel of the heathen, and bringeth to nought the devices of the people. But the counsel of the Lord shall stand for ever, and the thoughts of his heart throughout all ages." For, as Salomon saith, "There is no wisdom, no forecast, no counsel, that can prevail against the Lord."

Why God is called almighty.

Isai. xliii.

Psal. xxxiii.

Prov. xxi.

Moreover, as concerning Christ's being in heaven only until the day of judgment, we are taught of the holy scriptures both so to believe and to teach. For in the word of God we find none other place appointed for the humanity of Christ than heaven, as we have tofore abundantly heard.

And as touching the body of Christ, although immortal and glorified, to be but in one place only at one time, you have heard before both the determination of the Holy Ghost, and also the consent of the ancient godly fathers in this behalf; which all, with one perfect agreement, teach and affirm that the body of Christ is but in one place at one time, although his godhead be every where, and fulfilleth all things. For this is diligently to be noted, that to be in many or in all places at once is only appropriated to the nature of God. For no creature, although never so glorious, pure, immortal, and spiritual, can be in more places at once than in one only. Yea, the very angels and invisible spirits, forasmuch as they be creatures, are only in one place at once, as Basilius Magnus testifieth, saying: "The angel which stood by Cornelius was not at the same time also with Philip, nor the angel which spake to Zachary at the altar was not the same time in his proper place in heaven. But the Holy Ghost was at one time in Abacuck, and in Daniel at Babylon, and with Jeremy in prison, and with Ezechiel in Chobar[1]." Of this sentence of Basil learn here two things: one is that all creatures, although never so pure and perfect, are only at one time in one place, and not in many and diverse places at once; again, that God alone, which is the Creator and Maker of all creatures, can be in many or in all places at once.

Note well.

Lib. de Spiritu Sanct. cap. xxii.

[1 Ὁ γὰρ τῷ Κορνηλίῳ ἐπιστὰς ἄγγελος οὐκ ἦν ἐν ταὐτῷ καὶ παρὰ τῷ Φιλίππῳ, οὐδὲ ὁ ἀπὸ τοῦ θυσιαστηρίου τῷ Ζαχαρίᾳ διαλεγόμενος κατὰ τὸν αὐτὸν καιρὸν καὶ ἐν οὐρανῷ τὴν οἰκείαν στάσιν ἐπλήρου. τὸ μέν τοι πνεῦμα, ὁμοῦ τε ἐν Ἀββακοὺμ ἐνεργεῖν, καὶ ἐν Δανιὴλ ἐπὶ τῆς Βαβυλωνίας πεπίστευται· καὶ ἐν τῷ καταῤῥάκτῃ εἶναι μετὰ Ἱερεμίου, καὶ μετὰ Ἰεζεκιὴλ ἐπὶ τοῦ Χοβάρ.—Basil. Op. Par. 1721—30. Lib. de Spir. Sanct. cap. xxiii. Tom. III. p. 46.]

And Didymus, in his book which he writeth of the Holy Ghost, proveth that the Holy Ghost is very God, because he is in many places at one time, which no creature can be. "For," saith he, "all creatures, visible and invisible, be circumscribed and environed either within one place (as corporal and visible things be), or within the property of their own substance (as angels and invisible creatures be); so that no angel," saith he, "can be at one time in two places. And forasmuch as the Holy Ghost is in many men at one time, therefore," saith he, "the Holy Ghost must needs be God[2]." Cap. xxii.

Who seeth not now, except he be wilfully blind, that forasmuch as the body of Christ is a creature, although glorified and clad with immortality, it is and can be but in one place at once? To teach the contrary is none other thing than to evacuate and utterly to destroy the nature of Christ's humanity, and to affirm, with certain heretics, that the body of Christ is deified, and so swallowed up of the godhead, that it is now in all places with the godhead at all times; which is a most heinous and detestable heresy.

For St Austin affirmeth plainly, that a body must needs be in some certain place; and saith moreover, that if it be not within the compass of a place, it is nowhere: and if it be nowhere, then is it not[3]. Ad Dardanum, Epist. lvii.

St Cyril likewise, considering the proper nature of a very body, said "that, if the nature of the godhead were a body, it must needs be in a place, and have quantity, greatness, and circumscription[4]." De Trinit. Lib. ii.

We may therefore right well conclude, both with the authority of the holy scriptures and with the testimonies of the ancient writers, that the body of Christ, although utterly estranged from corruption and mortality, and now glorified and immortal, is and remain still a perfect and true body, circumscribed, compassed, and measured, and cannot be in divers places at one time.

[5]This doctrine is now so plain and evident, so open and manifest, that it cannot be denied; and I much marvel how the papists, specially the learned sort, durst ever maintain so damnable heresy, and teach that the body of Christ is in an infinite number of places at one time. For by this means they make his body to be God (whose property alone it is to be in many or in all places at once), and so confound the two natures of Christ, attributing to his human nature that thing which belongeth only to his divinity; which is a most heinous and abominable heresy.

Father. But what is then to be said concerning these words, which the papists continually object, and to the which they cleave with tooth and nail, and the which they defend with stocks and chains, with fire and fagot, with sword and halter, and with all other kind of tyranny?

Son. Of what words speak you? *Father.* Of these: *Hoc est enim corpus meum.* For thus read we: "Christ took the bread, thanked, brake it, and gave it to his disciples, saying, Take, eat: this is my body, which is given for you," &c. Spake he these words, "This is my body," of the bread, or rather of his own natural body, which he received of Mary the virgin? The words of consecration, as they call them, considered.

Son. I know what some hold and teach in this behalf. Some say that Christ, delivering the bread to his disciples for to eat, pointed to his own body and said: "This is my body, which is given for you;" and afterward said unto them: "Do that," that is to say, break the bread and eat it, "in the remembrance of me." But I rather approve and allow the judgment of them which teach that Christ spake these words, *Hoc est corpus meum*, "This is my body," of the bread, which he had now made and appointed the mystery of his body.

[2 The following is probably the passage intended: Ipse vero Spiritus sanctus, si unus de creaturis esset, saltem circumscriptam haberet substantiam; sicut universa quæ facta sunt. Nam etsi non circumscribantur loco et finibus invisibiles creaturæ, tamen proprietate substantiæ finiuntur. Spiritus autem sanctus, cum in pluribus sit, non habet substantiam circumscriptam...Angelus quippe qui aderat, verbi gratia, apostolo in Asia oranti, non poterat simul eodem tempore adesse aliis in ceteris partibus mundi constitutis. Spiritus autem sanctus non solum sejunctis a se hominibus præsto est, sed et singulis quibusque angelis, principatibus, thronis, dominationibus inhabitator assistit.—Did. Alex. in Biblioth. Vet. Patr. Stud. Galland. Venet. 1765—81. De Spirit. Sanct. Lib. 6. Tom. VI. p. 265.]

[3 See before, page 278, note 2.]

[4 *Εἰ γὰρ ὅλως τομῆς τε καὶ μερισμοῦ, καὶ ὧν ἐκεῖνοι φασὶν, ἡ θεία φύσις ἀνέχεται, νοείσθω καὶ σῶμα· εἰ δὲ τοῦτο, καὶ ἐν τόπῳ πάντως που, καὶ ἐν μεγέθει, καὶ ποσῷ. καὶ ἐπειδὰν πεπόσωται, μὴ φευγέτω περιγραφήν.*—Cyril. Alex. Op. Lut. 1638. De S. Trin. Dial. II. Tom. V. Pars I. p. 447.]

[5 *Father*, prefixed in Folio.]

Father. If Christ spake these words of the bread, then is the bread his body. *Son.* His body, I grant, in mystery and figure, but not in nature and substance. For the body of Christ was made of the substance of Mary the virgin, and not of the substance of bread. Though Christ called the bread his body, yet doth it not therefore follow, that the bread is his natural body; but so termed for certain resemblances and likenesses between the body of Christ and the creature of bread, as we have tofore heard. Christ in divers places of the holy scripture diversly nameth himself. He calleth himself "a vine," "a door," "a stone," &c. and is called of St Paul "a rock;" not that he is a natural vine, door, stone, rock, &c. but for certain resemblances and properties which he hath with them. Christ calleth his Father a plowman, his disciples vine-branches; the good seed, the children of the kingdom; the tares, the sons of the wicked; the field, the world; the harvest, the end of the world; the reapers, the angels, &c.; not that they are so indeed, but for certain properties and resemblances which are between them. Even after the same manner Christ calleth the bread his body; not that it is his natural body indeed, but because it representeth, signifieth, declareth, preacheth, and setteth forth his body unto us; and hath also, as I may so speak, certain properties with the body of Christ. For as the bread is broken of the faithful in the action of the Lord's supper, so was Christ's body broken on the altar of the cross. And as the bread nourisheth, preserveth, and comforteth the body, when it is eaten, so likewise ☞ the body of Christ nourisheth, preserveth, and comforteth both the body and the soul of the faithful communicants; as Christ himself testifieth: "I am the bread of life: he that cometh unto me shall not hunger, and he that believeth in me shall never thirst." "I am that living bread which came down from heaven. If any man eat of this bread, he shall live for ever; and the bread which I shall give for the life of the world is my flesh." "He that eateth my flesh, and drinketh my blood, hath everlasting life; and I shall raise him up in the last day. For my flesh is very meat, and my blood is very drink. He that eateth my flesh, and drinketh my blood, dwelleth in me, and I in him," &c. For these and such like properties and resemblances did Christ call the bread his body.

How the bread is Christ's body.

John xv. John x. Matt. xxi. 1 Cor. x. John xv. Matt. xiii.

Why Christ called the bread his body.

John vi.

Father. It is then no proper, but a figurative speech, when Christ calleth the bread his body. *Son.* You say truth. And that the breaking of Christ's body on the altar of the cross for our redemption might the more surely be fixed in our hearts, when we come together to eat the Lord's supper, Christ enabled[1] the sacramental bread with the name of his body, when notwithstanding it is the figure and sign of his body.

Neither is this a rare and seldom-found thing, but rather common and usual in the holy scriptures, to call the sign by the name of the thing that it signifieth, as St Austin saith: "The thing which signifieth is wont to be called by the name of that thing which it signifieth, as it is written, 'The seven ears are seven years.' It saith not, They signify seven years. And, 'Seven kine are seven years;' and many other like. And so said St Paul, that 'the stone was Christ,' and not, that it signified Christ, but even as it had been he indeed, which nevertheless was not Christ by substance, but by signification[2]," &c.

In Lev. xvii. quest. 57.

Again: "In such wise is blood the soul, as the stone was Christ; and yet the apostle saith not, that the stone signified Christ, but saith, 'it was Christ.' And this sentence, 'Blood is the soul,' may be understand to be spoken in a sign or figure. ☞ For Christ did not stick to say, 'This is my body,' when he gave the sign of his body[3]."

Contra Adimant. cap. 12.

Lev. xvii.

[[1] Folio, *ennabled*. Perhaps *ennobled*.]

[[2] Solet autem res quæ significat, ejus rei nomine quam significat nuncupari; sicut scriptum est, Septem spicæ septem anni sunt: non enim dixit, septem annos significant: et, Septem boves septem anni sunt: et multa hujusmodi. Hinc est quod dictum est, Petra erat Christus. Non enim dixit, Petra significat Christum, sed tamquam hoc esset, quod utique per substantiam non hoc erat, sed per significationem.—August. Op. Par. 1679—1700. Quæst. in Heptat. Lib. III. Quæst. lvii. 3. Tom. III. Pars II. col. 516.]

[[3] Non enim Dominus dubitavit dicere, Hoc est corpus meum, cum signum daret corpus sui...... tamen illud quod lex dixit, fundendum esse sanguinem, nec in escam assumendum, quia sanguis est anima, esse positum dicimus, sicut alia multa; et pene omnia scripturarum illarum sacramenta signis et figuris plena sunt futuræ prædicationis, quæ jam per Dominum nostrum Jesum Christum declarata est. Sic est enim sanguis anima, quomodo petra erat Christus......nec tamen ait, Petra significabat Christum: sed ait, Petra erat Christus.—Id. Cont. Adimant. cap. xii. 3, 5. Tom. VIII. cols. 124, 6.]

Once again he saith: "We customably use to say, when Easter draweth nigh, To-morrow or the next day is the Lord's passion. And yet it is many years since he suffered, and that passion was never done but once. And upon the Sunday we say, This day the Lord did rise again; and yet it is many years since he rose from death. Why then do not men reprove us as liars when we speak in this sort, but because we call these days by a similitude of those days wherein these things were done indeed? And so it is called that day, which is not that day indeed, but by the course of the year it is a like day. And such things be said to be done that day, for the solemn celebration of the sacrament, which things indeed were not done that day, but long before. Was Christ offered any more but once? And he offered himself; and yet in a sacrament or representation, not only every solemn feast of Easter, but every day he is offered to the people, so that he doth not lie that saith he is every day offered. For if sacraments had not some similitude or likeness of those things whereof they be sacraments, they could in nowise be sacraments. And for their similitude and likeness, commonly they have the name of the things whereof they be sacraments. Therefore, as after a certain manner of speech the sacrament of Christ's body is Christ's body, the sacrament of Christ's blood is Christ's blood; so likewise the sacrament of faith is faith. And to believe is nothing else but to have faith. And therefore when we answer for young children in their baptism that they believe, which have not yet the mind to believe, we answer that they have faith, because they have the sacrament of faith. And we say also that they turn unto God, because of the sacrament of conversion unto God; for that answer pertaineth to the celebration of the sacrament. And likewise speaketh the apostle of baptism, saying that 'by baptism we be buried with him into death.' He saith not, that we signify burial, but he saith plainly that 'we be buried.' So that the sacrament of so great a thing is not called but by the name of the thing itself[4]."

Ad Bonif. Epist. xxiii.

Rom. vi.

Of these words of St Austin it manifestly appeareth, that the sacraments are called by the names of those things whereof they be sacraments; as the sacrament of faith, which is baptism, is called faith. And the sacrament of Christ's body and blood is called the body and blood of Christ, not that they be the things themselves, but they be so called, because they be the figures, sacraments, and representations of the things which they signify, and whereof they bear the names.

Likewise in the old testament was it said of the paschal lamb, "This is the Lord's pass-by, or passover:" and yet that paschal lamb was not the Lords very passover or passing-by, but it was a figure, which represented his passing by: even after the same manner in the new testament the sacramental bread is called the body of Christ, and the sacramental wine the blood of Christ; not that they be Christ's very body and blood indeed, but they be figures, which by Christ's institution be unto the godly receivers thereof sacraments, tokens, significations, and representations of his very flesh and blood; instructing their faith, that as the bread and wine feed

[4 Nempe sæpe ita loquimur, ut pascha propinquante dicamus, crastinam vel perendinam Domini passionem, cum ille ante tam multos annos passus sit, nec omnino nisi semel illa passio facta sit. Nempe ipso die dominico dicimus, Hodie Dominus resurrexit; cum ex quo resurrexit tot anni transierint. Cur nemo tam ineptus est, ut nos ita loquentes arguat esse mentitos, nisi quia istos dies secundum illorum, quibus hæc gesta sunt, similitudinem nuncupamus, ut dicatur ipse dies qui non est ipse, sed revolutione temporis similis ejus; et dicatur illo die fieri, propter sacramenti celebrationem, quod non illo die, sed jam olim factum est? Nonne semel immolatus est Christus in seipso? et tamen in sacramento non solum per omnes paschæ solemnitates, sed omni die populis immolatur, nec utique mentitur, qui interrogatus eum responderit immolari. Si enim sacramenta quamdam similitudinem earum rerum, quarum sacramenta sunt, non haberent, omnino sacramenta non essent. Ex hac autem similitudine plerumque etiam ipsarum rerum nomina accipiunt. Sicut ergo secundum quemdam modum sacramentum corporis Christi corpus Christi est, sacramentum sanguinis Christi sanguis Christi est, ita sacramentum fidei fides est. Nihil est autem aliud credere, quam fidem habere. Ac per hoc cum respondetur parvulus credere, qui fidei nondum habet affectum, respondetur fidem habere propter fidei sacramentum, et convertere se ad Deum propter conversionis sacramentum, quia et ipsa responsio ad celebrationem pertinet sacramenti. Sicut de ipso baptismo apostolus, Consepulti, inquit, sumus Christo per baptismum in mortem. Non ait, sepulturam significavimus: sed prorsus ait, Consepulti sumus. Sacramentum ergo tantæ rei nonnisi ejusdem rei vocabulo nuncupavit.—Id. Epist. xcviii. 9. ad Bonifac. Tom. II. cols. 267, 8.]

them corporally, and continue this temporal life; so the very flesh and blood of Christ feedeth them spiritually, and giveth everlasting life.

Neither ought this phrase or manner of speaking seem strange to any man that hath but a spark of reason, seeing it is not only used in the scriptures of God, but also in our familiar and daily talk. When we behold the images of king Edward the sixth, or of queen Elizabeth, our most gracious queen and governess at this present, use we not to say, This is king Edward, and this is queen Elizabeth? Looking upon the pictures of Hercules, or Hector, our manner is also to say, This is Hercules, or this is Hector; whom notwithstanding they only represent those persons whom we name.

Contra Maximin. Lib. iii. cap. 22.

It is well and learnedly said of St Austin: "In sacraments we must not consider what they be, but what they signify. For they be signs of things, being one thing and signifying another[1]." Which thing he doth shew specially of this sacrament of the body and blood of Christ, saying: "The heavenly bread, which is Christ's flesh, by some manner of speech is called Christ's body, when in very deed it is the sacrament of his body. And that offering of the flesh, which is done by the priest's hands, is called Christ's passion, death, and crucifying, not in very deed, but in a mystical signification[2]."

In Sent. Prosp.

De Consec. Dist. 2. Hoc est.

Again he saith, as it is recited in the pope's decrees: "As the heavenly bread, which is Christ's flesh, after a manner is called the body of Christ, when in very deed it is a sacrament of Christ's body, that is to say, of that body which, being visible, palpable, mortal, was put upon the cross; and as that offering of the flesh, which is done by the priest's hands, is called the passion, the death, the crucifying of Christ, not in truth of the thing, but in a signifying mystery; so is the sacrament of faith (which is baptism) faith[3]."

Upon these aforesaid words writeth the expositor on this manner: "The offering which the priest maketh is called improperly the passion, death, or crucifying of Christ, not that it is that, but that it signifieth it." "And the heavenly sacrament, which truly representeth Christ's flesh, is called Christ's body, but improperly. And therefore it is said 'after a manner, but not in the truth of the thing, but in the signifying mystery;' so that the sense is this: It is called the body of Christ, that is, signifieth[4]."

De Consec. Dist. 2. cap. Cœlest.

Father. These things, which thou hast alleged out of the ancient writers, are so evident and plain, that no man can with a good conscience (except he will wilfully resist the truth), deny that these words of Christ, "This is my body," "This is my blood," are figuratively to be understand, and not so grossly as the words sound; yea, and that so much the more, because, if they should literally be taken, they should utterly dissent from many other texts of the holy scriptures, which most evidently declare, that Christ as concerning his corporal presence is not in earth, but in heaven only, and there shall remain until the day of judgment.

Notwithstanding, I would be glad to hear how the ancient fathers of Christ's church have understand and taken these words of Christ, that by this means leaving error, and embracing truth, I might from henceforth walk with a quiet conscience in this behalf, and no more be carried about with every wind of doctrine. For it much grieveth me to see in these our days such and so great dissension to be raised up of Satan among men about this sacrament of the body and blood of Christ; which holy and heavenly sacrament the Lord Christ ordained to be not only a pledge of his

Why Christ instituted the sacrament of his body and blood.

[1 Hæc enim sacramenta sunt, in quibus non quid sint, sed quid ostendant semper adtenditur: quoniam signa sunt rerum, aliud exsistentia, et aliud significantia.—Id. Cont. Maxim. Arian. Lib. II. cap. XXI. 3. Tom. VIII. col. 725.]

[2 This appears to be the same passage with that cited immediately after.]

[3 See before, page 250, note 1.]

[4 Immolatio quæ fit a presbytero, improprie appellatur Christi passio, vel mors, vel crucifixio: non quod sit illa, sed quia illam significat.—Ibid. col. 2387. And again: Cœleste sacramentum, quod vere repræsentat Christi carnem, dicitur corpus Christi, sed improprie. Unde dicitur suo modo, sed non rei veritate, sed significati mysterio, ut sit sensus, Vocatur Christi corpus, id est significat.—Decret. Gratiani, Par. 1583. Decr. Tert. Pars, De Consecr. Dist. ii. Gloss. in can. 48. col. 2388.]

love toward us, but also a sure and an unloosable bond of hearty love and singular good will, which we that profess Christ, and are partakers of those holy mysteries, ought to have and continually to nourish among ourselves, all contention, strife, debate, envy, hatred, malice, and all uncharitableness utterly laid aside and cast away.

Son. How the ancient fathers took and understood these words of Christ, "This is my body," "This is my blood," it may easily be known by their own writings.

First, Tertullian, which lived in the year of our Lord one hundred and sixty, hath these words, writing against the heretic Marcion, which denied the verity of Christ's body, affirming it not to be a natural but a fantastical body: "Christ, taking bread and distributing it to his disciples, made it his body, saying, 'This is my body,' that is to say, a figure of my body. But this bread could not have been a figure of it, except Christ had had a true body. For a vain thing or a fantasy can take no figure[5]." Again he saith, writing against the aforesaid heretic: "Christ himself did not reprove or discommend bread, which doth represent his body[6]."

Adversus Marcionem, Lib. iv.

Contra Marcionem, Lib. ii.

St Ambrose, which lived in the year of our Lord three hundred and eighty, saith: "Before the consecration another kind is named, but after the consecration the body of Christ is signified, &c[7]." Again he saith: "Make unto us, O Lord, this oblation to be acceptable, which is the figure of the body and blood of our Lord Jesu Christ[8]."

De Mysteriis initiandis, cap. ult.

De Sacram. Lib. iv. cap. 5.

St Jerome, which lived in the year of our Lord four hundred and twenty-two, writeth on this manner: "After the mystical Easter lamb fulfilled, and that Christ had eaten the lamb's flesh with the apostles, he took bread, which comforteth the heart of man, and passeth to the true sacrament of the Easter lamb; that as Melchisedech brought forth bread and wine prefiguring him, so might he likewise represent the truth of his body[9]."

In Matt. cap. xxvi.

Psal. civ.

Gen. xiv.

St Austin, which lived in the year of our Lord four hundred and thirty, writeth on this wise: "The Lord doubted not to say, 'This is my body,' when he gave the sign of his body[10]." Again he saith: "The Lord admitted Judas unto the maundy, wherein he did betake and deliver unto the disciples the figure of his body and blood[11]."

Contra Adimant. cap. 12.

In Psal. iii.

St Cyprian, which lived in the year of our Lord two hundred and sixty, in a certain sermon writeth on this manner: "The Lord gave at the table, in the which he made his last banquet with the apostles, bread and wine with his own hands; but on the cross he gave his body to be wounded with the hands of the soldiers[12]," &c.

In Serm. de Unctione Christi.

[[5] Professus itaque se concupiscentia concupisse edere pascha ut suum (indignum enim ut quid alienum concupisceret Deus), acceptum panem, et distributum discipulis, corpus illum suum fecit, Hoc est corpus meum dicendo, id est, figura corporis mei. Figura autem non fuisset, nisi veritatis esset corpus. Ceterum vacua res, quod est phantasma, figuram capere non posset.—Tertull. Op. Lut. 1641. Advers. Marcion. Lib. IV. 40. p. 571.]

[[6] Sed ille quidem usque nunc nec aquam reprobavit creatoris, qua suos abluit; nec oleum, quo suos unguit; nec mellis et lactis societatem, qua suos infantat; nec panem, quo ipsum corpus suum repræsentat; etiam in sacramentis propriis egens mendicitatibus creatoris.—Id. ibid. Lib. II. 14. pp. 439, 40.]

[[7] Ante benedictionem verborum cœlestium alia species nominatur, post consecrationem corpus significatur.—Ambros. Op. Par. 1686—90. De Myster. Lib. cap. ix. 54. Tom. II. col. 339. There is much doubt of the genuineness of this work.]

[[8] Dicit sacerdos: Fac nobis, inquit, hanc oblationem adscriptam, ratam, rationabilem, acceptabilem: quod figura est corporis et sanguinis Domini nostri Jesu Christi.—Id. de Sacram. Lib. IV. cap. v. 21. col. 371.]

[[9] Postquam typicum pascha fuerat impletum, et agni carnes cum apostolis comederat, assumit panem, qui confortat cor hominis, et ad verum paschæ transgreditur sacramentum; ut quomodo in præfiguratione ejus Melchisedec, summi Dei sacerdos, panem et vinum offerens fecerat, ipse quoque veritatem sui corporis et sanguinis repræsentaret.—Hieron. Op. Par. 1693—1706. Comm. Lib. IV. in Matt. cap. xxvi. Tom. IV. Pars I. col. 128.]

[[10] See before, page 282, note 3.]

[[11] ......eum tamdiu pertulit tamquam bonum, cum ejus cogitationes non ignoraret, cum adhibuit ad convivium, in quo corporis et sanguinis sui figuram discipulis commendavit et tradidit.—August. Op. Par. 1679—1700. Enarr. in Psalm. iii. 1. Tom. IV. col. 7.]

[[12] Dedit itaque Dominus noster in mensa, in qua ultimum cum apostolis participavit convivium, propriis manibus panem et vinum: in cruce vero manibus militum corpus tradidit vulnerandum; ut in apostolis secretius impressa sincera veritas, et vera sinceritas, exponeret gentibus, quomodo vinum et panis caro esset et sanguis, et quibus rationibus causæ effectibus convenirent, et diversa nomina vel species ad unam reducerentur essentiam, et significantia et significata eisdem vocabulis censerentur, ut sacramentum et res sacramenti.—Cypr. Op. Oxon. 1682. De Unct. Chrism. (Arnold.) Appendix, p. 48.]

Ad Mag. Lib. i. ep. 6. Again: "The Lord called bread, made of many corns and joined together, his body; and the wine, pressed out of many grapes and made into wine, he named his blood[1]." Ad Cæcil. Lib. ii. ep. 3. Also in another place: "It was wine that the Lord called his blood[2]."

Hilarius, which lived in the year of our Lord three hundred and fifty, saith: Dist. 2. cap. Corpus. "There is a figure; for bread and wine be outwardly seen. And there is also a truth of that figure; for the body and blood of Christ be of a truth inwardly believed[3]."

In Catalo. Sanctorum. Petrus de Natalibus saith: "The body of Christ is corporally contained in heaven, but in the host it is contained sacramentally[4]."

St Bernard, which lived in the year of our Lord one thousand one hundred and In Serm. de S. Mart. forty, saith: "The flesh of Christ even at this present day is exhibited and given to us, notwithstanding spiritually, not carnally[5]."

Beda, which lived in the year of our Lord seven hundred and thirty-two, writing upon the gospel of Luke, hath these words: "After the solemnity of the old Easter lamb was finished, which was observed in the remembrance of the old deliverance out of Egypt, he goeth unto the new, which the church gladly observeth in the remembrance of his redemption; that he, in the stead of the flesh and blood of the lamb, might institute and ordain the sacrament of his flesh and blood in the figure of bread Psal. cx. and wine, and so declare himself to be the same unto whom the Lord sware, 'Thou art an everlasting priest, after the order of Melchisedech.' And he himself brake the bread which he gave, to shew that the breaking of his body should not be done without his own will. And likewise he gave them the cup after he had supped. Psal. civ. And because bread doth confirm or strength the flesh, and wine worketh blood in the flesh, therefore is the bread mystically referred unto the body of Christ, and the wine referred unto his blood[6]."

In Matt. Christianus Druthmarus hath these words: "The Lord gave to his disciples the sacrament of his body unto the remission of sins, and unto the conservation of charity, that they, being mindful of that act, should always do that in a figure which he should do for them, and not forget this charity or love. 'This is my body,' that is to say, Psal. civ. in a sacrament or holy sign[7]." Again he saith: "Wine maketh merry, and increaseth blood, and therefore not unaptly the blood of Christ is figured by it; for whatsoever cometh to us from him maketh us merry with a true mirth, and increaseth all our goodness[8]."

Lib. Inst. i. cap. 31. Rabanus Maurus saith: "Forasmuch as corporal bread confirmeth the heart, there-

---

[[1] See before, page 267, note 6.]

[[2] Qua in parte invenimus calicem mixtum fuisse quem Dominus obtulit, et vinum fuisse, quod sanguinem suum dixit.—Cypr. Op. Oxon. 1682. Epist. lxiii. ad Cæcil. p. 152.]

[[3] Corpus Christi, quod sumitur de altari, figura est, dum panis et vinum extra videtur; veritas autem, dum corpus et sanguis Christi in veritate interius creditur.—Hilar. in Decret. Gratiani, Par. 1583. Decr. Tert. Pars, De Consecr. Dist. ii. Can. 79. cols. 2411, 12.]

[[4] ...... nec tamen ex hostiarum multitudine corpus unicum plurificatur: quod etiam in cœlo et in altare, tamen diversimode, continetur. In cœlo enim corporaliter; in hostia sacramentaliter.—Petr. de Natal. Catalog. Sanct. Lugd. 1508. De Fest. Corp. J. Christ. Lib. v. cap. xlv. fol. 125.]

[[5] Videtur tamen etiam in hoc mane de carnibus agni nonnihil esse servatum: sed quod residuum est, utique jam datur igni: quod videlicet usque hodie eadem caro nobis, sed spiritualiter utique, non carnaliter exhibeatur.—Bernard. Op. Par. 1690. In Fest. S. Martin. Serm. Vol. I. Tom. III. col. 1052.]

[[6] Finitis paschæ veteris solenniis, quæ in commemorationem antiquæ de Ægypto liberationis agebantur, transiit ad novum, quod in suæ redemptionis memoriam ecclesia frequentare desiderat. Ut videlicet pro carne agni vel sanguine suæ carnis sanguinisque sacramentum in panis ac vini figura substituens, ipsum se esse monstraret, cui juravit Dominus et non pœnitebit eum, Tu es sacerdos in æternum, secundum ordinem Melchisedech. Frangit autem ipse panem quem porrigit, ut ostendat corporis sui fractionem non sine sua sponte futuram, sed sicut alibi dicit, potestatem se habere ponendi animam suam, et iterum sumendi eam. ...... Similiter et calicem, postquam cœnavit, dedit eis. Quia ergo panis carnem confirmat, vinum vero sanguinem operatur in carne; hic ad corpus Christi mystice, illud refertur ad sanguinem.—Ven. Bed. Op. Col. Agrip. 1612. In Luc. Evang. cap. xxii. Lib. VI. Tom. V. col. 424.]

[[7] Dedit discipulis suis sacramentum corporis sui in remissionem peccatorum, et in conservationem caritatis; ut memores illius facti, semper hoc in figura facerent; quod pro eis acturus erat, non obliviscerentur. Hoc est corpus meum: id est in sacramento.—Christ. Druthmar. Expos. in Math. Evang. Argent. 1514. fol. 84.]

[[8] Vinum namque et lætificat et sanguinem auget. Et idcirco non inconvenienter sanguis Christi per hoc figuratur; quoniam quicquid nobis ab ipso venit lætificat lætitia vera, et auget omne bonum nostrum.—Id. ibid.]

fore it is aptly called the body of Christ; and because wine worketh blood in the flesh, therefore is it referred unto the blood of Christ[9]."

Isidorus writeth on this manner: "The bread and wine through mystical prayer and pronouncing of Christ's words are consecrate unto the remembrance of the Lord's passion, which he suffered for us[10]." Etym. Lib. vi.

Father. These words of the ancient fathers are so open, plain, and evident, that no man can with a good conscience deny, but that these words, "This is my body," "This is my blood," are not carnally but spiritually, not properly but figuratively, not naturally but significatively to be understand.

But forasmuch as all these testimonies which thou hast hitherto alleged are borrowed out of the Latin writers, I desire also to know and understand the minds of some Greek authors, and by this means learn the truth of God's word not only of the Latin, but also of the Greek fathers; that I, being confirmed through their authority in the true understanding of Christ's words concerning his holy supper, may from henceforth eschew falsehood and lies, and embrace the truth of God's most holy word, and continue in the same unto the end.

Son. God give us all grace so to do!

First, Origen, which lived in the year of our Lord two hundred and thirty, offereth himself unto us, and saith: "Consider that these things written in God's books (he speaketh of the eating of Christ's body, and of the drinking of Christ's blood) are figures; and therefore examine and understand them as spiritual, and not as carnal men. For if you understand them as carnal men, they hurt you and feed you not. For even in the gospel is there found a letter that killeth. And not only in the old testament, but also in the new, is there found letter that slayeth him that doth not spiritually understand that which is spoken. For if thou follow the letter or words of this that Christ said, 'Except ye eat my flesh and drink my blood,' this letter killeth[11]." John vi.

Like unto this writeth Chrysostom: "If any man understand the words of Christ carnally, he shall surely profit nothing thereby. For what mean these words, 'The flesh profiteth nothing?' He meant not of his flesh (God forbid!), but he meant of them that fleshly and carnally understood those things that Christ spake. But what is carnal understanding? To understand the words simply as they be spoken, and nothing else. For we ought not so to understand the things which we see; but all mysteries must be considered with inward eyes, and that is spiritually to understand them[12]." In Joan. Hom. 46. For, as he saith in another place: "If thou were spiritual or without a body, Christ would have given unto thee nakedly those gifts (which are signified by baptism, and the sacrament of thanksgiving) even spiritual and without a body. But forasmuch thy soul is joined to the body, things worthy of understanding are delivered unto thee in sensible things[13]." In Matt. cap. xxvi. Hom. 83. Again: "What do I call the communion? Even the In 1 Cor. cap. x.

[[9] Ergo quia panis corporis cor firmat, ideo ille corpus Christi congruenter nuncupatur. Vinum autem quia sanguinem operatur in carne, ideo ad sanguinem Christi refertur.—Raban. Maur. Op. Col. Agrip. 1626—7. De Inst. Cler. Lib. I. cap. xxxi. Tom. VI. p. 12.]

[[10] Sacrificium dictum, quasi sacrum factum; quia prece mystica consecratur in memoriam pro nobis Dominicæ passionis: unde hoc eo jubente corpus Christi et sanguinem dicimus, quod dum sit ex fructibus terræ, sanctificatur, et fit sacramentum, operante invisibiliter Spiritu Dei, cujus panis et calicis sacramentum Græci eucharistiam dicunt.—Isidor. Hispal. Op. Col. Agrip. 1617. Orig. sive Etymol. Lib. VI. cap. xix. p. 52.]

[[11] Agnoscite quia figuræ sunt, quæ in divinis voluminibus scripta sunt; et ideo tanquam spiritales et non tanquam carnales examinate, et intelligite quæ dicuntur. Si enim quasi carnales ista suscipitis, lædunt vos, et non alunt. Est enim et in evangeliis litera quæ occidit; non solum in veteri testamento occidens litera deprehenditur. Est et in novo testamento litera, quæ occidat eum, qui non spiritaliter quæ dicuntur adverterit. Si enim secundum literam sequaris hoc ipsum quod dictum est, Nisi manducaveritis carnem meam, et biberitis sanguinem meum, occidit hæc litera.—Orig. Op. Par. 1733—59. In Levit. Hom. vii. 5. Tom. II. p. 225.]

[[12] Ἐὰν γὰρ αὐτὸ σαρκικῶς τὶς ἐκλάβοι, οὐδὲν ἀπώνατο. τί οὖν, οὐκ ἔστι ἡ σὰρξ αὐτοῦ σάρξ; καὶ σφόδρα μὲν οὖν. καὶ πῶς εἶπεν, ἡ σὰρξ οὐκ ὠφελεῖ οὐδέν; οὐ περὶ τῆς ἑαυτοῦ σαρκὸς λέγων· μὴ γένοιτο· ἀλλὰ περὶ τῶν σαρκικῶς ἐκλαμβανόντων τὰ λεγόμενα. τί δέ ἐστι τὸ σαρκικῶς νοῆσαι; τὸ ἁπλῶς εἰς τὰ προκείμενα ὁρᾷν, καὶ μὴ πλέον τι φαντάζεσθαι. τοῦτο γάρ ἐστι σαρκικῶς. χρὴ δὲ μὴ οὕτω κρίνειν τοῖς ὁρωμένοις, ἀλλὰ πάντα τὰ μυστήρια τοῖς ἔνδον ὀφθαλμοῖς κατοπτεύειν· τοῦτο γάρ ἐστι πνευματικῶς.—Chrysost. Op. Par. 1718—38. In Joan. Hom. xlvii. Tom. VIII. p. 278.]

[[13] Εἰ μὲν γὰρ ἀσώματος εἶ, γυμνὰ ἂν αὐτά σοι τὰ ἀσώματα παρέδωκε δῶρα· ἐπεὶ δὲ σώματι συμπέπλεκται ἡ ψυχὴ, ἐν αἰσθητοῖς τὰ νοητά σοι παραδίδωσι.—Id. In Matt. Hom. lxxxii. Tom. VII. p. 787.]

very same body are we. What signifieth the bread? The body of Christ. What [In Matt. Hom. 83. cap. xxvi.] are they made which receive it? The body of Christ[1]." Once again: "If Christ died not, whose symbol and sign is this sacrifice? So [see] what an earnest study he had, [In Opere imperfecto in Matt. Hom. 11.] that we should alway remember that he died for us[2]." Also in another place: "If it be perilous to put these hallowed vessels unto private uses, in the which the true body of Christ is not, but a mystery of his body is contained; how much more the vessels of our body, which God hath prepared a dwelling-place for himself, ought [In Sermo de Euch. in Encæniis.] we not to give over to the devil for to do in them what he will[3]?" Item: "When ye come to these mysteries, think not that ye receive the divine body (he meaneth the [In Psal. xxii.] body of Christ) at the hand of man[4]." Once again he saith: "He prepared this table, that daily, for a similitude or likeness of the body and blood of Christ, he should shew unto us in a sacrament bread and wine, after the order of Melchisedech[5]."

[In Dio. i.] Theodoretus also saith: "Our Saviour Christ without doubt changed the names, and gave to the body the name of the sign or token, and to the token he gave the name of the body. And so when he called himself a vine, he called that blood which was the token of blood." And a little after he saith: "The cause is manifest to them that be expert in true religion. For he would that they which be partakers of the godly sacraments should not set their minds upon the nature of things which they see; but by the changing of the names should believe the things which be wrought in them by grace. For he that called that which is his natural body corn and bread, and also called himself a vine; even he also did honour the visible tokens and signs with the names of his body and blood; not changing the nature, but adding grace to nature[6]."

[In Ancor.] Epiphanius saith: "Christ speaking of a loaf, which is round in fashion, and cannot see, hear, nor feel, said of it: 'This is my body'[7]."

[In Joan. Lib. iv. cap. 14.] Cyril saith: "Christ gave to his disciples pieces of bread, saying: 'Take and eat: this is my body.'[8]"

[Lib. i. de Pasch.] Theophilus Alexandrinus saith: "The mystical waters in baptism are consecrate through the coming of the Holy Ghost; and the Lord's bread, wherein the body of our Saviour is shewed and represented, and the which we break for our sanctifying, and the holy cup, which is set on the table of the church, being things without

---

[1 Τί γὰρ λέγω κοινωνίαν, φησίν; αὐτό ἐσμεν ἐκεῖνο τὸ σῶμα. τί γάρ ἐστιν ὁ ἄρτος; σῶμα Χριστοῦ. τί δὲ γίνονται οἱ μεταλαμβάνοντες; σῶμα Χριστοῦ· οὐχὶ σώματα πολλὰ, ἀλλὰ σῶμα ἕν.—Id. In Epist. I. ad Cor. Hom. xxiv. Tom. X. p. 213.]

[2 Εἰ γὰρ μὴ ἀπέθανεν ὁ Ἰησοῦς, τίνος σύμβολα τὰ τελούμενα; ὁρᾷς ὅση γέγονε σπουδὴ, ὥστε ἀεὶ ἀναμιμνήσκεσθαι ὅτι ἀπέθανεν ὑπὲρ ἡμῶν;—Id. in Matt. Hom. lxxxii. Tom. VII. p. 783.]

[3 Si enim vasa sanctificata ad privatos usus transferre peccatum est et periculum, sicut docet nos Balthasar, qui bibens in calicibus sacratis de regno depositus est et de vita: si ergo hæc vasa sanctificata ad privatos usus transferre sic periculosum est, in quibus non est verum corpus Christi, sed mysterium corporis ejus continetur: quanto magis vasa corporis nostri, quæ sibi Deus ad habitaculum præparavit, non debemus locum dare diabolo agendi in eis quod vult?—Id. Op. Imperf. in Matt. Hom. xi. Tom. VI. p. 63.]

[4 Διὸ καὶ προσερχόμενοι, μὴ ὡς ἐξ ἀνθρώπου νομίσητε μεταλαμβάνειν τοῦ θείου σώματος, ἀλλ' ὡς ἐξ αὐτῶν των σεραφὶμ τῃ λαβίδι του πυρὸς, ἥνπερ Ἡσαΐας εἶδε, τοῦ θείου σώματος μεταλαμβάνειν νομίζετε. Id. De Pœnit. Hom. ix. Tom. II. p. 350. See also Op. Lat. Basil. 1547. De Euch. in Encæn. Admon. Sum. Tom. III. col. 919.]

[5 Et quia istam mensam præparavit servis et ancillis in conspectu eorum, et quotidie in similitudinem corporis et sanguinis Christi panem et vinum secundum ordinem Melchisedec nobis ostenderet in sacramento, ideo dicit: Parasti in conspectu meo mensam adversus eos qui tribulant me.—Id. Op. Basil. Expos. Psal. xxii. Tom. I. col. 712.]

[6 Ὁ δέ γε σωτὴρ ὁ ἡμέτερος ἐνήλλαξε τὰ ὀνόματα· καὶ τῷ μὲν σώματι τὸ τοῦ συμβόλου τέθεικεν ὄνομα, τῷ δὲ συμβόλῳ τὸ του σώματος. οὕτως ἄμπελον ἑαυτὸν ὀνομάσας, αἷμα τὸ σύμβολον προσηγόρευσεν ...... δῆλος ὁ σκοπὸς τοῖς τὰ θεῖα μεμυημένοις. ἠβουλήθη γὰρ τοὺς τῶν θείων μυστηρίων μεταλαγχάνοντας, μὴ τῇ φύσει τῶν βλεπομένων προσέχειν, ἀλλὰ διὰ τῆς τῶν ὀνομάτων ἐναλλαγῆς πιστεύειν τῇ ἐκ τῆς χάριτος γεγενημένῃ μεταβολῇ. ὁ γὰρ δὴ τὸ φύσει σῶμα σῖτον καὶ ἄρτον προσαγορεύσας, καὶ αὖ πάλιν ἑαυτὸν ἄμπελον ὀνομάσας, οὗτος τὰ ὁρώμενα σύμβολα τῇ τοῦ σώματος καὶ αἵματος προσηγορίᾳ τετίμηκεν, οὐ τὴν φύσιν μεταβαλὼν, ἀλλὰ τὴν χάριν τῇ φύσει προστεθεικώς.—Theod. Op. Lut. Par. 1642—84. Immut. Dial. I. Tom. IV. pp. 17, 18.]

[7 Τὸ μὲν γάρ ἐστι στρογγυλοειδὲς καὶ ἀναίσθητον, ὡς πρὸς τὴν δύναμιν. καὶ ἠθέλησεν χάριτι εἰπεῖν, τοῦτό μου ἐστὶ τόδε, καὶ οὐδεὶς ἀπιστεῖ τῷ λογῳ.—Epiphan. Op. Par. 1622. Ancorat. 57. Tom. II. p. 60.]

[8 Τοῖς γὰρ ἤδη πεπιστευκόσι διακλάσας τὸν ἄρτον ἐδίδου, λέγων· λάβετε, φάγετε· τοῦτό ἐστι τὸ σῶμά μου.—Cyril. Alex. Op. Lut. 1638. In Joan. Evang. Lib. IV. cap. ii. p. 360. It may be observed that in the old Latin version of Georg. Trapezont. from which most likely Becon quoted, the expression is rendered: fragmenta panis dedit.]

sense or understanding, are sanctified through the invocation and coming of the Holy Ghost[9]."

Gregorius Nazianzenus saith: "Let us be partakers of the passover, and notwithstanding as yet in a figure, although this passover be more plain and evident than the old passover. For the passover of the law, I speak boldly, was a more obscure figure of the figure; but not long hence we shall enjoy it more perfectly and more manifestly, when the Son of God shall drink with us that new (wine) in the kingdom of his Father, revealing and teaching us those things which he hath now but little declared unto us[10]." In Oratione de Pasch.

Athanasius, entreating of the eating of Christ's flesh and drinking of his blood, saith that "for this cause he made mention of his ascension into heaven, to pluck them from corporal phantasy, that they might learn hereafter, that his flesh was called the celestial meat that came from above, and a spiritual food, which he would give. 'For those things which I speak to you,' saith he, 'be spirit and life.' Which is as much to say as, that thing which you see shall be slain and given for the nourishment of the world, that it may be distributed to every body spiritually, and be to all men a conservation unto the resurrection of eternal life[11]." De Peccato in Spiritum Sanctum.

Theophylact saith: "Behold the foolishness of these people (he speaketh of the Capernaites). For it had been their duty to ask and to learn those things which they knew not. But they ran back, and expounded nothing spiritually, but all things as they appeared. For when they heard of flesh, they imagined that he would compel them to become devourers of flesh and blood. But forasmuch as we understand of it spiritually, we are no devourers of flesh, and moreover we are sanctified by such meat." Again he saith: "Forasmuch as we have oftentimes said, they expounding carnally those things which Christ spake were offended, he saith: 'When the things which I speak are spiritually understanded, then do they profit.' For the flesh, that is to say, carnally and fleshly to expound those things, profit nothing, but is made an occasion of offence, &c. The words therefore that I speak are spirit; that is to say, they are spiritual, and life, having in them no carnal and fleshly thing, and bringing everlasting life[12]." In Joan. vi.

These aforesaid authorities alleged out of the books of the ancient learned fathers, both of the Latin and Greek church, do evidently declare, that these words of Christ, "This is my body," "This is my blood," are spiritually and figuratively to be understand, and that they themselves did alway so take and expound them; and in that

---

[9 Dicit enim Spiritum sanctum non operari ea quæ in anima sunt, nec ad irrationabilia pervenire. Quod asserens non recogitat aquas in baptismate mysticas adventu sancti Spiritus consecrari, panemque dominicum, quo Salvatoris corpus ostenditur, et quem frangimus in sanctificationem nostri; et sacrum calicem; quæ in mensa ecclesiæ collocantur, et utique inanima sunt; per invocationem et adventum sancti Spiritus sanctificari.—Theophyl. Alex. in Mag. Biblioth. Vet. Patr. Col. Agrip. 1618—22. Epist. Pasch. i. Tom. IV. p. 712.]

[10 Μεταληψόμεθα δὲ τοῦ πάσχα, νῦν μὲν τυπικῶς ἔτι, καὶ εἰ τοῦ παλαιοῦ γυμνότερον· τὸ γὰρ νομικὸν πάσχα, τολμῶ καὶ λέγω, τύπου τύπος ἦν ἀμυδρότερος· μικρὸν δὲ ὕστερον, τελεώτερον καὶ καθαρώτερον, ἡνίκα ἂν αὐτὸ πίνῃ καινὸν μεθ' ἡμῶν ὁ Λόγος ἐν τῇ βασιλείᾳ τοῦ Πατρὸς, ἀποκαλύπτων καὶ διδάσκων, ἃ νῦν μετρίως παρέδειξεν.—Gregor. Nazianz. Op. Par. 1778—1840. In Sanct. Pasch. Orat. lv. 23. Tom. I. p. 863.]

[11 'Αλλὰ διὰ τοῦτο τῆς εἰς οὐρανοὺς ἀναβάσεως ἐμνημόνευσε τοῦ υἱοῦ τοῦ ἀνθρώπου, ἵνα τῆς σωματικῆς ἐννοίας αὐτοὺς ἀφελκύσῃ, καὶ λοιπὸν τὴν εἰρημένην σάρκα βρῶσιν ἄνωθεν οὐράνιον, καὶ πνευματικὴν τροφὴν παρ' αὐτοῦ διδομένην μάθωσιν· ἃ γὰρ λελάληκα, φησὶν, ὑμῖν, πνεῦμά ἐστι καὶ ζωή· ἴσον τῷ εἰπεῖν, τὸ μὲν δεικνύμενον καὶ διδόμενον ὑπὲρ τῆς τοῦ κόσμου σωτηρίας, ἐστὶν ἡ σὰρξ ἣν ἐγὼ φορῶ· ἀλλ' αὕτη ὑμῖν καὶ τὸ ταύτης αἷμα παρ' ἐμοῦ πνευματικῶς δοθήσεται τροφὴ, ὥστε πνευματικῶς ἐν ἑκάστῳ ταύτην ἀναδίδοσθαι, καὶ γίνεσθαι πᾶσι φυλακτήριον εἰς ἀνάστασιν ζωῆς αἰωνίου.—Athanas. Op. Par. 1698. Epist. iv. ad Serapion. 19. Tom. I. Pars II. p. 710.]

[12 "Ορα δὲ ἀνοησίαν· δέον γὰρ ἐρωτῆσαι, καὶ μαθεῖν τὰ ἀγνοούμενα, οἱ δὲ ἀποπηδῶσι, καὶ οὐδὲν πνευματικῶς ἐκλαμβάνονται, ἀλλὰ πάντα κατὰ τὸ φαινόμενον. ἐπεὶ γὰρ σάρκα ἤκουον, ἐνόμιζον, ὅτι σαρκοφάγους αὐτοὺς ἀναγκάζει γενέσθαι καὶ αἱμοβόρους. οἱ δὲ πνευματικῶς νοοῦντες ἡμεῖς οὔτε σαρκοφάγοι ἐσμὲν, καὶ μᾶλλον ἁγιαζόμεθα διὰ τῆς τοιαύτης τροφῆς...... ἐπειδὴ, ὡς πολλάκις εἴπομεν, σαρκικῶς ἐκλαμβάνοντες τὰ λεγόμενα παρὰ τοῦ Χριστοῦ ἐσκανδαλίζοντο, φησὶν, ὅτι τὸ πνευματικῶς νοεῖν τὰ λεγόμενα παρ' ἐμοῦ, τοῦτό ἐστι τὸ ὠφελοῦν. ἡ δὲ σὰρξ, τουτέστι, τὸ σαρκικῶς αὐτὰ ἐκδέχεσθαι, οὐδὲν ὠφελεῖ, ἀλλὰ σκανδάλου ἀφορμὴ γίνεται. οὕτω δὴ αὐτοὶ σαρκικῶς ἀκούοντες τῶν παρὰ Χριστοῦ λεγομένων, ἐσκανδαλίζοντο. ἐπιφέρει οὖν, ὅτι τὰ ῥήματα ἃ ἐγὼ λαλῶ, πνεῦμά ἐστι, τουτέστι, πνευματικά ἐστι, καὶ ζωή ἐστιν, οὐδὲν ἔχοντα σαρκικὸν, καὶ ζωὴν προξενοῦντα αἰώνιον.—Theophyl. Op. Venet. 1754—63. In Joan. Comm. cap. vi. Tom. I. p. 597.]

sense their words remained in the church of Christ a long time after, even unto the time of pope Nicholas the second, which lived in the year of our Lord one thousand[1] and fifty-eight, which first of all taught the gross and corporal presence of Christ in the sacrament, affirming that after the words of consecration the body of Christ was so present, that it was handled and broken with the hands of the priest, and crushed and torn on pieces with teeth of the faithful communicants. Afterward, about the year of our Lord one thousand two hundred and fifteen, pope Innocentius the third did not only affirm that the body of Christ lurked under the kinds of bread and wine, and was handled and broken with the hands of the priest, yea, and crushed and torn on pieces with the teeth of the communicants, according to the doctrine of pope Nicholas the second; but also he decreed by general council, that the sacramental bread was turned into the natural substance of Christ's body, and the sacramental wine into the natural substance of the blood of Christ; so that from that time unto this present age this wicked doctrine of Christ's bodily presence in the sacrament hath so prevailed, that few have espied the truth of God's holy word in this behalf: which thing is the alone occasion that many even at this present day remain and abide still in their old error and blindness.

Father. God have mercy on us and bless us, and lighten his countenance upon us, that we here on earth may know his ways and his saving health among all nations! *Son.* Amen.

Father. Methink that this one rule, which the learned inculk and beat in all their preachings and writings, might seem to appease the contention of all men in this behalf.

Son. What is that?

Note this well. *Father.* When one sentence of the holy scripture seem to repugn a multitude of sentences, the one sentence ought to give place to the multitude, and not to destroy the verity of the other. As for an example, this one sentence, "This is my body," grossly taken and fleshly understand, yea, and received after the literal sense, seemeth to teach that the natural, corporal, real, substantial, and essential body of Christ is in the sacrament: but if we consider the other places of the holy scripture, which are many in number, affirming plainly that Christ as concerning his corporal presence is not on earth, but in heaven, and so in heaven that he neither is or yet shall be in any other place until the day of judgment; we shall easily grant that it is but a sacramental and figurative speech, and confess that this one sentence ought to give place to a multitude; so that the sacrament is called Christ's body, because it signifieth and representeth to us the body of Christ, and not that it is so in deed and in truth.

Son. It is truly said. For sacraments and signs in the holy scripture, yea, and in our daily speech also, are called by the names of the things which they signify, as we have tofore heard. But as we may draw to an end in this matter, would God all men would at all times remember this good lesson of St Augustine!

De Doctrina Christ. Lib. iii. cap. 6. "Seldom," saith he, "is any difficulty in proper words, but either the circumstance of the place, or the conferring of divers translations, or else the original tongue wherein it was written, will make the sense plain; but in words that be altered from their proper[2] signification, there is great diligence and heed to be taken. And specially we must beware that we take not literally any thing that is spoken figuratively." "Nor contrariwise we must not take for a figure any thing that is spoken properly. Therefore must be declared," saith St Austin, "the manner how to discern a proper speech from a figurative. Wherein," saith he, "must be observed this rule, that if the thing which is spoken be to the furtherance of charity, then is it a proper speech, ☞ and no figure." "So that if it be a commandment that forbiddeth any evil or wicked act, or commandeth any good or beneficial thing, then it is no figure. But if it command any evil or wicked thing, or forbid any thing that is good and beneficial, then John vi. is it a figurative speech. Now this saying of Christ, 'Except ye eat the flesh of the

[[1] The folio has 158.—For popes Nicholas and Innocentius, see before, p. 260, note 2, and 264, n. 3.]
[[2] Folio, *prayer*.]

Son of man, and drink his blood, ye shall have no life in you,' seemeth to command an heinous and a wicked thing; therefore it is a figure, commanding us to be partakers of Christ's passion, keeping in our minds to our great comfort and profit, that his flesh was crucified and wounded for us[3]." Again he saith: "The Lord and the teaching of his apostles hath given to us a few signs for many, and those most easy to be done, most excellent in understanding, and in performing most pure; as the sacrament of baptism, and the celebration of the body and blood of the Lord; which every man, when he receiveth, knoweth whereunto they be referred, being taught that he worship not them with a carnal bondage, but rather with a spiritual freedom. And as it is a vile bondage to follow the letter, and to take the signs for the things signified by them; so to interpret the signs to no profit is an error that shrewdly spreadeth abroad[4]."

De Doctrina Christ. Lib. ix. cap. 9.

Father. These sentences of St Augustine, if they were diligently noted, weighed, pondered, and considered, might soon put away the too much uncharitable contention, strife, and debate, which (alas for sorrow!) reigneth now-a-days among men concerning the corporal presence of Christ in the sacrament; while every one with tooth and nail goeth about to defend his own assertion, little regarding what the apostles of Christ and the ancient fathers of Christ's church have taught in this behalf. But come off, my son, seeing we have sufficiently talked for this present of this matter, let us fall in hand with the third error, which thou notedst in the doctrine of the papists concerning the Lord's supper.

Son. The papists teach, that not only the faithful and godly, but also the unfaithful and wicked, eat and drink in the sacrament the body and blood of Christ.

The third error of the papists in the doctrine of the sacrament.

Father. And what sayest thou, my son, to this their doctrine? Is it to be allowed?

Son. Nothing less; forasmuch as it is contrary both to the doctrine of Christ and to the teaching of the ancient fathers. And, notwithstanding, the papists are fallen to such impudency and unshamefacedness, while they affirm the corporal presence of Christ in the sacrament, that they shame not to say, that not only the wicked and ungodly, but also the brute beasts, as the mouse, the cat, the rat, the weasel, &c. eating the sacrament, eat also the very true and natural body of Christ, as he was born of Mary the virgin, and hanged on the cross; which is so monstrous doctrine, that nothing can be invented more prodigious or monster-like.

Father. Let me hear it proved by the word of God, that the wicked and ungodly eat not the flesh of Christ, nor drink his blood. *Son*. Christ himself, which is not only true, but also the self truth, saith thus: "I am that living bread which came down from heaven. If any man eat of this bread, he shall live for ever. And the bread which I shall give is my flesh, which I shall give for the life of the world." "Verily, verily, I say unto you, Except ye eat the flesh of the Son of man, and drink his blood, ye shall not have life in you. But whosoever eateth my flesh, and drinketh

John vi.

[[3] Rarissime igitur et difficillime inveniri potest ambiguitas in propriis verbis, quantum ad libros divinarum scripturarum spectat, quam non aut circumstantia ipsa sermonis qua cognoscitur scriptorum intentio, aut interpretum collatio, aut præcedentis linguæ solvat inspectio. Sed verborum translatorum ambiguitates, de quibus deinceps loquendum est, non mediocrem curam industriamque desiderant. Nam in principio cavendum est, ne figuratam locutionem ad literam accipias...... Huic autem observationi, qua cavemus figuratam locutionem, id est translatam, quasi propriam sequi, adjungenda etiam illa est, ne propriam quasi figuratam velimus accipere. Demonstrandus est igitur prius modus inveniendæ locutionis, propriane an figurata sit. Et iste omnino modus est, ut quidquid in sermone divino neque ad morum honestatem neque ad fidei veritatem proprie referri potest, figuratum esse cognoscas...... Si præceptiva locutio est aut flagitium aut facinus vetans, aut utilitatem aut beneficentiam jubens, non est figurata. Si autem flagitium aut facinus videtur jubere, aut utilitatem aut beneficentiam vetare, figurata est. Nisi manducaveritis, inquit, carnem Filii hominis et sanguinem biberitis, non habebitis vitam in vobis. Facinus vel flagitium videtur jubere: figura est ergo, præcipiens passioni dominicæ communicandum, et suaviter atque utiliter recondendum in memoria, quod pro nobis caro ejus crucifixa et vulnerata sit.—August. Op. Par. 1679—1700. De Doctr. Christ. Lib. III. 8, 9, 14, 24. Tom. III. Pars I. cols. 47, 9, 52.]

[[4] ...... quædam pauca pro multis, eademque factu facillima, et intellectu augustissima, et observatione castissima ipse Dominus et apostolica tradidit disciplina: sicuti est baptismi sacramentum, et celebratio corporis et sanguinis Domini. Quæ unusquisque cum percipit, quo referantur imbutus agnoscit, ut ea non carnali servitute, sed spiritali potius libertate veneretur. Ut autem literam sequi, et signa pro rebus quæ iis significantur accipere, servilis infirmitatis est; ita inutiliter signa interpretari, male vagantis erroris est.—Id. Ibid. 13. col. 49.]

my blood, hath everlasting life; and I will raise him up at the last day. For my flesh is meat indeed, and my blood is drink indeed. He that eateth my flesh, and drinketh my blood, dwelleth in me, and I in him. As the living Father hath sent me, even so live I by my Father; and he that eateth me shall live by me. This is the bread which came down from heaven; not as your fathers have eaten manna, and are dead: he that eateth of this bread shall live for ever." Again he saith: "I am that bread of life. He that cometh to me shall not hunger, and he that believeth on me shall never thirst," &c.

The wicked and unfaithful neither eat nor drink the body and blood of Christ.

Of these words of our Lord and Saviour Jesus Christ it is manifest, plain, and evident, that the virtue and power of his flesh and blood is so great and mighty, that whosoever eateth and drinketh thereof shall live for ever, and have everlasting life. But the wicked and unfaithful, although they eat the sacramental bread and drink the sacramental wine, have not everlasting life, as we have Judas for an example: therefore it followeth, that the wicked and unfaithful do not eat nor drink the body and blood of Christ.

Again Christ saith: "He that eateth my flesh, and drinketh my blood, dwelleth in me, and I in him." But the wicked and unfaithful dwell not in Christ, nor Christ in them; therefore the wicked and unfaithful neither eat nor drink the body and blood of Christ, although they daily receive the sacraments and signs of them, as

In Sententiis Prosp.

St Augustine saith: "He receiveth the meat of life, and drinketh the everlasting cup, that dwelleth in Christ, and in whom Christ dwelleth. For he that agreeth not with Christ doth neither eat the flesh of Christ, nor drink his blood, although to the condemnation of his presumption he receive every day the sacrament of so high a matter. ☞ For this is to eat that bread of life, even to believe in Christ, that is to say, by love to be incorporate in him. Therefore, forasmuch as the reprobate hath not believed in him, he hath not eaten him; and so he had not the faith of the Christians, whereby alone sins are released[1]."

Father. These words are very plain, and cannot justly be denied; of the which we learn truly, that not the unfaithful, but the faithful, not the wicked, but the godly-disposed only, eat and drink the body and blood of Christ. Notwithstanding, I would also in this behalf gladly hear the judgment of the ancient fathers and old writers, that we may be well assured, even by their testimonies also, that this is no new doctrine, to teach that the godly only eat Christ, and not the wicked; the faithful, and not the unfaithful; the members of Christ, and not the members of Satan.

In Matt. cap. xv.

Son. The ancient writer Origen hath these words: "The Word was made flesh and very meat, which whoso eateth shall surely live for ever, which no evil man can eat. For if it could be that he that continueth evil might eat the Word made flesh, seeing that he is the Word and bread of life, it should not have been written,

John vi.
In Levit. cap. vi. Hom. 4.

'Whosoever eateth this bread shall live for ever[2]'." Again he saith: "The one and perfect sacrifice is Christ offered. If any man touch the flesh of this sacrifice, he is made holy straightways[3]."

In Serm. de Cœna Dom.

St Cyprian saith: "None do eat of this Lamb, but such as be true Israelites[4]," that is to say, pure christian men, without colour or dissimulation.

In Esai. cap. lxvi.

St Hierome saith: "All that be lovers more of pleasure than of God eat not the

---

[[1] Escam vitæ accipit, et æternitatis poculum bibit, qui in Christo manet, et cujus Christus habitator est. Nam qui discordat a Christo, nec carnem ejus manducat, nec sanguinem bibit: etiam si tantæ rei sacramentum ad judicium suæ præsumptionis quotidie indifferenter accipiat.—Id. Prosp. Lib. Sentent. ex August. cccxli. Tom. X. Appendix, col. 247. See also In Johan. Evang. cap. vi. Tractat. xxvi. 18: below, page 293, note 11.]

[[2] Πολλὰ δ' ἂν καὶ περὶ αὐτοῦ λέγοιτο τοῦ Λόγου, ὃς γέγονε σὰρξ, καὶ ἀληθινὴ βρῶσις, ἥν τινα ὁ φαγὼν πάντως ζήσεται εἰς τὸν αἰῶνα, οὐδενὸς δυναμένου φαύλου ἐσθίειν αὐτήν· εἰ γὰρ οἷόν τε ἦν ἔτι φαῦλον μένοντα ἐσθίειν τὸν γενόμενον σάρκα, Λόγον ὄντα καὶ ἄρτον ζῶντα, οὐκ ἂν ἐγέγραπτο, ὅτι πᾶς ὁ φαγὼν τὸν ἄρτον τοῦτον ζήσεται εἰς τὸν αἰῶνα.—Orig. Op. Par. 1733—59. Comm. in Matt. Tom. xi. Tom. III. p. 500.]

[[3] Igitur sacrificium, pro quo hæc omnia sacrificia in typo et figura præcesserant, unum, et perfectum, immolatus est Christus. Hujus sacrificii carnem si quis tetigerit, continuo sanctificatur.—Id. In Levit. Hom. iv. 8. Tom. II. p. 203.]

[[4] Una est domus ecclesiæ, in qua agnus editur; nullus ei communicat, quem Israelitici nominis generositas non commendat.—Cypr. Op. Oxon. 1682. De Cœn. Dom. (Arnold.) Appendix, p. 42.]

flesh of Jesu, nor drink his blood, of the which himself saith: 'He that eateth my flesh, and drinketh my blood, hath everlasting life[5].'" Again he saith: "Heretics eat not the flesh of Jesu, whose flesh is the meat of faithful men[6]." Also in another place he saith: "They eat this bread which are strong in Christ, &c. And they drink this wine which are virgins, holy both in body and in spirit[7]." John vi. In Hiere. cap. xxii. In Zach. cap. ix.

St Ambrose saith: "Jesus is the bread, which is the meat of saints, and he that taketh this bread dieth not the death of a sinner. For this bread is the remission of sins[8]." And in another place he saith: "He that did eat manna died; but he that eateth this body shall have remission of his sins, and shall not die for ever[9]." De Bened. Patriarch. cap. ix. De Sac. Lib. iv. cap. 5.

St Augustine saith: "They cannot be both the members of Christ and the members of an harlot. For he saith: 'He that eateth my flesh, and drinketh my blood, dwelleth in me, and I in him.' Here doth he shew what it is, not sacramentally, but truly and effectually, to eat the body of Christ, even to dwell in him. He that dwelleth not in Christ, let him not say or think that he eateth the body of Christ, forasmuch as he is not of his body. He is not a member of Christ, which maketh himself a member of an harlot[10]." Also in another place he saith: "This is to eat that meat, and to drink that drink, even for a man to dwell in Christ, and to have Christ dwelling in him. And therefore he that dwelleth not in Christ, and in whom Christ dwelleth not, without doubt he neither eateth spiritually his flesh, nor drinketh his blood, although carnally and visibly[11] he bite the sacrament of Christ's body and blood; but he rather eateth and drinketh the sacrament of so worthy a thing unto his own damnation." Item: "They judge truly that say, that he eateth not the body of Christ, which is not in the body of Christ. Neither are they counted to eat the body of Christ, forasmuch as they are not reckoned among the members of Christ[12]." Once again he saith: "The heretics that are without the church may have the sacrament; but the matter of the sacrament they cannot have[13]." De Civ. Dei, Lib. xxi. c. 25. John vi. In Joan. Tract. 26. De Civit. Dei, Lib. xxi. c. 25. Ad Bonifacium.

Hilarius saith: "These things taken and received (he speaketh of the body and blood of Christ) make that both we are in Christ, and Christ in us[14]." De Trinit. Lib. viii.

[5 Omnes voluptatis magis amatores, quam amatores Dei......nec comedunt carnem Jesu, neque bibunt sanguinem ejus. De quo ipse loquitur: Qui comedit carnem meam, et bibit sanguinem meum, habet vitam æternam.—Hieron. Op. Par. 1693-1706. Comm. Lib. XVIII. in Isai. cap. lxvi. Tom. III. col. 506.]

[6 Possumus autem hunc locum juxta anagogen contra hæreticos accipere...Quodque infert, Non comedent et non bibent, subauditur corpus et sanguinem Salvatoris.—Id. Comm. Lib. IV. in Jerem. Proph. cap. xxii. cols. 630, 1.]

[7 Hunc panem comedunt, qui in Christo robusti sunt...Qui frumentum est electorum, sive juvenum, ipse est et vinum quod lætificat cor hominis; et bibitur ab his virginibus, quæ sunt sanctæ et corpore et spiritu.—Id. Comm. Lib. II. in Zach. Proph. cap. ix. col. 1763.]

[8 Hic ergo panis factus est esca sanctorum......qui autem accipit, non morietur peccatoris morte, quia panis hic remissio peccatorum est.—Ambros. Op. Par. 1686—90. De Bened. Patriarch. Lib. cap. ix. 38, 9. Tom. I. cols. 524, 5.]

[9 Deinde manna qui manducavit, mortuus est: qui manducaverit hoc corpus, fiet ei remissio peccatorum, et non morietur in æternum.—Id. De Sacram. Lib. IV. cap. v. 24. Tom. II. col. 372.]

[10 Ut enim alia taceam, non possunt simul esse et membra Christi et membra meretricis. Denique ipse dicens, Qui manducat carnem meam, et bibit sanguinem meum, in me manet, et ego in eo; ostendit quid sit non sacramento tenus, sed re vera corpus Christi manducare, et ejus sanguinem bibere: hoc est enim in Christo manere, ut in illo maneat et Christus. Sic enim hoc dixit, tamquam diceret, Qui non in me manet, et in quo ego non maneo, non se dicat aut existimet manducare corpus meum, aut bibere sanguinem meum. Non itaque manent in Christo, qui non sunt membra ejus. Non sunt autem membra Christi, qui se faciunt membra meretricis.—August. Op. Par. 1679-1700. De Civ. Dei, Lib. XXI. cap. xxv. 4. Tom. VII. cols. 646, 7.]

[11 Folio, *invisibly*.—Hoc est ergo manducare illam escam, et illum bibere potum, in Christo manere, et illum manentem in se habere. Ac per hoc qui non manet in Christo, et in quo non manet Christus, procul dubio nec manducat spiritaliter carnem ejus, nec bibit ejus sanguinem, licet carnaliter et visibiliter premat dentibus sacramentum corporis et sanguinis Christi; sed magis tantæ rei sacramentum ad judicium sibi manducat et bibit.—Id. In Johan. Evang. cap. vi. Tractat. XXVI. 18. Tom. III. Pars II. col. 501. See the 29th Article of our Church.]

[12 .... recte intelligunt, non dicendum esse eum manducare corpus Christi, qui in corpore non est Christi......Nec isti ergo dicendi sunt manducare corpus Christi; quoniam nec in membris computandi sunt Christi.—Id. De Civ. Dei, Lib. XXI. cap. xxv. 3, 4. Tom. VII. col. 646.]

[13 Isti autem cum quibus agimus, vel de quibus agimus, non sunt desperandi: adhuc enim sunt in corpore: sed non quærant Spiritum sanctum, nisi in Christi corpore, cujus habent foris sacramentum, sed rem ipsam non tenent intus cujus est illud sacramentum; et ideo sibi judicium manducant et bibunt. —Id. Lib. de Corr. Donatist. seu Epist. ad Bonifac. clxxxv. 50. Tom. II. col. 663.]

[14 De veritate carnis et sanguinis non relictus est ambigendi locus. Nunc enim et ipsius Domini pro-

In Joan. cap. x.

Cyril saith: "The fathers which did eat manna died, because they received thereby no strength to live ever (for it gave no life, but only put away bodily hunger); but they that receive the bread of life shall obtain immortality, and shall eschew all evils of destruction, and for ever live with Christ[1]." Again: "He that eateth the flesh of Christ hath everlasting life[2]." Once again: "When we eat the flesh of Christ, then have we life in us. For if through the touching of Christ's body alone things corrupt were made whole, how then shall we not live, which both taste and eat his flesh[3]?"

In Joan. cap. xv. In Joan. cap. xiv.

And in a certain gloss recited in the pope's law, we read thus: "As in baptism Christ is put on sometime sacramentally, and sometime unto the sanctification of life (the first is common both to good and bad, but the second is proper only to the ☞ good); so likewise Christ is eaten of evil persons sacramentally only: but of the good he is received both sacramentally and spiritually, and of all the faithful spiritually[4]."

All these testimonies of the ancient writers, diligently considered, declare manifestly that not the wicked and unfaithful, but the godly and faithful persons only eat the body and drink the blood of Christ. The ungodly eat the sacrament; but they eat not Christ, which is signified by the sacrament, as St Augustine writeth of Judas: "The apostles," saith he, "did eat bread, that was the Lord; but Judas did eat but the bread of the Lord, and not the bread that was the Lord[5]." For whosoever eateth Christ liveth for ever, dwelleth in Christ and Christ in him, is incorporated and made all one with Christ, is made a member of Christ's body, is sanctified and made holy, is made clean both in body and soul, dieth not the death of a sinner, hath remission of his sins, obtaineth immortality, escheweth all evils of death, and for ever liveth with Christ. But none of all these things chance to the unfaithful and wicked persons; therefore eat they not the body of Christ, nor yet drink his blood.

In Joan. Tract. 59.

What it is to eat Christ.

Father. I would gladly hear what it is to eat Christ. *Son.* Christ is eaten or received two manner of ways; that is to say, sacramentally and spiritually. He is received or eaten sacramentally, when we eat and drink the sacramental bread and wine, according to the institution of Christ; which thing is done not only of the faithful, but also of the unfaithful. He is also eaten or received spiritually, when we believe in Christ, embrace him as our alone Saviour, put our whole hope, trust, and confidence of our redemption and salvation in that one and alone sacrifice, which Christ offered upon the altar of the cross, having his body there broken, and his blood there shed, for the remission of our sin: again, when we earnestly consider in our minds the passion and death of Christ, with all the benefits thereof, chawing and digesting them with the stomach of our heart, be thankful for them to God the Father, and labour to the uttermost of our power to live worthy his kindness, daily increasing more and more in all godliness and honesty. And after this manner

---

fessione et fide nostra vere caro est, et vere sanguis est. Et hæc accepta atque hausta id efficiunt, ut et nos in Christo, et Christus in nobis sit.—Hilar. Op. Par. 1693. De Trin. Lib. VIII. 14. col. 956.]

[1 Οὐκοῦν οἱ μὲν φαγόντες τὸ μάννα, φησὶ, τετελευτήκασιν, ὡς οὐδεμιᾶς δηλονότι ζωῆς μετουσίαν παρ' αὐτοῦ δεξάμενοι· οὐ γὰρ ἦν ὄντως ζωοποιὸν, λιμοῦ δὲ μᾶλλον ἐπίκουρον σαρκικοῦ, καὶ ὡς ἐν τύπῳ τοῦ ἀληθεστέρου παραληφθέν. οἱ δὲ τὸν ἄρτον ἐν ἑαυτοῖς εἰσκομίζοντες τῆς ζωῆς, γέρας ἕξουσι τὴν ἀθανασίαν, φθορᾶς τε καὶ τῶν ἐκ ταύτης κακῶν παντελῶς ἀλογήσαντες, πρὸς ἀμήρυτόν τε καὶ ἀτελεύτητον βίου τοῦ κατὰ Χριστὸν ἀναβήσονται μῆκος.—Cyril. Alex. Op. Lut. 1638. In Joan. Evang. Lib. IV. cap. ii. Tom. IV. p. 351.]

[2 Οὐκοῦν ὁ τρώγων τὴν ἁγίαν σάρκα Χριστοῦ ζωὴν αἰώνιον ἔχει.—Id. ibid. p. 363.]

[3 Καὶ ἐπείπερ ζωοποιὸς γέγονε τοῦ Σωτῆρος ἡ σὰρξ, ἅτε δὴ τῇ κατὰ φύσιν ἡνωμένη ζωῇ, τῷ ἐκ Θεοῦ δηλονότι λόγῳ, ὅταν αὐτῆς ἀπογευσώμεθα, τότε τὴν ζωὴν ἔχομεν ἐν ἑαυτοῖς συνενούμενοι καὶ ἡμεῖς αὐτῇ, καθάπερ οὖν αὐτὴ τῷ ἐνοικήσαντι λόγῳ ......καὶ εἰ διὰ μόνης ἀφῆς τῆς ἁγίας σαρκὸς ζωοποιεῖται τὸ ἐφθαρμένον, πῶς οὐχὶ πλουσιωτέραν ἀποκερδανοῦμεν τὴν ζωοποιὸν εὐλογίαν, ὅταν αὐτῆς καὶ ἀπογευσώμεθα;—Id. ibid. p. 361.]

[4 Nam sicut in baptismo induitur Christus interdum sacramento tenus, interdum quoad vitæ sanctificationem (primum bonorum et malorum est commune, secundum bonorum et piorum: sed secundum est proprium bonorum); sic a malis manducatur Christus sacramentaliter tantum, a bonis vero sacramentaliter et spiritualiter, et ab omnibus credentibus spiritualiter.—Decret. Gratiani, Par. 1583. Decr. Tert. Pars, De Consecr. Dist. ii. Glossa in can. 59. col. 2396.]

[5 Illi manducabant panem Dominum, ille panem Domini contra Dominum: illi vitam, ille pœnam.—August. Op. Par. 1679-1700. In Johan. Evang. cap. xiii. Tractat. LIX. 1. Tom. III. Pars II. col. 663.]

the godly and faithful only eat and receive Christ. Other eating or receiving of Christ there is none.

Father. Why, is not the very natural body of Christ eaten of the communicants both faithful and unfaithful at the Lord's supper? *Son.* Christ is only received and eaten of the faithful communicants: the unfaithful receive not the body and blood of Christ, but the sacraments of the same only, yea, and that unto their damnation. 1 Cor. xi.

Father. And is Christ received corporally with the corporal mouth of the faithful communicants? *Son.* The natural body of Christ is only in heaven; and, notwithstanding, the soul of the faithful communicant with her mouth, that is to say, with faith, doth truly and unfeignedly feed upon it unto her great joy and comfort, and feeleth no less true refection than the body doth by receiving corporal food; yea, the faithful communicant, thus eating and receiving Christ, receiveth both in body and soul an heavenly nourishment, a singular comfort, and an unoutspeakable joy.

Father. Faith then is the mouth of the soul, wherewith Christ is received and eaten. *Son.* Yea, verily, as Christ saith: "I am that bread of life. He that cometh John vi.
unto me shall not hunger, and he that believeth in me shall never thirst."

Hereto pertaineth the saying of St Augustine: "Why dost thou prepare thy teeth In Joan. Tract. 25.
and thy belly? Believe, and thou hast eaten[6]." "For to believe in him is to eat the bread of life. He that believeth in him eateth him[7]."

Likewise saith St Cyprian: "So oft as we do these things (he speaketh of receiv- In Serm. de Cœna Dom.
ing the mysteries of the body and blood of Christ), we whet not our teeth to bite, but with pure faith we break the holy bread[8]."

Hereto agreeth the saying of Eusebius Emissenus, which lived about three hundred years after Christ's ascension: "When thou dost go up to the reverend altar to feed In Serm. de Euchar.
upon spiritual meat, look upon the holy body and blood of thy God with thy faith, De Consec. dist. 2.
honour him, touch him with thy mind, take him with the hand of thy heart, and chiefly drink him with the draught of thy inward man[9]."

Chrysostom also saith: "'Where the dead corpse is', saith Christ, 'thither will the In 1 Cor. cap. x.
eagles resort'. The dead corpse is the body of the Lord, because he died. For Hom. 24.
except he had fallen, we had never risen again. He nameth eagles, to declare that he that cometh to this body, must climb up on high, and have nothing to do with the earth, nor to be drawn unto the things beneath and to creep; but always to fly up unto the things that are above, and to look upon the Sun of righteousness, and to have a most quick and sharp eye of the mind. For this is a table of eagles, and not of jays[10]".

And in the Nicene council we are admonished "not to look down unto the bread Concil. Nicen.
and the cup that are set on the Lord's table; but to lift up our minds, and with our faith to consider the Lamb of God that taketh away the sins of the world[11]".

Bertrammus saith, speaking of the body and blood of Christ: "It is a spiritual In Lib. de Corp. et
meat, and a spiritual drink, spiritually feeding the soul, and giving the life of ever- Sang. Dom.

[6 Ut quid paras dentes et ventrem? Crede, et manducasti.—Id. In Johan. Evang. cap. vi. Tractat. xxv. 12. Tom. III. Pars II. col. 489.]

[7 Credere enim in eum, hoc est manducare panem vivum. Qui credit, manducat: invisibiliter saginatur, quia invisibiliter renascitur.—Id. Tractat. xxvi. 1. col. 494.]

[8 Hæc quotiens agimus, non dentes ad mordendum acuimus, sed fide sincera panem sanctum frangimus et partimur.—Cypr. Op. Oxon. 1682. De Cœn. Dom. (Arnold.) p. 44.]

[9 ...... ita cum reverendum altare cœlestibus cibis satiandus ascendis, sacrum Dei tui corpus et sanguinem fide respice, honora, mirare, mente continge, cordis manu suscipe, et maxime haustu interiore assume.—Euseb. Emiss. in Decret. Gratiani, Decr. Tert. Pars, De Consecr. Dist. ii. can. 35. cols. 2377, 8.]

[10 Ὅπου γὰρ τὸ πτῶμά, φησιν, ἐκεῖ καὶ οἱ ἀετοὶ, πτῶμα καλῶν τὸ σῶμα διὰ τὸν θάνατον. εἰ μὴ γὰρ ἐκεῖνος ἔπεσεν, ἡμεῖς οὐκ ἀνέστημεν. ἀετοὺς δὲ καλεῖ, δεικνὺς ὅτι καὶ ὑψηλὸν εἶναι δεῖ τὸν προσιόντα τῷ σώματι τούτῳ, καὶ μηδὲν πρὸς τὴν γῆν κοινὸν ἔχειν, μηδὲ κάτω σύρεσθαι καὶ ἕρπειν, ἀλλ' ἄνω πέτεσθαι διηνεκῶς, καὶ πρὸς τὸν ἥλιον τῆς δικαιοσύνης ἐνορᾷν, καὶ ὀξυδερκὲς τὸ ὄμμα τῆς διανοίας ἔχειν. ἀετῶν γὰρ, οὐ κολοιῶν, αὕτη ἡ τράπεζα. Chrysost. Op. Par. 1718—38. In Epist. I. ad Cor. Hom. xxiv. Tom. X. p. 216.]

[11 'Επὶ τῆς θείας τραπέζης πάλιν κἀνταῦθα μὴ τῷ προκειμένῳ ἄρτῳ καὶ τῷ ποτηρίῳ ταπεινῶς προσέχωμεν· ἀλλ' ὑψώσαντες ἡμῶν τὴν διάνοιαν, πίστει νοήσωμεν κεῖσθαι ἐπὶ τῆς ἱερᾶς ἐκείνης τραπέζης τὸν ἀμνὸν τοῦ Θεοῦ, τὸν αἴροντα τὴν ἁμαρτίαν τοῦ κόσμου, ἀθύτως ὑπὸ τῶν ἱερέων θυόμενον.—Gelas. Hist. Concil. Nic. in Concil. Stud. Labbei. Lut. Par. 1671-2. cap. xxx. Tom. II. col. 233.]

John vi. lasting satiety, as our Saviour himself, commending this mystery, saith: 'It is the Spirit that quickeneth; for the flesh profiteth nothing[1].'"

De Consec. Dist. 2. Glossa in cap. Quid est. In the pope's own law we read thus: "Christ is eaten two manner of ways: one way sacramentally, which chanceth both to the good and to the bad: another way, when he is received by faith and love working together; and this belongeth only to the good[2]."

Father. I perceive now right well, that Christ's natural body is not eaten, as the papists teach, with the mouth of the body, but with the mouth of the soul, which is faith. *Son*. It is truth. For thus read we in the book of the pope's canons: De Consec. Dist. 2. cap. Utrum. *Christum fas vorari dentibus non est;* that is to say, "Christ cannot be devoured with teeth[3]."

In Joan. Tract. 25. As St Austin likewise saith, as we tofore heard: "Why dost thou prepare the teeth and the belly? Believe, and thou hast eaten." "For to believe in him is to eat
In Ps. xcviii. the bread of life. He that believeth in him eateth him[4]." Again he saith: "When
John vi. the Lord spake of his flesh, and said, 'Except a man eat my flesh, he hath not everlasting life in him,' his disciples were offended (peradventure they were seventy), and said, 'This is an hard saying: who can away with this? And they went away from him, and walked no more with him.' This seemed hard unto them, that he saith: 'Except a man eat my flesh, he shall not have everlasting life.' They took it foolishly: they understood it carnally: they thought that the Lord would have cut off certain pieces from his body and given them; and therefore they said, 'This is an hard saying.' Notwithstanding they were hard, and not the saying. Yet he instructed them, and said unto them: 'It is the Spirit that quickeneth: the flesh profiteth nothing. The words which I have spoken to you are spirit and life.' Understand you spiritually the thing that I have spoken unto you. This body that ye see shall ye not eat, neither shall ye drink that blood which they shall shed that shall crucify me. I have set forth unto you a certain sacrament, which, being spiritually understanded, shall quicken you, or make you alive[5]."

Father. If Christ be not otherwise truly eaten than with the mouth of the soul, which is faith, and if the faithful alone eat the body of Christ, and drink his blood, how cometh it to pass that we sometime read in ancient fathers, that the wicked
De Bapt. contra Donat. cap. 8. also eat the body of Christ? St Austin saith on this wise: "Judas received the body and blood of the Lord[6]," &c. *Son*. You heard before, that sacraments in the holy scripture have the names of the things that are signified by them. After the same

---

[1 ......quoniam spiritualis est esca, et spiritualis potus, spiritualiter animam pascens, et æternæ satietatis vitam tribuens; sicut ipse Salvator mysterium hoc commendans, loquitur: Spiritus est, qui vivificat, nam caro nihil prodest.—Ratram. Lib. de Corp. et Sang. Dom. Oxon. 1838. cap. ci. pp. 51, 2.]

[2 Duobus modis manducatur Christus. uno modo sacramentaliter, quod competit bonis et malis: alio modo spiritualiter, cum per fidem et dilectionem cooperantem accipitur. hoc est tantum bonorum. —Decret. Gratiani, Decr. Tert. Pars, De Consecr. Dist. ii. Glossa in can. 46. col. 2386.]

[3 Sed quia Christum vorari dentibus fas non est, voluit Dominus hunc panem et vinum in mysterio vere carnem suam et sanguinem suum consecratione Spiritus sancti potentialiter creari, et quotidie pro mundi vita mystice immolari.—Id. Dist. ii. can. 72. cols. 2405, 6.]

[4 See the preceding page, notes 6, 7.]

[5 Tunc autem, quando hoc Dominus commendavit, de carne sua locutus erat, et dixerat, Nisi quis manducaverit carnem meam, non habebit in se vitam æternam. Scandalizati sunt discipuli ejus quidam, septuaginta ferme, et dixerunt, Durus est hic sermo, quis potest eum intelligere? Et recesserunt ab eo, et amplius cum eo non ambulaverunt. Durum illis visum est quod ait, Nisi quis manducaverit carnem meam, non habebit vitam æternam: acceperunt illud stulte, carnaliter illud cogitaverunt, et putaverunt quod præcisurus esset Dominus particulas quasdam de corpore suo, et daturus illis, et dixerunt, Durus est hic sermo. Ipsi erant duri, non sermo....... Ille autem instruxit eos, et ait illis, Spiritus est qui vivificat, caro autem nihil prodest: verba quæ locutus sum vobis, spiritus est et vita. Spiritaliter intelligite quod locutus sum: non hoc corpus quod videtis, manducaturi estis; et bibituri illum sanguinem, quem fusuri sunt qui me crucifigent. Sacramentum aliquod vobis commendavi; spiritaliter intellectum vivificabit vos. Etsi necesse est illud visibiliter celebrari, oportet tamen invisibiliter intelligi.—August. Op. Par. 1679—1700. Enarr. in Psalm. xcviii. 9. Tom. IV. cols. 1065, 6.]

[6 The following, though not couched in precisely the language above given, is probably the passage intended. Sicut enim Judas, cui buccellam tradidit Dominus, non malum accipiendo, sed male accipiendo locum in se diabolo præbuit: sic indigne quisque sumens dominicum sacramentum non efficit, ut quia ipse malus est, malum sit, aut quia non ad salutem accipit, nihil acceperit.—Id. De Bapt. cont. Donatist. Lib. v. 9. Tom. IX. col. 146. But see In Johan. Evang. cap. xiii. Tractat LXII. 3. Tom. III. Pars II. col. 669.]

manner speaketh St Austin in this place. He saith, that Judas received the body and blood of the Lord, when he meaneth the sacrament of the body and blood of the Lord. For that Judas received not the body and blood of Christ, it appeareth manifestly by these words of St Austin: "The apostles," saith he, "did eat bread that was the Lord; but Judas did eat but the bread of the Lord, and not that bread that was the Lord[7]." Here St Austin affirmeth plainly that the apostles, receiving the sacramental bread, received also Christ himself; but Judas, which was wicked and unfaithful, received only the sacramental bread, and not Christ; so far is it off that he received the very body and blood of Christ, which cannot be eaten nor drunken, but only of the faithful, yea, and that none otherwise than with the mouth of the soul, which is faith, which faith the believing alone have; and therefore they alone eat and drink the body and blood of Christ. For this cause, when we read in the old fathers that the wicked receive the body and blood of Christ, it is to be understand of the sacrament of the body and blood of Christ; remembering always that figures, signs, or sacraments bear the names of the things which they signify and represent. "All mysteries," saith St John Chrysostom, "are to be considered with inward eyes, that is to say, spiritually[8]."

In Joan. Tract. 59.

A good lesson.

In Joan. Hom. 46.

Father. Hitherto thou hast declared, my son, what the Lord's supper is, who did institute the Lord's supper, why the Lord's supper was instituted, how we ought to prepare ourselves unto the Lord's supper, and what abuses and errors have crept into the church of Christ through the wicked doctrine of the papists about the Lord's supper; so that nothing almost concerning the supper of the Lord hath escaped thee, whereof thou hast not sufficiently spoken, yea, and confirmed the same both by the authority of the holy scriptures, and by the testimonies of the ancient fathers. Notwithstanding, let me ask thee one or two questions, although not of so great and weighty importance. What thinkest thou, is it more meet to receive the supper of the Lord at a table, or rather at an altar? *Son*. At a table.

Father. Why so? *Son*. For our Saviour Christ did both institute this holy supper at a table, and the apostles of Christ also did receive it at a table. And what can be more perfect than that which Christ and his apostles have done? All the primitive church also received the supper of the Lord at a table. And St Paul, speaking of the Lord's supper, maketh mention not of an altar, but of a table. "Ye cannot be partakers," saith he, "of the Lord's table, and of the devils' table also." Tables for the ministration of the Lord's supper continued in the church of Christ almost three hundred years after Christ universally, and in some places longer, as histories make mention[9]; so that the use of altars is but a new invention, and brought in, as some write, by pope Sixtus, the second of that name[10].

A table is more meet for the ministration of the Lord's supper, than an altar.

1 Cor. x.

Moreover, an altar hath relation to a sacrifice. And altars in the old law were built and set up at the commandment of God, to offer sacrifice upon them. But all those sacrifices do now cease (for they were but "shadows of good things to come"); therefore the altars ought to cease with them. Christ alone is our altar, our sacrifice, and our priest. Our altar is in heaven. Our altar is not made of stone, but of flesh and blood; of whom the apostle writeth thus: "We have an altar, whereof it is not lawful for them to eat which serve in the tabernacle."

Heb. x.

Heb. xiii.

Furthermore, the papists have greatly abused their altars, while they had such confidence in them, that without an altar, or in the stead thereof a *superaltare*, they were persuaded that they could not duly and truly, and in right form, minister the sacrament of the body and blood of Christ. And this their altar and *superaltare* likewise must be consecrate, have prints and characters made therein, washed with oil, wine, and water, be covered with a cloth of hair, and be garnished with fine white linen cloths, and other costly apparel; or else whatsoever was done thereon was counted vain and unprofitable. The use also of altars hath greatly confirmed and maintained

[7 See before, page 294, note 5.]

[8 See before, page 287, note 12.]

[9 For a full account of the custom of the primitive church, and the use of the terms *altar*, and *table*, see Bingham, Orig. Eccles. Book VIII. chap. vi. 11—14.]

[10 See Stella, Vit. Pontif. Basil. 1507. Sixtus II. fol. B.]

the most wicked error and damnable heresy, which the papists hold, concerning the sacrifice of the mass; while they teach that they offer Christ in their mass to God the Father, an oblation and sacrifice for the sins of the people, both of the living and of the dead, and by this means they greatly obscure and deface that most sweet-smelling and alone true, perfect, and sufficient sacrifice of Christ's death. And therefore all the altars of the papists ought now no less to be thrown down and cast out of the temples of the Christians, than in times past the altars of the priests of Baal; so far is it off that they be meet to be used at the celebration of the Lord's supper.

Finally, who knoweth not that we come unto the Lord's table, not to offer bloody sacrifices, to the performance whereof we had need of altars, but to eat and drink and spiritually to feed upon him that was once crucified and offered up for us on the altar of the cross, a sweet-smelling sacrifice to God the Father, yea, and that once for all? Now if we come together to eat and drink these holy mysteries, and so spiritually to eat Christ's body, and to drink his blood, unto salvation both of our bodies and souls, who seeth not that a table is more meet for the celebration of the Lord's supper than an altar?

Of gestures to be used at the Lord's table.

Father. Thy reasons are good, and not to be discommended. But what sayest thou concerning the gestures to be used at the Lord's table? Shall we receive those holy mysteries kneeling, standing, or sitting? *Son*. Albeit I know and confess that gestures of themselves be indifferent; yet I would wish all such gestures to be avoided as have outwardly any appearance of evil, according to this saying of St Paul: "Abstain from all evil appearance." And first of all, forasmuch as kneeling hath been long used in the church of Christ at the receiving of the sacrament, through the doctrine of the papists, although of itself it be indifferent to be or not to be used, yet would I wish that it were taken away by the authority of the higher powers.

1 Thess. v.

Of kneeling.

Father. Why so? *Son*. For it hath an outward appearance of evil. When the papists, through their pestilent persuasions, had made of the sacramental bread and wine a god, and had taught and commanded the people to take and worship it as God, then gave they in commandment straightways that all people should with all reverence kneel unto it, worship, and honour it. And by this means this gesture of kneeling crept in, and is yet used in the church of the papists, to declare that they worship the sacrament as their Lord God and Saviour. But I would wish with all my heart, that either this kneeling at the receiving of the sacrament were taken away, or else that the people were taught that that outward reverence was not given to the sacrament and outward sign, but to Christ, which is represented by that sacrament or sign[1]. But the most certain and sure way is utterly to cease from kneeling, that there may outwardly appear no kind of evil, according to this commandment of St Paul, "Abstain from all evil appearance:" lest the enemies, by the continuance of kneeling, should be confirmed in their error, and the weaklings offended and plucked back from the truth of the gospel. Kneeling with the knowledge of godly honour is due to none but to God alone. Therefore, when Satan commanded our Saviour Christ to kneel down before him and worship him, he answered, "It is written, Thou shalt worship the Lord[2]"...

1 Thess. v.

Matt. iv.

Of standing.

Standing, which is used in the most part of the reformed churches in these our days, I can right well allow it, if it be appointed by common order to be used at the receiving of the holy communion. And this gesture of standing was also used at the commandment of God of the old Jews, when they did eat the paschal lamb, which was also a sacrament and figure of Christ to come, as our sacrament is a sign and figure of Christ come and gone. Neither did that gesture want ☞ his mystery. For the standing of the Jews at the eating of the Lord's passover signified, that they had a further journey to go in matters of religion, and that there was a more clear light of the gospel to shine than had hitherto appeared unto them, which

Exod. xii.

[[1] A notice to the effect here mentioned had appeared in the second book of king Edward VI. It was laid aside under queen Elizabeth, but restored with some slight alterations at the last review of the Liturgy, in 1662.]

[[2] It seems probable that there is some omission here; as the sense is confused.]

were wrapped round about with the dark shadows of ceremonies: again, that other, yea, and those more perfect, sacraments were to be given to God's people; which all things were fulfilled and came to pass under Christ, the author of the heavenly doctrine of the gospel, and the institutor of the holy sacraments, baptism and the Lord's supper.

Now, as concerning sitting at the Lord's table, which is also used at this day in certain reformed churches, if it were received by public authority and common consent, and might conveniently be used in our churches, I could allow that gesture best. For as it is not to be doubted but that Christ and his disciples sat at the table, when Christ delivered unto them the sacrament of his body and blood, which use was also observed in the primitive church, and long time after[3]; so likewise it is most comely that we Christians follow the example of our Master Christ and of his disciples. Nothing can be unreverently done, that is done after the example of Christ and of his apostles. We come together to eat and drink the holy mysteries of the body and blood of Christ: we have a table set before us: is it not meet and convenient that we sit at our table? The table being prepared, who standeth at his meat? Yea rather, who sitteth not down? Of sitting.

When Christ fed the people, he bade them not kneel down, nor stand upon their feet, but he commanded them to sit down; which kind of gesture is most meet when we assemble to eat and drink, which thing we do at the Lord's table. Neither doth the sitting of the communicants at the Lord's table want her mystery. For as the standing of the Jews at the eating of the Lord's passover signified that there was yet to come another doctrine than the law of Moses, even the preaching of the glorious gospel of our Lord and Saviour Christ Jesu, and other sacraments than circumcision and the passover, even the sacraments of baptism and the Lord's supper; so in like manner the sitting of the christian communicants at the Lord's table doth signify, preach, and declare unto us, that we are come to our journey's end concerning religion, and that there is none other doctrine nor none other sacraments to be looked for than those only which we have already received of Christ the Lord. And therefore we, sitting down at the Lord's table, shew by that our gesture that we are come to the perfection of our religion, and look for none other doctrine to be given unto us. Notwithstanding, as I said before, gestures are free, so that none occasion of evil be either done or offered. In all things which we call indifferent, this rule of St Paul is diligently to be obeyed: "Abstain from all evil appearance." John vi. 1 Thess. v.

Father. I do not disallow thy judgment in this behalf. But come off, tell me, what sayest thou concerning the vestures which the ministers use at the ministration of the Lord's supper? Of vestures at the ministration of the Lord's supper.

Son. In some reformed churches the ministers use both a surplice and a cope; in some only a surplice; in some neither cope nor surplice, but their own decent apparel.

Father. And what thinkest thou in this behalf? *Son*. When our Lord and Saviour Christ Jesus did minister the sacrament of his body and blood to his disciples, he used none other but his own common and daily apparel, and so likewise did the apostles after him, and the primitive church likewise used that order; and so was it continued many years after, till superstition began to creep into the church. After that time, fond foolish fancy of man's idle brain devised, without the authority of God's word, that the minister in the divine service and in the ministration of the holy sacraments should use a white linen vesture, which we now commonly call a surplice. Until this time, the church of God continued in the simplicity of Christ and of his apostles, requiring no painted visors to set forth the glory and beauty of our religion; which is then most glorious and most beautiful when it is most simple, and none otherwise set forth than[4] it was used and left unto us of Christ and of his apostles. And contrari- Surplice.

[3 On the posture observed in receiving the sacrament of the Lord's supper in church, see Bingham, Orig. Eccles. Book xv. chap. v. 3., who gives numerous quotations from the fathers to shew "that the ancients received sometimes standing, sometimes kneeling, but never sitting."]

[4 Folio, *whan*.]

wise, it is then most obscured and defaced when it is daubed over with the vile and vain colours of man's wisdom, although outwardly never so gorgeous and glorious.

Afterward, as superstition grew and increased, so likewise the people began more and more to be liberal in giving to the church, and in adorning, decking, and trimming the temples of the Christians; yea, and that so much the more, because they were now persuaded that such temple and will-works pleased God, deserved remission of sins and everlasting life. By this means came it to pass that the simple and plain tables, which were used in the apostolic and primitive church, were taken away, and standing altars set up and gorgeously decked with sumptuous apparel, and garnished with gold, pearl, and precious stone. And because that he which should minister at that gorgeous and sumptuous altar should answer in some point to the glory thereof, therefore it was devised that the minister also should have on his back gallant and

Vestments. gorgeous apparel, as an amice, an alb, a tunicle, a girdle, a fannel[1], a stole, a vestment, &c., whereof some were made of silk, some of velvet, some of cloth of gold; yea, and those garnished with angels, with images, with birds, with beasts, with fishes, with flowers, with herbs, with trees, and with all things that might satisfy and please the vain eye of the carnal man. And all these things, being before but voluntary, grew afterward unto matters of so great weight and importance, yea, unto such necessity, that it was made a matter of conscience, yea, it was become deadly sin to minister the holy communion without these scenical, histrionical, and hickscorner-like garments; so that now to sing mass or to consecrate, as they use to say, without these popish robes, is counted in the church of the papists more than twice deadly sin; so far is it off that these missal vestures are now things of indifferency.

Note. Wherefore, in my judgment, it were meet and convenient that all such disguised apparel were utterly taken away; forasmuch as it is but the vain invention of man,

2 Cor. vi. and hath been greatly abused of the massing papists. For "what hath the temple of God to do with idols?" "What concord is there between Christ and Belial?" What have the vestments of a popish altar to do with the table of the Lord Christ?

Whether it be lawful to wear a surplice. *Father.* But what thinkest thou of the surplice, which is now commonly used in the most part of the reformed churches? is it lawful to wear a surplice, or not? *Son.* In things indifferent we may use our liberty, which we have gotten by Christ. Therefore if a magistrate, being godly, command that the minister in the time of his administration wear a surplice, not for the maintenance of superstition, but for a seemly and decent order, his commandment in this behalf is to be obeyed, and no godly minister ought to resist it. For in all matters that are not contrary to God's word the magis-

Rom. xiii. trate is to be obeyed, "not only for fear of punishment, but also for conscience sake." But if the magistrate command any thing directly against God's word, in this behalf he is not to be obeyed, nor his commandment to be accomplished; but we must answer

Acts v. with the apostles: "We must obey God more than men." "Whether it be righteous in the sight of God to hear you rather than God, judge ye." But in things that be indifferent, we must take heed that we clog no man's conscience, nor make that a thing of necessity which is mere voluntary.

Of receiving the sacrament with the hands. *Father.* It is well said. But what thinkest thou of the receiving of the mysteries of Christ's passion and death? In the church of the papists the lay people can by no means be suffered with their hands to touch either the Lord's bread or the cup; but the sacrificing priest put the bread into the people's mouth and give them the wine, as though the people were unworthy either to touch the bread or the cup. In the reformed churches they take both the sacramental bread and cup in their own hands, delivered unto them by the minister.

Son. When the popish priests had exalted themselves too far above the laity, and counted the common people, in comparison of themselves, profane and unclean persons; again, when they had made of the sacrament a god, and had taught the people to worship it, and to kneel unto it; then, that the sacrament might be had in the greater estimation, they decreed among themselves that the laity should by no means touch with their unclean hands the body of their Lord God, as they call it;

[1 Fannel, or fanon: a sort of small scarf worn by a priest on his arm while saying mass.]

again, that they with their profane hands should not touch the sacred and hallowed chalice, wherein notwithstanding not the mystery of Christ's blood, but mere wine is contained. For as the papists, like thieves, have stolen away from the common people the Lord's cup, contrary to Christ's institution. And although I know, that it is a matter neither of salvation or damnation, as they use to say, the laity either to take the sacrament into their own hands, or else to receive it at the hand of the minister into their mouths; yet is it more agreeable to the institution of Christ, and to the order of the primitive church, to take the sacraments into their own hands, both the bread and the cup. For what hath the hand more offended than the lips, the tongue, the mouth, the teeth, &c.? Hath not he sanctified the hand which hallowed the mouth? Be not both of like holiness before God? A layman to touch the sacramental bread or cup with his bare hand is counted in the parish church a grievous sin; but if the layman have a glove on his hand, made of a sheep's skin, then he may be bold to touch it: as though there were more holiness or worthiness in a sheep's skin than in a christian man's hands. O hypocrites, swallowing in a camel and straining out a gnat!

When Christ delivered the signs of his body and blood to his disciples sitting at the table, he said not unto them, Gape, hold, eat, &c. and so thrust the bread into their mouths; but he delivered the bread into their hands, and said: "Take ye, and eat." Neither said he, Hold, open your mouths, I will pour wine into them; but he delivered the cup into their hands, saying: "Take, and divide this among you." And this order continued many years after Christ's time, as we may find both in histories, and also in the monuments of the ancient writers[2]. This popish custom therefore, of thrusting the sacramental bread into the mouths of the communicants, ought utterly to be abolished, lest that by the maintenance thereof the popish and wicked error of Christ's corporal presence be established and confirmed.

Father. Is the sacramental bread to be worshipped, as the papists have heretofore taught? *Son.* Nothing less. For it is written: "Thou shalt worship the Lord thy God, and him alone shalt thou serve." To worship any creature as God is plain idolatry. Christ said: "Take, eat," "divide among you." He said not, Behold, fall down and worship. The worshipping therefore of the sacrament ought utterly to be forbidden and to be abolished, as mere idolatry and most execrable abomination before the Lord our God, to whom alone all worship, honour, and glory is due. Whether the sacrament ought to be worshipped.

Father. Well, my dear son, thou hast not only satisfied, but also overcome mine expectation in all things wherein I have hitherto talked with thee. Five parts of the Catechism have we passed over: one part now remaineth behind to be entreated of, which is concerning the offices of all degrees. *Son.* You say truth, most loving father.

[[2] See Cypr. Op. Oxon. 1682. De Lapsis, p. 132; De Bon. Patient. p. 216; August. Op. Par. 1679—1700. Cont. Lit. Petil. Lib. II. 53. Tom. IX. col. 233. An abundance of other authorities may be seen in Bingham, Orig. Eccles. Book xv. chap. v. 6.]

THE SIXTH PART OF THE CATECHISM.

OF THE OFFICES OF ALL DEGREES.

Father. WHAT order wilt thou observe in this sixth and last part of the Catechism? *Son.* I will first entreat of the offices and duties of the higher powers, both temporal and ecclesiastical; and afterward of all other degrees in order, that are stablished and grounded in the word of God.

Father. Thou wilt then begin first with the temporal magistrate? *Son.* Yea, verily.

OF THE OFFICE AND DUTY OF THE TEMPORAL MAGISTRATE.

What a magistrate is.

Father. First of all tell me, my son, what a temporal magistrate is. *Son.* A temporal magistrate is a public person, to whom the sword is committed for the defence of the good, and for the punishment of the evil.

The office of a magistrate is the ordinance of God.

Father. Is the magistrate appointed of God an officer, or is he rather a tyrant, usurping power and authority over other persons, against all right and law? *Son.* He is ordained of God to be a ruler over his people; and no man hath justly rule and authority in any commonweal, which is not ordained of God.

Father. Let me hear this proved by the word of God. For there are, as I hear, which utterly deny the magistrate to be of God, that is to say, of God's ordinance and appointment. *Son.* Ye speak of the anabaptists, which are so enemies to this noble degree and honourable estate, that they are almost friendly to none having their foundation in the religion of Christ. But that magistrates rule at the appointment of God, Prov. viii. it is thus proved. God by the mouth of Salomon speaketh on this manner: "Through me kings reign: through me princes make just laws. Through me lords bear rule; Wisd. vi. and all judges of the earth execute judgment." And the wise man saith: "Hear, O ye kings, and understand: give ear, ye that rule the multitudes. For the power is given you of the Lord, and the strength from the most high God." St Paul also saith: Rom. xiii. "There is no power but of God. The powers that be are ordained of God. Therefore whoso resisteth the power resisteth the ordinance of God; and they that resist get 1 Pet. ii. to themselves damnation." St Peter likewise exhorteth us to "honour the king, and be subject unto him as the supreme governor, and to the other rulers that are sent of him," yea, and that "for the Lord's sake;" that is to say, because they are God's officers, "ordained of him for the punishment of the evil, but for the praise of the good."

Wicked princes are given of God to punish the wickedness of the people.

Father. But what if the magistrates be evil, wicked, ungodly, tyrants, haters of the truth, oppressors of the poor, &c.? Are they also appointed of God? *Son.* In Job it is thus written: "For the sins of the people doth God make an hypocrite to reign over them." And God himself saith by the prophet: "I shall give them children to be their princes; and babes shall have the rule of you. The people also shall be pilled Psal. ix. and polled," &c. The psalmograph prayeth against the ungodly on this manner: "Set, O Lord, a tyrant over them, that the heathen may know themselves to be but men." John xix. And our Saviour Christ confessed that the authority which Pilate had, although a wicked and ungodly person, was from God, and he willingly suffered death under that tyrant. Neither do we read, that the apostles at any time did reject and cast away the regiment of the heathen rulers as a thing unlawful; but they rather exhorted the subjects to obey them, so far as they commanded nothing contrary to God's word, to honour them, to pray for them, to give them tribute, custom, toll, &c. Thus see we that not only godly, but also ungodly princes, not only righteous, but also unrighteous and wicked rulers are given us of God: the one, I mean the good, for the favour which God beareth toward us, when we labour to walk in his holy ways; the other, I mean the evil, for anger and displeasure that he hath toward us, when he seeth us disobedient to his laws and ordinances.

Christ and his apostles never withstood the authority of wicked rulers.

Father. What manner of men should magistrates be? *Son.* Men of activity, and such as fear God; true men, and hating covetousness; wise and politic; and whose conversation is allowed of all men.

Exod. xviii. Num. xi. Deut. i.

What manner of men magistrates ought to be.

Father. What is the office of a temporal magistrate? *Son*. It consisteth chiefly in two points. The first is, that he, banishing out of his kingdom all false religion and idolatry, do avance, set forth, and maintain God's true religion and holy word. The second is, that he govern his people justly, defend them from all perils, preserve their goods, maintain the good, and punish the evil.

What the office of a magistrate is.

Father. Have civil magistrates also to do with matters of religion? *Son*. Yea, verily. For God hath appointed temporal rulers not only keepers and maintainers of the works of the second table of the law, which concern the body, but also of the works of the first table of the law, which belong unto God and unto the soul. As the magistrate by the virtue of his office is bound to provide that, so much as in him is, there be no manslaughter, no whoredom, no theft, no false witness-bearing, none unjust coveting of other men's goods, &c., in his land or dominion; so likewise is his duty to aforesee, that there be no false religion, no idolatry, no superstition, no invocation of strange gods, no dishonouring of the Lord's name, no wicked doctrine, &c., used in his country or kingdom.

Whether the temporal rulers ought to meddle with matters of christian religion.

And for this purpose, because he should not be deceived of the wily and subtile hypocrites, which desire above all things to lead the higher powers in ignorance and blindness, that they may do what they list without check, the magistrate is commanded of God to be learned himself in the laws and ordinances of God, that he may do all things according to God's book, and not after his own fancy or will, nor yet after the crafty persuasions of the subtile hypocrites. "The king," saith God, "when he is set upon the seat of his kingdom, he shall write him out a copy of this law in a book. And it shall be with him, and he ought to read therein all the days of his life, that he may learn to fear the Lord his God, and to keep all the words of this law," &c. And to Josua God said likewise: "Let not the book of this law depart out of thy mouth; but record[1] therein day and night, that thou mayest observe and do according to all that is written therein. For then shalt thou make thy way prosperous, and then shalt thou do wisely." The prophet David also exhorteth the kings and rulers of the earth to get them understanding, and to be learned in the law of the Lord, yea, and to "kiss the Son," that is to say, to embrace Christ the Son of God and his holy gospel; lest, if they do the contrary, God be angry with them, and so they perish from the right way. The like thing read we in the sixth and ninth chapters of the book of Wisdom.

Magistrates ought diligently to read God's word.

Deut. xvii.

Josh. i.

Psal. ii.

Wisd. vi. ix.

Father. Prove by the word of God, that the temporal rulers have to do with matters of christian religion. For there want not at this present day which think, that civil magistrates ought not to meddle with matters pertaining unto the soul, but unto the body only. As for all spiritual causes and matters of religion, they belong, say they, to the bishop of Rome and to his adherents. *Son*. These are the papists, which desire alone to reign in the consciences of men, and to have rule over their faith. But that temporal rulers ought to meddle with matters of God's religion, and that it appertaineth unto their office to weed out all false worshipping of God and all wicked doctrine, it is probable enough by divers histories of the holy scripture.

The fancy of the papists.

As I may pass over king David and Salomon his son, which travailed not a little in avancing God's true religion, and in setting forth his holy word, what shall I speak of Asa king of Juda? Did not he, being a worldly prince, take away strange altars, and break down the images, and cut down the groves, and command Juda to seek the Lord God of their fathers, and to do according to the law and commandment of God? Did not he also put away all the abominable idols that his father had made? Again, did not he put down Maacha his mother from bearing rule, because she had made images in groves? yea, Asa destroyed all her images and burnt them by the brook Cedron. And all these doings of Asa did so greatly please God, that he gave him and all his land rest and quietness; so far is it off that God was angry with Asa for these his enterprises in matters of religion.

1 Kings xv. 2 Chron. xiv.

[[1] Record: call to remembrance, meditate.]

2 Chron. xix. Read we not also of Jeosaphat king of Juda, that, after that God had placed him in his kingdom, perceiving that God was greatly dishonoured through false religion brought in by his wicked forefathers and by the false prophets, he straightways commanded a visitation to be had for the speedy redress of all enormities, both in matters of religion and also in worldly affairs, and for the performance of the same he sent forth his lords, and with them certain priests and Levites to go throughout all the cities of Juda to teach the people, having with them the book of the law of God; so that by this means the fear of the Lord fell upon all the kingdoms of the lands that were round about Juda, and the king and his people lived in great joy, quietness, and wealth, having abundance of riches and honour?

Father. Methink this is both a noble and notable history, to declare and shew, that all princes in their dominions have authority and power to redress abuses and errors in matters of religion, and that for that purpose they may at all times appoint visitations to be had in their kingdoms for a reformation of all enormities, both in spiritual and temporal matters. *Son.* You say truth. But this cannot the papists abide. But as they alone will be called spiritual, so likewise do they challenge to themselves all spiritual jurisdiction and the determination of all matters concerning religion, leaving to the magistrates authority and power only over the body and bodily matters, making them in this behalf no better than swineherds and shepherds. But not only cure of body, but also charge of soul is committed of God to the secular powers; and they ought to seek the salvation of both, if they will avoid God's great anger and heavy displeasure, as we may perceive by the histories aforesaid.

The papists make the magistrates no better than swine-herds and shepherds.

Father. Were there any other kings that shewed themselves zealous in God's religion also? *Son.* To whom are the noble acts and godly enterprises of king Hezekia unknown? Did not he put away the hill-altars, and break the images, and cut down the groves, and all-to brake the brasen serpent that Moses had made? Did he not renew the feast of the passover? Did not he ordain priests and Levites to serve the Lord God, providing honest living for them, that they might substantially apply themselves to the study of the law of the Lord? and the Lord was with Hezekia, so that he prospered in all things which he took in hand.

2 Kings xviii. 2 Chron. xxxi.

The most worthy and most glorious acts of that most noble and most godly king Josia are more famous and known than that they need here to be recited. He purged all Juda and all Hierusalem from hill-altars, groves, carved images, and images of metal, and such other kinds of idolatry. He repaired the house of the Lord his God. He renewed the feast of the passover. He read in the ears of all the people the words of the law of the Lord, and made a faithful promise to the Lord, that he and all his people should walk according to the statutes of that book; so that they turned not aside from the Lord God of their fathers so long as he lived. The Lord God therefore deferred his plague that he had threatened to Juda, suffered Josia to live in much honour, and brought him to his grave in peace; so that his eyes did not see the mischief that the Lord God afterward brought immediately upon Hierusalem and upon the inhabiters of the same.

2 Chron. xxxiv.

2 Kings x. What shall I speak of Jehu, king of Israel, which caused all the priests of Baal to be slain, all the images to be fet[1] out of the temple of Baal, and to be burnt? He commanded also his captains and men of war to break the image of Baal, and to destroy the house of Baal; so that Baal's house was made a draught-house unto this day. And because Jehu thus sought the glory of God, and destroyed idolatry with the maintainers thereof, he lived in his kingdom unto his dying day; and his children unto the fourth generation sat on the seat of Israel.

And as these aforesaid most noble kings shewed themselves valiant and courageous magistrates in matters of God's religion, by banishing all idolatry and wicked doctrine, and by erecting and setting up the true worshipping of God and the sincere preaching of his most holy word; so likewise read we in ecclesiastical histories of certain noble christian princes, which attempted the like enterprises in avancing the true

[[1] Fet: fetched.]

religion of God, and in driving out of their dominions all idolatry, false worshipping of God, wicked doctrine, &c.

Of this sort was that godly emperor Constantinus Magnus[2], whom when God had called unto the empire and unto the knowledge of his holy word, he straightways commanded that the temples of the idols should be shut up, and from henceforth to be no more frequented, nor sacrifice to be offered any more in them unto those false gods. He commanded also that the gospel of our Saviour Christ should be preached openly, and he gave to the preachers thereof large stipends and honourable rewards. And when the wicked and damnable heresy of Arius began to spread abroad, the most noble emperor with his great labour and cost gathered together a great number of learned bishops, and celebrated an holy and honourable council at Nice, for the suppression of that too much detestable heresy. How godly and prince-like he behaved himself at the council, histories do abundantly declare. God therefore blessed him many and divers ways. Constantinus Magnus.

What shall I speak of Gratianus, Valentinianus, and Theodosius, most holy and worthy emperors, which gave out strait commandment throughout all their dominions, that all their subjects should receive and admit none other doctrine than that only which the holy and blessed apostle St Peter had preached and taught? And they commanded, that all the temples of the idols should utterly be thrown down and rooted out, that the idolaters might have none occasion after their time to set up again their wicked sacrifices[3]. Gratianus. Valentin. Theodosius.

In a certain city of Phrygia Adauctus, lieutenant of that country under Diocletian, that tyrant-like emperor, toppled down all the idols, and persuaded the whole multitude to receive the doctrine of Christ[4]. Adauctus.

Again, in the city Nicomedia a certain nobleman, receiving the letters of that wicked tyrant Diocletian, which he had sent for the abolishing of christian religion, rent them all on pieces and trod them under his feet, the people looking on[5].

Divers such like examples we read in ecclesiastical writers, which declare manifestly with what and how fervent zeal a christian magistrate ought to be led toward christian religion; so that his chief study and labour should be to seek the honour and glory of God, to avance his holy religion, to set forth his blessed word, and to procure the salvation of his subjects' souls, all idolatry, superstition, hypocrisy, and whatsoever is contrary to wholesome doctrine, utterly excluded and put away. And for this cause are they called in the holy scripture "gods," that is to say, persons appointed of God to conserve, keep, and maintain true religion, and to forbid and abolish idolatry, superstition, wicked doctrine, &c. Psal. lxxxii.

And that they may this do the more conveniently, it is meet and necessary that they add these two things, without the which true religion cannot long stand. What is to be done of the magistrates for the conservation of the true religion.

The first is, that they provide godly and learned preachers in all parts of their dominions, which more truly and unfeignedly teach their subjects the way of the Lord, that they may from their very heart fear the Lord God, honour him, serve him, worship him, call on his holy name, thank him for his benefits, and lead a life worthy their profession. And that the preachers may labour in the vineyard of the Lord the more gladly, and have the better courage to do their duty, it is the office of a good magistrate to provide honest and quiet stipends for the preachers, that they may have whereof to feed both themselves and their family, yea, and also to give somewhat to the poor. And to encourage the godly magistrates to do this, it shall be good for them always to set before their eyes this saying of the wise man: "When the preaching of God's word faileth, the people perish and run out of order." Preachers. Prov. xxix.

[2 Euseb. de Vit. Constant. in Hist. Eccles. Script. Amst. 1695—1700. Lib. II. capp. xlv. xlvii. Lib. III. cap. vi. pp. 382, 3, 400.]

[3 Theodoret. in eod. Lib. v. cap. xxi. pp. 226—28. See also Cod. Justin. in Gothofr. Corp. Jur. Civil. Amst. 1663. Lib. I. Titt. i. l. xi. Tom. II. pp. 1. 37, 38.

An account of the steps taken by the christian emperors for the overthrow of heathenism may be read in Beugnot, Hist. de la Destruction du Paganisme en Occident. Paris, 1835.]

[4 Nicephor. Callist. Hist. Eccles. Lut. Par. 1630. Lib. VII. cap. x. Tom. I. pp. 452, 3.]

[5 Id. ibid. cap. v. p. 445.]

Schools. The second is, that forasmuch as preachers be mortal, and cannot alway remain in their function and office, but must needs give over to nature, and change this life after the manner of all men, the magistrates erect and set up schools, where the youth of the christian commonweal may be brought up in good letters and godly manners, but specially in the knowledge of God's true religion; that the young children, being trained up even from their cradles in the mysteries of God's most holy word, may in time to come supply the rooms of the departed pastors, and become good shepherds of the Lord's flock, feeding them, not with the pestiferous leaven of Pharisees, but with the sweet and comfortable wheat of Christ's gospel. And that *Books of the holy scriptures ought to be read in christian schools. 2 Tim. iii.* they may be the more able this to do, the magistrate must diligently provide that the books both of the old and new testament be read every day to the young ones, with some short exposition of the same; that they may learn holy letters from their infancy, as we read of bishop Timothy, and not spend all their childhood or young age in man's doctrine, doctrine many times more meet for the children of the Turks *1 Cor. vii.* than for the children of the Christians, which, as St Paul saith, are "holy and clean." And that they may wax the sooner ripe in the knowledge of godliness, it shall be *Sermons.* convenient that the scholars do oftentimes repair unto the temples to hear the sermons, and afterward to render accompts of those things that they have heard, lest they become forgetful hearers. And it shall not a little profit unto the increase of *Orations.* godly knowledge, that the scholars sometime have some theme of the holy scripture offered unto them privately in their schools, and so prove their wits, what they are able to do in dilating that text, sometime by tongue, sometime by pen.

School-masters. And that those things may be done of the scholars with the more fruit, a christian magistrate must diligently provide, that such as shall be chosen and appointed schoolmasters, be men of gravity, wisdom, knowledge, learning, of an honest and godly conversation, of an approved life, of uncorrupt manners, diligent and painful in their office, favourers of true and pure religion, earnest lovers of God's word, haters of idolatry and superstition, and such in all points as may be to their scholars, not only teachers of good and godly doctrine, but also example-givers of honest and virtuous conversation; that as in doctrine, so likewise in manners, they may proceed and go forward, and afterward become profitable members of the christian commonweal.

Provision for schoolmasters. And that the schoolmasters may be the better encouraged to do their office, and to bring up the youth of the Christians in the nurture and doctrine of the Lord, that they may afterward become good and profitable members of the commonweal, whether they be called unto temporal or spiritual affairs, it shall be necessary that the magistrates provide liberally for the teachers and bringers up of youth, that they may have whereof honestly to live. For if we think it a thing unfitting and unreasonable not to provide for our swineherds and shepherds, which attend upon our brute beasts; what a shame were it to leave our schoolmasters, which bring up our children, made like to the image of God, in virtue and learning, unprovided!

The very heathen in times past have liberally entertained the teachers of their children; and shall Christians be negligent in this behalf?

The Turks at this present day shew themselves very bounteous and of great liberality to such as bring up their children in the knowledge of tongues; and shall the teachers of christian men's children be either left[1] unprovided, or at the least slen- *Matt. x. 1 Tim. v.* derly recompensed? "The workman is worthy of his reward." And "they that rule well are worthy of double honour."

Father. These things which thou hast spoken, my dear son, if they were diligently considered and put in practice, would make a flourishing christian commonweal, so that God should be truly honoured, and his holy church garnished with all kind of good and godly officers, both in spiritual and temporal matters. But come off, and tell me what the office and duty of the magistrate is in worldly affairs. *Son.* *What the duty of a magistrate is in worldly matters.* As the duty of a magistrate is to avance the glory of God, to set forth the gospel of our Saviour Christ, to plant true religion in all his dominions, to banish idolatry and false worshippings of God, to weed out unfaithful teachers and false prophets,

[[1] The folio has *least*.]

and instead of them to appoint godly and learned preachers, which may attend upon "the flock of Christ, whom he purchased with his most precious blood," and for their godly travails to appoint them such stipends as shall be liberally sufficient both for them and for their family, yea, of the same also to give somewhat to the poor; again, to erect and set up schools for the virtuous bringing up of youth, and to appoint godly, grave, and learned schoolmasters for the right institution of them, yea, and those also bounteously recompensed for their painful travails; so likewise is it his office and duty to govern his people, whom God hath committed to his charge, justly, to defend them from all perils, to preserve their goods, to maintain the good and godly, and to punish the evil and wicked. Acts xx.

Father. Are the people over whom the magistrates reign God's people? *Son.* Yea, verily, God's people, his workmanship, and the sheep of his pasture; for so are they termed in the word of God. Exod. iii.

Father. And are the magistrates appointed of God to govern his people? *Son.* The magistrate is God's minister, appointed to this end, that he may govern and rule the people of God. And for this cause they be called in the holy scriptures "gods," "princes," "kings," "rulers," "governors," "shepherds," "guides," "captains," &c.

Father. And this their regiment ought to be just and righteous? *Son.* Yea; for they must render an accompts to him that is King of kings and Lord of lords of their regiment and governance. To govern justly is required of a magistrate above all things. **Magistrates ought to rule justly.**

Father. What is it to govern justly? *Son.* To do all things according to equity and justice, and by no means to decline from the way of righteousness, neither unto the right nor unto the left hand; to cast away all partiality in judgments; not to pervert justice for bribes' sake; not to judge neither for favour nor for hatred; to hear both parts indifferently; and neither to justify the wicked nor to condemn the innocent. **What it is to rule justly.**

Father. Is it thus commanded of God? *Son.* To whom is that unknown? God saith: "Ye shall do no unrighteousness in judgment. Thou shalt not favour the poor nor honour the mighty; but in righteousness shalt thou judge thy neighbour." "Hear the cause of your brethren," said Moses to the judges, "and judge righteously between every man and his brother, and the stranger that is with him. See that ye know no faces in judgment; but hear the small as well as the great, and be afraid of no man; for the judgment is God's." "He that saith to the ungodly," saith Salomon, "Thou art righteous, him shall the people curse, yea, the commenty[2] shall abhor him. But they that rebuke the ungodly, in them doth God delight; and a rich blessing shall come upon them." "Judge the thing that is right, O ye sons of men," saith the psalmograph. "O love righteousness, ye that are the judges of the earth." Notable is the exhortation that king Josaphat gave to the judges: "Take heed that ye do," saith he; "for ye execute not the judgment of men, but of God, which is with you in the judgment. Wherefore now let the fear of the Lord be upon you, and take heed, and be doing the thing that pleaseth him. For there is none unrighteousness with the Lord our God, that should have any respect of persons, or take reward." Lev. xix. Deut. i. Prov. xxiv. Psal. lviii. Wisd. i. 2 Chron. xix.

Father. Would God all magistrates would obey these most righteous commandments of God! Then should not so many deal unjustly, as they do now-a-days. For gifts, rewards, and bribes do so rule in the hearts of many rulers in this our age, that they utterly weigh down and suppress justice, and make it of no force. *Son.* Where bribe-taking is used, justice is utterly refused; and where money is set by, there right loseth the mastery. Therefore God in his law commandeth that such should be made rulers over the people as hate covetousness and abhor bribes. Would God that all such bribe-takers and gift-eaters would set before their eyes these commandments of God: "Thou shalt take no gifts; for gifts blind the sight, and pervert the words of the righteous." "Wrest not thou the law, nor know any person, neither take any reward; for gifts blind the wise," &c. Against such bribe- **Bribe-taking.** Exod. xviii. Exod. xxiii. Deut. xvi.

[[2] Commenty: community.]

Isai. v. takers and gift-eaters the prophet crieth out on this manner: "Wo be unto them that give sentence with the ungodly for rewards, but condemn the just cause of the righteous! Therefore, like as fire licketh up the straw, and as the flame consumeth the stubble, even so their root shall be as corruption, and their blossom shall vanish away like dust." Job also saith: "The fire shall consume the houses of such as are greedy to receive gifts." (Job xv.)

Friendship. *Father.* As gifts and bribes cause the subversion of justice, likewise doth friendship many times; so truly is it said in our common proverb: "As a man is friended, so is his matter ended." *Son.* Neither friendship nor favour ought to prevail against justice.

Both parties ought to be heard indifferently. *Father.* Some magistrates are so undiscreet, that, when matters of controversy be brought before them, the first tale doth so prevail that the other party cannot be heard, although his cause be never so just and good. *Son.* These judges forget the work of nature, which hath created in them two ears, one to hear the accusant, the other to hear the defendant.

☞ King Alexander. And in this behalf I would wish that they were like to king Alexander the Great, which, when any man complained to him of another being absent, used to stop the other ear with his hand. Being demanded why he did so, he answered that, as he left open one ear to the accusant, so he would keep one ear stopped and close for the defendant. Here even of an heathen prince may rulers learn to hear both parts indifferently.

Father. If the magistrates would thus behave themselves in all their sessions and courts, the commonweal should be better ordered in many places than it is now; neither should the poor people so grievously complain of injuries and wrongs done unto them. I pray God give the magistrates grace according to their office to govern the people of God justly. *Son.* Amen.

Father. It is the duty of magistrates also to defend their subjects from all perils, ☞ and to keep such goods as they have harmless? *Son.* That is their office. They are called in God's book "shepherds;" because, as a good shepherd doth not only feed his flock, but also defend his flock, and mightily fight for the conservation of his flock against the wolves, so likewise a true magistrate ought to seek all means possible to save his people, to keep them harmless, to save their goods, and to be as careful for them as for themselves. For, as St Paul saith: "The magistrate is God's minister, appointed for thy wealth." (Rom. xiii.) Yea, to save and to defend the lives and goods of their subjects, they ought to put their own lives and goods in jeopardy. Their own private commodity ought to give place to the safeguard of the commonweal. What a fatherly care Moses, Josua, Samuel, David, and other noble princes had for their people, the holy scriptures do evidently declare.

Magistrates ought not to oppress their subjects. *Father.* If it be the duty of princes to defend their subjects from all perils, and to keep such goods as they have harmless; then ought they not to use their subjects as slaves, villains, and peasants, nor to spoil them of their goods, which were either left unto them of their parents, or else they have gotten with their hard labour, at their pleasure. *Son.* The wise man saith: "If thou be made a ruler, pride not thyself therein; but be thou as one of the people. Take diligent care for them, and look well thereto; and when thou hast done all thy duty, sit thee down, that thou mayest be merry with them, and receive a crown of honour." (Ecclus. xxxii.) Salomon also saith: "Mercy and faithfulness preserve the king; and with loving-kindness his seat is holden up." (Prov. xx.) ☞ The richer and the wealthier that the commons are in any realm, the richer and the wealthier is the prince of that realm, yea, and the stronger also is he, and the further from all jeopardy and danger. But, contrariwise, the poorer and the baser that the commons are in any realm, the more feeble and the less valiant is the prince against his enemies. This considered the wise man, which writeth on this manner: "The increase and prosperity of the commons is the king's honour; but the decay of the people is the confusion of the prince." (Prov. xiv.) Notable is this saying of Marcus Curius[1], that most noble consul of Rome: "I had rather," saith he, "bear rule over them that are rich than to be rich myself." (Marcus Curius.)

[[1] Valer. Max. Lib. IV. cap. iii. 5.]

Moreover, that a magistrate may not unjustly take away his subjects' goods, the history of Nabot and of wicked king Achab declareth that most manifestly. 1 Kings xxi.

And who knoweth not how vehemently God thundereth by his prophets against such wolvish and tyrant-like rulers, which poll and pill the people, and oppress them against all equity and right? Are not these the words of God by the prophet Amos? "O hear this word, ye that do poor men wrong, and oppress the needy: ye that say to your lords, Bring hither, let us drink. Therefore the Lord hath sworn by his holiness, the days shall come upon you, that the enemies shall carry you away," &c. Again by the same prophet he saith: "O wo be to the proud wealthy, to such as think themselves so sure, even them which hold themselves for the best of the world, and rule the house of Israel as they lust!" "Ye are taken out for the evil day; even ye that sit in the stool of wilfulness; ye that lie upon beds of ivory, and use your wantonness upon your couches; ye that eat the best lambs of the flock, and the fattest calves of the drove; ye that sing at the lute, and in playing of instruments compare yourselves unto David; ye that drink wine out of goblets, and anoint yourselves with the best oil; but as for Joseph's hurt, none of you all are sorry for it. Therefore now shall ye be the first of them that shall be led away captive; and the lusty cheer of the wilful shall come to an end, &c. The Lord is minded to smite the great houses." "For ye have turned true judgment into bitterness, and the fruit of righteousness into wormwood." Once again by the same prophet he saith: "O ye that oppress the poor, and destroy the needy in the land:. . . shall not your destruction come upon you as a water-stream?" &c. And by the prophet Micha God also speaketh on this manner: "O ye heads of the house of Jacob, and ye leaders of the house of Israel, should not ye know what were lawful and right? But ye hate the good, and love the evil. Ye pluck off men's skins, and the flesh from their bones. Ye eat the flesh of my people, and flay off their skin. Ye break their bones: ye chop them on pieces, as it were into a caldron, and as flesh into a pot. Now the time shall come that, when they call unto the Lord, he shall not hear them, but hide his face from them; because that through their own imaginations they have dealt so wickedly," &c.

Amos iv. Amos vi. Amos viii. Micah iii.

Father. It is to be wished that all princes would remember this saying of the most wise prince and king Salomon: "With true judgment," saith he, "the king setteth up the land; but if he be a man that oppresseth the people with gatherings, he turneth it upside down. For when the righteous bear rule, the people are in prosperity; but when the ungodly have the overhand, then the people are in beggary." *Son*. Yea, it is to be wished that all magistrates, from the highest to the lowest, might so behave themselves in their office, that they might justly say with Samuel on this wise: "Behold, here am I: bear record of me before the Lord, and before his anointed. Whose ox have I taken? whom have I done wrong to? whom have I hurt? or of whose hand have I received any bribe, to blind mine eyes therewith? and I will restore it you again. The people answered Samuel and said, Thou hast done us no wrong, nor hurt us, neither hast thou taken ought of any man's hand. He said unto them again, The Lord is witness against you, and his anointed is witness this day, that ye have no evil in my hands."

Prov. xxix. 1 Sam. xii.

Father. It were not out of the way for all princes to remember what chanced to Rehoboam, king Salomon's son, for the ungentle entreating of his commons. And how unfortunately it hath gone with many princes in times past for their insatiable polling and pilling of their subjects, histories in all places make mention: "Like as a roaring lion, and as an hungry bear, even so is an ungodly prince over the poor people," saith Salomon. But let us hear more of the magistrate's office, which, thou saidst, is not only to govern the people justly, to defend them from all perils, and to preserve their goods, but also to maintain the good, and to punish the evil. *Son*. So is it.

1 Kings xii. Prov. xxviii.

Father. What is it to maintain the good? *Son*. To defend them from the violence of the wicked, not to suffer them to be oppressed of the tyrants, to help them unto their right, to defend their cause, to maintain their good name, to provide for them, to suffer them not to lack any good thing, to promote them, to place them in offices about the matters of the commonweal, to have them in reverence for virtue's sake,

Magistrates ought to maintain good and godly people.

although they be never so poor and base, &c. And this is it that God saith by the
Isai. i. prophet: "Learn to do right, apply yourselves to equity, deliver the oppressed, help
Jer. xxi. the fatherless to his right, let the widow's complaint come before you." Again: "Hear
the word of the Lord, O thou house of David; for thus saith the Lord, Minister
righteousness, and that soon: deliver the oppressed from violent power, or ever my
terrible wrath break out like a fire and burn, so that no man may quench it, because
Jer. xxii. of the wickedness of your imaginations." Also in another place: "Thus the Lord
commandeth, Keep equity and righteousness: deliver the oppressed from the power of
the violent: do not grieve nor oppress the stranger, the fatherless, nor widow; and
Zech. vii. shed no innocent blood." Item: "Thus saith the Lord of hosts, Execute true judgment: shew mercy and loving-kindness every man to his brother. Do the widow, the
fatherless, the stranger, and poor no wrong; and let no man imagine evil in his heart
Psal. lxxxii. against his brother." The psalmograph also saith: "How long will ye give wrong
judgment, and accept the persons of the ungodly? Defend the poor and fatherless:
see that such as be in need and necessity have right. Deliver the outcast and poor:
save them from the hand of the ungodly."

Magistrates ought to punish the wicked. *Father*. As the duty of the magistrate is to maintain the good and godly, so
likewise is it his office to punish the wicked and ungodly. It is not so? *Son*. Yes,
Gen. ix. verily: for so are we taught by the word of God. God himself saith: "Whoso
sheddeth man's blood, by man (he speaketh of the magistrate) shall his blood be shed."
Deut. xix. Again: "Thine eye shall have no compassion, but life for life, eye for eye, tooth for
tooth, hand for hand, foot for foot, shalt thou require." Likewise saith St Paul:
Rom. xiii. "Rulers are not fearful to them that do good, but to them that do evil. Wilt thou
be without fear of the power? Do well then, and so shalt thou be praised of the
same. For he is the minister of God for thy wealth. But and if thou do that which
is evil, then fear. For he beareth not the sword for nought. For he is the minister
1 Pet. ii. of God, to take vengeance on him that doth evil." St Peter also saith: "Submit
yourselves to all manner ordinance of man for the Lord's sake; whether it be unto
the king as unto the chief head; either unto the rulers, as unto them that are sent
of him for the punishment of evil-doers, but for the praise of them that do well."

Lev. xxiv. Deut. xiii. Lev. xix. Lev. xx. Lev. xxiv. Deut. xxii. Deut. xxxii. Lev. xx. Deut. xxi. xxxii. God in the law of Moses straitly commanded that the magistrates should by no means suffer these kind of persons to live; that is to say, the blasphemer of God's holy name, the false prophet, the idolater, the witch, the necromancer, the sorcerer, the murderer, the man-stealer, the adulterer, and the adulteress, the willingly-deflowered maid before she was married, he that hath to do with a brute beast, a stubborn child against father and mother, a false witness, &c. And every godly magistrate did punish the wicked in every age according to the laws of the realm where they dwelt, both among the people of God and among the heathen. And this order is observed at this day in all nations, both faithful and unfaithful.

☞ That magistrate which suffereth the wicked to escape unpunished is guilty of all the mischief that is done by them, and doth nothing else than seek the subversion and utter destruction of the commonweal, unto his own damnation. God commandeth that the malefactor shall not be spared. That ruler therefore, which spareth the malefactor, is first disobedient to God, and afterward injurious to himself, and last of all
Note. a wolf and an enemy to the commonweal. For to suffer the wicked to live is nothing else than to destroy the good. Of the prosperity of the evil what followeth but the destruction of the good? Not to pluck away the wolf from the lamb, what other thing is than to murder the lamb? Those magistrates are unworthy to reign, which, being moved with childish, yea, rather foolish pity, favour and pardon[1] open malefactors, and suffer them to live unto the great hindrance of the commonweal, according to the common proverb: "Foolish pity marreth the city." The magistrate hath not a peacock's tail given unto him when he is made a ruler, but a sword; which sword he ought to pluck out and exercise whensoever occasion is given, lest the weeds over-
Rom. xiii. grow the corn, and the wicked triumph against the righteous. "He beareth not the sword in vain," saith St Paul; "for he is the minister of God, to take vengeance on

[[1] The folio has *pardon and*.]

him that doeth evil." King David saith: "I will destroy out of hand all the ungodly that are in the land, that I may root out all wicked doers from the city of the Lord." Psal. ci.

Did not God command Moses to hang up those wicked princes and rulers, which of a foolish pity would not punish and put to death the wicked offenders, but rather spared them? "Take," saith he, "all the heads of the people, and hang them up before the Lord against the sun, that the wrath of the Lord's countenance may be turned from Israel." By this one history it appeareth evidently, how greatly God is displeased with these magistrates which cease to punish the wicked. Num. xxv.

And albeit that these sheepish, sluggish, and sleepy rulers escape in this world unpunished, for this their negligence and dissolute or loose regiment, yet shall they not avoid the hands of the most high Magistrate in the world to come; but they shall so much the more suffer punishments, because that they have not ministered due correction to the wicked and ungodly, as their duty was. For thus saith the wise man, speaking to the magistrates: "Give ear, ye that rule the multitudes, and delight in much people. For the power is given you of the Lord, and the strength from the Highest; which shall try your works, and search out your imaginations: how that ye, being officers of his kingdom, have not executed true judgment, have not kept the law of righteousness, nor walked after the will of God. Horrible, and that right soon, shall he appear unto you; for an hard judgment shall they have that bear rule. Mercy is granted unto the simple; but they that be in authority shall be sore punished. For God, which is Lord over all, shall accept no man's persons, neither shall he stand in awe of any man's greatness. For he hath made the small and great, and careth for all alike. But the mighty shall have the sorer punishment." Wisd. vi.

Father. But let me ask thee one question, my son: in punishing the wicked and ungodly, may the temporal rulers also punish the idolaters and false prophets or preachers of corrupt and wicked doctrine? *Son*. The magistrate hath the sword committed unto him, not only to punish the transgressors of the second table, but also such as offend and break the commandments of the first table. For if the temporal ruler ought not to suffer any person to escape unpunished that offendeth man, much less ought he to suffer any to escape unpunished that offendeth his Lord God, specially by idolatry and false doctrine. Is not this the commandment of God given to all high powers? "If there arise among you a prophet, or a dreamer of dreams, and give thee a sign or a wonder, and that sign or wonder which he hath said come to pass, and then say, Let us go after strange gods, which thou hast not known, and let us serve them; hearken not thou unto the words of that prophet or dreamer of dreams. For the Lord thy God proveth you, to wit whether ye love the Lord your God with your heart, and with all your soul. Ye shall walk after the Lord your God, and fear him, keep his commandments, and hearken unto his voice, serve him, and cleave unto him. And that prophet or dreamer of dreams shall die; because he hath spoken to turn you away from the Lord your God, &c. And therefore thou shalt put the evil away from thee. If thy brother, the son of thy mother, or thine own son, or thy daughter, or the wife that lieth in thy bosom, or thy friend, which is as thine own soul unto thee, entice thee secretly, saying, Let us go and serve strange gods, which thou hast not known, nor yet thy fathers, &c.; thou shalt not consent unto him, nor hearken unto him: thine eye shall not pity him, neither shalt thou have any compassion on him, nor keep him secret, but cause him to be slain. Thine hand shall be first upon him to kill him, and then the hands of all the people. And thou shalt stone him with stones that he die; because he hath gone about to thrust thee away from the Lord thy God, which brought thee out of the land of Egypt, and from the house of bondage. And all Israel shall hear, and fear, and shall do no more any such wickedness as this is among you."

Whether the magistrate may lawfully punish idolaters and false teachers.

Deut. xiii.

Again God saith: "The prophet which shall presume to speak a word in my name, which I have not commanded him to speak, or that speaketh in the name of strange gods, the same prophet shall die." Also in another place: "Whosoever curseth his God shall bear his sin. And he that blasphemeth the name of the Lord, let him be slain; and all the multitude shall stone him to death: whether he be born in the land or a stranger, when he blasphemeth the name of the Lord, let him be slain." Deut. xviii. Lev. xxiv.

Can there be a greater cursing of God, than to fall from him which is the alone true God, and to turn unto creatures, and to crave all things of them, as of God? And can there be a more heinous blasphemy done or spoken against the most glorious name of the Lord our God, than to preach and set forth doctrine contrary to God's word; and by this means to bring the people into error, and to lead them from the way of truth unto falsehood, and so finally unto everlasting damnation? "Wo be unto them," saith the prophet, "that call evil good and good evil, which make darkness light and light darkness, that make sour sweet and sweet sour! Wo be unto them that are wise in their own sight, and think themselves to have understanding!"

Isai. v.

But we have not only an expressed commandment to kill and put out of the way all idolaters and false prophets, I mean such as wilfully and obstinately resist the truth, and will by no means be reformed; but we read also of divers kings and rulers which did put the same commandment in execution and practice; and God blessed them greatly for it.

2 Kings x.

Read we not that Jehu king of Israel caused all the priests of Baal to be slain, all the images to be fet out of the temple of Baal, and to be burnt? He caused also his captains and men of war to break the image of Baal, and to destroy the house of Baal; so that Baal's house was made a draught house. And did not the Lord bless Jehu for thus doing; so that he lived quietly in his kingdom unto his dying day, and his children sat on the seat of Israel unto the fourth generation? Read we not also that king Josia put down the ministers of Baal, whom the kings of Juda had founded to burn incense in the hill-altars and cities of Juda that were round about Jerusalem, and also them that burnt incense unto Baal, to the sun, to the moon, to the planets, and to all the host of heaven? Read we not also that king Josia did slay all the priests of the hill-altars that were there, even upon the altars, and burnt men's bones upon them, that were idolaters and false preachers? Moreover, read we not that Nabuchodonozor, although an heathen king, set out a proclamation, and commanded that all people, kindreds, and tongues, which spake any blasphemy against the God of Israel, should die the death, and that their houses should be prised[1], &c.? Read we not again that king Darius gave out a commandment that whosoever did hinder the glory of the God of Israel, there should be a beam taken from his house and set up, and he hanged thereon, and his house be made a dunghill? What shall I speak of king Artaxerses, which commanded also, that whosoever would not fulfil the law of the God of Israel and obey his voice, he should have his judgment without delay, whether it were unto death, or to be rooted out, or to be condemned in goods, or to be put in prison?

2 Kings xxiii. Dan. iii. Ezra vi. Ezra vii.

Furthermore, we read that these noble emperors, Constantinus, Valentinianus, and Theodosius, did not only by their laws forbid the worshipping of idols, but also they made certain penal statutes against the idolaters, so that whosoever would presume to offer sacrifice to any idol contrary to their decrees, they should die the death. Likewise read we of Leo the third, emperor of Greece, which commanded all images to be taken out of churches and openly to be brent. He made a law also, that whosoever resisted his proceedings in this behalf, he should suffer death[2]. Ecclesiastical histories minister unto us divers such like examples, which declare manifestly that princes have not only authority by the word of God to meddle with matters of christian religion, but also to punish the enemies and hinderers of the same, but specially idolaters and false prophets.

Constant. Valentin. Theodosius. Leo the emperor.

Whether it be lawful to kill heretics.

Father. And what sayest thou of heretics? *Son*. Even the same that I have said of idolaters and false prophets.

Father. May the magistrate also punish them? *Son*. Yea, and also take them out of this life, if they will not repent, amend, and come to the truth.

Father. What if they keep their errors and heresies in their breasts secretly, and publish them not abroad? *Son*. Then hath the magistrates nothing to do with them. God alone seeth and judgeth the heart.

[1 Prised: overturned, destroyed.]

[2 See before, page 69, note 2; and page 305, note 2. See also Cod. Justin. in Gothofr. Corp. Jur. Civil. Amst. 1663. Lib. I. Tit. viii. p. 36.]

Father. What if the heretics publish their heresies, and go about to infect other with their pestilent doctrine? *Son.* They ought not straightways to be ungently entreated, to be thrown into prison, to be condemned, and so to be carried unto the place of execution; but first of all to have them convented before the godly magistrates and learned ministers, bishops, or pastors, and so friendly and lovingly to confer with them, without scorns, checks, or taunts, that their conference may seem to proceed not of anger, malice, hatred, or displeasure, but rather of amity, friendship, love, and good will, yea, of such an heart as wisheth rather their salvation than their damnation. And forasmuch as heresy is a spiritual thing, and cannot be weeded out with any corporal violence; therefore ought such as be godly learned to travail with heretics, and to convince them, not with fire and fagot, with sword and halter, or with law will I[3], nor yet with old customs and ancient fathers, but with the sincere and pure word of God, with the faithful testimonies of the old godly writers, and with the perfect consent of the apostolic and primitive church.

These are the armours[4] which we must use against the heretics and enemies of God's truth, as St Paul saith: "The weapons of our warfare are not carnal things, 2 Cor. x. but things mighty in God to cast down strong holds; wherewith we overthrow counsels, and every high thing that exalteth itself against the knowledge of God, and bring into captivity all imagination to the obedience of Christ, and are ready to take vengeance on all disobedience." For it is required of a spiritual minister not only to Tit. i. be able to exhort by wholesome doctrine, but also to improve, convince, and overcome them that speak against it. "The servant of the Lord," saith St Paul, "must not 2 Tim. ii. strive, but be gentle unto all men, apt to teach, and one that can suffer the evil with meekness, and can inform them that resist (the truth), if that God at any time will give them repentance for to know the truth; and that they may come to themselves again out of the snare of the devil, which are holden captive of him at his pleasure." Again he saith: "Brethren, if a man be taken in any fault, ye which are spiritual Gal. vi. help to amend him in the spirit of meekness, considering thyself, lest thou also be tempted." St James also saith: "Brethren, if any of you do err from the truth, James v. and another convert him, let the same know that he, which converteth the sinner from going astray out of his way, shall save a soul from death, and shall hide the multitude of sins."

Father. What if they, after friendly conference had, do persevere and continue still stubborn and obstinate in their erroneous opinions and blasphemous doctrine? *Son.* I would wish that, according to the common proverb, every stone should be moved, and every occasion sought to win them unto the truth; but if they remain incorrigible, and will by no means leave and give place to the truth, then let this commandment of St Paul be obeyed: "A man that is an heretic, or an author of sects, Tit. iii. after the first and second admonition, avoid; knowing that he (that is such) is perverted, and sinneth even damned by himself." Or as our Saviour Christ biddeth: "Tell it to the congregation. And if he hear not the congregation, let him be unto Matt. xviii. thee as an heathen man and as a publican."

Father. Now then is the heretic avoided; he is to the congregation as an heathen and publican; he is given to Satan; he is excommunicate; he is cut off from the congregation of God: what is now to be done? Shall he straightways be put to death? *Son.* St Paul saith: "The magistrate beareth not the sword in vain." If Rom. xiii. he that beareth false witness against man be worthy of death by the commandment of God; is he worthy of less punishment that beareth false witness against God? If he that speaketh evil of a king, which is but a mortal man, yea, but earth, dust, and ashes, dieth the death without remedy; shall he escape unpunished, that openeth his mouth to speak blasphemies against the Most Highest, that King of kings and Lord of lords? If that member be worthily cut off from the body, which is corrupt, and not only unprofitable, but also perilous, yea, pernicious and hurtful to the whole body; is such one to be suffered in a commonweal, which by his pestilent doctrine

[3 Law will I: arbitrary law. Sic volo, sic jubeo, &c.]

[4 The folio reads *armonies*, which is most probably a misprint.]

corrupteth both body and soul, and bringeth them to everlasting damnation? If that magistrate be counted worthy of praise and commendation, which doth so defend his country with his sword from the invasion of a foreign enemy, that his subjects may live in his realm quietly both with bodies and goods; how much more worthy to be commended is that ruler, which with his authority and power doth so drive away the masters of errors and the teachers of false doctrine either by banishment or by sword out of his realm, that his people, retaining the wholesome doctrine of the gospel, may be sound in faith and good works, and so living with a quiet conscience before God and man in this world, obtain everlasting joy in the world to come! If that shepherd be counted wise and discreet, which putteth away the scabby and diseased sheep from the residue of the flock which is whole and sound; is not that magistrate to be counted prudent and wise which separateth such as are infected with error and heresy from them that are yet sound in doctrine and judgment?

1 Tim. ii. Notwithstanding it is to be wished that, forasmuch as God "would have all men to be saved and to come unto the knowledge of the truth;" again, forasmuch as
Matt. xx. God alone giveth faith and right judgment, and calleth some at this hour, some at that hour, even when his godly pleasure and blessed will is; the magistrate would first of all gently and lovingly deal with heretics, and see unto what conformity he could bring them with his wisdom and counsel, and also suffer them to have access unto such as be godly learned, which may yet once again have conference with them.

It were not unfitting also, that the magistrate should enforce and compel the heretics to resort unto the hearing of sermons, in the which sermons the heresies of those sectaries should be declared, refelled[1], and confuted by the word of God of the preachers; if peradventure by this means it may come to pass, that they may be called unto repentance, and unto the knowledge of their errors, and so be saved. For who knoweth not, that this is the ordinary way which God useth in calling sinners unto
Rom. x. repentance and faith; even the preaching of his word, as St Paul saith: "Faith cometh by hearing, and hearing cometh by the word of God?" The psalmograph
Psal. li. also saith: "I will teach the unrighteous thy ways; and the ungodly shall turn unto thee."

If the heretics will not hear, but still obstinately resist the truth, and go forth to spread abroad their errors and heresies, yea, their blasphemies against God and his holy word, and by this means seduce the subjects and lead them out of the way of truth, and move sedition in the commonweal, setting them at variance which ought to remain in one mind, as citizens of one city and subjects of one magistrate; then may the head ruler with a good conscience punish those heretics, not only as heretics, but as seditious persons and troublers of commonweal, whether it be by imprisonment, loss of goods, banishment, sword, or otherwise. For this sentence of St Paul must
Rom. xiii. for ever and ever abide true: "If thou do evil, then fear. For the higher power beareth not the sword in vain. For he is the minister of God to take vengeance on
1 Pet. ii. him that doth evil." St Peter also testifieth, that "the rulers are appointed of God unto the praise of them that do well, but unto the punishment of evil-doers."

But if the magistrates be so sheepish, sleepy, and sluggish, and led with such childish and foolish pity, that they will not punish these wicked blasphemers of God's truth, and seditious troublers of the commonweal, but let them run at large, or suffer all men to have free access unto them, and so they poison the minds of the simple and innocent with their pestilent errors and blasphemous heresies; let those rulers be well assured that, as they do not the duty of a good magistrate, so shall they not escape unpunished at the hand of God; and so many as perish through their negligence and their dissolute or loose regiment, their blood shall be required at those
1 Sam. ii. unrighteous magistrates' hands before the judging-seat of God's majesty. "Them that worship me," saith God, "I will worship; and they that despise me shall come to shame."

Father. Albeit I do not disallow these things which thou hast spoken concerning heretics, and the punishment of them, specially if they be incorrigible, sowers of

[[1] Refelled: the same as *confuted.*]

wicked doctrine, corrupters of men's minds, seducers from God and his truth, seditious persons, troublers of the commonweal, authors of schisms and divisions, breakers of the public peace, &c.; yet I would wish that all magistrates should be ware and circumspect in handling such as be called heretics, and specially those magistrates which bear rule in the kingdom of the pope. For hitherto the tyranny of the pope and of his papists have so prevailed in many kingdoms, that whosoever hath spoken against the lessest of the pope's decrees and ceremonies, he hath been counted for an heretic, accused and condemned, yea, and with fire consumed unto ashes; although he believed and confessed all things to be true that are comprehended within the holy bible. These smeared pill-pates[2], I would say, prelates, first of all accused him, and afterward pronounced the sentence of death upon him, and straightways delivered him to the temporal magistrate for to be put to execution; making the magistrate their hangman and bond-slave, to hang, to draw, to quarter, to burn, to drown, &c. as it pleased them to appoint. O slavery! O misery! O unnoble nobility! Note.

In such places therefore, where the devil and the pope yet reign, it shall be necessary for all magistrates, if they will avoid the heavy indignation and fierce displeasure of God, to take heed unto these bloody antichrists, and from henceforth no more to be their hangmen or slaughtermen, but to know the cause themselves, and to examine the person themselves, yea, and to judge the matter themselves, and afterward pronounce as it shall seem good to their wisdom and discretions, yet so that they shall at all times seek rather the salvation of the person than the destruction, the life than the death; evermore remembering that their power is given them from above to edify and not to destroy. Let the destruction of errors rather than of men be sought. He that is this day a Saul may be to-morrow a Paul. Beware, ye temporal rulers, betimes, and be no longer the pope's hangmen.

If that noble doctor, Saint Augustine, had been taken away either by halter, fire, or sword, when he was infected with the heresy of the Manichees; verily he had not left to the church of Christ so many noble and learned works, unto the great profit of his posterity. St Austin.

Neither are they straightways to be counted heretics, which do err peradventure of ignorance and for lack of knowledge; but such as through the instinct and motion of the devil have drunken in damnable errors directly against the manifest word of God, and obstinately, maliciously, and willingly defend them, and by no means will suffer themselves to be plucked from them, either with the authority of God's word, or with the testimonies of the ancient writers, or yet with probable reasons and arguments.

And therefore must those magistrates, which live under the tyranny of the Romish bishop, that antichrist, that son of perdition, and that Babylonical strumpet, take heed that they be no more deceived with the glistering visor of feigned holiness, nor yet become any longer the hangmen and butchers of those spiteful, I would say, spiritual generation, which condemn men, not for resisting the truth of God's word, nor yet for dissolution of life, although never so wicked and detestable; but for impugning their feigned holiness and counterfeit religion, wherewith they go about to lead their captives, not to salvation, but to destruction; not to life, but to death; yea, death everlasting. If those whom the bloody and cruel papists, that adders' spawn and generation of vipers, do accuse and condemn for heretics, be found only to resist antichrist and his antichristian decrees, let the magistrates take heed that they join not hands with the adversaries, and consent to the shedding of innocent blood, as their predecessors have done in times past, unto the great peril of their everlasting damnation; but rather, washing their hands from their wicked conspiracy, withstand those bloody papists, yea, and remembering themselves to be called "gods" and "God's ministers" in the holy scripture, make those whelps of Rome rather to obey them, than they any more to be in subjection and slavery to so wolvish and Nero-like generation, a generation sprung out of hell, whose heart imagineth nothing but mischief, whose mouth speaketh nothing but blasphemies, whose hands are imbrued with the blood of saints, whose feet are swift to run to do mischief, whose parts, both inward and outward, only imagine and practise sin, wickedness, tyranny, and abomination. The description of the papists.

[2 Pill-pates: pilled or polled, i.e. shaven or shorn, heads. Synonymous with *shavelings*. Folio, *pylpates*.]

But if they whom these Babylonical merchants have condemned for heretics, (which seldom chance,) be heretics indeed, and obstinately persist in their errors and heresies; then would I with all my heart wish that all such should be ordered as thou, my son, hast heretofore godly declared. Let all means possible be sought for their salvation before any extremity be shewed. Let the cruel sentence of the papists move the godly magistrates nothing at all to attempt extremities; but let them rather remember with themselves that they be the ministers of God, which willeth not the death of a sinner, but rather that he turn and live; which will have all men to be saved, and to come unto the knowledge of the truth; which call some unto him in the cock-crowing, some in the dawning of the day, some in the morning, some at high noon-day, some in the evening, some at midnight, &c. Let them also consider that power is given them, not to destroy but to edify.

How the old godly magistrates handled heretics in times past.

Let them also follow the practices of the noble ancient magistrates, which lived in the church of Christ before the tyranny of the bishop of Rome was known. They most diligently at all times laboured to suppress heresies and to confound heretics, that the church of Christ might in the unity of the christian faith, and in the sincerity of God's true word, continually remain and abide. They called councils both general and national, they gathered together learned men in the holy scriptures, they commanded the heretics to be present, disputations were had, the heretics were suffered quietly, and without any mocks or taunts, to speak, and to shew their learning and reasons. Answer was made again soberly, charitably, and temperately, yea, and that not out of the pope's decrees, or law will I, but out of the word of God, which at that time was judge alone of all controversies. The learned bishops and godly pastors in all their disputations behaved themselves so gravely and lovingly, so quietly and learnedly, that whatsoever came from them seemed to proceed from the spirit of humility, meekness, gentleness, love, and good will, yea, from such a spirit as tendered nothing more than their amendment, conversion, and salvation; whereby it came to pass many times, that they which before erred, seeing the great gentleness of the learned fathers toward them, both in quiet disputation and in friendly exhortation and in godly counsel-giving (as I may speak nothing of their true and sincere allegations of the holy scripture, and of their arguments and reasons grounded on God's word), gave over their errors, repented, converted unto God, embraced the truth of God's word, praised God, thanked the good magistrates and godly ministers, and for ever after remained in the unity of the apostolic faith and doctrine; insomuch that St Austin

Epist. 48. ad Vincent.

write of such on this manner: "We now rejoice of the correction and amendment of many which so truly hold and defend the catholic unity, and are glad that they are delivered from their old errors; so that now we may well marvel at them, yea, and that with great gratulation and rejoicing[1]."

The godly magistrates and learned bishops at that time sought nothing else but the conversion and salvation of men. The errors, not the men, they sought to extirp and weed out. Of the heresies, and not of the heretics, they laboured to see the de-

Lib. i. contra Literas Petil. cap. 29.

struction, as St Austin admonisheth, saying: "Love the men, kill the errors, strive for the truth without cruelty[2]." Yea, many of the magistrates were so loving and friendly, so gentle and long-suffering, and so desirous of the heretics' conversion and salvation, that although they seemed incorrigible and too much obstinate in the defence of their damnable errors and heresies, after that they were convinced and overcome by the word of God, yet if they did abstain from sparsing abroad the seeds of their wicked doctrine, and from corrupting other, and lived quietly, and otherwise behaved themselves honestly and peaceably in the commonweal, they would not minister unto them any extreme punishment at the first, but quietly bare with them, patiently abiding their conversion. But if they passed these bounds, so that by publishing their errors they gathered to them a church, and so sowed sedition among the people unto the great

[1 Nam de multorum jam correctione gaudemus, qui tam veraciter unitatem catholicam tenent atque defendunt, et a pristino errore se liberatos esse lætantur, ut eos cum magna gratulatione miremur.—August. Op. Par. 1679—1700. Ad Vincent. Rogatist. Epist. xciii. 1. Tom. II. col. 230.]

[2 Diligite homines, interficite errores: sine superbia de veritate præsumite, sine sævitia pro veritate certate.—Id. Cont. Lit. Petil. Lib. I. 31. Tom. IX. col. 218.]

disturbance of the christian public weal; then the magistrates, perceiving these great enormities, according to their authority and power given them of God, some they deprived of their liberties, livings, promotions, and honours; some they banished, some they punished by the purse; and such as were the chief seductors and deceivers of the people they kept in prison, till that they remembering themselves came unto amendment, otherwise they continued still in prison. Few did they put to death, except they added to their heresies commotions, tumults, seditions, insurrections, and such other plagues and pestilences of the commonweal.

And for my part I would wish with all my heart that this order were used universally in the church of Christ at this present day: then should not the men, but the errors, be destroyed, slain, and made out of the way; yea, many should then peradventure be saved, which now dying in their errors be damned. Notable is this sentence of St Austin: "This pleased no good men in the catholic church, if cruelty extend itself so far that it killeth any man, yea, though he be an heretic.[3]"

Son. Lenity, clemency, and gentleness is to be shewed to all men, specially to such as err in matters of faith, if peradventure hereafter through the benefit of God they may be called unto repentance and amendment, and so be saved. Notwithstanding, both in this and in all other matters the magistrate must always set before his eyes the glory of God, the avancement of his true religion, the setting forth of Christ's gospel, the salvation of his subjects, the public peace, the conservation of the commonweal, the avancement of virtue, and the suppression of vice. Whatsoever shall make unto the setting forth of these things, that must the magistrate with all diligence perform; but whatsoever shall hinder these things, that shall the godly magistrate weed out and take away, and by no means suffer to remain in his realm, lest it be made of the church of Christ the synagogue of antichrist, and a cage of all foul and unclean birds. For this sentence of St Paul must always abide true: "If thou do evil, then fear. For the higher power beareth not the sword in vain. For he is the minister of God to take vengeance on him that doth evil." And St Peter saith, that "the rulers are appointed of God unto the praise of them that do well, but unto the punishment of them that do evil." And David saith: "I will destroy out of hand all the ungodly that are in the land, that I may root out all wicked doers from the city of the Lord."

Rom. xiii.

1 Pet. ii.

Psal. ci.

Father. God give all magistrates his holy Spirit, which may direct them in all their ways, and so govern them in all their affairs, that they attempt nothing contrary to the glory of God and the benefit of the commonweal! *Son.* Amen.

Father. Now that we have heard the office of the temporal magistrate, let us hear also what the duty is of the spiritual magistrate, I mean, the minister of the Lord's word, whether he be called bishop, deacon, minister, pastor, overseer of the Lord's flock, &c. *Son.* Agreed. For it followeth next in order.

OF THE OFFICE AND DUTY OF THE MINISTERS OF GOD'S WORD.

Father. First of all, tell me what a bishop or spiritual pastor is. *Son.* He is the minister of Christ, and the dispensator of the mysteries of God.

What a bishop or spiritual pastor is. 1 Cor. iv.

Father. Why is he called "the minister of Christ"? *Son.* Because he is Christ's servant and embassador, to speak and to do those things which he hath received in commission of his Master Christ.

Father. May not a spiritual pastor speak and preach, do and work, what he will? *Son.* Whosoever preacheth and teacheth any otherwise than he hath learned of his Master Christ, or worketh any thing that is contrary to his Master's will, he is not the minister of Christ, but the bond-slave of antichrist. St Paul saith: "Although we ourselves, or an angel from heaven, should preach unto you any other gospel than that which we have preached, hold him accursed. As we said afore, even so say we

Gal. i.

[[3] Augustine repeatedly expresses his unwillingness that harsh measures should be used against heretics. See Ad Donat. Procons. Epist. c. Tom. II. cols. 269, 70, in which the idea, though not the exact words above cited, may be found.]

again now, If any man preach unto you any other gospel than that which ye have
1 Pet. iv. received, hold him accursed." St Peter also saith: "If any man speak, let him so
speak, that it be agreeable to the word of God." Hitherto belongeth the saying of
2 John. St John: "If any man come unto you, and bring not this doctrine, receive him not
into that house, neither bid him God speed. For he that biddeth him God speed, is
partaker of his evil works." Christ commandeth his ministers to preach the gospel,
that is to say, remission and forgiveness of sins, in his name, and not men's traditions
and his own dreams. And as the minister of Christ ought to preach nothing but
Christ's word, so ought all his acts, deeds, and enterprises tend unto this purpose
only, to set forth the glory of God and the honour of his holy name, both in life
John xiii. and doctrine, both in work and word, as Christ saith: "I have given you ensample,
that, as I have done, so likewise ye should do."

Father. Why is a spiritual pastor called "a dispensator of the mysteries of God"?
Son. For as the steward of a nobleman hath the treasures and riches of his master
and lord, to bestow and distribute them where his master's good will and pleasure
is; so likewise he that is a spiritual pastor and an overseer of the Lord's flock hath
the heavenly riches and most blessed treasures of God in possession, not to hide them
under a bushel, nor to couch them in the ground, but to communicate them to other,
even to such as the Lord hath committed to his spiritual charge, as it is written by
Mal. ii. the prophet: "The lips of a priest keep knowledge, and at his mouth shall they
require the law; for he is the angel of the Lord of hosts."

Father. What are these "mysteries of God"? *Son*. The knowledge of his holy and
blessed will, the gift of his word and sacraments, the opening of his Son Christ Jesus
to mankind, and of their salvation by him alone.

Father. Why are they called "mysteries"? *Son*. Because they be the secrets of
Matt. xi. God, hid from the prudent and wise of this world, and revealed only to such as the
good will and pleasure of God is.

The ministry of the word is God's ordinance. *Father*. And is a spiritual pastor an officer in the church of Christ at the
appointment of God, or doth he usurp that authority uncalled and unappointed of
God? *Son*. Even as the temporal magistrate is God's ordinance, and hath his sword
given of him, of God for the maintenance of the good and for the suppression of the
evil; so likewise is the spiritual magistrate, I mean the minister of God's word, the
ordinance of God, and hath a sword also committed to him for the comfort of the
good and for the chastisement of the evil.

Eph. vi. *Father*. What is his sword? *Son*. The word of God, which St Paul calleth "the
sword of the Spirit."

Father. Shew me by the word of God, that the spiritual minister ruleth in the
church of Christ at God's appointment. *Son*. A little before our Lord and Saviour
Christ ascended with his body into the kingdom of his Father, he said to his
apostles, and also to all their successors, which are all spiritual ministers that labour
Matt. xxviii. in word and doctrine: "Teach all nations, baptizing them in the name of the Father,
and of the Son, and of the Holy Ghost, teaching them to keep all things that I
have commanded you. And behold I am with you continually unto the world's end."
Mark xvi. Again: "Go ye throughout the world, and preach the gospel to every creature. He that
believeth and is baptized shall be saved: but he that believeth not shall be con-
John xx. demned." Once again: "As my Father sent me, so send I you. Take the Holy
Ghost. Whose sins ye shall forgive are forgiven them: whose sins ye do retain are
John xxi. retained." Item: "Feed my lambs." "Feed my sheep." And St Paul saith: "God
1 Cor. xii. hath ordained in the church, first apostles, secondarily prophets, thirdly teachers," &c.

Father. May every man that will take upon him this ecclesiastical function or
Rom. x. office of spiritual ministry? *Son*. Nothing less. For St Paul saith: "How shall
they preach, except they be sent?" Aaron and the prophets, Christ and his apostles,
preached not till they were sent. Those that take upon them the ministry before
they be called are of the number of those whom God by the prophet describeth on
Jer. xxiii. this manner: "I sent them not, and they ran: I spake not unto them, and they
preached."

Of calling unto the ministry. *Father*. How many ways may the ministers be called unto the ministry? *Son*.
Two. One is, when they be called immediately of God, as the prophets and apostles

were, which were raised up of God to prophesy and to teach without any vocation or calling of man. And this kind of vocation God useth customably outwardly to approve and confirm with wonderful testimonies and signs, as we may more see in Moses, Helias, &c. But this calling is now ceased. The other is, when the ministers be called mediately, as they say, and in order of men, that is to say, of the magistrate and of the people. They that are thus called unto the ministry may right well persuade themselves that they are called of God, and that their calling is lawful, and that they living in that vocation please God, and their service is acceptable unto God.

Father. May not a man offer himself to the church, and desire to be admitted unto the ministry? *Son.* Yes, verily, so that it rise not of ambition and of the desire of ease and worldly lucre: again, so that he submit himself to the judgment of the congregation, either to be admitted, or to be refused. For thus writeth St Paul: "If any man desire the office of a bishop, he desireth a good work." Again: 1 Tim. iii.
"Covet spiritual gifts; but most chiefly that ye may prophesy," that is to say, teach 1 Cor. xiv.
the congregation. Whosoever therefore perceived himself to be apt and meet to rule in the congregation, both in life and doctrine, and feeleth in himself to be moved thereunto by the instinct of the Holy Ghost, and hath in himself also an ardent zeal and fervent desire to help and profit the church of Christ, and to avance God's true religion; the same man may with a good conscience desire the ministry.

Father. What difference is there between a bishop and a spiritual minister? *Son.* None at all: their office is one, their authority and power is one[1]. And therefore St Paul calleth the spiritual ministers sometime bishops, sometime elders, sometime pastors, sometime teachers, &c.

The ministers of God's word have all one authority.

Father. What is "bishop" in English? *Son.* An overseer or superintendent, as St Paul said to the elders or bishops of Ephesus: "Take heed unto yourselves, and to all the flock over whom the Holy Ghost hath made you bishops, overseers, or superintendents, to rule, or feed, the congregation of God, which he hath purchased with his blood."

Bishop. Acts xx.

Father. What manner of man ought he to be, that should be chosen to be a minister? *Son.* St Paul, in his letters unto Timothy and Titus, declareth this evidently. Unto bishop Timothy he writeth thus: "A bishop (he meaneth every spiritual minister) must be blameless, the husband of one wife, diligent, sober, discreet, a keeper of hospitality, apt to teach; not given to overmuch wine, no fighter, not greedy of filthy lucre; but gentle, abhorring fighting, abhorring covetousness, one that ruleth well his own house, one that hath children in subjection with all reverence. For if a man cannot rule well his own house, how shall he care for the congregation of God? He may not be a young scholar, lest he swell, and fall into the judgment of the evil-speaker. He must also have a good report of them which are without, lest he fall into rebuke and snare of the evil-speaker." And unto bishop Titus he writeth thus: "For this Tit. i.
cause left I thee in Creta, that thou shouldest reform the things that are unperfect, and shouldest ordain elders in every city, as I had appointed thee: if any be blameless, the husband of one wife, having faithful children, which are not slandered of riot, neither are disobedient. For a bishop must be blameless, as the steward of God; not stubborn, not angry, not given to much wine, no fighter, not given to filthy lucre; but a keeper of hospitality, one that loveth goodness, sober, righteous, godly, temperate,

What manner of man a spiritual minister ought to be. 1 Tim. iii.

[1 It may be proper to say, that the Romanists, apparently in order to exalt the pope as the sole fountain of ecclesiastical power, did much to depress the authority and office of bishops. Sometimes in enumerations of the orders of the church bishops seem hardly admitted to be a distinct order. Discussions upon this point occurred at the council of Trent; when those who held that all the apostles, and by consequence all bishops, derived their authority from Christ were told that they took away the due authority of the pope. See Fra. Paolo. Hist. Conc. Tr. Lib. vii. In Burnet, Hist. Ref. Vol. I. Records Addenda v., may be found a Declaration subscribed by many bishops and other divines, in which they express their belief that "in the new testament there is no mention made of any degrees or distinctions in orders, but only of deacons or ministers, and of priests or bishops." This notion was hence, it would seem, introduced into the book called "The Institution of a Christian Man," which appeared in 1537. This will shew that Becon was not singular in the opinion he expresses in this place. It is of course not intended to discuss the matter here: it may, however, be observed that Bingham produces abundant evidence from the early Fathers to shew that "the order of bishops was always owned to be superior to that of presbyters." Orig. Eccles. Book ii. chaps. i. ii. See also Burnet, Vol. I. Addenda.]

and such as cleaveth unto the true word of doctrine, that he may be able also to exhort by wholesome learning, and to improve them that say against it."

Father. I would gladly that this rule of St Paul were observed in the election and admission of our spiritual ministers in this our age. Then should not the ministry be so evil spoken of as it is at this present. *Son.* It were good in this behalf for the bishops
1 Tim. v. and elders of the congregation to remember this commandment of the apostle: "Lay hands
1 Tim. iii. suddenly on no man, neither be partaker of other men's sins." Again: "Let them first be proved, and then let them minister, so that no man be able to reprove them."

The office of a spiritual pastor.

Father. Let me now hear what the office and duty of a bishop or spiritual minister is. *Son.* It consisteth principally in three points: first, in teaching the word of God, and in ministering the sacraments: secondly, in praying for the people: thirdly, in leading a good life, unto the example of his parishioners. There are also that add to these aforesaid things the maintenance of hospitality, and say that it appertaineth also unto the office of a bishop or spiritual pastor to maintain hospitality. And St
Tit. i. Paul, in the description of a bishop, saith that he ought "not to be given to filthy lucre; but to be a keeper of hospitality."

Hospitality decayed among bishops.

Father. Verily, a virtue worthy of so noble estate. And would God that our bishops and spiritual pastors were more diligent in this behalf, that they might feed not only with word, but also with work! But come off, tell me, is the first and principal point of a bishop's and a spiritual minister's office to teach and preach the word of God? *Son.* Yea, truly.

Of preaching God's word.

Father. What if he preach not, neither can preach? *Son.* Then is he a Nicholas bishop[1] and an idol, and indeed no better than a painted bishop on a wall: yea, he
Isai. lvi. is, as the prophet saith, a "dumb dog, not able to bark;" he is also, as our Saviour
Matt. v. Christ saith, "unsavoury salt, worth for nothing but to be cast out, and to be trodden under foot of men." Wo be to those rulers that set such idols and white daubed walls over the flock of Christ, whom he hath purchased with his precious blood! Horrible and great is their damnation.

Father. Let me hear it proved by the word of God, that it is the duty of a spiritual pastor to preach and teach the word of God. *Son.* The scripture is full of this matter
Isai. xl. in every place. By the prophet Esay God himself saith: "Go up unto the high hill, thou that bringest good tidings: lift up thy voice with power, O thou preacher:
Isai. lviii. lift it up, and be not afraid." "Cry now as loud as thou canst. Leave not off, lift up thy voice like a trumpet, and shew my people their offences, and the house of Jacob
Isai. lxii. their sins." Again: "I have set watchmen upon thy walls, O Jerusalem, which shall neither cease day nor night to preach the Lord." By the prophet Ezechiel God saith
Ezek. iii. thus: "Thou son of man, I have made thee a watchman unto the house of Israel; therefore take good heed to the words of my mouth, and give them warning at my commandment. If I say unto thee concerning the ungodly man, that without doubt he must die, and thou givest him not warning, nor speakest unto him that he may turn from his evil way and so to live, then shall the ungodly man die in his own unrighteousness; but his blood will I require at thy hand. Nevertheless, if thou give warning unto the wicked, and he yet forsake not his ungodliness, then shall he die in his own wickedness; but thou hast discharged thy soul."

John xx. Our Saviour Christ saith to his disciples: "As my Father sent me, so send I
Isai. lxi. Mark i. you." Now who knoweth not, that Christ was sent of his heavenly Father to preach
Luke iv. the gospel, as we may see in divers and sundry places of the holy scripture? It therefore followeth, that such as are sent of Christ are sent to preach the gospel. If they preach not, it is an evident token that Christ sent them not, but antichrist

The dregs of the pope. A rabble of rotten eggs.

and the devil. When Christ sent forth his apostles, he commanded them not to baptize bells; nor to hallow churches, copes, vestments, chalices, altars, altar-cloths, &c.; nor to consecrate oil and cream; nor to butter children in the forehead; nor to sing matins, mass, and even-song in Latin; nor to make holy bread and holy water; nor to hallow

[[1] Nicholas bishop: a mock bishop. The allusion is to the boy-bishop, who was elected and inaugurated on St Nicholas's day (Dec. 6), or the evening before. The practice of appointing this mock prelate was abrogated in the earlier years of the reformation, but revived under queen Mary, in 1556. See Strype, Eccles. Mem. Vol. III. chap. xxxix.]

palms, ashes, candle, fire, &c.; nor to hear auricular confession, and to give private absolution in a tongue which the penitent understandeth not; nor to enjoin penance to say five *Ave Marias* in the worship of the five joys of our lady, and five *Pater Nosters* in the honour of the five wounds of our Lord, and one creed in the worship of the twelve apostles, &c., to go on pilgrimage, to buy the pope's pardons, to purchase masses of *Scala Cœli*, to go woolward[2], to fast bread and water, &c.; nor to vow chastity and to lead an unpure single life; nor to wear shaven crowns, long gowns, tippets, copes, vestments, albs, surplices; nor to cense images; nor yet to make new decrees and constitutions for other to observe and keep, &c.; but he commanded them to keep[3]. Matt. xxviii.

And when Christ was ready to ascend into the kingdom of the Father, he commanded Peter and his fellow-apostles, yea, and all spiritual ministers, to feed his flock, (John xxi.) his lambs, and his sheep. St Peter also saith: "The elders which are among you (1 Pet. v.) I exhort, which am also an elder, and a witness of the afflictions of Christ, and also a partaker of the glory that shall be opened: feed ye Christ's flock, as much as lieth in you, taking the oversight of them, not as compelled thereto, but willingly; not for the desire of filthy lucre, but of a good mind; not as though ye were lords over the parishes, but that ye be an example to the flock. And when the chief Shepherd shall appear, ye shall receive an uncorruptible crown of glory." Likewise saith St Paul to every spiritual minister: "Give attendance to reading, to exhortation, to doctrine." (1 Tim. iv.) "Preach thou the word: be fervent in season and out of season: improve, rebuke, (2 Tim. iv.) exhort with all long-suffering and doctrine." And in the description of a bishop he saith: "A bishop must be meet to teach." (1 Tim. iii.) He requireth not only in a bishop or spiritual minister, that he be learned both in divine and human letters; again, that he have some mean knowledge at the least of tongues, Greek, Hebrew, and Latin; but also ☞ that he be endued with such gifts of grace from above, that he be apt to teach and to inform other. Not learning therefore alone, and the knowledge of tongues, is to be considered in him that shall be appointed to the ministry; but also the aptness of teaching.

Father. We may then lament in this our age the state of the church, which have such guides to rule over them as be neither learned nor apt to teach. *Son*. They be the blind guides of the blind. And "if the blind lead the blind, both fall into (Matt. xv.) the ditch."

Thus see we, that the holy scripture requireth of a bishop and spiritual pastor, that he be diligent in preaching the word of God at all times; seeing that "when the (Prov. xxix.) preaching of God's word fail, the people perish."

Father. What if they preach not? *Son*. Then nothing abideth them but everlasting damnation, as St Paul saith: "Wo unto me, if I preach not the gospel!" (1 Cor. ix.) And against such dumb dogs and blind guides God himself crieth out on this manner by the prophet, saying: "Wo be unto the shepherds of Israel that feed themselves! (Ezek. xxxiv.) Should not the shepherds feed the flocks? Ye have eaten up the fat, ye have clothed you with the wool, the best fed have ye slain; but the flock have ye not nourished. The weak have ye not holden up, the sick have ye not healed, the broken have not ye bound together, the outcasts have ye not brought again, the lost have ye not sought; but churlishly and cruelly have ye ruled them. Thus are they scattered here and there without a shepherd: yea, all the beasts of the field devour them, and they go astray, &c. Therefore, O ye shepherds, hear the word of the Lord. Thus saith the Lord God, As truly as I live, forasmuch as my sheep are robbed and devoured of all the wild beasts of the field, having no shepherd; and seeing that my shepherds take no regard of my sheep, but feed themselves only, and not my sheep; therefore hear the word of the Lord, O ye shepherds: thus saith the Lord God, Behold, I myself will upon the shepherds, and require my sheep from their hands, and make them cease from feeding of my sheep: yea, the shepherds shall feed themselves no more. For I will deliver my sheep out of their mouths; so that they shall not devour them after this," &c.

Father. Is it the duty of a spiritual pastor only by his preaching to exhort?

[2 Woolward: clad in wool.] [3 i.e. to keep *them*, the decrees, &c. as in Matt. xxviii. 20.]

Tit. i. *Son.* The minister of the Lord's word must not only be able, as St Paul saith, to exhort by wholesome doctrine, but also to improve, refel, confute, and put to silence such as speak against it. "The devil" in all ages "goeth about like a roaring lion, seeking whom he may devour," and ceaseth not at all times to sow his weeds, tares, and cockle in the Lord's field; I mean, to plant heresies, wicked opinions, and corrupt and false doctrine in the hearts of men by his false prophets, which transfigure and change themselves into angels of light, that they may the more easily creep into the consciences of the people, and so deceive them. It is therefore necessary and convenient that such be chosen unto the ministry, as shall be able to drive away these wolves from the Lord's flock; yea, and that not with fire and fagot, not with sword and halter, not with stocks and chains; but with the authorities of the holy scripture, with the testimonies of the ancient fathers, and with arguments agreeable to the word of God. Such a noble warrior in the Lord's battle was Apollos, that man of great eloquence and learning. He was "mighty in the scripture," saith Luke, "and spake fervently in the spirit," "and overcame the Jews mightily, shewing by the scriptures that Jesus was Christ." Such a warrior also was St Stephen, St Paul, St Austin, &c. These stoutly and strongly resisted the adversaries of God's truth, and defended the sheep of Christ from the teeth of the ravening wolves. Such ought all spiritual ☞ pastors to be. For it is the duty of a good shepherd not only to drive his flock unto good and wholesome pasture, but also to defend them from the ravening beasts; that no hurt chance unto them.

1 Pet. v. Matt. xiii. 2 Cor. xi. Acts xviii.

Father. God send us once such shepherds! We may sooner wish them than have them; so great ignorancy and blindness occupieth the hearts of the most part of our pastors at this present. *Son.* Besides doctrine, there is also required of a spiritual overseer due and faithful ministration of the sacraments. For of baptism thus saith the Lord Christ: "Baptize all nations in the name of the Father, and of the Son, and of the Holy Ghost." Of the mysteries of his body and blood he saith: "Do this in the remembrance of me," &c. The sacraments are then duly and faithfully ministered, when they be delivered unto the people according unto Christ's institution, ☞ without any adding or putting to of the pope's beggarly ceremonies, even simply and plainly; and when the true use of them is preached, declared, and set forth to the people, that the simplest and plainest among them may understand what they are, * what they signify, and what profit is received by the worthy taking of them. For sacraments received and not perceived profit little.

Of praying for the people.

Father. Rehearse unto me now the second point of the office and duty of a bishop or spiritual pastor. *Son.* That consisteth in praying for the people.

Lev. ix. *Father.* How provest thou that by the word of God? *Son.* God commanded the priests of the old law to pray for the people, which thing they used daily and diligently.
John xvii. Our Saviour Christ also prayed for his holy congregation and church. So likewise did the apostles of Christ. The holy and blessed apostle St Paul maketh mention in many places of his epistles how he prayed for the faithful continually. To the Romans
Rom. i. he writeth thus: "I thank my God, through Jesus Christ, for you all, that your faith is spoken of in all the world. For God is my witness (whom I serve with my spirit in the gospel of his Son) that without ceasing I make mention of you always
Phil. i. in my prayers," &c. To the Philippians also he writeth on this manner: "I thank my God with all remembrance of you always in all my prayers for you, and pray with gladness, because ye are come into the fellowship of the gospel," &c. Again: "God is my record how greatly I long after you from the very heart-root in Jesus Christ. And this I pray, that your love may increase yet more and more in know-
Col. i. ledge, and in all understanding," &c. To the Colossians he thus writeth: "We give thanks to God the Father of our Lord Jesus Christ always for you in our prayers." Again: "We have not ceased to pray for you, and to desire that ye might be fulfilled with the knowledge of his will in all wisdom and spiritual understanding, that ye
1 Thess. i. might walk worthy of the Lord," &c. To the Thessalonians he hath these words: "We give God thanks always for you all, making mention of you in our prayers without
2 Tim. i. ceasing," &c. To Timothy he writeth thus: "Without any ceasing I make mention of thee in my prayers night and day."

Thus see we, that as the duty of a good spiritual pastor is to preach the holy word of God to the people, so likewise is it his office to pray for the people.

Father. How shall he pray for the people? Shall he daily say, as the manner in the pope's church is, our lady's matins, matins of the day, mass, even-song, seven psalms, fifteen psalms, litany, suffrages, &c., and all in Latin, which for the most part neither the priests themselves nor the people understand?

Son. With a pure conscience, and in the Spirit, shall they call upon God our heavenly Father, in the name of Jesus Christ, his dearly-beloved Son, that he of his fatherly goodness will vouchsafe to defend his church against all heretics and tyrants, and to keep those, whom he hath committed to his spiritual charge, in the true love and study of the heavenly doctrine of the gospel, and to nourish and confirm in them faith and the true invocation of his holy and blessed name, that they may garnish the doctrine of the gospel with godly manners and virtuous examples. Thus did Christ and all the apostles, yea, and the godly bishops and pastors of the primitive church, pray for the people of God continually. And this also ought to be the exercise of all godly ministers at this present day, that the Lord may give good success to their labours, and make their doctrine to be fruitful in their hearers. For except God also teacheth inwardly by his holy Spirit, the outward ministry profiteth little, as St Paul: "I have planted, Apollo watered; but God gave the increase. 1 Cor. iii.
So then neither is he that planteth any thing, neither he that watereth; but God that giveth the increase." And as the psalmograph saith: "Except the Lord build Psal. cxxvii.
the house, their labour is but lost that build it. Except the Lord keep the city, the watchman waketh but in vain."

Father. What is the third point of the office and duty of a bishop or spiritual Of leading a godly and virtuous life.
pastor? *Son.* As it is the duty of a true spiritual and godly minister to preach the word of God, and to minister the holy sacraments to the people; again, to pray unto God also for the health and safeguard of his church; so likewise is it required of him, that he lead such a life, and so godly a conversation, that all his parishioners, beholding him and his manners, may take an ensample to live soberly, righteously, and godly in this present world.

To this end are the pastors called of our Saviour Christ "the light of the world." Matt. v.
For as the light sheweth unto us how we may safely walk, and without dangers; so likewise the spiritual ministers ought so to shine with all kind of virtues, that whosoever beholdeth the godliness of their life may know how to walk in all their conversation, and so please God. For this cause St Paul, in the description of a 1 Tim. iii. Tit. i.
bishop, doth principally and first of all require, that he be irreprehensible, that is to say, such one as no man can justly accuse, or lay any notable crime to his charge; again, to whom it cannot be worthily said, when he reproveth any sin, "Physician, Luke iv.
heal thyself;" or as St Paul hath: "Thou believest that thou thyself art a guide of Rom. ii.
the blind, a light of them which are in darkness, an informer of them which lack discretion, a teacher of the unlearned, which hast the ensample of knowledge and of the truth by the law. Thou therefore, which teachest another, teachest not thyself. Thou preachest a man should not steal, yet thou stealest. Thou that sayest a man should not commit advoutry, yet thou breakest wedlock. Thou abhorrest images, and yet robbest God of his honour. Thou, that makest thy boast of the law, through breaking the law dishonourest God. For the name of God is evil spoken of among the gentiles through you."

In consideration whereof, God in the old law commanded that none should minister unto him that had any deformity in his body. "Whosoever," saith he, "hath any Lev. xxi.
blemish shall not come near; as, if he be blind, or lame, or that hath a bruised nose, or that hath any misshapen member, or is broken-footed, or broken-handed, or have no hair on his eye-brows, or have a web or other blemish in his eye, or be mangy, or scald, or hath his stones broken," &c.

What other thing meant God by this, than that such as should be appointed to the ministry should be sound and faultless, both in doctrine and life, having none imperfection nor insufficiency in them, whereof they may be justly accused of the adversary. For look, what the eye is to the body, the same should the spiritual minister

Matt. vi. be to the flock of Christ. "The light of the body," saith our Saviour Christ, "is the eye. Wherefore if thine eye be single, all thy body shall be full of light: but and if thine eye be wicked, all thy body shall be full of darkness. Wherefore if the light that is within thee be darkness, how great is that self darkness!" "Be unto them that believe," saith St Paul, "an ensample in word, in conversation, in love, in spirit, in faith, in pureness." Again: "Keep thyself pure." Also in another place: "Study to shew thyself laudable unto God, a workman that needeth not to be ashamed, distributing the word of truth justly." Item: "In all things shew thyself an ensample of good works, in the doctrine with honesty, gravity, and with the wholesome word, which cannot be rebuked; that he which withstandeth may be ashamed, having no evil thing to speak of you."

1 Tim. iv. 1 Tim. v. 2 Tim. ii. Tit. ii.

1 Pet. v. St Peter also saith: "Feed ye Christ's flock as much as lieth in you, taking the oversight of them, not as compelled thereto, but willingly; not for the desire of filthy lucre, but of a good mind; not as though ye were lords over the parishes, but that ye be an ensample to the flock. And when the chief Shepherd shall appear, ye shall receive an uncorruptible crown of glory." Again, in setting forth what manner a man a bishop and overseer of the Lord's flock should be, saith not the apostle that he ought to be "blameless, as the steward of God, sober, discreet, righteous, godly, temperate, one that loveth goodness, no drunkard, no fighter, not given to filthy lucre, but abhorring covetousness, and in fine, such as no man shall be able to reprove, neither in doctrine nor life?"

1 Tim. iii. Tit. i.

Father. I see now right well, that a good life is also required of God in the minister. *Son.* To such as teach well and live evil God speaketh on this manner by the psalmograph: "Why dost thou preach my laws, and takest my covenant in thy mouth? whereas thou hatest to be reformed, and hast cast my words behind thee. When thou sawest a thief, thou consentedst unto him, and hast been partaker with the advouterers. Thou hast let thy mouth speak wickedness, and with thy tongue thou hast set forth deceit. Thou satest and spakest against thy brother, yea, and hast slandered thine own mother's son. These things hast thou done, and I held my tongue, and thou thoughtest (wickedly) that I am even such one as thyself; but I will reprove thee, and set before thee the things that thou hast done." Our Saviour Christ saith: "Whosoever doeth and teacheth, the same shall be called great in the kingdom of heaven." To teach well and to live evil is nothing else than to defile the doctrine that is taught, and to persuade the people that whatsoever is preached is vain and untrue. True doctrine profiteth not so much as corrupt life marreth and destroyeth.

Psal. l. Matt. v.

Father. If the preachers live evil and teach well, shall we therefore contemn and despise the word of God which they preach? *Son.* God forbid. Seneca saith: "Not who speaketh, but what is spoken, see that thou mark." Although the godliness of the preacher's life doth well commend and set forth the word of God, specially to the weaklings; yet the dignity and worthiness of the Lord's word consisteth not in the life of the preacher, whether it be godly or ungodly. Therefore where they preach well and live evil, let us follow the counsel of our Saviour Christ, which saith: "The scribes and the Pharisees sit in Moses' seat. All therefore whatsoever they bid you observe, that observe and do; but do not ye after their works; for they say, and do not." Notable is this saying of St John Chrysostom: "If the priests live well," saith he, "it is their avantage; but if they teach well, it is yours. Be not curious to boult out that which pertaineth to another man. For oftentimes good learning cometh forth from an evil man, as evil earth bringeth forth precious gold. Is precious gold despised for the vile earth? Therefore, as the gold is chosen, and the earth forsaken; so likewise take you the learning, and leave the manners." Again he saith: "Let us take the doctrine, but not the manners. Herbs are not necessary for the bees, but the flowers are. So ye likewise gather the flowers of doctrine, and leave their fashions of living[1]."

Matt. xxiii. In Matt. cap. xxiii.

[[1] Chrysost. Op. Par. 1718–38. Opus Imperf. in Matt. Hom. xliii. ex cap. xxiii. Tom. VI. p. clxxxiii. See Vol. I. page 387, note 5.]

Father. God give us all grace to be the same in life and conversation that we are in name and profession! *Son.* Amen.

Father. But what sayest thou of hospitality? Doth that also pertain unto the office of a bishop or spiritual pastor? *Son.* St Paul, as you heard in the description of a bishop, saith, that he ought to be "a maintainer of hospitality." Again he saith: "Distribute unto the necessity of the saints. Be ready to harbour." Once again he saith: "Forget not hospitality; for thereby have divers men lodged angels unwares." Likewise saith St Peter: "Be ye harborous one to another without grudging." God in the old law commanded that tithes should be paid to the priests, not only that they should have whereof to live themselves, but also to have whereof they might give to the poor, and relieve the necessity of their needy brethren. By the prophet Malachy he saith: "Bring ye every tithe into my barn, that there may be meat in my house." The bishop's house, the parson's house, the vicar's house, the priest's house, the archdeacon's house, the dean's house, the prebendary's house, &c., all these are God's houses; and tithes and offerings be brought into these houses, not for the incumbents' sake only, but also for the maintenance of the poor, and that the needy may have whereof to be relieved at their hands. The spiritual ministers are called in the Latin tongue *pastores*, that is to say, "feeders;" not for this cause only, that they should feed themselves, but rather that they should feed the flock of Christ, both spiritually and corporally.

Of hospitality. 1 Tim. iii. Tit. i. Rom. xii. Heb. xiii. 1 Pet. iv. Mal. iii.

And hereof also have we a goodly example, I mean, of hospitality and relieving the poor, in our Saviour Christ, which, when he lived here on earth and preached the gospel, did not only feed the people with the word of God, but also with corporal sustenance; so that he fed them both corporally and spiritually. This did he, without doubt, to give an example to all bishops and spiritual ministers, that they should be careful for the people, namely for such as be in necessity, and harbour them and relieve them in all their need, and by no means to suffer them to lack any good thing to the uttermost of their power. And some say, that when Christ commanded Peter, and in him all pastors, to feed his flock thrice, he meant that he should, first, feed them with the word of God; secondly, with example of good life; and thirdly, with hospitality. Of this I am sure, that both Peter and all his fellow-apostles were always careful for the poor, and made provision for them both by themselves and by other. And as touching that holy and blessed apostle St Paul, how careful and diligent he was for the poor, it is easy to see, both in his own writings and others'.

Matt. xiv. Mark vi. Luke ix. John vi. John xxi. Acts iii. iv. vi. xi. Rom. xv. 1 Cor. xvi. Gal. ii. Acts xi.

What shall I speak of the honourable bishops and holy fathers which lived after the apostles' time? Their houses were always open, and ready to receive strangers, to harbour the poor, to relieve the miserable afflicted saints of God, to comfort so many as were in necessity, &c. This to do was their glory. When their houses were full of poor people, then joyed they and rejoiced. Yea, many of those holy bishops and godly fathers were so wholly given to the maintenance of hospitality and relieving the poor, that when they had not sufficient of their own goods to succour them withal, they laboured with their own hands to get more, that the poor people might lack no good thing; as we read of St Paul: "Ye know," saith he, "that these hands have ministered unto my necessities, and to them that were with me. I have shewed you all things, how that so labouring ye ought to receive the weak, and to remember the words of the Lord Jesu, how that he said, It is more blessed to give than to receive."

Note well. Acts xx.

St Jerome saith: "Whatsoever the clerks have (he meaneth the bishops and ministers of Christ's church), that is the poor's; and their houses ought to be common to all men, and they ought to apply themselves to the receiving of pilgrims and strangers[2]." And in the pope's law it is thus found written: "Hospitality is so necessary for bishops, that if they be found to be no maintainers thereof, they may lawfully be deposed[3]." In consideration whereof Gregory writeth to bishop John, how

Quæst. i. can. Quoniam. Dist. 85. can. Archidiaconum.

[[2] Hieron. Op. Par. 1693—1706. Reg. Monachor. ex scriptis ejusdem per Lupum de Oliveto collecta. Tom. V. col. 382. See Vol. I. page 23, note 9.]

[[3] Decret. Gratiani, Par. 1583. Decr. Prima Pars, Dist. lxxxv. cols. 511, 12. See Vol. I. page 23, note 10.]

they did put out and depose a certain bishop at Antioch, because of his tenacity and niggardliness, and did choose another in his place, called Rusticus, a man not greatly learned, notwithstanding liberal, and a great maintainer of hospitality for the poor[1]. Dist. 81. can. Episcopus. Again: "A bishop to the uttermost of his power ought to minister to the poor and to the sick, which through weakness are not able to labour with their own hands, Dist. 86. can. Fratrem. meat, drink, and clothe[2]." Also in another place: "A bishop should have a liberal hand: he should help them that be in need, and think other men's necessity to be his own necessity: if he be not thus affected and minded, he beareth the name of a bishop in vain[3]."

Father. Hospitality is a noble virtue, seemly for all men, but namely for bishops and spiritual pastors, whose goods are the goods of the poor, that they may be found pastors and feeders, not only of the soul, but also of the body, and so answer to their name.

OF THE OFFICE OF DEACONS.

But what is to be said of the office and duty of deacons? Are not they also ministers in the church of Christ? *Son.* Yes, verily, and necessary ministers also, if their office were rightly and truly executed and used.

Father. What is "deacon" in English? *Son.* A minister or servant.

Father. What manner a man ought he to be, that should be a deacon? *Son.* St 1 Tim. iii. Paul describeth him on this manner, and saith, that "a deacon should be the husband of one wife, and such as ruleth his children well, and his own household," "honest, not double-tongued, not given unto much wine, neither greedy of filthy lucre; but holding the mystery of the faith with a pure conscience." "For they that minister well get themselves a good degree, and great liberty in the faith which is in Christ Jesu."

The office of a deacon. *Father.* What is the office of deacons? *Son.* If we consider and mark well what blessed Luke writeth of this matter in his chronicle of the apostles' acts, we shall Acts vi. soon perceive what their office and duty is. These are his words: "In those days, when the number of disciples grew, there arose a grudge among the Greeks against the Hebrews, because their widows were despised in the daily ministration. Then the twelve called the multitude of the disciples together, and said, It is not meet that we should leave the word of God, and serve tables. Wherefore, brethren, look ye out among you seven men of honest report, and full of the Holy Ghost and wisdom, to whom we may commit this business. But we will give ourselves continually to prayer, and to the ministration of the word. And the saying pleased the whole multitude. And they did choose Stephen," &c.

Here is it evident to be seen, that deacons in the primitive and apostolic church were chosen to this end, that they should daily serve at the table in the ministry of corporal food, that the apostles might not be hindered from the ministry of the word. Those deacons were the almners and distributers of such things as were given of the faithful, in their ecclesiastical assembly or otherwise, for the behoof, use, commodity, and profit of the poor people, of pilgrims and strangers, of widows and fatherless children. The true office therefore of a deacon is to minister unto the necessity of the saints things necessary for their corporal sustenance, whether they be goods freely and willingly offered of the congregation for that purpose, or whether they be things otherwise by their wisdom procured unto that end. We read also that the deacons Acts vi. viii. xxi. did preach the gospel, as we may see, in the Acts of the Apostles, of Stephen and Philip: which thing, I think, they began first to practise by the authority and appointment of the apostles, after that the communion of things began to cease at Jerusalem, and the Christians were dispersed into divers countries. Of this may we gather that, although the chief and principal office of a deacon be to provide for the poor, and

[1 See Vol. I. page 23, note 8.]

[2 Decret. Gratiani, Dist. lxxxii. can. 1. cols. 497, 8. See Vol. I. page 23, note 11.]

[3 Decret. Gratiani, Dist. lxxxvi. can. 6. cols. 515, 6. See Vol. I. page 24, note 1.]

to minister unto their necessities; yet may they also, if they be godly learned, be admitted of the rulers of Christ's church unto the ministry of the word.

Moreover, in the ecclesiastical writers we read that deacons afterward were admitted not only to preach the word, but also to minister the sacraments, and to do all things whatsoever the bishop or pastor did in the ecclesiastical ministry[4]; which seemeth unto me to be a confusion of the orders, and far to dissent from the first institution. In the church of the pope the name of a deacon remaineth still; but the office of a deacon, as it was used in the apostles' time, is utterly abolished. They are now appointed, as their chief office, daily to say matins of the day, and to sing the gospel at mass, and to stand nearest to the priest. Here is all their solemn business that they have to do, one thing excepted, which is to sing, *Ite missa est*, on principal feasts, when high mass is done. As touching the poor, and the provision for them, the popish deacons do not so much as once dream of the matter; so far are they fallen away from the true office of a deacon. And would God that even in the reformed churches, which have forsaken the wicked doctrine of the bishop of Rome, the office of a deacon were restored unto the right use, that our churches might go right up, and not halt in any condition! Then should the state of the poor be in much better case than it is at this present.

The office of a deacon in the pope's church.

Father. We have now talked of the chief and principal offices of such as bear rule in the christian commonweal. Let us now hear the duties and offices of the inferior degrees. And first of all, the duty of subjects toward their superiors, namely the temporal magistrates. *Son*. Agreed.

OF THE OFFICE AND DUTY OF SUBJECTS.

Father. What is the duty of subjects toward their superiors? *Son*. It consisteth principally in five points. The first is that they even from the very heart love and reverence the civil magistrates as the ministers and vicars of God, whom God himself doth vouchsafe to adorn and garnish with his own name, saying: "Ye are gods."

The duty of subjects.

Psal. lxxxii.

Father. If it be the duty of subjects not only with outward gesture and words to love, reverence, and honour the higher powers, but also with a true and inward affection of the heart, then may they not hate them, and unworthily speak of them. *Son*. You say truth. For God saith by Moses: "Thou shalt not rail upon the gods (that is to say, the temporal magistrates, which execute the office of God), neither blaspheme the ruler of thy people." And the wise man saith: "Wish the king no evil in thy thought, and speak no hurt of the rich in thy privy chamber; for a bird of the air shall betray thy voice, and with her feathers shall she bewray thy words." When the people of Israel began to hate Moses, and unreverently to speak of him, being appointed of God to be their magistrate, Moses answered and said unto them: "Your murmurings are not against us, but against the Lord. For what are we, that ye have murmured against us?" And God said to Samuel, when the people desired a king, and would have him no more to be their magistrate: "They have not cast thee away, but me, that I should not reign over them." Whatsoever displeasure is done against the magistrate, whether it be in thought, word, or deed, that same is done against God, and it shall not escape unplagued, as Salomon saith: "The king ought to be feared as the roaring of a lion: whoso provoketh him unto anger offendeth against his own soul." Likewise saith St Paul: "Let every soul submit himself unto the authority of the higher powers. For there is no power but of God. The powers that be are ordained of God. Whosoever therefore resisteth power resisteth the ordinance of God. And they that resist shall receive to themself damnation." Again: "He (the magistrate) beareth not the sword in vain. For he is the minister of God, to take vengeance on him that doth evil."

Exod. xxii.

Eccles. x.

Exod. xvi.

1 Sam. viii.

Prov. xx.

Rom. xiii.

Secondly, the duty and office of subjects is, not only with the very heart to love and reverence the civil magistrates, but also fervently and heartily to pray for them,

Prayer for the magistrates.

[4 A full account of deacons and of the offices and duties to which they were admitted may be found in Bingham, Orig. Eccles. Book II. chap. xx.]

that God may be present with them, assist them, defend them, rule and govern all their counsels, studies, devices, enterprises, affairs, &c., unto the glory of his name, and unto the tranquillity and quietness of the christian public weal.

Father. Where are we taught to pray for the magistrates? *Son.* St Paul saith: "I exhort that, above all things, prayers, supplications, intercessions, and giving of thanks be had for all men; for kings, and for all that be in authority; that we may live a quiet and a peaceable life with all godliness and honesty. For that is good and accepted in the sight of God our Saviour." And Jeremy the prophet commanded the Jews that were led away captive unto Babylon under king Nabuchodonozor, that they should pray for the city (he meaneth the magistrates and all the inhabitants thereof), wherein they were prisoners. "Seek," saith he, "after peace and prosperity of the city wherein ye be prisoners, and pray unto the Lord for it. For in the peace thereof shall your peace be." Baruch the prophet also saith: "Pray for the prosperity of Nabuchodonozor king of Babylon, and for the welfare of Balthazar his son; that their days may be upon earth as the days of heaven, that God also may give us strength, and lighten our eyes, that we may live under the defence of Nabuchodonozor king of Babylon, and under the protection of Balthazar his son, that we may long do them service, and find favour in their sight." And in Esdras we read thus: "Let them offer sweet savours unto the God of heaven, and pray for the king's life, and for his children."

1 Tim. ii. Jer. xxix. Bar. i. Ezra vi.

Obedience toward the magistrates.

Thirdly, it is required of all faithful subjects that they do not only love and reverence their magistrates, and pray for them, but also that they humbly obey them, yea, and that not for fear of punishment, but for conscience sake. For as God hath appointed the magistrate to rule, so hath he commanded to obey. This commandment of God may by no means be disobeyed. For to disobey the magistrate is none other thing than to disobey God, whose minister the magistrate is, and whose office he executeth.

Father. Where is obedience in the holy scriptures required of subjects toward their superiors? *Son.* Are not these the words of blessed St Paul? "Let every soul submit himself to the higher powers. For there is no power but of God. The powers that be are ordained of God. Whosoever therefore resisteth the power resisteth the ordinance of God. But they that resist shall receive to themselves damnation," &c. Again: "Ye must obey, not only for fear of punishment, but also for conscience sake." Also in another place: "Warn the subjects, that they submit themselves to rule and power, that they obey the officers, that they be ready unto every good work, that they speak evil of no man, that they be no fighters, but gentle, shewing meekness unto all men." Likewise saith St Peter: "Submit yourself unto all manner ordinance of man for the Lord's sake; whether it be to the king, as unto the chief head; either unto rulers, as unto them that are sent of him for the punishment of evil-doers, but for the praise of them that do well."

Rom. xiii. Tit. iii. 1 Pet. ii.

Father. If this obedience were thoroughly grafted in the hearts of subjects, all murmurings, tumults, commotions, seditions, insurrections, &c., should soon cease in the commonweal. *Son.* They should soon cease; for they should never be attempted. But whosoever, through the motion of the devil, enterprise such things against the magistrates, they alway come unto a miserable end; so far is it off that they have good success in their wicked and damnable attempts, as histories of all ages do evidently declare. To what end Dathan and Abiron, Zambri and Baasa, with such other like came, it is well known to them that read the holy histories. The wise man giveth a good lesson, and saith: "Fear the king, and keep no company with seditious persons." All subjects ought to be so affected toward their rulers as the people of Israel were toward Josua, when they said: "All that thou hast commanded us we will do, and whithersoever thou sendest us we will go." "And whosoever he be that doth disobey thy mouth, and will not hearken unto thy words in all that thou commandest him, let him die. Only be strong and of good courage."

Seditions and insurrections have never good success.

Num. xvi. 1 Kings xvi. Prov. xxiv. Josh. i.

Magistrates commanding contrary to

Father. But what if the magistrates command such statutes, acts, decrees, and proclamations to be observed of their subjects, as be contrary to the laws and commandments of God? Shall the subjects obey the higher powers in this behalf also? *Son.* Nothing less. Here we owe them no obedience. We must say with the apostles: "Whether it be right in the sight of God to hear you rather than God, judge ye." "We must obey God more than men." But of this matter we have tofore sufficiently spoken, when we entreated of the fifth commandment.

God's word are not to be obeyed.

Acts v.

Father. Well remembered, my son. Go forth therefore to declare whatsoever remaineth of the duty of subjects toward their superiors.

Son. Fourthly, the office of subjects is willingly and without grudging to bear such burdens, and to pay such charges, as the magistrates shall reasonably require of them, either for the provision and maintenance of their prince-like estate, or else for the safeguard of the commonweal.

Of payments to princes.

Father. Where is that commanded in the word of God? *Son.* Our Saviour Christ saith: "Give unto Cæsar that is due unto Cæsar." And St Paul saith: "Give to every man his duty; tribute to whom tribute belongeth; custom to whom custom is due; fear to whom fear belongeth; honour to whom honour pertaineth." Hereof we have also in the holy scriptures divers examples, which teach that subjects ought not to deny the magistrates such tributes, customs, tolls, tenths, rents, subsidies, &c., as the head rulers reasonably and justly require of them, urgent and necessary causes provoking them thereunto. In the new testament we read that Joseph and Mary his espoused wife went into their own city to be taxed at the commandment of Augustus the emperor. Our Saviour Christ paid tribute both for himself and for his disciples to the officers of the emperor.

Luke ii.

Matt. xvii.

Father. May the magistrate take away the subject's goods at his pleasure? *Son.* Nothing less. For there is a propriety of goods and possessions as well in the subject as in the magistrate; so that, if the magistrate do unjustly take away his subject's goods, he is a tyrant, and shall not escape the terrible indignation and fierce plagues of God; as we may see in the history of king Achab, and Naboth the Israelite, whose vineyard the king wrongfully took away; and therefore both he and all his posterity were most grievously punished. St Paul saith that "the magistrate is the minister of God, ordained for our wealth," and not for our destruction; for the maintenance of our goods, and not for the unjust taking away of them. For this is to play the tyrant, and not to do the part of God's minister. It was wittily and wisely said of a certain emperor[1]: "It is the property of a good shepherd to shear, and not to devour the sheep." The higher powers are called in the word of God "shepherds," and not "wolves." The property of a good shepherd is to take that only from the sheep which they may well forbear, yea, and that without any damage or hurt to themselves, as the wool and milk in time of the year. But the nature of a wolf is, without any respect, to rent, to tear, to destroy, to kill, to murder, to devour, and to swallow up whatsoever cometh to hand. The rulers that are so disposed are called of the prophet "wicked," and "companions of thieves." Yea, they are termed in God's book "ravening wolves," and "roaring lions." But a godly magistrate shall not abuse his authority and power, which he hath received of God for the wealth of his subjects. He shall require of his people just tributes and just exactions, even such as necessity rather than riot shall ask; and above all things beware that they do not waste and con sume his subjects' goods with unmeasurable and unreasonable exactions and pollages. He may not rule over his people as though they were brute beasts or bond-slaves, as the Turks and barbarous princes do, which know not the gospel; but as their brethren in Christ, and fellow-inheritors of everlasting life.

Note.

1 Kings xxi.

Rom. xiii.

Isai. i. Ezek. xxii. Zeph. iii.

Father. Remaineth there any thing of the duty of subjects toward their rulers?

Son. Fifthly and finally, it is required of the subjects that they do not blaze nor publish abroad, but rather conceal and hide, the faults, oversights, and negligences of the magistrates, seeing that "charity covereth the multitude of sins." For it is not almost possible but that, in so great weight and multitude of matters, the magistrate shall sometime omit and let pass that which of necessity he ought to have done, or sometime do that which had been better to have been left undone. For who almost

The faults of the magistrates ought to be dissembled of the subjects.

[[1] Tiberius. See Sueton. in Vit. 32.]

in his own private causes do not many times overshoot himself? What marvel is it then, though he which is a ruler over an whole city, yea, over an whole country or kingdom, do sometime err, fail, or do amiss in some things? The duty therefore of all faithful subjects is to interpret all the doings of the prince unto the best; foras-
Prov. xxi. much as they know that the heart of every magistrate "is in the hand of God, and
Exod. xxii. he turneth it whithersoever he will." And this is it that God saith by Moses: "Thou shalt not rail upon the gods, neither blaspheme the ruler of thy people."

What profit we have by the temporal rulers.

Father. If the subjects did diligently consider with themselves, what benefits and commodities they have by the temporal magistrates, they would not only take in good part all the doings of their rulers, but also give God most humble thanks for them. For by them is public innocency, honest behaviour, godly learning, virtuous knowledge, sincere erudition, necessary arts, fruitful occupations, maintained. By them we live in tranquillity and peace. By them we enjoy our own possessions without any disturbance. By them we are preserved from all injuries and cruel oppressions. By them our realms are defended from the invasion of bloody tyrants. By them the glory of God flourisheth. By them the gospel of Christ triumpheth, and all sects and heresies are extirped and plucked up by the roots. To conclude, by them all good things chance to us, and all evil things are removed from us. *Son.* Fire and water are not more necessary unto the conservation of this our mortal life, than the office of a magistrate is for the preservation and maintenance of good order in a commonweal.

Father. It is true, my son; and God make us thankful for this his benefit! *Son.* Amen.

Father. Now that thou hast opened unto me the office and duty of subjects toward the civil magistrates, my desire is, that thou likewise declare what the duty of such as be hearers of God's word toward their bishops and other spiritual pastors, which go about no less diligently to defend the souls of their parishioners from the tyranny of the devil, the world, and the flesh, with their sword, which is "the sword of the Spirit," I mean the word of God, and to preserve and keep them in the favour of God, than the temporal magistrates, with their corporal sword, study to keep their lives, bodies, and goods safe and free from all danger and disturbance. *Son.* I will do it gladly.

OF THE DUTY OF PARISHIONERS TOWARD THEIR PASTORS AND MINISTERS.

Parishioners owe unto their pastors, by the word of God, four things.

Spiritual pastors are to be honoured and reverenced. Mal. ii. 1 Cor. iv. Heb. xiii. Acts xvi. What profit we have by the spiritual ministers.

Father. Which are they? *Son.* The first is outward honour and reverence.

Father. Why so? *Son.* For they are the angels, ambassadors, and ministers of Christ. They are also the dispensators of the mysteries of God. They watch and take care for the salvation of our souls. They shew unto us the way of truth. They comfort the weak. They confirm the strong. They stablish and make strong the wavering and doubtful. They make the blind to see, and the halt to go right up. They set the prisoners at liberty. They bring joy and quietness to troubled consciences. They drive away Satan with his subtile suggestions. They plant the faith of Christ in us. They feed our souls with the heavenly food of Christ's gospel. They by their prayers asswage the wrath of God kindled against us through sin. In fine, they by their ministry bring unto us a sea of good things; so that without them we can none otherwise but perish and fall from the way of salvation, as Salomon saith:
Prov. xxix. "When the preaching of God's word fail, the people perish and run clean out of order." Who honoureth not the ambassador of an earthly prince, and have him in great reverence? And shall we leave them without honour, which are the ambassadors of him which is King of kings and Lord of lords? We esteem him greatly that bringeth us good and joyful news concerning our body and this present life; and shall we not think him worthy of much more estimation, which bringeth unto us blessed and heavenly news concerning the salvation of our souls, and life everlasting? as the
Isai. lii. prophet saith: "O how beautiful are the feet of them which bring tidings of peace,
Rom. x. and bring tidings of good things!" St Paul writeth that the Galatians, for the word's

sake which he preached unto them, received him "as an angel of God, yea, as Christ Jesus himself." He addeth, moreover, that they loved him so dearly, that to pleasure him they could have been contented to dig out their own eyes, and to give them unto him. In what great estimation all good and godly men in times past had the prophets, apostles, and preachers of God's word, the histories declare manifestly. Certes they that do dishonour the ministers of Christ dishonour Christ himself, as Christ testifieth, saying: "He that despiseth you despiseth me, and he that despiseth me despiseth him that sent me." Gal. iv. Luke x.

Father. What honour and reverence is it that we owe unto the ministers of God's word? *Son.* Honourably and reverently both to think and to speak of them, namely for the ministry sake, which they use at the appointment of God; to attribute unto them the opinion of wisdom and learning; to be persuaded that, as they are garnished with divers gifts of the Spirit far passing the common sort of men, so likewise they are preserved, kept, and defended of God; to give them outward honour and reverence with our body, as to put off our caps, to bow the knee unto them, to give them the upper hand in all places, to give them audience when they speak, &c.

What honour we owe to the spiritual ministers of God's word.

Father. Prove by the word of God that we owe this honour and reverence to the ministers of Christ's gospel. *Son.* The wise man saith: "Fear the Lord with all thy soul, and honour his ministers. Love thy Maker with all thy strength, and forsake not his ministers. Honour God with all thy soul, and reverence his priests. Give them their portion of the first-fruits and increase of the earth, like as it is commanded thee." St Paul saith: "The priests or elders that rule well are worthy of double honour, most specially they which labour in the word and teaching." Again: "We beseech you, brethren, that ye know them which labour among you, and have the oversight of you in the Lord, and give you exhortation, that ye have them in high reputation through love for their work's sake, and be at peace with them." Also in another place: "Let a man this wise esteem us, even as the ministers of Christ, and stewards of the mysteries of God." Item: "He that despiseth (the minister of God's word) despiseth not man, but God." And our Saviour Christ himself saith: "He that receiveth you receiveth me, and he that receiveth me receiveth him that sent me. But he that despiseth you despiseth me, and he that despiseth me despiseth him that sent me."

Ecclus. vii. 1 Tim. v. 1 Thess. v. 1 Cor. iv. 1 Thess. iv. Matt. x. Luke x.

Father. What is the second thing that parishioners are bound to do unto the ministers of God's word? *Son.* Plentifully and liberally to give unto them whatsoever is necessary for the maintenance of them and of theirs, and of their degree and estate, that they may quietly, and without any disturbance or thought-taking for worldly things, give their minds to the study of godly letters, to prayer, to the preaching of God's word, and to the ministration of the holy sacraments. And this ought to be the study and care of princes, to provide and aforesee that the pastors of Christ's church be not neglected or forsaken; but that provision be made for them in all things that concern their bodily sustenance and living, either of the common treasury, or else of private collections, or of tenths, or else of their own liberality, according to this saying of the prophet: "Kings shall be thy nursing-fathers, and queens shall be thy nursing-mothers." For how is it possible that they, which are daily occupied in the public ministry, may travail about things appertaining unto their living? The office of a minister requireth an whole man, and not such one as is distracted and occupied partly about spiritual and partly about temporal affairs. "No man that warreth," saith St Paul, "entangleth himself with worldly business; and that because he may please him which hath chosen him to be a soldier. And though a man strive for a mastery, yet is he not crowned, except he strive lawfully." Therefore as God hath appointed the subjects to pay to the temporal magistrate tribute, toll, custom, &c. that he may the more freely attend upon his office, and see to the commonweal; so likewise hath he ordained that "they which preach the gospel should live of the gospel."

Parishioners owe to their preachers all things necessary for their living. Isai. xlix. 2 Tim. ii. Rom. xiii.

Father. Where is that proved? *Son.* The Lord Christ saith himself: "The workman is worthy of his meat." Again: "The workman is worthy of his reward." And the holy apostle St Paul saith, speaking of the Jews and of the gentiles: "If the

Matt. x. Luke x. Rom. xv.

gentiles be made partakers of their spiritual things, their duty is to minister unto them
1 Cor. ix. in bodily things." Again: "It is written in the law of Moses, Thou shalt not muzzle
Deut. xxv. the mouth of the ox that treadeth out the corn. Doth God take thought for oxen?
Saith he it not altogether for our sake? For our sake, no doubt, this is written:
that he which eareth should ear in hope; and he which thresheth in hope should
be partaker of his hope. If we sow unto you spiritual things, is it a great thing if
we reap your bodily things?" "Do ye not know how that they which minister about
holy things live of the sacrifice? and how that they which stand at the altar are
partakers of the altar? Even so also did the Lord ordain, that they which preach
the gospel should live of the gospel." For "who goeth a warfare at any time at
his own cost? Who planteth a vineyard, and eateth not of the fruit thereof? Or
who feedeth a flock, and eateth not of the milk of the flock?" &c. Also in another
Gal. vi. place he saith: "Let him that is taught with the word minister unto him that
1 Tim. v. teacheth him in all good things. Be not deceived. God is not mocked." Item: "The
priests that rule well are worthy of double honour, most specially they which labour
Deut. xxv. in the word and doctrine. For the scripture saith, Thou shalt not muzzle the mouth
Luke x. of the ox that treadeth out the corn. And, The labourer is worthy of his reward."

Father. Rehearse the third part of the office and duty which the parishioners are
Obedience toward the spiritual ministers. bound by the commandment of God to do unto their pastors. *Son*. Their duty is not
only to reverence and honour the ministers of God's word, and to make sufficient provision for their living, but also to obey them.

Father. What meanest thou by that? *Son*. Not to wince, kick, and spurn
against their sayings, although sometime they seem to reprove them sharply for their
misbehaviour, but to suffer themselves to be admonished and warned of them, and
to be called again home to the sheepfold, yea, and also to obey them, and to follow their
most wholesome admonitions and precepts; forasmuch as they know that their pastors
Heb. xiii. and preachers are appointed of God to attend upon the health of their souls, as they
which shall render an accompt at the great day of judgment to the high Shepherd
Christ for the state of them all: again, whatsoever wholesome doctrine they teach
them out of the word of God, gladly to receive it, and humbly to obey it, and
most diligently to practise it in their life and conversation.

Father. Where are we commanded to obey the spiritual pastors? *Son*. St Paul
Heb. xiii. saith: "Obey them that have the oversight of you, and submit yourselves unto
them; for they watch for your souls, even as they that must give accompts, that they
Deut. xvii. may do it with joy, and not with grief." And in the old law we read thus: "That
man that will do presumptuously, and will not hearken and obey the commandment
of the priest, which standeth before the Lord thy God to minister, that man shall die;
and thou shalt put away evil from Israel. And all the people shall hear, that they may
fear, and do no more presumptuously."

Father. But what if the minister command things contrary to the word of God;
Ministers teaching contrary to the word of God are not to be obeyed. shall we also obey them in this behalf? *Son*. Nothing less. So long as they sit in
the chair of Moses, that is to say, so long as they teach the word of God purely,
truly, sincerely, and without the mingling of man's doctrine, they are to be heard
and obeyed as the angels and ambassadors of God; but, if they once sit in the chair
of pestilence, that is, if they teach men's traditions, strange doctrine not contained
in the holy bible, but forged of their own idle brains, or devised by other without
the authority of God's word, they are by no means to be obeyed, but to be abhorred
Gal. i. as extreme enemies of our soul's health, according to this saying of St Paul: "If
we ourselves, or an angel from heaven, preach any other gospel unto you than that
which we have preached unto you, let him be accursed." And as St John saith:
2 John. "If there come any unto you, and bring not this learning, him receive not to house,
neither bid him God speed. For he that biddeth him God speed is partaker of all
his evil deeds." But of this matter we have tofore sufficiently spoken in the declaration
of the fifth commandment. No doctrine, no commandment is to be obeyed, that
fighteth with the word of God.

Father. Well said. Therefore let me now hear the last part of the duty of
parishioners toward their pastors and preachers. *Son*. Forasmuch as we be all men,

and no man liveth without fault, it is required of the parishioners that, if the ministers do at any time offend, or commit that thing which is unseemly for their degree, and unworthy their estate, either in word or deed, they do not publish and declare the same abroad, to their infamy and shame, and to the dishonour of their ministry; but rather that they for the word's sake, which they preach, do bear with them, dissemble the matter, conceal and hide the fault, according to the order of charity, which "covereth the multitude of sins." And in this behalf let them follow the godly example of the most godly emperor Constantine the Great, whose gentle behaviour in covering the vices and faults of ecclesiastical persons is marvellous and almost to be wondered at. Among all other, this his saying is notable, which we read in chronicles: "Certes," saith he, "I owe such reverence and honour to the ministry of God's word, which ye profess, and to you, ye bishops and priests, for the word's sake, that if I saw any of your order sin with a woman, I would cover him with my mantle; because men should have none occasion to speak evil of your religion for any unseemliness committed on your behalf[1]." Let them also follow God the Father, if they will be his children, which doth not straightways, when we have offended him, publish and punish us and our sins; but he rather dissembleth and cloketh them, patiently abiding our conversion and amendment. As we would that God should deal with us, so likewise ought we to deal one with another. Every one of us ought to be to other not a wolf, but a god. "Brethren," saith St Paul, "if a man be taken in any fault, ye which are spiritual, help to amend him in the spirit of meekness; considering thyself, lest thou also be tempted. Bear ye one another's burden, and so fulfil the law of Christ. For if any man seem to himself that he is somewhat, when indeed he is nothing, the same deceiveth his own mind. Let every man prove his own work, and then shall he have rejoicing only in hisself, and not in another. For every man shall bear his own burden."

The faults of the ministers are to be dissembled of their parishioners.

Constantine the Great.

Wisd. xi. Rom. ii. 2 Pet. iii.

Gal. vi.

If the pastors teach the word of God purely and faithfully, and otherwise do their office well, though they sometime, through the frailty of man's nature, do amiss and offend, yet ought the parishioners quietly to bear with them, to speak the best of them, lovingly and charitably to admonish them secretly, to pray for them, and to do all things that may maintain their good name, yea, and that for the glory of the ministry of the gospel, which they profess. "Above all things," saith St Peter, "have love among yourselves. For love shall cover the multitude of sins."

1 Pet. iv.

Father. Although, my son, I do not discommend thy judgment concerning the hiding of the minister's faults (for "all of us offend in many things"), yet I would wish, that all bishops and preachers should so order their life according to their doctrine, that they might not only be "the salt of the earth," but also "the light of the world," that God may be glorified both by their doctrine and conversation. *Son*. It is greatly to be wished. For, as our Saviour Christ saith, "whosoever doth and teacheth, the same shall be called great in the kingdom of heaven." Notwithstanding, better is it for the christian people to have a true and faithful teacher of God's word, with a life not altogether faultless and pure, than to have an hypocrite, outwardly glistering with the visor of holiness, and the same to be a sower of wicked doctrine, and a corrupter of men's souls. For, as Chrysostom saith: "If the priests live well, it is their avantage; but if they teach well, it is the people's profit[2]."

James iii.

Matt. v.

Matt. v.

In cap. Matt. xxiii.

Father. Let us go forth with the offices of other degrees. What followeth? *Son*. The next in order that followeth to be entreated of is the duty of husbands unto their wives.

Father. What sayest thou of that matter? Let me hear now the office of a married man.

[1 Οὐ γὰρ ἔφη χρῆναι τῶν ἱερέων τὰ πλημμελήματα δῆλα γίνεσθαι τοῖς πολλοῖς, ἵνα μὴ σκανδάλου πρόφασιν ἐντεῦθεν λαβόντες, ἀδεῶς ἁμαρτάνωσι. φασὶ δὲ αὐτὸν καὶ τόδε προσθεῖναι, ὡς εἰ αὐτόπτης ἐπισκόπου γάμον ἀλλότριον διορύττοντος γίνοιτο, συγκαλύψαι ἂν τῇ πορφυρίδι τὸ παρανόμως γινόμενον, ὡς ἂν μὴ βλάψῃ τοὺς θεωμένους τῶν δρωμένων ἡ ὄψις.—Theodoret. in Hist. Eccles. Script. Amst. 1695—1700. Lib. I. cap. xi. p. 36.]

[2 See before, page 324, note 1.]

OF THE DUTY OF HUSBANDS TOWARD THEIR WIVES.

Son. Four things are necessarily required of every true and godly christian married man, if he will do the duty of a faithful husband toward his wife.

The duty of an husband is to love his wife.

Father. Which are they? *Son.* The first is, that he love his wife.

Father. How should he love her? *Son.* Even as himself, and as Christ loved his congregation.

Eph. v.

Father. Where findest thou that? *Son.* St Paul saith: "Ye husbands, love your wives, even as Christ also loved the congregation, and gave himself for it, to sanctify it, and cleansed it in the fountain of water through the word, to make it unto himself a glorious congregation, without spot or wrinkle, or any such thing; but that it should be holy and without blame. So ought men to love their wives as their own bodies. He that loveth his wife loveth himself. For no man ever yet hated his own flesh, but nourisheth and cherisheth it, even as the Lord doth the congregation." Again he
Col. iii. saith: "Ye husbands, love your wives, and be not bitter to them."

Certain causes why the husband ought to love his wife.

Father. Wherefore should the husband love his wife? *Son.* First, because God hath so commanded, as we tofore heard; whose commandment to disobey is more than double wickedness. The husband, in loving his wife according to the will of God, doth with his obedience greatly avance the glory of God, and the honour of his holy name; and it is also a testimony to his own conscience, that God was the author of his marriage, and that he, living quietly with his wife in that state, pleaseth God.

Secondly, the husband ought to love his wife, because his marriage, which he hath made with his wife in the fear of God, is an holy mystery of that spiritual marriage and true love, which Christ the Son hath made with every true faithful soul, as
Hos. ii. he saith by the prophet: "I will marry thee unto me in faith." For as a faithful husband brenneth with true and unfeigned love toward his dear wife, so likewise is the love of Christ toward his holy congregation most fervent and brenning; insomuch
Eph. v. that "we are now become members of his body, of his flesh, and of his bones": which thing he hath most manifestly declared by taking man's nature upon him.

Thirdly, the married man ought to love his wife, not for the satisfying of his carnal pleasure, not for nobility of parentage, not for beauty, nor for properness of personage, nor yet for riches, &c., (for such love is between ruffians and harlots); but because she is his sister in the christian faith, and inheritor with him of God's most glorious kingdom: again, because she is given him of God to be an helper unto him, and a faithful yoke-fellow, as well in adversity as in prosperity. Moreover, he shall
Gen. ii. Matt. xix. Eph. v. love her because she is flesh of his flesh, and bone of his bones; and in fine, because she is endued through the Spirit of God with noble and godly virtues, as shamefacedness, chastity, modesty, sobriety, diligence, sadness[1], patience, temperance, silence, obedience, and such other ghostly virtues. All these things, diligently considered, shall easily provoke a true christian married man dearly and heartily to love his wife, although she be never so poor and base in beauty.

Father. Must the love of a married man toward his wife excel his love toward all other persons? *Son.* Yea, verily. For we read that, so soon as God at the beginning
Gen. ii. had brought the woman unto Adam, he brast out into these words, and said: "This is now bone of my bones, and flesh of my flesh. She shall be called woman, because
Matt. xix. she was taken out of man. For this cause shall a man leave his father and his mother, and shall be joined with his wife; and they shall become one flesh."

Father. How long ought this love to continue between man and wife? *Son.* So
Matt. xix. long as they live together, as Christ saith: "Let not man put asunder that which
Rom. vii. God hath coupled together." "The woman," saith St Paul, "which is in subjection to a man, is bound by the law to the man as long as he liveth. But if the man be dead, she is loosed from the law of the man," &c. So likewise may it be said of ☞ the man. So long as God blesseth the man and wife together with life, ought unfeigned love to remain between them, yea, and if it be possible, daily to increase more and more; so far is it off that it ought in any point to be diminished.

[[1] Sadness: gravity.]

Father. What is required more of a married man? *Son*. That he so dearly love his wife, that he do not only not touch any other woman, but also that he refrain both his eyes and the thoughts of his heart from coveting any strange flesh.

Father. Where is that commanded? *Son*. Yea, rather where is it not commanded? Is not this the commandment of God, "Thou shalt not covet thy neighbour's wife?" Exod. xx. Deut. v.

Father. Is it not enough, if I do abstain from the act of gross whoredom, except I also keep my heart pure from filthy and unclean thoughts? *Son*. Christ saith: "Whosoever looketh on another man's wife to lust after her hath committed advoutry with her already in his heart." Matt. v.

Father. Must I also keep mine eyes pure and chaste, and refrain them also from lascivious and wanton sights? *Son*. That is our duty.

Father. But it is hard so to do.

Son. I grant. In our power it lieth not so to do. We must therefore pray unto God with the psalmograph for the cleanness of the heart, and say: "Make me a clean heart, O God, and renew a right spirit within me." (Psal. li.) And for the stableness of the eyes pray must we on this manner with the psalmograph also: "O turn away mine eyes, lest they behold vanity; and quicken thou me in thy way." (Psal. cxix.) It shall also profit us greatly to consider alway in our mind these sentences of the holy scripture: "Apply not thyself to the deceitfulness of a woman. For the lips of an harlot are a dropping honey-comb, and her throat is more glistering than oil. (Prov. v.) But at the last she is as bitter as wormwood, and her tongue as sharp as a two-edged sword. Her feet go down unto death, and her steps pierce through hell, &c. Keep thy way far from her, and come not nigh the doors of her house, &c. Be glad with the wife of thy youth. Loving is the hind, and friendly is the roe. Let her breasts always satisfy thee, and hold thee ever content with her love. My son, why wilt thou have pleasure in an harlot, and embrace the bosom of another woman? For every man's ways are open in the sight of God; and he pondereth all their goings. The wickedness of the ungodly shall catch himself, and with the snares of his own sins shall he be trapped," &c. "Keep thee from the evil woman, and from the flattering tongue of the harlot, (Prov. vi.) that thou lust not after her beauty in thy heart, and lest thou be taken with her fair looks. An harlot will make a man to beg his bread; but an honest married wife will hunt for the precious life. May a man carry fire in his bosom, and his clothes not be brent? Or can one go upon hot coals, and his feet not be hurt? Even so, whosoever goeth in to his neighbour's wife and toucheth her cannot be unguilty." "Therefore let not thine heart wander in the ways of an whore, and be (Prov. vii.) not thou deceived in her paths. For many one hath she wounded and cast down; yea, many a strong man hath been slain by the means of her. Her houses are the way unto hell, and bring men down into the chambers of death." Old Toby said to his son: "My son, keep thee well from whoredom; and beside thy wife, see (Tob. iv.) that no fault be known of thee." Job also saith: "I made a covenant with mine (Job xxxi.) eyes, that I would not look upon a damsel. For how great a portion shall I have of God, and what inheritance from the Almighty on high? As for the ungodly, and he that joineth himself to the company of wicked doers, shall not destruction and misery come upon him?" St Paul saith: "If any that is called a brother (that is (1 Cor. v.) to say, a Christian) be an whoremonger, see that ye eat not with him." "Flee fornication," (1 Cor. vi.) for "neither fornicators, neither advouterers, neither weaklings, neither abusers of themselves with mankind, shall inherit the kingdom of God." Again he saith: "Wedlock is honourable among all persons, and the bed undefiled. (Heb. xiii.) But whoremongers and adulterers God shall judge."

Moreover, it shall not be unfitting nor out of the way to consider how grievously God in all ages hath punished whoredom. For whoredom the whole world almost (Gen. vi.) was drowned with waters. For whoredom Sodom and Gomorre, with certain other (Gen. xix.) cities, were consumed with fire and brimstone from heaven. For whoredom all the (Gen. xxxiv.) citizens of Sichem were slain with sword. For whoredom there were slain in the (Num. xxv. 1 Cor. x.) wilderness on one day twenty-three thousand of the Israelites. For whoredom the (Judg. xx.) whole tribe of Benjamin was almost slain and destroyed. For whoredom the sons of (1 Sam. ii.)

2 Sam. xi. Hely the priest perished in battle. For whoredom David and his whole kingdom fell 1 Kings xi. into great miseries. For whoredom Salomon fell into idolatry, and into other grievous sins.

Not only the holy scriptures, but also human histories, do set forth unto us many and horrible examples of God's wrath and fierce vengeance against whoremongers and adulterers, which ought at all times to be remembered, but specially when the devil and the flesh move and tempt us unto the uncleanness of the body. The consideration of these things shall easily drive away Satan and his subtile suggestions, with that pestiferous mermaid the flesh, and all her deceitful pleasures, and cause the godly married man to rest in the love of his wife, all strange women utterly refused.

Father. How adultery and whoredom, with all other uncleanness of the body, may be avoided, thou declaredst very godly in the exposition of the seventh commandment. Therefore go forth, and let me hear more of the duty of a married man toward his wife. *Son*. Thirdly, it is required of every godly married man, that he make provision for his wife, children, and family, that they lack nothing that is necessary for their living, but that he minister unto them all good things. For if any man be negligent in this behalf, and "provide not for his household, he hath denied the faith," saith St Paul, "and he is worse than an infidel."

The husband is bound to make provision for his wife and family. 1 Tim. v.

Father. Ought the man to labour for his wife and family? Where doth the word of God teach that? *Son*. Did not God, after the transgression of his commandment in paradise, enjoin penance both to man and to woman? As he spake thus to the woman, "In multiplying I will multiply thy sorrow and thy conceiving; in sorrow shalt thou bring forth children, and thy lust shall pertain to thy husband, and he shall have the rule of thee:" so likewise saith he to the man, "In the sweat of thy face shalt thou eat thy bread, till thou be turned again into the ground, out of the which thou wast taken; for dust thou art, and into dust thou shalt be turned again." Here is a general commandment given to all men, that no man be idle, but that every man work some good and necessary thing, profitable both for himself and for other. Who seeth not then, even of this one commandment of God, that the married man is bound to labour, both for himself and for all such as belong unto him? As St Paul writeth of himself, that he with his own hands got all things necessary, not only for himself, but also for so many as were with him.

Of labour. Gen. iii. Acts xx.

Psal. cxxviii. Likewise saith the psalmograph: "Thou shalt eat the labours of thine hands. O well is thee, and happy shalt thou be. Thy wife shall be as the fruitful vine upon the walls of thy house: thy children like the olive-branches round about thy table. Lo, thus shall the man be blessed that feareth the Lord." St Paul commandeth, that "every man should labour some good thing, that he may have to give unto him that lacketh and is in need." How much more is it the duty of a godly married man to labour, that he may have wherewith to feed his hungry wife and children! The man is bound to "love his wife, as Christ loved the congregation." Now who knoweth not, that of Christ we receive all good things, whatsoever we have need of? Nothing is expedient for us, but that he giveth it unto us abundantly. Likewise, after the example of Christ ought the husband to provide all good and necessary things for his wife. Again: "The husband ought to love his wife as himself, yea, as his own flesh." The husband "hateth not his own flesh," neither doth he suffer it to perish for hunger, "but he feedeth it and cherisheth it," and bestoweth upon it all good things: so likewise ought he to do unto his wife, and to suffer her to lack no good thing. Item, the husband and the wife are one flesh and one body; the husband therefore ought to make no less provision for his wife than for himself. To be short, this sentence of St Paul shall for ever and ever abide true, yea, and that unto the condemnation of all sluggish and negligent husbands, and such like: "If any man do not provide for such as belong unto him, he hath denied the faith, and is worse than an infidel."

Eph. iv. Eph. v. The husband ought to be the same to his wife that he is to himself. Eph. v. 1 Tim. v.

How careful husbands ought to be for their wives and children, the examples of Abraham, Isaac, Jacob, David, Toby, and such like do sufficiently declare. Therefore ☞ whosoever intendeth to marry in the fear of God, he ought first of all to consider if he have whereof to nourish his wife, and to bring up his children. If he have not, let him abstain from marriage, till he have learned some honest and virtuous occupation, whereby he shall be able to feed both himself and his. They that are otherwise minded fall for the most part after their marriage unto beggary, and from beggary unto stealing, and from stealing to hanging. And in the mean season they give an occasion to their wives to give themselves to uncleanness of life, and to play the whores, not knowing otherwise how to live, for lack of provision. Better had it been for such husbands to have had a mill-stone tied about their necks, and to be cast into the midst of the sea, than so loosely to marry, and afterward to be the authors of so many and so grievous evils.

Father. Is it the duty of an husband only to provide for his wife things necessary for the body? *Son*. Not only. His duty is also to provide things necessary for her soul's health, as right institution in the mysteries of Christ's religion, knowledge of God's holy word, the true understanding of the holy sacraments, and all other things that be necessary for the salvation of her soul. Husbands ought to provide for the safeguard of their wives, both body and soul.

Father. How provest thou that the man is thus bound to teach his wife the way of truth, and to inform her from time to time in all such matters as appertain unto salvation and unto everlasting life? *Son*. St Paul hath these words: "Let 1 Cor. xiv.
your women keep silence in the congregations. For it is not permitted unto them to speak; but to be under obedience, as the law saith. If they will learn any thing, Gen. iii.
let them ask their husbands at home: for it is a shame for women to speak in the congregation." Again: "Let the woman learn in silence with all subjection." Here 1 Tim. ii.
is it evident, that if the wife lack knowledge in spiritual and heavenly things, she ought to ask her husband, and to learn of him. If the wife be bound to learn of her husband, then is the husband bound to teach his wife, and to inform her with the knowledge of God's mysteries. Is not the unbelieving wife many times sanctified by the believing husband? "How knowest thou, O man," saith St Paul, "whether 1 Cor. vii.
thou shalt save thy wife or no?" How can the faithful man save his unfaithful wife, but by teaching her the word of salvation? The man is bound to "love his wife, as Eph. v.
Christ loved the congregation." Christ loveth so his congregation, that when he was here corporally on earth, he himself taught it; and now that he is gone from us concerning his bodily presence, he sendeth unto the faithful his holy Spirit, to instruct and to teach them, and to lead them into the way of truth, as he saith by the prophet: "I will pour out of my Spirit upon all flesh; and your sons and your Joel ii.
daughters shall prophesy," &c. Again he saith: "That Comforter, that Holy Spirit, Acts ii. John xiv.
whom the Father shall send in my name, he shall teach you all things, and lead and xvi.
you into all truth." After the example of Christ ought the husband to instruct his wife, and to seek all means possible to bring her unto the truth. Again, the man is bound to "love his wife as himself." Is there any man so estranged from all wit Eph. v.
and reason, that he desire to be ignorant of those things which concern his salvation? Will not he rather seek all means possible to be taught, and to come unto the knowledge of those things? Even that care ought the man also to have for his wife, that she in like manner may have the perfect knowledge of the way of salvation. We are commanded to "teach and warn one another": and shall not the husband Col. iii.
teach his wife, and warn her of those things that belong unto her salvation? Every man is a bishop in his own house. Who seeth not then that the householder is bound to teach his household, the chief member whereof the wife is, and therefore necessarily to be instructed and taught of her husband?

But it is to be noted in this part of the husband's duty, that the man is not only bound to provide for his wife both bodily and ghostly, but also to defend her from all injury and displeasure. Her life, her honesty, her good name, and her health ought he to conserve, keep, and maintain, yea, to put himself in danger and peril for the safeguard of his wife, rather than any harm should chance unto her; following in this behalf the example of Christ, which for the defence of his church bestowed his blood and life. The husband is bound to defend his wife from all injuries.
And for this cause "is man head of the wife, even as Christ is head Eph. v.
of the congregation;" namely, to govern, rule, defend, preserve, and maintain her in all godliness and honesty, and to tender her and her wealth, even as the head studieth, deviseth, and compasseth all means possible how to conserve and keep all the members of the body in safety, health, and wealth. Why man is appointed to be the head of the woman.

Father. It is meet and convenient that the man should this do. But now, my son, tell me what is the fourth and last part of the office and duty of a husband toward his wife. *Son.* To bear and forbear his wife; to dissemble the faults of his wife; not to see, but to wink sometime at her negligences; to cover her vices; to forgive her sins; not to be churlish and cruel toward her, but quiet, gentle, modest, patient, long-suffering, kind, and soft in all his behaviour toward her, and even such one as a gentle and tender father is toward his most dear and sweet child; ever remembering that that sex, (I mean the feminine kind,) is more weak both in body and mind than the man is, and therefore is called in the holy scripture "the weaker vessel." And this is it that St Paul saith: "Love your wives, ye husbands, and be not bitter unto them." Hereto agreeth the saying of St Peter: "Ye men, dwell with your wives according to knowledge, giving honour unto the wife, as unto the weaker vessel, and as unto them that are heirs of the grace of life; that your prayers be not hindered."

The husband ought to bear with his wife. 1 Pet. iii. Col. iii. 1 Pet. iii.

☞ That Christ is to the congregation, that same ought every husband to be to his wife. Now who knoweth not in what state Christ took the congregation to his wife? and how many of her faults he doth daily dissemble, and will not see, but rather cover them, never laying them to her charge, and for his love sake toward her recounteth her faultless, fair, and beautiful, although in herself and of herself spotted with divers blemishes, as it is written: "I am black, O ye daughters of Jerusalem, like as the tents of Cedarnes, and as the hangings of Salomon; but yet I am fair and well-favoured withal." The congregation in herself is black and deformed; but in Christ she is fair and well-favoured. Again, though the congregation runneth sometime astray, and followeth strange lovers, yet is not he so angry with her, but that he patiently abideth her conversion; and if she at any time return again unto him, he receiveth her most joyfully, and embraceth her most lovingly, never laying to her charge afterward whatsoever tofore she hath done amiss; as he himself saith by the prophet: "Commonly when a man putteth away his wife, and she goeth from him, and marrieth with another, then the question is, should he resort unto her any more after that? Shall not that woman be then defiled and unclean? But as for thee, thou hast played the harlot with many lovers; yet turn again to me, saith the Lord, and I will receive thee." For "I, yea, even I only, am he that for mine own self's sake do away thine offences, and forget thy sins, so that I will never think upon them any more."

Cant. i. Jer. iii. Isai. xliii.

After this manner ought the husband to deal with his wife, and, as I may so speak, be even a Christ unto her. Moreover, who knoweth not that such as are strong are commanded in the word of God to bear the infirmities of those that are weak; yea, not only to bear patiently what is done against them, but also to forgive it, and for evil to recompense good? Ought not the man much more to do this to his wife, which is his own flesh and his own bones? If the foot chance sometime ☞ to stumble, so that the body do fall, and is put in jeopardy, do all the other members of the body rise up against the foot, and either grievously smite it, or else cut it off? Nothing less, but rather bear it both quietly and patiently, and are afterward more circumspect, that the foot may no more stumble. Whatsoever one member is to another member of the same body, even the very same ought the husband to be to his wife; forasmuch as "they two are one flesh." "Men," saith St Paul, "ought so to love their wives as their own bodies. He that loveth his wife loveth himself. No man at any time hath hated his own flesh; but he rather cherisheth it, and nourisheth it, even as the Lord doth the congregation. So ought men to do to their wives."

Rom. xv. Gal. vi. Col. iii. Rom. xii. Eph. v.

Father. There can be no long concord between man and wife, except one bear with another, and one wink at another's faults. Therefore in this behalf the currish and doggish behaviour of some loose-bands, rather than husbands, is greatly to be reproved, which will nothing at all bear with their wives, but all things take to the worst part; yea, be the fault never so little, they make of a fly an elephant, and of a mole-hill a mountain; making such a stir in the house, as though heaven and earth should go together. *Son.* These husbands are much worse than the heathen philosopher Socrates, which, to maintain peace and quietness in his house, was well contented to bear all kinds of displeasures at his wife's hand.

Socrates.

Father. They entreating their wives evil have always this saying of God: "Thou shalt be under the power of thy husband; and he shall rule thee," and keep thee under. And hereof they gather that they may do with their wives what they lust, and use them, yea, rather abuse them, at their pleasure. *Son.* Husbands are not appointed heads and rulers of the women unto this end, that they should reign over their wives like lords, or bridle them like horses, or make them to couch down like dogs, or to tumble before them in the mire like swine; but to be the very same to their wives that Christ is to the congregation, that is to say, such as should at all times defend their wives from all perils and dangers, and provide for them all good things, as we have tofore heard; and whatsoever the wives lack either in counsel or wisdom, the husbands to supply it and to make it good; so that the husband shall evermore be that to the wife which the head is to the body. And as the head doth not compass nor imagine how to hurt the body, but rather how to conserve the body and to keep it harmless; so likewise ought the man, whom God hath appointed head of the woman, not to abuse his power, but to use it unto the conservation and health, unto the quietness and safeguard, of his wife; ever setting before his eyes this commandment of God by the apostle: "Ye men, love your wives, and be not bitter unto them." St Peter also exhorteth all husbands that they "dwell with their wives according to knowledge;" that is to say, modestly, soberly, quietly, and, as it become christian men, with all patience and long-suffering. And to move the men to be the more gentle, the holy apostle putteth them in remembrance that their wives be no dish-clouts, nor no hand-basket-sloys, nor no drudges, nor yet slavish people, but fellow-heirs with them of everlasting life, and so dear to God as the men; forasmuch as they also be made like unto the image of God, redeemed by the blood of Christ, and sanctified by the Holy Ghost.

Gen. iii. Note. Col. iii. 1 Pet. iii.

Father. Some husbands also be so churlish, and so wedded to their own fancy, that, although their wives be both sober, wise, and prudent, and also able to give good counsel; yet will they by no means hear them, nor follow their counsel and advice, but rather do that which their brain-sick heads have determined, although foolish and worthy to be laughed at. [*Son.*] These husbands err and go out of the way. For women also many times can give better counsel than men, and are able to determine what is good and what is otherwise, no less than their husbands. Their counsels therefore and devices are not to be neglected and despised, as the wise and sage Cato monisheth, saying:

Uxoris linguam, si frugi est, ferre memento[1].

"If thy wife," saith he, "be able to give good counsel, be content to hear her, and to suffer her to speak."

Read we not that when Sara, Abraham's wife, willed her husband to put away Agar, the bond-maid, and her son Ismael, which she had borne to Abraham, Abraham was loth so to do? But God said unto Abraham: "Let it not be grievous in thy sight because of the lad, and of thy bond-maid. All that Sara hath said unto thee, hear her voice," &c. Did not Isaac also follow the counsel of his wife Rebecca, in sending away their son Jacob from the fury of his brother Esau into Mesopotamia, unto his uncle Laban? Let husbands therefore know that godly and sage matrons have no less the Holy Ghost than the men have, and be endued no less with the fruits of God's Spirit than they are; and therefore are they and their counsels worthy also to be had and to be followed.

Gen. xxi. Gen. xxviii.

Father. If all husbands would thus behave themselves toward their wives, as thou hast declared, then should there be continual concord and perfect agreement at all times between married folk, and so a most sweet and pleasant life. *Son.* It is greatly to be wished. For there is nothing that pleaseth God better than amity and concord between husband and wife: which thing God grant, for his mercy's sake!

Father. Amen. Now, my son, seeing thou hast shewed the office of an husband toward his wife, let me now hear also what the duty of a wife is unto her husband. *Son.* I will do it gladly, mine own dear father.

[[1] Caton. Dist. Moral. Lib. III. 49.]

OF THE DUTY OF WIVES TOWARD THEIR HUSBANDS.

Divers things are remembered in the holy scripture, which do belong unto the office and duty of a true, honest, and godly wife, which I will recite in order. The first is, that she submit herself to the will of her husband, and be content to be admonished, ruled, and governed by him, knowledging him to be her head and lord, and giving him such reverence and honour as the wife oweth to the husband by the word of God.

Wives ought to be in subjection to their husbands.

Father. How provest thou that wives ought to be in subjection to their husbands? *Son.* God himself at the beginning said to the woman: "Thou shalt be under the power of thy husband; and he shall rule thee." St Paul saith: "Ye women, submit yourselves unto your own husbands, as unto the Lord. For the husband is the wife's head, even as Christ is head of the congregation; and the same is he that ministereth salvation to the body. Therefore as the congregation is in subjection to Christ, even so let the wives be in subjection to their husbands in all things." Again: "Ye wives, submit yourselves unto your own husbands, as it is comely in the Lord." Also in another place: "Let the women learn in silence with all subjection. But I suffer not a woman to teach, neither to usurp authority over the man, but to be in silence. For Adam was first formed, and then Eve. Adam also was not deceived, but the woman, and was subdued to the transgression. Notwithstanding, through bearing of children she shall be saved, if they continue in faith, and love, and holiness, with discretion." St Peter also saith: "Ye wives, be in subjection to your husbands, that even they which obey not the word may without the word be won by the conversation of the wives; while they behold your chaste conversation coupled with fear."

Gen. iii. Eph. v. Col. iii. 1 Tim. ii. Gen. ii. 1 Pet. iii.

Father. Where is the man called the head of the woman? *Son.* St Paul saith: "The husband is the wife's head, even as Christ is the head of the congregation." Again, in that God hath made man ruler over the woman, it evidently appeareth that man by God's ordinance is head of the woman.

Eph. v. Gen. iii.

Father. Where is it commanded that women should reverence their husbands? *Son.* St Paul saith: "Let the wife reverence her husband." And St Peter saith: "In old time holy women.... were obedient to their husbands, even as Sara obeyed Abraham, and called him lord."

Eph. v. 1 Pet. iii. Gen. xviii.

Father. The stubbornness then and the unreverence which some froward wives use against their husbands is by no means to be commended. *Son.* Yea, rather most highly to be discommended. For God by no means can abide that the wife should ☞ grow up unto such arrogancy, pride, and haughtiness of mind, that she should in any condition lout or flout, contemn and despise her husband, whom God hath appointed her head, although he be never so simple, homely, plain, and of slender wit or policy; as we may see in the history of Michol, Saul's daughter and David's wife, which despised David, and laughed him to scorn as a light-brained fellow, because he danced before the ark of the Lord. But God did plague her for her unreverence toward her husband; so that she had no child unto the day of her death. And as this Michol escaped not unpunished for the abusing of herself against her husband David, no more shall those unreverent, scornful, and disobedient wives go away unplagued from the face of God. God by no means can abide that his ordinance should be neglected and despised. Look what subjection, reverence, obedience, worship, and honour the congregation oweth to Christ her head; even the very same, as I may so speak, oweth the wife unto her husband, as St Paul saith: "Ye women, submit yourselves unto your own husbands, as unto the Lord. For the husband is the wife's head, even as Christ is the head of the congregation." "Therefore as the congregation is in subjection to Christ, even so let the wives be in subjection to their husbands in all things." And look, what great offence the congregation committeth, when unreverently she disobeyeth Christ her head; even the like offence committeth the wife, as I may so speak, when she disobeyeth her husband, whom God hath appointed to be her head. For it is written: "Let the wives be in subjection to their husbands in all things."

2 Sam. vi. Eph. v.

Father. But what if the husbands should command their wives to do things contrary to the commandment of God? shall they also obey them in this behalf; seeing it is said, "Let the wives be in subjection to their husbands in all things?" *Son*. Here the wives owe no obedience to their husbands. "We must obey God more than men." If the husband, for fear of the loss of his goods or life, should command his wife to commit idolatry, and to defile herself with image-service; or for lucre's sake move his wife to play the harlot; here the wife ought not by any means to obey her husband, nor to satisfy his commandment, but rather to forsake him, or to suffer death, if the cruelty of the time should so require. Obedience to God and to his holy word ought to be preferred before all obedience to be shewed unto man and unto his commandments. Therefore, if the man will challenge of the woman the obedience, subjection, and reverence that the congregation oweth to her Head; let the man provide that he be the same to his wife that Christ is to the congregation, and that he command nothing, but that may stand with the word of God, and work God's favour and everlasting salvation to his wife so obeying; as Paul writeth of Christ: "Christ," saith he, "is the head of the congregation; and the same is he that ministereth salvation to the body."

Wives owe no obedience to their husbands commanding wicked things.

Eph. v.

Father. Godly spoken. But what followeth concerning the office of the wife? *Son*. The second point of an honest and godly matron is that she truly, dearly, faithfully, and unfeignedly love her husband. And this her love toward her husband shall not rise of any carnal pleasure, beauty, riches, strength, nobility, goodliness of personage, or of any outward thing; but only of obedience toward the commandment of God. For God hath commanded that wives should love their husbands. If we ought to love all men as ourselves, how dear then ought the love to be that should be between man and wife, whom God hath coupled together, and which are one flesh, and members one of another's body! The married woman therefore shall love her husband as herself, and think her own husband in her eyes to be most fair, most beautiful, most proper, most handsome, most amiable, most honest, most garnished with all virtues and qualities that become a godly husband; which opinion the husband also ought to have of his wife, that one may unfeignedly rejoice in another, and heartily love one another. "In three things," saith the wise man, "hath my spirit ever had pleasure, which also are allowed before God and man: the concord of brethren, the love of neighbours, and man and wife that agreeth well together." This love, grafted in the wife's heart toward her husband by the Holy Ghost, shall make her to do all things willingly, and to seek all means possible to please her husband, and by no means to offend and displease him. This love shall so work in her, that she shall accommodate and apply herself and all her studies, labours, and travails wholly unto the contentation of her husband's mind in all honest and godly things; yea, and that not only at commandment, but also, as they use to say, at a beck. For the nature of true and hearty love is such, that it need no prescription of laws; for freely and of itself it doth more than any law can require of it. This love shall be of such efficacy, virtue, might, power, and strength, that no persuasions, no flattering words, no fair promises, no gifts, no tokens, &c., shall be able to turn her mind from her husband, and to entangle her with strange love, and so to make her to defile her husband's bed, and to cast away her first faith and promise that she made to her husband.

Tit. ii.

Wives ought to love their husbands.

[Ecclus. xxv.]

The nature of love.

Father. Would God this love were in the hearts of all married women in these our days! Then should not holy and honourable matrimony be so defiled with adultery, whoredom, and all other uncleanness, as it is now (alas, for pity!), yea, and that almost without check or punishment. *Son*. The devil, which "goeth about like a roaring lion, seeking whom he may devour," is enemy to all degrees that God hath ordained; but specially to the christian state of holy matrimony, as we may see from the beginning. He can by no means abide that this holy order should be kept of the married folk unspotted and without blemish. Therefore a thousand ways deviseth he to pollute and defile the honourable state of matrimony, and specially by fornication, adultery, incest, and such other most damnable uncleanness. It shall therefore, as we have tofore spoken of the man, be necessary for every godly married woman ever to set before her eyes

1 Pet. v.

Gen. iii.

all those commandments of God which forbid whoredom and adultery, and also all those most terrible histories of God's anger against whores and whoremongers, that be mentioned in the holy bible.

It shall not be unprofitable also to consider with herself her marriage promise, that she hath made to her husband before God and before his holy congregation; from the which to fall, and the which to transgress and break, is more than double wickedness, and deserveth not only horrible plagues in this world, but also everlasting damnation.

Neither shall it be unfitting or out of the way to remember secretly with herself, what a great diversity there is between an honest married wife and a strumpet or whore. The blessing of God is upon the godly married woman: the curse and vengeance of God is upon the whore. The honest married woman hath a free and joyful conscience: the whore hath an unrestful mind in her, tormenting her continually with the remembrance of her wicked living, as with the painful pains of hell-fire. The faithful married woman delighteth in the presence of her husband: the whore abhorreth her husband, and hath all her pleasure in the company of strange lovers. The true married woman seeketh how to enrich her husband: the whore deviseth all means possible to impoverish him. The godly married woman hath great joy when she beholdeth her true and natural children, being well assured that they are the blessings of God, forasmuch as they are the fruit of her matrimony by her lawful husband: the whore hath no delight in her children, forasmuch as, so oft as she beholdeth them, they are witnesses against her, both of her most detestable whoredom, and also of her damnation, putting her in remembrance of her unfaithfulness against her husband, and of her wicked behaviour with strange lovers; again, that her children were not begotten in true matrimony, but are bastards and misbegotten, and therefore they were both begotten, conceived, and born in the heavy anger, wrath, and displeasure of God; so that by this means they cannot prosper, but have short continuance on the earth, as the wise man saith: "Thus shall it also go with every wife that leaveth her husband, and gets the inheritance by the strange marriage (that is to say, she shall be openly punished in the streets of the city, and she shall be chased abroad like a young horse-foal; and when she thinketh least upon it, then shall she be taken: thus shall she be put to shame of every man, because she would not understand the fear of the Lord). For first, she hath been unfaithful unto the law of the Most Highest. Secondly, she hath forsaken her own husband. Thirdly, she hath played the whore in advoutry, and gotten her children by another man. She shall be brought out of the congregation; and her children shall be looked upon. Her children shall not take root; and as for fruit, her branches shall bring forth none. A shameful report shall she leave behind her, and her dishonour shall not be put out. And they that remain shall know that there is nothing better than the fear of God, and that there is nothing sweeter than to take heed unto the commandments of the Lord. A great worship it is to follow the Lord; for long life shall be received of him."

The diversity between an honest woman and an whore.

Ecclus. xxiii.

Again, the honest married woman is satisfied and well contented with the alone company of her husband, neither doth she desire to be entangled with the love of strangers: "The whore is never satisfied, but is like as one that goeth by the way and is thirsty; even so doth she open her mouth, and drink of every next water that she may get. By every hedge she sits down, and opens her quiver against every arrow." The godly married woman cannot be enticed, neither with fair words nor with gifts, to defile her husband's bed: the whore is easily moved to all kind of dishonesty, yea, for a morsel of bread or a pot of beer. The true married woman is not ashamed to shew her face in the presence of all men: the whore lurketh in corners, and dare not appear in the company of such as be godly and honest, as our Saviour Christ saith: "All that do evil hate the light." The honest married woman hath a good name, and cometh to wealth and worship: the whore is of every man evil reported, and she is despised of men, as dung in the street; and the best end of her is extreme beggary with shame. The godly married woman maketh peace and quietness wheresoever she becometh: the whore causeth strife and dissension, and setteth men

Ecclus. xxvi.

John iii.

together by the ears. The virtuous married woman is sure always to have God her helper and aider in all her honest travails: the whore hath God ever an enemy unto her, and all that ever she goeth about cometh unto confusion, and hath no good success. The honest married woman dare with a good conscience in all her necessity and trouble call upon God, with this perfect persuasion and assured hope, that he will both hear her and help her: the whore is so confounded in her conscience, and so feeleth the hot wrath and fierce vengeance of God kindled against her for her whoredom, that she dare not once lift up her eyes unto God, but in her heart wisheth that there were no God, that she might go forth to sin freely and without punishment. The godly married woman, while she liveth in this world, is at rest and peace in her conscience with God and man, and after this life she is well assured to be heir of everlasting glory: the whore in this world is "like a raging sea, which findeth no rest;" and when she is once dead, she hath "her portion in that lake that brenneth with fire and brimstone." Isai. lvii. Rev. xxi.

If a godly married woman set these things continually before her eyes, she shall easily both repel Satan and his fiery darts, and quietly repose herself in the love of her husband, according to her bounden duty.

Father. I allow thy sayings well, my son. Go forth now to open unto me the office and duty of an honest and godly wife toward her husband. *Son*. The third point of a virtuous matron is to look unto her house; to provide that nothing perish, decay, or be lost, through her negligence; to see that whatsoever be brought into the house by the industry, labour, and provision of her husband, be safely kept and warely bestowed; not only to command other to do things, but also to set hand to the business herself; never to be idle, but always to be well occupied; to be an example of all godliness and honesty to her household; to reprove vice sharply in her servants, and to commend virtue; not to meddle with other folks' business abroad, but diligently to look upon her own at home; not to go unto her neighbours' houses, to tattle and prattle after the manner of light housewives; not to be tavern-hunters; not idly and wantonly to gad abroad, seeking new customers; not to resort unto places where common plays, interludes, and pastimes be used; not to accompany herself with any light persons, but only with such as be sober, modest, grave, honest, godly, virtuous, housewifely, thrifty, of good name, well reported, &c.; and in fine, continually to remain at home in their house diligently and virtuously occupied, except urgent, weighty, and necessary causes compel her to go forth, as to go unto the church, to pray or to hear the word of God, to visit her sick neighbours or to help them, to go to the market to buy things necessary for her household, &c. Wives ought to look well to their houses. Note well.

Father. If all married women were such housewives, my son, as thou hast here pointed and set forth, many husbands should be in better case than they be at this present. For many women be of such disposition, that they can almost no more abide their own house, than an hare can away with a tabret. Whatsoever meat and drink they have at home, be it never so good, they think it as bitter as gall. And whatsoever company they have at home, although never so honest and virtuous, yet are they none other but thorns and pricks in their eyes; abroad must they. Their house is a wild cat. They shall easily find it again at their return. Set cock on the hoop. Let the devil pay the malt-man. But, my son, let me hear if ought yet remain of the wife's duty.

Son. The fourth point of an honest and godly matron is patiently and quietly to bear the incommodities of her husband; to dissemble, cloke, hide, and cover the faults and vices of her husband; not to upbraid nor to cast them in his teeth; not to exasperate or sharpen her husband's mind through her churlishness, but rather with her soft, gentle, and sober behaviour to quiet him, to pacify his anger, to mitigate his fury, and, as they use to say, to make him of a lion a lamb. So saith St Peter: "Ye wives, be in subjection to your husbands, that even they, which obey not the word, may without the word be won of the conversation of the wives, while they behold your chaste conversation coupled with fear." Wives ought to forbear their husbands. 1 Pet. iii.

This thing practised a certain virtuous woman called Monica, the mother of St Austin, with her husband. She, having such an husband as was not only of a fierce Monica, St Austin's mother.

nature, churlish, cruel, unpatient, angry, drunken, and replenished with all kind of vice, but also an heathen man, and given to idolatry, yea, and a very enemy to her religion, and to her likewise for her religion sake, did use him with such gentleness of words, and with so sweet, kind, and loving behaviour, that at the last she overcame him, brought him from rudeness and vice unto civility and virtue; and in fine, she brought him from gentility unto christianity, so that he became a Christian and a professor of godliness. And all this came to pass through her godly conversation. For when her husband was drunk, she was sober. When he was angry, she was patient. When he blowed out many furious and unseemly words, she either held her peace, or else gave him fair and gentle language. When he in his manners was more like a brute beast than a man, she shined in her house as a mirror of virtue, in whom there appeared nothing but true godliness. Moreover, this was also her property, not to fall at words with her husband in his anger or drunkenness, or to upbraid him by it in the presence of other, but to conceal and hide his fault at all times, so much as lay in her power; and, when his fury and drunkenness was past, to warn him of it by sweet words, and gently to exhort him unto better things. Thus did she not only through her virtuous behaviour win her husband from vice to virtue, from wickedness to godliness, from gentility to christianity, yea, from hell to heaven, but also she became a noble example of most noble virtues to other women and a good counsel-giver; insomuch that, when a certain woman complained to her of her husband's churlishness, and of his cruel handling of her, she very modestly and soberly answered and said unto her: "I fear much lest your husbands be so bitter, sharp, and churlish against you, not so much of their own crooked nature, as through your own fault. For I doubt not but, if you would sometime give place to your husbands in their anger, and bear with them in their drunkenness, and conceal and hide their faults at a time, rather than fall out with them, and upbraid them by their wicked life, ye should have more gentle and more profitable husbands than ye now have; and all this cometh to pass because of your rashness and lack of sobriety, forasmuch as ye bear not with your husbands sometime, when ye see them out of the way, and wait your time, when ye may conveniently admonish them of their vices and faults, yea, and that gently and lovingly, that they may perceive that your admonitions and counsels proceed not from an hateful and evil will, but rather of a loving and well-desiring mind toward them. For I myself also had sometime a churlish and a froward husband; but by entreating him gently, by bearing with him patiently, and by giving him sweet words and wholesome exhortations, I brought him from that rude behaviour, and converted him unto the christian faith; so that now he is become a true professor of godliness, and a profitable citizen of the christian public weal[1]."

Father. O most worthy and noble matron! O most goodly spectacle for all women to behold! O most godly example to be followed!

Son. If all women would address themselves unto the practice of this godly act[2]

[[1] The substance of what is here stated may be found as follows: Educata itaque pudice ac sobrie, potiusque a te subdita parentibus, quam a parentibus tibi, ubi plenis annis nubilis facta est, tradita viro servivit veluti Domino, et sategit eum lucrari tibi, loquens te illi moribus suis, quibus eam pulcram faciebas, et reverenter amabilem atque mirabilem viro. Ita autem toleravit cubilis injurias, ut nullam de hac re cum marito haberet umquam simultatem. Expectabat enim misericordiam tuam super eum, ut in te credens castificaretur. Erat vero ille præterea sicut benevolentia præcipuus, ita ira fervidus. Sed noverat hæc non resistere irato viro, non tantum facto, sed ne verbo quidem. Jam vero refracto et quieto, cum opportunum videret, rationem facti sui reddebat, si forte ille inconsideratius commotus fuerat. Denique cum matronæ multæ, quarum viri mansuetiores erant, plagarum vestigia etiam dehonestata facie gererent, inter amica colloquia illæ arguebant maritorum vitam, hæc earum linguam, veluti per jocum graviter admonens, ex quo illas tabulas quæ matrimoniales vocantur, recitari audissent, tamquam instrumenta, quibus ancillæ factæ essent, deputare debuisse; proinde memores conditionis, superbire adversus dominos non oportere. Cumque mirarentur illæ, scientes quam ferocem conjugem sustineret, numquam fuisse auditum, aut aliquo indicio claruisse, quod Patricius ciderit uxorem, aut quod a se invicem vel unum diem domestica lite dissenserint, et caussam familiariter quærerent, docebat illa institutum suum, quod supra memoravi. Quæ observabant, expertæ gratulabantur: quæ non observabant, subjectæ vexabantur....... Denique etiam virum suum jam in extrema vita temporali ejus lucrata est tibi, nec in eo jam fideli planxit, quod in nondum fideli toleraverat.—August. Op. Par. 1679—1700. Confess. Lib. IX. 19, 22. Tom. I. cols. 164, 5.]

[[2] Act. Qu. *art?*]

of this most godly matron Monica, and use the like gentleness and sober behaviour toward their husbands, more love, peace, amity, quietness, and concord, should be found among married folk than is at this present day. But some women are more like the furies of hell than Monica, St Austin's mother. For their whole delight and pleasure is to scold, to brawl, to chide, and to be out of quiet with their husbands; so far is it off that with their godly conversation and gentle behaviour they go about to maintain amity and concord in their houses. And when they are reproved for their misdemeanour toward their husbands, they shame not to answer: 'A woman hath none other weapon but her tongue, which she must needs put in practice. They have been made dolts and fools long enough: it is now high time to take hart of grease[3] unto them. There is no worm so vile, but if it be trodden upon it will turn again, &c.'

Father. These furies are far unlike the godly ancient matrons which are commended to us in the holy scriptures and in other histories; and yet will they be called and counted Christians, being indeed worse than the pagans' wives in their behaviour. *Son.* Of such women speaketh the wise man on this manner: "It is Prov. xxi.
better to dwell in a wilderness, than with a chiding and an angry woman." Again:
"It is better to sit in a corner under the roof, than with a brawling woman in a Prov. xxv.
wide house." Jesus, the son of Sirach, also saith: "There is not a more wicked Ecclus. xxv.
head, than the head of the serpent; and there is no wrath above the wrath of a woman. I will rather dwell with a lion and a dragon, than to keep house with a wicked wife. The wickedness of a woman changeth her face: she shall muzzle her countenance, as it were a bear, and as a sack shall she shew it among the neighbours. Her husband is brought to shame among his neighbours; and when he heareth it, it maketh him to sigh. All wickedness is but little to the wickedness of a woman: the portion of the ungodly shall fall upon her. Like as to climb upon a sandy way is to the feet of the aged, even so is a wife full of words to a still quiet man. The wrath of a woman is dishonour and great confusion. If a woman get the mastery, then is she contrary to her husband. A wicked wife maketh a sorry heart, an heavy countenance, and a dead wound. Weak hands and feeble knees is a woman, that her husband is not the better for. Of the woman came the be- Gen. iii.
ginning of sin; and through her all we are dead. Give thy water no passage, no 1 Tim. ii.
not a little; neither give a wicked woman her will. If she walk not after thy hand, she shall confound thee in the sight of thine enemies. Cut her off then from thy flesh, that she do not alway abuse thee."

Father. God give all wives grace so to behave themselves, as it becometh women that profess godliness!

Father. Where is that commanded in the word of God? *Son.* St Paul hath these words: "I will that women array themselves in comely apparel, with shame- 1 Tim. ii.
facedness and discreet behaviour; not with broided hair, either gold, or pearls, or costly array; but, as becometh women that profess godliness, through good works." Hereto agreeth St Peter: "Women's apparel," saith he, "shall not be outward, with 1 Pet. iii.
broided hair and hanging on of gold, either in putting on gorgeous apparel; but let the hid man, which is in the heart, be without all corruption, so that the spirit be at rest and quiet; which spirit before God is a thing much set by. For after this manner, in the old time, did the holy women which trusted in God tire themselves, and were obedient to their husbands, even as Sara obeyed Abraham, and called him lord; whose daughters ye are, so long as ye do well."

Father. Why doth the Holy Ghost give so strait a charge concerning women's apparel? *Son.* The Spirit of God knoweth right well the vanity that lurketh in women's hearts, and how desirous they are of vain things, but special of gorgeous apparel and precious jewels. Therefore, to restrain them from this vanity, and to keep them in a comely order concerning their apparel, such godly lessons are left unto us by the holy apostles, which both wrote and spake as the Holy Ghost taught

[[3] A "hart of grease" means a *fat* one: hence, one of spirit. It is sometimes corrupted in old writers into *Greece.* See Nares's Glossary, v. *Greece*, and the ballad there quoted.]

them. And notwithstanding, who seeth not in this our age how little this commandment of God is regarded of a number of vain women, which are so addict unto vanity, that they little esteem what either God or man commandeth, so that they may satisfy their vain desire and carnal lusts?

Father. Why, is it not lawful for women to be honestly apparelled? *Son.* Honestly, but not sumptuously; cleanly, but not vainly. It is the part of an heathenish woman, and not of a christian matron, to be decked and trimmed like a mare-lady[1], or the queen of a game. And to say the truth, it is much to be feared that that woman, which so trimmeth and setteth forth herself, passing her degree and estate in costly apparel, keep herself within the bounds of honesty. If she seek only to please her husband with her apparel (which is the duty of every honest woman), what need she then to set out herself, as it were to sell, so minion-like when she goeth abroad? Is this to please her husband, which is at home, or rather to stir up the lusts of other toward her, which are abroad? For who doubteth but that many women, thus disguising themselves, wound the hearts of many, infect the eyes of many, and give also occasions of much evil to many? A measure therefore ought to be kept in their apparel. Neither ought any woman to go apparelled otherwise than their degree and estate require: the prince's wife according to her degree, being a prince's wife; and so forth orderly even to the poor husbandman's
1 Cor. xiv. wife, that all things may be comely done and in order, as the apostle saith: "For God is the author of peace, and not of confusion." And whether the women be of high or low degree, nobly apparelled or otherwise, let none of them all glory in their
Ecclus. xi. apparel, according to this commandment of the wise man, "Never rejoice thou in thine apparel;" but even those that are most sumptuously arrayed, let them be like-
[Esth. xiv. Apocrypha.] minded to that most virtuous and godly queen Hesther, which in her prayer made unto God confesseth that she hated the token of pre-eminence and worship which she bare upon her head what time she must shew herself and be seen, and abhorred it like an unclean cloth; again, that she did not wear it when she was quiet and
1 Tim. vi. alone by herself. "If we have to eat and drink," saith St Paul, "and wherewith we may be covered (he saith not, wherewith we may be gorgeously, gallantly, sumptuously, and finely apparelled), let us be content." "For nothing brought we into the world, neither shall we carry anything out of it." Let the godly matrons therefore be content with honest and comely apparel, every one according to their degree, without any gorgeousness or niceness, always remembering that clothes were first of all provided of God to cover our filthy, shameful, and miserable nakedness, and not to deck and trim us like peacocks: and above all things let them provide that the inward man be decked and garnished with all kind of godly and goodly virtues, which may brast out into godliness of life, that by this means they may shew themselves to be such women as profess godliness, and also garnish the doctrine of our Saviour Christ Jesu through their good works, and glorify the most glorious name of the Lord our God.

Father. God give all women, and us likewise, grace so to do! *Son.* Amen.

Now followeth in order the duty of parents, or fathers and mothers, toward their children: will it please you to hear that also?

Father. Yea, most gladly, my dear son.

OF THE OFFICE AND DUTY OF FATHERS AND MOTHERS TOWARD THEIR CHILDREN.

Son. In the office and duty of parents toward their children, many things are to be considered.

The man ought to be circumspect in choosing his wife. First of all, whosoever intendeth to have good, godly, and virtuous children, and the continuance of them and of their posterity upon the earth, it is necessary that he be wary and circumspect in choosing his wife, and also in ordering his own life. And

[1 Mare-lady: perhaps Mayer-lady, or May-lady, queen of the May. Unless it be rather an allusion to the "mare" in the harvest-home festivals; for which see Brand's *Popular Antiquities*, Vol. I.]

forasmuch as the man is the principal part, it shall be expedient that he himself live in the fear of God, and garnish his life with all kind of godly virtues, that he may be an ensample of godliness and honesty to so many as are under him. And as the man shall dispose and give himself wholly to virtuous and godly exercises, that he may please God, and procure God's blessing in time to come, not only to himself, but also to his wife, whom he intendeth to marry in the fear of the Lord, and likewise to his children, which he trusteth to receive of the liberality of God, as tokens and pledges of God's dear love and singular good will toward him; so in like manner shall he, in choosing a wife, of whom through the blessing of God he may receive children, use a discretion, and take heed whom he take unto him to be his wife; and in this behalf not to respect (as the manner of the world is) riches, beauty, favour, nobility, friendship, &c., but rather the godly qualities of the mind, the honesty of her parentage, her virtuous bringing up, her housewifeliness, and ready disposition to do good. This thing greatly considered the holy ancient fathers in times past, both in their own marriages, and also in the marriages of their children. To obtain godly and virtuous wives for their children, they sent into far countries, not so greatly respecting the riches as the godliness of the maid. For it is diligently to be considered whom a man shall take to wife, by whom he looketh to have children. Every tree bringeth forth fruit like unto itself, according to the common proverb: "Of an evil crow cometh an evil egg." He that chooseth such one to be his wife as cometh of wicked parents, have been wickedly brought up, and is wicked herself, void of all fear, faith, love, and knowledge of God, destitute of virtue, full of vice, &c.; what children are to be looked for of such a monster of wickedness, but monstrous and wicked children, like to their mother? And what good thing can come unto them from God? Or who dare promise to himself long posterity of such fruit? It shall therefore be meet and convenient for him that will marry in the Lord, and have children in whom he may delight, and of whom he may hope good things, to choose him such a wife as unfeignedly feareth God, and bendeth herself to live according to her profession, and afterward crave of God to have children by her. That fruit wherewith God shall bless those married folk, so coupled together in the fear of the Lord, shall surely take root and prosper, as it is written: "Blessed is the man that feareth the Lord: he hath great delight in his commandments. His seed shall be mighty upon earth: the generation of the faithful shall be blessed."

Gen. xxiv. Gen. xxviii.

Psal. cxii.

Secondly, when God hath blessed christian parents with children, the father shall provide that the infants in convenient time and place be consecrated to God by holy baptism, and offered to God by fervent prayer; at the which time and place it is the duty of a godly father to be present, and diligently to note what is there promised for the children, both by him and by other, that he may train and bring them up according to the vow and promise there made.

The father ought to be present at the baptism of his children.

Thirdly, it is the duty of a good and natural mother not to put forth her children to other women to be nourished, fostered, and brought up with strange milk, except very necessity compel her; but to nurse them herself, yea, and that with her own milk. For to what end hath God given her milk in her breast, but that she with the same milk should nourish and bring up her children? If God hath created nothing in vain, then hath he not given that milk into the mother's breast without cause; verily to nourish and to bring up her infants. Those mothers therefore, which, either of niceness or for ease, put out their children from them to other, when they themselves have abundance of milk, and might well bring them up, if they would take the pain; as they be but half mothers indeed, so likewise do they greatly offend God, and corrupt the nature of the infants. They offend God, in that they resist his ordinance and workmanship by putting away their milk, and by the refusing the labour of nursing their children, which God as a penance hath laid upon them. They corrupt also the nature of the infants, in that they be fostered and brought up not of their mothers, but of strange women; not with the natural, but unnatural milk. And by this means it many times comes to pass, that children, being brought forth of gentle and godly parents, prove churlish and wicked, and utterly estranged from the nature and good disposition of the parents. For children, by drinking in strange milk, drink in also

Mothers ought to nurse their own children.

strange manners and another nature. Therefore, as it is the duty of a good and natural mother to nurse her child herself, yea, and that with her own milk; so likewise is it the part of a true father to provide that his wife, having abundance of milk, do not refuse the labour of fostering her infant, according to the work and commandment of God, knowing that in so doing she shall greatly please God, and satisfy the office of a true and natural mother.

Father. The holy scripture declareth that the ancient godly matrons of the old testament nursed their children themselves. So likewise did the mother of Christ, Mary the virgin. *Son.* Yea, and all godly women, from the beginning unto this day for the most part, a few nicelings excepted, which are born to do no good, but only to consume idly the good fruits of the earth.

Father. In divers countries, where I have travelled in times past, I have known and proved, that those women which are most noble, and of most excellent parentage, and of greatest renown, and of highest authority, do not put forth their children abroad, but nurse them at home with their own milk, only having certain honest and godly matrons otherwise to attend upon the infants. *Son.* A custom much commendable, and worthy to be practised of all godly, true, and natural mothers.

Father. Go forth, my son, and declare more of the office and duty of good parents toward their children.

Son. Fourthly, in the time of nursing the infants, the father and the mother must provide, that no bodily harm chance to the children, either by fire, water, overlaying, or otherwise; but that they be kept warely and diligently both by night and day. But this is chiefly the office of the mother, which ought principally to attend upon the young ones in their infancy; forasmuch as the father is occupied abroad, about the provision for his family. And it shall be necessary that the parents do many times commend their little children to God in their prayers, beseeching him for his mercy to send them his holy angel, which may attend and wait upon them, guard and preserve them from all evil, and evermore conduct them unto all goodness, that they may live, prosper, and become creatures worthy such a Creator.

Father. This is godly.

Son. Fifthly, when the little children begin to learn to speak, the parents must diligently take heed that neither they themselves nor any other by the reason of niceness or wantonness learn them to stammer, to lisp, and to pronounce their words by halves; but let them teach their young ones to speak plainly and distinctly, and to utter every word and syllable truly and perfectly. For many in their youth learn such unapt manner of speaking and pronouncing their words, that when they come to age they cannot leave it. So soon as the children be able to speak plainly, let them even from their cradles be taught to utter not vain, foolish, and wanton, but grave, sober, and godly words; as, God, Jesus Christ, faith, love, hope, patience, goodness, peace, &c. And when they be able to pronounce whole sentences, let the parents teach their children such sentences as may kindle in them a love toward virtue, and an hatred against vice and sin; as for an ensample: God alone saveth me. Christ by his death hath redeemed me. The Holy Ghost sanctifieth me. There is one God. Christ alone is our Mediator and Advocate. The blood of Christ cleanseth us from all sin. There is no damnation to them that are in Christ Jesu, which walk not after the flesh, but after the Spirit. Depart from evil, and do good. Seek peace. Pray without ceasing. Be thankful in all things. Be swift to hear, and slow to speak. Walk in love, as Christ hath loved us. Trust in God, and work that is good. Flee idleness. Spend thy time fruitfully. Be humble and lowly; for such doth God love. Abhor pride; for God is an enemy to the proud. Learn to die, &c.

Children ought to be brought up in the knowledge of God's word.

After these and such like godly sentences drunken in of the young ones, it shall be profitable to teach them the Lord's prayer, the articles of the christian faith, and the ten commandments, with such other wholesome doctrine, as is contained in the catechism, or principles of christian religion; that even from their very young and tender age they may learn to drink in godliness. It is also the duty of faithful parents to teach their children to say grace both at dinner and supper, that they may learn to know of whom they have all good things both for soul and body, and to be thankful for them. In these and such like godly exercises the parents must daily and diligently train up their youth, that they, being thus acquainted with virtue from the beginning, may the more easily for ever after abstain from all sin and vice.

Father. If parents would labour thus to bring up their children, virtue should soon increase, and vice decrease.

Son. Sixthly, forasmuch as children be naturally given to play, and are desirous of pastimes, it shall be convenient that such pastimes and plays be devised for them as may not hurt their tender bodies, nor yet infect the mind with any lewdness. In their pastimes the parents must take heed that one of them hurt not another; again, that they use no swearing, no vain talk, nor babbling, but use a certain kind of gravity and modesty, even in the midst of all their most pleasant pastimes and merry conceits, that gravity, sobriety, and modesty may grow up with them even from the very cradles, all lightness, lewdness, and wantonness of manners utterly repelled and laid aside. The plays or pastimes of children.

Seventhly, the parents also must take heed with whom they do accompany their young ones, both in earnest studies and in merry pastimes; for as great profit is to be gotten of company-keeping with honest and godly persons, so likewise by keeping fellowship with the wicked and naughty packs all evils are possessed. And as the company of the virtuous is to be recounted more precious than gold or pearl; even so the fellowship of the sinful and ungodly is to be eschewed, as the plague and pestilence, yea, as hell and the devil. For as the one bringeth health and salvation, so likewise the other bringeth death and damnation. With such as a man keepeth company, even such shall he himself also prove, as the psalmograph saith: "With the holy thou shalt be holy, and with a perfect man thou shalt be perfect. With the clean thou shalt be clean, and with the froward thou shalt learn frowardness." The wise man also saith: "Whoso toucheth pitch shall be defiled withal: and he that is familiar with the proud shall clothe himself with pride." Again: "Depart from the wicked; and no misfortune shall chance unto thee." Salomon also saith: "He that keepeth company with wise men shall be wise; but whoso is a companion of fools shall come to misfortune." Of company-keeping for children. Psal. xviii. Ecclus. xiii. Ecclus. vii. Prov. xiii.

Father. The godly matron Sara, Abraham's wife, could by no means abide that her son Isaac should play and keep company with Ismael, her handmaid's son, but she drave both him and his mother out of the doors. Jacob also would not in any condition keep company with his ungodly brother Esau. Old Toby, among other most godly and wholesome admonitions, charged his son young Tobias, that he should not keep company, neither eat nor drink with the sinners. This saying of Sara, young Tobias' wife, in her prayer unto God, is so notable, that it is right well worthy to be written in letters of gold: "Thou knowest, O Lord, that I never had desire unto man, and that I have kept my soul clean from all uncleanly lust. I have not kept company with those that pass their time in sport, neither have I made myself partaker with them that walk in light behaviour." And we are commanded in the word of God, that we should not eat nor keep company with such as be of a lewd and wicked disposition. Gen. xxi. Gen. xxviii. Tob. iv. [Vulgate.] Tob. iii. [Vulgate.] 1 Cor. v. vi. 2 Cor. vi.

Son. Not without a cause. For, as the wise man saith: "Look what way a child tradeth in his youth, he will not depart from the same in his age." Whatsoever liquor is first of all put in a box, it will smell of the same continually. It is an hard point to leave things accustomed: for custom is another nature. Good parents therefore ought above all things to provide, that their children at all times accompany themselves with none but with such only as be honest, godly, and virtuous; lest by the company-keeping of the evil their good disposition be altered and corrupted. For, as St Paul saith: "Evil words corrupt good manners." Prov. xxii. 1 Cor. xv.

Eighthly, it is the duty of godly and christian parents to teach their children good manners, yea, and that even in their very tender age and young years, lest they prove rude and barbarous in their behaviour, and so become savage people, and unprofitable members of the christian commonweal. Let them first of all be taught, that whensoever God, Christ, or the Holy Ghost be named of them, or of other in their presence, they shew some outward reverence, either by putting off their cap, or else by bowing their knee. Again, if they be present in the time of prayer, or when the holy scripture is read or preached, or else when the holy and blessed sacraments are ministered, or when any other godly mysteries be in hand, let them Good manners.

either kneel down or stand up, as the manner and custom of the place is, yea, and that with their caps put off. Let them also be taught to reverence their elders, to rise against them, to make courtesy unto them, to put off their caps, and to give them the way. If any man speak unto them, let them salute them again, and uncover their heads. If any man talk with them, let them stand right up, hold up their heads, and look them in the face with a modest and cheerful countenance, mixed with gravity. Let them hold their hands and feet still: let them not bite their lips, nor scratch their head, nor rub their elbows, nor pore in their ears; but, all the parts of the body being set in a comely order, let them diligently mark what is said unto them, that they may make an apt and discreet answer. Let them also be taught to behave themselves mannerly at the table, whether they do sit at it or wait and attend upon it. This also is not to be neglected, that the children be accustomed both evening and morning to humble themselves unto their parents, to kneel before them, and so with all reverence to ask them blessing, and to desire their continual favour; yea, and daily also to pray for the prosperous preservation of their parents.

Father. If children from their infancy were accustomed to these and such like good and virtuous manners, then should not such rudeness, grossness, and barbarousness of behaviour, nor such disobedience and unreverence to their elders, be found in them as is at this present day. For civility and comely behaviour is now-a-days so neglected, that it is almost despised. There is no reverent obedience nor obedient reverence used of the youth toward their superiors in this our age. Parents are not had in such honour and worship of the children as they ought. Mere[1] barbarousness occupieth the hearts of all youth almost at this present.

Son. No marvel. For christian discipline is exiled out of the church; neither are parents so diligent in doing their office as they are bound by the commandment of God. But I will proceed with my matter.

Ninthly, when the children be come to the age of six or seven years, let the parents provide that they be sent to school, yea, and that unto such a school-master as feareth God, is learned, well-mannered, and is able with discretion to judge of the nature and capacity of the children, and so according to the same to teach, instruct, trade, rule, and govern them. But in this education and bringing up of the children in good letters this must be provided, that the children be not, after the common custom of schools, continually nousled[2] in reading and learning heathen and pagan writers, of whom many times is drunken in more wickedness than godliness, more sin than virtue, (for the tongue may not so be filed that the mind be defiled, nor the speech so polited that the heart be polluted;) but rather that with eloquence they learn also godliness. For those schools, wherein nothing is taught but the doctrine of paganism, are more meet for the youth of the Turks and of the Saracens, and of such other miscreants and cast-aways, than for the children of the Christians. Neither can I see what great profit can come to a christian commonweal of such schools. "Vain are all they," saith the wise man, "in whom there is no knowledge of God." Yea, where there is no knowledge of God and of his holy word, there hath the soul no pleasure. "To know thee, O God, is perfect righteousness; and to know thy righteousness and truth is the root of immortality." And as our Saviour Christ saith: "This is everlasting life, to know thee to be the alone true God, and whom thou hast sent, Jesus Christ." Likewise saith St Paul: "I shewed myself among you to know nothing but Jesus Christ, even him that was crucified." Without this knowledge, I mean of Christ and of his gospel, all other knowledge is not greatly profitable, yea, it rather hindereth than profiteth.

Children sent to school.

Wisd. xiii.

Wisd. xv.

John xvii.

Porphyry with his logic, Aristotle with his philosophy, Homer with his poetry, Ptolomy with his astronomy, Hippocrates with his physic, &c. without the knowledge of Christ crucified, are ignorant and blind men, neither knowing or seeing any thing that is allowable before God, or is profitable for their souls' health. For "vain are all they," saith the wise man, "in whom there is no knowledge of God." Therefore godly parents must earnestly provide, that their children, going to school, do above all things learn to know God, that he is their Maker and Father, that they

Wisd xiii.

[1 Folio, *more*.] [2 Nousled, or nuzzled, differently written: nursed.]

receive of him all good things necessary both for body and soul, and that he hath not made them to this end, that they should alway remain here, but rather that they, leaving this transitory life at his appointment, should for ever after dwell with him in his glorious kingdom, and have such joys as eye never saw the like, ear never heard the like, no tongue is able to express the like, nor no heart is able to conceive or to think the like. They must also learn to know, that all the benefits which they receive of God the Father are not given unto them for their own dignity and worthiness, for their own merits and deserts, but only for the dignity and worthiness, for the merits and deserts of our alone Mediator Christ Jesus, our alone Saviour, our alone Redeemer, our alone Peace-maker, our alone Advocate, our alone High Priest, our alone Law-fulfiller, and our alone Righteousness; for whose sake God the Father is well pleased with us, so that through him we obtain all good things both worldly and heavenly of our most dear Father; so that now we are become the sons and heirs of God, and heirs annexed with Christ Jesus of everlasting life. Rom. viii.

Moreover, they must be taught that, for this most loving kindness of their heavenly Father toward them for Jesus Christ's sake, they labour to the uttermost of their power to please God, to fear God, to love God, to believe in God, to call on the glorious name of God by fervent prayer in all their necessities, to be thankful to God for all his benefits, to walk worthy of their profession, to lead a new life, to become new creatures, to be fruitful in doing good works, to live according to their vocation and calling, to shine as mirrors of virtue, and in fine, to be such as shall resemble their heavenly Father and their elder brother Christ in all their life and conversation, as it is written: "He that saith he dwelleth in Christ ought to walk as Christ hath walked." For we are "delivered from the power of our enemies" to this end, that we should "serve the Lord our God in holiness and righteousness all the days of our life." And Christ hath "purged our conscience from dead works," saith St Paul, "to serve the living God." 1 John ii. Luke i. Heb. ix.

Furthermore, that the children may learn these things the more commodiously, it is the duty of parents to prepare for them, not idle and wanton, not vain and trifling books, but wholesome, holy, and godly books, as the new testament of our Saviour Christ Jesu, the parables of Salomon, the book of Jesus the son of Sirach, and such like, that they may be trained and brought up in them, and by this means drink in the knowledge of godliness from their young and tender years. Books for children.

It shall profit also very much unto true godliness, that the children be brought unto the church to hear the godly psalms, prayers, and chapters that be there read, but specially to hear the sermons and preachings of God's word; and, when they come home, to require of them an accompts of such things as they have heard in the church, but namely concerning the sermon. If they can well call the doctrine of the preacher to remembrance, and make true report thereof, let then the parents praise and commend them, that by this means the children may be encouraged to continue, yea, to increase in well-doing. For, as the common saying is, "virtue praised increaseth." But if the parents shall find them negligent in this behalf, let them be rebuked, yet not too sharply, and exhorted to do better, and to give more diligence hereafter.

It shall also help greatly forward unto the increase of true godliness, if the parents take this order with their children, that whensoever they come home from school unto dinner or supper, so soon as they themselves be set down at the table, and grace said, one of their children read a chapter of the old or new testament, the other giving good ear thereunto; and, the chapter once done, reverently to talk of the same, that such as be present may be edified, as St Paul saith: "Let no filthy communication proceed out of your mouth, but that which is good to edify withal, as oft as need is; that it may minister grace unto the hearers." Again: "Let your speech be always well savoured and powdered with salt, that ye may know how ye ought to answer every man." Chapters of the bible read at dinner and supper of the children. Eph. iv. Col. iv.

Father. Is it the duty of parents thus to train up their children in the knowledge of God, and of his holy word? *Son*. It is the principal office of a christian father and mother. The principal office of a christian parent is to bring up his children godly.

Father. Yet the common sort of parents think that they have done their duty toward their children abundantly, if they keep them from fire and water, and from other dangers; if they cleanly apparel them; if they give them meat and drink enough; if they provide to leave them richly after their departure. *Son.* The Turks and Saracens, and the other infidels, do this also for their children. They therefore, which only make ☞ provision for the bodies of their children, and neglect their souls, are none other than Turkish and Saracen-like fathers; and in this behalf no better than the brute beasts, which also provide for the bodily conservation of their young ones. But it is required of christian parents, yea, and that most chiefly, that they study also for the health and wealth, for the conservation and preservation of the souls of their children; forasmuch as they know that their children are appointed of God after this life to be the citizens of heaven, and there to remain for ever and ever in glory. Neither is it with christian men's children as it is with the younglings of brute beasts, whose bodies being once dissolved, there remain no part of them unperished. But when the bodies of the children return again unto the earth, their souls are taken up into the glorious kingdom of heaven through the ministry of God's angels, and there remain in joy unto the day of judgment, when their bodies by the mighty power of God shall be restored unto them; and so, their bodies and souls linked and joined together, they shall continue with their Lord God for ever after in joy and glory, worlds without end. In consideration whereof, the parents ought to provide, not only for the bodies, but also for the souls of their children, that they may be made citizens worthy of such and so glorious a city.

Father. I would gladly hear it proved by the word of God, that it is the duty of christian parents to see their children brought up in the knowledge of God and of his holy word. *Son.* The probation is so easy as that which is most easy. God
Deut. iv. himself gave this commandment to all parents: "Take heed to thyself, and keep thy soul diligently, that thou forget not the things which thine eyes have seen, and that they depart not out of thine heart all the days of thy life; but teach them thy
Deut. vi. sons, and thy sons' sons." Again: "These words which I command thee this day shall be in thine heart; and thou shalt shew them unto thy children, and shalt talk of them when thou art at home in thine house, and as thou walkest by the way, and when thou liest down, and when thou risest up; and thou shalt bind them for a sign upon thine hand. And they shall be warning between thine eyes; and thou shalt write them upon the posts of thy house, and upon thy gates." The psalmo-
Psal. lxxviii. graph also saith: "I will open my mouth in a parable: I will declare hard sentences of old; which we have heard and known, and such as our fathers have told us; that we should not hide them from the children of the generations to come; but to shew the honour of the Lord, his might, and wonderful works that he hath done. He made a covenant with Jacob, and gave Israel a law, which he commanded our fathers to teach their children, that their posterity might know it, and the children which were yet unborn; to the intent that, when they came up, they might shew their children the same; that they might put their trust in God, and not to forget the works of God, but to keep his commandments." And king Ezechias, in his thanksgiving unto
Isai. xxxviii. God, saith: "The father shall declare thy truth to his children." The wise man also
Ecclus. vii. saith: "If thou have sons, bring them up in nurture and learning, and hold them in
Ecclus. xxx. awe from their youth up." Again: "He that teacheth his son shall have joy in him, and need not to be ashamed of him among his acquaintance." Likewise saith St
Eph. vi. Paul: "Ye fathers, move not your children to wrath; but bring them up in the doctrine and information of the Lord."

All these sentences of the holy scripture declare manifestly that parents are bound by the commandment of God, and as they will avoid the danger of everlasting damnation, to teach their children the law of God and the true worshipping of him, that they, in their young years drinking in the knowledge of God's most holy will, may
Luke i. learn to serve their Lord God "in holiness and righteousness all the days of their life." And according to these commandments of God, all good and godly parents from the beginning have travailed from time to time to bring up their children, as we have divers examples in the holy scripture.

Examples of the godly bringing up of youth. Rom. iv. *Father.* Recite to me part of them. *Son.* Abraham, which in the holy scripture is called "the father of the faithful", brought up his children both godly and virtuously, and taught them the law of God, as he himself had learned of the Holy Ghost; as these words do manifestly declare: "Shall I hide from Abraham," saith God, "the Gen. xviii. thing which I intend to do; seeing that Abraham shall be a great and a mighty people, and all the nations of the earth shall be blessed in him? I know this also, that he will command his children and his household after him, that they keep the way of the Lord, and do after right and conscience." And as Abraham trained up his children in godliness and virtue, so likewise did all the other godly patriarchs that succeeded him from time to time.

How diligent king David was in the godly bringing up of his children, and specially of Salomon, that he might worthily succeed him in his prince-like estate, as many other, so likewise these words which he spake to Salomon lying on his death [bed] do sufficiently shew: "Behold," saith he, "I must walk by the way of all the world; 1 Kings ii. nevertheless, be strong and quit thyself manfully, and see thou keep the appointment of the Lord thy God, that thou walk in his ways, and keep his commandments, ordinances, laws, and testimonies, as it is written in the law of Moses," &c.

The travail of the godly ancient father Tobias, in bringing up his son in the fear Tob. i. [Vulgate.] and knowledge of God even from his infancy, is more known to such as read the holy histories than it need here to be rehearsed. His exhortations are such, that they Tob. iv. are worthy at all times to be remembered of all men, specially of youth.

That godly and virtuous lady Susanna, having righteous parents, was brought Hist. Sus. up by them from her very cradles in the law of Moses, and taught to fear the Lord her God.

Blessed Luke, in the chronicle of the apostles' acts, maketh mention of the four Acts xxi. daughters of Philip the evangelist, which did prophesy; that is to say, they were so godly brought up in the knowledge of God's most blessed law, that they were able to declare and expound the holy scriptures and mysteries of God, according to this prophecy: "I will pour out of my Spirit upon all flesh; and your sons and your Joel ii. Acts ii. daughters shall prophesy." Read we not also that blessed St Paul doth greatly commend bishop Timothy, because he had "known the holy scriptures even of a 2 Tim. iii. child?"

These and divers other like histories shew evidently that all godly parents, from time to time in all ages, have been diligent according to the commandment of God to bring up their children in the knowledge of God's most holy word, yea, and that from their very cradles and tender infancy; so that whosoever will do the part of a good and godly father, may not only make provision for the wealth of the bodies, but also for the health of the souls of his children, which cannot be brought to pass without the knowledge of God's word. Yea, more blessed and happy is that ☞ child, to whom his father hath procured the knowledge of God and of his holy word, with other virtues and good sciences, than that son to whom his father departing leaveth a thousand pounds by the year. For the possessions of the one are constant and immortal: the possessions of the other are inconstant, transitory, and subject to the vanity of frowning fortune.

Moreover, St Paul saith: "Exercise thyself rather unto godliness. For bodily exercise 1 Tim. iv. profiteth little; but godliness is profitable unto all things, as a thing which hath promises of the life that is now, and of the life to come. This is a sure saying, and by all means worthy to be allowed." Our Saviour Christ saith also: "First of all seek the Matt. vi. kingdom of God and the righteousness thereof; and all these things (he meaneth necessaries for the sustentation of the life) shall be cast unto you." Likewise saith the psalmograph: "I have been young, and now I am waxen old; and yet never saw Psal. xxxvii. I righteous man forsaken, nor his seed begging their bread on the earth."

Father. I see now right well, that the office of a godly father is to see that his children be virtuously brought up and in the knowledge of God's most holy word. But let me ask thee one question. What if, the father doing his duty, the Parents ought to correct their children, if they do amiss. children be negligent and will not learn; or if they learn, they will not frame their life according to their knowledge; may not the father with a good conscience correct those children? *Son*. Yes, most lawfully. For moderate correction is as necessary for children as meat and drink. "He that spareth the rod," saith Salomon, "hateth Prov. xiii.

Prov. xxii. his son; but whoso loveth him chasteneth him betimes." "Foolishness sticketh in Prov. xxiii. the heart of the lad; but the rod of correction shall drive it away." "Withhold not correction from the child; for if thou beatest him with the rod, he shall not die Prov. xxix. thereof. If thou smite him with the rod, thou shalt deliver his soul from hell." "The rod and correction minister wisdom; but if a child be not looked to, he bringeth his mother to shame." "Nurture thy son with correction, and thou shalt be at rest; Ecclus. vii. yea, he shall do thee good at the heart." Jesus, the son of Sirach, also saith: "If thou have sons, bring them up in nurture and learning, and hold them in awe from their youth up. If thou have daughters, keep their body, and shew not thy face Ecclus. xxx. cheerful toward them." Again he saith: "Whoso loveth his child holdeth him still under correction, that he may have joy of him afterward. He that teacheth his son shall have joy in him, and need not to be ashamed of him among his acquaintance. Whoso informeth and teacheth his son grieveth the enemy, and before his friends he may have joy of him. Though the father die, yet is he as though he were not dead; for he hath left one behind him that is like him. In his life he saw him, and had joy in him, and was not sorry in his death, neither was he ashamed before his enemies; for he left behind him an avenger against his enemies, and a good doer unto his friends. He that chasteneth his child bindeth the wounds together, that his heart may fear every word. An untamed horse will be hard; and a wanton child will be wilful. If thou bring up thy son delicately, he shall make thee afraid; and if thou play with him, he shall bring thee to heaviness. Laugh not with him, lest thou weep with him also, and lest thy teeth be set on edge at the last. Give him no liberty in his youth, and excuse not his folly. Bow down his neck while he is young: hit him on the sides while he is yet but a child, lest he wax stubborn, and give no more force of thee; and so shalt thou have heaviness of soul."

Deut. xxi. Moreover, who knoweth not that God in the law of Moses commanded, that the children which were stubborn and disobedient to their parents should be stoned unto death? To whom also is it unknown unto what miserable end the priest Hely came, because he brought up his children dissolutely, and corrected them not[1]...forward, and brake his neck? Perished not his sons also in battle? Again, did not Adonia the [1 Kings i. 6.] son of Hagith exalt himself, and said, "I will be king?" "And his father would not displease him in any condition, nor said so much to him as, Why doest thou so?" What was the end of him? was he not slain? Fathers therefore ought not to be slothful nor negligent in the correction of their children, when they see them do amiss, lest the vengeance of God fall both upon them and upon their children.

Father. Notwithstanding, the correction ought to be gentle and favourable. *Son.* According to the fault, and also according to the nature of the child that offendeth. If the fault be little, correction by word is sufficient, or else little punishment. But if the fault be great, let correction be done according to the fault. Some children also be brought as soon to amendment by words as by stripes. But this is to be observed of all parents in all their corrections, that first of all, before they punish their children which have offended, they lay the fault openly before them, declare unto them how greatly they have offended and broken God's commandment, and exhort them from thenceforth to do better; that the children may evidently perceive that both the words and stripes, which they suffer at their parents' hands, proceed from such an heart as heartily wish and desire not their destruction, but their salvation; not their loss, but their profit. And this meaneth the apostle, when he saith: "Fathers, provoke not your children to wrath, lest they be of a desperate mind." The good-will of the father toward his child ought to appear and shine even in the midst of his anger, and a moderation is to be had both in words and stripes; that the wits of the children be not dulled, nor they driven to such an hatred with their parents, that they begin no more to love them as parents, but to hate them as tyrants, and hereof take an occasion to run away from them.

Things to be observed in correction.

Father. As those fathers are not to be commended which are so tender over their children that they cannot abide the wind to blow upon them, nor, though they

[[1] This sentence is imperfect. *That he fell*, or words of the like meaning, should be supplied.]

offend, once to frown upon them, or to give them a sharp word; even so are those parents greatly to be discommended which furiously rage against their children, and without consideration beat them as stock-fish. These parents are rather butchers than fathers.

Son. It become all parents to use a moderation in correcting their children; but now that I have answered to your question, I will go forth with the office of the parents. *Father.* Let it so be.

Son. Tenthly, after the children have consumed certain years in the school of godliness, virtue, and learning, it is convenient that the parents do now consider with themselves, to what kind of honest and godly exercise they will put their children, that they may be able hereafter to live as good and profitable members of the commonweal, and by their own industry and labour to get their living, yea, and to have also whereof to give unto the needy. For God hath appointed no man to be idle in this world; but every man to eat his own bread in the labour of his own hands, and to drink his own drink in the sweat of his own brows. And who knoweth not, what a sure patrimony and strong defence against the cruel darts of poverty and beggary an honest and good occupation is? according to this common proverb: *Artem quævis terra alit;* that is to say, "A man having an occupation shall be able to live wheresoever he become." Therefore shall it be wisdom for godly parents to determine with themselves betimes, how they will bestow their children, that they may be able afterward to live. If any of their children shall be found apt in time to come to be spiritual ministers in the church of God, pastors, and preachers, or to be schoolmasters, or magistrates in the public weal; then shall it be convenient, that they continue still in their studies, and be sent unto some university, where they may exercise themselves in such kind of learning as shall be most meet for that vocation which they intend afterward openly to profess unto the glory of God, and unto the profit of their country. The residue of their children let the parents appoint to some honest and virtuous occupation, that they may be able afterward truly and honestly to live of themselves; and by no means suffer them to live idly, nor to be of the number of such Sim Shakebucklers[2], as in their young years fall unto serving, and in their old years fall unto beggary, if not unto worse. An honest and profitable occupation is a rich and wealthy patrimony. But in this behalf also this consideration must be had of the parents, that their children be set to such occupations as they of nature be most apt and inclined unto: so shall the science which they learn prosper the better with them, and they also shall so much the sooner come unto the knowledge and perfection of the same. For by striving against nature nothing cometh well and fortunately to pass.

Furthermore, after the children be set in such estate, that by their knowledge, industry, and labour, they be able to live of themselves, yea, and to make provision for other also, if God shall call them to be rulers of households, and the time doth now require that they give themselves to marriage, whereof also they shew themselves very desirous, that they may be fruitful in the earth, and leave seed behind them, as their ancestors tofore have done according to the commandment of God; it is the office and duty of good and godly parents to provide marriages for them, that they may marry in the Lord, and with the consent of their parents, to whom also in this behalf they are obedient, and without whose counsel and advice they ought not rashly to enterprise any thing concerning matrimony. Children in the state of matrimony ought not to follow their own blind judgment, foolish fancy, carnal appetite, sensual pleasure, &c. but the grave, sage, prudent, and wise counsel of their parents, as persons which both for their wisdom and experience know, will, and can better provide for them in this case, than they can or may provide for themselves. Those children, which of their own brain and fancy attempt marriage without the good-will and consent of their parents, do grievously offend; and seldom cometh to pass that such marriages come unto a fortunate and prosperous end. What can prosper, where fear toward God and obedience toward the parents is cast aside, and fleshly sensuality followed? If God's blessing be not present, what can have good success?

Gen. i.

Parents ought to provide marriages for their children.

And as the duty of children is, not to entangle themselves with the bond of matri-

[[2] Blusterers and bullies were called *swash-bucklers*, or *shake-bucklers*, from shaking their bucklers (which were used by serving-men) in a noisy threatening manner.]

mony without both the consent and counsel of their fathers and mothers; so likewise is it the office of all godly parents, understanding the desire, will, and mind of their children, to provide such yoke-fellows for them as fear God, come of an honest parentage, have been godly brought up from their infancy, love virtue, hate vice. Let them not so much respect nobility, riches, friendship, &c., after the manner of the world, as the riches of the mind, I mean honest and godly qualities. Let them in this behalf follow the holy and ancient patriarchs, which, because they would couple their children to such as feared God, sent into far countries; whereas, if they had only considered and tendered wealth, riches, promotions, nobility of blood, friendship, beauty, strength, &c., they might have been provided at home at their own doors, yea, and that with less pain and charge.

What manner of wife a father ought to provide for his son. Tob. iii. [Vulgate.]

If they be sons whom they intend to set forth in marriage, let them provide such honest, godly, and virtuous maids to be their wives, as may truly say with Sara, young Tobias' wife: "Thou knowest, O Lord, that I never had desire unto man, and that I have kept my soul clean from all uncleanly lust. I have not kept company with those that pass their time in sport, neither have I made myself partaker with them that walk in light behaviour. Nevertheless, an husband have I consented to take, not for my pleasure, but in thy fear." Let them be no delicate minions, nor no white-fingered housewives, which can do nothing else but trick up themselves like puppets, and prick upon a clout without any gain, swift to command, but ready to do nothing, except it be to eat and drink, to keep company with some he-saint, to play at the dice and cards, to dance, to play upon a lute or upon a pair of virginals, &c.; but rather let them be such as will lay their hands to work, help to get the penny, save such things as the man bringeth in, dress meat and drink, spin and card, look to her family, nurse her own children, suffer nothing to perish, and in fine, even such one as Salomon describeth in the thirty-first chapter of his proverbs.

What manner of husband a father ought to provide for his daughter.

If they be daughters whom the parents intend to set forth in marriage, let them above all things take heed that such as shall marry their daughters be men that fear God, love his word, come of an honest stock, have been well brought up, have honest occupations to get their livings, are desirous to live with truth and honesty, abhor riot, hate dicing, carding, and such other vain pastimes, love their own houses, are ☞ careful for their families, &c. For better it is for a man to couple his daughter to such one as feareth God, although poor and base, than to a rich man without the fear of God and without the virtuous qualities of the mind, as Themistocles said: "I had rather marry my daughter to a man without money, than to money without a man.[1]" * For nothing can want where God is friend: neither can any thing long prosper where God is enemy. If the parents do thus set forth their daughters to men of a good disposition, then have they done that which is the duty of honest and godly fathers and mothers, as the wise man saith: "If thou have daughters, keep their body, and shew not thy face cheerful toward them. Marry thy daughter, and so shalt thou perform a weighty matter; but give her to a man of understanding."

Ecclus. vii.

But this is also seemly, that parents, giving their children to marriage, give unto them also, according to their ability, some honest portion of substance, that they may be the more able to live: which thing also shall not a little increase, maintain, and confirm love and friendship between the married folk, when they consider the liberality and free heart of the parents toward them. Notwithstanding, let them so give that ☞ they themselves lack not: for better it is that children crave of their parents, than that parents should ask of their children.

Moreover, as all these things heretofore rehearsed appertain unto the office of christian parents, and may by no means be neglected; so likewise is this also the duty of fathers and mothers, so uprightly to live, and so innocently to behave themselves in all their words and acts, that they offend not their children, nor be unto them example-givers of evil; but rather that in all their doings they shine as mirrors of virtue in the presence of their children. For, as nothing doth more profit and edify the children than the virtuous, honest, and innocent life of the parents; so likewise

Parents ought to give good example to their children in godliness of life.

[[1] Plut. Apophth. Valer. Max. VII. ii. Extern. 8.]

nothing corrupteth and hurteth more both the bodies and minds of the children than the wicked and naughty manners of fathers and mothers. For the children think that nothing is unlawful in them that is lawful in the parents; again, that they may boldly do that which they see their parents enterprise, use, and practise before their face. Let all parents therefore think, that fear God, that it is not sufficient for * them to provide that their children be brought up in godliness and virtue, except they also confirm the same with their examples and manners, that their children, beholding their innocency and quiet behaviour, may study with all diligence to practise the same in their life and conversation. For, as the common proverb is, "The young cock croweth as he heareth the old." Again, "The child followeth the father." It were good for all fathers to have this saying of Christ ever before their eyes: "Whosoever doth offend one of these little ones which believe in me, it were better for him that a mill-stone were hanged about his neck, and that he were drowned in the depth of the sea." Matt. xviii.

Finally, this is the duty of all parents at all times, with their fervent and earnest prayers to commend their children to God, that he may preserve, keep, and govern them with his holy Spirit in his faith, fear, and love, and bless all their doings, giving good success to all their godly and honest enterprises, and so endue them with the abundance of his grace, that they, in this world serving him in holiness and righteousness all the days of their life, may, after their departure from this vale of misery, enjoy the heavenly inheritance purchased not with corruptible gold and silver, but with the precious blood of that pure and undefiled Lamb Christ Jesus our Lord; to whom be glory for ever. *Father.* Amen.

Now, my child, seeing thou hast so godly and fruitfully set forth the office of parents toward their children, I also greatly desire to hear of thee on the other part the duty of children unto their parents. *Son.* It followeth next in order.

OF THE DUTY OF CHILDREN TOWARD THEIR PARENTS.

As concerning the duty of children toward their parents, we talked of that matter in the declaration of the fifth commandment; so that it may seem now almost superfluous any more to speak of it: notwithstanding, forasmuch as the place and order requireth that we speak somewhat also now of the office and duty of children, and it is your pleasure that I should so do, I will gladly express unto you whatsoever I have to say in this behalf. *Father.* I allow thy diligence.

Son. The most worthy apostle St Paul describeth the office and duty of children toward their parents on this manner: "Children, obey your fathers and mothers in the Lord; for that is right. Honour thy father and mother (the same is the first commandment in the promise), that thou mayest prosper, and live long on the earth." Eph. vi. Again he saith: "Ye children, obey your fathers and mothers in all things; for that is well-pleasing to the Lord." Col. iii. Here see we, that the office and duty of children toward their parents consisteth in two things.

Father. What two things are they? *Son.* Honour and obedience. That child, which will do his office truly and faithfully according to the commandment of God, must both honour and obey his father and mother. Children ought to honour and to obey their parents.

Father. In what points doth the honour of parents consist? *Son.* First of all, in having a reverent opinion of them, of their prudence and wisdom, of their state and vocation, of their regiment and governance; being persuaded that they are our parents, not by fortune and chance, but by the singular providence and good-will of God, given unto us of God for our great commodity, profit, and wealth. Of honouring parents.

Secondly, in loving them, yea, and that not feignedly, but from the very bottom of the heart; and in wishing unto them all good things from God, as unto persons which, next unto God, have and do best deserve of us.

Thirdly, in giving them that reverence and honour outwardly, which by the commandment of God is due from children to their parents; as to bow the knee unto them, to ask them blessing, to put off their cap, to give them place, reverently and meekly to speak unto them, and with all outward gestures to shew a reverent honour and honourable reverence toward them, as persons representing the majesty of God.

Fourthly, in labouring to the uttermost of their power to be thankful, and to requite their parents for such and so great benefits as they have received of God by them and their labours. As for an example, if their parents be aged and fallen into poverty, so that they are not able to live of themselves, nor to get their living by their own industry and labour, then ought the children, if they will truly honour their parents, to labour for them, to see unto their necessity, to provide necessaries for them, and by no means, so much as in them is, to suffer them for to lack any good thing; forasmuch as their parents cared and provided for them, when they were not able to care and provide for themselves.

Fifthly and finally, in concealing, hiding, covering, and in interpreting all their parents' faults, vices, and incommodities unto the best, never objecting nor upbraiding them by any thing done amiss; but quietly and patiently to bear all things at their hands, considering that in thus doing they greatly please God, and offer unto him an acceptable sacrifice; and by no means to follow the wicked manners of the most wicked Ham, which, when Noah his father was drunken and lay uncovered[1] in the tent, went and told his two brethren without; but rather to practise the godly behaviour of Sem and Japhet, which, taking a garment, laid it upon their shoulders, and, coming backward, covered the nakedness[2] of their father, namely, their faces being turned away, lest they should see their father's nakedness[2]. By this means were they blessed, and Ham cursed.

Gen. ix.

It becometh a good and godly child, not to display, but to conceal the faults of his father, even as he wisheth that God should cover his own offences, as the wise man saith: "Rejoice not when thy father is reproved; for it is not honour unto thee, but shame. For the worship of a man's father is his own worship; and where the father is without honour, it is the dishonesty of the son. My son, make much of thy father in his age, and grieve him not as long as he liveth. And if his understanding fail, have patience with him, and despise him not in thy strength. For the good deed that thou shewest to thy father shall not be forgotten; and when thou thyself wantest, it shall be rewarded thee," &c.

Ecclus. iii.

Father. Wherein consisteth the obedience of a child toward his father? *Son*. In two things principally.

Of obeying parents.

First, in shewing himself obedient, not feignedly, but from the very heart, to the will and commandment of his father in executing, performing, and accomplishing the same with all diligence, evermore seeking to do that which may please him, and eschewing again at all times whatsoever in any point may displease him.

Father. But what if the father command the child to do that thing which is contrary to the word of God? *Son*. Here the child oweth unto the father no obedience. For "we must obey God more than men." But of this matter we spake when we talked of the fifth commandment.

Acts v.

Secondly, in attempting no grave or weighty matter without the counsel of his father, but to desire and crave his father's advice and judgment in all things; as not to enterprise marriage without his consent, nor to entangle himself with any weighty cause without the counsel and consent of his father; always preferring his father's judgment before his own, as one of more experience, larger wisdom, and greater knowledge, yea, as one that tendereth his commodity and profit no less than his own.

Children ought not to enterprise marriage without the counsel and consent of their parents.

Father. What ought to move children to shew this honour and obedience unto their parents? *Son*. First, the commandment of God, which saith: "Honour thy father and thy mother." Again: "Ye children, obey your fathers and mothers in the Lord."

Exod. xx.

Eph. vi. Col. iii.

Secondly, the promise which is annexed to the commandment; even this, that they which honour and obey their parents shall prosper and live long on the earth.

Thirdly, the commination or threatening of God's anger and vengeance against all disobedient children. "Whoso laugheth his father to scorn, and setteth his mother's

Prov. xxx.

[[1] Three words are omitted.] [[2] A word is substituted.]

commandment at nought," saith the wise man, "the ravens pick out his eyes in the valley, and devoured be he of the young eagles." How miserably perished Absolon for his disobedience against his father! Is not the commandment of God, that such children as are stubborn and disobedient to their parents should be stoned unto death? 2 Sam. xviii. Deut. xxi.

Fourthly, the great labours and pains which the parents take, and the infinite charges and costs which they also bestow, in bringing up of them.

These and such like things, diligently considered, shall easily move the heart of any natural and well-disposed child to shew true honour and unfeigned obedience unto his parents, and cause him to seek all means possible to gratify his parents again, and to answer kindness for kindness.

Father. God for his mercy work this good disposition in the hearts of all children toward their parents! *Son.* Amen.

Father. Go forth now, my son, to recite the offices of such degrees as remain. *Son.* Next in order followeth the office of householders or masters toward their servants.

OF THE OFFICE OF MASTERS OR HOUSEHOLDERS TOWARD THEIR SERVANTS.

Forasmuch as every householder or master, that keepeth servants, maintaineth them unto this end, that by their labour and work things may be provided and gotten that be necessary for himself and for his family; and forasmuch as all labour and pain is taken in vain, except God blesseth the labours, and giveth good success to the travails; therefore the first and principal office of a master or householder is to bring up his servants and family in virtue and in the true knowledge of God, and to train them daily in the exercises of true godliness at certain hours appointed, that by this means God may prosper their labours and travails, and bless his household, and enrich every corner of his house, giving him abundance of all things. For "it is the blessing of the Lord that maketh men rich:" and, "except the Lord build the house, they labour in vain that build it." Masters ought to govern their servants godly, and to train them up in godliness. Prov. x. Psal. cxxvii.

In the morning before they go unto labour, let the master of the house call all his servants together, and, meekly kneeling down upon their knees, let one in the name of them all give thanks unto our heavenly Father, that it hath pleased him of his merciful goodness to preserve and defend them that night from all evil, and to give them sweet sleep and comfortable rest; and desire him also to keep and save them that day from all perils and dangers, and graciously to prosper their labours which they intend to enterprise, and always to assist them with his holy Spirit, that they take nothing in hand, but that may be acceptable in his sight, profitable to their christian brethren, and healthful to their souls. Let the rest of the family mark diligently what is said, consent to it in their hearts, and when it is ended say, Amen. Exercises of godliness. Prayer in the morning.

Afterward, all the servants rising up again together, let them all with one voice recite the articles of the christian faith: that done, let them all fall down again upon their knees, and one of them rehearse the ten commandments of God, the residue giving ear unto them, and saying together at the end of every commandment these words: "Lord, have mercy upon us, and incline our hearts to keep this law." And when all the commandments be ended, let them say together with one voice on this wise, lifting up their hearts, eyes, and hands unto heaven: "Lord, have mercy upon us, and write all these thy laws in our hearts, we beseech thee." These things done, if convenient leisure will serve, let a chapter be read in the presence of them all, even such one as the master of the house shall think most expedient and profitable for his family.

After these things, let the master give his servants some little exhortation, to move them to live in the fear of God, to avoid sin, to embrace virtue, and in all points to frame their life according to their vocation and calling, every one in his office, doing their work so as though they did it unto God, which beholdeth all their doings, and will reward every man according to his deeds; and so let them depart every man unto his work in the peace of God.

Prayer before dinner or supper.

When the time requires that the servants shall take their repast, whether it be breakfast, dinner, or supper; before they sit down, let them all reverently stand before the table, and one in the name of them all pray unto God to bless them and those his gifts which they shall there receive of his bounteous liberality, and so mannerly sit down together every man in his place, so behaving themselves all the time of their repast as it become the guests of God, all wanton talk, all scolding words, and all swearing utterly laid aside. Let all their communication either be of godly matters pertaining unto their salvation, or else of such things as belong unto their vocation and calling. Let them not eat and drink unto surfeiting and drunkenness, but unto the satisfaction of nature, which is content with a little; always remembering, that we live not to eat, but we eat to live. For a belly too much burdened is not meet unto labour.

☞ Grace after meat.

Their repast taken, let one of them in the name of all say grace, and give thanks to God for his benefits so liberally bestowed upon them, and desire him to give them grace to walk worthy of his loving-kindness, that they neither in thought, word, or deed commit any thing displeasant to his divine Majesty; but unfeignedly serve him in holiness and righteousness all the days of their life. Afterward saluting one another, let them repair unto their work in the fear of God, doing that diligently that their vocation requireth.

And let this be their exercise at all times, both at breakfast, dinner, and supper. For every householder's house ought to be a school of godliness; forasmuch as every householder ought also to be a bishop in his own house, and so to oversee his family, that nothing reign in it but virtue, godliness, and honesty. After this manner did the holy patriarchs and all godly householders both of the old and new testament rule and order their families in times past; yea, and many other godly persons, as the ecclesiastical histories do manifestly shew.

And after this manner also ought every true and faithful householder to govern and rule his family and household, that God may be honoured in his house, and his holy name magnified of all the inhabitants thereof.

Moreover, the days appointed unto work godly and virtuously passed over, when the Sunday come, and such other days as are consecrate to spiritual exercises, the householder, when convenient time require, shall repair unto the church with all his family attending upon him, and there both he and his whole household earnestly pray unto God, with his most humble thanks for his benefits so bounteously bestowed upon him and his family. They shall also give good advertence to the things that be read in the church, and specially to the chapters of the holy bible. And if there be a sermon, let the householder provide, that both he and his family sit in such convenient place nigh unto the pulpit, that they may well hear the preacher, and the better note what is spoken. Again, if the holy and blessed communion be ministered that day, let both the householder and such as belong unto him, being prepared thereunto, address themselves unto the receiving thereof with all humility and worthiness. And when the householder with his company be returned home, and he is set down at the table, let him call before him all his servants that were with him at church, and require of them an accompts of those things that they have there heard. Such as can well report the sermon, and such other like godly things uttered in the church, let the master commend them; but such as be negligent and forgetful, let him exhort them to be more diligent hereafter: and so with godly and virtuous talk pass over the time, till the hour calleth again to the church, whither he and his ought with all reverence to resort, and to do such things as the worthiness of the place requireth. The evening prayer done, it shall not be unseemly for the householder to license his servants to take some honest pastime for the recreation of their wearied bodies, so that it be done with sobriety and christian modesty, all lightness and wanton toys set aside. The householder, thus training up his household in the exercises of true godliness, shall so obtain the favour of God, that all things shall right well prosper with him.

Secondly, as it is the duty of a good master or householder to provide that godliness be planted in the hearts of his servants; so is it his office likewise to see diligently that no vice take root in them. For commonly, wheresoever God buildeth a church, the devil will build a chapel just by. And wheresoever the goodman of the Matt. xiii. house sow wheat, there will the enemy also sow tares.

Therefore the householder must have a diligent and watching eye, that no vice creep into his house. But above all things, let him take heed that there be no swearing used in his house. For that offendeth God greatly, and provoketh the vengeance of God to fall upon that house where it is used, as the wise man saith: "A man that useth much swearing shall be filled with wickedness; and the plague," Ecclus. xxiii. that is to say, the hot wrath and the fierce vengeance of God, "shall never go from his house." Again he saith: "The words of the swearer bringeth death. God grant that it be not found in the house of Jacob!" And the prophet Zachary saith, that he saw "a flying book," of twenty cubits long and ten cubits broad, in Zech. v. the which were contained the curses and plagues that shall fall upon the house where swearing is used. "I will bring it forth," saith the Lord of hosts, "so that it shall come to the house of the swearer, and consume it with the timber and stones thereof."

Let him also take heed that there be no whoring nor uncleanness of body, no, not so much as a filthy word used in his house; but all cleanness and purity of life, as St Paul saith: "As for fornication and all uncleanness, let it not once be named Eph. v. among you, as it becometh saints, or filthiness, or foolish talking, or jesting, which are not comely; but rather giving of thanks. For this ye know, that no whoremonger, either unclean person, hath any inheritance in the kingdom of Christ and of God." Let no filthy ballads or songs of love be sung in his house, that might stir up the filthy desires of the flesh; but rather songs of the holy scripture, and the psalms of David, set forth in metre in our English tongue, very apt for that purpose. In these things let them exercise themselves, whensoever they intend to sing, that they may rejoice in God, as St Paul saith: "Be ye filled with the Spirit, speaking unto your- Eph. v. selves in psalms and hymns and spiritual songs, singing and making melody to the Lord in your hearts, giving thanks alway for all things unto God the Father in the name of our Lord Jesus Christ."

David's psalms set forth in English metre.

Again, let him provide that there be no quarrelling, scolding, chiding, and fighting used in his house; but rather all love, charity, quietness, amity, and concord. If there chance to fall any variance betwixt the servants, let the master of the house call for them that be at debate, hear the matter quietly, declare unto them how unseemly a thing it is for the servants of one master, dwelling in one house, wearing one livery, feeding upon one table, sleeping together, &c., to fall at variance one with another, which ought to take all one part, draw all by one line, speak all one thing, love together as brethren, &c. And before they depart from their master's presence, let such reconciliation be made between them that they ask one another forgiveness, and desire the good-will one of another, and promise before their master, that they will for ever after continue in hearty friendship one toward another.

Moreover, let him take heed that there be no picking nor stealing used in his house, but all truth; no lying, but all fidelity; no dissimulation, but all simplicity; no craft and subtilty, but a plain and right-up dealing with all men; no wickedness, but godliness; no sin, but virtue; no vice, but integrity of manners; no corruption of life, but purity of conversation; that in all things they may garnish the doctrine of our Lord and Saviour Jesus Christ.

Thirdly, as it is the duty of a master or householder to train their servants in all points of godliness, and to exercise them in all virtue and goodness; so likewise is it his duty to give a good example of virtue and godliness to his servants in life and conversation; lest that he, commanding good things, and working the contrary, destroy more by his wickedness of life than he edify with the godliness of words. Nothing maketh the men-servants so good as the goodness of the master, and nothing maketh the maid-servants so honest as the honesty of the mistress. It is a vain thing for the master to say unto his servant, "Be good ones," when he himself is continually evil. What shall it profit a mistress to exhort her maid unto honesty, when she herself is an harlot? Let a master and a mistress be the same in their houses, that they would wish their household servants to be. For nothing doth so much allure unto godliness as good example-giving. Let masters and mistresses therefore shine in their houses as great lights, full of godliness and virtue, that their servants, seeing their good works, may take an occasion to practise the like, and to glorify our Father which is in heaven. After this sort did the holy patriarchs and all godly persons use themselves in their houses from the beginning. I would wish all householders to have these words of the psalmograph ever before their eyes, and according to the doctrine of the same to rule and govern his house.

The words are these:

Psal. ci. 1. "I will walk in my house with a perfect heart."

2. "I will take no wicked thing in hand."

3. "I hate the sins of unfaithfulness: there shall no such cleave unto me."

4. "A froward heart shall depart from me."

5. "I will not know a wicked person."

6. "Whoso privily slandereth his neighbour, him will I set nought by."

7. "Whoso hath a proud look and an high stomach, I will not suffer him."

8. "Mine eyes look unto such as be faithful in the land, that they may dwell with me."

9. "Whoso leadeth a godly life, he shall be my servant."

10. "There shall no deceitful person dwell in my house: he that telleth lies shall not tarry in my sight."

Father. If all householders with their servants were such as the prince-like prophet David doth here describe, then should godliness and virtue reign in more men's hearts than they do at this present. But let me hear if ought remain of the householder's office.

Son. Fourthly, it is the duty of a godly householder or master not to be rigorous and hasty with their servants, but rather to be gentle and quiet with them; so that, if the servants sometime through negligence or oversight leave any thing undone, or do not things in such order as they ought to do, they quietly and patiently bear with them, exhorting them from henceforth to be more diligent and circumspect in doing their duty, and by no means like a madman fall out with them, curse, and lame them, cast dishes and pots at their heads, beat them, put them in danger of their life, &c. This becometh not christian modesty nor civil sobriety. It becometh every godly master or householder ever to set before his eyes this saying of the wise man:
Ecclus. iv. "Be not as a lion in thine own house, destroying the household folks, and oppressing
Eph. vi. them that are under thee." Hereto agreeth the saying of St Paul: "Ye masters, put away threatenings, knowing that your Master also is in heaven; neither is there
Col. iv. any respect of persons with him." Again: "Masters, do unto your servants that which is just and equal, knowing that ye also have a Master in heaven."

Father. Why, is it not lawful for a master to correct his servants that offend, as well by stripes as by words? *Son*. If words may do good, what need stripes? Who offendeth not sometime? If a servant be so negligent or wilful that he will not amend his fault, although many times heretofore admonished and rebuked for the same, the master may use his discretion in this behalf, and minister such moderate correction to the offender, as shall seem meet to his wisdom; this always considered, that measure be observed in all things, and that correction be ministered with discretion and favour. We be bought all with one price, and we be all inheritors of one glory. Christian men may not handle their servants as the unfaithful Turks do, which entreat their servants as bond-slaves, yea, as beasts, without any respect of manhood.

Fifthly and finally, it pertaineth unto the office of a master or householder to give unto their servants such covenants as were agreed of between them; meat, drink, lodging, apparel, wages, &c., and to put unto them such labours as are tolerable, and that they can well bear; and by no means to charge them with such burdens as they cannot bear, nor with such pains as they are not able to suffer, nor yet to defraud them of their necessary food or rest, whereby they should be the less able to do their work. It is the duty also of a good master not only to provide that his servant shall have all things necessary for him so long as he remaineth with him, and all his covenants at his departure; but also, if he be of ability, to make some provision for him, that he may afterward be the more able to live, as the wise man saith: "Whereas thy servant Ecclus. vii. worketh truly, entreat him not evil, nor the hireling that is faithful unto thee. Love a discreet servant as thine own soul: defraud him not of his liberty, neither leave him a poor man."

Father. God make all masters thankful to their servants, and give them grace to consider the painful labours of their faithful servants! But, my son, as thou hast now opened unto me the office of masters or householders, so likewise declare thou now unto me the duty of servants toward their masters. *Son.* I will gladly do it, mine own dear father.

OF THE DUTY OF SERVANTS TOWARD THEIR MASTERS.

The chief and principal point of the duty of servants consisteth in honouring and obeying their masters. Of honouring masters.

Father. What is it to honour the masters? *Son.* Reverently to think of them; honourably to speak of them; heartily to pray for them; stedfastly to defend their good name; and in all points so to esteem of them as of persons appointed of God to rule over them, by whom God feedeth them, clotheth them, governeth them, and teacheth them. This honour toward their masters, although never so simple and base, may the servants by no means neglect, nor deny to their rulers. For to dishonour the master is none other thing than to dishonour God, who hath straitly commanded thee, that art a servant, to honour thy master, and to have him in reverence.

Father. Where is it commanded? *Son.* God, by the holy apostle St Paul, saith: "Let as many servants as are under the yoke count their masters worthy of all honour, 1 Tim. vi. that the name of God and his doctrine be not evil spoken of."

Father. Owe servants also obedience unto their masters? *Son.* Yea, verily.

Father. What is it to obey the masters? *Son.* Faithfully and with a good heart Of obeying masters. to do that which the master commandeth, and diligently to take heed that nothing be either enterprised or neglected, that may in any point offend the master; but rather to seek how to pleasure him, and to satisfy his commandment.

Father. Where is this obedience commanded? *Son.* St Paul saith: "Ye servants, Eph. vi. obey them that are your bodily masters with fear and trembling, even with the singleness of your heart, as unto Christ; not doing service unto the eye, as they that go about to please men; but as the servants of Christ, doing the will of God from the heart; with good-will serving the Lord, and not men; knowing this, that whatsoever good deed any man doth, the same shall he receive again of God, whether he be bond or free." Again: "Ye servants, be obedient unto them that are your bodily masters in Col. iii. all things; not with eye-service, as men-pleasers; but in singleness of heart, fearing God. And whatsoever ye do, do it heartily, as though ye did it to the Lord, and not unto men; knowing that of the Lord ye shall receive the reward of inheritance; for ye serve the Lord Christ. But he that doth sin shall receive for his sin. Neither is there any respect of persons with God." Once again he saith: "Exhort servants to be obedient Tit. ii. unto their own masters, and to please them in all things; not answering again; neither to be pickers; but that they shew all good faithfulness; that they may do worship to the doctrine of God our Saviour in all things."

Father. But what if the masters be unkind, churlish, and shrewd? must the servants obey them also? *Son.* So teacheth us St Peter, saying: "Servants, obey your masters 1 Pet. ii. with fear; not only if they be good and courteous, but also though they be froward. For this is thank-worthy, if a man for conscience toward God endure grief, and suffer wrong undeserved. For what praise is it, if, when ye be buffeted for your faults, ye take it patiently? But and if, when ye do well, ye suffer wrong, and take it patiently, then is there thanks with God."

Masters commanding contrary to God's word are not to be obeyed.

Father. What if the master command their servants to do that which is contrary to the will of God? shall they obey them also in this behalf? *Son.* Nothing less; for "we must obey God more than men." But of this matter we spake in the declaration of the fifth commandment. Notwithstanding, whatsoever the master commandeth his servant to do, not being repugnant to the word of God, it ought to be done with all diligence and cheerfulness of mind; as we have Jacob for an ensample, which served Laban, his uncle and master, in keeping his flocks of sheep many years, yea, and that
Gen. xxxi.
with great pains, as these his words declare, which he spake to his wives: "I have served your father with all my might." To Laban he also said: "Behold, these twenty years have I been with thee: thy sheep and thy goats have not been barren; and the rams of thy flock have I not eaten. Whatsoever was torn of beasts, I brought it not unto thee, but made it good myself: of my hand didst thou require it, even as it that was stolen by day or night. By day the heat consumed me, and the frost by night, and my sleep departed from mine eyes," &c.

Father. We have few Jacobs at this present day. Such diligence and faithfulness, such labours and pains, as Jacob took, are not now-a-days found in our servants; unto such dissolution of life, stubbornness of heart, and haughtiness of mind are they come.

How servants may become good.

Son. It is the more to be lamented. To become right Jacobs, that is to say, faithful and painful servants, this shall help greatly; if such as serve consider with themselves, that God hath cast them into that kind of life, that God hath made them servants and subject unto other, and that therefore they ought with all diligence and faithfulness, with all labour and pain, to satisfy their masters' commandment; yea, and that not with eye-service, as men-pleasers, but in singleness of heart; forasmuch as they know that, in doing faithful service unto their masters, they serve and please God. They ought also to set this before their eyes, that if they walk truly and faithfully in their vocation, serving their bodily masters according to the will and commandment of God, they shall not escape unrewarded; if not at man's hand, yet at the hand of God, which for his promise sake will leave no good work unrewarded, as St Paul
Eph. vi.
saith: "Whatsoever good deed any man doth, the same shall he receive again of God,
Rom. ii.
whether he be bond or free." "God will reward every man according to his deeds; that is to say, praise, honour, and immortality to them which continue in good-doing and seek immortality. But unto them that are rebels, and do not obey the truth, but follow unrighteousness, shall come indignation and wrath, tribulation and anguish upon the soul of every man that doth evil." How beneficial God is to those servants
Gen. xxxi. xli.
which truly and faithfully, diligently and painfully serve their bodily masters, the histories of Jacob and Joseph shew manifestly. Neither shall faithful and painful servants be rewarded only in this world with the abundance of all temporal things; but also in the
Col. iii.
world to come they shall "receive the reward of" heavenly "inheritance." Again, this they ought also to consider, that as they serve their masters now, so shall they be served of other, when they be householders and masters. If they be true, faithful, trusty, and
☞ diligent servants to their masters, God shall give unto them in time to come true, faithful, trusty, and diligent servants again. But if they be untrue, unfaithful, untrusty, and negligent servants to their masters, even with such shall God pay them home again.
Luke vi.
For this saying of our Saviour Christ shall for ever and ever abide true: "With what
Matt. vii.
measure that ye mete withal, shall other men mete to you again." "Therefore, whatsoever ye would that men should do to you, do ye even so to them also. For this is the law and the prophets." If servants would remember these things, it should encourage them to do their duty, and to live according to their vocation and calling.

Father. Is there any thing behind of the servants' duty? *Son.* The chief point of their duty ye have heard. This only remaineth, that every servant, where many be in house together, do strive and labour to the uttermost of their power to excel other in virtue, godliness, honesty, and in all kind of well-doing, being certainly persuaded, that in thus doing they please God, which will abundantly acquit this their faithfulness toward their masters, both in this world and in the world to come. Let them be faithful and true to their master. Let them pick, steal, or bribe nothing from their master. Let them study by all means possible honestly and truly to enrich their master, and not in any condition to hinder him. Let them use no lying, swearing, nor whoring in their master's house; but rather with Joseph embrace all godliness, honesty, and virtue, and in all points so behave themselves, that their master may rejoice in them, and they in their master, and God in them both. So shall it go well with all parties.

Father. Well said, my son. What followeth now? *Son.* The offices and duties of the chief degrees and estates we have already heard. It now remaineth that we talk somewhat of the inferior degrees, as of widows, of young men, of maids, of old men, of old women, &c.

Father. What sayest thou of widows and of their office?

OF THE OFFICE OF WIDOWS.

Son. St Paul describeth two kinds of widows; the younger, and the elder. The office of the elder or ancient widow is to be occupied about matters of God and about businesses of the congregation, and wholly to give herself to the exercises of the spirit, as to frequent the temple in the time of prayer, to be present at the sermons, to visit the sick, to relieve the needy, to wash the feet of the saints, to be rich in good works, to continue in prayers and supplications both day and night, and to be holy both in body and mind. Such a virtuous and holy widow was that noble matron Judith, which in the higher parts of her house made herself a privy chamber, where she dwelt, being closed in with her maids. She ware a smock of hair, and fasted all the days of her life, except the sabbaths and new moons, and the solemn days that the people of Israel keep. She was a woman of a very good report with every one; for she feared the Lord greatly, and there was nobody that spake any evil word of her. Such a godly widow also was Anna, of whom St Luke writeth, that she "departed not from the temple, but served God with fasting and prayers night and day."

1 Tim. v. The office of the elder widows. Judith viii. Luke ii.

As touching the younger widows, forasmuch as many of them wax wanton against Christ, and follow Satan, breaking their first faith and promise, which they made to God at their baptism (which is to abstain from all uncleanness both of body and mind, and to lead a pure and honest life), and so cast themselves into the danger of everlasting damnation; it is convenient, by the doctrine of St Paul, that they "marry again, bring forth children, guide their house" virtuously, and so live in the holy state of matrimony, that no man[1] may have just occasion to speak evil of them.

The office of the younger widows. 1 Tim. v.

Father. Where writeth St Paul this? *Son.* In his first epistle to Timothy. These are his words: "The younger widows refuse. For when they have begun to wax wanton against Christ, they will marry, having damnation, because they have cast away their first faith. And also they learn to go from house to house idle, yea, not idle only, but also prattlers and busy-bodies, speaking things which are not comely. I will therefore, that the younger woman marry, to bear children, to guide the house, and give none occasion to the adversary to speak evil."

1 Tim v.

Father. The counsel of the holy apostle is good and necessary. For what is more convenient and meet for such widows as are ancient, old, aged, and (as they use to say) past the world, than to apply their minds unto the exercises of spiritual and heavenly things, always meditating death, and their departure from this vale of misery, wishing with St Paul to be loosened out of this mortal and wretched body, and to be with Christ? Again, what is more seemly for a young widow, which is apt to be a wife and to bring forth children, than to marry in the fear of God, and to take unto her an husband, by whom she may have children, and godly to bring them up, and to govern her household virtuously, and to do such other things as appertain unto an honest and godly wife? For how light, vain, trifling, unhonest, unhousewife-like, young widows have been in all ages, and are also at this present day, experience doth sufficiently declare.

Phil. i.

[[1] The folio has *woman*.]

☞ Nothing therefore is better for young widows than to marry again, so that it be done in the Lord. By this means they shall answer to their age, live honestly with their husbands, be free from all suspicion of uncleanness, and pass over their time among their neighbours in good name and fame.

Son. Old widows also in this our age are not free from fault. For many of them, which by the course of nature are not only past child-bearing, but also ready to go to their grave, do so doat and are so mad in these our days, that when they ought to leave the world, they begin to think anew of the world, and when they should only meditate and consider spiritual and heavenly things, they set their mind on fleshly pleasures; insomuch that some of them, being almost fourscore years old, have been known to marry with boys of eighteen years old: another sort, being so plagued with diseases that they were not almost able to stir in their beds, have notwithstanding given themselves to marriage, being far grown in age, yea, and that unto such husbands as, the riches once past, have little esteemed their wives; but, leaving them in all misery whom they found rich and wealthy, they have entangled themselves with strange love, utterly forsaking the company of their old and toothless wives.

Old widows doat in these our days.

* *Father.* Fruits worthy such monstrous marriages; marriages in times past hated even of the very heathen and infidels. It is good for so many as have the gift of continency to keep themselves free from marriage, that they may the more freely serve God; but specially for old women, which by the course of nature are past children-bearing: for their marriages are prodigious marriages. *Son.* You say truth. But I will go forth to recite the office and duty of young men that be unmarried.

Father. Let it be so, my son.

OF THE OFFICE AND DUTY OF YOUNG MEN UNMARRIED.

Son. The office and duty of such young men as be unmarried consisteth chiefly in these points.

First, that they, both with their words, works, and outward gestures, do shew reverence, worship, and honour unto them that be their elders.

Lev. xix. *Father.* Where is that commanded? *Son.* God himself saith: "Thou shalt rise up before the hoar head, and reverence the face of the old man, and dread thy God. I am the Lord."

Secondly, that they do not only outwardly reverence their elders, but also be ruled by them, ask counsel of them, and suffer themselves to be admonished and rebuked by them; being persuaded, that there is more wisdom, knowledge, understanding, learning, and experience in the elders, than in themselves, which are but young and of small practice. And therefore ought young persons to have a great delight and singular pleasure to frequent the company of such as be ancient and of good experience and wisdom, that by this means they may come by knowledge, as the wise man saith: "My son, keep company with the multitude of such elders as have understanding, and consent unto their wisdom with thine heart, that thou mayest hear all godly sermons, and that the worthy sentences escape thee not. And if thou seest a man of discreet understanding, get thee soon unto him; and let thy foot tread upon the steps of his doors." Again he saith: "Think scorn of no man in his old age; for we wax old also." "Despise not the sermons of such elders as have understanding, but acquaint thyself with the wise sentences of them; for of them thou shalt learn wisdom and the doctrine of understanding, and how to serve great men without complaint. Go not from the doctrine of the elders; for they have learned it of their fathers. For of them thou shalt learn understanding, so that thou mayest make answer in the time of need."

Ecclus. vi.

Ecclus. viii.

Thirdly, that they be not proud, nor stand in their own conceit, nor brag or boast themselves of such gifts as God hath endued them with; but rather that they be sober-minded, humble, meek, lovely, gentle, and ready to hear other, and also to give place unto their elders, as St Peter saith: "Ye young folk, submit yourselves unto the elders. Submit yourselves every man one to another. Knit yourselves together

1 Pet. v.

in lowliness of mind. For God resisteth the proud, and giveth grace to the humble." St Paul also saith: "Exhort the younger men that they be sober-minded." Tit. ii.

Fourthly, that they be not idle, no tavern-hunters, no users of unhonest or unlawful pastimes, no pickers of quarrels, no drunkards, no keepers of evil company; but rather well occupied, content with the houses where they dwell, using honest and lawful pastimes, quiet, sober, keeping company with the godly and virtuous, and ever having God before their eyes.

Fifthly and finally, forasmuch as they intend once to marry, if God bless them with life, it is the duty of young men also to keep their bodies unpolluted, undefiled, unspotted, free and utterly estranged from all whoredom and uncleanness, that they may come with pure bodies unto the holy state of honourable wedlock; following in this behalf the godly example of the most godly young man Joseph, Jacob's son, which did rather choose to lose all his promotions and wealthy livings, yea, to be cast into prison, and there to suffer many and great miseries, than he would transgress the commandment of God and abuse his body in any kind of uncleanness, before God called him unto the blessed state of matrimony.

This example let all young men that be unmarried have continually before their eyes, and remember how graciously God dealt with Joseph afterward, how he blessed Gen. xli. him, and made him greatest and of highest authority in all Egypt, the king only excepted. Therefore, when the devil, the world, and the flesh shall move them unto uncleanness, either to deflower maids, or to corrupt men's wives, or to defile widows, or otherwise unhonestly to behave themselves either in thought, word, and deed, let them say with Joseph: "How can I do this wickedness, and sin against God?" Gen. xxxix. Let them eschew idleness, vain talk, and evil company, and give themselves to prayer, and to the reading of the holy scriptures; and they shall easily avoid and escape the flattering and deceitful songs of that pleasant, but poisonful mermaid, the flesh. "Watch and pray," saith our Saviour Christ, "that ye fall not into temptation." "I Matt. xxvi. have hidden up thy words in my heart," saith the psalmograph, "that I might not Psal. cxix. sin against thee."

Father. Thy counsel is good, my son. God give us all grace to follow it! But what sayest thou concerning the duty of maids and young women that be unmarried?

OF THE DUTY OF MAIDS AND YOUNG UNMARRIED WOMEN.

Son. The maids, whether they be in their fathers' houses, or abroad at service, must diligently take heed, that they have continually before their eyes the fear of God, and above all things seek to please him, and to frame their life according unto his holy word. And that they may the better this do, they ought many times to call upon God for his holy Spirit and grace, that he may keep them safe and sound both in mind and body. For without his help and favour nothing can prosper or have good success: without his grace, and without the comfort of his holy Spirit, neither the bodies nor the minds of the maids can continue pure, chaste, continent, and honest, but rather fall into all kind of uncleanness. God therefore is at all times to be called upon with fervent prayers, that he may preserve and keep them in all godliness, honesty, and virtue, as we have Sara, young Tobias' wife, for an example; which, when she was a maid, gave herself busily unto prayer, insomuch that we read, that at a Tob. iii. [Vulgate.] certain time she went up into an high chamber of her father's house, and there continued in prayer unto God by the space of three days and three nights, neither eating nor drinking in the mean time.

Secondly, the duty of honest and godly maids is to be obedient to their masters and mistresses, and diligently to do in the household affairs whatsoever they are commanded, and always to have an eye unto the godly doings of their mistresses, and studiously learn to do the like; that, when the time comes that they also shall be householders, they may know the better how to rule and govern their own house.

Thirdly, it appertaineth unto the office of virtuous maids never to be idle, but alway to work some good thing. For idleness is a great occasion of many evils, as the wise man saith: "Idleness bringeth much evil." So soon as idleness occupieth the mind of any person, vain and evil thoughts brast in straightways, out of the which springeth all mischief, as pride, slothfulness, banqueting, drunkenship, whoredom, adultery, vain communication, bewraying of secrets, cursed speaking, &c. To avoid these pestilences, it shall become honest and virtuous maids to give themselves to honest and virtuous exercises, to spinning, to carding, to weaving, to sewing, to washing, to wringing, to sweeping, to scouring, to brewing, to baking, and to all kind of labours without exception, that become maids of their vocation, of whatsoever degree they be, rich or poor, noble or unnoble, fair or foul. This thing shall help greatly in time to come to get their living, if need require.

King Salomon, in the description of an honest faithful woman, saith on this manner: "She occupieth wool and flax, and laboureth gladly with her own hands. She is like a merchant's ship, that bringeth her victuals from afar. She is up in the night season, to provide meat for their household, and food for her maidens." "She layeth her fingers to the spindle; and her hand taketh hold of the distaff," &c. (Prov. xxxi.)

Thus were divers godly maids brought up in their tender years, which be mentioned in the holy scripture, and they practised the same when they were wives. Anna, old Tobias' wife, learned to weave when she was a maid; and therefore, when her husband was blind and could not work, she went daily to the weaving work: and look, what living she could get with the labour of her hands, she brought it home for the relief of her family. Hanna also, the wife of Helcana, wrought with her own hands, and made cloth, so that every year she brought a coat of the cloth that she had made to Samuel her son, when she came up with her husband to offer unto the Lord. Tabitha also is greatly commended in the holy scripture, for coats and garments that she made both for her own family and also for the poor. Again, Lydia, a godly and faithful woman, occupied selling of purple. Priscilla also, a virtuous woman, made tents with her husband Aquila; of the which occupation St Paul was, and laboured with them for his living. (Tob. ii. 1 Sam. ii. Acts ix. Acts xvi. Acts xviii.)

Not only the divine histories, but also the ecclesiastical and other human writings minister unto us abundance of such and the like examples, which declare sufficiently that in all ages all godly women from time to time have learned and practised some art or occupation, whereby they might get at the least some part of their living, if necessity should require. And what is more brittle than brittle and flattering fortune, or more inconstant and flitting than the transitory possessions of the world? An occupation is a most certain patrimony.

Fourthly, not only idleness is to be eschewed of those maidens which intend to prove godly and virtuous, but also the running about unto vain spectacles, games, pastimes, plays, interludes, &c., where rather vice than virtue, sin than soul-health, wickedness than godliness, is to be learned. Let them remember what chanced to Dina, Jacob's daughter, through going abroad to see vain sights. Was she not deflowered, and lost her virginity? ☞ Virginity once lost, what remaineth safe and praise-worthy in a maid? The highest, best, and greatest dowry that a maid can bring to her husband is honesty; the which if she lack, though she might strive with king Crœsus in riches, yet is she more miserable than Irus. Let the maids therefore above all things seek to maintain their honesty, and eschew all such things as might work the corruption thereof. (Gen. xxxiv.)

Fifthly, forasmuch as nothing doth so greatly hinder the good name and fame of maids, as keeping company with naughty packs, and persons of a dissolute and wanton life (for every man proveth such as he is with whom he is conversant); and contrariwise, nothing doth so much commend, avance, and set forth their good name and fame, as resorting unto such as are well reported, and of an honest disposition; therefore shall it be requisite that all godly maids do refrain themselves from keeping company with light, vain, and wanton persons, whose delight is in fleshly and filthy pastimes, as singing, dancing, leaping, skipping, playing, kissing, whoring, &c. All such must they avoid, if they tender their good name; which once lost, they are no more of estimation, but contemned and despised of all good and godly persons. The wise man saith: "Like as the clearness of the eyes rejoiceth the heart, so doth a good (Prov. xv.)

name feed the bones." Again: "A good name is more worth than great riches, and loving favour is better than silver and gold." Once again he saith: "A good name is more worth than a precious ointment." Jesus, the son of Sirach, also saith: "Labour to get thee a good name; for that shall continue surer by thee than a thousand great treasures of gold. A good life hath a number of days; but a good name endureth for ever."

Prov. xxii. Eccles. vii. Ecclus. xli.

Sixthly, this also must honest maids provide, that they be not full of tongue, and of much babbling, nor use many words, but as few as they may, yea, and those wisely and discreetly, soberly and modestly spoken, ever remembering this common proverb: "A maid should be seen, and not heard." Except the gravity of some matter do require that she should speak, or else an answer is to be made to such things as are demanded of her, let her keep silence. For there is nothing that doth so much commend, avance, set forth, adorn, deck, trim, and garnish a maid, as silence. And this noble virtue may the virgins learn of that most holy, pure, and glorious virgin Mary, which, when she either heard or saw any worthy and notable thing, blabbed it not out straightways to her gossips, as the manner of women is at this present day; but, being silent, she "kept all those sayings" secret, and "pondered them in her heart," saith blessed Luke.

Silence in a maid is greatly commendable. Luke ii.

Seventhly, forasmuch as maids, no less than young men, after they once come to fourteen years of age, are so desirous to be married, and to have the company of other, to this end that they may be fruitful according to the work of God and nature; and notwithstanding such untimely marriages are not to be commended, seeing that through them the bodies of the persons so too soon married are greatly enfeebled, and the fruit that cometh of them prove weaklings, of small stature, and almost of no strength, and so unprofitable for the commonwealth; it shall be convenient for all honest maids, if they tender the health and conservation of their bodies, and the prosperity of the fruit wherewith God shall bless them afterward, and the continuance of the same, that they labour to the uttermost of their power to suppress that lust and desire in them, by moderate eating and drinking, by using a temperate diet, and by avoiding all superfluity, and by keeping their bodies low, either by fasting or by receiving of such meat and drink as shall least of all inflame the body or provoke it unto lust. It shall be necessary in this behalf, that the maids use no fine and exquisite meats, but homely and usual, even such as may slay hunger, and not kindle lust; satisfy nature, and not pamper the body. The drink also that they shall use ought either to be pure water, or else thin ale, or small beer; that it may slake thirst and not kindle lust. For nothing doth so tame the raging lusts of the flesh as slender and moderate diet; and contrariwise, nothing doth so inflame and set on fire carnal concupiscence, as fine fare and hot wines; as St Paul saith: "Be not drunk with wine, wherein is excess." Again: "Let us walk honestly, as it were in the day-light; not in eating and drinking, not in chambering and wantonness; but put ye on the Lord Jesus Christ: and make not provision for the flesh, to fulfil the lusts of it." "For if ye live after the flesh, ye shall die. But if ye through the Spirit do mortify the deeds of the body, ye shall live." Our Saviour Christ saith also: "Take heed to yourselves, lest at any time your hearts be overcome with surfeiting and drunkenness." If the ancient Romans did forbid their women the use of wine and delicate fare, lest by the reason thereof they might fall into any uncleanness and dishonesty, and so bring shame both to themselves, to their husbands, and to their family; how much less tolerable is it for maids to accustom themselves to such meat and drink as shall excite and stir up carnal concupiscence and fleshly lust in them, and provoke them peradventure unto lewdness and dishonesty, and so by this means they shame themselves for ever after, and dishonest their whole stock and kindred! What wicked uncleanness and unclean wickedness hath in times past brast out from delicate fare, both divine and human histories abundantly declare; neither want we experience hereof at this present day. Let the maids therefore above all things use slender, simple, and homely diet. By this means shall they keep their bodies in good temperature, conserve their health, quiet their minds, suppress carnal lusts, avoid unclean desires,

Untimely marriages hurt greatly. The diet of maids. Eph. v. Rom. xiii. Rom. viii. Luke xxi.

eschew evil company, and set themselves in a goodly order against the time that God shall call them unto the holy state of honourable wedlock.

Of maids' apparel. Eighthly, seeing that, as experience teacheth, maids desire nothing so greatly as gallant apparel and sumptuous raiment, and covet that so greatly, that many times not a few of them labour to come by it, not only with the loss of their truth, but also of their honesty; it shall not be unfitting that all honest and godly-disposed maids content themselves with comely and seemly apparel, even such as becometh their degree, state, vocation, and calling, utterly rejecting and casting away all nice vanity and vain niceness of apparel, according to the doctrine of the gospel. "I will," saith St Paul, "that the women (he meaneth also maids and all of the woman-kind) array themselves in comely apparel, with shamefacedness and discreet behaviour; not with broided hair, gold, or pearls, or costly array; but, as becometh women that profess godliness, through good works." Likewise saith St Peter: "Women's apparel shall not be outward, with broided hair, and hanging on of gold, either in putting on of gorgeous apparel; but let the hid man, which is in the heart, be without all corruption, so that the spirit be at rest and quiet; which spirit is before God a thing much set by. For after this manner in the old time did the holy women, which trusted in God, tire themselves," &c.

Esth. xiv. [Apocrypha.] Ester, a most noble and virtuous queen, confesseth in her prayer unto God, that she utterly abhorred and hated that prince-like and gorgeous apparel, even as an unclean cloth, which she was compelled to wear when she must shew herself to the people; and that when she was quiet and alone by herself, she did not wear it. If a princess of so noble estate, of so great dignity, and of so high pre-eminence did not gladly wear costious apparel, but wished rather to go simply apparelled, and so used when she was alone by herself; how unseemly a thing then is it for homely and base maids, for maids far inferior to her degree, so to tire themselves, so to trick and trim their bodies, as though they were mare-ladies[1] or puppets in a game! Vain and nice apparel becometh the daughters of the heathen, and not the children of the Christians, which profess godliness.

☞ The lightness of apparel is a plain demonstration of the lightness of the mind; so that, whatsoever woman delight in gorgeous garments, she setteth forth herself to sale, and declareth evidently her incontinency both of body and mind. Look, how much the body is beautified with the gallantness of apparel, so much is the mind deformed with the corruption of arrogancy and vain-glory. And the more humbly that the body is outwardly clad, the more humble is the mind within, and the better garnished with the riches of godly virtues. The decking and trimming of a Christian is inward, not outward: it consisteth in mind, and not in body; in virtue and godliness, and not
Psal. xlv. in gold and pearl; as it is written: "The king's daughter is all glorious within."

Fulgentius saith: "Let the garment of an holy maid be such as may be a witness of her inward chastity. (Note well.) Let no gallantness be sought to set forth the outward man, lest the fashion of the inward man be deformed. The maid, that desireth the garnishing of the bodily vesture, spoileth her soul of the beauty of virtues; neither hath she true chastity that goeth about with her gallant apparel to allure the eyes of other to behold her; neither keepeth she her promise with Christ, that seeketh rather to please the people than her husband. And thus must it needs follow that she, which soweth lust to the eye of man, do reap wrath in the sight of God[2]." Let not the maid therefore say, when she is so gorgeously apparelled, The garment or the jewel will do no harm. I grant. Notwithstanding, by this means the malefactor
1 Tim. vi. and suggester of an evil will (he meaneth the devil) will enter in. St Paul saith: "We

---

[[1] See the note, page 346.]

[[2] Vestis quoque talis sit sacræ virginis, quæ testis existat intimæ castitatis: Nihil nitoris in habitu exterioris hominis quæratur, ne interioris hominis habitus sordidetur. Virgo quæ ornatum corporeæ vestis affectat, animam suam virtutum splendore despoliat: nec habet castitatem veram, quæ intuentibus parat illecebram: nec fidem servat Christo, quæ populo quærit magis placere quam sponso. Consequenter autem necesse est, ut quæ humano conspectui concupiscentiam seminat, in divino conspectu iracundiam metat.—Fulgent. Op. Venet. 1742. Ad Prob. de Virg. et Humil. Epist. iii. 22. p. 79.]

brought nothing into the world, neither can we carry any thing out of it. Having food and wherewith we may be covered (he saith not, garnished, decked, trimmed, and gallantly set out in our apparel, like May-lords and May-ladies), let us be content." All the godly from the beginning, both men, women, and maids, even so many as professed godliness, have been contented with simple and seemly apparel; being rather desirous to garnish the inward man with the beauty of virtues, than the outward man with the gallantness of fine apparel. Let all maids, therefore, that are studious of virtue, and desire rather to please God and all godly men than the world and the wicked worldlings, utterly sequester their minds from the filthy desires of vain and light apparel, and content themselves with such vestures as become maids that profess godliness, every one according to their vocation and calling; and above all things seek to garnish and trim their inward man with the goodliness and beauty of virtues; that their whole life may be nothing else than a very mirror of virtue and godliness.

Of maids' marriages.

Finally, when the time cometh that they feel themselves apt unto marriage, and are desirous to contract matrimony, to the end that they may avoid all uncleanness, and bring forth fruit according to God's ordinance, as their parents have done before them, they must diligently take heed, that they presume not to take in hand so grave, weighty, and earnest matter, nor entangle themselves with the love of any person, before they have made their parents, tutors, friends, or such as have the governance of them, privy of their intent; yea, and also require their both counsel and consent in the matter, and by no means to stablish or appoint any thing in this behalf without the determination of their rulers. For this is part of the honour that the children owe to their parents and tutors by the commandment of God, even to be bestowed in marriage as it pleaseth the godly, prudent, and honest parents or tutors to appoint; with this persuasion, that they, for their age, wisdom, and experience, yea, and also for the tender love, singular benevolence, and hearty good-will that they bear toward them, both know and will better provide for them than they be able to provide for themselves.

Children ought not to contract matrimony without the consent of their parents.

The histories of the holy bible teach evidently that the godly fathers in times past appointed the marriages of their children, and that the children attempted nothing in this behalf without the counsel, consent, determination, and appointment of their parents. And that authority, which parents at that time had over their children, have fathers and mothers also at this present. And as the children then did not take upon them to marry without the consent of their parents, no more ought they to do in this our age. The children, which presume to marry without the counsel of their parents, do greatly offend God, and are fallen away from the obedience which they owe to their parents or tutors in this behalf by the commandment of God. Let all godly maids take heed therefore that they snarl not themselves with the love of any other, nor marry with any person before they have the good-will of their parents. Let them receive no tokens of any man, nor be too much familiar with any person in the way of marriage; but if any be suitors unto them for to marry with them, and they could well be contented for their godly qualities and honesty of life to take them unto their husbands in the fear of God, let them first of all open the matter to their parents or tutors, being contented to be ruled by them, submitting their own judgment to the judgment or wisdom of their superiors, and praying also unto God that he may rule and govern the hearts of their parents on such sort, that they may appoint that thing which he knoweth to make most unto his glory, and unto the salvation of their souls. If their parents do agree unto their desire, let them thank God for it, and know that God is the author of this their marriage, and that, as he hath brought them together, so will he bless both them and their marriage, and give good success unto them in all their godly and honest attempts, so that they shall lack no good thing. But if their parents do not consent, let the children be content, and think that it is for the best, and that they see more in the matter than they themselves can perceive, being far inferior to them in age, wisdom, discretion, knowledge, reason, experience, &c. And let them think that this also cometh of God, which ruleth the hearts of their parents, and turneth them which way it pleaseth him, and all for their commodity and profit, for their health and wealth; yea, let them think that God is their Father, and they his children; again, that he is their Creator, and they his creatures; and therefore that he will not neglect them, but so provide for them as a father for his children, and never forsake them so long as they live in the obedience of his holy word.

Of the consent of the children in marriage. *Father.* Thou holdest then, that parents ought to place their children in marriage, and that children in this behalf also owe obedience unto their parents. *Son.* Yea, verily.

Father. Ought not the consent of the children also to be considered in this behalf no less than the authority of the parents? *Son.* God forbid else! For we read, that when Rebecca was promised that she should go with Abraham's servant to be married
Gen. xxiv. unto Isaac, they said: "We will call the damosel, and inquire at her mouth. And they called forth Rebecca, and said unto her, Wilt thou go with this man? and she
☞ answered, I will go," &c. Here see we, that though the authority of the parents be great over their children, yet in the matter of marriage the consent of the children may not be neglected. For parents must so use their authority, that they do not abuse it. They abuse it, when it turneth unto the hinderance, incommodity, and destruction of their children. The parents therefore must so place their children in marriage, as may profit, and not hinder them, yea, and that with the good-will and consent of the children, to whom the matter chiefly pertain; that the authority of the parents and the consent of the children may go together, and make perfect an holy and blessed marriage.

Father. This is commendable. But some parents greatly abuse their authority, while they sell their children to other for to be married for worldly gain and lucre, even as the grazier selleth his oxen to the butcher to be slain, having no respect to the person, whether he be godly or ungodly, honest or unhonest, wise or foolish, &c. If money, if riches, if the muck of the world come, let the child go. The person is godly enough, honest enough, wise enough, &c., though he be never so ungodly, without all honesty, and a very fool. *Son.* These be wicked parents, and marriages thus made for the most part have never good success, as experience daily teacheth. It becometh therefore all godly and christian parents to provide for their children such mates and yoke-fellows as fear God, love his word, and will diligently provide for their family; and, such ones provided, it becometh all faithful children to obey the authority of their parents, and to take such unto them to be their companions in matrimony as their fathers and mothers have appointed, and so to live together in the fear of God, loving one another as Christ loveth the congregation.

Father. Thou speakest godly, my son. What followeth now? *Son.* That we speak of the office and duty of old and ancient men.

OF THE OFFICE OF OLD AND ANCIENT MEN.

First, those men which be ancient and grown in age ought above all things so to behave themselves, that both in their words and works they may shine as great lights among the younger folks; so that, when their inferiors in age do behold them, they may truly seem to look upon mirrors of virtue and glasses of godliness, having nothing in them that they may justly accuse and condemn, but many things that they ought of duty both to allow and to follow. And in this behalf, forasmuch as the duty of godliness is a thing most worthy to be embraced and practised of the younger sort, it shall be fitting and convenient that old and ancient men give a good example of the same in their outward behaviour, by resorting unto the sermons and preachings of God's word, by reading the holy scriptures, and by accompanying such as be lovers and avancers of God's true religion; that the younger folk, beholding this their earnest zeal toward the truth of God's most holy word, may be kindled unto the like exercises, and from their youth drink in true godliness, and so at the last wax ancient in
John xvii. the knowledge of God and of his Son Christ Jesu our Lord; which knowledge bringeth everlasting life. For what is more comely for old age, whose departure from

this world by the course of nature is at hand, than the consideration and meditation of heavenly things, and an utter sequestration of their mind from the study of earthly things, wholly reposing themselves in the delight, not of transitory and mortal pleasures, but of constant and immortal joys, contrary to the disposition of the most part of our ancients in this our age, whose property is, the longer they live the more covetous they are, and the less need they have of worldly things the more desirous they are of the same?

Father. Covetousness is a vice appropriated as it may seem to old men, according to this old saying: *Cum omnia vitia senescunt, sola avaritia juvenescit:* "When all vices wax old, covetousness alone waxeth young." For men of this our time, when they be come to that age that they are ready to depart out of the world, then begin they to purchase land; and when they be ready to be carried out of house into grave, then fall they to buying of houses and building of gorgeous mansions. O vain madness and mad vanity! *Son.* It is truth. And therefore, as I said before, nothing is more fitting for old age than the meditation of their hasty departure from this world, and the continual consideration of the heavenly joys. **Covetousness reigneth chiefly in old men.**

Secondly, the duty of old and ancient men is to declare their good affection and tender zeal toward God's holy word in their talk and communication; so that their chief speaking be always of the holy scriptures, and of such things as make unto edifying, that such as be present at their communication may learn godliness, knowledge, and wisdom. They must take heed that no light and wanton words proceed out of their mouth, which may infect the ears of the hearers, and minister unto them occasion of lewdness; but let their talk be such as shall provoke unto virtue, godliness, and honesty. "God," saith the wise man, "hateth an old body that doateth and is unchaste:" not only unchaste in body, but also in words. For as many as profess Christ, specially the ancient, ought to be so far estranged from all uncleanness, that it should not once be named among them. "Let no filthy communication proceed out of your mouth," saith St Paul, "but that which is good to edify withal, as oft as need is, that it may minister grace unto the hearers." Our Saviour Christ saith, that "at the day of judgment" we shall "render an account of every idle word that we have spoken." And who knoweth not that "evil words corrupt good manners?" **Ecclus. xxv.** **Eph. v.** **Eph. iv.** **Matt. xii.** **1 Cor. xv.**

Thirdly, the old men ought to avoid the whole lump of sin, and utterly to cast it away from them, and so purely and innocently to live, that their life may be blameless and an example to the younger folk of all godliness and honesty, replenished with all kind of virtues, and garnished with all manner of good works. For as nothing doth more dishonour old age than wicked and corrupt life, so likewise nothing doth more beautify and garnish old age than innocency of life and godliness of conversation, as the wise man saith: "Age is an honourable thing: nevertheless it standeth not only in the length of time, nor in the multitude of years; but a man's wisdom is the grey hair, and an undefiled life is the old age." St Paul requireth of the elder men that they be "sober, sage, discreet, sound in the faith, in love, in patience." **Wisd. iv.** **Tit. ii.**

He would have them "sober," that is to say, no drunkards, no tavern-hunters, not given to much wine, not sitting all day at the ale-house tippling and quaffing. For old age is much given to belly-cheer, and soon falleth into drunkenness; which vice greatly disgraceth all men, but the older sort specially, whose life ought to be unspotted, and a mirror of virtue to all young folk. For drunkenness maketh of a reasonable man a brute beast, spoiling him of all his senses, so that no part of his body can do his office; and by this means is he made a vile dung-hill of Satan, to be used, yea, rather abused at his pleasure unto all sin and wickedness.

Again, he would have them "sage" and grave; that is to say, such persons as neither in countenance, gestures, words, behaviour, or apparel, should shew any point of lightness, incontinency, impudency, or whatsoever is contrary to the dignity of old age; but rather so behave themselves in all points as becometh their age, state, and vocation, unto the good example of other.

Furthermore, he requireth of them that they be "discreet;" that is to say, temperate, quiet, not rash, not uncircumspect, not furious, not doing any thing of head and without judgment; but using such temperance in all their affairs as shall become men of good consideration and gravity, and such discretion in all their enterprises as shall not be counted unworthy nor unseemly for their age; that the younger folk, beholding this their discretion and temperance, may be occasioned to follow and practise the like in all their attempts, utterly rejecting and casting away all rashness and headlong judgment.

Moreover, the holy apostle commandeth that old men be "sound in the faith;" that is to say, that they truly and constantly believe in God, embrace his holy word, continue in the same unto the end, and by no means suffer themselves to be carried about with every wind of doctrine, as the apostle saith: "Be not carried about with divers and strange learning; for it is good that the heart be stablished with grace:" that the younger sort, seeing this their constancy in God's religion, may be occasioned the rather at their example to do the like, and grow daily more and more in the knowledge of godliness, till at the last they also more wax ancient in Christ.

Heb. xiii.

Item, it is required of ancient men that they be also sound "in love;" he meaneth toward their neighbour. For out of their faith toward God ought true, perfect, and unfeigned love issue toward their christian brother, yea, toward their very enemy, for God's sake; not only inwardly or with lips to love him, but also outwardly and with deeds, ready at all times to succour his necessity, and to do for him whatsoever lieth in their power, as St John saith: "Let us not love in word, nor in tongue; but in work and truth." For he that is sound in love loveth his neighbour as himself, and is the very same to his neighbour that Christ is to him, as St John saith: "Hereby perceive we love, because he (Christ) gave his life for us; and we ought to give our lives for the brethren. But whoso hath this world's good, and seeth his brother have need, and shutteth up his compassion from him, how dwelleth the love of God in him?"

1 John iii. ☞ 1 John iii.

In fine, the blessed apostle St Paul chargeth the old and ancient men that they also be sound "in patience;" that is to say, if God at any time sendeth them adversity either for the trial of their faith, or for the correction of their manners, that they grudge not against God, but patiently and thankfully bear his loving visitation, being fully persuaded that that cross which God hath laid upon them cometh not from an angry but from a loving heart, even such an heart as seeketh not their destruction, but their salvation. "For what son is he whom the father chasteneth not?" "If ye endure chastening," saith the apostle, "God offereth himself unto you as unto sons. But if ye be not under correction, whereof all are partakers, then are ye bastards, and not sons. For whom the Lord loveth, him he chasteneth: yea, he scourgeth every son that he receiveth." Again, if their neighbour at any time offend them either in word or deed, that they seek not straightways to be avenged of them, and to acquit evil for evil, but rather patiently and quietly to bear it at their neighbour's hand, obeying this counsel of St Paul, which saith: "If it be possible (as much as is in you), live peaceably with all men. Dearly beloved, avenge not yourselves, but rather give place unto wrath. For it is written, Vengeance is mine: I will reward, saith the Lord. Therefore be not overcome of evil, but overcome evil with goodness." And as St Peter saith: "Christ suffered for us, leaving us an ensample, that we should follow his steps: which did no sin, neither was there guile found in his mouth: which, when he was reviled, reviled not again; when he suffered, he threatened not, but committed the vengeance to him that judgeth righteously." Patience is a present remedy against all evils, with the which except we be enarmed, we can neither live godly before God nor charitably before our neighbours. Patience is the bond of perfection, without the which all neighbourly love doth decay, and all quietness, both of body and mind, cease and goeth away. "Through your patience," saith our Saviour Christ, "shall ye possess your souls." And the apostle saith: "Ye have need of patience, that, after ye have done the will of God, ye might receive the promise." Again: "Let us run with patience unto the battle that is set before us, looking unto Jesus the captain and finisher of our faith; which for the joy that

Heb. xii. Prov. iii. Rom. xii. Deut. xxxii. 1 Pet. ii. Patience. Luke xxi. Heb. xii.

was set before him abode the cross, and despised the shame, and is set down on the right hand of the throne of God."

Thus have I set forth the office and duty of old and ancient men, even as I have learned out of the word of God.

Father. Godly hast thou declared all things. Let me now hear what is the duty of old and ancient women. *Son.* I will do it gladly.

OF THE OFFICE AND DUTY OF OLD AND ANCIENT WOMEN.

First, such as be godly and ancient matrons are commanded of the holy apostle St Paul, that they wear such raiment as becometh holiness. Old women for the Tit. ii.
most part, if they be rich and of ability, are greatly desirous, when favour and beauty faileth them, to garnish and set forth themselves with sumptuous apparel, that by this means at the least they may commend themselves to the people, and allure their eyes unto the consideration and beholding of them, that in some part they may stick in the eyes of men, and not utterly be rejected for their wrinkled forehead and withered face: whereas they ought not to seek how they may please men by their vain and light apparel, but how they may please God by the decking and trimming of their inward man with the beautiful array of virtues; forasmuch as they know that they, being aged, cannot long continue in this world, but must shortly depart. "For 1 Pet. iii.
after this manner," saith blessed Peter, "in the old time did the holy women, which trusted in God, tire themselves." Therefore the holy apostle, willing to bridle this foolish, vain, and carnal affection of trimming themselves in their old age, commandeth all sage and ancient matrons, that they, laying aside all light and girl-like apparel, array and tire themselves with such raiment as becometh the women that profess godliness.

Father. Not without a cause. For to what end should they go about to please the world, that are ready to go out of the world? If they be old women and married, not light apparel, but sad[1] raiment pleaseth a godly husband. If they be unmarried, what is more comely than to wear such array as becometh their state, profession, and age? An old woman to be decked with gallant apparel is none other thing than to daub over an old rotten tottering wall with new plastering. Therefore those women are most of all to be commended, which, considering their age, apparel themselves according to the same, all vanity and lightness laid aside. *Son.* Truth it is; but I will go forth with the office of old women, as St Paul describeth it.

Secondly, forasmuch as old age is naturally bent to much babbling, and specially such as be of the feminine kind, whom, by the judgment of all wise and learned men, silence doth rather commend than speech; St Paul, willing to restrain this their immoderate manner of talking, commandeth that the ancient women by no means do abuse their tongue, either by prating or by false accusing and evil reporting of other; but that they rather give themselves to silence, or, when they speak, so speak as it becometh women of gravity, wisdom, and knowledge, without reproach or ignominy to other, always remembering that at the day of judgment they must render an account before the high Judge Christ of "every idle word" that they have Matt. xii.
spoken.

Thirdly, forasmuch as nothing doth so greatly provoke old women unto babbling, as too much drinking (for when the wine is in, the wit is out), and old women naturally love well tippling; the holy apostle commandeth that the ancient matrons shall not give themselves to much wine, but rather embrace sobriety and temperancy, being content with that that sufficeth, and not oppresseth nature. For as sobriety is the nurse of many noble virtues, so likewise drunkenness is the mother and nurse of many lewd vices. And where drunkenness taketh place, neither body nor mind doth his office. The mind is void of memory, and altogether without understanding. The body is so intoxicate and out of all order, that neither eye, tongue, hand, nor

[1 Sad: grave.]

foot can do their office. And albeit that drunkenness is vile and discommendable in all creatures, yet in old women, which ought to be mistresses of sobriety and mirrors of all virtue, it is not only vile and discommendable, but also horrible and detestable. For an old woman overcome with drunkenness is made a sink of all evils. There is no sin which easily floweth not into her. There is no virtue whereof she maketh not shipwreck. In consideration whereof, the blessed apostle St Paul chargeth the old women soberly and temperately to behave themselves in their diet, that they may give good ensample to the younger women, and be the more apt to do such things as belong unto their vocation and calling; lest that they, doing the contrary, forget christian modesty and gravity, and fall unto such lewdness and lightness as is unseemly for their estate.

Fourthly and finally, forasmuch as it is not sufficient for true Christians not to do evil, except they also do good, as the psalmograph saith, "Depart from evil and do good;" therefore the holy apostle, after that he hath dissuaded the old women from vanity of apparel, from much babbling, and from drunkenness, declareth what good they ought to do, lest that they, being trees without fruit, "be hewn down and cast into the fire." And this good work that he requireth of them is that they "teach honest things."

Psal. xxxiv.

Matt. iii.

1 Tim. ii.

Father. But St Paul in another place saith: "I suffer not a woman to teach, neither to usurp authority over the man, but to be in silence." *Son*. The same St Paul also, in another place, expounding what is meant by those words which you now recited, saith: "Let your women keep silence in the congregations. For it is not permitted unto them to speak, but to be under obedience, as saith the law. If they will learn any thing, let them ask their husbands at home: for it is a shame for women to speak in the congregation." Of these words of St Paul we learn that it is not lawful for women to teach in the congregation openly, which only appertain unto men, yea, and unto such men alone as are appointed by public authority unto the ministry: notwithstanding, women to preach and teach in their own houses, it is not only not forbidden, but also most straitly commanded. For who knoweth not that every man and every woman is a bishop in their own house, and ought to teach their family, and to bring them up in the doctrine and nurture of the Lord our God? It is therefore lawful also for old and ancient matrons to teach.

1 Cor. xiv.

Gen. iii.

Father. Whom should they teach? *Son*. "Young women," saith St Paul.

Father. What should they teach them? *Son*. "To be sober-minded, to love their husbands, to love their children, to be discreet, chaste, housewifely, good, obedient to their husbands; that the word of God be not evil spoken of."

Father. I looked that thou shouldest have said unto me, that the ancient matrons should teach the young women trimly to dance, minionly to play upon the lute or virginals, cunningly to work with the needle, finely to apparel themselves, handsomely to play the serving maids, pleasantly to entertain strangers, younkers, and gentlemen, &c. *Son*. These be things of vanity, rather provoking unto lewdness than unto virtue, heretofore abhorred and hated of all modest and sober women. The works and qualities which St Paul here setteth forth, that the ancient matrons should teach the young women, are necessary works and godly qualities. Can any thing be more necessary or godly in a christian commonweal, than to bring up maids and young women virtuously, and to teach them "to be sober-minded, to love their husbands, to love their children, to be discreet, chaste, housewifely, good, obedient to their husbands?" &c.

Father. If all our maids and young women were thus brought up, we should not have so many idle, unhonest, and lewd women, as we have at this present day. *Son*. To bring this thing to pass, it is expedient that by public authority schools for women-children be erected and set up in every christian commonweal, and honest, sage, wise, discreet, sober, grave, and learned matrons made rulers and mistresses of the same, and that honest and liberal stipends be appointed for the said school-mistresses, which shall travail in the bringing up of young maids, that by this means they may be occasioned the more gladly and willingly to take pains. And to this end without doubt at the beginning were the monasteries of solitary women, whom we heretofore called nuns, built and set up, and endowed with possessions of our godly ancestors,

Schools for women-children ought to be set up.

although in process of time they were greatly abused; so that they were made of christian and free schools prisons of antichrist, and, as St John saith, "habitations of devils, and holds of all foul spirits, cages of all unclean and hateful birds." Rev. xviii.

The young maids were not enforced to wear this or that apparel; to abstain from this or that kind of meats; to sing this or that service; to say so many prayers; to shave their heads; to vow chastity; and for ever to abide in their cloister unto their dying day. But, contrariwise, they might wear what apparel they would, so that it were honest and seemly, and such as becometh maidens that profess godliness. They might freely eat all kinds of meats according to the rule of the gospel, avoiding all excess and superfluity, yea, and that at all times. Their prayers were free and without compulsion, every one praying when the Holy Ghost moved their hearts to pray; yea, and that such prayers as present necessity required, and that also not in a strange tongue, but in such language as they did right well understand. To shave their heads, and to keep such-like superstitious observances as our nuns did in times past, and yet do in the kingdom of the pope, they were not compelled. For all that they were commanded to do of their school-mistresses and governesses was nothing else than the doctrine of the gospel, and matters appertaining unto honest and civil manners; whom they most willingly obeyed. Moreover, it was lawful for them to go out of the cloister when they would, or when they were required of their friends; and also to marry when and with whom they would, so that it were in the Lord. And would God there were some consideration of this matter had among the rulers of the christian commonweal, that the young maids might be godly brought up, and learn from their cradles "to be sober-minded, to love their husbands, to love their children, to be discreet, chaste, housewifely, good, and obedient to their husbands," according to the doctrine of St Paul!

Father. It is a matter most worthy to be considered. For if it be thought convenient, as it is most convenient, that schools should be erected and set up for the right education and bringing up of the youth of the male kind, why should it not also be thought convenient that schools be built for the godly institution and virtuous bringing up of the youth of the female kind? Is not the woman the creature of God so well as the man? and as dear unto God as the man? Is not the woman a necessary member of the commonweal? have not we all our beginning of her? Are not we born, nursed, and brought up of a woman? Do not the children for the most part prove even such as the mothers are of whom they come? Can the mothers bring up their children virtuously, when they themselves be void of all virtue? Can the nurses instil any goodness into the tender breasts of their nurse-children, when they themselves have learned none? Can that woman govern her house godly which knoweth not one point of godliness? Who seeth not now then, how necessary the virtuous education and bringing up of the woman-kind is? Which thing cannot be conveniently brought to pass, except schools for that purpose be appointed, and certain godly matrons ordained governesses of the same, to bring up the maids and young women in the doctrine and nurture of the Lord. And verily, in my judgment, they do no less deserve well of the christian commonweal, that found and stablish schools with honest stipends for the education and bringing up of the women-children in godliness and virtue, than they which erect and set up schools for the institution of the men-children in good letters and godly manners. Note.

Son. It is truly said. But if it shall please you, I will go forth to recite the offices and duties of the other degrees. And forasmuch as we have now last of all talked of schools, I will first of all rehearse the duty and office of school-masters, that they also may learn how to behave themselves in their vocation and calling. *Father.* Let it so be.

OF THE OFFICE AND DUTY OF SCHOOL-MASTERS.

Son. I have heard our preacher and our catechist also many times say, that that commonweal, where a good magistrate, a faithful preacher, and a diligent school-master is, cannot decay and perish, but rather greatly prosper and flourish. For through the magistrate public peace is maintained, virtue is avanced, vice is depressed. Through the preacher true religion is known, the word of God, which is the food of our souls, is taught, and the holy mysteries of Christ's church are ministered, unto the great consolation and joy of all the faithful. Through the school-master the youth of the christian commonweal is brought up in the knowledge of God and of his holy word, and also in the science of good letters and virtuous manners; and so trained up in them from their very cradles, that as they grow in age, so likewise they increase in godliness, virtue, learning, knowledge, good manners, and innocency of life; and afterward become the faithful servants of God, and profitable members of the commonweal, yea, and good citizens of the country where they inhabit. Therefore those rulers and magistrates, in whose power it is to choose and appoint school-masters, ought above all things to take heed that they elect and ordain such school-masters, such teachers and instructors of the christian youth, as unfeignedly and from the very bottom of the heart fear God, love his word, embrace his religion, tender the glory of God, wish the increase of true godliness in all persons, are learned, are virtuous in their life and conversation, desire well to the christian public weal, and above all things seek how best to profit, further, avance, promote, and set forward the youth committed to their charge in all godliness, learning, knowledge, and virtue.

Magistrate. Preacher. School-master. What men school-masters ought to be.

Father. God grant us many such school-masters! But now declare unto me, according to thy promise, the office and duty of a school-master.

Son. First, forasmuch as the most noble treasures and most precious jewels of the christian commonweal are committed to a school-master to be kept and preserved in safety, yea, to be kept and preserved in such sort, that he may render them home again much more noble, precious, and glorious, than he received them (I mean the children of the Christians, in whom our Saviour Christ so greatly delighted, that he commanded them to be brought unto him; yea, "he took them up in his arms, lovingly embraced them, and blessed them," pronouncing that the kingdom of heaven pertaineth unto them; whom also St Paul calleth clean, pure, and holy); and seeing that nothing doth so adorn, deck, garnish, trim, set forth, and make beautiful and glorious in the sight of God, of his holy angels, and of all good men, any person, as the knowledge and practice of true godliness; it is the office and duty of a good and godly school-master, first of all, and above all things, to instil into the minds of the young christian children true persuasions of God, and of his holy religion, according to this commandment of Christ: "First of all seek the kingdom of God, and the righteousness thereof;" that even from their tender infancy, and (as the proverb is) from the very cradles, they may drink in that new sweet wine of Christ's gospel, while they yet are new and sweet bottles, not corrupt with the filthy savours of old Adam, nor made drunken with the poisonful wine of the whore of Babylon, that stinking strumpet and blasphemous bawd, yea, that murdering mother of whoredom and all abominations of the earth, which is guilty of "the blood of the prophets, and of the saints, and of all that are slain upon the earth." And that the school-master may do this thing the more aptly, and with the greater fruit, it shall be convenient that he read unto his scholars some godly and learned catechism, containing the principles or chief points of christian religion, and that he exercise them in the same daily, diligently searching whether they truly understand the things which they read. If they understand them not, so is it the duty of a good school-master to declare it unto them, and to shew them the true understanding of all things, lest they pronounce after the manner of a parrot, without any understanding, and profit nothing by their ☞ studies. For what doth hasty pronouncing profit, where understanding is absent?

Matt. xix. Mark x. Matt. vi. Matt. ix. Rev. xvii. Rev. xviii. Christian children ought to be brought up in christian doctrine.

After that the school-master hath diligently exercised his scholars in the doctrine of the catechism, so that now they understand the principles of christian religion, it shall greatly profit unto the increase of godly knowledge, if he once in the day read unto them a lesson out of the new testament of our Saviour Jesu Christ.

And albeit the whole book, being the word of life and the food of our souls, be most worthy to be learned so perfectly that it may readily be recited by heart; yet, forasmuch as tender wits are not to be accumbered with many things, lest they be there dulled where they ought to be quickened, it shall be good that the school-master do acquaint his scholars principally with these parcels of the new testament; that is to say, with the gospel of St Matthew and of St John, and with those epistles which St Paul wrote to the Romans and to the Galatians. For whoso understandeth these parcels well, he shall easily understand the residue of the new testament, yea, of the whole bible. For in them is contained whatsoever is taught in the whole scripture necessary for our salvation. In those writings therefore of St Matthew, John, and Paul, let the school-master exercise his scholars both daily and diligently.

And in these their lessons, as occasion shall serve, let them sometime handle and set forth unto them some common-place of the holy scripture, as of God, of God's word, of the law, of the gospel, of faith, of charity, of hope, of good works, of our justification by Christ, of baptism, of the Lord's supper, of remission of sins, of the last judgment, of the resurrection, of the everlasting joys of the faithful, of the endless pains of the unfaithful, &c. Likewise let them sometime entreat of some virtue, or of some vice. And in the treatise of virtue, let them declare how acceptable it is to God, and how God in all ages hath blessed them that have practised that virtue in their life and conversation, whether it be humility, modesty, sobriety, concord, peace, patience, or any other virtue. Let them allege certain histories concerning that matter out of the holy scriptures, that the scholars by this means may the better be acquainted with the word of God, and be the sooner brought unto the love and practice of the same virtue. When they shall entreat of any kind of sin, let them paint and set forth the abomination of that sin, how horrible and grievous it is in the sight of God, how pestiferous, noisome, and hurtful it is to man, how grievously it hath been plagued and punished in every age, and how the practisers of that sin have always come unto a most miserable end in this world, as they may speak nothing of the intolerable pains which they now suffer, and worlds without end shall suffer, "in that lake that brenneth with fire and brimstone."

And here also let them call to remembrance some histories of the holy scripture, which manifestly declare the great anger of God against all such as use that sin, or any other kind of wickedness, as the psalmograph saith: "Thou art the God that Psal. v.
hath no pleasure in wickedness; neither shall any evil dwell with thee. Such as be foolish shall not stand in thy sight: thou hatest all them that work vanity," &c. These things shall marvellously kindle and stir up the minds of the scholars, both unto the love of virtue, and also unto the hate of vice; and shall so plant godliness in their young and tender breasts, that as they grow in age, so likewise shall they increase in all godliness and virtue, and never depart from it so long as they live; so greatly doth it profit to be acquainted with good things from the tender years: for whatsoever is then drunken in abideth stedfastly, and falleth not lightly away.

Moreover, forasmuch as the education and bringing up of a child doth either make or mar him, whether it be in religion, doctrine, or manners; it shall be necessary, that a good and godly school-master enarm the breasts of his scholars against all heresies and wicked opinions with the sound and wholesome doctrine of the holy scripture; yea, and that so much the more, because this our age is most miserably vexed with divers and sundry damnable sects, as papists, anabaptists, Arians, Davidians, Adamites, libertines, epicures[1], &c., which every one of them go about to defend their vain opinions, false errors, and wicked heresies with tooth and nail, and shame not also many times to allege the scriptures for the confirmation and maintenance of their devilish doctrine, as the devil played with Christ, that they may the easlier deceive Matt. iv.
the minds and blind the eyes of the simple and unlearned.

But forasmuch as the sect of the papists hath heretofore many years been accepted and taken, and yet is of some either ignorant or obstinate papists, "whose minds 2 Cor. iv.

[[1] Several of these sects have been before mentioned. The Davidians emanated from the anabaptists, and had their name from David George, a native of Delft. The Adamites were a Bohemian sect, and were so called as they professed to imitate the state in which the first man was created. See Mosheim, Eccles. Hist. Cent. xv. Part II. chap. v. 2. and Cent. xvi. Sect. III. Part II. chaps. ii. 38, 39, iii. 24.]

the god of this world hath blinded, that the light of the gospel of the glory of Christ (which is the image of God) should not shine unto them," for the only true religion of God; being enforced thereunto either by education, or by long custom, or by crafty persuasions of the subtile adversaries, or by the names of our mother holy church, ancient fathers, general councils, constitutions provincial, &c., or by the glistering visor of hypocrisy and feigned holiness, or by ignorance, or by malice, or by hope of gain and wealth of living, &c.; when notwithstanding no sect is more pernicious and hurtful, no faction more pestiferous and damnable, nor more contrary to the glory of God and to the salvation of men, as it is evident to them that are taught of God, and have tasted of the sweet waters that flow out of the heavenly fountains of our Saviour Christ Jesu; it shall be very needful and expedient, that the godly school-master fortify and make strong the minds of their disciples, against this wicked sect of the papists and all their poisonful darts, with the spiritual armours of God's word, which, as the apostle saith, are "mighty in God to cast down strong holds, and to overthrow counsels, and every high thing that exalteth itself against the knowledge of God, and to bring into captivity all imagination to the obedience of Christ, and to take vengeance on all disobedience;" and prepare against every error and heresy of the papists a remedy out of the holy scriptures; as for an ensample:

The sect of the papists is most wicked and damnable.

2 Cor. x.

God alone saveth.

The papists teach that we are not saved by Christ alone, but also by the intercession of saints, by the merits of other, by the prayers, fastings, and watchings of the religious persons, as monks, friars, canons, nuns, priests, hermits, &c., by the works of penance, by our own merits and deservings, by the pope's pardons, by masses of *Scala Cœli*, &c. Against this damnable heresy set these sentences of the holy scripture. Our Saviour Christ saith by the prophet: "I am he, yea, I am he indeed, which put away thy sins, yea, and that for mine own sake, and will remember them no more. Tell me if thou hast any thing wherewith thou mayest be justified. Come, let us reason together." Again: "O Israel, forget me not. As for thine offences, I have driven them away like the clouds, and thy sins as the mist." Once again: "I am the Lord, and there is no saviour but I alone." Item: "Thy destruction, O Israel, cometh of thyself; but thy salvation cometh only of me." The angel said to Joseph of Christ: "Thou shalt call his name Jesus (that is to say, a Saviour): for he it is that shall save his people from their sins." St Peter saith: "There is salvation in none other (he speaketh of Christ). Neither is there any name under heaven given unto men wherein we must be saved," but only the name of Christ Jesu. Again: "To him (Christ) give all the prophets witness, that through his name whosoever believeth in him shall receive remission of sins." St Paul saith: "If righteousness come by the law, then died Christ in vain." Also in another place: "Christ Jesus came into the world to save sinners."

Isai. xliii. Isai. xliv. Isai. xliii. Hos. xiii. Matt. i. Acts iv. Acts x. Gal. ii. 1 Tim. i.

The papists teach that Christ alone is not our mediator, advocate, and intercessor; but if we will have our prayers heard, and our petitions granted of God, we must also desire the help of Mary the virgin, of Paul, Peter, James, Christopher, Katherine, Margaret[1], &c. and make them our mediators, advocates, and intercessors unto God, that they may pray for us. Against this wicked error of the papists set these sentences of the holy scripture. Our Saviour Christ saith: "I am the way, and the truth, and the life. No man cometh unto the Father, but by me." "And whatsoever ye shall ask in my name, that will I do, that the Father may be glorified by the Son. If ye ask any thing in my name, I will do it." "If ye abide in me, and my words abide in you, whatsoever ye will, ask, and ye shall have it." "Ye have not chosen me, but I have chosen you, and have ordained you, that ye should go and bring forth fruit, and that your fruit may abide; that, whatsoever ye shall ask the Father in my name, he may give it you." "Verily, verily I say unto you, Whatsoever ye shall ask the Father in my name, he will give it you. Hitherto ye have asked nothing in my name. Ask, and ye shall receive, that your joy may be perfect." St Paul saith: "There is one God, and one Mediator between God and man, even the man Christ Jesus, which gave himself a ransom for all men." Again: "Christ is on

Christ alone is our mediator and advocate. John xiv. John xv. John xvi. 1 Tim. ii. Rom. viii.

[[1] See Vol. I. page 139, note 4.]

the right hand of God, and maketh intercession for us." Also in another place he saith: "Christ is able ever to save them to the uttermost that come unto God by him, seeing he ever liveth to make intercession for us." St John also saith: "If any man sin, we have an Advocate with the Father, Jesus Christ the righteous. He it is that obtaineth grace for our sins; not for our sins only, but also for the sins of the whole world."

Heb. vii.
1 John ii.

The blood of Christ is the alone purgatory for our souls.

The papists teach that there is a place of punishment after this life, called "purgatory," in the which christian men's souls are most miserably tormented with the most grievous pains of fire, and shall not be delivered from those intolerable torments, till they have either satisfied themselves by suffering there worthy and condign punishments for their offences, or else be redeemed from thence by the sacrifice of the popish mass, by the prayers and merits of the monks, or by doing the works of almose; where the holy scripture teacheth us none other purgatory for the soul, but only the precious blood of our Lord and Saviour Christ Jesu. Therefore against this their devilish dream of purgatory, bring forth these armours[2] of God's word. St John saith: "The blood of Jesus Christ maketh us clean from all sin." Again: "Christ washed us from our sins in his own blood, and made us kings and priests unto God his Father." St Paul saith: "Jesus Christ gave himself for us, to redeem us from all unrighteousness, and to purge us a peculiar people unto himself, fervently given unto good works." Again: "The blood of Christ, which through the everlasting Spirit offered himself unspotted to God, hath purged our conscience from dead works to serve the living God." Once again: "We have liberty to enter into the holy place (that is to say, heaven) by the blood of Christ." St Peter also saith: "Ye were not redeemed with corruptible things, as silver and gold, from your vain conversation; but with the precious blood of Christ, as of a lamb undefiled and without spot." Again: "Christ himself bare our sins in his body on the tree, that we, being delivered from sin, should live unto righteousness; by whose stripes ye were healed." The prophet Esay also saith: "He (Christ) only hath taken on him our infirmity, and borne our pains." "He was wounded for our offences, and smitten for our wickedness. For the chastisement of our peace was laid upon him; and with his stripes are we healed. As for us, we have all gone astray like sheep: every one hath turned his own way. But the Lord hath heaped together upon him the iniquity of us all." The prophet Zachary also saith: "Thou through the blood of thy covenant shalt let thy prisoners out of the pit wherein is no water."

1 John i.
Rev. i.
Tit. ii.
Heb. ix.
Heb. x.
1 Pet. i.
1 Pet. ii.
Isai. liii.
Zech. ix.

Thus[3] shall a godly and diligent school-master gather such flowers out of the holy bible for his scholars, from time to time, as occasion shall serve, with the sweet and strong savour whereof they may repel and put away the pestiferous and mortal odours of the errors and heresies, not only of the papists, but also of all other sectaries whom the devil hath already raised up, or hereafter shall raise up unto the great disturbance of Christ's church; that with whatsoever error or heresy any sectary shall assail them, they, thus defenced with the armours of the Holy Ghost, may not be seduced, but continue constant and stedfast in the wholesome doctrine of Christ, that master and teacher of truth, unto the end, and so be made his true disciples, as Christ himself saith: "If ye continue in my word, then are ye my worthy disciples; and ye shall know the truth, and the truth shall make you free."

John viii.

Let the school-master therefore be diligent to gather together the wicked opinions of all sectaries, and the holy scriptures that do impugn and condemn them, and deliver them to the scholars to commend to memory; that they, being thus enarmed against the subtile assaults of Satan and of his ministers, which many times change themselves into angels of light, that through the glistering visor of feigned holiness and "through sweet and flattering words they may deceive the hearts of the simple," may stand strong and stedfast against all the infernal army, and like valiant soldiers mightily conquer, vanquish, and overcome all our enemies, unto the glory and praise of our grand Captain Jesus Christ, King of kings and Lord of lords.

Rom. xvi.

Father. If the youth of the Christians were thus brought up from their tender

---

[2 The folio has *armourers.*] [3 Folio, *This.*]

years in the knowledge of God's most holy and blessed word, and had their breasts thus furnished with the armours of the holy scriptures against the damnable opinions of the papists, and of such other wicked sectaries as the devil hath raised up in this our time, the christian commonweal should soon have another face both in doctrine and manners. For the alone occasion of all the evils wherewith we are troubled most miserably now-a-days, whether we respect learning or life, cometh only of the naughty ☞ and wicked education of the youth. If the youth were godly and virtuously brought up, and in the fear of God trained from their young years, and were taught diligently the word of God from time to time, not only all contention of doctrine, but also all corruption of life, should soon fall away, and all godliness and virtue succeed in the places thereof.

Son. That is most true. Therefore, as I said before, the principal point of a good school-master is even from the very cradles to sow the seeds of godliness and virtue in the tender breasts of the young children, that, as they grow in age, so they may increase in all godliness and virtue, and never depart from them so long as they live, Prov. xxii. according to the saying of the wise man: "It is a common saying, that a child, when he is old, shall not go away from such things as he learned in his youth." For to teach them nothing but the doctrine of heathen and profane writers is not to edify, but to destroy, not to correct, but to corrupt, the youth of the Christians. And such school-masters are more meet to teach and bring up the children of the Turks and of such other miscreants, than the children of them that profess Christ. This commandment Matt. vi. of Christ ought the school-masters continually to have before their eyes: "First of all seek the kingdom of God and the righteousness thereof."

Father. After that the school-master have diligently planted the religion of Christ in the tender breasts of the children, by teaching them the word of God, what is then his duty to do? *Son.* To teach them good letters, I mean poets, orators, historiographers, philosophers, &c.; not that they should be mates with God's word, but Note. rather handmaids unto it, and serve to set forth the honour and glory thereof. For unto this end ought all liberal sciences to be studied and learned, even that they might not depress, but avance the true religion of God. For eloquence without godliness is as a ring in a swine's snout; yea, all arts and sciences, not coupled with the love of religion, are rather instruments of wickedness than of godliness; and, as Tully saith, "To give to a lewd man eloquence without wisdom is none other thing than to give unto him armours to destroy the commonweal."

But, in reading these kinds of authors to his disciples, the school-master must diligently take heed that he read those only to his scholars that be most profitable, and contain in them no matter that may either hinder the religion of God or the innocency of manners. Some writers in many places of their works are wanton and unhonest, as Martialis, Catullus, Tibullus, Propertius, Cornelius Gallus, and such-like; some wicked and ungodly, as Lucianus, &c. From the reading of these and such-like filthy writers, is convenient that the youth do abstain; lest by the reading of them they make shipwreck both of their faith and manners, and in their tender years drink in such corruption as shall be noisome unto them all their life after. For, as 1 Cor. xv. he saith: "Evil words corrupt good manners."

The very heathen were so ware and circumspect in the virtuous and honest bringing up of their youth, that they by no means would suffer the breasts of their children to be infected with the reading of unclean and wanton writers, although Valer. Max. Lib. vi. cap. 3. never so wise, learned, and eloquent. Read we not that the Lacedæmonians commanded that the books of the poet Archilochus should be carried out of their city, because they entreated of vain, foolish, light, wanton, and trifling matters; and that they by no means would suffer their children to read them, lest by the reading of them they should get more hurt to their manners than profit to their wits? They esteemed eloquence nothing in comparison of virtue and honesty. Eloquence is to be embraced, but not with the loss of virtue. All things ought to give place to virtue and to innocency of life. Plato, that most divine and noble philosopher, also expelled all poets out of his commonweal, as persons occupied about vain, false, lying, and wanton matters, unworthy to be read of such as tender the avancement of virtue.

Was not the poet Ovidius banished of Augustus Cæsar for the books which he made *De Arte Amandi* (he might more justly have termed them *De Arte Meretricandi*, because that through the reading of them he corrupted the minds of the youth); yea, and so banished, that he could never after obtain favour to return into his country, notwithstanding the making of his books to the contrary, *De Remedio Amoris;* but after his long and miserable banishment and life among the barbarous and rude Getians, most miserably perished and died in that most savage and wild country? A punishment worthy of such fact. If the wise heathen thought it a thing unfitting to have their youth corrupted with the reading of vain and wanton books, and therefore banished both them and their authors out of their cities; how much more ought the Christians to be ware and circumspect, that nothing be read to their youth that may infect them with any lewdness, or work corruption either to their faith or to their manners!

It was well said of our countryman, master Lilly, sometime school-master of Paul's in London[1]: *Puerum nil nisi pura decent.* It were not out of the way for the school-master to have these verses of the poet always before his eyes, to put him in remembrance that a child ought neither to hear nor to see any thing which is not good, godly, honest, and commendable: Master William Lilly.

> Nil dictu fœdum visuque hæc limina tangat
> Intra quæ puer est: procul hinc, procul inde puellæ
> Lenonum, et cantus pernoctantis parasiti.
> Maxima debetur puero reverentia, &c.

Juvenalis Satira xiv.

This also is to be considered, that the school-master in all his lessons and readings do seek an occasion to speak of virtue and godliness, always inculking and beating into the heads of his scholars, that which may provoke them unto virtue and fray them away from vice, that from their tender years godliness may grow up with them.

Father. To interlace godliness in the lessons of profane writers maketh greatly unto the avancement of virtue; and heathen authors so read profit very much. But what remaineth of the office of a school-master? *Son.* After that the school-master have sown in the tender breasts of his scholars the seeds of godliness and doctrine, it shall be necessary that he also plant in them good manners, and bring them up in humanity and civility of life; that they may know how to behave themselves in all places and toward all persons, lest the wildness and rusticity of manners destroy that in them which virtue and learning have built and set up, always having before his eyes these our common proverbs: "A child were better unborn than untaught." Again: "Manners make a man." Let the school-master instruct them how they shall behave themselves in the temples, abroad in the streets, at home in the houses, in their plays and pastimes, at the table in dinner or supper, toward their parents, magistrates, superiors, elders, citizens, school-fellows, and generally toward all men and in all things; that their behaviour may answer in all points to their knowledge and learning, and that their life may be blameless before men, so that they may prosper in wisdom and age, and in favour with God and man. Good manners.

Father. This is a good point of a diligent school-master. For I see not what the excellency of learning profiteth, if civility of manners lacketh. Verily, learning without manners is as a gold ring in a swine's snout. But is there any other thing behind, that belongeth unto the duty of a school-master? *Son.* Yea, forsooth. It is not sufficient that a school-master do his endeavour to make his scholars virtuous and well-mannered, except he himself also be virtuous and well-mannered. For examples in the eyes of children move more than words. If the master teacheth virtue and good manners, and he himself be vicious and lewd, what profiteth it? What he edifieth in words he destroyeth in manners. And as a certain man saith: "It is an uncomely thing for a teacher to reprove that vice in another, whereof Cato.

[[1] Born about 1468, died 1523. He was the first master of the school, on its being founded by dean Colet.]

he himself is guilty[1]." It becometh a good school-master to do that he commandeth, and not to think that he hath done his duty sufficiently, when he hath taught well, although his life be never so lewd and wicked. Such school-masters are like to the scribes and Pharisees, of whom the Lord speaketh in the gospel on this manner: Matt. xxiii. "The scribes and the Pharisees sit in Moyses' seat. All therefore whatsoever they bid you observe, that observe and do; but do not ye after their works. For they Rom. ii. say, and do not." And as St Paul saith: "Thou that teachest another teachest not thyself."

A godly and an honest school-master therefore must not only provide that he teach his scholars good and godly things, but also that he practise the same in his life and conversation, unto the good ensample of his disciples; forasmuch as the property and nature of youth is to follow the manners of their superiors, whether they be good or evil, being persuaded that it is lawful for them to do whatsoever they see their school-master do before their eyes. In consideration whereof, let the teacher diligently take heed that no vain or light communication proceed out of his mouth; that he use no unseemly gesture; again, that all his behaviour be such, so godly, so honest, so virtuous, that his scholars may see nothing in him worthy to be reprehended, but many, yea, all things most worthy to be followed; ever having before his Matt. xviii. eyes this saying of Christ: "Whosoever doth offend one of these little ones which believe in me, it were better for him that a mill-stone were hanged about his neck, and that he were drowned in the depth of the sea:" remembering also, that the hope of the christian commonweal is committed unto him of special trust, to be brought up in godliness and virtue, which to frustrate were more than double wickedness: again, not forgetting, that in teaching the youth he hath God and his holy angels which do behold him and all his doings; so that, if he do well, he shall not go unrewarded, but shall have manifold blessings poured upon him both in this world and in the life to come; contrariwise, if he behave himself evil in his office, he shall not escape unplagued, neither in this world nor in the world to come.

Father. If school-masters would diligently do their duty, we should have a blessed commonweal, replenished with all knowledge, godliness, wisdom, learning, innocency of life, civility of life, civility of manners; all barbarousness, rudeness, ignorancy, superstition, papistry, idolatry, utterly banished and driven out of the bounds of Christianity. But come off, my dear son, and tell me if any thing yet remain, that pertaineth unto the Of the chastising of scholars. duty of a school-master. *Son.* One thing is yet behind, and this it is; that he, which is a school-master, keep a measure in chastising his scholars. For the most part of teachers do overshoot themselves in this behalf, and have no mean in punishing. They think themselves then best school-masters, and most faithful to do their office, when they teach little and beat much. But a good school-master must use both wisdom and discretion in this matter.

He must consider the nature of his scholars. Some be so gentle and corrigible, that words may seem abundantly to suffice, and that without stripes. Some are so stubborn, stiff-necked, and almost incorrigible, that to bring them into the way, and to make them to prosper in their studies, there is need not only of words but also of stripes. The children, which either are tender, or tender-witted, or fearful, or easy to be reclaimed, the school-master ought gently to entreat, and to rebuke them only with words, or at the least, if they offend oft, to minister unto them easy punishment. But those children which are negligent, froward, stubborn, and rather given to play than to studies, yea, and that of set purpose, the master ought not only with words sharply to reprove them, but also with stripes largely to chastise them. Notwithstanding, in all punishments a measure is to be observed, lest through too much severity wits rather be dulled than quickened, studies rather oppressed than excited, and learning rather hated than embraced.

☞ And this also ought to be considered in punishments, that, before the school-master beat his children, he first of all lay their faults before them, so that they

[[1] Lib. I. See Vol. I. page 15, note 1.]

themselves are compelled to grant that they have grievously offended, and have justly deserved to be punished; and shew unto them out of the word of God, that they have done amiss, and that God is angry with them, and will grievously plague them, if they will not amend; again, that he himself is loth to punish them, as one that rather rejoiceth in their well-doing than otherwise; and if it were not so well for the amendment of themselves, which have so offended, as for the example of other, he could right well be content to let them go unpunished. These things thus handled, let him punish the offenders; yet so that they may think that that punishment, which their master minister unto them for their faults, cometh rather of love than of hatred toward them.

And that they may the better be persuaded thus to think, let the school-master, as I said before, use a moderation in punishing, and not beat them like stock-fishes, as a great number of school-masters do; which, like frantic men, when any thing offend them, be it never so little, so furiously behave themselves toward their scholars, that a man, beholding them, may right well think that they are vexed with some infernal fury. Let the school-master therefore keep a measure in chastising, and follow the example of a good father, which neither with too much softness marreth his children by making them too wanton, nor yet with too much severity dulleth them, their wits, and their memory; but rather so useth his correction, that the children are more amended than hindered, according to this commandment of St Paul: "Ye fathers, move not your children unto wrath, lest they be of a desperate mind; but bring them up in the doctrine and nurture of the Lord." And when the school-master hath punished his scholars measurably and according to the rule of reason, let him give them immediately some gentle and loving exhortation, to beware that they fall no more into the same or the like fault, and declare unto them how goodly and pleasant a thing it is, both before God and man, to do well; contrariwise, how wicked a thing it is, vile, displeasant, and abominable in the sight of God and of all good men, to do evil.

Father. If all school-masters would thus behave themselves, both in teaching and correcting, as thou, my son, hast now declared, there were a good hope that our children should prosper and go forward in their studies better than they do now-a-days. But forasmuch as thou hast set forth the office of a school-master toward his scholars, I would also gladly hear the duty of a scholar toward his teacher and master. *Son*. I will do it, yea, and that most gladly.

OF THE OFFICE AND DUTY OF SCHOLARS.

As a school-master is bounden by his office, first and above all things, to plant in the breasts of his disciples true religion and the knowledge of God, that, as they grow in age, they likewise may increase in godliness and virtue, and so lead a life worthy of their profession; even so is it the duty of all good scholars, and of such as intend to prosper in their studies, and to have God their merciful Lord, to endeavour themselves unto the uttermost of their power, even from their tender years, to drink in godliness, and to learn how they may truly and faithfully serve, honour, and worship God, call on his holy name by fervent prayer, be thankful unto him for his benefits, and lead a life worthy of his kindness. And that they may do these things with the more fruit, it shall be convenient that the scholars always at their uprising in the morning, after thanks given for their quiet sleep, do commend themselves to God, and most humbly beseech him to preserve them that day and evermore from all evil, to keep them in his fear, faith, and love, to prosper them in their studies, and so to direct all their travails, that both they and their enterprises may turn unto the glory of his holy name, and unto the profit of the christian commonweal.

Again, after that the hearts of scholars be stablished in God and in his holy word, so that now their chief and principal delight is in the study of godliness and of true religion, the next point that appertaineth unto their duty is to love, reverence, **Scholars ought to love and to reverence their school-masters.**

and honour their school-master, even as another father; honourably to think and speak of him, and to conceal and keep secret his faults, if he have any; also quietly, patiently, thankfully, and in good part to take his both admonitions and corrections, being persuaded that they come from such an heart as tendereth both them and their commodity. For if that father which only begetteth the gross body, in this point not much differing from the brute beasts, be worthy of honour; how much more is he to be honoured and reverenced, which tilleth, trimmeth, decketh, and garnisheth both body and mind with honest virtues and godly qualities! Verily, look how much the mind passeth the body (the one we have common with brute beasts, the other with the heavenly spirits), so much doth the father of the mind pass the father of the body.

This considered right well Philip, king of Macedonia, which, when Alexander his son was born, wrote unto Aristotle, that famous philosopher, and in his letters thanked God, not so much that he had given him a son, as that it chanced that he was born in the time of so noble a philosopher, which might instruct, teach, and bring him up in virtue and learning, and through his good advertisements to make him such one as is worthy both of so noble a father, and of so worthy a kingdom[1]. This most puissant and worthy prince knew right well, that the nobility of the father, the good disposition of the child, and all other good gifts of nature, profit little unto the furniture of a true man, except there be a cunning artificer to frame the mind aright, and to adorn it with the wholesome precepts both of doctrine and of manners.

In what great honour and reverence learned and diligent school-masters were had in times past, even among the very heathen, histories abundantly declare; as I may speak nothing of the exceeding great liberality which they at all times shewed to the teachers of their children. Christian children therefore may not deny that honour and reverence to their school-masters, which the very heathen in times past most willingly gave to their teachers; yea, and that so much the more, because they taught vain and worldly matters, but ours teach profitable and heavenly things, things necessary unto everlasting salvation.

Moreover, the duty of scholars is earnestly and diligently to apply their books, and to give their minds to the studies of good letters, remembering with themselves that that is their vocation, whereunto they are called of God; and therefore with all their industry, labour, and diligence, they ought to follow it, and by no means to be negligent therein, lest God be angry with them and punish them. Whatsoever their master teacheth them, let them diligently note it, and commend it to memory. Let not their bodies be in the schools, and their minds in the fields; but let them most earnestly do that which the place requireth. Above all things they ought to take heed that they spend not their time in vain; but rather that there escape no day with them, wherein they have not somewhat profited, both in learning and manners. Let them oftentimes repeat that they have learned, that nothing be forgotten. Let them confer with other in doubtful matters. Let them not be ashamed to be taught of other. Let them strive with all main to excel their fellows in virtue, learning, knowledge, and good manners. If any of their age and continuance do pass them in doctrine, let them bear it heavily, and never cease till they have overtaken him, yea, and overcome him. Let them diligently mark the best and purest words and phrases of the Latin tongue, and use them in their daily speech. And that they may do this thing the more aptly, let them make paper books, and in them diligently note both the best and most notable sentences and phrases of the Roman tongue, and practise them both in their speaking and writing; and according to the words and phrases of that writer to frame both their tongue and style.

And although we lack not authors whom the scholars may worthily follow in this behalf, yet, by the judgment of all learned men, Cicero, which is the father of eloquence and the prince of the Latin speech, is most worthy to be embraced, and both in tongue and pen to be followed. In this author therefore, for the right framing of the Latin tongue, let the scholars most diligently exercise themselves, and labour to the uttermost of their power to express both his words and phrases in their speaking and writing,

[1 See before, page 5, note 2.]

and by no means, so much as is possible, admit any other or strange phrases. Let the scholars also call themselves oftentimes to an account, and see how they prosper in the studies of good letters and manners, but specially of godliness. If they find themselves negligent in any point, let them redress that is amiss, and always take heed that they do not neglect their vocation whereunto God hath called them, but labour with all diligence to do that which their calling requireth; that is to say, to become learned, eloquent, wise, prudent, cunning, &c.

Finally, it is the duty of good and godly scholars not only to be learned, but also to have their lives so garnished with good manners and godly virtues, that there appear nothing in them worthy of reproach. In the temples let them shew themselves devout, holy, and religious, both in praying and in hearing the holy sermons. In their houses at home let them behave themselves modestly, soberly, honestly, and temperately. In the streets abroad let their behaviour be gentle, quiet, amiable, pleasant, friendly, and loving toward all men, all contention, disquietness, strife, and debate set apart. In their plays and pastimes let them shew no point of childish lightness, but remember christian modesty. In their words let them be ware and circumspect, that they abuse not themselves in vain, foolish, trifling, and wanton communication. In countenance let gravity, sobriety, modesty, and shamefacedness appear. In going let no pride, no stateliness, be shewed. In all their gestures let there be an honest comeliness and sober behaviour, that whosoever behold them may conceive a good opinion of them. To end, let them so compose their life and manners, let them so appoint their travails and studies, that in time to come they may be good and profitable members of the christian public weal, unto the glory of God, and unto the profit of his holy congregation.

Father. Amen. Remain there yet behind any other degrees, whose offices are also to be declared? *Son.* Two only; the duties of the rich man, and of the poor labouring man: which once finished, we will in few words knit up the office of all degrees in common, and so make an end. And first I will begin with the office of rich men.

Father. Let it so be.

OF THE OFFICE AND DUTY OF RICH MEN.

Son. First, it is the duty of rich men to consider of whom they have received their temporal goods and possessions.

Father. Of whom have they received their riches? *Son.* Verily not of themselves, nor by their own industry, labour, diligence, wisdom, policy, forecast, &c.

Father. Of whom then? *Son.* Of God, from whom "cometh down every good and perfect gift."

Father. How provest thou that? *Son.* By the word of God, which is the faithful testimony of the Lord. Salomon saith: "The blessing of the Lord maketh men rich; as for careful travail, it doth nothing thereto." Jesus, the son of Sirach, saith thus: "Prosperity and adversity, life and death, poverty and riches, come all of the Lord."

Father. Saith not Salomon, "An idle hand maketh poor; but a quick labouring hand maketh rich?" *Son.* I grant. For as God feedeth us, and notwithstanding by means; even so God enricheth us, and yet by a mean: which mean is labour. For though we labour never so much, yet, except God blesseth our labours, our travail is vain, as the psalmograph saith: "Except the Lord build the house, their labour is but lost that build it. Except the Lord keep the city, the watchman waketh but in vain. It is but lost labour that ye haste to rise up early, and so late take rest, and eat the bread of carefulness." Prov. x. Psal. cxxvii.

Father. When the rich men have considered that their goods are the gift of God, what is then their duty to do? *Son.* To be thankful unto God for them, and not to glory in themselves, as though they had gotten them by their own policy and wit. For if we ought to be thankful to God for all his benefits, verily we ought not to be unthankful for the gift of riches, which is one of the principal gifts that appertain unto the body. For without them the life that is led is a miserable life, yea, in a manner no life. Who wisheth not rather not to live, than miserably, wretch- The rich men ought to be thankful to God for their riches.

edly, beggarly, and painfully to live? The life that is passed over in penury and wretchedness, is it any other thing than sorrow and pain? He is therefore twice ingrate, ungentle, and churlish, that giveth not thanks to God for the riches and possessions wherewith he is endued.

It is lawful to possess the goods of the world.

Father. It is lawful then to possess worldly goods? *Son.* Why not? Are they not the gifts of God? May we not lawfully possess that God liberally giveth?

Father. Yet have I heard that some have condemned riches as things unlawful to be had in the possession of Christians. Some also have counted it a point of great perfection to leave the goods of the world, and to profess wilful poverty, as they call it. *Son.* As touching the first, I answer, that riches may lawfully be possessed of the Christians. Abraham, Isaac, Jacob, Joseph, David, Salomon, Ezechias, Josias, Job, Toby, Nicodemus, Zacheus, Joseph of Arimathea, with many other, were rich men, and endued with great possessions; yet were they dearly beloved of God, and are now glorious and blessed saints in heaven.

As concerning the second sort, which brag that they forsake the goods of the world and profess wilful poverty, these are those subtile hypocrites and double dissemblers, which, forsaking nothing, possess all things; which, spending their time idly, live of the labour of other men's hands, and of the sweat of other men's brows; which
Rom. xvi. "serve not the Lord Jesus Christ, but their own bellies, and with sweet and flattering words deceive the hearts of the simple." Is this perfection? yea, rather most high
Matt. v. imperfection. Christ said not only, "Blessed are the poor"; but he added, "in
☞ spirit." They are poor in spirit, not that have nothing, but they which, having riches, are notwithstanding content to depart from their riches, whensoever the glory of God or the commodity of the christian brother doth require; as St Paul saith:
1 Cor. vii. "Brethren, the time is short. It remaineth that they which have wives be as though they had none; and they that weep be as though they wept not; and they that rejoice be as though they rejoiced not; and they that buy be as though they possessed not; and they that use this world be as though they used it not: for the fashion of this world goeth away."

1 Tim. vi. And in another place St Paul commandeth Timothy to "charge them which are rich in this world," not that they should profess wilful poverty, and forsake their worldly goods, but "that they be not high-minded, nor put their trust in uncertain riches, but in the living God, which giveth us abundantly all things to enjoy them; that they do good; that they be rich in good works; that they be ready to give, and gladly to distribute; laying up in store for themselves a good foundation in time
Psal. lxii. to come, that they may obtain everlasting life." Likewise saith David: "If ye have abundance of riches, set not your heart upon them." The psalmograph commandeth not the rich men to forsake their goods and to run into a cloister, there to profess wilful poverty, and to live idly of the labour of other men's hands; but he willeth them not to set their hearts upon them, to delight in them, to trust in them, and
Matt. vi. to serve them. For, as our Saviour saith: "Ye cannot serve God and mammon."

Matt. xix. *Father.* Are not these the words of Christ? "Verily I say unto you, It shall be hard for the rich to enter into the kingdom of heaven. And again I say unto you, It is easier for a cable rope to go through the eye of a needle, than for the rich to enter into the kingdom of God." Who would desire now to be rich, seeing that riches are such an obstacle and let unto the heavenly inheritance? Who wisheth not rather to be poor in this world, and so enter into glory, than to be rich here,
James ii. and afterward to be damned? "Did not God choose the poor of this world, and
Matt. xix. made them heirs of his glorious kingdom?" Did not the apostles "forsake all things and follow Christ?" Who seeth not now that poverty is a ready way unto everlasting salvation?

Son. Neither riches nor poverty of themselves help us any thing at all unto the
Rom. vi. kingdom of God; for "everlasting life is the gift of God through Jesus Christ our
Ecclus. xi. Lord." And "both riches and poverty come from God," as the wise man saith. And where you do allege the saying of Christ, to declare that it is an hard thing for rich men to enter into the kingdom of heaven, you shall understand that that sentence of our Saviour Christ doth no more exclude the rich than the poor out of the kingdom

of heaven; inasmuch as blessing is the riches of God. Christ speaketh of that kind of rich men which have their hearts glued unto their riches, contrary to this saying of the psalmograph, "If ye have abundance of riches, set not your heart upon them:" which put their trust in their riches; which serve mammon and are money-slaves; which delight in nothing but in their worldly goods; which seek help in all their adversities rather of their money than of God; which repose all their affiance in their riches, and not in the living God, &c. That Christ speaketh of such rich men, blessed Mark declareth manifestly in these his words: "Jesus said to his disciples, How uneasily shall they that have money enter into the kingdom of God! And the disciples were astonied at his words. But Jesus answered and said unto them, Children, how hard is it for them *that trust in money* to enter into the kingdom of God!" Riches, if they be not abused, hinder men no more from the kingdom of heaven, than poverty impatiently borne doth further them. Prov. x. Psal. lxii. 1 Tim. vi. Matt. vi. Mark x.

And as touching the apostles, in effect, heart, and mind they had given over their worldly goods so soon as Christ called them unto the ministry of his holy word: that is to say, rather than they would leave their vocation whereunto they were called, they were content not only to leave their goods, but also their life, so great desire had they to win all men unto the gospel; but the possession and use of their goods they did not refuse and cast away, but continued still owners of them, for the relief of their own necessity, and for the comfort of other also.

Father. Said not Peter thus unto Christ of himself and of his fellow-disciples, "Behold, we have forsaken all things, and we have followed thee?" *Son.* Truth it is. But this forsaking consisted rather in effect and mind than otherwise, as St Paul said of himself: "None of these things move me, neither is my life dear unto myself, so that I may finish my course with joy, and the ministration (of the word) which I have received of the Lord Jesu, to testify the gospel of the grace of God." For he that said, "Behold, we have forsaken all things," &c., even the very same had notwithstanding, being Christ's disciple, a house of his own and a family, and also meat and drink in his house, and all other things necessary to entertain such as came unto him. Matt. xix. Acts xx. Matt. viii. Mark i. Luke iv.

We read also of St Matthew, that, after Christ had called him to be his disciple and preacher of his holy word, yet had he still his goods in possession, insomuch that he feasted Christ and his disciples with divers other. Read we not thus also in the gospel, "The disciples went away again unto their own home?" Read we not also that the apostles had ships of their own, and that they laboured in them for to get their living, but namely after the death of Christ? Who seeth not now that the evangelical poverty consisteth not in the lack or want of worldly goods, or in forsaking nothing and possessing all things, after the manner of the monstrous monks; but rather in effect, spirit, and mind?—so that to forsake all things for Christ's sake, or to be poor after the doctrine of the gospel, is not to possess nothing and to have all things ministered by the painful labours of other; but to have a mind so estranged from the desire and love of worldly things, that it can alway be content, prest[1], and ready to forsake whatsoever is upon the earth, yea, the very life itself, whensoever the glory of God or the commodity of the christian brethren require. Matt. ix. Mark ii. Luke v. John xx. John xxi.

Father. I see now right well that, as the riches are the gift of God, so likewise may a christian man lawfully possess and enjoy them, yea, and that with a good conscience. But to what end hath God given to rich men their riches? *Son.* After that the rich men have considered with themselves, that they have received their riches of God's free liberality, and according to their bounden duty have given him thanks for them, it is their duty also to weigh with themselves, for what[2] purpose and to what end God hath endued them with their possessions and worldly substance; lest, by the abuse of them, they be put out of office with that unrighteous steward, fall from the favour of God, and lose the inheritance of everlasting glory. That they may spend their goods aright and according to the blessed pleasure of God, it shall be expedient that the rich men consider with themselves, that the riches which they have are Why God hath given the rich men their goods. Luke xvi.

[[1] Prest: ready, prepared.] [[2] The folio has *that*.]

Hag. ii. not theirs, but God's, as God himself saith by the prophet: "Gold is mine, silver is Psal. xxiv. mine." The psalmograph saith: "The earth is the Lord's, and all that is contained in it." And by the same psalmograph God himself saith again: "All the beasts of Psal. l. the forest are mine, and so are the cattle upon a thousand hills." "The whole world is mine, and all that therein is."

And as their riches are God's, so likewise will he call them to an account how Luke xvi. Matt. xxv. Luke xix. they have bestowed them, as we may see in the gospel of St Luke, and in other places of the holy scripture. They must therefore also consider with themselves, that they are not the proper owners of the goods which they have in possession, but only the dispensators and distributers of God's goods; and that therefore they ought to be ware and circumspect how they spend those goods that God have committed unto them. The foolish world thinketh that they may bestow their goods as they lust, and recounteth no sin wastefully to spend them in riot and excess: but the godly rich ☞ man knoweth that they be the goods of God, and that therefore they must be bestowed according to the will of God. Such therefore as fear God may not spend away their goods in dicing, and carding, and such other vain, foolish, and fleshly pleasures; neither in eating, drinking, and banqueting; nor yet in gorgeous apparel and costious buildings; Luke xvi. but as God hath appointed. Read we not in the gospel, that the ungodly rich man was damned and cast down into the deep dungeon of hell-fire, because he abused his riches in consuming them upon delicate fare, sumptuous apparel, &c.? We read not that he was any briber, poller, piller, extortioner, usurer, or wrong-doer to any man; but only that he abused his goods, and spent them otherwise than the will of God was.

Father. How shall the rich men then bestow their goods according to God's good How rich men shall use their goods. will and pleasure? *Son*. First of all, in the ware using of them about their own necessities, without excess. For whatsoever is spent superfluously and without necessity is consumed contrary to the will of God, and deserveth everlasting damnation. The rich therefore, that fear God, shall take with thanksgiving so much of the goods which they have received of God liberally, as shall abundantly suffice the necessity both of 1 Tim. v. themselves and of so many as belong unto him. For "if any man make not provision for his own family, he hath denied the faith, and is worse than an infidel."

Father. What shall he do with the rest of his goods? *Son*. All rich men ought to consider with themselves that they are, as I said before, not proper owners of the goods, but only the dispensators and distributers of God's goods, which he hath committed to their hands. Their own necessary expenses deducted, they ought to distribute the residue as time and occasion shall serve.

Unprofitable members of the commonweal. *Father*. To whom shall they distribute those goods? to monks, friars, canons, nuns, anchors[1], anchoresses, pardoners, soul-priests, &c., that they by their masses of *Scala Cœli* may deliver souls out of purgatory? or to carvers, gilders, and painters, to make, gild, and paint images? or to wax-chandlers, to make candles, tapers, and torches, to set up in the churches before idols and mawmets? or to singing-men, that they in churches or chapels may roar, bool[2], bleat, yell, grunt, cry out, &c., some a bass, some a countertenor, some a mean, some a treble, yea, and altogether without the affection of the mind, or without any edifying to the hearers? *Son*. The word of God speaketh nothing at all of these kind of people, neither are the rich men by the commandment of God charged with the provision of such. For such are no necessary members of the christian commonweal.

Upon whom the rich men shall bestow their goods *Father*. To whom then ought the distribution to be made? *Son*. To the poor, to the feeble, to the lame, and to the blind.

Luke xiv. *Father*. Where is that commanded? [*Son*.] Our Saviour Christ saith: "When thou makest a feast, call the poor, the feeble, the lame, and the blind, and thou shalt be happy; for they cannot recompense thee: but thou shalt be recompensed at the Isai. lviii. resurrection of the righteous." God by the prophet also saith: "Break thy bread to the hungry, and the needy and wandering bring home into thy house: when thou seest a naked man, cover him; and hide not thy face from thy neighbour, neither despise Ecclus. iv. thou thine own flesh." The wise man saith: "My son, defraud not the poor of his

[[1] Anchors: anchorites.] [[2] Bool: bawl.]

alms, and turn not away thine eyes from him that hath need. Despise not an hungry
soul, and defy not the poor in his necessity: grieve not the heart of him that is helpless,
and withdraw not thy gift from the needful," &c. The Lord Christ saith: "If thou Matt. xix.
wilt be perfect, go and sell all that thou hast, and give it to the poor." Again: "Sell Luke xii.
that ye have, and give alms. And prepare you bags which wax not old, even a
treasure that faileth not in heaven, where no thief cometh, neither moth corrupteth.
For where your treasure is, there will your heart be also." Also in another place:
"Make you friends of the unrighteous mammon, that, when ye shall have need, they Luke xvi.
may receive you into everlasting habitations." Item: "Verily I say unto you, What- Matt. xxv.
soever ye have done to one of the least of these my brethren, ye have done it to me."

Likewise saith St Paul: "Distribute unto the necessity of the saints: be ready Rom. xii.
to harbour." "For God loveth a cheerful giver." "He that soweth little shall reap 2 Cor. ix.
little, and he that soweth largely shall reap largely." "For whatsoever a man soweth, Gal. vi.
that shall he also reap." "Let us not be weary of well-doing; for, when the time is
come, we shall reap without weariness. While we have therefore time, let us do good
unto all men; but specially unto them which are of the household of faith." St Peter
saith: "Be ye harbourers one to another, without grudging. As every man hath 1 Pet. iv.
received the gift, even so minister the same one to another, as good ministers of the
manifold grace of God." St John saith: "Whoso hath the goods of this world, and 1 John iii.
seeth his brother have need, and shutteth up his compassion from him, how dwelleth
the love of God in him?" To conclude, old Tobias said to his son: "Give alms of thy goods, and turn never thy face from the poor; and so shall it come to pass that the face of the Lord shall not be turned away from thee. Be merciful after thy power. If thou have much, give plenteously: if thou have little, do thy diligence gladly to give of that little. For so gatherest thou to thyself a good reward in the day of necessity. For mercy delivereth from all sin and from death, and suffereth not the soul to come in darkness. A great comfort is mercy before the high God, unto all them that shew it."

Father. Are not the poor widows and needy fatherless children to be considered
also? *Son*. Yes, verily, and so many besides as have need of help, as we are taught Luke x.
in the gospel. But as concerning widows and fatherless children, God giveth the
rich men a special charge of them, as persons which have most need of help, and
are most of all unable to defend themselves. St James also saith: "The pure and James i.
undefiled religion before God the Father is to visit the fatherless and widows in their
adversity, and to keep himself unspotted in the world."

Father. What reward shall the rich man have at the hand of God for the faithful
distribution of their goods to the poor people? *Son*. Our Saviour Christ saith: "When Luke xvii.
ye have done all those things which are commanded you, say, We are unprofitable
servants: we have done that which was our duty to do." Notwithstanding, so gentle
and loving is our heavenly Father to us for Christ's sake, that look, whatsoever we
are to the poor people, even the very same will he be unto us; yea, for worldly gifts
(although the gifts be his own) he will give us heavenly gifts and uncorruptible
treasures, as our Saviour Christ saith: "Blessed are the merciful; for they shall Matt. v.
obtain mercy." And in another place, where Christ setteth forth the form of his last
judgment, we read that he shall say to the merciful on this manner: "Come, ye Matt. xxv.
blessed of my Father, possess ye the kingdom which was prepared for you from the beginning of the world. For I was an hungred, and ye gave me meat: I was thirsty, and ye gave me drink: I was harbourless, and ye took me in; naked, and ye clothed me; sick, and ye visited me: I was in prison, and ye came unto me. Then shall the righteous answer him, saying, Lord, when saw we thee an hungred, and fed thee? or thirsty, and gave thee drink? when saw we thee harbourless, and took thee in? or naked, and clothed thee? or when saw we thee sick, or in prison, and came unto thee? And the King shall answer and say unto them, Verily I say unto you, Inasmuch as ye have done it unto one of the least of these my brethren, ye have done it to me. And these shall go into everlasting life."

"Blessed is the man," saith David, "that considereth the poor (and needy): the Psal. xli.
Lord shall deliver him in the time of trouble. The Lord shall preserve him, and keep

him alive, that he may be blessed on earth, and not be delivered into the will of his
enemies. The Lord shall comfort him when he lieth sick upon his bed," &c. Again:
Psal. cxii. "He hath sparsed abroad and given to the poor; and his righteousness remaineth for
ever. His horn shall be exalted with honour." Salomon saith: "He that is merciful
Prov. xi. doth himself a benefit; but whoso hurteth his neighbour is a tyrant." "He that is
liberal in giving shall have plenty, and he that watereth shall be watered also himself.
Whoso hoardeth up his corn shall be cursed among the people; but blessing shall light
Prov. xiv. upon his head that giveth food." Again: "Whoso despiseth his neighbour doth amiss;
but blessed is he that hath pity on the poor." "He that doth a poor man wrong
blasphemeth his Maker; but whoso hath pity on the poor doth honour unto God."
Prov. xvi. Also in another place: "Through mercy and faith are sins purged." Item: "He that
hath a loving eye shall be blessed; for he giveth of his bread to the poor." Once
Prov. xxviii. again: "He that giveth unto the poor shall not lack; but he that turneth away
Prov. xix. his eyes from such as be in necessity shall suffer great poverty himself." Item: "He
that hath pity upon the poor lendeth unto the Lord; and look, what he layeth out,
Ecclus. iii. it shall be paid him again." Jesus, the son of Sirach, also saith: "Water quencheth
Ecclus. xvii. burning fire; and mercy reconcileth sins." Again: "The mercy that a man sheweth
Ecclus. xxix. is as it were a purse with him." Also in another place: "Lay up thine alms in the
hand of the poor; and it shall keep thee from all evil. A man's alms is as a purse
with him, and shall keep a man's favour as the apple of an eye, and afterward shall
it arise and pay every man his reward upon his head. It shall fight for thee against
thine enemies, better than the shield of a giant or spear of the mighty." Daniel said
Dan. iv. to king Nabuchodonosor: "Redeem thy sins with alms, and thine offences with mercy
to poor people; for this shall be an healing of thine error." Our Saviour Christ saith:
Luke xi. "Give alms of that ye have; and behold all things are clean unto you." The holy apostle
1 Tim. vi. St Paul exhorteth the rich men "to do good, to be rich in good works, to be ready to
give, and gladly to distribute, that by this means they may lay up in store for themselves
a good foundation against the time to come, that they may obtain everlasting life."

Thus see we, that the reward which is laid up for them that deal mercifully with the poor is great and unoutspeakable, whether we respect things appertaining unto the soul or unto the body.

Father. But what reward shall those rich men have, that be unmerciful to the poor, and shew no liberality unto the needy? *Son.* Their reward shall be in this world the wrath of God, and in the world to come everlasting damnation.

Matt. xxv. *Father.* How provest thou that? *Son.* Read we not that that "unprofitable
servant, which abused his master's goods," was "cast into utter darkness, where weeping
Luke xvi. and gnashing of teeth is?" Read we not that the wicked steward was put out of
his office? Doth not our Saviour Christ call out upon the unmerciful rich men, and
Luke vi. say: "Wo unto you that are rich! for ye have your consolation. Wo unto you
that are full! for ye shall hunger. Wo unto you that now laugh! for ye shall wail
and weep." In the description of the last judgment, read we not that the Lord Christ
Matt. xxv. shall on this manner speak unto the unmerciful rich worldlings? "Depart from me,
ye cursed, into everlasting fire, which is prepared for the devil and his angels. For
I was an hungred, and ye gave me no meat: I was thirsty, and ye gave me no drink:
I was harbourless, and ye took me not in: I was naked, and ye clothed me not:
I was sick, and in prison, and ye visited me not. Then shall they answer him, saying,
Lord, when saw we thee an hungred, or athirst, or harbourless, or naked, or sick, or in
prison, and did not minister unto thee? Then shall he answer them, saying, Verily I say
unto you, Inasmuch as ye did it not to one of the least of these, ye did it not to me.
And these shall go into everlasting pain." An example hereof have we in the gospel
Luke xvi. of St Luke, where we see evidently that that gorgeous rich glutton was condemned
only because he would shew no mercy to the poor miserable beggar Lazarus, which
craved succour at his hand, but he could get none; neither could that rich glutton
obtain any mercy at the hand of God when he cried; that that may be found true which
Prov. xxi. the holy scripture hath: "He that stoppeth his eyes at the crying of the poor, he shall
James ii. cry himself, and shall not be heard." Again: "The judgment shall be without mercy
to him that sheweth no mercy."

Father. We may therefore well say with the wise man: "Blessed is the rich, which is found without blemish, and hath not gone after gold, nor hoped in money and treasures. Where is there such a one? and we shall commend him, and call him blessed; for great things doth he among his people. Whoso is tried and found perfect in such things shall be commended and praised. Therefore shall his good be stablished; and the whole congregation shall declare his alms." *Son.* God make all wealthy men rich toward God! Ecclus. xxxi.

Father. Amen. But come off, tell me, my son, when the rich men ought to distribute their goods to the poor. For many use to keep their goods straitly together so long as they live, and when they are ready to die, then they appoint after their death, by will and testament, large dole to be given to the poor, that they may pray for their souls, that they may be delivered out of the bitter pains of purgatory. *Son.* These people gather riches to themselves, but they are "not rich toward God." They follow not the counsel of our Saviour Christ, which saith: "Make you friends of unrighteous mammon, that, when ye shall have need, they may receive you into everlasting habitations." When the rich men ought to distribute their goods. Luke xii. Luke xvi.

But to come unto your question. They that are rich in God ought not to defer their alms till death come; but, whensoever an occasion is given, straightways to shew their liberality toward the poor. A christian man in the holy scripture is compared to "a tree planted by the river-side, which bringeth forth her fruit in due season," or in her time. So likewise ought a christian man, whensoever the glory of God or the commodity of his neighbour require, to do good, and not to defer the time, not to tarry till another occasion be offered, as St Paul saith: "Let us not be weary of well-doing: for when the time is come, we shall reap without weariness. Therefore, while we have time, let us do good unto all men, and specially unto them which are of the household of faith." And our Saviour Christ saith: "Walk while ye have light, lest the darkness come upon you." Salomon also saith: "Withdraw no good thing from them that have need, so long as thine hand is able to do it. Say not unto thy neighbour, Go thy way, and come again, to-morrow will I give thee; whereas thou hast now to give him." Jesus, the son of Sirach, saith: "Despise not an hungry soul, and defy not the poor in his necessity: grieve not the heart of him that is helpless, and withdraw not thy gift from the needful. Refuse not the prayer of one that is in trouble: turn not away thy face from the needy," &c. Again, the preacher saith: "Let thy garments be alway white, and let thine head lack no ointment:" "whatsoever thy hand is able to do, do it out of hand; for in the grave that thou goest unto, there is neither work, counsel, knowledge, nor wisdom." Psal. i. Gal. vi. John xii. Prov. iii. Ecclus. iv. Eccles. ix.

Thus are the rich men taught in the holy scripture not to defer their alms unto their dying day, or until the time after their death, to be distributed by their executors or by their friends; but out of hand, even so soon as an occasion is offered, to minister unto the poor and needy persons all good things. There is an old verse worthy to be remembered:

Da tua, dum tua sunt: post mortem tunc tua non sunt.

"Give thy goods while they be thine; for, when thou art once dead, they be none of thine." There is also an old distinction not worthy to be forgotten, and it is this:

Quod sibi quisque serit præsentis tempore vitæ,
Hoc sibi messis erit, cum dicitur, Ite, venite.

"Look, whatsoever a man soweth in the time of this present life, that shall he reap, when Christ shall say, 'Get ye hence, ye cursed, into everlasting fire,' &c. 'Come, ye blessed of my Father, possess the kingdom,'" &c. Likewise saith St Paul: "Whatsoever a man soweth, that shall he also reap. For he that soweth in his flesh shall of the flesh reap corruption: but he that soweth in the Spirit shall of the Spirit reap life everlasting." Again: "He that soweth little shall reap little; and he that soweth largely shall reap largely." "For God loveth a cheerful giver." Gal. vi. 2 Cor. ix.

Father. It is good then for a man to bestow his goods himself upon the poor before he die. *Son.* Yea, verily; so is the counsel of the wise man, which saith: "Do good unto thy friend before thou die, and according to thine ability reach out thine hand, and give unto the poor. Be not disappointed of the good day, and let not Ecclus. xiv.

portion of the good day overpass thee. Shalt thou not leave thy travails and labours unto other men? In the dividing of the heritage give and take, and sanctify thy soul. Work thou righteousness before thy death; for when thou art once dead, there is no meat to find." Moreover the apostle saith that "every man shall bear his own burden," and "receive his reward according to his own labour;" again, that "God shall give to every man after his own deeds, even those deeds which he hath done in his own body, whether they be good or evil." As God findeth us, so shall he judge us. If he find us at the hour of death unfruitful and without good works, we may be sure to receive the curse of everlasting damnation, though never so many good works be done for us of other after our death; neither can the purgatory-rakers, with all their trentals, dirigies[1], commendations, masses of *Scala Cœli*, &c., profit us any thing at all.

Gal. vi. 1 Cor. iii. Rom. ii.

Father. Then are many deceived which, although they have been unfruitful fig-trees all the days of their life, hope notwithstanding to be saved by such means. *Son.* From whence should they be saved?

The holy scripture knoweth no purging-place after this life. Luke xvi.

Father. They say, out of purgatory. *Son.* The scripture knoweth no such place. Hell and heaven are set forth in the word of God: more places after this life the scripture knoweth not. And as two places only in the holy scripture are declared, that is to say, heaven and hell; so likewise are there set forth unto us only two kinds of people, that is to say, good and bad, faithful and unfaithful, as our Saviour Christ saith: "He that believeth on the Son of God hath everlasting life: but he that believeth not on the Son of God hath not life; but the wrath of God abideth upon him." Again: "He that believeth and is baptized shall be saved; but he that believeth not shall be condemned." So soon as the faithful depart, they are carried straightways by the ministry of the angels into the bosom of Abraham. And as for the unfaithful, the devils after their death carry them straightways into hell-fire; as we may see in the history of poor Lazarus and of the rich glutton.

John iii. Mark xvi. Note well. Luke xvi.

St Austin saith, that "the catholic faith believeth that there are two places after this life. One is the kingdom of heaven, a place appointed for the faithful: the other is hell-fire, where the unfaithful shall be tormented. As for the third place," saith he, "we utterly know none; neither do we find in the holy scriptures that there is any[2]." And in another place he saith that "the souls of all the saints since the ascension of Christ, so soon as they be departed from the body, go straightways unto heaven, and are there with Christ, looking for the resurrection of their bodies; even as the souls of sinners go unto hell, and abide the rising again of their bodies[3]," &c. Again he saith: "There are two dwelling-places; one in everlasting fire, the other in the everlasting kingdom[4]."

Lib. v. Hypog. De Differ. Eccles. Dogmat. De Verbis Apostoli. Serm. 181.

Father. If the matter stand thus, I do not see what large legacies bequeathed of the rich men to soul-priests to sing for them when they are dead, or any other good works done for them, profit the dead any thing at all. *Son.* You say truth. Hear what St Jerome saith: "While we are in this present world, we may help one another, whether it be by prayer or by counsel. But when we come once before the judging-place of Christ, not Job, not Daniel, nor Nohe can pray or entreat for any man, but every man shall bear his own burden[5]."

In Galat. cap. vi.

[[1] Dirigies: dirges.]

[[2] Primum enim locum fides catholicorum divina auctoritate regnum credit esse cœlorum, unde, ut dixi, non baptizatus excipitur; secundum, gehennam, ubi omnis apostata vel a Christi fide alienus æterna supplicia experietur: tertium penitus ignoramus, immo nec esse in scripturis sanctis inveniemus.—August. Op. Par. 1679-1700. Cont. Pelag. et Cœlest. Hypogn. Lib. v. cap. v. Tom. X. Appendix, col. 40.]

[[3] Post adscensionem Domini ad cœlos omnium sanctorum animæ cum Christo sunt, et exeuntes de corpore ad Christum vadunt, exspectantes resurrectionem corporis sui, ut ad integram et perpetuam beatitudinem cum ipso pariter immutentur: sicut et peccatorum animæ in inferno sub timore positæ exspectant resurrectionem sui corporis, ut cum ipso ad pœnam detrudantur æternam.—Id. De Eccles. Dog. Lib. cap. xlvi. Tom. VII. Appendix, col. 80.]

[[4] Duæ quippe habitationes sunt; una in igne æterno, alia in regno æterno.—Id. Serm. clxi. 4. De Verb. Apost. Tom. V. col. 776.]

[[5] Obscure licet docemur per hanc sententiolam, novum dogma quod latitat: dum in præsenti sæculo sumus, sive orationibus, sive consiliis invicem posse nos coadjuvari: quum autem ante tribunal Christi venerimus, non Job, non Daniel, nec Noe rogare posse pro quoquam; sed unumquemque portare onus suum.—Hieron. Op. 1693—1706. Lib. III. in Epist. ad Gal. cap. vi. Tom. IV. Pars I. col. 311.]

Like unto this writeth St John Chrysostom, saying: "Let us not think that when we come thither mercy shall be granted us, which do not so behave ourselves that we may deserve to receive forgiveness, although Abraham should pray for us, yea, although Noe, although Job, although Daniel should entreat for us. Therefore while the time is in our hands, let us prepare for ourselves much confidence with God[6]." In Hom. de Lazaro et Divite.

"Such as God findeth thee," saith St Cyprian, "when he calleth thee, even such also doth he judge thee. The righteous are called unto joy: the unrighteous are plucked unto punishment. Comfort is out of hand given to the faithful, and pain to the unfaithful[7]." In Serm. de Mortalitate.

"The time that we have in this world," saith Gregorius Nazianzenus, "is the time of working; but that which is to come is the time of reward[8]." In Orat.

Likewise saith Hisychius: "In this world to come there is no working; but they that have wrought now come there unto reward[9]." In Levit. Lib. vi. cap. 19.

"Prepare thy works," saith Chrysostom, "against thy departure, and address thyself unto thy journey. If thou hast taken ought from any man, give it him again, and say with Zacheus, 'If I have defrauded any man of any thing, I give him four times as much.' If thou be enemy to any man, reconcile thyself before thou come unto the judgment. Despatch all things here, that thou mayest behold that judging-seat without grief. So long as we be here, there is good hope and enough; but if we be once gone that way, it lieth not in our power afterward to repent, nor to put away our offences[10]." Hom. de Lazaro. Luke xix.

For, as St Ambrose saith: "He that receiveth not remission of his sins here, shall not have it there. He shall not have it indeed, for he cannot come unto everlasting life; for everlasting life is remission of sins. Therefore David, as a pilgrim making haste unto that common country of all the saints, desireth that his sins may be forgiven him before he depart out of this life, saying: 'Forgive me, that I may be refreshed, before I go hence[11].'" De Bono Mortis. cap. 2. Psal. xxxix.

Father. I see now that it is a vain thing to trust unto the good deeds of other, when a man is departed. *Son.* St Austin saith: "Every one sleepeth with his own cause, and shall rise again with his own cause[12]." In Joan. Tract. 49.

And Theophylact saith, that "the virtue of my neighbour shall scarcely be enough In Matt. cap. xxv.

[6 This passage is quoted in the Catalog. Test. Gen. 1608: Nec putemus nobis, quum illuc venerimus, misericordiam esse tribuendam, qui non agimus ut veniam mereamur accipere, etsi Abraham pro nobis roget, etsi Noe, etsi Job, etsi Daniel. Igitur, dum tempus est in manibus, plurimam nobis apud Deum fiduciam præparemus. col. 409. The editor has not, however, succeeded in discovering it in Chrysostom's works. There are passages *implying* what is here asserted, in Chrysost. Op. Par. 1718-38. De Lazar. Conc. iii., iv. Tom. I. pp. 741, 752.]

[7 Hoc quod sine ullo discrimine generis humani cum injustis moriuntur et justi; non est quod putetis bonis et malis interitum esse communem: ad refrigerium justi vocantur, ad supplicium rapiuntur injusti: datur velocius tutela fidentibus, perfidis pœna....... Qualem te invenit Dominus cum vocat, talem pariter et judicat; quando ipse testetur et dicat: Et scient omnes ecclesiæ quia ego sum scrutator renis et cordis.—Cypr. Op. Oxon. 1682. De Mortal. pp. 161-3.]

[8 Ἐργασίας γὰρ ὁ παρὼν, ὁ δὲ μέλλων ἀνταποδόσεως.—Gregor. Naz. Op. Par. 1778-1840. Orat. xix. 6. Tom. I. p. 367.]

[9 Dies autem tertia, quia in ipsa a mortuis Dominus noster resurrexit, figuram futuri seculi et mortuorum resurrectionis gerit, in quo jam non licet operari: sed qui nunc operati sunt, illic ad retributionem veniunt.—Isych. in Levit. Basil. 1527. Lib. vi. in cap. xix. fol. 110, 2.]

[10 Καὶ πάλιν, ἑτοίμαζε εἰς τὴν ἔξοδον τὰ ἔργα σου, καὶ παρασκευάζου πρὸς τὴν ὁδόν. εἴ τινος ἥρπασάς τι, ἀπόδος, καὶ εἰπὲ κατὰ τὸν Ζακχαῖον· δίδωμι τετραπλασίονα τὰ ἁρπαγέντα· εἴ τινός τι ἐσυκοφάντησας, εἴ τινος γέγονας ἐχθρὸς, καταλλάγηθι πρὸ τοῦ δικαστηρίου. πάντα ἴνταῦθα διάλυσαι, ἵνα χωρὶς πραγμάτων τὸ βῆμα ἴδῃς ἐκεῖνο. ἕως ἂν ἐνταῦθα ὦμεν, ἐλπίδας ἔχομεν χρηστάς· ἐπειδὰν δὲ ἀπέλθωμεν ἐκεῖ, κύριοι λοιπὸν μετανοίας οὐκ ἐσμὲν, οὐδὲ τοῦ τὰ ἡμαρτημένα ἡμῖν ἀπονίψασθαι.—Chrysost. Op. De Lazar. Conc. ii. Tom. I. p. 730.]

[11 Et ideo tamquam peregrinus ad illam sanctorum communem omnium patriam festinabat, petens pro hujus commorationis inquinamento remitti sibi peccata, priusquam discederet e vita. Qui enim hic non acceperit remissionem peccatorum, illic non erit. Non erit autem qui ad vitam æternam non poterit pervenire, quia vita æterna remissio peccatorum est. Ideoque dicit: Remitte mihi, ut refrigerer, priusquam abeam, et amplius non ero.—Ambros. Op. 1686-90. De Bon. Mort. Lib. cap. ii. 5. Tom. I. col. 391.]

[12 Sic unusquisque hominum cum caussa sua dormit, cum caussa sua surgit.—August. Op. In Johan. Evang. cap. xi. Tractat. xlix. 9. Tom. III. Pars ii. col. 623.]

to defend himself; so far is it off that it can be sufficient for me also. For every man," saith he, "shall be justified by his own works, and not by the works of his neighbours." And he compareth them that hope to be relieved by the good works of other, after they be dead, to the five foolish virgins, which would have begged oil of the five wise virgins, but all in vain; insomuch that they were not suffered to enter

In Luc. cap. xvi.

into the bridegroom's chamber[1]. "For it shall be no time then," saith he, "to work; neither shall it be honest to beg. For they are foolish virgins that beg[2]."

Father. Would God all rich men knew these things, that while they have time, they might do good, and shew mercy unto the poor! *Son.* "The god of this world hath blinded the minds of many rich men which believe not, lest the light of the glorious gospel should shine unto them," and they by this means, being merciful, should be saved, and be made heirs of everlasting glory.

Basilius Magnus, in a certain sermon, grievously rebuketh those covetous rich men, which, so long as they live, will depart from nothing to the poor; and when they see none other remedy, but die thou must, then make they their will, and bequeath largely to the poor. "Thou sayest," saith he, "I will enjoy my goods so long as I live; but I will remember the poor in my testament after I am dead. Ah, wretch!" saith he, "wilt thou then be gentle and liberal to men when I shall see thee [a] dead corpse? Shall I then call thee a lover of thy brother? Ah! know thou, know thou, there is no more buying when the mart is done, and when the shop-windows are shut up[3]."

Hope of long life maketh many unmerciful.

Father. The hope of long life doth much harm in this behalf. For the rich men persuade themselves that they shall live long; and therefore they are loth to depart from any thing while they live, lest, if they should be liberal to the poor, they themselves should want and have need.

Infidelity is the root of all evil.

Son. Infidelity, unfaithfulness, mistrust, or lack of belief is the occasion of all this mischief, as it is the only cause of all evils besides. If the rich men had a true faith in God, and were thoroughly persuaded of God's liberality and good-will toward them, they would soon give over this their covetousness, and become merciful to the poor

Prov. xix.

people. Salomon saith: "He that hath pity upon the poor lendeth unto the Lord; and look, what he layeth out it shall be paid him again." Also in another place he

Prov. xxviii.

saith: "He that giveth unto the poor shall not lack; but he that turneth away his eyes from such as be in necessity shall suffer great poverty himself."

Luke vi.

Our Saviour Christ saith: "Give, and it shall be given unto you: good measure, and pressed down, and shaken together, and running over, shall men give into your bosoms. For with the same measure that ye mete withal shall other men mete to you again." If the covetous rich worldlings did believe these promises and such-like, which God hath made and set forth in the holy scriptures to all such as are liberal to the poor, they would never be so unmerciful as they are, nor defer their alms so much as one hour, but freely and plenteously give whensoever occasion is offered. Is not this

---

[1 Νυσταγμὸς δὲ, ὁ θάνατος. χρονισμὸς δὲ τοῦ νυμφίου, τὸ μὴ συντόμως γίνεσθαι τὴν δευτέραν παρουσίαν...μωραὶ δὲ ὄντως εἰσὶν αἱ παρθένοι καὶ κατὰ τοῦτο, καθὸ τότε ἐζήτουν τὸ ἔλαιον, ὅτε οὐκ ἔτι καιρὸς πραγματείας. αἱ δὲ φρόνιμοι φασὶ, μήποτε οὐκ ἀρκέσῃ ἡμῖν καὶ ὑμῖν· ἡ γὰρ ἀρετὴ τοῦ πλησίον μου μόλις ἀρκέσει ἐκείνῳ πρὸς ἀπολογίαν, μήτιγε καὶ ἐμοί· ἕκαστος γὰρ ἐκ τῶν ἔργων αὐτοῦ δικαιωθήσεται, οὐχὶ τῶν τοῦ πλησίον· ἀλλ' αἱ μωραὶ πρὸς τοὺς πωλοῦντας ἀπέρχονται, τουτέστι, πρὸς τοὺς πένητας...ἀλλὰ γὰρ ἐκλείσθη αὐταῖς ἡ θύρα· μεταμελείας γὰρ καὶ ἐργασίας καιρὸς οὐκ ἔστι μετὰ τὴν ἐνθένδε ἀποβίωσιν.—Theophyl. Op. Venet. 1754-63. In Matt. Comm. cap. xxv. Tom. I. pp. 136, 7.]

[2 'Αλλ' ὀψὲ γοῦν συναισθώμεθα, ποῖ φερόμεθα, καὶ ὅτι ἐν τῇ ἡμέρᾳ ἐκείνῃ οὔτε κάμνειν δυνάμεθα, ἐργασίας γὰρ οὐκ ἔστι τότε καιρὸς, οὔτε ἐπαιτεῖν εὐπρεπές.—Id. In Luc. Comm. cap. xvi. p. 413.]

[3 'Αλλ' ἀπολαύσας αὐτῶν παρὰ πᾶσάν μου τὴν ζωὴν, μετὰ τὴν τελευτὴν τοῦ βίου διαδόχους ποιήσομαι τῶν ἐμοὶ προσόντων τοὺς πένητας, γράμμασι καὶ διαθήκαις κυρίους αὐτοὺς τῶν ἐμῶν ἀποδείξας. ὅτε οὐκέτι ἔσῃ ἐν ἀνθρώποις, τότε γενήσῃ φιλάνθρωπος· ὅταν νεκρόν σε ἴδω, τότε σε εἴπω φιλάδελφον; πολλή σοι χάρις τῆς φιλοτιμίας, ὅτι ἐν τῷ μνήματι κείμενος, καὶ εἰς γῆν διαλυθεὶς, ἁδρὸς γέγονας ταῖς δαπάναις καὶ μεγαλόψυχος. ποίων, εἰπέ μοι, καιρῶν τοὺς μισθοὺς ἀπαιτήσεις, τῶν ἐν τῇ ζωῇ, ἢ τῶν μετὰ τὴν ἀποβίωσιν; ἀλλ' ὃν μὲν ἔζης χρόνον, καθηδυπαθῶν τοῦ βίου καὶ τῇ τρυφῇ διαῤῥέων, οὐδὲ προσβλέπειν ἠνείχου τοὺς πένητας· ἀποθανόντος δὲ, ποία μὲν πρᾶξις; ποῖος δὲ μισθὸς ἐργασίας ὀφείλεται; δεῖξον τὰ ἔργα, καὶ ἀπαίτει τὰς ἀνταποδόσεις. οὐδεὶς μετὰ τὸ λυθῆναι τὴν πανήγυριν πραγματεύεται.—Basil. Op. Par. 1721-30. Hom. in Divit. Tom. II. p. 60.]

the saying of the psalmograph? "I have been young, and now am old; and yet saw I the righteous never forsaken, nor his seed begging their bread. He is always merciful, and lendeth; yet his seed hath God's plenty and enough." Psal. xxxvii.

As touching the hope of long life, who knoweth not how short and uncertain the life of man is? "What is your life?" saith St James, "it is even a vapour, that appeareth for a little time, and then vanisheth away." The history of the rich man set forth in the gospel sheweth evidently how vain it is for rich men to gather great heaps of worldly goods, and to promise themselves long life to enjoy the same. "The ground of a certain rich man," saith our Saviour Christ, "brought forth plentiful fruits; and he thought within himself, saying, What shall I do, because I have no room where to bestow my fruits? And he said, This will do. I will destroy my barns, and build greater, and therein will I gather all my goods that are grown unto me, and I will say to my soul, Soul, thou hast much goods laid up in store for many years: take thine ease, eat, drink, be merry. But God said unto him, Thou fool, this night will they fetch away thy soul again from thee. Then whose shall those things be which thou hast provided?" Our Saviour Christ concludeth, and saith: "So is it with him that gathereth riches to himself, and is not rich toward God." "Take heed therefore," saith he, "and beware of covetousness. For no man's life standeth in the abundance of things which he possesseth." James iv. Luke xii.

Here see we what great preparation this covetous rich worldling made, yea, and that for a great number of years, and promised himself many joyful days and long life, when notwithstanding even out of hand he lost both life and goods, leaving all his possessions, he knew not to whom; so truly is it said of the psalmograph: "He (the covetous man) heapeth treasure upon treasure, and cannot tell for whom he gathereth his treasure." Psal. xxxix.

Father. It is to be wished that all rich men were so mercifully disposed toward the poor, that they might freely and with a good conscience say with Job: "When the poor have desired any thing at me, have I denied it them? Have I caused the widow to stand waiting for me in vain? Have I eaten my portion alone, that the fatherless hath had no part with me? For mercy grew up with me from my youth, and compassion from my mother's womb. Have I seen any man perish through nakedness and want of clothing? Or any poor man for lack of raiment, whose sides thanked me not, because he was warmed with the wool of my sheep? Did I ever lift up mine hand to hurt the fatherless? Yea, in the gate, where I saw myself to be in authority? Then let mine arm fall from my shoulder, and mine arm-holes be broken from the joints. For I have ever feared the vengeance and punishment of God, and knew very well that I was not able to bear his burden. Have I put my trust in gold? Or have I said to my finest gold of all, Thou art my confidence? Have I rejoiced because my power was great, and because my hand gat so much? Did I ever greatly regard the rising of the sun? Or had I the going down of the moon in great reputation? Hath my heart meddled privily with any deceit? Or did I ever kiss mine own hand? That were a wickedness worthy to be punished; for then should I have denied the God that is above. Have I ever rejoiced at the hurt of mine enemy? Or was I ever glad that any harm happened unto him? O no! I never suffered my mouth to do such a sin, as to wish him evil." "I have not suffered a stranger to lie without; but I opened my doors unto him that went by the way." Job xxxi.

Son. If our rich men would follow this godly rich man Job, whose words ye have now recited, then should they better do their duty toward the poor than many of them do at this present day, which rather poll and pill the poor people, and seek how to undo them, than succour, comfort, and relieve them: yea, then should they shew themselves true dispensators, faithful administrators, and good stewards of the Lord's goods, and "lay up in store for themselves a good foundation against the time to come," as the apostle saith, "that they may obtain everlasting life." 1 Tim. vi.

Father. God give them grace so to do, and always to have this admonition of our Saviour Christ before their eyes! "Take heed and beware of covetousness. For no man's life standeth in the abundance of things which he possesseth." But now, my son, seeing we have so largely conferred of the office of rich men, I would now gladly Luke xii.

hear the duty of the poor labouring man, that we may also call to remembrance what he ought to do, that he be no unprofitable member of the christian commonweal. *Son.* Order requireth that we should now entreat of that matter; therefore I will do it gladly.

OF THE OFFICE AND DUTY OF POOR LABOURING MEN.

First, it is the duty of them which are poor, and by the reason of their poverty are compelled to labour (although no man in a christian commonweal ought to be idle, but to work some good thing unto the glory of God, and unto the relief of the poor, be he never so rich or wealthy), not to disdain, nor to bear it heavily, that they are enforced to get their living with the labour of their hands and with the sweat of their brows, nor to think that God hateth them because they live not in this world so easily and delicately as the wealthier sort do, nor yet to envy such as be rich, or unjustly to take away other men's goods; but rather quietly and patiently to live in their vocation, being assured that they are called thereunto by the providence of God, diligently to labour for their living, truly to eat their own bread, faithfully to dispose themselves in all their doings, and charitably to behave themselves toward all men, with this faithful persuasion and assured hope, that God will so bless and fortunate
Tob. iv. their labours, that they shall want no good thing, as Tobias said to his son: "My son, be not afraid: truth it is we lead here a poor life; but great good shall we have if we fear God, and depart from all sin, and do well."

Father. The state then of a labouring man, of an artificer, or of a common citizen, that eateth his bread in the sweat of his face, pleaseth God, and is acceptable unto him. *Son.* No less than the state of a king or of an emperor. For it is the Lord from whom cometh both riches and poverty. It is the Lord that enricheth and impo-
Psal. cxiii. verisheth, as it is written: "The Lord maketh poor and maketh rich, bringeth low, and heaveth up on high. He raiseth up the poor out of the dust, and lifteth up the beggar from the dung-hill; to set him among princes, and to ennoble him with the
☞ seat of glory." And to speak plainly, there is no condition of life more pleasant in the sight of God, than that which is passed over in labour and honest exercises. Did
Gen. ii. not God appoint man even in the state of his innocency to dress and keep the garden of Eden, otherwise called paradise? Did not God also command man, after he had
Gen. iii. offended, that he should eat his bread in the sweat of his face, till he returned unto the earth?

And this commandment was not only given to Adam, but also to all his posterity. Therefore according to this commandment all the holy men and women of the old testament gave themselves to labour, and did eat their bread and drink their drink in the labour of their hands and in the sweat of their brows. Likewise in the new
Mark vi. testament none refused labour. Our Saviour Christ was a carpenter. His apostles
Matt. iv. were fishermen. St Paul was a tent-maker, and rejoiceth in many places of his epistles
Acts xviii. xx. that he gained his bread with the labour of his hands. And so forth, from time to time, all godly persons in every age gave themselves to some godly exercise, that they might not be unprofitable members of the christian commonweal: whereof we may easily conclude that no life pleaseth God better than that which is passed over in labour; as I may speak nothing, how that there is no meat eaten more merrily and with a better conscience than that which is gotten with labour, as the psalmograph
Psal. cxxviii. saith: "Thou shalt eat the labours of thine hands: O well is thee, and happy shalt thou be."

And although the poor labouring men have not such abundance of worldly goods, nor so delicate fare, as the rich and voluptuous worldlings have; yet let them be content and praise God in their frugality, which hath promised that they, labouring according to his will, shall want no good thing, neither will he suffer them to perish for hunger, but minister unto them all good things; so that they shall lack nothing
Psal. xxxiv. that is necessary for them and theirs. "They which seek the Lord," saith David,

"shall want no manner of thing that is good." For "behold, the eye of the Lord is upon them that fear him, and upon them that put their trust in his mercy, to deliver their souls from death, and to feed them in the time of dearth." Again: "I have been young, and now am old; and yet saw I never the righteous forsaken, nor his seed begging their bread." And who knoweth not, that "a small thing which the righteous hath is better than great riches of the ungodly? For the arms of the ungodly shall be broken; but the Lord upholdeth the righteous." Are not these the words of Salomon? "Better is a little with the fear of the Lord, than great treasure with sorrow." Again: "Better is it to have a little thing with righteousness, than great rents wrongfully gotten." And Salomon in his prayer desired of God, that he would give him neither poverty nor riches, but only a necessary living. Jacob desired of God no more but bread to eat, and clothes to put on. St Paul saith: "Godliness is great riches, if a man be content with that he hath. For we brought nothing into the world, neither may we carry any thing out. If we have food and raiment, let us therewith be content. For they that will be rich fall into temptation and snares, and into many foolish and noisome lusts, which drown men into perdition and destruction. For covetousness of money is the root of all evil, which while some men lusted after, they erred from the faith, and tangled themselves with many sorrows. But thou, man of God, flee such things. Follow righteousness, godliness, faith, love, patience, meekness, &c." Again he saith: "Let your conversation be without covetousness, and be content with such things as ye have already. For he hath said, I will not fail thee, neither forsake thee: so that we may boldly say, The Lord is my helper, and I will not fear what man may do unto me."

Psal. xxxiii. Psal. xxxvii. Prov. xv. Prov. xvi. Prov. xxx. Gen. xxviii. 1 Tim. vi. Heb. xiii. Josh. i. Psal. cxviii.

Secondly, it is the duty of all godly labourers, of whatsoever art or occupation they be, diligently, truly, and faithfully to labour, always setting before their eyes that God beholdeth all their doings, and will reward them according to their acts. Again, that in all their travails, labours, and exercises, they use no craft, wiliness, and subtilty with their neighbours; but that they deal with all men honestly, justly, uprightly, and brotherly, all fraud and guile, all falsehood and dissimulation, utterly laid aside; forasmuch as they know that God can abide no such wickedness, but will most extremely punish it, as the psalmograph saith: "Thou art the God that hath no pleasure in wickedness; neither shall the evil dwell with thee. The unrighteous shall not abide in thy sight; for thou hatest all them that work iniquity. Thou shalt destroy them that speak leasing: the Lord will abhor both the bloodthirsty and deceitful man." The holy apostle also saith: "This is the will of God, that no man oppress or defraud his brother in bargaining; because that the Lord is the avenger of all such things."

Psal. v. 1 Thess. iv.

How the labouring man shall use his goods.

Thirdly, such goods as the labouring men get by their industry and diligence, which also is the blessing and gift of God, they must take heed that they spend them warely and honestly, and not wastefully and wickedly. Many, whatsoever they win all the whole week past, they lash it out prodigally at the tavern or ale-house on the Sunday, and never cease riotously to waste their gains, till all be brought to nought; no care in the mean while had for their careful wife, poor children, and miserable family. Another sort consume their goods in dicing and carding, and in such-like wicked pastimes. Another company bestow all that ever they have in gallant apparel and fine array, far passing their degree and estate, without any respect had to their necessary charges. Another sort are so hard and niggardly, so hold-fast and wedded to the world, that whatsoever they can get, they so hoard it up, that they had rather that their wife and children should perish for hunger than they gladly would spend a groat for their relief, like unto him which said: "The savour of lucre is good, howsoever a man come by it[1]," yea, and that of every thing.

Thus may not the godly labouring man be affected and minded; but whatsoever God send him by the labour of his hands and by the sweat of his brows, let him give God thanks for it, and make merry with it, he, his wife, his children, and his family; nothing doubting, but that Lord, which is "rich enough for all them that

Rom. x.

[[1] Juv. xiv. 204, 5.]

call on him," will abundantly provide for him and his, if he go forth diligently to labour according to his vocation and calling, as St Paul saith: "The Lord is at hand. Be careful for nothing." Also St Peter: "Cast all your care upon the Lord; for he careth for you." "There is a sore plague," saith the wise man, "which I have seen under the sun, even riches kept to the hurt of him that hath them in possession. For oftentimes they perish with his great misery and trouble; and if he have a child, it getteth nothing. Like as he came naked out of his mother's womb, so goeth he thither again, and carrieth nothing away with him of all his labour. This is a miserable plague, that he shall go away even as he came. What helpeth it them then, that he hath laboured in the wind? All the days of his life also he did eat in the dark, with great carefulness, sickness, and sorrow. Therefore methink it is a better and fairer thing, a man to eat and drink, and to be refreshed of all his labour, that he taketh under the sun, all the days of his life which God giveth him; for this is his portion. For unto whomsoever God giveth riches, goods, and power, he giveth it him to enjoy it, to take it for his portion, and to be refreshed of his labour: this is the gift of God. For he thinketh not much how long he shall live; forsomuch as God filleth his heart with gladness."

Phil. iv. 1 Pet. v. Eccles. v.

Moreover, let him eschew all superfluous expenses, all riotous company, all vain pastimes, all banqueting, &c. and think, that it is the part of an honest man rather ¶ to spend a pound in his own house with his wife and children, than a penny in the tavern or ale-house. "Be merry with the wife of thy youth," saith Salomon, "as with a loving hind and friendly roe. Let her breasts always satisfy thee, and hold thee content with her love." "Keep not company with wine-bibbers and riotous eaters of flesh; for such as be drunkards and riotous shall come to poverty, and he that is given to much sleep shall go with a ragged coat." "Who hath wo? who hath sorrow? who hath strife? who hath brawling? and who hath wounds without cause? or who hath red eyes? Even they that be ever at the wine and seek excess. Look not thou upon the wine, how red it is, and what a colour it giveth in the glass. It goeth down softly, but at the last it biteth like a serpent, and stingeth as an adder. So shall thine eyes look unto strange women, and thine heart shall muse upon froward things," &c. "He that hath pleasure in banquets shall be a poor man; and whoso delighteth in wine and delicates shall not be rich." "For wine maketh a man lecherous, and strong drink causeth a man to be unquiet: whoso delighteth therein shall never be wise."

Prov. v. Prov. xxiii. Prov. xxi. Prov. xx.

Of the apparel of labouring men.

Again, as concerning his apparel, let the labouring man provide that it be not too much sumptuous, but honest, grave, seemly, and meet for his degree, and such in all points as becometh him that profess godliness, ever setting before his eyes this saying of Job: "Naked came I out of my mother's womb, and naked shall I return unto the earth again." The apostle saith: "If we have food, and wherewith we may be covered (he saith not, garnished and trimmed), let us be content;" "for nothing brought we into the world, neither shall we carry any thing out of it." The aforesaid apostle saith, that many godly men in times past "walked up and down in sheeps-skins and goats-skins, being destitute, troubled, and vexed." The raiment of St John Baptist was made of camel's hair, and his girdle was of leather. And our Saviour Christ, speaking of St John Baptist, saith: "What went ye out to see? A man clothed in soft raiment? Behold, they that wear soft clothing are in kings' houses." The wise man's counsel is, that we should not glory nor delight in gallant apparel; but if we have wherewith to cover our nakedness, it is sufficient, so it be seemly and honest.

Job i. 1 Tim. vi. Heb. xi. Matt. iii. Matt. xi.

But this is also to be considered, that the labouring man or artificer do so bestow his gains that he getteth with his labours, that, sufficient provision made for his household (for, as the apostle saith, "he that provideth not for his family hath denied the faith, and is worse than any infidel"), some portion thereof may more be ministered to the poor and needy, which lack and have not whereof to live, but only of the charitable alms of good and godly people. So admonisheth St Paul, saying: "Let him that stole steal no more; but let him rather labour with his hands the thing which is good, that he may give unto him that needeth." Yea, he shall sometime spare it from his own belly and back to give it unto the poor; forasmuch

1 Tim. v. Eph. iv.

as we all be members of one body. And this is it which God saith by the prophet: "Break thy bread to the hungry, and bring the poor wandering man into thy house: when thou seest a naked man, cover him, and despise not thine own flesh." Isai. lviii.

Fourthly, let every labouring man, of what condition soever he be, take heed that, although through his labour God have endued him with wealth and with abundance of possessions, he give not himself to idleness and to dissolution of life; but rather do his endeavour daily more and more to conserve and keep together his goods that he hath gotten, yea, to augment, increase, and enlarge them, that he may be the more able both to live himself, and also to give unto other that have need. For as the sage and wise Cato saith: "That which a man hath be long in getting is quickly spent and consumed[1]." And things come soon to nought that are not in time renewed. And albeit there are many things which bring hasty destruction to a man's substance, yet idleness excelleth all, as a most ready and present shipwreck of all good things, as the wise man saith: "He that tilleth his land shall have plenteousness of bread; but he that followeth idleness shall have poverty enough." "Idleness," as the gnomagraph[2] saith, "bringeth much evil." For the avoiding therefore of idleness, and for the continuance of work and labour so long as he liveth, it shall be convenient that the labourer or artificer do alway set before his eyes these sentences of the holy scripture. God saith: "In the sweat of the face shalt thou eat thy bread, till thou returnest unto the earth. For earth thou art, and unto earth thou shalt return." The godly man Job saith: "As the bird is born to fly, so is man born to labour." The psalmograph saith: "Thou shalt eat the labours of thine hands: O well is thee, and happy shalt thou be." Jesus, the son of Sirach, saith: "Let no laborious work be too tedious unto thee, neither the husbandry which the Almighty hath created." St Paul saith: "We beseech you, brethren, that ye increase more and more, and that ye study to be quiet, and to meddle with your own business, and to work with your own hands, as we commanded you; that ye may behave yourselves honestly toward them that are without, and that nothing be lacking unto you." Again: "When we were with you, this we warned you of, that if any would not work, the same should not eat." Once again: "We have heard say, that there are some which walk among you inordinately, working not at all, but being busy-bodies. Them that are such we command and exhort by our Lord Jesus Christ, that they work with quietness, and eat their own bread. Brethren, be not ye weary in well-doing."

Idleness of all men is to be eschewed. Prov. xxviii. Ecclus. xxxiii. Gen. iii. Job v. Psal. cxxviii. Ecclus. vii. 1 Thess. iv. 2 Thess. iii.

These and such-like sentences shall greatly encourage the labouring man to eschew idleness, and to go forth according to his vocation to labour and travail, that he may have the more abundantly both to feed his own family, and also to give to such as have need.

Fifthly and finally, forasmuch as we live not only before God, but also before man, and we are commanded so to live, that with our godly conversation we may beautify and "garnish the doctrine of our Saviour Christ Jesus," and "stop the mouths of foolish and ignorant men;" it shall be convenient that the labouring man or artificer seek diligently to live with his neighbours honestly, quietly, and uprightly, and not to be a busy-body among them, or to stir up dissension, contention, strife, and debate; but to the uttermost of his power to conserve and maintain unity, peace, and concord, both public and private, as the apostle counselleth: "Provide," saith he, "aforehand things honest, not only before God, but also in the sight of all men. If it be possible, as much as is in you, live peaceably with all men." Likewise saith St Peter: "Be ye all of one mind, of one heart, love as brethren, be pitiful, be courteous, not rendering evil for evil, or rebuke for rebuke; but contrariwise bless; knowing that ye are thereunto called, even that ye should be heirs of the blessing. For he that doth long after life, and liveth to see good days, let him refrain his tongue from evil, and his lips that they speak no guile. Let him eschew evil, and do good: let him seek peace, and ensue it."

Tit. ii. 1 Pet. ii. Rom. xii. 1 Pet. iii. Psal. xxxiv.

[1 Labitur exiguo, quod partum est tempore longo. —Caton. Dist. Mor. Lib. II.]

[2 Gnomagraph: proverb, or maxim writer.]

Therefore, seeing we are all men, and cannot at all times so circumspectly live, but sometime one of us offend another; if any such thing chance between his neighbour and him, let the labouring man or artificer straightways seek a reconciliation, and procure the renewing of love and amity so soon as is possible, as the holy apostle

Eph. iv. saith: "Be angry, and sin not. Let not the sun go down upon your wrath; neither give place unto the backbiter." Let no grudge nor malice long remain, lest, being festered and cankered, it be hard to be put away; but straightways remove it, and

Reconciliation. in the stead thereof place again love and friendship. If any possessed with an evil spirit would sow dissension between him and his neighbour, by making false report, let him not be light of credit, but straightways repair to his neighbour, and lovingly and friendly break the matter to his neighbour; and, when he have once proved it contrary, desire him to shew him the like kindness, if any chance to bring any slanderous reports of him also. But if it so be that the matter be found true, as it is reported, then let him charitably admonish his neighbour, and exhort him from henceforth to behave himself more christianly and neighbourly, and none otherwise to report of him than he himself would be reported. By no means let him seek to be avenged, nor to render evil for evil; but rather follow the counsel of St Paul, which

Rom. xii. saith: "Dearly beloved, avenge not yourselves, but rather give place unto wrath.

Deut. xxxii. For it is written, Vengeance is mine, and I will reward, saith the Lord. Therefore, if thine enemy hunger, feed him; if he thirst, give him drink: for in so doing thou shalt heap coals of fire on his head. Be not overcome of evil, but overcome evil

Col. iii. with goodness." Again: "If any man have a quarrel against another, as Christ forgave you, even so do ye. Above all things put on love, which is the bond of perfection. And the peace of God rule in your hearts, to the which peace ye are called in one body."

Furthermore, in all his labours and travails, in all his buyings and sellings, and in all his other businesses which he hath to do with his neighbour, let him do to another as he would be done to; not seeking his own profit, to the hurt and damage

1 Cor. x. of other, as St Paul saith: "Let no man seek that which is [his] own; but let every man seek that which belongeth to another;" for "we are all brethren and members of one body." In fine, let him be that to his neighbour that he wisheth God to be unto him.

Father. If the common people would thus behave themselves one toward another, then should we have a joyful and a quiet commonweal; then should hatred, malice, and all displeasure be soon banished, and love, amity, and concord quickly enter in; then should penury, scarceness, and dearth of things, wherewith, through the covetousness of certain insatiable covetous men, the poor people are now most miserably grieved and oppressed, be utterly taken away from us; and in their place succeed abundance and plenty of all good things, according to the abundant and plenteous blessings of

1 Tim. vi. God, wherewith he daily most richly enricheth us, as St Paul saith: "God giveth us abundantly all things to enjoy them." But now, my son, let me hear the duty of all degrees in common, according to thy promise, and so make an end. *Son*. Most gladly.

OF THE OFFICE AND DUTY OF ALL DEGREES AND ESTATES GENERALLY.

Of our duty toward God. Of faith. Heb. xi. Rom. xiv. Heb. xi.

First of all and above all things, all men owe unto God faith, which is the ground and foundation of the christian religion, "without the which faith it is not possible to please God;" yea, without the which faith, all that ever we do is plain sin, and abominable before God. "For he that cometh unto God must believe that God is, and that he will reward them that seek him."

Father. How provest thou that it is the duty of all men generally to believe in

Prov. iii. God? *Son*. The wise man saith: "Have faith in the Lord with all thine heart, and

2 Chron. xx. lean not unto thine own wisdom." Jehosaphat saith: "Believe in the Lord your

Ecclus. xxxii. God, and ye shall be without jeopardy." Jesus, the son of Sirach, saith: "In all thy works believe thou in the Lord from thy whole heart; for that is the keeping of the commandments. Whoso believeth God's word taketh heed to the commandments; and he that putteth his trust in the Lord shall want nothing." Again: "O ye that fear the Lord, believe him; and your reward shall not be empty." Our Saviour Christ saith: "Ye believe in God, believe ye also in me." "For this is the will of him that sent me, that every one that seeth the Son and believeth in him have everlasting life." And St John saith: "This is his commandment, that we believe on the name of his Son Jesus Christ." "Abraham believed God," saith the scripture; "and it was counted unto him for righteousness." Ecclus. ii. John xiv. John vi. 1 John iii. Gen. xv. Rom. iv.

Father. What owe we unto God more than faith, that is to say, to believe him and his holy word, and by no means to doubt of it?

Son. Secondly, forasmuch as "faith worketh by charity" or love, we must provide that we do not only believe in the Lord our God with our whole heart, but also that we most entirely love him, and have all our delight and pleasure in him. Of love. Gal. v.

Father. Where are we commanded so to do? *Son.* Moses saith: "Hear, O Israel: the Lord our God is Lord only; and thou shalt love the Lord thy God with all thine heart, and with all thy soul, and with all thy might." Josua saith: "Take good heed unto yourselves, that ye love the Lord your God." David saith: "Love the Lord, all ye his saints; for the Lord preserveth them that are faithful." Deut. vi. Josh. xxiii. Psal. xxxi.

Father. Doth the Lord our God require of us any more, but to believe in him and to love him? *Son.* Yea, verily.

Thirdly, as out of faith love, so likewise out of love springeth the fulfilling of God's holy law; at the least an earnest study and fervent desire to frame our lives according to the same, whereby we also shew even before men, that our faith and love which we have inwardly toward God, and which are only known to God, are true and unfeigned. This also is therefore required of us, that, as we believe and love God, so likewise we address ourselves with all our power unto the accomplishment of his holy will; which both necessarily and orderly followeth, as our Saviour Christ saith: "If any man love me, he will keep my word; and my Father will love him; and we will come unto him, and dwell with him; but he that loveth me not keepeth not my word." Again: "If ye love me, keep my commandments." For "he that hath my commandments, and keep them, he it is that loveth me." "Abide in my love. If ye keep my commandments, ye shall abide in my love, even as I have kept my Father's commandments, and I abide in his love." "Ye are my friends, if ye do things which I command you." This obedience and earnest study to address our conversation according to the blessed will of God must be coupled with a reverent fear toward God, which, as a bit, may restrain us from all evil, and, as a spur, may prick us forward unto all goodness and virtue. A new life. John xiv. John xv. Of fear.

Father. Where is that commanded? *Son.* The preacher saith: "Fear God, and keep his commandments; for that belongeth unto all men." The psalmograph saith: "O fear the Lord, all ye his saints; for they that fear him shall lack nothing." The prophet Micheas saith: "What acceptable thing shall I offer unto the Lord? Shall I bow my knee to the high God? Shall I come before him with brent-offerings, and with calves of a year old? Hath the Lord a pleasure in many thousand rams, or innumerable streams of oil? Or shall I give my first-born for mine offences, and the fruit of my body for the sin of my soul? I will shew thee, O man, what is good, and what the Lord requireth of thee; namely, to do right, to have pleasure in loving-kindness, to be lowly, and to walk with thy God." And by another prophet himself saith: "The son honoureth his father, and the servant feareth his lord. If I now be a father, where is mine honour? if I be the Lord, where is my fear? saith the Lord of hosts." Eccles. xii. Psal. xxxiv. Mic. vi. Mal. i.

Father. Requireth God any thing of us besides those things which thou hast now recited? *Son.* There yet remaineth one thing behind.

Father. What is that?

Son. Fourthly and finally, our duty toward the Lord our God is, forasmuch as sometime in this wretched world we be assaulted with the bitter storms of adversity, and so oppressed with them that we know not what to do; to resort unto God, Of prayer.

which is a present helper in all troubles, be they never so many and grievous, with fervent prayer, and earnestly to call upon him, that he may be our defence, shield, and buckler against all assaults of our enemies, and against all the bitter storms of adversity, nothing doubting but that, as he hath promised, so likewise he both can and will hear and deliver us from all evil: again, whensoever fortune smileth upon us, not to be proud and arrogant, and to forget God; but rather to be thankful unto him for those his benefits, to use them unto the glory of his holy name, and ever to walk worthy the loving-kindness of so loving and kind a Father.

Of thanksgiving.

Father. Where are we commanded to pray unto God in our adversity? *Son*. God saith by the psalmograph: "Call on me in the time of thy trouble, and I will deliver thee, and thou shalt glorify me." Salomon also saith: "The name of the Lord is a mighty strong tower: unto that the righteous flieth, and findeth succour;" as the prophet saith: "Whosoever calleth on the name of the Lord shall be safe." "For there is one Lord of all, rich enough for all that call on him: he that putteth his trust in him shall never be confounded."

Psal. l. Prov. xviii. Joel [ii.] Acts [ii.] Rom. x. Isai. xxviii.

Father. And where are we commanded to give thanks to God in our prosperity? *Son*. The psalmograph saith: "Offer unto God the sacrifice of praise." Again: "I will praise the name of God with a song, and magnify it with thanksgiving. This shall please the Lord better than a bullock that hath horns and hoofs." God himself: "Whoso offereth me thanks and praise, he honoureth me; and to him that ordereth his conversation aright will I shew the salvation of God."

Psal. l.

Father. This is the duty of all Christians toward their Lord God, that thou hast now recited. *Son*. Yea, verily.

Father. What now remaineth? *Son*. That I declare the duty of all men toward their neighbours.

Of our duty toward our neighbours.

Father. What is that? *Son*. To love our neighbour as ourself, and to do none otherwise to other than we would that other should do to us.

Father. Where is that commandment? *Son*. As concerning love toward our neighbour, the holy scripture hath this commandment in divers places: "Thou shalt love thy neighbour as thyself." And our Saviour Christ saith: "A new commandment give I unto you, that ye love together; as I have loved you, that even so ye love one another. By this shall all men know that ye are my disciples, if ye have love one to another." St Peter saith: "Above all things have fervent love among you; for love shall cover the multitude of sins." St John saith: "If any man say, I love God, and yet hateth his brother, he is a liar; for he that loveth not his brother, whom he hath seen, God, whom he hath not seen, how can he love? And this commandment have we of him, that he which loveth God, should also love his brother." Hereto agreeth the saying of St Paul: "Owe nothing to any man, but this, that ye love one another. For he that loveth another hath fulfilled the law. For these commandments, Thou shalt not commit adultery, Thou shalt not kill, Thou shalt not steal, Thou shalt not bear false witness, Thou shalt not lust, and so forth; if there be any other commandment, it is all comprehended in this saying, namely, Love thy neighbour as thyself. Love hurteth not his neighbour. Therefore is love the fulfilling of the law." And touching that this is also our duty, none otherwise to do unto our neighbour than we would he should do unto us, this saying our Saviour Christ maketh most plain and evident: "Whatsoever ye would that men should do to you, do ye even so to them also. For this is the law and the prophets." Likewise saith old Tobias: "Look that thou never do to another man that thing which thou wouldest not that another should do to thee." With this agreeth the saying of the heathen philosopher Cleobulus Lindius: "Do not that unto another which thou thyself hatest."

Of love toward our neighbour. Lev. xix. Matt. xxii. Rom. xiii. Gal. v. John xiii. 1 Pet. iv. 1 John iv. Rom. xiii. Exod. xx. Deut. v. Matt. v. Luke xviii. Matt. vii. Luke vi. Tob. [iv.]

Father. Now have we heard what all men ought to do both toward God and toward their neighbour. Is there yet any thing remaining? *Son*. Now that we have heard what all sort of us without exception ought to do both unto God and unto our neighbour, it only remaineth that we now express, declare, shew, and set forth, what our duty is every man unto himself, that we may walk with joyful and merry consciences before God and man.

Of the duty of every man toward himself.

Father. What is that? *Son.* First, forasmuch as God desireth nothing of us so greatly as the heart, as he saith by Salomon, "My son, give me thine heart;" and the scripture saith, "Thou shalt love the Lord thy God with all thy heart," &c.; again: "Turn unto the Lord your God with all your heart," &c.; item: "They honour me with their lips, but their heart is far from me; verily they worship me in vain," &c.; it is convenient above all things that we keep our heart pure and clean, and utterly estranged from all corruption of wickedness, according to the admonition of the wise man: "Keep thine heart with all diligence; for thereupon hangeth life." Likewise saith God by the prophet: "Wash thine heart from wickedness, that thou mayest be saved." For God detesteth, abhorreth, and hateth nothing more than an unpure and unclean heart, as he delighteth and hath pleasure in nothing so greatly as in an heart that is pure, as our Saviour Christ saith: "Blessed are the pure in heart; for they shall see God." This may we evidently see in the history of Abel and Cain. The sacrifices of Abel were accepted and allowed of God, because they came from a pure and clean heart; but the oblations of Cain were utterly rejected and cast away, because they came from an unpure and unclean heart. Likewise the works of the scribes and Pharisees and of such-like hypocrites were highly allowed of men, because outwardly they glistered with a certain shine of holiness: but our Saviour Christ, which knew the filthy uncleanness of those most filthy and unclean hypocrites, compared them unto "painted sepulchres, which appear beautiful outward, but are within full of dead men's bones;" and said unto them: "Even so ye also outwardly appear righteous unto men; but within ye are full of hypocrisy and wickedness." Again: "Ye are they which justify yourselves before men: but God knoweth your hearts. For that which is highly esteemed amongst men, is abominable in the sight of God."

Prov. xxiii. Deut. vi. Matt. xxii. Mark xii. Joel ii. Isai. xxix. Matt. xv. Mark vii. Of the heart. Prov. iv. Jer. iv. Prov. vi. Matt. v. Matt. xxiii.

Now, forasmuch as nothing doth so defile the heart as unclean thoughts ("for froward thoughts separate a man from God," saith the wise man, "and the Holy Ghost withdraweth himself from the thoughts that are without understanding, and where wickedness hath the upper hand he flieth from thence;" yea, "inquisition shall be made at the day of judgment for the thoughts of the ungodly"), we must above all things take heed of Satan, which "goeth about like a roaring lion, seeking whom he may devour;" and of the flesh, which "always lusteth against the Spirit;" and also of the world, which ceaseth not with her vain pleasures and deceivable riches to allure men's hearts from the true, constant, and immortal goods unto the desire of vain and transitory things. If these at any time go about to occupy and possess our hearts, and to estrange them from the most wholesome considerations of God and of his holy law, and to allure them unto the meditation of wicked, unclean, and godless things, and so pollute and defile the inward man, which is "the temple of the Holy Ghost;" let us by no means consent to their subtile suggestions and crafty persuasions, but rather manfully resist them, and not so much as once suffer them to enter into our hearts, no, not with one evil thought, but in all things keep our hearts so pure and so clean both toward God and our neighbour, that the Holy Ghost may vouchsafe to make his mansion and dwelling-place in us for ever.

Matt. xv. Mark vii. Wisd. i. Of thoughts. 1 Pet. v. Gal. v. 1 John ii.

And that this thing may the more fortunately come to pass, let us at all times, so much as is possible, sequester our minds from all worldly and carnal things, and so "use the world as though we used it not," and so live in the flesh as persons wholly mortified to the flesh, as St Paul saith, "They truly that are Christ's have crucified the flesh with the affections and lusts:" again, forasmuch as of ourselves we are frail vessels, and are soon overcome of these our so mighty enemies, as we may see in Adam, David, Salomon, Lot, Noah, Peter, Magdalen, and in divers other the elect people of God; it shall be necessary that we give ourselves oftentimes to prayer, and crave help at the hand of our Lord God against these cruel and fierce adversaries, according to the most wholesome counsel of our Saviour Christ, which saith: "Watch and pray, that ye fall not into temptation. The spirit is ready; but the flesh is weak." Let us pray unto our heavenly Father, as the Lord Christ taught us: "O heavenly Father, lead us not into temptation, but deliver us from evil." Let us also pray with David: "Make me a clean heart, O God, and renew a right spirit within me.

1 Cor. vii. Gal. v. Gen. iii. 2 Sam. xii. 1 Kings xi. Gen. xix. Gen. ix. Matt. xxvi. Luke vii. Matt. xxvi. Matt. vi. Psal. li.

Cast me not away from thy presence, and take not thy holy Spirit from me. O give me the comfort of thy help again, and stablish me with thy free Spirit."

[Note well.] It shall also profit greatly unto the keeping of our heart pure and estranged from vain, wicked, carnal, worldly, and idle thoughts, if every one of us do consider with ourselves unto what vice we are most of all bent, and when we are provoked thereunto, either of the devil, of the world, or of the flesh, straightways to resist those temptations with some sentence of the holy scripture. For there is not a better armour against [Eph. vi.] the infernal army than "the sword of the Spirit, which is the word of God." Therefore [Psal. cxix.] said David: "In my heart have I hidden thy words, that I might not sin against thee." And to give us an example hereof, our grand Captain and Lord Jesus Christ [Matt. iv.] took unto him this armour when Satan assaulted him, and so put him to flight. [Prov. xxx.] "The word of God is pure and clean; yea, it is a shield unto all them that trust [Rom. i.] unto it." "It is the power of God to save so many as believe." Let us therefore furnish our breasts with this armour of the holy scripture, and we shall become valiant and glorious conquerors.

[Idleness is above all things to be eschewed.] Moreover, to be ever well, virtuously, and godly occupied, and at all times to eschew idleness, is also a necessary thing to keep our hearts pure and clean. For idleness openeth a window to Satan and to all his satanical army, and encourageth them to assail us with their temptations; but such as are godly and virtuously occupied easily escape all such dangers.

Furthermore, this shall also greatly help unto the conservation of the cleanness of our hearts, if we, so soon as Satan, or the flesh, either the world, go about to assail us and to occupy our minds with their vile and vain suggestions, call straightways [Of death.] unto remembrance our death and departure from this world; and again, the terrible judgment of God against all wickedness; which God shall call us unto an account for every wicked thought, idle word, and sinful work, that we have done. To set these things before the eyes of our mind continually shall keep the inward man in a most goodly and godly order, so that not so much as a vain thought shall find any dwelling-place in us; so far is it off that we shall run headlong into all kind [Ecclus. vii.] of sin, as the wise man saith: "Remember thy latter end, and thou shalt never do amiss." If we on this wise labour to keep our hearts pure and clean, so that we suffer not so much as an ill thought to rule in them, whereby either God should be dishonoured, or our neighbour hindered, or our soul defiled; O who is able to express what a joy, yea, what a heaven we shall find in our consciences! as the wise [Prov. xv.] man saith: "A quiet heart is a continual feast." Again: "A merry heart maketh a cheerful countenance; but an heavy heart compelleth a man to sigh."

[Matt. xii.] Secondly, forasmuch as our Saviour Christ saith, "A good man out of the good [Of speech.] treasure of the heart bringeth forth good things," and "out of the abundance of the heart the mouth speaketh;" it is necessary that we out of a pure heart bring forth [Eph. iv.] pure words, even such words as may neither offend God nor man, but rather "edify and minister grace to the hearers;" yea, and that so much the more, because we are [Matt. xii.] taught in the gospel that at the day of judgment we "shall render an account of every [Prov. xxi.] idle word that we speak." The wise man saith: "Whoso keepeth his mouth and his [Prov. xiii.] tongue, the same keepeth his soul from troubles." Again: "He that keepeth his mouth [Eph. iv.] keepeth his life; but whoso openeth his lips to evil destroyeth himself." "Let no [Eph. v.] filthy communication proceed out of our mouths." "As for fornication and all uncleanness, or covetousness, or filthiness, or foolish talking, or jesting, which are not comely, let them not once be named among us, but rather giving of thanks, as it [James iii. Of the tongue.] becometh saints." And forasmuch (as St James saith) as "the tongue is a little member, and boasteth great things," and is so "set among our members that it defileth the whole body, and setteth afire all that we have of nature, and is itself set afire even of hell; yea, it is an unruly evil, full of deadly poison, and cannot be tamed of the nature of man (for therewith bless we God the Father, and therewith curse we men, [Gen. i.] which are made like unto the image of God);" it is meet that we, for the taming and ordering of so great an evil, flee unto God with hearty prayer, and beseech him so to dispose and govern our mouth, that nothing may flow out of it which shall not turn unto the glory of God, the profit of our neighbour, and the salvation of our souls. Let us pray with David, and say: "Set a watch, O Lord, before my mouth, and keep the doors of my lips." Psal. cxli.

Let us pray also with Salomon: "O God, remove from me vanity and lies." Let us likewise have this saying of the wise man ever before our eyes: "Put away from thee a froward mouth; and let the lips of slander be far from thee." "A man full of words," saith David, "shall not prosper upon the earth: evil shall hunt the wicked person to overthrow him." Prov. xxx. Prov. iv. Psal. cxl.

Thirdly, as it is our duty godly and virtuously to use our tongue, and with judgment so to dispose our words that no evil follow thereof; so likewise it becometh us soberly and modestly, gravely and temperately, to use all the other parts of the body. In our eyes let there neither appear pride nor wantonness. For "the Lord," saith Salomon, "abhorreth a proud look." Neither can he abide adulterous and whorish eyes. In consideration whereof the wise man, for a redress of both these evils, prayeth unto God on this manner: "O Lord, let me not have a proud look, but turn away all voluptuousness from me: take from me the lusts of the body: let not the desires of uncleanness take hold upon me, and give me not over into an unshamefaced and obstinate mind." It shall be good always to have in remembrance this saying of the wise man: "Let thine eyes behold the thing that is right; and let thine eye-lids look straight before thee." And that we may this do the more perfectly according to the will of God, it shall be convenient that we pray with David, and say: "O turn away mine eyes, lest they behold vanity; and quicken thou me in thy way." Of eyes. Prov. vi. Ecclus. xxiii. Prov. iv. Psal. cxix.

Moreover, with our hands let us work no wickedness. For "the Lord abhorreth ... those hands that shed innocent blood," saith Salomon. He also detesteth those hands which are guilty of theft or robbery, or of any other lewdness. The hands of the Christians ought not to be exercised in any point of wickedness, but in honest and godly travails and labours, as it is written: "Thou shalt eat the labours of thine hands." Again: "Let him that stole steal no more; but let him rather labour with his hands the thing which is good, that he may give unto him that needeth." St Paul glorieth and rejoiceth that he with the labour of his own hands fed both himself and such also as were with him. And who knoweth not, that "a man is born to labour, even as the bird is to fly?" And unto this end God hath given us our hands, even that we should work some good thing with them, profitable to ourselves and to our neighbours, and by no means to abuse them with any vain, wanton, ungodly, or wicked exercises, nor to suffer them to be idle; forasmuch as "an idle hand maketh poor, but a quick labouring hand maketh rich." Prov. vi. Of hands. Psal. cxxviii. Eph. iv. Acts xx. Job v. Prov. x.

Furthermore, our feet we ought so to direct, that they by no means haste unto wickedness. For "the Lord abhorreth ... the feet that be swift in running to do mischief." Unto taverns, ale-houses, play-houses, whore-houses, dancing-houses, and such other places of wickedness, let us by no means direct our steps; but rather unto such places where the word of God is to be heard; where the poor people are to be relieved and succoured; where honest and virtuous company do resort; where virtue is to be learned; where vice and all sin is abhorred; where we need not to be ashamed of our being; where we dare avouch both the place, the company, and the exercise, &c.; ever having before our eyes this saying of Salomon: "Ponder the path of thy feet; and let all thy ways be ordered aright. Turn not aside, neither to the right hand nor to the left; but withhold thy foot from evil. For the Lord knoweth the ways that are on the right hand. As for the ways that be on the left hand, they be froward; but he shall direct thy goings, and thy ways shall he guide in peace." Again: "The path of the righteous is to eschew evil; and whoso looketh well to his ways keepeth his own soul." Of feet. Prov. vi. Prov. iv. Prov. xvi.

And that we may thus trade our steps in all godliness and honesty, let us with the psalmograph pray on this manner, and say: "Thou, O Lord, hast charged that we shall diligently keep thy commandments. O that my ways were made so direct that I might keep thy statutes! So shall I not be confounded, while I have respect unto all thy commandments." "O make me to go in the path of thy commandments; for therein is my desire," &c. Psal. cxix.

And as it is our duty thus to use these members of our body which I have now spoken of, so in like manner are we bound by the commandment of God honestly and We ought to use godly all the members of our body.

godly to use the residue of the same, that our whole body may be the temple of the
1 Cor. iii. Holy Ghost, as St Paul saith: "Know ye not that ye are the temple of God, and how that the Spirit of God dwelleth in you? If any man defile the temple of God, him shall God destroy. For the temple of God is holy, which temple ye are." Again:
1 Cor. vi. "Know ye not how that your bodies are the temple of the Holy Ghost which dwelleth in you, whom ye have of God, and how that ye are not your own? For ye are dearly bought. Therefore glorify God in your bodies, and in your spirits, which are
2 Cor. vi. God's." Once again: "Bear not ye the yoke with the unbelievers. For what fellowship hath righteousness with unrighteousness? Or what company hath light with darkness? Or what concord hath Christ with Belial? Either what part hath he that believeth with an infidel? Or how agreeth the temple of God with images? For ye are the temple of the living God; as God said, I will dwell among them, and
Exod. xix. Lev. xxvi. Ezek. xxxvii. Isai. lii. walk among them; and will be their God, and they shall be my people. Wherefore come out from among them, and separate yourselves from them, saith the Lord, and touch none unclean thing. So will I receive you, and will be a Father unto you; and ye shall be my sons and daughters, saith the Lord Almighty."

Fourthly and finally, we shall then do our duty toward ourselves, and live with a merry conscience both before God and man, if we be that indeed that we are called; if our life answer to our profession; if we garnish the doctrine of God our Saviour with good works; if we "do all thing," as the apostle saith, "without murmuring and disputing, that we may be such as no man can complain on, and unfeigned sons of God, without rebuke in the midst of a crooked and perverse nation, and shine as great lights in the world, holding fast the word of life;" yea, to be short, then shall we do our duty toward ourselves, when we so live, that our conscience do never accuse us of any evil thing, neither in thought, word, nor deed; but rather at all times testify with us, that whatsoever we do is good and pleasant in the sight of God, and acceptable
2 Cor. i. before his divine Majesty. For "our rejoicing is this," saith the apostle, "even the testimony of our conscience, that in singleness (of heart) and godly pureness, and not in fleshly wisdom, but by the grace of God, we have had our conversation in the world."

To end, let every one of us so live that we may say with St Paul on this manner:
Acts xxiii. Acts xxiv. Heb. xiii. "I have lived in all good conscience before God until this day." Again: "I study to have alway a clear conscience toward God and toward men." Item: "We trust we have a good conscience among all men, and desire to live honestly." For no man is able to express what a precious jewel and noble treasure, yea, what a paradise and heaven,
Horat. Lib. i. Ep. 1. a good, pure, and clear conscience is. It is, as the poet saith, *Murus aheneus*, that is to say, "a wall of brass," a strong tower, and an invincible fortress.

Thus have I, most loving father, according to your commandment and will, declared unto you all the parts of the Catechism, and in such order as I learned them of our preacher and catechist. If I have not in all points satisfied your expectation, I shall desire you to consider my young and tender age, and my small exercise as yet in matters of christian religion. As I increase in age, so I trust also to increase in the knowledge of God's most holy will, that at the last I, through the Spirit of God, may grow and wax ancient in Christ, and so at the last become a perfect man in faith and truth; which thing I most humbly beseech God for his mercy, yea, for his dear Son Christ's sake, to grant me.

Father. Amen. O my most dear and dearly-beloved son, I thank God for thee, and I bless his holy name for the good gifts that he hath bestowed upon thee. And I most humbly beseech him for his holy name's sake, that, as he hath begun in this thy young and tender age to pour a good spirit into thee, and to bring thee unto the knowledge of the gospel of his Son Christ Jesu (which knowledge bringeth everlasting life); so it may please him of his fatherly goodness to continue this his favour toward thee, and daily more and more to multiply and increase these his heavenly benefits in thee; that in this world thou mayest be a good and profitable citizen of the christian commonweal, and in the world to come an inheritor of everlasting glory. For this I say unto thee, my dear son, thou hast not only satisfied mine expectation, but thou hast also greatly overcome it, and rendered a reason of thy faith and knowledge, far passing both mine opinion and thine age. But it is truly said of the psalmograph, in his prayer unto God: "Out of the mouth of babes and sucklings thou hast ordained praise, because of thine enemies, that thou mightest still the enemy and the avenger." And God himself saith by the prophet: "I will pour out of my Spirit upon all flesh; and your sons and your daughters shall prophesy." The psalmograph also saith: "I have had more understanding than the old men, because I sought after thy commandments." Our Saviour Christ likewise giveth thanks to his heavenly Father, that it pleased him to "hide the mysteries of his blessed will from the prudent and wise of this world, and to reveal and open them to little ones." For "not many wise men after the flesh, not many mighty, not many of high degree, are called; but God hath chosen the foolish things of the world, to confound the wise; and God hath chosen the weak of the world, to confound things which are mighty; and vile things of the world, and things which are despised, hath God chosen, yea, and things of no reputation, for to bring to nought things of reputation, that no flesh should rejoice in his presence."

Psal. viii. Joel ii. Acts ii. Psal. cxix. Matt. xi. 1 Cor. i.

The doctrine, that thou hast now in the declaration of the Catechism uttered unto me, is in all points sound, true, godly, faithful, wholesome, and substantially grounded upon "the foundation of the apostles and prophets, Jesus Christ himself being the head corner-stone;" so that "the gates of hell shall never be able to prevail against it:" yea, though a shower of rain descend, and the floods come, and the winds blow, and beat upon this doctrine, yet shall it not fall; for it is grounded on the rock Christ Jesus; and though it be tried with fire, yet shall it not consume and perish; for it is not hay and stubble, but gold, silver, and precious stones, built upon a foundation, which is Jesus Christ: again, although heaven and earth perish, and all flesh, with the glory thereof, wither and fade away, yet shall this doctrine endure for ever, so that not one jot or one tittle of it shall perish; as God himself saith by the prophet: "What hath chaff and wheat to do together? saith the Lord. Is not my word like a fire? saith the Lord; and like an hammer, that breaketh the hard stone?"

Eph. ii. Matt. xvi. Matt. vii. 1 Cor. iii. Isai. xl. Matt. v. Jer. xxiii.

And as this doctrine is agreeable to the word of God, so likewise doth it not dissent from the teaching of the true catholic and apostolic church; but concordeth and agreeth therewith in all points, yea, and with so many as from the beginning unto this our age have taught the truth of God's word. And I doubt not, but that so many as are content with the voice of their Shepherd Christ, and regard not the voice of strangers, both do and will approve and allow this doctrine. As for such as follow strange doctrine, and will "not consent unto the wholesome words of our Lord Jesu Christ, and to the doctrine which is according to godliness, as they be puffed up and know nothing, but waste their brains about questions and strife of words, whereof spring envy, strife, railings, evil surmisings, vain disputation of men that have corrupt minds, and that are robbed of the truth, which think that lucre is godliness;" even so from them that are such and so minded ought we to separate ourselves, and to have nothing to do with them; forasmuch as "they be the blind guides of the blind."

John x. 1 Tim. vi. Matt. xv.

And although, "as Jannes and Jambres withstood Moses, these men of corrupt minds, and lewd, as concerning the faith, resist the truth; yet shall they prevail no longer: for their madness shall be uttered unto all men, even as theirs was." "The God of peace shall tread Satan under our feet shortly." "Great Babylon," that wicked whore, that stout and strong strumpet, that blasphemous bawd, that murdering "mother of all the whoredoms and abominations of the earth," that painted and glorious "harlot, with whom the very kings of the earth have committed fornication, and the inhabiters of the earth are drunken with the wine of her whoredom;" this whore, this strumpet, this bawd, this harlot, shall shortly have a fall, with all her marked[1] merchants, and she shall become "the inhabitation of devils, and the hold of all foul spirits, and a cage of all unclean and hateful birds. For her sins are gone up to

2 Tim. iii. Rom. xvi. Rev. xvii. Antichrist shall shortly be confounded with all his antichristian doctrine.

[[1] Having the mark of the beast. Rev. xiii. 17.]

heaven, and God hath remembered her wickedness. Her plagues shall come in one day, yea, and that suddenly, death, and sorrow, and hunger; and she shall be brent with fire; for strong is the Lord God which shall judge her." Insomuch that with great joy and triumph the elect and chosen people of God shall cry out, and say, Rev. xix. "Alleluia: Salvation, and glory, and honour, and power, be ascribed to the Lord our God; for true and righteous are his judgments; for he hath judged the great whore, which did corrupt the earth with her fornication, and he hath avenged the blood of his servants of her hand. Alleluia."

Therefore, my dear and sweet child, as thou hast begun to taste of the most wholesome, sweet, and comfortable waters of God thy Saviour, unto my great joy and unto the singular consolation of thine own soul, yea, and unto the wonderful hope of all thy dear friends and hearty well-willers; even so go forth unto the end, Jer. ii. utterly rejecting and casting away those vile and stinking puddles, "which are able to hold no water," yea, which rather poison than refresh the thirsty soul. Stir up 2 Cor. vi. this grace that God hath given thee, and by no means seem to receive it in vain. Go thou oft unto the throne of God's majesty with most humble supplications, and entirely beseech him to increase thee in the fruits of his holy Spirit, to lighten thy senses, to teach thee the truth of his holy word, to conduct thee in all thy doings, and, in fine, to confirm and finish that same perfectly in thee, which he most graciously hath begun in thee; that whatsoever thou thinkest, breathest, speakest, or doest, may turn unto the glory of his most blessed name, and unto the profit of his holy congregation.

John xv. Rom. vii. *Son.* I confess, most loving father, that of myself I have no good thing, neither am I able any thing to do that may be pleasant in the sight of God, which of myself 2 Cor. iii. am not able so much as to think a good thought (all "our ability is of God," which Phil. ii. "worketh in us both to will well and to do well"): therefore, according to your good advertisement, I will to the uttermost of my power endeavour myself to have God my gracious Lord, both by prayer and godly life, that he may go forth daily more and more to bless me with his benefits, and to make me a vessel of mercy and an inheritor of his glorious kingdom, through Jesus Christ, his only-begotten and dearly-beloved Son, and mine alone Saviour.

Father. I commend thy good and godly disposition. And I beseech God to confirm thee in his truth unto the end. *Son.* Amen.

Father. Come, my dear child, let us go and see what thy mother doth.
2 Tim. iv. "The Lord Jesus Christ be with thy spirit." And the grace of God
be with us all, both now and ever. *Son.* Lord, let it
so come to pass, for thy name's sake, that we
never fall from thy truth, but stedfastly
abide in the same unto the end.
Father. Amen.

Give the glory to God alone.

THE

JEWEL OF JOY,

BY

THOMAS BECON.

The Jewel of Joy:

by

Thomas Becon.

TO THE

MOST EXCELLENT PRINCESS AND VIRTUOUS LADY ELIZABETH[1]

HER GRACE, SISTER TO THE KING HIS MAJESTY, HER MOST HUMBLE AND FAITHFUL ORATOR, THOMAS BECON, WISHETH TRUE KNOWLEDGE OF GOD'S MOST HOLY WORD, AND A LIFE AGREEABLE TO THE SAME.

WHOSOEVER considereth and deeply weigheth the state of this our time, most gracious Lady, shall easy espy out urgent causes both of joy and sorrow. For what is he (except an enemy to true and godly religion, a friend to superstition and papistry) that, considering the too much miserable state wherein we lived under the tyranny of the Roman bishop, rejoiceth not to see the most comfortable light of Christ's glorious gospel in these our days to brast out of the thick clouds of popish ignorancy, and clearly to shine among us unto the great consolation of the faithful?

Before God lightened his holy countenance upon us by restoring the light of his most blessed word to this realm of England, how wretchedly were we led captive of that Romish antichrist, whom we reputed not only a man of great excellency and singular virtue, passing all other mortal creatures, but almost a god, calling him Christ's vicar, Peter's successor, supreme head of the universal church throughout christendom, and at the last, what not! The tyranny of the Romish bishop.

How was his power believed to be equal with God's! How took he upon him to forgive sin, to dispense with the law of God, nature, and man, to bless and curse, to interdict lands for not obeying his tyrannical power, to depose kings and emperors, to appoint rulers at his pleasure, to deliver souls out of purgatory, (a place of his own making,) to stablish new religion, to make saints, chiefly such as maintained his antichristian[2] kingdom, &c.!

Again, what a swarm of popish shavelings brought he forth, as it were out of the bottomless pit of hell, some white, some black, some grey, some russet, some blue, some red, some bearded, some unbearded, some shaven, some unshaven, some booted, some shoed, some crossed, some uncrossed, some close, some open, some flesh-cormorants, some fish-devourers, some Dominicans, some Augustinians, some Minorites, some Carmelites, some Bernardines, some Benedictines, some Antonians, some Paulians, some Clarians, some Brigidians[3], some and all altogether monstrous,—I mean, monks, friars, canons, nuns, hermits, anchors, anchoresses, votaries, vowesses, lewd brethren, lewd sistren, &c.; which were divided into more than five hundred sects among themselves; whom we esteemed to be of so angelic perfection, that at their hands, at their prayers, watchings, fastings, yea, at their lousy cowls and beggarly observances, we sought salvation and remission of sins, thinking that to do God most high sacrifice, when we were most beneficial to those monstrous sects, idle lubbers, bellied hypocrites, careless caterpillars, and unprofitable clods of the earth, although we robbed our heirs of their right inheritance, spoiled our neighbours, neglected the poor, and despised our needy parents and friends! Monastical sects.

How ran we from post to pillar, from stock to stone, from idol to idol, from place to place, to seek remission of our sins, and to make God amends for our sinful living! How called we upon dead mawmets for relief and succour! How gilded we images, painted their tabernacles, and set up candles before them, thinking in so doing to do a more meritorious deed than if we had bestowed our goods in helping the poor members of Christ! Pilgrimages. Images.

[1 Afterwards queen Elizabeth.]

[2 The folio has *antichristie*. Perhaps, therefore, it should be *antichristy*.]

[3 In one of his other treatises, the Reliques of Rome, Becon gives a detailed account of these and many other religious orders.]

Men's traditions. Intercession of saints. How hoped we to have God merciful unto us for keeping the traditions of men, and unmerciful if we neglected them! How fled we in our prayers to such as are departed, for the relief of our necessity, sickness, care, trouble, loss of goods, forgiveness Purgatory. of sins, &c.! What confidence had we to be delivered out of the pope's pinfold after our departure, though we lived never so ungodly, through the popish prattling of Masses. monstrous monks, and the mumbling masses of those[1] lazy soul-carriers! What trust reposed we in the masking masses of the momish mass-mongers, believing to have as plenteous remission of all our sins in them, as in the precious death of our Lord and Saviour Jesu Christ, that immaculate and undefiled Lamb of God! Into how foolish a paradise were we brought, through the crafty juggling of the spiritual sorcerers, to believe that the work of a sinful man (I mean, saying of the popish private mass for the quick and dead) was a propitiatory, satisfactory, expiatory[2] sacrifice for the sin of so many as it was offered for, yea, and of greater strength and virtue than the sweet-smelling sacrifice of the high bishop Christ Jesu! For was not this the doctrine of the papists, and now renewed by the apish anabaptists, that Christ satisfied only for original sin by his death; and all other sins, say the pope's chaplains, both venial and mortal, are put away by the sacrifice of the mass, and by our own works of penance?

Auricular confession. What affiance did we put in auricular confession, and in the whispering absolution of the papists, believing our sins straightways to be forgiven, if *ego absolvo* were once spoken! How believed we to please God highly, if at the pope's commandment Fasting. certain days we abstained from a piece of gross smoky bacon, or salt withered beef, and pampered our bellies with all kind of dainty fish, and such other delicate fare! Ceremonies. How were we bewitched to believe, that in observing the pope's ceremonies there was everlasting salvation, and in neglecting them eternal damnation! Who among the Vows. popish votaries thought it not a less offence to deflower virgins, to defile wives, to corrupt widows, yea, unnaturally to abuse themselves, than godly and honestly to marry? In fine, we were so overwhelmed with the clouds of blind ignorance and ignorant blindness, that we neither knew God nor ourselves aright, neither did we understand what the will of God is, nor what we ought to do to please him, nor how to walk in his holy and blessed ways.

Who seeth not in how miserable state we lived under the Romish bishop? Who perceiveth not our captivity to be no less grievous under that Roman antichrist, concerning our souls, than the corporal servitude of the Israelites was under that most cruel king Pharao in Egypt? How fervent occasion therefore have we to rejoice, and to thank our most valiant captain Jesu Christ, for this our deliverance from spiritual Egypt, that vile cage and stinking house of intolerable bondage, and for the restoring of the glorious light of his most blessed gospel to the world in these our days, that we may learn to know him, to honour, worship, and serve him aright, and to do that thing which is pleasant in his most godly sight! It may truly be verified of Isai. ix. us that was spoken so many years past by the prophet, saying: "The people which sat in darkness saw a great light; and to them which sat in the region and shadow of death, light is sprung."

Col. i. 1 Pet. i. 1 John i. Rev. i. Isai. liii. Matt. viii. 1 Pet. ii. Heb. vii. ix. x. Mark ii. Luke v. Rom. viii. 1 Tim. ii. 1 John ii. Eph. v. Col. i. 1 Pet. ii. James i. We sat in darkness indeed. For we knew not Christ's most precious blood to be a sufficient purgatory for all our sins. We knew not that by the one and alone sacrifice of Christ's most blessed body a perfect ransom, even at the full, was paid for all our wickednesses. We knew not that we were justified by faith alone in Christ's blood. We knew not that God alone absolveth and freely forgiveth us for Christ's sake all our sins, if we repent and believe. We knew not that Christ alone is our intercessor, mediator, and advocate. We knew not that Christ alone is the supreme head of the universal church of christendom, and under him every prince in his own realm. We knew not that the "pure and undefiled religion before God the Father is to visit the comfortless and widows in their trouble, and for a man to 1 Pet. ii. keep himself unspotted from the world." We knew not that the true pilgrimage is Matt. xxv. to sequester ourselves from carnal affects, from worldly lusts, and to visit and to help needy prisoners, and the poor succourless people. We knew not that God re-

[[1] The folio reads *that*.] [[2] Folio, *expediatory*.]

quired of us "rather mercy than sacrifice." We knew not that the worshipping of God with the traditions and commandments of men was but vain and unprofitable. We knew not that the true and christian fast is moderately to taste the gifts of God appointed to be eaten with thanksgiving, to be the more sparing of our meats from our own bellies, that we may have to give the more largely to the hungry, and to keep our minds and bodies free from sins. We knew not that the priests might lawfully marry, and ought rather so to have done, according to the law of God, than to fall into any fleshly uncleanness, and that it is chastity for a man, be he priest or otherwise, if he cannot contain, to lie with his own wife. To be short, the way of truth was unknown unto us; therefore trode we weary and tedious ways, unto the great discomfort of weak consciences,—would God not unto the loss of many souls!

Hos. vi. Matt. xii. Matt. xv. Matt. vi. Isai. lviii. 1 Tim. iv.

Lev. xxi. Ezek. xxiv. 1 Cor. vii. 1 Tim. iii. Tit. i. Heb. xiii. 2 Tim. ii.

Wo worth thee, thou antichrist, thou son of perdition, thou deceiver of the people, thou corrupter of men's minds, thou robber of God's glory, thou murderer of christian men's souls; wo worth thee, wo worth thee, for this thy tyranny and cruelty, which thou hast shewed against the poor and ignorant Christians! but the Lord shall destroy thee "with the breath of his mouth," yea, the Lord himself shall give judgment on thee. Thou that wast clothed in raynes[3], and purple, and scarlet, and decked with gold, and precious stone, and pearls, shalt come to nought even at one hour. For with thine enchantments were all nations deceived; and "in thee hath been found the blood of the prophets, and of the saints, and of all that were slain on the earth."

Isai. xi. 2 Thess. ii. Rev. xviii. The destruction of the Romish bishops.

O how blessed and godly fortunate are we, to whom it hath chanced, through the singular benefit of God, to see the fall of this Romish antichrist in this our realm, to have the dark clouds of papistical ignorance dispelled and put away from us, that the true light of God's most holy truth may shine unto us, and that we walk in it without stumbling! God hath beautified England with many goodly benefits and singular gifts; but this restoring of the glorious gospel of his Son and our Lord, Christ Jesu, is a gift incomparable, a benefit inestimable, a treasure most precious; so that all the true-hearted Christians of this our nation may joyfully say with the holy psalmograph: "Thou hast blessed, O Lord, thy land, and hast turned away the captivity of Jacob. Thou hast forgiven the iniquity of thy people: thou hast covered all their sins. Thou hast mitigated all thy wrath, and turned away the heavy displeasure of thine indignation."

England blessed.

Psal. lxxxv.

But as we have an urgent cause to rejoice for the restoring of the true light of Christ's gospel unto us, seeing by it we receive so many commodities and singular profits for the health of our souls; so likewise have we no mean cause to lament that with this precious wheat, the food of our inward man, [un]wholesome tares and noisome cockle riseth and springeth up, through the envy of Satan our enemy; whereby we may learn how studious and diligent the devil, that old adversary of mankind, is to molest, disquiet, and trouble the congregation of Christ, and to take away from us the most comfortable food of our souls.

Matt. xiii.

1 Pet. v.

What wicked and ungodly opinions are there sown now-a-days of the anabaptists, Davidians, libertines, and such other pestilent sects, in the hearts of the people, unto the great disquietness of Christ's church, moving rather unto sedition than unto pure religion, unto heresy than unto things godly! Again, what a number of false Christians live there at this present day, unto the exceeding dishonour of the christian profession, which "with their mouth confess that they know God, but with their deeds they utterly deny him, and are abominable, disobedient to the word of God, and utterly estranged from all good works!" What a swarm of gross gospellers have we also among us, which can prattle of the gospel very finely, talk much of the justification of faith, crack very stoutly of the free remission of all their sins by Christ's blood, avance themselves to be of the number of those which are predestinate unto eternal glory, &c.; but how far doth their life differ from all true Christianity! They are puffed up with all kind of pride: they swell with all kind of envy, malice, hatred, and enmity against their neighbour: they bren with unquenchable lusts of

Sectaries.

False Christians.

Tit. i.

Gross gospellers.

[[3] Raynes: fine cloth made at Rains, or Rheims.]

carnal concupiscence: they wallow and tumble in all kind of beastly pleasures: their greedy covetous affects are insatiable, the enlarging of their lordships, the increasing of their substance, the scraping together of their worldly possessions infinite, and knoweth no end. In fine, all their endeavours tend unto this end, to shew themselves very ethnicks, and utterly estranged from God in their conversation, although in words they otherwise pretend. As for their alms-deeds, their praying, their watching, their fasting, and such other godly exercises of the Spirit, they are utterly banished from these rude and gross gospellers. All their religion consisteth in words and disputations, in christian acts and godly deeds nothing at all. [Matt. xxv.] They are like the five foolish virgins, which had lamps, and no oil. [Matt. xxi.] They are like to the fig-tree, which had flourishing leaves, but no fruit at all. They are like to that son, which promised his father to work in his vineyard, and yet did not. [Matt xxvi.] They are like unto Judas, which in words pretended to love his Master, but in act he unrighteously betrayed him even unto the death.

O who lamenteth not to hear these things? to see them, to feel them, who is ☞ not utterly dismayed? This dissolution of life, this impiety of manners maketh the gospel of our salvation to be evil-spoken of: yea, it driveth away the papists and such as be weaklings in christian religion from embracing the word of God, and confirmeth them in their ungodly and superstitious opinions. How can it otherwise be? For when they see an alteration in religion, and no alteration in manners, but a continuance in the old, or else a practice of much more ungodliness than heretofore hath been used, the adversaries of God's truth take easily an occasion to blaspheme the christian doctrine, calling it heresy and new learning, and report the preachers thereof to be heretics, seditious persons, teachers of strange doctrine, authors of new sects, despisers of all laudable customs, enemies of our mother holy church, disturbers of the commonweal, breakers of all good order, and at the last, what not!

To consider these things bringeth no little sorrow to a true christian man's heart, which wisheth nothing more than the fortunate success and free progress of God's most blessed word.

[The want of the fear of God is the root of all evil.] But whence cometh this corruption of manners, and dissolution of life? Certes of the want of the fear of God in their hearts. For as "the beginning of wisdom is the fear of the Lord," so the mother and nurse of all wickedness is the want of that godly fear. That prince-like prophet David, describing the unsavoury manners of men, [Psal. xiv.] affirmeth that they be corrupt, and abominable in their devices. "There is none," saith he, "that doth good, no, not one. All are swerved from the true way: they are all together become unprofitable. Their throat is an open grave: they work deceit with their tongues: the poison of adders is under their lips. Their mouth is full of cursing and bitterness: their feet are swift to shed blood. Weariness and wretchedness do they follow; but the way of peace have they not known." Why men fall into this filthy sink of evils, he declareth immediately, saying: *Non est timor Dei ante oculos eorum:* "There is no fear of God before their eyes."

For, where the fear of God wanteth, there is no faith in God. Where there is no faith in God, there is no love of God. Where there is no love of God, there is no rejoicing in God. Where there is no rejoicing in God, there is no working of God's good pleasure, nor yet any following of his most godly commandments, but an headlong falling down into all kind of abominable wickedness. And hereof cometh it to pass that so many, leaving the way of truth, embrace this present world and the transitory pleasures of the same, rejoice not in God, but in things of vanity, delight not in the spiritual treasures of the soul, but repose their delectation in frail things, serving the filthy lusts of the most frail flesh: so that the rejoicing in the Lord our God is almost banished from the hearts of men; the embracing of worldly vanities doth so wholly occupy their breasts.

[Note.] Neither can any man truly rejoice in God, except he first of all sequester his mind from the love and desire of worldly things, according to this commandment of [1 John ii.] blessed John: "Love not the world, nor those things that are in the world. If any man loveth the world, the love of the Father is not in him. For all that is in the world, as the lust of the flesh, the concupiscence of the eyes, and the pride of the life, is not of the Father, but it is of the world. And the world passeth away, and the lust thereof: but he that doth the will of God abideth for ever." Hereto agreeth the saying of St Paul: "If ye be risen again with Christ, seek for those things that are above, where Christ is sitting on the right hand of God. Set your mind on things above, and not on things that are on the earth." Col. iii.

To the intent, therefore, that such as fear God, believe in God, love God (whereof I have abundantly entreated in my other works), yea, to the intent that they also which hitherto have lived without the true knowledge of God may at the last learn truly to savour their Lord God, greedily to taste how sweet he is, desirously to know how liberal he is and merciful, that by this means they all may be occasioned to sequester their minds from worldly things, and only to rejoice in the Lord our God, that fountain and head-spring of all goodness, I have selected and chosen out of the godly letter of St Paul to the Philippians one sentence, which is this: "Rejoice in the Lord alway: yea, once again I say, Rejoice." In the declaration Phil. iv. whereof, that the readers may be the more provoked unto the hearty rejoicing in the The contents of this book. Lord our God, and have their minds sequestered and utterly estranged from worldly things, I have shewed by the word of God that there is nothing under the high heavens, appear it in the sight of the world never so glorious, goodly, excellent, and praiseworthy, wherein the faithful Christians may worthily rejoice (every thing is so Eccles. i. subject and bond unto vanity, yea, the things themselves are mere vanity), but in God alone which filleth both heaven and earth, according to the saying of St Paul: "He that rejoiceth let him rejoice in the Lord." 1 Cor. i. Afterward I have declared many urgent and weighty causes, why we ought to rejoice in the Lord our God, where I have opened, as the time and matter requireth, the inestimable benefits that God hath shewed unto man through Jesu Christ our Lord; which things whoso shall advisedly read, and diligently note, I doubt not but all worldly things shall soon wax vile unto him; his heart shall so fervently be kindled with earnest love toward his Lord and Saviour. Other godly matters be interlaced not altogether unworthy the reading.

And because the matter should be the more pleasant and less tedious to the readers, I have set it forth dialogue-wise, yea, and that as plainly and as simply as I could devise, without adding of any strange or unused words, whereby the unlearned reader should be barred from the true understanding of the sentence, speaking[1] by this means to edify such as have not the knowledge of tongues.

This treatise, entitled "The Jewel of Joy," I offer unto your grace, most noble and virtuous lady, moved hereunto of godly zeal, through the notable fame that is universally spread abroad of your grace's most godly disposition, and hearty love toward the word of God, daily practised both in your grace' most virtuous behaviour, and also in the godly order of your household[2], unto the great comfort of all true-hearted Christians, and the notable example of so many as seek the glory of God unfeignedly; most humbly beseeching your grace favourably to accept this my rude labour. And I shall most instantly pray unto the Lord our God, that that good work, which he hath through his holy Spirit begun in your grace, even in these your young and tender years, he may go forth to finish the same, unto the glory of his blessed name, and the singular comfort of so many as love the gospel of our salvation unfeignedly; that your grace, being a mirror and exemplar of virtue to the faithful in this world, may grow up to full and perfect holiness in the fear of God, and be found blameless at the great day of the glorious appearance of the Lord Christ Jesu, who mought ever preserve your grace in all godliness, and increase of honour! Amen.

Your grace's most humble and faithful orator,
Thomas Becon.

[1 Perhaps *seeking*.] [2 The folio has *house should*.]

THE

JEWEL OF JOY.

PHILEMON, EUSEBIUS, THEOPHILE, AND CHRISTOPHER TALK TOGETHER.

Phil. So oft as I call to remembrance (which for the most part I do every hour) this commandment of our Lord and Master, "Occupy yourselves till I come;" whereby we are admonished diligently to employ our talent committed unto us, every one according to our vocation, in the avancement of God's glory and in the edification of our christian brethren, whose health and salvation, not only with the loss of our temporal possessions, but even of our life also (if need so require), we are bound, under pain of damnation, to seek, seeing that God, as the wise man testifieth, "hath given to every man charge over his neighbour;" again, seeing that, according to the doctrine of blessed John, as Christ gave his life for us, so likewise are we bound to bestow our life to win our brethren to Christ; forasmuch as we all are members of one body, and are commanded without dissimulation to love our neighbour as ourself, and to seek his commodity, profit, and furtherance in all godliness no less than our own; I can none otherwise than reprove and accuse mine own sluggishness, which almost these five years past have omitted my duty toward my neighbours, not going forth as I began in my "Christmas Banquet," in my "Potation," in my "Nosegay," and in my "New-year's Gift," to exhort them to godliness, and to encourage them valiantly to go forth in the same, and to persevere unto the end, but, training my life in other exercises, I trust not altogether ungodly, nor unprofitable to the christian public weal, I have neglected the neighbourly office which I ought to have practised toward them.

Luke xix.
Ecclus. xvii.
Rom. xii. 1 Cor. xii. 1 Tim. i. 1 John iii. Lev. xix. Matt. xxii. Rom. xiii.

Yea, I fear lest, through the neglecting of my duty toward my neighbours, I have not shewed myself an obedient servant in all points concerning the diligent accomplishment of my Lord and Master's precept, which straitly chargeth me not only to occupy myself privately in virtuous studies and godly exercises, but also openly, that his holy and glorious congregation may be edified and brought to the true and perfect knowledge of his most godly will.

Certes, the omission and leaving of this my duty toward my neighbours doth not a little disquiet me, seeing that so long time I have had no familiar talk with them of godly matters, no, nor yet once seen them since I gave them a new-year's gift; being unwillingly, through the furious and Nero-like cruelty of certain persons (whose tyranny since that time God hath not left unpunished), driven away from them, to the great and continual disturbance of my mind, for lacking the company of so loving neighbours and sweet friends.

But I have sent my servants for them, that I may talk with them after mine old sort, renew our acquaintance, and be merry together. For it is a sweet thing when friends meet, and merry when old acquaintance flock together-ward. I marvel that they tarry so long. I fear lest my servant doeth not his message expeditely; or else that they have some great letting. For I am well ascertained, that, if they once have knowledge of my return into the country, no worldly affairs can withdraw them long from my company.

But behold, where they come flocking together. O pleasant and comfortable sight! Tears distil out of mine eyes for very joy; yet can I not withhold myself from them, but must needs with meeting arms embrace them, lovingly salute them, and sweetly kiss them.

O most dear neighbours, and christian brethren, so heartily welcome as heart can think! Blessed be God, which hath preserved us alive unto this day, that we may yet once again see one another, talk one with another, and freely rejoice in the Lord our God. Come, come unto me. Let me embrace you, kiss you, and once again bid you heartily welcome.

Eus. O most true-hearted friend, and unfeigned brother, we praise God for your safe return into the country. *Theo.* This day, most sweet neighbour, hath replenished us all with joy unspeakable; forasmuch as it hath offered you again to our sight. *Chris.* O dear brother Philemon, your repairing into this country, your sight, your company, your talk hath even now suddenly so revived us, that we seem to have put on a certain kind of immortality. And as for all other his benefits, so likewise for this, do we render to the immortal God most hearty thanks, and with one voice we all bid you most heartily welcome home. *Phil.* I know, dear neighbours, your unfeigned love and ready bent good-will toward me. And you do not more rejoice at my return, than I am entirely glad that I have found you all in good health.

Eus. But, I pray you, tell us of good fellowship, brother Philemon, in what parts[1] of the world have ye travelled so long time? For neither by letters, nor yet by report of any credible persons, since your departure, could we learn where you trained your life. We feared lest, in so perilous time, ye had been swallowed up of the greedy cormorants and insatiable locusts, which are never satisfied nor filled with the shedding of innocent blood. Neither was the liberty of your speech, nor the swiftness of your pen unknown to us, which the swarm of antichrist's sect, since you first of all travailed in the Lord's harvest, could never abide, but extremely persecute, blaspheme, and condemn. *Phil.* What gentleness I found for my godly travails at the hands of some men in these parts, ye know right well. Therefore, when neither by speaking nor by writing I could do good, I thought it best not rashly to throw myself into the ravening paws of these greedy wolves, but for a certain space to absent myself from their tyranny according to the doctrine of the gospel.

The malice of the papists against the author's both preachings and writings.

Matt. x.

For as there is "a time to speak," so is there "a time to keep silence." When the poor are oppressed and trodden under the foot, then "shall the wise man," saith the prophet, "hold his peace; for the time is evil." And we have a manifest commandment of our Saviour Christ, that we should "not give that which is holy unto dogs, nor cast pearls before swine, lest they tread them under their feet, and they turn again and all-to rent" us.

Eccles. iii. [Amos v. 13.] Matt. vii.

For there be some kind of men so greatly infected with the nature of Suffenus[2], and accombered with the properties of Mevius[3], two foolish and vain-glorious poets, that they think nothing well spoken, nothing truly written, except they themselves be the authors and doers thereof. They are those same very hypocrites, which find fault at a little mote in another man's eye; but they cannot perceive a great beam in their own eyes. They are those same Pharisees, which spar up the kingdom of heaven before men. They are those same "lawyers, which take away the key of knowledge: they themselves enter not in, neither suffer they other that would to enter in." They are those same Babylonical backsliders, and lying children, which will not hear the law of the Lord, but daily cry: *Loquimini nobis placentia;* "Tell us pleasant things:" provide us of errors: "care not for the right way; but away with the Holy One of Israel from our face." They are those same false Christians, of whom St Paul prophesied, which should be "lovers of themselves, covetous, high-minded, proud, evil-speakers, disobedient to their elders, unthankful, ungodly, unkind, false of their promise, false accusers, rioters, fierce, despisers of them that are good, traitors, heady, standing in their own conceit, lovers rather of pleasures than lovers of God, having an outward appearance of godliness, but denying the power thereof." "Like as Jannes and Jambres withstood Moyses, even so do they also resist the truth. Men are they of corrupt minds, and lewd as concerning the faith: but they shall prevail no longer; for their foolishness shall be manifest unto all men, as theirs was."

Matt. vii. Matt. xxiii. Luke xi. Isai. xxx. 2 Tim. iii.

Where things be so ordered that the truth can bear no place, nor the professors thereof be thankfully received, but rather blasphemed, persecuted, imprisoned, and ungently handled; what should men do but shake off the dust of their feet, for a witness against them at the day of judgment, and depart into some other place, where they may do good, as Christ and the apostles did, and quietly to abide the

Matt. x. Matt. xv. Acts xiii. John iv. vi.

[1 The folio here, and in a few other places, has *parties.*]

[2 Catull. xiv. 19.] [3 Virg. Eclog. iii. 90.]

Lam. iii. pleasure of God, as the prophet saith, "It is good to look for the saving health of the Lord with silence?" After this sort did I appoint myself, and, leaving mine own native country, I travelled into such strange places as were unknown to me, and I to them. And yet I thank the Lord my God, which never leaveth his servants succourless, I, although an unprofitable servant, in that exile and banishment wanted no good thing. Let the voluptuous worldlings take thought for the belly, and be careful for this present life: I have learned, in that my journey, to cast my care upon the Lord my God, which abundantly feedeth so many as trust in him and depend on his liberality and goodness. For one house, I found twenty; and for one friend, an hundred. I could wish nothing for the provision of this my life, but I had it plenteously; God so aforeseeing for me his unprofitable and wretched servant.

Psal. xxxiii. xxxiv. xxxvii. Matt. vi. Luke xii. 1 Pet. v.

Matt. xix. Luke xviii. *Theo.* The promise of God is even so. "Every one," saith he, "that forsaketh house, or brethren, or sistern, or father, or mother, or wife, or children, for my name's sake, and for the kingdom of God," that is to say, for the love that he beareth toward the gospel of Christ, "he shall receive an hundred-fold as much in this present time, and in the world to come life everlasting."

Chris. Truth it is; but you have not yet declared to us in what countries ye have been here in England, since your departure from hence.

Phil. After I departed from you, and had taken my leave of my most sweet mother, and of my other dear friends, I travelled into Derbyshire, and from thence into the Peak, whither I appointed my books and my clothes to be brought.

Derbyshire. The Peak.

Eus. Into the Peak? Lord God, what made you there? That is a marvellous and a barren country, and, as it is thought, such a country that neither hath learning, nor yet no spark of godliness. *Phil.* Mine intent was, by exercising the office of a school-master, to engraft Christ and the knowledge of him in the breasts of those scholars whom God should appoint unto me for to be taught. *Theo.* I think you found there very peakish people.

Phil. Not so. I confess to you that I found there very good wits, and apt unto learning. *Chris.* But how favour they christian religion in those parts? *Phil.* I will tell you. Coming into a little village, called Alsop in the Dale, I chanced upon a certain gentleman called Alsop, lord of that village, a man not only ancient in years, but also ripe in the knowledge of Christ's doctrine.

Master Alsop.

Theo. By what means had ye knowledge of his godly disposition? *Phil.* After we had saluted one another and taken a sufficient repast for that present, he shewed me certain books which he called his jewels and principal treasures.

Eus. I pray you, what books were they? *Phil.* To rehearse them all by name I am not able; but of this am I sure that, among all other, there was the new testament, after the translation of the godly learned man Myles Coverdale, which seemed to be as well worn by the diligent reading thereof as ever was any portass or mass-book among the papists.

Myles Coverdale.

Chris. A rare thing, and almost a miracle to find an old man, namely in those parts where Christ, I think, as yet was never truly preached, to be so well affected toward the reading of the sacred scriptures. *Eus.* Yea, and a gentleman also. For gentlemen now-a-days for the most part delight so much in reading the word of God, as a true Christian doth in reading the pope's decretals; they are altogether so addict to the vain pleasures of this world.

Gentlemen.

Theo. Many think it to be an unseemly thing for a man of nobility to be studious of holy letters: hawks and dogs, dice and cards (as I may speak nothing of their service to lady Venus) is their pastime and delectation. If they read any thing, it is some vain trifle of love, or, when they be best occupied, an history or chronicle.

Phil. I grant many gentlemen little answer their vocation, neither are they studious of God's word as they ought: notwithstanding (praised be God for it!) I know many both men and women of nobility, which greatly delight in reading the holy scriptures, and do not only love, but also live the gospel. *Eus.* I pray God increase the number daily; for then shall it go well with christian religion, when noblemen shall be learned in those books, which are fountains and head-springs of all true, perfect, and christian religion. Notable is the sentence of Plato, which affirmeth that the

Plato.

public weal is most fortunate and greatly avanced, if such as be the governors thereof be either wise or studious of wisdom. Therefore doth the scripture in so many places exhort to civil magistrates to be learned in the law of God. But, I pray you, tell us, had the gentleman none other books but only the new testament? Deut. xvii. Josh. i. Psal. ii. Wisd. i. vi.

Phil. Yes, verily. I remember right well that he had many other godly books, as "The Obedience of a Christian Man," "The Parable of the Wicked Mammon[1]," "The Revelation of Antichrist," "The Sum of Holy Scripture," "The Book of John Frith against Purgatory," all the books published in the name of Thomas Becon, with divers other learned men's works. In these godly treatises this ancient gentleman among the mountains and rocks occupied himself both diligently and virtuously.

Chris. I would not lightly have believed that such a man could have been found in so barbarous and rude a country, nor that so fruitful works had been placed in so unlearned a region. *Phil.* Neither would the prophet Helias have believed that there had been any godly men left alive besides himself, when king Achab and his wicked wife Jesabel had cruelly murdered such great number of the Lord's prophets and servants; till God made him answer and said: "I have yet reserved to me seven thousand men which have not bowed their knees before Baal." When the papists and antichrists think their kingdom most strongest, and most like to continue, then is it most nigh unto downfal; so worketh God for the avancement of his glory, and for the profit of his poor afflicted congregation. When the enemies of God burn good men, and consume their books unto ashes, then are these martyrs the better credited, their doctrine the more regarded, and their books both the more warely kept, and hold in the greater reverence. 1 Kings xix. Rom. xi. Mark, ye papists.

Theo. I believe it right well. For there be certain books, whose remembrance had fallen away long before this time from the minds of the people, if they had not furiously and without consideration been condemned for heresy. But when the people saw them condemned, and no cause why, but plain tyranny, *Sic volo, sic jubeo, stat pro ratione voluntas*[2], it caused them to have the more respect unto the books; and when they had read them, perused them, and compared them with the scriptures of God, perceiving that in all points they did agree with them, it caused the readers to have an evil opinion of the adversaries, and to embrace and safely keep the books as holy reliques and precious treasures. So that, where the papists sought a final destruction to the books by burning them, contrary to their expectation, they have made them as it were immortal, and won to the authors of them a noble fame, and glorious renown. Very truly is it said of Salomon: "There is no wisdom, no forecast, no counsel, that can prevail against the Lord." Prov. xxi.

Eus. Truth it is; but to return unto the Peak, of what sort, I pray you, are the people concerning christian religion? *Phil.* When I was there, all their religion consisted in hearing matins and mass, in superstitious worshipping of saints, in hiring soul-carriers to sing trentals, in pattering upon beads, and in such other popish pedlary. Feigned religion.

Theo. The history of the gentleman caused me not so much to rejoice, as the hearing of this maketh me sorry. I wonder that the common people be so ignorant. *Chris.* Do ye wonder? What wonder is it, when such as should lead them in the light of Christ's gospel are the very self darkness? "The eye," that is to say, the preacher of God's word, "is the light of the body," that is, of the whole congregation of Christ. "If the eye be single," that is to say, if the curate or preacher be godly learned, "then shall all the body be full of light," that is, the christian congregation shall have the word of God dwell in them plenteously, and truly walk in the light of God's most blessed will, without halting on both parts." "But if the eye be darkness," that is to say, if the preacher be unlearned, "how great then shall the darkness be!" that is, how ignorant and blind shall the gross and rude people be! Is not this the saying of Salomon? "When the preaching of God's word faileth, the people perish and come to nought." The priests are "the salt of the earth; but if the salt be unsavoury, and have lost his saltness, what can be salted therewith? It Ignorant priests. Matt. vi. Luke xi. Prov. xxix. Matt. v.

[1 These treatises were by William Tindal. Simon Fish translated from the Dutch the "Sum of the Scriptures:" the "Revelation of Antichrist" was Frith's.]

[2 Juv. Sat. vi. 222.]

is afterward good for nothing but to be cast out, and to be trodden under foot of men." *Phil.* I cannot deny, but that the priests in that country are very basely learned,
Isai. lvi. and in a manner such as are painted of the prophet, saying: "The curates are blind every one of them: they are altogether without knowledge: they are dumb dogs not able to bark," &c. *Eus.* The priests for the most part universally through the realm
Ezek. xxxiv. are such as Ezechiel crieth out on, saying: "Wo be to the shepherds of Israel which feed themselves! Should not the shepherds feed the flock? Ye have eaten up the milk: ye have clothed you with the wool: the best-fed have ye slain; but the flock have ye not nourished: the weak have ye not holden up: the sick have ye not healed: the broken have ye not bound together: the outcasts have ye not brought again: the lost have ye not sought up; but churlishly and cruelly have ye ruled them," &c.

Chris. Where such unlearned pastors bear rule, no marvel though papistry be not
Matt. xv. exiled. "If the blind lead the blind, both fall into the ditch." *Phil.* The people where I have travelled for the most part are reasonable and quiet enough, yea, and very conformable to God's truth. If any be stubbornly obstinate, it is for fault of knowledge, and because they have been seduced of blind guides.

Counsel worthy to be followed. *Theo.* It should help very much unto an uniformity in religion, and unto the salvation of christian men's souls, if there were learned curates appointed in every parish; if so many cannot be found, then to place in every country certain learned and godly preachers, which may go from parish to parish, preaching to the people the good-will and pleasure of God. And let the other priests be ministers under the super-attendents, or overseers, and in their absence read to the people the said scriptures, and the homilies, reverently minister the sacraments, visit the sick people, make collections for the poor, and virtuously bring up the youth of the town. If this were brought to pass, what a flourishing realm should we have! How should learning and virtue prosper! How purely should we honour God! How faithfully should one of us love another! What christian works should issue out of our daily conversation and living! *Phil.* I doubt not but that the king's majesty, with his most honourable council, will very graciously consider these things, yea, and that with expedition.

Chris. But, sir, once again to the Peak. I pray you, continued you there still to this return into the country? *Phil.* I will tell you. While I was in the Peak,
Robert Wisdom. I learned that R. Wisdom[1] was in Staffordshire: ye know the man, I am sure. *Eus.* We know him to be a godly man in his conversation, and a faithful preacher in his doctrine, and such one as hath not been altogether free from persecution for the maintenance of God's truth.

Col. iv. *Phil.* He was the same to me that Aristarchus was to Paul. Desiring greatly to see him I bade my friends in the Peak farewell, and made haste toward him. When I came to him, I did not only rejoice to see him in health, but also gave God thanks that he was so well placed and provided for. For I found him in the house of a
John Olde. certain faithful brother, called John Olde, a man old in name, notwithstanding young
Acts xvii. in years, and yet ancient in true godliness and christian life. He was to us as Jason was to Paul and Silas. He received us joyfully into his house, and liberally, for the Lord's sake, ministered all good things to our necessities. And as he began, so did he continue a right hearty friend, and dearly loving brother, so long as we remained in the country. Even as blessed Paul wished to Onesiphorus, so wish I to him, and
2 Tim. i. with the same words pray for him: "The Lord grant to him that he may find mercy with the Lord in that day!" After that we had passed over certain days in the house of that most loving brother, refreshing ourselves with the comfort of the holy scriptures, after so many grievous tempests, troublous storms, and painful labours, I know not of what friend our dear brother Robert Wisdom was called away by letters, which was to us both no small pain and grief. Notwithstanding, we submitted ourselves to the good pleasure of God, with this hope and comfort, that his return to his old familiars should make greatly to the avancement of God's glory, and to the quietness of his christian studies, whereof might spring hereafter no small commodity to the christian public weal. And so we, wishing one to another the assist-

[[1] An account is given of Wisdom, Old, and Aylmer, Vol. I. pages viii. ix., notes 4, 7.]

ance of God's Spirit, repentance of our former life, strength of faith, and perseverance in all godliness to our last end, departed, yea, and that not without tears.

Chris. Did he write nothing all the time that he was in those parts? *Phil.* He was ever virtuously occupied, and suffered no hour to pass away without good fruit. He is a man in whom the fear of God reigneth unfeignedly. Besides his other works, of this I am sure, that he hath written very godly and fruitful expositions upon certain psalms of David, of the which also he translated some into English metre very learnedly. He hath written also many godly and learned sermons upon the epistles and gospels, that are read in the temples on Sundays, part whereof I have both seen and read. Moreover, he hath translated the postill of Antonius Corvinus[2], and divers other learned men's works. And, which I had almost forgotten, he hath made a confutation of those errors which were imputed and laid to his charge very unjustly of his adversaries, a book farced[3] with all kind of godly learning. *Theo.* These his works are not printed nor commonly published abroad. *Phil.* Truth it is: would God they were! They should without doubt bring great profit to the readers, and highly avance the glory of God. The books of Robert Wisdom.

Eus. But, I pray you, what exercise did you practise in Staffordshire after his departure? *Phil.* According to my talent I brought up youth in the knowledge of good literature, and instilled into their breasts the elements and principles of Christ's doctrine, teaching them to know their Lord God, to believe in him, to fear and love him, and studiously to walk in his holy ways, from their very cradles even to the yielding up of their last breath. I doubt not but that Christ was so deeply graven in their hearts at that time, that he is not yet worn out, neither, as I trust, shall be so long as they live. *Eus.* How savoured the people Christ and his doctrine in those parts, when you were there? *Phil.* Not altogether unlike the people of the Peak, but that they were not in all points commonly so superstitious: they savoured somewhat more of pure religion. This, I think, came to pass through certain English books that were among them, and through travellers to and fro London. Staffordshire.

Chris. What of the priests? *Theo.* Ye should ask what of the moving of mountains. *Phil.* Indeed when I was there, they were all massmongers, applying their portass and mass-book very diligently, but the holy bible very little. *Eus.* Were they not, as he writeth of men of Crete, "evil beasts and slow bellies?" *Phil.* It becometh me to dispraise no man. "For charity covereth the multitude of sins." Notwithstanding, I would wish more learned pastors to be appointed for to feed the flock of Christ. For they are not such priests, as whose "lips keep knowledge," neither can their "mouth utter the law of God," if any man should require it of them. Priests. Tit. i. Prov. x. 1 Pet. iv. Mal. ii. 1 Pet. iii.

Chris. If I should rehearse here to you the childish ignorance that was found in priests at the king's majesty's visitation, it would make your heart to bleed for to consider that such blind curates should have the oversight and charge of Christ's congregation. *Phil.* Their blindness is rather to be lamented than to be derided; notwithstanding, this must I needs say by the way, I wish with all my heart that the church of Christ may be purged of such unprofitable clods of the earth, at the least, that they may not occupy the room and enjoy the living of a preacher; they themselves being altogether unlearned, and more meet to be taught than to teach. He that should be a curate, after St Paul's rule ought to be a man able to teach the people God's word, yea, and such a man as should not only be "able to exhort, but also to convince and overcome all such as speak against the truth." Tit. i.

Theo. A great fault in this behalf is to be imputed unto the bishops, which admitted such unlearned asses unto the order of priesthood. *Eus.* The patrons of the benefices are not altogether blameless for giving the livings to such ignorant men, whether it be for affection or for rewards; neither shall their punishment, I fear, be small at the day of judgment. For if, "when the blind leadeth the blind, both fall into the ditch," what shall we then say of them which are the occasion that the blind guide with his blind flock fall into the ditch, that is to say, into everlasting damnation? Shall not the blood of them that perish be required at the patrons' hands in the dreadful Bishops. Patrons of benefices. Matt. xv. Note.

[[2] A Hessian divine. This postill was published in 1549. See Herbert's Ames' Typ. Ant. Vol. I. p. 600.]

[[3] Farced: stuffed, filled.]

day of judgment? If I put a sword in a madman's hand, which with the same immediately killeth another man, am not I guilty of the blood of him that is slain? *Phil.* Let these things pass; for doubt ye not the king's highness with his most honourable council will most graciously provide for the redress of such abuses.

Theo. Did you tarry, I pray you, continually in Staffordshire until ye returned into your country? *Phil.* Nay, forsooth. After that I had consumed a year in that country and somewhat more in the virtuous education and godly bringing up of youth, I departed into Warwickshire, where in like manner as afore I freely enjoyed the liberality of my most sweet and dear friend, John Olde, which, impelled by urgent causes, departed into that country for to inhabit. There likewise taught I divers gentlemen's sons, which I trust, if they live, shall be a beauty to the public weal of England, both for the preferment of true religion and for the maintenance of justice.

Eus. How fancied you that country? *Phil.* I travelled both in Derbyshire, in the Peak, in Staffordshire, and in Leicestershire; yet Warwickshire was to me most dear and pleasant. *Chris.* How so? *Phil.* In Leicestershire (as I may pass over the other), I had familiarity only with one learned man, a countryman of ours, called John Aylmer, a master of arts of the university of Cambridge, a young man singularly well learned both in the Latin and Greek tongue, teacher to my lord marquis Dorset his children; but Warwickshire ministered unto me the acquaintance and friendship of many learned men.

M. John Aylmer.

Chris. What are their names, I pray you? For nothing delighteth me more than to hear of learned men. *Phil.* First cometh to my remembrance a man worthy to be loved and reverenced of all true-hearted christian men, not only for the pureness of his life, which hath always before the world been innocent and blameless, but also for the sincerity and godliness of his evangelic doctrine, which since the beginning of his preaching hath in all points been so comfortable[1] to the teaching of Christ and of his apostles, that the very adversaries of God's truth, with all their menacing words and cruel imprisonments, could not withdraw him from it; but whatsoever he had once preached, he valiantly defended the same before the world, without fear of any mortal creature, although of never so great power and high authority, wishing and minding rather to suffer not only loss of worldly possessions, but also of life, than the glory of God and the truth of Christ's gospel should in any point be obscured or defaced through him. His life was not dear unto him, so that he might fulfil his course with joy, and the office that he received of the Lord Jesu to testify the gospel of God's favour. He might well say with the holy psalmograph: "I spake, O Lord, of thy testimonies and ordinances in the presence of kings, princes, and rulers, and I was not abashed."

Master Latimer.

Psal. cxix.

Eus. I much desire to know his name: tell it us, I pray you. *Phil.* Ye have heard, I am sure, of Master Latimer, sometime bishop of Worcester? *Chris.* His noble fame and virtuous renown is more known, not only in this realm of England, but also in foreign countries among both learned and unlearned, than it can be hid. I, for my part, have known him before twenty years in the university of Cambridge, to whom next unto God I am specially bound to give most hearty thanks for the knowledge, if any I have, of God and of his most blessed word.

Phil. How so? *Chris.* I was sometime a poor scholar of Cambridge, very desirous to have the knowledge of good letters; and in the time of my being there, this godly man preached many learned and christian sermons both in the Latin and English tongue, at the which all I for most part was present; and, although at that time I was but a child of sixteen years, yet I noted his doctrine so well as I could, partly reposing it in my memory, partly commending it to letters, as most faithful treasures unto memory.

I was present when, with manifest authorities of God's word and arguments invincible, besides the allegations of doctors, he proved in his sermons, that the holy scriptures ought to be read in the English tongue of all christian people, whether they were priests or laymen, as they be called; which thing divers drowsy duncers, with certain false flying flattering friars, could not abide, but openly in their unsavoury

Bible in English.

[[1] Perhaps *conformable.*]

sermons resisted his godly purpose, even as Alexander the coppersmith, and Elymas 2 Tim. iv.
the sorcerer, with many other, resisted blessed Paul and his godly doctrine; notwith- Acts xiii.
standing, he (yea, rather God in him, whose cause he handled) gat the victory; and it came to pass according to his teaching.

Neither was I absent when he inveighed against temple-works, good intents, Will-works.
blind zeal, superstitious devotion, &c.; as the painting of tabernacles, gilding of images, setting up of candles, running on pilgrimage, and such other idle inventions of men, whereby the glory of God was obscured, and the works of mercy the less regarded.

I remember also how he was wont to rebuke the beneficed men with the authority Beneficed
of God's word for neglecting and not teaching their flock, and for being absent from men.
their cures, they themselves being idle, and masting[2] themselves like hogs of Epicurus' flock, taking no thought though their poor parishioners miserably pine away, starve, perish, and die for hunger.

Neither have I forgotten how he at that time condemned foolish, ungodly, and Vows[3].
impossible vows to be fulfilled, as the vow of chastity, wishing rather that liberty of marriage might be granted to them which have so vowed, by the higher powers, than so to continue through single life in all kind of abominable uncleanness.

O how vehement was he in rebuking all sins, namely idolatry, false and idle swearing, covetousness, and whoredom! again, how sweet and pleasant were his words in exhorting unto virtue! He spake nothing but it left as it were certain pricks or stings in the hearts of the hearers, which moved them to consent to his doctrine. None, except they were stiff-necked and uncircumcised in heart, went away from his sermons which were not led with a faithful repentance of their former life, affected with high detestation of sin, and moved unto all godliness and virtue. I did know certain men which, through the persuasion of their friends, went unto his sermons swelling, blown full, and puffed up like unto Esop's frog, with envy and malice against him; but when they returned, the sermon being done, and demanded how they liked him
and his doctrine? they answered with the bishops' and Pharisees' servants: *Nunquam* John vii.
sic locutus est homo, sicut hic homo: "There was never man that spake like unto this
man." So sharp a two-edged sword is the word of God (it "entereth through even Heb. iv.
unto the dividing of the soul and the spirit, and of the joints and the marrow"), so Jer. i.
watcheth God upon his word, so causeth the Father of heaven his "word not to Isai. lv.
return unto him void, but to do whatsoever his good pleasure is," and to take root
and bring forth fruit in them that are afore ordained unto everlasting life, "in some Acts xiii.
an hundred-fold, in some three-score-fold, in some thirty-fold." Matt. xiii.

I leave off to report his free speech against buying and selling of benefices, against Benefices.
the promoting of them unto the livings of spiritual ministers which are unlearned and Unlearned ministers.
ignorant in the law of God, against popish pardons, against the reposing our hope Pardons.
in our own works or in other men's merits, against false religion, &c. Neither do I Vain hope.
here rehearse how beneficial he was, according to his possibility, to poor scholars and Alms-deeds.
other needy people; so conformable was his life to his doctrine, so watered he with good deeds whatsoever tofore he planted with godly words, so laboured he with all main both in word and deed to win and allure other unto the love of Christ's doctrine and his holy religion. There is a common saying which remaineth unto this day: "When Master Stafford[4] read, and Master Latimer preached, then was Cambridge blessed."

Eus. What was that Stafford? *Chris.* A man whom the unthankful world was Master
unworthy any longer to have. As I may pass over the gifts of nature and such George Stafford.
goodly qualities as win unto them that have them the favour and commendation of men, wherewith he was plenteously endued, this I unfeignedly say unto you, he was a man of a very perfect life, and (if I may so speak) of an angelic conversation, approvedly learned in the Hebrew, Greek, and Latin tongues, and such one as had, through his painful labours, obtained singular knowledge in the mysteries of God's most blessed word.

[[2] Masting: feeding on mast.] [[3] The folio has *Jews.*] [[4] See Vol. I. page vii., note 5.]

I doubt whether he was more bound to blessed Paul for leaving those godly epistles behind him, to instruct and teach the congregation of God, whereof he was a dear member, or that Paul, which before had so many years been foiled[1] with the foolish fantasies and elvish expositions of certain doting doctors, and, as it were, drowned in the dirty dregs of the drowsy duncers, was rather bound unto him, seeing that by his industry, labour, pain, and diligence, he seemed of a dead man to make him alive again, and putting away all unseemliness to set him forth in his native colours; so that now he is both seen, read, and heard not without great and singular pleasures of them that travail in the studies of his most godly epistles. And as he beautified the letters of blessed Paul with his godly expositions, so likewise did he learnedly set forth in his lectures the native sense and true understanding of the four evangelists, vively restoring unto us the apostle's mind, and the mind of those holy writers, which so many years before had lien unknown and obscured through the darkness and mists of the Pharisees and papists.

Matt. xxiv. He was a faithful and prudent servant, giving meat to the Lord's household in due time. 1 Tim. iv. He did cast away profane and old wives' fables, and as the good servant of Jesu Christ he exercised himself unto godliness. He was an example to the faithful in word, in conversation, in love, in spirit, in faith, in purity. He gave his mind to reading, to exhorting, to doctrine. 2 Tim. ii. He studied to shew himself unto God a laudable workman, that needeth not to be ashamed, dividing the word of truth justly. He was gentle unto every man, and with meekness informed them that resisted the truth, if God at any time would give them repentance for to know the truth, and to turn again from the snare of the devil. 2 Tim. iv. He fought a good fight, he fulfilled the course, he kept the faith; 1 Pet. v. therefore is there laid up for him a crown of righteousness, which the Lord, that righteous Judge, shall give him in that day, not to him only, but to all them that love his coming.

Phil. I am glad, brother Christopher, that ye have spoken no less truly than friendly of these two men of God, of the which one reigneth with the high Bishop Christ in glory (for "the wise," as the prophet Daniel saith, "which have taught other shall glister as the shining of heaven; and those that have instructed the multitude unto godliness shall be as the stars, world without end"), the other is yet alive, worthy, if God's good pleasure so were, to live the years of Mathusalath, both for his godly doctrine and christian conversation. With this true preacher of God's word I chanced in Warwickshire to be somewhat acquainted (which was to me no small comfort); not with him only, but with divers other, whereof some were men of worship well bent toward the holy scriptures, some were men very godly learned in the laws of the Most Highest, and professors of the same. So oft as I was in their company, methought I was clean delivered from Egypt and quietly placed in the new glorious Jerusalem, which is described in the Revelation of blessed John; so sweet a thing is it to be in the company of godly learned men.

Dan. xii.

M. Latimer was afterward most cruelly brent at Oxford, for the confession of God's truth, by the bloody and wicked papists, with the godly martyr, Doctor Ridley, sometime bishop of London.

Rev. xxi.

Eus. Travelled you into none other country afterward? *Phil.* While I was training up of youth, and fashioning their minds unto true godliness in that country, behold, unlooked for, were letters sent unto me from my most dear mother, in the which she required me to return into my native country, and to be a staff of her old age; Tob. v. forasmuch as my father-in-law was departed from this vale of misery. In considering my duty and the honour which I owe unto her by the manifest commandment of God, Exod. xx. Deut. v. immediately after, not without the friendly consent of my well-willers, [I] departed from Warwickshire, and with all haste repaired home. And forasmuch as I have now quietly reposed myself (thanks be to the high Lord), I, remembering our old friendship, thought it my bounden duty to send for you, and after mine accustomed manner to talk with you of some part of the holy scripture. For therein are we commanded by the mouth of God to meditate ourselves both day and night; Psal. cxix. for, as David saith: "It is a lantern to our feet, and a light unto our paths."

Chris. The rehearsal of this your travel by divers countries hath so delighted us, that we seem now to have been with you in all your journeys. *Theo.* We magnify God

[[1] Foiled: trampled on, or perplexed, puzzled. See Todd's Johnson.]

most heartily, that he by his holy angel hath safe conduct you in all your ways, preserved you in health, gotten you dear friends, and now, at the last, brought you home again into your native country.

Eus. But, I pray you, did you write nothing in this your long absence? *Phil.* I wrote divers treatises, but as yet there are published only these three: "The Governance of Virtue;" "An Invective against Whoredom;" "A Dialogue of Christ's Nativity between the Angel and the Shepherds." The other shall be set forth, if the Lord will, hereafter, at a convenient time. I translated out of Latin into English divers little treatises: "The Shield of Salvation;" "The Solace of the Soul;" "The Commendation of Death," &c.

Thus have I declared unto you, neighbours, how I spent my time whiles I have been from you. It now remaineth that, forasmuch as heretofore I have perceived your gentleness in accepting the poor and homely gifts that I have given you, I go forth to use still mine accustomed liberality toward you, and to enrich you with more gifts, which may no less garnish your souls than the other have done in times past, howsoever the papists and antichrist's soldiers have judged of them. For as the blind owls cannot away with the sun-light, no more can these cankered papists away with the light of God's word, or any godly book that is drawn forth of the holy scriptures.

The gift which I will now give you is called "The Jewel of Joy," and not without a cause. For in it you shall receive much true joy and perfect solace, much godly pleasure and spiritual comfort. In it ye shall see in what thing alone ye ought to rejoice, and how vain and transitory those things are wherein the foolish and fantastical worldlings repose their chief pleasure and delectation. This jewel have I borrowed of the blessed apostle, St Paul; and it is among his treasures couched in the fourth chapter of his epistle to the Philippians. *Chris.* I pray you, what is it? let it be brought forth. The Jewel of Joy.

Phil. Lo! here it is:

"Rejoice in the Lord alway, and again I say, rejoice." Phil. iv.

How like you this jewel? Is it not both goodly and precious? Is it not worth the looking on, as they say? Is it not a jewel worthy to be worn of every true-hearted christian man? *Eus.* It is a jewel indeed, not only amiable and pleasant in aspect, but also very comfortable and wholesome to a christian man's conscience.

Theo. It is no apt jewel for the wicked worldlings and bellied hypocrites, which, like to Esop's cock, set more by a barley-corn than by all the precious stones in the world, of this sort chiefly. *Phil.* Truth it is. For if men, estranged from the public weal of the true Israelites, carnally-minded, uncircumcised in heart, disobedient to the yoke of Christ, not regenerate by the Spirit of God, nor renewed by the holy baptism, but in all points led captive at the devil's pleasure with the affects of the world, should hear this aforesaid sentence of the holy apostle recited to them, and chiefly of such one as is imprisoned, fettered, bound in chains (as blessed St Paul was, what time he Phil. i. wrote this epistle unto the Philippians), which are instruments to the voluptuous worldlings of no gladness, but of sadness, of no joy and pastance[2], but of sorrow and grievance, they would no less than marvel at his fondness; yea, it is to be thought, that they would laugh him to scorn as a person transposed and far set beyond the limits of witty reason and reasonable wit, seeing he exhorteth unto that which, in so great storms and tempests of troublous adversity, no heart led with human wisdom can easily approve; so blind, foolish, ignorant, and of no capacity, feeling, or understanding in spiritual things, is the wisdom of this world, as St Paul saith: "A natural 1 Cor. ii. man doth not perceive those things that pertain to the Spirit of God. For they are foolishness to him; neither can he come to the knowledge of them, because they are spiritually judged." The head rulers among the Jews, the bishops, the priests, the scribes, the Pharisees, the Sadducees, the lawyers, with many other which were in Christ's time, prove this thing evidently true enough, which, although in their own John vii. conceit puffed up with the excellent knowledge of God's mysteries, perceived nothing at all of Christ's blessed doctrine; so truly is it said of the holy apostle: "The wisdom 1 Cor. iii. of this world is foolishness before God." Neither want we examples at this present.

[[2] Pastance: pastime; or rather perhaps, feasting, the state of one *bene pastus*.]

To know Christ truly is the gift of God. *Eus.* To know Christ and Christ's doctrine aright is the singular gift of God, wrought in our hearts by his holy Spirit, as Christ himself testifieth, saying: "No man can come unto me, except the Father which sent me draw him; and I will raise him up in the last day. It is written in the prophets, All shall be taught of God; therefore every one that hath heard of the Father, and hath learned, he cometh to me." John vi. Isai. liv. Jer. xxxi.

Matt. xi. *Theo.* In the gospel of blessed Matthew our Saviour Christ giveth thanks to his heavenly Father, because he hath hidden the knowledge of his mysteries from the wise and prudent of this world, which gloried in their own wisdom, and hath revealed them to the little ones; that is to say, to them that be humble-minded, meek in spirit, lowly in heart, and even such as ascribe all glory and honour to God, and not to themselves. "Forsooth, Father," saith he, "even so was it thy good pleasure. All things are given over unto me of my Father. And no man knoweth the Son but the Father, neither knoweth any man the Father save the Son, and he to whomsoever the Son will open him."

Rom. i. Gal. i. 1 Tim. ii. *Phil.* But this our apostle and faithful ambassador, sent from God the Father to be a doctor to the gentiles in faith and verity, a true citizen of the new celestial Hierusalem, abundantly replete with the fruits of the Holy Ghost, and plenteously endued with wisdom from above to understand and declare the excellent mysteries of God's most high providence, hid in the bosom of his divine secrets from everlasting, and now in this last angle[1] revealed, published, and set abroad to the great comfort of all faithful penitent sinners, through his Son Jesu Christ our Lord—this our apostle, I say, even in the midst of his chains and fetters, writeth to the Philippians, and by them to all other true Christians, and exhorteth them to be merry and to rejoice in the Lord. He is nothing dismayed, nor yet abashed, of his bonds, chains, and fetters, of Acts xxi. his imprisoning, locking, and stocking; but being of a frank courage and lusty stomach, not only to suffer chains, but also death, if the good-will of God so be, he with a vehemency of spirit and stoutness of heart commandeth us not to be discouraged, with whatsoever kind of adversity we be assailed, but valiantly and unfeignedly to repose, fix, and set the eyes of our mind on the Lord, and in him, in him alone, to rejoice at all times. "Rejoice in the Lord alway," saith he, "and once again I say, rejoice."

The covetous man. *Eus.* Every man moveth other to delight in that thing specially wherein he himself hath reposed his chief delectation. The covetous man hath his greatest delight in temporal possessions, and as he is only bent to the accumulating and heaping up together of worldly goods, so in like manner doth he exhort so many as he tenderly loveth to set their minds on gathering together the goods of this world, being not Prov. xxx. unlike them, which are ever crying, *Adfer, adfer*: "Bring hither, bring hither." The The papist. papist hath his mind altogether set on papistry; therefore laboureth he to the uttermost of his power to allure other unto his pernicious and damnable doctrine.

Phil. Truth it is that you say. Therefore the blessed apostle, having his principal joy in the Lord our God, exhorteth, moveth, and stirreth us earnestly to rejoice in the Lord, that we may be partakers with him of one and the same glory. He is not content himself only to be in the favour of God, except he have other also Phil. i. to be "in the bowels of Jesus Christ." *Chris.* In the epistle unto the Romans he wished Rom. ix. himself to be cursed from Christ, so that his brethren the Israelites, which were his kinsmen as pertaining to the flesh, might be saved. *Theo.* He dissented not much from the manners of Moses, that most excellent prophet of God, which, perceiving that God was minded to destroy the children of Israel for their abominable idolatry Exod. xxxii. in worshipping the golden calf, desired God very heartily that he would either forgive them that fault, or else wipe him out of the book of life. *Eus.* O most faithful herdman, which wished the salvation of his flock no less than his own!

Phil. But we shall note that St Paul pricketh not us forward unto the rejoicing in worldly and carnal things, but unto a perfect joy in the Lord our God, which ☞ endureth for ever. For what thing is comprehended in the whole circle of the world,

[[1] Angle: perhaps an error for *age*; or if correct, it must mean *corner*, i.e. of time.]

wherein we may worthily rejoice? Consider the air above, the earth underneath, with the deep waters in the secret and inferior parts of the world, and mark diligently, if in them any thing be contained that may bring to us true and perfect joy. They may delight our fancies, and move our affects for a certain space unto delectation, while we behold, hear, feel, or taste them; but how soon doth this carnal delectation and worldly joy vanish away! yea, how soon are we weary of them, if measure be exceeded! Musical instruments feed the ear with very sweet and pleasant harmony, and for a time greatly exhilarate, cheer, and comfort our wearied spirits; but in how short space do we loathe them, if they be continually played upon or exercised out of time! and though we delight never so greatly in them, doth not the sound straightway perish, and we receive none other commodity than loss of time? Music.

Theo. The wise man saith: "Like as the carbuncle stone shineth that is set in gold, so is the sweetness of music by the mirth of wine." Again: "Wine and minstrels rejoice the heart." *Phil.* Yea, but what followeth? The best is behind, as they say. "But the love of wisdom is above them both." This sentence of the wise man doth not condemn music nor wine, so that the use of them be moderate and exceedeth not measure: notwithstanding, it preferreth the love of wisdom, that is to say, a fervent desire to know the will of God, and advanceth that above both wine and music. Ecclus. xxxii. Ecclus. xl.

Chris. I wish that all men, but chiefly such as be of nobility, did know and would practise this aforesaid sentence. For many delight in music, but few in the love of wisdom: many covet to excel in singing, playing, and dancing, but in the knowledge of God's word very few. Many can abide to spend whole days and whole nights in musical exercises, but in hearing or reading the holy scriptures, they think one holy day in a week a great matter; when the one moveth unto virtue, the other unto vice; the one getteth the favour of God, the other provoketh his wrath, indignation, and vengeance; the one lifteth up unto heaven, the other detrudeth and thrusteth down into hell-fire.

Phil. To say the truth, music is a more vain and trifling science than it becometh a man, born and appointed to matters of gravity, to spend much time about it. And although I have learned of histories, that divers have exercised minstrelsy, both kings and philosophers, which I think used it as a remedy against the tediousness of their painful labours, and to make them the more apt to return unto matters of great importance; yet I remember well that it was counted a reproach in many. King Philip, when he heard his son Alexander, that triumphant conqueror, sing and play very pleasantly, checkingly rebuked him, saying: "Art thou not ashamed that thou canst play and sing so cunningly?" Meaning that other arts and sciences are more worthy a king. An heathen prince thought that a great fault in his son, which christian rulers count worthy of high commendation and singular praise. Sextus Nero the emperor, lying on his death-bed, greatly lamented that he was so excellent in the science of music, wishing that he had spent that time in good letters and virtuous exercises, whereby he might have been made the more able justly and truly to govern his realm. King Philip. Sextus Nero.

Eus. Would God that his repentance might be a warning to all noble men! There have been, (would God there were not now!) which have not spared to spend much riches in nourishing many idle singing-men to bleat in their chapels, thinking so to do God an high sacrifice, and to pipe down their meat and their drink, and to whistle them asleep; but they have not spent any part of their substance to find a learned man in their houses to preach the word of God, to haste them to virtue and to dissuade them from vice. Therefore swarmed their houses with pride, ambition, vain-glory, covetousness, whoredom, swearing, stealing, polling, picking, envy, malice, fighting, flattery, superstition, hypocrisy, papistry, idolatry, and all kind of abomination, as it must needs come to pass where the word of God is banished, though there be never so much massing and masking, according to the saying of Salomon: "When the preaching of God's word faileth, the people perish and come to nought." Prov. xxix.

Theo. It becometh kings, princes, and rulers rather to hear the preacher of God's Note.

word, and to give ear unto the lamentable voices and humble supplications of their poor afflict and oppressed subjects, than to hearken to the sound of vain instruments, and to delight in hearing the filthy and trifling songs of drunken musicians, which rather provoke unto fleshly fantasies than unto virtuous exercises. A christian man's melody, after St Paul's mind, consisteth in heart, while we recite psalms, hymns, and spiritual songs, and sing to the Lord in our hearts, "giving thanks always for all things unto God the Father, in the name of our Lord Jesus Christ." All other outward melody is vain and transitory, and passeth away and cometh to nought. *Phil.* Vain and transitory is it indeed: notwithstanding, music may be used, so it be not abused. If it be soberly exercised and reputed as an handmaid unto virtue, it is tolerable; otherwise it is execrable, and to be abhorred of all good men. So that ye perceive, that music is not so excellent a thing, that a christian man ought earnestly to rejoice in it. *Chris.* It is evident enough; seeing that it endureth not, but passeth away like other things subject to vanity.

Eph. v.

Gorgeous houses.

Phil. There are that greatly delight in building gorgeous houses and sumptuous mansions; but how vain is their delectation! When they have spent innumerable riches in erecting their pleasant and fair houses, what have they but a great heap of stones couched one upon another, which for a little season feedeth the eye well, but, ☞ when we be once gone, what profit carry we away with us? The holy patriarchs of the old time, remembering how vain it is to delight in gorgeous houses, built them tents, and in those safely dwelt, considering with themselves that they were but strangers and pilgrims, and therefore prepared them houses not for this world, but for the world to come, by couching their treasures in the bosoms of poor men.

Eus. To build necessary and convenient houses for our use is not ungodly, as I judge; but to repose our delight in them, or so to spend our goods on building that the poor people are the less regarded, succoured, relieved, and holpen, this is wicked, this is ungodly. *Chris.* Building is the daughter of fancy, and may in a manner be compared to the web of Penelope. For that one setteth up, another, after the disbursing of many pounds, destroyeth, and buildeth it up again with double expences; the third succeedeth, and, his fantasy not fully satisfied, he again altereth the building and addeth threefold charge: so that to build (I speak of too much gorgeous and not necessary houses) is nothing else than to dally with the world and to be led with fancy.

Theo. What was in time past more gorgeous than Rome, when she was called the lady and head of the world? What was more sumptuously built than the temple of Salomon, yea, and that at God's commandment? as I may pass over many ancient and famous cities: what is become of them? how are they decayed! Many are come to such and so great downfal, and to so extreme ruin, so deformed, so destroyed, so consumed to dust, that there remaineth not so much as a step, neither is there left of them any mention at all. Well were it with christian religion, if christian men would remember this sentence of blessed Paul: "We have no dwelling-place in this world, but we look for another to come." Then should the heavenly mansion be more desired and sought after. But now many build and they know not who shall inherit, and in the midst of these their gorgeous buildings the poor people are not considered nor provided for. *Eus.* Would God all such as so greatly delight in costious buildings, would sometime set this sentence of the wise man before their eyes: "If thou keepest not thyself," saith he, "in the fear of the Lord continually, thy house shall soon be subverted, toppled over, and brought to nought."

Heb. xiii.

Ecclus. xxvii.

Chris. Methink that this curious building, which almost universally is used now-a-days among us, is a great token of the day of judgment being at hand. For Christ in the gospel, among other tokens, recited building to be one of the chief, whereby we may learn that the coming of the Son of man unto the terrible judgment is at hand, as St James saith: "Behold, the judge standeth before the door."

Luke xvii.

James v.

Phil. I perceive now right well, ye are fully persuaded that no man ought to rejoice in gorgeous buildings, wherein many delight now-a-days. *Theo.* Yea, verily. The history of the rich man in the gospel maketh us afraid, which was a builder also; and when he had finished his building, and couched his goods in his fair and

Luke xii.

large houses, thinking that he should have lived many years, suddenly it was said unto him: "Thou fool, this night shall they take away thy life from thee; and then whose shall these things be thou hast gathered together?"

Phil. To enjoy great possessions in this world seemeth, not to a few, a singular commodity and high profit, but with how many cares and troubles are they accompanied! With what great labour are they gotten and scraped up together! With what carefulness and disquiet of mind are they kept, the hoarders up of them being at all hours in more fear lest they should be taken away from them either by robbing, polling, pilling, burning, or by some other chance! How shortly are they consumed and brought to nought, which were not gathered together without long time and great sweat! So vain and transitory be the goods of the world. Again, are not the worldly possessions many times left to such heirs, as spend them no less prodigally, than their ancestors got them hardly, and keepeth them niggardly? What just cause also hath any man to rejoice in temporal riches, seeing that, at the dreadful day of judgment, they shall render a strait accompts of every farthing to the high and everlasting Judge, Christ, how they have bestowed them? For God hath not endued the rich men with their possessions that they should spend them at their pleasure and fancy, but according to his most godly commandment, will, and pleasure. "Silver is mine, and gold is mine, saith the Lord of hosts." Hereto agreeth the saying of the psalmograph: "The earth is the Lord's, and all that is contained in it." The Lord hath committed his goods to the rich men, and he will call them to accompts again, to see how they have bestowed them, and what they have won and gotten by the exercise of them for the Lord's avantage, as we may see in the gospel. If they be found unprofitable servants, and have not bestowed them in setting forth the glory of God, and in the helping of their christian brethren, but have hid them up in the ground, that is to say, kept them niggardly to their own use, or spent them about vain and wicked things; they may be sure to be bound feet and hands, to be cast into utter darkness, where shall be weeping and gnashing of teeth.

Of riches. Hag. ii. Psal. xxiv. Matt. xxv. Luke xix.

Chris. O that these things were well considered, pondered, and weighed in the just balance of reasonable discretion! then should the right[1] men of this world have little occasion to glory in their terrestrial and worldly possessions, but rather recount them most happy, wealthy, and fortunate, to whom least is committed. For every man shall render accounts of the talents received, be they few or many.

Theo. "Blessed is the rich which is found without blemish," saith the wise man, "and hath not gone after gold, nor put his trust in money and treasures. Where is there such a one? and we shall commend him, and call him blessed. For great things doeth he among his people. Whoso is tried and found perfect in such things shall be commended and praised. Yea, his good shall be stablished, and the whole congregation shall declare his alms." "Make you friends," saith our Saviour Christ, "of the unrighteous mammon, that, when ye shall have need, they may receive you into everlasting habitations."

Ecclus. xxxi. Luke xvi.

Eus. To see the inordinate affection and insatiable desire which the more part of men have unto the goods of the world, it is a world. Ancient authors complain of the covetousness used in their time; but if they were now alive they would marvel, and with high indignation wear their pen, and write satires and invectives against our covetous worldlings. For their covetous affects know no end, neither are they at any time satiate, be their abundance [of] temporal possessions never so much overflowing and passing all measure. O, good God, good God, how do our spiritual men tumble benefice upon benefice, and prebend upon prebend! And yet are they led with no care of feeding Christ's flock, neither corporally nor spiritually: Christ's threefold *Pasce* is turned into the Jews' double *Tolle*. They feed nothing, except themselves: they toll and catch whatsoever catch they may: would God they once would be obedient to this commandment of God given by the wise man, "Let not thine hand be stretched out to receive, and shut when thou shouldest give!" "A bishop," saith St Paul (he meaneth every spiritual overseer), "ought to maintain

Spiritual men. [John xxi. 15-7. xix. 15.] Ecclus. iv. 1 Tim. iii.

[[1] Perhaps *rich*.]

Heb. xiii. Hospitality. hospitality." Again he saith: "Forget not hospitality and household-keeping: for thereby have divers men received into their houses angels unwares." Hereto agreeth 1 Pet. iv. the saying of St Peter: "Be ye harbourous one to another without grudging. As every man hath received the gift, even so minister the same one to another, as good ministers of the manifold grace of God." God in the old law, greatly tendering the maintenance of hospitality in his ministers, gave this commandment to his people for Mal. iii. paying their tithes, saying: "Bring ye in all tithes into my barn, that there may be Why tithes were paid. meat in my house." Here God commanded tithes to be paid, but for what cause? that the ministers should spend them in the court or at the university? or about whoring? or in keeping of hawks or dogs, or in maintaining a sort of idle valiant lubbers, which do nothing but consume the good fruits of the earth? Nay, verily, but that there should be meat in his house, (for the parsonage or vicarage is God's house.) For whom? for the covetous worldlings and rich men which have no need of it? Nay, sir, not so; but for the poor Christians, as Christ prescribeth, saying: Luke xiv. "When thou makest a dinner or supper, call not thy friends, nor thy brethren, neither thy kinsmen, nor thy rich neighbours, lest they also bid thee again, and a recompence be made thee. But when thou makest a feast, call the poor, the feeble, the lame, and the blind, and thou shalt be happy; for they cannot recompense thee: but thou shalt be recompensed at the resurrection of the righteous."

Why priests are despised. *Chris.* I think the greatest cause why priests be contemned at this time is, that they neither regard their office in preaching God's word, nor[1] yet their duty in Mal. ii. maintaining hospitality. *Eus.* Truth it is; for God saith by the prophet: "I have made you, O ye priests, to be despised and to be of no reputation among all the people, because ye have not kept my ways, but have been partial in the law." The duty of priests. The ways and ordinances of God, which he hath prescribed to priests for to observe, is truly to preach his holy doctrine, reverently to minister his blessed sacraments, and bounteously to maintain hospitality. If they would do these things, they should recover their honour which is due to faithful ministers by the word of God, as St Paul 1 Tim. v. saith: "The priests that rule well are worthy double honour, specially they that labour in word and doctrine."

Theo. But covetousness reigneth not only in the spiritualty? *Eus.* In the spiri- Temporal men. tualty only! No, God knoweth. For the temporalty is not behind, for their part. If ever heretofore, in this our time specially, is[2] this saying of the prophet found true: Jer. vi. "From the least unto the most they hang upon covetousness, and from the prophet unto the priest they go all about with falsehead and lies." How join they lordship to lordship, manor to manor, farm to farm, land to land, pasture to pasture, house to house, and house for a vantage! How do the rich men, and specially such as be Sheepmongers. sheepmongers, oppress the king's liege people by devouring their common pastures with their sheep; so that the poor people are not able to keep a cow for the comfort of them and of their poor family, but are like to starve and perish for hunger, if there be not provision made shortly! What sheep-ground scapeth these caterpillars of the commonweal? How swarm they with abundance of flocks of sheep! and yet when was wool ever so dear, or mutton of so great price? If these sheepmongers go forth as they begin, the people shall both miserably die for cold, and wretchedly perish for hunger. For these greedy wolves and cumberous cormorants will either sell their wool and their sheep at their own price, or else they will sell none. Oh, what a diversity is this in the sale of wools, a stone of wool sometime to be sold at eight groats, and now for eight shillings! And so likewise of the sheep. God have mercy on us!

If the king his majesty, with his most honourable council, do not provide for the redress of these things, God himself will surely see a remedy, as he saith by the Psal. xii. psalmograph: "For the wretchedness of the needy, and the bewailing of the poor, even Isai. xxxiii. now will I rise, saith the Lord." Again he saith: "Wo be to thee that spoilest! shalt not thou thyself be likewise spoiled? And thou that despisest the poverty, shalt not thou in like manner be despised? When thou hast made an end of polling and pilling, then shalt thou be polled and pilled thyself: and when thou ceasest to despise

[1 Folio, *not*.] [2 Folio, *in*.]

other, then shalt thou be despised and nought set by. O Lord, have mercy upon us: for all our whole trust is in thee. Be thou our defence, yea, and that shortly. Be thou our saving health in the time of our trouble."

Chris. Rich men were never so much estranged from all pity and compassion toward the poor people, as they be at this present time: "They devour the people as it were a morsel of bread." If any piece of ground delight their eye, they must needs have it, either by hook or by crook. If the poor man will not satisfy their covetous desire, he is sure to be molested, troubled, and disquieted on such sort that, whether he will or will not (though both he, his careful wife, and miserable children, with his whole family, should perish for hunger), he shall forego it; or else it were as good for him to live among the furies of hell as to dwell by those rich carles and covetous churls. There is no end of enlarging their grounds, neither are they led with any fear of God's indignation, expressed by the prophet, saying: "Wo and everlasting damnation be unto them that join house to house, and couple land to land so nigh together, that the poor can get no more ground! Shall ye alone dwell in the midst of the earth? These things are in mine ears, saith the Lord of hosts. Surely, saith he, many great and fair houses shall be made so desert and waste, that no man shall dwell in them." Hereto agreeth the saying of another prophet: "Wo and everlasting damnation be unto him that heapeth up other men's goods! How long will he lade himself with thick clay unto his own damnation? O how suddenly will they stand up that shall bite thee, and awake that shall tear thee in pieces! Yea, thou shalt surely be their prey. Seeing thou hast spoiled many people, therefore shall they that remain spoil thee, because of men's blood, and for the wrong done in the land, in the city, and unto all them that dwell therein. Wo and everlasting damnation be unto him that covetously gathereth evil-gotten goods into his house, that he may set his nest on high to escape the power of misfortune! Thou hast devised the shame of thine own house; for thou hast slain too much people, and hast wilfully offended; so that the very stones of the wall shall cry out of it, and the timber that lieth betwixt the joints of the building shall answer," &c.

Psal. xiv.

The unmercifulness of rich men.

Isai. v.

Hab. ii.

Theo. These be grievous threats of God's vengeance against the covetous worldlings.

Phil. They be no less true than grievous, and shall undoubtedly chance as it is threatened, except the covetous worldlings repent and amend; for "God is faithful in all his sayings"; and "the word of the Lord abideth for ever." He is the self truth: therefore can he not lie. Whatsoever he threateneth he will surely bring to pass, except faithful repentance be a mean. Are not these his words? "Wo and everlasting damnation be unto them that sin, and keep not my commandments, saith the Lord: I will not surely spare them." And the wise man saith: "Wo be unto you, O ye wicked persons, which have forsaken the law of the Lord, that most high God! If ye be born, ye shall be born to cursing: if ye die, the curse shall also be your portion." David saith: "Upon the ungodly the Lord shall rain snares, fire and brimstone, storm and tempest: this shall be their portion to drink." How doth our Saviour Jesus Christ thunder against the ungodly rich in the holy gospel: "Wo unto you that are rich!" saith he, "for ye have your consolation. Wo unto you that are full! for ye shall hunger. Wo unto you that now laugh! for ye shall wail and weep."

Psal. cxl.

Isai. xl.

John xiv.

2 Esdr. xv.

Ecclus. xli.

Psal. xi.

Luke vi.

Chris. These be grievous words against the covetous worldlings and voluptuous epicures: but full little do such things sink into the breasts of men now-a-days; the devil hath so blinded their eyes, that they think that God is a childish God, and will be pleased with this apple at the last end: 'I am sorry for my sins: good Lord, forgive me: I trust to be saved by Christ's passion,' and many good morrows. So long as they live, they never repent their wicked living: they go forth daily more and more to provoke the wrath of God against them, they heap sin upon sin, they wallow all in pleasures like filthy swine, they have not the fear of God before their eyes, they are without all mercy toward their christian brethren, they grievously oppress their needy neighbours, they make no end of raking together the goods of the world, they follow the lusts of the flesh as miserable and bond captives; to conclude, their whole life is nothing else but a serving of the devil: how can these men at the last end truly repent and convert unto God, leading afore a life abominable,

Psal. cxlv. so wicked, so stinking, so hateful both to God and to all good men? I grant "the mercy of God is great, and excelleth all his works;" but how can they, which have led their whole life altogether displeasant unto God, be bold to crave mercy of God at the last end, whom all the days of their life they have so despised by disobeying his most godly will and pleasure? Are not these his words spoken by king Salomon? Prov. i. "I have called; and ye refused it: I have stretched out my hand; and no man regarded it; but all my counsels have ye despised, and set my correction at nought. Therefore shall I also laugh in your destruction, and mock you, when that thing that ye fear cometh upon you; even when the thing that ye be afraid of falleth in suddenly like a storm, and your misery like a tempest, yea, when trouble and heaviness cometh upon you. Then shall they call upon me; but I will not hear: they shall seek me early, but they shall not find me; and that because they hated knowledge, and received not the fear of the Lord, but abhorred my counsel, and despised all 1 Pet. iv. my correction." "If the righteous shall scarcely be saved," saith blessed Peter, "where shall the ungodly and the sinner appear?"

Destroyers of towns. *Eus.* Satan, through covetousness, doth so possess the hearts of many men in these our days, that they do not only link house to house, but, when they have gotten many houses and tenements into their hands, yea, whole townships, they suffer the houses to fall into utter ruin and decay; so that by this means whole towns are become desolate, and like unto a wilderness, no man dwelling there, except it be the shepherd and his dog.

Phil. Truth it is. For I myself know many towns and villages sore decayed; so that, whereas in times past there were in some town an hundred households, there remain not now thirty; in some fifty, there are not now ten; yea (which is more to be lamented), I know towns so wholly decayed, that there is neither stick nor stone standing, as they use to say.

Where many men had good livings, and maintained hospitality, able at all times to help the king in his wars, and to sustain other charges, able also to help their poor neighbours, and virtuously to bring up their children in godly letters and good sciences, now sheep and conies devour altogether, no man inhabiting the aforesaid places. Those beasts which were created of God for the nourishment of man do now devour man. Psal. viii. The scripture saith that God made "both sheep and oxen with all the beasts of the field" subject unto man; but now man is subject unto them. Where man was wont to Beasts above men. bear rule, there they now bear rule. Where man was wont to have his living, there they now only live. Where man was wont to inhabit, there they now range and graze.

And the cause of all this wretchedness and beggary in the commonweal are the Gentlemen sheepmongers. greedy gentlemen, which are sheepmongers and graziers. While they study for their own private commodity, the commonweal is like to decay. Since they began to be sheep-masters and feeders of cattle, we neither had victual nor cloth of any reasonable price. No marvel; for these forestallers of the market, as they use to say, have gotten all things so into their hands, that the poor man must either buy it at their price, or else miserably starve for hunger, and wretchedly die for cold: for they are touched Phil. ii. with no pity toward the poor. It is found true in them that St Paul writeth: "All seek their own advantage, and not those things which belong unto Jesu Christ." They which in times past were wont to be fathers of the country, are now pollers and pillers of the country. They which in times past were wont to be the defenders of the poor, are now become the destroyers of the same. They by whom the commonweal sometime was preserved, are now become the caterpillars of the commonweal, and such as seem by their manners to have made a solemn vow utterly to subvert the commonweal, and to procure the final destruction of the same. They are insatiable wolves. They know no measure. So they may reign, they care not who suffer pain. So they may abound, they care not who fall to the ground. So they may be enriched, they care not who be impoverished. They are right brothers of Cain, which had rather Gen. iv. slay his brother Abel, than he should have any part with him of worldly possessions.

Ecclus. xxxiv. The wise man saith: "The bread of the needy is the life of the poor: he that defraudeth him of it is a manslayer." Do not these rich worldlings defraud the Bread, what it signifieth. poor man of his bread, whereby is understand all things necessary for a man's life, which, through their insatiable covetousness, sell all things at so high price, and suffer towns so to decay, that the poor hath not what to eat, nor yet where to dwell? What other are they then, but very manslayers? They abhor the names of monks, friars, canons, nuns, &c.; but their goods they greedily gripe. And yet, where the cloisters kept hospitality, let out their farms at a reasonable price, nourished schools, brought up youth in good letters, they did none of all these things. They lightly esteem, and in a manner contemn priests, parsons, vicars, prebendaries, &c.; yet their possessions they gladly embrace and niggardly retain. So that now they are become in effect, although not in name, very monks, friars, canons, priests, parsons, vicars, prebendaries, and, at the last, what not? and yet how vainly those goods be spent, who seeth not? Mark well.

The state of England was never so miserable as it is at this present. Good Lord, have mercy upon us, and put in the hearts of the king and of his council to redress these intolerable pestilences of the commonweal, or else make haste to dissolve this wretched world by thy glorious coming unto the judgment; where thou shalt "render to every man according to his deeds;" lest, if we long remain in this too much wretchedness, we be compelled through poverty to attempt unrighteous things, and forswear the name of thee, our Lord God. Rom. ii. Prov. xxx.

Well, of these things aforesaid, I trust ye perceive that no man ought to rejoice in the riches of this world, seeing they are none of ours, but God's, and we, as the treasurers and stewards of God, must at the dreadful day of judgment render accompts to the high Judge Christ for all that we have received, be it much or little; seeing also they are very transitory and flitting from one to another, insomuch that he which is this day a lord highly in favour, and a man of great possessions, is to-morrow a traitor, and not worth a gally half-penny[1]. Again, if they be abused, they are very enticements unto all mischief and naughtiness; they pluck our hearts from God to the devil; they make us idolaters, by serving that wicked mammon; they provoke the vengeance of God against us; they make us to be abhorred of God and of all good men; they pluck from our bodies rest, from our minds quietness, from our eyes sleep, from our face natural colour, and add to all the parts of man distemperance, making man a slave unto that which ought to be obedient unto him. Riches abused.

Theo. We perceive these things right well. For the wise man saith: "There is nothing worse than a covetous man; neither is there a more wicked thing than to love money. For such one hath his soul to sell, and yet is he but filthy dung while he liveth." And the preacher saith: "He that loveth money will never be satisfied with money; and whoso delighteth in riches shall have no profit thereof. Where as much riches is, there are many also that spend them away. And what pleasure more hath he that possesseth them, saving that he may look upon them with his eyes? A labouring man sleepeth sweetly, whether it be little or much that he eateth; but the abundance of the rich will not suffer him to sleep; yea, many times riches are kept to the hurt of him that hath them in possession. For ofttimes they perish with his great misery and trouble; and if he have a child, it getteth nothing." "Like as he came naked out of his mother's womb, so goeth he thither again, and carrieth nothing away with him of all his labour," &c. Ecclus. xx. Eccles. v. Job i.

Eus. It were wisdom for the rich men, if they tender their own salvation, and be led with any hope of the life to come, to hear what blessed Paul writeth unto bishop Timothy, and earnestly to follow that. His words are these: "Charge them which are rich in this world, that they be not high-minded, nor trust in uncertain riches, but in the living God, which giveth us abundantly all things to enjoy them; that they do good works, that they be ready to give, and glad to distribute; laying up in store for themselves a good foundation against the time to come, that they may obtain eternal life." 1 Tim. vi.

Phil. O that they would be advertised by this apostle! Then should God be their defender in all their affairs, and cause both them and their posterity long to enjoy their possessions, with the favour and blessing of all good men. But let us go forth, and search whether any thing can be found in this transitory world wherein we may worthily rejoice. What say ye unto nobility? Of nobility.

[[1] See Vol. I. page 235, note 6.]

Chris. Not a few do greatly rejoice in that, magnifying themselves because they descend of noble parentage, and in comparison of themselves they greatly despise other.

Phil. O foolish, rude, ignorant people! Why rather do they not consider that both rich and poor, noble and unnoble, high or base, do consist and are made of the same Gen. iii. elements, subject unto like diseases, and bond to the same affects? Earth we are all and dust, and unto earth and dust shall we return. As we were made to live, so likewise are we all appointed to die. Bodies have we all corruptible, and bond to mortality. There is no exception among us. Neither hath any of us obtained such privilege of God, that we may escape the bondage of frail nature. Seeing then that, as touching our corporal creation, there is no difference, no prerogative, what nobility or worthiness of blood can there be more in the noble personage than in the base slave? Their beginning is like: their end is all one. Twice mad are they, therefore, that brag of their noble blood, and esteem themselves the more worthy because they descend of noble parentages; neither do such any other-thing than boast of that which is none of Psal. xxx. theirs. King David saith: "What profit is there in my blood, seeing I go down unto Ecclus. x. corruption?" And the wise man saith: "Why art thou proud, O thou earth and ashes?" We are all earth and ashes, both noble and unnoble. We all shall return unto corruption, and be so consumed as concerning our bodies, as though we had never been. Isai. xl. The prophet also saith: "All flesh is grass, and all his glory is like a flower of the field:" where is any mention made here of noble blood? "I know," saith St Paul, "that Rom. vii. there dwelleth in me, that is to say, in my flesh, no goodness:" where is carnal nobility then become? Doth not the same loathsome vileness come from the noble, that issueth out of the unnoble? Are not the carcases of all personages meat for worms alike? Pour the blood of the villain[1] in one basin, and the blood of the gentleman in another: what difference shall there be proved? Dig up the bones out of the sepulchres both of the noble and unnoble; and who can discern of the sight of them, which was the servant, which the lord, who was rich and who was poor, who beautiful and who deformed, which were noble, and which unnoble? "There is no difference," as St Ambrose saith, "between the carcases of the dead, except peradventure it be this, that the dead corpse of the rich stink more grievously than the poor, because it was more daintily fed[2]".

Titled gentlemen. *Eus.* So far as I perceive, they err greatly that boast of their kindred, and esteem themselves the more worthy because they come of worthy parents, although they themselves be never so great drunkards, gluttons, dice-players, whoremongers, swearers, fighters, thieves, ruffians, pickers of quarrels, riotous persons, &c. For little doth it profit a man to descend of a noble house, if he himself be of base and vile manners, and lead a life defiled with wickedness; yea, it rather bringeth unto him ignobility than In Matt. nobility. Well is it said of our golden-mouthed doctor: "The nobility and goodness of our kinsfolk availeth nothing, except we ourselves be good. For what doth noble generation profit him whom his manners do defile? Or what doth vile generation hurt him whom good manners do garnish and adorn? Certes he sheweth himself void of all goodness, that glorieth in his parents[3]." "To glory upon the nobility of other," saith Petrarch, "is a boasting even to be laughed at[4]." And such as have nothing but the badges, cognisances, and arms of their ancestors to set out their nobility withal, they differ not much from Esop's crow, which decked himself with other birds' feathers, he himself being altogether black and unamiable.

Wherein true nobility consisteth. *Theo.* The true nobility consisteth neither in strength, beauty, nor riches, no, nor yet in any other external and bodily thing, but in the suppressing of vice and embracing of virtue. "Virtue is the alone and only nobility," as Antisthenes was wont to say: "They that are endued with virtue, they have the true nobility." Notably is it said In Matt. of the golden-mouthed doctor, John Chrysostom: "He is a man of great renown, he

[1 Villain: bondman or servant.]

[2 Nulla discretio inter cadavera mortuorum; nisi forte quod gravius fœtent divitum corpora distenta luxurie.—Ambros. Op. Par. 1686-90. Hexaem. Lib. VI. cap. viii. 51. Tom. I. col. 133.]

[3 Quid enim prodest ei quem sordidant mores, generatio clara? Aut quid nocet illi generatio vilis, quem mores adornant? Ipse se vacuum ab omnibus bonis actibus ostendit, qui gloriatur in patribus.—Chrysost. Op. Par. 1718-38. Opus Imperf. in Matt. Hom. iii. ex cap. iii. Tom. VI. p. xxxvii.]

[4 Alieno gloriari ridiculosa jactantia.—Petrarch. Op. Basil. 1581. De Remed. Utriusq. Fort. Lib. I. Dial. xvi. De Orig. Generos. p. 13.]

is a worthy personage, he is the true nobleman, that disdaineth to serve vices, and by no means will be overcome of them[5]." And Cocceius Nerva the emperor said that the virtue of a man, and not his kindred nor his country, is to be considered. *Chris.* Would God all men of nobility were persuaded that virtue and godly conversation were the alone and only true nobility! Then would they not repose their glory in their ancestors, as many very foolishly do at this present; but rather endeavour themselves so to train their life in all godliness and virtue, that even for their own godly and virtuous enterprises they should be counted noble and worthy of praise.

Eus. But what say you unto beauty? *Phil.* Even as Salomon saith: "Favour is deceitful, and beauty is a vain thing." Beauty. Prov. xxxi. They are much estranged from the course of true reason, that rejoice in so frail a thing. For it is more brittle than glass, more transitory than the flower, more inconstant than the wind, more vain than the smoke, and more flitting away than the time. Beauty is a thousand manner of ways corrupted and defaced. How doth one little fever make the fairest woman in the world the foulest and the most unpleasant in aspect! And to say the truth, is beauty any other thing than "a little thin skin well coloured? If the inward parts might be seen, how great filthiness would there appear even in the most beautiful person[6]!" Neither is the fairest body in the world any other thing than a dunghill covered with a cloth, as it were, of white and purple colour. And what a madness is this, for any person to glory in beauty! seeing that the beholder of it hath more delectation and pleasure in it, as one that hath the use and fruition thereof, than such as are endued with the beauty. I leave off to speak that beauty is an enticement unto uncleanness, and a very enemy to chaste and pure conversation, as we read in divers histories. Beauty is an enticement to uncleanness.

Chris. This seemeth to be true by the saying of the wise man: "Look not too narrowly," saith he, "upon the beauty of a woman, lest thou be provoked in desire toward her." Ecclus. xxv. Again he saith: "Turn away thy face from a beautiful woman, and look not upon the fairness of other. Ecclus. ix. Many a man hath perished through the beauty of women; for through it the desire is kindled, as it were fire." Hereto agreeth the saying of Salomon: "Let not thine heart lust after the beauty of a woman, lest thou be taken with her fair looks." Prov. vi. What kindled David's heart with love toward Bethsabe, the wife of Urias, and caused him to commit adultery with her, but only her beauty? "David," saith the scripture, "arose out of his bed, and walked upon the roof of the king's palace, and from the roof he saw a woman washing herself; and the woman was very beautiful to look on." 2 Sam. xi. Again, how came it to pass that the two judges burned so fervently with the love of Susanna, Joachim's wife, and sought all means possible to have defiled her, but that they were drowned with the sight of her beauty? Hist. Sus. The scripture saith she was "a very fair woman;" but there is a goodly addition, she was also "such one as feared God." When beauty and the fear of God are linked together, beauty is not to be discommended: Note well. otherwise it is but a net, wherewith the devil useth to catch the foolish people. "A fair woman without discreet manners," saith Salomon, "is like a ring of gold in a swine's snout." Prov. xi. And that we may be well ascertained that it was her beauty that moved them without shame to provoke her to uncleanness, these words of that history declare it manifestly: "Susanna was a tender person, and marvellous fair of face. Therefore the wicked men commanded to take the cloth from her face, that at the least they might so be satisfied in her beauty."

Phil. God send us more Susans! Beauty reigneth in many: would God it were accompanied with the fear of God, Follow, ye wives. that the beautiful persons might not abuse their beauty, but choose rather to be stoned unto death with Susan, than once to defile their husbands' bed.

Eus. God send us the beauty of the mind, which consisteth in godly virtues and honest qualities; for that is the true beauty, the other is but frail, vain, transitory, and doth not long endure. But what say you unto gallant apparel, whereof so many brag and boast now-a-days? Of gallant apparel. Is it not a thing wherein we may worthily rejoice?

Phil. Nothing less, for the wise man saith: "Glory not in thine apparel at any time." Ecclus. xi. Vestures were given us of God to cover our filthy nakedness, and not that Why clothing was given unto us.

[5 See Hom. ix. Tom. VII. p. 136; Hom. xliv. p. 468; Hom. lviii. p. 589.]

[6 Lod. Vivis Valent. Op. Basil. 1555. Introd. ad Sap. 61. Tom. II. cols. 72, 3. See Vol. I. page 203, note 5.]

we should glory in them, and make them instruments of pride. We ought rather, when we put on our garments, to lament our mischance, our mortality, and uncleanness, ☞ than to rejoice in them. For, so long as our grandfather Adam continued in the state of innocency, he needed no kind of apparel to cover his body (for he was altogether clean, beautiful, good, holy, innocent, and perfect); but after he had broken the commandment of God by giving ear to Satan's subtile persuasions, perceiving his misery and wretchedness whereinto he was fallen through his disobedience, he was ashamed of himself, and both he and his wife, perceiving that they were naked, sewed fig-leaves together and made themselves aprons to cover their filthy and shameful nakedness withal. Afterward, when God drove them out of paradise, because their feeble and mortal bodies, which now were subject to all kind of diseases, tempests, and blasts, should not perish for cold; again, that they might have wherewith to cover their filthy nakedness, that they might walk the more honestly; he made them leathern garments, and clothed them therewith. Here, even from the beginning, do we learn both what garments were given unto man of God, and for what purpose. Neither with fine clothe, nor with satin, damask, velvet, nor with cloth of gold, did God apparel Adam, neither did he trim and set forth our grandmother Eve with sumptuous apparel of cloth of silver, or cloth of gold, neither did he set upon her head a French hood with an edge of gold, besides pearls and precious stones, and such other trim-trams, I cannot tell what; but he clothed them both with simple garments of leather, not that they should rejoice and be proud of them, but to use them as things necessary to cover their wretched nakedness, and to defend them from the cruel storms and fierce tempests of wind, rain, snow, hail, &c.

Gen. iii.

Note.

Eus. As in other things, so likewise in apparel, is[1] the world at this present wonderfully fallen from the first institution of things. For if we should compare the children with the father, I mean, if we should consider what apparel God appointed unto Adam, and what is used now-a-days, a man should find as great difference between them, as is between the sun and the least star in light and brightness.

The madness of Englishmen in their apparel.

To behold the vain and foolish light fashions of apparel used among us, it is too much wonderful. I think no realm in the world, no, not among the Turks and Saracens, doth so much in the vanity of their apparel, as the Englishmen do at this present. Their coat must be made after the Italian fashion, their cloak after the use of the Spaniards, their gown after the manner of the Turks: their cap must be of the French fashion; and at the last their dagger must be Scottish, with a Venetian tassel of silk. I speak nothing of their doublets and hoses, which for the most part are so minced, cut, and jagged, that shortly after they become both torn and ragged. I leave off also to speak of the vanity of certain light-brains, which, because nothing should want to the setting forth of their fondness, will rather wear a Martin chain[2], the price of eight-pence, than they would be unchained. O what a monster and a beast of many heads is the Englishman now become! To whom may he be compared worthily, but to Esop's crow? For as the crow decked herself with the feathers of all kind of birds to make herself beautiful, even so doth the vain Englishman, for the fond apparelling of himself, borrow of every nation to set forth himself gallant in the face of the world. He is an Englishman: he is also an Italian, a Spaniard, a Turk, a Frenchman, a Scot, a Venetian, and, at the last, what not? He is not much unlike a monster called chimæra, which hath three heads, one like a lion, another like a goat, the third like a dragon.

The apparel of women.

I pass over the light and wanton apparel of women now-a-days, partly because it is so monstrous, and partly because I have not been nor yet am very much acquainted

[1 The folio has *in*.]

[2 Martin chain: of counterfeit or base metal. So also St Martin's rings. "They are like rings and chaines bought at St Martin's, that were faire for a little time, but shortly after will prove alchimy, or rather pure copper." Minshull, Essay, p. 23, cited by Nares, v. Alchimy. See also Brand's Popular Antiquities, Vol. II. p. 26, note, v. St Martin's Rings. It appears from Maitland's History of London, p. 770, that St Martin's Le Grand had a right of sanctuary, and became in consequence such a resort of various disreputable characters, that a royal ordinance was issued Feb. 5th, 35 Hen. VI., directing among other things, "That subtle pickers of Locks, Counterfeitors of Keys, Contrivers of Seals, Forgers of false Evidences, *Workers of counterfeit Chaines*, Beades, Brouches, Ouches, Rings, Cups, Spoons silvered, and Plates of Copper gilt, *uttered for Gold*, unto the common hurt of the people, be not suffered in the said Sanctuary."]

with them, whereby I might be the more able to describe their proud peacocks' tails, if not at the full, which were an infinite labour, yet at the least somewhat to set it forth as a painter doth, before he do lay on colours. But of this am I certain, that they observe not in their apparel the rule of the holy scriptures. For St Peter saith, that "the apparel of honest and virtuous women should not be outward with broided hair, and hanging on of gold, either in putting on of gorgeous apparel; but let the hid man," saith he, "which is the heart, be without all corruption, so that the spirit be meek and quiet, which spirit is before God a thing much set by. For after this manner in the old time did the holy women which trusted in God tire themselves, and were obedience to their husbands; even as Sara obeyed Abraham and called him lord, whose daughters ye are as long as ye do well." Hereto agreeth the saying of St Paul to Timothy: "Let the women array themselves in comely apparel, with shamefacedness and discreet behaviour; not with broided hair, either gold, or pearls, or costly array; but, as it becometh women that profess godliness, through good works." Again to Titus he saith: "Speak to the women, that they be in such raiment as becometh holiness." Salomon, in the description of an unhonest woman, among other proprieties rehearseth sumptuous and gallant apparel, calling it whorish apparel, fit to deceive souls, signifying that this too much costly and proud apparel is more meet for whores that lie await to allure men unto their love, than for honest women which profess godliness.

[1 Pet. iii.] [Gen. xviii.] [1 Tim. ii.] [Tit. ii.] [Prov. vii.]

Phil. As filthy, beggar-like, and sluttish apparel becometh not christian women, if they have, or righteously and with honesty may have other; so likewise is it not convenient for them to wear too much sumptuous, costly, and gallant array.

It is enough for chaste and pure maids to wear clean and simple apparel, as a testimony of the uncorruption and cleanness both of their mind and body, without the flaring out and colouring of their hair, without the painting of their faces, without the putting on of wanton and light array, whereby they be enticed rather to pride and whoredom than to humility, shamefacedness, and cleanness of life. [Maids.]

It is sufficient also for honest married wives, that they be so apparelled that they please their husbands: they that deck themselves to please the fancies of other, and to make themselves gazing-stocks to the world, practise rather the manners of whores, than the conditions of honest women. There is nothing that doth better adorn, garnish, and set forth an honest woman, than sobriety, shamefacedness, cleanness of life, honest conversation, integrity of manners, silence, fear toward God, loving obedience toward her husband, comely behaviour in countenance, in looking, in going, in speaking, in doing, and at the last to wear such apparel as serveth for her state and degree. She that is endued with these goodly and godly virtues aforesaid, is a very fair and beautiful woman, though her face may right well be resembled to the colour of an Ethiope, and she may say as it is written in Salomon's ballads: "I am black, yet am I fair." For though she be black in colour of face, yet is she beautiful in mind. And look, how much the mind excelleth the body, even so much doth the beauty of the mind exceed the fairness of the face. [Married women.] [Cant. i.]

Chris. Hester was a very godly and virtuous woman, yet did she wear glorious apparel. *Phil.* I grant; but ye must consider that she was no private person, nor one of the base sort, but she was the most worthy woman in the realm, even the king's wife: notwithstanding, how little she delighted in that gorgeous apparel, which she was compelled to wear for to serve her state and degree, these her words do evidently shew: "Thou knowest, O Lord," saith she, "my necessity, that I hate the token of pre-eminency and glory or worship, which I bear upon my head, what time as I must shew myself and be seen, and that I abhor it as an unclean cloth, and that I wear it not when I am quiet and alone by myself." Do we not also read that, when she prayed to the Lord, she laid away her glorious apparel, and put on the garments that served for sighing and mourning? Again, do we not also read, that when the Jews at any time did humble themselves in the sight of God, and would obtain any thing at his hand, that they laid aside their gallant apparel, and put on sackcloth? Laid they not away thair precious ointments, and scattered ashes and dung upon their heads? This meant somewhat. [Esth. xiv. [Apocr.]]

Eus. Of this am I sure, that holy John Baptist did wear very homely apparel.

Matt. iii. "His raiment," saith the scripture, "was of camel's hair, and he had a girdle of leather about his loins." It is to be thought also that Christ and his apostles, which were but poor men, had not very sumptuous apparel to wear. And St John writeth: "He that saith that he dwelleth in Christ, ought to walk even as Christ walked." How can gorgeous and gallant apparel then agree with christian profession? Is the disciple above his master, or the servant above his Lord? Doth not St Paul, in his epistle to the Hebrews, declare that certain faithful and godly persons "walked up and down in sheep-skins and goat-skins," and were highly commended of God? Doth not St James rebuke the rich men, that have such plenty of garments that they be moth-eaten? Doth he not also reprove such as will accept and make much of them that be clothed in goodly apparel, and neglect the poor which are but homely apparelled? Was it for nought that Christ said to the people of St John Baptist, "What went ye out to see? a man clothed in soft raiment? Behold, they that wear soft clothing are in kings' houses." Is it in vain that St Luke, in the description of the rich glutton, declareth, that "he was clothed in purple and fine white?" Do we not read also that king Herod was arrayed in royal apparel, when the angel of the Lord smote him; so that he died a very miserable death? To rehearse what the doctors of Christ's church write of the vanity of[1] gorgeous apparel; again, to declare out of profane histories, how greatly the noble princes and mighty emperors even among the ethnicks, abhorred sumptuous raiment, both time and tongue should fail me.

[Margin: 1 John ii. — Heb. xi. — James ii. — Matt. xi. — Luke xvi. — Acts xii.]

[Margin: A rule for apparel.] *Phil.* It is very fitting and praiseworthy enough for all degrees of persons to wear apparel according to their state and calling, so that vanity, excess, and rejoicing therein be banished. But confusedly every man or woman to wear as them liketh is both without order and greatly discommendable, and ought by the higher powers to be redressed. To be short in this behalf, it shall be convenient for so many as profess Christ always to set before the eyes of their mind this saying of the apostle: "Having food, and wherewith we may be covered, let us be content." "For we brought nothing into the world, neither shall we carry any thing out of it." And he apparelleth himself well, which forgetteth not to clothe the poor, according to this commandment of God: "When thou seest the naked, clothe him;" as we read of the noble and virtuous woman Tabitha, which made coats and garments for the poor.

[Margin: 1 Tim. vi. — Isai. lviii. — Acts ix.]

Theo. If these things were deeply weighed and considered, they that so greatly delight in sumptuous apparel would soon cease from that vanity, and no more repose their delectation in it. For these garments which we now set by very much, within few years we put them to vile offices, and throw them away upon the dunghill; so that we have little occasion to rejoice in them.

Phil. Truth it is, as these things aforesaid be proved to bring no perfect felicity nor true joy to men, so likewise these that remain, whatsoever they be, make a man no more truly joyful than the other. To pamper the belly and to fare deliciously is reputed among the voluptuous epicures an high and singular pleasure; yet these meats and drinks, which are so dearly bought, and wherein many so greatly delight, become afterward so vile and loathsome, that we can neither abide the sight nor the smell of them. What doth yesterday feasting profit the greedy appetite of the day following? O short and vain pleasure! *Chris.* This belly-cheer and banqueting bringeth not only to man a transitory delectation, and such pleasure as soon passeth away, but it also wasteth[2] a man's substance, and pierceth him with the darts of poverty, as Salomon saith: "He that hath pleasure in banquets shall be a poor man, and whoso delighteth in wine and delicates shall not be rich." Again he saith: "Keep not company with wine-bibbers and riotous eaters of flesh; for such as be drunkards and riotous shall come to poverty."

[Margin: Of banqueting. — Prov. xxi. — Prov. xxiii.]

Eus. They shall not only come to poverty, but such as are riotous persons shall get to themselves through their distemperance and excess of eating and drinking divers sicknesses and diseases very hard to be put away; as the same Salomon saith: "Who hath wo? who hath sorrow? who hath strife? who hath brawling? and who hath wounds without a cause? or who hath red eyes? Even they that be ever at the wine, and seek excess. Look not thou upon the wine, how red it is, and what colour

[Margin: Prov. xxiii.]

[1 Folio, *or*.] [2 Folio, *wasted*.]

it giveth in the glass. It goeth down softly, but at last it biteth like a serpent, and stingeth like an adder." Hither maketh the saying of the wise man: "Be not greedy in every eating, and be not too hasty upon all meats. For excess of meats bringeth sickness; and gluttony cometh at the last to an unmeasurable heat. Through surfeit have many one perished; but he that dieteth himself temperately prolongeth his life." Our Saviour Christ commandeth us to beware of excess in eating and drinking, when he saith: "Take heed that your hearts be not overcharged with surfeiting and drunkenship." St Paul also saith: "Be not drunken with wine, wherein is excess." *Phil.* Of these holy sentences may ye gather, that there is no cause why any man should rejoice in banqueting, except he have a pleasure to procure his own destruction; which cometh by no means sooner than by poverty and sickness, which springeth out of delicate fare; as I may leave off to speak of other inconveniences, yea, and pestilences to man's life, which issue from banqueting in like manner.

Ecclus. xxxvii. Luke xxi. Eph. v.

Eus. It is an easy thing to gather out of the holy scriptures not only sentences, but histories also, which declare what destruction to man banqueting, drunkenship, and the study of the belly bringeth. Did not Adam and Eve through eating the forbidden fruit cast not only themselves, but all their posterity, into damnation? How was Noe much laughed to scorn even of his own son, when through his drunkenship he fell on sleep and lay naked[3]! Into what abominable uncleanness did Lot fall through drunkenness, when he committed incest with his own daughters! Did not the children of Israel give themselves to banqueting, and afterward fell to the worshipping of the golden calf, committing most shameful idolatry? Was not Holofernes, that mighty and valiant captain, in his drunkenness slain of a woman? Is not that rich man, which would have no pity upon Lazarus, and therefore was after his death carried into hell-fire, described of blessed Luke to fare daintily every day? What shall I speak of king Herod, which in the midst of his banqueting was content to grant that holy John Baptist's head should be stricken off? It is therefore convenient for a christian man to remember in all his eating and drinking christian sobriety, and always to avoid excess, lest he fall into some of those inconveniences whereof is made mention afore.

Gen. iii. Gen. ix. Gen. xix. Exod. xxxii. Judith xiii. Luke xvi. Matt. xiv.

Theo. But what say ye to the favour of noble men? may we not rejoice in that? *Phil.* There are not a few which covet nothing so greatly as to be in favour with great men, and to be placed in their houses, thinking by this means to avoid the cruel darts of fortune, to obtain wealthy livings, and to have all things at their own will and pleasure; but I see not why any man should repose his chief delectation in the favour of any noble man, seeing the holy scripture saith: "Put not your trust in princes nor in the children of men, in whom there is no health." And the prophet saith: "Cursed be he that putteth his trust in man, and maketh flesh his arm."

Of the favour of great men. Psal. cxlvi. Jer. xvii.

Chris. How vain a thing the favour of great men is, the history of Aman declareth, which was so high in his king's favour, that he might do what he list, kill, save, exalt, depress, lift up, pluck down, and, as we say commonly, bind bears; and yet was he not shortly after cast out of favour on such sort, that he was immediately hanged on the same gallows which he had newly prepared for another?

Esth. vii.

Eus. There is nothing more uncertain than the good-will of great men. For whom they now love straightways they hate, and such as have done most for them are many times least regarded and most cruelly entreated. How handled king Alexander his most trusty counsellors, which so oft had put their lives in jeopardy for him! How tyrant-like did he slay them, and yet no cause why! I leave to speak of Nero, that monster of nature, which caused his own mother to be slain, and such as had done most for him. Who was so much in favour with the emperor Justinian as Belisarius and Narses? which being most noble warriors, subdued divers kingdoms to the empire; but how were they recompensed? Belisarius, that most valiant captain, without desert had at the emperor's commandment both his eyes plucked out, and afterward was compelled to beg his bread from door to door, and at the last died miserably a most wretched beggar. Narses also, if he had not fled, had been most

Alexander. Nero. Justinian.

[[3] Three words are omitted.]

unworthily handled: so are good men many times recompensed for their intolerable pains and painful service. Of such ensamples the books of histories are full. Whereof we may learn, how vain and too much foolish a thing it is to trust in the favour of noble men; so far it is off that any man may worthily rejoice in it.

Chris. I can none otherwise do but marvel at the madness of some men, which rather choose idly to spend their time in great men's houses, with this hope, to have somewhat at the last to live withal (which many times chanceth never), than in their youth to learn some honest occupation, which may defend them at all times from the bitter storms of needy and cruel fortune. Of all creatures are they slaves most miserable, and for the most part come to the most wretched end: a young courtier, an old beggar. Ah, how many have I known, which after twenty or thirty years' service have been with great displeasure driven away, and so died most wretchedly! And thus is that common saying found true: "Service is no heritage."
Serving-men. Serving-men may well be compared to Esop's toothless greyhound, which, so long as he could hunt well, follow and get his prey, was much made of; but when he began to wax old and could catch no more, he was no more loved of his master, but rather hated, despised, and beaten. Nothing now-a-days is dear where profit is absent. If these things were well pondered, men would not so headlong and without consideration run unto service, there to spend the flower of their youth, and, when crooked old age cometh, either to go a begging, or else to be put in some alms-house. But howsoever the matter goeth, of this am I sure, that no man ought to rejoice neither in men, nor yet in men's services, seeing that nothing is more uncertain than their favour, seeing also that cruel fortune doth oppress so suddenly noble men many times, that they, being turned to a base state, have neither to succour themselves, nor yet to help their poor servants.

Phil. Well, thus have we searched the principal things that pertain unto man outwardly, wherein the foolish world doth most chiefly rejoice; and we have found among them all not one thing wherein we may worthily glory and repose our delectation.

Theo. Truth it is; but what say you to the inward natural gifts of man, as wisdom, strength, knowledge, and such other gifts of the mind? *Phil.* Hear what
Jer. ix. God saith by the prophet: "Let not the wise man rejoice in his wisdom, nor the strong man in his strength, neither the rich man in his riches: but whoso will rejoice, let him rejoice in this, that he understandeth and knoweth me; for I am the Lord which do mercy, equity, and righteousness upon the earth. Therefore have I pleasure in such things, saith the Lord." Whether we have respect to the body or to the mind, if we find any good thing in them, it is the gift of God, as St James saith:
James i. "Every good gift and every perfect gift is from above, and cometh down from the Father of lights;" and therefore ought no man to glory neither in himself nor in
1 Cor. iv. the gifts, but in God alone the giver, as St Paul saith: "What hast thou that thou hast not received? If thou hast received it, wherefore dost thou rejoice and glory as though thou hadst not received it?" But wherefore do we tarry long before we come to our matter, while we labour to shew that there is nothing in the world wherein
Of man. we may worthily rejoice, seeing that man himself, which is the principal creature that ever God made in this world, is but vanity, and not worthy wherein any true and perfect delectation ought to be set? Are not these the words of the holy scripture,
☞ "Every man that liveth is altogether vanity?" What is the body of man, cometh it of never so noble house, but earth, dust, and ashes? Or, as St Bernard saith: "A
Of the body. stinking sperm or seed, a sack of dung, and the meat of worms[1]." Who will rejoice in such a body, to garnish such a body with gold, silver, pearls, precious stones, ouches, gallant apparel, sumptuous garments, &c.? What other thing is it than to
Of the soul. cover a dunghill with cloth of gold? Now as touching our inward man, I mean the soul, what are we? What have we received of Adam? In what case hath he set us before we be regenerate by Christ? Are we any other thing than flesh, and
Rom. viii. fleshly-minded? As Christ saith: "That which is born of the flesh is flesh." And
John iii. Eph. ii. saith not blessed Paul, that "we are the children of wrath?" Is not our heart un-

---

[[1] Bernard. Op. Par. 1690. Medit. Piis. cap. iii. 8. Vol. II. Tom. v. col. 322. See Vol. I. page 204, note 1.]

clean, lewd, wicked, and unsearchable? Are not our senses, imaginations, and thoughts, even from our infancy, evil and naught? Are not all our righteousness like a cloth defiled [2]? Are we not all hypocrites, lying children, workers of iniquity, unprofitable servants, sinners, ungodly, and of ourselves all that naught is? What have we then either of ourselves, or in ourselves (I mean before our regeneration), whereof we may worthily rejoice? *Chris.* Truly nothing at all. Prov. xx. Jer. xvii. Gen. viii. Isai. lxiv. Isai. ix. Luke xvii.

Phil. It is convenient therefore, seeing hitherto we have found nothing wherein we may worthily rejoice, to sequester our joy, our mirth, our delectation, from worldly things, and to transfer it unto the Lord our God, according to this admonition of the holy apostle: "Rejoice in the Lord alway: yea, once again I say, Rejoice." Phil. iv.

Theo. But we would gladly hear what earnest occasion we have to rejoice in God. *Phil.* My desire is to declare this thing abundantly unto you, if ye will hear. *Eus.* We all will gladly give ear.

Phil. God, in whom we are so instantly motioned to rejoice, even from the beginning had such favour to man, that when the angels, for their disobedient pride and proud disobedience, were worthily cast down headlong into hell, there perpetually to remain in most grievous and intolerable pains, he, willing again to furnish the celestial mansions with other creatures, made man, not like unto other brute beasts, but according unto his own similitude, likeness, and image; not to be a fire-brand of hell, but heir of his most glorious and regal palace; not to perish for hunger, but to enjoy all kind of pleasures most abundantly; not to be subdued of other, but as lord and chief ruler under God his Creator and Maker, to have the dominion of all beasts, fishes, and fowls, of all lands, meadows, and pastures, of all trees, herbs, and flowers, and whatsoever other thing is comprehended in this great and unmeasurable world. Yea, the high element, the sun, the moon, the stars, the day, the night, the water, the fire, the cold, the heat, the rain, the wind, and whatsoever other thing ye can reckon besides, did he make, not only to shew forth his glory, might, and power, but also for man's comfort, wealth, joy, and pleasure. *Chris.* O the unoutspeakable goodness of God toward man! The benefits of God toward man. Job iv. 2 Pet. ii. Gen. ii.

Phil. Have we not here a great occasion unfeignedly to rejoice in the Lord our God, and for ever and ever to glorify, celebrate, and magnify his most glorious and blessed name? To make us like to his own similitude! to appoint us heirs of his most glorious mansion! to endue us with the fruition of so many goodly and sweet pleasures! to make us rulers and lords over all his creatures in the world! to prepare all things for our solace, joy, and comfort! Who is so flint-hearted that melteth not at the hearing of these things so pleasant and sweet? Who is so estranged from God, that he applieth not with all main to embrace so gentle, so kind, so loving a Lord, yea, such a Lord as is altogether set to magnify man, to exalt him unto the high heavens, to place him among the holy angels and blessed spirits, to kiss and kull him as his dear darling and well-beloved heir? Can that man rejoice enough in his Lord and Master, which of a base slave maketh him a man of honour, of a beggar a man of great possessions, of a vile condition a man of high and noble renown? *Eus.* Truly the goodness of God toward man cannot be expressed.

Phil. Yet are these benefits which one man giveth to another more vile than dust, if they be compared to the precious gifts heretofore rehearsed, which God gave to man. But mark what followeth. *Theo.* Say on, we beseech thee.

Phil. Satan, that old and subtile serpent, perceiving man to be made of God for this intent, that he should inherit that glory, from the which for his intolerable arrogancy he was most worthily deject and cast down, craftily, subtilly, and like himself, with many sweet promises and fair flattering words, at the last allured our grandmother Eve to the transgression of God's commandment, and she likewise her husband; so that by this means both they and their postery were not only deprived of those pleasures and commodities which I rehearsed heretofore, but also utterly damned for their disobedience. And all this came to pass through the envy of Satan, as the wise man saith: "God created man to be undestroyed, yea, after the image Gen. iii. Wisd. ii.

[[2] Two words are omitted.]

of his own likeness created he him. Nevertheless through envy of the devil death entered into the world."

Chris. O lamentable chance! Now is man become of the image of God the image of the devil, of the heir of glory the inheritor of everlasting pain, of immortal mortal, of good and godly wicked and devilish, of free a bond-slave with all his powers to Satan, sin, death, hell, desperation, &c.

Eus. But what, enjoyed that ravening wolf his prey? *Phil.* Nothing less; for God, which is gentle, and the self gentleness, moved with loving compassion, tender zeal, and fatherly pity toward man, forgetting the displeasure that man had done to him through his disobedience, casting all his sins behind his back, inflamed with no less love toward man concerning his salvation (behold what grace and mercy doth!) than he was before the transgression, and minding to shew himself of no less puissance and strength to recover and save man, than Satan was to destroy and condemn man, came into paradise, sought him up, made garments for him to cover his nakedness, sent him into this world, made him lord over all, and promised him that the seed of a woman, even Jesus Christ, his own Son, born of Mary the virgin, should deliver him from the power of Satan, reconcile him to his godly favour, satisfy for his wickedness, make him a new man, endue him with his holy Spirit, finally, through his merits and good works, bring him unto the celestial inheritance, from the which Satan at that present had exiled him. This promise was so faithful (for God himself spake it, which is the self truth, "which cannot lie," which is "just in all his words"), and again so comfortable, that so many (I mean Adam and his posterity), as did apprehend and lay hand on that with earnest faith, were free from that miserable thraldom, whereinto they were cast through Satan's wiliness, received into favour, taken as most dear children, and recounted perfectly righteous, for the assured persuasion and undoubted faith that they conceived in the blessed seed Jesus Christ at the time promised of God the Father; so that, so long as they lived in this present world, they lived in the favour of God, and when they departed from hence God appointed their bodies to rest in the earth, placed their souls where his good pleasure was unto the coming of his Son, then to receive that blessed joy and heavenly felicity that they had lost through their disobedience, Jesu Christ, that most blessed seed, working this salvation for man, not for any good deeds that we had done, but of his own mere mercy and tender pity.

Gen. iii.

John xiv. Tit. i. Psal. cxlv.

Theo. O here is the good shepherd that sought up the lost sheep, and when he had found it, laid it lovingly upon his shoulders, and tenderly brought it home again to the sheepfold. O here is that most sweet, loving, and tender father, which with so great joy and embracing arms received home again the lost son. O here is that merciful Samaritan, which, pitying the wounded man being half dead, poured wine and oil into his wounds, bound them up, laid him upon his beast, carried him to an inn, and paid for his healing. O here is that most puissant king, which of his own liberality forgave his servant the ten thousand talents which he ought. O here is that mighty lord which trod down the wine-press alone, alone, neither was there any at all that holp him. O here is that most loving Saviour that saveth his people from all their sins. O here is that diligent physician that is ready at all times to help the diseased, to refresh them that labour and are laden. O here is that mighty David that slew Golias, and delivered the Israelites from the cruel Philistians. O here is that most valiant emperor, which for our sakes hath conquered Satan, hell, death, sin, desperation, damnation, with all the powers infernal. O here is that tender-hearted lover, that can no more forget us, than a mother can forget the child of her womb, and though she forget her child, yet cannot he forget us. For he hath written up us in his hands, so that we are always in his sight. To whom is not here opened an exceeding great and large window to rejoice in the Lord our God, except we be estranged from all that is God or godly?

Luke xv. Luke x. Matt. xviii. Isai. lxiii. Matt. i. Matt. ix. Matt. xi. 1 Sam. xvii. Hos. xiii. 1 Cor. xv. Isai. xlix.

Phil. I am glad, brother Theophilus, to hear you speak on this manner. But let us go forth. After so many pleasures shewed to man, which all through his own fault he so wickedly lost; after so great a sin committed against the divine Majesty, so freely to forgive man, so to accept him into his favour, so to love him, that he promiseth to send down from his most glorious throne his own dearly-beloved Son to make a perfect reconciliation and everlasting agreement between him and man, that they may for ever and ever dwell together in joyful glory: O what a fervent charity and unmeasurable love of God is this! Who can worthily either by heart think, or by tongue express, or yet by pen set forth the exceeding greatness of God's kind hearty love toward man?

The King of all kings, the Lord of all lords, yea, that Lord to whose majesty all Rev. xix. Phil. ii. things are obedient both in heaven, earth, and hell, so to set his mind on man, being but a poor, vile, and miserable creature, yea, of all mortal creatures most sinful, most disobedient, most frail, and ready to fall; so to love and tender him, that, to do him good, to bring him unto glory and honour, he disdaineth not, but most willingly vouch- Rom. viii. safeth to send down his only-begotten and dearly-beloved Son; yea, and that into this John iii. sinful vale of misery, here to become man, to be circumcised, to be made obedient to the law, to be baptized, to preach, to work miracles, to hunger, to thirst, to watch, to fast, to pray, to suffer all kind of adversity, to be persecuted, to be laid wait for, to be snatched at, to be blasphemed, to be railed upon, to be convented before worldly tyrants, bishops, priests, lawyers, &c., to be scorned, mocked, buffeted, whipped, crowned with thorn, nailed on the cross, scourged, pierced to the heart with a spear, and at the last dying the most spiteful and shameful death that could be invented of the wicked worldlings, unto the utter defacing of this blessed seed Christ, and of his godly doctrine; yea, and all this for the love that he beareth toward man: O what a kindness is this! what love, what amity, what hearty friendship! Far be it from us, dear brethren, to be so stony-hearted and ungodly, that we feel not this tender love of God toward us.

Chris. There is, in mine opinion, no faithful man, no true professor of Christ, that doth not earnestly rejoice at the hearing of these most heavenly benefits promised to man of God in this blessed seed Christ Jesu.

Phil. Moreover, after the promise made to our first parents concerning their reconciliation to be made by the blessed seed Jesu Christ, whereby they, with all their posterity, were in the mean season well comforted, enarmed against Satan, blessed, and saved, how friendly ever after dealt God with man! What benefit was there, whereof man was not made partaker? In what kind of benignity did man at any time (I speak of the faithful congregation) perceive the tender bowels of God to be sparred against him? What desired he, and obtained not his request? How oft did God familiarly talk with man by his holy angels! Was he not so loving to Gen. xviii. xxii. &c. man, that he sent his angels to eat and drink and to be merry with him? If any plague or misfortune were imminent and at hand for the ungodly, did he not declare Gen. viii. it to man, and so provided for him that he was free from all danger? How many victorious battles gave he to man against his enemies! How did he so accompany him at all times, that he ever found favour even among the barbarous and strangers! How wonderfully delivered he his people from the Egyptians! How marvellously fed Exod. xii. he them with the meat of angels from heaven! How mightily did he subdue the Gen. xii. xv. xvii. heathen kings, and brought his people into the land of behest, a land that flowed with milk and honey, a land full of all plenty and pleasure!

But what shall I speak of this most singular benefit, that he gave his law to man, yea, such a law as is pure, turneth souls, giveth wisdom to babes, maketh hearts merry, Psal. xix. lighteneth eyes, and is sweeter than the honey and honey-comb? Prophets also gave he to man, to premonish and afore warn him if any mischief were at hand, to teach him his holy ordinances, to renew the promise of sending the blessed seed Jesu Christ Isai. vii. liii. for man's salvation, that he might not wax faint in faith, but with valiant hope look for that blessed Saviour.

And when the time predefined and tofore appointed from everlasting was come of sending down this blessed seed and glorious Messias, how faithfully and no less lovingly Gal. iv. sent he him into the womb of the most blessed virgin Mary through the wonderful Isai. vii. Matt. i. operation of the Holy Ghost, there to take very flesh without the seed of man, there Luke ii. Rom. i. to take on him human nature, and to become of that holy maid perfect and true man, Gal. iv. John i. as he was before of God perfect and true God!

Chris. Would God this thing were no less of all men truly believed, than it is in the holy scriptures abundantly proved! *Eus.* The anabaptists in this our time do vehemently impugn this article of our faith, and affirm obstinately that Christ took no flesh of the blessed virgin Mary, but brought his body with him from heaven.

The anabaptists.

Theo. Of this matter, if I remember well, ye taught us, neighbour Philemon, in your New-year's Gift.

Phil. This article, that Christ took natural flesh of Mary the virgin, is so necessary unto salvation, that whosoever believeth it not believe the other in vain, neither is he of God, but of the devil, as St John saith: "Dearly beloved, believe not every spirit, but prove the spirits whether they be of God; for many false prophets are gone forth into the world. By this know ye the Spirit of God. Every spirit that confesseth that Jesus Christ came in the flesh is of God. And every spirit that doth not confess that Jesu Christ came in the flesh is not of God. And this is that spirit of antichrist, of whom ye have heard that he should come, and he is now already in the world." And this most pestilent heresy which the apish anabaptists have renewed in these our days (as Satan is never idle, nor ceaseth in his members to disquiet the congregation of Christ) was holden many hundred years past of divers heretics, as Marcion, Cerdon, Manicheus, Valentinus, Apelles[1], and such other offsprings of the devil, and was condemned and confuted by divers great learned men.

1 John iv.

The denying of Christ's incarnation is an old heresy.

But to our matter. And because we should not fear to come unto this our Lord and Saviour Jesu Christ, all that ever he did was done in such humility and lowliness, both of outward behaviour and mind, that it would allure any reasonable creature in the world with high boldness and faithful courage to come unto him. He was not born of a noble empress, nor of a devout vowess, nor yet of an holy nun; but of a poor maid in a poor stable, and poorly wrapped in poor clouts. Instead of a mighty and gallant guard of men, he was accompanied with oxen and asses. "Thus became Christ poor, when he was rich," and the King of glory; "that we through his poverty should be made rich." Moreover, he, being without all sin and Lord of the law, became subject to the law, and was circumcised according to the law. He was obedient to his mother Mary and to Joseph her husband, and led a poor life with them unto the age of thirty years, and wrought diligently for his living after the manner of other men. At the age of thirty years he was baptized of blessed John, son to Zachary the priest. After his baptism was he led of the Holy Ghost into wilderness, where he fasted forty days and forty nights, and was grievously tempted of Satan. Immediately after, humbly and lowly at the commandment of his heavenly Father, he took on him the office of preaching, declaring free remission of sins to so many as repent in faith. And as he was poor in worldly riches, and lowly in mind, so did he choose poor and humble men to be his disciples, that they might go and bear abroad, like faithful ministers, the heavenly riches of his exceeding mercy toward man.

Luke ii. Isai. i. 2 Cor. viii. Luke ii. Luke iii. Matt. iii. Matt. iv. Mark i. Luke iv. Matt. iv. 1 Cor. i. James ii.

Chris. Not without a cause. For the rich, gallant, and pompous worldlings are not fit vessels to carry the treasures of the kingdom of heaven; so unequally matched are Christ and mammon, heaven and earth, gold and God's word, light and darkness. They may pretend, and bear an outward face to the world, as though they were the apostles and ministers of Christ, as Judas, Simon Magus, and such other did; but inwardly and afore God they are the apostles and ministers of Satan; and when they seem most of all to talk of Christ, of Christ's doctrine and of his glory, then are they most of all enemies of the cross of Christ, seek the condemnation both of his doctrine and glory, and labour to stablish their own drowsy dreams, lousy laws, crooked constitutions, devilish decrees, antichristian acts, and all for their god, the belly; so sweet a thing is it to these false ministers and crafty apostles of Satan, to tumble and wallow in all kinds of carnal pleasures and worldly riches. Christ, therefore, knowing all such belly-gods[2] to be unapt for the preaching of the gospel, as he was poor and humble himself, so did he choose to be his ministers and apostles poor humble men, fishers, day-labourers, toll-gatherers, and such other vile persons and abjects of the world. These appointed he unto the office of preaching his heavenly Father's will. These made he

Matt. vi. Luke vi. Matt. x.

The disciples of Christ.

[1 See Vol. I. page 412, note 1.] [2 Folio, *belly goddes.*]

dispensators and stewards of the mysteries of God. These commanded he to go forth and preach the gospel, the joyful and glad tidings, the favour of God toward man, repentance, faith, free remission of sins in his blood, peace, tranquillity of conscience, everlasting life, &c. 1 Cor. iv.

Theo. These your words doth blessed Paul affirm, saying: "The foolishness of God is wiser than men, and the weakness of God is stronger than men. Brethren, ye see your calling, how that not many wise men after the flesh, not many mighty, not many of high degree, are called: but God hath chosen the foolish things of the world to confound the wise; and God hath chosen the weak things of the world to confound the things which are mighty; and vile things of the world and things which are despised hath God chosen, yea, and things of no reputation, for to bring to nought things of reputation; that no flesh should rejoice in his presence." 1 Cor. i.

Phil. Again, to shew his humility and lowliness, how was he content at every man's desire to go whither they would have him, and gladly to do whatsoever they requested him! Did he not heal the diseased? restore the blind to their sight? the deaf to their hearing? the dumb to their speaking? the dead to their life? Yea, the very lepers did he not disdain to purge and cleanse of their leprosy, and to touch with his own hands, whom the fine Pharisees, the lusty lawyers, the solemn Sadducees, the saucy scribes, the bragging bishops, the pattering priests, with the whole rabble of the hypocritish sort, disdained once to look upon; so far is it off that these holy fathers sought any remedy at all to help the poor diseased. Matt. iv. Matt. viii.

After many tragedies had between Christ and the spiritual sorcerers, with the other pompous worldlings, for his doctrine and miracles, when the time came, appointed of his heavenly Father from everlasting, that he, for man's reconciliation and pacifying of the divine wrath, should offer himself a sweet and everlasting sacrifice to God his Father, whereby he might redeem man from the tyranny of Satan, pay his ransom by the price of his dear heart-blood, satisfy for his offences, set a perpetual peace between God the Father and man, and by his death and passion bring an whole sea of heavenly treasures to the faithful penitent sinners, with what alacrity and cheerfulness of mind, with what desire and readiness, went he to his glorious passion! The passion of Christ.

No kind of pain
Did he disdain
For to sustain,
  To do man pleasure:
His own heart blood
To shed on the rood,
It did him good,
  To make man all pure.

Eus. O the unoutspeakable favour of God toward man! If he had sent down faithful Abraham, or any other of the old patriarchs or ancient holy prophets, to have suffered for man's salvation, it had, without all doubt, been a token of singular great favour toward man; but to send down his only-begotten and dearly-beloved Son from his glorious throne, yea, and that for his enemies, for their health and salvation, it is love passing all love, it is charity far exceeding all charity, it is favour rather to be deeply marvelled at than able worthily to be expressed. The Son of God to become man, and suffer death for our sake! O how can we otherwise than earnestly, and from the very heart, rejoice in the Lord our God! Rom. v.

Chris. Truly, too much iron-hearted are all they which rejoice not in the blessed incarnation and glorious death of this most blessed seed Jesu Christ our Lord, by whom so many and so excellent treasures of heavenly goods have freely chanced unto us. All things, even unto the very death, did he for our health and salvation, yea, and that so consummate and perfect, that there was nothing left behind unaccomplished that might turn unto our wealth, commodity, and profit, concerning our redemption. Let the Turks boast their Mahumet, and rejoice in him so much as they list: let the papists avance their pope, and triumph in him so much as is possible: let the rich worldlings magnify their wicked mammon, and rejoice in it full The Turks. The papists.

their hearts: let the glistering hypocrites delight in their god, the belly, even unto the uttermost: yet let us, let us, I say, that profess Christ aright, only rejoice in Christ, in Christ's nativity, passion, blood, and death, as St Paul saith: "God forbid that I should rejoice in any thing, but in the death of our Lord Jesu Christ." For so loving and gentle a Saviour can nowhere be found; so favourable a liberal a Lord can nowhere be sought out. In this Saviour and Lord, therefore, let us rejoice, and in none other.

The Christians. Gal. vi.

Theo. The papists cannot brook this doctrine, that Christ alone (the most high and everlasting Priest) hath by his death and passion, in offering up his own blessed body a sweet-smelling sacrifice to God the Father, so plenteously, so omnisufficiently, so at the full, made satisfaction for our sins, that we need none other sacrifice satisfactory to put away our wickednesses.

The papists. Eph. v.

Phil. No marvel; for, in defacing the glory and honour of the true and only sacrifice Jesu Christ, they set up and magnify an idol of their own making, which is the mass, and presume in that to offer sacrifice daily for the sins of the quick and dead, and crack that it is of no less price, valor, strength, and virtue, than the passion and death of Christ is: again, that whatsoever Christ did for the salvation of man upon the altar of the cross, they do the very same at the mass.

Of the mass. Mass-mongers.

Chris. O extreme blasphemy! Who ever "denied the Lord that bought them," if these popish massmongers do it not? Who justly may be called "the enemies of the cross of Christ," if the mumbling mass-hunters be not the very same? Who at any time hath "trodden under foot the Son of God, and counted the blood of the testament, wherewith the faithful are sanctified, as an unholy thing, and do dishonour to the Spirit of grace," if these shameless sacrificers have not done it? And yet it is a world to see what a number there are, not only of the ignorant and unlearned, but of them also which brag both of wisdom and learning, that cleave to this idolatrous mass with tooth and nail; that defend it to the uttermost with sword, fire, and halter; that maintain it with their riches and possessions; that strive for it with as strong reasons and arguments as they can; partly because they are afraid (I speak of the popish priest) lest this common whore, their mass, should be driven out of the game-place, and by this means their kitchen should wax cold, and their idle bellies be no more fed with the labours of other men's hands; partly because they think, if this abominable strumpet, the mass, were banished out of the temples (I speak of the rude and ignorant people), all true religion were gone, all christian devotion were perished, insomuch that they could not tell what to do for to please God, nor yet how to worship him; partly (I speak of the worldly wise), because they will give no place to the truth, lest, if they should consent to the putting away of this most stinking and filthy whore the mass, that old bawd and grandmother of whoredom and abominations of the earth, they should be compelled to grant, as they think, to their great shame and ignominy, that both they have been blind, and also led other blind these many years, and so they should lose their estimation, renown, and fame among the people, which thing they most chiefly hunt and hawk after. For "they love the praise of men more than the glory of God."

2 Pet. ii. Phil. iii. Heb. x. Mass-hunters. Why the papists are loth to forego the mass. Rev. xvii. John xii.

Eus. Certes, so long as that popish mass shall be continued in the church and believed to be a sacrifice for the sins of the quick and dead, idolatry shall bear rule among us, infidelity shall lie couched in the hearts of men, superstition shall never be exiled from the bounds of Christianity, hypocrisy shall still sit in the consciences of men, the usurped power of the bishop of Rome shall not lose her strength, the fruits of Christ's death shall never be truly known, neither our heavenly Father worthily thanked for them, the purging furnace of the Italian bishop shall never be quenched, the idle shaven nation of the popish massmongers shall still be maintained in their dissolute and beastly manner of living, the papistical sacrifices shall not cease to blaspheme that most sweet-smelling sacrifice Jesu Christ, that most high and everlasting Bishop, the holy and blessed supper of the Lord shall never be truly frequented and used in the church of Christ; to be short, an whole sea of evils shall reign, flourish, and triumph in the christian congregation.

What incommodities follow the mass.

Phil. Truly I think there is no christian heart, which, considering these things tofore rehearsed, lamenteth not to see so great an evil and pestilence as the mass is to reign among them that profess Christ, yea, and to be had in so high price that it is believed to be of no less strength and virtue than the glorious passion of our Lord and Saviour Jesus Christ.

But let us see how this wicked opinion of the sacrifice of the mass agreeth with God's most holy word. The papists affirm that the sins of the quick and dead are put away by the sacrifice of their masses, which they mumble daily. Against this devilish doctrine must we set (as an invisible[1] bulwark) this text of blessed St Paul: "It became us to have such an high priest as is holy, innocent, undefiled, separate from sinners, and made higher than heaven; which needeth not daily, as the other priests, to offer sacrifice, first for his own sins, and then for the sins of the people: for this did he," that is to say, Christ, "once for all when he offered up himself." Let these sacrificers here note, that no priest can offer any sacrifice for our sins but such a one as is holy, innocent, undefiled, &c., which is Jesus Christ alone. Seeing then that they want this holiness, innocency, purity, &c., it is evident by St Paul's words, that they cannot sacrifice neither for the quick nor for the dead. Again, blessed Paul saith that this everlasting priest, Jesus Christ, "needeth not daily (as the other priests) to offer sacrifice," which by one oblation of himself hath delivered for evermore so many as believe in him from all their sins. Verily these missars are altogether amiss. What will they say now?

The sacrifice of the mass.

Heb. vii.

If Christ need no more to offer sacrifice, much less need the priests. If one oblation of Christ be altogether sufficient, then are the daily oblations of the popish massmongers vain and unprofitable. If Christ offered himself once for all, then cannot the papists offer him so often as it pleaseth them. Whereof it may be concluded, that they do nothing in their satisfactory masses but blaspheme the Lord and his Anointed, seeing they so arrogantly arrogate unto themselves power to offer sacrifice for the sins of the people, when this one oblation of our Saviour and Lord Christ Jesus is all wholly sufficient, and throughly able in every point even unto the uttermost to save all the elect and chosen people of God; yea, and that so abundantly and at the full, that henceforth there needeth no reiteration nor no renewing thereof.

If there were no more scriptures to condemn this wicked opinion of the sacrifice of the mass but this one tofore recited, it might seem to any christian judgment sufficient to subvert, overthrow, and topple down whatsoever the papists have builded upon the sand of their own inventions these certain hundred years. "What is chaff in comparison to wheat? saith the Lord. Is not my word like fire? saith the Lord, and like a twibytte[2] cleaving the rock of stone?" But let us rehearse more scriptures.

Jer. xxiii.

The blessed apostle saith: "Christ, being a bishop of good things to come, came by a greater and more perfit tabernacle, not made with hands, that is to say, not of this manner building; neither by the blood of goats or calves, but by his own blood, entered he once for all into the holy place, and found eternal redemption." Again, in the latter end of the same chapter: "Christ is not entered into the holy places that are made with hands (which are but similitudes of true things); but into the very heaven, for to appear now before the face of God for us: not to offer himself oft, as the high priest entereth into the holy place every year with strange blood; for then must he often have suffered since the world began: but now in the end of the world hath he appeared once for all to put sin to flight by the offering up of himself. And as it is appointed unto men that they shall once die, and then cometh the judgment; even so Christ was once offered to take away the sins of many." Blessed Paul hath no shift of descant, but singeth ever one song, nothing less than pleasant to the ears of these sacrificers. He affirmeth that "Christ by his own blood entered into heaven once for all, and found eternal redemption." Where we may learn that Christ is so sweet a smelling sacrifice to God the Father, that by the once offering up of himself he hath found everlasting redemption. Redemption and remission of sins is so plenteously purchased by the death of Christ, that it remaineth for evermore. The papistical sacrificers do greatly err therefore, which take upon them daily to sacrifice for

Heb. ix.

Eph. v.

[1 Probably *invincible*.] [2 Twibytte or twibill: a two-edged bill or mattock.]

the sins of the quick and dead; as though Christ's sacrifice endured no longer and were of no more effect and virtue.

Chris. O blasphemous hypocrites!

Phil. Again he saith that "now in the end of the world Christ hath appeared once for all to put sin to flight, by the offering up of himself;" as though he should say, Many sacrifices were offered of the priests of the old law; but none of them could put sin to flight. Therefore Christ, the high priest in these last days, became man, and was not offered of any other, but he offered himself, yea, and that once for all for the sins of so many as unfeignedly repent and truly believe; and his oblation for ever and ever abideth of so great strength, virtue, and power, that that alone, and none other, chaseth away and putteth to flight the sins of many, both of Jews and gentiles, if they believe. Once again he saith: "We are sanctified and made holy by the oblation of Christ's body once for all." Are not these words plain enough? How oft doth St Paul recite the oblation of Christ's body, yea, and that "once for all," and stiffly affirmeth that by that once offering up of himself we are perfectly sanctified and made holy! What need then have we of the sacrifice of the mass to be made holy, if there were any such sacrifice as the papistical sacrificers feign? It followeth also in the same chapter: "Every priest is ready daily ministering, and oftentimes offereth one manner of offering, which can never take away sins. But this man," that is to say, Christ, "when he had offered for sins one sacrifice, which is of value for ever, sat him down on the right hand of God, and from thenceforth tarrieth, till his foes be made his foot-stool. For with one offering hath he made perfect for ever them that are sanctified." This one sentence maketh to fall flat upon the ground all that ever the papists have builded for the maintenance of their missal sacrifice.

Heb. x.

Note this, yea, note it well.

First, he saith that all the sacrifices which the other priests offer "can take away no sin." Secondly, that Christ offered one sacrifice for our sins, which is of value for ever, by the which one sacrifice he excludeth all other. Thirdly, that he sat him down on the right hand of God the Father, and there tarrieth till the day of judgment. Then can he be offered and sacrificed no more, whatsoever the pedlar-like papists chatter, as St Paul saith: "Christ, raised from the dead, dieth no more. Death shall have no more power over him. For as touching that he died, he died as concerning sin once; but as touching that he liveth, to God." Fourthly, that "with one offering he hath made perfect for ever them that are sanctified." If we be made perfect with one offering, which is the oblation of Christ's body upon the altar of the cross, what imperfection remaineth there in us, that we should have need of the missal sacrifice? If one sacrifice make us perfect for ever, what need we to have so many sacrifices offered daily in the popish masses? All these scriptures tofore alleged shew evidently, that the death of Christ is a sacrifice so omnisufficient, so perfect, so absolute, so consummate, so plenteous at the full, that it alone maketh clean for ever the faithful from their sins, without any repetition or renewing.

Rom. vi.

Eus. Cursed therefore are these papistical sacrificers, which so arrogantly dare presume to offer and sacrifice Christ again, as though the first oblation and sacrifice were imperfect.

Phil. God amend them, turn their hearts, and give them grace to know his truth! For what other thing is it to set up a new oblation, than to annul the old, to make God a liar, to deny Christ, as St Peter right well prophesied of such subtile sacrifices? For he that saith that sins are forgiven by the mass, and that the mass is a sacrifice for the sins both of the living and of the dead, he must either grant that the alone sacrifice of Christ upon the cross is not sufficient for the faithful, or else that the missal sacrifice is a mocking of Christ, and a plain scorning of God the Father. O abomination! Why is Christ called "an everlasting priest," but that his sacrifice, once done on the altar of the cross, endureth for ever in full strength and power for so many as believe, (though they sin never so oft,) if they return unto God, and seek remission of their sins in the precious blood of our alone Saviour Jesus Christ? As St John saith: "If any man sin, we have an advocate with the Father, Jesus Christ the righteous; and he it is that obtaineth grace for our sins; not for our sins only, but also for the sins of the whole world." What need we then more

2 Pet. ii.

Psal. cx.

1 John ii.

oblations? St Paul saith: "Without effusion or shedding of blood there is no remission of sins." If the papists therefore will have their mass a sacrifice, so is it proved by the words of the apostle that they crucify Christ again, and shed his blood. Heb. ix.

Chris. O bloody sacrificers! What christian heart can abide to be present where such ignominy is done to Christ the Lord?

Phil. He that sacrificeth is greater than the sacrifice: so doth it follow that the priests are greater than Christ the King of glory. He offered us a sacrifice to God; and go we about to offer him? Again, he that sacrificeth ought to be so pure as the sacrifice; and who, I pray you, can be so pure as Christ our sacrifice? "Who is able to say, My heart is clean, and I am free from sin?" To presume to offer sacrifices for the sins of the people, is it any other thing than to make themselves Christs and saviours, and to say with that most proud angel, as it is written by the prophet, "I will climb up above the clouds, and will be like the Highest of all?" Do not they go about to shew themselves equal to Christ, yea, Christ himself, which take upon them to offer sacrifice for the sins of the people? What other thing did Christ, but take away our sin? If our massmongers do the same, are they not Christs indeed? Prov. xx. Isai. xiv.

A comparison between Christ and the massmongers.

And yet this prerogative have they above Christ, that, whereas Christ could not obtain pardon for our sins but by suffering great pains, yea, and very death, they do it without any pains-taking at all. Christ was mocked and scorned: they be praised and much made of. Christ was accused of heresy and treason: they be counted good catholic men and full devout fathers. Christ was pricked to the brains with a crown of thorn: they have a bald patch upon their heads instead of crowns, and some have on their caps and mitres for catching cold. Christ was stripped naked of all his clothes: they be clad in silk, satin, damask, velvet, and cloth of gold. Christ bare his own cross of wood upon his shoulders, when he went to suffer: they have crosses of gold and silver borne before them. Christ was nailed unto the cross: they stand at the altar with turn, return, and half-turn[1]. Christ, hanging on the cross, prayed for his very enemies: they, standing at the altar, pray for such as be their patrons, founders, benefactors, and for such as hire them for money. Christ patiently suffered the blasphemies and opprobrious words that causeless were spoken against him: they, if any man offend them, straightways accuse, condemn, curse, and excommunicate them. Christ with his sacrifice sought to do good to other: they with their sacrifices seek to bring men to superstition, to wrap them in idolatry, to graff in them wicked opinions, but above all things to enrich Corban, Corban, that they may have plenteously wherewith to feed their idle and beastly bellies. Christ at his passion had vinegar and gall given him to drink; but they have bread of the finest and wine of the best to eat and drink. Christ offered his own blessed body a sweet-smelling sacrifice to God the Father for the sins of the people: they offer a wafer-cake and a spoonful of wine, making the people to believe that it is a sacrifice, which they offer *pro salute vivorum et requie omnium fidelium defunctorum*, "for the health of them that be alive, and the rest of all the faithful that are dead." Christ, after he had offered his sacrifice, said, *Consummatum est:* "Every thing is done" and perfectly finished, that maketh unto the salvation of man, yea, and that by this my one oblation. They cannot say so, neither bring they any thing unto perfection. For their sacrifices are so imperfect, that they are as ready to offer to-morrow as to-day, and never the better. Christ, after the oblation of his most blessed body, commended his spirit into the hands of his heavenly Father, and died straightways: they, after they have offered their new-found oblation, fall to banqueting, drinking, gulling, and glossing, to hunting, whoring, dicing, and carding, and all the days of their life they live dissolutely in most vain pleasures, both of the flesh and of the world. What fellowship and agreement is there here, I pray you, between Christ and the massmongers? between the oblation of Christ and the popish sacrifice? between the mass and the death of Christ? Ye may see into what absurdities and too much inconveniences these pedlar-like papists fall, while they stablish John xix.

[1 Gestures and changes of position used in celebrating mass.]

an idol of their own making. How say ye? are they not goodly Christs and pretty saviours?

Theo. Christs! They are even such Christs as the true Christ himself speaketh of [Matt. xxiv.] in the gospel of St Matthew. "There shall arise," saith he, "false Christs and false prophets." Here be they called "Christs", but there is added unto it "false;" so that they be false Christs, feigned Christs, lying Christs, deceitful Christs.

[Matt. xxiv.] *Chris.* Of such Christs Christ gave us warning, and bade us take heed, saying: "If any man shall say unto you, Behold, here is Christ, or there is Christ, believe him not. If they shall say unto you, Behold, he is in the wilderness, go not out. Behold, he is in the pix, believe them not. Lo, I have told you aforehand." These popish mass- [2 Cor. xi.] mongers are the "ministers of Satan, which change themselves into angels of light." [1 Tim. vi.] These are those men that have "corrupt minds, which are without all truth, which [2 Pet. ii.] think that lucre is godliness." These are those "false prophets" and "false teachers," which, saith St Peter, "shall privily bring in damnable sects, even denying the Lord that hath bought them, and bring upon themselves swift damnation; and many shall follow their damnable ways, by whom the way of truth shall be evil spoken of, and through covetousness shall they with feigned words make merchandise of you; whose [2 Pet. iii.] judgment is now not far off, and their damnation sleepeth not."

Phil. We have texts almost innumerable contained in the holy scriptures, which declare that Christ alone by his blood hath perfectly wrought our redemption, satisfied for our sins, pacified the wrath of God, and brought us again into favour. But if there were no more places of the scripture to condemn the sacrifice of the mass but this [John xix.] one, which Christ hanging upon the cross said, "Every thing is made perfect," it were sufficient. For if Christ by his death have made all things perfect, then left he nothing imperfect. So doth it truly follow that the papistical sacrificing for the sins of the quick and dead is damnable, injurious, and despiteful to the blessed passion of Christ, seeing Christ made all things consummate and perfect by his precious death, and by ☞ that alone obtained perpetual remission for all the sins of the faithful. For his glorious death and bitter passion is even now of as full strength and of as much virtue as it was what time he suffered, and so shall continue unto the world's end, as blessed Paul [Heb. xiii.] saith: "Jesus Christ yesterday, and to-day, and the same continueth for ever." Therefore is he called an everlasting priest, because he doeth all things perfectly, and requireth [Isai. lxiii.] none other to help him, as he himself saith by the prophet: "I am he that teacheth righteousness, and am of power to help." The congregation of the faithful speaketh: "Wherefore then is thy clothing red, and thy raiment like his that treadeth in the wine-press?" Christ answereth: "I have trodden the press alone, and of all people there is not one with me." Neither Abraham nor Isaac, neither Zachary nor John Baptist, neither Mary nor Elizabeth, neither Peter nor Paul, neither man nor angel, [1 Pet. i.] hath paid our ransom by his blood-shedding; but Christ alone, alone, that most pure [John i.] and undefiled "Lamb, which taketh away the sins of the world."

[Acts iv.] In him alone, and in none other, is all our health and salvation; "neither is there any other name given unto men, wherein they must be saved," but only the name of our most blessed Lord and bounteous Saviour Christ Jesu, that King of glory. He [Isai. liii. Matt. viii. 1 Pet. ii. Isai. liii. Psal. cxix.] only "hath taken on him our infirmities and borne our pains." "He was wounded for our offences, and smitten for our wickedness. The chastisement of our peace was laid upon him; and with his stripes we are healed. As for us, we have gone all astray: like sheep every one hath turned his own way. But the Lord hath heaped together upon him the iniquity of us all. He suffered violence and was evil entreated, and did not [Jer. xi. Matt. xxvi. Acts viii.] yet open his mouth. He was led as a sheep to be slain: yet was he as still as a lamb before the shearer, and did not open his mouth. He was had away from prison, his [2 Cor. v.] cause not heard, and without any judgment." All this suffered he for our sake, and to put away our iniquities. Yea, "he was cut off from the ground of the living, which punishment did go upon him (saith God) for the transgression of my people," which indeed had deserved that punishment. "It pleased the Lord thus to burst him with plagues, and to smite him with infirmities, that when he had made his soul an offering for sin, he might see long-lasting seed. He hath justified the multitude, and borne away their sins."

These words are spoken by the prophet, which teach us manifestly that there is no sacrifice that deserveth remission of sins to us, or pacifieth the wrath of God stirred up against us through sin, but only the death of Jesus Christ. Isai. liii.

"By the means of Jesu Christ," saith St Paul, "ye, which sometime were far off, are made nigh by the blood of Christ." "By Christ we have redemption through his blood, even the forgiveness of sins, according to the riches of his grace." "God hath delivered us from the power of darkness, and hath translated us into the kingdom of his dear Son; by whom we have redemption through his blood, even the forgiveness of sins." "It pleased the Father, that in him should all fulness dwell, and by him to reconcile all things unto himself, and to set at peace by him through the blood of his cross both things in heaven and things in earth." "This is a true saying, and by all means worthy to be received of us, that Christ Jesus came into the world to save sinners." "There is one God, and one mediator between God and man, even the man Christ Jesus, which gave himself a ransom for all men." "Ye know," saith blessed Peter, "how that ye were not redeemed with corruptible things, as silver and gold, from your vain conversation; but with the precious blood of Christ, as of a lamb undefiled and without spot." "The blood of Jesus Christ, God's own Son, maketh us perfectly clean," saith St John, "from all sin." Again he saith: "Christ loved us and washed us from our sins in his own blood." If these sentences were truly known of the lay people and unfeignedly believed, they would soon give over their popish sacrifices, and only cleave, as they ought, to the alone sacrifice of the high and everlasting priest Jesus Christ, which he once for all offered upon the altar of the cross. They would leave to run gadding to the masking mass of the papists, and make more haste unto godly sermons, and unto the holy and blessed supper of the Lord.

Eph ii. Eph. i. Col. i. 1 Tim. ii. 1 Pet. i. 1 John i. Rev. i. Heb. ix.

Eus. Methink these massmongers, which make of the Lord's supper a private churlish breakfast, forasmuch as they eat and drink alone, and make the people believe that in their mass they offer sacrifice for their sins both of the living and of the dead, and boast that their mass is of as great virtue and strength as the passion of Christ for the satisfaction of our wickednesses, besides their intolerable blasphemies against the Lord and his Anointed, offend greatly against the dignity and the right use of the Lord's supper. For Christ, when he instituted this blessed supper to be celebrated with bread and wine, and appointed them to be the holy mysteries of his body and blood, gave no commandment to offer and sacrifice for the sins of the quick and the dead, but to eat and drink these holy mysteries in the remembrance of his death, as he himself saith: "Do this in the remembrance of me." Hereto agreeth St Paul: "So oft," saith he, "as ye shall eat of this bread, and drink of this cup, ye shall shew the death of the Lord till he come." So that the Lord's supper was not instituted of Christ to be a sacrifice propitiatory, satisfactory, expiatory, and I cannot tell you what; but only a commemoration or remembrance of that sacrifice which could not but once be offered, and a certain confirmation or seal for the infirm and weaklings, that they be redeemed by Christ, by Christ's passion, blood, and death, that thereby they may be assured of the favour of God, of remission of sins, if they stedfastly believe that Christ hath satisfied for their sins upon the cross, and in this faith eat and drink the mysteries of his body and blood. For whensoever the true Christians eat and drink the body and blood of Christ in faith, and with a believing spirit, their sins are forgiven them no less than if Christ even at that present had died upon the cross; not for the eating and drinking, but for the faith's sake in Christ's blood: so mighty in operation is Christ, and so present is he at every hour unto so many as believe in him, and are gathered together in his name. For he is the eternal God; therefore hath his death an eternal and everlasting fruit.

Of the Lord's supper. Luke xxii. 1 Cor. xi. Mark well.

Chris. Ye have taught us, neighbour Philemon, many goodly and godly things concerning the sacrifice of Christ, which beat down the sacrifice of the popish mass even unto the ground; yea, they drive it down even unto the pit of hell, from whence it first came. Now will I rehearse unto you again what I have read and heard of the papists concerning this matter, that ye may see what their opinion was and is of the mass and of the sacrifice thereof. *Phil.* I pray you, speak on.

The doctrine of the papists concerning the mass.

Chris. The mass, say they, maketh men holy, yea, it maketh them righteous, and delivereth them from sins. The mass is a sacrifice, and not the sign of a sacrifice only. In the mass is the body and blood of Christ truly offered for the quick and dead. The mass of a priest, be he never so naughty, is profitable *ex opere operato.* Christ with his passion satisfied for original sin, and instituted the mass to be an oblation for the sins committed daily, both mortal and venial. To hear mass is the honouring of God, whether the hearer understandeth it or not. *Missa* soundeth "sacrifice:" ergo the mass is a sacrifice. *Missa* is derived of *mitto*, "to send;" for in the mass the Lamb, that is to say, Christ, is sent unto the Father to forgive our sins. The mass delivereth souls from purgatory, forasmuch as it is a satisfactory sacrifice for sins. Not only the sacrifice of Christ, wherein he offered himself, was a sacrifice for sin, but we also offer for our sins a continual sacrifice in the mass. The sacrifice of Christ obtaineth mercy only for original sin, and for the sins past. The sacrifice of the mass every day is the true sacrifice for sins.

Although Christ was once offered on the cross in the open likeness of flesh, yet is the same Christ daily offered on the altar at mass. The words of consecration duly spoken of the priest, there is made a transubstantiation of wine into the blood of Christ, and of the bread into his body. Every man may lawfully worship the host consecrated. Although Paul calleth the sacrament of the supper "bread," yet may we not believe therefore that the substance of bread remaineth in the sacrament. Christ said: *Hoc est corpus meum:* "This is my body;" therefore must we needs hold that there is a transubstantiation, and that the substance of bread is changed into the body of Christ. The body of Christ is present in the mass so great and large as it was when it hanged on the cross. Forasmuch as Christ, that most high majesty of God, is present at the mass, therefore it is very godly to appoint many ceremonies, that Christ may be entertained honourably. Mass ought not to said but in an holy place, and upon an altar of stone; for Christ himself is called a stone. The mass, among all the suffrages for the dead, doth profit most of all for the deliverance of souls out of purgatory.

By hearing of mass we may obtain not only spiritual goods, but all manner of corporal and temporal goods also. The canon of this mass is godly and catholic, and it was ordained of the apostles. The mass, *ex opere operato*, justifieth and taketh away the guiltiness of the fault and pain in them for whom it is done. With the sacrifice of the mass the satisfactions of the dead are redeemed. The mass, *ex opere operato,* giveth grace, and being applied for other deserveth unto them, *ex opere operato*, forgiveness of the fault and pain, and obtaineth whatsoever we have need of in all our life. In the old testament there was a bishop that offered sacrifices for the sins of the people; therefore in the new testament must there be priests and bishops to offer sacrifices for sins. The body of the Lord, once offered on the cross for original sin, is continually offered for daily sins upon the altar, that by this means the church may have a gift, wherewith they may pacify the wrath of God. It is an heresy of the Arians to hold that the mass is not a sacrifice for the quick and the dead.

How say ye, neighbours, to this doctrine of the masking papists? Is it not good stuff?

Theo. God have mercy on us! I have not heard more blasphemous doctrine in my life against the truth of God's most blessed word, nor more injurious and despiteful against the glorious passion of our only Lord and Saviour Jesu Christ. O too much miserable is that realm where such doctrine is taught! Bond-slaves and wretched captives are they to Satan and to his antichristian synagogue, where such teachers reign and bear rule. O when will these papists cease to speak blasphemies against the Son of the living God? The teachers of this doctrine are right chaplains to that
Rev. xiii. beast which had seven heads and ten horns, and opened her mouth to speak blasphemies against God and his name, and against his holy congregation, with so many
Rev. xviii. as inhabit the heavens. These are those marked merchants, which have committed abominable whoredom with that filthy and unclean strumpet Babylon, and weep now because no man will buy their merchandise nor their pedlary any more, their gold, silver, and precious stones, their pearl raines, purple and scarlet, their ornaments, their frankincense, wine, and oil, their fine flour and wheat, with the bodies and souls of men.

Phil. I have spent the more time in declaring unto you the wicked opinion of the papists concerning the sacrifice of the mass, and confuting of the same, because ye should rejoice in none other thing, as touching your redemption and satisfaction for your sins, and a perfect atonement made between God and us, but only in the death and passion of our Lord and Saviour Jesu Christ, as St Paul saith: "God forbid that I should rejoice in any thing, but in the death of our Lord Jesu Christ." Gal. vi.

Now, the sacrifice of the mass being reproved, and proved of no force and virtue to put away the sins of the quick and dead, as the papists have falsely taught and made the foolish simple people to believe for lucre's sake, of what price, I pray you, is the mass now to be esteemed? It agreeth no more with Christ's supper than Christ and Belial, light and darkness, truth and falsehood.

An antithesis between the Lord's supper and the pope's mass. John xiv. xv. xvi. Matt. xxvi. Mark xiv. Luke xxii.

1 Christ made a sermon before he ministered the sacrament of his body and blood to his disciples: the papists say masses, the devil and all, and yet no sermon at all.

2 Christ sat at the table, and turned his face to his disciples, when he gave them the mysteries of his body and blood: the papists sequester themselves from the people, they stand at an altar, and turn their backs to the multitude.

3 Christ rehearsed the words of the institution of his supper openly, yea, and that in such a tongue as all his disciples understood: the papists whisper to themselves, playing silence gloom[1], and utter all things in a strange tongue, that no man understandeth what is spoken, nor for the most part themselves neither.

4 Christ gave the sacrament of his body and blood to his disciples for to eat: the papists give nothing to any man, but eat and drink all together themselves.

5 Christ ministered the mystery of his body in common bread: the papists minister printed wafer-cakes, otherwise not commonly used.

6 Christ ministered wine to be a commemoration of his blood-shedding to his disciples: the papists minister to the people not only wine, but water also mingled therewith.

7 Christ gave the sacrament of his body and blood into the disciples' hands: the papists put in the people's mouths, not suffering them to touch it with their hands for their too much base filthiness.

8 Christ delivered the sacrament to his disciples sitting at the table: the papists compel the people to receive it kneeling upon their knees.

9 Christ, delivering the bread and wine to his disciples, said unto them: "Take ye, eat ye, and drink ye:" the papists said, "Behold, honour, worship, and reverence your Maker here."

10 Christ instituted his supper to be a remembrance of his death and passion, which is the only sacrifice for the sins of the people: the papists affirm that their masking mass is a perfect sacrifice for the quick and the dead, and of as great virtue and strength as the blessed passion of our Saviour Christ is.

11 Christ, delivering the mysteries of his body and blood to his disciples, told them that his body should be broken for them, and his blood shed for them and many into the remission of sins: the papists shame not to lie that Christ by his death satisfied only for original sin and the sins past; as for all our sins, whatsoever they be, venial or mortal, committed after baptism, they be put away by the sacrifice of the mass.

12 Christ delivered the sacrament of his body and blood under both kinds to his disciples: the papists steal away from the common people the mystery of Christ's blood.

13 Christ gave to his disciples the sacrament to be eaten for a remembrance of his death: the papists hold it up above their heads, and command the people to worship it as God.

14 Christ ministered the sacrament in such apparel as he did customably wear: the papists put on masking apparel, albs, girdles, vestiments, copes, subdeacon, deacon, tunicle, and what not.

15 Christ plainly and purely ministered the sacrament to his disciples, without any ceremonies: the papists must have censers, bells, candles, candlesticks, paxes, corporasses, superaltaries, altar-cloths, cruets, napkins, besides their dowkings[2] and loutings, their turnings and returnings, their gaspings and gapings, their kneelings and winkings, their mockings and mowings, their crossings and knockings, their kissings and lickings, their noddings

[1 Silence gloom: probably a character in an old drama.] [2 Dowkings: i. e. duckings.]

and nosings, their washings and wipings, their bowings and bleatings; as I may speak nothing of their prostrations and inclinations, of their commemorations and histrionical gesticulations, more meet for mad-brains and drunkards than for grave and sober honest men.

16 Christ commanded his disciples to receive the sacrament so oft as they would: the papists appoint the common people only to receive it at Easter, or when they be in peril of death.

17 Christ willed disciples, so oft as they eat of that sacramental bread, to remember his death till he come; he meaneth, unto the judgment: the papists say they have him already in their hands and in their mouths, in their boxes and in their pixes.

18 Christ did not appoint any part of the sacrament to be reserved after the communion: the papists reserve it, and hang it up with an halter in the pix, cense it, carry it about in procession, and make a pageant of it.

19 Christ appointed his sacrament to be eaten in the remembrance of his passion: the papists keep it so long that it corrupteth, waxeth mould, and breedeth full of worms.

20 Christ, in the institution of the mystery of his body, said: "This is my body, which is given for you. Do this in the remembrance of me." The papists in their consecration, as they call it, mangle the words of Christ, in some place adding of their own to the words of Christ, and in another place leaving altogether out. In the consecration of the bread they have *enim*, which Christ hath not, nor any word for in the Hebrew tongue. And herein do they grievously offend against God, which commandeth that nothing should be added to his word. Again, they leave out this comfortable promise, *Quod pro vobis datur*, "Which is given for you," wherein our chief consolation, joy, and comfort is contained[1]. And here again do they not a little offend against the high majesty of God, seeing they pluck so many words from the institution of Christ. They are also very thieves and enemies to us, seeing they deprive us of so sweet and comfortable promise, wherein is comprehended the mystery of our salvation.

Luke xxii.

Deut. xii. Prov. xxx. Rev. xxii.

21 Christ, in delivering the cup of the mystery of his blood, spake these words: "Drink ye all of this. This cup is the new testament in my blood, which is shed for you and for many into the remission of sins." The papists rehearse not the words in the consecration of the wine (as I may go forth to use their term in all points), as Christ did, but add more unto them; as though there were a certain imperfection or insufficiency in the words of Christ. Their words are these: "This is the chalice of my blood, a new and everlasting testament, the mystery of faith, which for you and many shall be shed for the remission of sins[2]." Although in the addition of these words there is no untruth, yet is not convenient for any man which is but flesh, earth, dust, and ashes, to put ought to the words of Christ, which is the Wisdom of the Father, and knoweth best what is most expedient for the setting forth of his glory. If a man add any thing to the testament and last will of any mortal man, or do pluck ought therefro, his fault is counted very great, and he himself for ever after discredited, because he hath so unjustly dealt with his neighbour's will. In what estimation then are they to be had, which corrupt the testament and last will, not of man only, but of God and man also, wherein are bequeathed not worldly and transitory things, but things heavenly and perpetual? Neither is this blessed testament sealed with wax, but with the precious and dear heart-blood of our Lord and Saviour Christ Jesus. To mangle this heavenly testament, to corrupt this blessed will, wherein is bequeathed unto us the favour of God, remission of all our sins, and eternal life, if we truly repent and earnestly believe, is much unfitting for any christian man; neither are such manglers and corrupters, such thieves and robbers, any more to be believed of the faithful congregation.

Matt. xxvi. Luke xxii.

John iii. Ecclus. x. Col. ii.

Note.

[[1] Qui pridie quam pateretur accepit panem in sanctas ac venerabiles manus suas: et elevatis oculis in cœlum ad te, Deum patrem suum omnipotentem, tibi gratias agens benedixit, fregit, deditque discipulis suis dicens, Accipite et manducate ex hoc omnes; hoc est enim corpus meum.—Missal. ad Us. et Consuet. Sar. Par. 1527. Canon Missæ. foll. 157, 8.]

[[2] Simili modo postea quam cœnatum est, accipiens et hunc præclarum calicem in sanctas ac venerabiles manus suas, item tibi gratias agens benedixit, deditque discipulis suis dicens, Accipite, et bibite ex eo omnes, hic est enim calix sanguinis mei, novi et eterni testamenti, mysterium fidei, qui pro vobis et pro multis effundetur in remissionem peccatorum.—Id. ibid.]

22 Christ (as I may once make an end), after he had fed his disciples with the holy mysteries of his body and blood, gave thanks to God the Father, and so prepared Matt. xxvi. Matt. xiv. himself, through earnest prayer, unto the death. John xvii. The papists, after they have once drunk and eat up all together, they give no thanks, whereby the common people are edified, except it be when they bless with the empty cup, or bid them go home with *Ite missa est.*

Well, thus may ye easily perceive how greatly the popish mass differeth from the true institution of the Lord's supper, and that they agree together as Christ and Belial, light and darkness, truth and falsehood, &c.

Chris. It shall therefore be convenient for all true christian hearts no more to repose the trust of their salvation in the sacrifice of their popish mass, nor in any thing appertaining to the same; but only in the blessed passion, in the precious blood, and glorious death of our Lord and Saviour Jesus Christ, which by the alone sacrifice of his most holy body hath, even unto the uttermost and at the full, paid our ransom, and brought us everlasting health.

Theo. This is a comfortable hearing for all faithful penitent sinners. But I pray you, neighbour Philemon, remain there no more causes of rejoicing in the Lord our God?

Phil. Yes, verily. For this our Lord and Saviour Jesus Christ did not only both Of Christ's resurrection. willingly and freely give himself unto the death of the cross for our sins and wickedness, and by this means paid our ransom to God the Father for our offences, that Satan might have no power over us; but he also, through the might of his godhead, rose again gloriously and triumphantly on the third day, according to the scriptures, for our justification, as the apostle saith: "He was betrayed unto the death for our Rom. iv. sins, and rose again for our justification." For as by the death of Christ our ransom is paid, the divine wrath is pacified, our sins are washed away in Christ's blood, a reconciliation and perfect atonement is made between God the Father and us, the obligation of our debt is rased out, the law is fulfilled, the curse of God's wrath is taken away, all things both in heaven and in earth are pacified; so in like manner by the resurrection of Christ we are made righteous, accepted into God's favour, recounted for just, holy, and virtuous, set at liberty from the tyranny of Satan, admitted into the celestial court of the new Hierusalem, and become fellow-citizens of the household of God with the saints and blessed spirits.

Eus. O inestimable treasures, brought to us by the glorious resurrection of our most blessed Saviour Jesu Christ! *Phil.* Yea, let us mark this also by the way, that, as our most valiant Lord and emperor Jesus Christ by his resurrection gat the victory over Satan, sin, death, hell, desperation, and all that is enemy to man's health; so in like condition have we in him and through him gotten a glorious victory over Satan and all his kingdom, that we may with a joyful voice say: "Death is 1 Cor. xv. swallowed up into victory. O death, where is thy sting? The sting of death is sin: the power of sin is the law. But thanks be to God, which hath given us the victory through our Lord Jesu Christ."

Chris. O what a joy and comfort is this to a christian man's heart, to see his enemies, which before so greatly sought his destruction, thus vanquished, subdued, and trodden under his foot! This have we gotten, as ye very truly have said, by Christ's resurrection, as Christ himself testifieth, saying: "Now is the judgment of John xii. the world: now shall the prince of this world be cast out." Again: "Be of good John xvi. comfort: I have overcome the world." By the prophet Osee he also saith: "I will Hos. xiii. deliver them from the power of death, yea, from death itself will I redeem them. O death, I will be thy death. O hell, I will be thy destruction."

Phil. Moreover, by Christ's resurrection have we obtained not only justification and victory over our enemies, but also resurrection of body and everlasting immortality. For as our Lord and Saviour Jesus Christ did put off the mortality of his body, and became immortal at his resurrection; so by the power of that his most glorious resurrection shall we also at the great day of judgment in our resurrection receive immortal and incorruptible bodies, even like unto the glorious body of our most mighty and valiant captain Jesu Christ. *Theo.* O who can express the worthiness and excellency of these heavenly gifts, which we obtain by the most victorious and triumphant resurrection of Jesus Christ our Lord and Saviour?

Phil. Let these things therefore, dearly beloved brethren, make you to rejoice in the Lord. Let these things provoke you to withdraw your mind from transitory things, and stedfastly to fix it on things constant and everlasting. Let these things sequester your joy and pleasure from the sweet enticing mermaids of this world, and call[1] you to the alone delectation in celestial treasures. *Chris.* O blessed is that man to whom it is given from above truly to savour these things, faithfully to believe them, and earnestly to rejoice in that Lord which is the alone giver of them! Sure may that man be that his name is written in the book of life.

Of Christ's ascension.

Phil. But let us go forth to declare more benefits of God toward man, that our joy in the Lord may be unfeigned, consummate, and perfect. After this most noble conquest and victorious triumph, which our most mighty emperor Christ Jesus had over Satan and his infernal ministers, he tarried here in this world certain days with his disciples, eating, drinking, and talking with them of the kingdom of his heavenly Father, and confirming them in the way of truth. And this did he not only to make them strong in the article of his resurrection, but also by the instruction of them to corroborate, fortify, and strength us in the same, seeking no less our health than the salvation of them. For, as the apostle saith: "If thou dost confess with thy mouth the Lord Jesus, and believe with thine heart that God raised him up from the dead, thou shalt be saved." Certain days past from his resurrection, Christ our Lord by the power of his godhead, in the sight of his apostles, ascended into heaven, God and man. Have we no cause to rejoice in this behalf? Hath this his marvellous ascension brought no commodity and profit to us? Have we a just cause to rejoice in his nativity, preaching, miracles, good works, cross, passion, blood, death, resurrection (which all are ours), and not in his ascension also? We read that the apostles were very sad when Christ told them that he should ascend unto his Father; but Christ said unto them: "I tell you truth: it is expedient and profitable for you that I go" and ascend unto my Father. Christ told the apostles that it was expedient and profitable for them that he should go up into heaven. If it were expedient for them, it is even so likewise for us. For we are saved by the very same way whereby they received salvation. Let us therefore consider what commodities and profits the apostles had by Christ's ascension, and let us with a constant faith and hope look for the same. For there is but "one Lord of all, rich enough for so many as call on him."

Rom. x. Acts i. John xvi. Rom. x.

Eus. I pray you, let us hear, that our joy may be full.

The fruits of Christ's ascension.

Phil. First, that we may truly rejoice in Christ's ascension, I will labour to shew you some of the commodities of it, as we are taught in the sacred scriptures. Christ in his last sermon said unto his disciples: "I go to prepare a place for you. If I go my way and prepare a place for you, I will come again and take you unto myself, that where I am ye may be also." Here have we one urgent cause why we ought earnestly to rejoice in Christ's ascension. For of this aforesaid sentence we learn that Christ is ascended unto his Father to prepare a place for us in heaven. Can any thing sound more pleasant and thank-worthy to our ears, than to hear that the Son of God came down from his heavenly throne, became man, suffered death, rose again for our sake, and is now ascended, very God and very man, into heaven to prepare a glorious mansion for us in the kingdom of heaven? What is more comfortable for a pilgrim than, after long travelling by strange countries, at the last to come home to his own house, and there to find all things well provided for him? Are not we "strangers and pilgrims" in this world? Do we not wander from place to place uncertainly, and look for another mansion more quiet and merry to come? If there were not such a dwelling-place to be looked for after this present life, of all creatures the true Christians were most miserable. But there is undoubtedly an heavenly palace prepared for the faithful, yea, and that by Christ's ascension.

John xiv. 1 Pet. ii. Heb. xiii.

Theo. Certes here have we, I confess, one great occasion to rejoice in the ascen-

[1 Folio: *all*.]

sion of Christ, seeing by it he hath prepared for us a dwelling-place among the holy saints and blessed angels, and promiseth that he will come once again, take us unto him, and place us even there where he himself is.

Phil. Another commodity that we have by Christ's ascension is the gift of the Holy Ghost. For Christ himself saith: "If I go not away, the Comforter shall not come unto you. But if I go my way, I will send him unto you." By this Comforter he understandeth the Holy Ghost, which comforteth and maketh strong with godly puissance, yea, and leadeth into all truth, the hearts of so many as he inhabiteth. What an inestimable treasure the gift of the Holy Ghost is, no man knoweth but he that is endued with wisdom from above. Whence come all these backsliders from God and his word, but only of the lack of the Holy Ghost? Whence come so many heretics, schismatics, anabaptists, sacramentaries, papists, with all the whole rabble of seditious sectaries, but only that they are destitute of this Comforter, of this holy Spirit, which should comfort them in faith, and lead them into all truth? David knew full well, what a singular and great treasure to a faithful man the having of the Holy Ghost is; again, what an utter decay and extreme destruction it is to that man that wanteth this Comforter, when he prayed on this manner: "Create in me a pure heart, O God; and a right spirit renew now in my inward parts. Cast me not away from thy face; and thy holy Spirit take not away from me." This holy Spirit do the faithful receive from God the Father through the ascension of Christ. Is this a small gift, to have the Holy Ghost given unto us to dwell within our breasts, and with him all the heavenly fruits of the Spirit, faith, love, hope, patience, joy, long-suffering, meekness, temperance, justice, goodness, gentleness, modesty, honest behaviour, peace, with an whole sea of good things more, yea, and at the last everlasting life? Who rejoiceth not in this most excellent gift, purchased for us by the ascension of the Lord Christ, our God and Saviour?

John xvi.

Psal. li.

Gal. v.

Chris. That such gifts should be given unto men of Christ after Christ's ascension, it was long before prophesied of the holy psalmograph: "Thou art gone up on high, thou hast led captivity captive, and received gifts for men." *Eus.* Of the gift of the Holy Ghost, plenteously to be given after Christ's ascension, God himself speaketh by the prophet Joel, saying: "It shall be in the last days, saith God, of my Spirit I will pour out upon all flesh. And your sons and your daughters shall prophesy, and your young men shall see visions, and your old men shall dream dreams. And on my servants and on my hand-maidens I will pour out of my Spirit in those days; and they shall prophesy."

Psal. lxviii. Eph. iv.

Joel ii. Acts ii.

Phil. Neither do here cease the commodities and profits that we enjoy by the ascension of Christ. For besides the preparation of the heavenly mansions, and the gift of the Holy Ghost (which without doubt are most high and singular treasures), Christ by his ascension is become our Intercessor, Mediator, and Advocate. He sitteth on the right hand of God the Father, making intercession for us. If we will obtain any thing of God the Father, he is straightways ready to be an advocate, and to plead our cause before his Father, and easily obtaineth whatsoever he desireth; so great is his dignity and excellency.

Christ our Intercessor, Mediator, and Advocate.

Again, if at any time we offend God (as "we all do amiss in many things"), and by our offence provoke the wrath of God unto vengeance, Christ our Advocate and Mediator is at hand immediately to pacify the ire and wrath of God, to reconcile us unto him, to purchase remission of our sins, and to recover the favour that we had lost through our weakness, as St John saith: "If any man sin, we have an Advocate with the Father, Jesus Christ that righteous one. And he is a mercy-stock[2] for our sins; not for our sins only, but for all the world's also." For the blood of Christ is not like the blood of Abel. For the blood of Abel crieth for vengeance upon his brother Cain, which unjustly slew him (as the blood of all innocents and martyrs do in like manner call for vengeance against them that have oppressed them, and shed their blood unjustly); but the blood of Christ crieth for grace, favour, and mercy, crieth for pardon, forgiveness, and remission of sins, crieth for joy, quietness, and

James iii.

1 John ii.

Heb. xii. Gen. iv.

[[2] Mercy-stock: propitiation.]

Rom. v. everlasting life. "God," saith St Paul, "setteth forth his love wonderfully toward us; for if, when we were yet sinners, Christ died for us, much more then we, being now justified in his blood, shall be saved from the wrath by him. If, when we were enemies, we were reconciled to God by the death of his Son, much more we, being reconciled, shall be made safe through his life."

No man can sufficiently express the worthiness of this commodity, that Christ is not only become by his ascension a preparer of an heavenly and glorious mansion for us, again, a purchaser of the Holy Ghost to comfort us and to lead us into all truth, but also an Intercessor, Mediator, and Advocate, whereby he obtaineth for us all good things, and putteth aback from us whatsoever should hinder the obtaining of God's favour and the heavenly inheritance. Christ purchaseth for us of his Father through his intercession so abundantly and so altogether sufficiently all things necessary for the conservation both of our body and soul, that we need not to pray unto any saint in heaven, as the papists have taught us, neither unto Mary, John, Peter, James, nor any
1 Tim. ii. other, to be our intercessor, mediator, or advocate. It is Christ's office alone to be a Mediator between God and us, as blessed Paul teacheth us in his epistle unto Timothy.

I doubt not, neighbours, but so many as are faithful are replete with exceeding joy to consider how manifold and divers benefits, gifts, and graces, chance to us by the wonderful ascension of Christ our Lord and Saviour.

Theo. Whosoever considereth deeply in his mind those things that ye have taught us hitherto, shall be occasioned unfeignedly to obey this commandment of the blessed
1 Cor. i. apostle: "He that rejoiceth, let him rejoice in the Lord;" so sweet and full of all heavenly pleasure are these commodities which we receive of God through Christ our Lord.

Phil. But let us make haste unto an end concerning this matter, that we may learn in few words whatsoever remaineth of God's goodness toward us in Christ; I mean so much as our wit can comprehend, and we be taught in the holy scripture, that we may earnestly rejoice in the Lord our God. We have heard heretofore many urgent and weighty causes, why we should of very right and bounden duty rejoice and be merry in the Lord. Now it remaineth orderly to declare the final and last cause, why we ought to be glad and rejoice in God. *Chris.* I pray you, let us hear.

Of Christ's coming to judgment. *Phil.* As Christ was born for us, wrought all good things in his manhood for us, suffered for us, died for us, rose again for us, ascended into heaven for us, purchased the Holy Ghost for us, prayeth for us, obtaineth all best things for us; so likewise at the last day shall he, being our head, come again from the right hand of his Father to fetch us his members, and to enunite us with him in the same glory, there ever to remain. And although to the wicked he shall come as a terrible and righteous judge, to revenge, and not to pardon; to punish, and not to forgive; to condemn, and not to save; yet to the faithful shall he come in his glorious majesty, and all the blessed angels with him, like a most loving and gentle Saviour, saying to them on this manner: "Come, ye blessed of my Father, possess ye the kingdom prepared for you from the beginning of the world." O who is able to express what joy and comfort this aforesaid sentence shall bring to the hearts of the faithful? But to the unfaithful it shall be said: "Get ye hence, ye cursed, into everlasting fire, which is prepared for the devil and his angels."

Zeph. i. *Eus.* O that day shall be to the wicked "a bitter day, a day of wrath, a day of tribulation and anguish, a day of calamity, misery, and wretchedness, a day of darkness and mist, a day of cloudiness and boistuousness, a day of fearful trumpets and shawms blowing."

Phil. I grant: notwithstanding, to the faithful it shall be a sweet day, a day of favour, a day of quietness and peace, a day of wealth and felicity, a day of clearness and light, a day of comfort and solace, a day of heavenly mirth, joy, and pleasure.
1 Cor. ii. Isai. lxiv. For, as blessed Paul saith: "The eye hath not seen, nor the ear hath not heard, neither can the heart of man think, what things God hath prepared for them that love
Matt. xxii. him." They "shall be as angels of God in heaven." "They shall shine as the clear-
Wisd. v. ness of the firmament, and as stars for ever and ever." They shall be "counted among the sons of God, and their lot shall be among the saints." "They shall receive of
Rev. vii. the Lord's hand an honourable kingdom and a beautiful diadem." They shall be "clad with long white garments." They shall be "before the throne of God, and serve him

day and night in his temple." "They shall hunger and thirst no more, neither shall the sun or any heat fall upon them; for the Lamb Christ[1], which is in the midst of the throne, shall govern them, and lead them unto the fountains of the water of life; and God shall wipe away every tear from their eyes." They shall dwell in a city that "needeth neither sun nor moon to shine in it; for the clearness of God shall Rev. xxi.
illumine it." "They shall behold the glorious face of God presently; and his name Rev. xxii.
shall be written in their foreheads." They shall "eat of the tree of life, which is in Rev. ii.
the paradise of God." To conclude, they shall have a crown of glory, and sit with Rev. iii.
Christ their elder brother in his throne, even as he sitteth with his Father in his throne; and shall live with God and his holy angels in all kind of honour and glory, joy and pleasure, world without end. O what can a christian man desire more of the Lord his God, than these things which I have heretofore rehearsed? Come off, tell me now, I pray you, if we have not many, yea, and innumerable both urgent and weighty causes why we should rejoice in the Lord our God. I doubt not, I doubt not, most dear brethren, but by the hearing of these things ye are now so rapt into the love of God for the most high and singular pleasures, which through Christ Jesus ye have already received, and hereafter shall receive a thousand times more abundantly, that from henceforth all worldly things shall wax vile unto you, and ye shall even from the very heart endeavour yourselves at all times to repose all your joy, comfort, pleasure, and felicity in the Lord our God alone, alone; so that ye shall rejoice in none, neither in heaven nor in earth, but in him alone, alone.

Chris. Neighbour Philemon, we all are kindled with so fervent and so hearty love toward God for these his most singular and inestimable benefits, that we do not only defy the world and all the vain pleasures of it, but we also are ready, for our stedfast love in God and for the perfect rejoicing in him, gladly to say with the blessed apostle: "Who shall separate us from the love of Christ? Shall tribulation, or Rom. viii.
anguish, or famine, or nakedness, or peril, or persecution, or sword? I am sure that neither death, nor life, nor angels, nor sovereignties, nor powers, nor things present, nor things to come, nor strength, height, nor depth, nor any other creature, shall be able to separate us from the love of God, which is in Christ Jesus our Lord."

Phil. I am glad to hear these your words, that I am fully persuaded that this your joy shall increase unto an exceeding and perfect rejoicing in the Lord our God, unto the great and singular comfort both of your bodies and souls. But ye shall note that the holy apostle doth not only bid us rejoice in the Lord, but he addeth unto it, "alway:" "Rejoice in the Lord alway," saith he.

Theo. What meaneth the blessed apostle by this word "alway?" *Phil.* Verily he will that our joy and rejoicing in the Lord be not flitting, transitory, and of small continuance (as the pleasure that is conceived of worldly things is, the end whereof is bitter and sorrowful, as Salomon saith, "The end of worldly joy is heaviness," mourn- Prov. xiv.
ing, and lamenting), but constant, stedfast, immutable, not diminishing, but increasing unto an high perfection of godly mirth, joy, felicity, and pleasure. For "he that con- Matt. x.
tinueth unto the end," saith Christ, "shall be saved." It is not enough to begin well and to continue in the same a certain space, except we persevere even unto the end of our life. The wife of Lot began well when she came out of sinful Sodom; but, because Gen. xix.
she did not go forth, but looked back again unto it, she was turned into a salt pillar. The wise men, that came from the east part of the world to worship Jesus Christ the Matt. ii.
new-born King of the spiritual Israelites, were commanded of God no more to return to the most bloody and wicked king Herod. Judas began well, and was one of Christ's disciples, and very earnest in setting forth the kingdom of God for a certain space; but seeing he did not persevere in that godly purpose, but became of a preacher a traitor, of a disciple a thief, of a minister a murderer, he is now the son of perdition, and damned for evermore.

He is not the true son, that promiseth his father that he will work in his vineyard, Matt. xxi.
and doth not; but he that manfully worketh in it indeed, and so persevereth to the end, he shall enjoy the inheritance of his father. For the kingdom of God shall

[[1] The folio reads, *Lamb of Christ*.]

be taken away from idle lubbers, and given to them that work and bring forth the fruits thereof. Not they which, when they hear the word first of all, do joyfully receive it, believe it for a time, talk of it, and in the time of temptation go away, slide back, and become other men, shall possess eternal life; but they which with great joy and gladness of mind hear it, receive it, believe it, cleave fast unto it in the time of persecution, and persevere in the same even unto the very last breath.

Matt. xiii. Mark iv. Luke viii.

"No man is crowned," saith St Paul, "except he fight lawfully;" that is, until he have gotten the victory by resisting the world, the devil, and the flesh, through Christ our Lord. And the Lord himself saith: "No man that putteth his hand to the plough, and looketh back, is meet for the kingdom of heaven." Hereto agreeth the saying of St Peter: "If, after they have forsaken the uncleanness of the world by the knowledge of the Lord and Saviour Christ Jesus, they yet again, being wrapped in them, are overcome, the last is worse than the first to them. For it had been better for them not to have known the way of righteousness, than after their knowledge to turn away from that holy commandment that was given them. But that is chanced to them that is wont to be spoken in a true proverb, The dog is returned unto his vomit; and the sow clean washed unto the wallowing in the mire."

2 Tim. ii. Luke ix. 2 Pet. ii. Prov. xxvi.

Of these things aforesaid may we learn, that it is not enough to begin well, except we persevere and continue even unto the giving up of the ghost, as they use to say. "He that continueth to the end," saith Christ, "shall be saved." Again he saith: "If ye abide in my word, truly ye shall be my disciples, and ye shall know the truth, and the truth shall deliver you." We must abide in the word of God, or else we cannot be Christ's disciples. "We are delivered from the rule of our enemies," saith holy Zachary the priest, father to that most excellent prophet of God, St John Baptist, "that we, being without fear, should serve God in holiness and righteousness before him all the days of our life." Note that he saith, "all the days of our life" must we serve God in such holiness and righteousness as is acceptable before him. The holy scripture requireth of us a continual progress and an unletted perseverance in the way of godliness. In consideration whereof the blessed apostle doth not only exhort us to rejoice in the Lord, but he addeth unto it "alway," requiring of us not a flitting and transitory rejoicing, but a constant, stedfast, sure, continual, and unchangeable rejoicing in the Lord. "Rejoice in the Lord alway," saith he.

Matt. x. John viii. Luke i.

Note well.

Eus. It is but a trifle to joy and rejoice in the Lord, in his word and ordinances, so long as prosperity endureth, and the world laugheth upon us; but to rejoice in the Lord, in his word and ordinances, when we be assailed with troublous adversity, when we be visited with grievous sickness, when we be impoverished through miserable misfortunes, when we be hated, blasphemed, persecuted, oppressed, imprisoned, punished of worldly tyrants for God, for his word and ordinances; this is a perfect joy, and christian rejoicing. To bear the cross of Christ, to suffer patiently all kind of adversity, to cleave fast to God in the time of temptation, to be content so well to abide troubles as prosperous things, and thankfully to take whatsoever plagues or punishments God shall lay upon us, either by his own loving visitation, or by the cruelty of the wicked worldlings, which are alway enemies to God's truth, and to all true lovers of the same; this is mine opinion to rejoice alway in the Lord, and to acknowledge him to be our most gentle Father and loving Saviour, whether he send prosperity or adversity.

A good lesson.

Phil. Truth it is that ye say, brother Eusebius. If therefore any of you at any time be visited with sickness or diseases of the body, murmur not, nor grudge not against God, blaspheme him not, nor speak not unreverently of him, nor yet wish not that sickness to be taken from you otherwise than his godly pleasure shall be, which knoweth much better what is expedient or profitable for you, than ye yourselves do; but with high patience, and most hearty thanksgiving, receive that loving visitation of your heavenly Father, as an holy emplasture and wholesome salve to heal all those pocky diseases, wherewith your souls are infected through the stinking corruption of old sinful Adam. "We are corrected and punished of the Lord," saith St Paul, "that we should not be damned with this world." David also saith: "It is good for me that thou hast thus humbled and brought me down full low, that I may learn thy righteous ordinances."

1 Cor. xi. Psal. cxix.

If thou therefore, in thy sickness, shalt feel thy flesh to be impatient, disobedient to the will of God, and at defiance with God for this his loving correction, pleasant to the spirit, but altogether bitter to the flesh for a season, restrain and pluck her back with the bit of patience, and never leave to fight against the furious and raging motions of the flesh, till thou hast made her obedient to the spirit, and willing to suffer whatsoever kind of adversity God shall lay upon her back.

Labour in thy sickness so to joy and rejoice in the Lord, that with high patience and cheerfulness of mind, even in the midst of thy most bitter vexation, thou mayest say with St Paul: "We are not wearied; but though our outward man perish, yet 2 Cor. iv.
the inward man is renewed day by day. For our tribulation, which is momentany, of short continuance, and light, prepareth an exceeding and an eternal weight of glory unto us; while we look not on the things which are seen, but on the things which are not seen. For things which are seen are temporal; but things which are not seen are everlasting." Again: "We know surely, if our earthly mansion, wherein we 2 Cor. v.
now dwell, were destroyed, that we have a building ordained of God, an habitation not made with hands, but eternal in heaven."

And that ye may with the more patient and thankful mind receive all kind of sicknesses and diseases, wherewith ye are at any time vexed, look that ye persuade yourselves and believe undoubtedly, that your punishments come not unto you by chance, but by the counsel, providence, and appointment of God, without whose will Matt. x.
an hair doth not fall from your heads; which also keepeth all your bones, so that Psal. xxxiv.
not one of them shall be bruised without the permission and sufferance of that our good God. "He made us, and we not ourselves: we are his flock, and the sheep Psal. c.
of his pasture:" therefore like a most gentle shepherd, considering the grievous diseases wherewith we are already infected, or else like to be, he prepareth his tar, and greaseth us with that, that we should be free from all contagious diseases, and be found whole and sound, whensoever we shall be searched. For God doth not visit us with sickness and other plagues that he might destroy us, cast us headlong into hell-fire, and damn us perpetually; but to call us to repentance, to provoke us to come home again unto the sheep-fold, to exercise, prove, and try our faith, that by this means he might save us. For that Lord, which is the searcher of reins and hearts, perceiving how old Adam beginneth to wax cruel and fierce in us, restraineth and plucketh him back with the bridle of sickness, that he shall not do what he himself would, but what the good-will of our heavenly Father is; which else, without all doubt, would so rage and grow unto such licentious riot, that with his vain pleasures and fleshly lusts he would deceive the most precious and noble soul, and so deceived throw it into the danger of eternal damnation.

Theo. Of these your words may we right well perceive, that affliction, troubles, sicknesses, and diseases, be no tokens of God's ire, wrath, and displeasure toward us; but of much high mercy, favour, love, and good-will, that he beareth to us. *Phil.* Truth. For if this most gentle Saviour and best God did not seek our salvation, our wealth, and health everlasting, he would not with so sharp and loving corrections call us home again unto the sheep-fold, but suffer us to run headlong into all kind of carnal voluptuousness and beastly pleasure, and afterward, for our dissolute living, reward us with pains eternal among the belly-gods and epicures.

Chris. O who is so far estranged from the right course of reason, that he had not rather have his carnal affects and beastly will mortified with temporal and short sicknesses in this world, than for a little space to tumble and wallow in all kind of carnal pleasures according to his fleshly desire, and afterward for ever and ever to be The pains of hell.
cast into such pains as are both intolerable and everlasting, where weeping and gnashing Matt. xiii.
of teeth is, where the darknesses are so great that they may be felt, where the fire shall Isai. lxvi.
never be quenched, where the worm that shall gnaw the conscience of the wicked shall never die, where there is a lake and stinking puddle that burneth continually with Rev. xxi.
fire and brimstone, where nothing shall be felt but pain, nothing remembered but sin, nothing tasted but bitterness, nothing seen but our most wicked enemies Satan with his infernal ministers; who shall not be grieved and led with a certain compassion toward the damned for the multitude of the most bitter pains, wherein they shall see them most

miserably tormented, but they shall rejoice, yea, they themselves shall never cease to minister intolerable punishments to the damned souls, world without end?

Eus. O whose heart is so inflamed with the fire of carnal pleasure, that waxeth not cold at the hearing of these things? Who had not rather in this world continually to be shaken with hot agues, grieved with bone-ache, eaten with cankers, pined away for hunger, and to suffer any other temporal disease that can be named, be it never so grievous and bitter to the flesh, than to fall into those most horrible pains that you named heretofore? The pains that are suffered in this world are great and bitter, I confess; but they have an end, and work health to the soul. And in like manner, the pains that are sustained in hell are both great and bitter also; but they have no end, and bring eternal damnation to the soul.

Phil. O what plague can be named like unto this? Who is now so stiff-necked
2 Cor. xii. and hard-hearted, that he will not say with the apostle, "I will with all my heart rejoice in my infirmities and weakness, that the virtue, power, and strength of Christ may dwell in me?" Who now is so blind, which seeth not that to be visited with sickness in this world is to receive a singular and high benefit of God? Who is so far from true faith, that will not be persuaded that afflictions, troubles, sicknesses, and diseases, be plain testimonies and evident signs of God's good favour toward us?
Prov. iii. as the wise man saith: "The chastening of God thou shalt not refuse; neither grudge thou, when he shall correct thee. For whom the Lord loveth, him he correcteth, and delighteth himself as the father in the son." David also saith: "O blessed is that man
Psal. cxix. which is under the law and nurture of the Lord." Again: "It is highly for my wealth, O Lord, that thou hast brought me under to learn thy ordinances." Hereto agreeth
Heb. xii. the saying of the apostle: "My son, despise not the chastening of the Lord; neither faint thou, when thou art rebuked of him. For whom the Lord loveth, him he chasteneth, yea, and he scourgeth every son that he receiveth. If ye endure chastening, God offereth himself unto you as unto sons. What son is that whom the father chasteneth not? If ye be not under correction (whereof all are partakers), then are ye bastards, and not sons. Wherefore, seeing we had fathers of our flesh which corrected us, and we have them in reverence, should we not much rather be in subjection unto the Father of spiritual gifts? And they verily for a few days nurtured us after their own pleasure; but he learneth us unto that which is profitable, that we might receive of his holiness. No manner of chastising for the present time seemeth to be joyous, but grievous: notwithstanding, afterward it bringeth quiet fruit of righteousness unto them which are exercised in the same."

Bear not therefore, dearly beloved, impatiently the cross of sickness, whensoever God layeth it on your back, neither strive ye against the good pleasure of your heavenly Father, which only seeketh your commodity and eternal salvation; but patiently suffer, and pray that his godly will (which is always best) may be done in you, and whether he sendeth sickness or health, ever glorify his name, and rejoice in him, being throughly persuaded that he will handle you none otherwise than shall make both unto his glory and your salvation, which to resist were extreme impiety and too much ungodliness.

A godly prayer. *Chris.* Forasmuch, O Lord, as we are thy workmanship, and are in thy hands, even as the clay is in the potter's, do with us according to thy most godly pleasure; only give us a patient and thankful heart, that whether thou sendest prosperity or adversity, sickness or health, quietness or trouble, we may at all times praise and magnify thy most blessed and glorious name. *Theo.* Let it so come to pass, O Lord.

Of poverty or loss of goods. *Phil.* Now, neighbours, even as I would wish you to rejoice in the Lord our God, whensoever he visit you with his loving correction and scourge of sickness; so would I gladly also have you to joy and rejoice in him, if he at any time sendeth poverty or loss of goods to any of you all. If therefore it so chanceth, that ye be accumbered with any misfortune, grudge not against God, but shew yourself conformable to his godly will in all points, nothing doubting but that loss of your temporal possessions shall turn unto your high commodity and furtherance in obtaining goods which are a thousand times more precious, I mean God's favour, quietness of conscience, and
James i. eternal glory. "Let the brother," saith St James, "that is poor and of low degree

rejoice in that he is exalted, and the rich in that he is made low. For even as the flower of the grass shall he vanish away. The sun riseth with heat; and the grass withereth, and his flower falleth away, and the beauty of the fashion of it perisheth: even so shall the rich man perish with his abundance." The goods of this world, wherewith ye be righteously endued, are God's: if therefore it shall be his good pleasure at any time to take them from you, grudge not against him for taking his own, but rather with a thankful and rejoicing heart say with the patient man Job: "The Lord gave it, the Lord hath taken it away again. As it pleased the Lord, so is it come to pass. Blessed be the name of the Lord." Job i.

Peradventure God perceiveth that thy mind is so much set on temporal possessions, that thou clean forgettest the spiritual riches and heavenly treasures of the soul: therefore he, minding to make thee his son and heir of eternal glory, and of much better and more excellent goods than this beggarly vale of misery can comprehend, taketh away from thee that muck of this world, that thou mayest the more freely aspire and breathe forward unto the getting of heavenly riches, wherewith the soul being gorgeously decked may after this transitory life sit gloriously in the glorious palace of heaven. "For what doth it profit a man," saith Christ, "though he winneth all[1] the world and loseth his soul?" Again: "Hoard not up treasures unto you on the earth, where rust and moths corrupt, and where thieves break through and steal. But hoard ye up treasures in heaven, where neither rust nor moths corrupt, and where thieves break not up nor yet steal. For where your[1] treasure is, there will your heart be also." And that ye[1] may bear the cross of poverty with the more patient mind, remember that though Christ was Lord over all, yet was he so poor from his infancy unto his departure out of this world, that he had not a place where once to rest his head. His mother and all the apostles, with many blessed martyrs, faithful ministers of God's word, and other innumerable that were good men and dearly beloved of God, escaped not the hard dart of poverty. Now seeing ye have Christ the Lord of lords and King of kings, his blessed mother, with the holy apostles and martyrs, &c., exemplars of poverty to follow and practise, if God at any time do lay the cross of necessity on your backs, suffer it both patiently and thankfully. Disdain not you, being servants, to bear that burden which your Lord and Master refused not to take upon him. "Ye know the liberality of our Lord Jesu Christ," saith St Paul, "that for your sake he became poor when he was rich, that ye through his poverty should wax rich."

Why God taketh away the worldly goods from them whom he loveth.

Matt. xvi. Matt. vi. Matt. viii. Luke ii. Acts iii. 2 Cor. viii.

Eus. Neighbour Philemon, although (thanks be to God!) we have our breasts so well furnished and fortressed with the weapons and armours of holy scriptures against the violence of all misfortunes, yet some perchance, not being throughly instructed of God's liberality toward his creatures, will object and say, as the common proverb is, necessity is an hard dart, and hunger is a sharp thorn; how then can we take poverty so patiently, that we may rejoice in the Lord our God, namely in so great penury and scarceness of things?

Phil. I answer with the psalmograph: "I have been young, and now I am old; yet never saw I righteous man forsaken, nor his seed begging their bread on the earth." If thou therefore be righteous, that is, faithful to God and just to thy neighbour, labouring diligently for thy living according to thy vocation and calling, as God hath commanded thee, thou mayest be sure not to want that shall suffice nature. Who ever trusted in God, and went away succourless? "Cast thy care on the Lord, and he shall nourish thee," saith David. "The Lord giveth meat to the hungry." "Behold, the eyes of the Lord are upon them that fear him, and upon them that trust in his mercy, that he may deliver their lives from death, and nourish them in the time of hunger." "They that fear the Lord shall have no scarceness." "They which seek the Lord shall want no good thing." "Fear not, my son," saith Tobias: "we lead a poor life: notwithstanding we shall have plenty of all good things, if we fear the Lord, depart from all sin, and do well." "God giveth us abundantly in all things to enjoy them," saith St Paul. God himself saith: "I will not fail thee nor yet forsake thee."

Psal. xxxvii. Psal. lv. Psal. cxlvi. Psal. xxxiii. Tob. iv. 1 Tim. vi. Josh. i. Heb. xiii.

Chris. Who, being a faithful man, although never so much oppressed with poverty,

[1 Folio has *at*, *you*, and *he*.]

will not rejoice in the Lord, which hath promised, and will no less perform, that he will not forsake so many as trust in him?

Phil. And that ye may be throughly persuaded of his faithfulness concerning the accomplishment of his promise, consider, I pray you, how friendly and faithfully he dealt in times past with his servants, and will no less favourably handle us, if we have like faith in him. Did he not feed the people of Israel with meat from heaven, and gave them drink out of the rock? Did he not send meat twice a day by the ravens to the prophet Helias, and so miraculously fed him when the unfaithful perished for hunger? Did not Christ turn water into wine at the marriage in Cana Galilee? Did not Christ with five barley loaves and two fishes feed five thousand men, besides women and children, and yet thereof remained twelve baskets full of the fragments? Do not all these histories teach us to have faith in God, and to believe that God hath a fatherly care for his servants? "Whatsoever things are written are written," saith blessed Paul, "for our learning, that through patience and comfort of the scriptures we should have hope."

Exod. xvi. xvii. 1 Kings xvii. John ii. Matt. xiv. John vi. Rom. xv.

It is not to be passed over at this present, that Christ hath in the gospel of Matthew: "Be not careful for your life, what ye shall eat, or what ye shall drink; nor yet for your body, what ye shall put on. Is not the life more worth than meat, and the body more of value than raiment? Behold the fowls of the air; for they sow not, neither reap, nor carry into the barns; and your heavenly Father feedeth them. Are ye not much better than they? Which of you by taking thought can put one cubit to his stature? And why care ye then for raiment? Consider the lilies of the field, how they grow. They labour not, neither spin; and yet I tell you that Salomon in all his royalty was not arrayed like unto one of these. Wherefore, if God so clothe the grass, which is to-day in the field and to-morrow shall be cast into the furnace, shall he not much more do the same to you, O ye of little faith? Take therefore no thought, saying, What shall we eat? or, What shall we drink? or, Wherewith shall we be clothed? After all these things seek the heathen. For your heavenly Father knoweth that ye have need of all these things. But seek ye first the kingdom of heaven, and the righteousness thereof; and all these things shall be cast unto you."

Matt. vi.

Theo. O sweet and comfortable scriptures! Let the heathen take thought for their living, which know not God; as for the faithful Christians, they have a Lord which will provide for them abundantly. Let adulterers, fornicators, thieves, drunkards, swearers, and such other wicked persons, take care wherewith they shall be fed and clad: as for the servants of God, they have an almighty Lord in heaven, which shall send them plenty of all good things. "If ye be loving and obedient," saith the prophet Esay, "ye shall enjoy the best thing that groweth in the land. But if ye be obstinate and rebellious, ye shall be devoured with the sword. For thus the Lord hath promised with his own mouth." The wicked therefore, and not the faithful, shall want and be oppressed with famine.

Isai. i.

Eus. If God taketh such fatherly care for his servants, how then cometh it to pass many times, that those, which seek most of all his glory, lead in this world the most base and miserable life, and often are found succourless and destitute of all man's help; when they, which be unfaithful, regard neither God nor any thing that is godly, despise his most blessed word, persecute the true preachers thereof, oppress their poor neighbours, deal unjustly with all men, &c., have overflowing abundance of all things, live like voluptuous epicures in all kind of pleasure, and possess whatsoever their hearts can wish or desire? This thing see we presently before our eyes; and, as it may be gathered of the holy scriptures, many good men in times past have complained of this thing unto God, and almost, as it were, accused God of unrighteousness. Are not these the words of the holy and patient man Job? "When I consider myself, I am afraid; and my flesh is smitten with fear. Wherefore do wicked men live in health and prosperity, come to their old age, and increase in riches? Their children live in their sight, and their generation before their eyes. Their houses are safe from all fear; and the rod of God doth not smite them. Their bullock gendereth, and that not out of time: their cow calveth, and is not unfruitful. They send forth their children by flocks; and their sons lead the dance. They bear with them tabrets and harps, and have instruments

Job xxi.

of music at their pleasures. They spend their days in wealthiness," &c. The holy prophet Jeremy, marvelling greatly at the prosperity of the wicked, speaketh to God on this manner: "O Lord, thou art more righteous than I should dispute with thee. Jer. xii. Nevertheless, let me talk with thee in things reasonable. How happeneth it that the way of the ungodly is so prosperous, and that it goeth so well with them which without any shame offend and live in wickedness? Thou plantest them; and they take root: they grow and bring forth fruit."

Are not these the words also of the blessed psalmograph? "Truly God is loving Psal. lxxiii. unto Israel, and unto such as are of a clean heart. Nevertheless my feet were almost gone: my treadings had well nigh slipped. And why? I was grieved at the wicked: I do see also the ungodly in such prosperity. For they are in no peril of death, but are lusty and strong. They come in no misfortune like other folk; neither are they plagued like other men. And this is the cause why they be so holden with pride and overwhelmed with cruelty: their eyes swell for fatness, and they do even what they lust. They corrupt other, and speak of wicked blasphemy: their talking is against the Most Highest. For they stretch forth their mouth unto heaven; and their tongue goeth through the world. Therefore fall the people unto them; and thereout suck they no small advantage. Tush, say they, how should God perceive it? Is there any knowledge in the Most Highest? Lo, these are the ungodly: these prosper in the world, and these have riches in possession."

Again, the apostles of Christ, even Christ himself being with them, were sometime so hungry and destitute of all kind of victual, that as they went by the way they were compelled even for very hunger to pluck the ears of corn and to eat it. And Matt. xii. Mark ii. doth not St Paul in these words declare the miserable state both of himself and of his fellow-apostles? "Even unto this time," saith he, "we hunger and thirst, and are 1 Cor. iv. naked, and are buffeted with fists, and have no certain dwelling-place, and labour, working with our hands. We are reviled, and yet we bless. We are persecuted, and suffer it. We are evil spoken of, and we pray. We are made as the filthiness of the world, the offscouring of all things, even unto this day." At the marriage in John ii. Cana Galilee, where Christ himself was present with the blessed virgin Mary his mother, and his disciples, was there not such scarceness, that they wanted wine before the wedding-feast was done? And yet it is to be thought that both they which were married, and the other there assembled, were Christ's friends, and dearly beloved of Christ. What shall I rehearse the history of the rich man which was gorgeously apparelled and Luke xvi. fared daintily every day, and of the poor Lazar, which died for hunger? The rich glutton lived pleasantly, and was damned in hell: the poor Lazar, living in all kind of worldly misery, after the death of his body reigneth in glory with God. The enemy of God hath after his own carnal lust all things: the friend of God wanteth that should suffice the necessary appetite of nature.

Phil. I confess that for the most part the wicked in this world have more abundance of temporal goods, and live a thousand times more pleasantly in the face of the world, than the true Christians do; God through his unsearchable wisdom so appointing, which aforeseeth much better than we what is necessary for us. Notwithstanding, though God doth not customably send to his servants such abundance of worldly treasures as voluptuous worldlings do possess, lest their minds, snarled with the love of them, should be withdrawn from the true and everlasting goodness (as it cometh to pass in many); yet very seldom or never doth he leave them succourless, but sendeth them whatsoever is necessary for the sustentation of their needy and poor life, according to his promise, as he said unto his disciples: "When I sent you without wallet, and scrip, Luke xxii. and shoes, lacked ye any thing? And they said, No." Truly no more shall we lack any necessary thing, if we love God and obey his word. The faithful may perchance sometime feel the dart of poverty; yet will not God leave them succourless and destitute of help. For God sendeth poverty sometime to the righteous for to prove his faith, and to stir him up to call on him which is the giver of all good things, that he may know by the exercise of his faith that they be the gifts of God, as the wise man saith: "Good and evil, life and death, poverty and riches, are of God." "Trust Ecclus. xi. in God, and abide in thy place. For it is an easy thing in the sight of God quickly to enrich a poor man."

Discomfort not yourselves therefore, dear brethren, though sometime ye feel the cross of poverty; but be on a good comfort, joy and rejoice in God. For God hath promised that he will not leave nor forsake you, but give you all good things abundantly for your present necessity. His delay is only to prove your faith, and to provoke you to flee unto him by fervent prayer, and to require of him all things necessary for your living. If ye do this (so ye be not idle, but work according to your calling), the earth shall sooner cease to give forth her fruit, than ye shall want your honest necessaries. "Rejoice therefore in the Lord alway; and once again I say, Rejoice."

Josh. i. Heb. xiii. 1 Tim. vi.

Chris. The Lord of heaven give us all grace so to order our life according to his holy word, so to repose our affiance in him; so to call on his most blessed name in all our adversity, and so to be thankful for his exceeding goodness toward mankind, that we be not found altogether unworthy the receipt of his benefits. *Theo.* So be it.

Of the cross. *Phil.* Finally, as I would have you to rejoice in the Lord, whensoever he sendeth you sickness, poverty, or any other cross, to nurture you, to mortify old Adam, to slay your carnal lusts, to make your bodies subject to the spirit, that they may be "a living and holy sacrifice to God;" so would I exhort you to rejoice also in the Lord, if at any time he raiseth up tyrants to persecute you for the fervent zeal and godly love that ye bear toward the verity and truth of his most blessed word. For as it came to pass in the time of Moyses and the prophets, in the days of Christ and his apostles, even so hath it been from their time unto this day, that the bellied hypocrites and wicked worldlings have ever hated, and still unto the world's end shall hate, the glorious light of God's word. Neither is it any marvel.

Rom. xii.

Hypocrites. For as concerning the bellied hypocrites, God's word condemneth their hypocrisy, superstition, feigned holiness, new-found religion, carnal ceremonies, outward sanctimony, and all the whole glittering face of their popish solemnity. It crieth out upon them, that they are so idle, and do not only not preach themselves, but also forbid other, that would both gladly and freely set forth the glory of Christ's gospel unto the exceeding comfort and great joy of all true Christians; yea, they persecute them, blaspheme them, imprison them, burn them, &c. It crieth out upon them that have so great multitudes of worldly possessions, and yet make no provision for the poor people, for the virtuous bringing up of youth in good letters and virtuous manners, but spend it upon gorgeous buildings, lusty horses, delicate fare, idle lubbers, yea, upon hawks, dogs, and whores. It crieth out upon them, that whereas they ought to be the light of the world, and to give example of virtuous living to all men, they are become of all men most abominable, most lewd, most ungodly, most given to idleness, most drowned in voluptuousness, and altogether sworn to do mischief. How can these belly-gods and swinish hypocrites, whose life is overwhelmed with the dark clouds of sin, abide the glorious light of Christ's gospel? How can these gluttonish epicures suffer their hypocrisy and feigned holiness to be rebuked of the poor abjects and villains of this world by the authority of God's word? It cannot be, it cannot be. For "every one that doth evil," saith Christ, "hateth the light; neither cometh he to the light, lest his works should be reproved."

John iii.

Worldlings. Now as concerning the wicked worldlings, they can favour no more the truth of God's word than the bellied hypocrites. For it condemneth their covetousness, their ambition, their vain-glory, their pride, their whoredom, their polling, their pilling, their falsehood, their oppression, their unmercifulness, their cruelty, their tyranny, and whatsoever abomination they use beside. How can it otherwise come to pass, but they which rebuke these vices must needs be hated, persecuted, imprisoned, and slain of the wicked worldlings, for telling them the truth, and for rebuking these their most abominable and outrageous sins?—as the prophet saith: "They hate him that reproveth them openly, and whoso telleth them the plain truth, they abhor him." Can light and darkness agree? Can Christ and Belial be at unity? No more can the workers of wickedness and the rebukers of the same be led with one consent. There must needs be dissension between them, as was between Abel and Cain, Jacob and Esau, Christ and the bishops, the apostles and the worldly tyrants.

Amos v. 2 Cor. vi.

And forasmuch as the same impiety and ungodliness, the same wickedness and abomination, reigneth now in the world that hath been used in times past, and it ought of very duty to be rebuked at this present with no less liberty of speech than it hath been in times past, except we will wink at so great abomination, and with the wicked worldlings and bellied hypocrites sink down to the devil for our labour; it is not to be doubted but they, that shall take upon them that office, shall prove and find even that same gentleness at their hands, that Moyses and the prophets, Christ and his apostles, the holy martyrs and blessed saints, received of their bloody predecessors.

Therefore, if the waves and surges of cruel persecution shall at any time rise against us (the good-will of our heavenly Father so providing, without whose sufferance all the hypocrites in the world can do nothing against us), let us not despair nor cast away our hope, but still go forth to rejoice in the Lord our God, and manfully abide by the verity of his word; remembering that it is called "the word of the cross," trouble, 1 Cor. i.
and persecution; remembering that no kind of adversity chanceth to us, but the same happened in times past to the prophets and apostles, yea, to Christ himself, that pure Lamb of God; remembering that all which will live godly in Christ Jesus shall suffer persecution; remembering that by the cross a way is prepared for us unto eternal life. And that we may with the more free spirit and frank courage rejoice in the Lord, whensoever the cross or persecution is laid on our backs for God's sake and for his gospel, let us enarm ourselves with the comfortable texts of the holy scripture, and call to remembrance the histories of the blessed men of God, which also suffered like or greater pains for the glory of the Lord, not forgetting that even from the beginning of the world the wicked began to persecute the godly, as we may see in Abel and Gen. iv.
such other.

Eus. Unto this patience and the following of the prophets doth blessed James exhort us, saying: "Be patient, brethren, to the coming of the Lord. Behold, the hus- James v.
bandman waiteth for the precious fruit of the earth, and hath long patience thereupon, until he receive the early and latter rain. Be ye also patient therefore, and settle your hearts; for the coming of the Lord draweth nigh. Grudge not one against another, brethren, lest ye be damned. Behold, the Judge standeth before the door. Take, my brethren, the prophets for an example of suffering adversity, and of patience, which spake in the name of the Lord. Behold, we count them happy which endure."

Chris. Our Saviour Christ saith also: "Blessed are ye, when men revile you, and Matt. v.
persecute you, and shall falsely say all manner of evil sayings against you for my sake. Rejoice and be glad; for great is your reward in heaven. For so persecuted they the prophets which were before you."

Phil. What pleasures the holy prophets of God found at the world's hand, it is The persecution of the prophets.
not hard to express. Esay, that most excellent prophet of God, for his liberty of speech in rebuking the sin of the princes and of the people, and for prophesying of the vengeance of God to fall upon the country and people for not receiving the word of God, was cut in two parts asunder with a saw of wood. *Theo.* O intolerable pain!

Phil. The prophet Jeremy was stoned unto death of his people at Taphnes in Egypt, Jeremy.
because he rebuked them of their wicked living, and exhorted them unto repentance and amendment of life. The prophet Amos, at the commandment of king Amasias, Amos.
for his preaching was cruelly beaten and grievously tormented, and at the last the king's son Ochosias caused him to be thrust into the temples of the head with a great nail of iron, and so shortly after died. The prophet Micheas was cruelly beaten, imprisoned, 1 Kings xxii. Micheas.
and fed with bread and water, because he spake the truth, and told the king what should chance unto him. The prophet Helias was grievously persecuted of queen Jesabel, king Helias.
Achab's wife, for speaking against Baal and his chaplains. The prophet Zachary, son Zachary.
of Barachias, was stoned to death for telling the king truth. The prophet Daniel was 2 Chron. xxiv.
cast into the den of lions, because that contrary to king Darius' commandment he prayed Dan. vi.
unto his Lord the God of Israel. Which of the prophets escaped without persecution?

And as the wicked worldlings and bellied hypocrites handled the prophets of God for telling the truth, so handled they all other that obeyed not their wicked laws and filthy requests. Were not Sidrach, Misac, and Abednago cast into a fiery furnace, Dan. iii.
because they would not worship the golden image that king Nabucodonosor had made, but only the God of Israel? Was not Achimelech, with certain other holy men of God, Achimelech.

1 Sam. xxii. slain at king Saul's commandment, because he shewed kindness to David the hearty-beloved servant of God? Was not Joseph cast into prison, because he would not lean to the filthy request of his lord's wife? Was not Susan the virtuous woman at the point to be stoned unto death, because she would not consent to the [un]lawful and filthy requests of the two judges? Was not Eleazarus miserably put to death, because he at the king's commandment would not eat swine's flesh contrary to the law of God? Was not a certain woman with her seven sons most cruelly put to death, because they would not obey the wicked precept of the most wicked king? I pass over many other of the old testament, which were unmercifully persecuted and slain for God's truth. Some, as the blessed apostle saith, "were tried with mockings and scourgings, with bonds and prisonment: some were stoned, some were hewn asunder, some were slain with sword:" all were troubled and vexed.

Joseph. Gen. xxxix. Susanna. Hist. Sus. Eleazarus. 2 Macc. vi. 2 Macc. vii. Heb. xi.

Wisd. iii. *Theo.* These are they of whom the wise man speaketh: "God proved them, and found them meet for himself; yea, as the gold in the furnace did he try them, and received them as a burnt-offering," &c.

Phil. As I may at the last come to the new testament, to whom is it unknown that Jesus Christ our Lord and Saviour, after many blasphemies, rebukes, slanders, and bitter torments, suffered the most spiteful death of the cross, and so entered into glory? Holy John Baptist, that blessed priest's son, for truth-telling to king Herod, for reproving him of his abominable living, was cast into prison and beheaded. James, the brother of John, had his head stricken off for preaching Christ to be Son of the living God. The holy martyr St Stephen was stoned unto death, because he preached Christ, and affirmed that God dwelleth not in temples made with man's hand. What kindness Peter and Paul with the other apostles found at the hands of them, whose salvation they most diligently sought, the histories make mention. Neither do I here speak of those blessed martyrs, which since their days have died for the confession of God's truth; so that the gospel of Christ is not without a cause called of St Paul, "the word of the cross." "For all that will live godly in Christ Jesu," saith he, "shall suffer persecution."

Christ. Matt. xxvii. Luke xxiii. Matt. xiv. John Baptist. Acts xii. James. Acts vii. Stephen. 1 Cor. i. 2 Tim. iii.

To consider these histories afore rehearsed shall stablish our faith greatly, and very much comfort us in the time of our tribulation; so that we shall not lightly slide from God and from his holy word, but rejoice in him, recounting ourselves most blessed, fortunate, and wealthy, that God hath vouchedsafe not only that we should believe in him, but also suffer for him. It shall be expedient for us also to remember that Christ calleth them "blessed which suffer persecution for righteousness sake," and saith, that "theirs is the kingdom of heaven:" again, that "the servant is not greater than his lord;" but, if they persecuted Christ our Lord and Master, they will also persecute us his servants and disciples. "If they have called the father of the household Belzebub, much more they will call them so that are of his household." If we were of the world, the world would love us; but forasmuch as we are not of the world, but Christ hath chosen us out of the world, therefore doth the world hate us. And did not Christ tell us afore that we should lament and weep, that is to say, be oppressed of tyrants, but the world should rejoice, and that in the world we should have affliction and trouble? Again, are we not taught that "by many tribulations we must enter into the kingdom of God?"

Matt. v. Matt. x. John xv. John xvi. Acts xiv.

Chris. The flesh abhorreth trouble and persecution, namely when death is like to follow.

Matt. xxvi. *Phil.* "The spirit," as Christ saith, "is ready," and of a good courage to suffer all things for the glory of God; "but the flesh is weak." The outward man is loth to die; but the inward man wisheth to be loosened out of this corruptible body, and to be with Christ. But if the good-will of our heavenly Father so be, that we must needs suffer death for Christ's sake, let us set this saying of St Paul before our eyes, and stedfastly believe it: "If we die with Christ, we shall live with him. If we suffer with him, we shall also reign with him." And our Saviour Christ saith: "Whosoever shall lose his life for my sake and for the gospel, he shall keep it." Hereto agreeth the saying of St Peter: "Dearly beloved, marvel not that ye are proved by fire (which thing is to try you), as though some strange thing happened unto you; but rejoice, inasmuch as ye are partakers of Christ's passion, that, when his glory

Phil. i. 2 Tim. ii. Mark viii. 1 Pet. iv.

appeareth, ye may be merry and glad. If ye be railed upon, happy are ye. For the glory and the Spirit of God resteth upon you." Again: "If any man suffer as a christian man, let him not be ashamed; but let him glorify God on this behalf." And "let them that are troubled according to the will of God commit their souls to him with well doing, as unto a faithful Creator." They that suffer trouble for the Lord's sake and for the gospel shall stand before the glorious seat of God, and before the Lamb Christ, and they shall be "clothed with long white garments and palms in their Rev. vii. hands." "They shall ever be in the presence of the seat of God, and serve him day and night in his temple; and he that sitteth in the seat shall dwell among them. They shall hunger no more, neither thirst; neither shall the sun light on them, neither any heat. For the Lamb which is in the midst of the seat shall feed them, and lead them unto fountains of living water; and God shall wipe away all tears from their eyes."

Furthermore, it shall be great comfort for us also to remember, with what willing hearts Christ and all the blessed martyrs suffered death for the glory of God. Christ our Lord and Saviour, when the time of his bitter passion began to draw nigh, and perceived that Judas went about to betray him to the bishops and priests, said: "That John xiii. thou intendest to do, do it quickly and out of hand." And when the bishops' servants came to lay hand on him, whereas he might have escaped their cruel hands, he willingly Matt. xxvi. offered himself unto them; whereby we may see, that he went unto his death with a merry and joyful heart.

Chris. These his words, which long before his passion he spake to the Jews, do also testify and witness his ready bent good-will to suffer for the salvation of mankind. "Therefore doth my Father love me, because I give over my life, that I may take it John x. again. No man taketh it away from me; but I give it over even of mine own good-will. I have power to give it over, and I have power to take it again." *Theo.* Of the willing oblation of himself it was prophesied by the holy prophets. The prophet Esay saith: "He was offered, because it was his good pleasure." David also saith Isai. liii. in the person of Christ: "I will offer sacrifice unto thee willingly." He speaketh of Psal. liv. the sacrifice of his body. Again, Christ himself saith by the foresaid prophet unto his heavenly Father: "As for sacrifice and offering, thou wouldest none; therefore Psal. xl. madest thou me a body. As for burnt-offerings for sin, thou hast not allowed them. Then said I, Behold, I am at hand. In the beginning of the book is it written of me, that I should do thy will, O God."

Phil. As the Lord Christ willingly suffered for the health of man, so likewise did the apostles suffer all kinds of torments joyfully for the glory of God, for the Acts v. setting forth of his blessed word, and for the name of Jesu Christ the Lord, as we read in the Acts of the Apostles. They were whipped of the bishops' servants, as St Luke testifieth, because they preached Christ, and so sent away. "But when Acts v. they came from the council, they rejoiced that they were counted worthy to suffer rebuke for the name of Jesu." How glad, joyful, and ready the blessed apostle St Paul was to suffer any kind of torment for Christ's sake, these his words do abundantly shew: "Behold, I being bound in the spirit, go forth unto Hierusalem, not knowing what Acts xx. things shall chance unto me there; but that the Holy Ghost in every city doth testify, saying that bonds and troubles do abide me. But I care not for them: neither is my life dear unto me, so that I may finish my course with joy, and the office which I have received of the Lord, to testify gospel of the grace of God." Again, when Agabus the prophet took Paul's girdle, and bound his hands and feet therewith, saying, "Thus saith the Holy Ghost, The man whose girdle this is, shall the Jews Acts xxi. thus bind at Hierusalem, and they shall deliver him into the hands of the heathen;" and when they that were with Paul, hearing these things, most instantly desired him that he should not go up unto Hierusalem, the blessed apostle answered, saying: "What do ye, weeping and troubling my heart? I am ready not only to be bound, but also to die at Hierusalem for the name of the Lord Jesu."

O faithful apostle! The Lord Jesu Christ was so dear unto him, that for his sake, for the avancement of his glory, for the setting forth of his most glorious gospel, he feared neither chains nor death. He always had before his eyes the short pains of this world and the everlasting joys of the world to come. He ever remembered this

Mark viii. Matt. x. saying of the Lord Christ: "Whosoever shall lose his life for my sake and for the gospel, he shall keep it." He never forgat these his Master's words: "Whosoever shall be ashamed of me and of my sayings in this whorish and sinful generation, the Son of man shall also be ashamed of him when he shall come in the glory of his Father with the holy angels. But whosoever shall confess me before men, I shall confess him also before my Father which is in heaven."

Ignatius. We read also that the blessed martyr Ignatius, after many grievous torments, was threatened, if he would not forsake Christ and his word, that he should be cast unto wild beasts, and so be devoured. But he, being nothing abashed with those threats, but perceiving his death to be deferred, which he so greatly desireth to suffer for Christ's name, wrote an epistle to the Romans, and desired them that they would keep him no longer from his martyrdom, but with all expedition bring to pass that they had so long threatened. In the which epistle, among many other words which declare his valiant faith and mighty courage in God, he writeth on this manner: "O wholesome beasts that are prepared for me! When shall they come? when shall they be sent out? when shall they eat my flesh? I would wish with all my heart that they might be more greedy; and I will bid them unto the devouring of me, and pray them, lest peradventure, as they have done in many, they fear to touch my body. Yea, if they shall make any delay, I myself will brast in to them, and offer myself to them. Give me liberty, I beseech you; for I know what is expedient for me. Now that I begin to be the disciple of Christ, let fires, gallows, wild beasts, breaking of my bones, racking of my members, pain throughout all my body, and all the punishments of the world that can be invented by the craft and subtilty of the devil, be ministered unto me. I will refuse none of them all, so that I may deserve to obtain Jesus Christ[1]."

Note.

Theo. O blessed and glorious martyr! O valiant and noble soldier of our most mighty captain Christ Jesu! O what a mirror-glass and spectacle is here offered unto us, wherein we may see and learn not only high patience, but also an exceeding desire to suffer all kind of torments for the glory of Christ!

Phil. Not only the blessed martyr Ignatius shewed himself willing and joyful to suffer all kind of adversity, yea, very death, for the confession of Christ and of his blessed truth, but other holy men innumerable, as we read in histories.

When Decius the emperor, that most cruel tyrant, had spoiled the blessed martyr Hippolitus. Hippolitus of his vestures, because he would not do sacrifice to false gods, the man of God spake boldly unto him, saying: "Thou hast not spoiled me of my garments, but thou hast rather begun to clothe me." And when the aforesaid tyrant commanded that he should be clothed again with his own accustomed kind of apparel, and said unto him, "Use thine old service which thou hast ever had in our sight, and be our friend;" the blessed martyr with a stout courage answered: "My service is this, faithfully to serve Christ, and, by serving him, speedily to come unto a fruitful victory." Shortly after the tyrant, seeing his stedfast and unshaken constancy, commanded him to be deprived of all his goods and to be headed, with divers other, about the number of nineteen, which all with joyful courage suffered death for Christ's sake[2].

[1 Ὀναίμην τῶν θηρίων τῶν ἐμοὶ ἡτοιμασμένων, καὶ εὔχομαι ἕτοιμά μοι εὑρεθῆναι· ἃ καὶ κολακεύσω συντόμως με καταφαγεῖν, οὐχ ὥσπερ τινῶν δειλαινόμενα οὐχ ἥψαντο. κἂν αὐτὰ δὲ ἄκοντα μὴ θελήσῃ, ἐγὼ προσβιάσομαι. συγγνώμην μοι ἔχετε, τί μοι συμφέρει ἐγὼ γινώσκω· νῦν ἄρχομαι μαθητὴς εἶναι. μηθέν με ζηλώσῃ τῶν ὁρατῶν καὶ ἀοράτων, ἵνα Ἰησοῦ Χριστοῦ ἐπιτύχω. πῦρ καὶ σταυρὸς, θηρίων τε συστάσεις, ἀνατομαὶ, διαιρέσεις, σκορπισμοὶ ὀστέων, συγκοπὴ μελῶν, ἀλησμοὶ ὅλου τοῦ σώματος, κακαὶ κολάσεις τοῦ διαβόλου ἐπ' ἐμὲ ἐρχέσθωσαν· μόνον ἵνα Ἰησοῦ Χριστοῦ ἐπιτύχω.—Ignat. ad Rom. Epist. cap. v. in Patr. Apost. Oxon. 1838. Tom. II. pp. 358-60.]

[2 Hippolitus is said to have buried the body of St Laurence. For this he was apprehended and carried before the emperor. Quem videns Decius Cæsar subridens dixit ei: Numquid et tu magus effectus es, qui corpus Laurentii abstulisti? Cui Ipolitus: Hoc feci non quasi magus sed quasi Christianus. Tunc Decius furore repletus præcepit ut habitu quo ut Christianus utebatur exspoliaretur, et os ejus lapidibus tonderetur. Cui Ipolitus: Non me exspoliasti: sed magis vestisti......Et cum tormenta hujusmodi derideret, veste militari qua antea utebatur eum vestiri fecit: hortans ut amicitiam et militiam pristinam retineret. Cui Ipolitus cum diceret se Christo militare: Decius ira repletus Valeriano prefecto eum tradidit, ut omnes facultates ejus acciperet et diris tormentis eum interficeret.—Opus Aureum et Legend. Insig. Sanct. Lugd. 1526. fol. 85. See also Pet. de Natal. Catal. Sanct. Lugd. 1508. Lib. VII. cap. lvi. fol. 91.]

The blessed martyr Tyburtius was apprehended of the cruel judge Fabian, and commanded either to offer sacrifice to the idols, or else to go with naked feet upon the hot burning coals. He boldly went on them barefooted, having no harm, and said to the tyrant: "Lay away thine unfaithfulness, and learn that he is the God alone, whom we confess to have power over all creatures. For through the might of my Lord Jesus Christ, methink that going upon burning coals I walk as it were upon red roses, without feeling of any pain or hurt of my feet. For the creature obeyeth the commandment of the Creator." When the tyrant saw that the fire did him no harm, he commanded that he should be slain with the sword. The blessed martyr went unto his death with a joyful heart, praising God that he would vouchsafe to give him strength for to confess his most blessed name and holy word before worldly tyrants[3]. Tyburtius.

When Galerius the proconsul commanded that St Cyprian should be headed, because he was an enemy to the gods of the Romans, and would serve none but Christ alone the Son of Almighty God, the blessed martyr, with a lusty courage and merry heart, brast out into these words, saying: "I thank Almighty God, which vouchethsafe to loosen me from the bands of this body;" and so died[4]. Cyprian.

When Maximianus, that most cruel emperor, commanded his soldiers to worship false gods, and to slay so many as professed Christ and his blessed word, Mauricius with his fellows answered, that either in worshipping false gods, or in slaying the true Christians, they by no means would obey the emperor. "We are," said [they,] "thy soldiers, O emperor; but yet we freely confess that we are the servants of God, which gave us this our life. We cannot follow the emperor so that we should deny God our Maker, yea, and thy Maker also, whether thou wilt or wilt not. We are christian men; therefore may we not persecute such as profess Christ. We are ready rather to die than to kill such. And we are more desirous to die innocents, than to live wicked and sinful. Know thou that the minds of this army by no means can be overcome. These worldly weapons we cast away. Our breast is enarmed with the faith of Christ, which is our shield, buckler, and defence against the fiery darts of the devil, and of all his soldiers. Therefore, slay thou, kill thou, murder thou, minister what kind of pain thou wilt; we, with a bold courage, offer ourselves to suffer for the glory of God." And shortly after that holy man of God, with a great number of blessed martyrs more, were slain with the sword[5]. Mauricius and his fellows.

Eus. These be notable examples and worthy to be practised of all faithful Christians, if God at any time calleth them unto this conflict with the worldly tyrants and feigned holy hypocrites, for the confession of his blessed truth.

Phil. I could rehearse many more godly histories to declare with what a ready will, with how rejoicing an heart, the blessed martyrs of Christ suffered all manner of bitter torments for the Lord's sake; but these at this present shall suffice. For hereof may ye learn to practise this word of the apostle, "alway:" I mean, to rejoice in the Lord our God, not only in prosperity, but also in adversity, be it in sickness, loss of goods, poverty, persecution, or any other cross, that God our Father layeth upon us. For this is the duty of a true christian man, to conceive that same faith, hope, and joy in God, when he is assailed in tribulation, that he had before, when all things were most prosperous to him. So meaneth the apostle when he saith: "Rejoice in the Lord alway." And because he would have us earnestly to rejoice in the Lord at all times, be it in prosperity or adversity, he doubleth this word, "rejoice," saying: "Rejoice in the Lord alway; yea, once again I say, Rejoice." Pithy and full of efficacy is this sentence of the apostle, and comprehendeth in it many godly mysteries, as ye have hitherto partly heard. St Paul desireth nothing Note.

[[3] Tyburtius is said to have suffered in the persecution of Diocletian and Maximian. A brief notice of his martyrdom as related more at length in the text may be found in the Catalogus Sanctorum: Jussit Fabianus carbones accendi: et ut Tyburtius aut thura super eos diis imponeret, aut nudis pedibus desuper ambularet. Qui invocato Christi nomine nuda planta super carbones incedens illæsus permansit: quem Fabianus......decollari præcepit.—Lib. VII. cap. xlvi. fol. 89.]

[[4] ......decretum ex tabella recitavit: Thascium Cyprianum gladio animadverti placet. Cyprianus episcopus dixit: Deo gratias.—Cypr. Op. Oxon. 1682. Cypr. Pass. p. 13.]

[[5] See before, page 91, note 1. See also Pet. de Natal. Catal. Sanct. Lib. VIII. cap. ciii. foll. 231, 2.]

more, than that we should rejoice in the Lord. His joy is altogether in God; therefore would he that yours should be so likewise. And unto this doth that prince-like prophet exhort you also, saying: "Be ye glad and rejoice in the Lord, O ye righteous; and all ye that are true-hearted, be merry in the Lord." Again: "Let so many as trust in thee, O Lord, be merry; yea, they shall be joyful for ever, and thou shalt dwell among them: and all that love thy name shall rejoice in thee." Therefore, if we love the name of God, if we trust to be saved by his mercy, if we look for good things at the hand of our heavenly Father through Jesus Christ, let us sequester our joy from all worldly things, which are but vanity, as ye have heard before, and repose it only in the Lord our God.

Psal. xxxiii. Psal. v.

Chris. That Lord, which is "the Father of mercies, and the God of all consolation," mought grant unto us his most holy Spirit, to work in us such a sweetness and delectation in spiritual things, that whatsoever is of the world may wax vile, unpleasant, and bitter unto us; and that we by this means may unfeignedly, and even from the very bottom of the heart, rejoice in the Lord our God alone, alone! *Theo.* The Lord might bring this thing to pass in us!

2 Cor. i.

Phil. Well, neighbours. Now, according to my promise, have I given you this Jewel of Joy; not so cunningly and workman-like, I confess, handled, as some other of better knowledge and more ripe judgment in the mysteries of God could have done it, notwithstanding truly and faithfully wrought according to the pure vein of the holy scriptures. But whatsoever this your gift is, I pray you take it to good worth, and accept my loving heart toward you. Though possibility faileth, yet good-will shall never want in me: but whatsoever the Lord shall give, at all times I will bestow it upon you, and upon his holy congregation, and by no means suffer the talent given unto me of my Lord God to lie idle by me; but for my power I will so employ it, that it may turn to the glory of God, and to the profit of his blessed church. For the history of the unprofitable servant, which hid up the money of his lord in the ground, and therefore was condemned and cast into utter darkness, where weeping and gnashing of teeth shall be, ought to make all men afraid that have received any gift at all of God, and to provoke them not to be sluggish and idle, but to use their talents according to the commandment of God, which saith: "Occupy yourselves till I come."

Matt. xxv. Luke xix.

Eus. Blessed is that man which so occupieth his talent, that God therewith is glorified, and his neighbour edified. Sure may he be, at that great and dreadful day of judgment, to hear of his Lord God this most sweet and joyful sentence: "O mine own good servant and faithful, thou hast been faithful in little: I will make thee ruler over much. Enter in into thy Lord's joy."

Matt. xxv.

Phil. Neighbours, I will disease you no longer; but as I have given you a spiritual jewel, joyful and comfortable for the soul, so will I in like manner, at this my coming home and return into my native country, bestow somewhat upon you, that shall not be unprofitable for the body. For I wish good both to your soul and body. And would God it lay in my power to gratify you in both alike! But that which shall want in worldly things shall, if I live, be recompensed in spiritual things.

But as I may at the last make an end, remember, brethren, remember, what ye have heard of me at this present. Remember that all things in this world be subject unto vanity, yea, they themselves are mere vanity, as the preacher saith: "All is but vanity, yea, altogether is plain vanity." What marvel, when man himself, for whose sake all worldly things were created, is very vanity? Remember that the end of all worldly joy, of all carnal pleasure, of all temporal felicity, is bitter sorrow and grievous pain. Remember that we are born to die: prepare therefore for your last end. Remember that the goods of this world are transitory, flitting away, and seldom tarry long with their old possessor and owner: "Gather not, therefore, treasure together on earth, where rust and moths corrupt, and where thieves break through and steal; but gather ye treasure together in heaven, where neither rust nor moths corrupt, and where thieves neither break up nor steal." "Make you friends of the wicked mammon, that, when ye shall have need, they may receive you into everlasting dwelling-places." Remember that whatsoever ye sow, that shall ye reap, whether it be of the flesh, corruption; or

Eccles. i. Matt. vi. Luke xvi. Gal. vi.

of the Spirit, eternal life. If ye on this wise judge both of the world and of worldly
things, doubt ye not but that your hearts shall burn with such an earnest and unfeigned
love toward God, that ye shall rejoice in him alone, alone, yea, and that alway, that is,
both in prosperity and adversity, and at all times have a quiet and a merry conscience,
which of all treasures is the most precious in this world.

And that ye may do this the more fortunately, consider your vocation, remember
your calling. Ye are called Christians: express Christ your Lord and Master in all
your conversation and living. "He that saith he dwelleth in Christ ought to walk 1 John ii.
even as Christ walked." Ye are called gospellers: love and live the gospel. "Let Matt. v.
your light so shine before men, that they may see your good works, and glorify your
Father which is in heaven." The papists rail on you, blaspheme you, call you heretics,
seditious persons, &c.: order so your life that the adversaries, seeing your godly con-
versation, may either be won to confess the same truth with you, or else be ashamed
to speak any evil of you. "For this is the will of God, that with well-doing ye should 1 Pet. ii
stop the mouths of foolish and ignorant men; as free, but not making liberty to be a
cloke of naughtiness, but even as the servants of God." Ye confess yourselves to be
justified before God by faith alone: provide that this your faith be not idle, sluggish,
nor dead, as St James saith, but livish, and mighty in operation, and full of all good James ii.
and christian works. "For in Christ Jesu neither is circumcision any thing worth, Gal. v.
neither yet uncircumcision; but faith, which worketh by charity:" and "the end of the 1 Tim. i.
commandment is charity, that cometh of a pure heart, and of a good conscience, and of
faith unfeigned." Ye believe to be saved by the alone sacrifice of Christ's most blessed Heb. ix. x.
body: commit nothing unworthy the gentleness of so kind and loving Saviour. Ye
confess to know God: deny him not in your deeds; but be always studious of good Tit. i.
works.

Ye profess that doctrine which requireth of you and of all subjects faithful and Rom. xiii.
humble obeisance to the king's majesty: answer to your profession, "obey unfeignedly, 1 Pet. ii. Rom. xiii.
not only for fear of punishment, but for conscience sake also." "For there is no power
but of God. The powers that be are ordained of God. Therefore whosoever resisteth
the power resisteth the ordinance of God; and they that resist shall get to themselves
damnation." "Fear God and the king," saith Salomon. "Fear God and honour the Prov. xxiv.
king," saith blessed Peter. Therefore fear, obey, love, and honour our most excellent prince. 1 Pet. ii.
Neither think, breathe, speak, or do any thing that may be prejudicial to the godly
doings of the king's highness; but be thou alway led with a reverent fear toward his
grace. Neither consent to any tumult, commotion, insurrection, sedition, conspiracy,
&c., neither conceal any thing whereby any dishonour to the king's majesty, any dis-
pleasure to his most honourable council, any unquietness to the public weal may be
wrought; but evermore set before your eyes this sentence of the preacher: "Wish the Eccles. x.
king no evil in thy thought, and speak no hurt of the nobleman in thy privy chamber.
For a bird of the air shall betray thy voice, and with her feathers shall she bewray
thy words." How grievously they have always be punished that were seditious, and
walked without any godly fear toward the civil magistrates, the histories of Dathan Num. xvi.
and Abiron, of Zambri and Baasa, of Bagathan and Thares, shew manifestly. Neither 1 Kings xvi.
have we wanted experience of this thing in those our days. And as unto the king's Esth. ii. 1 Pet. ii.
majesty, so likewise submit yourselves unto the "other rulers that are sent of him, for
the punishment of evil-doers, but for the praise of them that do well."

Ye have a pleasure to hear the preachers of God's word: reverence them as the
ministers of God, giving them no less honour than the child giveth the father, remem-
bering that they be "the angels of God," "the messengers of Christ," "the light of Mal. ii.
the world," "the salt of the earth," "the dispensators of the mysteries of God," the 1 Cor. i. Matt. v.
feeders of christian men's souls, the comforters of the weak, the physicians of the 1 Cor. iv John xxi.
sick, the upholders of the whole, the exhorters unto the virtue, the frayers away from
vice, which watch continually for the health of our souls. Be not unthankful to the Heb. xiii.
preachers; but to such as minister spiritual things to you disdain not to give corporal
things, that the preachers may the more freely give their mind to the studies of the
holy scriptures. "If we sow unto you spiritual things," saith St Paul, "is it a great 1 Cor. ix.
thing if we reap your carnal things? The Lord hath ordained that they which preach

Gal. vi. the gospel should live of the gospel." Again he saith: "Let him that is taught with the word minister unto him that teacheth him in all good things. Be not deceived: God is not mocked."

Eph. v. Moreover, ye that are married, "love your wives, even as Christ loved the congregation. Nourish and cherish them as your own bodies," remembering that they be Col. iii. your own flesh and your own bones; and see that "by no means ye be bitter unto 1 Pet. iii. them," but "give honour unto them, as to the weaker vessels, and as to them that are Tit. ii. fellow-heirs also of the grace of life." Teach your wives to be obedient unto you as 1 Tim. iii. unto the Lord, to love you as their own selves, to be of honest behaviour, chaste, housewifely, good, no evil speakers, but sober and faithful in all things. Learn them 1 Pet. iii. to keep silence with all subjection, and to "array themselves in mannerly apparel, with shamefacedness and honest behaviour; not with broided hair, either gold, or pearls, or costly array; but with such as becometh women that profess the worshipping of God, through good works; that the hid man of the heart may be uncorrupt with a meek and quiet spirit, which spirit is before God a thing much set by. For after this manner in the old time did the holy women, which trusted in God, tire themselves, and were Gen. xviii. obedient to their husbands; even as Sara obeyed Abraham, and called him lord." Eph. vi. "Bring up your children with the nurture and information of the Lord," and teach them to obey and honour you. "Do that unto your servants which is just and equal, remembering that ye also have a Master in heaven." Exhort your servants to be Col. iii. obedient unto you in all godly things; "not with eye-service, as men-pleasers; but in singleness of heart, fearing God."

Phil. iv. Love all men as yourselves, in few: "Whatsoever things are true, whatsoever things are honest, whatsoever things are just, whatsoever things are pure, whatsoever things pertain to love, whatsoever things are of honest report, if there be any virtuous thing, Col. iii. if there be any laudable thing, those same have ye in mind." "And all things whatsoever ye do in word or deed, do in the name of the Lord Jesu, giving thanks to God the Father by him." So shall ye in this world live with a merry conscience, and after this present life joy and rejoice in eternal glory with God the Father; to whom, with his Son Christ Jesu, our most precious jewel, and the Holy Ghost, that sweet Comforter, be all honour and praise for evermore. *Theo.* Amen. *Chris.* So be it.

Phil. Now, dear neighbours, come with me, that I may deliver you those jewels which I have also prepared for your bodies; that ye, being enriched both in mind and body, may go forth to conceive a good opinion of my friendship toward you, which I wish to keep unspotted so long as my life endure.

Eus. We know, brother Philemon, your good-will toward us; and although we confess ourselves much indebted to you for all your other benefits, yet for this your Jewel of Joy, wherein we have found so great comfort, we most heartily thank you, and wish that God may be merciful to you in all your affairs.

Phil. Well, come and go with me.

Chris. We follow gladly.

Theo. Blessed be God for his benefits.

Eus. Amen.

Give the glory to God alone.

THE

PRINCIPLES OF CHRISTIAN RELIGION,

BY

THOMAS BECON.

¶ The Principles of Christen Religion necessary to be knowen of the faythfull newly sette forth to the great profit of al the readers. By *Thomas Becon.*

Iohn.xiii.

¶ *If ye knowe these thynges, blessed are ye if ye do them.*

THE CONTENTS OF THIS BOOK.

OF FAITH.

What faith is.
What benefits we receive of God through faith.
The articles of the christian faith, with confirmations of the same out of the holy scriptures.

OF PRAYER.

What prayer is.
What benefits we receive of God by prayer.
The Lord's prayer, called the *Pater noster*, with confirmations of every petition out of the holy scripture.

OF THE LAW.

What the law is.
To what use the law was given.
The ten commandments of God, with confirmations of every commandment out of the holy scripture.

OF REPENTANCE.

What repentance is.
Of the fruits of repentance, declared by the word of God.

OF BAPTISM.

What baptism is.
To what use baptism was ordained.

OF THE LORD'S SUPPER.

What the Lord's supper is.
To what use Christ did institute it.

The duty of all estates and degrees, according to the doctrine of God's holy word.
The duty of the high powers, and of the other temporal magistrates.
The duty of subjects toward the high powers.
The duty of bishops and ministers of God's word.
The duty of parishioners unto the ministers of God's word.
The duty of husbands unto their wives.
The duty of wives unto their husbands.
The duty of fathers and mothers unto their children.
The duty of children toward their fathers aud mothers.
The duty of masters to their servants.
The duty of servants to their masters.
The duty of widows.
The duty of old men.
The duty of old women.
The duty of young folk.
The duty of all degrees and estates generally both toward God and their neighbour.

TO THE

MOST GENTLE AND GODLY DISPOSED CHILD, MASTER THOMAS CECIL[1],

SON TO THE RIGHT HONOURABLE SIR WILLIAM CECIL, KNIGHT, AND SECRETARY TO THE KING'S MAJESTY, THOMAS BECON WISHETH THE FAVOUR OF GOD WITH INCREASE OF VIRTUE AND LEARNING.

If of holy letters we be not sleepy nor vain readers, but diligently mark what we read, we shall easily perceive that among other commandments of God this is not at the last nor the least, which he giveth concerning the bringing up of youth in the knowledge of his blessed will. For the godly wisdom knoweth right well, that except the younglings of a commonweal be virtuously brought up, and faithfully framed according to the right rule of God's holy appointment, it cannot come to pass, but that his glory (the good parents being once deceased) must needs be obscured in this world, the invocation of his name cease, and all godly religion decay: yea, the men themselves (if they be worthy that name) must needs become brute-like, be carried about with every strange doctrine, comtemn all laudable laws, break all good orders, follow their fleshly appetites, like unreasonable beasts, and so at the last bring both themselves and their realms unto utter destruction.

Therefore as God in his holy law requireth of parents nothing more earnestly than to bring up their children virtuously and according to his word; so likewise all godly fathers and mothers have ever from the beginning done their uttermost endeavour to train up their younglings, even from the very cradles, in the nurture, fear, and doctrine of the Lord; supposing themselves then best to please God, and most to do the true office of godly and natural parents, when they study how to garnish, not their children's bodies with gay and sumptuous vestures, but their minds with noble and precious virtues; not how to lift them up unto transitory dignities and

[[1] The Cecils are descended from the ancient family of Sitselt, who were early seated in the principality of Wales. Robert Sitselt aided Robert Fitzhamon in the conquest of Glamorganshire, (A.D. 1091, the 4th year of king William Rufus,) and for his services was rewarded by Fitzhamon with lands in Herefordshire and Gloucestershire. Fourteenth in direct lineal descent from this Robert Sitselt was David Cyssel of Stamford in the county of Lincoln, made by Henry VIII. one of his sergeants-at-arms. He was grandfather to Sir William Cecil, afterwards lord Burleigh, whose son it was to whom this treatise is inscribed. Of a personage so well known as lord Burleigh, who, after previously filling high employments, was principal minister of queen Elizabeth for forty years, from her accession till the period of his death in 1598, it is not necessary here to say any thing. The character of this sagacious statesman is delineated in every history of England. By his first wife Mary, daughter of Peter Cheke, and sister to Sir John Cheke, lord Burleigh had his eldest son Thomas, who succeeded him in his title, and afterwards became the first earl of Exeter. He was yet but a youth when Becon dedicated to him the Principles of the Christian Religion. He served as a volunteer, in the 16th year of queen Elizabeth, in the expedition sent into Scotland, when the castle of Edinburgh was besieged and taken. The next year, having waited on the queen at the earl of Leicester's, he received from her majesty the honour of knighthood. He distinguished himself in the wars of the Low Countries, and was in 1585 made governor of the Brille, one of the cautionary towns which the states of Holland pledged to the English queen: this command he held for about two years. In 1588, the memorable year of the Spanish attempted invasion, he and his brother Sir Robert Cecil were both volunteers on board the fleet. He afterwards took a part in the suppression of the insurrection made by the earl of Essex, and was one of the commanders of the force that obliged that ill-fated nobleman to surrender. For these and other services he was appointed a knight of the order of the Garter, and was installed at Windsor in 1601. His credit did not decline in the ensuing reign: indeed fresh honours were heaped upon him. Having been one of king James' privy-council, he was raised by that monarch in 1605 to the dignity of earl of Exeter, this being, it it said, the first instance of the earldom of the principal *town* or *city* being conferred when the earldom of the *county* was already possessed by another. Lord Exeter was now advanced in years; but we find him employed even to the verge of his long life; for so late as 1620 he was put in commission with the archbishop of Canterbury against heresies and errors in matters of religion; and was also at the same time in another commission with the archbishop of York for matters of ecclesiastical jurisdiction in that province. On Feb. 7, 1622, he died at the age of 80, and was buried in Westminster Abbey, where a monument still existing was erected to his memory. He was married, first, to Dorothy Nevil, one of the co-heirs of John Nevil, lord Latimer, by whom he had five sons and eight daughters; secondly, to Frances, relict of Sir Thomas Smith, master of requests to James I., and daughter to William Brydges, 4th Lord Chandos: by her he had an only daughter. It may be added that lord Exeter was a benefactor to Clare Hall, Cambridge, to which he gave lands for the maintenance of three fellows and eight scholars.]

worldly honours, which, as daily experience teacheth, are more brittle than glass and fade away like the grass, but how to make them honourable and praiseworthy in the sight of good men, and profitable to the commonweal, through virtue, learning, wisdom, and counsel. And the more the parents themselves did excel other in knowledge, wisdom, and learning, the greater desire had they to bring their children unto the like perfection, bearing heavily that theirs should in any point degenerate from their fathers' virtues, and not orderly answer to the godly qualities of their noble parents.

Histories, both godly and ethnick, do minister unto us examples abundantly in this behalf, which I would here gladly recite, if I had not attempted the like enterprise already in my preface unto the Governance of Virtue; again, if I were not fully persuaded, that you have heretofore both read and also heard of your teacher the same or else the like histories. Your right honourable and most worthy father, knowing the good pleasure of God in this behalf, hath also, after the example of all other noble and godly parents, painfully travailed, both by himself and by learned teachers, to bring you up even from your cradles in the knowledge of God's will and of good letters, that you might, as in age, so likewise in virtue and learning, grow and increase unto his comfort, unto your own commendation, and unto the profit of the commonweal hereafter. And as your father is learned, and hath a breast stuffed with all godly virtues, so is his desire to have you both learned and virtuous; that when he shall give over to nature (God so disposing), he may leave behind him his own image, yea, as I may so speak, himself, not only in lineaments of body, but also in virtue, in godliness, in wisdom, in knowledge, and by this means be counted of his posterity a worthy member of the commonweal, both in himself and in his son.

It is your duty, therefore, to satisfy the godly desire of so natural a father, and to answer the expectation of many which look to find [in] you hereafter that virtue, learning, wisdom, and gravity, that is evidently perceived in your most worthy father. This shall be brought to pass, if according to your beginning ye go forth diligently to call on the name of God, to apply your mind to good letters, to give ear to the wholesome admonitions of your most dear father, and to take heed to the daily exhortations of your teacher, ever framing your life according to your knowledge.

And that ye may do this the more conveniently, I give you this little treatise, which shall abundantly instruct you in those points of christian religion, which at this present do most of all become your age. In it are contained the principles of our profession, which I have so opened with the conference of the other scriptures, that they may worthily seem to strive with large commentaries. I have also set forth the duties of all estates and degrees, as they be taught in God's word, that all ages and all kinds of people may here learn to know their duty both toward God and their neighbour. Neither is any thing taught in this treatise, that is not sufficiently fortressed with the authorities of the holy scriptures; so that I doubt not but the godly learned, which love to hear the voice of their Shepherd Christ, will not disallow this my diligence. Let other entreat of high mysteries, and climb up to the highest heaven: I shall be content to write of things according to my knowledge and your capacity, and to creep upon the ground. Let other talk of the unknown secrets of the blessed Trinity, of predestination, of the state of the souls departed, &c.: I will speak of the articles of the christian faith, of the Lord's prayer, of the ten commandments, of the sacraments of Christ's church, &c. Let other be counted the flowers of learning, for opening I know not how secret mysteries: I force not to be called unlearned, so that I may know Christ crucified, and in teaching him, either by my writings or sermons, win some unto God.

But to end: embrace virtue, love learning, garnish your breast with the fruits of God's Spirit, be not idle, flee vain and too much childish pastimes, spend your time fruitfully, exercise yourself in reading God's word. So shall God bless you, multiply your years on earth, and give you joyful days, unto the great comfort of yourself, and the singular joy of your honourable parents, whom with you I wish alway prosperously to do.

Fare ye well.

THE

PRINCIPLES OF CHRISTIAN RELIGION.

OF FAITH.

WHAT FAITH IS.

FAITH is a sure persuasion and an undoubted belief of the heart in the merciful promises of God, made to all faithful penitent sinners in Christ's blood, and freely performed of God the Father for Christ's sake.

WHAT BENEFITS WE RECEIVE OF GOD THROUGH FAITH.

Eph. ii. By faith we, which afore by nature were the children of wrath, are made the sons and children of God.

Probations out of the holy scriptures.

John i. "As many as received him, to them gave he power to be the sons of God, even them that believed on his name, which were born, not of blood, nor of the will of the flesh, nor yet of the will of man, but of God."

Gal. iii. "All ye are the sons of God, because ye have believed on Christ Jesu."

Rom. iv. By faith we, which afore were sinners, are justified and counted righteous in the sight of God for Christ's sake.

Probations out of the holy scripture.

Rom. iii. "We plainly affirm that a man is justified by faith, without the works of the law."

Rom. v. "We, being justified by faith, have peace toward God through our Lord Jesu Christ."

Gal. ii. "We know that a man is not justified by the deeds of the law, but by the faith of Jesu Christ; and we have believed on Jesu Christ, that we might be justified by the faith of Christ, and not by the deeds of the law; because by the deeds of the law no flesh shall be justified."

Gal. v. "As many of you as are justified by the law are fallen from grace. We look and hope for in the Spirit to be justified through faith. For in Jesu Christ neither is circumcision any thing worth, neither yet uncircumcision, but faith which worketh by love."

By faith we are married unto Christ.

Probations out of the holy scriptures.

Hos. ii. "I will marry thee unto myself in faith; and thou shalt know the Lord."

Matt. xxii. Faith is the "wedding garment," wherewith we be married unto Christ according to the parable, which we read in the gospel.

By faith our prayers are accepted and heard of God.

Probations out of the holy scripture.

Matt. xxi. "All things whatsoever ye ask in prayer, if ye believe, ye shall receive them."

James i. "Let him that pray ask in faith, and doubt not. For he that doubteth is like a wave of the sea, which is tossed of the winds and carried with violence. Neither let that man think that he shall receive any thing of the Lord."

By faith Christ's fulfilling of the law is counted our fulfilling.

Probations out of the holy scripture.

"Christ is the fulfilling of the law to justify all that believe." Rom. x.

"Christ hath delivered us (he speaketh of the faithful) from the curse of the law; Gal. iii.
inasmuch as he was made accursed for our sake."

"Be it not known unto you, ye men and brethren, that through this man (Christ) is Acts xiii.
preached unto you the forgiveness of sins, and that by him all that believe are justified from all things, from the which ye could not be justified by the law of Moses?"

By faith our works are allowed before God for Christ's sake.

Probations out of the holy scripture.

"Whatsoever is not of faith is sin." Rom. xiv.

"Thine eyes, O Lord, look upon faith." Jer. v.

Abel's sacrifice was allowed of God; because it was done in faith. And so like- Gen. iv.
wise were all the sacrifices which the holy patriarchs and other godly men offered in the old law.

By faith everlasting life is given unto us for Christ's sake.

Probations out of the holy scripture.

"As Moses lifted up the serpent in the wilderness, so must the Son of man be John iii.
lifted up, that every one that believeth on him may not perish, but have everlasting life. For God hath so loved the world, that he gave his only-begotten Son, that every one that believeth in him may not perish, but have everlasting life."

"He that believeth on the Son hath everlasting life. But he that believeth not on the Son shall not see life, but the wrath of God abideth on him."

"He that heareth my word, and believeth on him that sent me, hath everlasting John v.
life, and shall not come into damnation, but is scaped from death unto life."

"This is the will of him that sent me, that every one which seeth the Son and John vi.
believeth on him have everlasting life."

THE ARTICLES OF THE CHRISTIAN FAITH, WITH CONFIRMATIONS OF THE SAME OUT OF THE HOLY SCRIPTURE.

THE FIRST ARTICLE.

I believe in one God the Father Almighty, Maker of heaven and earth.

The Confirmations.

I believe.

"Without faith it cannot be that any man should please God. For he that cometh Heb. xi.
to God must believe that God is, and that he is a rewarder of them that seek him."

In one God.

"Hear, O Israel: the Lord our God is the Lord only." Deut. vi.

"I am God, and there is none but I." Deut. xxxii.

"I am the Lord, and there is else none." Isai. xlv.

"I am the Lord, besides whom there is none other."

"I am the Lord, besides whom there is none other God; a true God, and such as saveth: there is [n]one but I alone."

"I am he before whom there was never any God, neither shall there be any after Isai. xliii.
me. I am, yea, I am Lord alone, and besides me there is no saviour."

"I am the first and the last, and besides me there is no God." Isai. xliv.

"We are sure that there is none other God but one." 1 Cor. viii.

The Father.

Isai lxiii. "Thou, O Lord, art our Father and Redeemer. Thy name is from everlasting."

Mal. ii. "Have not we all one Father? Hath not one God created us? Why then doth every one of us despise his own brother, and so break the covenant of our Father?"

Matt. xxiii. "Call no man your father upon the earth: for one is your Father, which is in heaven."

1 Cor. viii. "We have but one God, even the Father, of whom all things are."

Eph. iv. "One Lord, one faith, one baptism, one God and Father of all, which is above all, and through all, and in you all."

Almighty.

Gen. xvii. "I am the Almighty God. Walk before me, and be thou perfect."

Jer. xxxii. "Thou, O Lord, art the great and mighty God, whose name is the Lord of hosts, great in counsel and excellent in work."

"Behold, I am the Lord God of all flesh: is there any thing too hard for me? Shall any thing be unpossible in my sight? saith the Lord of hosts."

Matt. xix. "With God all things are possible."

Rev. xvi. "O Lord God Almighty, true and righteous are thy judgments."

Maker of heaven and earth.

Gen. i. "In the beginning God made heaven and earth."

Psal. lxxxix. "The heavens, O Lord, are thine, the earth also is thine: thou hast laid the foundation of the round world, and all that therein is."

Isai. xlii. "The Lord made the heavens, and spread them abroad, and set forth the earth with her increase, which giveth breath unto the people that is in it, and spirit to them that dwell therein."

Jer. xxxii. "O Lord God, it is thou that hast made heaven and earth with thy great power and high arm; and there is nothing hid from thee."

Acts iv. "O Lord, thou art God, which hast made heaven and earth, the sea, and all that in them is."

Eph. iii. "God made all things through Jesu Christ."

THE SECOND ARTICLE.

And in Jesu Christ his only-begotten Son our Lord.

The Confirmations.

And in Jesus Christ.

John iii. "He that believeth on the Son hath everlasting life. But he that believeth not on the Son shall not see life; but the wrath of God abideth upon him."

John vi. "This is the work of God, that ye believe on him whom he hath sent."

John viii. "If ye believe not that I am he, ye shall die in your sins."

John ix. Christ said to the blind man whom he had made to see: "Dost thou believe on the Son of God? He answered and said, Who is it, Lord, that I might believe on him? Jesus said unto him, Thou hast seen him, and he it is this that talketh with thee. And he said, Lord, I believe. And he worshipped him."

John xi. Christ said unto Martha: "He that believeth on me, yea, though he were dead, yet shall he live, and whosoever liveth and believeth on me shall never die. Believest thou this? She said unto him, Yea, Lord, I believe that thou art Christ the Son of God, which should come into the world."

John xiv. "Ye believe in God, believe also in me."

1 John iii. "This is God the Father's commandment, that we believe on the name of his son Jesu Christ."

1 John v. "He that believeth on the Son of God hath the witness in himself. He that believeth not God hath made him a liar; because he believed not the record that God gave of his Son. And this is that record, how that God hath given unto us eternal life; and this life is in his Son. He that hath the Son hath life; and he that hath not the Son hath not life."

His only-begotten Son.

"The Lord said unto me, Thou art my Son, this day have I begotten thee." Psal. ii.

"This is my well-beloved Son, in whom I am well pleased." Matt. iii.

"Thou art Christ, the Son of the living God." Matt. xvi.

"God hath so loved the world, that he gave his only-begotten Son, that every one that believeth on him may not perish, but have everlasting life. For God sent not his Son into the world to condemn the world, but that the world should be saved by him." John iii.

"He that believeth on him is not condemned. But he that believeth not is already condemned; because he hath not believed on the name of the only-begotten Son of God." John iii.

"In this appeareth the love of God toward us, because that God sent his only-begotten Son into the world, that we might live through him." 1 John iv.

Our Lord.

"I am the Lord, and this is my name. My glory will I give to none other, neither mine honour to graven images." Isai. xlii.

"God is faithful, by whom ye are called unto the fellowship of his Son Jesus Christ our Lord." 1 Cor. i.

"There is but one Lord, even Jesu Christ, by whom are all things, and we by him." 1 Cor. viii.

"Ye call me Master and Lord, and ye say well; for so am I in deed." John xiii.

THE THIRD ARTICLE.

Which was conceived by the Holy Ghost, born of the virgin Mary.

The Confirmations.

Which was conceived by the Holy Ghost.

"Joseph, the son of David, fear not to take unto thee Mary thy wife. For that which is conceived in her cometh of the Holy Ghost." Matt. i.

"The Holy Ghost shall come upon thee, and the power of the Highest shall overshadow thee. Therefore that holy thing which shall be born shall be called the Son of God." Luke i.

Born of the virgin Mary.

"Behold, a virgin shall conceive and bear a son; and thou shalt call his name Emmanuel." Isai. vii.

"Unto us a child is born, and unto us a Son is given." Isai. ix.

"There shall come a rod forth of the kindred of Isay, and a blossom shall flourish out of his root." Isai. xi

"Jacob begat Joseph the husband of Mary, of whom Jesus was born, which is called Christ." Matt. i.

"She shall bring forth a son, and thou shalt call his name Jesus. For he shall save his people from their sins."

"Behold, thou shalt conceive in thy womb, and bear a son, and shalt call his name Jesus." Luke i.

"When the time was full come, God sent his Son, made of a woman, and made bond unto the law." Gal. iv.

THE FOURTH ARTICLE.

He suffered under Ponce Pilate, was crucified, dead and buried. He descended unto hell.

The Confirmations.

He suffered under Ponce Pilate, &c.

"The kings of the earth stood up, and the rulers took counsel together, against the Lord and against his Anointed." Psal. ii.

Acts iv. "Of a truth, O Lord, against thy holy child Jesus (whom thou hast anointed), both Herod, and also Ponce Pilate, with the gentiles and the people of Israel, gathered themselves together in this city, for to do whatsoever thy hand and thy counsel determined before to be done."

1 Tim. vi. "I give thee the charge in the sight of God, which quickeneth all things, and before Jesu Christ (which under Ponce Pilate witnessed a good witnessing), that thou keep the commandment, and be without spot," &c.

Was crucified.

Psal. xxii. "They pierced my hands and my feet."

Isai. liii. "He was wounded for our offences, and smitten for our wickedness."

Zech. xii. "They shall look upon me whom they have pierced."

John iii. "As Moyses lifted up the serpent in the wilderness, so must the Son of man be lifted up, that every one which believeth on him may not perish, but have everlasting life."

Matt. xxviii. "Ye seek Jesus that was crucified."

1 Cor. i. "We preach Christ crucified."

1 Pet. ii. "Christ his own self bare our sins in his body on the tree, that we, being delivered from sin, should live unto righteousness: by whose stripes ye were healed."

Dead.

Dan. ix. "After this sixty-two weeks shall Christ be slain; and they shall have no pleasure in him."

Rom. v. "When we were yet sinners, Christ died for us."

1 Cor. xv. "Christ died for our sins, according to the scriptures."

Buried.

Isai. liii. "His grave was given him with the condemned."

1 Cor. xv. "First of all I delivered unto you that which I received, how that Christ died for our sins, agreeing to the scripture, and that he was buried."

John xix. Joseph and Nicodemus took Jesus' body, and buried it in a new grave.

He descended into hell.

Psal. xvi. "Thou shalt not leave my soul in hell, neither shalt thou suffer thy Holy One to see corruption."

Zech. ix. "Thou through the blood of thy covenant shalt let thy prisoners out of the pit, wherein is no water."

Hos. xiii. "O death, I will be thy death: O hell, I will be thy destruction."

1 Pet. iii. "Christ hath once suffered for sins, the just for the unjust, to bring us to God, and was killed as pertaining to the flesh, but was quickened in the Spirit: in which Spirit he also went, and preached unto the spirits that were in prison."

THE FIFTH ARTICLE.

The third day he rose again from the dead.

The Confirmations.

Psal. iii. "I laid me down and slept, and rose up again; for the Lord sustained me."

Hos. vi. "After two days shall he quicken us, and in the third day shall he raise us up, so that we shall live in his sight."

Acts iii. "Ye slay the author of life, whom God hath raised up from the dead."

Rom. i. "Jesus Christ our Lord rose again from the dead."

Rom. iv. "Christ died for our sins, and rose again for our justification."

1 Cor. xv. "Jesus Christ rose again the third day, according to the scriptures."

2 Tim. ii. "Remember that Jesu Christ, of the seed of David, rose again from death, according to my gospel."

THE SIXTH ARTICLE.

He ascended into heaven, and sitteth on the right hand of God the Father Almighty.

The Confirmations.

He ascended into heaven.

"God is gone up with a merry noise, and the Lord with the sound of the trump." Psal. xlvii.

"Thou art gone up on high, thou hast led captivity captive, and received gifts for men." Psal. lxviii.

"It came to pass, as he blessed them, he departed from them, and was carried up into heaven." Luke xxiv.

"Jesus was taken up on high; and a cloud received him up out of their sight. And while they looked stedfastly up toward heaven as he went, behold, two men stood by them in white apparel, which also said, Ye men of Galilee, why stand ye gazing up into heaven? This same Jesus, which is taken up from you into heaven, shall so come, as ye have seen him go into heaven." Acts i.

"When he went on high, he led captivity captive, and gave gifts unto men. That he ascended, what meaneth it, but that he also descended first into the lowest parts of the earth? He that descended is even the same also that ascended up above all heavens, to fulfil all things. Eph. iv.

And sitteth on the right hand, &c.

The Confirmations.

"The Lord said unto my Lord, Sit thou on my right hand, until I make thine enemies thy footstool." Psal. cx.

"When the Lord had spoken unto them, he was received into heaven, and is sitting on the right hand of God." Mark xvi.

"Christ...is on the right hand of God, and maketh intercession for us." Rom. viii.

"If ye be risen again with Christ, seek those things which are above, where Christ sitteth on the right hand of God." Col. iii.

Christ "hath by his own person purged our sins, and sitteth on the right hand of the Majesty on high." Heb. i.

THE SEVENTH ARTICLE.

From thence he shall come to judge the quick and dead.

The Confirmations.

"The Lord shall judge the world with righteousness, and the people with equity." Psal. xcviii.

Read the twenty-fifth chapter of St Matthew's gospel.

"The Father hath committed all judgment unto the Son, because that all men should honour the Son as they honour the Father." John v.

Christ "was ordained of God to be judge of quick and dead." Acts x.

"We must all appear before the judgment-seat of Christ, that every man may receive the works of his body according to that he hath done, whether it be good or bad." 2 Cor. v.

"Our conversation is in heaven, from whence we look for a Saviour, even the Lord Jesus Christ; which shall change our vile body, that he may make it like unto his glorious body, according to the working, whereby he is able to subdue all things unto himself." Phil. iii.

"The Lord Jesus Christ shall judge the quick and dead at his appearing in his kingdom." 2 Tim. iv.

God "is ready to judge the quick and the dead." 1 Pet. iv.

THE EIGHTH ARTICLE.

I believe in the Holy Ghost.

The Confirmations.

"The Spirit of God moved upon the face of the waters." Gen. i.

Psal. li. "Take not thy holy Spirit from me."

Matt. iii. "When Christ was baptized, the Holy Ghost came down upon Christ in the likeness of a dove."

Matt. xxviii. "Christ commanded his disciples to baptize in the name of the Father, and of the Son, and of the Holy Ghost."

John xvi. The Holy Ghost shall "reprove the world of sin."

1 John v. "There are three which give witness in heaven, the Father, the Son, and the Holy Ghost; and they three are one."

THE NINTH ARTICLE.

I believe the holy universal congregation, which is the fellowship of saints.

The Confirmations.

Matt. xviii. "If he will not hear the congregation, let him be unto thee as an heathen man, and as a publican."

Eph. v. "Christ loved the congregation, and gave himself for it to sanctify it, and cleansed it in the fountain of water through the word, to make it unto himself a glorious congregation, without spot or wrinkle or any such thing, that it should be holy and without blame."

1 Tim. iii. "I write these things unto thee,...that thou mayest know how thou oughtest to behave thyself in the house of God, which is the congregation of the living God, the pillar and ground of truth."

Acts ii. "All that believed kept themselves together, and had all things common, and sold their possessions and goods, and parted them to all men, as every man had need. And they continued daily with one accord in the temple, and brake bread from house to house, and did eat their meat together with gladness and singleness of heart, praising God."

Acts iv. "The multitude of them that believed were of one heart and of one soul: neither said any of them that ought of the things which he possessed was his own; but they had all things common." "And great grace was with them all. Neither was there any among them that lacked. For as many as were possessors of lands or houses sold them, and brought the price of the things that were sold, and laid it down at the apostles' feet. And distribution was made unto every man according as he had need."

THE TENTH ARTICLE.

I believe the forgiveness of sins.

The Confirmations.

Isai. xliii. "I am he, yea, I am he, which put away thine iniquities, and that for mine own sake, and will remember them no more."

Mic. vii. "The Lord shall put down our wickednesses, and cast all our sins into the bottom of the sea."

Psal. ciii. "Look, how wide the east is from the west, so far hath he set our sins from us. Yea, like as a father pitieth his own children, even so is the Lord merciful unto all them that fear him. For he knoweth perfectly whereof we be made: he remembereth that we are but dust."

Isai. liii. Christ "hath taken upon him our infirmities, and borne our diseases."

Matt. viii. Luke xix. "The Son of man came to seek and save that was lost."

John iii. "All that believe in Christ shall not perish, but have everlasting life."

1 Tim. i. "This is a true saying, and worthy to be noted, that Christ Jesus came into the world to save sinners."

1 John i. "The blood of Jesus Christ maketh us clean from all sin. If we say we have no sin, we deceive ourselves; and the truth is not in us. But if we confess our sins, God is faithful and righteous to forgive us our sins, and to make us clean from all iniquity."

THE ELEVENTH ARTICLE.

I believe the resurrection of the body.

The Confirmations.

"I believe that my Redeemer liveth, and that I shall rise out of the earth in the latter day, and that I shall be clothed again with this skin, and see God my Saviour in my flesh. Yea, I myself shall behold him, not with other eyes, but with these same eyes. This hope is stedfastly set [in] my heart." Job xix.

"Thy dead men shall live, even with my body shall they rise again. Awake and sing, ye that dwell in the dust. For thy dew is even as the dew of herbs; and the earth shall cast out them that be under her," &c. Isai. xxvi.

"O ye dry bones, hear the word of the Lord. Thus saith the Lord God unto these bones: Behold, I will put breath unto you that ye may live, I will give you sinews, and make flesh grow upon you, and cover you over with skin, and so give you breath, that ye may live, and know that I am the Lord." Ezek. xxxvii.

"Behold, I will open your graves, O my people, and take you out of your sepulchres."

"The hour shall come, in the which all that are in the graves shall hear the voice of the Son of God, and shall come forth; they that have done good unto the resurrection of life, and they that have done evil unto the resurrection of damnation." John v.

"If Christ be preached how that he rose from the dead, how say some among you that there is no resurrection of the dead? If there be no rising again of the dead, then is Christ not risen again. If Christ be not risen again, then is our preaching in vain, and your faith also is in vain." 1 Cor. xv.

Read the whole chapter.

"We know that he which raised up the Lord Jesus shall raise us up also by the means of Jesus." 2 Cor. iv.

"If we believe that Jesus died and rose again, even them also which sleep by Jesus will God bring again with him." [1 Thess. iv.]

Read the latter end of the chapter.

THE TWELFTH ARTICLE.

I believe everlasting life.

The Confirmations.

"Many of them that sleep in the dust of the earth shall awake, some to everlasting life, some to perpetual shame and reproof. The wise (such as have taught other) shall glister as the shining of heaven, and those that have instructed the multitude unto godliness shall be as the stars world without end." Dan. xii.

Read the second chapter of the fourth[1] book of Esdras. 2 Esdr. ii.

"The righteous shall go into everlasting life." Matt. xxv.

"My sheep hear my voice, and I know them, and they follow me, and I give them everlasting life." John x.

"This is everlasting life, even to know thee the alone true God, and whom thou hast sent, Jesus Christ." John xvii.

"O Father, these that thou hast given me, I will that where I am there also be they with me, that they may see my glory, which thou hast given me."

"The eye hath not seen, and the ear hath not heard, neither have the things entered into the heart of man, which God hath prepared for them that love him." 1 Cor. ii.

"We know that, if our earthy mansion of this dwelling were destroyed, we have a building of God, an habitation not made with hands, but everlasting in heaven." Amen. 2 Cor. v.

All these articles aforesaid I with my whole heart believe, and with my mouth unfeignedly confess to be true and agreeable to God's holy word.

[[1] That is, 2 Esdras; the books of Ezra and Nehemiah being formerly called 1 and 2 Esdras.]

THE PRAYER OF THE APOSTLES.

"Lord, increase our faith."

OF PRAYER.

WHAT PRAYER IS.

Prayer is a lifting up of a pure mind unto God, wherein we ask somewhat of God that is agreeable to his holy will.

Probations out of the holy scripture.

Rom. viii. "We know not what we should desire and pray for as we ought; nevertheless the Spirit itself maketh intercession mightily for us with unoutspeakable groanings. Howbeit he that searcheth the heart knoweth what the mind of the Spirit is; for he maketh intercession for the saints, according to the pleasure of God."

John iv. "The time cometh, and is now already, that the true worshippers shall worship in spirit and truth. For the Father will have such to worship him. God is a spirit, and they that worship him must worship him in spirit and truth."

Phil. iii. "We are the circumcision, even we that serve God in spirit."

1 Tim. ii. "I will that all men pray in all places, lifting up pure hands without wrath and strife."

Matt. xv. "This people honoureth me with their lips, but their heart is far from me: verily, they worship me in vain."

Matt. vii. "Ask, and it shall be given you. Seek, and ye shall find. Knock, and it shall be opened unto you. For whosoever asketh receiveth, and he that seeketh findeth, and to him that knocketh it shall be opened."

1 John v. "This is the trust that we have in God, that, if we ask any thing according to his will, he heareth us. And if we know that he heareth us, whatsoever we ask, we know that we have the petitions that we desire of him."

WHAT BENEFITS WE RECEIVE OF GOD BY PRAYER.

By prayer we are delivered out of trouble.

Probations out of the holy scripture.

Psal. cxx. "When I was in trouble, I called on the Lord; and he graciously heard me."

Psal. l. "Call on me in the day of trouble, and I will deliver thee, and thou shalt honour me."

Psal. xci. "He shall call upon me, and I will hear him; yea, I am with him in trouble. I will deliver him, and bring him to honour," &c.

2 Chron. xv. "When any man in his trouble did turn unto the Lord God of Israel, and sought him, he was found of him."

By prayer we are preserved from our enemies.

Probations out of the holy scripture.

Psal. xviii. "I will call upon the Lord, which is worthy to be praised; so shall I be safe from mine enemies."

2 Kings xix. King Ezechias by prayer was delivered from the proud wicked tyrant Sennacherib, both he and all his.

So likewise were Joseph, Daniel, Susanne, Peter, &c.

By prayer we get the victory of our enemies in battle.

Probations out of the holy scripture.

Exod. xvii. The people of Israel got the victory over the Amalechites so long as Moyses prayed for them.

When the black Moors came out to fight against Asa king of Juda, Asa prayed unto the Lord, and the Lord gave him the victory; so that all his enemies were destroyed in battle. Read the chapter. 2 Chron. xiv.

Judas Machabeus, after he had called on the name of the Lord, got a noble victory of Gorgias and his company. 1 Macc. iv.

By prayer we obtain health of body.

Probations out of the holy scripture.

The miracles which Christ wrought upon them that were diseased, and fled unto him for help with faithful prayer, prove this true.

By prayer we obtain all thing necessary for the body.

Probations out of the holy scripture.

Moses by prayer obtained manna from heaven for the Israelites. Exod. xvi.

Helias by prayer obtained rain of God to water the earth. 1 Kings xviii.

By prayer our sins are forgiven us.

Probations out of the holy scripture.

"I said, I will confess my sins unto the Lord; and thou forgavest the wickedness of my sin. For this shall every one that is godly make his prayer unto thee in a time when thou mayest be found." Psal. xxxii.

"I forgave thee all that debt, when thou desiredst me." Matt. xviii.

The sinful publican, praying for remission of his sins, went home more righteous in the sight of God than the proud Pharisee. Luke xviii.

"If any be diseased among you, let him call for the elders of the congregation, and let them pray over him, and anoint him with oil in the name of the Lord: and the prayer of faith shall save the sick, and the Lord shall raise him up; and if he be in sins, they shall be forgiven him." James v.

By prayer we overcome the devil and all our ghostly enemies.

Probations out of the holy scripture.

"This kind of devils is not cast out but by prayer and fasting." Matt. xvii.

"Watch and pray, that ye fall not into temptation. The spirit is willing, but the flesh is weak." Matt. xxvi.

By prayer we obtain of God the Holy Ghost.

Probations out of the holy scripture.

"If ye which are evil can give your children good gifts, how much more shall your Father which is in heaven give the Holy Ghost to them that desire it of him?" Luke xi.

As the disciples of Christ were gathered together in one place, and continued in prayer, they were all filled with the Holy Ghost. Acts i. ii.

By prayer we obtain all good things, both for the body and the soul.

Probations out of the holy scripture.

"What things soever ye desire when ye pray, believe that ye receive them, and ye shall have them." Mark xi.

"The harvest is much, but the labourers are few. Pray ye therefore the Lord of the harvest, that he will send labourers into his harvest." Matt. ix.

James i. "If any of you lack wisdom, let him ask of him that giveth it, even God, which giveth to all men indifferently, and casteth no man in the teeth; and it shall be given him. But let him ask in faith," &c.

Phil. iv. "The Lord is even at hand. Be careful for nothing, but in all prayer and supplication let your petitions be known unto God with thanksgiving."

Many other benefits receive we of God through prayer, which here to rehearse were too long. Read diligently my book called "The Pathway unto Prayer;" and that shall sufficiently instruct thee in all things concerning prayer.

The Pathway unto Prayer.

THE LORD'S PRAYER, CALLED THE *PATER NOSTER*, WITH CONFIRMATIONS OF EVERY PETITION OUT OF THE HOLY SCRIPTURE.

Luke xi. Deut. xxxii. The disciples said unto Christ: "Lord, teach us to pray." Christ said unto them: "When ye pray, say on this manner, Our Father, which art in heaven, hallowed be thy name," &c.

THE PREFACE OF THE LORD'S PRAYER.

Our Father, which art in heaven.

The Confirmations.

Our Father.

Isai. lxiii. "Is not the Lord God the Father and thine honour? Hath he not made thee and ordained thee? Thou, O Lord God, art our Father and Redeemer."

Mal. ii. "Have we not all one Father? Hath not God made us? Why doth every one of us then despise his own brother?"

Mal. i. "Should not the son honour his father, and a servant his master? If I be now a father, where is my honour? If I be a lord, where is my fear?"

Rom viii. "Ye have not received the spirit of bondage to fear any more; but ye have received the Spirit of adoption, whereby we cry, Abba (that is to say) Father. The same Spirit certifieth our spirit, that we are the children of God. If we be children, then are we heirs also; yea, heirs of God, and fellow-heirs with Christ."

Which art in heaven.

Isai. lxvi. "Heaven is my seat, and the earth is my footstool."

Psal. ciii. "The Lord hath prepared his seat in heaven."

Psal. cxv. "Our God is in heaven: he doth whatsoever pleaseth him."

Psal. cxxiii. "Unto thee lift I up mine eyes, which dwellest in the heavens."

Matt. xxiii. "Call no man father upon earth; for one is your Father, which is in heaven."

THE FIRST PETITION.

Hallowed be thy Name.

The Confirmations.

Ezek. xxxix. "I will make the name of my holiness to be known among my people of Israel, and I will not let my holy name to be evil spoken of any more; but the very heathen also shall know that I am the Lord, the Holy One of Israel."

Joel ii. "The time shall come, that whosoever calleth on the name of the Lord shall be saved."

Mal. i. "From the rising up of the sun unto the going down of the same my name is great among the gentiles; yea, and that in all places."

Job i. "The Lord gave, and the Lord hath taken away. Now blessed be the name of the Lord."

"Sing unto the Lord, and praise his name: be telling of his salvation from day to day. Declare his honour among the heathen, and his wonders among all people." Psal. xcvi.

"I will declare thy name unto my brethren: in the midst of the congregation will I praise thee." Psal. xxii.

"The name of the Lord is a strong tower: the righteous fleeth unto it, and shall be saved." Prov. xviii

"By Christ do we offer the sacrifice of prayer always unto God, that is to say, the fruit of those lips which confess his name. Heb. xiii.

THE SECOND PETITION.

Thy kingdom come.

The Confirmations.

"Seek first the kingdom of God and the righteousness thereof; and all things shall be ministered unto you." Matt. vi.

"The kingdom of heaven suffereth violence; and the violent pluck it unto them." Matt. xi.

"Whosoever receiveth not the kingdom of God as a child, he shall not enter into it." Luke xviii.

"Except a man be born of water and of the Spirit, he cannot enter into the kingdom of God." John iii.

"The kingdom of God is no meat and drink, but righteousnesses, peace, and joy in the Holy Ghost." Rom. xiv.

"The kingdom of God is not in words, but in power." 1 Cor. iv.

THE THIRD PETITION.

Thy will be done, as in heaven so likewise in earth.

The Confirmations.

"Teach me, O Lord, to do thy will; for thou art my God." Psal. cxliii.

"Not every one that saith unto me, Lord, Lord, shall enter into the kingdom of heaven; but he that doth the will of my Father which is in heaven." Matt. vii.

"Whosoever doth the will of my Father which is in heaven, he is my brother, and sister, and mother." Matt. xii.

"This is the will of him which sent me, that whosoever seeth the Son, and believeth on him, have everlasting life." John vi.

"Fashion not yourselves like unto this world; but be ye changed through the renewing of your mind, that ye may prove what thing that good, and acceptable, and perfect will of God is." Rom. xii.

"This is the will of God, even your sanctifying, that ye abstain from whoredom, that every one of you know how to keep his vessel in holiness and honour, and not in the lust of concupiscence, as the heathen do, which know not God." 1 Thess. iv.

"Forasmuch as Christ hath suffered for us in the flesh, arm ye yourselves likewise with the same mind. For he which suffereth in the flesh ceaseth from sin, that he from henceforth should live, as much time as remaineth in the flesh, not after the lusts of men, but after the will of God. For it is sufficient for us, that we have spent the time that is past of the life after the will of the gentiles, walking in wantonness, lusts, excess of drinking, and abominable idolatry." 1 Pet. iv.

THE FOURTH PETITION.

Give us this day our daily bread.

The Confirmations.

"I have been young, and now am old; and yet saw I never the righteous forsaken, nor his seed begging their bread. He is ever merciful, and lendeth; and yet have his children God's plenty and enough." Psal. xxxvii.

Psal. cxlv. "The eyes of all wait upon thee, O Lord; and thou givest them their meat in due season. Thou openest thy hand, and fillest every living creature with thy blessing."

Prov. x. "The blessing of the Lord maketh men rich: as for careful travail, it doth nothing thereto."

"The Lord will not let the soul of the righteous suffer hunger; but he taketh away the riches of the ungodly."

Prov. xxx. "Two things have I required of thee, that thou wilt not deny me before I die. Remove from me vanity and lies: give me neither poverty nor riches: only grant me a necessary living; lest, if I be too full, I deny thee, and say, Who is the Lord? and lest I, being constrained through poverty, fall unto stealing, and forswear the name of my God."

Matt. vi. "Be not careful for your life, what ye shall eat or drink; nor yet for your body, what raiment ye shall wear. Is not the life more worth than meat, and the body more of value than raiment?" Read forth the chapter.

1 Pet. v. "Cast all your care on God; for he careth for you."

THE FIFTH PETITION.

And forgive us our debts, as we forgive our debtors.

The Confirmations.

And forgive us.

Isai. xliii. "I am he, yea, I am he, which put away thine iniquities, and that for mine own sake, and will remember thy sins no more."

Isai. xliv. "As for thine offences, I drive them away like the clouds, and thy sins as the mist. Turn thee again unto me; and I will deliver thee."

Matt. xviii. God is that king which forgiveth his servant the ten thousand talents.

Mark ii. Luke v. "No man can forgive sin, but God alone."

Luke xv. God is the most loving father which joyfully receiveth home again his lost son, when he repent and convert.

Our debts.

Psal. xiv. "They are all gone out of the way, they are all together become abominable: there is none that doth good, no, not one."

Psal. xix. "Who can tell how oft he offendeth? O cleanse thou me from my secret faults!"

Prov. xx. "Who can say, My heart is clean, I am free from sin?"

Eccles. vii. "There is not one righteous man in all the earth, that doth good and sinneth not."

Job iv. xv. xxv. "Behold, God hath found unfaithfulness among his own saints; yea, the very heavens are unclean in his sight. How much more then abominable and vile man, which drinketh wickedness like water!"

1 Esdr. iv. "All the children of men are wicked; and all their works are naught: neither is there any truth in them."

Isai. ix. "All are hypocrites and wicked."

Isai. lxiv. "We are all become unclean; and all our righteousnesses are as a cloth polluted[1]."

Luke xvii. "We are all unprofitable servants."

Rom. iii. "All have sinned, and want the glory of God."

1 John i. "If we say we have no sin, we deceive ourselves, and the truth is not in us. But if we confess our sins, God is faithful and righteous to forgive us our sins, and to make us clean from all iniquity."

As we forgive our debtors.

Ecclus. xxviii. "He that seeketh vengeance shall find vengeance of the Lord, which shall surely keep him his sins. Forgive thy neighbour the hurt that he hath done thee, and so

[1 Two words are omitted.]

shall thy sins be forgiven thee also when thou prayest. A man that beareth hatred against another, how dare he desire forgiveness of God? He that sheweth no mercy to a man, which is like himself, how dare he ask forgiveness of his sins? If he that is but flesh beareth hatred and keepeth it, who will entreat for his sins? Remember the end, and let enmity pass."

"If ye forgive other men their trespasses, the heavenly Father shall forgive you. Matt. vi.
But if ye will not forgive men their trespasses, no more shall your Father forgive you your trespasses."

"When ye stand and pray, forgive, if ye have ought against any man, that your Mark xi.
Father also which is in heaven may forgive you your trespasses."

"Forgive, and it shall be forgiven unto you." Luke vi.

"Forbear one another, and forgive one another. If any man have a quarrel against Col. iii.
another, like as Christ hath forgiven you, even so do ye likewise."

Christ forgave his persecutors, and prayed for them, saying: "Father, forgive them; Luke xxiii.
for they know not what they do."

St Stephen forgave his enemies, and prayed for them on this manner: "O Lord, lay Acts vii.
not this sin to their charge."

THE SIXTH PETITION.

And lead us not into temptation.

The Confirmations.

"My son, if thou wilt come into the service of God, stand fast in righteousness and Ecclus. ii.
fear, and arm thy soul to temptation," &c.

"Watch and pray, that ye fall not into temptation. The spirit is willing, but the Matt. xxvi.
flesh is weak."

"Blessed is the man that standeth fast in temptation. For when he is tried, he shall James i.
receive the crown of life, which the Lord hath promised to them that love him. Let no man say, when he is tempted, that he is tempted of God. For as God cannot be tempted with evil, so neither he himself tempteth any man unto evil. But every man is tempted, when he is drawn away and enticed of his own concupiscence. Then when lust hath conceived, she bringeth forth sin; and sin, when it is done in deed, bringeth forth death."

THE SEVENTH PETITION.

But deliver us from the evil.

The Confirmations.

"Satan hath desired after you, that he might sift you even as wheat. But I have Luke xxii.
prayed for thee, O Simon, that thy faith may not fail. And when thou art converted, strength thy brethren."

"God is faithful, which will not suffer you to be tempted above your strength, 1 Cor. x.
but shall in the midst of the temptation make a way to come out, that ye may be able to bear it."

"Be sober and watch; for your adversary the devil walketh about like a roaring 1 Pet. v.
lion, seeking whom he may devour: whom resist stedfast in the faith."

"The Lord knoweth how to deliver the godly out of the temptation." 2 Pet. ii.

"We know that whosoever is born of God sinneth not; but he that is begotten 1 John v.
of God keepeth himself, and that wicked toucheth him not."

THE CONCLUSION OF THE LORD'S PRAYER.

For thine is the kingdom, and the power, and the glory, for ever and ever.

The Confirmations.

"Blessed be thou, Lord God of Israel our Father, for ever and ever. Thine, O 1 Chron. xxix.

Lord, is might, power, glory, victory, and praise. For all that is in heaven and in earth is thine. O Lord, thine is the kingdom, and thou excellest above all, even as the head of all. Thine are the riches, treasures, honour, and dominion over all. And in thy hands is the virtue, might, power, excellency, empire, and rule, upon and above all things. Wherefore now, O our God, we give laud, praise, and glory to thy most noble name."

Rom. xi. "Of him, and through him, and in him, are all things. To him be praise for ever."

Rom. xvi. "To God, which alone is wise, be glory through Jesus Christ for ever."

Eph. iii. "Unto him that is able to do exceeding abundantly above all that we ask or think, according to the power that worketh in us, be praise in the congregation by Christ Jesus throughout all ages, world without end."

1 Tim. i. "Unto God, King everlasting, immortal, invisible, alone wise, be honour and glory for ever and ever!"

Rev. iv. "Thou art worthy, O Lord, to receive glory, and honour, and power; for thou hast created all things, and for thy will's sake they were and are created."

Rev. v. "Blessing, honour, glory, and power, be unto him that sitteth upon the seat, and unto the Lamb for evermore. Amen."

All these petitions I undoubtedly believe that I shall enjoy, whensoever I ask them in faith of God, my heavenly Father, through Jesus Christ our Lord.

OF THE LAW.

WHAT THE LAW IS.

The law of God is a doctrine prescribing unto us what we ought to do, and what to eschew, both toward God and our neighbour.

The Confirmations.

Exod. xx. "Thou shalt love the Lord thy God with all thy heart."
"Thou shalt not take the name of thy Lord God in vain."
"Thou shalt love thy neighbour as thyself."
"Thou shalt not kill: thou shalt not steal."

TO WHAT USE THE LAW WAS GIVEN.

First, that it should declare unto us the will of God, how we ought to live, and what works we ought to do, that we may please the Lord our God.

The Confirmations.

Psal. xix. "The law of the Lord is an undefiled law, converting souls: the testimony of the Lord is sure, and giveth wisdom to the simple. The statutes of the Lord are right, and rejoice the heart. The commandment of the Lord is pure, and giveth light to the eyes."

Psal. cxix. "Thy word is a lantern to my feet, and a light to my pathways."

Psal. cxlvii. "He sheweth his word unto Jacob, his statutes and ordinances unto Israel. He hath not dealt so with any nation, neither have the heathen knowledge of his laws."

Secondly, that it should reveal and open unto us our sin and wickedness, while we consider how unable we be of ourselves to do that which the holy, righteous, and good law of God requireth of us to be done.

The Confirmations.

Rom. iii. "By the law cometh the knowledge of sin."

Rom. v. "The law entered in, that sin should increase."

Rom. vii. "What shall we say? Is the law sin? God forbid. But I knew not what sin meant but by the law: for I had not known what lust had meant, except the law had said, Thou shalt not lust. But sin took an occasion by the means of the commandment, and wrought in me all manner of concupiscence. For without the law sin was dead. I once lived without law: but when the commandment came, sin revived, and I was dead. And the very same commandment, which was ordained unto life, was found to be unto me an occasion of death. For sin took occasion by the means of the commandment, and so deceived me, and by the self commandment slew me."

"The sting of death is sin, and the strength of sin is the law." 1 Cor. xv.

"The letter," that is to say, the law, "killeth." 2 Cor. iii.

The law is "the ministering of condemnation."

"Moses," saith Christ, "gave you a law; and yet none of you fulfilleth the law in deed." John vii.

Thirdly, after we have learned our weakness, our wretchedness, our sin, our wickedness, by comparing our strength and life with the law of God, which proveth us all sinners and worthy of eternal damnation, lest we should fall into desperation, and so be damned, the law was given of God to be a school-master unto us to lead us unto Christ, the alone end and perfect fulfiller of all the laws of God; that we, through faith taking upon us his righteousness, and his fulfilling of the law, might be found blameless through him in the sight of God, and so be made inheritors of everlasting glory.

The Confirmations.

"The law was our school-master unto Christ, that we should be justified by faith. But after that faith is come, we are no longer under the school-master. For ye are all the children of God, because ye believe in Christ Jesu." Gal. iii.

"The law brought nothing to perfection, but was an introduction to a better hope, by the which we draw nigh unto God." Heb. vii.

"Be it known unto you, ye men and brethren, that through this man Christ is preached unto you the forgiveness of sins, and that by him all that believe are justified from all things, from the which ye could not be justified by the law of Moses." Acts xiii.

"Why tempt ye God, to put on the disciples' necks the yoke which neither our fathers nor we were able to bear? But we believe that through the grace of the Lord Jesu Christ we shall be saved." Acts xv.

"Christ is the fulfilling of the law, to justify all that believe." Rom. x.

"Christ hath delivered us from the curse of the law, inasmuch as he was made accursed for us." Gal. iii.

THE TEN COMMANDMENTS OF GOD, WITH CONFIRMATIONS OF EVERY COMMANDMENT OUT OF THE HOLY SCRIPTURE.

THE FIRST TABLE OF THE LAW, CONTAINING FOUR COMMANDMENTS, WHEREIN IS DECLARED OUR DUTY TOWARD GOD.

THE FIRST COMMANDMENT.

I am the Lord thy God. Thou shalt have no strange gods before me. Exod. xx.

The Confirmations.

"The Lord he is God, and there is none other but he alone." Deut. iv.

"Understand and think it in thy heart, that the Lord he is God in heaven above, and upon the earth beneath; neither is there any other."

"Hear, O Israel, the Lord our God is God alone. Thou shalt love the Lord thy God with all thine heart, and with all thy soul, and with all thy might." Deut. vi.

"Thou shalt fear the Lord thy God, and serve him alone."

Deut. viii. "If thou forget the Lord thy God, and walk after strange gods, and serve them, and worship them, I testify unto you that ye shall surely perish."

Deut. x. "Now, O Israel, what doth the Lord thy God require of thee, but that thou shouldest fear the Lord thy God, and walk in his ways and love him, and serve the Lord thy God with all thy heart and with all thy soul, and keep the commandments of the Lord?"

Deut. xxx. "If thine heart turn away from God, so that thou wilt not hear his word, but go astray and worship strange gods, and serve them, I pronounce unto you this day that ye shall surely perish, and not live long on the earth."

Deut. xxxii. "See now how that I, yea, that I am God, and there is none but I."

Psal. lxxxi. "I will assure thee, O Israel, if thou wilt hearken unto me. There shall no strange god be in thee, neither shalt thou worship any other god. I am the Lord thy God."

Isai. xliii. "Besides me there was never any God, neither shall there be after me: I am, I am the Lord alone, and besides me there is no saviour."

Isai. xlv. "There is none other God but I. A true God, and such one as saveth; there is none but I alone."

Matt. xxii. "Thou shalt love the Lord thy God with all thy heart, and with all thy soul, and with all thy mind. This is the first and greatest commandment."

John xvii. "This is the everlasting life, even to know thee the alone true God, and whom thou hast sent, Jesus Christ."

1 Cor. viii. "There is none other God but one. And although there be that are called gods, whether in heaven, either in earth (as there be gods many and lords many), yet unto you there is but one God."

1 Tim. ii. "There is one God and one Mediator."

THE SECOND COMMANDMENT.

Exod. xx. *Thou shalt make thee no graven or carved image, nor likeness at all of any thing that is in heaven above, or in the earth beneath, or in the waters under the earth: thou shalt not bow before them, nor worship them. For I the Lord thy God am a jealous God, punishing the wickedness of the parents in the children, unto the third and fourth generation, if they hate me, and shew mercy unto the thousands, even unto those that love me, and keep my commandment.*

The Confirmations.

Lev. xix. "Ye shall not turn unto idols, nor make you gods of metal."

Deut. iv. "Take heed unto yourselves, that ye forget not the appointment of the Lord your God, which he made with you, and that ye make you no graven image, nor any picture that the Lord thy God hath forbidden thee. For the Lord thy God is a consuming fire, and a jealous God. If ye do wickedly, and make any manner of graven image, and work evil in the sight of the Lord thy God to provoke him to anger, I call heaven and earth to record against you this day, that ye shall shortly perish."

Deut. vii. "Ye shall overthrow the altars of the idols, and break down their pillars, cut down their groves, and burn their graven images with fire. For thou art an holy nation unto the Lord thy God."

Deut. xxvii. "Cursed be the man that maketh any carved or molten image, an abomination unto the Lord, the work of the hands of the craftsman, and putteth it in a secret place. And all the people shall answer and say, Amen."

Psal. xcvii. "Confounded be all they that worship carved images, and that delight in vain gods."

Isai. xlii. "I am the Lord, this is my name; my glory will I give to none other, neither mine honour to graven images."

Read the forty-fourth and forty-sixth chapters of Esay.

Ezek. xiv. "Be converted, and forsake your idols."

Wisd. xiv. "The seeking out of idols is the beginning of whoredom, and the bringing up of them is the destruction of life. For they were not from the beginning, neither shall they continue unto the end. The wealthy idleness of men hath found them out upon the earth; therefore shall they come shortly to an end."

"The honouring of abominable images is the cause, the beginning, and the end of all evil."

Read the thirteenth, fourteenth, fifteenth, and sixteenth chapters of Wisdom.

Read also the sixth chapter of the prophet Baruch.

"We preach unto you that ye should turn from these vanities unto the living God, which made heaven, and earth, and the sea, and all things that are therein." Acts xiv.

"My sentence is, that we trouble not them, which from among the gentiles are turned to God; but that we write unto them that they abstain themselves from the filthiness of images." Acts xv.

"They are not gods which are made with hands." Acts xix.

"Be not worshippers of images." 1 Cor. x.

"No worshippers of images shall inherit the kingdom of God." 1 Cor. vi.

"Babes, keep yourselves from images." 1 John v.

THE THIRD COMMANDMENT.

Thou shalt not take the name of the Lord thy God in vain. For the Lord will not hold him guiltless, that taketh his name in vain. Exod. xx.

The Confirmations.

"Ye shall not swear by my name in vain, neither shalt thou defile the name of thy God. I am the Lord." Lev. xix.

"He that hath not sworn to deceive his neighbour, he shall receive blessing from the Lord, and mercy from God his Saviour." Psal. xxiv.

"He that blasphemeth the name of the Lord, let him be slain; and all the multitude shall stone him to death." Lev. xxiv.

"Thou shalt swear, The Lord liveth, in truth, in equity, and righteousness." Jer. iv.

"My curse and vengeance," saith the Lord, "shall fall upon his house, that falsely sweareth by my name, and shall remain in his house, and consume it with the timber and stones thereof." Zech. v.

"Ye have heard how it was said to them of old time, Thou shalt not forswear thyself, but shalt perform unto the Lord those things that thou swearest. But I say unto you, Swear not at all; neither by heaven, for it is God's seat; neither by the earth, for it is his footstool; neither by Jerusalem, for it is the city of the great King; neither shalt thou swear by thy head, because thou canst not make one hair white or black. But your communication shall be yea, yea, and nay, nay; for whatsoever is added more than these, it cometh of evil." Matt. v.

"Above all things, my brethren, swear not, neither by heaven, nor by earth, neither any other oath. Let your yea be yea, and your nay, nay, lest ye fall into dissimulation." James v.

"Let not thy mouth be accustomed with swearing; for in it there are many falls. A man that useth much swearing shall be filled with wickedness; and the plague shall never go from his house. He that sweareth in vain shall not be found righteous; for his house shall be full of plagues. The words of the swearer bring death: God grant that be it not found in the house of Jacob; but they that fear God eschew all such, and lie not weltering in sin." Ecclus. xxiii.

"O praise the Lord with me, and let us magnify his name together." Psal. xxxiv.

"All our glory is in God all the day long; and we will praise thy name for ever." Psal. xliv.

"Call on me in the time of trouble, and I will deliver thee, and thou shalt honour me." Psal. l.

"Forasmuch as he hath trusted in me, I will deliver him, yea, I will defend him, because he hath known my name. He shall call upon me, and I will hear him: yea, I am with him in trouble: I will deliver him, and bring him to honour. With long life will I satisfy him, and shew him my salvation." Psal. xci.

"The name of the Lord is a strong castle: the righteous flieth unto it, and is in safeguard." Prov. xviii.

"Whosoever calleth on the name of the Lord shall be saved." Joel ii.

THE FOURTH COMMANDMENT.

Exod. xx. *Remember that thou keep holy the sabbath-day. Six days shalt thou work and do all thy business. But in the seventh day is the sabbath of the Lord thy God, wherein thou shalt do no work, neither thou, nor thy son, nor thy daughter, nor thy servant, nor thy maid, nor thy beast, nor thy stranger that is within thy gates. For in six days the Lord made heaven and earth, sea, and all that is therein, and the seventh day he rested; and therefore the Lord blessed the sabbath-day, and made it holy.*

The Confirmations.

Exod. xxxi. "In any wise see that ye keep my sabbaths; for it is a sign between me and you in your generations, for to know that I the Lord am he that doth sanctify you," &c.

Num. xv. The man that was found gathering sticks on the sabbath-day was stoned to death at the commandment of God.

Isai. lvi. "Blessed is the man that taketh heed that he unhalloweth not the sabbath, that is to say, keepeth himself so that he do no evil."

"All they which keep themselves that they unhallow not the sabbath, I mean that they fulfil my covenant, them will I bring to my holy mountain, and make them joyful in my house of prayer."

Isai. lviii. "If thou on the sabbath-day turn thy feet, so that thou do not the thing which pleaseth thyself in my holy day, but givest God the honour, so that thou do not after thine own imagination, neither seek thine own will, nor speak thine own words, then shalt thou have thy pleasure in the Lord; and I will carry thee high above the earth, and feed thee with the heritage of Jacob thy father. For the Lord's own mouth hath so promised."

Isai. lxvi. "There shall be a new sabbath for the other old sabbath; and all flesh shall come to worship before me, saith the Lord."

Heb. iv. "There remaineth yet a rest to the people of God. For he that is entered into his rest hath ceased also from his own works, as God did from his. Let us study therefore to enter into that rest, lest any man fall after the same ensample of unbelief."

WHAT IT IS TO KEEP HOLY THE SABBATH-DAY.

To keep holy the sabbath-day is not to cease from bodily labour, that thou shouldest the more licentiously give thy mind to the wearing of gallant apparel, to banqueting, to idle talk, to vain pastimes, and such other filthy pleasures of the flesh; but that thou, setting aside all worldly businesses, shouldest the more freely apply thyself to read, hear, and learn the word of God, to pray in the temple with the congregation, to be thankful to God for his benefits, to be present at the ministration of the holy sacraments, to be partaker of the mysteries of the Lord's body and blood, to give some good thing to the relief of the poor, to visit and comfort the sick and them that are in prison, and, casting away the works of the flesh, wholly to exercise thyself in the fruits of the Spirit.

THE SECOND TABLE OF THE LAW OF GOD, CONTAINING SIX COMMANDMENTS, WHEREIN IS DECLARED OUR DUTY TOWARD OUR NEIGHBOUR.

THE FIFTH COMMANDMENT.

Exod. xx. *Honour thy father and mother, that thy days may be made long upon the land which the Lord thy God giveth thee.*

The Confirmations.

Lev. xix. "Ye shall reverence every man his father and his mother."

Lev. xx. "Whosoever he be that curseth his father or his mother, let him die; for he hath cursed his father and mother: his blood be upon him."

"He that smiteth his father or mother, let him be slain for it." Exod. xxi.

"If any man have a son that is stubborn and disobedient, that he will not hearken unto the voice of his mother, and they have chastened him, and he would not hearken unto them; then shall his father and his mother take him and bring him out unto the elders of that city, and unto the gate of the same place, and say unto the elders of the city, This our son is stubborn and disobedient, and will not hearken unto our voice: he is a rioter and a drunkard. And all the men of that city shall stone him with stones unto death." Deut. xxi.

"Cursed be he that curseth his father and his mother. And all the people shall say, Amen." Deut. xxvii.

"My son, hear thy father's doctrine, and forsake not the law of thy mother. For that shall bring grace to thy head, and shall be as a chain about thy neck." Prov. i.

"A good child will hearken to his father's warning; but he that is scornful will not hear when he is reproved." Prov. xiii.

"He that hurteth his father, or shutteth out his mother, is a scornful and an unworthy son." Prov. xix.

"Whoso robbeth his father and mother, and saith it is no sin, the same is like unto a destroyer." Prov. xxviii.

"Whoso laugheth his father to scorn, and setteth his mother's commandment at nought, the ravens pick out his eyes in the valley, and devoured be he of the young eagles." Prov. xxx.

"The Lord will have the father honoured of the children; and look, what a mother commandeth her children, he will have it kept." Ecclus. iii.

"Whoso honoureth his father shall have a joy of his own children, and when he maketh his prayer he shall be heard. He that honoureth his father shall have long life, and he that is obedient for the Lord's sake, his mother shall have joy of him. He that feareth the Lord honoureth his father and mother, and doth them service, as it were unto the Lord himself. Honour thy father in deed, in word, and in all patience, that thou mayest have God's blessing; and his blessing shall abide with thee at the last. The blessing of the father buildeth up the houses of the children; but the mother's curse rooteth out the foundations. Rejoice not when thy father is reproved; for it is not honour unto thee, but a shame. For the worship of a man's father is his own worship; and where the father is without honour, it is the dishonesty of the son. My son, make much of thy father in his age, and grieve him not as long as he liveth. And if his understanding fail, have patience with him, and despise him not in thy strength. For the good deed that thou shewest to thy father shall not be forgotten, and when thou thyself wantest,' it shall be rewarded thee (and for thy mother's offence thou shalt be recompensed with good, yea, it shall be founded for thee in righteousness), and in the day of trouble thou shalt be remembered: thy sins also shall meale[1] away, like as the ice in the air and warm weather. But he that forsaketh his father shall come to shame, and he that despiseth his mother is cursed of God."

"Children, obey your fathers and mothers in the Lord; for that is right. Honour thy father and mother; the same is the first commandment in the promise; that thou mayest prosper, and live long on earth." Eph. vi.

THE SIXTH COMMANDMENT.

Thou shalt not kill. Exod. xx.

The Confirmations.

"Whoso sheddeth man's blood, by man shall his blood be shed. For in the image of God did God make man." Gen. ix.

"Thou shalt not hate thy brother in thy heart," &c. Lev. xix.

[[1] Meale: melt.]

"Thou shalt not avenge thyself, nor be mindful of wrong against the children of my people; but shalt love thy neighbour as thyself: I am the Lord."

Lev. xxiv. "He that killeth any man, let him die the death."

Deut. xxvii. "Cursed be he that smiteth his neighbour secretly. And all the people shall say, Amen."

Matt. v. "Ye have heard that it was said unto them of the old time, Thou shalt not kill: whosoever killeth shall be in danger of judgment. But I say unto you, That whosoever is angry with his brother shall be in danger of judgment," &c.

"Ye have heard that it was said, Thou shalt love thy neighbour, and hate thine enemy. But I say unto you, Love your enemies, bless them that curse you, do good to them that hate you, pray for them which hurt you and persecute you; that ye may be the children of your Father which is in heaven. For he maketh his sun to arise on the evil and on the good, and sendeth rain on the righteous and on the unrighteous."

Luke vi. "Be ye merciful, as your Father is merciful. Judge not, and ye shall not be judged. Condemn not, and ye shall not be condemned. Forgive, and ye shall be forgiven. Give, and it shall be given to you, good measure, and pressed down, and shaken together, and running over shall men give into your bosom. For with the same measure that ye mete withal, shall other men mete to you again."

Rom. xii. "Recompense to no man evil for evil."

"If it be possible (as much as is in you), live peaceably with all men. Dearly beloved, avenge not yourselves, but rather give place unto wrath. For it is written,
Deut. xxxii. Vengeance is mine, and I will reward, saith the Lord. Therefore if thine enemy hunger, feed him: if he thirst, give him drink. For in so doing thou shalt heap coals of fire upon his head. Be not overcome of evil, but overcome evil with goodness."

Eph. iv. "Be angry, and sin not. Let not the sun go down upon your wrath, neither give place unto the backbiter."

"Let all bitterness, and fierceness, and wrath, and roaring, and cursed speaking be put away from you, with all maliciousness. Be ye courteous one to another, merciful, forgiving one another, even as God for Christ's sake hath forgiven you."

1 John iii. "He that hateth his brother is a manslayer. And ye know that every manslayer hath not everlasting life dwelling in him."

1 John iv. "This commandment have we of God, that he which loveth God should also love his brother."

THE SEVENTH COMMANDMENT.

Exod. xx. *Thou shalt not commit advoutry.*

The Confirmations.

Lev. xviii. "Thou shalt not lie with thy neighbour's wife to defile her[1]."

Lev. xix. "Thou shalt not make thy daughter common, that thou wouldest cause her to be an whore, lest the land also fall to whoredom, and be full of wickedness."

Deut. xxii. "If a man be found lying with a woman that hath a wedded husband, they shall die both of them, both the man that lay with the wife and also the wife; and so shalt thou put away evil from Israel."

Deut. xxiii. "There shall be no whore of the daughters of Israel, nor whore-keeper of the sons of Israel."

Deut. xxvii. "Cursed be he that lieth with his neighbour's wife. And all the people shall say, Amen."

Prov. v. "The lips of an harlot are a dropping honey comb, and her throat is more glistering than oil. But at the last she is a[s] bitter as wormwood, and her tongue as sharp as a two-edged sword. Her feet go down unto death; and her steps pierce through unto hell."

"Be glad with the wife of thy youth. Loving is the hind, and friendly is the roe.

[[1] Two words are omitted.]

Let her breasts alway satisfy thee, and hold thee ever content with her love. O my son, why wilt thou have pleasure in an harlot, and embrace the bosom of another woman? Every man's ways are open in the sight of the Lord, and he pondereth all their goings. The wickedness of the ungodly shall catch himself, and with the snares of his own sins shall he be trapped."

"Keep thee from the evil woman, and from the flattering tongue of the harlot, that thou lust not after her beauty in thy heart, and lest thou be taken with her fair looks. An harlot will make a man to beg his bread; but an honest woman will seek about to get her living. May a man carry fire in his body, and his clothes not be brent? or can one go upon hot coals, and his feet not be hurt? Even so whosoever goeth in to his neighbour's wife and toucheth her cannot be unguilty." Prov. vi.

"Whoso committeth advoutry with a woman, he is a fool, and bringeth his life to destruction. He getteth himself also shame and such dishonour as shall never be put out."

Read the seventh chapter of the Proverbs.

"An whore is a deep grave, and an harlot is a narrow pit. She lurketh like a thief, and bringeth unto her such men as be full of vice." Prov. xxiii.

"He that keepeth company with harlots shall come to beggary." Prov. xxix.

Read the twenty-third chapter of Ecclesiasticus.

"My son, keep thee well from all whoredom; and beside thy wife, see that no fault be known of thee." Tob. iv.

"If my heart hath lusted after my neighbour's wife, or if I have laid wait at his door, O then let my wife be another man's whore, and let other men lie with her. For this is a wickedness and sin that is worthy to be punished; yea, a fire that should utterly consume and root out all my substance." Job xxxi.

"Whoredom, wine, and drunkenness, take the heart away." Hos. iv.

"Ye have heard that it was said to them of old time, Thou shalt not commit adultery: but I say unto you, That whosoever looketh on another man's wife to lust after her hath committed advoutry with her already in his heart." Matt. v.

"If any that is called a brother be a fornicator, with him that is such see that ye eat not." 1 Cor. v.

"Neither fornicators, neither advouterers, neither weaklings, neither abusers of themselves with mankind, shall inherit the kingdom of God." 1 Cor. vi.

"Let us not be defiled with fornication, as some of them were defiled with fornication, and fell in one day twenty-three thousand." 1 Cor. x.

"As for fornication and all uncleanness, let it not once be named among you, as it becometh saints; or filthiness, or foolish talking, or jesting, which are not comely; but rather giving of thanks. For this ye know, that no whoremonger, nor unclean person, hath any inheritance in the kingdom of Christ and of God." Eph. v.

"This is the will of God, even your holiness, that ye should abstain from fornication; and that every one of you should know how to keep his vessel in holiness and honour, and not in the lust of concupiscence, as do the heathen, which know not God." 1 Thess. iv.

"Wedlock is honourable among all men, and the bed undefiled. As for whoremongers and advouterers, God shall judge them." Heb. xiii.

"Whoremongers have their part in the lake that burneth with fire and brimstone." Rev. xxi.

THE EIGHTH COMMANDMENT.

Thou shalt not steal. Exod. xx.

The Confirmations.

"Thou shalt not do thy neighbour wrong, neither rob him violently; neither shall thy workman's labour abide with thee till the morning." Lev. xix.

"Ye shall not steal, neither lie, neither deal falsely one with another."

"Ye shall do no unrighteousness in judgment, in meteyard, in weight, or in measure: true balances and true weights shall ye have. I am the Lord."

Lev. xxv. "If thou sellest ought unto thy neighbour, or buyest of thy neighbour's hand, ye shall not deceive one another."

"If thy brother be waxen poor, and fallen in decay with thee, thou shalt relieve ☞ him, that he may live with thee....Thou shalt not give him thy money upon usury, nor lend him thy corn for increase....Thou shalt not take usury of him for vantage."

Deut. xv. "If one of thy brethren among you be poor within any of thy gates in thy land which the Lord God giveth thee, thou shalt not harden thy heart, nor shut thine hand from thy poor brother; but open thine hand unto him, and lend him sufficient for his need which he hath."

"The land shall never be without poor; and therefore I command thee, saying, Thou shalt open thine hand unto thy brother that is needy and poor in thy land."

Prov. xxix. "Whoso keepeth company with a thief hateth his own soul."

Isai. xxxiii. "Wo be to thee that spoilest; for thou thyself shalt be spoiled."

Isai. lviii. "Break thy bread to the hungry, and bring the poor wandering into thine house. When thou seest a naked man, cover him, and so shalt thou not despise thy flesh."

Zech. v. "The thief is cursed of God; and all that he hath shall come to nought."

Ecclus. v. "Shame and sorrow goeth over the thief."

Tob. ii. Anna, old Toby's wife, went daily to the weaving work; and look, what living she could get with the labour of her hands, she brought it home. And it happened that she took a kid, and brought it home. And when her husband heard it cry, he said: "Look that it be not stolen: if it be, restore it again to the owners. For it is not lawful for us to eat or touch any thing that is stolen."

Tob. iv. "Give alms of thy goods, and turn never thy face from the poor; so shall it come to pass that the face of the Lord shall not be turned away from thee. Be merciful after thy power. If thou hast much, give plenteously: if thou hast little, do thy diligence gladly to give of that little; for so gatherest thou thyself a good reward in the day of necessity. For mercy delivereth from all sin and from death, and suffered not the soul to come in darkness."

L ke xix. "Behold, Lord," said Zacheus, "the half of my goods do I give to the poor: and if I have done any man wrong, I restore him fourfold."

1 Cor. vi. "Neither thieves, neither pillers, shall inherit the kingdom of God."

Eph. iv. "Let him that stole steal no more; but let him rather labour with his hands the thing which is good, that he may give unto him that needeth."

THE NINTH COMMANDMENT.

Thou shalt not bear false witness against thy neighbour.

Exod. xxiii. "Thou shalt not accept a vain tale, neither shalt thou put thy hand with the wicked to be an unrighteous witness."

Deut. xix. "If an unrighteous witness rise up against a man to accuse him of trespass, then both the men which strive together shall stand before the Lord, before the priests and the judges, which shall be in those days; and the judges shall make diligent inquisition. ☞ And if the witness be found false, and that he hath given false witness against his brother, then shall ye do unto him as he had thought to do to his brother. And thou shalt put away evil from thee."

Deut. xxvii. "Cursed be he that taketh a reward to slay the soul of innocent blood. And all the people shall say, Amen."

Prov. vi. "The Lord hateth a false witness that bringeth up lies."

Prov. xix. "A false witness shall not escape unpunished, and he that speaketh lies shall perish."

Prov. xxi. "A false witness shall perish; but he that is a true man boldly speaketh that he hath heard."

Prov. xxv. "Whoso beareth false witness against his neighbour, he is a very club, a sword, and a sharp arrow."

Wisd. i. "The mouth that lieth slayeth the soul."

Psal. v. "Thou, O Lord, wilt destroy all them that speak lies."

Ecclus. iv. "In no wise speak against the word of truth; but be ashamed of thy lying."

"Use not to make any manner of lie; for the custom thereof is not good." Ecclus. vii.

"A thief is better than a man that is accustomed to lie; but they both shall have destruction to heritage." Ecclus. xx.

The two elders that bare witness against Susanna were stoned unto death. Hist. Sus.

"Out of the heart come false witnesses,...and those defile man." Matt. xv.

"Evil speakers shall not inherit the kingdom of God." 1 Cor. vi.

"Put away lying, and speak every man truth unto his neighbour; forasmuch as we are members one of another." Eph. iv.

"All liars shall have their part in the lake that brenneth with fire and brimstone." Rev. xxi.

THE TENTH COMMANDMENT.

Thou shalt not covet thy neighbour's house. Thou shalt not covet thy neighbour's wife, his servant, his maid, his ox, his ass, nor any thing that is thy neighbour's. Exod. xx.

The Confirmations.

"Keep thy heart with all diligence; for thereupon hangeth life." Prov. iv.

"God hateth an heart that goeth about with wicked imaginations." Prov. vi.

"Take heed that thou lust not in thy heart after the beauty of a strange woman."

"Evil thoughts are abomination to the Lord." Prov. xv.

"Whosoever looketh upon another man's wife, lusting after her, hath committed advoutry with her already in his heart." Matt. v.

"Out of the heart proceed evil thoughts,...and those defile man." Matt. xv.

"The cares of this world, and the deceitfulness of riches, and the lusts of other things, choke the word, and make it unfruitful." Mark iv.

"Take heed to yourselves, lest at any time your hearts be overcome with the cares of this life." Luke xxi.

"I had not known what lust had meant, except the law had said, Thou shalt not lust." Rom. vii.

"Make not provision for the flesh, to fulfil the lusts of it." Rom. xiii.

"Mortify your earthy members, fornication, uncleanness, unnatural lust, evil concupiscence," &c. Col. iii.

"Godliness is great riches, if a man be content with that he hath. For we brought nothing into the world, neither can we carry any thing out. But when we have food and raiment, let us be content therewith. They that have a mind to be rich fall into temptation and snares of the devil, and into many foolish and noisome lusts, which drown men into perdition and destruction. For covetousness is the root of all evil, which while some lusted after, they erred from the faith, and tangled themselves with many sorrows. But thou, man of God, flee such things. Follow righteousness, godliness, faith, love, patience, meekness," &c. 1 Tim. vi.

"Let your conversation be without covetousness; and be content with such things as ye have already." Heb. xiii.

"Love not the world, nor those things that are in the world. For all that is in the world, as the concupiscence of the flesh, and the lust of the eyes, and the pride of the life, is not of the Father, but it is of the world. And the world passeth away, and the lust thereof. But he that doeth the will of God, abideth for ever." 1 John ii.

THE SUM OF THESE TEN COMMANDMENTS, AND ALL OTHER LAWS OF GOD.

"Thou shalt love the Lord thy God with all thy heart, with all thy soul, with all thy mind, and with all the uttermost of thy power. This is the first and greatest commandment. The other is like unto this, Love thy neighbour as thyself. In these two commandments are contained the whole law and prophets." Matt. xxii.

"Owe nothing to any man, but that ye love one another. For he that loveth the other hath fulfilled the law. For these commandments, Thou shalt not commit advoutry, Thou shalt not kill, Thou shalt not steal, Thou shalt bear no false witness, Thou shalt Rom. xiii.

not lust, and all other commandments are briefly comprehended in these words, Love thy neighbour as thyself."

1 Tim. i. "The end of the law is charity, that cometh out of a pure heart, and a good conscience, and a faith not feigned."

Matt. vii. "Whatsoever ye would that men should do unto you, do ye even the same to them also; for this is the law and the prophets."

OF REPENTANCE.

WHAT REPENTANCE IS.

Repentance is an inward sorrow of the mind, wrought by the Holy Ghost, for the sins tofore committed against God, joined both with a perfect faith to be forgiven for Christ's sake, and also with a full determined purpose from henceforth to amend, and to lead a new life.

Probations out of the holy scripture.

2 Cor. vii. "I now rejoice, not that ye were sorry, but that ye so sorrowed that ye repented. For ye sorrowed godly, so that in nothing ye were hurt by us. For the sorrow that is wrought by God causeth repentance unto salvation not to be repented of; contrariwise, worldly sorrow causeth death."

2 Tim. ii. "The servant of God must inform them that resist, if that God at any time will give them repentance for to know the truth, and that they may come to themselves again out of the snare of the devil, which are holden captive of him at his will."

Jer. xxxi. "Convert thou me, O Lord, and I shall be converted; for thou art my Lord God. Yea, as soon as thou turnest me, I repented, and as soon as thou shewest (my sins) unto me, I smote my thigh: yea, I was confounded and right greatly ashamed."

Lam. v. "O Lord, turn thou us unto thee; and so shall we be turned."

Ezek. xxxvi. "I will pour clean water upon you, and ye shall be clean: yea, from all your uncleannesses and from all your idols shall I cleanse you. A new heart also will I give you, and a new spirit will I put into you. As for that stony heart, I will take it out of your body, and give you a fleshy heart. I will give my Spirit among you, and cause you to walk in my commandments, to keep my laws, and to fulfil them. And ye shall be my people; and I will be your God."

Psal. lxxx. "O thou God of hosts, turn thou us, and shew us the light of thy countenance; and so shall we be whole."

OF THE FRUITS OF REPENTANCE DECLARED BY THE WORD OF GOD.

Isai. lv. "Seek the Lord while he may be found, and call upon him while he is nigh. Let the ungodly man forsake his own ways, and the unrighteous his own imaginations, and turn again unto the Lord; so shall he be merciful unto him; and to our God; for he is very ready to forgive."

Jer. iv. "O Israel, if thou wilt turn thee, then turn unto me, saith the Lord. And if thou wilt put away thine abominations out of my sight, thou shalt not be moved."

"Be circumcised in the Lord, and cut away the foreskin of your hearts, that my indignation break not forth like fire, and kindle, so that no man may quench it, because of the wickedness of your imaginations."

Ezek. xviii. "If the ungodly will turn away from all his sins that he hath done, and keep all my commandments, and do the thing that is equal and right, doubtless he shall live and not die. As for all his sins that he did before, they shall not be thought upon; but in his righteousness that he hath done he shall live. For have I any pleasure in the death of a sinner? saith the Lord God; but rather that he convert and live.

"Be converted, and turn you clean from all your wickedness; so shall there no sin do you harm. Cast away from you all your ungodliness that ye have done. Make you new hearts and a new spirit. Wherefore will ye die, O ye house of Israel, seeing I have no pleasure in the death of him that dieth? saith the Lord God. Turn ye then, and ye shall live."

"As truly as I live, saith the Lord God, I have no pleasure in the death of the wicked; but much rather that the wicked turn from his way and live. Turn you, turn you from your ungodly ways, O ye house of Israel. O wherefore will ye die? Ezek. xxxiii.

"The wickedness of the wicked shall not hurt him, whensoever he converteth from his ungodliness."

"Turn you unto me, saith the Lord of hosts, and I will turn me unto you." Zech. i.

"Turn you unto me with all your hearts, with fasting, weeping, and mourning. Rent your hearts, and not your clothes. Turn you unto the Lord your God; for he is gracious and merciful, long-suffering, and of great compassion, and ready to pardon wickedness." Joel ii.

"Repent of the life that is past; for the kingdom of heaven is at hand." Matt. iii.

"Bring forth the fruits that belongeth to repentance. For even now is the axe put unto the root of the tree; so that every tree which bringeth not forth good fruit is hewn down and cast into the fire."

"I am not come to call the righteous, but sinners to repentance." Matt. ix.

"Come unto me, all ye that labour, and are laden; and I will ease you." Matt. xi.

"Repent, and believe the gospel." Mark i.

"I say unto you, that joy shall be in heaven over one sinner that repenteth, more than over ninety and nine just persons, which need no repentance." Luke xv.

"The Son of man is come to seek and to save that which was lost." Luke xix.

"Repent and convert, that your sins may be done away." Acts iii.

"As ye have given your members servants to uncleanness and to iniquity (from one iniquity to another), even so now give over your members servants unto righteousness, that ye may be sanctified." Rom. vi.

"Put off that old man, which is corrupt according to the deceivable lusts, and be ye renewed in the spirit of your mind, putting on that new man, which after God is shapen in righteousness and true holiness," &c. Eph. iv.

"Mortify your earthy members; fornication, uncleanness, unnatural lust, evil concupiscence, and covetousness, which is worshipping of idols; for which things' sake the wrath of God useth to come on the disobedient children: among whom ye walked sometime, when ye lived in them. But now put ye also away from you all such things; wrath, fierceness, maliciousness, cursed speaking, filthy communication. Lie not one to another, seeing that ye have put off the old man with his works, and have put on the new man, which is renewed into the knowledge and image of him that made him. Therefore, as the elect of God, holy and beloved, put on tender mercy, kindness, humbleness of mind, meekness, long-suffering, forbearing one another, and forgiving one another, if any man have a quarrel against another. As Christ forgave you, even so do ye. Above all these things, put on love, which is the bond of perfection. And whatsoever ye do in word or deed, do all in the name of the Lord Jesu, giving thanks to God the Father by him." Col. iii.

OF BAPTISM.

WHAT BAPTISM IS.

Baptism is the ordinance of Christ, to wash every believing Christian with water in the name of the Father, and of the Son, and of the Holy Ghost.

St Paul calleth baptism "the fountain of the new birth, and renewing of the Holy Ghost." Tit. iii.

Probations out of the holy scripture.

"All power is given unto me in heaven and in earth. Go ye therefore, and teach all nations, baptizing them in the name of the Father, and of the Son, and of the Holy Ghost, teaching them to observe all things whatsoever I have commanded you." Matt. xxviii.

"Go ye into all the world, and preach the gospel to every creature. He that believeth and is baptized shall be saved: but he that believeth not shall be damned." Mark xvi.

"Except a man be born from above, he cannot see the kingdom of God." John iii.

"Verily, verily, I say unto thee, Except a man be born of water and of the Spirit, he cannot enter into the kingdom of God. That which is born of the flesh is flesh; and that which is born of the Spirit is spirit."

TO WHAT USE BAPTISM WAS USED.

First, to be a sure seal and an evident testimony unto us that God the Father for his Son Jesus Christ's sake hath freely forgiven us all our sins, received us into his favour, and given us the Holy Ghost; by whom we are born anew, not of mortal, but of immortal seed; by whom also we are made the sons and heirs of God, and through faith reckoned pure and holy in his godly sight.

Probations out of the holy scripture.

Mark xvi. "He that believeth and is baptized shall be saved."

Acts ii. "Repent you of your sins, and be baptized every one in the name of Jesus Christ, for the remission of sins; and ye shall receive the gift of the Holy Ghost."

Eph. v. "Christ loved the congregation, and gave himself for it, to sanctify it, and cleansed it in the fountain of water through the word, to make it unto himself a glorious congregation, without spot or wrinkle or any such thing, but that it should be holy and without blame."

Tit. iii. "Not by the deeds of righteousness which we wrought, but according to his mercy hath he saved us, by the fountain of the new birth, and renewing of the Holy Ghost, which he shed on us abundantly through Jesus Christ our Saviour; that we, justified by his grace, should be made heirs according to the hope of eternal life."

1 Pet. iii. "Baptism saveth us, not the putting away of the filth of the flesh, but in that a good conscience consenteth to God by the resurrection of Jesus Christ, which is on the right hand of God, and is gone into heaven."

Secondly, to put us in remembrance that, forasmuch as we are become the soldiers of Christ, we ought, so long as we live, valiantly to fight against the devil, the world, and the flesh, to mortify all unclean lusts, to die unto sin, and to rise again new men, bearing the image of Christ, and fashioning our conversation and manners after his example, that we may learn[1] the Lord our God in such holiness and righteousness as is allowed before him all the days of our life.

Probations out of the holy scriptures.

Rom. vi. "Know ye not that all we which are baptized into Jesu Christ are baptized to die with him? We are buried then with him by baptism for to die; that, like wise as Christ was raised from death by the glory of the Father, even so we also should walk in a new life. For if we be graft in death like unto him, even so shall we be partakers of the resurrection; knowing this, that our old man is crucified with him also, that the body of sin might utterly be destroyed, that henceforth we should not be servants unto sin. For he that is dead is justified from sin. Wherefore if we be dead with Christ, we believe that we shall also live with him."

Gal. iii. "All ye that are baptized have put on Christ."

Col. ii. "Ye are buried with Christ through baptism, in whom ye are also risen again through faith that is wrought by the operation of God, which raised him from death."

Col. iii. "If ye then be risen again with Christ, seek those things which are above, where Christ sitteth on the right hand of God. Set your affection on heavenly things, and not on earthly things. For ye are dead; and your life is hid with Christ in God. Whensoever Christ, which is our life, shall shew himself, then shall ye also appear with him in glory."

OF THE LORD'S SUPPER.

WHAT THE LORD'S SUPPER IS.

The Lord's supper is an holy and heavenly banquet, in the which the faithful Christians, besides the corporal eating of the bread, and the outward drinking

[[1] Perhaps *serve*.]

of the wine, do spiritually through faith both eat the body of Christ and drink his blood, unto the confirmation of their faith, the comfort of their conscience, and the salvation of their souls.

TO WHAT USE CHRIST DID INSTITUTE HIS HOLY SUPPER.

First, to put us in remembrance that his body was broken and his blood shed for our redemption.

Probations out of the holy scripture.

"The Lord Jesus the same night in the which he was betrayed took bread; and when he had given thanks, he brake it, and gave it to his disciples, saying, Take ye and eat: this is my body, which is broken for you. This do ye in the remembrance of me. After the same manner also he took the cup, when supper was done, saying, This cup is the new testament in my blood. This do, as oft as ye drink it, in remembrance of me. For as oft as ye shall eat this bread, and drink of this cup, ye shall shew the Lord's death till he come." 1 Cor. xi.

"When they were eating, Jesus took bread, and when he had given thanks, he brake it, and gave it to his disciples, and said, Take, eat: this is my body. And he took the cup, and thanked, and gave it them, saying, Drink ye all of this. For this is my blood (which is of the new testament), that is shed for many for the remission of sins." Matt. xxvi.

"As they did eat, Jesus took bread; and when he had given thanks, he brake it, and gave it to them, and said, Take, eat: this is my body. And he took the cup; and when he had given thanks, he took it to them; and they all drank of it. And he said unto them, This is my blood of the new testament, which is shed for many." Mark xiv.

"He took bread; and when he had given thanks, he brake it, and gave unto them, saying, This is my body which is given for you. This do in the remembrance of me. Likewise also, when he had supped, he took the cup, saying, This cup is the new testament in my blood, which is shed for you." Luke xxii.

Secondly, to stir us up unto thanksgiving, while we consider how precious, great, and inestimable benefits we have received of God the Father by the death of his Son; as deliverance from Satan, freedom from the curse of the law, forgiveness of sins, the favour and good-will of God, quietness of conscience, the Holy Ghost, righteousness, victory against sin, death, and hell, salvation, and finally everlasting life. That we should not be unthankful, but rather joyfully brast out into all kind of spiritual praises, lauding and magnifying God the Father for these his most high and singular free gifts, the Lord Christ did institute this holy supper. Therefore is it called of the ancient doctors *Sacramentum Eucharistiæ:* "The sacrament of thanksgiving."

Probations out of the holy scriptures.

"All that believed continued daily with one accord in the temple, and brake bread from house to house, and did eat their meat together with gladness and singleness of heart, praising God." Acts ii

"Is not the cup of thanksgiving, for the which we give thanks, partaking of the blood of Christ? Is not the bread which we break partaking of the body of Christ?" 1 Cor. x.

Thirdly, to put us in remembrance, that as the bread, which we eat at the Lord's table, is made of many grains one loaf, and the wine pressed together of sundry grapes is made one wine; so we being many are one body, whereof Christ is the head. And because we all are one body, we ought all to be beneficial one to another, one to love another, one to bear with another, one to wish well unto another, and one to do for another whatsoever we be able, even to the uttermost of our power, as our head Christ for our health and for our salvation disdained not to bestow his very life, and to suffer death, even the death of the cross, for our redemption. And as we presently, at the receiving of the holy mysteries of Christ's body and blood, do enjoy, through faith in God's promises, all the benefits which Christ obtained for us by his blessed death and glorious passion; so likewise ought they that be partakers of the Lord's table (every one according to their ability), at that present to be beneficial to the poor members of Christ, and somewhat to give that may relieve them, and ever after also, when occasion is given, gladly to distribute unto the needy some portion of their goods, wherewith God hath endued them. That this was the custom in the apostles' time, and in the primitive church, yea, and long after, till the popish mass had driven out of the church the right use of the Lord's supper, it is evident enough by divers testimonies both of the holy scriptures and of ancient histories.

THAT WE ARE ALL ONE BODY.

Probations out of the holy scriptures.

Rom. xii. "As we have many members in one body, and all members have not one office, so we being many are one body in Christ, and every man among ourselves one another's members."

1 Cor. x. "We, though we be many, yet are one bread and one body; inasmuch as we all are partakers of one bread."

1 Cor. xii. "As the body is one, and hath many members; and all the members of one body, though they be many, yet are but one body; even so is Christ. For by one Spirit are we all baptized to make one body, whether we be Jews or gentiles, whether we be bond or free; and have all drunk of one Spirit. For the body is not one member, but many, &c.; therefore if one member suffer, all suffer with him: if one member be had in honour, all members be glad also. Ye are the body of Christ, and members one of another."

OF THE DISTRIBUTION TO THE NEEDY.

Acts ii. "All that believed kept themselves together, and had all things common, and sold their possessions and goods, and parted them to all men, as every man had need."

Acts iv. "Great grace was there with all them that believed. Neither was there any among them that lacked. For as many as were possessors of lands or houses sold them, and brought the price of the things that were sold, and laid it down at the apostles' feet; and distribution was made unto every man according as he had need."

Rom. xii. "Distribute unto the[1] necessity of the saints. Be ready to harbour."

1 Cor. xvi. "As concerning the gathering for the saints,...let every one of you upon some sabbath-day put aside and lay up whatsoever is meet," &c.

2 Cor. viii. "It is not my mind that other be set at ease and ye brought into cumbrance; but that there be egalness[2] now at this time, and that your abundance may succour their lack, and that their abundance may supply your lack, that there may be equality:
Exod. xvi. agreeing to that which is written, He that had much had not the more abundance; and he that had little had never the less," &c.

Read the chapter.

2 Cor. ix. "Of the ministering to the saints, it is but superfluous for me to write unto you. For I know the readiness of your mind, &c. Yet this I say, He that soweth little shall reap little; and he that soweth (in giving) largely and freely shall reap plenteously. And let every man do according as he hath purposed in his heart, not grudgingly or of necessity: for God loveth a cheerful giver. God is able to make you rich in all grace, that ye, in all things having sufficient unto the uttermost, may be rich unto all manner
Psal. cxii. of good works; as it is written, He hath sparsed abroad and hath given to the poor: his righteousness remaineth for ever."

[[1] Folio, *unto thee the.*] [[2] Egalness: equality.]

"The office of this ministration not only supplieth the need of the saints, but also 2 Cor. ix.
is abundant herein, that for this laudable ministering thanks might be given to God of many; which praise God for the obedience of your consenting to the gospel of Christ, and for your singleness in distributing to them and to all men, and in their prayers for you, which long after you for the abundant grace of God in you. Thanks be unto God for his unspeakable gift.

THE DUTY OF ALL ESTATES AND DEGREES.

THE DUTY OF THE HIGH POWERS AND OF THE OTHER TEMPORAL MAGISTRATES.

The duty of the high powers and of the other temporal rulers is to be learned in the law of God, to maintain pure and christian religion, to nourish and defend the preachers and students of God's word, to banish all false religion and idolatry, to punish, yea, and if they will not turn, to kill the preachers and maintainers of false doctrine, to judge equally and indifferently without partiality, to take no bribes, nor to oppress the common people, but to care for them as a father for his children, to defend the good, to correct the evil, to avance virtue, and to punish vice.

THAT THEY OUGHT TO BE LEARNED IN THE LAWS OF GOD.

Probations out of the holy scripture.

"The king shall not multiply horses to himself,...neither ought he to multiply wives Deut. xvii.
unto himself, lest his heart turn away: neither shall he gather him silver and gold too much. And when he is set upon the seat of his kingdom, he shall write him out a copy of this law in a book. And it shall be with him; and he ought to read therein all the days of his life, that he may learn to fear the Lord his God, and to keep all the words of this law and these ordinances for to do them, and that his heart arise not above his brethren, and that he turn not from the commandment to the right hand or to the left, but that he may prolong his days in his kingdom."

"Let not the book of this law depart out of thy mouth, but record therein day and Josh. i.
night, that thou mayest observe and do according to all that is written therein. For then shalt thou make thy way prosperous, and then shalt thou do wisely."

"Get ye understanding now, O ye kings: be learned, ye that judge the earth. Psal. ii.
Serve the Lord in fear, and rejoice (unto him) with reverence. Kiss the Son, lest he be angry, and so ye perish from the right way."

"If your delight be in royal seats and sceptres, O ye kings of the people, set your Wisd. vi.
lust upon wisdom, that ye may reign for evermore." "O love the light of wisdom, all ye that be rulers of the people."

Read the ninth chapter of the Book of Wisdom.

THAT THEY OUGHT TO MAINTAIN PURE AND CHRISTIAN RELIGION.

Probations out of the holy scripture.

How greatly king David avanced God's religion, and sought his glory, the holy 1 Chron. xxiii. xxiv. xxvi. and xxviii.
scriptures make mention.

"Asa, king of Juda, did that was good and right in the eyes of the Lord his God. 2 Chron. xiv.
For he took away strange altars and the hill-altars[3], and brake down the images and cut down the groves, and commanded Juda to seek the Lord God of their fathers, and to do according to the law and commandment." "Yea, he put away all the abominable 1 Kings xv.
idols that his father had made. And he put down Maacha his mother for bearing rule, because she had made images in groves. And Asa destroyed her images, and

[3 Folio, *wyll alters.*]

burnt them by the brook Cedron." The Lord God therefore gave him and all his land[1] rest and quietness."

2 Chron. xvii. "Jeosaphat, king of Juda, sent to his lords...that they should teach in the cities of Juda, and with them he set Levites and priests. And they taught in Juda, and had the book of the law of God with them; and went about throughout all the cities of Juda, and taught the people. And the fear of the Lord fell upon all the kingdoms of the lands that were round about Juda, and they fought not against Jeosaphat." "And the Lord stablished the kingdom in his hand, and all they that were in Juda brought king Jeosaphat presents, so that he had abundance of riches and honour."

2 Kings xviii. King Hezekia put away the hill-altars, and brake the images, and cut down the groves, and all-to brake the brasen serpent that Moses had made. He renewed the feast 2 Chron. xxxi. of the passover. He ordained priests and Levites to serve the Lord God, and provided honest livings for them, that they might substantially apply themselves to the law of the Lord. And the Lord was with him; so that he prospered in all things which he took in hand.

2 Chron. xxxiv. The good king Josia, besides the purging of Juda and Jerusalem from hill-altars, groves, carved images, and images of metal, and such other kinds of idolatry, repaired the house of the Lord his God, renewed the feast of the passover, read in the ears of all the people the words of the law of the Lord, and made a faithful promise unto the Lord that he and all his people should walk according to the statutes of that book. And they turned not aside from the Lord God of their fathers, so long as he lived. The Lord God therefore deferred his plague that he had threatened to Juda, suffered Josia to live in much honour, and brought him to his grave in peace, so that his eyes did not see the mischief that the Lord God afterward brought immediately upon Jerusalem and upon the inhabiters of the same.

Isai. xlix. "Kings shall be thy nursing-fathers; and queens shall be thy nursing-mothers."

THAT THEY OUGHT TO PUNISH, YEA, AND IF THEY WILL NOT TURN, TO KILL THE PREACHERS AND MAINTAINERS OF FALSE DOCTRINE.

Probations out of the holy scriptures.

Deut. xiii. "If there rise among you a prophet, or a dreamer of dreams, and give thee a sign or wonder, and that sign or wonder which he hath said come to pass, and then say, Let us go after strange gods, which thou hast not known, and let us serve them; hearken not thou unto the words of that prophet or dreamer of dreams. For the Lord thy God proveth you, to wete, whether ye love the Lord your God with all your heart and with all your soul. Ye shall walk after the Lord your God, and fear him, and keep his commandment, and hearken unto his voice, serve him, and cleave unto him. And the prophet or dreamer of dreams shall die, because he hath spoken to turn you away from the Lord your God."

Deut. xviii. "The prophet which shall presume to speak a word in my name, which I have not commanded him to speak, or that he speaketh in the name of strange gods, the same prophet shall die."

2 Kings x. Jehu, king of Israel, caused all the priests of Baal to be slain, all the images to be fet out of the temple of Baal, and to be burnt. He caused also his captains and men of war to break the image of Baal, and to destroy the house of Baal; so that Baal's house was made a draught-house unto this day. And because Jehu thus sought the glory of God, and destroyed idolatry with the maintainers thereof, he lived quietly in his kingdom unto his dying day, and his children unto the fourth generation sat on the seat of Israel.

2 Kings xxiii. King Josia "put down the ministers of Baal, whom the kings of Juda had founded to burn incense in the hill-altars and cities of Juda that were round about Jerusalem, and also them that burnt incense unto Baal, to the sun, to the moon, to the planets, and to all the host of heaven."

[[1] Folio *lane*.]

THAT THEY OUGHT TO JUDGE EQUALLY.

Probations out of the holy scripture.

"Ye shall do no unrighteousness in judgment. Thou shalt not favour the poor, nor honour the mighty; but in righteousness shalt thou judge thy neighbour." Lev. xix.

Moses said to the judges: "Hear the cause of your brethren, and judge righteously between every man and his brother, and the stranger that is with him. See that ye know no faces in judgment; but hear the small as well as the great: and be afraid of no man; for the judgment is God's." Deut. i.

King Jehosaphat said also to the judges: "Take heed what ye do; for ye execute not the judgments of man, but of God, which is with you in the judgment. Wherefore now let the fear of the Lord be upon you, and take heed, and be doing the thing that pleaseth him. For there is no unrighteousness with the Lord our God, that should have any respect of persons, or take rewards." 2 Chron. xix.

"A king that sitteth in the throne of judgment, and looketh well about him, driveth away all evil." Prov. xx.

"He that saith to the ungodly, Thou art righteous; him shall the people curse, yea, the commenty shall abhor him. But they that rebuke the ungodly, in them doth God delight, and a rich blessing shall come upon them." Prov. xxiv.

"Judge the thing that is right, O ye sons of men." Psal. lviii.

"O love righteousness, ye that are the judges of the earth." Wisd. i.

THAT THEY OUGHT TO TAKE NO BRIBES.

Probations out of the holy scriptures.

"Thou shalt take no gifts; for gifts blind the sight, and pervert the words of the righteous." Exod. xxiii.

"Wrest not thou the law, nor know any person, neither take any reward; for gifts blind the wise, and pervert the words of the righteous. That which is just and right shalt thou follow, that thou mayest live, and enjoy the land which the Lord thy God giveth thee." Deut. xvi.

"Thou shalt seek out among all the people men of activity, and such as fear God, true men, hating covetousness; and make them heads over the people." Exod. xviii.

"The fire shall consume the houses of such as are greedy to receive gifts." Job xv.

"Wo be unto them that give sentence with the ungodly for rewards, but condemn the just cause of the righteous! Therefore, like as fire licketh up the straw, and as the flame consumeth the stubble, even so their root shall be as corruption, and their blossom shall vanish away like dust." Isai. v.

"He that keepeth his hand, that he touch no reward, and he which stoppeth his ears, that he hear no counsel against the innocent blood, he it is that shall dwell on high." Isai. xxxiii.

THAT THEY OUGHT NOT TO OPPRESS THE COMMON PEOPLE.

Probations out of the holy scripture.

"The increase and prosperity of the commons is the king's honour; but the decay of the people is the confusion of the prince." Prov. xiv.

"Like as a roaring lion, and as an hungry bear, even so is an ungodly prince over the poor people. Where the prince is without understanding, there is great oppression and wrong; but if he be such a one as hateth covetousness, he shall long reign." Prov. xxviii.

"When the righteous have the over-hand, the people are in prosperity; but when the ungodly bear rule, then that people mourn." Prov. xxix.

"With true judgment the king setteth up the land; but if he be a man that oppresseth the people with gatherings, he turneth it upside down."

Amos iv. "O hear this word, ye that do poor men wrong, and oppress the needy, ye that say to your lords, Bring hither, let us drink. Therefore the Lord hath sworn by his holiness, The days shall come upon you, that the enemies shall carry you away," &c.

Amos vi. "O wo be to the proud wealthy, to such as think themselves so sure, them which hold themselves for the best of the world, and rule the house of Israel even as they list!" "Ye are taken out for the evil day, even ye that sit in the stool of wilfulness. Ye that lie upon beds of ivory, and use your wantonness upon your couches; ye that eat the best lambs of the flock, and the fattest calves of the drove; ye that sing at the lute, and in playing of instruments compare yourselves unto David; ye that drink wine out of goblets, and anoint yourselves with the best oil; but as for Joseph's hurt, none of you all are sorry for it. Therefore now shall ye be the first of them that shall be led away captive; and the lusty cheer of the wilful shall come to an end, &c. The Lord is minded to smite the great houses. For ye have turned true judgment unto bitterness, and the fruit of righteousness into wormwood."

By Joseph is here understand the common people.

Amos viii. "O ye that oppress the poor, and destroy the needy in the land, shall not your destruction come upon you as a water-stream?" &c.

Mic. iii. "O ye heads of the house of Jacob, and ye leaders of the house of Israel, should not ye know what were lawful and right? But ye hate the good, and love the evil. Ye pluck off men's skins, and the flesh from their bones. Ye eat the flesh of my people, and flay off their skin, ye break their bones, ye chop them in pieces as it were into a cauldron, and as flesh into a pot. Now the time shall come that, when they call unto the Lord, he shall not hear them, but hide his face from them; because that through their own imaginations they have dealt so wickedly," &c.

1 Sam. xii. "Behold, here am I," said Samuel to the children of Israel: "bear record of me before the Lord, and before his anointed. Whose ox have I taken? or whose ass have I taken? whom have I done wrong to? whom have I hurt? or of whose hand have I received any bribe to blind mine eyes therewith? and I will restore it you again. They said, Thou hast done us no wrong, nor hurt us, neither hast thou taken ought of any man's hand. He said unto them again, The Lord is witness against you, and his anointed is witness this day, that ye have no evil in my hands."

A mirror for magistrates.

1 Kings xii. What chanced to Rehoboam, king Salomon's son, for the ungentle entreating of his commons, the holy histories do testify.

Read 1 Kings xii.

THAT THEY OUGHT TO CARE FOR THE COMMONS, AS A FATHER FOR HIS CHILDREN.

Probations out of the holy scripture.

Prov. xx. "Mercy and faithfulness preserve the king; and with loving-kindness his seat is holden up."

Ecclus. xxxii. "If thou be made a ruler, pride not thyself therein; but be thou as one of the people. Take diligent care for them, and look well thereto; and when thou hast done all thy duty, set thee down, that thou mayest be merry with them, and receive a crown of honour."

With how fatherly a care Moyses, Samuel, David, and divers other noble princes governed their people, the holy scriptures do evidently declare.

THAT THEY OUGHT TO DEFEND THE GOOD, AND TO CORRECT THE EVIL, TO AVANCE VIRTUE, AND TO PUNISH VICE.

Probations out of the holy scripture.

Isai. i. "Learn to do right: apply yourselves to equity: deliver the oppressed: help the fatherless to his right: let the widow's complaint come before you."

Jer. xxii. "Thus the Lord commandeth, Keep equity and righteousness: deliver the oppressed from the power of the violent: do not grieve nor oppress the stranger, the fatherless, nor the widow; and shed no innocent blood."

"Execute true judgment: shew mercy and loving-kindness every man to his brother. Do the widow, the fatherless, the stranger, and poor no wrong; and let no man imagine evil against his brother in his heart." Zech. vii.

"Deliver him that suffereth wrong from the hand of the oppressor, and be not faint-hearted when thou sittest in judgment. Be merciful unto the fatherless as a father, and be instead of an husband unto their mother; so shalt thou be as an obedient son of the Highest, and he shall love thee more than thy mother doth." Ecclus. iv.

"My song shall be of mercy and judgment: unto thee, O Lord, will I sing. O let me have understanding in the way of godliness. When wilt thou come unto me? I will walk in my house with a perfect heart. I will take no wicked thing in hand: I hate the sins of unfaithfulness: there shall no such cleave unto me. A froward heart shall depart from me: I will not know a wicked person. Whoso privily slandereth his neighbour, him will I destroy. Whoso hath also a proud look and an high stomach, I will not suffer him. Mine eyes look unto such as be faithful in the land, that they may dwell with me. Whoso leadeth a godly life, he shall be my servant. There shall no deceitful person dwell in my house: he that telleth lies shall not tarry in my sight. I shall soon destroy all the ungodly that are in the land, that I may root out all wicked doers from the city of the Lord." Psal. ci.

"Rulers are not fearful to them that do good, but to them that do evil. Wilt thou be without fear of the power? Do well then, and so shalt thou be praised of the same. For he is the minister of God for thy wealth. But and if thou do that which is evil, then fear; for he beareth not the sword for nought: for he is the minister of God to take vengeance on him that doeth evil." Rom. xiii.

THE DUTY OF SUBJECTS UNTO THE HIGH POWERS.

The duty of subjects unto the high powers is honourably to speak of them, heartily to love and reverence them, humbly to obey them for conscience sake in all things that fight not with God's word, fervently to pray for them, and willingly to pay such charges unto them as they reasonably require, either for the maintenance of their prince-like estate, or else for the safeguard of the commonwealth.

Probations out of the holy scriptures.

"Thou shalt not rail upon the gods," that is to say, the temporal magistrates, which execute that office of God, "neither blaspheme the ruler of thy people." Exod. xxii.

"Wish the king no evil in thy thought, and speak no hurt of the rich in thy privy chamber; for a bird of the air shall betray thy voice, and with her feathers shall she betray thy words." Eccles. x.

"Let every soul submit himself unto the higher powers. For there is no power but of God: the powers that be are ordained of God. Whosoever therefore resisteth the power resisteth the ordinance of God; but they that resist shall receive to themselves damnation. For rulers are not fearful to them that do good, but to them that do evil. Wilt thou be without fear of the power? do well then, and so shalt thou be praised of the same. For he is the minister of God for thy wealth. But if thou do that which is evil, then fear; for he beareth not the sword for nought: for he is the minister of God to take vengeance on him that doth evil. Wherefore ye must needs obey, not only for fear of punishment, but also for conscience sake. And for this cause pay ye tribute. For they are God's ministers, serving for the same purpose. Give to every man therefore his duty; tribute to whom tribute belongeth; custom to whom custom is due; fear to whom fear belongeth; honour to whom honour pertaineth." Rom. xiii.

"I exhort that above all things prayers, supplications, intercessions, and giving of thanks, be had for all men; for kings, and for all that are in authority; that we may live a quiet and peaceable life with all godliness and honesty. For that is good and accepted in the sight of God our Saviour." 1 Tim. ii.

"Warn the subjects that they submit themselves to rule and power, that they Tit. iii.

obey the officers, that they be ready unto every good work, that they speak evil of no man, that they be no fighters, but gentle, shewing meekness unto all men."

1 Pet. ii. "Submit yourselves unto all manner ordinance of man for the Lord's sake; whether it be unto the king, as unto the chief head; either unto rulers, as unto them that are sent of him for the punishment of evil-doers, but for the praise of them that do well, &c. Fear God, honour the king."

THE DUTY OF BISHOPS AND MINISTERS OF GOD'S WORD.

The duty of bishops and ministers of God's word is, first, to feed Christ's flock with the sweet bread of Christ's gospel, without mingling of the Pharisees' leaven: secondly, to lead a life agreeable to their doctrine, that they may teach both with word and work: thirdly, to relieve the poor and needy with such goods as they receive of the church, either by maintaining hospitality, or else by some other godly means.

Probations out of the holy scripture.

OF DOCTRINE.

Isai. xl. "Go up unto the high hill, thou that bringest good tidings: lift up thy voice with power, O thou preacher, lift it up, and be not afraid."

Isai. lviii. "Cry now as loud as thou canst. Leave not off, lift up thy voice like a trumpet, and shew my people their offences, and the house of Jacob their sins."

Isai. lxii. "I have set watchmen upon thy walls, O Jerusalem, which shall neither cease day nor night to preach the Lord."

Jer. i. "Behold, I put my words in thy mouth; and behold, this day do I set thee over the people and kingdoms; that thou mayest root out, break off, destroy, and make waste, and that thou mayest build up and plant."

Ezek. iii. "Thou son of man, I have made thee a watchman unto the house of Israel: therefore take good heed to the words of my mouth, and give them warning at my commandment. If I say unto thee concerning the ungodly man, that without doubt he must die; and thou givest him not warning, nor speakest unto him that he may turn from his evil way, and so to live; then shall the same ungodly man die in his own unrighteousness; but his blood will I require of thy hand. Nevertheless, if thou give warning unto the wicked, and he yet forsake not his ungodliness, then shall he die in his own wickedness; but thou hast discharged thy soul."

John xxi. If thou lovest me, "feed my sheep."

1 Cor. ix. "Wo unto me if I preach not the gospel!"

2 Cor. iv. "We preach not ourselves, but Jesus Christ our Lord."

2 Cor. ii. "We are not as the most part are, which chop and change with the word of God; but out of pureness, and by the power of God, in the sight of God, so speak we in Christ."

Gal. i. "Though we ourselves, or an angel from heaven, preach any other gospel unto you, than that which we have preached unto you, let him be accursed."

1 Tim. iii. "A bishop must be meet to teach."

1 Tim. iv. "Give attendance to reading, to exhortation, to doctrine."

2 Tim. iv. "Preach thou the word: be fervent in season and out of season: improve, rebuke, exhort with all long-suffering and doctrine," &c.

OF LIFE AND CONVERSATION.

Psal. l. "God said to the ungodly, Why dost thou preach my laws, and takest my testament in thy mouth? where thou hatest to be reformed, and hast cast my words behind thee. When as thou sawest a thief, thou consentest unto him, and hast been partaker with the advouterers."

Matt. v. "Whosoever doeth and teacheth, the same shall be called great in the kingdom of heaven."

"Be unto them that believe an ensample in word, in conversation, in love, in spirit, in faith, in pureness." 1 Tim. iv.

"Keep thyself pure." 1 Tim. v.

"Study to shew thyself laudable unto God, a workman that needeth not to be ashamed, distributing the word of truth justly." 2 Tim. ii.

"In all things shew thyself an ensample of good works, in the doctrine with honesty, gravity, and with the wholesome word, which cannot be rebuked; that he which withstandeth may be ashamed, having no evil thing to say of you." Tit. ii.

"Feed ye Christ's flock, as much as lieth in you, taking the oversight of them not as compelled thereto, but willingly; not for the desire of filthy lucre, but of a good mind; not as though ye were lords over the parishes, but that ye be an ensample to the flock. And when the chief Shepherd shall appear, ye shall receive an incorruptible crown of glory." 1 Pet. v.

OF HOSPITALITY.

"Distribute unto the necessity of the saints. Be ready to harbour." Rom. xii.

"A bishop must be a maintainer of hospitality." 1 Tim. iii.

"Forget not hospitality. For thereby have divers men lodged angels unwares." Heb. xiii.

THE DUTY OF PARISHIONERS UNTO THE MINISTERS OF GOD'S WORD.

The duty of parishioners unto the ministers of God's word is outwardly to honour and reverence them, to receive them as the angels and embassadors of God, to regard them as the ministers and stewards of God's mysteries, and liberally to give unto them whatsoever is necessary for the maintenance of their degree and estate; that they may quietly give their minds to the study of godly letters, to prayer, to the preaching of God's word, and to the ministration of the sacraments.

Probations out of the holy scriptures.

"Fear the Lord with all thy soul, and honour his ministers. Love thy Maker with all thy strength, and forsake not his ministers. Honour God with all thy soul, and reverence his priests. Give them their portion of the first-fruits and increase of the earth, like as it is commanded thee." Ecclus. vii.

"The priests that rule well are worthy of double honour, most specially they which labour in the word and teaching." 1 Tim. v.

"We beseech you, brethren, that ye know them which labour among you, and have the oversight of you in the Lord, and give you exhortation, that ye have them in high reputation through love for their work's sake, and be at peace with them." 1 Thess. v.

"Obey them that have the oversight of you, and submit yourselves unto them; for they watch for your souls, even as they that must give accompts; that they may do it with joy, and not with grief." Heb. xiii.

"In the priest's lips should be sure knowledge, that men may seek the law at his mouth; for he is the angel of the Lord of hosts." Mal. ii.

"Ye despised me not, neither did ye abhor me; but ye received me as an angel of God, yea, even as Christ Jesus. For I bear you record, that, if it had been possible, ye would have plucked out your own eyes, and have given them to me." Gal. iv.

"He that receiveth you receiveth me, and he that receiveth me receiveth him that sent me," &c. Matt. x.

"He that heareth you heareth me. He that despiseth you despiseth me, and he that despiseth me despiseth him that sent me." Luke x.

"Let a man this wise esteem us, even as the ministers of Christ and stewards of the mysteries of God." 1 Cor. iv.

"Bring every tithe into my barn, that there may be meat in my house." Mal. iii.

"The workman is worthy of his meat." Matt. x.

"If the gentiles be made partakers of their spiritual things, their duty is to minister unto them in bodily things." Rom. xv.

1 Cor. ix. "It is written in the law of Moses, Thou shalt not muzzle the mouth of the ox that treadeth out the corn. Doth God take thought for oxen? Saith he it not altogether for our sake? For our sake, no doubt, this is written; that he which eareth should ear in hope; and that he which thresheth in hope should be partaker of his hope. If we sow unto you spiritual things, is it a great thing if we reap your bodily things?...Do ye not know how that they which minister about holy things live of the sacrifice? They which wait of the temple are partakers of the temple. Even so also did the Lord ordain, that they which preach the gospel should live of the gospel."

"Who goeth a warfare any time at his own cost? Who planteth a vineyard, and eateth not of the fruit thereof? Or who feedeth a flock, and eateth not of the milk of the flock?" &c.

Gal. vi. "Let him that is taught in the word minister unto him that teacheth him in all good things. Be not deceived. God is not mocked," &c.

1 Tim. v. Deut. xxv. 1 Cor. ix. Matt. x. "The priests that rule well are worthy of double honour, most specially they which labour in the word and teaching. For the scripture saith, Thou shalt not muzzle the mouth of the ox that treadeth out the corn: and, The labourer is worthy of his reward."

THE DUTY OF HUSBANDS UNTO THEIR WIVES.

The duty of a faithful husband unto his wife is to forsake all other for her sake, to cleave only to his wife, to love her as Christ loved the congregation, to cherish her as he would cherish his own body, to provide for her, to teach her the law of God, to dwell with her according to knowledge, and to give honour unto her, although the weaker vessel, as to one that is fellow-heir with him of the grace of life.

Probations out of the holy scripture.

Gen. ii. "This is now bone of my bones, and flesh of my flesh. She shall be called woman, because she was taken out of man. For this cause shall a man leave his father and mother, and shall be joined with his wife, and they shall become one flesh."

Prov. v. "Be glad with the wife of thy youth." "Let her breasts alway satisfy thee, and hold thee ever content with her love. My son, why wilt thou have pleasure in an harlot, and embrace the bosom of another woman?" &c.

Eph. v. "Ye husbands, love your wives, even as Christ also loved the congregation, and gave himself for it, to sanctify it, and cleansed it in the fountain of water through the word, to make it unto himself a glorious congregation, without spot, or wrinkle, or any such thing; but that it should be holy and without blame. So ought men to love their wives as their own bodies. He that loveth his wife loveth himself. For no man ever yet hated his own flesh, but nourisheth and cherisheth it, even as the Lord doth the congregation," &c.

Col. iii. "Ye husbands, love your wives, and be not bitter to them."

1 Pet. iii. "Ye men, dwell with your wives according to knowledge, giving honour unto the wife, as unto the weaker vessel, and as unto them that are heirs also of the grace of life."

THE DUTY OF WIVES UNTO THEIR HUSBANDS.

The duty of an honest faithful woman unto her husband is to knowledge her husband to be her head, to be subject unto him, to reverence him, to obey him, quietly to learn of him, to lead a blameless life, to use much silence, peaceably and circumspectly to look unto her household, and to tire herself with such apparel as becometh a sober christian woman.

Probations out of the holy scripture.

Eph. v. "Ye women, submit yourselves unto your own husbands, as unto the Lord. For the husband is the wife's head, even as Christ is the head of the congregation; and the same is he that ministereth salvation to the body. Therefore, as the congregation is in subjection to Christ, even so let the wives be in subjection to their husbands in all things."

"Ye wives, submit yourselves unto your own husbands, as it is comely in the Lord." Col. iii.

"Let the women learn in silence with all subjection. But I suffer not a woman 1 Tim. ii.
to teach, neither to usurp authority over the man, but to be in silence."

"I will that women array themselves in comely apparel, with shamefacedness and discreet behaviour; not with broided hair, either gold, or pearls, or costly array; but as it becometh women that profess godliness through good works."

"Ye wives, be in subjection to your husbands; that even they which obey not 1 Pet. iii.
the word may without the word be won by the conversation of the wives; while they behold your chaste conversation coupled with fear. Whose apparel shall not be outward with broidered hair and hanging on of gold, either in putting on of gorgeous apparel; but let the hid man, which is in the heart, be without all corruption, so that the spirit be at rest and quiet, which spirit before God is a thing much set by. For after this manner in the old time did the holy women, which trusted in God, tire themselves, and were obedient to their husbands; even as Sara obeyed Abraham, and called him lord: whose daughters ye are, so long as ye do well."

THE DUTY OF FATHERS AND MOTHERS UNTO THEIR CHILDREN.

The duty of fathers and mothers unto their children is to train them up in the law of God, to teach them to know God and his holy word even from their cradles, to bring them up in good learning and necessary acts, to bridle them from the foolish and noisome lusts of youth, and to garnish their life with sober and grave manners.

Probations out of the holy scripture.

"Set your hearts unto all the words which I testify unto you this day, and ye Deut. xxxii.
shall command them unto your children, that they may observe and do all the words of this law."

"If thou have sons, bring them up in nurture and learning, and hold them in Ecclus. vii.
awe from their youth up. If thou have daughters, keep their body, and shew not thy face cheerful toward them. Marry thy daughter, and so shalt thou perform a weighty matter; but give her to a man of understanding."

"He that teacheth his son shall have joy in him and need not to be ashamed of Ecclus. xxx.
him among his acquaintance."

"He that spareth the rod hateth his son; but whoso loveth him chasteneth him Prov. xiii.
betimes."

"Ye fathers, move not your children to wrath; but bring them up through the Eph. vi.
doctrine and information of the Lord."

How godly Salomon, young Thoby, Susanna, Philip the evangelist's daughters, Timothy, and such like, were brought up of their parents, the holy scriptures bear witness.

THE DUTY OF CHILDREN TOWARD THEIR FATHERS AND MOTHERS.

The duty of children toward their parents is in their mind to love them, outwardly to reverence and honour them, to obey them in all things that are agreeable to God's will, and if they chance to fall into poverty, to help them, and to give them whereof to live.

Probations out of the holy scriptures.

"Honour thy father from thy whole heart, and forget not the sorrowful travail Ecclus. vii.
that thy mother had with thee. Remember that thou wast born through them; and how canst thou recompense them the things that they have done for thee?"

"Children, obey your fathers and mothers in the Lord; for that is right. Honour Eph. vi.
thy father and mother (the same is the first commandment in the promise); that thou mayest prosper, and live long on earth."

Read the confirmations of the fifth commandment.

THE DUTY OF MASTERS TO THEIR SERVANTS.

The duty of masters to their servants is to entreat them gently, to give them their covenants, and to help them, that they may afterward be able to live.

Probations out of the holy scripture.

Ecclus. vii. "Where as thy servant worketh truly, entreat him not evil, nor the hireling that is faithful unto thee. Love a discreet servant as thine own soul: defraud him not of his liberty, neither leave him a poor man."

Col. iv. "Ye masters, do unto your servants that which is just and equal, putting away threatenings; knowing that ye also have a Master in heaven, neither is there any respect of persons with him."

THE DUTY OF SERVANTS TO THEIR MASTERS.

The duty of servants to their masters is willingly and with a free courage to serve them even for conscience sake, not with the eye but with the heart, to obey them, to honour them, gently to answer them, not to pick or steal away their goods, but to be faithful unto them in all things.

Probations out of the holy scripture.

Eph. vi. "Ye servants, obey them that are your bodily masters with fear and trembling, even with the singleness of your heart, as unto Christ; not doing service unto the eye, as they that go about to please men; but as the servants of Christ, doing the will of God from the heart, with good-will serving the Lord, and not men; knowing this, that whatsoever good deed any man doth, the same shall he receive again of God, whether he be bond or free."

1 Tim. vi. "Let as many servants as are under the yoke count their masters worthy of all honour, that the name of God and his doctrine be not evil spoken of."

Tit. ii. "Exhort servants to be obedient unto their own masters, and to please them in all things, not answering again, neither to be pickers, but that they shew all good faithfulness; that they may do worship to the doctrine of God our Saviour in all things."

THE DUTY OF WIDOWS.

The duty of true ancient widows (besides the looking to their own household, and provision-making for their living) is to put their trust in God, to give themselves to the exercises of the Spirit, to frequent the temple, to be present at the sermons, to visit the sick, to relieve the needy, to be rich in good works, and to continue in supplications and prayers both day and night. But as touching the younger widows, lest they should wax wanton against Christ and follow Satan, breaking their first faith and promise that they made to God at their baptism (which is to abstain from all uncleanness both of body and mind, and to lead a pure and honest life), and so cast themselves into the danger of everlasting damnation, it is convenient that they marry again, bring forth children, guide their house virtuously, and so live in the holy state of matrimony, that no man may have occasion to speak evil of them.

Probations out of the holy scripture.

1 Tim. v. "She that is a true widow and friendless putteth her trust in God, and continueth in supplications and prayers day and night."

Judith viii. Judith, that virtuous widow, "in the higher parts of her house made herself a privy chamber, where she dwelt, being closed in with her maids. She ware a smock of hair, and fasted all the days of her life, except the sabbaths and new moons and the solemn days that the people of Israel kept.... She was a woman of a very good report with every one; for she feared the Lord greatly, and there was nobody that spake an evil word of her."

The godly ancient widow Anna "departed not from the temple, but served God with fastings and prayers night and day." Luke ii.

OF THE YOUNGER WIDOWS.

"The younger widows refuse. For when they have begun to wax wanton against Christ they will marry, having damnation, because they have cast away their first faith. And also they learn to go from house to house idle; yea, not idle only, but also tattlers and busy-bodies, speaking things which are not comely. I will therefore that the younger women marry, to bear children, to guide the house, and give none occasion to the adversary to speak evil." 1 Tim. v.

THE DUTY OF OLD MEN.

The duty of old men is to avoid all lightness, both in word, deed, and countenance, to talk of wisdom and grave matters, to be sober, sage, and discreet, and to lead a pure and undefiled life, that they may be an ensample of true godliness to the younger folk.

Probations out of the holy scripture.

God hateth "an old body that doteth, and is unchaste." Ecclus. xxv.

"Age is an honourable thing: nevertheless it standeth not only in the length of time, nor in the multitude of years; but a man's wisdom is the gray hair, and an undefiled life is the old age." Wisd. iv.

"Exhort the elder men to be sober, sage, discreet, sound in the faith, in love, in patience." Tit. ii

THE DUTY OF OLD WOMEN.

The duty of old women is, as in age, so in manners, to be sober, sage, and ancient; to wear no light apparel, but such raiment as become their age and profession; to be no tattlers, but to order their tongues discreetly; to be no tavern-hunters, nor given to drunkenness, but to lead a sober life; to provoke no young women unto lewdness and dishonesty, but rather to shew themselves lively glasses and natural mirrors of all godliness and honesty.

Probations out of the holy scriptures.

"Exhort the elder women that they be in such raiment as becometh holiness; not being false accusers, not given to much wine, but that they teach honest things; to make the young women sober-minded, to love their husbands, to love their children, to be discreet, chaste, housewifely, good, obedient to their husbands, that the word of God be not evil spoken of." Tit. ii.

THE DUTY OF YOUNG FOLK.

The duty of young folk is not to be proud, but humble, lowly, and gentle; gladly to hear the discreet talk of their elders, and to be ordered by them; not to be rash, but sober-minded in all their doings.

Probations out of the holy scriptures.

"Ye younger folk, submit yourselves unto the elders. Submit yourselves every man one to another, knit yourselves together in lowliness of mind. For God resisteth the proud, and giveth grace to the humble." 1 Pet. v.

"Thou young man, keep company with the multitude of such elders as have understanding, and consent unto their wisdom with thine heart, that thou mayest hear all godly sermons, and that the worthy sentences escape thee not," &c. Ecclus. vi.

"If thou be among men of higher authority, desire not to compare thyself unto them; and when an elder speaketh, make not thou many words." Ecclus. xxxii.

"Exhort the young men that they be sober-minded."

THE DUTY OF ALL DEGREES AND ESTATES GENERALLY, BOTH TOWARD GOD AND THEIR NEIGHBOUR.

The duty of all degrees and estates generally, both toward God and their neighbour, is to believe in God, to fear God and to keep his commandments, to love God above all things, and our neighbour as ourself, and to do none otherwise unto other than we wish to be done unto ourself.

Probations out of the holy scripture.

John xiv. "Ye believe in God, believe also in me," saith Christ.

Eccles. xii. "Fear God, and keep his commandments. For that belongeth to all men."

Matt. xxii. "Thou shalt love the Lord thy God with all thy heart, with all thy soul, and with all thy mind. This is the first and great commandment. The second is like unto this: Thou shalt love thy neighbour as thyself. In these two commandments are contained the whole law and prophets."

Matt. vii. "Whatsoever ye would that men should do to you, do ye even the same to them also. For this is the law and the prophets."

Give the glory to God alone.

A FRUITFUL

TREATISE OF FASTING,

BY

THOMAS BECON.

A fruitfull treatise of fasting, wherin is declared what ye Christen fast is, how we ought to fast, & what the true vse of fasting is. New lye made by *Thomas Becon.*

Mathew. vi.

When ye fast, be not sad, as the hipocrites are.

Luke. xxi.

Take hede to your selues, lest at anye tyme your heartes be ouercome with surfetyng and dronkennes.

Roma. xiii.

Make not prouisyon for the flesh to fulfyll the lustes, of it.

ii. Cor. vi.

Let vs giue no occasion of euil, that our office be not euyll spoken of, but in al thinges let vs behaue our selues as the ministers of God in muche pacience in watchynges and fastynges.

Ephe. v.

Be not dronke wyth wyne, wherin is excesse, but be fylled with the spirit.

TO THE

MOST REVEREND FATHER IN GOD,

THOMAS[1], ARCHBISHOP OF CANTERBURY,

PRIMATE OF ALL ENGLAND, AND METROPOLITAN, THOMAS BECON, HIS HUMBLE AND FAITHFUL SERVANT, WISHETH THE FAVOUR OF GOD, LONG LIFE, CONTINUAL HEALTH, AND PROSPEROUS FELICITY.

OUR Lord and alone Saviour Jesu Christ declareth in a parable of the gospel, that after a certain householder had sowed good seed in his field, while his servants slept, Matt. xiii. his enemy came and sowed tares among the wheat, and went his way. This householder is Christ the Lord. The good seed is the children of God and God's word. The servants that slept are negligent prelates and sleepy shepherds, which watch not over the Lord's flock. The enemy is the devil. The tares are the children of the wicked, and errors and heresies, which Satan soweth in the hearts of the unbelieving.

Of this parable, as we learn the goodness of Christ toward us in begetting us anew, "not of mortal seed, but of immortal by the word of God, which liveth and lasteth for 1 Pet. i. ever," so likewise learn we the maliciousness of Satan, which, like a subtile serpent and old enemy of mankind, never sleepeth, but continually "walketh up and down 1 Pet. v. like a roaring lion, seeking whom he may devour," and warely watcheth his time to destroy, whensoever any occasion is given, be it never so little. Not without a great cause therefore did our Saviour Christ exhort us to watch and pray, that we fall not into temptation.

And albeit in this our frail and sinful life many occasions of doing mischief be offered Matt. xxvi. to the enemy on our behalf, such is our negligence and uncircumspect behaviour; yet the greatest occasion, wherein Satan most glorieth and soonest hopeth for the victory, is when the shepherds of Christ's flock give no attendance to their charge, but lie sleep- Isai. lvi. ing and snorting, wallowing and weltering in their pleasures, and suffer the wolf to John x. scatter, yea, to catch, to kill, and to destroy the sheep. For although the devil letteth go no proffer which may move him to do evil, but layeth hand on it straightways; yet, as the histories both of the holy scriptures and of credible writers do testify, he never sheweth himself so right a devil, nor so lively setteth forth himself in his true colours, as when the guides of the Lord's flock be either absent from their sheep, or else are negligent in doing their duty,—I mean, in preaching God's word, and in writing godly books, if need require, for the confutation of errors and heresies, and for the establishment of God's holy religion.

How soon had the people of Israel forgotten God and his goodness toward them, after Moses was gone from them into the mount Sinai to talk with God, and to receive Exod. xxxii. the law! Fell they not straightways from the one and alone true and living God unto abominable idolatry, and worshipped a golden calf? After the days of Moses and of other godly prophets and preachers, when wicked kings reigned, and the preaching of God's word ceased, did not the people of Israel fall to the worshipping of strange gods, and made of the brasen serpent, which was but a sacrament and figure of Christ, a god, John iii. and brent sacrifice unto it? Certain years before the coming of Christ into this world, 2 Kings xviii. into how many sects and sundry religions were the Jews divided among themselves, which notwithstanding counted themselves only the people of God, and hated all other nations as abominable idolaters! Yea, in the time of the apostles, were there not

---

[1 Archbishop Cranmer.]

that denied Christ to be either true God or true man? How soon were the Corinthians and Galatians seduced by false apostles, after that the most worthy apostle St Paul was departed from them! How many kind of heretics rose there up in the church of Christ after the apostles' time! What great and how many contentions, both in sermons, disputations, and writings, had the holy bishops and godly fathers of the primitive church with the heretics of their time, for the maintenance of God's truth, and for plucking up the enemy's tares! Since the time that those virtuous bishops and learned fathers of Christ's church died, into how many sects have the people that profess God be divided! The number of sects and counterfeit religions, which yet live under the bishop of Rome, are almost innumerable. Neither ceaseth Satan, even in this most clear light of the gospel, to play the right devil, and to cast mists before the eyes of the unfaithful. Into how many sects is Christendom yet divided! Are not some called papists, some protestants, some anabaptists, some sacramentaries? Whence come all these abominations but only from Satan, the author of all evil? Moreover, in what field, where good seed hath been sowed, hath not the enemy sowed his tares also? how pestilently hath he corrupted the pure wheat of God's word with mingling his chaff, dross, darnel, cockle, and tares, I mean the false gloses and unsavoury expositions of the papists, anabaptists, and such other sectaries! How wickedly hath he perverted the right use of the sacraments, specially the sacrament of Christ's body and blood! fasting, prayer, and alms-deed, how hath he made to be abused! There is no point of christian religion, which Satan hath not attempted to overthrow by his ministers.

And albeit, as I said before, the enemy laboureth at all times to sow his tares in the Lord's field; yet, when the shepherds of Christ's flock be negligent in doing their duty, fall asleep, and look not to the Lord's field, then doth he most of all play his part, and bestir him like a right devil, as Salomon saith: "When the preaching of God's word faileth, the people perish." Prov. xxix.

It therefore becometh all men that tender the glory of God, but specially the Lord's ministers, to look diligently unto their Lord's field, and earnestly to take heed that the enemy sow not his tares among the Lord's wheat. If any be sowed, it is their duty to labour even to the uttermost of their power, not with violence and corporal armours, (for the use of the secular sword is not committed to the preachers of God's word, but to the temporal rulers only, to punish malefactors;) but with "the sword of the Spirit, which is the word of God," with prayers, supplications and tears, to weed them out. "The weapons of our warfare," saith St Paul, "are not carnal things, but things mighty in God to cast down strong-holds, wherewith we overthrow counsels, and every high thing that exalteth itself against the knowledge of God, and bring into captivity all imagination to the obedience of Christ." Luke xxii. Rom. xiii. Eph. vi. 2 Cor. x.

And in this behalf, (I mean, in plucking up the enemy's tares, and in purging the Lord's field that nothing may grow therein but pure wheat,) your both godly and unrestful pains, most reverend father, are well known in this church of England, and thankfully accepted of all faithful christian hearts; insomuch that very many do daily render unto God most humble and hearty thanks for the singular and great benefits, which they have received of him through your virtuous travail, in attaining unto the true knowledge of justification, of the sacrament of Christ's body and blood, and such other holy mysteries of our profession. And albeit the devil roar, the world rage, and the hypocrites swell at these your most christian labours, which you willingly take for the glory of God and the edifying of his congregation; yet as ye have godly begun, so without ceasing continue unto the end. By this means shall it come to pass, that "when the chief Shepherd shall appear, ye shall receive an incorruptible crown of glory." 1 Pet. v.

And forasmuch as so many as the Lord hath appointed watchmen over his flock ought, every one according to their talent, to follow your godly example in weeding out errors, and planting true and christian opinions in the hearts of the people, seeing that Satan hath not a little corrupted the true use of fasting, which being rightly used doth highly please God, and abused displeaseth him, I thought it good against this time of Lent, which of long continuance hath been appointed to abstinence, to write somewhat of fasting, that might both open a way to the faithful how they may fast to please God, and also disclose the false manner of fasting brought in by the devil and his ministers.

And in this my treatise I have, first, declared what the christian fast is; secondly, how we ought to fast; and, thirdly, what the true use of fasting is. I took this labour upon me the more gladly, partly because no man hitherto hath written of that matter in our English tongue; partly to satisfy the hearty requests of divers faithful brethren, which ceased not to require me in the Lord's name to write somewhat that might instruct them in the true use of fasting. The matter, I grant, requireth a workman of riper judgment, and more exercised in the Lord's harvest than I am, which might, according to the worthiness of the matter, have set it forth pleasantly and learnedly; but, seeing no man hath hitherto taken it in hand, I thought it my part not to deny the godly requests of the brethren, but gladly to bestow upon them whatsoever the Lord hath given me in this behalf. The contents of this book.

This treatise, whatsoever it is, I your humble and faithful servant, not having otherwise wherewith to testify the thankfulness of my heart toward your most honourable lordship, for the manifold benefits which ye have bounteously bestowed upon me, do dedicate to your name, most humbly beseeching you, according to your accustomed gentleness, to take in good part this my rude and gross work, which to polish and to make neat, if ability had served, shortness of time would not suffer. God, whose honour you most desirously seek, mought vouchsafe to preserve your grace in continual health and prosperous felicity unto the glory of his most blessed name, and the profit of his holy congregation! Amen.

A

TREATISE OF FASTING.

WHAT THE TRUE AND CHRISTIAN FAST IS.

The First Chapter.

The definition of the true fast.

THE true and christian fast is freely and willingly to abstain not only from all kind of meats and drinks, but also from all those things wherein the flesh hath pleasure and delectation; which abstinence or forbearing of meats, drinks, and other pleasures, wherein the outward man delighteth, riseth either of an heart contrite and sorrowful for the sins committed against God, or else of a mind fervently given to godliness.

The fast of the fathers of the old law.

That this is a true definition of the christian fast, it may be easily proved out of the holy scriptures. First, to whom is it unknown, that when the holy men in times past fasted, their manner was, so long as the fast continued, to abstain from all kind of meats and drinks, and from all pleasures wherein the flesh delighteth, and wholly to give themselves (all worldly affairs set apart) to godly exercises; as to the hearty and unfeigned lamenting of their sins, wherewith too much unkindly they had offended their Lord God, and provoked his fierce wrath and vengeance to fall on them; to fervent prayer and diligent calling on the name of God for turning away his heavy displeasure from them, and for remission of their sins through faith in the holy sacrifice to come of that blessed Seed of the woman, which by his own and alone oblation they believed should reconcile mankind to God the Father, pacify his wrath, and make him a merciful Lord; to the hearing and reading of God's word; to the comforting of one another; to the study of amendment of life; to the provision-making for the poor; to the redress of abuses in the commonweal; to the planting of true godliness, and abolishing of all wicked and strange religion? Of this manner of fasting speaketh the prophet, when he saith, "Hallow ye a fast;" meaning that they which fast should, in the time of their fasting, occupy themselves in spiritual, and not in worldly exercises; or else is it no fast before God.

Spiritual exercises in the time of fasting.

Joel i. ii.

The Second Chapter.

THIS abstinence, or forbearing of meats, did always continue at the least one whole day without receiving of any corporal sustenance, many times two or three days, as the histories of the holy scripture teach us.

Judg. xx.

The Israelites, when they saw so great a multitude of their people slain of the Benjamites in the battle, went up and came unto Bethel, where the ark of the appointment of God was in those days, wept, sat there praying before the Lord, and fasted the same day unto even, and offered burnt-offerings and peace-offerings before the Lord. Again, when the Israelites gathered together at Mizpha, lamenting their sins and praying unto the Lord for help against the Philistines, they fasted the whole day. So likewise did David and they that were with him, when they heard that Saul and his sons were slain in battle. Nehemiah fasted two days together or more: for he said, as it is written of him: "I sat me down and wept, and mourned certain days, and fasted and prayed before the God of heaven." We read that Queen Esther and her maidens, with all the Jews that were found at Susan, fasted three days and three nights together, and did neither eat nor drink. Moses, Elias, and Christ, fasted forty days and as many nights, without receiving of any corporal food: but such fasts are not to be practised, forasmuch as they are marvellous and past the bonds of men's

1 Sam. vii.

2 Sam. i.

Neh. i.

Esth. iv.

nature, and are done only by the unsearchable power and mighty working of God in few of his creatures.

But the common manner of fasting among the true godly was, when they did fast, to abstain from all meat the whole day till night, that they might the more freely give their mind to spiritual exercises, and at night to take some refection moderately, yea, and that with thanksgiving. And on this manner, as some fasted but one or two days together, so some fasted many, every one as they were moved by the Spirit of God, and as occasion required. We read that the prophet Daniel fasted thus three weeks together. His words are these: "I Daniel mourned for the space Dan. x. of three weeks, so that I had no lust to eat bread: as for flesh and wine, there came none within my mouth. No, I did not once anoint myself, till the whole three weeks were out." The scripture testifieth that the virtuous woman Judith "fasted all the Judith viii. days of her life, except the sabbaths and new moons, and the solemn days that the people of Israel kept." Likewise read we of Anna, the daughter of Phanuel, "which Luke ii. departed not from the temple, but served God with fastings and prayers night and day." On this manner did the apostles after Christ's ascension, and many other godly men in the primitive church, fast. So that their custom was on that day that they did fast to eat nothing till night, but to occupy themselves about such godly exercises, as heretofore are mentioned.

The Third Chapter.

And as the godly men, in the time of their fasting, did abstain from meat and drink, so did they from all other things that might delight the flesh, and behaved themselves outwardly according to the sorrow and trouble of their heart inwardly. Out of a mourning and sorrowful heart did spring outward, yea, and those unfeigned tokens of sorrow and mourning.

For we heard before that, when Daniel fasted three weeks, and prayed unto the Lord his God, although he did eat bread every night for the comfort of his weak body, yet he neither eat flesh nor drunk wine, nor yet once anointed himself. And Dan. x. in another place he saith: "I turned me unto God the Lord for to pray, and to Dan. ix. make mine intercession with fasting, sackcloth, and ashes." "The people of Ninive," Jonah iii. when they heard the preaching of Jonas, which threatened them and their city destruction after forty days, repented, "believed God, and proclaimed fasting, and arrayed themselves in sackcloth, as well the great as the small of them. And when the tidings came unto the king of Ninive, he also arose out of his seat, and did his apparel off, and put on sackcloth, and sat him down in ashes." Again, the children of Israel (as we read in Esdras), when they fasted, did put on sackcloth, and Neh. ix. sprinkled earth upon their heads, knowledged their sins, prayed unto God, and read in the book of the law of the Lord their God. Queen Esther also, when she fasted, Esth. iv. laid away her glorious apparel, and put on the garments that served for sighing and mourning. In the stead of precious ointment, she scattered ashes and dung upon her head; and as for her body, she humbled it with fasting, and brought it very low. Likewise king Achab, when he was reproved of the prophet Helias for killing Naboth, 1 Kings xxi. fell to fasting; and as he fasted, so did he "put sackcloth about his flesh, lay in sackcloth, went barefoot, and hanging down his head."

The Fourth Chapter.

Whatsoever might make to the humbling and taming of the flesh, that did the godly men use for the most part in the time of their fasting. Neither did those corporal exercises displease God, seeing they came from a contrite heart and troubled spirit, wholly depending with strong faith on the great mercies of God. For David saith: "A troubled spirit is a sacrifice to God; neither doth he despise a contrite Psal. li. and humbled heart."

But these outward signs of humiliation God utterly abhorreth when they come not from a penitent and faithful heart, and casteth them away as hypocritish and

Isai. lviii. devilish, as we read in the prophet Esay: "Wherefore fast we," say the hypocrites, "and thou, O God, seest it not? We put our lives to straitness, and thou regardest it not. Behold," saith God, "when ye fast, your lust remaineth still; for ye do no less violence to your debtors. Lo, ye fast to strife and debate, and to smite with the fist of wickedness. Now ye shall not fast thus, that your voice might be heard above. Think ye this fast pleaseth me, that a man should chasten himself for a day, and to writhe his head about like an hoop, and to lie upon the earth in an hairy cloth? Should that be called fasting, or day that pleaseth the Lord? Doth not this fasting rather please me; that thou loose him out of bondage that is in thy danger? that thou break the oath of wicked bargains? that thou let the oppressed go free, and take from them all manner of burdens? to deal thy bread to the hungry, and bring the poor wandering home into thy house? when thou seest the naked, that thou cover him, and hide not thy face from thy neighbour, and that thou despise not thine own flesh?" (If thou thus fastest), "then shall thy light break forth as the morning, and thy health flourish right shortly; thy righteousness shall go before thee, and the glory of the Lord shall embrace thee. Then, if thou callest, the Lord shall answer thee; if thou criest, he shall say, Here I am. Yea, if thou layest away from thee thy burdens, and holdest thy fingers, and ceasest from blasphemous talking; if thou hast compassion upon the hungry, and refreshest the troubled soul; then shall thy light spring out in the darkness, and thy darkness shall be as the noon-day. The Lord shall ever be thy guide, and satisfy the desire of thine heart in the time of drought, and fill thy bones with marrow. Thou shalt be like a fresh watered garden, and like the fountain of water that never leaveth running." Again, God saith by the
Joel ii. prophet Joel: "Turn you unto me with all your heart, with fasting, weeping, and
1 Cor. vii. mourning: tear your hearts and not your clothes." Moreover, albeit St Paul counselleth that married folk should not "withdraw themselves one from another any long time, lest Satan tempt them to incontinency and uncleanness;" yet, that they might be the more apt to fast and to pray, he would have them some time to withdraw themselves one from another. Hereunto pertaineth the saying of the prophet Joel:
Joel ii. "Blow out with the trumpet in Sion, proclaim a fasting, call the congregation, and gather the people together, warn the congregation, gather the elders, bring the children and sucklings together. Let the bridegroom go forth of his chamber, and the bride out of her closet."

The Fifth Chapter.

The true fast. THUS have we learned out of the holy scriptures, that the true and christian fast is to abstain not only from all kind of meats and drinks (during the time of fasting), but also from all those things wherein the flesh hath pleasure and delectation, and to occupy ourselves in all godly and spiritual exercises unto the glory of God, the comfort of our neighbour, and the health of our own souls.

Constrained fasts please not God. But it is to be noted, that this abstinence or fast must be freely and willingly done, or else can it by no means please God. For whatsoever cometh from an unwilling and constrained mind, God abhorreth, appear it never so godly and praise-worthy
2 Cor. ix. before the world. "God loveth a cheerful giver," saith St Paul. And the psalmo-
Psal. liv. graph saith: "An offering of a free heart will I give thee, and praise thy name, O Lord, because it is so comfortable." They therefore that fast for custom sake or at the commandment of man only, and not of a good-will and free spirit, do neither please God nor profit themselves. Therefore shall that chance unto them that God
Jer. xiv. threateneth by the prophet, saying: "When they fast, I will not hear their prayers."

The Sixth Chapter.

Fast commanded of the high powers. HERE peradventure some man will say, Is it ungodly to fast at the commandment of man? What if the magistrates cause a fast to be proclaimed? Ought it not to be observed of their subjects? I answer, If the high powers at any time commandeth fasting, so that it be done unto a godly end, and riseth not of superstition, it ought to be observed of the subjects. For we have examples hereof in the holy scriptures, which do both set forth the authority of magistrates in commanding fasting, and also the obedience of subjects in observing the same.

When the Israelites were in great fear and danger of the Philistines, Samuel, which at that time judged the people, called all the house of Israel together, proclaimed a fast, exhorted them unto prayer, willed them to put away the strange gods from among them, and with their whole heart to turn again unto the Lord their God, and he of his mercy would surely rid them out of the hands of the Philistines. The people gladly obeyed Samuel's commandment, put away their idols, confessed their sins, served the Lord only, and fasted the same day unto even. And God saved them from the hand of the Philistines all the days of Samuel. 1 Sam vii.

King Jehosaphat, hearing that the Moabites and Ammonites came with an exceeding great multitude against him to battle, was in great fear, sought for help at the Lord's hand, proclaimed fasting throughout all Juda, and called the people together to pray unto the Lord. The people willingly obeyed the king's commandment. All Juda came and stood before the Lord, with their young ones, their wives, and their children, to ask counsel of the Lord. They both fasted and prayed unto the Lord their God for help against their enemies: and the Lord gave them a wonderful and glorious victory. 2 Chron. xx.

Esdras, returning unto Jerusalem with the children of Israel, proclaimed a fast, and exhorted them to call on the name of God, that he might give them a prosperous journey. The people obeyed, fasted and prayed unto the Lord their God, and they had good success in all their doings. Ezra viii.

The king of the Ninivites, hearing of the most terrible and grievous plague that was threatened unto them and their city by Jonas the prophet of God, humbled himself, and sent forth a proclamation unto all his people, commanding that neither man nor beast, ox or sheep, should taste any thing at all, and that they should neither eat nor drink water, but put on sackcloth, both man and beast. He commanded them also, in his proclamation, to repent, to believe God and his word, to turn from their wicked ways, and mightily to cry unto God for mercy. The people did according to the king's proclamation; so that both the king and his subjects together repenting, fasting, believing, turning from their wicked ways, and mightily calling on the Lord for mercy and forgiveness of their sins, were saved, both they and their city with all that they had. Jonah iii.

Esther, hearing of the proclamation that king Ahasuerus, at the subtile suggestion of wicked Haman, had sent forth for the destruction of the Jews, commanded Mardocheus to gather together all the Jews that were found at Susan, and to fast for her, so that they should neither eat nor drink by the space of three days and three nights, but spend all that time in fasting and praying. Her commandment was fulfilled. It came to pass that God preserved the Jews alive, and brought their enemies to a shameful end. Esth. iv.

Thus have we learned out of the holy scriptures, that the rulers have authority given them of God to command their subjects to fast, whensoever any urgent cause is offered; as in the time of battle, hunger, drought, plague, pestilence, &c.; and that the people are bound by God's commandment to obey the magistrates and their ordinances in all such things, as they tender the glory of God, the conservation of the commonweal, and the health of their own souls. This meaneth the prophet Joel, speaking unto the heads of the people on this manner: "Proclaim fasting, call the congregation, gather the elders and all the inhabiters of the land together into the house of the Lord your God, and cry unto the Lord," &c. Again: "Blow out with the trumpet in Sion, proclaim fasting, call the congregation, and gather the people together." Joel i. Joel ii.

The Seventh Chapter.

FURTHERMORE the true and christian fast riseth either of an heart contrite and sorrowful for the sins committed against God, or else of a mind fervently given to godliness. As touching that fast which cometh from a contrite and sorrowful heart for the *The fast that cometh of a sorrowful heart.*

sins committed against God, it is a worthy and noble fast in the sight of God, and cannot but highly please him.

Psal. li. For the psalmograph saith: "A troubled spirit is a sacrifice unto God; neither doth he despise a contrite and humbled heart." And God himself saith by the pro-
Isai. lxvi. phet: "Whom shall I regard and favour? Even him that is poor, and of a lowly and troubled spirit, and such one as standeth in awe of my words." Whosoever doth
Mark well. so fear God and stand in awe of his indignation and heavy displeasure, that he is loth to offend him, and therefore seeketh all means possible to please him; and if at any time through frailness of nature he chanceth to offend, he is straightways angry with himself, repenteth of his former misdeeds, and conceiveth such an inward sorrow in his heart, that he delighteth in no worldly thing, neither in meat, drink, apparel, riches, pastimes, pleasures, &c., but continually sorroweth for his disobedient unkindness and unkind disobedience against God our heavenly Father; so that the very trouble of his heart will not suffer him to eat or drink till, through continual calling on the name of the Lord, he feeleth in his mind some token of God's goodness, grace, and favour toward him, and is through faith in Christ's blood fully persuaded that all his sins are forgiven him, and he again received into favour; the fast of such one is an acceptable sacrifice unto God.

Of this inward sorrow of the heart did the fasts of many good men heretofore rise, as the holy scriptures do declare, and therefore did they highly please God; insomuch that God granted them their requests, and was their merciful and most loving Lord. Examples hereof are the Israelites, that were gathered together at Mispha; the Ninivites; Esther and her company; Judith with the citizens of Bethulia; Achab, and divers other, whose fasts God allowed, because they proceeded from the hearts of such as humbled themselves in his sight, repented them of their sins, asked forgiveness, and promised amendment of life.

The Eighth Chapter.

The fast that cometh of a mind given to godliness. Now as touching that fast which springeth of a mind given to godliness, it cannot be disallowed of God. For he that seeketh to please God, and to avance his glory by any godly means, and, that he may have the grace so to do, fasteth, prayeth, studieth, laboureth; his fasting, his praying, his studying, his labouring cannot but please God, and have good and fortunate success.

Dan. ix. On this manner fasted Daniel, that he might be the more apt to receive the knowledge of God's mysteries, which were afterward declared unto him of the angel. So
2 Esdr. v. likewise did Esdras. Of this godly manner of fasting spake Christ, when the disciples of John came unto him, and demanded why his disciples fasted not, as they and the
Matt. ix. Pharisees did. To whom Christ answered and said: "Can the bridegroom's children mourn so long as the bridegroom is with them? But the days will come, when the bridegroom shall be taken from them, and then shall they fast." According to this prophecy, when Christ, which is the bridegroom, was taken from them, (I speak con-
Matt. xxviii. cerning his corporal presence, for by his Spirit he is with the faithful unto the end
Acts i. of the world,) they mourned, fasted, and prayed for the gift of the Holy Ghost, which
John xiv. xv. xvi. was promised to be sent unto them for to be their comforter and teacher, and to lead them into all truth; and the Holy Ghost was given unto them according to the promise of Christ and their expectation. They fasted also and prayed after they had received the Holy Ghost, that they might worthily fulfil that office which was committed unto them, that by their preaching many thousands might be converted and
Acts ii. iii. saved; and it so came to pass.

Luke ii. The holy and devout widow Anna fasted and prayed continually in the temple for the
Acts x. coming of the promised Messias, and she saw him before her death. Cornelius, that godly man, being troubled in his mind, as it may be thought, with the multitude of religions which at that time reigned in the world, as the religion of the gentiles, of the Jews, of the Pharisees, of the Sadducees, of the Essees, and the late sprung up religion of the Christians, humbled himself in the sight of God, mourned, fasted, gave almess, and prayed that it would please God to declare unto him which among them all was the

true religion, that he might observe the same, frame his life according unto that, and so please God. And to obtain this thing of God, he continued long fasting and praying. God therefore accepted his fast, heard his prayer, and granted him his request.

The prophets and preachers at Antioch fasted and prayed, that both they themselves might preach with fruit, and that other also might be sent of God, and appointed unto that office, that the glory of God might be set forth, that his word might be received, and that all nations of the earth might believe in him, and in his Son Jesu Christ. Their fasting and praying were allowed before God, and their desires were satisfied. For "the Holy Ghost said unto them, Separate me Barnabas and Saul for the work whereunto I have called them. And when they had fasted, and prayed, and laid their hands on them, they let them go." Paul and Barnabas also fasted when they prayed for the congregations of Lystra, Iconium, Antioch, and Pisidia, and when they ordained them elders in every congregation to teach and instruct them in their absence, and to confirm them in the faith and doctrine, which they had already received. And God gave good success to their doctrine and ministration. All these fasted of a mind fervently given unto godliness.

Acts xiii.

Acts xiv.

Hitherto have we learned out of the holy scriptures, what the true and christian fast is. Now let us see, in few words, whether the popish manner of fasting, *which we have so many years unfruitfully observed, be like unto that trade of fasting[1]* which the word of God hath painted and set forth unto us.

The Ninth Chapter.

Of the popish manner of fasting.

THE true and christian fast is done freely and willingly, and cometh from the fervent motion of the spirit. The popish and superstitious fast serveth the custom only, and is done at the commandment of man with a grudging and unwilling mind; which, being loth to fast if the custom and man's ordinance were not, wisheth both the fast and the commander of the fast at the devil. And if any in so great a multitude do willingly fast, yet is it done partly to satisfy the custom; partly because they will be counted good, devout, and catholic men; partly to honour some saint; partly to deserve remission of their sins, and to win everlasting life. Can this kind of fasting please God? "They worship me in vain," saith Christ, "teaching doctrines that are the commandments of men." St Paul also saith: "Whatsoever is not of faith is sin."

Matt. xv.

Rom. xiv.

The true and christian fast, during the time of fasting, is to abstain from all kind of meats and drinks (except very necessity requireth the contrary), and from all those things wherein the flesh delighteth. For that was the manner of fasting among the fathers of the old law, as we heard afore. Hierome confirming the same, "The Jews," saith he, "on those days that they fast took no meat, till they see the evening star up[2]." And a certain council, called *Concilium Chalcedonense*, ordained that such should not be counted to fast that did eat before evensong was done[3]; which at that time was not celebrated, as it is now, at two or three at the clock after dinner, but at night, about the eighth or ninth hour, when the day was all past.

Lib. ii. contra Jovinianum.

The popish and superstitious fasters persuade themselves to fast well, and to do a meritorious deed, if they only abstain from flesh; though in the morning, so soon as they rise out of their beds, they enfarce and stuff their bellies with as many fine cakes and toasts of white bread as they be able to eat, and with as much good ale, full of spices, or else burnt malmsey, as their paunches can hold. And when dinner

O worthy fast

The papists' drinking in the morning.

[1 The words between asterisks are printed twice over in the folio.]

[2 Perhaps the following is the passage intended: Petrus apostolus non expectans stellam more Judaico, sed hora sexta in solarium pransurus ascendit.—Hieron. Op. Par. 1693-1706. Adv. Jovin. Lib. II. Tom. IV. Pars II. col. 198.]

[3 There is probably an error in the reference which should be to the council of Châlons, instead of Chalcedon. *Ex Concilio Cabilonensi.* Solent plures, qui se jejunare putant, in quadragesima, mox ut signum audierint ad horam nonam, comedere. Qui nullatenus jejunare credendi sunt, si ante manducaverint, quam vespertinum celebretur officium. —Decret. Gratiani. Par. 1583. Decr. Tert. Pars. De Consecr. Dist. i. can. 50, cols. 2345, 6. But even among the canons of Châlons this does not appear; and Gratian adds: Habetur in capitulis Theodulphi Aurelianensi episcopi, c. 39.]

come, if they abstain from a smoky piece of bacon, or hard salted and powdered beef, or such-like, though they eat the most delicious fishes that can be gotten, and enfarce their beastly bodies with all the sweet meats that can be invented and sought out; yea, and that so unmeasurably, that, after they have once dined, they are provoked either to the pleasure of the body, or else like beasts of the belly fall straightways unto sleep, so that they are not able to serve God, nor themselves, nor any other; yet think they that they fast well, and do God a great pleasure.

The papists' manner of dining.

A story of a monk which was a great faster.

This manner of fasting among many other used a certain monk in my country, which, notwithstanding, was counted the greatest and devoutest faster in all those quarters. His manner was for the most part to make but one meal a day, as they use to say, yet such a meal as the meat of that one meal might have seemed sufficient to any reasonable creature to have served six godly fasters at a meal. When he came unto dinner, and was set down at the table, his use was ever to unbuckle and let slack his girdle a great quantity, which before was strait girded to his body. He fell to his meat as the hungry wolf to his prey, and never left off devouring the best meats that were set before him, till he had so stuffed his religious paunch, that his girdle, being afore loose, was so hard to his body that he could not put his little finger between the girdle and his clothes. He sat so swelling and sweating at the table through the too much devouring of pleasant meats and hot wines, which if Apelles had been present with his pencil, he might have had a jolly pattern to paint a right epicure. And notwithstanding both he and such like were counted good, holy, devout, religious, and catholic fasters.

To consume at one dinner so much as would serve three was no breaking of a fast. To devour unmeasurably all kind of pleasant fishes, or whatsoever dainties besides could be devised, was fast good enough in the pope's kingdom: but to eat a piece of flesh, although never so gross, was twice a deadly sin, and punished with fire. The eater of the flesh was called a Lollore, and adjudged to be brent with fire for his (I know not how great) offence, as though God abhorred more the eating of flesh than of fish; or as though fish were clean in the sight of God, and flesh vile
Matt. xxiii. and abominable. O bellied hypocrites, which strain out a gnat and swallow down a
1 Tim. iv. camel! O spirits of error and teachers of devilish doctrines, which "speak false through hypocrisy, and have their conscience marked with an hot iron, forbidding to marry and commanding to abstain from meats, which God hath created to be received with thanksgiving of them which believe and know the truth! For all the creatures of God are good, and nothing to be refused, if it be received with thanksgiving:
Tit. i. for it is sanctified by the word of God and prayer." "Unto the pure all things are pure; but unto them that are defiled and unbelieving is nothing pure; but even the mind and conscience of them is defiled." Why do not those blind guides remember this saying of our Saviour Christ, and cease to condemn the innocent?
Matt. xv. "That which goeth into the mouth defileth not the man; but that which cometh out of the mouth defileth the man. For whatsoever entereth in at the mouth goeth into the belly, and is cast out into the draught; but those things which proceed out of the mouth come from the heart, and they defile the man. For out of the heart proceed evil thoughts, murders, breaking of wedlock, whoredoms, thefts, false witness, blasphemies. These are the things which defile a man."

The Tenth Chapter.

The papists' drinking at night.

AGAIN at night, albeit the popish fasters eat no meat, yet make they such a drinking, as might justly seem a costious kind of banqueting. Besides their white bread and fine cakes, they have their figs, raisins, almonds, apples, pears, nuts, carroways, biscuits, succat, marmalade, cherries condite, quinces condite, and I know not what. And besides their nappy ale and heady beer, they have sundry wines, some spiced, and some brewed with a cup of ipocras[1] at the latter end to make up their mouth withal, and to finish their holy and religious fast. Is it not to be thought

[[1] Ipocras, or hippocras was a kind of piment or spiced wine.]

that these men take great pains in their fasting? Do not such fasts please God greatly, think you? O abominable mockers of christian abstinence!

These are those epicures which, as the poet saith, *Curios simulant et Bacchanalia vivunt*[2]. These are those hypocrites which "bind heavy burdens and grievous to be borne, and lay them on men's shoulders; but they themselves will not heave at them with one of their fingers." And as the wealthy worldlings and rich epicures think themselves to fast well if they make but one meal on a day, though otherwise they enfarce their bellies with never so many dainties, even so judge the baser kind of people that they fast well if they eat no meat, though they stuff their paunches with never so much bread and drink. Matt. xxiii. Luke xi.

Notable is this sentence of St Hierome against all such belly-gods. "What availeth it," saith he, "to eat no oil, and to seek about for such meats as are most dainty and hardest to come by, as dry figs, pepper, nuts, dates, fine cakes, honey, and pistacies? All the dainties that gardens can bring forth are sought, that we should not eat the usual bread. And while we seek deliciously to live, we are plucked back from the kingdom of heaven. Moreover, I hear say, that there be some which, contrary to the rule and nature of men, drink no water, nor eat bread; but sup not out of a cup, but out of a shell, dainty broths, and herbs brayed, and the juice of beets. Fie for shame! are we not ashamed of such fondness, nor weary of the superstition? Yea, we, living in all deliciousness, seek to be praised for our abstinence. The mightiest fast is water and bread; but because it hath no glory nor notable fame, and because we all live with bread and water, it is not counted as the public and common fast[3]." Ad Nepot. Pistacium is a kind of nuts. Nice and fine fasters in St Hierome's time.

Would God that all they that fast, yea, and so many as profess Christ, would remember and continually set before their eyes this saying of St Austin! "It nothing profiteth," saith he, "to have passed an whole day in long fasting, if afterward the soul be oppressed with deliciousness or superfluity of meats; for so is the mind much filled soon dulled, and the earth of our body so watered will bring forth thorns of wicked lusts. Let therefore our meat be temperate and no more than is sufficient; and let our belly never be too full. And let us always have more mind of the meat for the heart than of meat for the body; because within the inward man we be made after the image of God, but in the flesh we are fashioned of the slime of the earth[4]." Ex Serm. lvi. De Tempore.

The Eleventh Chapter.

FURTHERMORE, the christian fast riseth of an heart contrite and sorrowful for the sins committed against God, as we have heard heretofore. The popish fast riseth either of custom, or else of superstition. For the papists, in their chief and solemn fasting days, are led with no true fear toward God, neither do they lament their sins, nor study by hearty repentance, true faith, and amendment of life, to appease the wrath of God kindled against them for their abominable living on those days that they fast, more than any other time. What papists among them forsaketh his

[2 Juv. II. 3.]

[3 Quid prodest oleo non vesci, et molestias quasdam difficultatesque ciborum quærere, caryCas, piper, nuces, palmarum fructus, similam, mel, pistachia? Tota hortorum cultura vexatur, ut cibario non vescamur pane; et dum delicias sectamur, a regno cœlorum retrahimur. Audio præterea quosdam, contra rerum hominumque naturam, aquam non bibere, nec vesci pane; sed sorbitiunculas delicatas et contrita olera, betarumque succum, non calice sorbere, sed concha. Proh pudor, non erubescimus istiusmodi ineptiis, nec tædet superstitionis? Insuper etiam famam abstinentiæ in deliciis quærimus. Fortissimum jejunium est aqua et panis. Sed quia gloriam non habet, et omnes pane et aqua vivimus, quasi publicum et commune jejunium non putatur.—Hieron. Op. Par. 1693-1706. Epist. xxxiv. ad Nepot. de Vit. Clericor. Tom. IV. Pars II. col. 364.]

[4 Nihil prodest tota die longum duxisse jejunium, si postea ciborum suavitate vel nimietate anima obruatur. Illico mens repleta torpescit, et irrigata corporis nostri terra spinas libidinum germinabit. Sit ergo temperatus cibus, et numquam nimium venter expletus; et plus semper de cibo cordis quam de cibo corporis cogitemus: quia intus in homine interiore facti sumus ad imaginem Dei; in carne autem de limo terræ formati sumus.—August. Op. Par. 1679-1700. Serm. cxli. 4. In Quadrages. ii. Tom. V. Appendix, col. 251. This sermon is not Augustine's. It has been with some probability assigned to Cæsarius.]

papistry, hypocrisy, superstition, and idolatry, and gladly receiveth the truth of God' word? What covetous worldling leaveth his covetousness, and exerciseth mercy toward the poor members of Christ? What proud man giveth over his pride, and embraceth humility? What adulterer forsaketh his adultery, and leadeth an honest conversation? What glutton or drunkard giveth over his gluttony or drunkenness, and leadeth a sober life? what usurer leaveth his usury? what briber his bribery? what catchpole his extortion? what tyrant his tyranny? what whore her whoredom? what ribald his ribaldry? what blasphemer his blasphemy? what envious man his envy? &c. As they begin their fast with an unrepentant and wicked heart, even so do they continue and end the same; so far is it off that they have any sorrow in their heart for their sins committed against God, which should earnestly move them to forsake their meat, and to give themselves wholly to be reconciled unto God, by repenting and calling on the name of God for mercy in Christ Jesu our Lord. Their fast, therefore, is abomination before God; forasmuch as in the time of their fasting they give not over their wickedness, and earnestly seek to please God.

In what things the godliness of the papists consisteth.

Moreover, the christian fast riseth also of an heart fervently given to godliness. In this behalf also the popish fast agreeth nothing with christian abstinence. For the papists' minds are set on no true godliness in the time of their fasting, but altogether on superstition and hypocrisy. Their godliness, yea, rather ungodliness, when they fast, consisteth in observing the pope's ceremonies and man's inventions. If they fulfil those, they think themselves godly enough, when, notwithstanding, they be furthest from all true godliness. Neither do they direct their fasts unto any godly end; but as every one fantasieth, so do they fast, yea, and that for sundry purposes.

The fondness of the papists in their fasting.

Some fast bread and water, some eat nothing but fruit, some taste no kind of meat or drink that is dressed with fire; some in their fast go woolward, bare-footed and bare-legged; some are so scrupulous and superstitious in their fasting, that in the time of their fast they will neither eat, nor drink, nor sleep, nor yet swallow down their own spittle: if they do, they think themselves damned: provided alway that they also must be first and last at church. If they observe these fasts, they promise themselves I know not how great rewards, and how high seats in heaven above other, and how many gay garlands of red roses and sweet violets, that God and our lady and the blessed saints shall give them after this life for their devout fasting and pretty pains. O fond foolishness and foolish fondness, worthy rather to be lamented than to be laughed at!

The superstitious worshipping of saints.

If it be done of a good intent, say they, all is well whatsoever we do. If we fast the blessed saints' evens, and worship them with a *Pater-noster*, *ave*, and creed, they will do for us whatsoever we ask. St George will defend us in battle against our enemies. St Barbara will keep us from thundering and lightning. St Agasse will save our house from burning. St Antony will keep our swine. St Luke will save our ox. St Job will defend us from the pox. St Gertrude will keep our house from mice and rats. St Nicholas will preserve us from drowning. St Loye will cure our horse. St Dorothe will save our herbs and flowers. St Sith will bring again whatsoever we lose. St Apolline will heal the pain of our teeth. St Sweetlad and St Agnes will send us maids good husbands. St Peter will let us in at heaven-gates,—with a thousand such-like[1].

This superstition and idolatry is the godliness of the papists. If they fast and

[[1] Of most of the saints mentioned here an account was given, Vol. I. page 139, note 4. To what is there said, it may be added that St George is described as having been a knight of Cappadocia. The legend of his slaying the dragon is well known. He suffered martyrdom by beheading in 287, or as some say, 291, under Diocletian. Nicholas is stated to have been born of rich parents. He became bishop of Myra, and was at the council of Nice. He preserved by miracle some mariners from shipwreck who invoked his help. Dorothy was of the noble lineage of Roman senators. She declared herself espoused to Jesus Christ. When led to martyrdom, Theophilus, a scribe, asked her in scorn for some of the roses and apples which grew in the garden of her spouse: upon which a child, just before her death, supernaturally appeared to bring them. So remarkable a prodigy converted Theophilus. Dorothy died in 288, under Diocletian and Maximian. Sweetlad seems to be a mock-saint invented by the author to be joined with St Agnes, in ridicule of the ceremonies practised on St Agnes' eve.]

serve the saints unto this end, and on their feastful days fare daintily and drink largely in the honour of the good saint, they think they have done much for the saint, and have shewed themselves good, godly, and devout persons. O double ungodliness!

What shall I speak of the spiritual exercises, which the true and christian fast requireth to be done in the time of fasting? If we mark well the manners of the papists, and note their behaviour on their fasting days, we shall easily perceive, that in the midst of their fasting they are no less wicked and ungodly, no less proud and envious, no less lecherous and covetous, no less backbiting and slanderous, no less polling and pilling, no less churlish and unmerciful, no less given to gluttony and drunkenness, than they were afore. They lament not their sins, they fall not to faithful prayer, they call not on the name of God as they ought, but flee unto creatures; they give not themselves to the hearing or reading of God's word, which many of them extremely abhor, they go not about to leave their idolatry and wish to be better instructed in the knowledge of God's law, &c.; but continuing still in their old superstition and idolatry, they think themselves godly enough and good enough. If they eat not flesh, if they forbear white meats, all is well whatsoever they do, though there be no repentance, no calling on the name of God, no correction of manners, no amendment of life. God have mercy on us! God open their eyes and give them grace to amend!

Hitherto have we learned out of the word of God, what the true and christian fast is. We have heard also, how greatly the popish manner of fasting differeth from the true use of fasting which the holy scriptures teach. Now the order requireth that we also declare how we ought to fast that we may please God, and not fast in vain, as the hypocrites do.

HOW WE OUGHT TO FAST.

The Twelfth Chapter.

In declaring how we ought to fast, whom should I rather follow than our Saviour Jesus Christ, the teacher of all truth? which saith: "When ye fast, be not sad, as the hypocrites are. For they disfigure their faces, that they might be seen of men to fast. Verily I say unto you, They have their reward. But thou, when thou fastest, anoint thy head, and wash thy face; that it appear not unto men that thou fastest, but to thy Father which is in secret; and thy Father which seeth in secret shall reward thee openly." Christ our Saviour in this place doth not only rebuke the hypocritical and superstitious manner of the ungodly fasters, but he also teacheth the true manner of fasting. Matt. vi.

Of these his words we learn, that whosoever intendeth to fast aright, he must observe three things. The first is that he anoint his head. The second, that he wash his face. The third, that he fast in secret. These phrases, "anointing of the head," and "washing of the face," with many other, seem very strange manners of speaking to such as are not perfectly exercised in the reading of the holy scriptures and of the ancient writers: it is convenient therefore that we learn to know what is meant by them. Three things are to be observed in fasting.

And no man in this behalf can satisfy your desire better than our golden-mouthed doctor, St John Chrysostom, whose words are these: "In the anointing of the head," saith he, "we know that mercy is signified. Therefore to anoint the head is to shew mercy to our neighbour. For that mercy that is done unto a poor man is referred unto God, which is the head of the man, as the apostle and the Lord himself saith: 'Whatsoever ye have done to one of my lessest brothers, ye have done it unto me.' In the stead of the which mercy, with the divine retribution, as with a certain heavenly oil, we are poured and shed over by him which saith: 'Blessed are the merciful; for God shall have mercy on them.' Holy David also did know the unction and anointing of the celestial oil in the head, when he said: 'As in the ointment which came down into the beard.' But in washing the face the purity of a clean body and of a sincere conscience is known to be signified; so that to wash the face is to make clean the face of our heart from all filthiness of sin, and from the uncomeliness of trespass, and Hom. xlvi. ex cap. vi. Matt. ix. What it is to anoint the head. 1 Cor. xi. Matt. xxv. Matt. v. Psal. cxxxiii. What it is to wash the face.

to have a very pure conscience, that we may truly have in us the gladness of celestial joy, and the familiarity and cheerfulness of the Holy Ghost[1]."

Hitherto have I rehearsed the words of St John Chrysostom, whereby we may learn that to "anoint our head" is none other thing than to shew ourselves beneficial to the poor members of Christ. Again, to "wash our face" is to make clean both body and soul from sin and wickedness. If we therefore will fast aright, after the mind of St John Chrysostom, we must first anoint our head, that is to say, comfort the poor people with such good as God hath committed unto us. For the riches that we have be not ours, but they be God's, as he saith by the prophet: "Gold is mine, silver is mine." The psalmograph also saith: "The earth is the Lord's, and all that is contained in it."

Hag. ii. Psal. xxiv.

The Thirteenth Chapter.

A spectacle for rich men.

God hath put the goods of this world into the rich men's hands, that they should distribute part of them to the poor people. They are the stewards of God and the dispensators of his treasures, that they, continually living of them, should also with the distribution of part of them comfort the needy members of Christ. If they spend them otherwise than God hath appointed in his word, they shall render a strait accounts for it to the high Judge Christ. They have nothing at all, but that they shall be called to accounts for it, even to the uttermost farthing.

If they be not found to have used their talent well, and unto the profit of other, they shall with that unprofitable servant of the gospel be cast into utter darkness, where weeping and gnashing of teeth shall be. If they be proved unmerciful and negligent in the distribution of the worldly goods, surely they shall be carried with the rich glutton, of whom blessed Luke speaketh in the gospel, unto hell, and there burn in such cruel and bitter flames, as the fire whereof shall never be quenched, "neither shall the worm," which shall gnaw the consciences of them that are there, "die at any time," as the prophet saith. What cause then have the rich men to boast themselves, and to glory of their worldly goods, or to avance themselves above other for their possessions' sake? Certes none at all, more than a great man's servant hath, to whom his lord and master hath committed his goods for a certain space to keep, the servant looking at every hour, when his master will call him to accounts, and require them of him again.

Matt. xxii. Luke xvi. Isai. lxvi.

Ser. i. in Divites Avaros. An hard saying for unmerciful rich men.

Basilius Magnus hath a notable sentence, and it is this: "He is a very thief and a robber," saith he, "which maketh that thing his own that he hath received to distribute and give abroad. For the bread that thou retainest and keepest is the bread of the hungry: the garment which thou keepest in thy chest is the garment of the naked: the shoe that is mould with thee is the shoe of him that is unshod; and the money which thou hidest in the ground is the money of the needy. Moreover thou doest injury and plain wrong to so many as thou forsakest, when thou art able to help them[2]."

Ecclus. xxxiv. Isai. lviii.

Hereto pertaineth the saying of the wise man: "The bread of the needy is the life of the poor: he that defraudeth him of it is a manslayer." God also by the prophet teacheth, that that fast pleaseth him best, which is accompanied with the works of mercy, saying: "Break thy bread to the hungry, and lead the needy and wayfaring into thy house. When thou seest a naked man, cover him; and despise not thy flesh." Mark that he saith: "Break thy bread to the hungry." Certain that expound this text say, that thou then breakest thy bread to the hungry, when thou so fastest that thou sparest from thine own belly to give to the poor hungry man. For a christian man ought to be no less careful for the poor than for himself. We therefore do break our bread to the hungry, when we give him that which we ourselves necessarily should have eaten. So that to "anoint our head" is to break our bread to

What it is to break thy bread to the hungry.

[[1] Chrysost. Op. Lat. Basil. 1547. Ex Var. in Matt. Loc. Hom. ix. ex cap. Matt. vi. Fer. Quart. Cin. Tom. II. col. 1162. See Vol. I. page 107, note 4.]

[[2] Basil. Op. Par. 1721-30. Hom. vi. in Luc. xii. 18. Tom. II. p. 50. See Vol. I. page 25, note 9.]

the hungry, to lodge the poor in our house, to give clothes to the naked, and to comfort according to our ability so many as have need of our help. Unto these works of mercy doth our Saviour Christ exhort us in the gospel, saying: "When thou makest a dinner or a supper, call not thy friends, nor thy brethren, neither thy kinsfolk, nor thy rich neighbours; lest they also bid thee again, and a recompence be made thee. But when thou makest a feast, call the poor, the feeble, the lame, and the blind; and thou shalt be happy: for they cannot recompense thee; but thou shalt be recompensed at the resurrection of the righteous." Again he saith: "Give alms of those things ye have; and behold, all things are clean unto you." But of this we shall entreat more largely, when we come to the true use of fasting.

Luke xiv.

Luke xi.

The Fourteenth Chapter.

Moreover, if we will fast aright, we are not only commanded to "anoint our head," that is to say, to shew mercy to the poor people, but also to "wash our face," that is, to make our hearts clean from all sin through faithful repentance, that we may have a pure conscience. For it is not enough to be beneficial to other, except we also be beneficial to ourselves. This shall come to pass, if we labour with all main to have a mind pure and clean from all carnal affects, a body void of wicked deeds, and a life garnished with good works. For what was the cause that God did cast away the fasts and solemn feasts of the Jews, but only that they washed not their face, that is, they went not about to put off their old conversation, and to become new men? "I hate and abhor," saith God, "your sacrifices, your solemn feasts, and your fasts. Offer me no more oblations; for it is but lost labour. Your incense is abomination unto me: I have no pleasure in your sacrifices. I may not away with your new moons, your sabbaths," &c. Why so? "For your hands," saith he, "are full of blood." Your hearts are full of vengeance, your consciences are spotted and defiled with all kind of sins, your life is abominable in my sight, ye walk having no fear of God before your eyes, &c. What is then to be done? "Be ye washed," saith he, "be ye clean, take away your evil thoughts from mine eyes. Cease to do evil: learn to do well. Seek judgment, help the poor oppressed, be favourable to the comfortless, defend the widow," &c. Again God saith: "Wash thine heart from wickedness, that thou mayest be helped. How long shall thy noisome thoughts remain with thee?" God hateth those fasts, those prayers, those good deeds, as they call them, that come from a bloody conscience, a spotted and pocky soul, a defiled body, and wicked life, as a certain man saith: "It profiteth a man nothing at all to fast and pray, and to do other good things of devotion, except the mind be refrained from ungodliness, and the tongue from backbitings[3]." For God hath ever a principal respect to the heart of the doer of the work, as we see in the history of the sacrifices of Abel and Cain. If the heart be pure, clean, and faithful, then doth God approve the work; but if it be spotted with sin, God casteth it away, appear it never so glistering and commendable in the sight of the world. "Offer not," saith the wise man, "wicked gifts; for God will not receive them." Salomon also saith: "The sacrifices of the ungodly are abominable." That fast therefore, that cometh not from a pure heart, from an uncorrupt conscience, and from a godly life, pleaseth not God, but is abomination unto the Lord our God, yea, it is by no means worthy the name of a fast.

Why God did cast away the sacrifices, feasts, and fasts of the Jews.

Isai. i.

Jer. iv.

Pius Pont. Rom.

Gen. iv.

God judgeth the work of the heart, and not the heart of the work.

Ecclus. xxxv.

Prov. xxi.

For Basilius Magnus saith: "The true and christian fast is not only to abstain from meats, but also to eschew evil things[4]."

Ser. i. de Jejunio.

And our golden-mouthed doctor saith: "He that abstaineth from meat, and not from evil works, appeareth to fast, but yet he fasteth not in deed. For look, how much he fasteth unto men, so much doth he eat before God; seeing he goeth forth still to sin[5]."

Hom. xv. in cap. vi. Matt.

[3 Pii Papæ I. Epist. i. in Concil. Stud. Labbei. Lut. Par. 1671-2. Tom. I. col. 562. See Vol. I. page 109, note 2.]

[4 Basil. Op. De Jejun. Hom. i. Tom. II. p. 9. See Vol. I. page 106, note 2.]

[5 Chrysost. Op. Par. 1718-38. Opus Imperf. in Matt. Hom. xv. ex cap. vi. Tom. VI. p. 80. See Vol. I. page 105, note 4.]

In Levit. Hom. i. cap. 6.

The ancient doctor Origen saith also: "Wilt thou that I shew unto thee what fast thou oughtest to fast? Fast from evil deeds, abstain from evil words, refrain from evil thoughts, &c. Such a fast pleaseth God[1]."

Again St Hierome saith: "Then is the abstinence of the body commendable before God, when the mind fasteth from vices. For what doth it profit to make weak the body with abstinence, when the mind swelleth with pride[2]?"

Ex Sermone clxxii.

Hereunto pertaineth the saying of St Austin: "The fasts of christian men," saith he, "are rather to be observed spiritually than carnally. In consideration whereof, let us fast principally from our sins, lest our fast be refused of the Lord, as the fast of the Jews were. What a fast is this, that an impostor or deceitful fellow, I cannot tell who, should abstain from meats which the Lord hath created, and yet waxeth fat with the fatness of sins! 'Have I chosen such a fast?' saith the Lord. Read the eight-and-fiftieth chapter of the prophet Esay." And a little after he saith: "The fast, which the Most Highest do approve and allow, is not only to leave off to refresh the body, but also to depart from evil deeds[3]." In another place he also saith: "The great and general fast is to abstain from iniquities and unlawful pleasures of the world, which is a perfect fast; that we, 'forsaking ungodliness and the lusts of the world, should live in this world soberly, righteously, and godly'[4]."

Isai. lviii.

Ex Tract. xvii. in Joan. Tit. ii.

Of these authorities of the holy doctors also do we learn, that the true christian fast doth not only consist in the abstinence of meats, but also in the forsaking of sin. Therefore, if we intend to fast aright, and to make our fast acceptable to God, let us provide earnestly that our fast proceed from a pure and clean heart, void of all carnal affects, stuffed full of faith and charity, and altogether studious of true innocency and unfeigned godliness. So shall it come to pass, that both our fasts and all that ever we do according to God's word shall highly please God. Hitherto have we heard what it is to "anoint the head and to wash the face." Now remaineth to declare what it is to "fast in secret."

The Fifteenth Chapter.

What it is to fast in secret.

To fast in secret is not to keep ourselves close from the sight of men, and so, hiding ourselves in privy corners, to abstain from meat; but not to hunt and hawk after vain-glory, and the praise of men, for our fasting, nor to seek to be seen of men while we fast, to the end that they may commend and praise us, as the hypocrites did, whom Christ reproveth for their vain-glory and ambition, and saith, "They have their reward," not of God, but of men. We are counted before God then to fast in secret, when we fast with such a mind, that we would fast in deed, though no man living did see us, and when we regard more the accomplishment of God's will and the subjection and taming of our body, than all the glory and praise that man can give unto us.

Matt. vi.

It is lawful to do any good deed in the sight of men, so the vain-glory be absent. Matt. v. Phil. ii.

It is lawful for a christian man to fast, to pray, to give alms, or to do any other good work before the world, so that the desire of worldly praise and vain-glory be not in his mind. For our Saviour Christ saith: "Let your light so shine before men, that they may see your good works, and glorify your Father which [is] in heaven." St Paul also saith: "Be such as no man can complain on, and the unfeigned sons

[1 Orig. Op. Par. 1733-59. In Levit. Hom. x. 2. Tom. II. p. 246. See Vol. I. page 105, note 7.]

[2 Magis a vitiis jejunemus quam a cibis. Serm. de Quadrages. xxxii. Tom. IX, p. 117. This may be the passage referred to. Or is Jerome an error for Ambrose? See the following quotation: Est enim interdum inutile et inane jejunium, quod licet ventrem et omnia viscera succo saturitatis exhaurit, non tamen acceptum est Deo, quia mentem et intimos sensus minime vinculo iniquitatis evacuat. Quid enim prodest jejunare visceribus, et luxuriare venatibus? abstinere cibis, errare peccatis? castigare corpus inedia, mentem exercere nequitia?—Ambros. Op. Par. 1614. Serm. xli. Dom. III. Quadrag. Tom. V. col. 68. The Benedictine editors omit this sermon, as certainly not the work of Ambrose. It is in their appendix to Augustine, where they ascribe it to Cæsarius; but they afterwards retracted this opinion.]

[3 August. Op. Par. 1679-1700. Serm. clxxv. 1, 2. Tom. V. Appendix, col. 300. See Vol. I. page 105, note 8.]

[4 Id. in Johan. Evang. cap. v. Tractat. XVII. 4. Tom. III. Pars II. col. 424. See Vol. I. page 106, note 1.]

of God, without rebuke in the midst of a crooked and perverse nation, among whom see that ye shine as lights in the world, holding fast the word of life." Again St Peter counselleth us that, "whereas some backbite us as evil-doers, we should lead an honest and godly life among them, that they seeing our good works may praise God in the day of visitation." But if we seek any praise of men, and desire to be magnified for our good deeds-doing, verily then have we our reward not of God but of the world. For there is not a more pestiferous infection to poison any good work, that it should lose the reward before God, than the desire of vain-glory and worldly praise. For that it is which Christ condemneth in the alms-deeds, prayers, and fasts of the hypocrites.

1 Pet. ii.

The desire of vain-glory poisoneth all good works.

Matt. vi.

St John Chrysostom saith: "They that so fast that they please men rather than God, they have a labour concerning the affliction of the body; but through vain-glory they can have no reward of their labour with God, which, when they ought to do it only for religion or faith's sake, had rather to seek the vain-glory of the world. And therefore saith the Lord, 'Verily I say unto you, They have received their reward[5].'"

Hom. xlvi. in Matt. vi.

St Austin also saith: "Some good thing may be done, and yet they not doing them well, of whom they are done. For it is a good thing to help a man that is in jeopardy and in danger, namely if he be an innocent. But he that doth this good deed, if he doth it because he loveth the praise of men rather than the glory of God, it is not good that he doth; forasmuch as he that doth it is not good. For God forbid that that should be, or be counted a good will, which glorieth in other or in itself, and not in the Lord[6]."

Lib. iv. contra Julianum, cap. 3. Mark well.

Hereto pertaineth the saying of St Ambrose: "When thou fastest, boast not thyself, nor brag not of it; for in so doing thy fast profiteth thee nothing. Those things that are done unto ostentation and boasting continue not to be recompensed in the world to come, but they are consumed and brought to nought with the reward of present things[7]."

In Lib. de Helia et Jejunio.

Of eschewing vain-glory our Saviour Christ gave us notable examples in all his doings. When he had healed the leper, he said unto him: "See thou tell no man." After that he had restored the two blind men to their sight, he charged them that no man should know of it. And when he had made whole the dumb and deaf man, he commanded them that were present that they should tell it no man. In all these his doings and such-like he gave us example to flee vain-glory and worldly praise, and only to seek the glory and honour of God, and that we should rejoice and glory in nothing but in God alone, as it is written: "He that rejoiceth, let him rejoice in the Lord." Therefore all the works that we do, whether they be prayer, fasting, alms-deed, watching, visiting of the sick, comforting of the prisoners, or any other that be agreeable to the word of God, we must do them with a single mind, and with such an heart as, being altogether estranged from vain-glory and worldly praise, seeketh only the honour of God, and the accomplishment of his most blessed will. So shall we do our works in secret; and our Father, which[8] seeth in secret, shall recompense us openly.

Matt. viii. Matt. ix. Mark vii.

Jer. ix. 1 Cor. i.

Matt. vi.

Thus have we heard both what the true and christian fast is, and also how we ought to fast. Let us now fall in hand with the third and last part of this treatise, and so make an end.

[5 Verum qui ita jejunant, ut magis hominibus quam Deo placeant, habent quidem laborem de corporis afflictione, sed per inanem gloriam mercedem laboris apud Deum habere non possunt: qui cum solummodo id causa religionis ac fidei agere debeant, humanam potius laudis gloriam quærere malunt, et ideo ait Dominus: Amen dico vobis, perceperunt mercedem suam.—Chrysost. Op. Lat. Basil. 1547. Ex cap. Matt. vi. Hom. ix. Fer. Quart. Cin. Tom. II. col. 1161.]

[6 Possunt ergo aliqua bona fieri, non bene facientibus a quibus fiunt. Bonum est enim ut subveniatur homini periclitanti, præsertim innocenti: sed ille qui hoc facit, si amando gloriam hominum magis quam Dei facit, non bene bonum facit; quia non bonus facit, quod non bona voluntate facit. Absit enim ut sit vel dicatur voluntas bona, quæ in aliis, vel in se ipsa, non in Domino gloriatur.—August. Op. Cont. Julian. Pelag. Lib. IV. 22. Tom. X. col. 596.]

[7 Noli ergo te jactare cum jejunas, noli gloriari, ne nihil tibi prosit jejunium. Quæ enim ad ostentationem fiunt, non in futurum fructum extendent suum; sed præsentium mercede consumunt.—Ambros. Op. Par. 1686-90. De Elia et Jejun. Lib. cap. xi. 40. Tom. I. col. 547.]

[8 Folio, *with*.]

OF THE TRUE USE OF FASTING.

The Sixteenth Chapter.

The manner of fasting in the pope's kingdom was wicked.

THE use, yea, rather the abuse of fasting in the pope's kingdom was very wicked, and worthy to be abhorred of the faithful. For, besides the fondness of the simple people in abusing the notable virtue of fasting, for want of knowledge, unto many and sundry superstitious and ungodly purposes, as partly heretofore we have heard; there have not wanted among them that profess divinity, which both in their sermons and writings corrupted the true and godly use of fasting. For they have taught that fasting of itself is so worthy a virtue, and of so great power, that it is able to satisfy for sins, to appease the wrath of God, to reconcile us to God, to deserve righteousness, and to win everlasting life.

The erroneous doctrine of the papists concerning fasting.

This doctrine is an enemy to the free grace of God, injurious to the fruits and merits of Christ's passion, and by no means to be received of the faithful Christians. For albeit fasting be without doubt a worthy fruit of repentance, and pleaseth God, when he that fasteth humbleth himself in the sight of God, confesseth his sin, repenteth him of his misdeeds, calleth for mercy, believeth to be forgiven for Christ's sake, and studieth earnestly from henceforth to lead a life comformable[1] to the rule of God's word; yet is it not of such virtue in itself, that it is able to bring unto us those good things which we look for at[2] the hand of God through Christ our Lord,—I mean the favour of God, the forgiveness of sins, the gift of the Holy Ghost, a new heart stuffed with spiritual affects, righteousness, peace, quietness of conscience, and everlasting life. These be the singular and free gifts of God, given only of him to so many as be born anew by the Holy Ghost, and believe in him.

Fasting is a fruit of repentance.

If the fasts of the holy men of whom we heard heretofore had been directed unto that end, that is, if by their fasts they had sought to be justified, and turned their eyes from that blessed Seed, in whom all nations of the earth were promised to be blessed, so had their fasts been not commended of God, not favoured but abhorred, not received but rejected. But their fasts came from a penitent and faithful heart toward God, and were exercised of them unto godly purposes, as we have heard, they seeking salvation only at the merciful hand of God for the promised Seed sake; therefore were both they and their fasts allowed of God. Let us therefore learn the true use of fasting, that we may know to what end our fasts ought to be directed, lest while we seek for medicine we find poison, and receive for salvation damnation.

Gen. xii. xxii. xxvi. and xxviii.

The fasts of the old fathers.

The Seventeenth Chapter.

Job vii.

Gal. v.

FIRST, forasmuch as the life of man upon earth is nothing else than a "warfare" and continual afflict[3] with her ghostly enemies; seeing also that "the flesh" without ceasing, through the subtile suggestion of Satan, "lusteth contrary to the Spirit," so that man in this vale of misery is never at quiet, nor hath so much leisure as once to breathe; so greatly on every side is he besieged and compassed about with cruel enemies, which assault him and tempt him vehemently, that, except he strongly fight against him with the weapons of the Lord, and also if he giveth not diligent watch, he straightways falleth into his adversaries' hands and is utterly undone; it is convenient, that whosoever intendeth to get a glorious and triumphant victory over his enemies, and not like a coward either to be put to flight, or else to be overcome, and for ever and ever perish, but rather valiantly to fight and never to cease till he hath subdued his enemies, that he striving courageously may obtain that reward which is promised to so many as fight lawfully, even the crown of glory and the inheritance of everlasting joy; it is convenient, I say, that he seeketh all means possible to avoid the danger of his enemies, and so to behave himself in all his doings, that his adversaries may have no interest in him, nor spy any void place about him, where they may give

2 Tim. ii.

[1 Folio, *comfortable*.] [2 Folio, *all*.] [3 Afflict: conflict.]

the first adventure, and by this means be encouraged not only to assail him, but also to vanquish him.

And forasmuch as the devil, our head enemy, "goeth about" not only himself "like a roaring lion, seeking whom he may devour," but, besides innumerable thousands of wicked spirits, which pertain to his army, and are ready at every moment to seek the destruction of man, hath also two special servants, which daily procure our utter subversion, I mean the world and the flesh, the one being his waiting-man, the other his hand-maid, ready at every hour to assail and to subdue man, if diligent watch be not given on our behalf; and forasmuch as among these our deadly adversaries the flesh is the most present and mortal foe, and an household enemy ever at home and never without, even within our own breast, carried about with us whereso-ever we go, and accompanying us whatsoever we do, and continually provoking us unto those wicked acts which strive against the heavenly motions of God's holy Spirit, that by this means she may do her master the devil great pleasure, by bringing us to destruction; if we intend to subdue and get the victory of this our household enemy the flesh, let us know for a certainty that there is not a more speedy way nor a more present remedy against her assaults, than godly fasting is; which enemy, that is the flesh, being once subdued, the foreign enemies shall the easilier be kept out, and we live in the more quietness by the help of God's Spirit and fervent prayer.

1 Pet. v. *The devil's army are the wicked spirits, the world, and the flesh.* *Gal. v.*

The Eighteenth Chapter.

And here begin we to learn the true use of fasting, and to know unto what end our fasts ought to be directed. The first true and godly use of fasting is to subdue the flesh, to mortify her beastly affects, and to repress the wild and rank motions thereof, that it may be subject and obedient to the spirit, as an hand-maid to her mistress, or a servant to his lord.

The first use of fasting.

For albeit God hath made us of two parts, that is, of body and spirit, yet hath he ordained the spirit to be ruler, and the flesh to be in subjection to the spirit. But, notwithstanding, the flesh (such is her wild disobedience and disobedient wildness) can by no means abide to submit herself to the rule of the spirit, but continually striveth to have the upper hand, and contrary to God's appointment to make the spirit subject unto her. The spirit provoketh unto humility, charity, patience, quietness, continency, pureness of life, moderate eating and drinking, &c. The flesh contrariwise calleth unto pride, haughtiness of mind, envy, malice, vengeance, discord, whoredom, avoutry, gluttony, drunkenship, &c. So that there is a continual conflict between the spirit and the flesh, who shall have the victory, as St Paul saith. If the flesh subdueth the spirit, then perish we; but if the spirit according to God's ordinance beareth rule, and hath the flesh in subjection, then well are we.

The rebellion of the flesh against the spirit. *Gal. v.*

Now that this may be brought to pass, godly and christian abstinence shall help greatly. For there is nothing that so tameth and bringeth under the wild and unruly lusts of the flesh, as fasting and abstinence, even as there is nothing that maketh a wild and fierce horse so tame and obedient to his master as the withdrawing of his[4] hay, oats, bread, and such other provender. They therefore, that will use their fast aright and unto a godly end, must first direct it unto this purpose; that by the exercise thereof they may bridle the wantonness of the flesh, and refrain their bodies from sin, that the "spirit, which is a precious thing before God," may be "quiet," or else all other exercises and travails, although never so painful, are vain.

Fasting tameth the flesh. *1 Pet. iii.*

To this use served the fasts of many godly both men and women in times past, that, the body being mortified, the spirit might the more freely attend on God. The prince-like prophet saith: "I put on sackcloth, and humbled my soul with fasting." This holy prophet and king used fasting to this end, that he might bring his body low and in subjection to the spirit, that the ungodly lusts thereof might no more rage and rule in him as they did, what time he took Bethsaba, the wife of Urias, and lay

Psal. xxxv. *2 Sam. xi.*

[4 Folio, *this*.]

with her, and that he might freely enjoy her, caused her husband to be slain in battle. In another place he also saith: "My knees are weak through fasting, my flesh dried up for want of fatness." We read likewise, that that most virtuous queen Esther brought her body very low with fasting. Again, St Paul saith of himself: "I chastise and tame my body, and bring it into subjection, lest by any means it come to pass that, when I have preached to other, I myself should be cast away." These with many other chastised and tamed their bodies with fasting, that the spirit might have free course unto God, and be occupied about heavenly things. After this manner ought all true Christians to do, that, the body being kept in subjection, the spirit may rule and have the over-hand; and by no means to follow the wicked manner of the papists, which in their fasts abstain from gross flesh, and devour all kind of dainty and fine fish, which make their bodies much more prone to lewdness than the eating of flesh, and also bringeth the spirit into miserable servitude and bondage. O ungodly manner of fasting!

Psal. cix. Esth. xiv. [Apocrypha] 1 Cor. ix.

The Nineteenth Chapter.

UNTO this taming, chastening, subduing, and mortifying of the flesh, by the true use of fasting, doth St Austin exhort us, saying: "Let our flesh be continually subject to our soul, and serve it as an hand-maid doth her mistress. Let us not suffer our body to be over-lusty, lest it war against the spirit; but always let the flesh be subject, that it obey the commandment of the Holy Ghost. Neither let us suffer the hand-maid to wax too rank, lest she set light by her mistress; but rather let her obey all her commandments and do her service. For as horses must be bridled, so must our bodies be restrained with fasting, watching, and prayer. For as, if the guides of chariots do give their horse the reins, they draw them into headlong downfalls; so if our body be not bridled, the soul and it both together slip into the deep pit of hell. Let us therefore be good and expert carters or chariot-drivers to our body, that we may go the right way[1]," &c. Again he saith: "Fasting swageth the intemperancy and unruliness of the body, and expresseth or keepeth under the troublous motions and raging lusts thereof. It causeth the soul to be at liberty, and not to be oppressed of the flesh, as the Lord saith: 'Take heed that your hearts be not overcome with surfeiting and drunkenness.' For when the soul is delivered from too much eating and drinking, then doth it consider itself the better, and weigheth in what case it standeth. For as a man in a filthy glass seeth not himself such one as he is indeed; so likewise, if he be overladen with too much eating and drinking, he[2] thinketh himself to be another manner of man than he is. Yea, then is he provoked unto sensuality and filthy lust, moved unto anger, puffed up with pride, and stirred unto lechery. In respect whereof the apostle saith: 'Be not drunk with wine, wherein is unhonest behaviour.' But if the body be kept in order, and accustomed with fasting, then doth the soul know the better with what devotion she ought to serve her Redeemer. Fasting, therefore, is very necessary.[3]"

De Salut. Docu. cap. xxxv. Gen. xvi. Quest. cxx. Vet. et Nov. Test. Luke xxi. Eph. v.

[1 Et semper atque semper caro nostra subjecta sit animæ, et sicut ancilla famuletur dominæ suæ. Ne præbeamus vires illicitas corpori nostro, ne committat bellum adversus spiritum nostrum: sed semper subjecta sit caro, ut obtemperet jussis sancti Spiritus. Neque incrassari permittamus ancillam, ne contemnat dominam suam; sed omnibus jussis ejus et obsequiis mancipetur. Sicut enim equis frena sunt imponenda; ita corpora nostra jejuniis et orationibus sunt infrenanda. Nam quemadmodum aurigæ, si frena laxaverint, per præcipitia ducuntur; ita et anima cum ipso corpore, si ei frenum non imposuerimus, ad inferni præcipitia delabitur. Simus ergo boni et edocti aurigæ corpori nostro, ut per viam rectam possimus incedere.—August. Op. Par. 1679-1700. De Salutar. Document. cap. xxxv. Tom. VI. Appendix, col. 200. This is not a genuine treatise of Augustine. It is ascribed with every appearance of reason to Paulinus, patriarch of Aquileia.]

[2 Folio, *be*.]

[3 Jejunia ergo intemperantiam corporis mitigant, motus adversos reprimunt, pressuram animæ auferunt, sicut ait Dominus, Nolite dediti esse in esca et crapula, ne graventur corda vestra. Cum enim anima ab esu et potu nimio fuerit liberata, tunc se melius recognoscit. Sicut enim in speculo sordido non se talem homo adspicit qualis est; ita et si esca et crapula fuerit gravatus, alterum se sentit quam est. Tunc exsuscitatur libido, accenditur ira, inflammatur superbia, generatur luxuria. Unde apostolus, Nolite, ait, inebriari vino, in quo est luxuria. Quod si temperatum fuerit corpus interposito jejunio, cognitione sui recepta anima intelligit qua devotione obsequi debeat Redemtori. Magna ergo ex parte jejunia sunt necessaria.—Id. Quæst. ex Utroq. Mixt. Quæst. cxx. Tom. III. Appendix, col. 130.]

Hereunto pertaineth the saying of St John golden-mouth: "The abstinence from meats is received for this purpose, that it should restrain the vigour and fierceness of the flesh, to make it obedient to the spirit, even as an horse is to his keeper. For he that fasteth must above all things refrain anger, learn meekness and gentleness, have an heart contrite, and such one as may repel and put back unclean concupiscences and lusts. He must also set before his eyes alway the eye of that everlasting Judge, and the judging-place that cannot be corrupted. Again, he must by his money be made the better by distributing it to the poor, and have rule over it. He must be liberal in giving alms, and receive into his heart no evil against his neighbour, as Esay, speaking in the person of God, saith: 'Have I chosen this fast?' saith the Lord. 'Though thou wry about thy neck like an hoop, and strawest under thee sackcloth and ashes, yet will not I regard thy fast,' saith the Lord. What fast then, tell me? 'Loosen,' saith he, 'the bonds of the wicked bargains, break thy bread to the hungry, bring the poor man that hath no house into thy house. If thou doest these things,' saith he, 'then shall thy light break forth as the morning light, and thy health shall spring right shortly.' Hast thou now seen, my well-beloved, what the true fast is? Let us look upon this fast, and let us not think, as many do, the fasting standeth in this point, if we continue without any dinner till it be night[4]."

In Gen. Hom. ix. Why we abstain from meats.

Isai. lviii.

St Hierome also saith: "Satiety or fulness is to be eschewed even of the most vile meats. For there is nothing that so overwhelmeth the mind as a full belly[5]."

Thus have we heard that the first and principal use of fasting is to tame, chastise, subdue, and mortify the flesh, that it resist not, but rather obey the rule of the spirit, as an hand-maid her mistress, or an horse his keeper. But this is to be considered in our fasting, that we do not with our unmeasurable fasts so make weak and feeble the body, that it be able to serve neither God, nor our neighbour, nor yet ourselves; and by this means utterly quench the use and working of the spirit, as we read that many in times past have done: such fasts please not God. This commandment therefore of St Paul is to be observed in all our fasts: "Make not provision," saith he, "for the flesh, to fulfil the lusts of it." An horse, that is too much delicately fed, casteth his master; again, if he be kept too hungry, he fainteth in the midst of the journey, and doth not his office. A mean therefore is to be had, as in feeding of the horse, so likewise in ordering of the body. We live not to eat, but we eat to live.

A rule to be observed in fasting.

Rom. xiii.

The Twentieth Chapter.

THE second cause why we ought to use fasting is that we, abstaining from meats, may have to give unto the poor and hungry the more liberally. For this kind of fasting pleaseth God greatly, when he seeth that we have so put on the bowels of tender mercy, and are led with such and so hearty compassion toward our poor neighbour, that we cannot find in our heart he should want; yea, rather than he should lack, we will spare it out of our own belly and give it him. God right well accepteth this fast, and blesseth the faster with plenty and abundance, as the wise man saith: "He that hath pity on the poor maketh the Lord his debtor; and look, what he layeth out, it shall be paid him again." Unto this manner of fasting doth God exhort us by the prophet, where he saith: "Break thy bread to the hungry, and lead the needy and wayfaring men into thine house. When thou seest a naked man, cover him; and despise not thy flesh." What it is to break thy bread to the hungry, we heard afore in the thirteenth chapter. The angel of God told Thoby, that when fasting, prayer, and alms-deeds go together, that is good and accepted in the Lord's sight.

To fast to give unto the poor.

Prov. ix.

Isai. lviii.

Tob. xii.

It is written in a certain book called "Pastor" (the author whereof they say Hermas, St Paul's disciple, was) on this manner: "On that day that thou shalt fast, thou shalt taste nothing at all but bread and water; and when thou hast counted the

Hermas. St Paul's disciple.

Mark and follow.

[4 Chrysost. Op. Par. 1718-38. In cap. i. Genes. Hom. viii. Tom. IV. pp. 62, 3. See Vol. I. page 105, note 6.]

[5 Sed ex vilissimis cibis vitanda satietas est. Nihil enim ita obruit animum, ut plenus venter et exæstuans.—Hieron. Op. Par. 1693-1706. Adv. Jovin. Lib. II. Tom. IV. Pars II. col. 205.]

quantity of the meat that thou wast wont to eat on the other days, the cost that thou shouldest make on that day that thou fastest, lay it up, and give it to the widow, to the fatherless child, or to the poor man, and so shalt thou fast a good fast; that he which hath received it of thee may fill his soul, and that his prayer may go unto the Lord for thee. If thou fulfillest thy fast on this manner, as I command thee, thy sacrifice shall be acceptable to the Lord, and thy fast shall be written in the book of life.[1]"

In Lev. c. vi. Hom. x. Origen saith: "We find in a certain book that the apostles said, Blessed is he that fasteth to this end, that he may nourish the poor man. The fast of such one is wonderfully accepted before God.[2]"

A notable sentence. Quest. cxx. Acts x. Hereto pertaineth the saying of St Austin: "Mercy did commend and greatly set forth the prayer and fasting of Cornelius. For he, being rich and a wealthy man, fasted. He did not only fast, but he also fed them that wanted, that their fulness might make Ser. lvi. de Tempo. his fast acceptable.[3]" Again in another place he saith: "Before all things, that which we were wont to eat at our dinner, on the fasting days let us bestow it on the poor.[4]"

In Gen. Hom. vii. Our golden-mouthed doctor in a certain homily counselleth us that, whensoever we fast, we should be liberal to the poor, and give them largely of our goods[5]. In another Hom. ix. in Gen. place he also saith: "He that eateth his meat and is not able to fast, let him give the larger alms: let him be the more diligent in praying: let him have the more fervent desire to hear the word of God[6]."

Here Chrysostom esteemeth almess among other virtues of so high price, that if there be any which cannot abide to fast for the weakness of their body, yet if they be plenteous in doing the works of mercy, and in praying and hearing the word of God, they are not refused of God, but accepted as good Christians. Mercy therefore and alms is a precious thing in the sight of God, and ought to be exercised of the Tob. xii. faithful, whensoever occasion is given, whether they fast or not. "Mercy," saith the angel, "is better than to hoard up treasures of gold. For mercy delivereth from death, cleanseth sin, and causeth to find everlasting life."

Thus have we heard that christian men ought to use their fast unto this end, that they, abstaining from meat and drink, might have whereof to give the more abundantly to the poor, to feed the hungry, to clothe the naked, to relieve the sick, to help the indebted, and to comfort the needy. O blessed are they that so fast! Rara avis in terris. But where are they? and we shall commend them, and call them blessed. For great and commendable things do such work among their neighbours and christian brethren.

The Twenty-First Chapter.

Fasting to serve prayer. THIRDLY, if we will use fasting aright, we must use it unto this end also, that by the diligent doing and often exercise thereof, we may be made the more apt to pray

[1 Peractis quæ supra scripta sunt, illo die quo jejunabis, nihil omnino gustabis, nisi panem et aquam; et computata quantitate cibi, quem ceteris diebus comesturus eras, repones, et dabis viduæ, pupillo, aut inopi; et sic consummabis humilitatem animæ tuæ; ut qui ex eo acceperit, satiet animam suam, et pro te adeat Dominum Deum oratio ejus. Si igitur sic consummaveris jejunium tuum, quemadmodum præcipio tibi; erit hostia tua accepta Domino, et scribetur hoc jejunium tuum.—Herm. Past. Lib. III. Sim. v. 3. in Patr. Apostol. Stud. J. B. Coteler. Antv. 1698. Vol. I. p. 105.]

[2 Invenimus enim in quodam libello ab apostolis dictum: Beatus est qui etiam jejunat pro eo ut alat pauperem. Hujus jejunium valde acceptum est apud Deum, et revera digne satis.—Orig. Op. Par. 1733-59. In Levit. Hom. x. 2. Tom. II. p. 246.]

[3 Denique orationem et jejunium Cornelii misericordia commendavit. Ipse enim, abundans copiis, jejunabat; sed et non habentes pascebat, ut illorum saturitas jejunium ejus faceret acceptabile.—August. Op. Par. 1679—1700. Quæst. ex Utroq. Mixt. Quæst. cxx. Tom. III. Appendix, col. 130.]

[4 Ante omnia in diebus jejuniorum quod solebamus prandere, pauperibus erogemus.—Id. Serm. cxli. 4. in Quadrag. ii. Tom. V. Appendix, col. 251.]

[5 Τὸν νηστεύοντα μάλιστα πάντων προσήκει... περὶ τὴν ἐλεημοσύνην πολλὴν τὴν δαψίλειαν ἐπιδείκνυσθαι.—Chrysost. Op. Par. 1718—38. In cap. i. Genes. Hom. viii. Tom. IV. p. 63.]

[6 Ὁ τροφῆς τοίνυν μεταλαμβάνων, καὶ νηστεύειν μὴ δυνάμενος, δαψιλεστέραν τὴν ἐλεημοσύνην ἐπιδεικνύσθω, εὐχὰς ἐκτενεῖς, τὴν προθυμίαν ἐπιτεταμένην ἐχέτω περὶ τὴν ἀκρόασιν τῶν θείων λογίων.—Id. Hom. x. p. 73.]

and to lift up our hearts unto the Lord our God with fervent prayers, humble supplications, and hearty thanksgiving.

For unto this end served fasting in times past, as divers histories of the holy scripture do declare. If any misfortune or grievous plague chanced at any time to the people of God, then straightways they fasted, as we read in the book of Judges. Judg. xx. Again, if any plague were threatened them by the prophets of God for their wickedness, as we read of the Ninivites; or if they perceived any great evil to be at hand, Jonah iii. as we read in the histories of the Israelites, of Jeosaphat, Judith, Esther, &c.; then 1 Sam. vii. 2 Chron. xx. fell they straightways to fasting. Judith iv. & viii. And their fasts were taken unto this end, that they might humble themselves in the sight of God, Esth. iv. and be made the more meet for to pray, and to swage the wrath of God. Why the godly men used fasting in times past. Neither do we read that any solemn fast was proclaimed at any time, but it was done to this end, that the fasters might the more quietly and freely serve God, and call on his holy name, by fervent and continual prayer.

And as we read this in the old testament, so lack we not the like examples in the new. Is it to be doubted, but that our Saviour Christ, in that time of his long and Matt. iv. solemn fast, joined to his fast prayer? He without doubt prayed unto God his Father all that time, that by his preaching, which was at hand, many might be turned from their ungodliness unto the true worshipping of God, from wickedness of life unto innocency of manners. We read also, that the godly matron Anne served God in the Luke ii. temple with fasting and prayer both day and night. The apostles likewise, after Acts xiii. & xiv. Christ's ascension, did always join to their fasting prayer. In like manner read we of the virtuous man Cornelius, which joined to his fasting both prayer and alms-deed. Acts x. And the angel said unto Toby: "Prayer is good with fasting." Tob. xii. Esdras said likewise to the Jews: "We fasted and prayed unto the Lord, and we had good luck." Ezra viii. Queen Esther also sent word to Mardocheus, saying: "Gather together all the Jews, Esth. iv. and pray for me; but see that ye neither eat nor drink three days and three nights; and I, with my maids, will fast and pray likewise." Again, Eliachim the priest said to the children of Israel, when they were in great sorrow and danger of their enemies: "Be ye sure that the Lord will hear your petitions, if ye continue stedfast in fastings Judith iv. [Vulgate.] and prayers in the sight of the Lord."

Thus see we that the godly people, both of the old and of the new testament, joined always for the most part fasting and prayer together, thinking themselves then to fast well, when their fast was accompanied with prayer, as it is written: "Prayer is Tob. xii. good with fasting." St Peter also saith: "Be ye sober, and watch unto prayer." 1 Pet. iv.

The Twenty-Second Chapter.

Moreover, our Saviour Christ also joineth prayer and fasting together, where he saith: "This kind of devils is not cast out but by fasting and prayer." Matt. xvii. Mark ix. To this kind of fasting doth St Paul exhort us, when he saith: 2 Cor. vi. "Let us give no occasion of evil, that in our office be found no fault; but in all things let us behave ourselves as the ministers of God, in much patience, in labours, in watchings, and fastings." Also St Peter: "Be ye sober," saith he, "and watch unto prayer." 1 Pet. iv. And from the contrary doth our Saviour Christ call us away, saying: "Take heed to yourselves, lest Luke xxi. at any time your hearts be overcome with surfeiting and drunkenness, and cares of this life; and so the day of judgment come on you unwares." The prophet Esay thundereth against them which, despising this godly manner of abstinence, set all their minds on banqueting and belly-cheer. "Wo be unto them," saith he, "that rise up Isai. v. early to follow drunkenness, and to them that continue so until night, and till they be set on fire with wine! In those companies are harps and lutes, tabrets, and pipes, and wine. But they regard not the work of the Lord." Again he saith: "Wo be unto them that are strong to sup out wine, and expert men to set up drunkenness! These give sentence with the ungodly for rewards, but condemn the just cause of the righteous. Therefore, like as fire licketh up the straw, and as the flame consumeth the stubble, even so their root shall be as corruption, and their blossom shall vanish away like dust; for they have cast away the law of the Lord of hosts, and blasphemed the word of the holy Maker of Israel." From beastly banqueting unto faithful fasting, and continual calling on the name of the Lord, doth the prophet Joel call these belly-gods, saying: "Wake up, ye drunkards, and weep; mourn, all ye wine-bibbers:" and not without a cause. For he that hath his body loaden with meat and drink, is no more meet to pray unto God than a dead man is to tell a tale; neither can the mind of such one any more fly unto God with heavenly desires, than a ship, too much cumbered with burdens and at the point to sink, can any longer float upon the waters.

Joel i.

A true and common proverb.

We have a proverb no less true than common among us, When the belly is full, the body would be at rest; meaning that he, which hath enfarced his belly with delicious meats and costious drinks, is more meet to sleep like a swine, than to take any earnest and weighty matter in hand.

Ser. de Tent. et Jejunio Christi.

"We have not read," saith St Cyprian, "that the godly men did ever take any great thing in hand, except they first fasted. So oft as they went about to obtain any thing of God, they fasted, and wept, and watched whole nights in prayer, and ware garments of hair next to their flesh, and so with all humbleness desired God to be beneficial to them. Neither wanted they of their purpose, when they most humbly fell down at the feet of God, and offered unto him the sacrifice of a contrite heart; but God was near unto them that called on him, and reached forth his hand to them that were in danger, and holp them that were in trouble[1]." Again he saith: "Prayer is of great virtue when fasting goeth afore[2]."

In Regul. Mon. cap. 1.

Basilius Magnus saith also, that fasting is necessary when we desire to obtain any thing of the Lord[3].

Why fasts were appointed of the fathers of Christ's church. Note.

The ancient fathers of Christ's church, godly considering how necessary a thing prayer is in the church of Christ, ordained certain feastful days in the year, on the which the people should resort and come together unto the temple for to pray unto the Lord God; and that they might come the more devoutly and pray with the greater fruit, they appointed also that the day before the solemn feast they should fast, that they might be the more apt to pray when they come together into the temple. For where the body is burdened with meat, there the mind can have no free passage unto God. Let them therefore that fast appoint their fasting also to this use, that by their abstinence they may be the more ready to pray, and not only to prepare themselves to pray, but also earnestly to give their minds unto prayer; or else what doth their fast profit them?

Ambrose.

To fast from meat and to go about worldly matters, what other thing is it than a mocking of God, and a derision of christian abstinence? as St Ambrose saith: "Dost thou think that he fasteth aright, which waking betimes in the morning goeth not unto the church to pray and to hear the word of God, but, as soon as he is up, gathereth together his servants, layeth abroad his nets, bringeth forth his dogs, and goeth running about the forests[4]?"

Therefore if we fast, let us fast aright; and, after the examples of the ancient holy fathers, let us alway couple prayer with our fasting. So shall both we, our fasts, and our prayers please God.

The Twenty-Third Chapter.

Psal. cxix.
Psal. xix.

FOURTHLY and finally, forasmuch as the word of God is the singular and unspeakable gift of God, given of him to be "a lantern to our feet and a light to our pathways," to turn souls from idolatry unto true godliness, to give wisdom to the humble,

[1 Quotquot viros virtutum vidimus, non sine jejunio legimus ascendisse: nec aliquid magnum moliti sunt, nisi prius abstinentia præcessisset. Quotiens aliquid a Deo obtinere conati sunt, jejuniis incubuere et lacrymis, et pernoctantes in orationibus, ciliciis carni hærentibus supplices beneficia postularunt. Nec defuit proventus, ubi ad pedes Dei sacrificium contriti cordis offerens, se prostravit humilitas; sed prope fuit invocantibus se Deus, et porrexit manum naufragis, et subvenit afflictis.—Cypr. Op. Oxon. 1682. De Jejun. et Tentat. Christ. (Arnold.) p. 35.]

[2 Id. ibid. See Vol. I. p. 162, note 2.]

[3 The editor has not discovered these precise words; but see Basil. Op. Par. 1721-30. Const. Monast. cap. i. Tom. II. p. 536.]

[4 An putatis illum jejunare, fratres, qui primo diluculo non ad ecclesiam vigilat, non beatorum martyrum loca sancta perquirit, sed surgens congregat servulos, disponit retia, canes producit, saltus silvasque perlustrat?—Ambros. Op. Par. 1614. Serm. xli. Dom. III. Quadrages. Tom. V. col. 58.]

to make the faithful penitent hearts glad, to lighten the eyes of the ignorant, to teach the true religion, to improve errors and heresies, to amend sinners, and to instruct all degrees in righteousness, "that the man of God may be perfect and prepared unto all good works;" (2 Tim. iii.) it is convenient, whether we hear it of other or read it ourselves, that we both hear and read it with great reverence and all humility, seeing that not man but the Holy Ghost is the author of it, which breathed into the hearts of holy men the knowledge of it, and put in their minds what they ought to write; as St Paul saith: "The whole scripture was given of God by inspiration." (2 Tim. iii.) And St Peter recordeth the same, saying: "The scripture came never by the will of man; (2 Pet. i.) but holy men of God spake as they were moved by the Holy Ghost." If the holy scripture then cometh from God, and God be the author of it, who dare presume either to hear or to read it, but with an humble reverence and reverent humility?

God's word is reverently to be both read and heard.

As St Austin saith: "By the books of the holy scripture God himself and our Lord speaketh unto us, and sheweth unto us the effect of a godly will. (Ad Julianum, Ep. cap. 11.) Let us then consider and mark well with what honour the message of that God and Lord ought to be received of us. What if a message came unto us very early in the morning from a king, would we not straightways (all other cares laid aside) receive the letters with a ready will and with all devotion, and, after we had read them, labour to fulfil the king's request to the uttermost? And behold, from the heaven of heavens the King of kings and Lord of lords, yea, and our Redeemer hath vouchedsafe to direct his letters unto us by the prophets and apostles, not that he should commit unto us any service necessary for him, but signify what things may do us good unto salvation and glory.[5]" O with what reverence and great honour ought we then to receive, read, or hear the letters of this[6] everlasting King and immortal God, sent for our glory and for our salvation, seeing that by them not man, but God speaketh unto us, as our Saviour Christ testifieth: "He that heareth you (he speaketh of the preachers of God's word) heareth me, and he that despiseth you despiseth me, and he that despiseth me despiseth him that sent me." Now that we may come reverently and humbly to the hearing of God's word, it shall not be unfitting to use our fast unto this end also, that we may come unto it with fasting and empty stomachs, that our mind and inward man may have the purer senses to understand, the clear sight to behold, the more open ears to hear, and the greedier stomachs to digest the holy mysteries of God. For likewise as he is no meet man to pray unto God, that cometh out of the tavern sweating and set on fire with drinking of hot wine and eating of delicious meats; so in like manner is he no fit man either to read or to hear the word of God, that hath a full gorge and stuffed belly. The more the body is filled, the more is the mind dulled, and made unapt to receive any message from God. "But albeit the outward man decay and be made feeble for a time, yet the inward man is renewed day by day, and made strong." (2 Cor. iv.) And this meant the holy fathers and godly bishops of Christ's church in times past, when they appointed fasting on the evens of solemn feasts, that the people by their fasting might be made the more apt the day following, when they came to the temple, to hear the blessed word of their salvation.

Why fasting was instituted on evens of solemn feasts.

The holy letters do testify that, when Moses received the law, he was in the mount with God, and fasted forty days and forty nights, before the tables of the law were delivered unto him: (Exod. xxiv.) whereof we may learn how reverently we ought to take the word of God, and not to come unto it with unwashed feet, as they use to say. And this is to be noted by the way, that, as Moses' fasting was found worthy to receive the law of God, so likewise when he came down from the mount and saw the people drunk and mad, singing and piping, dancing and leaping, he threw down the tables (Exod. xxxii.)

Belly beasts are not meet to receive the word of God.

[5 In quibus libris tua dignitas optime exercere se novit: quia per illos nobis loquitur ipse Deus et Dominus noster, et piæ voluntatis nobis demonstrat affectum. Recognoscamus et recogitemus, quali honore nobis illius legatio sit accipienda. Quid si a rege legatio aut indiculus ad nos veniret, numquid non mox aliis curis postpositis prompta voluntate et cum omni devotione literas acciperemus, et legentes implere satageremus? Et ecce de cœlo Rex regum et Dominus dominantium, immo et Redemtor noster, per prophetas et apostolos dignatus est nobis dirigere literas suas: non ut aliquod servitium sibi necessarium nobis demandet, sed quæ ad salutem et gloriam nobis prodesse possint innotescat.—August. Op. Par. 1679—1700. De Salutar. Document. cap. ix. Tom. VI. Appendix, col. 194.]

[6 Folio, *his*.]

of the law, and brake them on pieces, by this declaring that epicures and belly-gods be no worthy and meet vessels to receive the new wine of God's word.

Neh. ix. When the children of Israel at a certain time came together to read the book of the law of the Lord, they fasted the whole day, that they might read the holy scriptures with the more reverence, and be made the more meet to have the Holy Ghost present with them to teach them by his godly inspiration.

2 Esdr. v. Esdras also, being greatly desirous to have certain secrets opened unto him, was commanded of Uriel the angel to fast seven days first of all. Which thing he did, and had his desire satisfied.

Dan. ix. x. In like manner, after the prophet Daniel had fasted and prayed unto the Lord for knowledge of certain mysteries, Gabriel, the angel of God, came and revealed unto him the secrets of Christ's incarnation, passion, death, &c.

Bar. i. When Baruch read his book before the king and the king's council, and before all the people, they all wept, fasted, and prayed before the Lord.

Matt. iv. Before that our Saviour Christ took upon him the office of preaching, to declare unto the people the joyful tidings that he brought from heaven, he fasted forty days and forty nights, and did eat nothing at all; giving us example by his fasting, not to fast the like fast, (which is impossible and above the natural strengths of any man,) but to come unto the word of God through fasting with all reverence and humility, whether we read or hear it.

Acts i. ii. The apostles of Christ likewise, before they universally preached the kingdom of Christ, fasted and prayed; and as they were fasting and praying, the Holy Ghost came down upon them, and endued them with the knowledge of all languages, and taught them the true understanding of God's holy mysteries.

Acts x. To end, Cornelius, being very desirous to know the true and approved religion before God, fasted and prayed unto the Lord; and God graciously satisfied his desire.

The Twenty-Fourth Chapter.

We must come to the word of God reverently.

THUS see we that all godly men both of the old and new testament used abstinence for the most part, when they should either preach, hear, or read the word of God, that they might come the more reverently unto it, and be made the more meet to handle so holy and worthy mysteries. It is convenient therefore that we also, if we will use fasting aright, do follow the examples of these holy men whensoever we intend either to preach, read, or hear the word of God; and not unreverently to come unto the holy scripture as unto profane writings, after the example of many ungodly persons, which without all humility and reverence read the word of God as though it were an ethnick chronicle, a book of man's statutes, of Bevis of Hampton, of Guy of Warwick, of Robin Hood, and such other like fond and foolish fancies; yea, there want not (the greater shall be our plague) which scorn the word of God, and most shamefully abuse it, some unto scoffing and jesting, some unto the taunting of other, some unto the upholding of their fleshly liberty and corrupt manners, some unto the maintaining of wicked opinions, &c., whose destruction sleepeth not, whose damnation is at hand.

Abusers of the word of God.

Matt. vii. For, if it be not lawful to "cast pearls before hogs, nor to give that is holy to dogs," neither is it lawful for hogs to touch pearls, nor dogs to taste that is holy.
Exod. xii. If they were punished that did eat unleavened bread at the feast of the passover, if
2 Sam. vi. Matt. xxii. Uza were stricken unto the death for touching the ark, if that guest that came unto the marriage, not having the wedding garment, was bound hand and feet, and cast
1 Cor. xi. into utter darkness, where weeping and gnashing of teeth is, if the Corinths were plagued for abusing the Lord's supper; let not those swinish epicures, doggish papists, licentious libertines, ungodly anabaptists, gross gospellers, and wicked worldlings think that they shall escape unpunished, if they go forth to abuse the word of God, or to come unreverently unto it. For the holy scripture is the message of God, brought unto us from heaven by his holy embassadors the prophets and apostles, yea, by his own dearly-beloved Son, that King of glory, which sealed and confirmed it with the

shedding of his most precious blood: it may not therefore be lightly regarded, nor unreverently handled. "For if he that despiseth Moses' law," saith St Paul, "dieth without mercy under two or three witnesses, how much sorer, suppose ye, shall he be punished, which treadeth under foot the Son of God, and counteth the blood of the testament, wherewith he was sanctified, as an unholy thing, and doth dishonour to the Spirit of grace?" Heb. x.

That we therefore may humbly, reverently, devoutly, and honourably come unto the preaching, hearing, or reading of the blessed word of God, let us not neglect this noble virtue of fasting; but, after the example of the aforesaid godly men, prepare ourselves by the diligent exercise thereof to be meet to handle so holy and heavenly mysteries. By this means shall it come to pass, that God, which is the author of the holy scripture, shall alway be present with us by his holy Spirit, and teach us the true knowledge of his godly will, unto the glory of his blessed name, the profit of his holy congregation, and the singular comfort of our conscience.

The conclusion of the book.

Now have we heard, first, what the true and christian fast is: secondly, how we ought to fast: thirdly, what the true use of fasting is. It remaineth that we be not like that negligent servant which knoweth his master's will, and doth it not, and therefore is beaten with many stripes; but rather that we be likened unto that good seed which bringeth forth her increase, some an hundred-fold, some three-score-fold, some thirty-fold. If we now know the true doctrine of the holy scripture concerning fasting, let us practise it in our conversation, whensoever any such occasion is offered as heretofore is declared; and at all times let us "live soberly, righteously, and godly[1] in this present world." Let us not with the abuse cast [a]way the use: but let us so much the more gladly exercise the godly manner of fasting, because the ungodly papists rail on us, and continually beat into the simple people's heads, that we, which profess the gospel, abhor and condemn all fasting and praying, all commendable customs and godly ordinances; that "by well-doing we may stop the mouths of foolish and ignorant men," and that "they, which backbite us as evil-doers, may see our good works and praise God in the day of visitation;" to whom be all honour and glory for ever and ever.

Luke xii. Matt. xiii. Tit. ii. 1 Pet. ii.

Give the glory to God alone.

[1 Folio, *goodly*.]

DIEU ET MON DROIT

The Castel of comfort, in the whyche it is euidently proued, that God alone absolueth, & frely forgeueth ye sins of so many as vnfaynedly repent & turne vnto hym, compyled by *Thomas Becon.*

Esaye. xliii.

I am he onely, that for myne owne selfes sake do awai thine offences, and forget thy synnes: so that I wyl neuer thyncke vpon them.

Johan. vii

If any man be thirsty, let him come vnto me and drynke.

Psal. xxxiiii.

Oh taste & se, howe swete the lorde is, blessed is that man that putteth hys trust in hym.

ARISE FOR IT IS DAY.

THE

CASTLE OF COMFORT,

BY

THOMAS BECON.

TO THE

MOST HONOURABLE AND VIRTUOUS LADY MARIE[1],

DUCHESS OF RICHMOND HER GRACE, THOMAS BECON WISHETH FROM GOD THE FATHER, THROUGH OUR LORD JESU CHRIST, A FAITHFUL PERSEVERANCE IN GOD'S MOST HOLY WORD UNTO THE END.

---

2 Thess. ii. It is not without a great cause, most godly lady, that the holy apostle St Paul desired the Thessalonians to hold fast the doctrine that he had taught them afore; and not suddenly to be moved from their knowledge and understanding, nor to be troubled, neither by spirit, neither by words, nor yet by letter. For he undoubtedly Matt. xxiv. did afore see, by the revelation of God's Spirit, that there should arise false anointed and false preachers, which should work great miracles and wonders, insomuch that, if it were possible, the very elect and chosen people of God should be brought into 2 Pet. ii. error; which also should say, Behold here is Christ, or, There is Christ; "bringing in damnable sects, and utterly denying the Lord that bought them," as Peter saith. He considered the imbecility, weakness, and childish hearts of men, which, except Heb. xiii. they be corroborated and fortified with the strength of God's Spirit, are soon "carried about with divers and strange learnings," embracing no less greedily that, that is to themselves noisome and pestiferous, than that which is good and profitable; as we at this present time see daily before our eyes, both in the papists and anabaptists, with such other damnable sectaries.

Therefore this most excellent apostle desired the Thessalonians, yea, and so many of us as profess Christ unfeignedly, to persevere and abide in the word of truth even

---

[[1] The Lady Mary, duchess of Richmond, was daughter of Thomas Howard, third duke of Norfolk, by Elizabeth, the daughter of Edward, duke of Buckingham; and was one of the most beautiful women of her time. She was affianced in very early life to Henry Fitzroy, natural son to king Henry VIII. by Elizabeth, daughter of Sir John Blount, knight, and widow of Gilbert, lord Talboys. As the parties were within the forbidden decrees of consanguinity, a dispensation was obtained for the marriage; which however, owing to the tender age of both, was not formally celebrated. Fitzroy had various honours heaped upon him. He was elected a knight of the garter, then created earl of Nottingham, and duke of Richmond and Somerset: he was made lieutenant-general of all the king's forces north of the Trent, warden of the marches of Scotland, and afterwards lieutenant of Ireland, sir William Skeffington being appointed his deputy, He was a youth of great promise, and died aged about 17, in 1536; his marriage with lady Mary Howard thus being never consummated. He was buried at Thetford; and, at the dissolution of the abbey there, his remains were transferred to St Michael's church at Framlingham. After the death of Richmond, the duke of Norfolk proposed marrying his daughter to Sir Thos. Seymour, brother to the earl of Hertford (afterwards the protector duke of Somerset); but, whatever the obstacles might be, no such union took place. On the indictment of the earl of Surrey for high treason, the duchess of Richmond incurred much opprobrium for appearing among her brother's accusers. She alleged that he had dissuaded her from going too far in reading the scriptures, and that he had set up an altar in a church at Boulogne. If it be allowed to put a charitable construction on her conduct, we may suppose that she was possessed, as Becon says, "of exceeding love and fervent zeal toward the word of God," and thought that her principles required of her this evidence. Possibly too she gave it with reluctance. Certain it is that she discharged in a most exemplary manner a mother's duty to the children of Surrey, two sons and three daughters, who were placed under her care after his unjust execution. She appointed Foxe, the martyrologist, their tutor, who spared no pains in the education of his pupils. So sensible were her own family of her excellent conduct, that the duke of Norfolk, her father, made a testamentary bequest to her on that account: "Unto my daughter the lady Mary, duchess of Richmond, the sum of £500., as well in consideration that she is my daughter, as that she hath been at great costs and charges in making suit for my delivery out of imprisonment, and in bringing up my said son of Surrey's children." She had besides a grant of £100. a year from the crown on the same account. Other grants of manors and lands were also made to her, both by Henry VIII. and Edward VI. The duchess died about the year 1555.]

unto the end, that we may be saved, and not lightly to be moved with the subtile and crafty persuasions of them that teach "weak and beggarly traditions" with human constitutions; which give heed to fables and men's commandments, "that turn away the followers of them from the truth;" "which profess that they know God, but with their deeds they deny him, inasmuch as they are abominable and disobedient, yea, and unmeet to all good works;" "which love their own pleasures more than God, having an utter appearance of godly living, but denying the power thereof;" "which run from house to house, and bring into bondage both men and women loaden with sin;" "which are led with divers lusts, ever learning, and never able to come unto the knowledge of the truth;" which are "enemies of the cross of Christ;" which "call that is evil good, and that is good evil," &c.; in few, which are "ravening wolves, not sparing the flock."

Matt. x. Gal. iv. Tit. i. 2 Tim. iii. Phil. iii. Isai. v. Acts xx.

Doth the world want these enemies of God's glory? Have not we also need to take heed unto the aforesaid wholesome admonition of the holy apostle St Paul? Doth not the world at this day nourish such ungodly monsters? What age hath been without them since the beginning of the world?

What need I to speak of that great whore of Babylon, "the mother of fornications and abominations of the earth," which hath made drunken with the wine of the wrath of her whoredom all the nations of the earth; yea, the very kings and rulers of the earth have played the advouterers with her? The fornication of that most filthy and stinking strumpet is so openly known, and made manifest unto us, both by godly books and learned sermons, that it needeth not here to be rehearsed. And would God that, as the name of this Babylonical strumpet is exiled out of men's mouths, and rased out of books among us; so in like manner her whoredom (I mean, the popish and devilish decrees, which fight with the manifest word of God) might once be utterly exiled, banished, and for ever driven away from the bounds of christendom; that all things in the christian public weal, both in this and in other foreign realms, might be instituted, ordered, and appointed, according to the verity of Christ's most blessed gospel!

Rev. xvii.

But besides this monstrous beast, are there risen not a few which are plain antichrists, and daily labour to obscure the glory of God. No marvel, seeing that in the apostles' time, blessed John confesseth that there were many antichrists and false prophets. What need I to speak of them, which teach that Christ by his most precious death delivered us only from original sin? Which teach that man is justified by his own works, and not by the faith alone that he hath in Christ's most blessed death? Which teach that by observing men's traditions everlasting life is gotten? Which teach that external ceremonies justify and put away sin? Which teach that man is able of his own strength to fulfil the law, and to satisfy the justice of God? Which teach that our prayers cannot be heard without the intercession of other? Which teach that all honour pertaineth not to God alone? Which teach that the blood of our Saviour Jesu Christ is not a sufficient purgatory for all our sins, except we be broiled, boiled, and parboiled in the pope's furnace? Which teach that the Lord Christ gave not himself so plenteously a sweet-smelling sacrifice to God the Father for us, that, with the one oblation of his most blessed body, he hath made them perfect for evermore, that are sanctified? Which teach that God alone forgiveth not sin, but sinful man also? Are not these very antichrists? enemies of the cross of Christ? defacers of God's glory, false anointed? false preachers, ravening wolves? "clouds without water? trees without fruit? raging waves of the sea, foaming out their own shame? wandering stars, to whom is reserved that mist of darkness for ever?" "men-pleasers, having men in great reverence for avantage sake? cursed children, which have forsaken the right way, and are gone astray?"

1 John ii. iv. 1 John i. Rom. iii. ix. Eph. ii. John vii. xv. 1 Tim. ii. 1 John i. Heb. vii. ix. x. Eph. v. Matt. ix. Mark ii. Luke v. 2 Pet. ii. [Jude.]

These are they doubtless, of whom both Christ and his apostles bid us take heed in so many places of the holy scriptures. Against these ought all men to fight, that tender the glory of God. To confound these antichrists, ought we to sell wallet, scrip, coat, with all that ever we have, and to buy us a sword: I mean that "sword of the Spirit, which is the word of God."

Luke xxii. Eph. vi.

And to this end, that I may provoke other valiantly and boldly to fight against

these aforesaid antichrists, I, according to the talent given me, have taken upon me to wrestle with those wicked papists which believe and teach that God alone doth not forgive sin, but man also with the same power, and like authority. Which thing I take in hand the more gladly, because I see that this kind of doctrine is a great defacing of God's glory, and that it throweth many into great danger; forasmuch as they look for that at the hand of man, which only is the gift of God; yea, it encourageth not a few to live dissolutely and without the fear of God, seeing they are persuaded, that if the priest layeth his hand once upon their head, and say, *Ego absolvo te*, they are quite delivered of their sinful burden; and, though they return straightways unto their filthy vomit, what skilleth it? *Ego absolvo te* will dispatch all together.
2 Thess. ii. If any man "sitteth in the temple of God, boasting himself as God," surely they do it, which take upon them the office of God, that is, to remit and forgive sin. But they
Isai. xi. shall be slain with the breath of the Lord's mouth.

The order of the doctrine contained in this treatise following. The order which I will observe in the treatise following is this. First, I will prove with manifest scriptures, that God alone forgiveth sin. Secondly, that the priest is but a minister appointed of God, to declare free remission of sins to the truly penitent, to declare, I say, and not to forgive. Thirdly, I will answer to the objections of the adversaries, and utterly wipe them away, restoring the scriptures to their native sense. At the last, lest I should seem to despise the true and christian absolution of a faithful minister, and the use of the keys, which consisteth in preaching, I will express my mind concerning them also, so that to any indifferent person I doubt not but that my judgment shall appear godly and conformable[1] to the true vein of the holy scriptures.

This little treatise, most virtuous lady, I send unto your grace, as a testimony of my ready bent good-will and serviceable heart toward your grace, being provoked hereunto through your exceeding love and fervent zeal, which your most honourable ladyship bear, both toward the word of God, and the true professors of the same; most humbly beseeching your grace to take in good part this my rude and simple gift. God, which by his holy Spirit hath wrought in your heart this entire love toward the gospel of his Son Christ Jesu, mought also bring forth in your grace plenteousness of good works, unto the glory of his blessed name, and the profit of his holy congregation! Amen.

(*)

Your grace's most humble and faithful
orator, THOMAS BECON.

[[1] Folio, *confyrmable*.]

THE

CASTLE OF COMFORT.

THAT God alone absolveth the truly penitent, and only forgiveth the sins of so many as with unfeigned faith and hearty repentance convert, turn, and flee unto his mercy, it is manifestly proved by divers texts of the holy scripture. (The first part.)

First, let us hear what God himself saith by the prophet: "I am he, yea, I am he in deed, which putteth away thy sins; yea, and that for mine own sake; and I will remember thy sins no more. Call to remembrance, and let us be judged together. Tell, if thou hast any thing that thou mayest be justified. Thy first father sinned; and thy prophets have trespassed against me." (Isai. xlii) Are not these words evident enough? God the Father, perceiving right well that there should arise false anointed and false preachers, which without all shame would arrogantly arrogate, and proudly challenge to themselves that power of forgiving sin which alone pertaineth to him, plainly here affirmeth that he alone putteth away our sins. (Matt. xxiv.) And because he would have us the more seriously and earnestly to believe it, he repeateth this word "I" twice, saying: "I am he, yea, I am he in deed, which putteth away thy sins; yea, and that for mine own sake." And lest any man should think that one may more forgive another his sins (I speak of those sins which are between God and our conscience, and not of the brotherly reconciliation), he affirmeth that our first father Adam, and all prophets and preachers have sinned, so that of them no remission of sins is to be looked for. (Rom. iii. Rom. xi.)

Can flesh purify the soul? "That which is born of flesh is flesh," saith Christ. (John iii.) "All have sinned," saith St Paul, "and want the glory of God." (Rom. iii.) Again: "God hath wrapped all nations," saith he, "in unbelief, that he might have mercy on all." (Rom. xi.) If all be sinners, flesh, and the children of wrath; if all be hypocrites, unprofitable servants, earth, dust and ashes; (Eph. ii. Luke xvii.) if all be the enemies of God, and unfaithful, how dare we be so bold, as to take upon us one to forgive another their sins? Is a traitor a meet man to purchase a pardon of a prince for another traitor? Can one traitor forgive another his treason? Can one sinner forgive another his sin? Of the unclean what can be made clean?—as Job saith: "Who can make him clean, that is conceived of unclean seed?" (Job xiv.) Is it not thou alone, O Lord? It is the Lord alone in deed, as David saith: Thou, O Lord, shalt "sprinkle me with hyssop, and I shall be made clean; yea, I shall be made whiter than snow." (Psal. li.) And as our Saviour Christ said unto Peter: "If I wash thee not, thou hast no part with me." (John xiii.) If God washeth us not from our filthiness, we have no part in the heritage of Christ.

Again, the aforesaid prophet saith: "The Lord is our judge, the Lord is our lawgiver, the Lord is our king; and he it is that shall save us." (Isai. xxxiii.) How oft is "the Lord" here repeated, to shew that it is he alone which worketh all good things in us, which forgiveth our sins, and saveth us; yea, and none but he alone.

Again, the Lord himself saith by the same prophet: "I am the Lord; and there is no Saviour besides me." (Isai. xliii.) Here God himself confesseth that he alone is the Lord, and that there is none other Saviour besides him; that is to say, none that forgiveth sin, and giveth eternal life, but he alone. By another prophet he also saith: "Thy destruction, O Israel, cometh of thyself: only of me cometh thy help and salvation." (Hos. xiii.) David, that holy king and godly prophet, knowing his deliverance from sin to be of God alone, stirreth up his inward man to magnify the Lord, saying: "Magnify the Lord, O my soul; and all that are within me, praise his holy name. O my soul, bless the Lord, and forget not all his benefits. For he it is that pardoneth all thine iniquities, and that healeth all thy diseases: yea, he it is that delivereth thy life from destruction, and crowneth thee in mercy and loving-kindness." (Psal. ciii.) Again: "Let Israel trust in the Lord; for with the Lord there is infinite mercy, and plenteous (Psal. cxxx.)

redemption. And he it is that redeemeth Israel from all their sins." Whosoever therefore taketh on him to forgive sin, maketh himself a saviour, and saith with the angel [Isai. xiv.] *apostata:* "I will climb up above the high clouds, and I will be like unto the Most [Isai. xlii.] Highest." But let him know that pride will have a fall, and that "the Lord is a jealous God, and will give his glory to none other."

[Gen. iii.] Who delivered Adam from everlasting damnation, when he with his wife had transgressed the commandment of the high Lord? Who absolved Nohe from his [Gen. xix.] drunkenness? Who delivered Loth from the uncleanness which he committed with [Exod. ii.] his daughters? Who saved Moyses, and forgave him his manslaughter? Who absolved [2 Sam. xi. Jonah iv.] David from his adultery? Who had compassion on the Ninivites when they repented, believed, and converted? To be short, who forgave and absolved all the patriarchs, kings, prophets, priests, &c., with all other of the old testament, when they knowledged their sins, and returned unto the Lord their God with faithful repentance, but only God alone? To whom did they flee for remission of sins, but to God alone? In whom did they put their affiance and trust, but in God alone, as the psalmograph testifieth, [Psal. xxii.] saying: "Our fathers trusted in thee, O Lord: yea, they trusted in thee; and thou deliverest them. They cried unto thee, and they were made safe: in thee, O Lord, they trusted, and were not confounded." Are not these the words of blessed David? [Psal. xxxii.] "I said, I will confess my sins unto the Lord; and thou forgavest the wickedness of my sin." Here is no mention made of Aaron, or of any of that priesthood; nor yet of pope, patriarch, cardinal, archbishop, bishop, priest, or of any other man to forgive us our sins, but of God alone. So followeth it, that the Lord alone remitteth the ungodliness of our sin, and that he alone absolve *a pœna et culpa.*

This was godly doctrine in the old testament; neither was he counted of godly men any heretic that taught this kind of learning at that time. God was then the Lord alone omnisufficient for all his people that truly repented and converted to his unmeasurable mercy; neither had he need at that time of any other to be conjoined with [Gen. xv.] him, as he himself said unto Abraham: "Fear not Abraham: I am thy defender, and [Isai. lix.] thine altogether sufficient rewarder:" and is the Lord's hand now so abbreviated and shortened, that he can save no more? or is his ear so stopped that he can not hear? Lord God, what a sudden change is this! But I stedfastly believe that he is the same Lord now, that he was in the old time, and of no less power to remit sin at this present, than he was many thousand years before these our days; inasmuch as he [Mal. iii.] abideth ever one, and is not changeable, as he saith by the prophet Malachi: "I am the Lord, and am not changed."

Hitherto have I been bold in few words to prove that in the time of the old law God alone forgave the sins of his people, without the help either of bishop, prophet, priest, Levite, or any other; that the whole glory of their salvation might be ascribed to him alone. Now let us also labour to declare that God alone doth the very same thing in the new testament; that he alone may still remain the God of health, against the pestilent doctrine of the wicked papists, which so boarishly sweat to maintain their usurped power and feigned authority in forgiving sin, to the great obscuring of God's [1 Tim. i.] glory; and that to him alone all honour and praise may be given.

We read in the holy gospel that, when a certain man being diseased of the palsy [Matt. ix.] was brought unto Christ to be made whole, Christ said unto him: "Son, be on a good comfort: thy sins are forgiven thee." The scribes, hearing these words of forgiving sin, thinking with themselves that Christ was not God, but man only, and that it was the office of God alone to remit and forgive sin, spake on this manner within themselves: *Hic blasphemat:* "This fellow blasphemeth;" or, as Mark and Luke [Mark ii. Luke v.] writeth: "Who is he that speaketh blasphemies? Who is able to forgive sin but God alone?" Here the scribes, tendering more the glory of God than our papists and Pharisees do at this time, could not abide that Christ, whom they judged only man, should challenge to him power to forgive sin, seeing that alone pertained to God. And upon this place of the scripture many write, that the scribes erred not in this confession that God alone forgiveth sin, but in this they say they were deceived, because they believed not that Christ was both God and man. If Christ had been nothing but man, he had blasphemed in deed; that is to say, taken that thing upon him which is the office of God alone: but forasmuch as he was not only man, but also God, he blasphemeth not, he challenged nothing but that was his right. So did the scribes, and not Christ, blaspheme. Let all men therefore learn of this history, that God alone forgiveth sin.

Doth not Christ also, in the aforesaid chapter of Matthew, call himself a physician, Matt. ix. and shew that he came to call sinners unto repentance, and to make them whole? Why calleth he himself a physician, but because it is his office to cure and heal? Jeremy prayed unto this physician, saying: "Heal me, O Lord, and I shall be healed: Jer. xvii. save thou me, and I shall be safe; for thou art he whom I will magnify." For he did know full well that all other physicians were unprofitable without his help, and no more meet to cure sick consciences of themselves, than the old lion was to heal the horse, of whom Esop writeth in his fables, which notwithstanding take on him to practise physic, when of that same science he was altogether ignorant.

Moreover, Christ calleth all them that labour and are laden to him, and promiseth Matt. xi. that he will refresh, ease, and comfort them. He sendeth them not away to other, but calleth them all, without exception, to him; whereby he sheweth that no creature, neither in heaven nor in earth, can truly and sufficiently heal our infirm and sick consciences, but he alone, which saith: "I am the resurrection and life. He that John xi. believeth in me, although he be dead, shall live; and every one that liveth and believeth in me shall never die." For who can forgive me my sin, but he alone, which is without 1 Pet. ii. all sin? Who can deliver me from death and hell, but he alone, which hath overcome Hos. xiii. them both? Who can make me good, but he alone, which only is good? Who can Matt. xi. make me wise, righteous, and holy, but he alone, which is appointed of God the Father to be our "wisdom, righteousness, and sanctification?" Finally, who can engraff in 1 Cor. i. Ecclus. xxiv. me life and virtue, but he alone, in whom is all hope of life and virtue? Therefore full well doth Christ call so many as labour and are loaden with the burden of sin to him, Matt. xi. and promiseth that he will refresh them, that is to say, absolve and deliver them from their sins.

Hereto belongeth the saying of blessed John Baptist: "Behold that Lamb of God, John i. which taketh away the sin of the world." Here blessed Baptist confesseth, that it is Christ alone which absolveth and taketh away the sin of the world. Doth not also the holy evangelist, St John, in the aforesaid chapter, call Christ that "true light, which lighteneth every man that cometh into this world?" What other thing is it to lighten, than to put away the clouds of sins, and to send into our hearts the radiant and glistering beams of the eternal Son, which is the knowledge of God's most holy will? And this, saith St John, is the office of Christ alone.

Why doth Christ call so many as thirst unto him, and promiseth that floods of Isai. lv. John vii. livish water shall flow out of their bellies; yea, and that he will give them the water Rev. xxii. of life freely; but only to shew that whosoever is thirsty, and heartily desireth remission of sins, must with all haste come to him, and say with the psalmograph, "Like as the Psal. xlii. hart desireth the water-brooks, so longeth my soul after thee, O God: my soul is athirst for God, yea, even for the living God," &c.? Furthermore, Christ commandeth that "repentance and remission of sins should be preached in his name." Where we Luke xxiv. may learn that forgiveness of sin cometh only by the name of Christ.

And in the Acts of the Apostles we find, that when any famous and notable act or miracle was done, the people, as many at this day, did ascribe it to the virtue and power of the apostles, willing to do sacrifice unto them for it; but the apostles did reject and cast away all such immerited honour and undeserved praise, contending and Acts iv. xiv. mainly labouring to persuade the people, that whatsoever was done came not to pass by their power, but by the virtue of Jesu Christ, whom God raised up from death. And when they made mention of remission of sins, they did never remember and rehearse their own power to forgive sin, but only preached that so many as believed and were baptized into the remission of sins should be absolved and freely forgiven by the name of Jesu Christ. And in the Acts of the Apostles blessed Peter plainly confesseth, that Acts x. there is no health, no life, no remission of sins, but in Christ alone, and that "there is Acts iv. none other name given unto men under heaven, wherein they must be saved," but the name of Jesu Christ alone.

Neither did the apostles absolve any otherwise than by the preaching of God's word, which when it was heard and believed, then were the diligent hearers and faithful believers of the same truly absolved, as Christ saith: "Now are ye clean for the word's sake that I have spoken unto you;" that is, "Now are ye delivered from your sins because ye have believed my preaching."

John xv.

"The faith of the heart justifieth," saith St Paul. Where it may be learned that, if faith be not given to the word, there is no absolution or deliverance from sin. "For whatsoever is not of faith is sin;" and where faith is not, there abideth the wrath of God, as holy John Baptist saith: "He that believeth the Son hath everlasting life; but he that believeth not the Son shall not see life, but the wrath of God abideth upon him." Therefore, before Christ absolved any man of his sins, he did behold and see whether he had faith or not. If Christ found true faith in his heart, then he always said, "Thy faith hath saved thee."

Rom. x. Rom. xiv. John iii. Matt. viii. ix. xv. Mark v. ix. Luke xvii. xviii. John xi.

Seeing then that none can search the heart, whether it be faithful or unfaithful, but God alone; seeing also that the absolution beareth no strength but where faith is, it followeth that none can absolve me of my sins, but that Lord alone which "searcheth the reins and the heart." The priest is only God's minister, appointed of God (if he be truly sent) to preach that absolution and free deliverance from my sin, through the name of Jesu Christ; which preaching if I believe, I am so sure to be delivered from all my sins, as though Christ himself had said unto me, "I freely absolve thee," or, "Thy sins are forgiven thee for thy faith's sake in my name." Are not these the words of Christ, which is the self truth and cannot lie, spoken to all faithful ministers? "He that heareth you heareth me; and he that despiseth you despiseth me; and he that despiseth me despiseth him that sent me."

Jer. xvii. Psal. vii. Rev. ii. John xiv. Tit. i. Luke x.

But let us rehearse more scriptures, although to any christian heart these, which hitherto I have recited, may seem abundantly to suffice. Blessed Paul, in his epistle to the Romans, proveth manifestly that God alone justifieth us. If our justification cometh from God alone, then followeth it well that the remission of our sins cometh from God alone also. For remission of sins goeth before justification. By Christ's death are we delivered from our sins; but by his resurrection are we justified and made righteous. So doth it evidently appear, that it is God alone which both remitteth the sin, and also justifieth the sinner for Christ's sake, which is our righteousness. Again, the aforesaid apostle saith that God hath not only given us his Son, but also all things with him: ergo, absolution of sins. So see we that God alone absolveth and forgiveth us our sins for Christ's sake.

Rom. viii. Rom. iv. 1 Cor. i. Rom. viii.

St Paul to the Galatians affirmeth, that Christ "gave himself for our sins, that he might deliver us from this present evil world;" that is to say, from all evil in this present world. Ergo, God alone it is which delivereth us from our sins in this vale of misery. "Ye are washed away from your sins," saith he, "yea, ye are sanctified and made righteous by the name of the Lord Jesu, and by the Spirit of our God." Ergo, our absolution, our deliverance from sin, our sanctification, our justification, and all that ever good is, cometh from God through Jesu Christ our Lord. Again he saith: "God the Father hath blessed us with all spiritual blessings:" ergo, with the blessing of absolution and free deliverance from all our sins. God "hath delivered us from the power of darkness, and carried us into the kingdom of his well-beloved Son, by whom we have redemption, even by his blood, remission of sins." Ergo, by Christ's blood are we absolved and delivered from our sins. "Every good gift and every perfect gift," saith James, "cometh from above, and descendeth from the Father of light." Ergo, absolution, which is a good and perfect gift, cometh down from the Father of light.

Gal. i. 1 Cor. vi. Eph. i. Col. i. James i.

Blessed John in his epistle saith: "If we confess our sins, God is faithful and righteous to forgive us our sins, and to make us clean from all iniquity." Here St John affirmeth that God forgiveth us our sins, and maketh us clean from all unrighteousness. He saith also, that "the blood of Jesu Christ, God's own Son, maketh us clean from all sin." And in the chapter following he saith: "If any man sinneth, we have an advocate with the Father, Jesu Christ, that righteous one. And he it is that obtaineth mercy for our sins, not for our sins only, but for all the world also." Again he saith:

1 John i. 1 John ii.

"I write unto you, O ye little children, that your sins are forgiven you for Christ's name sake." Here see again that by Christ remission of sins cometh to us from God the Father. Moreover, blessed John in his Revelation writeth on this manner. Christ hath "loved us, and washed us from our sins by his blood." Here see we that all our Rev. i. sins be washed away by Christ's blood alone.

What should I write more? If I go forth to gather together all the places of holy scripture that prove the absolution of our sins to come from God alone, I should not only trouble the most godly reader, but also write a volume longer than the Iliads of the Greek poet Homer, when to any christian judgment I may justly seem already to have proved my article true and sufficiently christian, unto the great shame of all these papists, which cease not with their stentoreous voices to speak evil of the true preachers of God's word, and to obscure or deface the glory of God.

Take away the power of only remitting sins from God; and what remaineth there wherefore we should confess ourselves bound to him? I speak of matters concerning the salvation of our souls. If all that be of the shaven nation have power to absolve men of their sins at their pleasure, and to remit or retain whose iniquities it pleaseth them, then is God well promoted, even out of the hall into the kitchen, as they use to say. So should it also follow, that so many as pleased the priests should have their sins forgiven them, and so be saved; otherwise not. O intolerable blasphemy! But as God alone remitted the sins of the fathers of the old testament, so in like manner doth he now in the new testament. Who absolved Mary Magdalene from Luke vii. her sins, but Christ? Who forgave the thief his robbery and manslaughter, but Christ? Who had compassion on Peter, when he had denied his Master Christ, but Luke xxii. Christ? Who made of Matthew, the publican and toll-gatherer, a faithful apostle and Matt. ix. preacher, but Christ? Who is that good shepherd that fetcheth home the stray Luke xv. sheep lovingly upon his shoulders unto the sheepfold? is it not Christ, which saith of himself, "I am that good shepherd: a good shepherd giveth his life for sheep?" John x. Who received home joyfully the lost son? was it not Christ? Who healed the wounded Luke xv. man? the priest or the Levite? or rather Christ the Samaritan? Luke x. Who made of Saul the persecutor Paul an apostle? was it not Christ? Who absolved all these, with many other in the scripture, from their sins, but Christ alone, the Son of the living God? Doth not all power belong to Christ, both in heaven and in earth? To him Matt. xxviii. therefore alone doth the power of remitting sin pertain. Seeing then that this is true, and nothing more true, why may we not be bold to say, maugre the papists, that God alone absolveth the truly penitent, and only remitteth the sins of so many as with an unfeigned faith convert and flee unto his mercy?

I could allege divers sentences out of the holy doctors of Christ's church, which maintain this doctrine; but, seeing I fight not for the avancement of man, but for the glory of God, I will not enfarce this my work with man's doctrine, but with the infallible verity of God's word. For I know that every man is a liar; but God is Psal. cxvi. true, and his word abideth for evermore. Isai. xl.

Now will I prepare myself to the second part of this[1] treatise, and afterward make answer to the objections of the adversaries, that God may still remain a glorious God in the presence of all men, and all other recounted dust and ashes in comparison of him.

The second part of this treatise is this: as concerning the priest, he forgiveth not The second part. the sin, but only is a minister of God, appointed to utter and declare that free remission of sins purchased for us of God the Father by the most precious blood of Jesu Christ. This maketh the papists to cry, *Ad ignem, ad ignem.* For this doctrine plucketh them down one staff lower than they were before. They may now become no more checkmate with God. For before they were not only not contented to be his ministers, but also they would be 'hail fellow well-met' with him. Now shall they be fain, either to be the messengers and servants of God, or else plain antichrists and papists. But let us see what the scripture saith. That the priest forgiveth not sin, but God alone, it is sufficiently proved before. Now must we learn

[1 So the edition of 1550: the folio has *his*.]

of the holy scriptures, whether the priest be but only a minister appointed of God to utter and declare that absolution and free deliverance from sin, or not. That this is his office, it is manifest by divers places of the new testament.

Mark xvi. When Christ sent forth his disciples, he said unto them on this manner: "Go into the universal world, and preach the gospel to every creature: whoso shall believe and be baptized, he shall be saved; but whoso will not believe shall be condemned." Here is it evident enough what authority priests have, and what their office is; verily to preach the gospel and to baptize. Mark that they must preach the gospel, as St

1 Cor. i. Paul saith: "Christ sent me not only to baptize, but to preach the gospel." Again:

1 Cor. ix. "Wo is unto me, if I preach not the gospel." And in the description of a spiritual minister he sheweth that such one ought to be chosen, as is not only learned, but

1 Tim. iii. Tit. i. also "apt to teach," "able to exhort with wholesome doctrine, and to convince or over-

1 Pet. v. come them that speak against the truth of Christ's gospel." And St Peter saith: "Ye elders, feed the flock of Christ, so much as in you is."

What it is to preach the gospel. What other thing is it to preach the gospel, than to declare unto the people that their sins be forgiven them freely of God, if they repent and believe in Christ, as it

John iii. is written, "He that believeth the Son hath everlasting life?" If sins be forgiven of God, and the ministers commanded to declare the same to the people, then doth it follow that they forgive not the sin, but only are ministers appointed of God to ☞ publish that benefit of our salvation. If a prince pardoneth his subject for his treason committed against his person, and sendeth his letters of favour to the traitor by one of his faithful servants, commanding him to declare his pitiful mercy to the guilty; who forgiveth the fault, the messenger or[1] the king? I am sure it will be answered, The king. And not unjustly. For the prince alone pardoneth: the messenger only declareth his prince's pleasure to the traitor. Even so all we have offended and worthily deserved eternal death. Now the good pleasure of our most mighty prince is to forgive us even of his own free mercy, without our deserts or merits, for Christ's sake; and that his unspeakable goodness toward mankind may be known, he hath appointed his ministers to publish it abroad. The sum of their commission is this, that whosoever will repent his former life, and believe to have remission of their sins, through the mercy of God in Jesu Christ our Lord, they shall be forgiven. The ministers of God publish these joyful news, exhort unto repentance and faith. The people repent and believe: their sins are forgiven. Who forgiveth the sins of the faithful repentant? The granter of the commission, or the declarer thereof? God or man? I doubt not but that ye will answer, God. If God alone, whom we offend, forgiveth the sin, and not the declarers of the forgiveness, I have gotten that I have desired for the probation of the second part of this little treatise.

John xx. But let us hear what Christ saith: "As my Father sent me, so send I you." Now, I pray you, how was Christ sent, and for what purpose? Let us hear what he himself saith; and then shall I be blameless. By the prophet Esay he speaketh

Isai. lxi. Luke iv. on this manner: "The Spirit of the Lord is upon me, because he hath anointed me; to preach the gospel to the poor he hath sent me, to heal the broken-hearted, to preach deliverance to the captive, and sight to the blind, freely to set at liberty them that are bruised, and to preach the acceptable year of the Lord." Again he saith:

Luke iv. "I must preach the glad and joyful tidings of the kingdom of God to other cities

Mark i. also; for therefore am I sent." Once again he saith: "Let us go into the next towns, that I may preach there also; for therefore am I come." All these sentences declare manifestly, that Christ was sent to preach the kingdom of God, that is to say, free deliverance from sin to so many as repent and believe. If they will not be above Christ, they must be contented to preach the will of the celestial Father as he was, and not to take upon them that thing whereof only they are ministers.

Doth not St Paul, James, Peter, and Jude, call themselves the servants of Jesu Christ in all their epistles, declaring thereby that they are not the self master, by whom remission and absolution of sins cometh; but only the ministers of him, which infundeth[2] and poureth into all men grace, favour, remission of sins, and everlasting

[1 Folio, *of*.] [2 Infundeth: the same as *poureth into*.]

life? There is but "one Master, that is to say, Christ:" the other are servants, as St Paul witnesseth: "We preach not ourselves, but Christ Jesu the Lord, and we your servants for Jesus' sake." Again: "Let a man on this wise esteem us, even as the ministers of Christ, and stewards of the secrets of God." Matt. xxiii. 2 Cor. iv. 1 Cor. iv.

All these texts declare manifestly that priests, if they be true ministers, and not rather idols, are nothing but ministers and servants appointed of God to declare unto the christian congregation, that free remission of sins cometh unto us from God alone, through the glorious name of Jesu Christ; so far is it off that the priests contrary to their commission can forgive sins, whose office consisteth in declaring, and not in giving, remission of sins. Therefore let them be contented no more from henceforth arrogantly to arrogate that unto them, which pertain to God alone, but humbly confess that God only forgiveth the sin, and that they are but commissioners, appointed of God, to publish and set forth the same, I mean the remission of sins given to the faithful penitent of God alone.

Neither let them frown at this doctrine, which setteth them in their right place, but rather (as it becometh good and faithful servants) let them give the glory of our salvation to God alone, and be glad that they are called unto so worthy and honourable office to declare the mysteries of God to the people, whose preachings or sermons whosoever believeth, may be so certainly assured of the remission of their sins, as though God himself had said unto them, Your sins are forgiven you. For this saying of Christ is an infallible verity: "He that heareth you heareth me." Luke x.

Now let us behold the objections of the papists, and briefly confute them, that all the glory may be the Lord's. First, they allege this saying of Christ: "Loosen him, and let him go away." Again: "Loosen them, and bring them unto me." Here is simple poor shift to prove their absolution, when they are compelled to flee unto the untying of a vile sheet, and loosening of a simple rude ass. Look, wheresoever the papists find any word that cometh of this verb *solvo*, that maketh for absolution straightways. I marvel how this escaped them, *Solve quod debes*. I think, if *Salve regina* had been turned into *Solve regina*, as some of them that be not very fine-mouthed pronounce it, they would not have been ashamed to have alleged it for absolution, even as some of the papists do, which, wheresoever they find *ignis*, take it for purgatory straightways. O noble doctors of tyrology[3], rather than of theology! The third part. John xi. Matt. xxi. Matt. xviii.

As concerning the first text, which is that Christ commanded that Lazarus should be let loose, and suffered freely to go his way; if they will gather their absolution of that, it may then be proved that all other men and women have that same power so well as they. For there were at that time present, not only the disciples of Christ, but also divers Jews with certain women, which I am sure were not all priests. Have they not made a good market? they have brought a shilling to ninepence, yea, rather to nothing. They have done fair by themselves, by my fay. While they labour to make themselves gods, and to excel all other in dignity, they go so wisely to work, that they have made themselves equal to the most inferior. O crafty daubers! Which of them all is able to prove that Christ spake these words, "Loosen him and let him go," rather to his disciples than to all the other indifferently? I think rather that he spake them to the women, as most commonly occupied about such things. But to whom he spake, the text maketh no mention; therefore can they prove nothing.

As touching the loosening of the ass, who seeth not their foolishness? The occasion why Christ sent the disciples for the ass was not to give them power to loosen men from their sins at their pleasure, but to fulfil the prophecy of Zachary, which so long before prophesied that Christ should come riding meekly upon an ass, contrary to the expectation of the ambitious and vain-glorious Jews. What is this to the purpose? Whereas Christ by this example teacheth humility, the papists gather pride. Christ submitteth himself even with the most lowest; and they exalt themselves with the Most Highest, yea, "above all that is called God or that is worshipped, and sit in the temple of God, and shew themselves as God." Tell me, good reader, are not these sweet allegory-makers? I would they would once cease to moralize; for they have lied too long. Matt. xxi. Zech. ix. 2 Thess. iii.

[[3] Tyrology: instruction for mere beginners. But is *pyrology* intended?]

Matt. xvi. Some of them also allege this saying of Christ: "Whatsoever thou shalt bind on the earth shall be also bound in heaven: and whatsoever thou shalt loosen on earth shall be loosened in heaven." Here they esteem themselves more than gods. By this text they think they may do whatsoever pleaseth them, save or condemn, bind or loose, hold up or cast down, build or subvert, bring to heaven or cast down to hell; but if the good men would take the pains to look what goeth before, their comb should soon be plucked down, they would not make so much of their painted sheath. Christ saith a little before: "I will give thee the keys of the kingdom of heaven." Note well. He saith not: "I give thee." Christ in this place only promised the keys to the congregation, and performed his promise after his resurrection, as we may see in the John xx. gospel of John. Hereof may the papists right well perceive that this text, whereof hitherto they have so greatly gloried, and out of the which they have sucked so great advantage, maketh little unto the advancement of their feigned power.

Their last and most strong bulwark, where the keys were given to the true mi- John xx. nisters, is this text: "Whosesoever sins ye forgive, they are forgiven unto them: and whosoever's sins ye retain, they are retained." Here they triumph and persuade themselves that they have gotten the victory, though they never fight stroke. But if they will be favourable to God, and work no injury to the other scriptures afore re- ☞ hearsed, they shall have no cause to lift up their bristles. Christ speaketh here after the manner of our speech, which diligently must be noted, unless we will deprive God of his glory. When we see a man restored to his health, which long before hath been vexed of some grievous disease, and is made whole through the diligence of some physician, we use to say, 'Doctor Turner made this man whole, or Doctor Byl, or some other,' which is expert in that kind of science; and yet is it not the doctor that made him whole, but rather the emplastures and medicines that he ministered unto him, yea, rather God, if we will speak truly, which gave such virtue to his creatures to work health unto the sick. So doth the scripture speak. Sometime it attributeth our health to the ministers of the word, as in this aforesaid place, sometime and most commonly to God himself, as we tofore have abundantly heard, and sometime to the John xv. word of God, as it is written: "Now are ye clean for the word's sake which I have Wisd. xvi. spoken unto you." Item: "Neither herb nor emplasture hath healed them; but thy word, O Lord, that healeth all things." Hereto pertaineth the saying of the psal- Psal. cvii. mograph: "He sent his word and healed them, and delivered them from their destructions;" and yet doth God only make us whole, and forgive us our sins; as he himself Hos. xiii. witnesseth by the prophet, saying: "Thy destruction, O Israel, cometh of thyself: only of me cometh thy help and salvation."

What can be more plainly spoken? Who is able once to hiss against these things? Who will once open his mouth to bark against this doctrine? No man, I suppose, Note. except he be altogether drowned in papism. This, therefore, is the true meaning of the aforesaid text. Whensoever the ministers of the Lord's word declare unto me the sweet promises of God the Father made to me in Christ's blood, and I believe them, then are my sins forgiven me at the very instant; but if I do not believe them, then are my sins retained, that is to say, not forgiven. And forasmuch as I either repent and believe, or else continue still in mine old damnable state, at the preaching of the Lord's ministers; therefore the scripture attributeth my deliverance from sin or otherwise to them, when notwithstanding God alone remitteth my sin, if I repent and believe. If I do not, the uncircumcision of my heart, that is, my incredulity and unfaithfulness, is the occasion that my sins are retained and not forgiven. For this saying alway must needs abide true: "Thy destruction, O Israel, cometh of thyself: only of me cometh thy help and salvation." So that the priests (I mean the ministers of God's word) are counted to forgive sin, when they preach to the truly repentant[1] remission of sins through Christ, and to retain sin, when they declare to the unfaithful damnation, and that the wrath of God abideth upon them, so long as they remain still in their John iii. incredulity and unfaithfulness, as it is written: "He that believeth not on the Son shall not see life; but the wrath of God abideth upon him."

[[1] So the smaller edition reads. Folio, *to thee truly repentance*.]

Thus see we that those texts of the holy scripture, which the papists allege for the maintenance of their feigned and usurped power in remitting sin, maketh nothing for their purpose, if they be truly alleged and understand, according to the vein of the holy scriptures. The scriptures of God may not be rent and torn, neither hacked nor wrested to serve the private affects of men; but every text must be so weighed, pondered, alleged, and understand, that it may agree with the other texts of the holy bible, that all the glory of our salvation may be ascribed to God alone, which is both the beginner and finisher of all our health: to him therefore be all honour and praise for ever. Amen.

The fourth and last part. Matt. xvi. John xx.

Now will I make haste to the last part of this treatise, which requireth that I should express my mind concerning the keys which Christ before his passion promised to his church, and after his resurrection performed his promise; and shew by the sacred scriptures that the gift of the keys is no vain and idle gift, but a necessary, joyful, and comfortable treasure. For the papists will here object, If remission of sins cometh from God alone, then were the keys given to the congregation in vain. But to the intent that I may stop the mouths of the adversaries, and that they may have no occasion to bark against the glory of God after this, mark well, good reader, what shall be spoken.

Isai. liv. Jer. xxxi. John vi. Heb. viii. Joel ii. Acts ii. Psal. i. John v. John viii. John x. John xviii.

Truth it is that God alone teacheth men his verity by the Holy Ghost, as it is written: "All shall be taught of God." Again: "I will pour out of my Spirit upon all flesh; and your sons and your daughters shall prophesy." The psalmograph also saith: "I will hear what the Lord speaketh in me;" yet will he that they should be studious of the holy scriptures, both day and night, as it is commanded of Christ, "Search the scriptures," and also diligently hear the preaching of his word, as it is written: "He that is of God heareth the words of God." "My sheep hear my voice." "Every one that is of the truth heareth my voice."

Luke xxiv. Rom. x. 1 Cor. iii. 2 Cor. v. Gal. iv. 1 Thess. iv. Exod. xvi. Matt. x. Luke x.

So in like manner, although God alone remitteth all sin, yet will he that remission of sins should be preached to the people, that by this means they may repent, believe, and be made whole, as Christ testifieth, saying: "It behoved Christ to suffer, and to rise again from death the third day, and that repentance and remission of sins should be preached in his name among all nations." "Faith cometh by hearing, and hearing by the word of God." For the ministers of the gospel are the organs and instruments of Christ, by whom God worketh through his holy Spirit health and salvation in so many as are predestinate unto eternal life. They are "God's labourers," and "ministers, by whom we believe, even as the Lord giveth every man grace." They are the orators, messengers, interpreters, angels, apostles, and embassadors of the Lord, as the apostle saith: "All things are of God, which hath reconciled unto himself by Jesu Christ, and hath given us the office to preach the atonement. For God was in Christ, and reconciled the world unto himself, and imputed not their sins unto them, and among us hath he set up the word of atonement. Now then are we messengers in the room of Christ, even as though God exhorted by us. We beseech you now therefore in Christ's stead, that ye be at one with God." Again to the Galatians he writeth on this manner: "Ye did not despise nor abhor me, but received me as an angel of God, yea, even as Christ Jesu." Hereto pertaineth his saying to the Thessalonians: "He that casteth away us casteth not away men, but God, which hath given his holy Spirit into us." Moyses also, in times past, said unto the people that murmured against him: "The Lord hath heard your grudging and murmuring, wherewith ye murmur against him. For what are we? your murmurings are not against us, but against the Lord." So likewise read we in the gospel, that the Lord spake of his ministers: "Verily, verily, I say unto you, He that receiveth whomsoever I shall send receiveth me: and he that receiveth me receiveth him also that sent me." Again he saith: "He that heareth you heareth me, and he that despiseth you despiseth me; and he that despiseth me despiseth him also that sent me."

The ministers of God's word ought to be had in honour. 1 Tim. v. What the absolution is.

Here see we that the ministers of God's word are not to be despised; for they are necessary instruments unto the health of men, and they are "worthy of double honour," as the apostle saith. Therefore may it be concluded that the absolution of the priest is not to be despised; seeing it is none other thing, if it be a true and christian absolution, than the preaching of free remission of our sins in Christ's name.

1 Cor. iii. And although he that planteth be nothing, and he that watereth be nothing, but God which giveth the increase; again, albeit the Lord blesseth us with all spiritual benediction; yet, inasmuch as the inestimable kindness and manifold benefits of God Rom. x. toward us cannot be known nor believed without preaching (for "faith cometh by hearing, and hearing by the word of God"), therefore hath God appointed his ministers to open and declare unto men those excellent mysteries, those comfortable and joyful promises of God's mercy and good-will toward mankind, that they may perceive, learn, and understand, what is given them of the Lord, what they ought to believe, how they should obtain the gifts of God, and lead a life worthy the kindness of so bounteous a Father: God also hath appointed the ministers to beget men in Christ Jesu by the Luke i. gospel, to open the eyes of the blind, to turn them from darkness to light, "to convert the hearts of fathers into children, and the disobedient to the wisdom of the Luke xxiv. righteous." He hath commanded them "to preach repentance and remission of sins in Mark xvi. his name unto all nations." "Go your way," saith he, "into the world universal, and preach the gospel to every creature. He that believeth and is baptized shall be saved: he that believeth not shall be condemned."

Matt. xvi. Moreover, he hath given to his faithful ministers the keys of the kingdom of heaven, that whatsoever they loosen in earth may be also loosened in heaven; and whatsoever they bind in earth may also be bound in heaven: that is to say, he hath committed to them the office of preaching the gospel, that they should go forth into the world, and preach unto all men the grace and favour that is given of God the Father for Christ's sake; yea, and that they should proclaim, publish, and set abroad unto all men, that so many as repent and believe are loosened from the captivity of Satan, purged from sin, delivered from death, and made inheritors of eternal life; again, that so many as believe not remain still the captives and bond-slaves of Satan, and continue bound in their sins and in the state of damnation, and that therefore they shall die the death, and for evermore be damned, except they repent, turn, and believe. And thus their preaching is so certain and sure before God, that whatsoever they pronounce, being conformable to the word of God, shall as certainly come to pass, as though God himself had spoken it.

As for an example, whensoever the ministers and preachers of God's word in this world shall declare to the faithful repentance, remission of sins, and tell them that they be loosened from the captivity of Satan, it is even as certain and sure, as though God himself had said these words unto them: "Thy sins are forgiven thee." In like manner, when they shall say to the unfaithful, that they remain still bound in their sin, and that the wrath of God abideth upon them, and therefore they shall be damned; God approveth their saying, and it shall undoubtedly come to pass according to their preaching. So that whatsoever the minister of God's word saith, according to the word of God, ought to be received with great reverence, and taken as an oracle sent down from heaven, and undoubtedly believed as a manifest and infallible verity of God.

What the keys of the kingdom of heaven are. Matt. xvi. John xx. And this preaching of remitting or retaining sins are the keys of the kingdom of heaven, which Christ promised his apostles before his death, as we may see in Matthew, and after his resurrection performed his promise, as we read in the gospel of St John.

Why the preaching of God's word is likened to a key. And by a metaphor Christ calleth the preaching of his word a key. For as a key hath two properties, one to shut, another to open, so hath the word of God. It openeth to the faithful the treasure of the gifts of God, grace, mercy, favour, remission of sins, quietness of conscience, and everlasting life; but to the unfaithful it shutteth all his treasures, and suffereth them to receive none of them all, so long as they persist and remain in their incredulity and unfaithfulness. These keys are given to so many as, being truly called unto the office of ministration, preach the word of God. They loosen, that is to say, they preach to the faithful remission of sins by Christ. They also bind, Note. that is, they declare to the unfaithful damnation. But he that preacheth not the word of God can neither bind or loose, though he challenge never so great dignity, autho-Luke xi. rity, and power. For Christ calleth it "the key of knowledge." And the prophet Mal. ii. saith: "The lips of a priest keep knowledge, and at his mouth shall they require the law; for he is the angel or messenger of the Lord of hosts." Therefore where there is no knowledge, there is no key: and where there is no key, there is neither opening nor shutting, that is, neither binding nor loosening.

Here let all men judge what is to be thought of the papists' absolution, whereof they crack so much, which also they sell so dearly. If no remission of sins cometh from them, but by preaching God's word, it followeth that their absolution availeth but little, seeing they never preach, neither the law of God, nor the sweet promises of him, but only mumble a few words in the Latin tongue, yea, and those, as not understanded, so likewise many times contrary to the divine scriptures and the glory of God. Miserable doubtless is that congregation which hath a blind guide to their curate, which hath neither the gift nor the knowledge of preaching. For "if the blind leadeth the blind, both fall into the ditch." Again, greatly fortunate is that parish, and highly blessed of God, to whom a learned shepherd hath chanced, which can feed them with knowledge and doctrine. Whatsoever they shall hear of such a learned and godly minister, let them believe it as a voice coming down from heaven. And so oft as by such a shepherd remission of sins in the blood of Christ is preached unto the congregation, let them esteem that preaching none otherwise than if the Lord himself had preached it. Let them stedfastly believe the word of God, and undoubtedly by their faith, through the grace of God, they shall obtain remission of all their sins. Contrariwise, if they believe not, their sins are retained and by no means forgiven. Matt. xv.

These things have I spoken concerning the absolution or the keys, which consisteth only in preaching God's word, that the papists may have no occasion justly to bark against me, as they have done hitherto both for my sermons and books. God forgive them, and send them a better mind!

Now, forasmuch as the true and christian absolution is nothing else but the preaching of free deliverance from sin by the death of Jesu Christ, it ought not to be contemned and despised, but rather to be received with great humility and reverence, even as a divine oracle, "sent down from the Father of lights." For no man can express how greatly it comforteth infirm and weak consciences, which are troubled with the fear of God's judgments. Absolution, what it is. James i.

When the prophet Nathan came unto king David, and rebuked him for slaying Urias the Hethite, and for taking his wife Bethsabe unto his wife, and told him how greatly God was angry with him, and what plagues should fall upon his house, yea, upon himself, for his wickedness, it is not to be doubted but that David was stricken with a wonderful great heaviness, and his heart pierced with an inward sorrow; insomuch that he was right ashamed of himself, of his fault, of his wickedness, and was compelled even of conscience to brast out into the knowledge of his sin, and to say: "I have sinned against the Lord." As David was now full of sorrow, grief, trouble, disquietness in his heart, and had joy of nothing, (unto such shame and confusion was he brought in his conscience,) so likewise it is not to be doubted but that he was wonderfully revived, marvellously restored unto the peace and quietness of his conscience, yea, and plenteously replenished with joy in his mind, when the prophet said these words unto him: "The Lord hath put away thy sin: thou shalt not die." 2 Sam. xii. David.

Mary Magdalene was a famous sinner; and when she heard her unclean conversation rebuked by the word of God, she heartily repented, and was replenished with an inward sorrow, lamenting greatly that she had offended so bounteous a Lord and merciful God; insomuch that a large fountain of tears flowed out of her tender eyes. All this time undoubtedly her sorrow was greater than it can be here expressed. But when she heard this comfortable absolution of our Saviour Christ, *Remittuntur tibi peccata;* "Thy sins are forgiven thee;" again, "Thy faith hath made thee safe; go thy way in peace," that is to say, with a quiet and merry conscience; O good God! who is able to express with how great joy and singular solace she was affected? So sure and comfortable is it to weak and troubled consciences to hear the sweet and comfortable words of our free deliverance from the grievous burden of sins by Christ's blood. Luke vii. Mary Magdalene.

The thief was full of great anguish and trouble in his conscience when he hanged upon the cross in the time of Christ's passion, and confessed that both he and his fellow-thief suffered worthily, even according to their deserts; and in the midst of his troubled conscience, he cried unto the Lord Christ on this manner, saying: "Lord, remember me, when thou comest into thy kingdom." But when Christ had made him answer and said, "Verily, I say unto thee, this day shalt thou be with me in Luke xxiii.

paradise," O with what a quiet conscience suffered he his pains, and with how glad an heart yielded he up his spirit into the hands of the eternal Father! So comfortable a thing is it to a troubled conscience for to hear any thing that may quiet it.

Again, when blessed Peter preached unto the Jews, and told them, that they had
Acts ii. crucified Christ the Lord, the scripture saith that "they were pricked in their hearts, and said unto Peter and unto the other apostles, Ye men and brethren, what shall we do? Peter said unto them, Repent, and be baptized every one of you in the name of Jesus Christ, for the remission of sins, and ye shall receive the gift of the Holy Ghost." As they were greatly dismayed when the holy apostle opened unto them their malicious fact in slaying Christ the Lord, so were they very much comforted when they heard of St Peter that there was hope of their sins to be forgiven, so that they repented them of their wickedness, and were baptized in the name of Jesu Christ.

With how entire and unspeakable sorrow is it to be thought that the famous and
1 Cor. v. notable adulterer among the Corinthians was overwhelmed, when at the commandment of St Paul he was delivered unto Satan, excommunicate, put out of the christian company, and reputed among them as an ethnick and publican! Contrariwise, with what exceeding joy was he replenished, when after his repentance and sorrow he heard the sweet promises of God's mercy declared unto him, that lieth bent out toward all
2 Cor. ii. sinners that repent in faith, and afterward was received into the company of the faithful Christians!

I pass over divers other histories, both of the old and new testament, which do abundantly declare what great comfort the faithful penitent sinners have alway had in hearing the comfortable promises of God's mercy.

Now the absolution being, as I said before, nothing else but the preaching of free deliverance from sin by the death of Jesu Christ (for God alone forgiveth sin and absolveth the faithful penitent), it ought not to be contemned and despised; but whensoever the minister of the Lord's word, be it privately or openly, shall rehearse unto men the sweet and comfortable words of God's mercy toward all them that repent in faith, they ought to give earnest faith unto them, being undoubtedly persuaded that their sins at that time be assuredly forgiven them, as though God himself had spoken
Matt. x. Luke x. these words, according to this saying of Christ: "He that heareth you heareth me."

But it were expedient that all true ministers should pray, that their form or manner of absolution be pure and agreeable to the vein of the holy scriptures, without the intermixtion of any man's authority in remitting sin, either of Peter, Paul, Francis, Dominick, Benet, or any other, or yet of themselves; again, that it be declared to the penitent that God alone forgiveth the sin, and that the priests are but the ministers of God, to whom he hath given the keys of the kingdom of heaven, for to shew to the true penitent loosening, that is to say, remission of their sins; to the obstinate and hard-hearted sinners binding, that is, that they remain still in the danger of damnation, and shall be damned, except they repent and believe.

It would also be provided, that when the faithful penitent is desirous to have his conscience confirmed, stablished, and comforted with the word of God, it should not be mumbled in the Latin tongue, as the papists have hitherto used in their absolutions, but in the mother tongue, that the idiot[1] and unlearned may understand it, and be edified. Or else what faith shall he conceive in his heart? How shall he repent? How shall he know the goodness of God toward sinners? How shall he arm himself with faith against Satan, sin, and desperation? How shall he prepare himself to give God thanks for his kindness, and live worthy of his profession? God grant that all things may be done unto his glory, and unto the profit of his holy congregation!

Here hast thou, most godly reader, my mind concerning the absolution and forgiveness of sins; which, if it be examined by the scriptures of God, all man's doctrine set apart, I doubt not but it will stand so strong that the gates of hell shall not once be able to prevail against it. Farewell, most gentle reader, and pray that the Lord's word may have free passage, that the name of the great God and our Saviour Jesu Christ may be glorified among all nations, and that, all dissension laid aside, we may agree in one faith and one truth. Amen.

Give the glory to God alone.

[[1] Idiot: a private or unlearned person.]

THE

SOLACE OF THE SOUL,

BY

THOMAS BECON.

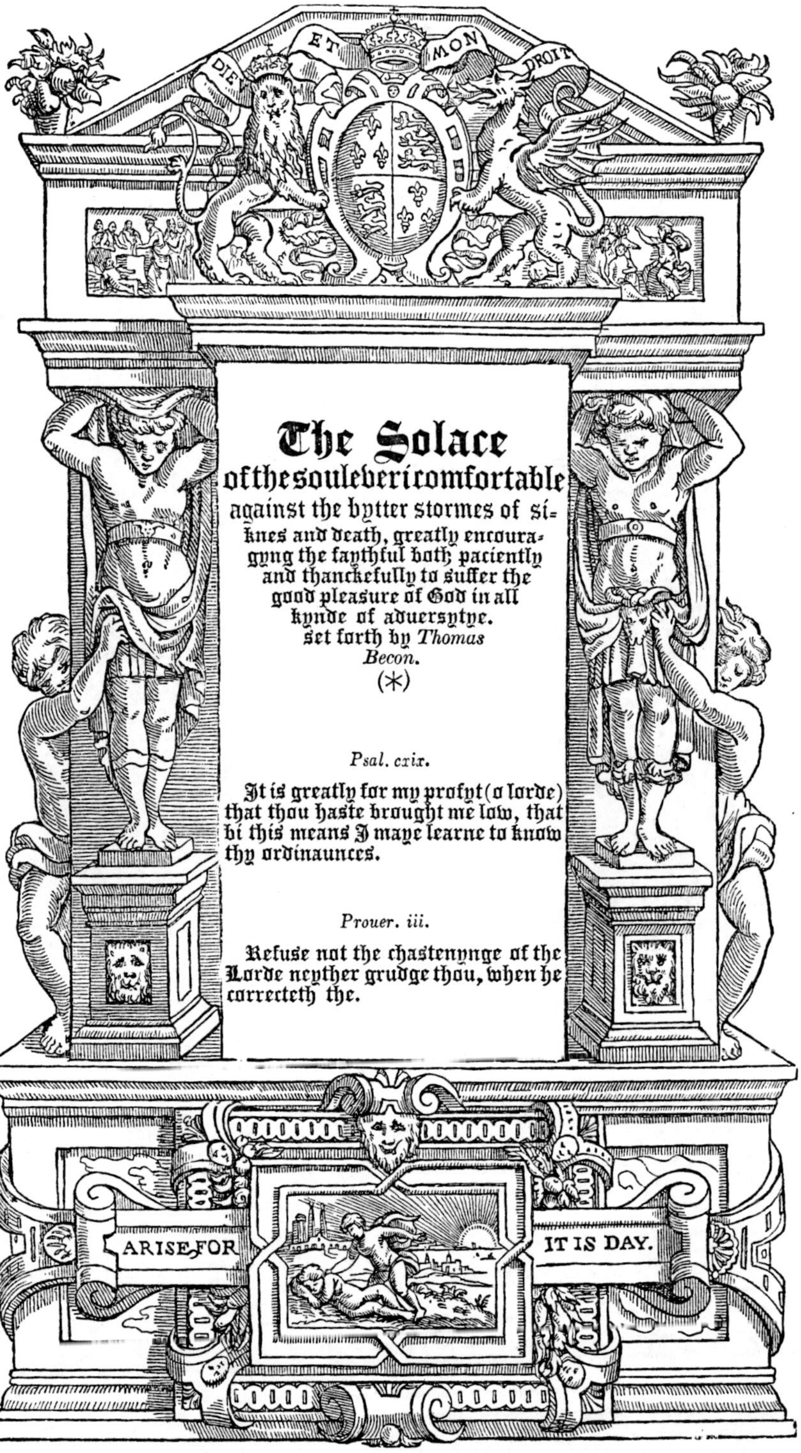

The Solace

of the soule veri comfortable against the bytter stormes of sikenes and death, greatly encouragyng the faythful both paciently and thanckefully to suffer the good pleasure of God in all kynde of aduersytye. set forth by *Thomas Becon.*

(*)

Psal. cxix.

It is greatly for my profyt (o lorde) that thou haste brought me low, that bi this means I maye learne to know thy ordinaunces.

Prouer. iii.

Refuse not the chastenynge of the Lorde neyther grudge thou, when he correcteth the.

THE PREFACE[1].

VERY notable is this saying of our Lord and Saviour Jesu Christ: "He that continueth unto the end shall be safe." For it declareth unto us, that though the most and greatest part of our life seemeth to be spent both faithfully and godly, yet if we persevere not in that faith and godliness even unto the last breath, but let slip our hold that we have had heretofore of faith and godly conversation in Christ Jesu, all the labours, pains, and travails, that we have sustained in the former part of our life, are frustrate and vain. For "no man that putteth his hand to the plough, and looketh back, is meet unto the kingdom of God." And it is written in the Revelation of St John: "Be faithful unto the death; and I shall give thee the crown of life." The crown of life is promised: but to whom? verily to those that be faithful even unto death, as St Paul saith: "No man is crowned except he striveth lawfully." To strive lawfully is not to play the coward in the battle of Christ our captain, and to give place to our adversaries, but at all times valiantly to fight again them with the strong and mighty shield of faith, and so to continue even unto the end. And albeit this conflict between the faithful Christians and their enemies be at all times jeopardous and full of peril, yet in the time of sickness, and when death beginneth to draw nigh, it is most dangerous. In health and prosperity Satan's assaults seem to be but trifles and things of[2] dalliance; but in adversity, trouble, sickness, and death, they appear most vehement, grievous, terrible, and not able to be resisted, at which time if we give place, we are undone; if we manfully resist, the victory is ours.

Matt. x. Luke ix. Rev. ii. 2 Tim. ii.

We must therefore, godly reader, against this so perilous time of sickness and death, so furnish ourselves unto this battle, that we be not put to flight, ever remembering that "our strife and fighting is not against blood and flesh, but against rulers, against powers, against the lords of the world, the governors of the darkness of this world, against spiritual subtilities or wilinesses in heavenly things," I mean Satan with all his infernal army and devilish warriors. And forasmuch as our principal conflict and chief battle is in the time of sickness and pains of death, and seeing we have then most need of consolation and comfort, that we be not overcome nor subdued of our enemies, but know how we shall both take the cross of Christ, appear it to the flesh never so painful, and put our adversaries to flight, and so continue faithful to the end; I have put forth this little treatise following, wherein thou shalt find most sweet and present comfort both for thyself and other, armours or weapons to defend thyself against all thine enemies, that not they over thee, but thou over them mayest full gloriously triumph, and get the victory through Jesus Christ our grand captain.

Eph. vi.

This little work I wish to be in the hands of all the faithful at all times, but specially in the time of their sickness, that they might learn unfeignedly to rejoice in tribulation, and valiantly to strive against their enemies, the flesh, the world, the devil, hell, sin, death, and desperation. Yea, I wish that all the faithful in the time of their sickness might have this treatise read unto them, either of their curates, or of some other faithful Christians: so should they, without all doubt, find exceeding great comfort, patiently and thankfully bear the cross that God layeth upon them, and with glad hearts wish with St Paul to be "loosened from this wretched body, and to be with Christ" in glory.

Phil. i.

Farewell, good reader, and pray that the gospel of our health, which is the mighty "power of God unto salvation for every one that believeth," may have free passage among us, unto the utter subversion of antichrist and his kingdom. Pray also that we may so lead our lives in all things conformable to the will of God, that through our godly manners and christian conversation we may garnish and beautify the doctrine of our Saviour and Lord Jesu Christ, to whom with the Father and the Holy Ghost be all glory, praise, and honour, worlds without end. Amen.

Rom. i.

[[1] It would seem that this treatise is a translation. See before, page 427.]

[[2] Folio, *or*.]

THE

SOLACE OF THE SOUL.

Thou shalt ever be at this point, O thou Christian, which art sick and diseased, faithfully to believe that thy punishment and trouble cometh not unto thee by chance or fortune, but by the appointment, counsel, and sufferance of God. Whatsoever sickness, calamity, or misery chanceth to the godly, all that come to pass at the ap-
Acts xvii. pointment, will, and pleasure of God. "For in him we live, move, and have our
Psal. c. being." "He hath made us, and not we ourselves." Neither shalt thou doubt but that of a right good and very fatherly mind he sendeth thee whatsoever disease thou hast, not to destroy thee, but to call thee unto repentance, and to exercise, prove, try, and stir up thy faith.

For afflictions are the sure signs and undoubted tokens of God's high mercy and
Prov. ii. Heb. xii. singular good-will. "Whom he loveth, him he correcteth," saith Salomon. "He scourgeth every son that he receiveth." That thy most tender and heavenly Father, which so dearly loveth thee, according to his singular good appointment, and of an earnest bent good-will toward thee, with this by adversity, even as it were with bonds, doth pluck back, refrain, and mortify thy old man, that thou mayest crucify with
Rom. xii. Christ the gladlier and more cheerfully thy body, and offer it as a sacrifice. This thy disease therefore, wherewith thou art vexed, is a fatherly chastisement laid upon thee, not that thou shouldest be destroyed, but that thou shouldest be amended, quickened, and made a new man.

Peradventure God the Father seeth that thy old Adam is fierce, stubborn, froward, unruly, take his pleasure, liveth more licentiously than behoveth him, followeth his own carnal affects, and can keep himself in no good order; therefore doth he cast this as an halter upon him, snarle him with these fetters and chains, speareth him in this prison and dungeon, overcometh him with this punishment, that he may bridle him, knock him down, and keep him under awe, that he cast not into peril, deceive, and put in extreme jeopardy thy most noble and precious soul. Flesh and blood reign and bear more rule in thee than the Spirit: here is God present with thy spirit, and helpeth her striving against the fierce, unruly, and rebellious flesh, that she may overcome, subdue, and tread under foot the flesh. If thou were in good health and in bodily prosperity now, peradventure the flesh (as it is alway naturally disposed, prone, and bent unto evil) should deceive thee and cast thee into many and grievous sins against God, wherewith God being displeased, thou shouldest be in danger of cursing and damnation. That thy heavenly Father therefore, preventing this incommodity and peril, and providing for thee and thy health, bringeth under and keepeth down thy flesh, which with all
Gal. v. main and fierceness waxeth wood against the Spirit, and is evermore contrary to it, that it be not wallowed forth into the most stinking and filthy puddle of sin, but be subject and obedient to the Spirit.

Forasmuch then as this is the pleasure of thy most loving Father; again, seeing that all things turn unto thy commodity and wealth; take heed diligently, O brother, that thou dost not strive against the good-will of God, but suffer and pray that the will of thy Father may be done in thee, that he may handle thee as he thinketh best, and that thou mayest not wish, covet, or desire any thing, but that he shall think good, that all things may turn to the glory and praise of God, and that he may assist thee with his grace, that thou mayest patiently and thankfully bear the cross that is laid
Rom. v. upon thee; for "patience bringeth experience, experience bringeth hope, and hope maketh not ashamed."

Here hast thou an occasion to exercise and learn patience in all thy troubles. For thou learnest that God of a fatherly mind punisheth thee, and this dost thou learn by experience; for except thou diddest prove in very deed how healthful it were to give over thyself wholly to God and to obey his will (as David saith, "It is highly Psal. cxix. for my profit, that thou hast punished me"), thou couldest not conceive a certain and sure hope of him, having no experience before that a mind so fatherly and wonderfully desirous of thee lieth[1] hid under this cross and rod. But seeing thou hast learned that before by experience, and hast now some taste of that thing, thou dost not despair in any trouble, but thy hope increaseth straightways, seeing thou hast before oftentimes proved the help of God present. And although he winketh at the matter, and sometime suffereth thee for a certain space to stick and stand fast in the mire, yet at the last he reacheth forth his helping hands, delivereth and saveth thee: he suffereth thee to swim for a certain space, yea, and to be overwhelmed with waters, but he suffereth thee not to be drowned. Hereof mayest thou gather a sure hope, that he will never leave thee succourless, nor cast thee away, seeing he hath preserved thee being so oft in jeopardy.

In afflictions and troubles therefore dost thou learn to conceive and nourish a good and undoubted hope of God, that even in the most grievous afflictions of all, where no help at all appeareth, thou mayest trust unto him, being now throughly taught his custom in delivering and saving his people. Thou hast learned that afflictions be sent not of displeasure, but of a fatherly love. Which thing thou believing and having experience thereof, dost patiently abide his help; neither despairest thou, but trustest stedfastly that he at the last will help thee, although he delayeth it never so long, hideth and keepeth himself secret never so much. And thus at the last dost thou know and understand that thy disease or trouble is no[t] sent unto thee for this purpose, that thou shouldest be destroyed, but that the glory of God may be set abroad, and that all things may turn unto thy health and salvation.

He that can give himself over and wholly commit himself to God on this manner, and put all his affiance and trust in his promises, truly that man never dieth; which thing Christ himself, even with an oath, because we should not doubt, affirming the same, saith: "Verily, verily, if any man keep my word, he shall never see death." John viii. And in another place he saith: "I am the resurrection and the life: he that believeth John xi. in me shall live, although he be dead. And he that liveth, and believeth in me, shall never die." These words of Christ, O brother, look that thou deeply repose them, and with all diligence keep them in thy mind; and whensoever thou perceivest that thy mind waver or is troubled, underprop and lift it up with these sweet aud comfortable sayings: He that believeth in Christ shall not taste death: "He that believeth in me hath everlasting life," saith Christ: "This is everlasting life, to know thee, even the true God, and whom thou hast sent, Jesus Christ." Everlasting life is begun in this world; for he that hath Christ hath the true life, for Christ is the life: he is also the John xiv. truth, therefore will not he mock us; but "all the promises of God are in him yea, 2 Cor. i. and are in him amen."

And that thou shouldest doubt nothing but that God will abide by his promises, he hath bound himself unto thee with a certain peculiar covenant and sign put unto Baptism. thy body. For when he, being greatly desirous of thy health, sent his Son into the world to offer himself unto death for thy sake, he did make and strike up a bargain of grace before through Christ, in whom he hath promised, if thou wilt believe and Mark xvi. be baptized, that he will give thee everlasting life freely, and never forsake thee; yea, that he will be thy Father, and crown thee with grace and mercy: thy baptism is a Psal. ciii. sign of this covenant. Now is it necessary for thee, that thou cleavest with tooth and nail to the promise, which are added to this sign. For God hath given this sign, that thou shouldest nothing doubt of the grace or favour that he hath promised, nor yet of his faith concerning the faithful performance of the same. Thou art baptized to die Rom. vi. with Christ, as Paul saith, that his death should be thy death, and that he should purify all things for thy sake; yea, thou hast put him on in baptism, that thou shouldest be whole in him, and he in thee.

[[1] Folio, *desirous of the lyght.*]

Baptism therefore is a covenant, which lifteth up, cheereth, and maketh quiet thy 1 Pet. iii. conscience before God (as Peter testifieth), that he will never damn thee for thy sins. Rom. v. For thou, being justified by faith, hast peace with God: a quiet, clear, and pacified conscience is the true peace. Thou hast received a most sure sign as a certain seal of this justification and remission of sins, even baptism; that thou shouldest believe for a certainty that God for Christ's sake will have pity on thee, preserve, and deliver thee. Now, seeing then that God favoureth thee, and will be thy Father and never forsake thee; seeing also that thou hast an undeceivable sign and witness on this thing, look that thou dost commit and wholly give over to him both thyself and all that ever pertain unto thee, obey his will, and patiently suffer his hand, whether he will that thou live or die; that his will, which is ever best, may be done in thee unto the glory Rom. viii. and praise of him; although it be impossible that thou shouldest perish, if thou dost faithfully trust on the mercy which he hath promised for Christ's sake. Therefore consecrate thyself wholly to him, obeying his most godly will in all points. For he hath promised that he will be thy Father; and, forasmuch as he is true, when thou knowledgest him to be thy Father, and dost hope and look for all good things of him, he can none otherwise but be thy Father, and save thee, although he handle thee for a certain time never so hardly.

Seeing then that he hath promised to be thy Father, and thou dost trust on his promises, without doubt he will care both for thee and thine at all times: wherefore thou shalt commend to him not only thy body, but also thy wife and children, thy kinsmen and friends, to be short, all that ever thou hast; and doubt not but that he will be a true father, a true husband, a true kinsman and friend: for he hath hitherto used thee in these things only as a steward and dispensator; but now, seeing he is minded that thou shouldest leave off the function and use of this office, he will appoint another in thy room, which, like a good steward, shall both faithfully and diligently look upon them.

If thou hopest this thing of him, and lookest for it with a full trust of heart, it is no doubt but he will do that I have spoken; wherefore put out of thy mind all sorrowful care of worldly things, and commend it to God. Rather take thought for thyself, how thou mayest provide for thy soul and send that unto God.

And seeing that God hath forgiven thee all thy sins freely for Christ's sake, he requireth nothing at all of thee for this exceeding great and inestimable benefit, but that thou shouldest again forgive, even from the very heart, them that have done thee Matt. vi. wrong; for he promiseth that he will forgive us our offences, if we forgive men their Matt. xviii. Mark xi. offences: therefore, when thou hast forgiven all offences even from the very heart, yea, and that so that thou never rememberest them afterward, pray also for them that Luke xxiii. have hurt thee according to the doctrine and example of Christ, yea, and if ever thou recoverest, help so much as lieth in thy power them that have need of thy help.

If that thou hast a mind void of dissimulation, privy displeasure, envy, malice, ill-will, and wrath, thou hast also a sign and earnest token that God hath forgiven Acts xv. thee thy sins; for faith, wherewith thy heart is purified, stretching out herself, and bringing forth her fruits for the infinite benefits of God, can none otherwise than forgive again, and do well to her neighbour. This fruit of charity beareth thee witness and maketh thee sure, that thy faith is true and livish, seeing it bringeth forth true 2 Pet. i. and good fruits. This meaneth Peter, where he commandeth that we should "make our vocation and election firm and sure" with good works. For he signifieth and plainly meaneth that these works are testimonies and signs that thou art elect of God, and purchased to be his son unto the joys of everlasting life.

Neither is there any cause, O brother, that God should forgive thee thy sins for 1 John ii. the grievousness of thy disease and cross; for there is none other satisfaction, none other recompence for thy sins, than the only death of Christ. God beholdeth none other thing in this cause, he accepteth none other thing here, than his dearly-beloved John i. Son: he is "that Lamb of God which taketh away the sins of the world." He is the Heb. x. sacrifice and oblation sufficient, absolute, and perfect for the sins of the whole world: thy disease and pains cannot satisfy before God for the least sin that thou hast committed, much less are they able to deserve health and everlasting salvation, as Paul testifieth, saying: "I do not think that the afflictions of this life are worthy of the glory which shall be shewed upon us." Rom. viii.

No creature, neither in heaven nor earth, no angel was able to appease, mitigate, and swage the wrath of the Father, much less shall this thy disease and short trouble pacify it. For he that should assuage that wrath, and reconcile God to man, he must needs be both God and man, seeing he must be an intercessor and advocate between God, being angry, and man condemned. 1 Tim. ii. Therefore was it convenient for the Son of God to become man, that he should appease the wrath of God the Father by suffering pains in his own body, and so preserve us from it, as the prophet testifieth, saying: "He hath taken upon him our diseases, and borne away our sorrows." "God hath laid the unrighteousness of us all on him." Isai. liii. "For the wickedness of my people have I stricken him." And Peter saith: "By his stripes were we made whole." 1 Pet. ii. Therefore for this Christ thy Lord are thy sins forgiven thee, and for none other thing neither in heaven nor in earth, nor for thy good works, nor for any affliction, although never so hard and bitter. Christ is our only righteousness, health, redemption, and satisfaction. 1 Cor. i. God "made him sin for us, which knew no sin, that we might be made righteous." Sin, that is to say, a sacrifice for sin. Wherefore if thou believest, thou art the son of God already: if thou be the son of God, then art thou also the heir of God, and fellow-inheritor with Christ. If everlasting life be inheritance and the "gift of God," as Paul calleth it, certes then shalt thou not deserve it with the sorrows of thy disease; Rom. vi. but God would have thee punished with this sickness, that thou mightest repress, break, restrain, and mortify thy old man, that it may once cease to sin, which thing shall come to pass at the last by the death of the body.

And for this cause must we die, that our soul may depart hence unto everlasting salvation; for this death is a gate and entrance unto eternal life: What the death of the body is. there at the last are we delivered from all wretchednesses, miseries, carefulness, disquietness, from all errors and juggling casts[1] of the devil; neither shall we any more be defiled with the most stinking filthiness of sin, neither shall we be seduced and led away into heresies or errors, nor yet be thrown headlong into desperation. For an end of all evils, adversities, and incommodities, is then come; yea, then shall we rest in the Lord, and enjoy eternal life and pleasure without end. Death therefore is not to be abhorred nor feared; yea, it is rather most fervently to be desired, seeing by that we pass hence unto eternal joys. Very true is that which Paul saith: "To the godly all things work for the best." Rom. viii. Death, in the sight of the world a thing of all things most odious, most hateful, most loathsome, and most horrible, yet to the faithful it is most sweet, most acceptable, and most pleasant. And although it be so, that our old Adam trembleth at it, escheweth and abhorreth it, yet the inward man is ready and willing to suffer it; forasmuch as he perceiveth and knoweth that by it he is delivered from all filthiness of sin, vice, and wretchedness, and departeth unto everlasting joys.

HOW THEY ARE TO BE COMFORTED WHICH ARE IN PERIL OF DEATH.

The best God and thy most loving Father, having pity on thee, O brother, calleth thee from this most wretched and miserable life, willing to remove thee unto him, and to carry thee into the perpetual joys of the heavenly life. Therefore yield, give over, and commend to him wholly thyself, and all that ever thou hast, and whatsoever his will is, let thy will be the same, and say, "Let thy will be done, O Father God," and not mine: Matt. xxvi. cry unto Christ with the thief fastened to the cross, "Remember me, O Lord, when thou comest into thy kingdom:" Luke xxiii. cry with the publican, "Lord, be merciful to me, wretched sinner:" Luke xviii. cry instantly with the ethnick woman the Canaanite, "O Son of David, have mercy on me." Matt. xv.

If thou criest thus, Christ will hear thee, doubt not; he will have mercy on thee, he will forgive thee thy sins, yea, thou shalt be with him in paradise: therefore lay hand on this Christ, cleave to him with tooth and nail, commit thy soul unto him, cry with

[1 Casts: contrivances.]

Psal. xxxi. this Christ crucified unto God the common Father: "O Lord, my trust is in thee, let me never be put to confusion, but rid me, and deliver me through thy righteousness: bow down thine ear unto me, make haste to deliver me. Be thou my God and stronghold, whereunto I may alway flee, that thou mayest help me; for thou art my strength and refuge: thou art my defender: into thy hands I commend my spirit."

Psal. xviii. Cry also with David: "O Lord, thou art my strength, my sure hold, my refuge, and my deliverer. O my God, thou art my helper, my defender, and the horn of my [Psal. xxv.] health and my protection." "Unto thee, O Lord, lift I up my soul: O my God, my trust is in thee, let me not be driven to shame:" "Direct me in thy truth, thou art the God my Saviour." "Remember, O Lord, thy tender mercies, and thy pitiful compassions, which thou hast ever used: remember not the trespasses of my youth: according to thy mercy remember me for thy goodness sake:" "For thy name's sake, O Lord, forgive my sin; for it is much: look on me, and have pity on me, deliver me from my necessities:" "Forgive me all my offences:" "Keep my soul, and deliver me: let me not be put to confusion; for my whole trust is in thee."

If on this manner thou wilt call for the help of God with an whole heart, God will surely help thee in time convenient, and he will say unto thee that which is in Psal. xci. the psalm: "Forasmuch as he hath put his trust in me, I will deliver him. I will defend him, because he hath known my name: he hath cried unto me; and I will favourably hear him. I am with him in his tribulation: I will deliver him and glorify him." Wherefore, O thou Christian, fight here a good fight, strive valiantly and with a good courage, as it becometh a true christian man: take heed thou givest not over, take heed thou turnest not thy back: there is no danger; thou strivest not here alone, but Jesus Christ the King is thy guide in this agony: this thy guide and captain shall be thine avenger, and in this battle he shall defend and deliver thee from all the enemies of thy soul, from all peril and from all misery and wretchedness: follow this captain going before thee in this conflict and battle: he is a king not like to other, but of an exceeding and infinite power: he hath already overcome and thrown under the Heb. ii. 1 Cor. xv. Hos. xiii. foot for thy sake death, Satan, and hell: "Death is swallowed up into victory." Christ died for thee. Therefore everlasting death hath no power in thee. Christ went down for thee unto hell, that he might deliver thee from these everlasting darknesses. Therefore be on a lusty and bold mind, and with a valiant courage brast into the army. Put away all fear: there is no danger in this behalf: there is no cause 1 Tim. ii. 1 John ii. Heb. x. why thou shouldest fear the fierce and strait judgment of God. Christ Jesus is a Mediator before God: the same is an advocate, yea, and thy patron, defender, bishop, and priest. He hath reconciled thee to God, and hath restored to thee his fatherly mind, which before was estranged from thee for thy sins. God for Christ's sake is now thy father: he taketh charge of thee, he entirely loveth thee as his most tender son.

Now seeing that so noble a King standeth on thy side, who shall put thee to any business, who shall be bold to assail thee or once fight against thee? Who, I pray Rom. viii. thee, shall do thee any wrong? What danger can there be? Hear Paul: "If God be on our side," saith he, "who can be against us? which spared not his own Son, but gave him for us all, how is it possible that with him he should not give us all things? Who shall lay any thing to the charge of God's elect? It is God that justifieth: Who is he that can condemn? It is Christ that died, yea, which rose again, which also is at the right hand of God, and maketh intercession for us: Who shall separate us from the love of God? I am sure that neither death, nor life, nor highness, nor deepness, nor any other creature can separate us from the love of God, which is in Christ Jesu our Lord."

Therefore, seeing that Christ is given to thee, with all that ever he hath, so followeth it that his righteousness, innocency, health, and everlasting life is given to 1 Cor. i. thee, as Paul witnesseth, saying: Christ "is made of God our wisdom, righteousness, sanctification, and redemption." Therefore put all thy hope, trust, and confidence in Psal. cxviii. 1 Pet. ii. Matt. xvi. this Christ, which is the head corner-stone. This stone is a valiant, strong, stedfast, and sure foundation, whereunto thou mayest safely trust and commit thyself. No tempest, although never so black and horrible, no showers, no storms can shake and topple over this foundation. In this Christ, I say, let all thy hope and confidence be set. Cast thyself wholly on him, yield thyself altogether to him, cleave to him with strong faith, let no trouble or temptation pluck thee from him, although all things seem never so much to thee to go to havoc; although flesh and blood tell thee never so much the contrary, and reason thinketh far otherwise; yea, although the devil sometime whisper in thy mind that thou art utterly undone, that God is an extreme enemy unto thee, and that thou hast deserved the punishment of hell-fire, and therefore thou must needs be damned.

For "faith is a sure confidence and a looking for of those things that are to be Heb xi.
hoped," that is to say, promised, "and a certainty and evident knowledge of those things that do not appear." With that holy patriarch Abraham thou must believe under hope against hope: thy faith and hope must needs resist and set themselves against all those things which either blind reason doth imagine, or that most subtile and crafty enemy do bring to remembrance and work against thee. Wherefore thou must throughly learn what custom God doth keep in saving his: whom he will lift up Deut. xxxii. 1 Sam. ii.
into heaven, him he bringeth down first unto hell: whom he will quicken, him doth Tob. xiii. Wisd. xvi.
he first kill: upon whom he will exercise his exceeding mercy, him will he first try, Psal. cxii.
and make as though he would damn him.

And this is that unfeigned purgatory and that true purging fire, into the which The true purgatory.
God casteth his servants and proveth them as gold in the fire. Wherefore, when thou Wisd. iii.
feelest none other thing than most present death, when God seemeth to be most angry with thee, to be gone away most furthest from thee, and to have forsaken thee utterly, yea, when he seemeth that he hath cast thee away and will condemn thee; even then think thou most certainly that he is most nigh unto thee, that he will defend thee and deliver thee, yea, that he then most entirely loveth thee, and careth most of all for thee. For when he doth lay affliction and trouble upon thee, then doth he remember his mercy, as the prophet saith: "His anger scarcely endureth the twinkling of an eye." "He is not angry for ever." "As the father hath pity of his Psal. ciii.
sons, so hath the Lord compassion of them that fear him; for he knoweth our making, and remembereth that we are but dust." "The mercy of the Lord endureth for ever and ever." "The Lord is a tender favourer and merciful, he is long-suffering and full of compassion."

Wherefore spare the eyes of thy senses, cast away the judgment of reason, and submit, yield, give over, and commend thyself wholly to Christ, and take it to good worth, howsoever he handleth thee: esteem not death and the dreadfulness and sorrows thereof after the judgment of the eyes, senses, or reason, but after the word of God. David saith: "Precious is the death of saints in the sight of the Lord." Again: Psal. cxvi.
"Blessed are the dead which die in the Lord." Christ also saith: "He that believeth Rev. xiv John viii.
in me shall not taste death."

Therefore, if any things come to remembrance which go about to turn thee from Christ, and to cast thee into desperation, cast them all out of thy mind: cleave to the lively word of God with tooth and nail, have thy meditation in that, and ever be whetting of that in thy mind. For thou shalt never by the perspicacity and quickness of thy own reason perceive how it may be possible, that by death thou shouldest go unto the true life; how, when thou givest up the ghost, thou shouldest depart unto a better state; how thy soul should be kept in the Lord and rest unto the last day; again, how thy body, being rotten, consumed, and eaten of worms, may rise again at the last judgment, and come forth in a new goodly form, shape, or fashion. This cannot reason comprehend. Faith alone is able to do it. Therefore call to thy remembrance continually the articles of thy faith, and boult out every parcel of them diligently, and weigh them earnestly in thy heart.

HOW HE IS TO BE SPOKEN UNTO, WHICH IS READY TO GIVE UP THE GHOST.

O brother in Christ, now look that thou fightest a good fight, look that thou abidest in the faith valiantly and stedfastly. Infix and deeply engrave in thy breast

John xi. the promises of Christ thy Redeemer. "I am the resurrection and life," saith Christ: "he that believeth in me shall live and never die." Christ took the nature of man
Heb. x. upon him, suffering many injuries and wrongs; and when he died he offered himself
1 John ii. a sacrifice for our sins on the altar of the cross: he with his holy blood thoroughly and in all points cleansed the sins of all mankind. This Christ will not forsake thee, this Christ will not leave thee succourless, this Christ careth for thee: Christ saveth
2 Tim. ii. thee and defendeth thee, so that no ill or misery shall chance unto thee. "The foundation of God standeth sure, having this seal, The Lord knoweth which are his." Christ
John x. saith: "My sheep hear my voice, and I know them, and they follow me, and I give them everlasting life, neither shall they perish for ever, nor yet shall any man pluck them out of my hand: my Father which gave them to me is greater than all; and no man can pluck them out of my Father's hand. I and my Father am one."

Wherefore, O brother in Christ, commend thy soul to God the Father, which
Luke xxiii. loveth thee so dearly: cry with Christ thy brother, when he hung on the cross, "O Father, into thy hands I commend my spirit." God, the Father of all mercy, mought lead thee into everlasting life, and save thee unto that most joyful resurrection at the last judgment! Amen.

Give the glory to God alone.

A PRAYER TO BE SAID OF THE SICK MAN, BEING IN PERIL OF DEATH.

O most merciful God, O Father of all mercy, the Father of our Lord Jesus Christ, be merciful to me a sinner: have pity on me, and quickly help me, poor wretch, for the most bitter and most precious passion and death of Jesus Christ thy only-begotten Son, and our alone Redeemer and Saviour. Amen.

Enter not into judgment with thy servant, O Lord, handle me not according to my deserts and merits, neither reward me after mine iniquity; but for thine infinite and unmeasurable bounty and exceeding great mercy receive me. I, miserable and weak creature, am in thy hand, I am thy bond-servant and thy debtor. O most gentle God, O most favourable Father, forsake me not, cast me not away, poor wretch that I am: I am thine with all that ever I can make. No man is able to confirm me, no man is able to deliver me, no man is able to help me, but thou alone. Thou art the true helper in adversity: thou art the most sure and present comfort in all necessity: thou alone art our help, our bulwark, our fortress, and our most mighty and strongly defenced tower: thou, O God, art our refuge, thou art our strength, thou art our helper in all our tribulations. In thee, O Lord, do I trust: let me not be confounded: let me never be put to shame: let me not be deceived of my hope; but preserve me for thine righteousness. Bow down thine ear unto me, make haste to deliver me. Be my defender, O God, and my strong hold, that thou mayest save me; for thou art my strength and my refuge: yea, thou art my God; and my destinies are in thy hands. Lighten thy countenance upon thy servant, save me for thy mercy's sake, O Lord.

And forasmuch, O sweet Father, as it is thy godly pleasure to call me from this miserable life and wretched world, I most entirely beseech thee so to defend me in this agony of death, that neither Satan nor his ministers prevail against me; but that I continue faithful and constant unto the end in the confession of thy holy name, looking for full remission of all my sins in the precious blood of thy well-beloved Son and my Saviour Jesus Christ, and that I, departing in this faith and perfect trust, may be placed among thy blessed saints and heavenly spirits, so for ever and ever to remain with thee in glory. Grant this, O most merciful Father, for thy Son Jesus Christ's sake.

Lord, receive my spirit. Father, into thy hands I commend my spirit; for thou that art the God of truth [which] hast redeemed me. To thee be all glory and honour. Amen.

Give the glory to God alone.

First, I believe in one God, Father of our Lord Jesu Christ, Judge of heaven Deut. vi. 2 Cor. i.
and earth, and Creator of all creatures; which also is our Father, and hath elected Luke xii. Heb. i.
us to be his children through Jesu Christ; and therefore ought we all to worship him Eph. iv. Eph. i.
only, and besides him to have none other gods; again, to fear him as an Almighty Deut. vi. Psal. xxxiv.
God, and to love him as a merciful Father with all our heart, with all our soul, Matt. xxii. Jer. xvii.
and with all the powers both of body and mind. Upon him also must stand all our James i. Acts xiii.
hope. For he is the Father of light, through whom all mankind liveth, and re- Prov. x. Psal. xxxvii.
ceiveth both bodily goods and everlasting salvation, with all other good and perfect James i.
gifts, which come down from him alone.

Furthermore, I believe in Jesu Christ, the Son of the living God, our Lord: Christ Matt. xvi.
is the very brightness of his Father's glory, and the very image of his substance, the 1 Cor. viii. Heb. i.
only-begotten Son of the Father, came forth of the mouth of the most highest God, John i. Ecclus. xxiv.
first-born before all creatures, through whom all things were created; in whom we Col. i. Heb. i.
have redemption, namely remission of sins through his blood, with the which he hath Col. i. Rev. i.
washed us, and reconciled us again to his most holy and glorious Father, which tofore Eph. ii.
were enemies to God. For after that God had made man like unto his own simili- Rom. v.
tude and image, he placed him in paradise, licensing him to eat of all the fruits in Gen. ii.
that garden of pleasure, the tree of knowledge of good and evil only excepted. But Gen. iii.
man disobeyed the Lord his God, and transgressed his holy commandment; through Rom. v.
the which disobedience and transgression of God's commandment, death and curse
came over all mankind. And when there was no help nor comfort for man, whereby
he might have been redeemed and delivered out of Satan's power, then God, the 2 Cor. i.
Father of mercies and God of all consolation, had pity upon mankind, and promised Gen. iii. 1 John ii. iii.
them a seed, even Jesus Christ his only-begotten Son, which should tread down the
head of the serpent, and overcome the devil, yea, and restore us to life again. And 2 Tim. i.
likewise, as God is righteous in all his ways, and holy in all his works, and true in Psal. cxlv. Psal. li.
all his words, so hath he kept all his promises truly; so that, when the time was Tit. i. Gal. iv.
fulfilled, God let his Word descend into the womb of the virgin Mary, and by the
working of the Holy Ghost to become flesh, as St John witnesseth, saying: "The John i.
Word became flesh, and dwelt among us, and we saw his glory, as the glory of the
only-begotten Son of the Father, full of all grace and truth." This only-begotten
Son of God became also like unto us in all things, sin alone except. Heb. iv.

Moreover, he hath suffered death for our sake, and hath taken away Satan's power, Isai. liii. 1 Tim. vi.
and restored life again; yea, he is made unto us wisdom, and righteousness, sancti- 1 Cor. i. Heb. ii
fying, and redemption. And likewise as he died for our sins, so is he risen again Rom. vi. Rom. iv.
through the power of his Father for our righteousness. And as he oftentimes shewed
himself after his resurrection unto his disciples, so likewise ascended he unto heaven Acts i. Rom. viii.
in their presence, and sitteth at the right hand of God the Father almighty, above Mark xvi. Luke xxiv.
all rule, and might, and dominion, and above all that may be named, not only in Eph. i.
this world, but also in the world to come, and hath subdued all things under his Heb. ii.
feet. To be short, he is a Lord above all lords, and a King above all kings: yea, Rev. xvii. xix.
he is Almighty God with his Father, and yet nevertheless he is our Advocate, Medi- 1 Tim. vi. Rev. xxii.
ator, and Intercessor, and our only High Priest. The sacrifice that he hath done for John x. 1 John ii.
our sins abideth in full strength unto our salvation for evermore. Furthermore, as 1 Tim. ii. Rom. viii.
Christ is ascended up into heaven, so shall he come again from heaven with the Heb. v. Heb. x.
dominion of his Father, and with the angels, to give to every man reward according Acts i. Matt. xxv.
to his works, yea, to judge the quick and dead. Acts x.

I believe also in the Holy Ghost, equal God with the Father and the Son; which
Holy Ghost is the teacher of the faithful to lead them into all truth, and he doth clothe John xiv. xv. xvi.
them with his gifts, and giveth every one the measure of faith according to his own 1 Cor. xii.
godly will, and keepeth them unmoveable in one faith. For he is the ruler of the Acts xx.
christian congregation. He is also the anointment wherewith all true Christians are 1 John ii.
anointed, and hereof are called "The anointed of the Lord." This Holy Ghost is Psal. cv.
given unto the Christians as an earnest of their inheritance unto their redemption; and Eph. i.
they again be his own unto the praise of his glory. To be short, it is impossible
without this Holy Ghost to know God truly, or with a faithful heart to believe on 1 Cor. ii.

Rom. viii. Gal. iv. him, or to call upon him as a Father. And therefore doth God pour this his Holy Ghost upon his children, whereby they may truly know him, truly believe on him, and faithfully call on him as a true Father. This is my belief in the Father, in the Deut. vi. Isai. lxvi. 2 Macc. i. Psal. cxlv. Rev. iv. Son, and in the Holy Ghost, which three I knowledge to be one God, whose seat is the heaven, and whose footstool is the earth, which is an everlasting and almighty God, alone worthy all honour and glory, forasmuch as he alone helpeth his and saveth his; Isai. xliii. which thing he doth for his name's sake, and not for our righteousness' sake.

Furthermore, as I have said, that all they that do believe are joined together, and through[1] the Holy Ghost knit in unity, so is there a living christian church which is 1 Pet. ii. Heb. iii. 1 Tim. iii. Eph. i. 1 Cor. x. 1 Cor. xii. Rom. xii. Eph. ii. builded of living stones, which church[2] is the house of God, and the house of God is the congregation of God, and the congregation of God is the body of Christ. And forasmuch as they which are true Christians are one body, in the which they all through one Spirit are baptized; so must it needs follow that there is also a communion of saints, that is to say, a congregation or company of true believers, which are so joined together in one faith, religion, and doctrine, as members in one body. And in this communion or company of saints is remission of sins, and without it is no sin forgiven, nor any hope of salvation. Yea, as it is unpossible that a member can live which is not in the body; so is it unpossible that any man may live in his soul, and be released out of Eph. ii. Eph. i. Eph. v. Isai. xliii. Mark ii. Luke v. death by remission of sins, which is not a member of the body of Christ; for Christ hath reconciled us all unto God his Father in one[3] body: and therefore must they all be out of the state of grace, that are no members of this body, of the which Christ is the head, to the which also he giveth salvation.

Now must we also know that, albeit God alone at all times forgiveth sins, yet hath Matt. xvi. John xx. Christ given to his congregation power to bind and to loose; which shall not be understand after antichrist's doctrine of the bishop of Rome, and of his adherents, which challengeth power to forgive sins, and to deliver such as buy his pardons, *a pœna et* Eph. i. Col. i. Acts xx. Rev. ii. Matt. xvi. xviii. Luke xxiv. John xx. *a culpa;* but of the christian congregation, whose head Christ is, and not that Romish antichrist; which also is ruled by the Holy Ghost, and not by that whorish spirit of the prophetess Jesabel. This christian congregation, I say, hath power to bind and to loose, that is to say, by the word of God to pronounce and declare to the impenitent and unfaithful the wrath of God and everlasting damnation; but to the penitent and faithful the favour of God and everlasting salvation. And whatsoever this holy con- 1 Cor. v. Acts xx. gregation bindeth or looseth, it is altogether done by the power of our Lord Jesu Christ, and through the Holy Ghost, which is the ruler of the christian congregation; so that we may undoubtedly hope and look for remission of sins in this holy company of the faithful.

Dan. xii. Matt. xxv. John v. There shall be also a general resurrection of the flesh at the last day; I mean, all they that are dead shall rise again, some to everlasting life and salvation, some to everlasting pain and damnation. And they that shall live and remain until the coming of our Lord Jesu Christ, shall be changed in the twinkling of an eye at the time of the 1 Cor. xv. last trumpet. "For the trumpet," saith St Paul, "shall blow; and the dead shall rise uncorruptible; and we shall be changed. For this corruptible body must put on uncorruptibility, and this mortal body must put on immortality."

John xvii. John vi. Rom. ii. Finally, there is also an everlasting life, which all they shall receive that believe on Jesu Christ, and stedfastly abide in good works, seeking praise, honour, and immortality.

This is the sum of the christian belief, through the which faith all righteous live, and without the which belief no man can please God. Blessed therefore be the everlasting God, which of his unmeasurable mercy and bounteous grace giveth us this faith, Hab. ii. Heb. ii. Eph. ii. and with the same faith everlasting life, through Jesu Christ our Lord and alone Saviour, to whom with the Father and the Holy Ghost be all glory, praise, and honour, worlds without end. Amen.

Give the glory to God alone.

[1 Folio, *though*.] [2 The folio here reads, *Christ*.] [3 Folio, *our*.]

THE

FORTRESS OF THE FAITHFUL,

BY

THOMAS BECON.

The fortresse
of the faythefull agaynst
the cruell assautes of pouer
tie and honger, newlye made
for the comforte of poore
nedye Chrystians, by
Thomas Becon.

Prouer. xviii.

A myghtye stronge fortresse is the name of the Lorde. Unto that flyeth the righteous, and is in sauegard.

Psal. xxxvii.

I haue bene young, and am nowe olde, and yet sawe I neuer the ryght-ous forsaken, nor hys chyldren beg-gynge theyr breade. The rightuous is euer mercifull and lendeth, and yet shall hys chyldren haue Goddes plen-ty and ynoughe.

TO THE

RIGHT WORSHIPFUL SIR JOHN ROBSART[1], KNIGHT,

THOMAS BECON WISHETH CONTINUAL HEALTH BOTH OF BODY AND MIND, FROM GOD THE FATHER IN CHRIST JESU OUR LORD.

So oft as I behold the wretched and too much miserable face of this needy and beggarly world, yea, so oft as I consider the lamentable and pitiful state of the poor people, which are now grown unto such a number, that they be almost innumerable, and so assailed with the cruel darts of poverty and hunger, that they in a manner despair of necessary food and convenient apparel for the sustentation of their poor wretched carcases, and by this means, for a redress of these their too manifold miseries, part of them whose brains are not perfectly settled, whose judgments are not throughly stayed in the way of perfect reason, not patiently bearing the cross of poverty, contrary to Christ's order and their bounden duty, attempt, unto the great dolour of all good men, ungodly and unlawful enterprises, as wicked counsels, unjust assemblies, abominable seditions, devilish insurrections, detestable commotions, unrighteous spoilings of other men's goods, uncharitable railings upon their superiors, &c., utterly defacing, so much as in them is, the face of the commonweal, not considering this plague of famine and hunger to be sent into the world for sin, according to the threatenings of God expressed in the holy scriptures—I can none otherwise than lament, and heartily wish better and more prosperous things to the needy and poor creatures of God universally.

Deut. xxviii. 1 Kings xvii. Jer. xviii. Ezek. iv. v. xiv. xxix. xxxii. xxxiii. Hos. ii.

For although, according to the common proverb,

Common proverbs.

Little wot the full sow, that is in the sty,
What the hungry sow aileth, that goeth by,

yet so many as are of God, and led with any natural or humane affection, they remember this old saying,

The nature of charity.

It is merry in hall,
When beards wag all;

and cannot, even in the midst of their wealth, but lament the misery of the miserable, the poverty of the poor, the famine of the famished, and to the uttermost of

[1 Sir John Robsart, or Robessart, was a gentleman of honourable lineage and large possessions in the county of Norfolk. An ancestor, John Robsart, distinguished himself under the seneschal of Hainault in the wars of Edward III. His son Robert, baron of Cannon in Hainault, was also a gallant soldier in the campaigns of those days, in both France and Spain. He left three sons, who were all in the English service. John, the eldest, having been knighted before the reign of Henry IV., received from that monarch a grant of £100. a year for life out of the exchequer. He was afterwards a knight of the garter, and was one of the commissioners appointed to negociate at Troyes the treaty which was to secure Henry V.'s succession to the French throne, and his marriage with the princess Catharine, on whom he was charged to attend till Henry should arrive to celebrate the nuptials. A more mournful service was not far distant. On his royal master's decease he attended his corpse to England. His descendant, Sir Terrey Robsart, married Elizabeth, daughter and heiress of Sir Thomas Kerdeston of Sidistern, Norfolk, by whom he had a daughter, Lucy, the wife of Edward Walpole, Esq. ancestor of the earl of Orford, and Sir John Robsart, to whom this treatise is dedicated, and of whom Becon makes such honourable mention. Sir John was the father of the unfortunate Anne or Amy Robsart, who was wedded with much pomp, June 4, 1550, (see king Edward VI.'s journal) to Sir Robert Dudley, afterwards earl of Leicester. This lady, having been sent to the solitary manor-house of Cumnor in Berkshire, belonging to Sir Richard Verney, died soon after, in consequence, it was reported, of a fall down a staircase. Her remains were hurried to the earth without an inquest; but her father, Sir John Robsart, came to the village, caused them to be disinterred, and a strict investigation to be made by the coroner. Nothing satisfactory however resulted; and her husband, on whom her singular death left a stain of suspicion, ordered her body to be re-buried with great solemnity in St Mary's Church, Oxford. As his daughter died without issue, Sir John Robsart's estates in Norfolk passed into the family of his sister above mentioned.]

their power study to relieve the distress of the needy, both with their goods and counsel. As a true christian man joyeth with them that are glad, even so sorroweth he with them that are sad.

Rom. xii.

Charity seeketh not her own, but both wisheth and doeth well to all men, even to her enemies. Charity putteth on the property of Christ, which became poor to make other rich. Charity joyeth not at her own joy, if other sorrow. Charity delighteth not in her own fulness, if other want. Charity abhorreth her own rest, if other be disquieted. "I am cumbered daily," saith St Paul, "and do care for all congregations. Who is weak, and I am not weak? Who is offended, and I am not grieved?" Yea, charity refuseth almost to be saved, if other enjoy not the like benefit. Did not that most excellent prophet Moses desire God either to forgive the children of Israel their sins, or else to wipe him out of the book of life? Did not blessed Paul wish to be accursed from God, so that the Israelites, his kinsmen after the flesh, might be saved? Did not the glorious martyr Stephen, according to the example of Christ, pray for his enemies? So wholly doth charity give herself to serve the health and wealth of other.

1 Cor. xiii. 2 Cor. viii. 2 Cor. xi. Exod. xxxii. Rom. ix. Acts vii. Luke xxiii.

And as touching the relief of the poor and needy, oppressed with the want of worldly things, what good and godly man hath not at all times, as occasion and ability hath served, sought it? Who, being godly-minded, seeing his christian brother or sister in necessity, seeketh not all means possible to help them? Can a Christian abound in worldly wealth, and suffer his neighbour to famish or to die for cold? He hath not put on the bowels and tender compassion of Christ, which is not moved with pity toward his needy neighbour.

Hospitality.

O what goodly and notable examples doth the holy scripture minister unto us of succouring the succourless! What a mirror to behold is that most reverend patriarch Abraham, the father of the faithful, unto the faithful! With what alacrity and cheerfulness of mind did he receive into his house the angels of God, being in men's likeness! With what diligence prepared he all things necessary for them, as he thought, weary bodies! When Lot saw the two angels of God, whom he judged to be men, coming unto Sodom at night, how reverently did he behave himself toward them, and instantly desired them to come into his house, and there lodged that night! "I beseech you, sirs," saith he, "turn into the house of your servant, and abide there: wash your feet, and in the morning ye shall go forth on your journey." "And afterward he made them a feast," saith the scripture. These two godly ancient fathers thought it not meet to suffer strangers and way-faring men to pass foreby their houses without relief. They did according to God's holy will expressed by the prophet, saying: "Break thy bread to the hungry, and lead the needy and the way-faring into thy house. When thou seest a naked man, cover him; so shalt thou not despise thy flesh." "Forget not hospitality," saith St Paul; "for by it certain unwares have received angels into their houses."

Gen. xviii. Gen. xix Isai. lviii. Heb. xiii.

How ready patient Job was to succour the succourless, and to relieve the needy, it is evident by these his words: "When the poor desired any thing of me, have I denied it them? Have I caused the widow to stand waiting for me in vain? Have I eaten my portion alone, that the fatherless hath had no part with me? For mercy grew up with me fro my youth, and compassion from my mother's womb. Have I seen any man perish through nakedness and want of clothing? or any poor man for lack of raiment, whose sides thanked me not because he was warmed with the wool of my sheep?" Again he saith: "I have not suffered a stranger to lie without; but I opened my doors unto him that went by the way."

Job xxxi.

As I may pass over many other examples contained in the old testament, which declare how merciful divers godly both men and women were toward strangers and poor people; how tender-hearted and full of most loving pity and unfeigned compassion did our Saviour Christ shew himself, when he fed so many people with seven loaves and a few small fishes: "I am inwardly moved with compassion toward the people," saith he, "because they have now been with me three days and have nothing to eat; and if I send them away fasting to their own houses, they shall faint by the way."

Mark viii.

Moreover, as I may let pass divers other miracles which he did for the relief of the poor, as turning water into wine at the marriage in Cana Galilee, and feeding five thousand with five barley loaves and two fishes; did he not shew himself to take great care for the poor, when he gave the rich men this commandment? "When thou makest a dinner or supper, call not thy friends, nor thy brethren, neither thy kinsmen, nor thy rich neighbours, lest they also bid thee again, and a recompence be made thee. But when thou makest a feast, call the poor, the feeble, the lame, and the blind, and thou shalt be happy; for they cannot recompense thee: but thou shalt be recompensed at the resurrection of the just men." In the description of the general judgment, which shall be at the last day, is not the reward of everlasting life set forth to the merciful, and eternal damnation to the merciless? "The judgment," saith St James, "shall be without mercy to them that hath shewed no mercy." "Blessed are the merciful; for they shall obtain mercy." "Give alms of that ye have; and behold, all things are clean unto you," saith our Saviour Christ. Was not the rich glutton damned because he was led with no pity toward the poor? John ii. John vi. Luke xiv. Matt. xxv. James ii. Matt. v. Luke xi. Luke xvi.

O how diligent were the apostles after Christ's ascension to appoint deacons to minister unto the poor, and to provide that they lack nothing! How earnest was blessed Paul in exhorting the Christians to make collections for the poor! Yea, how wrought he with his own hands, that he might have whereof to give unto the needy! What a friendly lesson in the poor people's behalf writeth he unto bishop Timothy, to be declared unto the rich worldlings! "Command them that are rich (saith he) in this world, that they be not high-minded, nor trust in uncertain riches, but in the living God, which giveth us abundantly all things to enjoy them; that they do good works, that they be ready to give and glad to distribute, laying up in store for themself a good foundation against the time to come, that they may obtain eternal life." Acts vi. xi. Acts xxiv. Rom. xv. 1 Cor. xvi. 2 Cor. viii. ix. Acts xx. 2 Thess. iii. 1 Tim. vi.

How is Dorcas, a noble and virtuous woman, commended in the holy scriptures! "She was full of good works and alms-deeds," saith blessed Luke. Yea, she with her own hands made coats and garments for the poor. An example worthy to be followed of our gentlewomen and ladies now-a-days, which in tiring and garnishing themselves know neither measure nor end; but of preparing garments for the poor, they for the most part do not so much as once dream. Dorcas could not abide that she herself should have a rich wardrobe full of sumptuous apparel, and see her christian brethren and sistern go naked and die for cold: yea, rather than they should want, she will set her own hands to work, which thing many of our fine white-fingered gentlewomen, yea, and some inferior to them, disdain to do. Acts ix. Mirrors for gentlewomen.

How instantly did a certain woman, named Lydia, desire St Paul and his companions to come into her house, and there to have all things necessary for them! "If ye think (saith she) that I believe on the Lord, come into my house, and abide there." Would God the like affection toward the preachers of God's word were found in our men and women at this present! then should not so many of them be oppressed with poverty, and wander abroad without livings, as they do now, unto the great slander of the gospel which they preach. Is it not a shame that they should want temporal things, which minister unto us spiritual and heavenly things? "Hath not the Lord ordained, that they which preach the gospel should live of the gospel?" Are not they that rule well, and labour in word and doctrine, worthy of double honour? Is it not convenient, that the husbandman which laboureth should first take of the fruits? Are we not forbidden to muzzle the mouth of the ox that treadeth out the corn? Is not a reward ordained for the workman? "If we have sown among you spiritual things, is it a great matter if we reap your carnal things?" "Do ye not know that they, which minister about holy things, live of the sacrifice? they, which wait of the temple, are partakers of the temple? Even so also did the Lord ordain that they, which preach the gospel, should live of the gospel," saith St Paul. Acts xvi. Preachers unprovided. 1 Cor. ix. 1 Tim. v. 2 Tim. ii. 1 Tim. v. Matt. x. 1 Cor. ix. Matt. x.

The apostle requireth that a bishop, that is, a spiritual minister, should maintain hospitality. How unseemly then is it for them that should feed other, either miserably to live on other men's trenchers, or else, like vagabonds, to hunt about for their living! Neither our ancestors, nor we in times past, have so dealt with the sorcerer-like sacrificers, with the prattling papists, with the monstrous monks, with the chattering canons, with the flattering friars, and such other mumming mummers as, under the visor 1 Tim. iii. Tit. i. Papists heretofore better provided for than preachers now.

of painted holiness, have deceived almost all the world, leading us from God's blessed word to man's trifling traditions, from the way of salvation unto the state of damnation, from heaven to hell, from God to the devil. But so hath it ever gone for the most part with the true preachers in this wicked and unthankful world. In the time 1 Kings xviii. of king Achab the true prophets of God were slain, and they that remained alive were secretly kept in caves, and there fed with bread and water of good Abdy, which unfeignedly feared God. If they had not been preserved by that godly man, they had either been slain, or else famished. But the priests of Baal abounded with all kind of wealth. Eight hundred and fifty, saith the scripture, "did eat of Jesabel's table."

Jer. xx. xxxviii. Who knoweth not that the prophet Jeremy was thrown into prison, cruelly entreated, and like to die for hunger, when Phashur, the priests, and such other false prophets, even man-pleasers, lived in all wealth and abundance of worldly things? Mark ii. With what poverty the disciples of Christ were grieved, it may easily be known, when they for very hunger were compelled to pluck the ears of corn and to eat. And how Matt. viii. xvi. poor Christ was, not a few places of the scripture do declare; when in the mean time John xviii. Zech. ix. Annas, Caiphas, Alexander, the scribes, the Pharisees, the lawyers, the bishops, the Matt. xxi. priests, the sacrificers, with all the rabble of hypocrites, lived in all pomp and pleasure. This ingratitude, churlishness, and illiberality[1] toward the ministers of God's word shall not escape unpunished. "He that despiseth you despiseth me," saith Christ, "and he that despiseth me despiseth him that sent me."

Luke x. Luke xix. Acts ix. Acts xvii. Acts xxi. xxviii. Gal. vi. But let us return unto our matter. What need I rehearse Martha, Zache, Simon the tanner, Jason, Aquila, Philip the evangelist, Publius, Philemon, Gaius, and such other, which all shewed themselves courteous, gentle, and beneficial toward all the poor, but "chiefly toward them that were of the household of faith," as St Paul warneth?

If we have recourse unto ancient histories, O how shall we learn of them the ☞ fatherly pity and godly glad affection which was in the bishops and deacons toward the poor people, when Christ's church began to flourish! Read we not that, for the Mirrors for our bishops. comfort of the poor and oppressed Christians, the godly ancient bishops did not only sell the ornaments, treasures, and jewels of the church, but also the very boxes of gold and silver, wherein the Lord's bread, which we commonly call the sacrament of the altar, was kept? They had rather keep the sacrament of Christ's body in a basket of wickers, and to sell that they made of gold for the relief of the poor, than they should want[2]. O godly bishops and faithful shepherds, which so diligently watched for the preservation of their sheep, both bodily and ghostly!

Is it not to be thought, that the sums of money, which the beneficed men yearly pay to the archdeacon of every diocese, were first of all freely granted and given of our predecessors to be distributed among the poor people of that diocese, as necessity required, and their discretion served? But how that money is now abused, who seeth The office of the archdeacon. not? The office of the archdeacon is yearly to visit every parish in the diocese where he dwelleth, and diligently to see what the poor people of every parish want, and to make provision for them; and unto that use, as I said before, was that money given, which every beneficed man payeth to the archdeacon: again, to see whether the parson or vicar be resident upon his benefice, and maintain such hospitality, as the poor of the parish be the better for it. But now-a-days the archdeacon ask not for the poor, nor in what condition they stand, but whether the hosts be well kept in the pix from moulding and furring, whether corporas cloths be clean washed, whether the chrismatory be safely locked up, whether the priest useth any unhallowed garments or chalice in his sacrificing, whether the copes, vestments, and albs be sufficiently repaired, whether the church, chancel, or church-yard be in case good enough, and such other trifles. God have mercy on us, and send us once a redress of these things!

Furthermore, with what a godly pity and charitable affection did our ancestors burn toward the poor members of Christ, which (as I may speak nothing of abbeys, Follow these forefathers. colleges, chantries, free chapels, &c.) built with their great cost hospitals, and such other houses, enduing the same with yearly revenues for the relief of the poor!

[1 So edition of 1550; folio, *liberality*.]

[2 See Vol. I. page 32, note 1.]

Men cry, "Fathers, fathers," but the manners of these fathers are clean forgotten. "All seek their own avantage, and not those things which pertain unto Jesu Christ." Phil. ii.

Thus see we that all good men have ever pitied the poor, and sought all means possible to do them good. But the contrary is found among us now-a-days. For men, according to St Paul's prophecy, are "the lovers of themselves," and not of the poor. They are covetous to themselves, and not liberal to the poor. They heap to themselves, they provide nothing for the poor. There be many signs of the last day to be at hand; but this cold affection, and more cold love, and most cold liberality toward the poor, prove evidently that it is not far off. 2 Tim. iii.

Among many other signs and tokens which Christ declareth to go before the day of judgment, is not this one of the most evident? "Forasmuch," saith he, "as iniquity shall abound, the love of many shall wax cold." When did iniquity ever so abound? When was the love of men ever so cold toward the poor? The rich worldlings in times past could build great monasteries for the bellied hypocrites, great colleges, chantries, and free chapels for soul-carriers and purgatory-rakers; but who buildeth so much as a cottage now for to harbour a silly poor man? Men in times past disherited their lawful heirs to nourish in idleness a number of idle bellies under the pretence of prayer; but who now even of his superfluities doeth any notable thing for Christ's poor members? A number of people heretofore hath decked idols and mawmets with silk, velvet, and other precious vestures, yea, with gold, silver, pearl, and precious stones: how many now, in so great a multitude, do clothe the poor naked creatures of God with canvas and rug? They gave shoes of silver and gold set with rich stones to dumb mawmets; but who now giveth shoes of leather to the poor? O too much unmercifulness! Can these things escape unplagued? If the Lord liveth, plagues be at hand, except we amend. This our ingratitude toward God, and unmercifulness toward the poor, will surely accelerate and haste forward the vengeance of God to fall upon us. For whether we respect and behold the spiritualty or temporalty, their love toward the poor, compared with the love of our ancestors, is very cold, yea, it is almost nothing. But if we compare their covetousness with the desire of our elders toward the goods of the world, we shall find it so far to excel and surmount as the high heavens do the low earth. Matt. xxiv.

How do many of our spiritual men, as they are called, heap promotion upon promotion, benefice upon benefice, deanery upon deanery, prebend upon prebend, and prebend for avantage! Ah, one filthy belly to devour so many wealthy livings! O abomination! And yet the careless swine are led with no pity toward the poor, whose sweat of their brows they lick up, whose labours of their hands they, cormorant-like, devour. Behold their pain in teaching, it is very small: behold their hospitality, it is nothing at all. "Wo be unto those shepherds," saith God by the prophet, "that feed themselves! Should not the shepherds feed the flocks? Ye have eaten up the fat, ye have clothed you with the wool, the best fed have ye slain; but the flock have ye not nourished. The weak have ye not holden up, the sick have ye not healed, the broken have ye not bound together, the outcasts have ye not brought again, the lost have ye not sought; but churlishly and cruelly have ye ruled them." Spiritual men covetous. Ezek. xxxiv.

Again, how do many of the temporal worldlings join farm to farm, office to office, lordship to lordship, pasture to pasture, land to land, house to house, and house for avantage! that the vengeance of God threatened by the prophets may come upon them: "Wo be unto you, that join house to house, and couple land to land, so nigh one to another, that the poor man can get no more ground! Shall ye dwell alone upon the face of the earth? These things are come up unto my ears, saith the Lord of hosts. Shall not many great and gorgeous houses be so waste that no man shall dwell in them?" Again: "Wo be unto him that heapeth up other men's goods! How long will he lade himself with the thick clay?" "Wo be unto him that covetously gathereth evil-gotten goods into his house, that he may set his nest on high, to escape from the power of misfortune! Thou hast devised the shame of thine own house." "The very stones of the wall shall cry out of it." O how doth our Saviour Christ thunder against the rich worldlings that live all in pleasure, and yet are not once Temporal men covetous. Isai. v. Hab. ii.

Luke vi. moved with pity and compassion toward the poor! "Wo be to you that are rich (saith he), which have your consolation! Wo be to you that are filled; for ye shall hunger! Wo be to you that laugh now; for ye shall mourn and weep!" Thus see we what unmercifulness reigneth in the world almost universally; and how all the threatenings of God's vengeance cannot quench in the wicked worldlings' hearts the insatiable thirst of gathering worldly goods, but that they go still forth to heap up thick clay against themselves, yea, and that beyond all measure, not considering how Psal. xxxix. vain and deceitful the possession of temporal things is in this world. "He heapeth treasure upon treasure," saith David, "and yet knoweth he not for whom he gathereth these things together."

Notable is the history that our Saviour Christ telleth of a certain rich man in Luke xii. the gospel of St Luke. "The ground of a certain rich man," saith he, "brought forth plentiful fruits, and he thought within himself, saying, What shall I do; because I have no room where to bestow my fruits? And he said, Thus will I do: I will destroy my barns and build greater, and then will I gather all my goods that are grown unto me, and I will say to my soul, O soul, thou hast much goods laid up in store for many years: take thine ease, eat, drink, and be merry. But God said unto him, Thou fool, this night will they fetch away thy soul again from thee. Then whose shall those things be which thou hast provided? So is it with him that gathereth riches to himself, and is not rich toward God."

What then remaineth but that they which are godly rich remember themselves to be the stewards of God, endued with worldly substance not to spend it voluptuously, or after their own foolish fancy about trifles, but upon their necessaries, and that they may conveniently spare to distribute unto the poor, which are their brothers in Christ, of the same flesh and blood, and fellow-inheritors with them of one and of Ecclus. xxxi. the same glory? "O blessed is the rich which is found without blemish, and hath not gone after gold, nor hoped in money and treasures! Where is there such a one? and we shall commend him, and call him blessed: for great things doeth he among his people."

Sentences for the godly rich to remember. And that the godly rich may be the more encouraged to gratify the poor, and to do good unto the needy in this wretched and beggarly time, let them ever set these and such like sentences of the holy scriptures before the eyes of their mind. Ecclus. iv. "My son, defraud not the poor of his alms, and turn not away thine eyes from him that hath need. Despise not an hungry soul, and despise not the poor in his necessity. Grieve not the heart of him that is helpless, and withdraw not the gift from the needful. Refuse not the prayer of one that is in trouble: turn not away thy face from the needy. Cast not thine eyes aside from the poor for any evil will, that thou give him none occasion to speak evil of thee. For if he complain in the bitterness of his soul, his prayer shall be heard; even he that made him shall hear him. Be courteous unto the company of the poor, humble thy soul unto the elder, and bow down thy head to a man of worship. Let it not grieve thee to bow down thine ear unto the poor; but pay thy debt, and give him a friendly answer, and that with meekness. Deliver him that suffereth wrong from the hand of the oppressor, and be not faint-hearted when thou sittest in judgment. Be merciful unto the fatherless as a father, and be instead of an husband unto their mother; so shalt thou be as an obedient son of the Highest, and he shall love thee more than thy mother doth." Ecclus. xxix. "Help the poor for the commandment's sake, and let him not go empty from thee because of his necessity. Lese[1] thy money for thy brother and neighbour's sake, and bury it not under a stone where it rusteth and corrupteth. Gather thy treasure after the commandment of the Highest; and so shall it bring thee more profit than gold. Lay up thy alms in the hand of the poor; and it shall keep thee from all evil. A man's alms is a purse with him, and shall keep a man's favour as the apple of an eye; and afterward shall it arise and pay every man his reward upon his head. It shall fight for thee against thine enemies better than the shield of a giant, or spear of Ecclus. xxxv. the mighty." "Whoso is[2] merciful and giveth alms, that is the right thank-offering."

[[1] Lese: lose.]

[[2] So ed. 1550: folio, *Who is so*.]

"Look, what thine hand is able, give with a cheerful eye. For the Lord recompenseth and giveth thee seven times as much again." "Give alms of thy goods, and turn never thy face from the poor; and so shall it come to pass that the face of the Lord shall not be turned away from thee. Be merciful after thy power. If thou have much, give plenteously: if thou have little, do thy diligence gladly to give of that little. For so gatherest thou thyself a good reward in the day of necessity. For mercy delivereth from all sin and from death, and suffereth not the soul to come in darkness. A great comfort is mercy before the high God unto all them that shew it." "Eat thy bread with the hungry and poor, and cover the naked with thy clothes." Tob. iv.

"He that is merciful doth himself a benefit; but whoso hurteth his neighbour is a tyrant. He that is liberal in giving shall have plenty, and he that watereth shall be watered also himself. Whoso hoardeth up his corn shall be cursed among the people; but blessing shall light upon his head that giveth food." "Whoso despiseth his neighbour doth amiss; but blessed is he that hath pity of the poor." "He that doth a poor man wrong blasphemeth his Maker; but whoso hath pity of the poor doeth honour unto God." "He that hath pity upon the poor lendeth unto the Lord; and look, what he layeth out, it shall be paid him again." "He that is bent unto mercy shall be blessed; for he giveth of his bread unto the poor." "He that giveth unto the poor shall not lack; but he that turneth away his eyes from such as be in necessity shall suffer great poverty himself." "Blessed is he that considereth the poor and needy: the Lord shall deliver him in the time of trouble: the Lord shall preserve him and keep him, and make him blessed upon earth, and not deliver him into the hands of his enemies: the Lord shall comfort him when he lieth sick upon his bed, yea, and make his bed in the time of his sickness." Prov xi. Prov. xiv. Prov. xix. Prov. xxii. Prov. xxviii. Psal. xli.

"Lay not up for yourselves treasure upon earth, where the rust and moth doth corrupt, and where thieves break through and steal. But lay up for you treasures in heaven, where neither rust nor moth doth corrupt, and where thieves do not break through nor steal. For where your treasure is, there will your heart be also." "He that hath two coats, let him part with him that hath none; and he that hath meat, let him do likewise." "Give to every one that asketh thee." "Be ye merciful, as your Father is merciful." "Sell that ye have, and give alms. And prepare you bags, which wax not old, even a treasure that faileth not in heaven, where no thief cometh, neither moth corrupteth." "Make you friends of the unrighteous mammon, that, when ye shall have need, they may receive you into everlasting habitations." "If thou wilt be perfect, go and sell all that thou hast, and give to the poor, and thou shalt have treasure in heaven." "He which soweth little shall reap little; and he that soweth (in giving) largely and freely shall reap plenteously. And let every man do according as he hath purposed in his heart, not grudgingly, or of necessity; for God loveth a cheerful giver." "While we have time, let us do good unto all men, but chiefly unto them which are of the household of faith." "To do good and to distribute forget not; for with such sacrifices God is pleased." "He that hath the goods of this world, and seeth his brother have need, and shutteth up his compassion from him, how dwelleth the love of God in him? My babes, let us not love in word, neither in tongue, but in work and truth." Matt. vi. Luke iii. Luke vi. Luke xii. Luke xvi. Matt. xix. 2 Cor. ix. Gal. vi. Heb. xiii. 1 John iii.

Again, that the ungodly rich may learn somewhat to bridle their covetous affects, and by that means be the more occasioned not to be altogether unmerciful to the poor, let them grave these and such like texts of the holy scripture in their hearts, and believe them to be as true as there is a God. "Trust not unto thy riches, and say not, Tush, I have enough for my life:...for it shall not help thee in the time of vengeance and temptation." "There is nothing worse than a covetous man. Why art thou proud, O thou earth and ashes? there is not a more wicked thing than to love money. And why? such one hath his soul to sell, yet is he but filthy dung while he liveth." "He that loveth riches shall not be justified, and whoso followeth corruption shall have enough thereof. Many one are come in great misfortune by the reason of gold, and have found their destruction before them. It is a tree of falling unto them that offer it up; and all such as be foolish fall therein." Sentences for the ungodly rich to remember. Ecclus. v. Ecclus. x. Ecclus. xxxi.

"He that trusteth in his riches shall have a fall; but the righteous shall flourish as Prov. xi.

Prov. xxiii. the green leaf." "Take not over-great travail and labour to be rich: beware of such a purpose. Why wilt thou set thine eyes upon the thing which suddenly vanisheth away? for riches make themselves wings, and take their flight like an eagle into the
Prov. xxviii. air." "He that giveth unto the poor shall not lack; but he that turneth away his eyes from such as are in necessity shall suffer great poverty himself."

Ecclus. xxxiv. "The bread of the needy is the life of the poor: he that defraudeth him of it is
Eccles. v. a man-slayer." "He that loveth money will never be satisfied with money; and whoso delighteth in riches shall have no profit thereof. Where as much riches is, there are many also that spend them away. And what pleasure more hath he that possesseth them, saving that he may look upon them with his eyes? A labouring man sleepeth sweetly, whether it be little or much that he eateth; but the abundance of the rich will not suffer him to sleep."

Matt. vi. "Ye cannot serve God and mammon," that is, the worldly riches. "Verily, I say
Matt. xix. unto you, a rich man shall hardly enter into the kingdom of heaven: and again I say unto you, it is easier for a cable rope to go through the eye of a needle, than a
Luke vi. rich man to enter into the kingdom of God." "Wo be to you rich men, which have your consolation! Wo be to you that are filled, for ye shall hunger! Wo be to you
Luke xii. that laugh now, for ye shall mourn and lament!" "Take heed and beware of covetousness. For no man's life standeth in the abundance of the things which he pos-
1 Cor. vi. sesseth." "Neither thieves, nor covetous persons, nor yet extortioners, shall inherit the
Eph. v. kingdom of God." "Let not covetousness...be once named among you, as it becometh saints. For this ye know, that no...covetous person, which is a worshipper of idols, hath
1 Tim. vi. any inheritance in the kingdom of Christ and of God." "Godliness is great riches, if a man be content with that he hath. For we brought nothing into the world, neither may we carry any thing out. But when we have food and raiment, we must therewith be content: they that will be rich fall into temptation and snares, and into many foolish and noisome lusts, which drown men into perdition and destruction; for covetousness of money is the root of all evil: which while some lusted after, they erred from the faith, and tangled themselves with many sorrows. But thou, man of God, flee
Heb. xiii. such things: follow righteousness, godliness, faith, love, patience, meekness." "Let your conversation be without covetousness, and be content with such things as ye have
James ii. already. For he hath said, I will not fail thee, nor forsake thee." "The judgment
James v. shall be without mercy to him that sheweth no mercy." "Go to now, ye rich men, weep and howl on your wretchedness that shall come upon you." "Your riches are corrupt, your garments are moth-eaten. Your gold and silver is cankered, and the rust of them shall be a witness unto you, and shall eat the flesh, as it were fire. Ye have heaped treasure together in your last days. Behold, the hire of labourers which have reaped down your fields, which hire is of you kept back by fraud, crieth; and the cries of them which have reaped are entered into the ears of the Lord of hosts. Ye have lived in pleasure on the earth, and been wanton. Ye have nourished your hearts, as in a day of slaughter: ye have condemned and killed the just; and he hath not resisted you."

If both the godly and ungodly rich would set these sentences before the eyes of their mind continually, surely it should go much better with the poor people than it doth at this present. For then would not the rich men so greedily gripe to themselves the goods of this world, nor so niggardly keep them after they have gotten them, as they do now. Then would not many gentlemen, as they are called, so grow out of kind from their name by shewing little gentleness to the poor, neither by enhancing their farms, by taking fines, by receiving great incomes, nor yet by putting the poor out of their houses, and suffering the tenements to fall down, as they do now: then would not the rich worldlings join farm to farm, and heave other men out of their livings, as they do now. Then
☞ would not many of our spiritual ministers, like insatiable wolves, get so many ecclesiastical promotions into their hands, as they do now; but, having one living and that sufficient, be content and remain upon it, teach their flock, lead a good life, and maintain hospitality among their parishioners, that the poor of their parish in time of need may
Mal. iii. have bread, broth, beef, and beer, as they say. "Bring every tithe into my barn,"
Note. saith the Lord, "that there may be meat in my house." The parsonage or the vicarage

is God's house; and tithes are paid unto them, that they should have meat in their houses to nourish and comfort the poor: but while "all men," as St Paul saith, "seek Phil. ii.
their own, and not Jesu Christ's," while all, as the prophet testifieth, "even from the Jer. vi. viii.
least to the greatest, give their minds to covetousness," and have no regard to the poor and to their commodity; the poor live miserably, the poor mutter in corners and grudge against the rich, the poor break the bond of peace, the poor run headlong into all kind of mischief, which thing we of late have seen unto our great sorrow, trouble, and disquietness: yea, some of the poor misers, for lack of bodily sustenance, fall to picking, robbing, stealing, and murdering of other; some kill, drown, hang themselves, because they do not presently see how they may be able to feed themselves, their careful wives, their lamentable children, and their altogether wretched family; wishing rather through desperation desperately to end this their needy, careful, and weary life, than so too much wretchedly for to live.

O what good man is not moved with pity to hear[1], see, and know these things? Yea, what good man thinketh not himself bound even of duty to help unto the redress of these inconveniences, yea, pestilences? They are enemies to God, to man, to the country, to the public weal, to our posterity, yea, to heaven and earth, which, wallowing in all kind of wealth like ethnish epicures, and living all in pleasure like effeminate Sardanapalus, and heaping the goods of the world together as though they should never hence depart, are nothing moved with the miseries of the poor miserable people.

Wo be to that glutton, which, enfarcing his own stinking and drafflesacked[2] belly with all kind of pleasant and dainty dishes, suffereth his poor needy neighbour to perish for hunger! Wo be to that covetous cankered churl, which so joineth house to house and land to land, that the poor man knoweth not where to hide his head, nor how to live! Wo be to that wicked worldling, which, decking himself gorgeously with sumptuous apparel, suffereth his poor christian brother to go naked, and to die for cold! Wo be to that rich ravening raker, which hath raked together plenty of worldly goods, and yet is unmerciful to the needy members of Christ! Wo be to that beneficed man, which, having whereof to cherish the poor of his parish, is absent from his benefice, nothing caring what becometh of them, so that he may live pleasantly and wealthily of the sweat of other men's brows! Yea, and wo be to all them, which, being able to help the need of the needy, and to relieve the misery of the miserable, refuse to do it! Great is their damnation.

But forasmuch as every man godly affected is by the order of charity, for his power, bound to seek and further a redress in things that are amiss, I for my part, considering that nothing in this world disquieteth a man more than pensive care and careful pensiveness for a living (if not too much, yet convenient), considering also how many incommodities do chance to a man that is continually vexed with grievous thought-taking for the provision of that belly; I thought good to gather together, as time hath suffered, certain sentences and histories of the holy scripture, which declare and set forth unto us the unmeasurable bounty and exceeding large liberality of God toward all them that cast their care on him, and travail according to their vocation and calling, that, by reading or hearing of them, the weak in faith may wax strong in faith, and be fully persuaded that God, which nourished them in their mother's womb, will not leave them now succourless, when they be able through his grace to cleave unto his promises, to call upon his name, and for their power endeavour[3] themselves by one honest godly means or other to get their living, ever casting their care on God, and yet not being idle, but labouring in their vocation according to God's good will and pleasure.

I doubt not but, if they diligently weigh and earnestly ponder these comfortable sentences and histories of the holy scripture, they shall not only cease to attempt any unlawful means, but they also shall find great quietness, procure much rest to their minds, and, so long as they live, live with a merry conscience.

[1 From edition of 1550: folio has *bear*.]
[2 Drafflesacked: filled with offal or swill.]
[3 From edition of 1550: folio, *to devour*.]

If I had been as able to redress the miserable state of the poor with worldly goods, as my will is to stay their consciences with the word of God, that they may not despair of a living, I would have been as ready to do the one, as I have laboured to do that other. But seeing froward fortune goeth forward to frown upon me, and daily ceaseth not to pierce me with that cruel darts of poverty, I must do that I may, when I may not that I would, laughing foolish fortune to scorn, with all her vanities and pleasures, thinking myself sufficiently rich, so long as I have such a Lord,
Rom. x. as is "plenteously rich for so many as call on him," so long as through God's grace I am endued with this faith to believe that, while I travail in my vocation for my power, according to God's will, I shall want no good thing that is necessary for the either covering or feeding of this my mortal body. And would God all men could so quiet themselves, and with Democritus the philosopher laugh this foolish world with all the voluptuous worldlings to scorn, or, with the blessed apostle, even from
Gal. vi. the very heart say: "The world is crucified to me, and I to the world!"

This little treatise, after I had once finished it, I thought meet to dedicate unto your right worshipful mastership, partly for the godly affection and christian zeal which both you and that good virtuous lady your wife have borne toward the pure religion of God these many years, partly for the good report that both you have among all good men for your charitable liberality and plentiful alms toward the poor people, unto the notable example of all rich men, specially of such as profess the
Gross gospellers. gospel; whereof many in these our days (alas for pity!) have the gospel swimming in their lips, and yet in their deeds live no part of the gospel, but abuse the name thereof to cloke their beastly living, and to shadow their carnal liberty, they themselves being the bond-slaves of Satan, further from the true faith than the very Turks and Jews, more estranged from all godly works, both[1] of fasting, praying, giving of alms, mortifying their carnal affects, &c., than the very papists, so covetous, proud, hateful, vain-glorious, dissembling, backbiting, lying, slandering, disdainful, uncharitable, unmerciful, wicked, and unclean in conversation, that I know not to whom I may
Tit. i. justly compare them. "They profess that they know God," as St Paul saith, "but with their deeds they utterly deny him, being abominable, disobedient, and wholly estranged from all good works." What shall we then look for, but (except we repent
Matt. xxi. and amend) even as Christ did prophesy, "The kingdom of God shall be taken from
Psal. cix. us, and given to a nation which shall bring forth the fruits thereof"? "He loved not blessing; therefore it shall be far from him," saith David. This unthankfulness toward God, this unmercifulness toward our neighbour, this dissolution of life toward ourselves, can by no means scape unpunished.

Luke i. The Lord have mercy upon us, and turn our hearts, that we may "serve him in holiness and righteousness all the days of our life!" God, which hath begun a good work in you, mought continue and finish the same, unto the glory of his holy name, and the profit of his christian congregation!

[[1] This correction is made from the edition of 1550: the folio has *but*.]

THE

FORTRESS OF THE FAITHFUL.

PHILEMON, CHRISTOPHER, THEOPHILE, AND EUSEBIUS, TALK TOGETHER.

Phil. WHOSOEVER, most dear brethren, with a single eye beholdeth the corrupt manners of this most corrupt world, he shall easily perceive that Satan, our old enemy, sleepeth not, but, as St Peter saith, "walketh about like a roaring lion, seeking whom he may devour." For if a tree may be known to be fruitful by her green leaves, flourishing blossoms, and pleasant fruit; if a workman may be proved by his labours and pains not to be idle; if the sun may be perceived to shine because of his fiery and glistering beams; surely Satan, by the works that he bringeth forth in the children of this world, may justly be judged not to be idle, not to sleep, not to slack his office, but to behave himself in all points like very Satan. 1 Pet. v.

For when at any time since the beginning of his infernal empire brought he forth so large testimonies of his devilish travails, and shewed himself so diligent and painful in procuring things meet for the enlarging of his empire, as he doth in these our days? Let our time be compared with any age that hath been from the beginning (I speak even of that age which was most ungodly, most wicked), and it shall more right well seem to be most godly, most virtuous. For although the pride, the covetousness, the whoredom, the unmercifulness, the malice, the banqueting, the building, the buying and selling, &c., exercised in the days of Noe, or at any other time, was without doubt great and abominable, and justly deserved the vengeance of God, as it came to pass; yet compared with the outrageousness of vices used in this our time, yea, and that so universally and unmeasurably, they may be judged but trifles, seeing the number of them, compared with the infinite multitude that now most wickedly live, is almost nothing. Gen. vii. Matt. xxiv. Luke xvii.

The pride of these our days is Lucifer-like, the covetousness is unsatiable, the whoredom is monstrous, the unmercifulness is butcher-like, the malice is immortal, the banqueting is too much epicure-like, the building is infinite, the buying and selling is full of falsehead, craft, and dissimulation; and so forth of other vices, which are already grown unto such an exceeding height, that they can stretch out their branches no further; so that it is truly said of St John: "The world is altogether set on wickedness." "They are corrupt, and become abominable in their doings: there is not one that doth good, no, not one," saith David. "The Lord looked down from heaven upon the children of men, to see if there were any that would understand and seek after God. But they are all gone out of the way: they are altogether become abominable: there is none that doeth good, no, not one." 1 John v. Psal. xiv.

And although every christian heart, beholding this most ungodly state of the world, cannot but lament and bewail the abominations used in these our days, and right heartily be sorry that the tares have so overgrown the good wheat, that vice doth so abound, that virtue can take no place, that sin hath so overflowed the whole world, that true godliness is not only neglected and contemned, but also hissed at and utterly abhorred, yet these traitorous conspiracies and hell-like commotions[2], which we of late have seen, wherewith also the commonweal of England hath both been disturbed, defaced, and greatly impoverished, who, except an enemy to all good order, sorrowfully sorroweth not? Who, if not an adversary to our succession, with large tears lamenteth not? The inferior members to envy the principal parts of the body! O unnatural disposition! The servant to rule the master, the inferior to rise against his sovereign, the subject to Insurrections and commotions come of the devil.

[[2] The insurrections in several counties, but chiefly Devonshire and Norfolk, in the year 1549. See with respect to these, and the alleged causes of them, the dearth, inclosures, &c., Strype, Eccles. Mem. Vol. II. Book I. chap. xxi.]

disobey his governor! O cumbrous confusion! The brainsick, yea, rather the brainless head to attempt redress of matters in a commonweal, unsent, uncalled! O preposterous order!

Chris. It cannot be denied but divers of the commons have gone far beyond their limits, and taken in hand that hath not become them; forasmuch as they, contrary to their calling, have presumed to do the office of magistrates, of men lawfully called to rule in the commonweal. *Theo.* Those their rash and disobedient behaviours can by no
1 Cor. xiv. means please God. *Phil.* Please! yea, it rather most highly displeaseth God, which is "the author of peace, and not of confusion;" which will "all things to be done seemly and in comely order;" which commandeth the subject to obey his superior in all things,
Rom. xiii. 1 Pet. ii. "not only for fear of punishment, but also for conscience sake." How greatly God is and ever hath been offended with disobedience and rebellion, with order-breaking and disturbance of a commonweal, the holy scriptures sufficiently do shew. Was not
Gen. iii. Disobedience. Adam our grandfather thrown out of paradise for his disobedience toward his Lord God, that most high and most excellent Magistrate, and both he and all we his offspring
1 Pet. i. damned for ever, if we had not been redeemed by the precious blood of the undefiled Lamb Jesu Christ? Thus from the beginning see we how greatly God abhorreth disobedience, though the fault in our eyes seemeth very little, and not to be passed of.
1 Sam. xv. *Eus.* Truly therefore is it said of Samuel: "Behold, to obey is better than sacrifice; and to hearken is better than the fat of rams. For rebellion is as the sin of whoredom; and stubbornness is as the sin of idolatry."

Phil. But that I may declare to you how God in commonweals hath ever punished
☞ Rebellion plagued. disobedience, rebellion, conspiracies, insurrections, commotions, &c. against lawful magistrates, I pray you give ear and mark what shall be said. *Chris.* We gladly hear.

Phil. Ye know right well that, when God determined to deliver his people the
Exod. xiii. Israelites out of Egypt, the land of bondage, he made Moses their guide and ruler under him. *Theo.* Ye say truth.

Phil. Here was Moses chosen and appointed of God to be the supreme magistrate and principal governor of God's people. And as he had here by God's commandment authority to rule, even so were the Israelites bound by God's word to obey; which thing so long as they did, they right well prospered, they lived quietly, God favoured them, Moses as a loving father cherished them. But when they shook off the yoke of obedience, sought carnal liberty, murmured against their magistrate, troubled the
Exod. xvi. commonweal, O how did God punish and plague them! "The Lord hath heard your murmurings," saith Moses, "which ye murmur against him. For what are we (he speaketh of himself and Aaron)? your murmurings are not against us, but against the Lord." The Israelites murmuring against Moses murmured against God, whose
Num. xi. officer Moses was. "Therefore," saith the scripture, "behold, the countenance of the Lord was moved against the people, and the Lord slew the people with an exceeding
Psal. lxxviii. great plague:" and, as David saith, "The heavy wrath of God came upon them and slew the wealthiest of them, yea, and smote down the chosen men that were in
Rom. xiii. Israel." "For there is no power," saith St Paul, "but of God: the powers that be are ordained of God. Whosoever therefore resisteth power resisteth the ordinance of
Num. xii. God. But they that resist shall receive to themselves damnation." With how grievous and horrible leprosy did God strike Miriam for murmuring against Moses! How
Num. xxi. plagued God the Israelites, for murmuring against him and Moses his servant, with fiery serpents, which stung them unto death! Corah, Dathan and Abiron, because they did not obey Moses, God's magistrate, but disdained that he should reign over them, although appointed of God, were they not swallowed up of the earth, both they, their wives, their children, and all their goods? Went not they, and all that they had, down alive unto hell, and the earth closed upon them, and they perished from among the congregation? *Chris.* A meet plague for rebellion.

Phil. On the morrow after, when the people of Israel murmured against Moses, saying, "Ye have killed the people of the Lord," and so unreverently railed on him, what, escaped they unpunished? The scripture saith: "There died in that plague fourteen thousand and seven hundred, besides them that died about the business of Corah." Thus see we that, in the beginning of the Israelites' public weal, God by no means could abide rebels and seditious persons, but punished them with most horrible and notable plagues. *Eus.* If God so grievously plagued them which did but murmur against his magistrates, how extremely will he punish them that do not only unreverently speak of the high powers, but also gather unlawful assemblies against them, and enarm themselves on such manner, as though they should rise against a common pestilence of the public weal! Surely the end of such must needs be too much miserable. Take heed, ye rebels.

Theo. These things were done to shew how greatly God approveth the office and dignity of a lawful magistrate, and that he will be avenged of all such as despise his holy ordinance; again, that we by these examples may learn to fear the high powers, to honour and obey them, and by no means to resist them, except we will prove the same or worse plagues.

Phil. Well said: Absolon, king David's son, made an insurrection against his father, and through the counsel of wicked Ahithophel wrought most villany against his father's honour. What followed? was not Absolon miserably slain? Did not his ungodly counsellor hang himself? Were there not also twenty thousand men slain in battle, that took Absolon's part? See to what point sedition bringeth both the authors, counsellors, and maintainers thereof. 2 Sam. xv. xvi. xvii. xviii.

Chris. It is therefore wisdom for all men to follow this counsel of the wise man: "My son, fear thou the Lord and the king, and keep no company with seditious persons; for their destruction shall come suddenly: and who knoweth the adversity that may come of them both?" Again: "Wish the king no evil in thy thought, and speak no hurt of the rich in thy privy chamber; for a bird of the air shall betray thy voice, and with her feathers shall bewray thy words." Prov. xxiv. Eccles. x.

Phil. Who knoweth not that Seba, the son of Bichri, which conspired also against David, and dissuaded the people of Israel from obedience to their liege sovereign lord, had his head cut off? *Eus.* A meet death for a traitor. 2 Sam. xx.

Phil. Baasa the son of Ahia conspired against Nadab king of Israel, slew him, and reigned in his stead. But what followed? Though Baasa in the sight of the world died no shameful death, yet died he in the displeasure of God, and afterward all his succession, with all his friends and kinsfolk, were all destroyed, so that there was not one left alive. Again, Zimri conspired against Ela king of Israel, slew him, and reigned in his stead: but shortly after he was driven to such misery and strait, that he fled into the king's palace at Thirza, and setting it on a fire, brent himself, and so wretchedly ended his life. *Theo.* An end worthy of such a beginning. 1 Kings xv. 1 Kings xvi.

Phil. What shall I rehearse unto you the histories of the two seditious men, Theudas and Judas of Galilee, of whom blessed Luke writeth in his book of the apostles' acts? The one boasted to do great things, and so allured much people to follow him: the other counselled the Jews by no means to pay tribute to Cæsar, but to maintain their old liberties, and by this means moved great sedition among the people. What became of them? were they not put to death, and so many as followed them either slain, or else scattered abroad, and so brought to nought? We read not in all the scriptures that any traitor or notable seditious person hath at any time escaped without notable punishment. God cannot suffer his magistrates to be disobeyed, his commonweals to be disturbed, his politic or civil laws to be condemned, his godly and honest orders to be broken, &c. Whosoever attempteth any such wickedness, God will be avenged of him; as it is evident not only in the holy scriptures, but also in the profane histories. For God, even among the heathen, cannot abide his ordinance to be despised. Acts v.

Chris. Would God that all they, which either were authors of sedition, or consented thereunto at any time in this our realm, had known these things! then would not they so greatly have forgotten themselves and their duty. *Eus.* If they had been as well trained up in learning such godly histories, as they were nousled in hearing popish masses, and such other trifling trumpery, they had raised up no such tragedies. If there had been but the tenth part of true and learned preachers, that there were of popish priests among them, they had never fallen to such disorder. But it is truly

Prov. xxix. said of the wise man: "When the preaching of God's word faileth, the people run out of order, perish, and come to nought."

Preachers. *Theo:* Yet have I heard it reported that these new preachers, as they call them, through their undiscreet sermons opened a large window unto dissolution of life, and by this means caused the common people to aspire and breach unto carnal liberty, which while they hunted, they forgot both themselves and their duty.

Phil. I will not excuse all preachers. For some, as I have heard, have taken upon them the office of preaching uncalled, unsent; and such disordered preachers, for the most part, bring all things to a disorder, yea, to an utter confusion, mask they with never so pleasant a visor, and babble they with never so painted eloquence in the
Rom. x. sight and ears of the simple and ignorant people. "How shall they preach, except
Jer. xxiii. they be sent?" saith St Paul. "I have not sent the preachers," saith the Lord; "and yet they run: I have not spoken to them; and yet they preached." But as I may speak in the faithful and discreet preachers' behalf, which are lawfully sent of the high powers, and called thereunto by the secret motion of God's Spirit in their hearts, howsoever they be reported, certain I am, they never taught such doctrine as should minister occasion to godly people to shake off the zeal of obedience, or to break any good order or politic law.

Chris. Yet have I heard some preachers, whom I know to be both prudent and faithful, slandered that they by their preaching have caused these uproars. *Phil.* Ye said well, "slandered." Were they preachers, or rather massmongers, that caused the insurrection in Devonshire? *Chris.* Massmongers and papists, as it is reported. *Phil.* Then are the godly preachers free from giving any occasion of that sedition.

Eus. But what of Norfolk? *Phil.* Even in Norfolk also, or elsewhere, I am sure the very rebels themselves will confess, as I have partly heard and known, that the preachers were not the authors nor provokers of their commotion. Can the sermons of them which teach all obedience, humility, and patience, move men unto disobedience, haughtiness of mind, and desire of revenging? Can light be the occasion of darkness, or truth of falsehead? But what is so prudently, godly, and circumspectly spoken, that envy cannot wrest and corrupt? Neither is it strange for the christian preachers to be misreported of the voluptuous worldlings and covetous carles.

How earnest a setter forth of God's glory was the prophet Elias, and yet how was he reported, not only of the baser sort, but even of the king and of the queen? "Art
1 Kings xviii. thou he," saith king Achab, "that troubleth Israel?" As though he should say: Art thou he which through thine undiscreet and rash sermons movest the people to sedition, makest them disobedient to me their king and to all my officers, causest them unlawfully to assemble together, and to make havoc of all things? But the prophet boldly answered: "It is not I that have troubled Israel, but thou and thy father's house, in that ye have forsaken the commandments of the Lord, and followed the way of Baal." As though he should have answered: Dost thou, O king, lay to my charge, that I troubled thy realm, which teach thy subjects to obey thee in all those thy commandments that fight not with God's word? Then untruly thou accusest me. There is, I grant, in thy realm sedition and much hurly-burly: what then? Impute not the fault to me, but coy[1] thyself on the head, and say: I myself and my wicked progenitors, which have not tendered the glory of God, nor loved to hear his blessed word, nor to maintain the preachers thereof, but rather have slain them and followed the way of that foul idol Baal, and nourished his priests at our own table, and have not ruled the realm with such justice and equity, with such clemency and gentleness, as becometh righteous and godly rulers, but have polled and pilled our subjects, oppressed the widows and fatherless, received bribes, condemned the guiltless for gifts, and shed innocent blood like unmerciful and butcher-like tyrants; we are only the occasion of all these tumults, seditions, conspiracies, &c., wherewith this my realm at this present is so greatly disquieted.

[[1] Coy, or in the edition of 1550, corle: to strike or pat with the hand.]

As I may let pass the other prophets, which for their godly sermons sustained the like displeasure at the worldly tyrants' hands, how was the self Master of truth, the Wisdom of the Father, I mean Jesu Christ our Lord, "in whose mouth was found no guile," no deceit, handled for his sermons? When they brought him before Pilate, did not his adversaries and accusers lay to his charge, that he sowed sedition among the people? that he corrupted and perverted the commons with his doctrine? that he forbad men to pay tribute to Cæsar, and that he said he himself was Christ a King? How unjustly Christ was here accused, the holy scriptures abundantly testify. How could he be the author of sedition, which came into this world to make peace? How could he corrupt and pervert the people with his doctrine, when he taught nothing but that which he had heard of his Father? Can heavenly things corrupt the minds of mortal men? Forbad he to pay tribute to Cæsar, which himself paid tribute to Cæsar, and commanded other so to do? Boasted he himself a king, which fled away from the people when they would have made him their king? Said he not unto Pilate, "My kingdom is not of this world?" Was he disobedient to the temporal rulers, which disdained not to be brought before them, to be judged of them, yea, and to suffer death under them?

Matt. v. 1 Pet. ii. Luke xxiii. Eph. ii. Luke ii. John viii. Matt. xvii. and xxii. John vi. John xviii. Matt. xxvii.

Moreover, was not the blessed martyr, St Stephen, accused that he spake blasphemous words against Moses and against God? when of God no man ever spake more godly, nor of Moses more reverently; yet must Stephen to the pot, and be condemned for an heretic, when Stephen deserved rather praise and promotion. But Stephen had offended enough, seeing it was the chief priests' pleasure, and the other ravening rabbins', that Stephen should live no longer.

Acts vi.

Again, when St Paul and Silas came to Thessalonica, and St Paul preached in the synagogue the passion and resurrection of Christ, how did certain of the Jews complain of them unto the heads of the city, and rushed into the house of Jason, the apostle's host, and violently plucked him out, saying: "These that trouble the world are come hither also, whom Jason hath received privily. And these all do contrary to the decrees of Cæsar, affirming another king, one Jesus." Here are the apostles accused both of sedition and treason, and yet were they neither seditious persons nor traitors. They troubled not the world, except the world here be taken for the devilish people of the world, to whom it is a trouble to hear any thing of Christ, or to hear their abominable living rebuked. The good people of the world they quieted, and made them merry in their conscience; forasmuch as they persuaded by the word of God, which the apostles preached, that they had gotten free remission of all their sins through faith in Christ's blood. The apostles did not contrary to the decrees of Cæsar, if they were not against God's word, but rather taught men to obey them. Although they preached Jesus to be a king, yet did this nothing derogate Cæsar's honour; for they taught Christ not to be a temporal, but a spiritual king; not to rule with sword or pole-axe, but with his Spirit and word; not to reign in princes' palaces, but in the hearts of the faithful. Is not here great sedition, great treason?

Acts xvii. Eph. ii. Col. i.

When St Paul was but seen at Hierusalem in the temple, how cried the Jews out, saying: "O ye men of Israel, help: this is the man that teacheth all men every where against the people, and the law, and this place," and violently drew[2] him out of the temple, smote him, and would have slain him if the high captain had not come. What had Paul offended? He spake nothing, he did nothing, but as other Jews did. It was enough to kill Paul, because he was that Paul which had preached Christ to be the Son of God. At another time, when he told the Jews that God appointed him to be a teacher of the gentiles, how lifted they up their voices, saying: "Away with such a fellow from the earth; for it is no reason that he should live!" Paul must die, because at the commandment of God he turneth the gentiles from idolatry to the true worshipping of God.

Acts xxi. Acts xxii.

And as the wicked worldlings cruelly entreated the apostles of Christ, so did the worldly tyrants handle the good bishops and faithful ministers in the primitive church. If any mischief, plague, or evil chanced in the country where they were, it was straight-

[[2] This is substituted from the edition of 1550: the folio has *drive*.]

way laid to their charge. Even so likewise doth the world at this time deal with the true preachers of the Lord's word. Dearth, famine, hunger, plague, pestilence, battle, insurrections, commotions, treasons, heresies, epicurism, licentious living, &c., all is imputed to the preachers of Christ's gospel. They, they, and none but they, are the occasion of all that naught is, when no kind of people is further from doing harm to a commonweal than they; neither doth a commonweal receive more benefits of any man than of the godly preacher.

Gen. vii. 2 Pet. ii. Gen. xix. If the old world had heard and obeyed the sermons of Nohe, they had not perished with waters. If the Sodomites and Gomorrians had hearkened to the sermons of Loth, they had not been consumed with rain, fire, and brimstone from heaven. If the Israelites had given ear to the warnings of the prophets, they had not so oft be plagued and led away into captivity. If the Jews had received the doctrine of Christ and his apostles, they and their city with all their posterity had not come to such a destruction. But when the Lord raiseth up his prophets and preachers to admonish ☞ the people of their wickedness, and to exhort them to repentance, and yet they will not amend, but cruelly entreat them, slander them, persecute them, kill them, then 2 Chron. xxxvi. cometh destruction. "The Lord God of their fathers," saith the scripture, "sent to them by his messengers, rising up betimes and sending; for he had compassion on his people and on his dwelling-place. But they mocked the messengers of God, and despised his words, and misused his prophets, until the wrath of the Lord arose against his people, and till there was no remedy. And so brought he on them the king of Chaldees, which slew their young men with the sword in their holy temple, and spared neither young man, maiden, old man, nor him[1] that stooped for age."

Matt. x. John xv. *Chris.* "The scholar is not above his master, nor the servant better than his lord." "If the world hate you," saith Christ, "ye know it hated me before it hated you. If ye were of the world, the world would love that is his: but forasmuch as ye are not of the world, but I have chosen you from the world, therefore the world hateth you."

Eus. Preachers are commanded of God, under pain of damnation, to tell the people their faults; and yet if they rebuke covetousness, then the covetous worldlings are mad. If they inveigh against pride, the proud are displeased. If they condemn whoredom, whores, bawds, and ruffians are wood. Look, whatsoever sin they reprove, the guilty Matt. viii. cannot abide, but malign the preacher, and seek to do[2] him displeasure. The Gergesenes had rather Christ should never come among them, yea, they had rather go to the Amos v. devil, than they would have their filthy swine drowned. *Theo.* "They owe him evil will," saith the prophet, "that reproveth them openly; and whoso telleth the plain truth, him they abhor."

Phil. Well, thus see ye it is no new thing for godly preachers to be slandered and burdened with those faults wherein they be nothing guilty.

Of gentlemen. *Chris.* I have heard it reported, that divers gentlemen have been the occasion of all these tumults and seditions, through the great oppressions and wrongs that they have done to the poor commons, as by making common pastures several to themselves, by inclosing more ground to their own use than heretofore hath been accustomed, and by this means take away the necessary food from the poor men's cattle, without the which they cannot live; again, by getting so many farms into their hands, and letting out their own lands unto the tenants and farmers for so great price, or else take such large fines and great incomes that they can never live of it. These and such like things have I heard.

Phil. Ye have heard my mind of preachers, which were slandered (I speak of the godly) in this behalf: I will now speak somewhat of gentlemen. As I do not allow all that be called preachers, so do I not approve the doings of all them that be called gentlemen. And as I do not condemn all preachers, so do I not dispraise all gentlemen. For as there are which are true preachers indeed, so likewise are there which are true gentlemen indeed. But some abuse the name of preachers, by teaching papistry, anabaptistry, epicurism, &c., and are no preachers indeed, but rather praters and deceivers of the people: so likewise are there many which are called gentlemen,

[[1] So edition of 1550: folio, *in*.] [[2] *do* is inserted from edition of 1550.]

and are no gentlemen indeed, but pollers and pillers, rakers and catchers, bribers and extortioners, yea, and very caterpillars of the commonweal. For they abuse the name of a gentleman, which is unfeignedly a name of much worship and great honour, and worthy to be had in reverence and high estimation. Without the true gentleman the commonweal can no more safely be than the body without eyes. For as the eyes are the principal comfort of an whole body, so likewise are the true gentlemen of the commonweal. And look, what the nose is without smelling, the tongue without speaking, the hands without feeling, the feet without going, the very same is a commonweal without them that are true gentlemen, as the wise man saith: "Where no good counsel is, there the people decay; but where as many are that can give good counsel, there is wealth." For such as are true gentlemen are fathers of the country, maintainers of the poor, defenders of the widows and fatherless, succourers of the needy, comforters of the comfortless, and upholders of the commonweal, in fine, gentlemen both in name and deed. These be pearls and jewels to a realm, and as necessary for the conservation of a public weal as fire, water, and heat is for the health of man's body. For their principal respect is not unto their own private lucre and singular commodity, but their whole study is how they may profit the commonweal and do good to many, as Salomon saith: "The righteous laboureth to do good; but the ungodly useth his increase unto sin." Not only their goods, but their very life also will they bestow to do good to other; so far is it off that for their own advantage they will impoverish or hinder any man.

Prov. xi.

Prov. x.

Eus. Would God we had many such gentlemen!

Phil. We have without all doubt many, although not so many as I would wish; for of good things we can never have enough.

Then is there another sort which glory in the title of gentlemen also, and they are such as this common proverb noteth:

As riseth my good,
So riseth my blood.

They think all nobility to consist in the abundance of worldly goods, in wearing of golden chains and costly apparel, in having fair houses and pleasant gardens. And to set forth this their gentlemanry they poll, they pill, they wake, they rake, they sweat, they fret, they gripe, they nip, they face, they brase, they semble, they dissemble; yea, they move every stone, as they say, to maintain and set forth their unnoble nobility, not caring how they come by it, so they have it. All is fish that cometh to the net: it is good to be taking. *Bonus est odor lucri ex re qualibet*[1]. These study not, as the true gentlemen do, to profit many, to do good to the country, to maintain the poor, to relieve the succourless, to nourish the weak, to cherish their needy tenants; neither seek they the commodity of the commonweal, but their own private advantage. They labour to possess much, but they distribute nothing. Their hand is stretched out to receive, but shut when they should give. If they once creep into a town or village, they for the most part never cease, till they have devoured and eaten up the whole town. Whatsoever is pleasant or profitable must be theirs, by hook or by crook; it lieth handsomely for them, and so near their nose, though it be a mile off. If there be either farm or sheep-ground, upon the which some honest poor man liveth, both he and his family, out he must. Had it must be, whatsoever it cost, though the poor man and all his should go a begging, it lieth so commodiously for our new-come gentleman. If they buy any tenement, and let it out again to the poor man, O how do they rack it and stretch out the rents thereof, almost from a penny to a pound! yea, and some of them, buying house and land in a town, suffer the houses to fall down, and turn the ground unto pasture, the poor man not having where to hide his head. Who will be troubled, say they, with such a sort of shake-ragged slaves in a town, which do nothing but burn up our hedges, eat up the common, fill the town full of beggars' brawls? Who? No man, I trow, namely where such fine and long-nosed gentlemen dwell. Some, buying the lordship of a town, handle the inhabitants thereof on such sort, that they lose divers of their liberties, being in much worse case than they were afore. Thus the poor people be so

Ecclus. iv.

[[1] Juv. xiv. 204, 5.]

wrung of these ungentle gentlemen, that the silly souls are like unto dry haddocks. Some Irishman, beholding them, might well think that they came lately out of St Patrick's purgatory: they are so withered away, even to the hard bones, for cold and hunger. Against such churlish gentlemen speaketh God by the prophet, saying: "O ye heads of the house of Jacob, and ye leaders of the house of Israel...should not ye know what were lawful and right? But ye hate the good, and love the evil: ye pluck off men's skins and the flesh from their bones: ye eat the flesh of my people, and flay off their skin: ye break their bones: ye chop them in pieces as it were into a cauldron, and as flesh into a pot."

Mic. iii.

Theo. These greedy gripes and hungry horse-leeches, by usurping the name of gentlemen, do much obscure the renown, worship, and honour of true gentlemen, and cause the name of a gentleman to be much disdained among the common people; as we have both heard and seen now of late days. And though they challenge to themselves never so much the name of a gentleman, by their goods, by their ancestors, by antiquity, by the worthiness of their stock[1], and many good morrows; yet, if they do degenerate and grow out of kind from the natural manners of a true gentleman, they are no gentlemen indeed, but carles and churls, yea, and in hurting their neighbours they are tyrants and murderers, as the holy scripture calleth them; and in polling and pilling them they are thieves, lions, and wolves, as the prophets term them. An ape shall be an ape, though she be clad in purple and gold. Esop's crow was still a crow, even when he had decked himself with the pleasant and goodly feathers of other birds.

Ecclus. xxxiv. Isai. i. Mic. ii. Zeph. iii.

True nobility.

It is virtue, and not gross flesh and blood, which thing we all are, that maketh the true noble and gentleman. It is a mind disposed to do good, yea, and doth good in deed when occasion serveth, and not sumptuous apparel and golden chains, that setteth forth true nobility. It is justice, mercy, liberality, kindness, gentleness, hospitality for the poor, and such other godly gifts of the mind, and not the multitude of riches, that declare who is a gentleman and who a churl, who is noble, who unnoble. He that can nighest approach unto lady virtue, and most lively set forth her natural disposition in his conversation and behaviour, he is the best gentleman, be his parents never so base, and his kindred never so vile in the judgment of the world.

Socrates.

Chris. Socrates, the philosopher, beholding a man very rich and wealthy indeed, but an ass-head in the knowledge of goodness, and notwithstanding gorgeous and gallant in apparel, said: "Behold a golden slave." Socrates, nothing esteeming the rich man for his riches and sumptuous raiment, called him a golden slave, meaning that, though he were laden with never so many golden chains, golden rings, golden apparel, yet so long as he himself is but filthy in his conversation, and hath a mind subject to carnal lusts, as covetousness, pride, ambition, &c., he is but a very slave, so far is it off that he is a gentleman. At another time that same philosopher, seeing a man both rich and gallantly apparelled, said: "Here is a horse trapped in silver." His apparel shewed him to be a gentleman; but his manners and conditions declared him to be but a horse and a beast. Diogenes, hearing a certain man bragging and boasting of his kindred, riches, beauty, costuous apparel, and such other worldly visors, knowing not one point of nobility to be in him, nor ought else worthy of praise, said: "Lo, here is a sheep with a golden fleece." Cato the elder was wont to say, that "the little thieves did wear fetters, but the great thieves went up and down gallantly apparelled with purple and gold." I pass over divers other sayings of the wise men, which, without any respect had to carnal nobility, worldly riches, gorgeous apparel, &c., called the wealthy worldlings by such names as their manners and behaviour deserved.

Diogenes.

Cato.

Eus. Would God all they which will be taken for gentlemen were gentlemen in deed! Then should it go much better with this realm of England.

Chris. This endless encroaching of worldly possessions shew evidently that they which use it are not friendly to the commonweal, seeing through it the poor com-

[[1] From the edition of 1550: the folio has *flock*.]

mons are brought to beggary. Salomon hath a notable saying, and would God all men would learn it! It is this: "The increase and prosperity of the commons is the king's honour; but the decay of the people is the confusion of the prince." *Theo.* Friendly to the commonweal? Marry, sir, they are not friendly to the king, by Salomon's saying, that impoverish the commons: if the commons' increase, wealth, and prosperity be the honour of the king, and if the decay and impoverishment of the commons be the confusion and destruction of the prince, then are they extreme enemies to the king, which, without any respect had to the commonweal, seek through their unsatiable covetousness to beggar the king's subjects, whereby they shall be the less able both to serve the king, and to bear for their portion the charges of the realm when time requireth. Prov. xiv.

Phil. Certes a king can never be poor so long as his subjects be wealthy. And better it is to have many that should help in time of need, than few; and easier is the burden and the gladlier it is borne, that many bear than few.

Chris. If that same gentleness and liberality were found at this present among the rich men of this world, that hath been heretofore in men of like degree, the commons should not only at all times be quiet, but also the realm should flourish with great wealth, yea, and that universally; whereas now it resteth in few men's hands. Gentlemen to be encroachers of farms, notable sheepmongers, graziers, butchers, clothiers, weavers, brewers, &c., as I may speak nothing of their parsonages, vicarages, prebends, &c., having otherwise whereof abundantly to live! O unworthy act! O unseemly sight! O abomination! What is it to beggar the realm, to famish the king's subjects, to bring slavery into this realm, if this be not? Do they not suck the poor men's blood, that suffer them not to have whereof to live? The wise man saith: "The bread of the needy is the life of the poor: he that defraudeth him of it is a murderer." Ecclus. xxxiv.

Phil. Well, neighbours, although I doubt not but that the king's majesty and his most honourable council will see redress in these things when they have convenient leisure, yet, if the world should go forth and continue as it is, and the rich worldlings more miserably oppress the poor than they heretofore have done, God forbid that the common people, or any kind of people, should raise up tumults, stir up seditions, lift up their hand against the high powers! For that is a sin which by no means can escape unplagued; yea, they that so do run into the danger of eternal damnation, as ye have heard afore. *Chris.* I say, God forbid also! but ye know the common proverbs: "The belly hath no ears:" "Hunger is sharper than thorn:" "Necessity is an hard dart:" "Need maketh the old wife trot." Proverbs.

Phil. St Paul had rather never to eat flesh nor drink wine, than he should offend his weak brother. Would he then, think you, trouble an whole commonweal, make uproars, raise up commotions, come armed in the field, assemble a sort of idle brains and brainless people together, rob men's houses, spoil their goods, break up their hedges, make several pastures common to all men, hunt carnal liberty, make a communion, yea, confusion of all things, and all for the belly? Paul would rather, like unto the poor Lazar, have died for hunger, than once violently and unjustly to take away other men's goods. Rom. xiv. 1 Cor. viii. Luke xvi.

Chris. Ye see the unmercifulness of the rich: what, would ye have the poor people starve and die for hunger? [*Phil.* Rather starve and die for hunger][2], as poor Lazar did, than to trouble a commonweal. As riches, so likewise poverty cometh from God: and both are to be taken thankfully, and not to be grudged at. If oppression be done to the poor of the rich worldlings, shall they avenge themselves? God forbid! yea, rather take that cross patiently, and think that they have deserved far worser things, which have so oft deserved hell; and pray to God to give those rich men merciful hearts, that according to their duty they may be moved with pity and compassion toward the poor. Again, if they have injuries done unto them, if they cannot otherwise be redressed, let them complain to the magistrates and officers of the commonweal, which are appointed to hear men's causes.

[[2] These words are supplied from the edition of 1550.]

Chris. If the poor oppressed complain to the justices of peace or such-like in the country where he dwelleth, that hath the injury done unto him, little redress, as I hear, can be had, one so serveth another's turn, even as the mules scratch one another's back.

Phil. If there be any such partial officers, which are not indifferent, but judge for favour, yet remaineth there another refuge, and that is to complain unto the king's majesty and his most honourable council, which without all doubt will both gladly hear their lamentable complaints, and redress their matters according to justice. But whoso leaveth godly means and attempteth wicked ways, both he and his enterprise must needs come to nought, as we have seen of late days. The Lord himself hath spoken it: "All they that take the sword shall perish with the sword." All they that are private men, and go about with force and violence to avenge their own cause, and to redress their own matters, shall surely come unto destruction. For they be order-breakers and despisers of God's holy ordinance, which hath appointed magistrates and head rulers justly to judge between man and man in all matters of controversy, that peace and quietness may be maintained in a commonweal.

Matt. xxvi.

Theo. If men were christian men in deed, as they profess in word, they would never for the belly's sake go about to disturb, trouble, and disquiet all the members of the body. There is a proverb no less true than common: "God never made mouth but he made meat." And truly I am thus persuaded that God, which made me a living soul, and fed me in my mother's womb, will not, after he hath brought me into this world, suffer me to perish for hunger, if I hang on his fatherly providence, cast my care on him, seek to please him, and live in my vocation according to his word.

Phil. I am glad, neighbour Theophile, thus to hear you speak; for I may tell you truth, the principal occasion why I so greatly desired to speak with you, and with my other neighbours here, was to comfort and strengthen you against this solicitude and thought-taking for the belly, wherewith many at this present are much vexed. For I am not ignorant what importune suitor the belly is, and how she is ever craving and casting doubts, fearing that she should never have enough, and therefore continually knocketh at the door of the mind to put him in remembrance to provide for her, saying, *Adfer, infer:* "Bring hither, bring in." For the idle belly continually consumeth, wasteth, but getteth, provideth nothing. Therefore is she full of thought and care for her living, even as a beggar is, which is so jealous over his drink, that he will not suffer the little fly to sit upon the brim of his cup, lest she should beguile him of his drink.

Of how great evils[1] belly-care is the author.

This belly-care causeth the lawyers to corrupt the law, the judge to give false sentence, the officers to be untrue to their lords and masters, the hypocrites to corrupt the holy scriptures, the rich men to be unliberal, unmerciful, the beneficed men to receive much and distribute little, the patrons of benefices[2] to sell to unlearned priests their benefices, parents to sell their children like calves and sheep for money, the papist to hate the truth of God's word, the merchant to forswear himself in selling his merchandise, the craftsman to make and utter false and sleighty wares, the temporal lord to raise his rents, or to take great fines and incomes, the inn-keepers to poll and pill his guests, the servant to rob his master, the maid her mistress, the single or married woman to play the whore, the single or married man to play the ruffian and the thief, the subject to rise against his superior, &c. Innumerable evils doth this belly-care bring unto men, against the which except they be well furnished both with strong faith in God's holy providence, and also fortressed with the knowledge of holy scriptures, wherein lie buried so great consolations for the faithful, they cannot abide the importune and continual suits of the sluggish belly, but must needs despair of satisfying her requests, and by this means not only have an unquiet mind, but also throw themselves into desperation, and so too much wretchedly finish this their careful life.

Chris. This belly-care without doubt is a great temptation to man, and very much disquieteth him, namely when he seeth all things so dear as they be now, and despair of a redress; forasmuch as they which should amend this thing are the cause of this

[[1] This is probably the word intended: the folio has *euines*. The note is not found in the edition of 1550.]

[[2] So the edition of 1550: the folio has *benefice*.]

dearth and famine—I speak of graziers, sheepmongers, and rich farmers. Therefore, neighbour Philemon, ye cannot entreat at this present in your communication among us of a thing more meet for this beggarly and needy wretched time, than to declare unto us by the holy scriptures, how merciful and bounteous Lord we have in heaven, which will not suffer us to perish for hunger, if we hang on his fatherly providence, and cast all our care on him.

Phil. This your bent good-will to hear doth not a little encourage me to speak that which I have purposed, yea, and that in few words, because I will not be tedious unto you. *Eus.* Speak, I pray you: we will give good ear.

Phil. That ye may be throughly persuaded of God's liberality toward his faithful servants, I pray you first of all consider God's order in the provision for his creatures. Before God made man, whom he was determined to make the high ruler under him over all things in this world, he made and prepared every thing necessary for him, and for the conservation of his body, that he might abundantly have whatsoever is expedient for him, and by no means perish for hunger and lack of food. First, placing him in Gen. ii. paradise, that garden of pleasure, he gave man liberty to eat of all the fruit that grew in the garden, except the tree of knowledge of good and evil. After the transgression of God's commandment, when man was justly driven out of paradise, and worthy for his disobedience not only to starve for hunger, but also to be condemned for ever, if God for his mercy's sake, promised in that blessed seed Christ Jesu, had not favoured Gen. iii. and forgiven him, God sending forth man into this vale of misery did not leave him comfortless and without provision for his bodily sustenance, neither sent he him into a barren desert, or salt ground void of all fruit, but into this world, where he found plenty and abundance of all things, and gave him liberty to eat of all fruits and seeds growing in it. "Increase," saith he, "and multiply, and replenish the earth, and Gen. i. subdue it, and have dominion of the fish of the sea, and the fowl of the air, and of every living thing that moveth upon the earth. And God said: Behold, I have given you every herb, sowing seed, which is in the upper face of all the earth, and in every tree in the which is the fruit of the tree, and that soweth seed, that they may be meat unto you." With this kind of food was Adam and his posterity content until the flood of Nohe. After the flood God, purposing, as it were, to repair mankind, and to be man's good and merciful Lord, and no less but much more bounteous to him than he was afore, said: "Bring ye forth, and multiply, and replenish the earth. The fear Gen. ix. of you, and the dread of you, shall be upon every beast of the earth, and upon every fowl of the air, and in all such as the earth bringeth forth, and in all the fishes of the sea: into your hand are they delivered. Every thing that moveth itself and that liveth shall be meat for you: even as the green herb have I given you all things." As God afore gave man liberty to eat all kind of herbs, seeds, and fruits that grow upon the earth, so likewise giveth he man authority now to eat all kind of fish or flesh as he listeth.

Chris. O exceeding great is the liberality of our Lord God, which dealeth so favourably with wretched man; not only to give him liberty to eat all kind of herbs, seeds, and fruits, but also all manner of flesh and fish. This is, without doubt, a singular benefit, and great token of God's inestimable goodness toward man.

Phil. Here, even from the beginning and repairing of man, doth the kindness of God brast out and shew forth itself toward man abundantly, so that now "all things Tit. i. are pure to them that are pure." Nothing is common or unclean, "neither is any kind 1 Tim. iv. of meat to be refused, if it be taken with thanksgiving." "For that which God hath Acts x. purified and made clean ought no man to call unpure, unclean." And all these things hath God given us to eat. Now, that ye may be thoroughly persuaded of God's truth in performing his promises, call to remembrance the histories of the holy scriptures, which do declare and evidently prove that God is faithful in all his words, and Psal. cxlv. dealeth no less favourably with his servants in deed, than he promiseth in word. God Gen. xii. commanded Abraham to get him out of his country and out of his nation, and from his father's house, unto a land that he would shew him. Abraham did as the Lord commanded him. If Abraham had not been fully persuaded of God's constancy and truth in accomplishing his promises, would he have forsaken his native country, and

gone out of his own house, where he was quietly placed and wealthily settled, and
wandered abroad like a masterless hound, he cannot tell whither?

Eus. A carnal and worldly-wise man would have thought it great madness to
leave a thing certain for that that is uncertain.

1 Cor. iii. *Phil.* So judgeth "the wisdom of this world, which is foolishness afore God."
Notwithstanding Abraham, nothing doubting of God's promise, forsook country, na-
tion, and house, and obeyed the voice and commandment of God. Neither was he
Gen. xiii. any thing at all thereby impoverished. The scripture saith, he was "very rich in cat-
tle, silver, and gold." For his native country God gave him a country that flowed
with milk and honey, that is, with the abundance of all things. For one house he
Rom. iv. gave him many houses. For one nation he made him a father of many nations. So
recompenseth God the losses that any man sustaineth for his sake.

Luke xviii. *Theo.* The like thing is promised of our Saviour Christ in the gospel. "There is
no man," saith he, "that hath forsaken house, either father or mother, either breth-
ren, or wife, or children, for the kingdom of God's sake, which shall not receive much
more in this world, and in the world to come life everlasting."

Phil. Who, even by this one example, is not greatly encouraged to believe the
promise of God, and to be fully persuaded, that as God dealt with Abraham, so in
like manner will he deal with us, if we obey the voice of God, as Abraham did?
Acts x. "For there is no respect of persons with him; but in all people he that feareth him
and worketh righteousness is accepted unto him." The promise of God is universal.
Whosoever therefore layeth hand on it with strong faith, he shall have of God what-
Rom. x. Joel ii. soever he hath promised. "There is no difference between the Jew and the gentile;
for one is Lord of all, which is rich unto all that call upon him. For whosoever
calleth on the name of the Lord, he shall be safe."

Luke xvii. *Chris.* It is not without a cause that the apostles prayed, "Lord, increase our
faith." For if true and undoubted faith were in the hearts of men, they would nei-
ther distrust the promise of God, nor yet despair of a convenient living.

Mark xi. *Phil.* Faith is much, yea, faith is altogether. "Whatsoever ye ask when ye pray,"
saith Christ, "believe to have it, and ye shall have it in deed." As God shewed him-
Rom. iv. self faithful in his promise to Abraham, which is the father of the faithful, so like-
wise did he to other, because no man should doubt of his liberality, which is com-
mon not to Abraham only, but to all the faithful in like manner: ye remember
Gen. xvi. that Hagar was the handmaid of Sara, Abraham's wife; and because Sara herself was
barren and childless, she gave to her husband her maid to be his wife, that she
might be edified by her. *Chris.* We remember it well.

Phil. This Hagar brought forth a son called Ismael, by her master Abraham,
Gen. xxi. which child was a mocker, insomuch that, after Sara had brought forth Isaac her
son, she would not suffer neither the lad nor his mother to tarry any longer in her
house, but caused Abraham to put them both out. *Eus.* Ye say truth.

Phil. Abraham rose up early in the morning, and took bread and a bottle of water, and gave it unto Hagar, putting it on her shoulders with the lad also, and sent her away. Now mark. Hagar is put out of her master's house with her child. She knoweth not whither to go. She hath no house wherein to hide her head, but wandereth up and down in the wilderness of Berseba. To comfort her no man is bent; for no man is present. As touching her victual, it is all spent: the bread is eaten, the water is drunk up. There remaineth now in sight no more, but utterly to despair of succour, and miserably to die. Which thing Hagar considering casteth the lad Ismael under a bush, goeth her way, and sitteth on the other side a great way, as it were a bow-shot off, because she would not see the death of the child. With how great sorrows her heart was stuffed, what plenty of tears gushed out of her eyes, what careful faintness occupied her whole body, no man is able to express. A child to die for hunger, the mother knowing of it, yea, and as it were in her sight, in her bosom! O dolour unspeakable! The mother likewise to be pierced with the same dart! O incomparable pain! All things are brought here to extreme desperation. There is no way to escape this present mischief. The child crieth, the mother weepeth: both look for present death. But what? Is God untrue, unjust, false in his promise?

Stoppeth he his ears, that he may not hear the lamentable complaints of the too much wretched? Despiseth he the tears of the mother, and the crying of the child? Yea, rather, when no remedy is looked for, God is present, God comforteth, God helpeth; because he will be found a God which is "faithful in all his words," which is the self truth and "cannot lie," which leaveth no man succourless that calleth on him. He sendeth his holy angel to the miserable woman, when no mortal creature is present to help. He comforteth her, and biddeth her not fear; "for God hath heard," saith he, "the voice of the child where he lieth." He sheweth her a well of water to comfort both her and her child withal, and afterward promiseth that the lad Ismael shall be a noble man, and great multitudes of people shall rise of him. Psal. cxlv. John xiv. Tit. i. Gen. xxi.

Theo. O history full of most sweet consolation! This is a comfortable and pleasant mirror for all people to behold, specially for them that are married, and yet see not (such and so great is their poverty) how they may be able to nourish them. If the married folk live according to their vocation, and travail in their estate in the fear of the Lord, though they have never so many children and great family, yet shall the sea sooner be without water and fish, and the land without grass and cattle, than any of them shall perish for hunger. If God provided for Ismael and his mother in the wilderness where no sustenance was to be gotten, where no man was present, but brute beasts and fowls of the air, will he leave them succourless that put their trust in him, being in cities, towns, and villages, and conversant with men where all things do abound?

Chris. If the poor married men did earnestly weigh and diligently ponder this most sweet and comfortable history, they should never despair of a living, neither for themselves, nor for their children and family; neither would they seek any unlawful means, as by stirring up commotions, making insurrections, spoiling other men's goods, &c., how to avoid their misery; but rather labour to answer their vocation, and without ceasing call on the name of the Lord, which will deal no less favourably with them, than he did with Hagar and Ismael. "Put thou thy trust," saith David, "in the Lord, and do good; so shalt thou dwell in the earth, and be fed with the best dainties thereof. Delight thou in the Lord; and he shall give thee thy heart's desire. Commit thy way to the Lord, and put thy trust in him; and he shall bring it to pass. He shall make thy righteousness as clear as the light, and thy just dealing as the noon-day. Hold thee still in the Lord, and abide patiently upon him," &c. Again: "Put your trust in God alway, O ye people: pour out your hearts before him; for he is our hope." [Psal. xxxvii.] Psal. lxii.

Phil. In the days of Isaac, Abraham's son, there fell a great dearth in the land where he dwelt, insomuch that he removed from that place, and took his journey toward Abimelech king of the Philistines, even unto Gerer. And while he was yet in his journey, God spake unto him, and said: "Go not down into Egypt, but abide in the land which I shall shew unto thee, sojourn in this land; and I will be with thee, and will bless thee. For unto thee and to thy seed I will give all these countries." Behold God's careful providence for his servants. Isaac, wishing to escape the cruel darts of hunger, hunteth about where he and his may conveniently dwell. And rather than he would die for hunger, he, after the example of his father Abraham, determineth to go down into Egypt. God, which is able to feed and to save his people in every place ("for the earth is the Lord's, and all that is contained therein"), forbiddeth Isaac to go down into Egypt, willeth him to tarry still in the country, and promiseth to bless him, yea, to give to him and to his seed all the countries of that land. Isaac, obeying the voice of God, tarried in that country, and waxed exceeding mighty, wealthy, and rich. For God gave him great abundance of corn, of sheep, and of oxen: yea, with a mighty household did the Lord bless him, insomuch that the king himself came unto him, and desired to make a covenant of peace and amity with him; unto such and so great power was Isaac grown. He which afore knew not where commodiously to live, and in the country which he would have forsaken for penury and hunger, even he now is become so rich that the king himself is glad to come to him, and to desire his favour. Gen. xxvi. Gen. xii. Psal. xxiv.

Eus. O wonderful works of God! *Chris.* Here find we that true which is spoken

Ecclus. xi. by the wise man: "Put thy trust in God, and abide in thine estate; for it is an easy thing in the sight of God to make a poor man rich, yea, and that suddenly. The blessing of God hasteth to the reward of the righteous, and maketh his fruits soon to flourish and prosper." *Theo.* This in deed was proved true in Isaac.

Phil. Not in Isaac only, but in so many as ever obeyed the voice of God, and lived[1] according to their vocation. God is the same God to us all that he was to Abraham and Isaac, if we by strong faith hang on him and on his fatherly providence, as they did, if the same integrity of manners and innocency of life appeareth in us that shined in them.

Eus. This beneficence and liberality of God toward Isaac ought to encourage all men to tarry at home in their own countries and houses, to be content with their estate and calling, and not to stray abroad for livings, as many idle brains do now-a-days, leaving their wives and their children in great care and misery, and many of them never returning unto them. Neither ought men to doubt but that God, which is almighty, and able to do whatsoever his good pleasure is, will as well provide for

Prov. x. them at home in their poor cottages, as in the halls of princes. "The blessing of the Lord maketh men rich; as for careful travail, it doth nothing thereto."

Phil. When Isaac sent his son Jacob to Mesopotamia, that he might take to

Gen. xxviii. wife one of the daughters of Laban, Jacob, as he passed forth on his journey, "made a vow, and said, If God will be with me, and will keep me in this journey which I go, and will give me bread to eat and clothes to put on, so that I come again unto my father's house in safety, then shall the Lord be my God, and this stone which I have set up an end shall be God's house, and of all that thou shalt give me will I give the tenth unto thee." Here Jacob desireth God's assistance in his journey, that he may go and come safe. And as touching worldly goods, he desireth no more but food and raiment. And so, nothing doubting of God's help, he goeth forward on his journey, according to the commandment of his father. Now behold the loving-kindness of God toward Jacob. God, which never leaveth them succourless that call on his holy name, appeareth unto Jacob in his sleep, and promiseth that he will give him and his seed the land that he sleepeth upon, and that his posterity shall be great and many, that they shall be as the dust of the earth, and shall spread abroad to the west, to the east, to the north, and to the south; yea, and that in his seed all kindreds of the earth shall be blessed.

Chris. Here are more benefits promised to Jacob than he asked. *Phil.* Yea, more than he durst have required of God. *Eus.* But what of the requests concerning his journey?

Phil. Ye shall hear. Whereas Jacob desired God to be with him, and to keep him in his journey, God said unto him on this manner: "Behold, I am with thee, and will be thy keeper in all places whither thou goest, and will bring thee again into this land, neither will I leave thee until I have made good all that I have promised thee." According to God's promise Jacob had a prosperous journey, travelling into Mesopotamia. Of whose coming when Laban heard, unto whom he was sent

Gen. xxix. of his father, Laban for very joy "came to meet him, embraced him, and kissed him, and brought him to his house."

Theo. This was good luck. *Chris.* Good luck indeed. *Phil.* So worketh God for his servants, which hath all men's hearts in his hand. *Theo.* But what entertainment had Jacob afterward?

Phil. Jacob tarried with Laban twenty years, in the which time God did not only send him bread and clothes according to his request, but also such wives as his

Gen. xxxi. heart desired, with many goodly children. Yea, God so blessed Jacob, that he was exceeding rich in gold and silver, in maid-servants, and men-servants, in sheep, camels, asses, goats, kine, &c. And afterward God brought him home again into his country both safely and wealthily. Who will now distrust the promise of such a Lord, so liberal, so bounteous, so beneficial?

☞ *Eus.* This history is greatly comfortable for all godly travellers by countries: hereof

[[1] The edition of 1550 is here followed: the folio reads *liveth*.]

may they learn that God will not forsake them nor leave them succourless, but send them all things necessary in their journey, defend them from their enemies, and safely bring them home again, if they call on his holy name, and cast their care on him. *Chris.* So saith the psalmograph: "He shall give his angels charge over thee, to keep thee in all thy ways. They shall bear thee in their hands, that thou hurt not thy foot against a stone." God "shall defend thee under his wing; and thou shalt be safe under his feathers. His faithfulness and truth shall be thy shield and buckler. Thou shalt not be afraid for any terror by night, nor for the arrow that flieth by the day." Again: "My help cometh even from the Lord, which hath made heaven and earth. He will not suffer thy foot to be moved, and he that keepeth thee will not sleep. Behold, he that keepeth Israel shall neither slumber nor sleep. The Lord himself is thy keeper: the Lord is thy defence upon thy right hand; so that the sun shall not burn thee by day, neither the moon by night. The Lord shall preserve thee from all evil: yea, it is even he that shall keep thy soul. The Lord shall preserve thy going out and thy coming in, from this time forth for evermore." Psal. xci. Psal. cxxi.

Theo. These be sweet and comfortable scriptures. *Phil.* I grant, to the faithful, which depend altogether on God, and on his fatherly providence. But the unfaithful, which trust on themselves, on their own wisdom and policy, feel no savour nor sweetness in them, as St Paul saith: "A natural man perceiveth not the things that belong to the Spirit of God; for they are foolishness unto him." 1 Cor. ii.

But let us behold more histories, which shall declare and set forth God's high providence and singular liberality toward his servants, that we may learn perfectly to hang on the Lord our God. Ye read in the first book of Moses, that in the time of Jacob, whom we spake of a little afore, there was a great dearth in all countries; insomuch that in the land of Canaan there was no victual to be gotten for money. Now behold the providence of God. God, aforeseeing this plague of famine, to the intent that his servants should not perish in time of hunger for lack of food, wonderfully sent Joseph afore into Egypt. And although his brothers sold him into a strange land, by this means seeking his destruction, yet God turned this his servitude unto his honour, and the evil that they did to their brother unto their profit, wealth, and commodity. For God exalted Joseph, and set up his honour above all the lords and princes of Egypt: even next unto the king was he in dignity, insomuch that he had the rule of all the king's dominions, and did what seemed him good in his own eyes; such favour found he in the sight of the king through God's working. Gen. xli. Gen. xxxvii.

Now, when this dearth was also felt in the land of Canaan, and Jacob with his family in great danger thereof, Jacob, hearing that corn was to be sold in Egypt (for through Joseph's wisdom was there corn enough laid up in the store-houses of every city in Egypt), sent his sons thither to buy corn for their money, that they might live, and not die. To be short, seeing the history is known, when the sons of Jacob came thither for victual, there was Joseph their brother in high authority, whom they judged either to be dead, or else to live like a bond-slave and drudge, not able either to do himself good or any other. In fine, they had victuals home with them and their money also, with many precious gifts, and at the last a commandment given them that they should bring their father and his household with all that he had, and provision should be made for them even in the best parts of the land of Egypt. Yea, the king himself sent chariots out of Egypt to fetch Jacob and all his family, and bade them not regard their stuff; "for the good of all the land of Egypt is yours," saith he. Jacob and all his were honourably brought thither, liberally and gently entertained of the king, quietly and wealthily placed in the land of Egypt. Gen. xlii. Gen. xli. Gen. xlii. xliii. xlv. Gen. xlvi.

And all this came to pass by the providence of God, which, aforeseeing things to come, worketh wonderfully for the safeguard and health of his servants. For the cause that Jacob and his children found such favour in the sight of king Pharao was not fortune, nor chance, but God's providence: again, that Joseph was exalted unto such dignity, the cause thereof was not Joseph's fair face, nor yet his goodly personage, but God's good-will, which gave him such wisdom as none had the like in all Egypt, neither Gen. xli.

was there any in all the dominions of king Pharao found like unto Joseph, whom the king might make governor over his realm.

And all these things wrought God for the preservation of his servants, as Joseph himself said to his brethren: "I am Joseph your brother, whom you sold into Egypt. Now therefore be not grieved therewith, neither let it seem a cruel thing in your eyes that ye sold me hither. For God did send me before you into Egypt for your wealth, and to save your lives. For this is the second year of dearth in the land; and five more are behind, in which there shall be neither earing nor harvest. Wherefore God sent me before you to make provision, that ye might continue in the earth, and to save your lives by a great deliverance. So now it was not you that sent me hither, but God, which hath made me a father unto Pharao, and lord of all his house, and ruler throughout all the land of Egypt." God himself also spake unto Jacob in a vision by night, saying: "I am God, the God of thy father: fear not to go down into Egypt; for I will there make of thee a great people. I will go down with thee into Egypt, and I will also bring thee again."

Gen. xlv.

Chris. O the unspeakable good-will of God toward all them that trust in him! "What other nation," saith Moses, "is so great that gods come so nigh unto, as the Lord our God is nigh unto us in all things, so oft as we call unto him?" "The Lord our God is a merciful God: he will not forsake us, neither destroy us, nor forget the appointment of our fathers, which he sware unto them." The Lord our God cherisheth us, even as a father doth his son. "Will a mother forget the child of her womb," saith God, "and not pity the son whom she bare? And though she doth forget, yet will not I forget thee. Behold, I have written thee up upon my hands," &c.

Deut. iv.

Isai. xlix.

☞

Theo. The last history which you rehearsed, neighbour Philemon, is very comfortable, and teacheth us, that although the plague of famine be cast upon any realm, and the wicked thereof perish for hunger, yet will God so provide for them that fear him, and call on his holy name, that they shall want no good thing. *Phil.* Well noted, neighbour Theophile. So would I have you both hear and read the histories of the holy scriptures, that ye should persuade yourself that whatsoever comfortable history ye find in the sacred bible, is there written for your comfort. And to prove your saying true, hear what God saith by the prophet: "Behold, my servants shall eat; but ye shall hunger. Behold, my servants shall drink; but ye shall suffer thirst. Behold, my servants shall be merry; but ye shall be confounded. Behold, my servants shall rejoice for a very quietness of heart; but ye shall cry for sorrow of heart, and complain for vexation of mind."

How the histories of the holy scriptures are to be read and considered.
Isai. lxv.

Eus. The saying of king David doth not much differ from this: "Behold, the eyes of the Lord are upon them that fear him, and upon them that trust in his mercy; that he may deliver their lives from death, and nourish them in time of hunger." Salomon also saith: "The Lord will not let the life of the righteous suffer hunger."

Psal. xxxiii.

Prov. x.

Phil. After God had delivered the Israelites out of Egypt with an out-stretched arm, and brought them into the wilderness of Sin, where they saw neither meat nor drink (for God was determined to prove them whether they were faithful or not), they grudged against Moses and Aaron, saying: "Would to God we had died by the hand of the Lord in the land of Egypt, when we sat by the flesh-pots, and when we did eat bread our bellies full! For ye have brought us out into this wilderness to kill the whole multitude with hunger." Ye see the unthankfulness of this people, for whom God had wrought so many wonders, and to whom God had shewed so great tokens of loving-kindness, even as a father doth to his child. Ye have heard how they murmured against Moses and Aaron, God's lawful ministers, which is nothing else than to murmur against God himself. Ye see their unfaithfulness, and how they are altogether swerved from God and from his holy providence; so that they are worthy no benefit at the hand of God: but what then? is God false of his promise? yea, rather, even for his promise sake (whereunto God hath ever chief respect), which he made to their fathers Abraham, Isaac, and Jacob, he wonderfully sent them down meat from heaven, even manna, and so fed them, as the wise man saith: "Thou hast fed thine own people with angels' food, and sent them bread ready from heaven without their labour, being very pleasant and

Exod. xvi.

God doth good for his promise sake even to the unworthy.

Wisd. xvi.

good of taste. And to shew thy riches and sweetness unto thy children, thou gavest every one their desire; so that every man might take what liked him best."

Theo. If God for his promises' sake feedeth the unfaithful and no less unthankful Israelites from heaven, we, that believe his promises, and hang only on him and on his fatherly providence, may be sure not to want, but abundantly to have whatsoever is necessary for us, as the psalmograph saith: "The eyes of all things look and wait upon thee, O Lord; and thou givest them meat in due time. Thou openest thy hand, and replenishest all things living with thy blessing." Again: "They that fear the Lord shall have no scarceness." "They which seek the Lord shall want no good thing." *Chris.* God shall sooner cease to be God, than such as unfeignedly trust in him shall perish for hunger.

Psal. cxlv.

Psal. xxxiv.

Phil. As the Israelites murmured for meat, so likewise did they for water. They came to Moses and chid with him; yea, they were almost ready to stone him, and said: "Give us water to drink." "Wherefore hast thou brought us out of Egypt to kill us and our children and cattle with thirst?" The Lord God, still considering his promises, and not weighing their infidelity nor unthankfulness, wonderfully, and against all natural and human expectation, gave them plenty of sweet waters out of the hard stony rock. *Eus.* O the marvellous works of God! He is not called Almighty without a cause; for he doth whatsoever his good pleasure is. It is truly said of David: "Great is our Lord, and great is his power: yea, his wisdom is infinity." Who will now doubt of necessary food, seeing God so marvellously feedeth the unfaithful, unthankful, and disobedient people?

Exod. xvii.

Psal. cxlvii.

Phil. At another time the rascal people that was among them, being weary of the meat sent down from heaven, fell a lusting, and turned themselves and wept (even as did also the children of Israel), and said: "Who shall give us flesh to eat? We remember the fish which we did eat in Egypt for nought, and the cucumbers, and melons, leeks, onions, and garlick. But now our soul is dried away; for we can see nothing else save manna: and our soul loatheth this light bread." Ye see that these people are still like themselves, that is, unfaithful, unthankful, disobedient. "O froward and crooked generation!" saith Moses; "do ye so reward the Lord, O ye foolish people and unwise?" *Chris.* It is not without a cause that St Stephen called that nation "stiff-necked, uncircumcised in hearts and ears, and such as alway resist the Holy Ghost."

Num. xi. xx. xxi.

Deut. xxxii.

Acts vii.

Phil. Well, yet note: notwithstanding their infidelity, unthankfulness, and disobedience, God continued still just in his promises, faithful in his words, and true in his dealings; for, according to their desire, for his promise' sake he would not suffer them to want, but gave them whatsoever they lusted for. "There went forth a wind from the Lord," saith the scripture, "and brought quails from the sea, and let them fall about the host, even a day's journey round about on every side of the host; and they did fly in the air as it were two cubits high over the earth. And the people stood up; and all that day, and all that night, and on the morrow, they gathered quails. And he that gathered a little gathered ten homers full. And they spread them abroad round about the host." Thus see ye how God for his promise' sake cherished the Israelites, although unfaithful, unthankful, and disobedient, even as the nurse doth her sucking babe; and fed them by the space of forty years in the wilderness, without their pain, care, travail, or labour.

Num. xi.

Theo. If God shewed such gentleness to the unfaithful and disobedient for his promise' sake, how much more will he shew himself a gentle and loving Father to them that fear him, believe in him, love him, and for their powers labour to walk in his holy pathways!

Phil. Such shall never want. Now mark what followeth. As God provided meat for the Israelites, so in like manner suffered he them not to go naked, nor to perish for cold; but all that time of forty years, when they were in the wilderness, he so preserved their clothes that they waxed not old, and so saved their shoes that they were not worn, but both garments and shoes so whole at the forty years' end, as they were at their first coming into wilderness: "I have led you forty years in the wilderness," saith God; "and your clothes are not waxed old upon you, neither are the shoes of your feet worn. Ye have eaten no bread, nor drunk wine, or strong drink, that ye

Deut. xxix.

Deut. viii. might know that I am the Lord your God." Moses also saith: "God humbled thee, and suffered thee to hunger, and fed thee with manna, which neither thou nor thy fathers knew of, to make thee to know that man doth not live by bread only; but by every word that proceedeth out of the mouth of the Lord, doth a man live. Thy raiment waxed not old upon thee, neither did thy foot swell those forty years." Hereof may ye perceive how bountiful God is in giving food and apparel, to them specially that fear him, and keep his holy commandments. Who will now be careful either for the belly, or for the back, as they say? God made them both, God will nourish them both.

Eus. These histories do so set forth the kindness of God toward man, that none except very infidels have just occasion to despair of God's liberality, if they call on his name, and travail according to their vocation.

Phil. There is nothing more certain. But lest any man should think that this kindness of God ceased in them of whom I have hitherto spoken, I will rehearse one or two histories more out of the old testament, and then allege certain out of the new, whereof ye may learn that other proved the like kindness at the hand of God, even as well in the new testament as in the old; that by this means ye may be perfectly persuaded God to be the Lord of the same liberality now that he was afore, and alike kind to his servants in all ages. Who knoweth not that Elias was an excellent prophet of God, fervent in spirit, vehement in word, and jealous for the glory of God?

Ecclus. xlviii. *Chris.* The scriptures testify no less of him. *Theo.* "Elias stood up as fire," saith the wise man; "and his word brent like a cresset[1]." While he lived, he was afraid of no prince; and no man might overcome him. Of his praise writeth Jesus, the son of Sirach.

Phil. This man of God lived in the time of Achab, king of Israel, in whose days God sent a great dearth into the world; for it rained not upon the earth by the space of three years and six months. In this plague of famine, whereof innumerable without doubt died, see how God provided for his servant Elias. First, when the waters 1 Kings xvii. began to be dried up, God sent him to the brook Cherith, where he promised to give him drink, which thing he unfeignedly performed; so that, when other perished for lack of drink, he had God's plenty and enough, as they use to say. Now, as touching his meat, behold the wonderful power of God, which commanded the ravens to feed him, and to bring him meat. "The ravens," saith the scripture, "brought him bread and flesh in the morning, and likewise bread and flesh in the evening; and he drunk of the brook." Behold, and mark well, how God provideth for his servant. He maketh the fowls of the air to be Elias' cooks, and to bring him meat; and God himself is butler, and giveth him drink at the brook Cherith. O what a God have the faithful! how tender and gentle, how loving and kind is he to all them that put their trust in him! Rather than his servant should die for meat, he maketh the fowls of the air to bring him things necessary for the sustenance of his body. O behold and diligently mark the fatherly care which the Lord God hath for his servants! Psal. ciii. "Even as a father pitieth his own children, even so is the Lord merciful to them that Psal. cxlv. fear him." It is truly said of the psalmograph: "The Lord is at hand to all them that call on him; yea, to all them that call on him in truth."

Psal. xxiii. *Theo.* Elias might right well say, as David writeth of himself: "The Lord guideth me; therefore can I lack nothing. He shall feed me in a green pasture, and lead me forth beside the waters of comfort." *Eus.* As God dealt with Elias and David, so will Rom. ii. Acts x. James ii. Rom. xv. he deal with us, if we labour to please him as they did. *Chris.* So I trust; "for there is no respect of persons with God." And "whatsoever is written is written for our learning, that through patience and comfort of the scriptures we may have hope."

Phil. Ye say truth. Neither did the care of God cease for his servant Elias with that benefit, whereof ye have hitherto heard. For God is no changeling: whom he 1 Kings xvii. loveth he loveth to the end. Therefore, when the brook was dried up because there fell no rain upon the earth, God, which never leaveth his servants succourless, said to Elias: "Up, and get thee to Sarepta, which is in Sidon, and dwell there: behold,

[[1] Cresset: a watch-fire, or beacon.]

I have commanded a widow there to sustain thee. So he arose, and went to Sarepta. And when he came to the gate of the city, the widow was there gathering sticks. And he called to her and said, Fet me, I pray thee, a little water in a vessel, that I may drink. And as she was going to fet it, he cried after her, and said, Bring me, I pray thee, a morsel of bread also in thine hand. She said, As truly as the Lord thy God liveth, I have no bread ready, but even an handful of meal in a barrel, and a little oil in a cruse. And, behold, I am gathering two sticks for to go in and dress it for me and my son, that we may eat and die. And Elias said unto her, Fear not, come and do as thou hast said; but make me thereof a little cake first of all, and bring it unto me, and afterward make for thee and thy son. For thus saith the Lord God of Israel, The meal in the barrel shall not be wasted, neither shall the oil in the cruse be diminished, until the Lord have sent rain upon the earth. And she did as Elias said. And she and her house did eat a good space; and the meal wasted not out of the barrel, neither was the oil spent out of the cruse, according to the word of the Lord, which he spake by the hand of Elias." Here again ye see what provision God made for Elias, and how beneficial he also was to Elias' hostess and to her household, because she entertained him so gently, and did whatsoever he commanded.

Theo. These be comfortable histories. *Eus.* And written for our comfort.

Phil. At another time, when he fled from wicked Jesabel, king Achab's wife, which sware that she would surely slay him, because he had killed all Baal's priests, whom she full daintily nourished at her own table, how did God, even when he was asleep, send his angel unto him with a loaf of broiled bread, and a vessel of water, and bade him eat! "For thou hast yet," saith he, "a great journey to go." "And in the strength of that meat," saith the scripture, "walked he forty days and forty nights, even unto Horeb, the mount of God." Here see ye that, when we sleep, God watcheth and careth for us, even as he cared for Peter, and sent his angel to deliver him out of prison, when Peter was in a sound sleep, and thought nothing at all of the matter. "Behold," saith the psalmograph, "he that keepeth Israel shall neither slumber nor sleep." Note again, that with one meal's meat God is able to preserve us forty days and forty nights, as he did the prophet Elias; yea, all our life-time, if it be his pleasure; so that it is truly said: "Man shall not live with bread alone, but with every word that cometh out of the mouth of God." And as God made provision for Elias, even so stirred he up Abdia, governor of wicked king Achab's house, to pity his prophets, and to provide for them; which, when devilish queen Jesabel destroyed the prophets of God, took an hundred of them, and hid them, fifty in one cave, and fifty in another, and provided bread and water for them; such and so great is the care which the Lord taketh for his servants universally.

1 Kings xix.

Acts xii.

Psal. cxxi.

Deut. viii.

1 Kings xviii.

Chris. It is therefore truly said of the prince-like prophet: "They that seek the Lord shall want no good thing." Again: "I have been young and am waxen old, and I have not seen the righteous forsaken, nor his children begging their bread on the earth."

Psal. xxxiv.

Psal. xxxvii.

Theo. These be comfortable histories for christian and godly preachers, whom for the most part the wicked and unthankful world neglecteth, despiseth, and set nought by, yea, and maketh less provision for them than for their malt-horses[2] and ban-dogs. Here may the true preachers see that, although the world regardeth them nothing at all, and suffereth them, so much as in them is, not only miserably to live, but also to perish for hunger, yet God, whose ministers they are, whose word they preach, will not suffer them extremely to want, but will either wonderfully feed them himself, as he did Elias, or else stir up some good Abdy to make provision for them, as this Abdy did for the prophets of the Lord, when he hid them in the caves from the tyranny of queen Jesabel, and provided things necessary for their living.

Preachers.

Phil. We read also, that a certain woman of the wives of the prophets came unto Heliseus the prophet, declaring unto him that her husband was dead, and that, for debt which she ought, and was not able to pay, the creditor was come to fet her two sons to be his bondmen. This woman was a prophet's wife. Her husband is dead, which

2 Kings iv.

[[2] Malt-horses: slow dull drudges of horses.]

left her both poor and in debt. Comfort hath she none, but only the company of her two sons, which also the creditor would take away and make his bondmen, because she is not able to discharge the debt. O in what misery is this careful woman! She hath nothing at all in her house but a pitcher of oil: but what is that to the dispatch of the debt? And if that be gone, there remaineth nothing whereof she and her sons may live. What is then to be done? Debt must be paid. Her substance will not reach so far. To make her children bond-slaves should be to her present death. This therefore remaineth. The sorrowful widow lamenteth, first of all, her cause secretly in her heart unto God, which is the helper and patron of all true widows and fatherless children, and afterward uttereth the same to Elizeus, the prophet of God, which, through God's blessing, of one pitcher of oil filleth so many empty vessels full of oil, that she, selling part of the same, was not only able to pay her debts at the uttermost, but also had enough of the rest to find her and her children.

Tob. iv. *Eus.* O notable miracle! Here find we true that holy Thoby said to his son: "My son, be not afraid. Truth it is we lead here a poor life; but great good shall we have if we fear God, and depart from all sin, and do well." *Chris.* This woman's husband was a prophet, and feared the Lord; therefore could not she and her children remain long comfortless. For God hath promised to be a husband to such widows, and a
Psal. xxxvii. father to such godly men's children. "I have not seen the righteous forsaken, nor their
Psal. cxii. children begging their bread on the earth," saith the psalmograph. Again: "Blessed is the man that feareth the Lord: he hath great delight in his commandments. His seed shall be mighty upon earth: the generation of the faithful shall be blessed. Riches and plenteousness shall be in his house; and his righteousness endureth for ever."

Preachers' wives. *Theo.* This is a comfortable history for such godly women as are christian preachers' wives. Hereof may they learn that, though their husbands be never so poor when they depart out of this world, yet, if they remain faithful and in the fear of God, and diligently call on his blessed name in their adversity, he will neither suffer them nor their children to lack necessaries for their living, but by one means or other send them
Josh. i. all good things; so that they shall not want. "I will not fail thee, nor yet forsake
Psal. cxlvi. Psal. xxxiii. thee," saith God. "The Lord giveth meat to the hungry." "Behold, the eyes of the Lord are upon them that fear him, and upon them that trust in his mercy, that he may
Ecclus. xxxv. deliver their lives from death, and nourish them in the time of hunger." "God despiseth not the desire of the fatherless, nor the widow," saith the wise man, "when she poureth out her prayer before him. Doth not God see the tears that run down the cheeks of the widow? or heareth he not the complaint over such as make her to weep? For from her cheeks do the tears go up unto heaven; and the Lord which heareth them doth accept them."

2 Kings iv. *Phil.* At another time also we read, that the aforesaid prophet in the time of dearth fed the prophets' children, and with a few loaves nourished a great number of men; insomuch that they did not only eat enough, but also left much of the bread; so greatly was it multiplied through the blessing of God, which is able of a little to make much, seeing of nothing he made all. "Give unto the people, that they may eat," saith the prophet. "The minister answered, What, should I set this before an hundred men? Set it before the people, saith he, and let them eat. For thus saith the Lord, They shall eat and leave. And he did set it before them; and they did eat and leave, according to the word of the Lord." See ye not here what the blessing of the Lord is, and
Psal. cxlv. how all things increase and abound when the Lord "openeth his hand?" If we depend on God's goodness, he will surely increase our victual in our store-houses, upon our table, yea, in our mouths and bellies. The prophet's servant thought it not possible
Matt. xix. that so great a number of men could be sustained with so few loaves. "But that which
Mark x. Luke xviii. is impossible with men is possible with God." Who therefore will doubt any more of God's liberality, have he much or have he little? It is all one before God to feed with much or to feed with little. If God bless us, we cannot want; but if God's blessing be taken from us, we must needs perish.

Psal. civ. *Eus.* So saith the psalmograph: "All creatures depend upon thee, O Lord, that thou shouldest give them their meat in due time. For, thou giving it them, they take it; and, thou opening thy hand, they are well satisfied. But, thou hiding thy face, they are sorrowful: thou taking away their breath, they are but dead, and turned into the earth that they came of."

Phil. How wonderfully did God feed Daniel the prophet, when he was cast into the lions' den of the high rulers, because he said that the great dragon, whom they of Babylon worshipped as God, was not God! Did not the angel of the Lord take the prophet Abacuck by the top, when he was going into the field to bear meat to the mowers, and carried him by the hair of the head, and through a mighty wind set him in Babylon, upon the den where Daniel was? "Go, carry thy meat," saith the angel, "that thou hast, into Babylon, unto Daniel, which is in the lions' den." And when Abacuck cried and said, "O Daniel, thou servant of God, have, take thy breakfast that God hath sent thee;" Daniel answered: "O God, hast thou thought upon me? well: thou never failest them that love thee." What a lively example is this of God's singular providence and fatherly care which he hath for his servants! Notable and worthy to be written in letters of gold is this saying of Daniel: "THOU NEVER FAILEST THEM THAT LOVE THEE." B. & Dr.

Chris. This history is very comfortable for all them that suffer imprisonment for the glory of God, and the confession of his truth. Hereof may they learn, that God will not leave them succourless nor destitute of help, as David saith: "The Lord is my light and my health: whom then shall I fear? The Lord is the defender of my life: of whom then shall I be afraid? When mine enemies came upon me to eat up my flesh, they stumbled and fell. Therefore, though an host of men were laid against me, yet shall not my heart be afraid; yea, and though there rose up war against me, yet will I put my trust in him." Psal. xxvii.

Phil. As I may leave off the histories of the old testament, and rehearse certain out of the new, that we may learn God's liberality toward his servants to be one and the same at all times and in all ages, let us call to remembrance the wonderful miracles that Christ wrought for the sustenance of his people. Read we not that our Saviour Christ at a certain time fed almost five thousand men, beside women and children, with five loaves and two fishes? And yet, when they all had eaten enough, they gathered up so much of the fragments that be left as filled twelve baskets full. At another time, when the people had been with Christ three days, and were ready to depart, having nothing to eat, and some of them had far to go, so that, if they had gone away without meat, they should have fainted by the way, what a friendly care had Christ for them! "I have compassion on the people," saith he, "because they have continued with me three days and have nothing to eat. And I will not let them depart fasting, lest they perish by the way." And when his disciples said, "Whence should we get so much bread in the wilderness, as should suffice so great a multitude?" and told him that they had but seven loaves and a few little fishes, "he commanded the people to sit down on the ground, and took the seven loaves and the fishes, and giving thanks, brake them, and delivered them to his disciples, and the disciples to the people; and they all did eat and were filled. And they took up of the broken meat that was left seven baskets full. And yet they that did eat were four thousand men, besides women and children." Here see ye that the loaves and fishes were multiplied in the hands of the disciples, and in the mouths and bellies of them that did eat, through Christ's blessing; so mighty is he to preserve the lives of his servants in the time of need. Matt. xiv. Mark vi. Luke ix. John vi. Matt. xv. Mark viii.

Theo. This is a comfortable history for all them that love to hear the word of God, and to frame their life according to the same. Such may be sure not to want the liberality of God in their necessity, which, as St Paul saith, "giveth us all things abundantly to enjoy them." *Chris.* This affirmeth that prince-like prophet, saying: "The rich shall want and suffer hunger; but they which seek the Lord shall want no good thing." 1 Tim. vi. Psal. xxxiv.

Phil. When Christ and his mother with his disciples were at the marriage in Cana, a city of Galilee, ye know that the guests wanted wine. What, spared he his liberality from them? Yea, rather did he not command the servitors to fill the water-pots with water? And when they had filled even unto the brim six water-pots of stone, containing two or three firkins a-piece, did not he turn all that water into John ii.

sweet wine? Certes they can want nothing, which have Christ present with them. Let us provide that we have Christ among us, and we may be sure to have abundance of all good things.

Married persons. *Eus.* This history is very comfortable for all married persons, which marry in the Lord. All such that so marry, and continue in the fear of God, may be sure, that the water in their wells shall sooner be turned into wine, and the stones of their walls into bread, and the clay of their floors into meat, and the thatch of their houses into cloth, than they shall extremely want necessary things, either for themselves or for their family. *Chris.* Would God all men believed this! Then should they have merry and quiet minds, where now through infidelity they be miserably disquieted
Psal. lv. with the care of worldly things. *Theo.* "Lay thy care on the Lord," saith David;
1 Pet. v. "and he shall nourish thee." Also St Peter: "Cast all your care on God; for he careth for you."

Matt. x. *Phil.* Again, how did our Saviour Christ provide for his disciples, when he sent them forth to preach, without money or meat! as he himself saith in the gospel of
Luke xxii. Luke: "When I sent you without wallet, and scrip, and shoes, lacked ye any thing? And they said, No." The disciples, according to their vocation, went forth and preached the gospel, nothing doubting but he that sent them would provide for them. For what master can find in his heart to see his servants lack?

Chris. This is very comfortable for the true preachers of God's word. Hereof may they well be ascertained that, if they do their Master's message faithfully, they shall not want, though the wicked world be never so unthankful and niggardly unto them.

Phil. O how comfortable are these words of our Saviour Christ to a faithful
Matt. vi. christian man! "I say unto you, be not careful for the life, what ye shall eat, or what ye shall drink; nor yet for your body, what ye shall put on. Is not the life more worth than meat, and the body more of value than raiment? Behold the fowls of the air; for they sow not, neither reap, nor yet carry into the barns; and yet your heavenly Father feedeth them. Are ye not much better than they? Which of you, though he took thought therefore, could put one cubit unto his stature? And why care ye then for raiment? Consider the lilies of the field, how they grow. They labour not, neither spin. And yet for all that, I say unto you, that even Salomon in all his royalty was not arrayed like unto one of these. Wherefore, if God so clothe the grass, which is to-day in the field, and to-morrow shall be cast into the furnace, shall he not much more do the same unto you, O ye of little faith? Therefore take no thought, saying, What shall we eat? or, What shall we drink? or, Wherewith shall we be clothed? After all these things seek the gentiles. For your heavenly Father knoweth that ye have need of all these things. But rather seek ye first the kingdom of God, and the righteousness thereof; and all these things shall be cast unto you."

Behold what goodly and natural examples our Saviour Christ bringeth forth here, that he may allure us to trust only on God's providence, and not to be careful for the necessaries of this life, which are not gotten by painful travail, but received of God's mere liberality. And because we should not be careful for meat, he first setteth before our eyes the fowls of the air for an example, whom seeing God the Father feedeth so plenteously that they want nothing, when they neither sow, nor reap, nor carry into the barns, much more will he feed us, and send us whatsoever is necessary for the preservation of this our natural life, if we call on his holy name, and live according to our vocation. If he feedeth the birds because they be his creatures, which notwithstanding so once die that they never live after, much more will he provide for us, which are not only his creatures, but also created after his own image, endued with an immortal soul, and made unto the end that we should set forth his glory, praise his blessed name, and after the general resurrection, our bodies and souls being knit together, live with him in glory, worlds without end, as his lawful heirs, through Jesus Christ our Lord. And as touching our apparel, to dissuade us from thought-taking for that, he biddeth us consider and diligently mark the lilies and flowers of the field; which, although they neither labour nor spin, are so clothed with fine and pleasant colours, that not king Salomon in all his royalty and glory was apparelled like unto one of them. If God so decketh the transitory flower, which this day is in the field pleasantly growing, and to-morrow shall be cut down and cast into the furnace, how much more will he send us convenient apparel for our bodies, which though they once die, yet shall they rise again, and for ever live with God in eternal glory! Christ therefore concludeth, that all these things shall be cast unto us, if we seek the kingdom of God and the righteousness thereof. Let us seek heavenly things; and things worldly shall abound unto us. Let us labour to garnish our minds with virtues; and God will not suffer our bodies to perish for lack of transitory things. For God is the Lord which "giveth meat to all flesh." "He giveth," as the psalmograph saith, "food to the cattle, and feedeth the young ravens that call upon him." He feedeth the Turk, the Saracen, the Jew, and all the rabble of infidels for their creation sake, and for his mercies' sake. He therefore will not leave them that be his faithful people unprovided, succourless, and destitute of help. He giveth the vile worms of the earth not only their being, but also whereof to live: he therefore will not see the faithful man lack, which is made like unto his own similitude and image. Let us therefore never despair either of food or of apparel. God gave us the life, God will preserve the life. God gave us the body, God will clothe the body. Away therefore with careful pensiveness and pensive care! Let us cast our eyes on God's most holy and infallible providence, which is certain and never faileth. "Take heed and beware of covetousness," saith our Saviour Christ; "for no man's life standeth in the abundance of the things which he possesseth."

Psal. cxxxvi. Psal. cxlvii. Luke xii.

Eus. I beseech God give us all grace so to do. *Theo.* Amen, good Lord, I most heartily beseech thee.

Phil. Furthermore, that we should be certain of corporal necessaries, Christ our Saviour hath commanded us, in that prayer which we commonly call the *Pater noster*, and so likewise taught us, that we should ask our bodily sustenance of our heavenly Father. This would he not have done, without doubt, if he had not been certain, that according to our requests our heavenly Father will deal with us, and give us our desires.

Matt. vi.

Chris. Of whom should the child crave, but of his father?

Phil. Again, to make us throughly assured of this thing, what comfortable promises have we in the holy scriptures! "Ask, and it shall be given you: seek, and ye shall find: knock, and it shall be opened unto you. For whosoever asketh receiveth; and he that seeketh findeth; and to him that knocketh it shall be opened. Is there any man among you, which, if his son asked him bread, would offer him a stone? or if he asked fish, would he proffer him a serpent? If ye then, which are evil, can give to your children good gifts, how much more shall your Father which is in heaven give good things to them that ask him!" "Whatsoever ye desire when ye pray, believe that ye shall have it; and it shall be done unto you." "Verily, verily, I say unto you, Whatsoever ye shall ask the Father in my name, he will give it you. Ask, and ye shall receive, that your joy may be full." "The Lord is at hand," saith St Paul: "be not careful, but in all things shew your petition unto God in prayer and supplication, with giving of thanks." Many other most sweet and comfortable promises have we in the holy scriptures, whereby we be assured to obtain of God whatsoever we ask of him, being agreeable to his most holy will.

Matt. vii. Mark xi. John xvi. Phil. iv.

Eus. To ask necessaries for our living is according to God's will. *Phil.* Truth. For God hath commanded us so to do, and promised that he will hear us. Jacob and Salomon, as the scripture witnesseth, asked of God necessaries for their living, and were heard.

1 John v. Gen. xxviii. Prov. xxx.

Chris. Although we ought to depend on God's providence, and by strong faith and fervent prayer look for all good things at his hand, yet may not we be idle, and lie wide open, gaping when God will put meat into our mouths, like careless swine.

Phil. God forbid. For, as the holy man Job saith: "A man is born to labour, even as the bird is to fly." From the beginning God appointed man to labour, saying: "In the sweat of thy face shalt thou eat thy bread until thou return unto the earth,

All men ought to labour in their vocation. Job v. Gen. iii.

whence thou wast taken. For earth thou art, and unto earth shalt thou return." Psal. cxxviii. David also saith: "Thou shalt eat the labours of thine own hands." The holy apostle 2 Thess. iii. St Paul giveth a commandment, that "if any man will not labour, the same should not eat," and giveth a charge that all men "work with quietness, and eat their own 1 Thess. iv. bread." "We beseech you, brethren," saith he, "that ye study to be quiet, and to meddle with your business, and to work with your own hands, as we commanded Eph. iv. you." Again: "Let him that stole steal no more; but let him rather labour with his hands some good thing, that ye may have to give unto him that needeth." St ☞ Paul calleth it theft for any man to live of the labour of other men's hands idly and without any certain vocation, and commandeth that all such should labour and get them some honest occupation, whereby they may be the more able both to find themselves, and also to distribute unto other that have need.

Examples of labour. Gen. iii. Gen. iv. Amos i. Gen. ix. Gen. xiii. xxvi. xxix. xli. Our first father Adam toiled in the earth, according to God's commandment, and so gat his living. Cain was a ploughman. Abel was a shepherd. Jubal exercised music. Tubalcain was a smith, and a graver in metal. Noe was a planter of vineyards. Abraham, Lot, Isaac, and Jacob were ploughmen and shepherds. Joseph was a magistrate, and a public minister in the commonweal of Egypt, under king Pha- Exod. iii. rao. Moses was a shepherd, and kept the sheep of Jethro his father-in-law, priest of Exod. i. Madian. The children of Israel got their living with hard and painful labour in 1 Sam. xvi. Egypt, under king Pharao. David, before he was anointed king of Israel, was a Exod. xxviii. shepherd. All the priests and Levites of the old law, every man according to his Luke i. vocation, laboured by giving attendance in the temple, by killing of beasts, and of- Mal. i. fering sacrifices, by studying the scriptures of God, and teaching the same unto the B. & Dr. people, &c. Amos the prophet was one of the shepherds at Therna. Abacuck the Mark vi. Matt. iv. Acts xx. prophet travailed in husbandry. Christ himself was a carpenter. The apostles of Christ were fishers. Paul laboured with his own hands, and gat both his own living, Col. iv. and others' that were with him. St Luke was a physician, and (as some writeth) a Acts xviii. painter also. Aquila was a maker of tents, of the which occupation St Paul was. Acts x. Acts ix. Simon, St Peter's host, was a tanner. Dorcas, that virtuous woman, made garments with her own hands, and gave them to the poor. There was no good and godly man even from the beginning of the world, which hath not practised somewhat to get his living, and lived in some certain honest and godly vocation, wherein he might with a good conscience eat his bread.

Magistrate. The magistrate is called of God to rule with the temporal sword, to be governor of the people, to promote God's word, to nourish the preachers of the same, to exercise justice, to defend the widow and fatherless, to conserve the commonweal, to banish all false religion out of his realm, and to seek the quietness and commodity of his subjects, even as a father seeketh the health and profit of his natural son.

Minister. The spiritual minister is appointed of God to rule with "the sword of the Spirit, which is the word of God," to rebuke sinners with the law, yea, and to excommunicate them, if they be obstinate and will not repent, to comfort and cherish the weak with the sweet promises of the holy scripture, to encourage the strong, and to exhort them to go forward until they wax ancient, and be perfect in Christ's religion, to minister the sacraments, to make collections for the poor, to maintain hospitality for the relief of the needy.

Subject. The subject is called of God to obey, and to be in subjection unto his superiors, and every one of them is bound by the commandment of God to live in their voca- Lawyer. tion. The lawyer in pleading and defending poor men's causes; the shoemaker in making shoes; the tailor in making garments; the merchant in occupying merchandise faithfully and truly; the school-master in bringing up his scholars godly and virtuously; the father of the household to provide for his family; the mother of the household to look upon things pertaining to the house, and to see her family well governed; and so forth in all other persons, in whatsoever state God hath called No man ought to live idly. them. Every man in his vocation ought to labour, and by no means to be idle. And who so doth, God will bless his labours, and send him wherewith abundantly to live.

Prov. xx. *Theo.* The wise man saith: "The sluggard plougheth not for cold; wherefore he beggeth in harvest, and getteth nothing." "He that gathereth in harvest is a wise son; but he that is idle in summer is the son of confusion." Again: "He that tilleth his field shall be satisfied; but he that is idle shall suffer hunger." Prov. xxviii.

Phil. God indeed hath promised to feed us, but yet so that we ourselves labour for our living. God hath promised us salvation in Christ Jesus, yet so that we believe his promise, and labour to the uttermost of our power to frame our lives according to his blessed will. David saith not only, *Spera in Domino*, "Trust in the Lord;" but he addeth unto it, *et fac bonitatem*, "and do good." All our affiance and trust must be reposed in God, and all good things must be looked for at his hand; yet must we do that lieth in our power concerning all those things that we desire to obtain of God. Therefore Christ saith: "Take no thought." He saith not, Labour not. The pensive care and thought-taking for our living, wherewith the heathen be so greatly disquieted, we must cast away from us, and lay it upon God, which careth for us; but as for labour, which is laid upon us of God as a cross for our sin and disobedience in Adam, we may not refuse, every man in his vocation, but joyfully take it upon us, and give God thanks that by such means, without our care and thought-taking, he will feed us according to his word. For what are all our pains, labours, and travails, if God bless them not? as the psalmograph saith: "Except the Lord build the house, their labour is but lost that build it. Except the Lord keep the city, he watcheth but in vain that keepeth it." Psal. xxxvii. Matt. vi. Careful pensiveness, and not labour, is forbidden of Christ.

Chris. Methink the occasion of this dearth[1], wherewith we are now oppressed, is not so greatly to be ascribed unto the covetousness of certain greedy gripes, as unto our own selves, unto our own ungodliness and dissolution of life, which so live as though there were no God at all, so behave ourselves as though there were neither heaven nor hell. They which have the gospel swimming in their lips, so live clean contrary to the doctrine of the gospel, as though there were no gospel at all. In ambition, in pride, in covetousness, in envy, in malice, in wantonness of life, &c., they give place to none. Another sort are so drowned in papistry, in superstition, in hypocrisy, &c., and burn with such an immortal hatred against God's word, that they can neither abide that (otherwise than it shall serve their fancy), nor the preachers of it, nor yet such as avance it. Can God do any otherwise than send his plagues where such impiety and ungodliness reign? It cometh from God's great mercies that we be not consumed, and handled as Sodom and Gomorre. But our own damnation sleepeth not, if we do not both shortly and earnestly repent and amend. Gross gospellers. Papists.

Phil. Truth it is indeed, that God many times sendeth the plague of famine into the world for sin, as it came to pass in the time of that most wicked and idolatrous king Achab, and at divers other times. And Moses, that most excellent prophet of God, saith: "If thou wilt hearken diligently unto the voice of the Lord thy God, to observe and do all his commandments, which I command thee this day, the Lord will set thee up on high above all nations of the earth. And all these blessings shall come on thee, and overtake thee, if thou wilt hearken unto the voice of the Lord thy God. Blessed shalt thou be in the town, and blessed in the fields. Blessed shall be the fruit of thy body, the fruit of thy ground, and the fruit of thy cattle, the fruit of thy oxen, and thy flocks of sheep. Blessed shall thy almary be, and thy store. Blessed shalt thou be both when thou goest out, and blessed when thou comest in, &c. The Lord shall command the blessing to be with thee in thy store-houses, and in all that thou settest thine hand to, &c. The Lord shall make thee plenteous in goods, in the fruit of thy body, in the fruit of thy cattle, and in the fruit of thy ground, &c. The Lord shall open unto thee his good treasure, even the heaven, to give rain unto thy land in due season, and to bless all thy[2] labours of thine hand, &c. But and if thou wilt not hearken unto the voice of the Lord thy God, to keep and to do all his commandments and ordinances, which I command thee this day, then all these curses shall come upon thee, and overtake thee. Cursed shalt thou be in the town, and cursed in the field. Cursed shall thine almary be, and thy store. Cursed shall the fruit of thy body and the fruit of thy land be, and the fruit of thy oxen, and the Deut. xxviii. Blessings. Cursings.

[[1] So edition of 1550; folio, *death*.] [[2] The edition of 1550 reads *the*.]

flocks of thy sheep. And cursed shalt thou be when thou goest in, and when thou goest out. And the Lord shall send upon thee famine, hunger, and going to nought in all things that thou settest thine hand to, until thou be destroyed and brought to nought quickly, because of the wickedness of thine inventions, in that thou hast forsaken the Lord." "And the heaven that is over thy head shall be brass, and the earth that is under thee iron. And the Lord shall turn the rain of thy land unto powder and dust: even from heaven shall they come down upon thee, until thou be brought to nought, &c. Thou shalt carry much seed out into the field, and shalt gather but little in; for the vermin shall destroy it." The prophet Esay also saith: "If ye be loving and obedient, ye shall eat the good things of the earth. But if ye be obstinate and rebellious, ye shall be devoured with the sword. For thus the Lord hath promised with his own mouth."

Isai. i.

These sentences, with many other in the holy scripture, do evidently shew that the plague of famine and hunger is sent unto us of God for our sins.

Eus. It is convenient therefore that we all hearken to the admonition of God, given by the psalmograph, which is, that there "be no strange god" among us, nor that we "worship any other god" but him alone, which only is the Lord our God that delivered us out of the spiritual Egypt, that is, from the servitude and tyranny of Satan. If we so do, God promiseth that he will give us whatsoever we ask of him. He will feed us with the finest wheat-flour, yea, and satisfy us with honey out of the stony rock. But to obtain of God this abundance and wealth, we may worship and have no strange gods.

Psal. lxxxi.

What is meant by strange gods.

These strange and new-found gods are not[1] only idols and mawmets made of wood or stone, which in times past the simple and foolish ignorant people worshipped as gods, but the abominable vices which reign so commonly now among us; I mean ☞ covetousness, pride, ambition, gluttony, lechery, malice, &c. These are strange gods. These must we put out of our breasts, if we will have God merciful and liberal unto us. For is this reasonable for us to serve strange gods, and to give over ourselves as bond-slaves to them, and yet to require our wages and reward of the true and only living God? "What fellowship hath righteousness with unrighteousness? What company hath[2] light with darkness? What concord hath Christ with Belial? Either what part hath he that believeth with an infidel? How agreeth the temple of God with idols?" "Know ye not," saith St Paul, "how that, to whomsoever ye commit yourselves as servants to obey, his servants ye are to whom ye obey, whether it be of sin unto death, or of obedience unto righteousness?" "Every one that doth sin is the servant of sin," saith Christ. We must first of all be God's servants, before we flatter ourselves with the obtaining of the good things promised by God; or else we deceive ourselves. If we be once the servants of God, and faithfully continue in his service, then may we be bold to ask of him our wages, and to persuade ourselves that all the comfortable histories and sentences which we read in the holy scriptures pertain unto us; otherwise we have no more to do with them than the Turk or the Jew. And if we receive any good thing at the hand of God, being not his servants, we reserve[3] it, as all other infidels do, unto our damnation.

2 Cor. vi.

Rom. vi.

John viii.

Phil. I confess, neighbour Eusebius, all this to be true which you have now spoken. Neither meant I, by talking so much of God's gentleness and liberality, and by alleging all these comfortable histories and sentences, to stablish the idolaters in their idolatry, the wicked in their wickedness, the covetous worldlings in their covetousness, the proud in their pride, the lecherous in their lechery, the idle bellies in their idleness, &c.; and yet notwithstanding to look for all those good things at the hand of God which belong unto his servants, as he witnesseth by the prophet; but to declare for your comfort and mine, that so many as give themselves over to God, believe in him, fear him, serve him, and live according to their vocation, shall never perish for hunger, but at all times have whatsoever is necessary for them. And if any should chance to famish (which seldom or never happeneth), God suffereth them so to do, partly that

Isai. lxv.

The merciful promises of God be made to the godly, and not to the ungodly.

[1 *Not* is supplied from the edition of 1550.]

[2 So edition of 1550. Folio, *have.*]

[3 This word, though not clearly printed in the edition of 1550, seems there to be *receive.*]

he may the sooner call them unto his glory, partly that their death may turn unto the greater damnation of such unmerciful monsters as suffered the servants of God to perish for hunger.

Theo. We know your godly intent, brother Philemon, neither doth our neighbour Eusebius otherwise take the matter. And I for my part thank you right heartily for your godly admonitions, freely confessing that I am much edified by your talk, and strongly enarmed against the darts of poverty and hunger, whensoever they shall go about to oppress me.

Chris. We all confess no less.

Eus. I spake that I spake to this end, that men should not flatter themselves with the sweet and comfortable promises of God, when they live in all wickedness and abomination; which promises pertain not unto them, but unto the faithful servants of God, which shall enjoy no less at the hand of God than he hath promised. If they will enjoy the like commodity, they must do the like service. They must away with their strange and new-found gods, I mean pride, covetousness, gluttony, whoredom, malice, &c., and serve the only true and living God.

Phil. Well, neighbours, to knit up your talk with few words, ye have heard how beneficial God is to them that put their trust in him, and live according to their vocation; so that those that be faithful need not to despair of comfort, seem the scarceness of things so great that it bringeth present death almost with it. For in that dearth and penury the faithful man that casteth his care on God, and hangeth wholly on his fatherly providence, may well say with the psalmograph: "If I walk in the midst of the shadow of death, I will not be afraid of any evil, for thou art with me." God is ever present with his people in all their tribulation, and he will undoubtedly deliver them, and save them harmless. This now remaineth, that when ye come among the poor needy Christians, ye comfort them with these sweet scriptures that ye have heard, which without all doubt shall greatly quiet their minds, and refrain them from attempting any unlawful redress of things after this. Again, according to your ability relieve their poverty with your riches. Exhort your rich neighbours likewise to be beneficial to the poor, as the faithful stewards of God, remembering that unto that end God hath endued them with their possessions. Pray unto God that he may give unto the covetous worldlings a merciful and liberal heart, that after this they may no less willingly seek the profit of their neighbours, than hitherto they have sought their own private lucre and singular commodity. To conclude, pray unto God that every one of us may so live and so frame our life according to his will, that he may vouchsafe to bless us, and send us necessaries for our living, that we may the more freely, and with the more quiet minds, "serve him in holiness and righteousness all the days of our life."

Psal. xxiii. Psal. xxi.

Luke i.

Well, neighbours, I pray you take the pains to come into the parlour with me. Ye shall take your part of such homely fare as I have. And I pray you, be no strangers: the ofter ye come, the more welcome shall you be.

Eus. We thank you, most gentle neighbour Philemon; and praised be the Lord for your godly and comfortable exhortations.

Chris. Amen.

Give the glory to God alone.

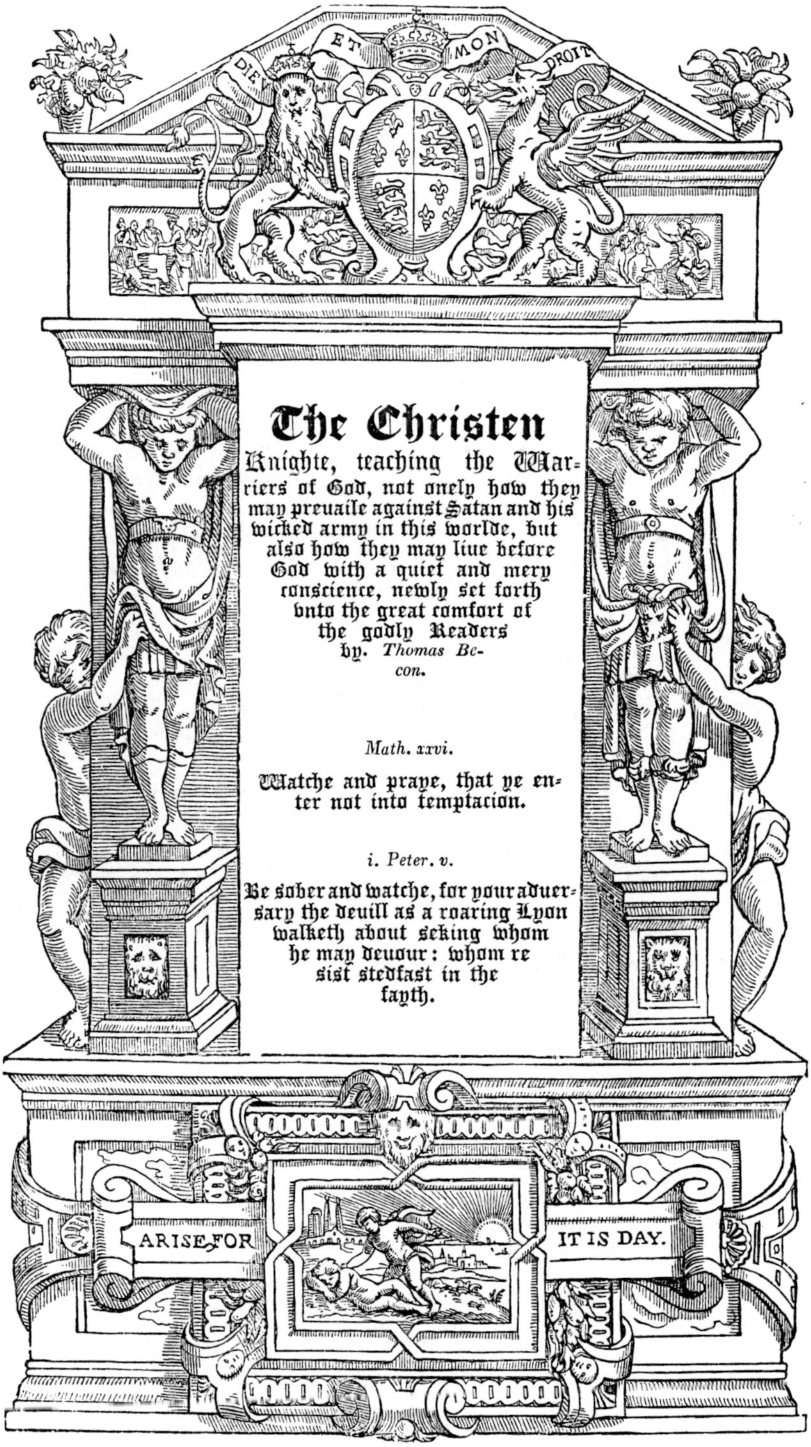

The Christen Knighte, teaching the Warriers of God, not onely how they may preuaile against Satan and his wicked army in this worlde, but also how they may liue before God with a quiet and mery conscience, newly set forth vnto the great comfort of the godly Readers by. *Thomas Becon.*

Math. xxvi.

Watche and praye, that ye enter not into temptacion.

i. Peter. v.

Be sober and watche, for your aduersary the deuill as a roaring Lyon walketh about seking whom he may deuour: whom resist stedfast in the fayth.

THE CHRISTIAN KNIGHT,

BY

THOMAS BECON.

TO THE RIGHT HONOURABLE

SIR FRANCIS RUSSELL, KNIGHT, LORD RUSSELL[1],

THOMAS BECON WISHETH THE FAVOUR OF GOD, CONTINUAL HEALTH, AND PROSPEROUS FELICITY.

If I had not by daily experience these few years past proved, yea, and that within mine own breast, right honourable lord, what disquietness, trouble, fear, anguish, the alone remembrance of sin, conjoined with the contemplation and stedfast beholding of the righteous and terrible judgments of God, set forth in the holy scriptures against all ungodly and wicked persons, bringeth to weak and troubled consciences; I think verily that no man living, although very excellent in persuading and moving affects, could have brought me in belief, that so great an hell lurk or rather lie buried in the breast of any mortal man, although overwhelmed never so much with the bottomless seas of sin, and estranged from all kind of virtue and godliness.

I have in times past heard by the relation of certain credible persons, how greatly divers godly and virtuous men have been troubled in their consciences by the consideration of their former life, which hath appeared to them so horrible and sinful,
Job iii. Jer. xv. that they have not only cursed the day of their birth, as we read of Job and Jeremy, but also been at the point of falling into desperation, and at utter defiance with God,
2 Cor. i. recounting him not as a "Father of mercy and God of all consolation," but rather as a terrible Judge and fierce Lord, which according to his righteousness will punish, smite, slay, and condemn without mercy all those that transgress his commandment, will, and pleasure. And I myself before few years did know certain men of an honest conversation and approved judgment (of whom some be yet living, worthy and valiant champions in the court of the Most Highest), which were so turmoiled and tossed with the raging and cruel waves of desperation, that scarcely there remained any hope of salvation in their breasts; so terrible and loathsome appeared the face of their life to the eyes of their mind; such fear conceived they of the righteous judgments of God. I have also read in the holy scriptures of God, and authentic histories, of divers holy men which have been grievously vexed and turmoiled in their consciences,

---

[1 Francis Russell, lord Russell, was the son of John Russell, first earl of Bedford, whose advancement was owing to his attendance on the archduke Philip, consort of Joanna of Spain. This prince having been compelled by stress of weather to land at Weymouth, was received by Sir Thomas Trenchard, a neighbouring gentleman. Sir Thomas dispatched the news of Philip's arrival to king Henry VIII., and meantime invited his relative, Mr Russell, of Kingston Russell near Burton in the county of Dorset, who had lately returned from foreign travel, to wait upon him. And so agreeable did Mr Russell prove himself to the archduke, that, having accompanied him to court, he was by him recommended to the king as a gentleman well qualified to serve him in some considerable station. Honours were accordingly heaped upon him: he was ennobled in 30th Henry VIII., as baron Russell of Cheneys in the county of Buckingham, and was subsequently created earl of Bedford. He died March 14, 1555. By his lady, Anne, relict of Sir John Broughton of Tuddington, Bedfordshire, and daughter of Sir Guy Sapcoates (nephew and heir to dame Agnes Cheney,) he had a son Francis, to whom Becon has inscribed this treatise. This nobleman was distinguished for his attachment to the reformed doctrines, and appears to have been intimately acquainted with many of the leading protestant divines. He was among those imprisoned on the accession of queen Mary; but was afterwards released, whether by any concession on his part seems not clearly ascertained. In the reign of queen Elizabeth he was frequently employed. He was more than once ambassador in France: he was also one of the peers who sat on the trial of the duke of Norfolk. He was so distinguished for hospitality and charity, that the queen used to say of him that he made all the beggars. He founded a school at Woburn; and bequeathed £20. per annum for the maintenance of two divinity students in University College, Oxford. Lord Bedford died July 28, 1585, at Bedford House, in the Strand; and was buried at Cheneys, where he ordered by his will twenty godly sermons to be preached within five months after his death; for which he allowed £20. The earl was twice married, first to Margaret, the sister of Oliver, first lord St John of Bletsoe, by whom he had several children, and secondly to Bridget, daughter of lord Hussey, and widow of Sir Richard Morrison and of the earl of Rutland: by her he had no issue. He was succeeded by his grandson, Edward, the third earl of Bedford.]

and almost ready to fall into the bottomless pit of desperation, if they had not been underset with the comfortable props of God's eternal mercy: but notwithstanding these things aforesaid, if I had not proved the very same thing in mine own breast which I have both heard and known of other, I would have thought the temptations of so many godly men to be but trifles, and things of no weighty importance; such carnal security and fleshly quietness concerning any grief of conscience reigneth in the heart of natural man, which, as Jeremy saith, is both lewd and so stuffed with the dunghill of sin, that the bottom of it cannot be searched but of him alone which trieth the hearts and reins. Jer. xvii.

If such trouble, anguish, disquietness, grief, and turmoiling be in the hearts of them which earnestly profess Christ, cleave unto God's mercy with strong faith, hang wholly on his most sweet promises made to us plenteously in Christ's dear blood, repent their wicked manners, mortify their carnal lusts, walk in a new life, and so appoint their conversation that in all their life they seem to seek nothing but the glory of God and the profit of their neighbour; what is to be thought of the false Christians which, professing[2] Christ only in name, are very antichrists in their deeds, painted sepulchres, full of all abomination and wickedness, glistering hypocrites, outwardly before men righteous, but inwardly before God full of hypocrisy, feigned holiness, dissimulation, and unrighteousness? O what an hell-like fire boileth in their breasts! how are they disquieted, troubled, tormented, grieved, and turmoiled! The sorrows and pains of their hearts are unspeakable, the trouble of their consciences is nothing inferior to the raging ocean sea. So that it is truly said of the prophet: "The wicked are like the raging sea that cannot rest, whose water foameth with water and gravel: the wicked have no peace, saith the Lord God." What marvel, seeing they find nothing in their breasts but sin, damnation, death, hell, desperation, and the devil and all? Matt. xxiii. Isai. lvii.

What quietness can there be where nothing is felt but the high indignation, hot wrath, heavy displeasure, and the sharp vengeance of God? If it be "a fearful thing to fall into the hands of the living God," which hateth all works of ungodliness, and threateneth eternal damnation to the transgressors of his law; yea, which condemneth without mercy them that willingly tread under foot Christ, his dearly-beloved Son, and counteth the blood of the testament, wherewith the faithful are sanctified, as an unholy thing, and do dishonour to the Spirit of grace; what quietness can such unfaithful and wicked people have in their hearts, seeing that God, his angels, and all his blessed saints are enemies to them? If God condemneth, who is able to save? if God casteth down to hell, who is able to lift up unto heaven? if God be an enemy, who can be a friend? Truly the wicked have against them whatsoever and whosoever is of God, not only good men, heavenly spirits, and glorious saints, but also the moon and seven stars, as they use to say. Heb. x.

But in this sharp agony and great disquietness of mind, as I may let the wicked pass, which, as they know not God aright, so likewise never flee they unto the throne of his gracious mercy, but continue unto the last day in the raging sea of troublous tempests, and after this life suffer much greater pains and torments; how shall the penitent sinner quiet his conscience, stablish his mind, comfort his spirit, strengthen his faith, recover his valiance in Christ Jesu, that he may be able to resist the fiery darts of Satan in the day of temptation? What shall he do? whither shall he turn him, that he may be free from the dangers of so cruel an enemy, which sleepeth not, which giveth no days of respite, which by no means will be reconciled, entreated, pacified, but "like a raging lion continually goeth about seeking whom he may devour?" He feared not to tempt many holy men in times past, yea, he feared not Christ Jesu, that most puissant Lord, but sought all means possible to allure him unto his most wicked will through his subtile suggestions; and is it to be thought that he will fear to assail us poor wretched sinners, which, if we be not strengthened by the Spirit of God, are ready to fall at every hour? O how ready is he at all times, namely in the time of adversity, trouble, and sickness, yea, most specially at the hour of death, when our memory faileth, out wits decay, our bodies are weak, our senses wax dull, our heart fainteth, our tongue faileth, and 1 Pet. v. Gen. iii. 1 Chron. xxi. Job i. ii. Matt. iv.

[[2] The folio has *professions*.]

whatsoever we have ceaseth to do the right office, to vex, trouble, disquiet, turmoil us, to lay before the eyes of our mind our sinful living, our wicked manners, our ungodly conversation, the breaking of God's precepts, the heavy displeasure of God against the wicked, the intolerable pains and exceeding torments of hell-fire, the eternal death and everlasting damnation, which all are prepared for the unfaithful!

What mortal man, being in the heavy and sharp agony of death, will not tremble at these things, and be ready to fall into desperation at the contemplation and beholding of so terrible a sight, if against so strong temptations he be not fortressed with the Spirit of God, and richly enarmed with the holy scriptures?

The common people have a saying among them, that "every man before he dieth shall see the devil." What is meant by this? Verily nothing else, but that Satan in the extreme agony and bitter pains of death will put man in remembrance of his most sinful and damnable living, accuse him of unrighteousness, reprove him of abominable wickedness, lay to his charge that he hath ever been and still is an outrageous sinner, an open malefactor, a shameless transgressor of God's most holy law, prove him worthy of eternal damnation by the righteous judgment of God, and justly committed to hell-fire for evermore. Therefore shall Satan say to the sinner, Despair, die, and be damned. To consider these things in the heart, to see these things presently with the eyes of the mind, wherein is nothing but wrath, displeasure, and damnation, what other things is it than to see the devil, and to feel the pains of hell? Now is man brought unto the brink of hell-pit, and seeth in himself nothing but sin, death, and damnation; again, Satan, sweating to the uttermost of his power, not only to lay things of most high wickedness to his charge, but also ready to accuse him before
Job xxv. the righteous throne of the divine Majesty, "in whose sight not the very stars are pure and clean:" what shall he now do? whither shall he turn him? to whom shall he flee? how shall he escape the devouring teeth of this most greedy and grievous wolf? Here are dangers more dangerous than can be expressed. How shall they be avoided? Here is salvation either gotten or lost: how shall it be gotten? O blessed is the man which getteth the victory over Satan in this most perilous conflict! If Satan be now overcome, he is driven to utter confusion, the infernal army is scattered abroad, hell-power is vanquished, the miserable afflict Christian is preserved, brought into the haven of quietness, carried unto eternal glory: the angels rejoice, and all the blessed saints and holy company of heaven are glad: God is glorified, praised, and magnified.

How this victory over Satan and his soldiers may be gotten, it is declared in this dialogue following, wherein the godly reader shall see how Satan sweateth to bring the christian knight unto desperation; again, how the christian knight defendeth himself against his enemy the devil, and valiantly putteth him to flight. It containeth without doubt much godly doctrine and spiritual, as they may easily see which read and mark it diligently. For whatsoever Satan can object against man is here confuted by the word of God, and the sinner set in salve estate; so that in this little treatise true knowledge may easily be gotten, both how to repel Satan and his cruel darts, and also how to obtain a joyful and quiet conscience before God in this life[1], which of all treasures is most precious.

After I had finished this little treatise, your lordship came first unto my remembrance as one right worthy, to whom I might dedicate my travail in this behalf. For to whom should I offer this christian knight, but to such one as is also both in word and work a true Christian and godly knight; yea, and a lord, not only in name and dignity, but also in virtue and godliness? Your lordship's hearty good-will and unfeigned favour both toward the setting forth of the glorious gospel of our Saviour Christ, and also the promoting of the true professors and faithful preachers of the same, is more known than it needeth here to be rehearsed. The works of love and tender compassion, which your lordship also continually bringeth forth, unto the great comfort of Christ's poor members, are not without a cause in this our days bruited and remembered of very many, unto the glory of God, the immortality of your name, and the godly example of other.

[[1] Folio, *litle*.]

These, right honourable lord, are the works of true nobility. And where these works want, though the parentage be never so ancient, famous, and honourable in the judgment of the worldlings, yet is not there the true nobility, which specially consisteth in the true knowledge, faith, love, and fear of God, in favouring and following his blessed word, in loving and living the holy gospel of Christ, in well-wishing and doing good to all men, in the innocency of life, in bridling carnal affects, in mortifying old Adam, and in putting on that new man, which after God is shapen in righteousness and true holiness.

These virtues, whereof springeth the true nobility, do livishly shine in your lordship's daily behaviour. And I doubt not but that God, which hath begun this good work in you, will also finish the same in you, unto the glory and praise of his blessed name, and unto the full reward of your faith which you have in Christ Jesu our Lord.

I therefore, considering these notable gifts wherewith God hath richly endued you, thought it not unfitting to give unto your lordship this little treatise, as a testimony of my serviceable heart and ready bent good-will toward your lordship, most humbly beseeching you, according to your accustomed gentleness, to take in good part this my old enterprise[2]. And I shall continually pray unto the Lord my God (whose blessed word you most entirely both favour and follow), to preserve your right honourable lordship in continual health, increase of honour, and prosperous felicity, unto the avancement of his glory, and the comfort of his holy congregation. Amen.

[[2] From the general style of this piece, as well as some particular expressions in it, it seems not improbable that it was a translation. And as above, p. 427, Becon mentions among his translations from the Latin "The Shield of Salvation," this may be the same piece under another title. See the note on the "Policy of War," p. 238, of the former Volume.]

THE DIALOGUE

BETWEEN

THE CHRISTIAN KNIGHT AND SATAN,

WHEREIN SATAN MOVETH UNTO DESPERATION, THE KNIGHT COMFORTETH HIMSELF WITH THE SWEET PROMISES OF THE HOLY SCRIPTURE.

SATAN.

Psal. lxvi. WHEREFORE goest thou so oft unto the church? Why hearest thou so many holy sermons?
John ix. For what cause prayest thou so fervently? In all these things thou labourest in vain; for "God heareth no sinners."

CHRISTIAN KNIGHT.

Matt. xxvi. God hath commanded me to hear the gospel, to believe and to pray; and therefore I pray and go unto the church, and believe that God is merciful unto me for
John iii. Christ's sake, and I trust that I shall have everlasting life, which God promiseth to so many as profess Christ and truly believe on him. And St Paul saith, that
1 Cor. xv. "the labour which we take in the Lord is not vain nor unprofitable." And as con-
John ix. cerning this saying, that "God heareth no sinners," it ought to be understand of such sinners as do not repent: the prayers of them God doth not hear; for their prayers
Rom. xiv. are no prayers, seeing they have not the true faith.

SATAN.

Thou pratest nothing to the purpose. Make God's ears deaf with thy prayers so long as thou wilt, yet canst thou never be throughly persuaded and truly believe that thou art heard and shalt be saved; for the righteous only shall be saved: he that fulfilleth not God's commandments is a sinner and
1 Cor. vi. unrighteous before God. And God saith by his apostle, that "the unrighteous shall not inherit the kingdom of God." It is therefore in vain that thou prayest: all the labour and pain that thou takest is of none effect, seeing thou art not righteous, nor satisfiest the law of God: wherefore there remaineth no hope of God's favour toward thee. Thou must needs despair; for here is no refuge, no succour: thou hast no place whither to stay, there is nothing that thou canst either lap[1] for thyself, or wherewith thou mayest rid thyself out of my hands; for thou art wholly in my power and altogether mine, seeing thou art unrighteous. Assay both what thou wilt and what thou art able; and yet remaineth there for thee no help nor succour.

THE KNIGHT.

The God of all mercy forbid this! thou hast no prey here for to hunt. I am far otherwise taught, and I know right well that the matter is much otherwise than thou babblest.

SATAN.

I care not what thou knowest, or what thou dreamest that thou knowest: hast thou not heard what I have said? thou art utterly undone: there is no cause why thou mayest look and trust for health and salvation; and that will I prove with open scriptures. Did not God himself say unto a certain Jew,
Luke x. being a lawyer, "Do this, and thou shalt live?" He meaneth the ten commandments, for he speaketh of the love of God and of thy neighbour, which in the ten commandments is required most pure and most perfect. Now canst thou not deny that thy God requireth of thee here the fulfilling of all his precepts,
Matt. xix. if thou despisest[2] to live with him for ever, as he saith [in] the gospel of Matthew: "If thou wilt enter into life, keep the commandments." Out of the which words of thy God it necessarily followeth that he, which keepeth not the commandments, shall not have everlasting life, but die for ever, and be eternally damned. Hear therefore how evil the matter goeth with thee, and in how great danger thou

---

[1 Lap: secure.] [2 Despise seems to be used in both these places in the sense of *desire*.]

art. But I will set[3] this matter before thee plainly in the form of a *syllogismus*, that thou mayest perceive it the better.

He that fulfilleth not perfectly the ten commandments cannot enter into life, but die the death Major.
everlasting.

These are the words of thy God, which follow of those words that he answered the scribe, by an Luke x.
argument of the contrary.

Thou hast not perfectly kept the commandments of God: thou art not righteous: thou hast trans- Minor.
gressed God's precepts.

Therefore it followeth necessarily, that thou shalt not live with Christ, but that thou shalt be damned Conclusion.
for ever.

What art thou able to answer to these things, being so strong and unable to be confuted? thou art taken, and so haltered on every part, that thou canst not escape.

THE KNIGHT.

The argument that thou hast proponed, no Jew, no ethnick, nor no unfaithful man is able to put away. But a true christian man can answer thee quickly, neither is he snarled with this thy reasoning, as thou boastest.

SATAN.

I despise [2] very greatly to hear what thou canst answer. Certes the two first propositions or premises are true, therefore the conclusion must needs be true; for of true premises a true conclusion doth follow: how then canst thou escape? thou must needs despair. For here is no help nor succour.

THE KNIGHT.

In this behalf I can easily set myself at liberty, and dispatch thy argument. For thou dost not dispute with a Jew, or with an unfaithful person (for I have both a faith and an hope in God, although I feel yet never so much weakness), but with a christian man, which cannot be snarled with such arguments. I answer therefore unto thy argument on this manner. As concerning the major or first proposition, which is, that he cannot enjoy everlasting life which keepeth not the commandments of God,
I grant and deny not but that it is true, for it followeth of the words of Christ my Luke x.
God and Redeemer. But the minor and second proposition, which is that I fulfil not the commandments of God, that I am not righteous, by no means do I grant, but plainly affirm that it is false; (for else should I do great injury and high despite to my Lord Christ, which at my baptism took me into his grace and favour:) wherefore thou canst not wrest thy conclusion against me.

SATAN.

What meneth[4] the minor much probation? ask thy conscience. Even that doth accuse thee, and evidently sheweth that thou art a sinner, and that thou hast not kept the precepts of God. Daily also
dost thou confess the same in the Lord's prayer, when thou sayest: "Forgive us our debts or trespasses;" Matt. vi.
and in the epistle of John it is read: "If we say we have no sin, we deceive ourselves, and the truth 1 John i.
is not in us:" these are the words of thy God. For the Spirit of thy God spake them by his apostles, neither do they lie unto thee, but these things are full true that they spake. But thou liest, when thou sayest that thou art righteous, that thou hast kept the commandments of God, that thou hast no sin: yea, besides all this thou art an hypocrite also, and dost trust in thyself, as though thou wast righteous; so that by this means thou art both the greater and also the more grievous sinner, as thy God teacheth
thee in the example of the Pharisee, that hypocrite. Therefore canst not thou escape out of my hands, Luke xviii.
thou must needs be mine. For I have proved that thou hast not kept the commandments of God, and that therefore thou art not righteous. I have proved that also out of the word of thy God, and the witness of thine own heart, of the prayer and the confession of thine own mouth. Why then dost thou cease to yield thyself unto me? despair straightways. No cause hast thou to look for salvation:
for the word of God cannot lie. Isai. xl. Matt. v.

THE KNIGHT.

Thou art no changeling, O Satan, and this thy lying is thine old trade and accustomed property. It is no newelty unto thee: thou art "a liar, and the father of John viii.
lying" from the beginning; yea, speaking the truth thou liest also. For if perchance

[[3] Folio, *let*.] [[4] Probably *needeth*.]

Matt. iv. at any time thou allegest any truth out of the scriptures, yet, according to thine old wont and malicious crafty and false quarrelling wit, either thou dost not speak altogether whole, or the things that thou allegest hang not together. For some things thou rehearsest, some things again subtilly thou dost omit and leave clean out, or else thou corruptest and depravest the scripture.

SATAN.

How canst thou justly say this? With what face dost thou accuse me of calumniating or depraving the scriptures? have I not word for word recited the words of the scriptures, even as they are read in the bible, not leaving out any parcel, nor yet depraving one little tittle? Thou shalt not therefore escape on this manner.

THE KNIGHT.

I do accuse thee worthily of calumniating and depraving the scripture, and of not reciting the same purely and wholly. For where my God hath spoken and taught those things that do agree and ought to be joined together, these dost thou partly allege, and partly omit or leave out. Thou dost allege, and with tooth and nail set forward, that which maketh for thee, and serveth thy turn to destroy men; but the other part thou castest behind and leavest clean out, as though it pertained nothing to the matter. Is not this to calumniate and deprave the scriptures? Thou layest many things against me concerning the law, because I have not fulfilled it; but of the gospel thou makest no mention at all, as though that pertained nothing unto me. God hath not only given a law, but also a gospel. If thou, therefore, wilt recite his word purely and not corruptly, use that manner and order that the scripture useth.
Law. For that, first of all, setteth forth unto us the law, whereof we may learn our sins, and the damnation that we have deserved. But it is not contented to have set forth
Gospel. the law unto us: it[1] setteth forth and offereth to us also the gospel, which teacheth us how we be delivered from our sins, and that the faith which we have in Christ saveth us. In the gospel therefore we find comfort and help, and of that we learn that the law cannot condemn us, if we believe.

SATAN.

Luke x. Thou speakest nothing to the purpose: are not these the words of thy God, "Do this, and thou
Matt. xix. shalt live"? "If thou therefore wilt enter into life, thou must needs keep the law." For this without all doubt is very true, that God gave not his precepts that they should be despised, or that a man might stubbornly and without punishment break them, but that they should be kept. And although thy fellow Paul disputeth and teacheth many things of faith, yet he concludeth and evidently declareth that the
Rom. iii. law is not abrogate or put away by the faith of the gospel, but that through the same it is rather stablished, that it may be performed and fulfilled. Thou knowest also that thy God throughout the gospel doth
Rom. ii. both teach his law, and also require the same to be done. Paul also saith that "upon them which do service unto unrighteousness indignation and wrath, affliction and anguishness" shall come. Here hearest thou in the gospel (if thou givest so much to the gospel, and wilt that any thing of that also be recited of me), here, I say, hearest thou out of that, that God will his precepts to be kept, except thou wilt
2 Thess. i. run into his indignation and displeasure. And Paul to the Thessalonians saith: "God shall render vengeance to them that know not God, and to them that obey not the gospel. All such shall be punished with everlasting damnation." And the gospel doth sufficiently bear witness in many places that no sinner can enter into the kingdom of heaven. Why then dost thou nourish a vain hope? Wherefore dost thou not despair? For doubtless thou art but cast away for ever and ever.

THE KNIGHT.

As concerning these things, which thou hitherto hast alleged out of the old and new testament, and reasoned with me, all these things are the law, or else belong unto the law: thou shalt therefore have none avantage here, neither shalt thou win any thing in this behalf. For I told thee before, that God hath set forth to sinful man two things: one is the law, the other is the gospel. And I confess with all my heart that the law is the word of my God; and according to this former word, I mean the law, I do knowledge and confess both frankly and with an open voice

[[1] Folio, *is.*]

(neither will I deny it at any time), that I am a sinner, guilty of everlasting damnation. For this is very true, that I, poor wretch, through mine own works and perfection have not fulfilled the law. Therefore, if there were none other way or mean here in this world to fulfil the law than by mine own works, yea, and those perfect and clean at the full, then must I needs grant the minor in the *syllogismus*, neither could I by any means escape, but be snarled and taken, I mean perish for evermore.

But I know and also have another manner of obtaining righteousness and fulfilling the law, which thou canst not cast away from me. For God himself hath taught me this manner and way in the gospel, even that I should believe in Christ, which alone hath most perfectly fulfilled the law, and all obedience for my sake. By this faith all my sins are forgiven me, and the Holy Ghost is given to me, which purifieth my heart, and beginneth to fulfil the law in me. If any thing wanteth in me (as we want many things in this sinful life, in many things are we inconstant and unpure, through the sinful flesh that we bear about), yet that he wanteth, I mean those sins or offences, are not imputed nor reckoned us unto damnation for the merits Psal. xxxii. and fulfilling of Christ which is ours. "For Christ is the fulfilling of the law for Rom. iv. Rom. x. every one that believeth unto righteousness," yea, Christ is our righteousness. Now 1 Cor. i. hast thou heard these things.

This is another word which God in like manner hath set forth to me, and he will that I believe this no less than the first. This second word is called *evangelium*, or gospel, that is to say, grace, favour, and remission of sins, promised in Christ. Thou understandest the gospel only after the letter, the very words of the gospel, but thou dost not believe the gospel; therefore shalt thou be damned, and not I. If I should Isai. xxxiii. bring forth to thee the absolution wherewith God himself did absolve me from all my Isai. xliii. sins that I ever committed against his law, wouldest thou then also reprove and accuse me of sin? But thou canst not do so by any means, when the judge doth absolve me and set me at liberty. Then lieth it not in thy power to condemn me. This know I for a certainty: therefore hear how I shall escape.

My sin ought not to be imputed to me only, but to thee also, yea, and that most Wisd. ii. of all. For thou first of all didst blow into our nature, being well made and pure, that hell-like poison of sins in Adam and Eva, whom after thou hadst deceived through Gen. iii. thy lying, thou threwest them headlong into sin and death. Hereof cometh it that all Eph. ii. Rom. v. we are born sinners from the time of Adam: hereof cometh it that thou hast so much John iii. power and rule over mankind: thereof cometh it that our nature is miserably corrupt, depraved, perverse, and froward; so that even from our mother's womb we are evil and lewd, blind in understanding, froward in will, as Moyses testifieth in Genesis, where he Jer. xvii. Gen. vi. viii. calleth us flesh, that is, men altogether carnal, fleshly, and void of God's Spirit. In like manner are we described in Hieremy, where the heart of man is called wicked, Jer. xvii. froward, or lewd: yea, our daily experience teacheth us what we have received of thee through our first parents; verily none other thing than an horrible depravation and corruption of our nature, sin, and death, and that we be the enemies of God, as Paul testifieth: "They that are carnal or fleshly-minded savour those things that pertain Rom. viii. unto the flesh:" "The wisdom of the flesh is enmity against God. For it is not obedient to the law of God, neither can it be: they that are in the flesh cannot please God."

To thee do we owe this our fault and wretchedness: thou art guilty of this evil, thou art the author to us of this misery; thou through thy guile, deceit[2], and lying broughtest us into this sea of wretched troubles, which are thine own crafts and subtilties. For thou canst do nothing but deceive, lie, hurt, and destroy. This our wretchedness we learn to know by the law. But the scripture ministereth to us also exceeding great comfort, even true redemption, how we be purged and made clean from our sins, 1 John i. but nature is made whole, how we may be delivered from death and dispatched out Matt. ix. of thy power. For our faithful God, when he saw this fault, and that we could not help ourselves, nor set ourselves at liberty from these evils; again, that our nature was

[[2] Folio, *decent*.]

so wholly corrupt, that we did neither understand nor know the will of God, nor yet
accomplish the same from the very heart, yea, rather to the uttermost of our power
we did fight with the will of God; he, having pity on us, promised, and sent to us
a true deliverer and valiant defender from all evils, which is both able and also will
Rom. i. strongly and mightily defend us. This is Jesus Christ, the natural Son of God, born of
the blood of Abraham and of David, of Mary the virgin, without sin, as God from the
Gal. iv. beginning had promised him by his prophets; and when the time was fulfilled, he sent
1 Tim. i. him also to become man, and that for this cause chiefly, that he might "save sinners,
of whom I am not the least."

This our Lord and Saviour talketh with us much more lovingly, familiarly, and
Moses. Deut. xxviii. gently, than Moyses his servant spake before in the law. Moyses required an high
and true perfect righteousness, and all that want that absolute righteousness he threat-
ened to condemn. But he found that perfect righteousness in no man born of the will
of man, but he proved all to be sinners; yet could he not deliver them by the doctrine
of the law from their sins, but only did[1] command those things that ought to be done,
and forbid those things that are not to be done, and to curse and condemn sinners.
Christ. But Christ Jesus our Redeemer comforteth us, and blesseth us with his gospel, and
delivereth us from sin and death, yea, in his gospel he absolveth us from sin, and plainly
affirmeth and recounteth us righteous.

Furthermore, thou frayest me with the words of St John, saying that we are all
sinners; but thou keepest in silence, and of a set purpose passeth over the absolution
1 John i. which is annexed in the very same place, where he saith: "If we confess our sins, God
is faithful and righteous, that he will forgive us our sins, and make us clean from all
unrighteousness." Fray me, therefore, by laying the law against me so long as thou
wilt; I will flee unto the gospel, wherein I find sure comfort and a way how I may
Deut. xxvii. scape out of thy hands. For although Moses saith unto me in the law, Thou art cursed,
because thou hast transgressed and broken the commandments of God, yet will I not
Matt. ix. despair for all that, but flee unto Christ, which saith unto me in the gospel: "Son, be
Isai. liii. Eph. v. on a good comfort, believe thy sins are forgiven thee. I myself have borne away thy
sins in mine own body upon the tree of the cross, yea, I have offered such a sacrifice
that I have made full satisfaction for them, and by this means reconciled thee to
Hos. xiii. Heb. ii. my Father. I have overcome death and Satan for thy sake. I have also perfectly
Rom. x. fulfilled the law for thee. All these things that I have done are thine, if thou believest
in me."

Hearest thou, Satan, what Christ saith? Thou layest Moyses against me: I again object Christ against thee: thou allegest the servant; but I bring forth the Lord himself. The servant accuseth me of maliciousness and unrighteousness, and will judge me to death. But the Lord himself defendeth and setteth me at liberty, and giveth me life of his own free will. I therefore set nothing by thine accusations; they cannot hurt me: thou mayest indeed lay my sins against me; but I again object and lay against thee infinite merits, even the satisfaction, the fulfilling of the law, the obedience, the death, and the resurrection of Christ my Redeemer. This now is my treasure, Christ's righteousness is my righteousness, yea, Christ himself is mine innocency and righteousness. If thou therefore canst accuse Christ of no sin, if thou canst not condemn him, neither canst thou have any power against me to condemn me, and that for Christ, which hath both fully put away and also forgiven me all my sins.

SATAN.

I neither can accuse nor condemn Christ of any sin. For he is righteous, I confess. But sinners are damned; and thou thyself hast confessed that thou art a sinner.

THE KNIGHT.

In myself I am a sinner, but in Christ, my righteous-maker, I am righteous. For
Note. he hath forgiven me all my sins, and hath taken me into his grace, favour, and tuition.

[1 Folio, *did and command*.]

He is always ready to help me, he forgiveth me the remnants of my sins, and purgeth them in me daily, till he maketh me altogether new. Wherefore go thy way unto the heathen that know not God, and to the Jews, which forsake Christ their Lord. On me thou hast no more power. For God my heavenly Father "hath delivered me from the power of darkness, and hath carried me into the kingdom of his well-beloved Son, in whom I have redemption by his blood, even remission of my sins." Behold, therefore, that thy accusation, which thou attemptest against me, cannot have place in me. For, although I fulfil not the commandments of God in the law with mine own works, yet fulfil I them in the gospel with the most perfect works and the satisfaction of Christ, in whom I believe. This faith is reckoned to me unto righteousness, although my works of themselves be imperfect. And this is the only and true manner of fulfilling the law of God, that I believe in Christ the only fulfiller of the law, and justifier, without whom the law can never be fulfilled, neither any man come unto God.

Col. i.

The fulfilling of the law.

All these things can I prove by the word of God. That teacher of the gentiles saith in his epistle to the Romans: "There is no condemnation in them that are in Christ Jesus, which walk not after the flesh, but after the Spirit. For the law of life in Christ Jesu hath delivered me from the law of sin and death. For that that was impossible to the law, forasmuch as it was weak because of the flesh, that performed God and sent his Son in the likeness of sinful flesh, and by sin condemned sin in the flesh, that the righteousness which is required of the law might be fulfilled in us." Here do I hear other words, and another manner of justifying, than thou bringest to me out of the law. Thou dost object against me that I have sins. I grant that in the law. But as concerning that thou dost hereof conclude, Therefore art thou damned; that the Holy Ghost denieth plainly. For though I have sin in mine own person never so much, which is subject to damnation in me, yet can it not condemn me: why so? because I am in Christ through faith; so that Christ and I are now "one spirit:" we are now one body. For he is my head, and I am his member, "of his flesh and of his bones;" and therefore was he of his own free will subject to the law, or became under the law, that he should redeem me from the accusation of the law, and he was made accursed for me, that he might deliver me from the curse of the law.

Rom. viii.

Mark well.

1 Cor. vi.

Eph. v.

Gal. iii.

With this do I comfort me, I have sins indeed, but yet for Christ's sake, in whom I believe, there is no damnation in me: why then dost thou accuse me? "For the law of the Spirit," that is the regiment and governance of the Holy Ghost in me, or the faith in Christ, "delivereth me from the law of sin and death," that sin can never condemn me, nor death swallow me up.

Rom. viii.

Verily the law is good and holy, but it can justify no man. It cannot change our stony heart, or give us a softer heart, or purify our sinful nature and renew it, or take away sins: this can the Spirit of Christ alone do. The nature or flesh of man is corrupt and bond to sin, having no strength of itself to accomplish the law of God: neither is it willing thereunto, but only prone and full bent to sin.

The law.

Notwithstanding, in this behalf God helpeth our weak nature, that it may come unto the fulfilling of the law; and he sent his Son that he might be born very man, even such as we are, sin alone except. Of a maid and a pure virgin was it convenient for him to be born, that he might be made a sacrifice of a pure and everlasting price for sin. For the cause why God became man was this, that he might condemn, purge, and put away our sins in his clean and innocent flesh by the true sacrifice for sin, that is to say, by himself, and deserve remission of sins for us, that so by this most holy and most innocent and perfectly clean sacrifice of the Son of God, both God and man, that might be fulfilled that the law required. For by this sacrifice for sin offered for us on the cross, first of all, he deserved for us remission of sins, and the Holy Ghost, which giveth faith and charity; and, those being once received, our righteousness and the fulfilling of God's commandments is begun in us: and although in this life we are not yet fully clean and perfect, and through the remnants of sins and maliciousness we never perfectly fulfil the precepts of God, yet nevertheless do we receive true righteousness before God, and all things that the law requireth for us, I mean righteousness which is of valor before God through faith in Christ. For he that believeth in Christ is righteous before God. This sentence is

Heb. iv.

Deut. xxviii.

the *evangelion*, that is to say, our glad and joyful tidings, our gospel, and that absolution which God himself pronounceth, and all the angels in heaven and the whole church say, Amen. So be it.

Note. He therefore that through faith hath Christ in his heart hath also the fulfilling of God's precepts, which Christ himself performed in his own person; and Christ is so become the righteousness of this faithful christian man, that that faithful Christian for Christ's sake is reputed before God righteous, as though he had perfectly fulfilled the law.

SATAN.

Thy friend Paul, in that place which thou allegest, addeth a certain thing which thou leavest out; Rom. viii. but I have noted and marked it diligently, and that is this, that he saith, they "that walk not after the flesh, but after the Spirit." God gave this promise or glad tidings, not to all manner of men generally, but to them only "which walk not after the flesh, but after the Spirit." But thou walkest after the flesh. For thou art covetous, proud, lecherous, and of a spiteful stomach, ready unto anger, intemperate, and altogether given to pleasures: what wilt thou answer me here? How wilt thou escape in this behalf?

THE KNIGHT.

I confessed before that in myself I am still a sinner; but this is not to walk after the flesh. For to walk after the flesh is without all fear, stubbornly, proudly, and ☞ malapertly to fulfil the lusts and desires of the flesh, and all that our sinful nature doth desire, and of itself is bent unto; again, with high will of the mind and cheerfulness to sin without repentance, and never to lament or once to be sorry for the sin committed, yea, to delight also in sinning, and with a certain pleasure of the mind to fulfil the desire of the flesh.

I fall indeed into sin; but yet after the inward man I hate sin, which boileth in the flesh, and I desire nothing more than to be clean and utterly delivered from sin, and I am sorry even from the very heart, that I have sinned and do sin against God. I pray God also daily, that he will increase my faith, that I may, as it were with a bit, restrain the flesh, so prone and ready unto sin. And although I be wonderfully weak, yet for that mine imbecility and weakness I am at utter defiance with myself, and I am sorry that so great infirmity reigneth in me; yet do I not therefore despair, but I put all my trust in Christ, doubting nothing at all but that he will forgive me my trespasses, and increase my faith daily more and more, that I may inhibit, knock down, quench, oppress, crucify, and kill the works of the flesh. Surely Esay
Isai. xlii. wrote of him not without a cause, that he should "not break a bruised reed, nor quench the smoking flax." I cannot of mine own natural strengths, without the Spirit of God, hate sin and resist it, seeing that even together with nature it is born into the world with me. He that hateth sin hath the Spirit of Christ, yea, he is Christ's, and not thine. St Paul therefore doth confess, that in all godly persons the remnants of sin do remain, against which the spirit striveth; but he addeth words full of high
Rom. viii. consolation, even that for all that there is [no] damnation in them. And this privilege and prerogative have they in Christ, that righteous One, in whom they are engraffed through faith, and whose merits they do enjoy, and by them are saved from their sins.

SATAN.

Thou hast not yet escaped, neither dost thou row in the haven, and art free from all jeopardy, as thou persuadest thyself or dreamest. For it is written: "He that continueth unto the end, he shall be saved." Many have fallen into my nets, which, notwithstanding, have with as bold courage, as thou dost now, set themselves against me in disputation, and would by no means consent unto me: first, they were very hot, but they could not continue in their purpose, so that at the last falling back they came into my hands. The very same thing shall chance to thee. After that thou hast striven against me much and a long time, yet at the last shall I overcome thee, and enjoy mine old possession.

THE KNIGHT.

The God of all mercy forbid! I know in very deed that we cannot stand, but must needs fall and decay, if God doth not give us faith, and confirm the same, yea,

and help us in temptation, that through his grace we may persevere. For to persevere or continue in goodness is no less the gift and work of God in us, than when we begin to believe and amend our life. But God hath commanded that we should ask of him perseverance and constancy or stedfastness in goodness and faith, and he hath promised me in Christ that he will both graciously hear me, and also help me; "in the which Christ all the promises of God are yea, and Amen," that is to say, 2 Cor. i.
highly perfect and very true: wherefore, with the help of God, I will pray that that which he hath mercifully begun in me, he may also finish in me, unto the glory of his holy name.

Here hast thou mine armours, darts, and sword. I am not able to resist thee with mine own strength and wisdom. But I can do all things through Christ Jesus, which hath overcome thee, and delivered me from thee. Even he teacheth, ruleth, governeth, confirmeth, strengtheneth, and defendeth me by his holy Spirit. Therefore Rom. viii.
seeing that God himself is on my side, who shall damn me?

SATAN.

If I cannot hinder nor let thy health and salvation, yet will I so trounce, turmoil, make lean, and trouble thee, and throw thee into so many misfortunes and calamities, and handle and vex thee on such miserable and cruel sort, unto the uttermost of my power, that thou shalt be weary of thy life, and wish rather to die than to live.

THE KNIGHT.

Certes I know right well that thou art the author of all evils and mischances, and that thou dost labour and imagine in every place none other thing than to hurt good men and vex them. And I know that I, being a wretched vessel, cannot enjoy continual pleasures in this life, in this ungracious world, thy most perilous and bloody June[1], but that I must be vexed divers ways; yet will I not despair and cast away all hope. For I have very plenteous comfort and such as cannot be overcome, wherewith I may confirm and make strong my mind, which neither thou nor all the whole world can take away from me. Thou art but a creature, as thou knowest right well, neither canst thou work any thing against me, nor do me more evil than my God suffereth thee. But he suffereth thee no more than is necessary unto my salvation and furtherance of godliness.

To abound with all kind of pleasures and commodities in this life is very danger- Mark well.
ous here in this world: neither can the godly be in the danger of greater misfortunes or perils here, than when all things chance to them in every condition after their own hearts' lust, when all things flow to them even as they would have it, when they abound with pleasures, and are heaped up with all the commodities of this life. For in so great wealth of living they forget both themselves and God their Father. Misfortunes, afflictions, and perils teach us for the merciful will of God to know ourselves, our infirmity, our weakness, our nothing, our wretchedness, and to fear God, to trust in God, and earnestly to call on him; which thing when we do, God is at hand and assist us with his present help, and so we learn both to know God and ourselves: what great harm then canst thou do me, if, God so providing and suffering thee, thou causest me to have loss and wretchedness in these corruptible and transitory things, which are not my true heritage?

My true inheritance is incorruptible, unable to be defiled, and an immortal and everlasting treasure in heaven. This treasure thou shalt not be so bold as once to handle, neither shalt thou at any time be able so to do. If thou killest my body, thou doest none other thing than bring me into the quietness of that true life that is to come; and he which gave me body and soul, and which redeemed me out of thy power, even very he shall also keep both my body and soul unto the day of redemption, wherein he shall raise up my body out of the earth into everlasting life. In the mean season, my soul is kept well and safely with Christ. Thou therefore canst not hurt me, while my God keepeth me constant and stedfast in the faith of Christ, I have

[[1] June: perhaps a misprint for *Inne*, that is, *inn*.]

Rom. viii. his word and promise. Those do not lie: "We know," saith St Paul, "that all things work for the best unto them that love God." John x. And my Saviour Christ saith: "I know my sheep: and I give them everlasting life; neither shall they perish for ever; nor yet shall any man pluck them out of my hand." And in the Psalm it is written: Psal. xci. "He that dwelleth in the help of the Most Highest, he abideth in the defence of the God of heaven. He saith to the Lord, Thou art my upholder and my refuge, yea, thou art my God in whom I trust. For he hath delivered me from the snare of the hunters, and from the sharp sword, or noisome pestilence." "He hath given his angels charge over thee, to keep thee in all thy ways: they shall bear thee in their hands, that thou hurt not thy foot against a stone." "He hath called unto me; and I will favourably hear him: I am with him in tribulation: I will deliver him and bring him to honour."

Dost thou hear how God himself do look upon and defend his people, and sendeth Psal. xxxiv. his holy angels from heaven to defend them? as David writeth: "The angel of the Lord pitcheth his tent round about them that fear the Lord, and delivereth them." Here hast thou on whom I trust, and wherefore I set thee[1] at defiance, and conceive Jer. ix. a good hope. I do nothing at all rejoice in myself, or of myself, but in my almighty Lord and God Jesus Christ do I glory and rejoice, yea, and that not without a cause. For he hath loved me and hath given himself for me, to deliver me from death, and that I should live and triumph with him in his everlasting kingdom without end. This is my comfort, and to this will I cleave by the grace of Jesus Christ. Amen.

Now assay thou, and imagine against me all that God my heavenly Father, which 1 John iv. is the self charity and goodness, doth suffer. That my Father will not leave me, his weak son, destitute and succourless in temptation. Christ will keep his little poor sheep, that it come not into the wolf's jaws. All the enemies of Christ and of the Christians shall be cast under our feet. This is as true as God is in heaven: wherefore, Satan, away, get thee hence from me. Thou hast no power on me. I pertain unto him, and am his for evermore, which bought me from thee with his precious blood, being undoubtedly a very great price, I mean my Lord Jesus Christ. He it is, and so will remain, which is a fiery wall unto me wheresoever I become. He it is that keepeth me as the apple of his eye. To him, with the Father and the Holy Ghost, be all glory and praise, worlds without end. Amen.

SATAN.

Thou speakest many things to dispatch thyself of me; but thou art not yet gone. Thou knowest that even from thy tender age thou wast always taught in the church, that it is high presumption to look for salvation and everlasting life without good works. But thou dost openly confess that thou hast not done, or do any good work, that thou art able to set against the judgment of God, or that can stand in God's judgment; yet (such is thy foolish rashness and extreme madness) without the fulfilling of the law, and the true good works, thou thinkest that thou shalt go up into heaven. What any other thing is this, than to make God most unrighteous? for that should be as though thou wouldest wallow thyself into a sink of all kind of ungraciousness, and desire of God that he would approve, accept, and allow that maliciousness, sinful wantonness, and thy wicked life, and that he should save thee, being so ungracious a fellow and lewd sinner. But this (know it for a truth) shall never come to pass. If thou dost think and hope that it will come to pass, thou thinkest in vain, and nourishest a vain hope.

Thou couldest away (so far as I hear), that thou shouldest get thee a great portion of other men's goods, and another man should pay thy debts, and that thou shouldest commit many robberies and another be hanged for thee. Thou wilt be a sinner and live naughtily at thy own pleasure, and yet, after this life, thou trustest to come unto heaven; but thou art clean deceived and hopest in vain: thou canst not go so easily and without any labour unto the stars: by this way canst thou not go up into heaven. God, for his infinite righteousness, cannot allow sin. If he would not have punished sin, for what use should he have made hell? Certes he should have laid forth and threatened the pains of hell in vain to ungodly and wicked persons. Thou knowest, if thou wilt know, that the matter is far otherwise: and yet thou thinkest that thou shalt pay to God with vain words those things that thou owest him, and by this mean escape from his judgment; which thing all you Lutherians and fellows of the new learning are wont to do, and, wresting the scriptures, ye expound them after the

[[1] Folio, *them*.]

fancies of your own brain: where the scripture requireth good works, there ye boast of your unfruitful and barren faith, and by that ye think that ye shall obtain all things. In other ye reprove sophistry, but ye yourselves use it more than any other, yea, and that in a cause which of all is most weighty. Where ye might use words that should make unto the edification of the simple, there of a set purpose do ye use manners of speaking which have not been used nor accustomed, yea, and those very slanderous; as when ye say, Faith alone justifieth: what manner of speaking, I pray thee, could be more perilous and more full of slander? For what other thing can any rude and simple man hereof understand, than that it maketh no matter how he liveth? ye, being instructed with this vain faith, do at your own pleasure what ye will, and after your hearts' lust live a pope's life, and yet nevertheless will ye be Christians and become saved; but your hope is vain and shall deceive you. This thing shall ye prove to be true and as I say in very[2] deed.

THE KNIGHT.

O thou most lying spirit, thou hatest the truth and canst not abide it; and, because thou canst bring nothing against it, thou assayest me another way, and dost loaden and invade us with those same reproaches, contumelies, and spiteful slanders, which we are compelled daily to hear of thine apostles, men full of venomous poison, and most unshamefaced sycophants, and unjust accusers of innocents. But lest thou shouldest think that thou hast gotten the mastery, I will answer thee to all thine objections.

And first, I confess with all my heart, that he is a very ungodly and naughty person, which continueth in a lewd and wicked life without repentance, and do not apply himself to good works, nor work no good thing, nor can be content to suffer any thing for Christ's sake, and yet nevertheless boasteth himself to be a christian man, and hopeth for salvation. This is to sin against the mercy of God; and verily that is an exceeding blindness and almost without hope of recovery, which neither perceiveth the peril and fierceness of sin, nor the mercy of God and the passion of Christ, and only dreameth to look for salvation, when notwithstanding it neither looketh for that truly, nor yet knoweth God aright. For what hope of health can there be where there is unrepentance of a self-will, where there is no fear of God, no love, no confidence in God, nor any knowledge of God? Many and all kinds of good works (Good works.) are to be done: we must apply our minds diligently to the study of good works, yet may we not put the[3] hope of health in our works, but in Christ only. For works, be they never so good, yet are they imperfect, and if God did not accept and approve them for Christ's sake, but judge and examine them according to the rigour, hard- (Note.) ness, severity, and sharpness of his law, they should be found very imperfect and sinful. He that giveth not his mind to good works, he believeth not God's word, and it is evident that he believeth not in Christ, and that he loveth not God, or hopeth and believeth truly to have everlasting life. But although true faith be not without good works, and though a man worketh never so much goodness, yet, forasmuch as his flesh boileth continually with evil thoughts and lusts, and fighteth against the Spirit, he fulfilleth not the law perfectly. In the exercise only of fulfilling the law we labour in this life: we only begin the law here, we do not fulfil it: certes the words of St Paul unto Titus are plain and evident, where he saith, "God saved us, not (Tit. iii.) for our own works, but of his mercy," and he addeth: "By the fountain of regeneration and the renewing of the Holy Ghost:" therefore whatsoever is against the will of God, as evil works and all sin, ought a christian man to abhor and eschew, and to work well. Neither may he remain in his old trade and living, but he must put off the old man with the works of darkness, and put out of him the old leaven; yet are we not recounted righteous before God for this newly-begun and imperfect fulfilling of the law, but of mercy, for the deserving and merit of Christ, if we believe in Christ.

To the second objection I answer that all our works are not in all points conformable to the commandments of God, and that we be and remain sinners; but this prerogative have we, that by baptism we are removed from that fierce judging-place into the court of mercy or throne of grace, where God will not deal with us accord-

[2 Folio, *every*.] [3 Folio, *to*.]

ing to the rigour of justice, but according to his mercy. There is therefore sin enough, yea, and (alas for sorrow!) too much in our life; but all our sins are smothered and drowned in the wounds and blood of Jesus Christ, which hath borne them away and satisfied for them, as though they had been his own.

To the third I answer, I will not ascend into heaven without good works and without the fulfilling of the law; for I know it is impossible: but I have the fulfilling of Christ through faith. That fulfilling of Christ through faith is mine and proper to me. And I[1] also, through the grace that I have received, give my mind to the exercise and study of good works, that I may go forward and be made perfect daily more and more. But when I am far from the perfect fulfilling, and seeing in many things I stumble and fall down, therefore do I believe in Christ, and call on the name of the Lord, and by this means do I receive remission of all my sins. And for my faith's sake in Christ God accepteth me for righteous, yea, and that for the Lord Christ, author of all righteousness, which hath most abundantly satisfied the law. For this benefit do I thank this my Lord Christ.

To the fourth objection I answer, I confess that I can abide, when I am greatly indebted, and so endangered, that I am not of sufficient ability to satisfy the same, that another should pay for me and dispatch my debt: what should a beggarly debtor[2], and a miserable captive or prisoner desire more, than to be redeemed and set at liberty? Seeing then that that most merciful God and my most favourable heavenly Father hath appointed and promised me in Christ this paying of my debt, this help and redemption without my deserving, yea, and that when I was his enemy and thy prisoner, even of his mere and gracious free mercy; why should I not most entirely desire, hope, and look for that exceeding mercy, and most necessary help for me, when it is offered? Why should I not accept it and gladly receive it? What greater madness were there, than if I should refuse it? In the payment of this my debt, or in this my redemption, God did plainly and evidently declare and shew the unsearchable and exceeding great riches of his fatherly affection, faith, and love toward us, and of the grace promised in Christ; in whom only he is truly known to be righteous and a righteous-maker: in Christ also is his unoutspeakable goodness, mercy, and tender love toward man espied and known; and therefore with hearty thanksgiving are his righteousness and
Rom. x. goodness highly avanced and magnified. He is rich in mercy, "rich toward all that call on him." But I am miserable and needy: I have therefore need of his help. Grace is promised of him: I have need of grace. Why should not I then with joy
John iii. and thanksgiving receive the grace offered? He "loved the world so entirely, that he gave his only-begotten Son" for us, to deliver us from all sorrowful chances and
1 Tim. ii. wretchedness; which also should be our mediator, our satisfier or sacrifice-offerer[3], and
1 John ii. John iii. our mercy-stock, "that every one which believe in him may not perish, but have everlasting life through him." If it hath so pleased my God, according to his ex-
Gal. iii. ceeding mercy, that his well-beloved Son should be "made accursed" for me, that I through him might be delivered from curse and damnation, surely I neither ought nor yet will refuse this high benefit, but, seeing it is offered, embrace it with both mine arms, and give everlasting and continual thanks to him for so noble a benefit. And although great weakness reigneth yet in me, notwithstanding, through the grace that I have received, I pray that not mine own ill will, but the good pleasure of God may be done in me; and I am sorry that I am not in all points pure and clean, and that I do not shew that obedience in all things to the commandments of God that I am bound. Neither do I doubt but that my Redeemer Christ, through his Spirit and his blood, will make me clean and a new man, so that no evil nor uncleanness shall remain or tarry in me. For he hath already begun to do that; and I know that his death, which bringeth salvation to us, and his mighty resurrection, shall not be unfruitful nor vain in me.

Psal. v. To the fifth I answer, I know that God will no wickedness, neither can he allow
Lev. xix. sin. For he is holy, and willeth that we also be holy. Certes he gave not his well-

---

[[1] Folio, *in*.] [[2] Folio, *debte*.] [[3] Folio, *offecer*.]

beloved Son unto the death for our sins, that we should remain in sin, but that we, being delivered and throughly made clean from sin, should as the holy sons of God "serve him in holiness and righteousness all the days of our life." For God gave not precepts in vain, neither hath he without a cause, or dallying, threatened those sinners that do not repent both temporal and everlasting pains. Luke i.

In the sixth place, thou playest the right devil throughout, and according to thine old wont and fashion, even for the endless bitterness and envy of thy most malicious stomach, thou loadest us with most cruel rebukes and shameless lies, calling us Lutherians and new gospellers. Such canst not thou abide. For they teach the plenteous and exceeding rich grace of perfect redemption in Christ, whereby alone we are justified and saved: and this do they very strongly, stedfastly, and plainly, against thy damned and most pestilent error brought in by the Pelagians, which trusted to their own works, and went about with their own works and strengths in the flesh to fulfil the law, to deserve (which notwithstanding was impossible) grace, to obtain righteousness and salvation; and so did they deny Christ and wholly buried him, and obscured[4] all his glory and benefits toward us. And this canst thou suffer. Thou canst have not greater pleasure done to thee. For with this doctrine thou fillest hell even full. But these words are not vain and of none effect, when a poor wretched sinner believeth the gospel, confesseth and knowledgeth his sins with true repentance, and, being sorry for them, laboureth to lead a better life, amendeth himself in those things wherein he hath offended, and doth not set against the fierce judgment of God his own imperfect works, but the infinite merits and works of Christ, and without presumption setteth all his trust on the grace of God promised in Christ. And this have all the true godly men ever done. In their greatest perils, in the extreme agony of death, they have even from the very heart knowledged themselves to be before God wretches and sinners worthy damnation; neither have they trusted to their own merits, but have said with the prophet: "Lord, enter not into judgment with thy servant; for no living creature shall be justified in thy sight;" and have removed very far their eyes from all their own merits into the merits of Christ, having a respect only and continually unto his death and resurrection. Note. Psal. cxliii.

So did St Bernard also, which, although he had done many good works, and had exercised himself diligently in the obedience of God's precepts, yet, when he should die, he trusted not to choose his own words, but called upon the tender mercy and favourable grace of God, saying: "Lord, unthriftily have I lived, and unthriftily have I spent my time; but this one thing comforteth me, that thou dost not despise a contrite and an humbled heart[5]." St Bernard.

And St Austin saith: "If thou wilt not be partaker of God's favour, boast thy merits[6]." Psal. xxxi.

Unto thy seventh and eighth objection, where as thou saidest that we after our own fancy do expound the holy scripture, and violently wrest it to stablish our opinions, I answer, that thou, according to thine old poisonful pleasure of lying and picking quarrels, dost without all shame lie. With these venomous lies dost thou go about to make all our labour which we spend in setting forth and teaching the doctrine of the gospel suspect, and to let that it bring forth no fruit; but those thy lies, be they never so glistering and many, shall at the last be uttered and come to light: so that the truth shall have the victory and abide for ever. For it is evident that we teach not dead or unfruitful faith, but true, constant, and livish faith in Christ, "which worketh by love," and bringeth forth many fruits. Where the scripture teacheth good works, there do we also teach good works; yea, and that much more diligently, more prudently, and in a better order, than the Pharisees and Sadducees, I mean the false hypocrites under the pope's kingdom, do. Gal. v. Note.

[4 Folio, *obserued*.]

[5 For expressions nearly similar to those in the text, used by Bernard in the near prospect of death, see Bernard. Op. Par. 1690. De Vit. Lib. I. cap. xii. 57. IV. cap. ii. 10. Vol. II. Tom. II. cols. 1084, 1154.]

[6 Si vis esse alienus a gratia, jacta merita tua.—August. Op. Par. 1679-1700. In Psal. xxxi. Enarr. II. 7. Tom. IV. col. 175.]

For we, first of all, lay a sure foundation, which is faith, whereof come forth and as out [of] a fountain issue all good works. When we have once laid this foundation, we teach all kind of good works, and what be the offices and duties of all men, every man in his calling. For God doth justify us through faith in Christ, for this cause, that we, being justified, may live alway righteously, and defend and maintain stedfastly innocency of life. To this true faith in Christ we give all those things that the scripture attributeth unto it.

Rom. iii. iv. Gal. ii. iii. This faith justifieth us.

John i. Gal. iii. By this faith are we adopted and purchased into the sons of God.

Acts x. By this faith we receive remission of sins.

Rom. v. This faith bringeth peace to the conscience.

John iii. This faith receiveth everlasting life.

Rom. x. This faith fulfilleth the law.

For it layeth hand on the true and only doer or fulfiller of the law, and challengeth him to be her own. It layeth hand also on the Spirit of Christ with his gifts, without whom the law cannot be fulfilled or accomplished.

John vi. This faith is the glorious and excellent work of God.

Heb. xi. Without this faith no man can please God.

Heb. xi. This faith is the only mean or instrument whereby, even from the beginning of the world, all holy men were justified and made acceptable to God; whereby also they wrought very great and wonderful things; again, whereby they laid hand on and did receive the promise of God.

Rom. iii. Matt. xvi. This alone faith is righteousness before God; yea, this alone obtaineth the kingdom of heaven.

1 John v. This faith is the victory of the godly, wherewith they overcome the world.

This faith in the evangelical history Christ doth very highly commend, where Luke vii. he saith: "Thy faith hath saved thee," &c.

Here thou seest, O most lying spirit, that we teach no dead, vain, and unfruitful faith; but that very same faith which the prophets taught, which Christ so highly Mark ix. commended, which the apostles preached, whereof St Mark also saith: "All things are possible to him that believeth." And even from the very beginning the true church both did and believed (which thou canst not condemn) even as we now do and believe, both as concerning the fulfilling of the law, and of good works and faith. Neither do we wrest the scriptures unto our fancies, nor do them any injury; but we understand and expound the scriptures according to the right trade of faith, that the sentence may be godly, and as the true church doth understand and take them.

Tract. iii. cap. i. Austin, writing upon John, agreeth with us, where he saith: "All that are justified by Christ are righteous, not in themself, but in him. For in themself, if thou dost ask what they be, they are Adam; in him, if thou dost ask, they are Christ's[1]." And 1 Retr. xix. again he saith, according to the mind of the holy letters: "All the commandments are counted done and perfectly fulfilled, when whatsoever is not done is forgiven[2]." Thou seest that our justification in this life can be no personal perfection and full accomplishment of the commandments of God, but a free merciful forgiving of our disobedience, and an imputation or reckoning of righteousness for Christ's sake.

In Rom. cap. iii. And Ambrose saith: "He fulfilleth the law that believeth in Christ[3]."

In Psal. iv. Also Gregory saith: "Faith is righteousness; without the which faith no man can be righteous[4]."

[1 Omnes qui ex Adam, cum peccato peccatores: omnes qui per Christum, justificati et justi, non in se, sed in illo. Nam in se si interroges, Adam sunt: in illo si interroges, Christi sunt.—Id. In Johan. Evang. cap. i. Tractat. III. 12. Tom. III. Pars II. col. 309.]

[2 Omnia ergo mandata facta deputantur, quando quidquid non fit ignoscitur.—Id. Retract. Lib. I. cap. xix. 3. Tom. I. col. 29.]

[3 Hic ergo servat legem, qui credit in Christo.—Ambros. Op. Par. 1686-90. Comm. in Epist. ad Rom. cap. ii. v. 25. Tom. II. Appendix, col. 41.]

[4 Justitia Dei fides est, sicut scriptum est: Credidit Abraham Deo, et reputatum est illi ad justitiam; quia justus ex fide vivit. Si ergo justi vita fides est, consequens est eamdem fidem esse justitiam, sine qua quisque esse justus non potest.—Gregor. Mag. Papæ I. Op. Par. 1705. In Psal. iv. Penitent. Tom. III. col. 504.]

Again Hierome: "They shall seek righteousness, which is none other than Christ himself[5]." In Sophon. cap. ii.

This without doubt was at that time the faith of the true godly men, when they, whom I have alleged, were the chief doctors of the church.

On this manner writeth Haymon upon Habacuke, where he giveth all the glory of our justification unto Christ, saying: "Christ is all my strength or virtue: Christ is all my righteousness, which is my God[6]." Cap. iii.

Thus do we understand the scripture as touching the justification of a sinner, even none otherwise than the holy church hath always understand and expounded it.

Unto the ninth objection I answer, If in these articles our doctrine be sophistical, as thou falsely layest against us, then did the holy doctors of the church at that time use sophistry or crafty dissembling with the scriptures, whom in this point thou dost also condemn, seeing for the very same matter thou condemned us. But thou dost falsely so accuse us; and when thou sayest that we use sophistry, thou liest full wickedly: when we will speak truly and rightly of the grace of God justifying us in Christ, then neither can nor ought any man speak of it otherwise than St Paul and other the chief doctors of the church have with one consent spoken of it. St Paul testifieth that a sinner is justified, not by works, but by faith; that is to say, by his trust and confidence that he hath in the grace of God promised in Christ; and that is as though he should say: A sinner is only saved and justified by the grace and mercy of Christ, and not for the worthiness of his good deeds, or of his own merit. This doctrine of Paul the old doctors [of] the church did right well understand, and therefore wrote they, the faith alone in Christ justifieth. For so speaketh Austin, Ambrose, Hilary, Chrysostom, Origen, Theophylact, Didymus Alexandrinus, with many other of the ancient doctors. And this manner of speaking of our justification was in times past so greatly used in the church, that the new or later doctors of the church have many times used the same, as Sedulius, Thomas Aquinas, Cricamus[7], Cardinalis, Bruno Carthusianus, Nicolaus Gorranus, and other. Rom. iii.

Therefore if this manner of speaking, where as we say that faith alone justifieth, were so slanderous and full of offences as thou sayest, surely those ancient catholic doctors and bishops would not have used the same. But seeing that they taught and wrote so unto the edifying and health of many men, why should not we then also use the same? But this is the matter: thou canst not abide any thing at all to hear of the free grace of God, neither is there any thing that doth more offend thee than when that is preached; therefore dost thou overwhelm us with picking of quarrels and slanderous reports. Hereof come those thy lamentations. This is it that troubleth and grieveth thee. Truth it is, if by this manner of speaking we would let or hinder the study of good works, we should not then so speak without grievous offence, yea, we should also teach very ungodly, and be heretics in deed; but we so speak for very weighty and most necessary causes. For it is our duty to keep unspotted above all things and in every place the grace of God, which we have in Christ, and royally to extol and set forth that even unto the uttermost. And that is done very goodly and most aptly by this manner of speaking. Neither is this our mind, when we use this manner of speaking, that faith ought to be or remain in a man alone or without fruit, but that it ought straightways to work by love and all kind of good works, unto the glory of God and the health of our neighbour. Therefore it is all one, whether we say, Faith justifieth without works, as Paul saith, God saveth us through his mercy, and not for our works; and as Peter saith, "We believe to obtain health through the grace of the Lord Jesus Christ;" or if we say with the ancient catholic doctors, Faith alone justifieth or saveth. For we mean none other thing by Note. Rom. iii. Tit. iv. Acts xv.

[5 Juxta Septuaginta autem præcipitur humilibus terræ, de quibus supra dictum est, ut operentur judicium, et quærant justitiam: quam non puto aliam esse præter Christum.—Hieron. Op. Par. 1693-1706. Comm. in Soph. Proph. cap. ii. Tom. III. col. 1659.]

[6 *Deus Dominus fortitudo mea.* Omnis mea virtus, omnis justitia Christus est, qui est Deus meus.—Haym. in XII Proph. Min. Enarr. Col. 1529. In Abac. cap. iii. fol. t. iiii.]

[7 The punctuation of the folio is retained here, as there seems to be some error. Is *Cricamus* a misprint for *Ochamus*?]

these words, than that our righteousness and everlasting health cometh of the free and mere grace of God promised in Christ; that Christ hath deserved these so great benefits for us, and not we ourselves; that we can none otherwise than by faith lay hand on the mercy of God or on Christ. And this is the confession and faith of all the catholic church.

For we have alway taught, and do teach, that the study of good works ought to be exercised with all main: we also are very earnestly diligent to shew how greatly we are bound to work well, and how large gifts the study of good works have; again, Mark well. how grievous pain, affliction, and all kinds of plagues do follow an ungodly and wicked dissolute life. Here seest thou that we and our cause do not lean on a vain and false trifling faith, but on a true, and such faith as worketh by charity and all good works, reneweth a man on such wise, that with high diligence he goeth about and covet to "live soberly, righteously, and godly in this present world."

Thou hast now my foundation whereunto I stick, and may safely so do. I grant thee, that the law hath worthily made me bond to malediction and cursing, because I have not shewed such obedience to the law as I ought, yet nevertheless I hope for Gal. iii. salvation. For "Christ my Redeemer hath delivered me from the curse of the law, when he became accursed" on the cross for my sake, and gave and brought to me everlasting blessing; so that now through him I have remission of all my sins, and am righteous before God, for he is become my righteousness before God. And the Isai. xxviii. Rom. x. word of God saith unto me, that no man shall be confounded that believeth in Christ. To this do I cleave, and still will cleave with tooth and nail, even unto the very death. I will lean on faith and hope, and I will fasten myself hard to this my Matt. xvi. rock, Jesus Christ, against whom "the very gates of hell shall not prevail."

Take these things for thine answer, which I know right well thou shalt never be able to confute. Get thee hence therefore from me. Where the Lord and my God Christ is and dwelleth, there shall I dwell also for evermore. Which mought vouchsafe to increase and keep my faith unto the glory and praise of his blessed and glorious name! Amen.

Give the glory to God alone.

AN

HOMILY AGAINST WHOREDOM,

BY

THOMAS BECON.

An homely against whordome, made by Thomas Becon.

Deute. xxiii.

There shalbe no whore amonge the doughters of Israel, neyther whore kepers among the sonnes of Israel.

Prouer. v.

The lips of an harlot are a droppinge hony combe, & her throte is softer then oile. But at the last she is as bitter as wormewood, and as sharpe as a two edged swerde. Her fete go down vnto death, and her steppes pearse through vnto hel. &c. Heare me therfore (O my son) and depart not from the words of my mouth. Kepe thy waye far from her, and come not nie the dores of her house.

Prouer. xxiii.

An whore is a depe graue, and an harlot is a narow pitte. She lyeth like a thefe, and such as be light and vncircumspect, she vtterly bringeth to destruction.

AN HOMILY[1]

AGAINST

WHOREDOM AND UNCLEANNESS.

Although there want not, good christian people, great swarms of vices worthy to be rebuked (unto such decay is true godliness and virtuous living now come), yet, above other vices, the outrageous seas of adultery, whoredom, fornication, and uncleanness, have not only brast in, but also overflowed almost the whole world, unto the great dishonour of God, and the exceeding infamy of the name of Christ, the notable decay of true religion, and the utter destruction of the public wealth; and that so abundantly, that through the customable use thereof this vice is grown into such an height, that in a manner among many it is counted no sin at all, but rather a pastime, a dalliance, and a touch of youth; not[2] rebuked, but winked at; not punished, but laughed at. Wherefore it is necessary at this present to entreat of the sin of whoredom and fornication, declaring unto you the greatness of this sin, and how odious, hateful, and abominable it is, and hath alway been reputed before God and all good men, and how grievously it hath been punished, both by the law of God, and the law[3] of divers princes: again, to shew you certain remedies whereby ye may (through the grace of God) eschew this most detestable sin of whoredom and fornication, and lead your lives in all honesty and cleanness.

And that ye may perceive that fornication and whoredom are in the sight of God most abominable sins, ye shall call to remembrance this commandment of God, "Thou shalt not commit adultery:" by the which word "adultery," although it be properly understand the unlawful commixtion of a married man with a woman beside his wife, or of a wife with any man beside her husband, yet thereby is signified also all unlawful use of those parts which be ordained for generation. And this one commandment, forbidding adultery, doth sufficiently paint and set out before our eyes the greatness of this sin of whoredom, and manifestly declareth how greatly it ought to be abhorred of all honest and faithful persons. How grievous a sin whoredom is in the sight of God. Exod. xx.

And that none of us all shall think himself excepted from this commandment, whether we be old or young, married or unmarried, man or woman, hear what God the Father saith by his most excellent prophet Moses: "There shall be no whore amongst the daughters of Israel, nor no whoremonger among the sons of Israel." Here is whoredom, fornication, and all uncleanness forbidden to all kinds of people, all degrees, and all ages, without exception. And that we shall not doubt but that this precept pertaineth to us in deed, hear what Christ, the perfect teacher of all truth, saith in the new testament. "Ye have heard," saith Christ, "that it was said to them of the old time, Thou shalt not commit adultery; but I say unto you, Whosoever seeth a woman to have his lust of her hath committed adultery with her already in his heart." Here our Saviour Christ doth not only confirm and stablish the law against adultery given in the old testament of God the Father by his servant Moses, and maketh it of full strength continually to remain among the professors of his name in the new law; but he also, condemning the gross interpretation of the scribes and Pharisees (which taught that the aforesaid commandment only required to abstain from the outward adultery, and not from the filthy desires and unpure lusts), teacheth us an exact and full perfection of purity and cleanness of life, both to keep our bodies

Deut. xxiii.

Matt. v.

[1 This homily is the same with that numbered 11 in the first part of the Book of Homilies set forth by authority in the reign of Edward VI. A.D. 1547. It was afterwards divided into three parts, and many minor variations occur in different editions. But, as with other treatises, the folio text printed under Becon's eye is here followed, except where there is reason to suppose a misprint in the folio.]

[2 So edition of 1547; folio, *but*.]

[3 Laws, 1547.]

undefiled, and our hearts pure and free from all evil thoughts, carnal desires, and fleshly consents.

How can we then be free from this commandment, where so great charge is laid upon us? May a servant do what he will in any thing, having a commandment of his master to the contrary? Is not Christ our Master? are not we his servants? How then may
John xv. we neglect our Master's will and pleasure, and follow our will and phantasy? "Ye are my friends," saith Christ, "if you keep those things that I command you." Now hath Christ our Master commanded us that we should forsake all uncleanness and lechery, both in body and spirit. This therefore must we do, if we look to please God.

Matt. xv. Mark vii. In the gospel of St Matthew we read that the scribes and Pharisees were grievously offended with Christ because his disciples did not keep the traditions of the forefathers; for they washed not their hands when they went to dinner or supper. And among other things Christ answered and said: "Hear and understand. Not that thing which entereth into the mouth defileth the man; but that which cometh out of the mouth defileth the man. For those things which proceed out of the mouth come forth from the heart, and they defile the man. For out of the heart proceed evil thoughts, murders, breaking of wedlock, whoredom, thefts, false witness, blasphemies. These are the things which defile a man." Here may we see that not only murder, theft, false witness, and blasphemy, defile men, but also evil thoughts, breaking of wedlock, fornication, and whoredom.

Who is now of so little wit, that he will esteem whoredom and fornication to
John xiv. be things of small importance, and of no weight before God? Christ (which is truth,
Tit. i. and cannot lie) saith, that evil thoughts, breaking of wedlock, whoredom, and fornication defile a man, that is to say, corrupt both body and soul of man, and make them of the temples of the Holy Ghost the filthy dunghill or dungeon of all unclean spirits; of the mansion of God the dwelling-place of Satan.

John viii. Again, in the gospel of St John, when the woman taken in adultery was brought unto Christ, said not he unto her, "Go thy way, and sin no more?" Doth not he
Rom. vi. here call whoredom sin? And what is the reward of sin, but everlasting death? If whoredom be sin, then is it not lawful for us to commit it: for St John saith,
1 John iii. John viii. "He that committeth sin is of the devil;" and our Saviour saith, "Every one that committeth sin is the servant of sin."

If whoredom had not been sin, surely St John Baptist would never have rebuked
Matt. xiv. king Herod for taking his brother's wife: but he told him plainly, that it was not lawful for him to take his brother's wife. He winked not at the whoredom of Herod, although he were a king of great power, but boldly reproved him for his wicked and abominable living, although for the same he lost his head. But he would rather suffer death than see God so dishonoured by the breaking of his holy precept, than to suffer whoredom to be [un]rebuked[1], even in a king. If whoredom had been but a pastime, a dalliance, and a thing not to be passed of (as many count it now-a-days), truly St John had been more than twice mad, if he would have had the displeasure of a king, if he would have been cast into prison and lost his head, for a trifle. But John knew right well how filthy, stinking, and abominable the sin of whoredom is in the sight of God; therefore would not he leave it unrebuked, no, not in a king. If whoredom be not lawful in a king, neither is it lawful in a subject: if whoredom be not lawful in a public officer, neither is it lawful in a private person: if it be not lawful neither in king, nor subject, neither in a common officer, nor private person, truly then is it lawful in no man nor woman, of whatsoever degree or age they be.

Acts xv. Furthermore, in the Acts of the Apostles we read, that when the apostles and elders, with the whole congregation, were gathered together to pacify the hearts of the faithful dwelling at Antioch (which were disquieted through the false doctrine of certain Jewish preachers), they sent word to the brethren, that it seemed good to the Holy Ghost, and to them, to charge them with no more than with necessary things: among other, they willed them to abstain from idolatry and fornication, "from which," said they, "if you keep yourselves, ye shall do well."

[[1] Folio, *rebuked.*]

Note here, how these holy and blessed fathers of Christ's church would charge the congregation with no more things than were necessary. Mark also, how among those things, from the which they command the brethren of Antioch to abstain, fornication and whoredom is numbered. It is therefore necessary, by the determination and consent of the Holy Ghost, and the apostles and elders, with the whole congregation, that, as from idolatry and superstition, so likewise we must abstain from fornication and whoredom. Is it necessary unto salvation to abstain from idolatry? so is it to abstain from whoredom. Is there any nigher way to lead unto damnation than[2] to be an idolater? no: even so neither is there a nearer way to damnation than to be a fornicator and an whoremonger.

Now where are those people which so lightly esteem breaking of wedlock, whoredom, fornication, and adultery? It is necessary, saith the Holy Ghost, the blessed apostles, the elders, with the whole congregation of Christ; it is necessary to salvation, say they, to abstain from whoredom. If it be necessary unto salvation, then wo be to them which, neglecting their salvation, give their mind to filthy and stinking sin, to so wicked vice, to such detestable abomination.

But let us hear what the blessed apostle St Paul saith to this matter: writing to the Romans, he hath these words: "Let us cast away the works of darkness, and Rom. xiii.
put on the armours of light. Let us walk honestly, as it were in the day-time; not in eating and drinking, neither in chamberings and wantonness, neither in strife, and envying; but put ye on the Lord Jesus Christ, and make not provision for the flesh, to fulfil the lusts of it." Here the holy apostle exhorted us to cast away the works of darkness, which, among other, he called gluttonous eating, drinking, chambering and wantonness, which all are ministers unto that vice, and preparations to induce and bring in the filthy sin of the flesh. He calleth them "the deeds and works of darkness," not only because they are customably done in darkness, or in the night-time (for "every one that doth evil hateth the light, neither cometh he to the John iii.
light, lest his works should be reproved"), but that they lead the right way unto that utter darkness, where weeping and gnashing of teeth shall be. And he saith in Matt. xiii.
another place of the same epistle: "They that are in the flesh cannot please God." Rom. viii.
"We are debtors to the flesh, not that we should live after the flesh; for if ye live after the flesh, ye shall die."

Again he saith: "Fly from whoredom. For every sin that a man committeth is 1 Cor. vi.
without his body; but whosoever committeth whoredom sinneth against his own body. Do ye not know that your members are the temple of the Holy Ghost, which is in you, whom also ye have of God, and ye are not your own? For ye are dearly bought. Glorify God in your body," &c. And a little afore he saith: "Do ye not know that your bodies are the members of Christ? Shall I then take the members of Christ, and make them the members of an whore? God forbid. Do ye not know that he which cleaveth to an whore is made one body with her? There shall be Matt. xix.
two in one flesh, saith he. But he that cleaveth to the Lord is one spirit." What godly reasons doth the blessed apostle St Paul bring forth here, to dissuade us from whoredom and all uncleanness! "Your members," saith he, "are the temple of the Holy Ghost, which whosoever doth defile, God will destroy him." If we be the temple of the Holy Ghost, how unfitting then is it to drive that Holy Spirit from us through whoredom, and in his place to set the wicked spirits of uncleanness and fornication, and to be joined and do service to them! "Ye are dearly bought," saith he; "therefore glorify God in your bodies." Christ, that innocent Lamb of God, 1 Pet. i.
hath bought us from the servitude of the devil, not with corruptible gold and silver, but with his most precious and dear heart-blood. To what intent? that we should fall again unto our old uncleanness and abominable living? Nay, verily, but "that Luke i.
we should serve him all the days of our life in holiness and righteousness," that we should glorify him in our bodies by purity and cleanness of life. He declareth also that our bodies are the members of Christ. How unseemly a thing is it, then, to cease to be incorporate and one with Christ, and through whoredom to be joined and made all one with an whore! What greater dishonour or injury can we do to Christ,

[2 So 1547; folio, *that*.]

than to take away from him the members of his body, and to join them to whores, devils, and wicked spirits? And what more dishonour can we do to ourselves, than through uncleanness to lose so excellent a dignity and freedom, and to become bond-slaves and miserable captives to the spirits of darkness? Let us therefore consider first the glory of Christ, and then our state, our dignity, and freedom, wherein God hath set us[1], valiantly defend the same against Satan and all his crafty assaults, that Christ may be honoured, and that we lose not our liberty, but still remain in one spirit with him.

Moreover, in his epistle to the Ephesians, the blessed apostle willeth us to be so pure and free from adultery, fornication, and all uncleanness, that we "not once name them among us (as it becometh saints), nor filthiness, nor foolish talking, nor jesting, which are not comely; but rather giving of thanks. For this ye know," saith he, "that no whoremonger, either unclean person, or covetous person (which is an idolater), hath any inheritance in the kingdom of Christ and God." And that we should remember to be holy, pure, and free from all uncleanness, the holy apostle calleth us "saints," because we are sanctified and made holy in the blood of Christ, through the Holy Ghost. Now if we be saints, what have we to do with the manners of the heathen? St Peter saith: "As he which called you is holy, even so be ye holy also in all your conversation: because it is written, Be ye holy; for I am holy."

Eph. v.

1 Pet. i.

Lev. xix.

Hitherto have we heard how grievous a sin fornication and whoredom is, and how greatly God doth abhor it, throughout the whole scripture. How can it any otherwise be than a sin of most abomination, seeing it once may not be named among the Christians, much less it may in any point be committed? And surely, if we would weigh the greatness of this sin, and consider it in the right kind, we should find the sin of whoredom to be that most filthy lake, foul puddle, and stinking sink, whereunto all kinds of sins and evils flow; where also they have their resting-place and abiding.

For hath not the adulterer a pride in his whoredom? as the wise man saith: "They are glad when they have done evil, and rejoice in things that are stark naught." Is not the adulterer also idle, and delighteth in no godly exercise, but only in that his most filthy and beastly pleasure? Is not his mind abstract and utterly drawn away from all virtuous studies and fruitful labours, and only given to carnal imaginations? Doth not the whoremonger give his mind to gluttony, that he may be the more apt to serve his lusts and carnal pleasures? Doth not the adulterer give his mind to covetousness, and to polling and pilling of other, that he may be the more able to maintain his harlots and whores, and to continue in his filthy and unlawful love? Swelleth he not also with envy against other, fearing that his prey should be allured and taken away from him? Again, is he not ireful, and replenished with wrath and displeasure, even against his best beloved, if at any time his beastly and devilish request be letted? What sin or kind of sin is it that is not joined with fornication and whoredom? It is a monster of many heads. It receiveth all kinds of vices, and refuseth all kinds of virtues.

Prov. ii.

If one several sin bringeth damnation, what is to be thought of that sin which is accompanied with all evils, and hath waiting on it whatsoever is hateful to God, damnable to man, and pleasant to Satan? Great is the damnation that hangeth over the heads of fornicators and adulterers.

What shall I speak of other incommodities which issue and flow out of this[2] stinking puddle of whoredom? Is not that treasure, which before all others is most regarded of honest persons, the good fame and name of man and woman, lost through whoredom? What patrimony, what substance, what goods, what riches, doth whoredom shortly consume and bring to nought! What valiantness and strength is many times made weak and destroyed with whoredom! What wit is so fine, that is not doted[3] and defaced through whoredom? What beauty (although it were never so

[1 "By giving us his holy Spirit," is here inserted in the edition of 1547.]

[2 So 1547; folio, *his*.]

[3 Doted: rendered doting.]

excellent) is not obscured through whoredom? Is not whoredom an enemy to the pleasant flower of youth, and bringeth it not grey hairs and old age before the time? What gift of nature (although it were never so precious) is not corrupted with whoredom? Come not the French pox, with other divers diseases, of whoredom? From whence come so many bastards and misbegotten children, to the high displeasure of God and dishonour of holy wedlock, but of whoredom? How many consume all their substance and goods, and at the last fall into such extreme poverty, that afterward they steal, and so are hanged, through whoredom! What contention and manslaughter cometh of whoredom! How many maids be deflowered, how many wives corrupted, how many widows defiled, through whoredom! How much is the public weal impoverished and troubled through whoredom! How much is God's word contemned and depraved by whoredom and whoremongers!

Of this vice cometh a great part of the divorces, which now-a-days be so commonly accustomed and used by men's private authority, to the great displeasure of God, and the breach of the most holy knot and bond of matrimony. For when this most detestable sin is once crept into the breast of the adulterer, so that he is entangled with unlawful and unchaste love, straightways his true and lawful wife is despised, her presence is abhorred, her company stinketh and is loathsome, whatsoever she doth is dispraised, there is no quietness in the house, so long as she is in sight. Therefore, to make short tale, must she away; for her husband can brook her no longer. Thus through whoredom is the honest and innocent wife put away, and an harlot received in her stead; and in like sort it happeneth many times in the wife towards her husband. O abomination!

Christ our Saviour, very God and man, coming to restore the law of his heavenly Father unto the right sense, understanding, and meaning, among other things reformed the abuse of this law of God: for whereas the Jews used, of a long sufferance, by custom, to put away their wives at their pleasure, for every cause, Christ, correcting that evil custom, did teach that, "if any man put away his wife, and marrieth another, **Matt. xix.** for any cause, except only for adultery (which then was death by the law), he was an adulterer, and forced also his wife, so divorced, to commit adultery, if she were joined to any other man; and the man also, so joined with her, to commit adultery." In what cause[4] then are those adulterers, which, for the love of an whore, put away their true and lawful wives, against all law, right, reason, and conscience? O damnable is the state wherein they stand! Swift destruction shall fall on them, if they repent not, and amend not; for God will not ever suffer holy wedlock thus to be dishonoured, hated, and despised. He will once punish this carnal and licentious manner of living, and cause that his holy ordinance shall be had in reverence and honour. For surely "wedlock," as the apostle saith, "is honourable among all men, **Heb. xiii.** and the bed undefiled: but whoremongers and fornicators God will judge," that is to say, punish and condemn.

But to what purpose is this labour taken, to describe and set forth the greatness of the sin of whoredom, and the incommodities that issue and flow out of it, seeing that breath and tongue shall sooner fail any man, than he shall or may be able to set it out according to the abomination and heinousness thereof? Notwithstanding, this is spoken to the intent all men should flee whoredom, and live in the fear of God: God grant that it may not be spoken in vain!

Punishments appointed for whoredom.

Now will I declare unto you in order, with what[5] grievous punishments God in times past plagued adultery; and how certain worldly princes also did punish it: that ye may perceive that whoredom and fornication be sins, no less detestable in the sight of God and all good men, than I have hitherto uttered. In the first book of Moyses we read, that when mankind began to be multiplied upon the earth, the men **Gen. vi.** and women gave their minds so greatly to carnal delectation and filthy pleasure, that they lived without all fear of God. God, seeing this their beastly and abominable living, and perceiving that they amended not, but rather increased daily more and more in their sinful and unclean manners, repented that he ever made man; and, to

[4 Case, 1547.] [5 So 1547; folio, *that*.]

shew how greatly he abhorred adultery, whoredom, fornication, and all uncleanness, he made all the fountains of the deep earth to burst out, and the sluices of heaven to be opened, so that the rain came down upon the earth by the space of forty days and forty nights, and by this means destroyed the whole world and all mankind,
2 Pet. ii. eight persons only excepted, that is to say, "Nohe the preacher of righteousness" (as St Peter calleth him), and his wife, his three sons, and their wives. O what a grievous plague did God cast here upon all living creatures for the sin of whoredom! for the which God took vengeance, not only of man, but also of beasts, fowls, and all
Gen. iv. living creatures. Manslaughter was committed before, yet was not the world destroyed for that; but for whoredom all the world (few only except) was overflowed[1] with waters, and so perished—an example worthy to be remembered, that ye may learn to fear God.

Gen. xix. We read again, that for the filthy sin of uncleanness Sodom and Gomorre, and the other cities nigh unto them, were destroyed with fire and brimstone from heaven; so that there was neither man, woman, child, nor beast, nor yet any thing that grew upon the earth there left undestroyed. Whose heart trembleth not at the hearing of this history? who is so drowned in whoredom and uncleanness, that will not now for ever after leave this abominable living, seeing that God so grievously punisheth uncleanness, to rain fire and brimstone from heaven, to destroy whole cities, to kill man, woman, and child, and all other living creatures there abiding, to consume with fire all that ever grew? What can be more manifest tokens of God's wrath and vengeance against uncleanness and impurity of life? Mark this history, good people, and fear the vengeance of God.

Gen. xii. Do we not read also that God did smite Pharao and his house with great plagues, because that he ungodly desired Sara, the wife of Abraham? Likewise read
Gen. xx. we of Abimelech, king of Gerar, although he touched her not by carnal knowledge. These plagues and punishments did God cast upon filthy and unclean persons before the law was given (the law of nature only reigning in the hearts of men), to declare how great love he had to matrimony; and again, how much he abhorred adultery, fornication, and all uncleanness.

And when the law that forbad whoredom was given by Moses to the Jews, did not God command that the transgressors thereof should be put to death? The words
Lev. xx. of the law are these: "Whoso committeth adultery with any man's wife shall die the death, both the man and the woman, because he hath broken wedlock with his
Deut. xxii. neighbour's wife." In the law also it was commanded that a damsel and a man taken together in whoredom should be both stoned to death. In another place we
Num. xxv. also read, that God commanded Moyses to take all the head rulers and princes of the people, and to hang them upon gibbets openly, that every man might see them, because they either committed, or did not punish whoredom. Again, did not God send such a plague among the people for fornication and uncleanness, that they died in one day twenty-three thousand?

I pass over, for lack of time, many other histories of the holy bible, which declare the grievous vengeance and heavy displeasure of God against whoremongers and adulterers. Certes this extreme punishment appointed of God sheweth evidently how greatly God hateth whoredom. And let us not doubt but that God at this present abhorreth all manner of uncleanness, no less than he did in the old law, and will undoubtedly punish it, both in this world and in the world to come. For he is a God that can abide no wickedness: therefore ought it to be eschewed of all that tender the glory of God and the salvation of their own souls.

1 Cor. x. St Paul saith: "All these things are written for our example," and to teach us the fear of God, and the obedience to his holy law. For "if God spared not the natural branches," neither will he spare us that be but grafts, if we commit like offences. If God destroyed many thousands of people, many cities, yea, the whole world, for whoredom, let us not flatter ourselves, and think we shall escape free and without
Deut. xxviii. punishment. For he hath promised in his holy law to send most grievous plagues upon them that transgress his holy commandments.

[[1] So 1547; folio, *overfloweth*.]

Thus have we heard how God punisheth the sin of adultery: let us now hear certain laws which the civil magistrates devised, in divers countries, for the punishment thereof; that we may learn how uncleanness hath ever be detested in all well-ordered cities and commonwealths, and among all honest persons.

The law among the Lepreyans was this, that when any were taken in adultery, they were bound, and carried three days through the city; and afterward, as long as they lived, were they despised, and with shame and confusion reputed as persons desolate of all honesty[2]. Laws devised for punishment of whoredom.

Among the Locrensians the adulterers had both their eyes thrust out[3].

The Romans in times past punished whoredom, sometime by fire, sometime by sword[4].

If a man among the Egyptians had been taken in adultery, the law was that he should openly, in the presence of all the people, be scourged naked with whips, unto the number of a thousand stripes. The woman that was taken with him had her nose cut off, whereby she was known ever after to be an whore, and therefore to be abhorred of all men[5].

Among the Arabians, they that were taken in adultery had their heads stricken from their bodies[6].

The Athenians punished whoredom by death, in like manner[7].

So likewise did the barbarous Tartarians[8].

Among the Turks, even at this day, they that be taken in adultery, both man and woman, are stoned straightways to death, without mercy[9].

Thus see we what godly acts were devised in times past of the high powers, for the putting away of whoredom, and for the maintaining of holy matrimony and pure conversation. And the authors of these acts were not Christians, but heathen. Yet were they so inflamed with the love of honesty and pureness of life, that, for the maintenance and conservation of that, they made godly statutes, suffering neither fornication nor adultery to reign in their realms unpunished. Christ said to the people: "The Ninevites shall rise at the judgment with this nation," meaning the unfaithful Jews, "and shall condemn them. For they repented at the preaching of Jonas; but behold," saith he, "a greater than Jonas is here," meaning himself; and yet they repented not. Shall not, think you, likewise the Locrensians, Arabians, Athenians, with such other, rise up at the judgment and condemn us; forasmuch as they ceased from whoredom at the commandment of man, and we have the law and manifest precepts of God, and yet forsake we not our filthy conversation? Truly, truly, it shall be easier at the day of judgment to those heathen than to us, except we repent and amend. Luke xi.

For although death of the body seemeth to us a grievous punishment in this world for whoredom, yet is that pain nothing in comparison of the grievous torments which adulterers, fornicators, and all unclean persons shall suffer after this life. For all such be excluded and shut out of the kingdom of heaven, as St Paul saith: "Be not deceived. For neither whoremongers, nor worshippers of images, nor adulterers, nor softlings, nor Sodomites, nor thieves, nor covetous persons, nor drunkards, nor cursed speakers, nor pillers, shall inherit the kingdom of God." And St John in his Revelations saith that whoremongers shall have their part with murderers, sorcerers, enchanters, liars, idolaters, and such other, in the lake which burneth with fire and brimstone, which is the second death. The punishment of the body, although it be death, hath an end; but the punishment of the soul, which St John calleth "the second death," is everlast- 1 Cor. vi. Rev. xxi.

[2 Various laws against adultery with the authorities, are enumerated, Loc. Com. Pet. Mart. Heid. 1613. Class. II. cap. ii. 20-23. pp. 318-21.]

[3 Ζάλευκος ὁ Λοκρῶν νομοθέτης προσέταξε τὸν μοιχὸν ἁλόντα ἐκκόπτεσθαι τοὺς ὀφθαλμούς.—Ælian. Var. Hist. L. Bat. 1731. Lib. XIII. cap. xxiv. Pars II. p. 891.]

[4 Adulterii convictam vir et cognati ut vellent necarent.—Orb. Terrar. Epit. per Joan. Boem. Auban. Pap. 1596. Lib. III. cap. xviii. p. 273.]

[5 In adulterio spontaneo deprehensus virgis cædebatur ad mille plagas, mulier naso mutilabatur.—Id. Lib. I. cap. v. p. 27.]

[6 Adulter capite plectitur.—Id. Lib. II. cap. i. p. 49.]

[7 Mœchum in adulterio deprehensum impune necari voluit.—Id. Lib. III. cap. ii. p. 162.]

[8 Castissime vivunt, nam in adulterio deprehensi tam vir quam mulier lege ipsa occiduntur.—Id. Lib. II. cap. x. p. 111.]

[9 In adulterio deprehensus cum adultera absque misericordia, absque mora lapidatur.—Id. Lib. II. cap. xi. p. 129.]

Matt. xiii. Isai. lxvi. ing: there shall be fire and brimstone, there shall be weeping and gnashing of teeth: the worm that shall there gnaw the conscience of the damned shall never die. O whose heart distilleth not even drops of blood, to hear and consider these things? If we tremble and shake at the hearing and naming of these pains, O what shall they do that shall feel them, that shall suffer them, yea, and ever shall suffer, worlds without end? God have mercy on us! Who is now so drowned in sin, and past all godliness, that he will set more by a filthy and stinking pleasure (which soon passeth away) than by the loss of everlasting glory? Again, who will so give himself to the lusts of the flesh, that he feareth nothing at all the pains of hell-fire?

How whoredom may be avoided. But let us hear how we may eschew the sin of whoredom and adultery, that we may walk in the fear of God, and be free from those most grievous and intolerable torments which abide all unclean persons. To avoid fornication, adultery, and all uncleanness, let us provide that above all things we may keep our hearts pure and clean from all evil thoughts and carnal lusts. For if that be once infected and corrupt, we fall headlong into all kind of ungodliness. This shall we easily do, if, when we feel inwardly that Satan our old enemy tempteth us unto whoredom, we by no means consent to his crafty suggestions, but valiantly resist and withstand him by strong faith in the word of God, objecting against him always in our heart this commandment of God: *Scriptum est, Non mœchaberis:* "It is written, Thou shalt not commit whoredom." It shall be good for us ever to live in the fear of God, and to set before our eyes the grievous threatenings of God against all ungodly sinners, and consider in our mind how filthy, beastly, and short that pleasure is whereunto Satan moveth us; and again, how the pain appointed for that sin is intolerable and everlasting. Moreover, to use a temperance and sobriety in eating and drinking, to eschew unclean communication, and to avoid all filthy company, to fly idleness, to delight in reading of holy scripture, to watch in godly prayers and virtuous meditations, and at all times to exercise some godly travails, shall help greatly unto the eschewing of whoredom.

And here are all degrees to be monished, whether they be married or unmarried, to love chastity and cleanness of life. For the married are bound by the law of God so purely to love one another, that neither of them seek any strange love. The man must only cleave to his wife, and the wife again only to her husband: they must so delight one in another's company, that none of them covet any other. And as they are bound thus to live together in all godliness and honesty, so likewise it is their duty virtuously to bring up their children; and to provide that they fall not into Satan's snare, nor into any uncleanness, but that they come pure and honest unto holy wedlock, when time requireth. So likewise ought all masters and rulers to provide that no whoredom, nor any point of uncleanness, be used among their servants. And again, they that are single, and feel in themselves that they cannot live without the company of a woman,
1 Cor. vii. let them get wives of their own, and so live godly together. For "it is better to marry than burn." And "to avoid fornication," saith the apostle, "let every man have his own wife, and every woman her own husband."

Finally, all such as feel in themselves a sufficiency and ability, through the operation of God's Spirit, to lead a sole and continent life, let them praise God for his gift, and seek all means possible to maintain the same; as by reading of holy scriptures, by godly meditations, by continual prayers, and such other virtuous exercises.

If we all on this wise will endeavour ourselves to eschew fornication, adultery, and all uncleanness, and lead our life in all godliness and honesty, serving God with a pure and clean heart, and glorifying him in our bodies by leading an innocent life, we may be sure to be in the number of those of whom our Saviour Christ speaketh in
Matt. v. the gospel on this manner: "Blessed are the pure in heart; for they shall see God:" to whom alone be all glory, honour, rule, and power, worlds without end.

Amen.

Give the glory to God alone.

INDEX.

ABSOLUTION, the power of unduly claimed, 556, 7; is of God alone, 557, &c.; what the true and christian is, 565, 7, 8; examples of it, 567, 8; it ought not to be mumbled in the Latin tongue, 568.

Adamites, a sect of heretics, 379; their origin, ibid., *n*.

Adauctus overthrew idols, 305.

Adoption, explained, 25.

Adultery, condemned, 98; plagued with punishment, 100, 1, 647, 8; remedies whereby to avoid it, 101, &c., 650; its prevalence lamented, 643, &c.; the incommodities that flow from it, 646, &c.; various laws against it, 649.

Adversity, the temptation of, 188, &c.; more profitable than that of prosperity, 188, 9; what we ought to do in it, 189, 191; God assails not only sinners but also his servants with it, 190.

Ælian, 649, *n*.

Æneas Sylvius, 245, *n*.

Afflict: conflict, 542.

Afflictions come not of chance but by the counsel of God, 572; they are sure signs of God's goodwill, ibid.; they are sent to subdue the old Adam in us, ibid.; to teach patience, ibid., 573; we must conceive a good hope in them, ibid.; what they teach us, 633.

Agape, the name anciently given to the Lord's supper, 231; see also 251.

Agasse, invoked to save persons from burning, 536.

Agde, council of, 71.

Age, what kind of is honourable, 373; covetousness reigns chiefly in it, ibid.; it is bent to much babbling, 375.

Agnes, invoked for good husbands, 536.

Albertus says that in times past all that came together to the church communicated together, 239, 40.

Alexander, 308, 441.

Alliaco, P. de (Cameracensis) allows it to be more agreeable to the truth of God's word to suppose that in the eucharist very bread and very wine remain, 269.

Alphonsus, king of Arragon, his speech about the flourishing state of his kingdom, 5; error in regard to him in Vol. I. corrected, ibid., *n*.

Alsop, Mr, 420.

Altars, objections against their use for ministration of the Lord's supper, 297; they are said to have been introduced by pope Sixtus II., ibid.

Ambrose numbers the second commandment among the ten, and holds it a moral law, 60; says Helena, having found the title, worshipped the king, not the tree, 72; calls Christ alone our mouth, our eye, and our hand to the Father, 135; says that to forgive sin and to give the Holy Ghost is only in the power of God, 173, 219, 27; declares that he alone forgives the sins which alone died for our sins, 173, 4, *n*.; says that the word of God forgives sin, the priest is the judge, 174; affirms that baptism ought necessarily to be given to young children, 210; proves that Valentinian, though he died unbaptized, yet died in the Lord, 224; speaks of baptism by trine immersion, 227; says that the flesh of Christ is offered for the salvation of the body, and the blood for our soul, 244; declares that we offer unto the remembrance of Christ's death, 249; says those things ought to be spoken which the hearers may understand, 254; exhorts to receive the Lord's bread daily, 259; says that, inasmuch as he always sins, he ought always to have the medicine, i.e. the sacrament, ibid.; declares that we lawfully condemn all new things which Christ has not taught, 261; warns against seeking Christ in the earth, or after the flesh, 274, 7; says that Christ here in image is there in truth, where as an advocate he intercedes for us, 277; speaks of the body of Christ as being signified after consecration of the bread, 285; calls the oblation the figure of Christ's body and blood, ibid.; says the bread is the meat of saints, 293; declares that he who eats this body shall never die, ibid.; asserts that he, who receives not remission of his sins here, shall not have it in another life, 395; declares that there is no difference between the carcases of the dead, except that the rich stink more than the poor, 436; cautions against boasting of a fast, else it will profit nothing, 541; asks whether he can be thought to fast aright, who, instead of going to the church, goes to the chase, 548; says he fulfils the law that believes in Christ, 638; speaks of faith alone justifying, 639.

Amen, what it signifies at the end of the creed, 51; and of the Lord's prayer, 197, 8.

Amendment of life, a disposition to it is necessary in preparation for the Lord's supper, 236; this disposition must continue for ever, 237.

Ames, 423, *n*.

Anabaptists, their opinion that sins after baptism are not forgiven refuted, 170, &c.; censured with their doctrines, 207, 15, 26; they untruly deny that the apostles baptized infants, 209; they revive the old heresy that Christ took no flesh of the virgin, 446.

Anacletus (bishop of Rome) commands all to communicate that will not be excommunicated, 238, 58.

Anchors: anchorites, 390.

Angels, honour is not to be given to them as to God, 58, 9.

Anger, strife, &c. forbidden, 95, 6.

Angle, see 428.

Antichrist, synagogue of, signs by which the church of Christ may be known from it, 42; his kingdom is large, 151; we desire in the Lord's prayer that his kingdom may be brought to confusion,

152 ; he shall shortly with his doctrine be confounded, 409, 10; many antichrists are risen up, 555 ; their doctrines must be fought against, ibid., 556.
Antioch (Ancona), a bishop deposed at, 325, 6.
Antisthenes, 436.
Antony, invoked for keeping swine, 536.
Apelles, a heretic, 446.
Apolline, invoked for healing the tooth-ache, 536.
Apostles first taught repentance, then faith, 13; —creed, why so called, 15; what Christ sent them to do, 320, 1; Christ commanded them to feed the flock, 320.
Appairing: impairing, 116.
Apparel, of maids must be seemly, 370, 1; lightness of it shews lightness of mind, 370; that of labouring men must be decent and seemly, 400; gallant not to be rejoiced in, 437, &c.; (or clothing) why it was given to us, 437, 8; madness of Englishmen in it, 438; that of women, what it should be, 438, 9; a rule for it, 440.
Aquilian church, how it worded the article of the creed respecting the resurrection of the body, 49.
Aquinas, Thomas, says that, though whole Christ be under both kinds, yet is he not given in vain under both kinds, 244; calls the sacrifice of the mass a memorial of the Lord's passion, 250; mentions various opinions as to the words used by Christ in the consecration of the eucharist, 263; used in speaking of justification the old manner of speech, that faith alone justifies, 639.
Arabians, their law against adultery, 649.
Archilochus, his books banished by the Lacedæmonians, 382.
Arians, the council of Nice convened by Constantine against them, 305.
Aristotle, Philip's letter to him, 5, 386.
Arnold, 226, *n.*; 267, *n.*; 285, *n.*; 292, *n.*; 295, *n.*
Athanasius numbers the second commandment among the ten, and holds it a moral law, 60; speaks of Christ's flesh as called celestial meat, and spiritual food, 289.
Athenians, their law against adultery, 649.
Augustine says that the prayer which is not made by Christ is very sin, 135; asserts that no man takes away the sins of the world but Christ alone, 173; says that the priests do not forgive sin, but the Holy Ghost through them, 174; affirms that the baptism of young children comes from the apostles to us, 210; declares that without the sanctifying of the invisible grace the visible sacraments do not profit, 218; says that the visible sign and the invisible grace may be present one without the other, ibid.; asserts that God has retained to himself alone the power in baptism to forgive sins, 219; says that it is fulfilled invisibly when not the contempt of religion but the article of necessity excludes the mystery of baptism, 224; declares that good and bad baptize visibly, but God baptizes invisibly by them, 227; says that to minister the word and sacrament the minister is somewhat, but to make clean and justify he is nothing, ibid.; speaks of baptism by trine immersion, 227; says images are wont to be called by the names of those things whereof they are images, 249; shews how the flesh and blood of Christ's sacrifice was promised, performed, and celebrated, 249; says (Lib. Sent. Prosp.) the heavenly bread is called the body of Christ, when it is indeed the sacrament or holy sign, 250; affirms (ibid.) that Christ was once offered in himself, and yet is daily offered in the sacrament, ibid.; says the bread is spent in receiving the sacrament, 252; speaks of the frequency of communicating in his time, 258; exhorts to communicate at least every Sunday, ibid.; insists on the authority of holy scripture, 261; says that which we see (in the sacrament) is the bread and the cup, 267, 8; declares that the sacrifice of the church consists of two things, of the sacrament, and of the thing signified thereby, 268; says the word comes to the element and thereof is made a sacrament, 270; proves that as concerning Christ's flesh he is not here, 273, 4, 8; says that to lay hand on Christ, who has carried his body into heaven, we must send up our faith, 274; proves that after the form of Christ's human nature we may not think that he is everywhere, 277, 8; declares that Christ is everywhere as God, but in a certain place of heaven because of the measure of a true body, 278; asserts that bodies must be in some certain places, and cannot be separated from their qualities, ibid., 281; says that Christ's body must be in one place, 278; declares we must believe that Christ's body is only in heaven, ibid.; shews how the thing which signifieth is wont to be called by the name of that thing which it signifieth, 282; says Christ did not stick to say, 'This is my body,' when he gave the sign of his body, ibid., 285; instances how, the sacraments having the name of the things whereof they are sacraments, the sacrament of Christ's body is Christ's body, 283; says that sacraments are signs of things, being one thing and signifying another, 284; shews that the heavenly bread is called Christ's body, when indeed it is the sacrament of his body, ibid.; says that Christ in the maundy delivered the figure of his body and blood, 285; explains how to distinguish literal from figurative expressions of scripture, 290, 1; teaches that the sacraments must be venerated not with a carnal bondage, but with a spiritual freedom, 291; says he that agrees not with Christ neither eats his flesh, nor drinks his blood, 292; distinguishes between sacramentally and truly eating the body of Christ, which is to dwell in him, 293; declares that he that dwells not in Christ neither eats spiritually his flesh, nor drinks his blood, ibid.; affirms the judgment of those who say that he eats not the body of Christ, who is not in the body of Christ, ibid.; says that heretics may have the sacrament, but the matter of it they cannot have, ibid.; declares that Judas did eat the bread of the Lord and not the bread that was the Lord, 294, 7; says if we believe we have eaten Christ, 295, 6; declares that he that believes in him eats him, ibid., 296; shews how the eating of Christ's flesh must be spiritually understood, 296; speaks of Judas (in one sense) receiving the body and blood of the Lord, ibid.; referred to to shew that in his time the bread and the cup were given into the hands of the com-

municants, 301, *n.*; rejoices when heretics were delivered from their old errors, 316; prescribes in respect of heretics to love the men but kill the errors, ibid.; says it pleases no good men in the catholic church for any one though a heretic to be killed, 317; recounts the behaviour as a wife of his mother Monica, 344, *n.*; says the catholic believes that there are but two places after this life, and knows no third, 394; declares that the souls of saints go straightways to heaven, and of sinners to hell, ibid.; asserts that there are two dwelling-places, one in fire, the other in the eternal kingdom, ibid.; says every one sleeps with his own cause, and with his own cause shall rise again, 395; declares it of no profit to pass a whole day in long fasting, if afterward the soul be oppressed with superfluity of meats, 535; says that the fasts of christian men are rather to be observed spiritually than carnally, 540; shews that the great and general fast is to abstain from iniquities and unlawful pleasures of the world, ibid.; says that good things (in themselves) may be done, and yet not be done well by those who do them, 541; recommends the taming and mortifying of the flesh, 544; shews the necessity of fasting to assuage the intemperancy of the body, ibid.; says mercy commended the prayer and fasting of Cornelius, who fed those that wanted, 546; recommends that what is not eaten on fasting-days be bestowed on the poor, ibid.; shews that God speaks to us in scripture, which must therefore be reverently received, 549; warns those who will be partakers of the grace of God not to boast their merits, 637; says all that are justified by Christ are righteous not in themselves but in him, 638; speaks of faith alone justifying, 639.

Auricular confession, the affiance that was placed in it, 414.

Aylmer, 424.

Backsliding, the danger of, 206, 7.

Banqueting, a vain pleasure, not to be rejoiced in, 440, 1; the evils it has brought, 441.

Baptism, sins after it may be forgiven, 170, &c.; its outward sign and its promise, 199; it ought to be administered openly, 200; what it is, 202; of how many parts it consists, ibid.; what it is to be baptized with the Holy Ghost, ibid.; that of water without the baptism of the Holy Ghost profits nothing, 203, 18; who instituted it, ibid.; what it is to be baptized in the name of the Father, the Son, and the Holy Ghost, ibid.; why we are baptized, ibid.; the fruit of it, ibid., &c.; we receive remission of sins and the Holy Ghost in it, 204; it declares we are in the favour of God, 205; it preaches not only the mortification of the flesh but the vivification of the Spirit, ibid., 206; ceremonies of it used in the pope's church, 207; of infants, ibid., &c.; proof of infant baptism from circumcision, 207, 8; proof from the fact that children have been from their cradle endued with the Holy Spirit, 208; proof because the apostles baptized households, 209; it may be ministered to children before they believe, 211; the case of children dying without it, 214, 5; a sacrament to be reverently received of all, 215; those that willingly reject it have no portion in God's kingdom, ibid., 224, 6; the doctrine that all are condemned that die without baptism of water is injurious, 215, &c., and dissents from the verity of God's word, 220, &c.; it is of the same necessity that circumcision was, 216; a seal of righteousness, 217; outward does not give grace by any power that it has, ibid.; of itself it brings not grace, but testifies that he who is baptized has received grace, 220; some may be spiritually baptized among the Turks and heathen, 221, 2; three kinds of it, yet but one, 225, 6; all who are contained in the visible church are not baptized alike, 225; it may not be ministered twice to one person, 226; the unworthiness of the minister does not hinder the worthiness of it, 226, 7; by trine immersion, 227; by affusion or sprinkling sufficient, ibid., 228; a commendable old custom to have godfathers and godmothers in it, 228; fathers should be present at that of their children, ibid.; what it is, with probations out of the scripture, 507, 8; to what use it was used, 508; a peculiar covenant and sign, 573; we must cleave strongly to the promise added to this sign, ibid.; a covenant which makes quiet the conscience, 574; by it we are removed from the fierce judging-place to the court of mercy, 635, 6.

Baptized in the name of Christ, what it is to be, 13.

Barbara, invoked to keep from thunder and lightning, 536.

Basil speaks of baptism by trine immersion, 227; says that the Holy Ghost is at one time in different persons, which angels cannot be, 280; rebukes covetous rich men who while alive will give nothing, but at their death bequeath largely to the poor, 396; calls him a thief who makes that his own which he has received to distribute, 538; defines the true and christian fast, 539; says that fasting is necessary when we desire to obtain any thing of the Lord, 548.

Beauty is a vain thing not to be rejoiced in, 437; an enticement to uncleanness, ibid.

Becon dedicates his Catechism to his children, 4; his desire to bring them up well, 6; his poverty and ill-fortune, 7; the malice of the papists against him and his writings, 419; travelled into the Peak of Derbyshire, ibid., 420; his books, 421; went into Staffordshire, 422; into Warwickshire and Leicestershire, 424; repaired home on hearing of the death of his father-in-law, 426; the books he wrote and translated while in the country, 427.

Bede says that Christ was taken up in his humanity, but concerning his divinity he abides still on the earth, 275; declares that Christ forsook those corporally whom concerning his divine majesty he never failed, ibid., 278; speaks of Christ instituting the sacrament of his flesh and blood in the figure of bread and wine, 286.

Beggars who can work and will not are thieves, 108; their duty, 115.

Belisarius, 441.

Bellarmine admits that the council of Basil allowed the cup in the eucharist to the Bohemians, 245, *n.*

Belly-care, the great evils of, 602.

Beneficed men, Latimer used to rebuke in his sermons, 425; see *Ministers*, *Pastors*.

Benefices, Latimer freely spoke against buying and selling of them, 425.

Berengarius, his recantation, 264, *n*.

Bernard says the will is taken for the deed (in baptism) when necessity excludes the deed, 224; exhorts daily to receive the sacrament as the medicine of the wound of sin, 259; says the flesh of Christ is given to us spiritually not carnally, 286; calls the body a stinking sperm and the meat of worms, 442; though he had done many good works, yet, when he should die, he acknowledged he had lived unthriftily, and called upon the favourable grace of God, 637.

Bertram says the substance of the creatures remains after consecration what they were before, 268; calls the body and blood of Christ a spiritual meat and a spiritual drink, 295, 6.

Beugnot, 305, *n*.

Bible in English, Latimer proved that it should be read by all, 424.

Bibliotheca Max. Vet. Patr. 91, *n*.; 256, *n*.; 267, *n*.; 289, *n*.

——— Mag. ——— 252, *n*.; 256, *n*.; 258, *n*.; 276, *n*.

——— Vet. Patr. Galland. 281, *n*.

Biel, Gab. 252, *n*.; says that how the body of Christ is under the kinds of bread and wine is not found expressed in the bible, 269.

Bingham, 9, *n*.; 297, *n*.; 298, *n*.; 301, *n*.; 319, *n*.; 327, *n*.

Bishops (or spiritual ministers) that neglect their duty are thieves, 107; their duty, 114; what they are, 317, &c.; differ not from spiritual ministers, 319; their order always owned to be superior to that of presbyters, ibid., *n*.; hospitality decayed among them, 320; they must shew hospitality, 325, &c.; their fault in ordaining unfit persons, 423; their duty, with probations of scripture, 516, 7; ancient, examples of their charity to the poor, 586; they sold the church utensils for the purpose of relieving the needy, ibid.

Blessings on those who obey God's word, 617.

Boemus, 649, *n*.

Bonaventure says that grace is not contained in the sacraments essentially as water in a vessel, 219.

Bool: bawl, 390.

Boy-bishop, 320, *n*.

Brand, 346, *n*.; 438, *n*.

Bread, what it signifies in scripture, 166; variously understood in the Lord's prayer, ibid., 167; holy, and holy water were ministered every Sunday by the papists instead of the sacrament, 260; and wine remain after consecration, 264; how it is Christ's body, 282; why Christ called it his body, ibid.; called Christ's body in the sacrament, when really a figure of his body, ibid.; and wine are figures, tokens, representations, ibid., 283; what it is to break it to the hungry, 538, 9.

Brethren, we are bound to seek their salvation, 176, 7.

Bribe-taking, its prevalence, 307.

Broke: breach, 94.

Bruno, 639.

Building, the daughter of fancy, 430; curious, practice of is a token that the day of judgment is at hand, ibid.

Burnet, bishop, 72, *n*.; 319, *n*.

Cæsarius, 535, *n*.; 540, *n*.

Careful pensiveness, not labour, is forbidden by Christ, 617.

Carefulness, proper, not forbidden, 164.

Carthaginian church, 49.

Cassander, Gregory in, 256, *n*.; Armen. Lit. in, ibid., *n*.; Vigilius in, 275, *n*.; 279, *n*.

Cassiodorus says not only singing but understanding we ought to give thanks, 255.

Casts: contrivances, 575.

Catalogus Testium, 261, *n*.; 395, *n*.

Catechism, what it means, 9; the teaching of it ancient, ibid.; the parts of Becon's, Part I. 10; II. 13; III. 53; IV. 125; V. 199; VI. 302; conclusion, 408.

Catechistæ, who they were, 9.

Catechumeni, 9, 256.

Catholic, why the church is so called, 42.

Cato, 339, 383, 384, 401, 600.

Catullus, 419, *n*.

Cave, 173, *n*.; 259, *n*.

Cecil, Thomas, dedication to, 480; account of his family, ibid., *n*.

Centur. Magdeb. 71, *n*.

Cerdon, a heretic, 446.

Ceremonies, how it was believed that in practising them was salvation, 414.

Charity, it must spring from repentance and faith in preparation for the Lord's supper, 235, 6; the nature of it, 583, 4.

Children, why God gives them, 4; the earnest study of the gentiles for bringing up theirs, 5; of God's people, ibid., 6; they are not punished for their fathers' sins, 75; they may have faith and please God, 211, 2; they may have the Holy Ghost, 213; those of unbelievers must be left to the judgment of God, 214; case of those dying without baptism, ibid., &c.; he who would have them virtuous must be cautious in choosing his wife, 346, 7; they must be brought up in the knowledge of God's word, 348, 9; their plays and pastimes, 349; company-keeping for them, ibid.; good manners must be taught them, ibid., 350; they must be sent to school, 350; good books must be provided for them, 351; chapters of the bible to be read by them at dinner and supper, ibid.; they must be corrected if they do amiss, 353, 4; they must not follow their blind judgment in matrimony, 355, 8, 71; they must honour and obey their parents, 357, &c.; what it is for them to honour their parents, 357, 8; what it is to obey, 358; reasons why they should so honour and obey, 358, 9; christian, must be brought up in christian doctrine, 378; their duty to their parents, with probations of scripture, 519.

Christ, his Godhead proved, 19, 20; he is alone a Saviour, 21, 2; what he is, 22; his kingdom is spiritual, ibid.; the profit of his kingdom, ibid.; he is alone our priest, 23; the profit of his priesthood, ibid.; he is our prophet, ibid.; the profit of this, 24; why he is called the only Son of God, ibid., 25; what his Godhead profits, 25; what profit we have in that he is our Lord, 26; of his humanity, ibid.; there are two natures in him, ibid.: what profit we have by his humanity, 27, 8; he received his humanity of the virgin, 28; what he did and suffered was for our sake, 29; what profit we have by his passion, ibid.; he suffered willingly, 30; what profit we have by his crucifixion, ibid., 31; his death and burial, 31, 2; what profit we have by his death and burial, 32, 3; his descent into hell, and our profit thereby, 33; his resurrection, ibid., 34; the profit we have by his resurrection, 34, 5; his ascension, 35, 6; the profit we have by it, 36; his sitting on the right hand of God, and the profit we have thereby, ibid., 37; his coming to judgment, 37, 8; what profit we have by this, 38; his church is but one only church, 42; for his sake God gives all good things, 45; prayer must be made in his name, 134; what it is to pray in his name, ibid.; he alone is the Son of God by nature, we by adoption, 145; he is the food of the soul, 166, 7; what it is to put him on, 206; the necessity of his death for us, 229, 30; by his death we are delivered from our sins, 230; his body is the nutriment of our soul, 232; the omnisufficiency of his sacrifice, 247, 8; his death the alone sacrifice for sin, 250; his natural body is only in heaven, 271; he is in his manhood in one place, in his Godhead everywhere, 272; the old fathers confirm this, ibid., &c.; the papists say that his natural body, though in heaven, is also in the sacrament, 276, 9; his body is not in divers places at once, 276, 7; the old fathers confirm this, 277, &c.; his humanity is in heaven only till the judgment, 280; to teach that his body is in several places evacuates his humanity, which is a heresy, 281; the wicked eat and drink not his body and blood, 291, 2, 5; the old fathers confirm this, 292, &c.; what it is to eat him, 294; he is received by faith, 295; the old fathers confirm this, ibid., &c.; passages which appear to controvert this explained, 296, 7; he alone saves, 380; the papists pervert this by introducing the merit of others, ibid.; he is the alone mediator and intercessor, ibid., 381; his blood is the alone purgatory for souls, 381; to know him truly is the gift of God, 428; commendation of him, 444; his alluring kindness, 446; his choice of his apostles, ibid.; his humility and lowliness, ibid., 447; his death, 447; Christians must rejoice in him, 448; his sacrifice makes clean for ever, 450, &c.; comparison between him and massmongers, 451; his resurrection and ascension a cause of rejoicing, 457, 8; our mediator, intercessor, and advocate, 459, 60; his coming to judgment a cause of rejoicing to the faithful, 460, 1; his death the only satisfaction for sin, 574, 5; he became sin, i.e. a sacrifice for sin for us, 575; we may have firm faith and trust in him against death, 576, 7; he reproves certain rich worldlings, 587, 8; he blesses those with the gospel whom the law has condemned, 630; by his sacrifice that is fulfilled which the law requires, 631; we are engraffed in him through faith, 632; he discharges our debt, 636.

Christians should consider their vocation, and seek to walk worthy of it, 475, &c.; false, what a fire boils in their hearts, 623.

Chrysostom numbers the second commandment among the ten, and holds it a moral law, 60; says that to deliver from the filthiness of sin is the mighty power of Christ, and that no man has power to forgive sin but God, 173; declares that the Lord's supper ought to be common, 239; says the things which belong to the eucharist, diverse from the old law, are common all between the priest and the people, 245; declares that when we offer that we do is to the remembrance of Christ's death, 249; speaks of the common supper after the communion, 251; says there can be no profit of a voice not understood, 254, 5; reference to the liturgy ascribed to him, 256; shews that none who do not communicate must be present at the sacrament, 257; the Lord's supper greatly frequented in his time, 258; says he that has a pure conscience ought every day to come to the communion, 258, 9; reproves his hearers for their slack coming to the holy table, 259; declares that the nature of bread tarries in the eucharist after it is sanctified, 265; cautions against understanding the words of Christ carnally, for that mysteries must be considered with inward eyes, 287, 97; explains why the gifts signified in the sacraments are not delivered nakedly, but in sensible things, 287; speaks of the bread and the receivers being or signifying the body of Christ, ibid., 288; calls the eucharistic sacrifice a symbol or sign of Christ, 288; says that not the true body but a mystery of Christ's body is contained in the hallowed vessels, ibid.; warns against the idea that the divine body is received at the hand of man, ibid.; speaks of bread and wine being shewn for a similitude of the body and blood of Christ, ibid.; says that he who comes to the body of the Lord must climb up on high, 295; declares that, if priests teach well but live ill, their doctrine, but not their manners, is to be taken, 324, 33; cautions against thinking that mercy will be granted us in another world at the prayers of any, if we do not behave ourselves so as to deserve to receive forgiveness, 395; advises men to prepare their works against their departure, as, when they are once departed, it lies not in their power to repent, or put away their offences, ibid.; says that the nobility and goodness of our kinsfolk avail nothing, except we ourselves be good, 436; calls him the true nobleman that disdains to serve vices, ibid., 437; explains what it is to anoint the head, and wash the face in fasting, 537, 8; says that he who abstains from meat and not from evil works, though he appears to fast, fasts not in deed, 539; declares that those, who so fast that they please men rather than God, through vain-glory have no reward of their labour, 541; says the abstinence from meats is received for this purpose, to make the flesh obedient to the spirit, 545; counsels that whenever we fast we should be liberal to the poor, 546; says that he who cannot fast must give the larger alms, and be more diligent in prayer, ibid.; speaks of faith alone justifying, 639.

Church, what it signifies, 41; why it is called

holy, ibid., 42; why called catholic or universal, 42; Christ's is one only church, ibid.; signs by which it may be known from the synagogue of antichrist, ibid.; why it is called the fellowship of the saints, 43; what profit there is in believing that there is a holy universal church, ibid.; there is no forgiveness of sins but in it, 44; its belief concerning faith and good works, 638, &c.

Cicero, scholars must exercise themselves in, 386.

Circumcision, some that died without were not condemned, 215, 22, 3; its spiritual character, 216.

Clement (of Rome) commanded that as many hosts should be offered on the altar as would suffice the people, 239, and forbad the reserving of what remained, 251.

Clichtoveus, 173, *n.*

Cod. Justin. in Gothofr. Corp. Jur. Civ. 305, *n.*; 312, *n.*

Colet, 383, *n.*

Comeracensis, or Cameracensis, see *Alliaco.*

Comestor, P., mentions different opinions as to the words of Christ in consecration of the eucharist, 263.

Come yer, or come er: come ere, or before, anticipate, 38.

Commandments, the ten, 56, with confirmations of scripture, 497, &c. the first, 56, 497, 8; what God requires of us in it, 57, &c.; the second, 59, 498, 9; the omission of the second and division of tenth into two, 59, 60; what God requires of us in it, 66; no particular takes away the virtue of the general law, 69; the third, 76, 499; what God requires and forbids in it, 76; the vengeance of God against the transgressors of it, 80; the fourth, 80, 500; what God requires in it, 80, 4; the fifth, 85, 500, 1; what is commanded in it, 85, &c.; the sixth, 94, 501, 2; what God requires of us in it, 94, 5, 7; the seventh, 97, 502, 3; what God forbids and requires in it, 97, &c., 103, &c.; the eighth, 104, 533, 4; what God forbids and requires in it, 104, &c., 111, &c.; the ninth, 116, 504, 5; God's will in it, and what he forbids and requires, 116, &c., 118, &c.; the tenth, 119, 505; what God requires in this, and in all, 120, &c., 123, &c.; the sum of them, 505, 6.

Commenty: community, 307.

Commons, the wrongful inclosure of, 599.

Commons (the people) their increase the honour of the king, and *vice versa,* 601.

Commonweal, that, where there is a good magistrate, a faithful preacher, a diligent school-master, not likely to decay, 377, 8.

Concil. Collect. 210, *n.*

Concupiscence is sin, 120, 1; why it is left and felt after baptism, 204; it does not condemn unless we give place to it, ibid., 205.

Confess and set forth true religion, we are commanded to, 79.

Confession of christian faith, 579, 80.

Conflict of Christians with their adversaries is most perilous in sickness, 571.

Conscience, of godly men, troubled, 622; how to be quieted declared in Christian Knight, 623, 4.

Consecration, the words of considered, 281, &c.; not to be grossly interpreted, 284; how the ancient fathers took them, 285, &c.

Constantine, the Great, his edict against idolatry, 71, 312; his godly laws and exertions for the furtherance of religion, 305; declared he would conceal the faults of the clergy, 333.

Constantine, Copronymus, forbids images to be adored, 71.

Constantine I. (pope) 71, *n.*

Content, we are required to be with what we have, 114.

Cornelia, her reply about her children, 5.

Corporal presence of Christ in the sacrament, 270, &c.; it follows of transubstantiation, 270; it establishes the Marcionite heresy, ibid.

Correction, things to be observed in it, 354, 5; how a school-master must use it, 384, 5.

Corvinus, his Postil translated by Wisdom, 423.

Cotelerius, 546, *n.*

Council, of Agde, 71, 259; of Elvira, 71; of Toledo, 71, 227, *n.*, 245; of Constance decreed that the cup should not be given to the laity, 244; of Basil allowed the Bohemians to receive in both kinds, 245; of Lateran, 253, 260, 2, 8; of Florence, 266; of Nice admonishes not to look down to the bread and cup, 295; this held by Constantine, 305; of Trent, 319, *n.*; of Chalcedon (Châlons) ordained that none should be counted to fast that ate before evensong was done, 533.

Covel, 266, *n.*

Coverdale, 420.

Covetous man, what his delight is in, 428.

Covetousness, of the age reprehended, 7; it is condemned in the Lord's prayer, 164; reigns chiefly in old men, 373.

Coy, or corle: to strike or pat with the hand, 596.

Cranmer, abp. dedication to, 525.

Creed, apostles', why so called, 15; its parts, 16.

Cresset: a watch-fire, or light on a beacon, 610.

Creyghton, 266, *n.*

Cricamus, (Ochamus?) 639.

Crinitus, 71, *n.*

Cross, hymn to, 72; of that of affliction, 468.

Curates, who neglect their duty are thieves, 107.

Cure: care, 112.

Curius, 308.

Cursings on those who disobey God's word, 617, 8.

Cyprian says the Lord alone may shew mercy and forgive sins, 172, 3; affirms plainly the baptism of infants, 209; refers to three kinds of baptism, 225, *n.*: says that, whether Judas or Paul baptizes, Christ puts away the sin, 226; resists the attempt to take away the mystery of the Lord's blood from the communion of the laity, 243; pronounces it sacrilege that by the appointment of man God's ordinance should be broken, 261; says the Lord called the bread his body and the wine his blood, 267, 86; declares that the hallowed bread entered into the wicked mouth of Judas, 267; says drink sanctified into the blood of Christ burst out of the defiled bowels, ibid.; declares that Christ gave bread and wine at the table, 285; says the Lord called wine his blood, 286; asserts that none but such as be true Israelites eat of this Lamb, 292; says that in the sacrament we whet not our teeth to bite, but with pure faith we break the holy bread, 295; referred to to shew that in his

time the bread and the cup were given into the hands of the communicants, 301, *n.*; says such as God finds men when he calls them, such does he judge them, 395; his exclamation when condemned to be beheaded, 473; denies that godly men ever took any great thing in hand except they first fasted, 548.
Cyril (of Alexandria), says that inwardly to quicken a sinner is the gift of God, 173; declares that Christ took away the presence of his body, though in the majesty of his Godhead he is ever here, 273; says that, if the nature of the Godhead were a body, it must needs be in a place, 281; declares that Christ distributed bread calling it his body, 288; says they that receive the bread of life shall obtain immortality, 294; asserts that he who eats the flesh of Christ has everlasting life, ibid.; declares that when we eat the flesh of Christ we have life in us, ibid.
Cyril (of Jerusalem), refers to three kinds of baptism, 225, *n.*; speaks of baptism by trine immersion, 227.

Damasus, (or Damascene ?), speaks of baptism by trine immersion, 227.
Davidians, a sect of heretics, 379, 415; their origin from David George, 379, *n.*
Deacons, their office, 326; in the pope's church, 327; account of them and their duties referred to, ibid., *n.*
Dearth, the prevalence of, 617; why it is sent, ibid., 618.
Death of the body, what it is, 575; it is not to be feared but desired, ibid.; how those are to be comforted who are in peril of it, ibid., 576; how he is to be spoken to who is at the point of it, 577, 8; a prayer for a sick man in peril of it, 578.
Debts to God, how we are to be delivered from, 178, 9.
Debtors, who will not pay when they can are thieves, 108; their duty, 115; we must forgive them, 179, 80.
Decretal epistles ascribed to the early bishops of Rome are not genuine, 238, *n.*
Desperation, how it is to be resisted, 577, 8; the godly are sometimes tossed with the waves of it, 622, 3.
Despise, used for desire, 626.
Devil the, his army are wicked spirits, the world, and the flesh, 543; a saying that every man sees him before he dies, 624. See *Satan*.
Dicers, carders, &c., are thieves, 108, 162.
Didymus Alexand., proves that the Holy Ghost is God, because he is in many places at one time which no creature can be, 281; speaks of faith alone justifying, 639.
Diet, temperance in, is a remedy against adultery, 102, 3; of maids, 369.
Diogenes, 600.
Dionysius, Areop., shews that in his time the bread and cup were not received of the minister alone, but distributed to all, 239; quoted to prove that the Lord's supper was called *Synaxis*, 240. *n.*; says that all that did not communicate were anciently not suffered to be present, 256.
Dirigies: dirges, 394.
Divorces, most of them are on occasion of adultery, 647.
Doctrine of Becon's Catechism is agreeable to the word of God, 409; it dissents not from the teaching of the true catholic church, ibid.
Dorothy invoked to save flowers, 536; account of her, ibid., *n.*
Doted: rendered doting, 646.
Dowkings: duckings, 455.
Drafflesacked: filled with offal or swill, 591.
Druthmarus Christ., speaks of Christ instituting the sacrament that the disciples might do that in a figure which he should do for them, 286; says the blood of Christ is aptly figured by wine, ibid.
Duns Scotus says the words of scripture might be expounded more easily without transubstantiation, 268, 9.
Durandus, 71, *n.*; explains how in the primitive church all that were present were wont to communicate, 239, 58.
Duty, of all men, to God, by exercising faith, 402, 3; love, 403; a new life, ibid.; prayer with thanksgiving, ibid., 404; to our neighbour, by shewing love, 404; to ourselves, we must keep the heart pure, 405; sequester it from worldly things, ibid.; call to remembrance our death, 406; we must keep our words pure, ibid.; and thereto pray for the taming of the tongue, ibid.; we must soberly use our eyes, 407; with our hands work no wickedness, ibid.; direct our feet that they haste not to wickedness, ibid.; use godly all our members, ibid., 408; we must take care that our life answer to our profession, 408; that of all estates, with probations of scripture, 511, &c.; of the high powers and temporal magistrates, that they should be learned in the laws of God, 511; maintain pure and christian religion, ibid., 512; punish, and, if they will not turn, kill preachers of false doctrine, 512; judge equally, 513; take no bribes, ibid.; not oppress the common people, ibid., 514; care for the commons as fathers, 514; defend the good and correct the evil, ibid., 515; of subjects, 515, 6; of bishops and ministers, 516, 7; in respect to doctrine, 516; life, ibid., 517; hospitality, 517; of parishioners to ministers, ibid., 518; of husbands to wives, 518; of wives to husbands, ibid., 519; of parents to children, 519; of children to parents, ibid.; of masters to servants, 520; of servants to masters, ibid.; of widows, ibid., 521; of old men, 521; of old women, ibid.; of young folk, ibid.; of all degrees and estates to God and their neighbour, 522.

Egalness: equality, 510.
Egypt, the deliverance out of, 57.
Election of God is not made frustrate by the want of outward baptism, 221.
Elizabeth (afterwards queen), dedication to, 413.
Elvira, council of, 71.
Endurance to the end is needful, 571.
Enemies of the Christian, 184; they can do no more than God suffers, 193.
England, once in darkness under popery, 414, 5; afterwards blessed with light, 415; miserable through the covetousness of the rich, 434, 5.

Epiphanius cut an image away, and said it was contrary to the authority of the holy scripture to have any in the church of Christ, 60, 1, 9, 71; says that Christ called a senseless loaf his body, 288.

Erasmus says Christ in the sacrament ought not to be carried about the fields on horseback, 253.

Eucherius, 91, *n.*

Eusebius speaks of the use of images as introduced from the heathen, 61; mentions Constantine's instruction and commands against idolatry, 71, *n.*; 305, *n.*; referred to, 140, *n.*

Eusebius Emissenus prescribes that we look upon the holy body and blood of our God with faith, 295.

Evagrius testifies that young children were called to eat the remains of the sacrament, 252.

Evils, of the soul, 195, 6; of the body, 196; of the times, displayed, 593.

Fabian (bishop of Rome) decreed that all should communicate at least thrice a year, 259.

Face, the command to wash, explained, 539, 40.

Faith is the companion of true repentance, 12; defined, 13; it is the gift of God, 14; without it all virtues are but sins, ibid.; the fruits of it, ibid., 15; the articles of christian faith, how many and what they are, 15; the first part, 16; the second, 19; the third, 38; the fourth, 41; by it we obtain all good things of God, 45, 6; it is needful in prayer, 132, 3; it is the will of God that it be exercised, 156; by it alone we are justified and saved, 176; it goes before baptism in those that have the use of reason, 211; infants may have it, ibid., 212; the ordinary way to it is the preaching of God's word, 212; it is the work of God, ibid.; it may dwell in children though not yet declared by works, 213, 4; it is necessary for worthy preparation for the Lord's supper, 234, 5; we must believe that Christ was born and gave himself *for us*, 235; it is the mouth of the soul wherewith Christ is received and eaten, 295; it is a duty which all men owe to God, 402, 3; what it is, 482; the benefits we receive of God through it, with probations of scripture, ibid., 483; the twelve articles of it, 483—9; confession of christian faith, 579, 80; encouraged to rely on the promises of God, 604; it is much, it is altogether, ibid.; through it Christ's fulfilling of the law is the believer's, 636; for it God accepts the Christian as righteous, ibid.; it must be laid as a sure foundation, 638; by it we are justified and receive other blessings, ibid; no unfruitful faith is taught, 638; it alone justifies without works, 639.

Faithful, what things are hoped for by them, 13, 14; they are the sons of God by adoption, 25; why they are called saints, 43; their final joy, 460, 1.

False witness forbidden, 116, 7.

Famine sent as a punishment for sins, 617, 8.

Fannel, or fanon: a sort of small scarf worn by a priest on his arm while saying mass, 300.

Farced: stuffed, filled, 423.

Fast, or fasting, how much it was trusted in, 414; used in Lent, 526; none have written of it in English, 527; definition of it, what the true and christian fast is, 528, &c.; that of the fathers in the old law, 528, 33; spiritual exercises in it, 528; how practised, ibid., 529; godly men abstained in it not only from meat, but from all that might delight the flesh, 529; that which is merely outward or constrained God abhors, ibid., 530; that which is commanded of the high powers is to be kept, 530, 1; the true fast rises of a heart contrite and sorrowful for sin, 531, 2; of a mind given to godliness, 532, 3; the popish manner of fasting, 533, &c.; story of a monk who was a great faster, 534; the popish fast rises of custom or superstition, 535, 6; the fondness of the papists in their's, 536; how we ought to fast, 537, &c.; three things to be observed therein, 537; that pleases God best which is accompanied by works of mercy, 538, 9; why God rejected the fasts and feasts of the Jews, 539; it consists not only in abstinence of meats but in forsaking of sin, ibid., 540; what it is to fast in secret, 540, &c.; the true use of it, 542, &c.; the manner of it in the pope's kingdom was wicked, 542; the erroneous doctrine of the papists concerning it, ibid.; it is a fruit of repentance, ibid.; it was not practised by the old fathers to be justified thereby, ibid.; its first use, to mortify and tame the flesh, 543, &c.; a rule to be observed herein, 545; its second use, to have more liberally to give to the poor, ibid., 546; its third use, that, as godly men of old, we may be more apt to pray, 546, &c.; Christ joined it and prayer, 547; why fasts were appointed of ancient fathers, 548; its fourth use, that we may the better hear and digest God's word, ibid., &c.; why it was instituted on the evens of solemn feasts, with examples, 549, 50.

Fathers of the church, some were in error in holding that all who died without baptism were lost, 214, 224; led with the Spirit of Christ they could teach nothing but that which is agreeable to the doctrine of Christ, 277.

Fathers and mothers, their duty towards their children, 346, &c.; they should be present at their baptism, 347; they must take care that no harm chance to them, 348; how they must teach them to speak, ibid.; they must train them in the knowledge of God's word, ibid., 349; they must devise convenient pastimes for them, ibid.; they must take heed with whom they keep company, ibid.; they must teach them good manners, ibid., 350; they must send them to school to a good school-master, 350, &c.; they must prepare them godly books, 351; they must let them read the bible at dinner and supper, ibid.; examples of their godly bringing them up, 352, 3; they should correct them if they do amiss, 353, 4; they must put them into some honest godly way of life, 355; they must provide proper marriages for them, ibid., 356; giving them a portion in marriage, 356; they must set them a good example, ibid., 357; they must commend them in prayer to God, 357; their duty to their children, with probations of scripture, 519.

Fear of God, the want of it is the root of all evil, 416.

Feastful days appointed by magistrates are to be observed, 83; of labour on them, ibid.

Fellowship of the saints, why the church is so called, 43.
Fet: fetched, 304.
Fidus, his opinion that infants should not be baptized before the eighth day disapproved by Cyprian and a council, 209.
File: defile, 62.
Finders of things who do not restore them to the owners are thieves, 108.
Fish, S., his translation of the Sum of the Scriptures, 421, *n*.
Flesh has a large kingdom, 150, 1; we desire in the Lord's prayer that its kingdom may be plucked up, 152; it is an enemy to the Christian, 184; the rebellion of it against the spirit, 543; it is tamed by fasting, ibid., 544; what it is to walk after it, 632.
Fliring: fleering, 7.
Foiled: trampled on, perplexed, puzzled, 426.
Forgiveness of sins, 43, 4; of others, examples of, 179; duty of it, ibid., 180, 574; not the cause of God's forgiving us, 181, 2; why we ought to practise it, 182.
Fornication forbidden, 98, 9; the sin of it plagued, 100, 1. See *Adultery*.
Frith, J. a book of his, 421.
Fronto Ducæus, 257, *n*.
Fulgentius says that, as concerning his man's substance, Christ was not in heaven when he was in earth, and forsook the earth when he ascended into heaven, 278, 9; advises that the garment of a holy maid be such as to be a witness of her inward chastity, 370.

Galley halfpenny, 435.
Gamesters, dicers, &c. who would overreach and win of their neighbours, are thieves, 108, 62; their duty, 115.
Gelasius Cyzic. Hist. Concil. Nic. 295, *n*.
Gelasius (bishop of Rome) commanded that the whole sacrament should be received in both kinds severally, 243; declared those accursed which receiving the body of Christ abstained from the communion of the cup, ibid.; the gloss upon pronounces it not superfluous to receive the sacrament under both kinds, ibid.; says that the nature of bread and wine in the sacrament does not go away, 267.
Gellius, A., 5, *n*.
Gennadius, 258, *n*.
Gentiles, their earnest study in bringing up their children, 5, 382, &c.
Gentlemen who unreasonably raise their rents are thieves, 108; their duty, 115; their little delight in reading the word of God, 420; their greediness censured in becoming sheepmongers, and causing the decay of towns, 434; their oppressions said to be the cause of rebellion, 598, 9; the character of those who are true gentlemen described, 598, &c.; of those which are not really so, ibid.
Gentlewomen, Dorcas an example to, 585.
George, David, 379, *n*.
George, invoked for defence in battle, 536; account of him, ibid., *n*.
Gertrude, invoked against mice and rats, 536.
Gestures to be used at the Lord's table, 298, 9; kneeling, 298; notice about this posture, ibid. *n*.; standing, 298, 9; sitting, 299; reference to the custom in the primitive church, ibid., *n*.
Gloss, upon Gelasius affirms the sacrament not to be superfluously received under both kinds, 243; of Nic. de Lyra says in the altar there is no doing again of Christ's sacrifice, 250; the ordinary declares that what we do is the commemorating of a sacrifice, ibid., *n*.; upon a canon in Gratian, explains, He is offered, that is, the offering of him is represented, ibid.; upon Paschasius in Gratian, says the offering of Christ is represented in the sacrament, ibid.; upon a canon in Gratian teaches that the consecration of the eucharist is effected when the last syllable of the words is uttered, 264; upon a canon in Gratian shews how the sacramental bread is called the body of Christ when it signifies it, 284; upon a canon in Gratian says that Christ is eaten of evil persons sacramentally only, 294; upon a canon in Gratian explains how Christ is eaten two manner of ways, 296.
Gluttony, proverb respecting it, 548.
Gnomagraph, proverb or maxim-writer, 401.
Goar, 257, *n*.
God, what he is, 16; why we call him Father, 17; why almighty, ibid., 18, 609; why called maker of heaven and earth, 18; comfort to be gathered of this, ibid., 19; all good things his gifts, ibid.; what it is to believe in him, 19; his love to mankind in giving his Son, 28; to sit on his right hand what it means, 37; he alone forgives sins, 45, 557, 60; what moves him to it, 45; he gives all good things for Christ's sake, ibid.; by faith we obtain them from him, ibid., 46; everlasting life is his free gift, 50; why called the Lord, 56; why he calls himself our God, ibid., 57; he did not give the Israelites his image to look on, 62; it is not lawful to make his image, 66, &c.; why he is called a strong and jealous God, 73, 4; his mercy greater than his anger, 76; he most chiefly detests idolatry and the abusing of his name, 79; of him only all good things are to be asked, 126, 7; how he is our Father, 145; what it profits us that he is, ibid., 146; what we learn by calling him our Father, 146; he is in heaven and why said so to be, ibid., 147; he is infinite and incomprehensible, 146; his name cannot be made more glorious than it is, 148; how to glorify him, ibid., 149; we desire his kingdom to be set up and enlarged, 152, 3; what is meant by praying that his will may be fulfilled in earth as in heaven, 154, 5; what his will is, 155, 6; he sends to his people for the best whatever comes upon them, 158; his fatherly care and good-will to them, 165, 6; why he is merciful to forgive sins, 175, 6; we are all debtors to him, 178; he remits sins of his free favour, 181, 2; what he is to us we must be to our neighbour, 182; how his temptations differ from Satan's, 185, 6; he tempts in two manner of ways, 186; why he lays his cross upon us, 189; why upon the faithful, 190; reasons why he tempts us, 191, &c.; he is not the author of temptation to evil and damnation, 194; the kingdom and power and glory are his, 196; his grace and Spirit are not bound to any external cere-

mony, 220; his election cannot be made frustrate by the want of outward baptism, 221, 2; he alone can be in all places at once, 271; his omnipotency explained, 280; his benefits towards man, in creation, 443; in the promise of redemption, 444; in giving the law and dealing friendly with him, 445; in sending his Son in the fulness of time, ibid.; he will supply his servants with necessary things, 466, 7; he judges the work of the heart, and not the heart of the work, 539; his liberality evidenced in the provision made for his creatures, 603; histories of scripture confirm this, 603, &c.; hereby he encourages poor married men, 605, 14; also men to stay at home and not wander, 606; and travellers that he will not forsake them, ibid., 607; he does good for his promise' sake to the unworthy, 608, 9; none should despair of his liberality, 610; to look for which godly preachers are encouraged, 611, 4; also their wives, 612; and those that are imprisoned for his glory, 613; and that love his word, ibid.; so that we should trust him for all things, 614, 5; his promises are made to the godly and not the ungodly, 618, 9; he is most beneficial to those that trust in him, 619; that he hears not sinners explained, 626; he sets forth to sinful men both the law and the gospel, 628; he upholds and defends his people, 633, 4; he gave his Son that we being cleansed from sin might serve him in holiness, 636, 7.

Godhead, three Persons in, 16, 17; of Christ, what it profits, 25.

God-fathers and god-mothers, a commendable old custom in baptism, 228.

Godly, nothing chances to them without the singular providence of God, 158; they have always acknowledged themselves sinners, 637.

Goods, there is a propriety of, so that they are not common, 110, 1.

Good works may be done in the sight of men, so vain-glory be absent, 540; they are to be done, but the hope of health not to be put in them, 635; the reformed doctrine teaches them where scripture teaches them, 637; they may be taught when faith is laid as a foundation, 638; the study of them is to be exercised, 640.

Gorgeous houses, the delight in them is vain, 430.

Gospel, what it is to preach it, 562; righteousness is set forth in and obtained by it, 629.

Gospellers, gross, censured, 206, 415, 16, 592, 617; new, teach the grace of perfect redemption, 637.

Governance of Virtue referred to, 481.

Gratian (emperor) his law for the establishment of St Peter's doctrine, 305.

Gratiani Decretum, 174, *n.*; 210, *n.*; Augustine in, 227, *n.*; Gregory to Leander in, 227, *n.*; fourth council of Toledo in, 227, *n.*; Gelasius to Majoricus and John in, 243, *n.*; gloss upon in, ibid.; Julius I. in, ibid.; Augustine in Lib. Sent. Prosp. in, 250, *n.*; 284, *n.*; Id. in, 250, *n.*; gloss upon in, ibid.; Paschasius in, ibid.; gloss upon in, ibid.; Fabian in, 259, *n.*; council of Agde in, ibid., gloss in, 264; August. in Lib. Sent. Prosp. in, 268, *n.*; gloss upon in, 584; Hilary in, 286; gloss in, 294; Eusebius Emissenus in, 295; gloss in, 296; canon in declares that Christ cannot be devoured with teeth, 296; canon in prescribes hospitality as necessary for bishops, 325; canon in commands a bishop to minister to the poor and sick, 326; canon in admonishes a bishop to have a liberal hand, ibid.; canon of council of Châlons in, 533.

Graziers, sheepmongers, and rich farmers the cause of a dearth, 603.

Greeks, they have no private masses, 239; they called the Lord's supper, *Synaxis*, 240; no man among them permitted to absent himself fourteen days from the sacrament, 258; they refused at the council of Florence to admit transubstantiation, 266.

Gregory Nazianzen numbers the second commandment among the ten, and holds it a moral law, 60; speaks of the passover as partaken of in a figure, though more plain than the old passover, 289; says the time we have in this world is the time of working, the future the time of reward, 395.

Gregory the Great considered images as laymen's books, 60, 3; reproved Serenus for breaking some images, 61; wrote to Leander against baptism by trine immersion, 227, *n.*; shews how non-communicants must go out before the celebration of the eucharist, 256; declares that Christ, though absent nowhere by the presence of his majesty, is not here by the presence of his flesh, 274, 5, 8; says the Word goes away in his body, but tarries in his Godhead, 275; speaks of the deposition of a bishop for niggardliness, 325, 6; says faith is righteousness, 638.

Gregory III. made a law that images should be worshipped, 60.

Gryft: graft, 214.

Guerricus, 259, *n.*

Hart of grease: a fat one, hence one of spirit, 345.

Hatred is manslaughter, 121.

Haymo says the speech ought to be understood, 255; gives all the glory of justification to Christ, 639.

Head, what it is to anoint, 537, 8.

Heart must be kept clean, 405; it is defiled by unclean thoughts, ibid.

Heathen authors, some ought not to be read, 382; some read warily, godliness being interlaced, profit much, 383.

Helena, 72.

Hell, affliction in the world is to keep us from the pains of it, 463, 4.

Herbert, 423, *n.*

Heresies and sects, great numbers of, 525, 6.

Heretics, whether it be lawful to kill them, 312, &c.; the course which must first be taken, 313.

Hermas prescribes that in fasting an account of the food commonly eaten should be had, and so much given to the poor, 545, 6.

Hesychius, or Isychius, testifies that the bread remaining of the sacrament was burned, 252; declares that in the world to come there is no working, 395.

Higinus, or Hyginus, commanded that infants when

brought to baptism should have at least one godfather and one god-mother, 210.
Hilary explains how there is a figure and a truth in the sacrament, 286; speaks of the receiving of the body and blood of Christ as causing us to be in Christ, and Christ in us, 293, 4; speaks of faith alone justifying, 639.
Hippolitus, his constancy in martyrdom, 472.
Holy Ghost, what it is to believe in him, 38; he is God, 39; the profit his Deity brings, 40, 1; the gift of him a commodity we have by Christ's ascension, 459.
Homilies, first book of, 643, *n.*
Honorius III., his decree respecting the carrying of the sacrament in procession, 253, *n.*
Honour, what the true to God is, 58; not to be given to angels as to God, ibid., 59.
Horace, 56, 162.
Hospitality, a noble virtue, necessary for all, especially for bishops, 326; the scripture gives examples to encourage to it, 584.
Housed, unhoused: with or without housings, a kind of stocking or boot, 65.
Humbertus says that, for a perfect remembrance of Christ, there must be distribution as well as blessing and breaking of the bread, 252.
Husbands must love their wives, and why, 334; they must not covet strange flesh, 335; they must make provision for their wives and families, 336; they must provide for the souls' health of their wives, 337; they must defend them from injuries, ibid.; they must bear with them after the example of Christ, 338; and not be tyrants or churlish to them, 339; what kind fathers must provide for their daughters, 356; their duty to their wives, with probations of scripture, 518.
Husbandmen, who sell their corn, &c., for unreasonable gain, are thieves, 108; their duty, 115.
Huss, John, burnt at the council of Constance, 244.
Hypocrites hate the light of God's word, 468.

Idiot: a private or unlearned person, 568.
Idleness, to be eschewed, 101, 401, 6; the evils thereof, 368; no man ought to live idly, 162, 616, 7.
Ignatius calls the Lord's supper Agape, 227, *n.*; exhorts oftentimes to come to the eucharist, 258; expressed his desire of martyrdom, 472.
Illyricus Flac., 245, *n.* See *Catalogus Testium.*
Images, honour as to God is not to be given to them, 58, 9; they are not lawful in christian temples, 60; Gregory III.'s law for them, ibid.; those in temples destroyed, ibid., 61; laws and decrees of princes, bishops and councils against them and idols, 61, 9, 71, 305, 12; the placing of them in churches came from idolaters, 61; they are not profitable as laymen's books, 61, &c.; they move not to devotion, 63, 4; they do not adorn the churches of the Christians, 65; those of God not lawful to be made, 66, &c.; in politic and civil matters they may be made, 68; lawful neither to make nor to worship them, 69, 70; service to them is an abomination, 70; what it is to bow before them, 72; what to honour or worship them, ibid., 73; their servants called God's enemies, 74; what great honours used to be paid to them, 413.
Incarnation of Christ by the Holy Ghost, 27.
Indulgences, granted by popes, 72.
Infant baptism. See *Baptism.*
Infidelity, the root of all evil, 396.
Infundeth: poureth into, 562.
Innocent III. invented the custom of hiding and closing the sacramental bread, 253; his decree affirming transubstantiation, 260, 8, 90; recounts various opinions as to the words of Christ in consecration, 263.
Institution of Christian Man, 319, *n.*
Insurrections and commotions come from the devil, 593; in Devonshire, Norfolk, &c., ibid., *n.*, 596; they are not to be excused, 601, 2.
Inward natural gifts are not to be rejoiced or gloried in, 442.
Ipocras, or hippocras, a kind of piment or spiced wine, 534.
Ireneus says the bread of the eucharist consists of two things, earthly and heavenly, 267; declares that of the eucharist the substance of our flesh is stayed and increased, ibid.
Isidore speaks of the bread and wine as consecrate to the remembrance of the Lord's passion, 287.

James, bishop of Jerusalem, 140.
Jerome, 49, *n.*; numbers the second commandment among the ten, and holds it a moral law, 60; approves the baptism of infants, 210; says the Lord's supper ought to be common to all, 240; testifies that whatever remained after the communion was consumed in the church, 251; speaks of the frequency of communicating in his time, 258; wishes that we could at all times receive the eucharist without a pricking conscience, 259; judges what councils may establish against the doctrine contained in the canonical letters a wicked error, 261; says that that which has not authority of the scriptures is despised with the same easiness with which it is proved, 263; declares that without authority of the scriptures garrulity has no faith, 264; expounds Matt. xxvi. 11., of Christ's corporal presence, 274; speaks of Christ in the sacrament as representing the truth of his body and blood, 285; says lovers of pleasure eat not Christ's flesh, nor drink his blood, 292, 3; declares that heretics eat not the flesh of Jesus, 293; describes the strong in Christ as eating this bread, and virgins (i. e. holy) as drinking this wine, ibid.; says whatever the clerks have, that is the poor's, 325; shews that while in this present world we may help one another, but not before the judging-place, 394; mentions the mode of the Jews' fasting, 533; reproves nice and fine fasters, 535; says that the abstinence of the body is commendable when the mind fasts from vices, 540; perhaps erroneously cited for Ambrose, ibid., *n.*; cautions against satiety, as nothing so much overwhelms the mind, 545; calls the righteousness which men shall seek none other than Christ himself, 639.
Jerome of Prague burnt at the council of Constance, 244.

Jesus, what the name means, and why given to Christ, 21; why he is called Christ, 22. See *Christ*.

Job, invocation of, 536.

Joy, and sorrow, cause for, to those who considered the state of the time, 413; Paul exhorts to joy, 428; ours should be in the Lord, 427, 8, 43; it should be continual, 461, 2, 73.

Judges who are corrupt in judgment are thieves, 108.

Judgment, Christ's coming to, 37, 8; a cause of joy to the faithful, and grief to the unfaithful, 460, 1.

Julius I. commanded that the people should receive both the bread and cup severally, 243.

June, query *inn*, 633.

Justification by faith, 638, 9; it is the doctrine of old authors, ibid.

Justin Martyr, 232, *n.*; describes the mode in his time of administering the Lord's supper, 239.

Justinian, his law commanding ministers to speak in a clear voice, 255, 441.

Justly, what it is to rule, 307.

Justus Orgelitanus shews how Christ is not always to be seen in the body, 275, 6.

Juvenal, 383, 99, 421, 535, 99.

Keys, the power of is no idle gift, 565; what those of the kingdom of heaven are, 566; why the preaching of God's word is likened to a key, ibid.

King, obedience to him enforced, 475.

Knowledge worldly without that of the gospel hinders rather than profits, 350.

Labbe, 60, *n.*; 71, *n.*; 244, *n.*; 245, *n.*; 253, *n.*; 259, *n.*; 260, *n.*; 264, *n.*; 266, *n.*; 295, *n.*

Labour, the yoke of laid on man's neck, 83, 4; examples of, 84, 5, 616; all men must labour in their vocation, 615, 6.

Labourers who do their work negligently are thieves, 106, 7; their duty, 115.

Lactantius says God cannot be truly worshipped where an image is, 61, 5, 9; reproves the use of images, 61.

Landlords, their duty, 115.

Lap: secure, 626.

Lashing: lavishing, 108.

Lateran, council of, 253, *n.*

Latimer, bishop, his character and preaching, 424, 5, 6.

Law the, what it is, 53; when and why it was given, ibid., &c., 496, 7; to be a certain doctrine, 53, 4; the names given to it in scripture, 54; called a light, ibid.; a glass, ibid., 55; to shew men their sinfulness, ibid.; to be a school-master to lead to Christ, 55, 6; to be a bridle to restrain the evil, 56; it contains ten commandments, ibid.; virtue of a general law is not taken away by a particular commandment, 69; it is spiritual, and why called so, 95, 120, &c.; the sum of it, 123; to obtain strength to walk in it, we must ask of God his holy Spirit, ibid.; what it is, with confirmations of scripture, 496; the first table of it, 497, &c.; the second, 500, &c.; the sum of all laws, 505, 6; a man is condemned by it, 628, 9; the true fulfilling of it, 631; it cannot justify, ibid.

Law will I: arbitrary law, 313.

Lawish sprinkling: that sprinkling which was prescribed and practised under the law, 227.

Lawyers who counsel wrongly for gain are thieves, 108; their duty, 114, 5.

Lay-people are members of Christ's church, for whose salvation he shed his blood as well as for that of the clergy, 241.

Leander, 227, *n.*

Lent, usually appointed to abstinence, 526.

Lent: offered, but perhaps an error for *bent*, 165.

Leo III. (emperor) his edict against images, 71, 312.

Leo, (pope) decree of, 210, *n.*

Lepreyans, their law against adultery, 649, 50.

Lese: lose, 588.

Life everlasting, 49, &c.; there is such a life, 50; it is God's free gift, ibid.; given only to the faithful, ibid., 51; to be enjoyed in body as well as soul, 51; the profit in believing it, ibid.

—— mortal, the shortness and uncertainty of it, 161; we are taught in the Lord's prayer that it is not maintained by our own forecast, 165; the hope of its being long makes many unmerciful, 396; the vanity thereof, 397; it is a warfare, 542.

Lilly, W., 383.

Liturgies referred to to shew that those who did not communicate must go out from the celebration of the Lord's supper, 256.

Locrensians, their law against adultery, 649.

Lombard, P., 174. *n.*; says that which is consecrated of the priest is called a sacrifice, because it is a remembrance and representation of the true sacrifice, 250; 264, *n.*; 278, *n.*

Lord's supper. See *Supper*.

Love, to our neighbour enjoined, 111, 2; examples of to each other, 177; it must be shewn, as is signified in the Lord's supper, 231, 5; its nature, 341, 8; a duty all men owe to God, 403; to their neighbour, 404.

Loye, invoked for cure of horses, 536.

Luke, invoked for saving oxen, 536.

Lusts, forbidden to be nourished in the heart, 121, &c.; evil punished, 122.

Lycurgus, his answer about the bringing up of his children, 5.

Lying forbidden, 117.

Lyra, N. de, 250, *n.*

Mabillon, Mus. Ital., 256, *n.*

Magistrates may lawfully require an oath of their subjects, 78; they ought to be honoured, 88, 9; examples of obedience to them, 89; the spiritualty not exempt therefrom, ibid.; disobedience to them punished, ibid., 90; they may lawfully kill offenders, 95; those who overcharge their subjects are thieves, 107; their duty, 114; the office and duty of temporal magistrates, 302, &c.; what they are, 302; their office is the ordinance of God, ibid.; when wicked they are given to punish the wickedness of the people, ibid.; Christ and his apostles never withstood their authority, ibid.; what manner of men they ought to be, 303; what their office is, ibid.; whether the temporal magistrates may meddle, which the papists deny, with matters of religion, ibid., &c.; they ought diligently to read God's word, 303; the papists make them no better than swineherds, 304; examples of their interference in matters of religion, ibid., &c.; what is to be done by them for the conservation of religion, 305, &c.; they must provide preachers, 305; and schools, 306; their duty in worldly matters, ibid. &c.; they must rule justly, 307; they must not oppress or plunder their subjects, 308, 9; they must maintain good and godly people, 309, 10; they must punish the wicked, 310, 1; whether they may lawfully punish idolaters and false teachers, 311, &c.; they should be circumspect whom they punish as heretics, 315; how the old godly magistrates handled heretics, 316; they were desirous of their conversion, ibid., 317; duty of spiritual magistrates, 317, &c. (See *Bishops, Ministers*); when commanding contrary to God's word they are not to be obeyed, 328, 9; they may not take away their subjects' goods at their pleasure, 329; the profit we have by them, 330; their duty, with probations of scripture, 511, &c. (See *Duties*); they have power to command their subjects to fast in urgent cause, 530, 1; they are called to rule with the temporal sword, 616.

Mahumet, the Turks rejoice and glory in him, 447.

Maids must have the fear of God before their eyes, and seek to please him, 367; they must be obedient to their masters and mistresses, ibid.; they must never be idle, ibid., 368; they must not run to vain spectacles, plays, &c., 368; they must not keep company with light persons, ibid.; they must observe a discreet silence, 369; they must avoid early marriages, ibid.; their diet, ibid.; they must content themselves with seemly apparel, 370, 1; they must not take in hand marriage without the counsel and consent of parents and guardians, 371.

Maitland, 438, *n.*

Malt-horses: slow dull drudges of horses, 611.

Man, why appointed the head of woman, 337; he is but vanity, 442. See *Old Men.*

Manicheus, a heretic, 446.

Marcion, a heretic, 446.

Mare-lady: may-lady, queen of May, 346, 70.

Maronis, F. de, denies that the sacraments of their own virtue cause grace, 219.

Marriage, a remedy against uncleanness, 103; untimely marriages are injurious, 369; they are not to be contracted without the consent of parents, 371; the consent of children is to be considered in them, 372.

Married persons must not break their marriage-vow, 97; their duty, 104, 476; married women should be so apparelled as to please their husbands, 439; poor married men should not despair of a living, or seek it by unlawful means, 605, 14.

Martin chain: of counterfeit or base metal, 438.

Martyr, P., 252, *n.*; 266, *n.*; 649, *n.*

Martyrs, baptized with blood, 225.

Masses, private, the ancient church of Rome knew none, 239; the Greeks have none, ibid.; the Armenians and Indians know none, 240; against the sacrifice of the mass, 246; they were believed to be propitiatory, 414; blasphemy of the mass, 448; why papists are loth to forego it, ibid.; the incommodities that follow of it, ibid.; the sacrifice of it agrees not with God's word, 449, 50; doctrine of the papists concerning it, 454; antithesis between the Lord's supper and it, 455, 6, 7.

Mass-hunters, how many there are, 448.

Massing papists make themselves to excel Christ in dignity, 246.

Mass-mongers and Christ, a comparison between, 451; they make the Lord's supper a private breakfast, 453; they caused the insurrection in Devonshire, 596.

Masters must govern their servants godly, 359; the order of prayers in their households, ibid., 360; they must carry them to church on Sundays, &c., 360; they must take care that no vice creep in, 361; that there be no filthy singing, but that psalms be sung, ibid.; they must set a good example, ibid., 362; imitating the pattern of David, 362; they must not be over-rigorous, ibid.; they must perform their covenants and not overburden their servants, ibid., 363; their commandments when contrary to God's word are not to be obeyed, 364; their duty to their servants, with probations of scripture, 520.

Masting: feeding on mast, 425.

Maurice, history of his martyrdom, 91, 473.

Meale: melt, 501.

Merchants and chapmen who deceive in trade are thieves, 108; their duty, 115.

Mercy-stock: propitiation, 459.

Mevius, 419.

Micrologus describes how communicants alone were wont to be present at the divine mysteries, 255, 6.

Ministers, spiritual, honour and obedience must be paid to them, 91; names given to them, ibid.; disobedience to them punished, 92; how far they are to be obeyed, ibid., 93; they all have one authority, 319; what sort of men they ought to be, ibid., 320; they must be vigilant that Satan sow not his tares, 526; they are to be had in honour, 565; they have the keys of the kingdom of heaven, 566; their words, when according to the word of God, are to be taken for an oracle, ibid.; they are appointed to rule with the sword of the Spirit, 616.

Ministry of the word is God's ordinance, 318; of calling unto, ibid., 319.

Minshull, 438, *n.*

Missa, why so called, 254; how derived, 454.

Missale ad us. Sar. 72, *n.*; quoted to shew that many should communicate with the priest, 240; and in both kinds, 245; calls the eucharist bread after consecration, 268; shews that the papists have changed the words of consecration, 456.

Missal sacrifice, injurious to the blood of Christ, 247.

Monasteries of solitary women, why they were first set up, 376.

Monastical sects, numbers of, 413.

Monica, her behaviour to her husband, 343, 4.

Monk, a story of one who was a great faster, 534.

Moses in the law requires a high and perfect righteousness, 630.

Mosheim, 379, *n.*

Mothers should nurse their own children, 347.
Murder wilful, unpardonable, 94.
Music, the delight of it is soon gone, 429; a vain and trifling science, ibid.; it may be used, if not abused, 430.

Name, a good passes all worldly riches, 116.
Nares, 345, *n.*; 438, *n.*
Narses, 441.
Natalibus (P. de) says the body of Christ contained corporally in heaven is contained sacramentally in the host, 286; 472, *n*; 473, *n.*
Natures, two in Christ, 26.
Necessaries corporal, God allows us to hope for the supply of them, 614, 5.
Necessities, every one may lawfully pray for his own, 160.
Nero, 429, 41.
Nerva, 437.
New life, it is the will of God that we should lead, 156.
New-year's Gift, referred to, 446.
Nicephorus, 305, *n.*
Nicholas, invoked to save from drowning, 536; account of him, ibid., *n.*
Nicholas bishop: a mock bishop, 320.
Nicholas II. (pope) his doctrine that Christ's body is torn in the sacrament, 264, 90.
Nicolaus Gorranus, 639.
Nobility, rejoicing in is vain, 435, 6; wherein it really consists, ibid., 437, 600.
Noblemen, their favour uncertain and not to be rejoiced in, 441, 2.
Nousled, or nuzzled: nursed, 350.
Nuns, 376.

Oaths, magistrates may lawfully require them of subjects, 78.
Offices and duties of all degrees, 302, &c.; of temporal magistrates, ibid.; of ministers of God's word, 317; of deacons, 326; of subjects, 327, &c.; of husbands to wives, 334, &c.; of wives to husbands, 340, &c.; of parents towards children, 346, &c.; of children towards parents, 357, &c.; of masters to servants, 359, &c.; of servants to masters, 363, &c.; of widows, 365, &c.; of young men unmarried, 366, 7; of maids and young unmarried women, 367, &c.; of old men, 372, &c.; of old women, 375, &c.; of schoolmasters, 377, &c.; of scholars, 385, &c.; of rich men, 387, &c.; of poor labouring men, 398, &c.; of all degrees generally, 402, &c. See *Duties.*
Old, J., 422, 4.
Old men must shine as lights among younger folks, 372; covetousness reigns chiefly in them, 373; they must declare their affection to God's word in their talk, ibid.; they must avoid the whole lump of sin, ibid.; what St Paul requires of them, ibid., 374; their duty, with probations of scripture, 521.
—women must wear becoming raiment, 375; they must not abuse their tongue, ibid.; they must not give themselves to wine, ibid., 376; they must teach honest things, but not in the congregation, 376; their duty, with probations of scripture, 521.
Opere operato, ex, the mass of a priest is held profitable, 454.
Opus Aureum, 472, *n.*
Ordo Romanus, 256, *n.*
Origen numbers the second commandment among the ten, and holds it a moral law, 60; affirms that the baptism of infants was the doctrine of the apostles, 209; says the Lord did not command the bread he gave to be reserved till the morrow, 251; in his time the bread that remained was burned, 252; says that without the witness of scripture our expositions are not to be believed, 261; speaks of the bread or symbolical body of Christ remaining as material substance, 265; proves that Christ as to his divinity is present every where, as to his humanity gone from us into heaven, 272, 3; declares that the words of eating Christ's flesh and drinking his blood must be understood spiritually, 287; says it cannot be that he that continues evil may eat the Word made flesh, 292; asserts that, if any man touches the flesh of Christ's sacrifice, he is made holy straightways, ibid.; declares what kind of fast pleases God, 540; recommends that fasting which leaves more to nourish the poor, 546; speaks of faith alone justifying, 639.
Ovid, 101, 383.

Panormitan (N. de Tudesch.) prefers a layman alleging scripture to a council or pope, 261.
Panormitan, Anton. 5, *n.*
Paolo Fra., 319, *n.*
Papists, call not on God in the name of Christ, but by the mediation of saints, 135; description of them, 315; their false doctrine, 380: what they delight in, 428; they advance and rejoice in the pope, 447; they cannot brook the doctrine that Christ has offered a sufficient sacrifice, 448; they are loth to forego the mass, ibid.; their doctrine concerning the mass, 454; their manner of dining, 534; of drinking at night, ibid., 535; in what their godliness consists, 536; their fondness in their fasting, ibid.; their erroneous doctrine as to the power of forgiving sins, 556, 8; their objections in behalf of priestly absolution answered, 563, &c.; they cannot abide God's word, or the preachers of it, 617.
Pardons granted by popes, 72; Latimer preached against them, 425.
Parents, they are wicked who neglect the godly bringing up of their children, 4; they are commanded of God to bring them up virtuously, and in the knowledge of his will, 8, 481; what it is to honour them, 85; commands in scripture to this, 86; examples of obedience to them, ibid.; how far they are to be obeyed, 87; their wicked commandments are not to be obeyed, ibid.; children disobedient to them ought to be punished, 88; it is their duty to lay up for their children, 164; some abuse their authority in marrying their children for gain, 372. See *Fathers and Mothers.*
Parishioners who withhold their lawful payments from ministers are thieves, 108; their duty, 114; they owe their pastors honour and reverence, 330, 1; and all things necessary for their living, 331, 2; also obedience, 332; they must dissemble

their pastors' faults, 333; their duty to ministers, with probations of scripture, 517, 8.
Paschasius says, Christ mystically is offered for us daily, 250; affirms that Christ did not give his body to be reserved, 252.
Pastance: pastime, or feasting, the state of one *bene pastus*, 427.
Pastors, the office of, first, to teach and minister the sacraments, 320; their condemnation if they preach not, 321; they must be able to drive away wolves, 322; they must administer the sacraments duly and faithfully, ibid.; secondly, to pray for the people, ibid.; how they must pray for the people, 323; thirdly, to lead a virtuous life, ibid., 324; Christ's charge to them, 325; they are to be honoured of parishioners, 330; teaching contrary to God's word, they are not to be obeyed, 332. See *Preachers*.
Pathway to Prayer referred to, 492.
Patience under the cross, the will of God, 156, 7; examples of it, 157.
Patrick's purgatory, 600.
Patrons of benefices blameable in presenting unfit persons, 423.
Paulus Diaconus, 71, *n*.
Peak of Derbyshire, Becon goes into, 420; the superstition and ignorance of the priests there, 421, 2.
Pearson on the Creed, 49, *n*.
Persecution for God's word, the faithful exhorted to rejoice in, 468, &c.; of the prophets, 469, 70; of Christ and his apostles, 470, 1; of martyrs in the early church, 472, 3.
Perseverance in the way of godliness necessary, 461, 2.
Persons, three in the Godhead, 16, 7.
Peter invoked to open heaven-gates, 536.
Petrarch calls glorying in the nobility of others, a boasting to be laughed at, 436.
Philip, 5, 386, 429.
Philip (Philippicus) emperor, removed images from St Sophia, 71.
Pilgrimages, how they were practised, 413.
Pill-pates: pilled or polled heads, shavelings, 315.
Pinsons: pincers, 65.
Pity, foolish, not to be shewn by magistrates, 310, 1.
Pius I. (bishop of Rome) says, it profits a man nothing to fast and pray, except the mind be refrained from ungodliness, 534.
Platina, 71, *n*.; 258.
Plato, 5, 137, 382, 420, 1.
Pleasures, to abound in them in this life is dangerous, 633.
Pœnitentes might not be present at the eucharist, 256.
Polydore Verg., 210, *n*.; 225, *n*.
Poor, in spirit, not simply poor, are blessed, 111; what we are to them, the same will God be to us, 391; they must not bear it heavily that they are forced to labour, 398, 9; they must labour faithfully without craft, 399; they must not spend what they get wastefully, but warily, ibid., 400; eschewing superfluous expences, 400; having their apparel decent and seemly, ibid.; they must beware of idleness, 401; they must seek to live honestly and quietly among their neighbours, ibid., 402; seeking, if any offences chance, reconciliation, 402; and checking false reports, ibid.; God can easily enrich them, 467; their miserable state through the dearth, 583, 91; godly men seek to relieve them, 584, 5; the coldness of love to them is a sign of the approach of the day of judgment, 587; they are to be comforted and relieved, 619.
Pope the, for a little money would deliver men from their sins, 174.
Portasses: breviaries, 135.
Poverty, against those that profess wilful, 388; we should not murmur against it, but rather rejoice, 464, &c.; why God sends it, or takes away goods, 465; when the faithful feel it, it is sent to prove their faith, 467.
Prayer, to be used as a remedy against adultery, 101; what it is, 125; the work of the spirit, ibid.; mouth-prayer proceeding from the heart is commendable, ibid.; in it we must ask somewhat, 126; the virtue of it, 127; how we shall prepare ourselves to it, 128, &c.; the cause which moves us to it must be diligently considered, 128; the commandment of God to it, 129; our unworthiness not to be objected against this, 130; the promise to hear it, ibid., 131; why God hears it, 131, 2; promises to be embraced in it, 132; faith in it, ibid., 133; it must be made in the name of Christ, 134; what it is to pray in his name, ibid.; those of Jews, Mahometans, &c. are not acceptable to God, 135; the papists do not make it in the name of Christ, ibid.; all things are to be asked in it according to the will of God, 136, 7; how to pray according to the will of God, 138, &c.; spiritual things may be asked in it without condition, 139; temporal things to be left to the will of God, ibid., 140; we must forgive if we hope to be forgiven in it, 140, &c.; no time of granting must be appointed in it to God, 142, 3; we must abide the Lord's leisure in it, 143; it must be offered to God alone and not to saints, 144; if not offered in love and charity, it is not acceptable to God, 180, 1; one for patience under affliction, 464; what it is, with probations out of scripture, 490; the benefit we receive of God in it, ibid., 491, 2; one for a sick man in peril of death, 578.
Prayer, the Lord's, the preface, 143, 492; why so called, 144; the excellency of it, ibid.; why we call God Father in it, 145; what we learn by calling him our Father, 146; why it is said that he is in heaven, ibid., 147; the 1st petition, 147, 492, 3; what we desire in it, 147, &c.; the 2nd petition, 149, 493; what we desire in it, 149, &c.; the 3rd petition, 154, 493; what we desire in it, 154, &c.; the 4th petition, 158, 493, 4; to what end we direct this to God, 158, 9; why we say give, 159; why we say us, ibid., 160; why we say this day, 160, 1; why we say our, 161, &c.; what is meant by daily, 163, &c.; what is understood by bread, 166, &c.; the 5th petition, 168, 494, 5; what we ask of God in it, 168, &c.; why we say forgive us, 176, 7; the 6th petition, 183, 495; why we are taught to pray against being led into temptation, 183, &c.; how we should understand the words of this petition, 194; the 7th petition, 195, 495; what evil we pray to be delivered from, 195; what treasures

we ask for in it, 196; the conclusion, 196, 495, 6; Amen, its meaning, 197, 8.

Preachers ought to be provided by magistrates, 305; if they live ill, but preach well, their word is not to be despised, 324; learned, should be placed in parishes, or sent to itinerate, 422; they are to be reverenced, 475; how inadequately they are provided for, 585; the papists and false prophets were better provided for formerly than true preachers now, ibid., 586; the want of them a cause of rebellion, 595; they are slandered as though they caused rebellion, 596; it was thus in the primitive church, 597, 8; when they rebuke sin, sinners are displeased, 598; they are encouraged by the comfortable histories of God's liberality, 611, 4; the world neglects and sets nought by them, 611; their wives encouraged that God will not let them lack, 612.

Preaching of God's word, 320.

Predestination, 481.

Prest: ready, prepared, 389.

Prester, called by Becon Precious, John, 258.

Priests, why those in the old law were to have no blemish, 323; the ignorance and superstition of the popish, 421, &c.; why they are despised, 432; their duty, ibid.; they forgive not sin, but are the ministers of God appointed to utter and declare forgiveness, 561, &c.

Princes, how far they should be obeyed, 90, 1. See *Magistrates.*

Prised: overturned, destroyed, 312.

Prisoners for God's glory encouraged by comfortable histories of God's liberality, 613.

Processions, public, brought in by Honorius III., 253.

Prodigal parents are thieves, 108.

Promises of God, to hear prayer, 130, 1; they are to be embraced when we pray, 132; they are made to the godly, and not to the ungodly, 618, 9.

Prosper, 250, 68, 84, 92. See *Augustine.*

Prosperity, the temptation of it, 186, 7; it is more dangerous than that of adversity, 187.

Proverbs, 583, 601, 2.

Provision, not to be carefully made for a long time to come, 161; necessary may be made, 164.

Psalms, set forth in English metre, 361.

Purgatory, the doctrine of it condemned, 175; the scripture knows none after this life, 394; it was believed that men could be delivered from it by masses, 414; what the true is, 577.

Rabanus Maurus, shews why bread is called the body of Christ, and the wine referred to his blood, 286, 7.

Raynes: fine cloth made at Rains or Rheims, 415.

Rebellion displeases God, 594; examples of its being plagued, 594, 5.

Record: call to remembrance, meditate, 303.

Refelled: confuted, 314.

Reformed: informed, 39.

Regeneration consists rather in the spirit than in the flesh, 224.

Rejoicing in the Lord is banished from the heart by embracing worldly vanities, 416; command to it, 417.

Religion true, we must confess and set it forth, 79.

Reliques of Rome referred to, 413, *n.*

Remission of sins, what it is to preach, 13; none but in the church, 44; what profit we have by believing it, 46.

Renaudot, 256, *n.*; 257, *n.*

Repentance, preached in the gospel, 10; its definition, ibid.; the fruit of the doctrine of it, 11; it is the gift of God, ibid., 12; that of the reprobate is not true repentance, 12; true has faith for its companion, ibid.; the will of God, 156; it is a part of preparation to the Lord's supper, 232; what it is, with probations of scripture, 506; the fruits of it declared by the word of God, ibid., 507.

Reservation of the sacramental bread, against, 251.

Resurrection of the body, 46, &c.; the truth of it proved, ibid.; the article of the creed respecting it differently worded in the Aquilian and Carthaginian churches, 49; what profit we have by it, ibid.

Revenge, those who seek, have not their sins forgiven, 183.

Rich men, their duty, 112, 3; they must consider of whom they have received their riches, 387; and be thankful to God, ibid., 388; they must consider why God has given them their goods, 389; how they are to bestow their goods, 390; not to distribute to monks, &c., ibid.; but to bestow them on the poor, ibid., 391; the reward to those who bestow their goods on the poor, 391, 2; to those who are unmerciful to the poor, 392; they should distribute in this life, 393, 4; since it is useless after death, 394; they must take heed and beware of covetousness, 397, 8; their oppression censured, 432, 3; threats against them, 433; they are the stewards of God, and must spend their goods as God has appointed in his word, 538; sentences of scripture for those who are godly to remember, 588, 9; for the ungodly, 589, 90; if these sentences were minded it would go much better with the poor, 590.

Riches, come from God, 387; delight in them is in vain, 431, &c.; they are fleeting, and must not be abused, 435.

Richmond, duchess of, dedication to, 554; account of her, ibid., *n.*

Right hand of God, what it is to sit on, 37.

Righteousness before God by faith in Christ, 631, 2.

Robsart, Sir J., dedication to, 583; account of him, ibid., *n.*

Rome, church of, the doctors say that men must hold as it has determined, 268, 9.

Romans, their law against whoredom, 649.

Romish bishop, his tyranny formerly in England, 413; he shall be destroyed, 415.

Ruffinus, 49, *n.*

Russel, lord, dedication to, 622; account of him, ibid., *n.*

Rusticus, set up in place of a deprived bishop, 325, 6.

Rutenes, Russians, 245.

Sabanus (Sabinus), condemned and abolished image-worship, 71.

Sabbath, what the word signifies, 80; what it is to sanctify it, ibid.; commands to sanctify it, 81;

whether Christians be bound to observe it as the Jews were, 82; the law of it is partly ceremonial, partly moral, ibid.; that of the Christians, ibid., 83.
Sacraments, two only in number, 199; but in the pope's church, seven, ibid.; what is required in them, ibid.; what they are, ibid.; why ordained, ibid., 200, 1; the need we have of them, 201; the difference between those of the old and those of the new testament, ibid., 202, 17; of themselves they give not grace, 218, &c.; each of them consists of the word and of the element, 270; they are called by the names of the things which they signify, 283, 90, 7.
Sacrifice of the mass, against, 246; it is injurious to the blood of Christ, 247; opposed to the omnisufficiency of Christ's sacrifice, ibid., 248; it agrees not with God's word, 449, 50.
Sad: grave, 375.
Sadness: gravity, 334.
Saints, why the faithful are so called, 43; honour is not to be given to them as to God, 58, 9; superstitious worshippers of them censured, 144; the papists teach us to invoke them, 380, 536; their intercession used frequently to be sought, 414.
Sarum, constitutions of Richard, bishop of, 253, *n.*
Satan, a great prince, 149, 50; we desire in the Lord's prayer that his kingdom may be subdued, 151; he is an enemy to the Christian, 184; termed the evil, 195; his malice illustrated by Christ in a parable, 525; he never shews himself so right a devil as when ministers are absent or negligent, 526; he has corrupted the true use of fasting, ibid.; his activity, 593, 623; insurrections come from him, 593; how victory over him is to be gotten, 624; he argues that God does not hear sinners, 626; and that he who has not kept the commandments must perish, ibid., 627, 8; is a liar from the beginning, so that speaking truth he lies, 627, 8; he calumniates and depraves the scriptures, 628; he is the author of man's sinful state, 629; he urges that sinners are damned, 630; he asserts that the promise is to those only that walk not after the flesh, 632; he alarms with the fear of backsliding, ibid.; he will disquiet if he cannot hinder the Christian's salvation, 633; he is the author of all evils and mischances, ibid.; his objections against christian doctrine and hope, 634, 5.
Satisfaction must be made to those who have been wronged, 105.
Scholars must attend sermons, 306; they must make orations or themes, ibid.; they must pray at their uprising, commending themselves to God, 385; they must love and reverence their schoolmasters, ibid., 386; they must be diligent in applying their books, 386; they must have their lives garnished with good manners and godly virtues, 387.
Schools ought to be established by the temporal magistrates, 306; the books of holy scripture must be read in them, ibid.; some should be set up for women-children, 376, 7.
School-masters, what kind they are to be, 306, 78; provision must be made for them, 306; they must instil into their scholars' minds true persuasions of God, 378; they must read some godly catechism to them, ibid.; also the scriptures, history, &c. ibid., 379; they must enarm them against heresies, 379; especially against the Romish, ibid., 380, 1; they must teach good letters, 382; and those authors that are profitable, ibid.; they must teach good manners, 383; they must shew a good example of conduct, 384; how they must chastise their scholars, ibid., 385; they are worthy of honour, 386.
Scriptures, in them are all things of necessity to be believed, 15; how we must understand if one sentence in them seems to repugn a multitude, 290; how they are to be read, 608.
Sects of monks, &c., how many among the papists, 415.
Seditions and insurrections never have good success, 328.
Sedulius, 639.
Seneca, 324.
Serenus, or Sirenus, broke images in pieces, 61, 71.
Serpent, the brasen, destroyed by Hezekiah, 69, 70.
Servants who do their work negligently are thieves, 106, 7; their duty, 115; they must honour their masters, 363; and obey them, ibid., 364; unless they command contrary to God's word, 364; how they may become good, ibid.; where many are in a house together, they must strive to excel each other in virtue and well-doing, ibid. See *Duty*, *Offices*.
Serving-men after long service often cast away, 442.
Sgyropulus, 266, *n.*
Shake-bucklers, or swash-bucklers: blusterers and bullies, 355.
Sheepmongers, their oppression of the people, 432.
Shorling: a sheep that has been shorn, a shaveling, 260.
Sickness, we must not murmur in it, but receive it with thanksgiving, 462, 3; the purpose of God in afflicting with it, 463; the conflict of Christians with their enemies is most perilous in it, 571; the Solace of the Soul is especially to be in the hands of the faithful in it, ibid.
Sicles: shekels, 109.
Sign is often called by the name of the thing signified, 282.
Silence in a maid is commendable, 369.
Silence gloom, 455.
Sin, those who repent after are not excluded from grace, 11; what it is to preach remission of sins, 13; no forgiveness of them but in the church, 44; God alone forgives them, 45, 172, &c., 557, &c.; of the forgiveness thereof, 168; the wicked opinion refuted that they are not forgiven after baptism, 170, 1, &c.; the bishop of Rome takes upon him unjustly to forgive them by bulls, 172, 3; priests have not power to forgive them, 174; God forgives both the fault and the pain of them, ibid., 175; verses to that effect, 174; why God is merciful to forgive them, 175, 6; a man may ask forgiveness of his own privately, 177; they are remitted by God of free favour, 181, 2; confession of them is necessary for those who come to the Lord's supper, 234; the papists' pestilent doctrine in respect to the forgiveness of them, 558; the apostles did not assume the power of remitting them, 559, 60; the priest forgives them not, but utters the free remission purchased of

God by Christ, 561, &c.; the remission of them is to be preached to the people, 565; they are not forgiven for the grievousness of disease, 574; Christ alone is the sacrifice for them, 574, 5; the sin of our nature is the work of Satan, 629.
Sinfulness of man, 27, 8, 44; it is shewn by the law, 54, 5; it is necessary to know this end of the law, 55.
Sinners, Satan's temptation that God does not hear them, 131, 626; all men are without exception, 168, 9.
Sith, invoked for bringing again lost things, 536.
Sixtus II. (pope) introduced altars, 297.
Slandering forbidden, 118.
Socrates, 137, 600.
Soul-priests, legacies to them are of no use, 394.
Spiritual men are covetous of rich benefices, 431, 587; they do not shew hospitality, 432; they should be more liberal to the poor, 590, 1.
Stafford, G., 425, 6.
Staffordshire, the superstition of the priests there, 423.
Stedfast we can be only if God give and confirm our faith, 632, 3.
Stella, 297, *n.*
Strabo, Walaf. (A. D. 842), his testimony to the frequency of communion among the Greeks, 258, *n.*
Strange gods, what is meant by, 618.
Strange tongue, it was not the ancient custom to minister in, 254.
Strype, 320, *n.*; 593, *n.*
Subjects who grudge to pay taxes are thieves, 107; their duty, 114; they must love and reverence the civil magistrates, 327; they must pray for them, ibid., 228; they must humbly obey them, 328, 9; they must pay tribute, 329; they must dissemble the magistrates' faults, ibid., 330; their duty, with probations of scripture, 515, 6; they are called on to obey, 616.
Suetonius, 329, *n.*
Suffenus, 419.
Superaltare, 297.
Superiors, of honour and obedience to, 88, 93; how far they are to be obeyed, 93, 4.
Supper, the Lord's, a spiritual nourishment, 167, 8; its signs and promises, 199; it ought to be administered publicly, 200; formerly administered to infants, 223; what it is, 228; who instituted it, and why, 229, 31, 2; called anciently *agape*, 231; also *sacramentum eucharisticæ*, 232; how we must prepare ourselves to the receiving of it, ibid., &c.; abuses that have crept into it, 237, &c.; the first, 238; it ought not to be a private repast, ibid., &c.; the second, the papists take away half, 240; lay people ought to receive under both kinds no less than ministers, 241; the objection that Christ spoke to consecrate priests answered, ibid., 242; receiving in both kinds was used in the church after the apostles, ibid., &c.; it is used in the Greek and other churches, 245; the third, the papists make it a sacrifice propitiatory, ibid., &c.; the fathers call it a sacrifice as a representative image of Christ's passion, 249; the fourth, the papists reserve it contrary to primitive practice, 251, &c.; the fifth, the papists carry it about in public processions, 253; the sixth, the papists minister in a strange tongue, 253, &c.; the seventh, the papists admit gazers at the communion against the primitive practice, 255, &c.; the eighth, the papists receive it contrary to primitive custom but once a year, 257, &c.; when the church was most pure it was most often received, and in both kinds, 259; whereas holy bread and holy water are given instead of it, 260; three errors about the matter of it have crept into the church, ibid.; the first, transubstantiation, 260, &c.; what the papists do if the bread corrupts or the wine is spilled, 262; it is destroyed by the doctrine of transubstantiation, 270; the second, the corporal presence, ibid.; the papists assert that the natural body of Christ though in heaven is yet invisibly in the eucharist, 276; the words of consecration considered, 281, &c.; why Christ instituted it, 284, &c.; the third, the papists teach that the wicked eat and drink the body and blood of Christ, 291, 2; a table is more meet for the ministering of it than an altar, 297, 8; vestures to be used at it, 299, &c.; of receiving it with the hands, 300, 1; it is not to be worshipped, 301; it is made a private breakfast by massmongers, 453; an antithesis between it and the pope's mass, 455, &c.; what it is, with probations of scripture, 508, 9; to what uses Christ instituted it, 509, 10; the first, 509; the second, ibid.; the third, ibid., 510.
Surplice, when introduced, and whether it may be used, 299, 300.
Swearing forbidden, 77; in what cases a Christian may swear, 76, 8.
Sweetlad, said to be invoked, 536.
Swinked: laboured, toiled, 7.

Table, the Lord's, gestures to be used at, 298, 9.
Talent entrusted to us, how it is to be employed, 418.
Tartarians, their law against adultery, 649.
Temperance in diet recommended, 102, 3.
Temptations, how those of God and Satan differ, 185, 6; of prosperity, 186; these are more dangerous than those of adversity, 187; of adversity, 188, &c.; why God sends them, 191, &c.; those with which he proves us are tokens of his good-will, 193; those of the devil, world, and flesh, God can make light if we ask his help, ibid.; what is to be done if we be overcome by them, 194, 5.
Temporal men, their covetousness, 432, 587.
Terence, 102.
Tertullian speaks of baptism by trine immersion, 227; mentions the common supper after the communion, 251; says Christ called the sacramental bread his body, meaning a figure of his body, 285; speaks of bread as representing Christ's body, ibid.
Theban legion, 91, *n.*
Theft and thieves, divers kinds of, 104, 5; theft punished, 109, 10.
Themistocles, 356.
Theodoret says that Christ honoured the symbols with the names of his body and blood, not changing the nature but adding grace to the nature, 266, 88; declares that the mystical

signs after the consecration depart not from their nature, ibid.; referred to for proceedings of emperors in establishing true religion, 305, *n.*; declaration of Constantine in, 333, *n.*
Theodosius, his edict against images, 71; his law for establishing St Peter's doctrine, and against idols, 305; his penal statutes against idolaters, 312.
Theodulphus, 533, *n.*
Theophilus (Alex.) speaks of the Lord's bread as that wherein the body of our Saviour is represented, 288, 9.
Theophylact says it belongs to God alone to forgive sins, and that priests have no power to remit them, 173, 4; speaks of baptism by trine immersion, 227; admonishes to frequent communion, 259; shews that Christ's words must be understood spiritually, for we are no devourers of flesh, 289; says that the virtue of our neighbour cannot be sufficient for us, for each must be justified by his own works, 395, 6; declares that then (in another world) it will be no time to work, nor honest to beg, 396; speaks of faith alone justifying, 639.
Tiberius, 329, *n.*
Tindal, W., books of his, 421.
Tithes, why they are commanded to be paid, 432.
Toledo, 12th and 16th councils of, 71; 4th, 227, *n.*; 11th, 245.
Tongue, the right use of, 118, 9.
Tooting: prying, peeping, 63.
Towns, how many have become desolate, 434.
Traditions, man's, how much they were observed, 414.
Transubstantiation, a papistical, wicked, and devilish error, 260, &c.; brought in by Innocent III., 260, 2; the meaning of the word, 262; reason denies the doctrine, ibid.; the scripture and old fathers never knew it, ibid., &c.; the papists agree not as to the words by which it is made, 263; Paul knew not of it, 264; there is this change neither of the bread nor of the wine, ibid.; the old doctors did not teach it, 265, &c.; it is not allowed of the Greek church, 266; it destroys the sacrament of Christ's body and blood, 270.
Trapezont, G., 288, *n.*
Travellers encouraged by the promises of God that they shall have necessary things, 606, 7.
Trinity of persons in the Godhead proved, 16, 7.
Turks will not suffer an image in profane or civil things, 68; their law against adultery, 649.
Turn and return, gestures at mass, 451.
Twlbytte or twibill: a two-edged bill or mattock, 449.
Tyburtius, his constancy in martyrdom, 473.
Tyrology: instruction for mere beginners, 563.

Uncleanness, all enticements to, forbidden, 99; that of the mind prohibited, ibid., 100.
Ungodly rich men in the Lord's prayer mock God, 163.
Unmarried persons forbidden to lead an incontinent life, 98, 9; their duty, 104.
Unmerciful rich men are thieves before God, 106.
Urban IV., (pope) the ministration of the Lord's supper under both kinds to the lay-people continued till his time, 243, 4.
Usurers are thieves before God, 106, 62.

Vain-glory, the desire of, poisons all good works, 541.
Valens published an edict against making images, 71.
Valentinian died without baptism, yet in the Lord, 224; his law for establishing St Peter's doctrine, and against idols, 305; he made penal statutes against idolaters, 312.
Valentinus, a heretic, 446.
Valerius Maximus, 5, *n.*; 137, *n.*; 308, *n.*; 356, *n.*; 382.
Verses, old, 174, 393, 447.
Vigilius proves that Christ touching the form of a servant is absent from us, but by the form of God he is present with us, 275; declares that Christ by his divine nature is everywhere, and by his human nature is contained in a place, 279.
Villain: a bondman or servant, 436.
Villany; servitude, 185.
Virgil, 419, *n.*
Virgin Mary confesses imperfections in calling God her Saviour, 170.
Virtues without faith are but sins, 14.
Vives, Lod. calls beauty a little thin skin well coloured, 437.
Vows, how they were observed, 414; Latimer preached against them, 425.

Wages, the unjust retaining of, is theft, 105.
Wanton or wicked company to be eschewed, 102.
Whoredom, see *Adultery*.
Wickliffe, condemned by the council of Constance, 244.
Widows, elder, their duty is to be occupied about matters of God and the congregation, 365; that of the younger to marry and guide the house, ibid.; old, frequently contract monstrous marriages, 366; their duty, with probations of scripture, 520, 1.
Will of man is naturally bent to evil, 154.
Will-works, Latimer's preaching against, 425.
Wisdom, R. 422; his books, 423.
Witness, false forbidden, 116, 7.
Wives must be subject to, and reverence their husbands, 340; owe no obedience to their husbands commanding wicked things, 341; they must love their husbands, ibid.; they must look well to their houses, 343; they must forbear their husbands, ibid.; they must array themselves in modest and comely apparel, 345, 6; why the Holy Ghost prescribes this, ibid.; men must be cautious in choosing them, 346, 7; what kind fathers should provide for their sons, 356; their duty to their husbands, with probations of scripture, 518, 9.
Woman, difference between an honest and a harlot, 342, 3; some are fond of brawling, 345; none are to teach in the congregation, 376. See *Old.*
Wool, high price of, 432.
Woolward, to go: to be clad in wool, 321.
Word of God where it lacks, superstitions reign, 54; it is to be read as a remedy against adultery, 101;

the will of God is revealed in it, 137, &c.; it is the nourishment of the soul, 167; to be reverently heard and come to, 549, 50; abusers of it censured, 550; those that love to hear it may be encouraged by comfortable histories of God's liberality, 613.

Works good, see *Good;* the trusting to obtain righteousness by them is the error of the Pelagians, 637.

World, a mighty prince, 150; we desire in the Lord's prayer that its kingdom may be dispersed, 151; an enemy to the Christian, 184; all things in it are subject to vanity, 474.

Worldlings hate the light of God's word, 468.

Worldly things, how they are to be used, 188; goods, it is lawful to possess, 388, 9; joys and delights soon pass, 428, 9.

Writhed with: turned away, 75.

Young unmarried men must reverence their elders, 366; and be ruled by them, ibid.; they must be not proud, but meek, ibid.; they must not be idle or tavern-hunters, 367; they must keep their bodies pure for honourable wedlock, ibid.; —folk, their duty, with probations of scripture, 521.

Youth must be brought up in the knowledge of God's will, 480.